Collins COBUILD

ILLUSTRATED BASIC

DICTIONARY

of American English

HEINLE
CENGAGE Learning

Australia • Brazil • Japan • Korea • Mexico • Singapore • Spain • United Kingdom • United States

Collins COBUILD Illustrated Basic Dictionary of American English

Heinle Cengage Learning

President: Dennis Hogan
Publisher: Sherrise Roehr
Senior Development Editor: Katherine Carroll
Technology Publisher: Mac Mendelsohn
Technology Project Manager: Shi-May Wei
Director of Global Marketing: Ian Martin
Director of U.S. Marketing: Jim McDonough
Senior Product Marketing Manager: Katie Kelley
Senior Content Project Manager: Dawn Marie Elwell
Associate Content Project Manager: Andrea Bobotas
Production Intern: Brooke Vinyard
Senior Frontlist Buyer: Mary Beth Hennebury
Cover Layout: Lisa Mezikofsky

In-text features including: Picture Dictionary, Sound Partners, Spelling Partners, Usage Notes, Word Builders, Word Worlds, and supplements including: Visual Guide to the Dictionary, List of Affixes, List of Vocabulary Builders, Headwords by Subject Area, Text Messaging and Emoticons, List of Basic Vocabulary, and Vocabulary Notebook.

Heinle Cengage Learning
20 Channel Center St.
Boston, MA 02210
USA

Cengage Learning products are represented in Canada by Nelson Education, Ltd.

Visit Heinle online at **elt.heinle.com**

Visit our corporate website at **www.cengage.com**

Collins

Founding Editor-in-Chief: John Sinclair
Publishing Management: Elaine Higgleton
Project Management: Lisa Sutherland
Senior Editor: Penny Hands
Contributors: Sandra Anderson, Carol Braham,
    Arline Burgmeier, Katharine Coates,
    Jamie Flockhart, Orin Hargraves,
    Kate Mohideen, Jane Solomon
Computing support: Thomas Callan
A-Z Typsetting: Davidson's Pre-Press

First Edition 2010

Harper Collins Publishers
Westerhill Road
Bishopbriggs
Glasgow
G64 2QT
Great Britain

www.collins.co.uk

Library of Congress Control Number: 2009935092

Softcover
ISBN 13: 978-1-4240-1940-3
ISBN 10: 1-4240-1940-0
Softcover + CD-ROM
ISBN 13: 978-1-4240-0081-4
ISBN 10: 1-4240-0081-5
Hard-cover
ISBN 13: 978-1-1110-3236-4
ISBN 10: 1-1110-3236-X
CD-ROM
ISBN 13: 978-1-4240-1941-0
ISBN 10: 1-4240-1941-9

Printed in China by China Translation & Printing Services Limited
1 2 3 4 5 6 7 8 9 10   13 12 11 10 09

CONTENTS

Acknowledgements

The publishers would like to acknowledge the following for their invaluable contribution to the original COBUILD concept:

John Sinclair
Patrick Hanks
Gwyneth Fox
Richard Thomas

Stephen Bullion, Jeremy Clear, Rosalind Combley, Susan Hunston, Ramesh Krishnamurthy, Rosamund Moon, Elizabeth Potter

Jane Bradbury, Joanna Channell, Alice Deignan, Andrew Delahunty, Sheila Dignen, Gill Francis, Helen Liebeck, Elizabeth Manning, Carole Murphy, Michael Murphy, Jonathan Payne, Elaine Pollard, Christina Rammell, Penny Stock, John Todd, Jenny Watson, Laura Wedgeworth, John Williams

We would like to acknowledge the assistance of the many hundreds of individuals and companies who have kindly given permission for copyright material to be used in the Bank of English™. The written sources include many national and regional newspapers in Britain and overseas; magazines and periodical publishers; and book publishers in Britain, the United States and Australia. Extensive spoken data has been provided by radio and television broadcasting companies; research workers at many universities and other institutions; and numerous individual contributors. We are grateful to them all.

Consultant
Paul Nation

Reviewers
Michael McGuire
Andrea O'Brien
Jolanta Olechowski
Juniace Senecharles
Cynthia Wiseman

John Sinclair

Founding Editor-in-Chief, Collins COBUILD Dictionaries
1933-2007

John Sinclair was Professor of Modern English Language at the University of Birmingham for most of his career; he was an outstanding scholar, one of the very first modern corpus linguists, and one of the most open-minded and original thinkers in the field. The COBUILD project in lexical computing, funded by Collins, revolutionized lexicography in the 1980s, and resulted in the creation of the largest corpus of English language texts in the world.

Professor Sinclair personally oversaw the creation of this very first electronic corpus, and was instrumental in developing the tools needed to analyze the data. Having corpus data allowed Professor Sinclair and his team to find out how people really use the English language, and to develop new ways of structuring dictionary entries. Frequency information, for example, allowed him to rank senses by importance and usefulness to the learner (thus the most common meaning should be put first); and the corpus highlights collocates (the words which go together), information which had only been sketchily covered in previous dictionaries. Under his guidance, his team also developed a full-sentence defining style, which not only gave the user the sense of a word, but showed that word in grammatical context.

When the first *Collins COBUILD Dictionary of English* was published in 1987, it revolutionized dictionaries for learners, completely changed approaches to dictionary-writing, and led to a new generation of corpus-driven dictionaries and reference materials for English language learners.

Professor Sinclair worked on the Collins COBUILD range of titles until his retirement, when he moved to Florence, Italy and became president of the Tuscan Word Centre, an association devoted to promoting the scientific study of language. He remained interested in dictionaries until his death, and the Collins COBUILD range of dictionaries remains a testament to his revolutionary approach to lexicography and English language learning. Professor Sinclair will be sorely missed by everyone who had the great pleasure of working with him.

VISUAL GUIDE TO THE DICTIONARY

Featuring all 2,845 of Dr. Robert Marzano's basic vocabulary words!

PRONUNCIATION

INFLECTED FORMS

GRAMMATICAL INFORMATION

PARTS OF SPEECH

MEANING SPLITS

SAMPLE SENTENCES IN NATURAL ENGLISH FROM REAL EXAMPLES OF ENGLISH IN THE BANK OF ENGLISH®

boot /but/ (boots, booting, booted)

1 NOUN Boots are shoes that cover your whole foot and the lower part of your leg. ❑ *He sat down and took off his boots.*

2 VERB TECHNOLOGY If you **boot** a computer, you make it ready to start working. ❑ *Put the CD into the drive and boot the machine.*

3 Boot up means the same as **boot**. ❑ *Go over to your computer and boot it up.*

→ look at **clothing**

FRIENDLY DEFINITIONS USE FULL SENTENCES

SUBJECT-AREA LABELS

VISUAL REPRESENTATIONS

CROSS REFERENCES

COLLOCATIONS

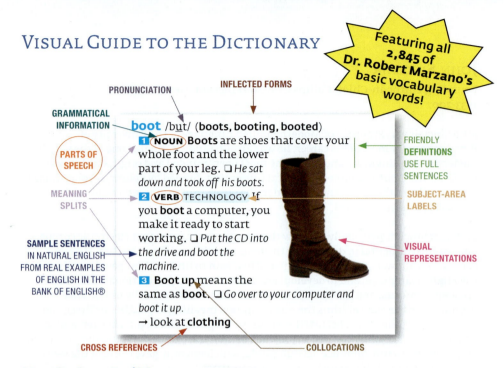

Vocabulary Builders:

Picture Dictionary
Understand new words on the same topic.

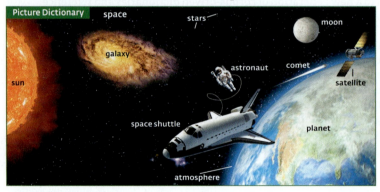

Picture Dictionary — space, stars, moon, galaxy, astronaut, comet, satellite, sun, space shuttle, planet, atmosphere

Spelling Partners
Learn words that are spelled the same but have different meanings.

Spelling Partners — chip

Spelling Partners — wave

Sound Partners
Learn words that sound alike but have different meanings.

Sound Partners — son, sun

Sound Partners — know, no

Word World
Discover words from the same topic.

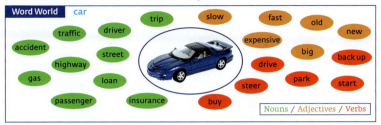

Usage
Remember tips for using words without making mistakes.

Word Builder
Learn word parts—prefixes, suffixes, and word roots.

Word Partners
Understand how words are used together.

CD-ROM

- **Search** definitions, example sentences, "Word Worlds", and "Picture Dictionary" boxes.
- **"PopUp" dictionary** finds the definition of a word while working in Microsoft Word, other programs, and web pages.
- **Audio pronunciation with record and playback** lets you practice your pronunciation.
- **"My Words"** lets you add your own words, definitions, and sample sentences.

LIST OF AFFIXES

Prefixes

auto-	in-	non-
bi-	ir-	over-
co-	inter-	part-
de-	kilo-	pre-
dis-	mega-	pro-
eco-	micro-	re-
extra-	mid-	semi-
hyper-	milli-	tri-
il-	mis-	ultra-
im-	mutli-	un-

Suffixes

-ability	-er	-less
-able	-ful	-ly
-action	-ibility	-ment
-al	-ic	-ness
-ally	-ication	-or
-ance	-ing	-ous
-cy	-ism	-sion
-ed	-ist	-tion
-ence	-ity	-y

Aa

a /ə, STRONG eɪ/ or **an** /ən, STRONG æn/

1 **ARTICLE** You use **a** or **an** before a noun when people may not know which particular person or thing you are talking about. ❑ *A waiter came in with a glass of water.* ❑ *He started eating an apple.*

2 **ARTICLE** You use **a** or **an** when you are talking about any person or thing of a particular type. ❑ *You should leave it to an expert.* ❑ *Bring a sleeping bag.*

3 **ARTICLE** You use **a** or **an** instead of the number "one" before some numbers or measurements. ❑ *...a hundred miles.*

4 **ARTICLE** **A** or **an** means "each" or "for each." ❑ *Cheryl goes to London three times a month.*

Usage   **a**

A is usually used before singular nouns beginning with consonants. Here are some examples: **a** car, **a** friend, **a** job, **a** phone, **a** teacher. An is usually used before words beginning with vowels. Here are some examples: **an** apartment, **an** elevator, **an** ice cream, **an** ocean, **an** umbrella

aban|don /əbǽndən/ (**abandons, abandoning, abandoned**)

1 **VERB** If you **abandon** a place, thing, or person, you leave them, especially when you should not. ❑ *His parents abandoned him when he was a baby.* ● **aban|doned** **ADJECTIVE** ❑ *They found an abandoned car.*

2 **VERB** If you **abandon** an activity or piece of work, you stop doing it before it is finished. ❑ *After several hours they abandoned their search.*

ab|bre|via|tion /əbriːvieɪʃᵊn/ (**abbreviations**) **NOUN** **LANGUAGE ARTS** An **abbreviation** is a short form of a word or phrase. ❑ *The abbreviation for Kansas is KS.*

ab|do|men /ǽbdəmən/ (**abdomens**)

1 **NOUN** **SCIENCE** Your **abdomen** is the part of your body below your chest. ❑ *The pain in my abdomen is getting worse.* ● **ab|domi|nal** /æbdɒmɪnᵊl/ **ADJECTIVE** ❑ *...the abdominal muscles.*

2 **NOUN** **SCIENCE** An insect's **abdomen** is the back part of the three parts that its body is divided into.

abil|ity /əbɪlɪti/ (**abilities**) **NOUN** An **ability** is a quality or skill that makes it possible for you to do something. ❑ *Her drama teacher noticed her acting ability.* ❑ *His mother had strong musical abilities.*

→ look at **disability**

able /eɪbᵊl/ (**abler** /eɪblər/, **ablest** /eɪblɪst/)

1 If you **are able to** do something, you have skills or qualities that make it possible for you to do it. ❑ *A 10-year-old should be able to prepare a simple meal.* ❑ *The company says they're able to keep prices low.*

2 If you **are able to** do something, you have enough freedom, power, time, or money to do it. ❑ *Are you able to help me?* ❑ *If I get this job, I'll be able to buy a new car.*

→ look at **disability**

ab|nor|mal /æbnɔrmᵊl/ **ADJECTIVE** Someone or something that is **abnormal** is unusual, especially in a way that is a problem. ❑ *She has an abnormal heartbeat.*

aboard /əbɔrd/

1 **PREPOSITION** If you are **aboard** a ship or plane, you are on it or in it. ❑ *He invited us aboard his boat.*

2 **ADVERB** **Aboard** is also an adverb. ❑ *It took two hours to get all the people aboard.*

abol|ish /əbɒlɪʃ/ (**abolishes, abolishing, abolished**) **VERB** If someone in authority **abolishes** a system or practice, they officially end it. ❑ *The committee voted Thursday to abolish the death penalty.*

● **abo|li|tion** /æbəlɪʃᵊn/ **NONCOUNT NOUN** ❑ *I support the total abolition of slavery.*

abo|li|tion|ist /æbəlɪʃᵊnɪst/ (**abolitionists**) **NOUN** **SOCIAL STUDIES** An **abolitionist** is someone who tries to stop people from being allowed to buy and sell slaves (= servants who are forced to work for someone). ❑ *He was a national leader in the abolitionist movement.*

about /əbaʊt/

1 **PREPOSITION** You use **about** to introduce a particular subject. ❑ *She knew a lot about food.* ❑ *He never complains about his wife.*

2 **ADVERB** **About** is used in front of a number to show that the number is not exact. ❑ *The child was about eight years old.* ❑ *It got dark at about six o'clock.*

3 If you are **about to** do something, you are going to do it very soon. ❑ *I think he's about to leave.*

above /əbʌv/

1 **PREPOSITION** If one thing is **above** another, it is over it or higher than it. ❑ *He lifted his hands above his head.* ❑ *Their apartment was above a clothing store.*

2 **PREPOSITION** If an amount or measurement is **above** a particular level, it is greater than that level. ❑ *The temperature rose to just above 40 degrees.*

3 **PREPOSITION** If someone is **above** you, they are in a higher position than you at work. ❑ *You have people above you making decisions.*

→ look at **location**

abroad /əbrɔd/ **ADVERB** If you go **abroad**, you go to a foreign country. ❑ *Many students go abroad to work for the summer.*

ab|rupt /əbrʌpt/ **ADJECTIVE** An **abrupt** change or action is very sudden, often in a way that is unpleasant. ❑ *His career came to an abrupt end in 1998.* ● **ab|rupt|ly** **ADVERB** ❑ *The horses stopped abruptly.*

ab|sence /æbs³ns/ (absences) **NOUN** Someone's **absence** from a place is the fact that they are not there. ❑ *Her absence from work is becoming a problem.*

ab|sent /æbs³nt/ **ADJECTIVE** If someone or something is **absent from** a place, they are not there. ❑ *Anna was absent from the meeting.*

absent-minded **ADJECTIVE** Someone who is **absent-minded** forgets things or does not pay attention to what they are doing. ❑ *She looked around the room in an absent-minded dream.* ● **absent-mindedly** **ADVERB** ❑ *Elliot absent-mindedly scratched his head.*

ab|so|lute /æbsəlut/ **ADJECTIVE** **Absolute** means total and complete. ❑ *No one knows anything with absolute certainty.*

ab|so|lute|ly /æbsəlutli/

1 **ADVERB** **Absolutely** means totally and completely. ❑ *Joan is absolutely right.* ❑ *I absolutely refuse to get married.*

2 **ADVERB** **Absolutely** is a way of saying yes or of agreeing with someone strongly. ❑ *"Do you think I should call him?"—"Absolutely."*

ab|sorb /əbsɔrb, -zɔrb/ (absorbs, absorbing, absorbed) **VERB** SCIENCE To **absorb** a substance means to take it in. ❑ *Cook the rice until it absorbs the water.* ● **ab|sorb|ent** /əbsɔrbənt, -zɔrb-/ **ADJECTIVE** ❑ *A real sponge is softer and more absorbent.*

→ look at **greenhouse effect**

ab|sorb|ing /əbsɔrbɪŋ, -zɔrb-/ **ADJECTIVE** An **absorbing** activity is very interesting and uses all your attention and energy. ❑ *This is a very absorbing game.*

ab|stract /æbstrækt/

1 **ADJECTIVE** **Abstract** thoughts are based on general ideas rather than on real things. ❑ *The students are intelligent and good at abstract thought.*

2 **ADJECTIVE** ARTS **Abstract** art uses shapes and patterns rather than showing people or things. ❑ *...Mondrian's abstract paintings, with their heavy black lines and bright blocks of color.*

abuse (abuses, abusing, abused)

> **PRONUNCIATION HELP**
> Pronounce the noun /əbyus/. Pronounce the verb /əbyuz/.

1 **NONCOUNT NOUN** **Abuse** of someone or something is cruel treatment of them. ❑ *There were reports of child abuse.*

2 **NONCOUNT NOUN** **Abuse** is very rude things that people say when they are angry. ❑ *I shouted abuse as the car drove away.*

3 **NOUN** **Abuse** of something is the use of it in a wrong way or for a bad purpose. ❑ *He wrote about his experience of drug abuse.*

4 **VERB** If someone **is abused**, they are treated cruelly. ❑ *The film is about her daughter, who was abused as a child.*

aca|dem|ic /ækədɛmɪk/ **ADJECTIVE** **Academic** means relating to the work done in schools, colleges, and universities. ❑ *Their academic standards are high.*

→ look at **school**

acad|emy /əkædəmi/ (academies) **NOUN** **Academy** is sometimes used in the names of schools. ❑ *He is an English teacher at the Seattle Academy for Arts and Sciences.*

ac|cel|er|ate /æksɛləreɪt/ (**accelerates,
accelerating, accelerated**)

1 **VERB** If something **accelerates**, it gets
faster. ❑ *Her heartbeat accelerated when she saw
him in the crowd.*

2 **VERB** When a moving vehicle
accelerates, it goes faster. ❑ *Suddenly the car
accelerated.*

ac|cent /æksɛnt/ (**accents**)

1 **NOUN** Someone who speaks with a
particular **accent** pronounces words in a
way that shows where they come from. ❑ *He
had a slight Southern accent.*

2 **NOUN** LANGUAGE ARTS An **accent** is a mark
written above a letter to show how it is
pronounced. ❑ *The word "café" has an accent on
the "e".*

ac|cept /æksɛpt/ (**accepts, accepting,
accepted**)

1 **VERB** If you **accept** something that
someone offers you, you say yes to it or agree
to take it. ❑ *She accepted his offer of marriage.*
❑ *Doctors may not accept gifts.* ● **ac|cept|ance**
/æksɛptəns/ **NONCOUNT NOUN** ❑ *We listened to
his acceptance speech for the Nobel Peace Prize.*

2 **VERB** If you **accept** an unpleasant fact or
situation, you recognize that it cannot be
changed. ❑ *People often accept noise as part of
city life.*

3 **VERB** If you **accept** responsibility for
something, you recognize that you are
responsible for it. ❑ *The company accepted
responsibility for the damage.*

ac|cept|able /æksɛptəbᵊl/

1 **ADJECTIVE** **Acceptable** activities and
situations are ones that most people
consider to be normal. ❑ *Asking people for
money is not acceptable behavior.* ● **ac|cept|ably**
ADVERB ❑ *They try to teach children to behave
acceptably.*

2 **ADJECTIVE** If something is **acceptable**, it
is good enough. ❑ *There was one restaurant that
looked acceptable.*

ac|cess /æksɛs/ (**accesses, accessing,
accessed**)

1 **NONCOUNT NOUN** If you have **access to** a
building or other place, you are allowed to
go into it. ❑ *The general public does not have
access to the White House.*

2 **NONCOUNT NOUN** If you have **access to**
information or equipment, you are allowed
to see it or use it. ❑ *Patients have access to their
medical records.*

3 **VERB** If you **access** information on a
computer, you find it. ❑ *Parents can see which
sites their children have accessed.*
→ look at **Internet**

ac|ces|sible /æksɛsɪbᵊl/ **ADJECTIVE** If a place
or building is **accessible** it is easy for people
to reach it or enter it. ❑ *The city center is easily
accessible to the general public.* ❑ *Most of the
bedrooms and bathrooms are accessible for
wheelchairs.*
→ look at **disability**

ac|ces|so|ry /æksɛsəri/ (**accessories**) **NOUN**
Accessories are small things such as belts
and scarves that you wear with your clothes.
❑ *We shopped for handbags, scarves and other
accessories.*

ac|ci|dent /æksɪdənt/ (**accidents**)

1 **NOUN** An **accident** happens when a
vehicle hits something and causes injury
or damage.
❑ *There were
14 highway
accidents
yesterday
afternoon.*

2 **NOUN** If
someone has
an **accident**, something bad happens to
them by chance, sometimes causing injury
or death. ❑ *She died in a car accident.*

3 If something happens **by accident**, it
happens by chance. ❑ *We met by accident at
a party in Los Angeles.*
→ look at **car**

Word Partners	Use **accident** with:
N.	**car** accident **1**
ADJ.	**bad** accident **1** **2**
V.	**cause an** accident, **killed in the** accident, **report an** accident **1** **2**
PREP.	**by** accident **3**

ac|ci|den|tal /æksɪdɛntᵊl/ **ADJECTIVE** An
accidental event happens by chance or as
the result of an accident. ❑ *He witnessed the
accidental death of his younger brother.*
● **ac|ci|den|tal|ly** /æksɪdɛntli/ **ADVERB**
❑ *They accidentally removed the names from the
computer.*

ac|com|mo|da|tion /əkɒmədeɪʃᵊn/
(**accommodations**) **NOUN** **Accommodations**
are buildings or rooms where people live or
stay. ❑ *Some people paid extra for luxury
accommodations.*

A

ac|com|pa|ny /əkʌmpəni/ (**accompanies, accompanying, accompanied**)

1 **VERB** If you **accompany** someone, you go somewhere with them. [FORMAL] ❑ *Ken agreed to accompany me on a trip to Africa.*

2 **VERB** MUSIC If you **accompany** a singer or a musician, you play one part of a piece of music while they sing or play the main tune. ❑ *Her singing teacher accompanied her on the piano.*

ac|com|plish /əkɒmplɪʃ/ (**accomplishes, accomplishing, accomplished**) **VERB** If you **accomplish** something, you succeed in doing it. ❑ *If we all work together, I think we can accomplish our goal.*

ac|com|plish|ment /əkɒmplɪʃmənt/ (**accomplishments**) **NOUN** An **accomplishment** is something unusual or special that someone has made or achieved. ❑ *This book is an amazing accomplishment.*

ac|cor|di|on /əkɔːrdiən/ (**accordions**) **NOUN** MUSIC An **accordion** is a musical instrument in the shape of a box, which you hold in your hands. You play it by pressing keys and buttons on the side, while moving the two ends in and out.

ac|cord|ing to

1 If something is true **according to** a particular person, that is where the information comes from. ❑ *They drove away in a white van, according to police reports.*

2 If something is done **according to** a particular set of rules, these rules say how it should be done. ❑ *They played the game according to the British rules.*

3 If something happens **according to plan**, it happens in exactly the way that it was intended to happen. ❑ *Everything is going according to plan.*

ac|count /əkaʊnt/ (**accounts, accounting, accounted**)

1 **NOUN** If you have an **account** with a bank, you leave your money there and take some out when you need it. ❑ *I have $3,000 in my bank account.*

2 **NOUN** **Accounts** are records of all the money that a person or business receives and spends. ❑ *He kept detailed accounts of all the money he spent.*

3 **NOUN** TECHNOLOGY An **account** is an arrangement you have with a company to use a service they provide. ❑ *... an email account.*

4 **NOUN** An **account** is a report of something that has happened. ❑ *He gave a detailed account of the events.*

→ look at **email**

▶ **account for** If you can **account for** something, you can explain it or give the reason for it. ❑ *How do you account for these differences?*

Word Partners	Use **account** with:
N.	account **balance**, **bank** account, account **number**, **savings** account **1**
V.	**open an** account **1**
	access your account **1** **3**

Word Builder	accountant

ant ≈ **someone who does**

account + ant = account**ant**
assist + ant = assist**ant**
attend + ant = attend**ant**
consult + ant = consult**ant**
contest + ant = contest**ant**

ac|count|ant /əkaʊntənt/ (**accountants**) **NOUN** An **accountant** is a person whose job is to keep financial accounts.

ac|cu|rate /ækyərɪt/

1 **ADJECTIVE** **Accurate** information is correct. ❑ *I can't give an accurate description of the man because it was too dark.* ● **ac|cu|ra|cy** **NONCOUNT NOUN** ❑ *Don't trust the accuracy of weather reports.* ● **ac|cu|rate|ly** **ADVERB** ❑ *He described it quite accurately.*

2 **ADJECTIVE** A person or machine that is **accurate** is able to work without making a mistake. ❑ *The car's steering is accurate, and the brakes are powerful.* ● **ac|cu|ra|cy** **NONCOUNT NOUN** ❑ *He questioned the accuracy of the story.* ● **ac|cu|rate|ly** **ADVERB** ❑ *He hit the golf ball powerfully and accurately.*

ac|cuse /əkyuz/ (**accuses, accusing, accused**) **VERB** If you **accuse** someone **of** something, you say that they did something wrong or dishonest. ❑ *They accused her of lying.*

ace /eɪs/ (**aces**)

1 **NOUN** SPORTS If you describe a sports player as an **ace**, you mean that they are very good at what they do. ❑ *...former tennis ace John McEnroe.*

2 **ADJECTIVE** **Ace** is also an adjective. ❑ *...ace film producer Lawrence Woolsey.*

3 **NOUN** SPORTS In tennis, an **ace** is a serve that is so fast that the other player cannot return the ball. ❑ *Federer served three aces in the final set of the tennis match.*

ache /eɪk/ (**aches, aching, ached**)

1 **VERB** If you **ache** or a part of your body **aches**, you feel a steady pain. ❏ *Her head was hurting and she ached all over (= in every part of her body).* ❏ *My leg still aches when I stand for a long time.*

2 **NOUN** An **ache** is a steady pain in a part of your body. ❏ *A hot bath will take away all your aches and pains.*

→ look at **sick**

achieve /ətʃiv/ (**achieves, achieving, achieved**) **VERB** If you **achieve** something, you succeed in doing it, usually after a lot of effort. ❏ *He worked hard to achieve his goals.*

achieve|ment /ətʃivmənt/ (**achievements**) **NOUN** An **achievement** is something that you have succeeded in doing, especially after a lot of effort. ❏ *Being chosen for the team was a great achievement.*

acid /æsɪd/ (**acids**) **NOUN** **SCIENCE** An **acid** is a chemical, usually a liquid, that can burn your skin and cause damage to other substances. ❏ *As you can see, the acid damaged the metal bowl.*

acid rain **NONCOUNT NOUN** Acid **rain** is rain that contains acid that can harm the environment. The acid comes from pollution in the air.

→ look at **pollution**

ac|knowl|edge /æknɒlɪdʒ/ (**acknowledges, acknowledging, acknowledged**) **VERB** If you **acknowledge** a fact or a situation, you agree that it is true or that it exists. [FORMAL] ❏ *He acknowledged that he was wrong.* ❏ *At last, the government has acknowledged the problem.*

ac|knowl|edg|ment /æknɒlɪdʒmənt/ (**acknowledgments**) also **acknowledgement** **PLURAL NOUN** **LANGUAGE ARTS** The **acknowledgments** in a book are the names of all the people who helped the writer. ❏ *There are two pages of acknowledgments at the beginning of the book.*

ac|quaint|ance /əkweɪntəns/ (**acquaintances**) **NOUN** An **acquaintance** is someone you have met, but don't know well. ❏ *He spoke to the owner, who was an old acquaintance of his.*

ac|quire /əkwaɪər/ (**acquires, acquiring, acquired**)

1 **VERB** If you **acquire** something, you obtain it. [FORMAL] ❏ *The club wants to acquire new sports equipment.*

2 **VERB** If you **acquire** a skill or a habit, you learn it or develop it. ❏ *Students on this program will acquire a wide range of skills.*

acre /eɪkər/ (**acres**) **NOUN** An **acre** is a unit for measuring an area of land. ❏ *He rented three acres of land.*

across /əkrɔs/

1 **PREPOSITION** If someone or something goes **across** a place, they go from one side of it to the other. ❏ *She walked across the floor and sat down.* ❏ *He watched Karl run across the street.*

2 **ADVERB** Across is also an adverb. ❏ *Richard stood up and walked across to the window.*

3 **PREPOSITION** If something is **across** something else, it goes from one side of it to the other. ❏ *The bridge across the river was closed.* ❏ *He wrote his name across the check.*

acryl|ic /əkrɪlɪk/ (**acrylics**)

1 **ADJECTIVE** **ARTS** Acrylic paint is a type of artist's paint that dries very quickly. ❏ *Most people prefer acrylic paint because it dries faster.*

2 **PLURAL NOUN** **ARTS** Acrylics are acrylic paints. ❏ *This book is a great introduction to painting with acrylics.*

act /ækt/ (**acts, acting, acted**)

1 **VERB** When you **act**, you do something for a particular purpose. ❏ *The police acted to stop the fight.*

2 **VERB** If someone **acts** in a particular way, they behave in that way. ❏ *The youths were acting suspiciously.* ❏ *He acts as if I'm not there.*

3 **VERB** **ARTS** If you **act** in a play or film, you have a part in it. ❏ *He acted in many films, including "Reds."*

4 **NOUN** An **act** is a single thing that someone does. [FORMAL] ❏ *As a child I loved the act of writing.*

5 **NOUN** An Act is a law passed by the government. ❏ *The organization was set up by an Act of Congress in 1998.*

6 **NOUN** An **act** in a play is one of the main parts it is divided into. ❏ *Act two has a really funny scene.*

act|ing /æktɪŋ/ **NONCOUNT NOUN** **ARTS** **Acting** is the activity or profession of performing in plays or films. ❏ *I'd like to do some acting some day.*

ac|tion /ækʃⁿn/ (**actions**)

1 **NONCOUNT NOUN** Action is doing something for a particular purpose. ❏ *The government is taking emergency action.*

2 **NOUN** An **action** is something that you do

on a particular occasion. ❑ *Peter could not explain his actions.*

ac|tive /ǽktɪv/

1 **ADJECTIVE** Someone who is **active** moves around a lot. ❑ *We've got three very active little kids.*

2 **NOUN** LANGUAGE ARTS In grammar, **the active** is the form of a verb that you use to show that the subject performs the action. For example, in "I saw him," the verb **see** is in the active. Compare with **passive**.
→ look at **disability**

ac|tiv|ity /æktɪ́vɪti/ (**activities**)

1 **NONCOUNT NOUN** Activity is when people do a lot of things. ❑ *Children are supposed to get physical activity every day.*

2 **NOUN** An **activity** is something that you spend time doing. ❑ *There were no activities for small children.*

ac|tor /ǽktər/ (**actors**) **NOUN** ARTS An **actor** is someone whose job is acting in plays or movies. ❑ *His father was an actor.*
→ look at **movie, performance**

ac|tress /ǽktrɪs/ (**actresses**) **NOUN** ARTS An **actress** is a woman whose job is acting in plays or movies. ❑ *She's a really good actress.*
→ look at **performance**

ac|tual /ǽktʃuəl/ **ADJECTIVE** You use **actual** to show that you are talking about something real, exact, or genuine. ❑ *The stories in this book are based on actual people.*

ac|tu|al|ly /ǽktʃuəli/ **ADVERB** You use **actually** to show that something really is true. ❑ *The judge actually fell asleep for a few minutes.*

acute /əkyút/ **ADJECTIVE** An **acute** situation or feeling is very severe or serious. ❑ *He was in acute pain.*

acute accent (**acute accents**) **NOUN** LANGUAGE ARTS An **acute** accent is a symbol that you put over vowels (= the letters a, e, i, o, and u) in some languages to show how to pronounce that vowel. For example, there is an acute accent over the letter "e" in the French word "café".

acute angle /əkyút ǽŋgəl/ (**acute angles**) **NOUN** MATH An **acute angle** is an angle of less than 90˚.
→ look at **geometry**

ad /ǽd/ (**ads**) **NOUN** An **ad** is an advertisement. [INFORMAL] ❑ *It costs $175.00 to place an ad in the newspaper for 30 days.*

AD /éɪ díː/ also **A.D.** SOCIAL STUDIES You use **AD** in dates to show the number of years that have passed since the year in which Jesus Christ was born. Compare with **BC**. ❑ *The church was built in 600 AD.*

a|dapt /ədǽpt/ (**adapts, adapting, adapted**)

1 **VERB** If you **adapt to** a new situation, you change your ideas or behavior in order to deal with it. ❑ *The world will be different in the future, and we will have to adapt to the change.*

2 **VERB** If you **adapt** something, you change it so that you can use it in a different way. ❑ *They adapted the library for use as an office.*

adapt|able /ədǽptəbəl/ **ADJECTIVE** Someone or something that is **adaptable** is able to deal with new situations. ❑ *Dogs and cats are easily adaptable to new homes.*

add /ǽd/ (**adds, adding, added**)

1 **VERB** If you **add** one thing **to** another, you put it with the other thing. ❑ *Add the grated cheese to the sauce.*

2 **VERB** MATH If you **add** numbers or amounts **together**, you calculate their total. ❑ *Add all the numbers together, and divide by three.*

3 **VERB** If you **add** something when you are speaking, you say something more. ❑ *"He's very angry," Mr. Smith added.*
→ look at **fraction, math**

▸ **add up** MATH If you **add up** numbers or amounts, you calculate their total. ❑ *Add up the number of hours you spent on the task.*

ad|dict /ǽdɪkt/ (**addicts**)

1 **NOUN** An **addict** is someone who cannot stop doing something harmful or dangerous, such as using drugs. ❑ *His girlfriend is a former drug addict.*

2 **NOUN** You can say that someone is an **addict** when they like a particular activity very much. ❑ *She is a TV addict.*

ad|dict|ed /ədɪ́ktɪd/ **ADJECTIVE** Someone who is **addicted to** a harmful drug cannot stop taking it. ❑ *Many of the women are addicted to heroin.*

ad|dic|tion /ədɪ́kʃən/ (**addictions**)

1 **NOUN** Addiction is the condition of not being able to stop taking drugs, alcohol, or some other substance. ❑ *She helped him fight his drug addiction.*

2 **NOUN** An **addiction** is a strong need to do a particular activity for as much time as possible. ❑ *...children's addiction to computer games.*

ad|di|tion /ədɪʃ°n/

1 **NONCOUNT NOUN** MATH Addition is the process of calculating the total of two or more numbers. ❏ *She can count to 100, and do simple addition problems.*

2 You use **in addition** when you want to mention another thing relating to the subject you are discussing. ❏ *In addition to meals, drinks will be provided.*

→ look at **math**

ad|dress (**addresses, addressing, addressed**)

> **PRONUNCIATION HELP**
> Pronounce the noun /ədrɛs/ or /ædrɛs/.
> Pronounce the verb /ədrɛs/.

1 **NOUN** Your **address** is the number of the building, the name of the street, and the town or city and state where you live or work. ❏ *The address is 2025 M Street NW, Washington, DC 20036.*

2 **NOUN** TECHNOLOGY The **address** of a website is its location on the Internet, for example, http://www.heinle.com. ❏ *Our website address is at the bottom of this page.*

3 **VERB** If something **is addressed to** you, your name and address have been written on it. ❏ *One of the letters was addressed to her.*

4 **VERB** If you **address** a group of people, you speak to them formally. ❏ *He addressed the crowd of 17,000 people.*

5 **NOUN** **Address** is also a noun. ❏ *Judge Richardson began his address to the jury.*

→ look at **email**

> **Word Partners**   Use **address** with:
> N.   **name and** address, **street** address **1**
> ADJ.   **permanent** address **1**

ad|dress book (**address books**)

1 **NOUN** An **address book** is a book in which you write people's names and addresses.

2 **NOUN** TECHNOLOGY An **address book** is a computer program that you use to record people's email addresses and telephone numbers.

ad|equate /ædɪkwɪt/ **ADJECTIVE** If something is **adequate**, there is enough of it or it is good enough. ❏ *One in four people worldwide do not have adequate homes.*

ad|he|sive /ædhiːsɪv/ (**adhesives**) **NOUN** An **adhesive** is a substance used for making things stick together. ❏ *Attach the mirror to the wall with a strong adhesive.*

ad|jec|tive /ædʒɪktɪv/ (**adjectives**) **NOUN**

LANGUAGE ARTS An **adjective** is a word such as "big," or "beautiful" that describes a person or thing. Adjectives usually come before nouns or after verbs like "be" or "feel".

→ look at **grammar**

ad|just /ədʒʌst/ (**adjusts, adjusting, adjusted**) **VERB** If you **adjust** something, you make a small change to it. ❏ *The company adjusts gas prices once a year.* ❏ *You can adjust the height of the table.*

ad|min|is|tra|tion /ædmɪnɪstreɪʃ°n/ (**administrations**)

1 **NONCOUNT NOUN** Administration is the job of managing a business or organization. ❏ *A private company took over the administration of the local jail.*

2 **NOUN** The **administration** is the government of a country. ❏ *Three officials in the Bush administration have resigned.*

ad|min|is|tra|tive /ædmɪnɪstreɪtɪv/ **ADJECTIVE** Administrative work involves managing a business or organization. ❏ *Administrative costs were high.*

ad|min|is|tra|tor /ædmɪnɪstreɪtər/ (**administrators**) **NOUN** An **administrator** is a person whose job is to help manage a business or organization. ❏ *Students and parents met with school administrators to discuss the problem.*

ad|mi|ra|tion /ædmɪreɪʃ°n/ **NONCOUNT NOUN** Admiration is a strong feeling of liking and respect. ❏ *I have great admiration for him.*

ad|mire /ədmaɪər/ (**admires, admiring, admired**) **VERB** If you **admire** someone or something, you like and respect them. ❏ *I admired her when I first met her.* ● **ad|mir|er** (**admirers**) **NOUN** ❏ *He was an admirer of her paintings.*

ad|mis|sion /ædmɪʃ°n/ (**admissions**)

1 **NONCOUNT NOUN** Admission is permission given to a person to enter a place. ❏ *One man was refused admission to the restaurant.*

2 **NOUN** An **admission** is when you admit that you have done something wrong. ❏ *By his own admission, he is not playing well.*

3 **NONCOUNT NOUN** Admission at a park, museum, or other place is the amount of money that you pay to enter it. ❏ *Gates open at 10:30 a.m. and admission is free.*

ad|mit /ædmɪt/ (admits, admitting, admitted)

1 **VERB** If you **admit** that you have done something wrong, you agree that you did it. ❑ *I am willing to admit that I made a mistake.*

2 **VERB** If someone **is admitted to** a place or organization, they are allowed to enter it or join it. ❑ *She was admitted to law school.* ❑ *Security officers refused to admit him.*

ado|les|cent /ædəlɛsᵊnt/ (adolescents)

1 **ADJECTIVE** **Adolescent** describes young people who are no longer children but who have not yet become adults. ❑ *Her music is popular with adolescent girls.*

2 **NOUN** An **adolescent** is an adolescent boy or girl. ❑ *Adolescents don't like being treated like children.* ● **ado|les|cence** /ædəlɛsᵊns/ **NONCOUNT NOUN** ❑ *Adolescence is often a difficult period for young people.*

→ look at **age**

adopt /ədɒpt/ (adopts, adopting, adopted)

1 **VERB** If you **adopt** a new attitude, plan, or way of behaving, you begin to have it. ❑ *You need to adopt a more positive attitude.*

2 **VERB** If you **adopt** someone else's child, you take it into your own family and make it legally your son or daughter. ❑ *There are hundreds of people who want to adopt a child.* ● **adop|tion** **NONCOUNT NOUN** ❑ *They gave their babies up for adoption.*

adore /ədɔr/ (adores, adoring, adored)

1 **VERB** If you **adore** someone, you feel strong love and admiration for them. ❑ *She adored her parents and would do anything to please them.*

2 **VERB** If you **adore** something, you like it very much. [INFORMAL] ❑ *Robyn adores university life.*

adult /ədʌlt/ (adults)

1 **NOUN** An **adult** is a fully grown person or animal. ❑ *Tickets cost $20 for adults and $10 for children.*

2 **ADJECTIVE** **Adult** is also an adjective. ❑ *I am the mother of two adult sons.*

→ look at **age**

ad|vance /ædvæns/ (advances, advancing, advanced)

1 **VERB** To **advance** means to move forward, often in order to attack someone. ❑ *Soldiers are advancing toward the capital.*

2 **VERB** To **advance** means to make progress, especially in your knowledge of something. ❑ *Science has advanced greatly in the last 100 years.*

3 **NOUN** An **advance** is a movement forward, usually as part of a military operation. ❑ *Hitler's army began its advance on Moscow in June 1941.*

4 **NOUN** An **advance** in a subject or activity is progress in understanding it. ❑ *There have been many advances in medicine and public health.*

5 If you do something **in advance**, you do it before a particular date or event. ❑ *The theater sells tickets in advance.*

ad|vanced /ædvænst/ **ADJECTIVE** Something that is **advanced** is modern. ❑ *This is one of the most advanced phones available.*

ad|van|tage /ædvæntɪdʒ/ (advantages)

1 **NOUN** An **advantage** is something that puts you in a better position than others. ❑ *Being small gives our company an advantage.*

2 **NOUN** An **advantage** is a way in which one thing is better than another. ❑ *The advantage of home-grown vegetables is their great flavor.*

3 If you **take advantage of** something, you make good use of it while you can. ❑ *People are taking advantage of lower prices.*

4 If someone **takes advantage of** you, they unfairly get what they want from you, especially when you are trying to be kind to them. ❑ *She took advantage of him—borrowing money and not paying it back.*

ad|ven|ture /ædvɛntʃər/ (adventures)

1 **NOUN** An **adventure** is an experience that is unusual, exciting, and perhaps dangerous. ❑ *I'm planning a new adventure in Alaska.*

2 **NOUN** An **adventure** story is a story about exciting, unusual, and dangerous events.

ad|verb /ædvɜrb/ (adverbs) **NOUN** LANGUAGE ARTS An **adverb** is a word such as "slowly," "now," "very," or "happily" that adds information about an action, event, or situation.

ad|ver|tise /ædvərtaɪz/ (advertises, advertising, advertised) **VERB** If you **advertise** something, you tell people about it in newspapers, on television, on signs, or on the Internet. ❑ *They are advertising houses for sale.* ❑ *We advertise on radio stations.*

ad|ver|tise|ment /ædvərtaɪzmənt/ (advertisements) **NOUN** An **advertisement** is information that tells you about a product, an event, or a job. [FORMAL] ❑ *They* saw an advertisement for a job on a farm. ❑ ...an advertisement for a new movie.

ad|ver|tis|ing /ˈædvərtaɪzɪŋ/ **NONCOUNT NOUN** Advertising is the business of creating information that tells people about a product or an event. ❑ I work in advertising.

ad|vice /ædvaɪs/ **NONCOUNT NOUN** If you give someone **advice**, you tell them what you think they should do. ❑ Take my advice and stay away from him! ❑ I'd like to ask you for some advice.

Word Partners	Use **advice** with:
V.	**ask for** advice, **give** advice, **need some** advice, **take** advice
ADJ.	**bad** advice, **expert** advice, **good** advice

ad|vise /ædvaɪz/ (**advises, advising, advised**) **VERB** If you **advise** someone **to** do something, you tell them what you think they should do. ❑ Passengers are advised to check in two hours before their flight.

ad|vis|er /ædvaɪzər/ (**advisers**) also **advisor** **NOUN** An **adviser** is an expert whose job is to give advice. ❑ Your college adviser will be happy to help you choose your classes.

aero|bics /ɛəroʊbɪks/ **NONCOUNT NOUN** SPORTS **Aerobics** is a form of exercise that makes your heart and lungs stronger. ❑ I'd like to join an aerobics class to improve my fitness. → look at **fitness**

aero|sol /ɛərəsɔl/ (**aerosols**) **NOUN** An **aerosol** is a metal container with liquid in it. When you press a button, the liquid comes out strongly in a lot of very small drops. ❑ ...an aerosol spray can.

aes|thet|ic /ɛsθɛtɪk/ also **esthetic** **ADJECTIVE** ARTS **Aesthetic** qualities relate to beauty and art. ❑ In this restaurant, eating is a truly aesthetic experience. ● **aes|theti|cal|ly** /ɛsθɛtɪkli/ **ADVERB** ❑ We want our product to be aesthetically pleasing.

af|fair /əfɛər/ (**affairs**)
1 NOUN An **affair** is an event or a group of related events. ❑ She has handled the whole affair badly.
2 NOUN If two people who are not married to each other have an **affair**, they have a sexual relationship. ❑ He was having an affair with the woman next door.
3 PLURAL NOUN Your **affairs** are things in your life that you consider to be private. ❑ Why are we so interested in the private affairs of famous people?

af|fect /əfɛkt/ (**affects, affecting, affected**) **VERB** If something **affects** a person or thing, it causes them to change in some way. ❑ This problem affects all of us. ❑ This area was badly affected by the earthquake.
→ look at **climate**

af|fec|tion /əfɛkʃən/ **NONCOUNT NOUN** If you feel **affection** for someone, you love or like them a lot. ❑ She thought of him with affection.

af|fec|tion|ate /əfɛkʃənɪt/ **ADJECTIVE** If you are **affectionate**, you show that you like someone very much. ❑ She's very affectionate, and she's always hugging the kids.
● **af|fec|tion|ate|ly** **ADVERB** ❑ He looked affectionately at his niece.

af|ford /əfɔrd/ (**affords, affording, afforded**) **VERB** If you **can afford** something, you have enough money to pay for it. ❑ Some people can't even afford a new refrigerator.

Word Partners	Use **afford** with:
ADJ.	**able to** afford, **unable to** afford
V.	afford **to buy**, **can** afford, **cannot** afford, afford **to pay**

afloat /əfloʊt/ **ADVERB** Someone or something that is **afloat** is floating. ❑ They tried to keep the ship afloat.

afraid /əfreɪd/
1 ADJECTIVE If you are **afraid** that something unpleasant will happen, you are worried that it may happen. ❑ I was afraid that nobody would believe me.
2 ADJECTIVE If you are **afraid of** someone or **afraid to** do something, you are frightened because you think that something very unpleasant is going to happen to you. ❑ I was afraid of the other boys.

af|ter /æftər/
1 PREPOSITION If something happens **after** a particular date or event, it happens later than that date or event. ❑ He died after a long illness. ❑ After breakfast Amy took a taxi to the station.
2 CONJUNCTION After is also a conjunction. ❑ The phone rang two seconds after we arrived.
3 PREPOSITION If you go **after** someone, you follow or chase them. ❑ Why don't you go after him? He's your son.
4 PREPOSITION After is used when you are telling the time. If it is **ten after six**, for example, the time is ten minutes past six.

after|noon /æftərnun/ (**afternoons**) **NOUN** The **afternoon** is the part of each day that

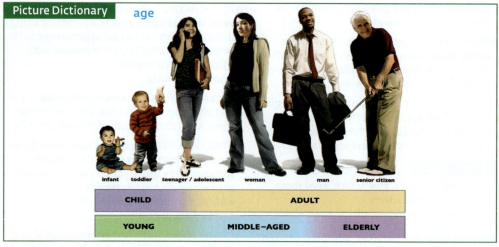

Picture Dictionary   age

infant   toddler   teenager / adolescent   woman   man   senior citizen

CHILD   ADULT

YOUNG   MIDDLE–AGED   ELDERLY

begins at lunchtime and ends at about six o'clock. ❑ *He's arriving in the afternoon.* ❑ *He stayed in his room all afternoon.*
→ look at **day, time**

after|ward /ˈæftərwərd/ also **afterwards**
ADVERB If something happens **afterward**, it happens after a particular event or time that you have already mentioned. ❑ *Shortly afterward, the police arrived.*

again /əˈgɛn, əˈgeɪn/
1 ADVERB You use **again** to say that something happens another time. ❑ *He kissed her again.* ❑ *Again there was a short silence.*
2 ADVERB You use **again** to say that something is now in the same state it was in before. ❑ *He opened his case, took out a folder, then closed it again.*

against /əˈgɛnst, əˈgeɪnst/
1 PREPOSITION If one thing is leaning or pressing **against** another thing, it is touching it. ❑ *She leaned against him.* ❑ *The rain was beating against the window panes.*
2 PREPOSITION If you are **against** something, you think it is wrong or bad. ❑ *He was against the war.*
3 ADVERB **Against** is also an adverb. ❑ *66 people voted in favor of the decision and 34 voted against.*
4 PREPOSITION If you compete **against** someone, you try to beat them. ❑ *This is the first of two games against Denver.*
5 PREPOSITION If you do something **against** someone or something, you try to harm them. ❑ *Security forces are still using violence against opponents of the government.*
6 PREPOSITION If you do something **against**

someone's wishes or advice, you do not obey them. ❑ *She left the hospital against the doctors' advice.*
7 PREPOSITION If something is **against** the law or **against** the rules, there is a law or a rule that says you must not do that thing. ❑ *It is against the law to help other people to kill themselves.*

age /eɪdʒ/ (**ages, aging** or **ageing, aged**)
1 NOUN Your **age** is the number of years that you have lived. ❑ *Diana left school at the age of 16.* ❑ *They have two children: Julia, age 8, and Jackie, age 10.*
2 NONCOUNT NOUN **Age** is the state of being old. ❑ *He refuses to let age slow him down.*
3 VERB When someone **ages**, or when something **ages** them, they seem much older. ❑ *Worry has aged him.*
4 NOUN An **age** is a period in history. ❑ *...the age of silent films.*
→ look at Picture Dictionary: **age**

agen|cy /eɪdʒənsi/ (**agencies**) **NOUN** An **agency** is a business that provides a service. ❑ *I work in an advertising agency.*

agen|da /əˈdʒɛndə/ (**agendas**)
1 NOUN Someone's **agenda** is a set of things they want to do. ❑ *They support the president's education agenda.*
2 NOUN An **agenda** is a list of things to be discussed at a meeting. ❑ *I'll add it to the agenda for Monday's meeting.*
→ look at **calendar**

agent /eɪdʒənt/ (**agents**)
1 NOUN An **agent** is a person whose job is to do business for another person or

company. ❑ *I am buying direct, not through an agent.*

2   **NOUN** An **agent** is a person who works for a particular government department. ❑ *He was arrested by FBI agents at his home in Hawaii.*

ago /əgoʊ/ **ADVERB** You use **ago** to talk about past time. For example, if something happened one year **ago**, one year has passed since it happened. ❑ *I got your letter a few days ago.*

ago|ny /ægəni/ **NONCOUNT NOUN** Agony is great physical or mental pain. ❑ *He tried to move, but screamed in agony.*

agree /əgri/ (**agrees, agreeing, agreed**)
1   **VERB** If people **agree with** each other about something, they have the same opinion about it. ❑ *I agree with you.* ❑ *Do we agree that there's a problem?*
2   **VERB** If you **agree to** do something, you say that you will do it. If you **agree to** a plan, you accept it. ❑ *He agreed to pay me for the drawings.*

agree|ment /əgrimənt/ (**agreements**)
NOUN An **agreement** is a plan or a decision that two or more people have made. ❑ *After two hours' discussion, they finally reached an agreement.*

ag|ri|cul|ture /ægrɪkʌltʃər/ **NONCOUNT NOUN** Agriculture is the business or activity of taking care of crops and farm animals.
● **ag|ri|cul|tur|al** /ægrɪkʌltʃərəl/ **ADJECTIVE** ❑ *...agricultural land.*

ah /ɑ/ **EXCLAMATION** People say **ah** to show that they understand something, or that they are surprised or pleased. ❑ *Ah, I see what you mean.*

aha /ɑhɑ/ **EXCLAMATION** People say **aha** to show that they are satisfied or surprised. ❑ *Aha! Here is the answer to my question.*

ahead /əhɛd/
1   **ADVERB** Someone or something that is **ahead** is in front of you. ❑ *The road ahead was blocked.*
2   **ADVERB** If you look **ahead**, you look directly in front of you. ❑ *Brett looked straight ahead.*
3   **ADVERB** If a person or a team is **ahead** in a competition, they are winning. ❑ *Dallas was ahead all through the game.*
4   **ADVERB** Ahead means in the future. ❑ *There are exciting times ahead.*

5   You say **go ahead**, when you are giving someone permission to do something. ❑ *"Can I borrow your dictionary?"—"Sure, go ahead."*
6   If someone is **ahead of** you, they are in front of you. ❑ *I saw a man thirty yards ahead of me.*
7   If something happens **ahead of** a planned time, it happens earlier than you expected. ❑ *We were a week ahead of schedule.*

aid /eɪd/ **NONCOUNT NOUN** Aid is money, equipment, or services that are given to people who do not have enough money. ❑ *They have promised billions of dollars in aid.*
→ look at **disability**

AIDS /eɪdz/ **NONCOUNT NOUN** AIDS is a disease that destroys the body's system of protection against other diseases. ❑ *Twenty-five percent of adults here have AIDS.*

aim /eɪm/ (**aims, aiming, aimed**)
1   **VERB** If you **aim for** something, you plan or hope to do it. ❑ *He is aiming for the 100 meter world record.*
2   **VERB** If you **aim** a weapon or object **at** something or someone, you point it toward them. ❑ *He was aiming the rifle at Wright.*
3   **NOUN** The **aim** of something that you do is the purpose of it. ❑ *The aim of the event is to bring parents and children together.*

ain't /eɪnt/ Ain't is short for "am not," "are not," "is not," "have not," and "has not." Many people think this use is wrong. [INFORMAL] ❑ *Well, it's obvious, ain't it?*

air /ɛər/
1   **NONCOUNT NOUN** SCIENCE Air is the mixture of gases all around us that we breathe. ❑ *Keith opened the window and felt the cold air on his face.*
2   **NONCOUNT NOUN** Air is used for talking about travel in aircraft. ❑ *Air travel will continue to grow at around 6% per year.*
3   **NONCOUNT NOUN** The **air** is the space around things or above the ground. ❑ *He was waving his arms in the air.*
→ look at **climate**

air-conditioned **ADJECTIVE** If a room or a vehicle is **air-conditioned**, a special piece of equipment makes the air in it colder. ❑ *All the rooms are air-conditioned, with private bathrooms and satellite TV.*

air-condition|ing **NONCOUNT NOUN** Air-conditioning is a system for keeping the air cool and dry in a building or vehicle.

air|craft /ˈɛɑrkræft/ (aircraft) **NOUN** An **aircraft** is an airplane or a helicopter. ❑ *The aircraft landed safely.*

air force (air forces) **NOUN** An **air force** is a military force that uses airplanes. ❑ *...the United States Air Force.*

air|line /ˈɛɑrlaɪn/ (airlines) **NOUN** An **airline** is a company that carries people or goods in airplanes. ❑ *Most low-cost airlines do not serve food.*

air|plane /ˈɛɑrpleɪn/ (airplanes) **NOUN** An **airplane** is a vehicle with wings that can fly through the air.
→ look at **transportation**

air pol|lu|tion **NONCOUNT NOUN** **SCIENCE** **Air pollution** is chemicals or other substances that have a harmful effect on the air. ❑ *We think that air pollution may be the cause of the illness.*

Word Builder   airport

port ≈ **carry**
    air + port = airport
    ex + port = export
    im + port = import
    port + able = portable
    trans + port = transport

---

air|port /ˈɛɑrpɔrt/ (airports) **NOUN** An **airport** is a place where airplanes come and go, with buildings and services for passengers. ❑ *Heathrow Airport is the busiest international airport in the world.*

aisle /aɪl/ (aisles) **NOUN** An **aisle** is a long narrow passage where people can walk between rows of seats or shelves. ❑ *You'll find the peas in the frozen food aisle.*

alarm /əˈlɑrm/ (alarms)
1 **NOUN** An **alarm** is a piece of equipment that warns you of danger, for example, by making a noise. ❑ *The fire alarm woke us at 5 a.m.*
2 **NOUN** An **alarm** is the same as an **alarm clock**. ❑ *Dad set the alarm for eight the next day.*

alarm clock (alarm clocks) **NOUN** An **alarm clock** is a clock that makes a noise to wake you up. ❑ *I set my alarm clock for 4:30.*

al|bum /ˈælbəm/ (albums)
1 **NOUN** An **album** is a collection of songs on a CD. ❑ *Oasis released their new album on July 1.*
2 **NOUN** An **album** is a book in which you keep things that you have collected. ❑ *Theresa showed me her photo album.*

al|co|hol /ˈælkəhɔl/
1 **NONCOUNT NOUN** Drinks that can make people drunk are sometimes called **alcohol**. ❑ *It is not legal to drink alcohol until you are 21.*
2 **NONCOUNT NOUN** **Alcohol** is a liquid that is found in drinks such as beer and wine. It is also used as a chemical for cleaning things. ❑ *Clean the wound with alcohol.*

al|co|hol|ic /ˌælkəˈhɔlɪk/ (alcoholics)
1 **NOUN** An **alcoholic** is someone who drinks alcohol too often and cannot stop. ❑ *He admitted that he is an alcoholic.*
2 **ADJECTIVE** **Alcoholic** drinks are drinks that contain alcohol. ❑ *Wine and beer are alcoholic drinks.*

alert /əˈlɜrt/ (alerts, alerting, alerted)
1 **ADJECTIVE** If you are **alert**, you are paying attention and are ready to deal with anything that might happen. ❑ *We all have to stay alert.*
2 **VERB** If you **alert** someone **to** a dangerous situation, you tell them about it. ❑ *He wanted to alert people to the danger.*

al|ge|bra /ˈældʒɪbrə/ **NONCOUNT NOUN** **MATH** **Algebra** is a type of mathematics in which letters and signs are used to represent numbers.
→ look at **math**

al|ien /ˈeɪliən/ (aliens)
1 **NOUN** An **alien** is someone who lives in a country where they are not a legal citizen. ❑ *He's an illegal alien.*
2 **NOUN** An **alien** is a creature from another planet. ❑ *Robin Williams plays the part of an alien from the planet "Ork."*

alike /əˈlaɪk/
1 **ADJECTIVE** If two or more things are **alike**, they are similar in some way. ❑ *They all look alike to me.*
2 **ADVERB** **Alike** means in a similar way. ❑ *They even dressed alike.*

alive /əˈlaɪv/ **ADJECTIVE** If people or animals are **alive**, they are not dead. ❑ *Is your father still alive?*

al|ka|li /ˈælkəlaɪ/ (alkalis) **NOUN** **SCIENCE** An **alkali** is a substance that is the opposite of an acid. It can burn your skin.

all /ɔl/

1 You use **all** or **all of** to talk about the whole of something. ❑ *Did you eat all of it?* ❑ *He watches TV all day.*

2 You use **all** or **all of** to talk about everyone or everything of a particular type. ❑ *Hugh and all his friends came to the party.*

3 **ADJECTIVE** All is also an adjective. ❑ *He loves all literature.*

4 **ADVERB** All means completely. ❑ *I went away and left her all alone.*

5 You use **at all** to make negative sentences stronger. ❑ *I never really liked him at all.*

Allah /ɑlə, ælə, ɑlɑ/ **NOUN** Allah is the name of God in Islam. ❑ *We thank Allah that the boy is safe.*

al|ler|gic /əlɜrdʒɪk/ **ADJECTIVE** If you are **allergic to** something, you become sick when you eat it or touch it, or breathe it in. ❑ *I'm allergic to cats.*

al|ler|gy /ælərdʒi/ (**allergies**) **NOUN** If you have an **allergy to** something, you become sick, or red marks appear on your skin when you eat it or touch it. ❑ *He has an allergy to nuts.*

al|ley /æli/ (**alleys**) **NOUN** An **alley** is a narrow street between the backs of buildings.

al|li|ance /əlaɪəns/ (**alliances**) **NOUN** An **alliance** is a group of people, countries, organizations, or political parties that work together. ❑ *The two parties formed an alliance.*

al|li|ga|tor /ælɪgeɪtər/ (**alligators**) **NOUN**

An **alligator** is a long animal with rough skin, big teeth, and short legs. ❑ *Do not feed the alligators.*

al|lo|cate /æləkeɪt/ (**allocates, allocating, allocated**)

1 **VERB** If something **is allocated to** a person, it is given to them. ❑ *Some of the tickets will be allocated to students.*

2 **VERB** If something **is allocated for** a purpose, it is used for that purpose. ❑ *They allocated one-billion dollars for malaria research.*

al|low /əlaʊ/ (**allows, allowing, allowed**)

1 **VERB** If someone **is allowed to** do something, they have permission to do it. ❑ *The children are allowed to watch TV after school.*

2 **VERB** If something is **allowed**, you have permission to do it, have it or use it. ❑ *Dogs are not allowed in the park.*

3 **VERB** If you **allow** something **to** happen, you give permission for it to happen. ❑ *Cellphone use is not allowed.*

ally /ælaɪ/ (**allies**)

1 **NOUN** A country's **ally** is another country that supports it, especially in war. ❑ *...the Western allies.*

2 **NOUN** An **ally** is someone who helps and supports another person. ❑ *He is a close ally of the president.*

al|mond /ɑmənd, æm-, ælm-/ (**almonds**) **NOUN** Almonds are nuts that you can eat or use in cooking. ❑ *She made a cake flavored with almonds.*

al|most /ɔlmoʊst/ **ADVERB** Almost means nearly but not completely. ❑ *We have been married for almost three years.* ❑ *He caught flu, which almost killed him.*

alone /əloʊn/

1 **ADJECTIVE** When you, or you and another person are **alone**, you are not with any other people. ❑ *She wanted to be alone.* ❑ *We were alone together.*

2 **ADVERB** Alone is also an adverb. ❑ *He lived alone in this house for almost five years.*

3 **ADVERB** When someone does something **alone**, they do it without help from other people. ❑ *Raising a child alone is very difficult.*

along /əlɔŋ/

1 **PREPOSITION** If you move **along** a road or other place, you move toward one end of it. ❑ *Pedro walked along the street.*

2 **PREPOSITION** If something is **along** a road or other long narrow place, it is in it or beside it. ❑ *There were traffic jams all along the roads.*

3 **ADVERB** When someone or something moves **along**, they keep moving. ❑ *He was talking as they walked along.*

4 **ADVERB** If you bring someone or something **along** when you go somewhere, you take them with you. ❑ *Bring along your friends and family.*

along|side /əlɔŋsaɪd/

1 **PREPOSITION** If one thing is **alongside** another thing, the first thing is next to the second. ❑ *He crossed the street and walked alongside Central Park.*

2 **ADVERB** Alongside is also an adverb. ❑ *He waited for a car to stop alongside.*

a

3 **PREPOSITION** If you work **alongside** other people, you all work together in the same place. ❑ *He worked alongside Frank and Mark.*

aloud /əlaʊd/ **ADVERB** When you speak, read, or laugh **aloud**, you speak, or laugh so that other people can hear you. ❑ *When we were children, our father read aloud to us.*

al|pha|bet /ælfəbɛt, -bɪt/ (**alphabets**) **NOUN** LANGUAGE ARTS An **alphabet** is a set of letters that is used for writing words. ❑ *The modern Russian alphabet has 31 letters.*
→ look at **language**

al|pha|beti|cal /ælfəbɛtɪkəl/ **ADJECTIVE** **Alphabetical** means in the normal order of the letters in the alphabet. ❑ *The books are arranged in alphabetical order.*
→ look at **dictionary**

al|ready /ɔlrɛdi/
1 **ADVERB** You use **already** to show that one thing happened before another thing. ❑ *The meeting had already finished when we arrived.*
2 **ADVERB** You use **already** to show that a situation exists now or that it started earlier than expected. ❑ *We've already spent most of the money.* ❑ *Most of the guests have already left.*

also /ɔlsoʊ/ **ADVERB** You can use **also** to give more information about something. ❑ *The book also includes an index of all U.S. presidents.* ❑ *We've got a big table and also some stools and benches.*

al|ter /ɔltər/ (**alters, altering, altered**) **VERB** If something **alters**, it changes. ❑ *World War II altered American life in many ways.*

al|ter|nate (**alternates, alternating, alternated**)

> **PRONUNCIATION HELP**
> Pronounce the verb /ɔltərneɪt/. Pronounce the adjective /ɔltɜrnɪt/.

1 **VERB** When you **alternate** between two things, you do one and then the other. ❑ *Alternate between walking and running.*
2 **VERB** When one thing **alternates with** another, the first thing happens, then the second thing, then the first thing again. ❑ *Rain alternated with snow.*
3 **ADJECTIVE** If something happens on **alternate** days, weeks, or years, for example, it happens on one, then it happens on every second one after that. ❑ *We go skiing on alternate years.*
4 **ADJECTIVE** **Alternate** describes a plan or

system that is different from the one that is being used now. ❑ *They were forced to turn back and take an alternate route.*

al|ter|na|tive /ɔltɜrnətɪv/ (**alternatives**)
1 **NOUN** If one thing is an **alternative to** another, the first can be used or done instead of the second. ❑ *The new treatment may provide an alternative to painkillers.*
2 **ADJECTIVE** An **alternative** plan or offer is different from the one that you already have. ❑ *Alternative methods of travel were available.*
3 **ADJECTIVE** **Alternative** describes something that is different from the usual thing. ❑ *Have you considered alternative health care?*

al|though /ɔlðoʊ/
1 **CONJUNCTION** You use **although** to introduce an idea that may seem surprising. ❑ *Their system worked, although no one knew how.* ❑ *Although I was only six, I can remember seeing it on TV.*
2 **CONJUNCTION** You use **although** to introduce information that slightly changes what you have already said. ❑ *They all play basketball, although on different teams.*

al|ti|tude /æltɪtud/ (**altitudes**) **NOUN** GEOGRAPHY **Altitude** is a measurement of height above the level of the ocean. ❑ *The aircraft reached an altitude of about 39,000 feet.* ❑ *The illness does not occur in areas of high altitude.*

al|to|geth|er /ɔltəgɛðər/ **ADVERB** If several amounts add up to a particular amount **altogether**, that amount is the total. ❑ *There were eleven of us altogether.*

alu|mi|num /əluːmɪnəm/ **NONCOUNT NOUN** **Aluminum** is a light metal used for making things such as cooking equipment and cans for food and drink. ❑ *We recycle aluminum cans.*

al|ways /ɔlweɪz/
1 **ADVERB** If you **always** do something, you do it whenever a particular situation happens. ❑ *She's always late for school.* ❑ *She always gave me socks for my birthday.*
2 **ADVERB** If you say that you will **always** do something, you mean that you will do it for ever. ❑ *I'll always love him.*
3 **ADVERB** If someone is **always** doing something, they do it a lot, and it annoys you. ❑ *Why are you always interrupting me?*

am /əm, STRONG æm/ **Am** is a form of the verb **be**.

a.m. /ˌeɪ ˈɛm/ also **am** You use **a.m.** after a number when you are talking about a time between midnight and noon. Compare with **p.m.** ❑ *The program starts at 9 a.m.*

ama|teur /ˈæmətʃər, -tʃʊər/ (**amateurs**) **NOUN** An **amateur** is someone who does something as a hobby and not as a job. ❑ *...an amateur golfer.*
→ look at **performance**

amaze /əˈmeɪz/ (**amazes, amazing, amazed**) **VERB** If something **amazes** you, it surprises you very much. ❑ *He amazed us with his knowledge of Colorado history.* ● **amazed ADJECTIVE** ❑ *I was amazed at how difficult it was.*

amaze|ment /əˈmeɪzmənt/ **NONCOUNT NOUN** Amazement is the feeling you have when something surprises you very much. ❑ *I looked at her in amazement.*

amaz|ing /əˈmeɪzɪŋ/ **ADJECTIVE** You say that something is **amazing** when it is very surprising and you like it. ❑ *It's amazing what we can remember if we try.* ● **amaz|ing|ly ADVERB** ❑ *She was an amazingly good cook.*
→ look at **science**

am|bas|sa|dor /æmˈbæsədər/ (**ambassadors**) **NOUN** An **ambassador** is an important official person who lives in a foreign country and represents his or her own country there. ❑ *We met the ambassador to Poland.*

am|bi|tion /æmˈbɪʃən/ (**ambitions**)
1 NOUN If you have an **ambition to** do something, you want very much to do it. ❑ *His ambition is to sail around the world.*
2 NONCOUNT NOUN Ambition is the desire to be successful, rich, or powerful. ❑ *These young people have hopes for the future and great ambition.*

am|bi|tious /æmˈbɪʃəs/
1 ADJECTIVE Someone who is **ambitious** has a strong feeling that they want to be successful, rich, or powerful. ❑ *Chris is very ambitious.*
2 ADJECTIVE An **ambitious** idea or plan needs a lot of work or money. ❑ *He has ambitious plans for the firm.*

am|bu|lance /ˈæmbyələns/ (**ambulances**) **NOUN** An **ambulance** is a vehicle for taking people to the hospital.

amend|ment /əˈmɛndmənt/ (**amendments**) **NOUN** SOCIAL STUDIES An

amendment is a change that is added to a law. ❑ *Do you know anything about the Fifth Amendment?* ❑ *They suggested an amendment to the defense bill.*

Ameri|can /əˈmɛrɪkən/ (**Americans**)
1 ADJECTIVE SOCIAL STUDIES American means belonging to or coming from the United States of America. ❑ *We spoke with the American ambassador at the United Nations.*
2 ADJECTIVE SOCIAL STUDIES You can call someone **American** when they come from North America, South America, or the Caribbean.
3 NOUN SOCIAL STUDIES An **American** is someone who is from the United States of America. ❑ *He's an American living in Israel.*
4 NOUN SOCIAL STUDIES You can call someone an **American** when they come from North America, South America, or the Caribbean.
→ look at **history**

among /əˈmʌŋ/
1 PREPOSITION Someone or something that is **among** a group of things or people is surrounded by them. ❑ *There were teenagers sitting among adults.*
2 PREPOSITION If something happens **among** a group of people, it happens within that group. ❑ *We discussed it among ourselves.*
3 PREPOSITION If something exists **among** a group of people, most of them have it or experience it. ❑ *There is concern among parents about teaching standards.*
4 PREPOSITION If something is shared **among** a number of people, some of it is given to all of them. ❑ *The money will be shared among family members.*

amount /əˈmaʊnt/ (**amounts, amounting, amounted**)
1 NOUN The **amount of** something is how much of it there is, or how much you have, need, or get. ❑ *He needs that amount of money to live.* ❑ *I still do a certain amount of work for them.*
2 VERB If something **amounts to** a particular total, all the parts of it add up to that total. ❑ *The payment amounted to $42 billion.*

am|pli|fi|er /ˈæmplɪfaɪər/ (**amplifiers**) **NOUN** An **amplifier** is a piece of electric equipment that makes sounds louder.

amuse /əˈmyuz/ (**amuses, amusing, amused**)
1 VERB If something **amuses** you, it makes you laugh or smile. ❑ *The thought amused him.*

A

2 **VERB** If you **amuse yourself**, you do something in order to not become bored. ❑ *I expect you'll find a way to amuse yourselves for another hour.*

amused /əmyuzd/ **ADJECTIVE** If you are **amused**, something makes you laugh or smile. ❑ *For a moment, Jackson looked amused.* ❑ *Alex looked at me with an amused expression on his face.*

amuse|ment /əmyuzmənt/ (**amusements**) **1** **NONCOUNT NOUN** Amusement is the feeling that you have when you think that something is funny. ❑ *Tom watched them with amusement.*
2 **NOUN** Amusements are ways of passing the time pleasantly. ❑ *People did not have many amusements to choose from in those days.*

amuse|ment park (**amusement parks**) **NOUN** An amusement park is a place where people pay to ride on machines for fun or to try to win prizes in games.

amus|ing /əmyuzɪŋ/ **ADJECTIVE** Someone or something that is **amusing** makes you laugh or smile. ❑ *It's an amusing program that the whole family can enjoy.*

an /ən, STRONG æn/ **ARTICLE** An is used instead of "a" before words that begin with vowel sounds.

> **Usage** **an**
> **An** is usually used before singular nouns beginning with vowel sounds **a, e, i, o, u.** Here are some examples. **an** apple, **an** egg, **an** island, **an** orange, **an** umbrella

analog /ænəlɔg/ **ADJECTIVE** TECHNOLOGY An **analog** clock or watch shows the time using hands (= the long parts that move around and show the time) instead of numbers. Compare with **digital.**
→ look at **time**

analy|sis /ənæləsɪs/ (**analyses** /ənæləsiz/) **1** **NOUN** Analysis is the process of considering something carefully in order to understand it or explain it. ❑ *Our analysis shows that the treatment was successful.*
2 **NONCOUNT NOUN** Analysis is the scientific process of finding out what is in something. ❑ *They collect blood samples for analysis.*

ana|lyze /ænəlaɪz/ (**analyzes, analyzing, analyzed**) **VERB** If you **analyze** something, you consider it carefully in order to fully understand it or to find out what is in it.

❑ *We need more time to analyze the decision.*
❑ *They haven't analyzed those samples yet.*

an|ces|tor /ænsɛstər/ (**ancestors**) **NOUN** SOCIAL STUDIES Your **ancestors** are the people in your family who lived before you. ❑ *Our daily lives are so different from those of our ancestors.*

an|chor /æŋkər/ (**anchors**) **NOUN** An **anchor** is a heavy object that you drop into the water from a boat to stop it moving away.

an|cient /eɪnʃənt/ **ADJECTIVE** Ancient means very old, or from a long time ago. ❑ *...ancient Jewish traditions.*
→ look at **history**

and /ənd, STRONG ænd/
1 **CONJUNCTION** You use **and** to connect two or more words or phrases. ❑ *She and Simon have already gone.* ❑ *I'm 53 and I'm very happy.*
2 **CONJUNCTION** You use **and** to connect two words that are the same, in order to make the meaning stronger. ❑ *Learning becomes more and more difficult as we get older.* ❑ *We talked for hours and hours.*
3 **CONJUNCTION** You use **and** when one event happens after another. ❑ *I waved goodbye and went down the steps.*
4 **CONJUNCTION** You use **and** to show that two numbers are added together. ❑ *Two and two makes four.*

anemia /ənimiə/ **NONCOUNT NOUN** Anemia is a condition in your blood that makes you feel tired and look pale. ❑ *She suffered from anemia.*

anemic /ənimɪk/ **ADJECTIVE** Someone who is **anemic** suffers from anemia. ❑ *Tests showed that she was anemic.*

an|es|thet|ic /ænɪsθɛtɪk/ (**anesthetics**) **NOUN** An anesthetic is a substance that doctors use to stop you feeling pain. ❑ *The operation was performed under a general anesthetic.*

an|gel /eɪndʒəl/ (**angels**)
1 **NOUN** Angels are beings that some people believe can bring messages from God. In pictures, angels often have wings.
2 **NOUN** An **angel** is someone who is very kind and good. ❑ *Thank you so much, you're an angel.*

an|ger /æŋgər/ (**angers, angering, angered**)
1 **NONCOUNT NOUN** Anger is the strong

emotion that you feel when you think that someone has behaved badly or has treated you unfairly. ❑ *He cried with anger.*

2 **VERB** If something **angers** you, it makes you feel angry. ❑ *The decision angered some Californians.*

anger man|age|ment **NONCOUNT NOUN**
Anger management is a way of helping people control their anger. ❑ *...an anger management program.*

an|gle /ˈæŋɡəl/ (**angles**)

1 **NOUN** MATH
An **angle** is the space between two lines or surfaces that meet in one place. Angles are measured in degrees. ❑ *...a 30 degree angle.*

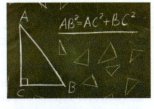

2 If something is **at an angle**, it is leaning so that it is not straight. ❑ *He wore his hat at an angle.*
→ look at **geometry**

an|gry /ˈæŋɡri/ (**angrier, angriest**) **ADJECTIVE**
When you are **angry**, you feel strong dislike about something. ❑ *We are very angry about the decision to close the school.* ❑ *An angry crowd gathered.*
→ look at **feeling**

ani|mal /ˈænɪməl/ (**animals**)
1 **NOUN** SCIENCE An **animal** is a creature such as a dog or a cat, but not a bird, fish, insect, or human. ❑ *He was attacked by wild animals.*
2 **NOUN** SCIENCE Any living creature,

including a human, can be called an **animal**.
→ look at Picture Dictionary: **animals**

ani|ma|tion /ˌænɪˈmeɪʃən/ **NONCOUNT NOUN**
ARTS **Animation** is the process of making films in which drawings appear to move. ❑ *...computer animation.*
→ look at **movie**

an|kle /ˈæŋkəl/ (**ankles**) **NOUN** Your **ankle** is the joint where your foot joins your leg. ❑ *John twisted his ankle badly.*
→ look at **body, foot**

an|ni|ver|sa|ry /ˌænɪˈvɜrsəri/ (**anniversaries**) **NOUN** An **anniversary** is a date that is remembered because something special happened on that date in an earlier year. ❑ *They just celebrated their fiftieth wedding anniversary.*

an|nounce /əˈnaʊns/ (**announces, announcing, announced**) **VERB** If you **announce** something, you tell people about it officially. ❑ *He will announce tonight that he is resigning.* ❑ *She was planning to announce her engagement.*

an|nounce|ment /əˈnaʊnsmənt/ (**announcements**) **NOUN** An **announcement** is information that someone tells to a lot of people. ❑ *The president is expected to make an announcement about his future today.* ❑ *An announcement told us that the train was going to be late.*

an|nounc|er /əˈnaʊnsər/ (**announcers**) **NOUN** An **announcer** is someone whose job is to talk between programs on radio or television. ❑ *The radio announcer said it was nine o'clock.*

a

Picture Dictionary　　**animals**

penguin　　panda　　frog　　ape　　lion

zebra　　rabbit　　shark　　mouse　　dog

Picture Dictionary	answer	

Check
Check the correct answer.
 	
"Small" is an ___.
  ___ noun
  ✓ adjective
  ___ verb
	Choose
	Choose the correct answer.
	
	_b_ Q: Is he a waiter?
	  A: Yes, he ___.
	    a. am
	    b. is
	    c. are
		Fill in the circle
		Fill in the circle.
		
		Ann ___ with her family.
		  ○ live
		  ○ living
		  ● lives

Cross out Cross out the word that doesn't belong. chicken ~~table~~ dog cow	**Fill in the blank** Fill in the blank. Q: Have you met Bill? A: Yes, I _have_.	**Underline** Underline the adjectives. The <u>young</u> woman was talking with a <u>tall</u> man.

an|noy /ənɔɪ/ (**annoys, annoying, annoyed**)
VERB If someone or something **annoys** you, they make you angry and upset. ❑ *Rosie said she didn't mean to annoy anyone.* ❑ *It annoyed me that she believed him.*

an|noyed /ənɔɪd/ **ADJECTIVE** If you are **annoyed**, you are angry about something. ❑ *She was annoyed that Sasha was there.*

an|noy|ing /ənɔɪɪŋ/ **ADJECTIVE** Someone or something that is **annoying** makes you feel angry and upset. ❑ *It's very annoying when this happens.*

an|nual /ænyuəl/
1 **ADJECTIVE** **Annual** events happen once every year. ❑ *They held their annual meeting May 20.* ● **an|nual|ly** **ADVERB** ❑ *The prize is awarded annually.*
2 **ADJECTIVE** **Annual** amounts or rates are for a period of one year. ❑ *The company has annual sales of about $80 million.* ● **an|nual|ly** **ADVERB** ❑ *El Salvador produces 100,000 tons of copper annually.*

anony|mous /ənɒnɪməs/ **ADJECTIVE** If you remain **anonymous** when you do something, you do not tell people that you were the person who did it. ❑ *You can speak to a police officer at any time, and you can choose to remain anonymous.* ● **anony|mous|ly** **ADVERB** ❑ *The photographs were sent anonymously to the magazine's offices.*

an|oth|er /ənʌðər/
1 **ADJECTIVE** **Another** person or thing means one more person or thing of the same type. ❑ *We're going to have another baby.*
2 **PRONOUN** **Another** is also a pronoun. ❑ *"These cookies are delicious."—"Would you like another?"*
3 **ADJECTIVE** **Another** person or thing is a different person or thing. ❑ *I'll deal with this problem another time.*
4 **PRONOUN** **Another** is also a pronoun. ❑ *He said one thing and did another.*
5 **PRONOUN** You use **one another** to show that each member of a group does something to or for the other members. ❑ *These women are learning to help one another.*

Word Partners	Use **another** with:
N.	another **one** **1**
	another **chance**, another **day** **3**

an|swer /ænsər/ (**answers, answering, answered**)
1 **VERB** When you **answer** someone, you say something back to them. ❑ *I asked him but he didn't answer.* ❑ *Williams answered that he didn't know.*
2 **VERB** When you **answer** the telephone, you pick it up when it rings. ❑ *Why didn't you answer when I called?*
3 **VERB** When you **answer** the door, you open it when you hear a knock or the bell.
4 **NOUN** **Answer** is also a noun. ❑ *I knocked at the front door and there was no answer.*
5 **VERB** When you **answer** a question on a test, you write or say what you think is correct. ❑ *Before you start to answer the questions, read the whole exam carefully.*
6 **NOUN** An **answer to** a problem is a way to solve it. ❑ *There are no easy answers to this problem.*
7 **NOUN** An **answer to** a question on a test is the information that you give when you are doing it. ❑ *I got three answers wrong.*
→ look at Picture Dictionary: **answer**
→ look at **math**

an|swer|ing ma|chine (**answering machines**) **NOUN** An **answering machine** is a small machine that records telephone messages.

ant /ænt/ (**ants**) **NOUN** Ants are small crawling insects that live in large groups.

an|ten|na /æntɛnə/ (**antennae** /æntɛni/ or **antennas**)

> **LANGUAGE HELP**
> **Antennas** is the usual plural form for meaning **2**.

1 **NOUN** **SCIENCE** The **antennae** of an insect are the two long, thin parts attached to its head that it uses to feel things with.

2 **NOUN** An **antenna** is a piece of equipment that sends and receives television or radio signals.

anti|bi|ot|ic /æntibaɪɒtɪk, æntaɪ-/ (**antibiotics**) **NOUN** Antibiotics are drugs that are used for killing bacteria and treat infections. ❏ *Your doctor may prescribe antibiotics.*

an|tici|pate /æntɪsɪpeɪt/ (**anticipates, anticipating, anticipated**) **VERB** If you **anticipate** an event, you think about it and prepare for it before it happens. ❏ *Organizers anticipate an even bigger crowd this year.*

an|tici|pa|tion /æntɪsɪpeɪʃən/
1 **NONCOUNT NOUN** Anticipation is a feeling of excitement about something that you know is going to happen. ❏ *The days before Christmas were filled with anticipation and excitement.*
2 If you do something **in anticipation of** an event, you do it because you believe that event is going to happen. ❏ *Some schools were closed in anticipation of the bad weather.*

an|ti|per|spi|rant /æntipɜrspɪrənt, æntaɪ-/ (**antiperspirants**) **NOUN** Antiperspirant is a substance that you use under your arms to keep that area dry. ❏ *Try using an antiperspirant for sensitive skin.*

an|tique /æntik/ (**antiques**) **NOUN** An **antique** is an old object that is valuable because of its beauty or because of the way it was made. ❏ *Jill started collecting antiques as a hobby about a year ago.*

anti|so|cial /æntisoʊʃəl, æntaɪ-/ **ADJECTIVE** Someone who is **antisocial** is not friendly toward other people. ❏ *...antisocial behavior.*

anti-virus also **antivirus** **ADJECTIVE** **Anti-virus** software is software that protects a computer from attack by viruses (= programs that enter your computer and stop it from working properly).

ant|ler /æntlər/ (**antlers**) **NOUN** Antlers are the horns that are shaped like branches on the head of a male deer (= a large brown animal with long thin legs).

an|to|nym /æntənɪm/ (**antonyms**) **NOUN** **LANGUAGE ARTS** An **antonym** is a word that means the opposite of another word.

anus /eɪnəs/ (**anuses**) **NOUN** **SCIENCE** A person's **anus** is the hole from which solid waste matter leaves their body.

anxi|ety /æŋzaɪɪti/ **NONCOUNT NOUN** Anxiety is a feeling of being nervous and worried. ❏ *Her voice was full of anxiety.*

anx|ious /æŋkʃəs/ **ADJECTIVE** If you are **anxious**, you are nervous or worried about something. ❏ *She became very anxious when he didn't come home.* ● **anx|ious|ly** **ADVERB** ❏ *They are waiting anxiously for news.*

any /ɛni/
1 **ADJECTIVE** You use **any** in negative sentences to show that no person or thing is involved. ❏ *I don't have any plans for the summer vacation yet.* ❏ *We made this without any help.*
2 **PRONOUN** Any is also a pronoun. ❏ *The children needed new clothes and we couldn't afford any.*
3 **ADJECTIVE** You use **any** in questions to ask if there is some of a particular thing. ❏ *Do you speak any foreign languages?*
4 **PRONOUN** Any is also a pronoun. ❏ *I will stay and answer questions if there are any.*
5 **ADJECTIVE** You use **any** in positive sentences when you want to say that it does not matter which person or thing you choose. ❏ *I'll take any advice.*
6 If something does not happen **any longer**, it has stopped happening or is no longer true. ❏ *I couldn't hide the tears any longer.*

any|body /ɛnibɒdi, -bʌdi/ **PRONOUN** Anybody means the same as **anyone**.

any|how /ɛnihaʊ/ **ADVERB** Anyhow means the same as **anyway**.

A

any|more /ɛnimɔr/ also **any more** ADVERB
If something does not happen or is not true **anymore**, it has stopped happening or is no longer true. ❑ *I couldn't trust him anymore.*

any|one /ɛniwʌn/

> **LANGUAGE HELP**
> You can also say **anybody**.

1 PRONOUN You use **anyone** or **anybody** in negative statements and questions instead of "someone" or "somebody". ❑ *I won't tell anyone I saw you here.* ❑ *Why would anyone want that job?*
2 PRONOUN You use **anyone** or **anybody** to talk about someone when the exact person is not important. ❑ *It's not a job for anyone who is slow with numbers.*
3 PRONOUN You use **anyone** or **anybody** to talk about all types of people. ❑ *Anyone could do what I'm doing.*

any|thing /ɛnɪθɪŋ/
1 PRONOUN You use **anything** in negative statements and questions instead of "something". ❑ *We can't do anything.* ❑ *She couldn't see or hear anything at all.* ❑ *Did you find anything?*
2 PRONOUN You use **anything** to talk about something when the exact thing is not important. ❑ *More than anything else, he wanted to become a teacher.*
3 PRONOUN You use **anything** to show that you are talking about a very large number of things. ❑ *He is young and ready for anything.*

any|time /ɛnitaɪm/ ADVERB You use **anytime** to mean a point in time that is not fixed. ❑ *The college admits students anytime during the year.* ❑ *He can leave anytime he wants.*

any|way /ɛniweɪ/

> **LANGUAGE HELP**
> You can also say **anyhow**.

ADVERB You use **anyway** or **anyhow** to suggest that something is true despite other things that have been said. ❑ *I'm not very good at golf, but I play anyway.*

any|where /ɛniwɛər/
1 ADVERB You use **anywhere** in negative statements and questions instead of "somewhere". ❑ *Did you try to get help from anywhere?* ❑ *I haven't got anywhere to live.*
2 ADVERB You use **anywhere** to talk about a place, when the exact place is not important. ❑ *I can meet you anywhere you want.*

apart /əpɑrt/
1 ADVERB When people or things are **apart**, they are some distance from each other. ❑ *Ray and his sister lived just 25 miles apart.* ❑ *Jane and I live apart now.*
2 ADVERB If you take something **apart**, you separate it into parts. ❑ *He likes taking bikes apart and putting them together again.*

apart|ment /əpɑrtmənt/ (**apartments**)
NOUN An **apartment** is a group of rooms where someone lives in a large building. ❑ *Christina has her own apartment at the top of the building.*

ape /eɪp/ (**apes**) NOUN An **ape** is a type of animal like a monkey that lives among trees in hot countries and has long, strong arms and no tail. ❑ *...wild animals such as monkeys and apes.*
→ look at **animal**

apolo|gize /əpɒlədʒaɪz/ (**apologizes, apologizing, apologized**)
1 VERB When you **apologize**, you say that you are sorry. ❑ *He apologized to everyone.*
2 VERB You can say "**I apologize**" as a formal or polite way of saying sorry. ❑ *I apologize for being late.*

apol|ogy /əpɒlədʒi/ (**apologies**) NOUN An **apology** is something that you say or write in order to tell someone that you are sorry. ❑ *I didn't get an apology.* ❑ *We received a letter of apology.*

apos|tro|phe /əpɒstrəfi/ (**apostrophes**)
NOUN LANGUAGE ARTS An **apostrophe** is the mark ' that shows that one or more letters have been removed from a word, as in "isn't" and "we'll." It is also added to nouns to show possession, as in "Mike's car."
→ look at **punctuation**

ap|par|ent /əpærənt/ ADJECTIVE If something is **apparent**, it is clear and obvious. ❑ *It's apparent that standards have improved.*

ap|par|ent|ly /əpærəntli/ ADVERB You use **apparently** to talk about something that seems to be true, although you are not sure whether it is true. ❑ *Apparently the girls are not at all talented.*

ap|peal /əpil/ (**appeals, appealing, appealed**)
1 VERB If something **appeals to** you, you find it attractive or interesting. ❑ *The idea appealed to him.*
2 VERB If you **appeal to** someone, you make a serious and urgent request to them.

❏ *Police appealed to the public for help.* ❏ *The president appealed for calm.*

3 **NOUN** An **appeal** is a serious and urgent request. ❏ *The police made an urgent appeal for help.*

ap|peal|ing /əpi̱lɪŋ/ **ADJECTIVE** Something that is **appealing** is pleasant and attractive. ❏ *The restaurant serves an appealing mix of Asian dishes.*

ap|pear /əpɪ̱ər/ (**appears, appearing, appeared**)

1 **VERB** When someone or something **appears**, it becomes possible to see them. ❏ *A woman appeared at the far end of the street.* ❏ *These small white flowers appear in early summer.*

2 **VERB** If something **appears to** be the way you describe it, it seems that way. ❏ *The boy appeared to be asleep.*

ap|pear|ance /əpɪ̱ərəns/ (**appearances**) **NOUN** Someone's or something's **appearance** is the way that they look. ❏ *She hates it when people make remarks about her appearance.*

ap|pen|dix /əpe̱ndɪks/ (**appendixes**)

1 **NOUN** SCIENCE Your **appendix** is a small closed tube in the right side of your body. ❏ *They had to remove his appendix.*

2 **NOUN** LANGUAGE ARTS An **appendix to** a book or document is extra information that is placed after the end of the main text. ❏ *...an appendix to the main document.*

ap|pe|tite /æ̱pɪtaɪt/ (**appetites**) **NOUN** Your **appetite** is the feeling that you want to eat. ❏ *He has a healthy appetite, so I cooked huge meals.*

ap|plaud /əplɔ̱d/ (**applauds, applauding, applauded**) **VERB** When people **applaud**, they clap their hands together to show that they like something. ❏ *The audience laughed and applauded.*

→ look at **performance**

ap|plause /əplɔ̱z/ **NONCOUNT NOUN** **Applause** is the noise that a group of people make when they all clap their hands together to show that they like something. ❏ *The crowd greeted the couple with loud applause.*

ap|ple /æ̱p³l/ (**apples**) **NOUN** An **apple** is a firm round fruit with green, red, or yellow skin. ❏ *I always have an apple in my packed lunch.*

→ look at **fruit**

ap|pli|ance /əpla̱ɪəns/ (**appliances**) **NOUN** An **appliance** is a machine that you use to do a job in your home. [FORMAL] ❏ *You can buy a DVD player from any electronic appliance store.*

ap|pli|cant /æ̱plɪkənt/ (**applicants**) **NOUN** An **applicant for** a job or a course is someone who formally asks to be considered for it. ❏ *The company keeps records on every job applicant.*

ap|pli|ca|tion /æ̱plɪke̱ɪʃ³n/ (**applications**)

1 **NOUN** An **application for** a job or a course is a written request to be considered for it. ❏ *We have not yet received your application form.*

2 **NOUN** TECHNOLOGY In computing, an **application** is a piece of software that is designed to do a particular task. ❏ *This is a software application that you can access via the Internet.*

Word Partners	Use **application** with:
v.	**fill out an** application **1**
N.	**college** application, application **form**, **job** application, **loan** application, **membership** application **1** application **software 2**

ap|ply /əpla̱ɪ/ (**applies, applying, applied**)

1 **VERB** If you **apply for** a job, you write a letter or write on a form in order to ask for it. ❏ *I am applying for a new job.*

2 **VERB** If a rule or a statement **applies to** a person or a situation, it is about them. ❏ *This rule does not apply to you.*

→ look at **job**

ap|point /əpɔ̱ɪnt/ (**appoints, appointing, appointed**) **VERB** If you **appoint** someone **to** a job or a position, you choose them for it. ❏ *The bank appointed Kenneth Conley as manager of its office in Aurora.*

ap|point|ment /əpɔ̱ɪntmənt/ (**appointments**)

1 **NOUN** An **appointment with** someone is an arrangement to see them at a particular time. ❏ *She has an appointment with her doctor.*

2 **NOUN** An **appointment** is a job or a position of responsibility. ❏ *I decided to accept the appointment as music director.*

ap|pre|ci|ate /əpri̱ʃieɪt/ (**appreciates, appreciating, appreciated**)

1 **VERB** If you **appreciate** something, you like it. ❏ *Everyone can appreciate this kind of art.*

2 **VERB** If you **appreciate** something that someone has done for you, you are grateful. ❏ *Peter helped me so much. I really appreciate that.*

● **ap|pre|cia|tion** **NONCOUNT NOUN** ❏ *He wants to show his appreciation for her support.*

ap|pren|tice /əprɛntɪs/ (**apprentices**) **NOUN**
An **apprentice** is a young person who works for someone in order to learn their skill. ❑ *Their son Dominic is an apprentice woodworker.*

ap|proach /əproʊtʃ/ (**approaches, approaching, approached**)

1 **VERB** When you **approach** something, you move closer to it. ❑ *He approached the front door.* ❑ *When I approached, the girls stopped talking.*

2 **VERB** When you **approach** a task, problem, or situation in a particular way, you deal with it or think about it in that way. ❑ *The bank has approached the situation in a practical way.*

3 **NOUN** Your **approach to** a task or problem is the way you deal with it or think about it. ❑ *There are two approaches: spend less money or find a new job.*

ap|pro|pri|ate /əproʊpriɪt/ **ADJECTIVE**
Something that is **appropriate** is correct for a particular situation. ❑ *Is it appropriate that they pay for it?* ❑ *Wear clothes that are appropriate to the job.* ● **ap|pro|pri|ate|ly** **ADVERB** ❑ *Try to behave appropriately and ask intelligent questions.*

ap|prov|al /əpruvᵊl/

1 **NONCOUNT NOUN** If you get someone's **approval for** something, they agree to it. ❑ *The chairman gave his approval for an investigation.*

2 **NONCOUNT NOUN** If someone or something has your **approval**, you like and admire them. ❑ *She wanted her father's approval.*

ap|prove /əpruv/ (**approves, approving, approved**)

1 **VERB** If you **approve of** someone or something, you like them or think they are good. ❑ *My father approves of you.*

2 **VERB** If someone in a position of authority **approves** a plan, they formally agree to it. ❑ *The directors have approved the change.*

ap|proxi|mate /əprɒksɪmət/ **ADJECTIVE** An **approximate** number, time, or position is near the correct number, time, or position, but is not exact. ❑ *The approximate value of the apartment is $300,000.* ● **ap|proxi|mate|ly** **ADVERB** ❑ *They've spent approximately $150 million.*

apri|cot /æprɪkɒt, eɪp-/ (**apricots**) **NOUN** An **apricot** is a small, soft, round fruit with

yellow flesh and a large seed inside. ❑ *...a bag of dried apricots.*

April /eɪprɪl/ **NOUN** April is the fourth month of the year. ❑ *I'm getting married in April.*

apron /eɪprən/ (**aprons**)
NOUN An **apron** is a piece of clothing that you wear over the front of your normal clothes, especially when you are cooking, in order to prevent your clothes from getting dirty.

aquar|ium /əkwɛəriəm/ (**aquariums**)

1 **NOUN** An **aquarium** is a building where fish and ocean animals live.

2 **NOUN** An **aquarium** is a glass box filled with water, in which people keep fish.

arch /ɑrtʃ/ (**arches**) **NOUN**
An **arch** is a structure that is curved at the top and is supported on either side. ❑ *The bridge is 65 feet at the top of the main arch.*
→ look at **foot**

ar|che|ol|ogy /ɑrkiɒlədʒi/ **NONCOUNT NOUN** SOCIAL STUDIES **Archeology** is the study of the past by examining the things that remain, such as buildings and tools. ● **ar|cheo|logi|cal** /ɑrkiəlɒdʒɪkᵊl/ **ADJECTIVE** ❑ *This is one of the region's most important archeological sites.* ● **ar|che|olo|gist** /ɑrkiɒlədʒɪst/ (**archeologists**) **NOUN** ❑ *Archeologists discovered buildings from an ancient culture in Mexico City.*

archi|tect /ɑrkɪtɛkt/ (**architects**) **NOUN** An **architect** is a person whose job is to design buildings.

archi|tec|ture /ɑrkɪtɛktʃər/

1 **NONCOUNT NOUN** **Architecture** is the art of designing buildings. ❑ *He studied architecture in Rome.* ● **archi|tec|tur|al** /ɑrkɪtɛktʃərəl/ **ADJECTIVE** ❑ *...architectural drawings.*

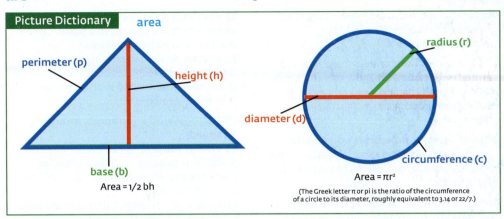

Picture Dictionary area

perimeter (p)

height (h)

base (b)

Area = 1/2 bh

radius (r)

diameter (d)

circumference (c)

Area = πr²

(The Greek letter π or pi is the ratio of the circumference of a circle to its diameter, roughly equivalent to 3.14 or 22/7.)

2 **NONCOUNT NOUN** The **architecture** of a building is the style of its design. ❏ ...*modern architecture.*

are /ər, STRONG ɑr/ **Are** is a form of the verb **be.**

area /ˈɛəriə/ (**areas**)
1 **NOUN** An **area** is a particular part of a town, a country, a region, or the world. ❏ *There are 11,000 people living in the area.*
2 **NOUN** A particular **area** is a piece of land or part of a building that is used for a particular activity. ❏ *We had lunch in the picnic area.*
3 **NOUN** MATH The **area** of a surface is the amount of flat space that it covers, measured in square units. ❏ *What's the area of this triangle?* ❏ *The islands cover a total area of 400 square miles.*
→ look at Picture Dictionary: **area**
→ look at **geometry**

area code (**area codes**) **NOUN** The **area code** for a particular city or area is the set of numbers at the beginning of a telephone number that represent that city or area. ❏ *The area code for western Pennsylvania is 412.*

arena /əˈrinə/ (**arenas**) **NOUN** An **arena** is a place where sports or entertainments take place. ❏ *This is the largest indoor sports arena in the world.*

aren't /ɑrnt, ˈɑrənt/ **Aren't** is short for "are not."

ar|gue /ˈɑrgyu/ (**argues, arguing, argued**)
1 **VERB** If you **argue with** someone, you disagree with them about something. ❏ *He was arguing with his wife about money.* ❏ *They are arguing over details.*
2 **VERB** If you **argue that** something is true, you give the reasons why you think it is

true. ❏ *Employers argue that the law should be changed.*

ar|gu|ment /ˈɑrgyəmənt/ (**arguments**)
1 **NOUN** An **argument** is a conversation in which people disagree with each other. ❏ *Annie had an argument with one of the other girls.*
2 **NOUN** An **argument** is what you say in order to try to convince people that your opinion is correct. ❏ *This is a strong argument against nuclear power.*

arise /əˈraɪz/ (**arises, arising, arose, arisen** /əˈrɪzən/) **VERB** If a situation or problem **arises**, it begins to exist. ❏ *When the opportunity finally arose, thousands of workers left.*

arith|me|tic /əˈrɪθmɪtɪk/ **NONCOUNT NOUN** MATH **Arithmetic** is basic number work, for example adding or multiplying. ❏ *We teach the young children reading, writing and arithmetic.*

arm /ɑrm/ (**arms, arming, armed**)
1 **NOUN** Your **arms** are the two parts of your body between your shoulders and your hands. ❏ *She stretched her arms out.*
2 **NOUN** The **arm** of a chair is the part on which you rest your arm when you are sitting down. ❏ *Mack held the arms of the chair.*
3 **NOUN** The **arm** of a piece of clothing is the part of it that covers your arm. ❏ *The coat was short in the arms.*
4 **PLURAL NOUN** **Arms** are weapons, especially bombs and guns. ❏ *Soldiers searched their house for illegal arms.*
5 **VERB** If you **arm** someone **with** a weapon, you provide them with a weapon. ❏ *She was so frightened that she armed herself with a rifle.*
→ look at **body**

arm|chair /ˈɑrmtʃɛər/ (**armchairs**) **NOUN** An **armchair** is a big comfortable chair that

supports your arms. ❏ *She was sitting in an armchair in front of the TV.*
→ look at **furniture**

armed /ɑrmd/ **ADJECTIVE** Someone who is **armed** is carrying a weapon, usually a gun. ❏ *City police said the man was armed with a gun.* ❏ *There were armed guards in the street outside their house.*

ar|mor /ɑrmər/ **NONCOUNT NOUN** In the past, **armor** was special metal clothing that soldiers wore for protection in battles. ❏ *...a suit of armor.*

arm|pit /ɑrmpɪt/ (**armpits**) **NOUN** Your **armpits** are the areas of your body under your arms where your arms join your shoulders. ❏ *The water came up to my armpits.*

army /ɑrmi/ (**armies**) **NOUN** An **army** is a large group of soldiers who are trained to fight battles on land. ❏ *Perkins joined the Army in 1990.*

arose /ərouz/ **Arose** is a form of the verb **arise**.

around /əraʊnd/
1 **PREPOSITION** Things or people that are **around** a place or object surround it or are on all sides of it. ❏ *She looked at the people around her.*
2 **PREPOSITION** If you move **around** a place, you go along its edge, and back to the point where you started. ❏ *We went for a walk around the lake.*
3 **ADVERB** Around is also an adverb. ❏ *They live in a little village with hills all around.* ❏ *They celebrated their win by running around on the football field.*
4 **PREPOSITION** If you move **around** something, you move to the other side of it. ❏ *The man turned back and hurried around the corner.*
5 **PREPOSITION** If you look **around** something, you look to see what is on the other side. ❏ *I looked around the door but the hall was empty.*
6 **PREPOSITION** You use **around** to say that something happens in different parts of a place or area. ❏ *Police say ten people have been arrested around the country.*
7 **ADVERB** Around is also an adverb. ❏ *Why are you following me around?*
8 **ADVERB** If you move things **around**, you move them so that they are in different places. ❏ *She moved things around so the table was under the window.*

9 **ADVERB** If someone or something is **around**, they are present in a place. ❏ *Have you seen my wife anywhere around?*
10 **ADVERB** Around means approximately. ❏ *My salary was around $45,000.*
11 **PREPOSITION** Around is also a preposition. ❏ *We're leaving around May 15.*

ar|range /əreɪndʒ/ (**arranges, arranging, arranged**)
1 **VERB** If you **arrange** an event, you make plans for it to happen. ❏ *She arranged an appointment for Friday afternoon.* ❏ *I've arranged to see him Thursday.*
2 **VERB** If you **arrange** things somewhere, you carefully place them in a particular position. ❏ *She enjoys arranging dried flowers.*

ar|range|ment /əreɪndʒmənt/ (**arrangements**)
1 **NOUN** Arrangements are plans that you make so that something can happen. ❏ *They're working on final arrangements for the meeting.*
2 **NOUN** An **arrangement** of things is a group of them that have been placed in a particular position. ❏ *...a flower arrangement.*

ar|rest /ərɛst/ (**arrests, arresting, arrested**)
1 **VERB** If the police **arrest** you, they take you to a police station, because they believe you may have broken the law. ❏ *Police arrested five young men in the city.*
2 **NOUN** Arrest is also a noun. ❏ *Police later made two arrests.*

ar|ri|val /əraɪvəl/ (**arrivals**) **NOUN** Your **arrival** is when you arrive somewhere. ❏ *It was the day after his arrival in Wichita.*

ar|rive /əraɪv/ (**arrives, arriving, arrived**)
VERB When a person or vehicle **arrives** at a place, they come to it from somewhere else. ❏ *Their train arrived on time.* ❏ *After a couple of hours, we arrived at the airport.*
→ look at **route**

ar|ro|gant /ærəgənt/ **ADJECTIVE** Someone who is **arrogant** behaves in an unpleasant way toward other people because they believe that they are more important than others. ❏ *Some rather arrogant people think they know everything.* ● **ar|ro|gance** **NONCOUNT NOUN** ❏ *...the arrogance of powerful people.*

ar|row /ærou/ (**arrows**)
1 **NOUN** An **arrow** is a long thin weapon that is sharp and pointed at one end. ❏ *They were armed with bows and arrows.*

2 **NOUN** An **arrow** is a written sign that points in a particular direction. ❏ *The arrow pointed down to the bottom of the page.*

art /ɑrt/ (**arts**)

1 **NONCOUNT NOUN** ARTS **Art** is pictures or objects that are created for people to look at. ❏ *...modern American art.*

2 **NONCOUNT NOUN** ARTS **Art** is the activity of creating pictures or objects for people to look at. ❏ *She decided she wanted to study art.* ❏ *...Savannah College of Art and Design.*

3 **PLURAL NOUN** ARTS The **arts** are activities such as music, painting, literature, film, theater, and dance. ❏ *She knew she wanted a career in the arts.*

ar|tery /ɑrtəri/ (**arteries**) **NOUN** SCIENCE **Arteries** are the tubes in your body that carry blood from your heart to the rest of your body. Compare with **vein**. ❏ *Many patients suffer from blocked arteries.*

art gallery (**art galleries**) **NOUN** ARTS An **art gallery** is a place where people go to look at art. ❏ *It is the most famous art gallery in the world.*

ar|thri|tis /ɑrθraɪtɪs/ **NONCOUNT NOUN** **Arthritis** is a medical condition in which the joints in your body swell and become painful. ❏ *I have arthritis in my wrist.*

ar|ti|choke /ɑrtɪtʃoʊk/ (**artichokes**) **NOUN** **Artichokes** or **globe artichokes** are round green vegetables that have thick leaves and look like flowers.

ar|ti|cle /ɑrtɪkᵊl/ (**articles**)

1 **NOUN** An **article** is a piece of writing in a newspaper or magazine. ❏ *I read about it in a newspaper article.*

2 **NOUN** LANGUAGE ARTS In grammar, an **article** is a word like "a," "an," or "the," which shows whether you are talking about a particular thing or things in general.

ar|ti|fi|cial /ɑrtɪfɪʃᵊl/ **ADJECTIVE** **Artificial** objects or materials are made by people, instead of nature. ❏ *The city has many small lakes, natural and artificial.* ❏ *Try to follow a diet that is free from artificial additives.*

● **ar|ti|fi|cial|ly** **ADVERB** ❏ *...artificially sweetened lemonade.*

ar|ti|fi|cial in|tel|li|gence **NONCOUNT NOUN** TECHNOLOGY **Artificial intelligence** is the way in which computers can work in a similar way to the human mind.

Word Builder	artist

ist ≈ **person who does this**

    art + ist = art**ist**
    guitar + ist = guitar**ist**
    journal + ist = journal**ist**
    novel + ist = novel**ist**

art|ist /ɑrtɪst/ (**artists**)

1 **NOUN** ARTS An **artist** is someone who draws, paints, or creates other works of art. ❏ *Each painting is signed by the artist.*

2 **NOUN** ARTS An **artist** is a performer such as a musician, an actor, or a dancer. ❏ *He was a popular artist, who sold millions of records.*

ar|tis|tic /ɑrtɪstɪk/ **ADJECTIVE** Someone who is **artistic** is good at drawing or painting. ❏ *The boys are sensitive and artistic.*

as /əz, STRONG æz/

1 **CONJUNCTION** If one thing happens **as** something else happens, it happens at the same time. ❏ *We shut the door behind us as we entered.*

2 **CONJUNCTION** You use **as** to say how something happens or is done. ❏ *Today, as usual, he was wearing a suit.* ❏ *Please do as you're asked first time.*

3 **CONJUNCTION** You can use **as** to mean "because." ❏ *As I was so young, I didn't have to pay.*

4 **PREPOSITION** You use **as** when you are talking about someone's job. ❏ *She works as a nurse.*

5 **PREPOSITION** You use **as** when you are talking about the purpose of something. ❏ *The fourth bedroom is used as a study.*

6 You use **as...as** when you are comparing things, or saying how large or small something is. ❏ *It's not as easy as I expected.* ❏ *I'm nearly as big as you.*

7 You use **as if** when you are saying that something appears to be the case. ❏ *Anne stopped, as if she didn't know what to say next.*

ash /æʃ/ (**ashes**) **NOUN** **Ash** is the gray powder that remains after something is burned. You can also call this substance **ashes**. ❏ *...the cold ashes of a log fire.*

ashamed /əʃeɪmd/ **ADJECTIVE** If you are **ashamed** of someone or something, you feel embarrassed or guilty because of them. ❏ *I was ashamed of myself for getting so angry.*

ashore /əʃɔr/ **ADVERB** Someone or something that comes **ashore** comes from the ocean onto the shore. ❏ *The hurricane came ashore south of Miami.*

ash|tray /ˈæʃtreɪ/ (ashtrays) NOUN An **ashtray** is a small dish for cigarette ash.

aside /əˈsaɪd/

1 ADVERB If you move something **aside**, you move it to one side of you. ❏ *Sarah closed the book and put it aside.*

2 ADVERB If you move **aside**, you move so that someone can pass you. ❏ *She stepped aside to let them pass.*

ask /æsk/ (asks, asking, asked)

1 VERB If you **ask** someone something, you say something to them in the form of a question. ❏ *"How is Frank?" he asked.* ❏ *I asked him his name.* ❏ *She asked me if I was enjoying my dinner.*

2 VERB If you **ask** someone **to** do something, you tell them that you want them to do it. ❏ *We politely asked him to leave.*

3 VERB If you **ask for** something, you say that you would like to know it or have it. ❏ *She asked for my address.*

4 VERB If you **ask** someone **to** an event or place, you invite them to go there. ❏ *I asked Juan to the party.*

asleep /əˈslip/

1 ADJECTIVE Someone who is **asleep** is sleeping. ❏ *My daughter was asleep on the sofa.*

2 When you **fall asleep**, you start sleeping. ❏ *Sam soon fell asleep.*

as|para|gus /əˈspærəgəs/ NONCOUNT NOUN **Asparagus** is a long, thin, green vegetable.
→ look at **vegetable**

as|pect /ˈæspɛkt/ (aspects) NOUN An **aspect** of something is a quality or a part of it. ❏ *He was interested in all aspects of the work here.*

as|pi|rin /ˈæspərɪn, -prɪn/ (aspirins) NOUN **Aspirin** is a mild drug that reduces pain and fever.

as|sas|si|nate /əˈsæsɪneɪt/ (assassinates, assassinating, assassinated) VERB
SOCIAL STUDIES When someone important is **assassinated**, they are murdered for political reasons. ❏ *Robert Kennedy was assassinated in 1968.* ● **as|sas|si|na|tion** /əˌsæsɪneɪʃ°n/ (assassinations) NOUN ❏ *Pope John Paul survived an assassination attempt in 1981.*

as|sault /əˈsɔlt/ (assaults, assaulting, assaulted)

1 NOUN An **assault** is a physical attack on a person. ❏ *There has been a series of assaults in the university area.*

2 VERB To **assault** someone means to physically attack them. ❏ *The gang assaulted him with baseball bats.*

as|sem|ble /əˈsɛmb°l/ (assembles, assembling, assembled)

1 VERB When people **assemble**, they come together in a group. ❏ *There was nowhere for students to assemble between classes.*

2 VERB To **assemble** something means to collect it together or to fit the different parts of it together. ❏ *Workers were assembling airplanes.*
→ look at **factory**

as|sem|bly /əˈsɛmbli/ (assemblies)

1 NOUN An **assembly** is a group of people gathered together for a particular purpose. ❏ *She made the announcement during a school assembly.*

2 NONCOUNT NOUN The **assembly** of something is the process of fitting its different parts together. ❏ *...an automobile assembly line.*

as|sess /əˈsɛs/ (assesses, assessing, assessed) VERB When you **assess** a person, thing, or situation, you consider them in order to make a judgment about them. ❏ *I looked around and assessed the situation.* ❏ *The doctor is assessing whether I am well enough to travel.* ● **as|sess|ment** (assessments) NOUN ❏ *We carry out an annual assessment of senior managers.*

as|set /ˈæsɛt/ (assets) NOUN An **asset** is something or someone that is considered to be useful or valuable. ❏ *He is a great asset to the company.*

as|sign|ment /əˈsaɪnmənt/ (assignments) NOUN An **assignment** is a task that you are given to do, especially as part of your studies. ❏ *We give written assignments as well as practical tests.*

as|sist /əˈsɪst/ (assists, assisting, assisted) VERB If someone or something **assists** you, they help you. ❏ *He was assisting elderly passengers with their baggage.*

as|sis|tance /əˈsɪstəns/ NONCOUNT NOUN If you give someone **assistance**, you help them. ❏ *Please let us know if you need any assistance.*
→ look at **disability**

a

Word Builder	assistant

ant ≈ **someone who does**

account + ant = account**ant**
assist + ant = assist**ant**
attend + ant = attend**ant**
consult + ant = consult**ant**
contest + ant = contest**ant**

as|sis|tant /əsɪstənt/ (**assistants**) NOUN
Someone's **assistant** is a person who helps
them in their work. ❑ *Kalan asked his assistant
to answer the phone while he went out.*

as|so|ci|ate (**associates, associating,
associated**)

> **PRONUNCIATION HELP**
> Pronounce the verb /əsoʊʃieɪt, -sieɪt/.
> Pronounce the noun /əsoʊʃiɪt, -siɪt/.

1 VERB If you **associate** someone or
something **with** another thing, you connect
them in some way. ❑ *Some people associate
money with happiness.*
2 NOUN Your **associates** are the people you
are closely connected with, especially at
work. ❑ *...business associates.*

as|so|ci|ate de|gree (**associate degrees**)
NOUN An **associate degree** is a college
degree that is given to a student who has
completed a two-year course of study. ❑ *She
has an associate degree in accounting.*

as|so|cia|tion /əsoʊʃieɪʃⁿn, -sieɪ-/
(**associations**) NOUN An **association** is an
official group of people who have the same
job, aim, or interest. ❑ *We're all members of the
National Basketball Association.*

as|sort|ed /əsɔrtɪd/ ADJECTIVE A group of
assorted things is a group of things that are
different from each other in some way. ❑ *We
have a selection of cotton sweaters in assorted
colors.*

as|sort|ment /əsɔrtmənt/ (**assortments**)
NOUN An **assortment** is a group of things
that are different from each other in some
way. ❑ *There was an assortment of books on the shelf.*

as|sume /əsum/ (**assumes, assuming,
assumed**) VERB If you **assume that**
something is true, you suppose that it is
true. ❑ *I assumed it was an accident.*

as|sure /əʃʊər/ (**assures, assuring, assured**)
VERB If you **assure** someone **that** something
is true or will happen, you tell them that it
is true or will happen. ❑ *He assured me that*

there was nothing wrong. ❑ *"Are you sure it's safe?"
she asked anxiously. "It couldn't be safer," Max
assured her.*

as|ter|isk /æstərɪsk/ (**asterisks**) NOUN An
asterisk is the sign *.

asth|ma /æzmə/ NONCOUNT NOUN Asthma
is a lung condition that causes difficulty in
breathing.

aston|ish /əstɒnɪʃ/ (**astonishes,
astonishing, astonished**) VERB If something
or someone **astonishes** you, they surprise
you very much. ❑ *The news astonished them.*
● **aston|ished** ADJECTIVE ❑ *They were
astonished to find the driver was a six-year-old boy.*

aston|ish|ing /əstɒnɪʃɪŋ/ ADJECTIVE
Something that is **astonishing** is very
surprising. ❑ *She found that fact astonishing.*
● **aston|ish|ing|ly** ADVERB ❑ *Andrea was an
astonishingly beautiful young woman.*

aston|ish|ment /əstɒnɪʃmənt/ NONCOUNT
NOUN Astonishment is a feeling of great
surprise. ❑ *He looked at her in astonishment.*

as|tro|naut /æstrənɔt/ (**astronauts**) NOUN
SCIENCE An **astronaut** is a person who is
trained for traveling in space.
→ look at **space**

as|trono|my /əstrɒnəmi/ NONCOUNT NOUN
SCIENCE **Astronomy** is the scientific study of
the stars, planets, and other natural objects
in space. ● **as|trono|mer** (**astronomers**)
NOUN ❑ *...an amateur astronomer.*

at /ət, STRONG æt/
1 PREPOSITION You use **at** to say where
something happens or is situated. ❑ *He will
be at the airport to meet her.* ❑ *I didn't like being
alone at home.* ❑ *They agreed to meet at a
restaurant.*
2 PREPOSITION You use **at** to say when
something happens. ❑ *The funeral will take
place this afternoon at 3:00.* ❑ *Zachary started
playing violin at age 4.*
3 PREPOSITION You use **at** to say how fast,
how far, or how much. ❑ *I drove back down the
highway at normal speed.* ❑ *There were only two
apartments at that price.*
4 PREPOSITION You use **at** when you direct
an action toward someone. ❑ *He looked at
Michael and laughed.*
5 PREPOSITION You use **at** to say that
someone or something is in a particular
state or condition. ❑ *The two nations are at war.*

6 **PREPOSITION** You are good **at** something if you do it well. ❑ *I'm good at my work.*

7 **PREPOSITION** You use **at** to say what someone is reacting to. ❑ *Mom was annoyed at the mess.*

Usage **at**

When you tell someone your email address you say this symbol @ as **at**. For example, you say @yahoo.com as **at** Yahoo **dot** com.

Sound Partners ate, eight

ate /eɪt/ **Ate** is a form of the verb **eat**.

ath|lete /ˈæθlit/ (**athletes**) **NOUN** **SPORTS** An **athlete** is a person who is good at any type of physical sports, exercise, or games, especially in competitions. ❑ *Jesse Owens was one of the greatest athletes of the twentieth century.*

ath|let|ic /æθˈlɛtɪk/ **ADJECTIVE** **Athletic** means relating to athletes and athletics. ❑ *He comes from an athletic family.*

at|las /ˈætləs/ (**atlases**) **NOUN** **GEOGRAPHY** An **atlas** is a book of maps.

ATM /ˌeɪ ti ˈɛm/ (**ATMs**) **NOUN** An **ATM** is a machine that allows people to take money from their bank account, using a special card. **ATM** is short for "automated teller machine."
→ look at Picture Dictionary: **ATM**
→ look at **city**

at|mos|phere /ˈætməsfɪər/ (**atmospheres**)
1 **NOUN** **SCIENCE** A planet's **atmosphere** is the layer of air or other gases around it. ❑ *The shuttle Columbia will re-enter the Earth's atmosphere tomorrow morning.*

● **at|mos|pher|ic** /ˌætməsˈfɛrɪk/ **ADJECTIVE** ❑ *...atmospheric gases.*
2 **NOUN** The **atmosphere** of a place is the general feeling that you get about it. ❑ *The rooms are warm and the atmosphere is welcoming.*
→ look at **climate, earth, greenhouse effect, space**

atom /ˈætəm/ (**atoms**) **NOUN** **SCIENCE** An **atom** is the very smallest part of something. ❑ *The simplest atom is the hydrogen atom.*

atom|ic /əˈtɒmɪk/ **ADJECTIVE** **SCIENCE** **Atomic** means relating to atoms or to power that is produced by splitting atoms. ❑ *...atomic energy.* ❑ *...the atomic number of an element.*

at|tach /əˈtætʃ/ (**attaches, attaching, attached**)
1 **VERB** If something is **attached to** an object, it is fastened to it. ❑ *There is usually a label with instructions attached to the plant.* ❑ *Please use the form attached to this letter.*
2 **VERB** If you **attach** a file **to** an email, you send it with the message. ❑ *I'm attaching the document to this email.*
→ look at **email**

at|tached /əˈtætʃt/ **ADJECTIVE** If you are **attached to** someone or something, you like them very much. ❑ *She is very attached to her family and friends.*

at|tach|ment /əˈtætʃmənt/ (**attachments**) **NOUN** **TECHNOLOGY** An **attachment** is a file that is attached to an email message and sent with it. ❑ *You can send your resume as an attachment to an email.*
→ look at **email**

Picture Dictionary ATM

automatic teller machine

ATM

insert card

enter your personal identification number (PIN)

buttons

screen

deposit money

get cash

cash dispenser

receipt

deposit slot

at|tack /ətæk/ (**attacks, attacking, attacked**)

1 **VERB** To **attack** a person or place means to try to hurt or damage them. ❑ *I thought he was going to attack me.* ❑ *He was in the yard when the dog attacked.*

2 **NOUN** Attack is also a noun. ❑ *There have been several attacks on police officers.*

3 **NOUN** An **attack of** an illness is a time when you suffer badly from it.

at|tempt /ətɛmpt/ (**attempts, attempting, attempted**)

1 **VERB** If you **attempt to** do something, you try to do it. ❑ *He attempted to enter law school.*

2 **NOUN** If you make an **attempt to** do something, you try to do it, often without success. ❑ *He made three attempts to rescue his injured colleague.*

at|tend /ətɛnd/ (**attends, attending, attended**)

1 **VERB** If you **attend** an event, you are present at it. ❑ *Thousands of people attended the wedding.* ❑ *I was invited but was unable to attend.*

2 **VERB** If you **attend** a school, college, or church, you go there regularly. ❑ *They attended college together.* ● **at|tend|ance** **NONCOUNT NOUN** ❑ *Attendance at the school is always high.*

→ look at **performance**

Word Builder　　　　**attendant**

ant ≈ **someone who does**

　　account + ant = accountant
　　assist + ant = assistant
　　attend + ant = attendant
　　consult + ant = consultant
　　contest + ant = contestant

---

at|tend|ant /ətɛndənt/ (**attendants**) **NOUN** An **attendant** is someone whose job is to serve people in a public place. ❑ *Tony Williams was working as a parking lot attendant in Los Angeles.*

at|ten|tion /ətɛnʃ°n/

1 **NONCOUNT NOUN** If you give someone or something your **attention**, you look at them, listen to them, or think about them carefully. ❑ *Can I have your attention?*

2 **NONCOUNT NOUN** If someone or something is getting **attention**, someone is dealing with them or caring for them. ❑ *Each year more than two million people need medical attention.*

3 If you **pay attention**, you watch and listen carefully. ❑ *Are you paying attention to what I'm saying?*

at|tic /ætɪk/ (**attics**) **NOUN** An **attic** is a room at the top of a house just under the roof.

→ look at **house**

at|ti|tude /ætɪtud/ **NOUN** Your **attitude** to something is the way that you think and feel about it. ❑ *You need to change your attitude to life.*

at|tract /ətrækt/ (**attracts, attracting, attracted**)

1 **VERB** If you are **attracted to** someone or something, you like them, and you are interested in knowing more about them. ❑ *I was attracted to her immediately.*

2 **VERB** If something **attracts** people or animals, they want to see or visit it. ❑ *The museum is attracting many visitors.*

3 **VERB** SCIENCE If one object **attracts** another object, it causes the second object to move towards it. ❑ *Opposite ends of a magnet attract each other.*

at|trac|tion /ətrækʃ°n/ (**attractions**)

1 **NONCOUNT NOUN** **Attraction** is a feeling of liking someone. ❑ *His attraction to her was growing.*

2 **NOUN** An **attraction** is something that people can visit for interest or enjoyment. ❑ *Disney World is an important tourist attraction.*

at|trac|tive /ətræktɪv/ **ADJECTIVE** An **attractive** person or thing is pleasant to look at. ❑ *She's a very attractive woman.* ❑ *The apartment was small but attractive.*

auc|tion /ɔkʃ°n/ (**auctions, auctioning, auctioned**)

1 **NOUN** An **auction** is a public sale where items are sold to the person who offers the most money. ❑ *The painting sold for $400,000 at auction.*

2 **VERB** If something **is auctioned**, it is sold in an auction. ❑ *Eight drawings by French artist Jean Cocteau will be auctioned next week.*

audi|ence /ɔdiəns/ (**audiences**) **NOUN** The **audience** of a performance, movie, or television program is all the people who are watching or listening to it. ❑ *There was a TV audience of 35 million.*

→ look at **performance**

audio /ɔdioʊ/ **ADJECTIVE** **Audio** equipment is used for recording and producing sound. ❑ *...audio and video files.*

A

audi|tion /ɔdɪʃⁿn/ (auditions) **NOUN** An **audition** is a short performance that an actor, dancer, or musician gives so that someone can decide if they are good enough to be in a play, film, or orchestra. ❑ *She went to an audition for a Broadway musical.*
→ look at **performance**

August /ɔgəst/ **NOUN** August is the eighth month of the year. ❑ *The movie comes out in August.* ❑ *My new job starts on August twenty-second.*

aunt /ænt, ɑnt/ (aunts) **NOUN** Your **aunt** is the sister of your mother or father, or the wife of your uncle. ❑ *She wrote to her aunt in Alabama.* ❑ *Aunt Margaret is coming to visit next week.*
→ look at **family**

> **Usage** **aunt**
>
> The pronunciation of **aunt** can be the same pronunciation as the word **ant**. An **ant** is a small insect. *My **aunt** saw an **ant** in the kitchen!*

authen|tic /ɔθɛntɪk/ **ADJECTIVE** An **authentic** person, object, or emotion is real. ❑ *They serve authentic Italian food.*

author /ɔθər/ (authors)
1 NOUN LANGUAGE ARTS The **author of** a piece of writing is the person who wrote it. ❑ *Jill Phillips is the author of the book "Give Your Child Music."*
2 NOUN LANGUAGE ARTS An **author** is a person whose job is writing books. ❑ *Haruki Murakami is Japan's best-selling author.*

author|ity /əθɔrɪti/ (authorities)
1 NONCOUNT NOUN Authority is the power to control other people. ❑ *Only the police have the authority to close roads.* ❑ *He is now in a position of authority.*
2 PLURAL NOUN The authorities are the people who are in charge of everyone else. ❑ *The authorities are investigating the attack.*
3 NOUN An **authority** is an official organization or government department. ❑ *...the Philadelphia Parking Authority.*

author|ize /ɔθəraɪz/ (authorizes, authorizing, authorized) **VERB** If someone **authorizes** something, they give their permission for it to happen. ❑ *Only the president could authorize its use.*
● **authori|za|tion** /ɔθərɪzeɪʃⁿn/ **NONCOUNT NOUN** ❑ *We didn't have authorization from the general to leave.*

auto|bi|og|ra|phy /ɔtəbaɪɒgrəfi/ (autobiographies) **NOUN** LANGUAGE ARTS Your **autobiography** is the story of your life, that you write yourself. ❑ *He published his autobiography last fall.* ● **auto|bio|graphi|cal** /ɔtoʊbaɪəgræfɪkⁿl/ **ADJECTIVE** ❑ *...an autobiographical novel.*

auto|graph /ɔtəgræf/ (autographs) **NOUN** An **autograph** is the signature of someone famous. ❑ *He asked for her autograph.*

auto|mat|ic /ɔtəmætɪk/
1 ADJECTIVE An **automatic** machine can continue to work when no one is operating it. ❑ *Modern trains have automatic doors.*
2 ADJECTIVE An **automatic** action is one that you do without thinking about it. ❑ *All of the automatic body functions, even breathing, are affected.* ● **auto|mati|cal|ly** /ɔtəmætɪkli/ **ADVERB** ❑ *You will automatically wake up after 30 minutes.*

auto|mo|bile /ɔtəməbil/ (automobiles) **NOUN** An **automobile** is a car. ❑ *...the automobile industry.*

autumn /ɔtəm/ (autumns) **NOUN** Autumn is the season between summer and winter when the weather becomes cooler and the leaves fall off the trees.
→ look at **season**

aux|ilia|ry /ɔgzɪlyəri, -zɪləri/ (auxiliaries) **NOUN** LANGUAGE ARTS In grammar, an **auxiliary** or **auxiliary verb** is a verb that you can combine with another verb to change its meaning slightly. In English, "be," "have," and "do" are auxiliary verbs.

avail|able /əveɪləbⁿl/
1 ADJECTIVE If something you want or need is **available**, you can find it or get it. ❑ *Breakfast is available from 6 a.m.*
2 ADJECTIVE Someone who is **available** is not busy and is free to do something. ❑ *Mr. Leach is not available for interviews today.*

ava|lanche /ævəlæntʃ/ (avalanches) **NOUN** SCIENCE An **avalanche** is a large amount of snow that falls down the side of a mountain.

av|a|tar /ævətɑr/ (avatars) **NOUN** TECHNOLOGY An **avatar** is an image that you can use to represent yourself on the Internet. ❑ *This site will create your avatar from any photo.*

av|enue /ævɪnyu, -nu/ (avenues)
1 NOUN Avenue is sometimes used in the

names of streets. The written short form **Ave.** is also used. ❑ *They live on Park Avenue.*

2 **NOUN** An **avenue** is a straight road, especially one with trees on either side.

av|er|age /ǽvərɪdʒ, ǽvrɪdʒ/ (**averages**)

1 **NOUN** MATH An **average** is the result that you get when you add two or more amounts together and divide the total by the number of amounts you added together. ❑ *The average age was 63.*

2 **ADJECTIVE** **Average** is also an adjective. ❑ *The average price of goods went up by just 2.2%.*

3 **NOUN** An amount or quality that is **the average** is the normal amount or quality for a particular group. ❑ *Rainfall was twice the average for this time of year.*

4 **ADJECTIVE** **Average** is also an adjective. ❑ *The average adult man burns 1,500 to 2,000 calories per day.*

5 **ADJECTIVE** **Average** means ordinary. ❑ *He seemed like a pleasant, average guy.*

avo|ca|do /ævəkɑ́doʊ/ (**avocados**) **NOUN** An **avocado** is a fruit with dark green skin and a large seed in the middle. ❑ *...crab and avocado salad.*

avoid /əvɔ́ɪd/ (**avoids, avoiding, avoided**)

1 **VERB** If you **avoid** something unpleasant, you do something to stop it from happening. ❑ *It was a last-minute attempt to avoid a disaster.*

2 **VERB** If you **avoid** doing something, you choose not to do it. ❑ *I avoid working in public places.*

3 **VERB** If you **avoid** a person or thing, you keep away from them. ❑ *She went to the women's restroom to avoid him.*

awake /əwéɪk/ **ADJECTIVE** Someone who is **awake** is not sleeping. ❑ *I stayed awake until midnight.*

award /əwɔ́rd/ (**awards, awarding, awarded**)

1 **NOUN** An **award** is a prize that a person is given for doing something well. ❑ *He again won the National Book Award for fiction.*

2 **VERB** If someone **is awarded** a prize, it is given to them. ❑ *She was awarded the prize for both films.*

aware /əwɛ́ər/ **ADJECTIVE** If you are **aware of** something, you know about it. ❑ *They are well aware of the danger.* ● **aware|ness** **NONCOUNT NOUN** ❑ *We are trying to raise awareness of the pollution problem.*

away /əwéɪ/

1 **ADVERB** If someone or something moves **away from** a place, they move so that they are no longer there ❑ *He walked away from his car.*

2 **ADVERB** If you are **away from** a place, you are not in the place where people expect you to be. ❑ *Jason was working away from home for a while.*

3 **ADVERB** When a sports team plays **away**, it goes to its opponents' ground to play. Compare with **home**. ❑ *Canada's Davis Cup team will play away against the Netherlands in February.*

4 **ADJECTIVE** **Away** is also an adjective. ❑ *Charlton are about to play an important away match.*

5 **ADVERB** If you put something **away**, you put it where it should be. ❑ *I put my book away and went to bed.*

6 **ADVERB** If an event is a week **away**, it will happen after a week. ❑ *Christmas is now only two weeks away.*

7 If something is a particular distance **away from** a person or place, it is not near that person or place. ❑ *Remember to stay a safe distance away from the car in front.*

awe|some /ɔ́səm/

1 **ADJECTIVE** An **awesome** person or thing is very powerful or frightening. ❑ *I love the awesome power of the ocean waves.*

2 **ADJECTIVE** If something is **awesome**, it is very good or special. [INFORMAL] ❑ *We all agreed the game was awesome.*

aw|ful /ɔ́fəl/ **ADJECTIVE** If someone or something is **awful**, they are very bad. ❑ *I thought he was an awful actor.* ❑ *There was an awful smell of paint.*

awhile /əwáɪl/ **ADVERB** **Awhile** means for a short time. ❑ *I waited awhile.*

awk|ward /ɔ́kwərd/

1 **ADJECTIVE** An **awkward** situation is embarrassing and difficult to deal with. ❑ *He kept asking awkward questions.* ● **awk|ward|ly** **ADVERB** ❑ *There was an awkwardly long silence.*

2 **ADJECTIVE** Something that is **awkward to** use or carry is difficult to use or carry because of its design. ❑ *The bicycle was small but awkward to carry.*

3 **ADJECTIVE** An **awkward** movement or position looks strange or uncomfortable. ❑ *Amy made an awkward movement with her hands.* ● **awk|ward|ly** **ADVERB** ❑ *He fell awkwardly.*

A

awoke /əw<u>ou</u>k/ Awoke is a form of the verb **awake**.

awok|en /əw<u>ou</u>kən/ Awoken is a form of the verb **awake**.

ax /æks/ (**axes**) NOUN An ax is a tool used for cutting wood. It has a heavy metal blade and a long handle.

axis /ˈæksɪs/ (**axes**)

1 NOUN SCIENCE An **axis** is an imaginary line through the middle of something. ❑ The Earth spins around its axis.

2 NOUN MATH An **axis** is one of the two lines that you mark points on to show measurements or amounts. ❑ We can label the axes: time is on the vertical axis and money is on the horizontal one.

→ look at **earth**

Bb

baa /bɑ/ (**baas, baaing, baaed**) **VERB** When a sheep **baas**, it makes its typical sound. ❑ *He sat by the tent, listening to the lambs baaing.*

baby /beɪbi/ (**babies**) **NOUN** A **baby** is a very young child. ❑ *He bathed the baby and put her to bed.* ❑ *My wife just had a baby.*

Word Partners	Use **baby** with:
N.	baby **boy**, baby **clothes**, baby **food**, baby **girl**, **new** baby, baby **sister**, baby **talk**
V.	**have a** baby

baby|sit /beɪbisɪt/ (**babysits, babysitting, babysat**) **VERB** If you **babysit for** someone, you look after their children while they are not at home. ❑ *I promised to babysit for Mrs. Plunkett.*

baby|sitter /beɪbisɪtər/ (**babysitters**) **NOUN** A **babysitter** is a person who looks after a child while the child's parents are not at home. ❑ *It can be difficult to find a good babysitter.*

bach|elor /bætʃələr/ (**bachelors**) **NOUN** A **bachelor** is a man who has never married.

Spelling Partners   back

back

❶ ADVERB USES
❷ OPPOSITE OF FRONT; NOUN AND ADJECTIVE USES
❸ VERB USES

---

❶ **back** /bæk/

1 **ADVERB** If you move **back**, you move in the opposite direction to the one in which you are looking. ❑ *She stepped back from the door.*

2 **ADVERB** If you go **back** somewhere, you return to where you were before. ❑ *I went back to bed.* ❑ *I'll be back as soon as I can.*

3 **ADVERB** If you put or give something **back**, you return it to the place where it was before. ❑ *Put the meat back in the freezer.*

4 **ADVERB** If you write or call **back**, you write to or call someone after they have written to or telephoned you. ❑ *I'll call you back after dinner.*

5 If someone moves **back and forth**, they move in one direction and then in the opposite direction. ❑ *He paced back and forth.*
→ look at **body**

❷ **back** /bæk/ (**backs**)

1 **NOUN** Your **back** is the part of your body from your neck to your waist that is on the opposite side to your chest. ❑ *Her son was lying on his back.*

2 **NOUN** The **back of** something is the side or part of it that is farthest from the front. ❑ *She was in a room at the back of the store.*

3 **ADJECTIVE** **Back** describes the side or part of something that is farthest from the front. ❑ *She opened the back door.* ❑ *Ann sat in the back seat of their car.*

4 If you say or do something **behind** someone's **back**, you do it without them knowing about it. ❑ *You shouldn't criticize her behind her back.*

❸ **back** /bæk/ (**backs, backing, backed**)

1 **VERB** When you **back** a vehicle somewhere, you move it backward. ❑ *He backed his car out of the driveway.*

2 **VERB** If you **back** someone, you support them. ❑ *We told them what we wanted to do, and they agreed to back us.*

▶ **back away** If you **back away**, you move away, often because you are frightened. ❑ *James stood up, but the girl backed away.*

▶ **back off** If you **back off**, you move away in order to avoid problems. ❑ *When she saw me she backed off, looking worried.*

▶ **back out** If you **back out**, you decide not to do something that you agreed to do. ❑ *They've backed out of the project.*

▶ **back up** **1** To **back up** a statement, means to show evidence to suggest that it is true. ❑ *He didn't have any proof to back up his story.*

2 **TECHNOLOGY** If you **back up** a computer file, you make a copy of it that you can use if the original file is lost. ❑ *Make sure you back up your files every day.*

back|bone /bǽkboʊn/ (backbones) NOUN
SCIENCE Your **backbone** is the line of bones
down the middle of your back.

back|ground /bǽkgraʊnd/ (backgrounds)
1 NOUN Your **background** is the type of
family you come from and the type of
education and experiences you have had.
❑ He came from a very poor background.
2 NOUN The **background** is sounds, such as
music, that you can hear but that you are
not listening to with your full attention.
❑ I heard the sound of music in the background.
3 NOUN ARTS The **background** of a picture
is the part that is behind the main things or
people in it. Compare with **foreground**.
❑ I looked at the man in the background of the
photograph.

back|pack /bǽkpæk/ (backpacks) NOUN A
backpack is a bag that you carry on your back.
→ look at **bag**

back|stroke /bǽkstroʊk/ NONCOUNT NOUN
SPORTS **Backstroke** is a way of swimming on
your back. ❑ Linda swam backstroke and Isabelle
swam breaststroke.

back|up /bǽkʌp/ (backups) also **back-up**
1 NONCOUNT NOUN **Backup** is extra help
that you can get if you need it. ❑ If you need
backup, just call me.
2 NOUN TECHNOLOGY A **backup** is a copy of
a computer file that you can use if the
original file is lost or damaged. ❑ It is very
important to make backups of your data.
→ look at **car**

back|ward /bǽkwərd/
1 ADJECTIVE A **backward** movement or look
is in the direction that your back is facing.
❑ He walked away without a backward glance.
2 ADVERB If you move **backward**, you move
in the direction that your back is facing.
❑ He took two steps backward.
3 ADVERB If you do something **backward**,
you do it in the opposite way to the usual
way. ❑ Kate counted backward from ten to zero.
4 If something moves **backward and
forward**, it keeps moving in one direction
and then in the opposite direction. ❑ Jennifer
moved backward and forward in time with the music.
5 ADJECTIVE A **backward** country does not
have modern industries and machines.
❑ ...backward nations.

back|yard /bǽkyɑrd/ (backyards) also **back
yard** NOUN A **backyard** is the land at the

back of a house. ❑ The house has a large backyard.

ba|con /béɪkən/ NONCOUNT NOUN **Bacon** is
strips of salted or smoked meat that comes
from a pig. ❑ We had bacon and eggs for breakfast.
→ look at **meat**

bac|te|ria /bæktíəriə/ PLURAL NOUN SCIENCE
Bacteria are very, very small living things
that can make people sick. ❑ There were high
levels of dangerous bacteria in the water.
● **bac|te|rial** ADJECTIVE ❑ Tuberculosis is a
bacterial disease.

bad /bǽd/ (worse, worst)
1 ADJECTIVE Something that is **bad** is
unpleasant or harmful. ❑ When the weather
was bad, I stayed indoors. ❑ When Ross and Judy
heard the bad news, they were very upset. ❑ Too
much coffee is bad for you.
2 ADJECTIVE Something that is **bad** is of a
very low standard, quality, or amount.
❑ ...bad housing. ❑ The school's main problem is
that teachers' pay is so bad.
3 ADJECTIVE Someone who is **bad at** doing
something is not good at doing it. ❑ He's a
bad driver.
4 ADJECTIVE If you are in a **bad** mood, you
are angry and behave unpleasantly to
people. ❑ She is in a bad mood because she is tired.
5 ADJECTIVE If you **feel bad about**
something, you feel sorry or guilty about it.
❑ I feel bad that he's doing most of the work.
6 ADJECTIVE If you have a **bad** back, heart, or
leg, for example, there is something wrong
with it. ❑ Joe has to be careful because of his bad
back.
7 ADJECTIVE **Bad** language is language that
contains rude or offensive words. ❑ I don't like
to hear bad language in the street.
→ look at **feeling, movie, news, play, sense**

badge /bǽdʒ/ (badges) NOUN A **badge** is a
small piece of metal or plastic that you wear
on your clothes to show people who you are.
❑ I showed him my police badge.

badg|er /bǽdʒər/ (badgers) NOUN A **badger**
is a wild animal that has a white head with
two wide black stripes on it. Badgers live
beneath the ground and come out to feed at
night.

bad|ly /bǽdli/ (worse, worst)
1 ADVERB If something is done **badly** or
goes **badly**, it is not very successful or
effective. ❑ I was angry because I played so badly.
❑ The whole project was badly managed.

2 ADVERB If someone or something is **badly** hurt or **badly** affected, they are seriously hurt or affected. ❑ *The fire badly damaged a church.* ❑ *One man was killed and another was badly injured.*

3 ADVERB If you want or need something **badly**, you want or need it very much. ❑ *Why do you want to go so badly?*

bad|min|ton /bædmɪntən/ **NONCOUNT NOUN** SPORTS **Badminton** is a game played by two or four players. The players get points by hitting a small object (= a shuttlecock) across a high net using a racket.

bag /bæg/ (**bags**) **NOUN** A **bag** is a container made of paper, plastic, or leather, used for carrying things. ❑ *He ate a whole bag of candy.* ❑ *The old lady was carrying a heavy shopping bag.*
→ look at Picture Dictionary: **bags**
→ look at **container**

bag|gage /bægɪdʒ/ **NONCOUNT NOUN** Your **baggage** is all the bags that you take with you when you travel. ❑ *He collected his baggage and left the airport.*

bag|gy /bægi/ (**baggier, baggiest**) **ADJECTIVE** **Baggy** clothes are big and loose. ❑ *He wore baggy pants and no shirt.*

bail /beɪl/ (**bails, bailing, bailed**)
1 NONCOUNT NOUN **Bail** is money that is paid to get a prisoner out of prison while he or she is waiting to go to court. ❑ *He was held without bail after a court appearance in Detroit.*
2 If a prisoner **is freed on bail**, or **released on bail**, or **makes bail**, he or she is let out of prison until they go to court, because someone has paid their bail. ❑ *When Guerrero made bail, he escaped to Colombia.*

3 VERB If you **bail** water from a boat, you use a container to take water out of it. ❑ *We kept the boat afloat by bailing with a cup.*

bait /beɪt/ **NONCOUNT NOUN** **Bait** is food that you put on a hook or in a trap to catch fish or animals. ❑ *This shop sells fishing bait.*

bake /beɪk/ (**bakes, baking, baked**) **VERB** When you **bake** food, you cook it in an oven. ❑ *How did you learn to bake cakes?* ❑ *Bake the fish in the oven for 20 minutes.*
→ look at **cook**

bak|er /beɪkər/ (**bakers**) **NOUN** A **baker** is a person whose job is to make and sell bread and cakes.

bak|ery /beɪkəri, beɪkri/ (**bakeries**) **NOUN** A **bakery** is a place where bread and cakes are baked or sold. ❑ *The town has two bakeries.*

bak|ing /beɪkɪŋ/ **NONCOUNT NOUN** **Baking** is the activity of cooking bread or cakes in an oven. ❑ *The children want to do some baking.*

bal|ance /bæləns/ (**balances, balancing, balanced**)
1 VERB If someone **balances**, they stay steady and they do not fall. ❑ *I balanced on Mark's shoulders.* ❑ *She balanced the chair on top of the table.*
2 NONCOUNT NOUN **Balance** is the ability to stay steady and not to fall over or to the side when you are standing or walking. ❑ *Dan lost his balance and started to fall.*
3 VERB If you **balance** one thing **with** something different, each of the things has the same importance. ❑ *Bob has difficulty*

Picture Dictionary bags

backpack   suitcase   purse / handbag   paper bag   plastic bag   messenger bag

briefcase   diaper bag   laptop bag   gym bag

balancing the demands of his work with the needs of his family.

4 **NOUN** A **balance** is when all the different parts of something have the same importance. ❑ It is important to have a balance between work and play.

5 **NOUN** The **balance** in your bank account is the amount of money you have in it. ❑ I'll need to check my bank balance first.

bal|anced /bǽlənst/
1 **ADJECTIVE** A **balanced** way of considering things is fair and reasonable. ❑ Journalists should present balanced reports.

2 **ADJECTIVE** A **balanced** diet has the right amounts of different foods to keep your body healthy. ❑ Eat a healthy, balanced diet and get regular exercise.
→ look at **eat**

bal|co|ny /bǽlkəni/ (**balconies**)
1 **NOUN** A **balcony** is a place where you can stand or sit on the outside of a building, above the ground.

2 **NOUN** In a theater, the **balcony** is the seats upstairs.

bald /bɔld/ (**balder, baldest**) **ADJECTIVE**
Someone who is **bald** has no hair, or very little hair, on the top of their head. ❑ He rubbed his hand across his bald head.

ball /bɔl/ (**balls**)
1 **NOUN** **SPORTS** A **ball** is a round object that is used in games such as tennis and soccer. ❑ Michael was kicking a soccer ball against the wall.

2 **NOUN** A **ball** is something that has a round shape. ❑ Form the butter into small balls.

3 **NOUN** A **ball** is a large formal party where people dance. ❑ My parents go to a New Year's ball every year.
→ look at **play**

Word Partners	Use **ball** with:
v.	bounce a ball, catch a ball, hit a ball, kick a ball, throw a ball **1**
N.	bowling ball, ball **field**, ball **game**, golf ball, **soccer** ball, **tennis** ball **1** snow ball **2**

bal|let /bælɛɪ/ (**ballets**)
1 **NONCOUNT NOUN** **ARTS** **Ballet** is a type of dancing with carefully planned movements. ❑ We saw a film about a boy who becomes a ballet dancer.

2 **NOUN** **ARTS** A **ballet** is a performance of this type of dancing that tells a story. ❑ Many people's favorite ballet is "Swan Lake."

ball game (**ball games**) also **ballgame**
NOUN **SPORTS** A **ball game** is a baseball match. ❑ They were listening to the ball game on the radio.

bal|loon /bəlún/ (**balloons**) **NOUN** A **balloon** is a small, thin, brightly-colored rubber bag that you blow air into so that it becomes larger. **Balloons** are used as decorations at parties. ❑ Large balloons floated above the crowd.

ball|park /bɔlpɑrk/ (**ballparks**) also **ball park**
1 **NOUN** **SPORTS** A **ballpark** is a field where baseball is played. ❑ He has watched baseball games in nearly every major-league ballpark.

2 **ADJECTIVE** A **ballpark** figure is an approximate figure. ❑ I can't tell you the exact cost, but $500 is a ballpark figure.

bam|boo /bæmbú/
NONCOUNT NOUN
Bamboo is a tall plant that grows in hot countries. It has hard, hollow stems that are sometimes used for making furniture. ❑ The family lived in a bamboo hut.

ban /bæn/ (**bans, banning, banned**)
1 **VERB** If someone **bans** something, they say that it must not be done, shown, or used. ❑ Ireland was the first country to ban smoking in all workplaces.

2 **NOUN** A **ban** is an official order that something must not be done, shown, or used. ❑ The report proposes a ban on plastic bags.

ba|na|na /bənǽnə/ (**bananas**) **NOUN**
Bananas are long curved fruit with yellow skins. ❑ I bought milk, bread and a bunch of bananas.
→ look at **fruit**

band /bænd/ (**bands**)
1 **NOUN** **MUSIC** A **band** is a group of people who play music together. ❑ Matt's a drummer in a rock band.

2 **NOUN** A **band** is a flat, narrow strip of material that you wear around your head or wrists, or that is part of a piece of clothing. ❑ Before treatment, doctors and nurses should always check the patient's wristband.

3 **NOUN** A **band** is a strip or circle of metal or another strong material that makes something stronger, or that holds several things together. ❑ He took out a white envelope with a rubber band around it.

band|age /bǽndɪdʒ/ (**bandages, bandaging, bandaged**)

1 **NOUN** A **bandage** is a long strip of cloth that is wrapped around an injured part of your body to protect or support it. ❏ *We put a bandage on John's knee.*

2 **VERB** If you **bandage** a wound or part of someone's body, you tie a bandage around it. ❏ *Mary finished bandaging her sister's hand.*

Band-Aid (**Band-Aids**) also **band-aid** **NOUN** A **Band-Aid** is a small piece of sticky material that you use to cover small cuts on your body. [TRADEMARK] ❏ *She had a Band-Aid on her ankle.*

ban|dit /bǽndɪt/ (**bandits**) **NOUN** A **bandit** is a person who robs people who are traveling. ❏ *The family was attacked by a gang of armed bandits.*

bang /bǽŋ/ (**bangs, banging, banged**)

1 **NOUN** A **bang** is a sudden loud noise. ❏ *I heard four or five loud bangs.*

2 **VERB** If you **bang on** something, you hit it hard, making a loud noise. ❏ *Lucy banged on the table with her fist.*

3 **PLURAL NOUN** **Bangs** are hair that is cut so that it hangs down above your eyes. ❏ *Both of them had blond bangs.*

→ look at **hair**

ban|jo /bǽndʒoʊ/ (**banjos**) **NOUN** MUSIC A **banjo** is a musical instrument that looks like a guitar with a round body, a long neck, and four or more strings.

bank /bǽŋk/ (**banks, banking, banked**)

1 **NOUN** A **bank** is a place where people can keep their money. ❏ *He had just $14 in the bank when he died.*

2 **NOUN** The **banks of** a river are the raised areas of ground along its edge. ❏ *We walked along the east bank of the river.*

→ look at **city**

▶ **bank on** If you **bank on** someone or something, you rely on them. ❏ *Everyone is banking on his recovery.*

bank card (**bank cards**) or **ATM card** **NOUN** A **bank card** is a plastic card that your bank gives you so that you can get money from your bank account using a cash machine.

bank|rupt /bǽŋkrʌpt/ **ADJECTIVE** People or organizations that go **bankrupt** do not have enough money to pay their debts. ❏ *If the company cannot sell its products, it will go bankrupt.*

ban|ner /bǽnər/ (**banners**) **NOUN** A **banner** is a long strip of cloth or plastic with something written on it. ❏ *The crowd danced and sang, and waved banners.*

bap|tism /bǽptɪzəm/ (**baptisms**) **NOUN** A **baptism** is a Christian ceremony in which a person is baptized. ❏ *Father Wright regularly performs weddings and baptisms.*

bap|tize /bǽptaɪz/ (**baptizes, baptizing, baptized**) **VERB** When someone **is baptized**, they are touched or covered with water, to show that they have become a member of the Christian church. ❏ *Mary decided to become a Christian and was baptized.*

bar /bɑ́r/ (**bars**)

1 **NOUN** A **bar** is a long, straight piece of metal. ❏ *The building had bars on all of the windows.*

2 **NOUN** A **bar of** something is a small block of it. ❏ *What is your favorite chocolate bar?*

3 **NOUN** A **bar** is a place where you can buy and drink alcoholic drinks. ❏ *Lyndsay met her boyfriend at a local bar.*

bar|becue /bɑ́rbɪkyu/ (**barbecues, barbecuing, barbecued**) also **barbeque, BBQ**

1 **NOUN** A **barbecue** is a piece of equipment that you use for cooking outdoors.

2 **NOUN** If someone has a **barbecue**, they cook food on a barbecue outdoors. ❏ *On Saturday we had a barbecue on the beach.*

3 **VERB** If you **barbecue** food, you cook it on a barbecue. ❏ *Tuna can be grilled, fried or barbecued.*

→ look at **cook, meat**

bar|ber /bɑ́rbər/ (**barbers**) **NOUN** A **barber** is a person whose job is to cut men's hair.

Sound Partners   bare, bear

bare /bɛ́ər/ (**barer, barest**)

1 **ADJECTIVE** If a part of your body is **bare**, it is not covered by any clothing. ❏ *Jane's feet were bare.*

2 **ADJECTIVE** A **bare** surface is not covered or decorated with anything. ❏ *The apartment has bare wooden floors.*

3 **ADJECTIVE** If a room, cupboard, or shelf is **bare**, it is empty. ❏ *His refrigerator was bare.*

bare|foot /bɛ̱ərfʊt/ **ADJECTIVE** If you do something **barefoot**, you do it without wearing shoes or socks. ❑ *He walked 10 miles barefoot to find help.*

bar|gain /bɑ̱rgɪn/ (bargains, bargaining, bargained)

1 **NOUN** Something that is a **bargain** is being sold at a lower price than usual. ❑ *At this price the dress is a bargain.*

2 **VERB** When two or more people **bargain**, they discuss what each of them will do, pay, or receive. ❑ *The workers have the right to bargain for better pay.*

barge /bɑ̱rdʒ/ (barges) **NOUN** A **barge** is a long, narrow boat with a flat bottom, used for carrying heavy loads. ❑ *The barges carried water, food, and medicines.*

bark /bɑ̱rk/ (barks, barking, barked)

1 **VERB** When a dog **barks**, it makes a short, loud noise. ❑ *Don't let the dogs bark.*

2 **NOUN** Bark is also a noun. ❑ *Your child may be afraid of a dog's bark, or its size.*

3 **NONCOUNT NOUN** SCIENCE Bark is the rough surface of a tree.

→ look at **tree**

barn /bɑ̱rn/ (barns) **NOUN** A **barn** is a building on a farm where animals and crops are kept.

→ look at **farm**

bar|racks /bæ̱rəks/ (barracks) **NOUN** A **barracks** is a building where soldiers or policemen live and work. ❑ *...an army barracks.*

bar|rel /bæ̱rəl/ (barrels)

1 **NOUN** A **barrel** is a large container, with curved sides and flat ends, for storing liquids. ❑ *The U.S. uses about 20 million barrels of oil a day.*

2 **NOUN** The **barrel** of a gun is the long metal part.

bar|ri|cade /bæ̱rɪkeɪd/ (barricades, barricading, barricaded)

1 **NOUN** A **barricade** is a line of things that have been put across a road to stop people from passing. ❑ *The street was blocked by a barricade.*

2 **VERB** If you **barricade** a road or an entrance, you put a barricade across it, to stop people from entering. ❑ *Police barricaded all entrances to the square.*

bar|ri|er /bæ̱riər/ (barriers) **NOUN** A **barrier** is a fence or a wall that prevents people or

things from moving from one area to another. ❑ *A police barrier blocked the road.*

bar|tender /bɑ̱rtɛndər/ (bartenders) **NOUN** A **bartender** is a person who makes and serves drinks in a bar.

Spelling Partners   base

base /be̱ɪs/ (bases, basing, based)

1 **NOUN** The **base** of something is its lowest part, or the part that it stands on. ❑ *They planted flowers around the base of the tree.* ❑ *The base of the statue weighs four tons.*

2 **VERB** If you **base** one thing **on** another thing, the first thing develops from the second thing. ❑ *The film is based on a novel by Alexander Trocchi.*

3 **NOUN** A military **base** is a place where soldiers live and work. ❑ *The army base is close to the airport.*

4 **NOUN** Your **base** is the main place where you work or live. ❑ *In the summer her base is her home in Connecticut.*

5 **NOUN** SPORTS A **base** is one of the four squares on a baseball field that runners touch. ❑ *The first runner to reach second base was John Flaherty.*

→ look at **area**

base|ball /be̱ɪsbɔl/ **NONCOUNT NOUN** SPORTS **Baseball** is a game that is played with a bat and a ball on a large field by two teams of nine players. Players must hit the ball and run around four bases to score.

base|ball cap (baseball caps) **NOUN** A **baseball cap** is a cap with a curved part at the front that sticks out above your eyes. ❑ *Joe often wears a baseball cap.*

→ look at **clothing**

base|ment /be̱ɪsmənt/ (basements) **NOUN** The **basement** of a building is a floor that is built below ground level. ❑ *They put the old toys in the basement.*

→ look at **house**

bases

PRONUNCIATION HELP
Pronounce meaning **1** /be̱ɪsɪz/.
Pronounce meaning **2** /be̱ɪsɪz/.

1 **Bases** is the plural of **base**.

2 **Bases** is the plural of **basis**.

bash /bæʃ/ (bashes, bashing, bashed) **VERB**
If you **bash** someone or something, you hit them very hard. [INFORMAL] ❑ *I bashed him on the head.*

bash|ful /bæʃfəl/ **ADJECTIVE** Someone who is **bashful** is shy and easily embarrassed. ❑ *He seemed bashful and awkward.* ❑ *She gave a little bashful smile.*

ba|sic /beɪsɪk/
1 **ADJECTIVE** **Basic** describes the simplest and most important part of something. ❑ *Everyone needs the basic skills of reading and writing.*
2 **ADJECTIVE** **Basic** goods and services are very simple ones that every person needs. ❑ *There were shortages of the most basic foods.*

ba|si|cal|ly /beɪsɪkli/ **ADVERB** You can use **basically** when you are talking about a situation in a general way. ❑ *Basically, he is a nice boy.*

ba|sin /beɪsᵊn/ (basins) **NOUN** A **basin** is a deep bowl that you use for holding liquids. ❑ *Water dripped into a basin at the back of the room.*

ba|sis /beɪsɪs/ (bases /beɪsiz/)
1 **NOUN** If something is done **on** a particular **basis**, that is the way that it is done. ❑ *We meet here for lunch on a regular basis.*
2 **NOUN** The **basis** of something is the most important part of it that other things can develop from. ❑ *The UN plan is a possible basis for peace talks.*

bas|ket /bæskɪt/ (baskets)
1 **NOUN** A **basket** is a container made from thin strips of wood, plastic, or metal, that is used for carrying or storing objects. ❑ *The picnic basket was filled with sandwiches and fruit.*
2 **NOUN** **SPORTS** A **basket** is the net that you throw the ball through in basketball.
3 **NOUN** **SPORTS** In basketball, if you **shoot** a **basket** you manage to throw the ball through the net. ❑ *The kids were outside shooting baskets.*
→ look at **laundry**

basket|ball /bæskɪtbɔl/ **NONCOUNT NOUN**
SPORTS **Basketball** is a game in which two teams of five players each try to throw a large ball through a round net hanging from a high metal ring.

bass /beɪs/ **ADJECTIVE** **MUSIC** A **bass** drum or guitar makes a very deep sound. ❑ *Dee Murray plays bass guitar in the band.*

bas|soon /bəsun/ (bassoons) **NOUN** **MUSIC**
A **bassoon** is a large musical instrument that is shaped like a tube. You play it by blowing into a curved metal pipe.

bat /bæt/ (bats, batting, batted)
1 **NOUN** **SPORTS** A **bat** is a long piece of wood that is used for hitting the ball in games such as baseball. ❑ *...a baseball bat.*
2 **VERB** **SPORTS** When you **bat**, you hit the ball with a bat in a game such as baseball. ❑ *Paxton hurt his elbow while he was batting.*
3 **NOUN** A **bat** is a small flying animal that looks like a mouse with wings. Bats hang upside down when they sleep during the day, and come out to fly at night.

batch /bætʃ/ (batches) **NOUN** A **batch** is a group of things or people of the same type. ❑ *I baked a batch of cookies.*

bath /bæθ/ (baths) **NOUN** When you take a **bath**, you sit or lie in a bathtub filled with water, and wash your body. ❑ *He took a bath before he went to bed.*

bathe /beɪð/ (bathes, bathing, bathed)
1 **VERB** When you **bathe**, you take a bath. ❑ *Most people bathe or shower once a day.*
2 **VERB** If you **bathe** a child, you wash them in a bathtub. ❑ *Back home, Shirley fed and bathed the baby.*

bathing suit (bathing suits) **NOUN** A **bathing suit** is a piece of clothing that you wear for swimming. ❑ *The children changed into their bathing suits.*
→ look at **wear**

bath|robe /bæθroʊb/ (bathrobes) **NOUN**
A **bathrobe** is a loose coat that you wear at home after taking a bath or shower.
→ look at **wear**

bath|room /bæθrum/ (bathrooms) **NOUN**
A **bathroom** is a room that contains a toilet. ❑ *She asked if she could use the bathroom.*
→ look at Picture Dictionary: **bathroom**
→ look at **house**

bath|tub /bæθtʌb/ (bathtubs) **NOUN** A **bathtub** is a long container that you fill with water and sit or lie in to wash your body. ❑ *She was lying in a huge pink bathtub.*
→ look at **bathroom**

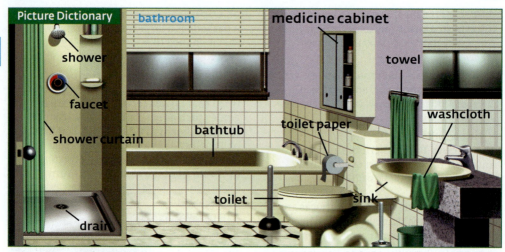

Picture Dictionary — **bathroom**

medicine cabinet

shower

faucet

towel

shower curtain

bathtub

toilet paper

washcloth

toilet

sink

drain

---

ba|ton /bətɑːn/ (batons)

1 NOUN MUSIC A **baton** is a light, thin stick that is used by a conductor (= a person who directs musicians).

2 NOUN SPORTS A **baton** is a short stick that one runner passes to another in a race.

bat|ter /bætər/ (batters)

1 NONCOUNT NOUN **Batter** is a mixture of flour, eggs, and milk, that is used for making cakes. ❏ *Pour the cake batter into a round pan.*

2 NOUN SPORTS In some sports, a **batter** is a person who hits the ball. ❏ *The batter hit the ball toward second base.*

bat|tery /bætəri/ (batteries)

1 NOUN **Batteries** are small objects that provide electricity for things such as radios. ❏ *The game requires two AA batteries.*

2 NOUN A car **battery** is a box containing acid. It provides the electricity that is needed to start the car. ❏ *Wendy can't take us because her car's battery is dead.*

bat|tle /bætəl/ (battles, battling, battled)

1 NOUN A **battle** is a violent fight between groups of people, especially between armies during a war. ❏ *The battle of Gettysburg took place in July 1863.*

2 NOUN A **battle** is a struggle for success or control over something. ❏ *Lance Armstrong won his battle against cancer.*

3 VERB If you **battle**, you try very hard to do something although it is extremely difficult ❏ *Doctors battled all night to save her life.* ❏ *Firefighters are still battling the two fires.*

bay /beɪ/ (bays) **NOUN GEOGRAPHY** A **bay** is a part of a coast where the land goes in and forms a curve. ❏ *We sailed across the bay in the morning.*

→ look at **landform**

BC /biː siː/ also **B.C.** SOCIAL STUDIES You use **BC** in dates to show the number of years before the year in which Jesus Christ was born. Compare with **AD**. ❏ *He probably lived in the fourth century BC.*

Sound Partners	be, bee

be

❶ AUXILIARY VERB USES
❷ OTHER VERB USES

❶ be /bi, STRONG biː/ (am, are, is, being, was, were, been)

LANGUAGE HELP
When you are speaking, you can use short forms of **be**. For example "I am" becomes "I'm" and "was not" becomes "wasn't."

1 VERB You use **be** with another verb to form the past or present continuous. ❏ *This is happening everywhere in the country.* ❏ *She was driving to work when the accident happened.*

2 VERB You use **be** with another verb to form the passive. ❏ *Her husband was killed in a car crash.*

3 VERB You use **be** with an infinitive to show that something is planned to happen. ❏ *The talks are to begin tomorrow.*

❷ be /bi, STRONG biː/ (am, are, is, being, was, were, been)

1 VERB You use **be** to introduce more information about a subject. ❏ *She's my mother.* ❏ *He is a very kind man.* ❏ *He is fifty years old.* ❏ *The sky was black.* ❏ *Dad's in the yard.*

Picture Dictionary beach

sun

lighthouse

rock

ocean

wave

shore

seaweed

shell

dune

sand

2 **VERB** You use **be**, with "it" when you are giving your opinion on a situation. ❏ *It was too cold for swimming.* ❏ *Sometimes it is necessary to say no.* ❏ *It's nice having friends to talk to.*
3 **VERB** You use **be** in expressions like **there is** and **there are** to say that something exists. ❏ *There are very few cars on this street.*

beach /biːtʃ/ (beaches) **NOUN** SCIENCE A **beach** is an area of sand or stones next to a lake or ocean. ❏ *The children played on the beautiful sandy beach.*
→ look at Picture Dictionary: **beach**
→ look at **ocean**

→ look at Picture Dictionary: **beach**
→ look at **ocean**

Word Partners Use **beach** with:

PREP.	**at the** beach, **on the** beach
N.	beach **chair**, beach **vacation**
V.	**lie on the** beach, **walk on the** beach
ADJ.	**private** beach, **public** beach, **sandy** beach

bead /biːd/ (beads) **NOUN** Beads are small pieces of colored glass, wood, or plastic that are used for making jewelry. ❏ *Victoria was wearing a purple bead necklace.*

beak /biːk/ (beaks) **NOUN** A bird's **beak** is the hard, pointed part of its mouth. ❏ *She pointed to a black bird with a yellow beak.*

Spelling Partners beam

beam /biːm/ (beams, beaming, beamed)
1 **VERB** If someone **is beaming**, they have a big happy smile on their face. ❏ *Frances beamed at her friend.*

2 **NOUN** SCIENCE A **beam** of light is a line of light that shines from something bright.
3 **NOUN** A **beam** is a long thick bar of wood or metal that supports the roof of a building. ❏ *The ceilings are supported by oak beams.*

bean /biːn/ (beans) **NOUN** Beans are the seeds of some plants that you can eat as a vegetable. ❏ *"More green beans, anyone?" Mrs. Parkinson asked.*

Sound Partners bear, bare

bear /bɛər/ (bears, bearing, bore, borne)
1 **VERB** If you **bear** an unpleasant experience, you accept it. ❏ *The loneliness was hard to bear.*
2 **VERB** If you can't **bear** someone or something, you dislike them very much. ❏ *I can't bear people being late.*
3 **VERB** If something **bears** your weight, it is able to support it. ❏ *The ice was not thick enough to bear their weight.*
4 **NOUN** A **bear** is a large, strong wild animal with thick fur and sharp claws.

bear|able /bɛərəbəl/ **ADJECTIVE** If something is **bearable**, you feel that you can deal with it without too much difficulty. ❏ *A cool breeze made the heat bearable.*

beard /bɪərd/ (beards) **NOUN** A man's **beard** is the hair that grows on his chin and cheeks. ❏ *He's 60 years old, with a long white beard.*
→ look at **hair**

→ look at **hair**

B

beast /bist/ (**beasts**) **NOUN** A **beast** is a large and dangerous animal. ❏ *He told the children that there were wild beasts in the woods.*

Sound Partners beat, beet

beat /bit/ (**beats, beating, beat, beaten**)
1 **VERB** To **beat** someone or something means to hit them very hard. ❏ *They beat him, and left him on the ground.* ❏ *We could hear the rain beating against the windows.*
2 **VERB** When your heart **beats**, it makes a regular sound and movement. ❏ *I felt my heart beating faster.*
3 **NOUN** **Beat** is also a noun. ❏ *He could hear the beat of his heart.*
4 **NOUN** MUSIC The **beat** of a piece of music is the rhythm that it has. ❏ *Play some music with a steady beat.*
5 **VERB** If you **beat** eggs, cream, or butter, you mix them quickly. ❏ *Beat the eggs and sugar together.*
6 **VERB** SPORTS If you **beat** someone in a competition or election, you defeat them. ❏ *The Red Sox beat the Yankees 5-2 last night.*
→ look at **music**

beau|ti|ful /byutɪfəl/
1 **ADJECTIVE** A **beautiful** person is very attractive to look at. ❏ *She was a very beautiful woman.*
2 **ADJECTIVE** Something that is **beautiful** is very attractive to look at or listen to. ❏ *New England is beautiful in the fall.* ❏ *It was a beautiful morning.* ● **beau|ti|ful|ly** /byutɪfli/ **ADVERB** ❏ *Karin sings beautifully.*
→ look at **music**

beau|ty /byuti/ **NONCOUNT NOUN** Beauty is the quality of being beautiful. ❏ *The hotel is in an area of natural beauty.*

beau|ty mark (**beauty marks**) **NOUN** A **beauty mark** is a small, dark spot on the skin.

beau|ty pag|eant /byuti pædʒənt/ (**beauty pageants**) **NOUN** A **beauty pageant** is a competition for young women in which judges decide who is the most beautiful.

bea|ver /bivər/ (**beavers**) **NOUN** A **beaver** is an animal with thick fur, a big flat tail and large teeth.

be|came /bɪkeɪm/ **Became** is a form of the verb **become**.

be|cause /bɪkɔz, -kʌz/
1 **CONJUNCTION** You use **because** when you are giving the reason for something. ❏ *He is called Mitch because his name is Mitchell.* ❏ *I'm sad because he didn't ask me to his birthday party.*
2 If an event or situation happens **because of** something, that thing is the reason or cause. ❏ *He's retiring because of ill health.*

be|come /bɪkʌm/ (**becomes, becoming, became, become**) **VERB** If someone or something **becomes** a particular thing, they start to be that thing. ❏ *The weather became cold and wet in October.* ❏ *Teresa wants to become a teacher.*

bed /bɛd/ (**beds**)
1 **NOUN** A **bed** is a piece of furniture that you lie on when you sleep. ❏ *We went to bed at about 10 p.m.* ❏ *Nina was already in bed.*
2 **NOUN** The ocean **bed** or a river **bed** is the ground at the bottom of the ocean or of a river.
→ look at **furniture**

Word Partners Use **bed** with:
ADJ.	**asleep in** bed, **ready for bed** **1**
V.	**get into** bed, **go to** bed, **lie in** bed, **put** *someone* **to** bed, **sick in** bed **1**
PREP.	**in** bed, **under the** bed **1**

bed|room /bɛdrum/ (**bedrooms**) **NOUN** A **bedroom** is a room that is used for sleeping in. ❏ *Emma, please clean your bedroom.*
→ look at **house**

bed|spread /bɛdsprɛd/ (**bedspreads**) **NOUN** A **bedspread** is a decorative cover that you put on a bed.

bed|time /bɛdtaɪm/ **NOUN** Your **bedtime** is the time when you usually go to bed. ❏ *It was eight-thirty, Peter's bedtime.*

Sound Partners bee, be

bee /bi/ (**bees**) **NOUN** A **bee** is a flying insect with a yellow-and-black striped body. Bees make a sweet food (= honey), and they can sting you. ❏ *Bees buzzed in the flowers.*

beef /bif/ **NONCOUNT NOUN** Beef is meat from a cow. ❏ *We had roast beef for lunch.*
→ look at **meat**

bee|hive /bihaɪv/ (**beehives**) **NOUN** A **beehive** is a container for bees to live in.

been /bɪn/
1 **Been** is a form of the verb **be**.
2 **VERB** If you have **been** to a place, you have gone to it or visited it. ❏ *Have you ever been to Paris?*

beep /biːp/ (beeps, beeping, beeped)

1 **NOUN** A **beep** is a short, high sound made by a piece of electronic equipment. ❑ *Please leave a message after the beep.*

2 **VERB** If a piece of electronic equipment **beeps**, it makes a short, high sound. ❑ *My cellphone beeps when I receive a text message.*

3 **NOUN** A **beep** is a short, loud sound made by a car horn.

4 **VERB** If a horn **beeps**, or if you **beep** it, it makes a short, loud sound. ❑ *He beeped the horn and waved.*

beer /bɪər/ **NONCOUNT NOUN** Beer is an alcoholic drink made from grain. ❑ *He sat in the kitchen drinking beer.*

Sound Partners	beet, beat

beet /biːt/ (beets) **NOUN** Beets are dark red roots that are eaten as a vegetable. They are often preserved in vinegar (= a sour liquid made from wine). ❑ *The duck was served with potato slices, beets and carrots.*

bee|tle /biːtᵊl/ (beetles) **NOUN** A beetle is an insect with a hard, shiny black body.

be|fore /bɪfɔr/

1 **PREPOSITION** If something happens **before** a particular date, time, or event, it happens earlier than that date, time, or event. ❑ *Annie was born a few weeks before Christmas.*

2 **CONJUNCTION** Before is also a conjunction. ❑ *Brush your teeth before you go to bed.*

3 **ADVERB** If someone has done something **before**, they have done it in the past. ❑ *I've never been here before.* ❑ *I have met Professor Lown before.*

beg /bɛg/ (begs, begging, begged)

1 **VERB** If you **beg** someone **to** do something, you ask them in a way that shows that you very much want them to do it. ❑ *I begged him to come to New York with me.* ❑ *I begged for help but no one listened.*

2 **VERB** If someone **is begging**, they are asking people to give them food or money because they are very poor. ❑ *Homeless people were begging on the streets.*

be|gan /bɪgæn/ **Began** is a form of the verb **begin**.

beg|gar /bɛgər/ (beggars) **NOUN** A beggar is someone who lives by asking people for money or food. ❑ *There are no beggars on the streets in Vienna.*

be|gin /bɪgɪn/ (begins, beginning, began, begun)

1 **VERB** To begin to do something means to start doing it. ❑ *Jack stood up and began to move around the room.* ❑ *David began to look angry.*

2 **VERB** When something **begins** or when you **begin** it, it starts to happen. ❑ *The problems began last November.* ❑ *He has just begun his second year at college.*

be|gin|ner /bɪgɪnər/ (beginners) **NOUN** A **beginner** is someone who has just started learning to do something. ❑ *The course is for both beginners and advanced students.*

be|gin|ning /bɪgɪnɪŋ/ (beginnings) **NOUN** The **beginning of** something is the first part of it. ❑ *This was the beginning of her career.* ❑ *The wedding will be at the beginning of March.* → look at **calendar**

be|gun /bɪgʌn/ **Begun** is a form of the verb **begin**.

be|half /bɪhæf/ If you do something **on** someone's **behalf**, you do it for that person. ❑ *She thanked us all on her son's behalf.*

be|have /bɪheɪv/ (behaves, behaving, behaved)

1 **VERB** The way that you **behave** is the way that you do and say things. ❑ *I couldn't believe Molly was behaving in this way.*

2 **VERB** If you **behave yourself**, you act in the way that people think is correct and proper. ❑ *Remember to behave yourself.*

be|hav|ior /bɪheɪvyər/ **NONCOUNT NOUN** A person's or animal's **behavior** is the way that they behave. ❑ *You should always reward good behavior.*

be|hind /bɪhaɪnd/

1 **PREPOSITION** If something is **behind** a thing or person, it is at the back of it. ❑ *I put a cushion behind his head.* ❑ *They were parked behind the truck.*

2 **PREPOSITION** If you are walking or traveling **behind** someone or something, you are following them. ❑ *Keith walked along behind them.*

3 **ADVERB** Behind is also an adverb. ❑ *The other police officers followed behind in a second vehicle.*

4 **PREPOSITION** If people or things are **behind**, or **behind** schedule, they are slower than they should be. ❑ *The work is 22 weeks behind schedule.*

b

5 ADVERB If you leave something or someone **behind,** you do not take them with you when you go. ❑ *The soldiers escaped into the mountains, leaving behind their weapons.*
→ look at **location**

beige /beɪʒ/ (beiges)
1 ADJECTIVE Something that is **beige** is pale brown in color. ❑ *The walls are beige.*
2 NOUN Beige is also a noun. ❑ *I like beige more than dark brown.*

be|ing /biɪŋ/ (beings)
1 Being is a form of the verb **be.**
2 NOUN A **being** is a person or a living thing. ❑ *Remember you are dealing with a living being—consider the horse's feelings too.*

be|lief /bɪliːf/ (beliefs) NOUN Belief is a powerful feeling that something is real or true. ❑ *Benedict has a deep belief in God.*

be|liev|able /bɪliːvəbəl/ ADJECTIVE If something is **believable,** you feel that it could be true or real. ❑ *Mark's excuse was believable.*

be|lieve /bɪliːv/ (believes, believing, believed)
1 VERB If you **believe** that something is true, you think that it is true. [FORMAL] ❑ *Scientists believe that life began around 4 billion years ago.* ❑ *We believe that the money is hidden here in this apartment.*
2 VERB If you **believe** someone, you feel sure that they are telling the truth. ❑ *Never believe what you read in the newspapers.*
3 VERB If you **believe in** something, you feel sure that it exists. ❑ *I don't believe in ghosts.*

bell /bɛl/ (bells)
1 NOUN A **bell** is a metal object that makes a ringing sound. ❑ *I was eating my lunch when the bell rang.*
2 NOUN A **bell** is a hollow metal object with a loose piece hanging inside it that hits the sides and makes a pleasant sound. ❑ *It was a Sunday, and all the church bells were ringing.*

bell pep|per (bell peppers) NOUN A **bell pepper** is a hollow green, red, or yellow vegetable with seeds.

bel|ly /bɛli/ (bellies) NOUN The **belly** of a person or animal is their stomach. ❑ *She put her hands on her swollen belly.*

be|long /bɪlɔŋ/ (belongs, belonging, belonged)
1 VERB If something **belongs to** you, you own it. ❑ *The house has belonged to her family for three generations.*
2 VERB If someone or something **belongs to** a group or organization, they are a member of that group or organization. ❑ *I used to belong to the tennis club.*
3 VERB If something or someone **belongs** somewhere, that is the right place for them to be. ❑ *After ten years in New York, I really feel that I belong here.*

be|long|ings /bɪlɔŋɪŋz/ PLURAL NOUN Your **belongings** are the things that you own. ❑ *I gathered my belongings and left.*

be|low /bɪloʊ/
1 PREPOSITION If something is **below** something else, it is in a lower position. ❑ *He came out of the apartment below Leonard's.* ❑ *We watched the sun sink below the horizon.*
2 ADVERB Below is also an adverb. ❑ *I could see the street below.*
3 PREPOSITION If something is **below** an amount, rate, or level, it is less than that amount, rate, or level. ❑ *Night temperatures can drop below 15 degrees.*
4 ADVERB Below is also an adverb. ❑ *Daytime temperatures were at zero or below.*

belt /bɛlt/ (belts) NOUN A **belt** is a strip of leather or cloth that you wear around your waist. ❑ *He wore a belt with a large brass buckle.*

bench /bɛntʃ/ (benches) NOUN A **bench** is a long seat made of wood or metal. ❑ *Tom sat down on a park bench.*

bend /bɛnd/ (bends, bending, bent)
1 VERB When you **bend,** you move the top part of your body down and forward. ❑ *I bent over and kissed her cheek.* ❑ *She bent down and picked up the toy.*
2 VERB When you **bend** a part of your body, you change its position so that it is no longer straight. ❑ *Remember to bend your legs when you do this exercise.*

3 **VERB** When something straight **bends**, it changes direction to form a curve. ❑ *The road bends slightly to the right.*

4 **NOUN** A **bend** in a road or a pipe is a curve or angle in it. ❑ *The accident happened on a sharp bend in the road.*

be|neath /bɪniθ/ **PREPOSITION** Something that is **beneath** another thing is under it. ❑ *She could see the muscles of his shoulders beneath his T-shirt.* ❑ *There are four levels of parking beneath the mall.*

ben|efit /bɛnɪfɪt/ (**benefits, benefiting, benefited**)

1 **NOUN** The **benefit** of something is the help that you get from it or the advantage that comes from it. ❑ *Parents need to educate their children about the benefits of exercise.*

2 **VERB** If you **benefit from** something, it helps you or improves your life. ❑ *You would benefit from a change in your diet.*

bent /bɛnt/

1 **Bent** is a form of the verb **bend**.

2 **ADJECTIVE** Something that is **bent** is not straight. ❑ *Keep your knees slightly bent.* ❑ *He found a bent nail on the ground.*

ber|ry /bɛri/ (**berries**) **NOUN** Berries are small, round fruit that grow on a bush or a tree.

be|side /bɪsaɪd/ **PREPOSITION** Something that is **beside** something else is next to it. ❑ *Can I sit beside you?*

be|sides /bɪsaɪdz/

1 **PREPOSITION** **Besides** something means in addition to it. ❑ *She has many good qualities besides being very beautiful.*

2 **ADVERB** You use **besides** when you want to give another reason for something. ❑ *The house is far too expensive. Besides, I don't want to leave our little apartment.*

best /bɛst/

1 **ADJECTIVE** **Best** is a form of the adjective **good**. If one thing is **best**, it is better than all the others. ❑ *Who is your best friend?* ❑ *Drink regularly through the day—water is best.*

2 **ADVERB** **Best** is a form of the adverb **well**. It means "in a way that is better than all the others." ❑ *I did best in physics in my class.* ❑ *J. R. R. Tolkien is best known as the author of "The Hobbit."*

3 **NOUN** If someone or something is **the best**, they are better than all other people or things. ❑ *We offer only the best to our clients.*

4 **NOUN** If you **do your best**, you try very hard to do something as well as possible. ❑ *If you do your best, no one can criticize you.* → look at **route**

bet /bɛt/ (**bets, betting, bet**)

1 **VERB** If you **bet on** a race or sports game, you give someone some money and say what you think that the result of the race or game will be. If you are correct, they give you your money back with some extra money, but if you are wrong they keep your money. ❑ *Jockeys are forbidden to bet on the outcome of horse races.* ❑ *I bet $20 on a horse called Bright Boy.*

2 **NOUN** **Bet** is also a noun. ❑ *Did you make a bet on the horse race?* ● **bet|ting** **NONCOUNT NOUN** ❑ *Betting is illegal in many countries.*

3 You say "**I bet**" to show that you are sure something is true. [INFORMAL] ❑ *I bet you were good at sports when you were at school.*

bet|ter /bɛtər/

1 **ADJECTIVE** **Better** is a form of the adjective **good**.

2 **Better** is a form the adverb **well**.

3 **ADVERB** If you like one thing **better than** another, you like it more. ❑ *I like your poem better than mine.*

4 **ADJECTIVE** If you are **better** after an illness or injury, you have recovered from it. ❑ *When I'm better, I'll talk to him.*

5 **ADJECTIVE** If you feel **better**, you no longer feel so ill. ❑ *He is feeling much better today.*

6 You use **had better** when you are saying what should happen. ❑ *I think we had better go home.*

be|tween /bɪtwin/

1 **PREPOSITION** If something is **between** two people or things, it has one of them on one side of it and the other on the other side. ❑ *Nicole was standing between the two men.*

2 **PREPOSITION** If you travel **between** two places, you travel from one place to the other and back again. ❑ *I spend a lot of time traveling between Waco and El Paso.*

3 **PREPOSITION** If something is **between** two amounts, it is greater than the first amount and smaller than the second amount. ❑ *Try to exercise between 15 and 20 minutes every day.*

4 **PREPOSITION** If something happens **between** two times, it happens after the first time and before the second time. ❑ *The house was built between 1793 and 1797.*

b

B

5 PREPOSITION When something is divided or shared **between** two people, they each have a part of it. ❑ *There is only one bathroom shared between eight people.*
→ look at **location**

bev|er|age /bɛvərɪdʒ, bɛvrɪdʒ/ (**beverages**) NOUN Beverages are drinks. [FORMAL] ❑ *Try to avoid beverages that contain a lot of sugar.*

be|ware /bɪwɛər/ VERB If you tell someone to **beware** of a person or thing, you are telling them to be careful because the person or thing is dangerous. ❑ *Beware of the dangers of swimming in the ocean at night.*

be|wil|dered /bɪwɪldərd/ ADJECTIVE If you are **bewildered**, you are very confused and cannot decide what you should do. ❑ *The shoppers looked bewildered by the huge variety of goods for sale.*

be|yond /bɪyɒnd/
1 PREPOSITION Something that is **beyond** a place is on the other side of it, or further away than it. ❑ *On his right was a garden and beyond it a large house.*
2 ADVERB Beyond is also an adverb. ❑ *The house had a fabulous view out to the ocean beyond.*

Bible /baɪbəl/ NOUN The **Bible** is the holy book of the Christian and Jewish religions.

bi|ceps /baɪsɛps/ PLURAL NOUN SCIENCE Your **biceps** are the large muscles at the front of the upper part of your arms.

bi|cy|cle /baɪsɪkəl/ (**bicycles**) NOUN SPORTS A **bicycle** is a vehicle with two wheels. You ride it by sitting on it and using your legs to make the wheels turn.
→ look at **transportation**

bid /bɪd/ (**bids, bidding, bid**)
1 NOUN If you make a **bid** for something that is being sold, you say that you will pay a certain amount of money for it. ❑ *Bill made the winning $620 bid for the statue.*
2 VERB If you **bid** for something that is being sold, you say that you will pay a certain amount of money for it. ❑ *Lily wanted to bid for the painting.*

big /bɪg/ (**bigger, biggest**)
1 ADJECTIVE Someone or something that is **big** is large in size. ❑ *Australia is a big country.* ❑ *Her husband was a big man.* ❑ *The crowd included a big group from Cleveland.*
2 ADJECTIVE Someone or something that is **big** is important or serious. ❑ *Mandy's problem*

was too big for her to solve alone. ❑ *He owns one of the biggest companies in Italy.*
3 ADJECTIVE Children often call their older brother or sister their **big** brother or sister. ❑ *I live with my dad and my big brother, John.*
→ look at **car, factory**

big bang theo|ry NOUN SCIENCE The **big bang theory** is a theory that states that the universe was created after an extremely large explosion.

bike /baɪk/ (**bikes**) NOUN SPORTS A **bike** is a bicycle or a motorcycle. [INFORMAL] ❑ *When you ride a bike, you exercise all your leg muscles.*
→ look at **fitness**

bi|ki|ni /bɪkini/ (**bikinis**) NOUN A **bikini** is a piece of clothing with two parts that women wear for swimming.

bi|lin|gual /baɪlɪŋgwəl/
1 ADJECTIVE Someone who is **bilingual** can speak two languages equally well. ❑ *He is bilingual in French and English.*
2 ADJECTIVE Something that is **bilingual** is written or spoken in two languages. ❑ *The company specializes in bilingual dictionaries.*
→ look at **dictionary**

bill /bɪl/ (**bills**)
1 NOUN A **bill** is a piece of paper that shows how much money you must pay for something. ❑ *They couldn't afford to pay their bills.*
2 NOUN A **bill** is a piece of paper money. ❑ *The case contained a large quantity of U.S. dollar bills.*
3 NOUN SOCIAL STUDIES In government, a **bill** is a written document that contains a suggestion for a new law. ❑ *The bill was approved by a large majority.*
→ look at **payment**

Word Partners	Use **bill** with:
N.	electricity bill, gas bill, hospital bill, hotel bill, phone bill **1**
	dollar bill **2**
V.	pay a bill **1**
	pass a bill, sign a bill, vote on a bill **3**

bill|board /bɪlbɔrd/ (**billboards**) NOUN A **billboard** is a very large board for advertisements at the side of the road.

bil|lion /bɪlyən/ (**billions**)

> **LANGUAGE HELP**
> The plural form is **billion** after a number.

A **billion** is the number 1,000,000,000.
❏ *The country's debt has risen to 3 billion dollars.*
❏ *The game was watched by billions of people around the world.*

bil|lion|aire /bɪlyənɛər/ (**billionaires**) **NOUN**
A **billionaire** is an extremely rich person who has money or property worth at least a billion dollars.

Bill of Rights **NOUN** SOCIAL STUDIES A **Bill of Rights** is a written list of the rights of people living in a particular country.

bin /bɪn/ (**bins**) **NOUN** A **bin** is a container that you keep things in. ❏ *...a plastic storage bin.*

bind /baɪnd/ (**binds, binding, bound**) **VERB** If you **bind** something, you tie rope or string around it to hold it firmly. ❏ *Bind the ends of the rope with thread.* ❏ *They bound his hands behind his back.*

bin|ocu|lars /bɪnɒkyələrz/ **PLURAL NOUN**
Binoculars are special glasses that you use to look at things that are a long distance away.

bi|og|ra|phy /baɪɒgrəfi/ (**biographies**)
NOUN LANGUAGE ARTS A **biography** of someone is the story of their life that is written by someone else. ❏ *I am reading a biography of Franklin D. Roosevelt.*

bio|logi|cal /baɪəlɒdʒɪkəl/ **ADJECTIVE** SCIENCE
Biological processes happen in the bodies and cells of living things. ❏ *...biological*

processes such as reproduction and growth.

bi|ol|ogy /baɪɒlədʒi/ **NONCOUNT NOUN**
Biology is the scientific study of living things. ● **bi|olo|gist** /baɪɒlədʒɪst/ (**biologists**) **NOUN** ❏ *The marine biologist was killed by a shark while diving.*
→ look at **science**

bird /bɜrd/ (**birds**) **NOUN** A **bird** is an animal with feathers and wings. ❏ *...a bird's nest.*
❏ *The bird flew away as I came near.*
→ look at Picture Dictionary: **birds**

bird|house /bɜrdhaʊs/ (**birdhouses**) **NOUN**
A **birdhouse** is a box placed in a tree or other high place that birds can build a nest in.
❏ *He showed us how to build a birdhouse.*

birth /bɜrθ/ (**births**)
1 **NOUN** When a baby is born, you call this moment his or her **birth**. ❏ *They are celebrating the birth of their first child.* ❏ *Alice weighed 5 lbs 7 oz at birth.*
2 When a woman **gives birth**, a baby comes out of her body. ❏ *She's just given birth to a baby girl.*

birth|day /bɜrθdeɪ, -di/ (**birthdays**) **NOUN**
Your **birthday** is the day of the year that you were born. ❏ *Mom always sends David a present on his birthday.*
→ look at **identification**

bis|cuit /bɪskɪt/ (**biscuits**) **NOUN** A **biscuit** is hard, dry bread in the form of a small round shape.

bish|op /bɪʃəp/ (**bishops**) **NOUN** A **bishop** is a leader in the Christian church whose job is to look after all the churches in an area.

b

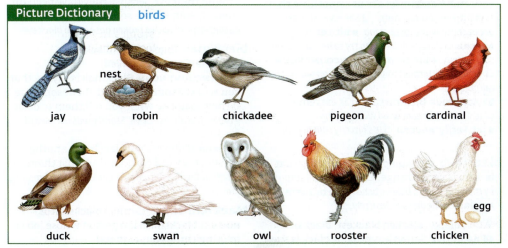

Picture Dictionary   **birds**

nest

jay   robin   chickadee   pigeon   cardinal

egg

duck   swan   owl   rooster   chicken

B

bit /bɪt/ (**bits**)

1 **NOUN** TECHNOLOGY A **bit** is a unit of information that can be stored on a computer.

2 **A bit of** something is a small amount of it, or a small part or section of it. ❑ *I do a bit of work at my children's school sometimes.* ❑ *Only a bit of the cake was left.*

3 **A bit** means a little. ❑ *This girl was a bit strange.* ❑ *I think people feel a bit happier now.*

4 **Quite a bit** means quite a lot. [INFORMAL] ❑ *Things have changed quite a bit.*

5 If you do something **a bit** or **for a bit**, you do it for a short time. ❑ *Let's wait a bit.*

6 **Bit** is a form of the verb **bite**.

bite /baɪt/ (**bites, biting, bit, bitten**)

1 **VERB** If you **bite** something, you use your teeth to cut into it or through it. ❑ *William bit into his sandwich.*

2 **NOUN** A **bite** of food is a small piece of it that you cut into with your teeth. ❑ *Dan took another bite of apple.*

3 **VERB** If a snake or an insect **bites**, it makes a mark or a hole in your skin with a sharp part of its body. ❑ *Do these flies bite?*

4 **NOUN** A **bite** is a painful mark on your body where an animal, a snake, or an insect has bitten you. ❑ *A dog bite needs immediate medical attention.*

→ look at **eat**

bit|ten /bɪtᵊn/ **Bitten** is a form of the verb **bite**.

bit|ter /bɪtər/ (**bitterest**)

1 **ADJECTIVE** A **bitter** food tastes unpleasantly sharp and sour. ❑ *The medicine tasted bitter.*

2 **ADJECTIVE** If someone is **bitter**, they feel very angry and upset about something that has happened to them. ❑ *She is very bitter about the way she lost her job.* ● **bit|ter|ly** **ADVERB** ❑ *"And he didn't even try to help us," Grant said bitterly.* ● **bit|ter|ness** **NONCOUNT NOUN** ❑ *I still feel bitterness toward the person who stole my purse.*

3 **ADJECTIVE** **Bitter** weather is extremely cold. ❑ *A bitter east wind was blowing.* ● **bit|ter|ly** **ADVERB** ❑ *It's bitterly cold here in Moscow.*

bi|zarre /bɪzɑr/ **ADJECTIVE** Something that is **bizarre** is very strange. ❑ *They were all surprised by their manager's bizarre behavior.* ● **bi|zarre|ly** **ADVERB** ❑ *She dresses bizarrely.*

black /blæk/ (**blacker, blackest, blacks**)

1 **ADJECTIVE** Something that is **black** is the color of the sky at night. ❑ *She was wearing a black coat with a white collar.* ❑ *He had thick black hair.*

2 **NOUN** **Black** is also a noun. ❑ *She was wearing black.*

3 **ADJECTIVE** A **black** person belongs to a race of people with dark skins, especially a race originally from Africa. ❑ *He worked for the rights of black people.*

4 **NOUN** **Black** people are sometimes called **blacks**, especially when comparing different groups of people. Other uses of the word could cause offense. ❑ *There are about 31 million blacks in the U.S.*

5 **ADJECTIVE** **Black** coffee has no milk in it. ❑ *A cup of black coffee contains no calories.*

→ look at **hair**

black and white also **black-and-white**

ADJECTIVE In a **black and white** photograph or film, everything is shown in black, white, and gray. ❑ *...old black and white films.* ❑ *...a black-and-white photo.*

black|berry /blækbɛri/ (**blackberries**)

1 **NOUN** A **blackberry** is a small, soft black or dark purple fruit.

2 **NOUN** TECHNOLOGY A **BlackBerry** is a small computer that can be used for receiving and sending email, and sometimes making phone calls. [TRADEMARK]

black|board /blækbɔrd/ (**blackboards**)

NOUN A **blackboard** is a big, dark-colored board for writing on in a classroom.

black eye (**black eyes**) **NOUN** If someone has a **black eye**, they have a dark-colored mark around their eye because they have been hit there by someone or something. ❑ *Jan arrived at the hospital with a broken nose and a black eye.*

black|mail /blækmeɪl/ (**blackmails, blackmailing, blackmailed**)

1 **NONCOUNT NOUN** **Blackmail** is saying that you will say something bad about someone if they do not do what you tell them to do or give you money. ❑ *Mr. Stanley was accused of blackmail.*

2 **VERB** If one person **blackmails** another person, they use blackmail against them. ❑ *Jeff suddenly realized that Linda was blackmailing him.*

black|smith /blæksmɪθ/ (**blacksmiths**)

NOUN A **blacksmith** is a person whose job is making things out of metal.

blad|der /blǽdər/ (bladders) NOUN SCIENCE
Your **bladder** is the part of your body where
liquid waste is stored until it leaves your body.

blade /bleɪd/
(blades) NOUN
The **blade** of a
knife is the flat,
sharp edge that
is used for
cutting. ❑ *The
ax blade cut deep
into the log.*

blame /bleɪm/ (blames, blaming, blamed)
1 VERB If you **blame** someone or something
for something bad, you say that they caused
it. ❑ *Police blamed the bus driver for the accident.*
2 NONCOUNT NOUN If you get the **blame for**
something bad that has happened, people
say that you caused it. ❑ *I'm not going to take
the blame for a mistake he made.*

bland /blænd/ (blander, blandest)
1 ADJECTIVE Someone or something that is
bland is dull and not interesting. ❑ *Their
music is bland and boring.*
2 ADJECTIVE Food that is **bland** has very
little flavor. ❑ *The pizza tasted bland, like warm
cardboard.*

blank /blæŋk/
1 ADJECTIVE Something that is **blank** has
nothing on it. ❑ *He tore a blank page from his
notebook.*
2 ADJECTIVE If you look **blank**, your face
shows no reaction. ❑ *Albert looked blank.
"I don't know him, sir."* ● **blank|ly** ADVERB ❑ *Ellie
stared at him blankly.*
→ look at **answer**

blan|ket /blǽŋkɪt/ (blankets) NOUN A
blanket is a large, thick piece of cloth that
you put on a bed to keep you warm.

blast /blæst/ (blasts) NOUN A **blast** is a big
explosion, especially one caused by a bomb.
❑ *250 people were killed in the blast.*

blaze /bleɪz/ (blazes, blazing, blazed)
1 VERB When a fire **blazes**, it burns
strongly and brightly. ❑ *Three people died as
the building blazed.*
2 NOUN A **blaze** is a large fire that destroys
a lot of things. ❑ *More than 4,000 firefighters are
battling the blaze.*

blaz|er /bleɪzər/ (blazers) NOUN A **blazer** is a
type of light jacket for men or women.

bleach /blitʃ/ (bleaches, bleaching, bleached)
1 VERB If you **bleach** something, you use a
chemical to make it white or lighter in
color. ❑ *These products don't bleach the hair.*
2 NONCOUNT NOUN **Bleach** is a chemical
that is used for making cloth white, or for
making things very clean.
→ look at **laundry**

bleak /blik/ (bleaker, bleakest)
1 ADJECTIVE If a situation is **bleak**, people do
not expect it to be happy or successful. ❑ *The
future looks bleak.*
2 ADJECTIVE When the weather is **bleak**, it
is cold, dull, and unpleasant. ❑ *The weather
can be quite bleak here.*

bleed /blid/ (bleeds, bleeding, bled) VERB
When part of your body **bleeds**, you lose
blood from it. ❑ *Ian's lip was bleeding.*
● **bleed|ing** NONCOUNT NOUN ❑ *We tried to
stop the bleeding from the cut on his arm.*
→ look at **sick**

blend /blɛnd/ (blends, blending, blended)
1 VERB If you **blend** substances together,
you mix them together. ❑ *Blend the butter with
the sugar.*
2 NOUN A **blend** of things is a mixture of
them. ❑ *Their music is a blend of jazz and rock'n'roll.*
3 VERB When different things **blend**, they
combine well. ❑ *All the colors blend perfectly
together.*

bless /blɛs/ (blesses, blessing, blessed)
1 VERB When a priest **blesses** people or
things, he or she asks for God's protection
for them. ❑ *The pope blessed the crowd.*
2 You can say "**bless you**" to someone when
they sneeze (= blow out air through their
nose and mouth suddenly and noisily).

Sound Partners	blew, blue

blew /blu/ **Blew** is a form of the verb **blow**.

blind /blaɪnd/ (blinds)
1 ADJECTIVE Someone who is **blind** is unable
to see. ❑ *My grandfather is going blind.*
2 PLURAL NOUN The **blind** are people who are
blind. ❑ *He's a teacher of the blind.* ● **blind|ness**
NONCOUNT NOUN ❑ *Early treatment can usually
prevent blindness.*
3 NOUN **Blinds** are a piece of cloth or other
material that you can pull down over a
window to cover it. ❑ *Susan pulled the blinds up
to let the bright sunlight into the room.*
→ look at **disability**

b

blind|fold /bl<u>aɪ</u>ndfoʊld/ (**blindfolds, blindfolding, blindfolded**)
1 **NOUN** A **blindfold** is a strip of cloth that is tied over your eyes so that you cannot see.
2 **VERB** If you **blindfold** someone, you tie a blindfold over their eyes. ❑ *Mr. Li was handcuffed and blindfolded.*

bling /blɪŋ/ or **bling-bling** **NONCOUNT NOUN**
Bling is expensive or fancy jewelry.
[INFORMAL] ❑ *Famous jewelers want celebrities to wear their bling.*

blink /blɪŋk/ (**blinks, blinking, blinked**) **VERB**
When you **blink**, you shut your eyes and very quickly open them again. ❑ *I stood blinking in bright light.*

blis|ter /bl<u>ɪ</u>stər/ (**blisters**) **NOUN** A **blister** is a raised area of skin filled with a clear liquid.
❑ *I get blisters when I wear these shoes.*

bliz|zard /bl<u>ɪ</u>zərd/ (**blizzards**) **NOUN** A **blizzard** is a very bad storm with snow and strong winds.
→ look at **disaster**

blob /bl<u>ɒ</u>b/ (**blobs**) **NOUN** A **blob** of thick liquid is a small amount of it. [INFORMAL]
❑ *Denise wiped a blob of jelly off Edgar's chin.*

Spelling Partners   block

block /bl<u>ɒ</u>k/ (**blocks, blocking, blocked**)
1 **NOUN** A **block of** a substance is a large, solid piece of it with straight sides.
❑ *Elizabeth carves animals from blocks of wood.*
2 **NOUN** A **block** in a town or city is a group of buildings with streets on all sides, or the distance between each group of buildings.
❑ *He walked around the block three times.* ❑ *She walked four blocks down High Street.*
3 **VERB** If someone or something **blocks** a road, there is something on it so that nothing can pass along it. ❑ *The police blocked a highway through the center of the city.* ❑ *A tree fell down and blocked the road.*

blocked /bl<u>ɒ</u>kt/ or **blocked up** **ADJECTIVE** If something is **blocked**, it is completely closed so that nothing can get through it. ❑ *The pipes are blocked and the water can't get through.*

blog /bl<u>ɒ</u>g/ (**blogs**) **NOUN** TECHNOLOGY A **blog** is a website that describes the daily life of the person who writes it, and also their thoughts and ideas. ❑ *His blog was later published as a book.* ● **blog|ger** (**bloggers**) **NOUN** ❑ *Loewenstein is a freelance author, blogger and journalist.* ● **blog|ging** **NONCOUNT NOUN** ❑ *Blogging is very popular.*

blogo|sphere /bl<u>ɒ</u>gəsfɪər/ or **blogsphere** /bl<u>ɒ</u>gsfɪər/ **NOUN** TECHNOLOGY The **blogosphere** is all the blogs (= personal records) on the Internet. ❑ *The blogosphere continues to expand.*

blonde /bl<u>ɒ</u>nd/ (**blonder, blondest**)
1 **ADJECTIVE** Someone who has **blonde** hair has pale-colored hair. ❑ *My sister has blonde hair.*
2 **ADJECTIVE** Someone who is **blonde** has blonde hair. ❑ *He's blonder than his brother.*
→ look at **hair**

blood /bl<u>ʌ</u>d/ **NONCOUNT NOUN** SCIENCE **Blood** is the red liquid that flows inside your body.
❑ *His shirt was covered in blood.*

blood ves|sel (**blood vessels**) **NOUN** SCIENCE
Blood vessels are the narrow tubes that your blood flows through.

bloom /bl<u>u</u>m/ (**blooms, blooming, bloomed**)
VERB When a plant or tree **blooms**, it grows flowers on it. When a flower **blooms**, it opens. ❑ *This plant blooms between May and June.*
→ look at **tree**

blos|som /bl<u>ɒ</u>səm/ (**blossoms, blossoming, blossomed**)
1 **NONCOUNT NOUN** **Blossom** is the flowers that appear on a fruit tree. ❑ *The cherry blossom lasts only a few days.*
2 **VERB** When a tree **blossoms**, it produces blossom. ❑ *The peach trees will blossom soon.*
→ look at **tree**

blot /bl<u>ɒ</u>t/ (**blots**) **NOUN** A **blot** is a drop of liquid on a surface. ❑ *The page was covered with ink blots.*

blouse /bl<u>aʊ</u>s/ (**blouses**) **NOUN** A **blouse** is a shirt for a girl or woman.
→ look at **clothing**

blow /bl<u>oʊ</u>/ (**blows, blowing, blew, blown**)
1 **VERB** When a wind or breeze **blows**, the air moves. ❑ *A cold wind was blowing.*
2 **VERB** If the wind **blows** something somewhere, it moves it there. ❑ *The wind blew her hair back from her forehead.*
3 **VERB** If you **blow**, you send out air from your mouth. ❑ *Danny blew on his fingers to warm them.*

4 VERB When someone **blows** a whistle, they make a sound by blowing into it. ❏ *When the referee blows his whistle, the game begins.*

5 VERB When you **blow** your nose, you force air out of it in order to clear it. ❏ *He took out a handkerchief and blew his nose.*

6 NOUN If someone receives a **blow**, they are hit hard with something. ❏ *He went to the hospital after a blow to the face.*

7 NOUN If something that happens is a **blow to** someone, it is very disappointing to them. ❏ *The increase in tax was a blow to the industry.*

▶ **blow out** If you **blow out** a flame, you blow at it so that it stops burning. ❏ *I blew out the candle.*

▶ **blow up** **1** If someone **blows** something up or if it **blows up**, it is destroyed by an explosion. ❏ *He was jailed for trying to blow up a plane.*

2 If you **blow** something **up**, you fill it with air. ❏ *Can you help me blow up the balloons?*

blown /bloʊn/ **Blown** is a form of the verb **blow**.

Sound Partners blue, blew
---

blue /blu/ (**bluer, bluest, blues**)
1 ADJECTIVE Something that is **blue** is the color of the sky on a sunny day. ❏ *We looked up at the cloudless blue sky.* ❏ *She has pale blue eyes.*
2 NOUN Blue is also a noun. ❏ *Julie and Angela wore blue.*
3 NOUN MUSIC The **blues** is a type of slow, sad music that developed among African American musicians in the southern United States. ❏ *I grew up singing the blues at home with my mom.*
→ look at **color, ocean**

blue|berry /bluʊbɛri/ (**blueberries**) NOUN A **blueberry** is a small dark blue fruit.

Blue|tooth /bluʊtuθ/ NONCOUNT NOUN TECHNOLOGY **Bluetooth** is a type of technology that allows devices such as cellphones and computers to communicate with each other without being connected by wires. [TRADEMARK] ❏ *This is the latest Bluetooth technology.*

blunt /blʌnt/ (**blunter, bluntest**)
1 ADJECTIVE If you are **blunt**, you say exactly what you think and you do not try to be polite.
2 ADJECTIVE A **blunt** object is not sharp or pointed. ❏ *...a blunt pencil.*

blurred /blɜrd/ ADJECTIVE When a picture is **blurred**, it is not clear. ❏ *She showed me a blurred black and white photograph.*

blush /blʌʃ/ (**blushes, blushing, blushed**)
VERB When you **blush**, your face becomes red because you are ashamed or embarrassed. ❏ *"Hello, Maria," he said, and she blushed again.*

board /bɔrd/ (**boards, boarding, boarded**)
1 NOUN A **board** is a flat, thin piece of wood. ❏ *There were wooden boards over the doors and windows.*
2 NOUN A **board** is a flat piece of wood or plastic that you use for a special purpose. ❏ *The picture was on the staff bulletin board.* ❏ *A wooden chopping board can be very heavy.*
3 NOUN The **board** of a company is the group of people who organize it and make decisions about it. ❏ *The board meets today, and it will announce its decision tomorrow.*
4 VERB When you **board** a train, a ship, or an aircraft, you get into it to travel somewhere. [FORMAL] ❏ *I boarded the plane to Boston.*
5 When you are **on board** a train, a ship, or an aircraft, you are on it. ❏ *All 25 people on board the plane were killed.*

board|ing pass (**boarding passes**) NOUN A **boarding pass** is a card that a passenger must show when they are entering an aircraft or a boat.

boast /boʊst/ (**boasts, boasting, boasted**)
VERB If someone **boasts** about something that they have done or that they own, they talk about it too proudly, in a way that annoys other people. ❏ *He boasted that the police would never catch him.* ❏ *Carol boasted about her new job.*

boat /boʊt/
(**boats**) NOUN
A **boat** is a small ship.
❏ *One of the best ways to see the area is in a small boat.*
❏ *...a fishing boat.*

body /bɒdi/ (**bodies**)
1 NOUN A person's or animal's **body** is all their physical parts. ❏ *Yoga creates a healthy mind in a healthy body.*
2 NOUN A person's or animal's **body** is the main part of them, but not their arms, head,

Picture Dictionary body

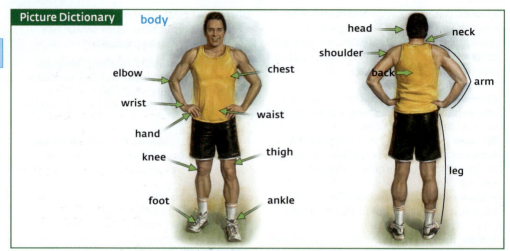

head → neck
shoulder →
elbow → ← chest
back →
wrist → arm
hand → ← waist
knee → thigh
foot → ankle
leg

and legs. ❏ *Lying flat on your back, twist your body onto one side.*

3 **NOUN** A **body** is a dead person or animal. ❏ *Two days later, her body was found in a wood.*

→ look at Picture Dictionary: **body**

body|guard /bɒdigard/ (**bodyguards**) **NOUN** A **bodyguard** is a person whose job is to protect someone important. ❏ *Three of his bodyguards were injured in the attack.*

boil /bɔɪl/ (**boils, boiling, boiled**)
1 **VERB** When a hot liquid **boils**, bubbles appear in it and it starts to change into steam. ❏ *I stood in the kitchen, waiting for the water to boil.* ❏ *Boil the water in the saucepan and add the salt.*

2 **VERB** When you **boil** food, you cook it in boiling water. ❏ *Wash and boil the rice.* ❏ *I peeled potatoes and put them in a pot to boil.*

→ look at **cook, water**

boil|ing point **NONCOUNT NOUN** SCIENCE
The **boiling point** of a liquid is the temperature at which it starts to change into steam.

bold /bould/ (**bolder, boldest**)
1 **ADJECTIVE** A **bold** action shows that you are not afraid to do dangerous things. ❏ *Their bold plan almost worked.*

2 **ADJECTIVE** A **bold** color or pattern is very bright. ❏ *Jill's dress was patterned with bold flowers in shades of red, blue or white.*

bo|lo|gna /bəlouni/ (**bolognas**) **NOUN**
Bologna is a type of sausage (= tube of meat). ❏ *Would you like a bologna sandwich?*

bolt /boult/ (**bolts, bolting, bolted**)
1 **NOUN** A **bolt** is a long piece of metal that you use with another small piece of metal with a hole in it (= a nut) to fasten things together. ❏ *Tighten any loose bolts and screws on your bicycle.*

2 **NOUN** A **bolt** on a door is a piece of metal that you move across to lock it. ❏ *Taylor went to the door and opened it.*

3 **VERB** When you **bolt** a door, you move the bolt across to lock it. ❏ *He locked and bolted the kitchen door.*

bomb /bɒm/ (**bombs, bombing, bombed**)
1 **NOUN** A **bomb** is a weapon that explodes and damages things nearby. ❏ *Bombs went off at two London train stations.* ❏ *The police do not know who planted the bomb.*

2 **VERB** When people **bomb** a place, they attack it with bombs. ❏ *Military airplanes bombed the airport.* ● **bomb|ing** (**bombings**) **NOUN** ❏ *The bombing of Pearl Harbor started World War II.*

bond /bɒnd/ (**bonds, bonding, bonded**)
1 **NOUN** A **bond between** people is a strong feeling of friendship, love, or shared beliefs. ❏ *The experience created a special bond between us.*

2 **VERB** When people **bond with** each other, they form a relationship based on love or shared beliefs and experiences. ❏ *Belinda quickly bonded with her new baby.*

bone /boun/ (**bones**) **NOUN** SCIENCE Your **bones** are the hard parts inside your body.

❏ *Many passengers suffered broken bones in the accident.*

bon|fire /bɒnfaɪər/ (bonfires) NOUN A **bonfire** is a large fire that you make outside. ❏ *Bonfires are not allowed in many areas.*

bo|nus /boʊnəs/ (bonuses)
1 NOUN A **bonus** is an extra amount of money that you earn, usually because you have worked very hard. ❏ *Each member of staff received a $100 bonus.*
2 NOUN A **bonus** is something good that you would not usually expect to get. ❏ *As a bonus, the CD comes with a free DVD.*

book /bʊk/ (books, booking, booked)
1 NOUN LANGUAGE ARTS A **book** is a number of pieces of paper, usually with words printed on them, that are fastened together and fixed inside a cover. ❏ *Her second book was an immediate success.* ❏ *I just read a new book by Rosella Brown.*
2 VERB When you **book** a hotel room or a ticket, you arrange to have it or use it at a particular time. ❏ *Laurie booked a flight home.*
→ look at **classroom**

book|case /bʊkkeɪs/ (bookcases) NOUN A **bookcase** is a piece of furniture with shelves that you keep books on.
→ look at **furniture**

book|let /bʊklɪt/ (booklets) NOUN A **booklet** is a very thin book that has a paper cover and that gives you information about something. ❏ *The travel office gave us a booklet about places to visit in Venice.*

book|mark /bʊkmɑrk/ (bookmarks, bookmarking, bookmarked)
1 NOUN TECHNOLOGY In computing, a **bookmark** is the address of a website that you add to a list on your computer so that you can return to it easily. ❏ *Use bookmarks to give you quick links to your favorite websites.*
2 VERB **Bookmark** is also a verb. ❏ *Do you want to bookmark this page?*

book|store /bʊkstɔr/ (bookstores) NOUN A **bookstore** is a store where books are sold.

boom /bum/ (booms, booming, boomed)
1 NOUN If there is a **boom** in the economy, there is an increase in the number of things that people are buying. ❏ *...an economic boom.*
2 VERB When something **booms**, it makes a loud, deep sound. ❏ *"Ladies," boomed Helena, "We all know why we're here tonight."*

3 NOUN **Boom** is also a noun. ❏ *We heard the boom of an explosion.*

boost /bust/ (boosts, boosting, boosted)
1 VERB If one thing **boosts** another, it causes it to increase, improve, or be more successful. ❏ *Lower prices will boost sales.*
2 NOUN **Boost** is also a noun. ❏ *The event would give the economy the boost that it needs.*
3 VERB If something **boosts** your confidence, it improves it. ❏ *If the team wins, it will boost their confidence.*
4 NOUN **Boost** is also a noun. ❏ *Scoring that goal gave me a real boost.*

boot /but/ (boots, booting, booted)
1 NOUN **Boots** are shoes that cover your whole foot and the lower part of your leg. ❏ *He sat down and took off his boots.*
2 VERB TECHNOLOGY If you **boot** a computer, you make it ready to start working. ❏ *Put the CD into the drive and boot the machine.*
3 **Boot up** means the same as **boot**. ❏ *Go over to your computer and boot it up.*
→ look at **clothing**

bor|der /bɔrdər/ (borders)
1 NOUN SOCIAL STUDIES The **border** between two countries is an imaginary line that divides them. ❏ *They drove across the border.* ❏ *Soldiers closed the border between the two countries.*
2 NOUN A **border** is a decoration around the edge of something. ❏ *The curtains were white with a red border.*

bore /bɔr/ (bores, boring, bored) VERB Someone or something that **bores** you is not at all interesting. ❏ *Dick bored me with stories of his vacation.*

bored /bɔrd/ ADJECTIVE If you are **bored**, you are not interested in something or you have nothing to do. ❏ *I am getting very bored with this television program.*

bor|ing /bɔrɪŋ/ ADJECTIVE Someone or something that is **boring** is not at all interesting. ❏ *Washing dishes is boring work.*
→ look at **television**

born /bɔrn/
1 VERB When a baby **is born**, it comes out of its mother's body and begins life. ❏ *She was born in Milan on April 29, 1923.*

B

2 ADJECTIVE **Born** describes someone who has a natural ability to do a particular activity or job. ❑ *Jack was a born teacher.*

borne /bɔrn/ **Borne** is a form of the verb **bear**.

bor|row /bɒroʊ/ (**borrows, borrowing, borrowed**) VERB If you **borrow** something that belongs to someone else, you use it for a period of time and then return it. ❑ *Can I borrow a pen please?*

boss /bɔs/ (**bosses**) NOUN Your **boss** is the person in charge of you at the place where you work. ❑ *He likes his new boss.*
→ look at **job**

bossy /bɔsi/ (**bossier, bossiest**) ADJECTIVE If someone is **bossy**, they enjoy telling people what to do. ❑ *Susan is a bossy little girl.*

bota|ny /bɒtəni/ NONCOUNT NOUN SCIENCE **Botany** is the scientific study of plants.
● **bo|tani|cal** /bətænɪkᵊl/ ADJECTIVE ❑ *The area is of great botanical interest.*

both /boʊθ/
1 ADJECTIVE You use **both** when you are saying that something is true about two people or things. ❑ *Stand up straight with both arms at your sides.* ❑ *Both men were taken to hospital.*
2 PRONOUN **Both** is also a pronoun. ❑ *Miss Brown and her friend are both from Brooklyn.* ❑ *They both worked at Harvard University.*
3 You use **both of** for showing that you are talking about two people or things. ❑ *Both of these women have strong memories of the war.* ❑ *Both of them have to go to London regularly.*
4 You use **both...and...** to show that each of two facts is true. ❑ *Now women work both before and after having their children.*

Usage both

In sentences with **both** and **and** use a plural verb. ***Both** Susan **and** her sister are teachers.*

---

both|er /bɒðər/ (**bothers, bothering, bothered**)
1 VERB If you do not **bother to** do something, you do not do it because you think it is not necessary. ❑ *Lots of people don't bother to get married these days.*
2 VERB If something **bothers** you, it makes you feel worried or angry. ❑ *Is something bothering you?*
3 VERB If someone **bothers** you, they try to talk to you when you are busy. ❑ *I'm sorry to bother you, but there's someone here to speak to you.*

bot|tle /bɒtᵊl/ (**bottles**) NOUN A **bottle** is a glass or plastic container in which drinks and other liquids are kept. ❑ *There were two empty water bottles on the table.* ❑ *She drank half a bottle of apple juice.*
→ look at **container**

bot|tom /bɒtəm/ (**bottoms**)
1 NOUN The **bottom** of something is the lowest or deepest part of it. ❑ *He sat at the bottom of the stairs.* ❑ *Answers can be found at the bottom of page 8.*
2 ADJECTIVE The **bottom** thing is the lowest one. ❑ *There are pencils in the bottom drawer of the desk.*

Word Partners	Use **bottom** with:
v.	**reach the** bottom, **sink to the** bottom **1**
N.	bottom **of a hill**, bottom **of the page**, bottom **of the pool**, **river** bottom, bottom **of the screen**, bottom **of the sea 1** bottom **drawer**, bottom **lip**, bottom **rung 2**
PREP.	**along the** bottom, **at the** bottom, **near the** bottom, **on the** bottom **1 2**

bought /bɔt/ **Bought** is a form of the verb **buy**.

boul|der /boʊldər/ (**boulders**) NOUN A **boulder** is a large round rock. ❑ *A passenger said that the train hit a boulder.*

boule|vard /bʊləvɑrd/ (**boulevards**) NOUN A **boulevard** is a wide street in a city. ❑ *The shop was on Lenton Boulevard.*

bounce /baʊns/ (**bounces, bouncing, bounced**)
1 VERB When an object such as a ball **bounces**, it hits a surface and immediately moves away from it again. ❑ *The ball bounced across the floor.* ❑ *Matthew came into the kitchen bouncing a rubber ball.*
2 VERB If you **bounce** on a soft surface, you jump up and down on it. ❑ *Some children were playing soccer; others were riding scooters or bouncing on the trampoline.*
3 VERB If an email **bounces**, it is returned to the person who sent it because the address was wrong, or because of a problem with one of the computers involved in sending it.

bound /baʊnd/ (**bounds, bounding, bounded**)
1 **Bound** is a form of the verb **bind**.

2 If something **is bound to** happen, it is certain to happen. ❑ *There are bound to be price increases next year.*

3 **VERB** If a person or animal **bounds** somewhere, they move quickly with large steps or jumps. ❑ *He bounded up the steps.*

bounda|ry /ba͟ʊndəri, -dri/ (**boundaries**) **NOUN** The **boundary of** an area of land is an imaginary line that separates it from other areas. ❑ *The river forms the western boundary of my farm.*

bou|quet /boʊke͟ɪ, bu-/ (**bouquets**) **NOUN** A **bouquet** is a bunch of flowers that have been cut. ❑ *The woman carried a bouquet of roses.*

bou|tique /buti͟k/ (**boutiques**) **NOUN** A **boutique** is a small store that sells fashionable clothes, shoes, or jewelry.

Spelling Partners bow

bow

❶ BENDING
❷ OBJECTS

❶ **bow** /ba͟ʊ/ (**bows, bowing, bowed**)
1 **VERB** When you **bow to** someone, you bend your head or body toward them as a formal way of greeting them or showing respect. ❑ *They bowed low to the king.*
2 **NOUN** Bow is also a noun. ❑ *I gave a theatrical bow and waved.*

❷ **bow** /bo͟ʊ/ (**bows**)
1 **NOUN** A **bow** is a knot with two round parts and two loose ends that is used in tying shoelaces and ribbons. ❑ *Add some ribbon tied in a bow.*
2 **NOUN** A **bow** is a weapon for shooting arrows. ❑ *Some of the men were armed with bows and arrows.*
3 **NOUN** MUSIC The **bow** of a violin or other similar instrument is a long thin piece of wood with threads stretched along it that you move across the strings.

bow|el /ba͟ʊəl/ (**bowels**) **NOUN** SCIENCE Your **bowels** are the tubes in your body where digested food from your stomach is stored before you pass it from your body. ❑ *Eating fruit and vegetables can help to keep your bowels healthy.*

bowl /bo͟ʊl/ (**bowls, bowling, bowled**)
1 **NOUN** A **bowl** is a round container that is used for mixing and serving food. ❑ *Put the soup in a bowl.*

2 **VERB** In a sport such as bowling, when a bowler **bowls**, he or she rolls the ball down a narrow track.

bowl|ing /bo͟ʊlɪŋ/ **NONCOUNT NOUN** Bowling is a game in which you roll a heavy ball down a narrow track toward a group of wooden objects and try to knock down as many of them as possible. ❑ *We go bowling every Saturday afternoon.*

Spelling Partners box

box /bɒ͟ks/ (**boxes, boxing, boxed**)
1 **NOUN** A **box** is a container with a hard bottom, hard sides, and usually a lid. ❑ *He packed his books into the cardboard box beside him.* ❑ *They sat on wooden boxes.*
2 **NOUN** A **box** is a square shape that is printed on paper. ❑ *For more information, just check the box and send us the form.*
3 **VERB** SPORTS To **box** means to fight someone according to the rules of boxing. ❑ *At school I boxed and played baseball.* ● **box|er** (**boxers**) **NOUN** ❑ *He wants to be a professional boxer.*
→ look at **container**

box|ing /bɒ͟ksɪŋ/ **NONCOUNT NOUN** SPORTS **Boxing** is a sport in which two people fight following special rules.

box of|fice (**box offices**) also **box-office** **NOUN** The **box office** in a theater or concert hall is the place where the tickets are sold. ❑ *There was a long line of people outside the box office.*

boy /bɔ͟ɪ/ (**boys**) **NOUN** A **boy** is a male child. ❑ *Did you have any pets when you were a little boy?*

boy|cott /bɔ͟ɪkɒt/ (**boycotts, boycotting, boycotted**)
1 **VERB** SOCIAL STUDIES If you **boycott** a country, a organization, or an activity, you refuse to be involved with it, because you disapprove of it. ❑ *Some groups threatened to boycott the meeting.*

b

2 NOUN SOCIAL STUDIES **Boycott** is also a noun. ❏ *The boycott of British beef was finally lifted in June.*

boy|friend /bɔɪfrɛnd/ (boyfriends) **NOUN** A **boyfriend** of a woman or a girl is a man or a boy that she is having a romantic relationship with. ❏ *Brenda came with her boyfriend, Anthony.*

Boy Scout /bɔɪ skaʊt/ (Boy Scouts)
1 NOUN The **Boy Scouts** is an organization that teaches children and young people practical skills, and encourages them to help other people. ❏ *I joined the Boy Scouts when I was ten years old.*
2 NOUN A **Boy Scout** is a member of the Boy Scouts. ❏ *He was a Boy Scout in his youth.*

bra /brɑ/ (bras) **NOUN** A **bra** is a piece of underwear that women wear to support their breasts.

brace|let /breɪslɪt/ (bracelets) **NOUN** A **bracelet** is a piece of jewelry that you wear around your wrist.

brack|et /brækɪt/ (brackets) **NOUN** LANGUAGE ARTS **Brackets** are curved ( ) or square [ ] marks that you can place around words, letters, or numbers when you are writing. ❏ *There's a telephone number in brackets under his name.*

brag /bræg/ (brags, bragging, bragged) **VERB** If you **brag**, you annoy people by proudly saying that you have something or have done something. ❏ *He's always bragging about winning the gold medal.*

braid /breɪd/ (braids, braiding, braided)
1 VERB You **braid** hair when you twist three lengths of it together. ❏ *She braided Louisa's hair with a red ribbon.*
2 NOUN A **braid** is a length of hair that has been twisted in this way. ❏ *Kelly wore her hair in two braids.*
→ look at **hair**

brain /breɪn/ (brains)
1 NOUN SCIENCE Your **brain** is the organ inside your head that controls your body's activities and allows you to think and to feel things.
2 NOUN Your **brain** is your mind and the way that you think. ❏ *Sports are good for your brain as well as your body.*
3 NOUN If someone has **brains**, they have the ability to learn and understand things quickly. ❏ *Scientists need brains and imagination.*

Sound Partners brake, break

brake /breɪk/ (brakes, braking, braked)
1 NOUN **Brakes** are the parts in a vehicle that make it go slower or stop. ❏ *He stepped on the brakes as the light turned red.*
2 VERB When the driver of a vehicle **brakes**, he or she makes it slow down or stop. ❏ *The driver braked to avoid an accident.*

branch /bræntʃ/ (branches) **NOUN** The **branches** of a tree are the parts that have leaves, flowers, and fruit. ❏ *We picked apples from the upper branches of a tree.*
→ look at **tree**

brand /brænd/ (brands) **NOUN** A **brand** is the name of a product that a particular company makes. ❏ *The store did not sell my favorite brand of cookies.* ❏ *... a new brand of cereal.*

brand-new **ADJECTIVE** A **brand-new** object is completely new. ❏ *Yesterday he bought a brand-new car.*

bran|dy /brændi/ (brandies) **NOUN** **Brandy** is a strong alcoholic drink that is made from wine.

brass /bræs/
1 NONCOUNT NOUN **Brass** is a yellow-colored metal. ❏ *Ritchie lifted the shiny brass door knocker.*
2 NONCOUNT NOUN MUSIC **Brass** is musical instruments that are made of brass. ❏ *...a piece of music for brass.*
3 NONCOUNT NOUN MUSIC The **brass** is all the musical instruments in an orchestra that are made of brass. ❏ *Suddenly the brass comes in with great power and intensity.*

brave /breɪv/ (braver, bravest) **ADJECTIVE** Someone who is **brave** is willing to do things that are dangerous, and does not show fear in dangerous situations. ❏ *A brave 12-year-old boy tried to help his friends.* ● **brave|ly** **ADVERB** ❏ *The army fought bravely.*

brav|ery /breɪvəri, breɪvri/ **NONCOUNT NOUN** **Bravery** is the ability to do things that are dangerous without showing fear. ❏ *He received an award for his bravery.*

bread /brɛd/ **NONCOUNT NOUN** **Bread** is a food made mostly from flour and water. ❏ *She bought a loaf of bread at the store.* ❏ *I usually just have bread and butter for breakfast.*
→ look at Picture Dictionary: **bread**

b

Picture Dictionary   bread

slice — loaf —

white bread

whole wheat bread

tortilla

bun

roll

rye bread

Sound Partners   break, brake

break /breɪk/ (**breaks, breaking, broke, broken**)

1 **VERB** When something **breaks**, it suddenly separates into pieces, often because someone has hit it or dropped it. ❑ *The plate broke.* ❑ *The plane broke into three pieces.*

2 **VERB** When you **break** something, you make it separate into two or more pieces, often because you have dropped it or hit it. ❑ *I'm sorry. I've broken a glass.*

3 **VERB** If you **break** a part of your body, a bone cracks in it. ❑ *She broke her leg in a skiing accident.*

4 **VERB** When a machine **breaks**, it no longer works. ❑ *The cable on the elevator broke, and it crashed to the ground.*

5 **NOUN** A **break** is a short period of time when you have a rest. ❑ *We get a 15-minute break for coffee.*

6 **VERB** If you **break** a rule or the law, you do something that you should not do. ❑ *We didn't know we were breaking the law.*

▶ **break down** **1** If a machine or a vehicle **breaks down**, it stops working. ❑ *Their car broke down.*

2 If someone **breaks down**, they start crying. ❑ *I broke down and cried.*

▶ **break in** If someone **breaks in**, they get into a building by force. ❑ *The robbers broke in and stole $8,000.*

▶ **break into** If someone **breaks into** a building, they get into it by force. ❑ *There was someone trying to break into the house.*

▶ **break off** If you **break** a part of something **off**, you remove it by breaking it. ❑ *Grace broke off a large piece of bread.*

▶ **break out** If something **breaks out**, it

begins suddenly. ❑ *He was 29 when war broke out.*

▶ **break up** If you **break up with** someone, your relationship with that person ends. ❑ *My girlfriend has broken up with me.*

Word Partners	Use **break** with:
N.	break *your* **arm**, break a **bone**, break *your* **leg**, break *your* **neck** **3**
	coffee break, **lunch** break **5**
	break **the law**, break **a rule** **6**
V.	**need** a break, **take** a break **5**

break|down /breɪkdaʊn/ (**breakdowns**)

1 **NOUN** The **breakdown of** a relationship, a plan, or a discussion is its failure. ❑ *Newspapers reported the breakdown of talks between the U.S. and European Union officials.* ❑ *Arguments about money led to the breakdown of their marriage.*

2 **NOUN** If a car or a piece of machinery has a **breakdown**, it stops working. ❑ *You should be prepared for breakdowns and accidents.*

break|fast /brɛkfəst/ (**breakfasts**) **NOUN** **Breakfast** is the first meal of the day. ❑ *Would you like eggs for breakfast?*
→ look at **eat**

break|through /breɪkθru/ (**breakthroughs**) **NOUN** A **breakthrough** is an important discovery that is made after a lot of hard work. ❑ *The scientist described a medical breakthrough in cancer treatment.*

breast /brɛst/ (**breasts**)

1 **NOUN** **SCIENCE** A woman's **breasts** are the two soft, round parts on her chest that can produce milk to feed a baby.

2 **NOUN** A **breast** is a piece of meat that is cut from the front of a bird. ❑ *For dinner I cooked chicken breast with vegetables.*

B

breast|stroke /brɛststroʊk/ **NONCOUNT NOUN** SPORTS **Breaststroke** is a way of swimming in which you pull both of your arms back at the same time, and kick your legs with your knees bent. ❑ *I'm learning to swim breaststroke.*

breath /brɛθ/ (breaths)
1 **NONCOUNT NOUN** Your **breath** is the air that you let out through your mouth when you breathe. ❑ *His breath smelled of onion.*
2 **NOUN** When you take a **breath**, you breathe in once. ❑ *He took a deep breath, and began to climb the stairs.*
3 If you are **out of breath**, you are breathing very quickly because your body has been working hard. ❑ *She was out of breath from running.*

breathe /brið/ (breathes, breathing, breathed) **VERB** SCIENCE When people or animals **breathe**, they take air into their lungs and let it out again. ❑ *He was breathing fast.* • **breath|ing** **NONCOUNT NOUN** ❑ *Her breathing became slow.*

breath|less /brɛθlɪs/ **ADJECTIVE** If you are **breathless**, you have difficulty in breathing properly, because you have been running, for example. ❑ *I was breathless after the race.*

breed /brid/ (breeds, breeding, bred)
1 **NOUN** SCIENCE A **breed** of animal is a particular type of it. ❑ *There are about 300 breeds of horse.*
2 **VERB** SCIENCE If you **breed** animals or plants, you produce more animals or plants with the same qualities. ❑ *He breeds dogs for the police.*
3 **VERB** SCIENCE When animals **breed**, they produce babies. ❑ *Birds usually breed in the spring.*

breeze /briz/ (breezes) **NOUN** A **breeze** is a gentle wind. ❑ *We enjoyed the cool summer breeze.*

bribe /braɪb/ (bribes, bribing, bribed)
1 **NOUN** A **bribe** is money or something valuable that one person offers to another in order to persuade them to do something. ❑ *The police took bribes from criminals.*
2 **VERB** If one person **bribes** another, they offer them money or something valuable in order to persuade them to do something. ❑ *He was accused of bribing a bank official.*

brib|ery /braɪbəri/ **NONCOUNT NOUN** Bribery is the act of offering someone money or something valuable in order to persuade them to do something for you. ❑ *He was arrested for bribery.*

brick /brɪk/ (bricks) **NOUN** Bricks are rectangular blocks used for building walls. ❑ *...a brick wall.*

bride /braɪd/ (brides) **NOUN** A **bride** is a woman who is getting married.

brides|maid /braɪdzmeɪd/ (bridesmaids) **NOUN** A **bridesmaid** is a woman or a girl who helps the bride on her wedding day.

bridge /brɪdʒ/ (bridges) **NOUN** A **bridge** is a structure that is built over a river or road so that people or vehicles can cross from one side to the other. ❑ *He walked over the bridge to get to school.*

brief /brif/ (briefer, briefest, briefs)
1 **ADJECTIVE** Something that is **brief** lasts for only a short time. ❑ *She once made a brief appearance on television.*
2 **ADJECTIVE** A **brief** speech or piece of writing does not contain many words or details. ❑ *The book begins with a brief description of his career.*
3 **PLURAL NOUN** Men's or women's underpants are sometimes called **briefs**. ❑ *...a pair of briefs.*

brief|case /brifkeɪs/ (briefcases) **NOUN** A **briefcase** is a small suitcase for carrying business papers in.
→ look at **bag**

brief|ly /brifli/ **ADVERB** Something that happens **briefly** happens for a very short period of time. ❑ *He smiled briefly.*

bright /braɪt/ (brighter, brightest)
1 **ADJECTIVE** A **bright** color is strong and noticeable. ❑ *She wore a bright red dress.*
2 **ADJECTIVE** A **bright** light is shining strongly. ❑ *He looked pale and tired under the bright lights of the TV studio.* • **bright|ly** **ADVERB** ❑ *The sun shone brightly in the sky.*
3 **ADJECTIVE** A **bright** place is full of light. ❑ *There was a bright room where patients could sit with their visitors.*
4 **ADJECTIVE** If someone is **bright**, they learn things quickly. ❑ *He seems brighter than most boys.*

bright|en /braɪt°n/ (brightens, brightening, brightened)

1 VERB If someone **brightens**, they suddenly look happier. ❑ *Seeing him, she seemed to brighten a little.*

2 VERB If someone or something **brightens** a place, they make it more colorful and attractive. ❑ *Pots planted with flowers brightened the area outside the door.*

bril|liant /brɪlyənt/

1 ADJECTIVE A **brilliant** person, idea, or performance is very clever or skillful. ❑ *She had a brilliant mind.* ● **bril|liant|ly** ADVERB ❑ *The movie was brilliantly written and acted.* ● **bril|liance** NONCOUNT NOUN ❑ *Mozart showed his brilliance at an early age.*

2 ADJECTIVE A **brilliant** light or color is extremely bright. ❑ *The woman had brilliant green eyes.*

brim /brɪm/ (brims) NOUN The **brim** of a hat is the part that sticks out around the bottom. ❑ *Rain dripped from the brim of his old hat.*

bring /brɪŋ/ (brings, bringing, brought)

1 VERB If you **bring** someone or something **with** you when you come to a place, you have them with you. ❑ *Remember to bring an old shirt to wear when we paint.* ❑ *Can I bring Susie to the party?*

2 VERB If you **bring** something that someone wants, you get it for them. ❑ *He poured a glass of milk for Dena and brought it to her.*

▶ **bring back** When you **bring** something **back**, you return it. ❑ *Please could you bring back those books that I lent you?*

▶ **bring in** Someone or something that **brings in** money earns it. ❑ *My job brings in about $24,000 a year.*

▶ **bring up** **1** When someone **brings up** a child, they take care of it until it is an adult. ❑ *She brought up four children.* ❑ *He was brought up in Nebraska.*

2 If you **bring up** a particular subject, you introduce it into a conversation. ❑ *Her mother brought up the subject of going back to work.*

brisk /brɪsk/ (brisker, briskest) ADJECTIVE A **brisk** activity or action is done quickly and with energy. ❑ *He gave me a brisk handshake.* ● **brisk|ly** ADVERB ❑ *Eve walked briskly through the park.*

bris|tle /brɪs°l/ (bristles)

1 NOUN **Bristles** are the short hairs that grow on a man's face.

2 NOUN The **bristles** of a brush are the thick hairs on it.

brit|tle /brɪt°l/ ADJECTIVE Something that is **brittle** is hard but easily broken. ❑ *I have very brittle finger nails.*

broad /brɔd/ (broader, broadest)

1 ADJECTIVE Something that is **broad** is wide. ❑ *His shoulders were broad and his waist was narrow.*

2 ADJECTIVE A **broad** smile is a big, happy smile. ❑ *He greeted them with a wave and a broad smile.*

3 ADJECTIVE **Broad** means including a large number of different things. ❑ *The library had a broad range of books.*

broad|band /brɔdbænd/ NONCOUNT NOUN TECHNOLOGY **Broadband** is a method of sending many electronic messages at the same time over the Internet. ❑ *They've announced big price cuts for broadband customers.*

broad|cast /brɔdkæst/ (broadcasts, broadcasting, broadcast)

1 NOUN A **broadcast** is a program, a performance, or a speech on the radio or on television. ❑ *We saw a live television broadcast of Saturday's football game.*

2 VERB To **broadcast** a program means to send it out so that it can be heard on the radio or seen on television. ❑ *The concert will be broadcast live on television and radio.* ❑ *CNN also broadcasts in Europe.*

broc|co|li /brɒkəli, brɒkli/ NONCOUNT NOUN **Broccoli** is a vegetable with thick green stems and small green flowers on top.
→ look at **vegetable**

bro|chure /broʊʃʊər/ (brochures) NOUN A **brochure** is a thin magazine with pictures that gives you information about a product or a service. ❑ *The city looked beautiful in the travel brochures.*

broil /brɔɪl/ (broils, broiling, broiled) VERB When you **broil** food, you cook it using very strong heat directly above it. ❑ *I'll broil the hamburgers.*

broke /broʊk/

1 **Broke** is a form of the verb **break**.

2 ADJECTIVE If you are **broke**, you have no money. [INFORMAL] ❑ *I don't have a job, and I'm broke.*

bro|ken /broʊkən/

1 **Broken** is a form of the verb **break**.

b

2 **ADJECTIVE** Something that is **broken** is in pieces. ❏ *She was taken to hospital with a broken leg.* ❏ *...a broken window.*

bronze /brɒnz/

1 **NONCOUNT NOUN** Bronze is a yellowish-brown metal that is a mixture of copper and tin. ❏ *...a bronze statue of a ballet dancer.*
2 **ADJECTIVE** Something that is **bronze** is yellowish-brown in color. ❏ *The sky began to fill with bronze light.*

bronze med|al (bronze medals) **NOUN** A **bronze medal** is an award made of brown metal that you get as third prize in a competition.

brooch /broʊtʃ/ (brooches) **NOUN** A **brooch** is a piece of jewelry that has a pin on the back so that it can be fastened on to your clothes.

brood /bruːd/ (broods, brooding, brooded) **VERB** If someone **broods** over something, they feel sad about it or they worry about it a lot. ❏ *She constantly broods about having no friends.*

broom /bruːm/ (brooms) **NOUN** A **broom** is a type of brush with a long handle. You use a broom for sweeping the floor.

broom|stick /bruːmstɪk/ (broomsticks) **NOUN** A **broomstick** is a long handle with a brush at the end that witches (= old women with magic powers) ride in children's stories.

broth|er /brʌðər/ (brothers) **NOUN** Your **brother** is a boy or a man who has the same parents as you. ❏ *Are you Peter's brother?*
→ look at **family**

brother-in-law (brothers-in-law) **NOUN** Someone's **brother-in-law** is the brother of their husband or wife, or the man who is married to their sister.
→ look at **family**

brought /brɔt/ **Brought** is a form of the verb **bring**.

brow /braʊ/ (brows)
1 **NOUN** Your **brow** is your forehead. ❏ *He wiped his brow with the back of his hand.*
2 **NOUN** Your **brows** are your eyebrows. ❏ *His glasses covered his thick dark brows.*

brown /braʊn/ (browner, brownest, browns)
1 **ADJECTIVE** Something that is **brown** is the color of earth or wood. ❏ *He looked into her brown eyes.*
2 **NOUN** Brown is also a noun. ❏ *Colors such as dark brown and green will be popular in the fashion world this fall.*
→ look at **hair**

brownie /braʊni/ (brownies) **NOUN** **Brownies** are small flat chocolate cakes. ❏ *She put a tray of chocolate brownies on the table.*

browse /braʊz/ (browses, browsing, browsed)
1 **VERB** If you **browse** in a store, you look at things in it. ❏ *I stopped in several bookstores to browse.*
2 **VERB** If you **browse through** a book or a magazine, you look through it in a relaxed way. ❏ *She was sitting on the sofa browsing through the TV magazine.*
3 **VERB** **TECHNOLOGY** If you **browse** the Internet, you search for information there. ❏ *The software allows you to browse the Internet on your cellphone.*
→ look at **Internet**

brows|er /braʊzər/ (browsers) **NOUN** **TECHNOLOGY** A **browser** is a piece of computer software that allows you to search for information on the Internet. ❏ *You need an up-to-date Web browser.*
→ look at **Internet**

bruise /bruːz/ (bruises, bruising, bruised)
1 **NOUN** A **bruise** is an injury that appears as a purple mark on your body. ❏ *How did you get that bruise on your arm?*
2 **VERB** If you **bruise** a part of your body, a bruise appears on it because you injured it. ❏ *I bruised my knee on a desk drawer.* ● **bruised** **ADJECTIVE** ❏ *...a bruised knee.*

brush /brʌʃ/ (brushes, brushing, brushed)
1 **NOUN** A **brush** is an object that has a lot of bristles or hairs attached to it. You use a brush for painting, for cleaning things, and for making your hair neat. ❏ *We gave him paint and brushes.* ❏ *He brought buckets of soapy water and scrubbing brushes to clean the floor.*
2 **VERB** If you **brush** something, you clean it or make it neat using a brush. ❏ *Have you brushed your teeth?* ❏ *She brushed the sand out of her hair.*

3 VERB If you **brush** something away, you remove it with movements of your hands. ❑ *He brushed the snow off his suit.*

4 VERB If one thing **brushes against** another, the first thing touches the second thing lightly. ❑ *Something brushed against her leg.*

brus|sels sprout /brʌsəlz spraʊt/ (**brussels sprouts**) NOUN Brussels sprouts are small round vegetables made of many leaves.

bru|tal /brut̬əl/ ADJECTIVE A brutal act or person is cruel and violent. ❑ *...a brutal military dictator.* ❑ *...brutal punishment.*
● **bru|tal|ly** ADVERB ❑ *Her parents were brutally murdered.*

BTW BTW is short for "by the way," and is often used in email. ❑ *BTW, the machine is simply amazing.*

bub|ble /bʌbəl/ (**bubbles, bubbling, bubbled**)
1 NOUN Bubbles are small balls of air or gas in a liquid. ❑ *Air bubbles rise to the surface.*
2 NOUN A bubble is a hollow ball of soapy liquid that is floating in the air or standing on a surface. ❑ *With soap and lots of bubbles children love bathtime.*
3 VERB When a liquid **bubbles**, bubbles move in it, for example, because it is boiling. ❑ *Heat the soup until it is bubbling.*

bub|bly /bʌbli/ (**bubblier, bubbliest**)
1 ADJECTIVE Someone who is **bubbly** is very lively and cheerful. ❑ *Sue is a bubbly girl who loves to laugh.*
2 ADJECTIVE If something is **bubbly**, it has a lot of bubbles in it. ❑ *When the butter is melted and bubbly, put in the flour.*

buck /bʌk/ (**bucks**) NOUN A buck is a U.S. or Australian dollar. [INFORMAL] ❑ *The food cost about fifty bucks.* ❑ *Why don't you spend a few bucks on a warm coat?*

buck|et /bʌkɪt/ (**buckets**) NOUN A bucket is a round metal or plastic container with a handle. Buckets are often used for holding and carrying water. ❑ *She threw a bucket of water on the fire.*

buck|le /bʌkəl/ (**buckles, buckling, buckled**)
1 NOUN A buckle is a piece of metal or plastic on one end of a belt or strap that is used for fastening it. ❑ *He wore a belt with a large silver buckle.*
2 VERB When you **buckle** a belt or a strap, you fasten it with a buckle. ❑ *The girl sat down to buckle her shoes.*

bud /bʌd/ (**buds**) NOUN SCIENCE A bud is a new growth on a tree or plant that develops into a leaf or flower. ❑ *Small pink buds were beginning to form on the bushes.*

Bud|dhism /budɪzəm, bʊd-/ NONCOUNT NOUN Buddhism is a religion that teaches that the way to end suffering is by controlling your desires.

Bud|dhist /budɪst, bʊd-/ (**Buddhists**)
1 NOUN A Buddhist is a person whose religion is Buddhism.
2 ADJECTIVE Buddhist means relating or referring to Buddhism. ❑ *...Buddhist monks.*

bud|dy /bʌdi/ (**buddies**) NOUN A buddy is a close friend, usually a male friend of a man. ❑ *We became great buddies.*

budge /bʌdʒ/ (**budges, budging, budged**)
1 VERB If someone will not **budge**, they refuse to change their mind. ❑ *The British will not budge on this point.*
2 VERB If someone or something will not **budge**, they refuse to move. ❑ *I tried to open the window, but it wouldn't budge.*

budg|et /bʌdʒɪt/ (**budgets, budgeting, budgeted**)
1 NOUN Your budget is the amount of money that you have available to spend. ❑ *She will design a new kitchen for you within your budget.* ❑ *The actress will star in a low budget film.*
2 VERB If you **budget** a certain amount of money for something, you decide that you can afford to spend that amount. ❑ *The company has budgeted $10 million for advertising.*
3 NOUN SOCIAL STUDIES The budget is a statement from the government about a country's financial situation. It gives details about changes to taxes, and the amount of money that will be spent on public services.

buf|fa|lo /bʌfəloʊ/ (**buffalo**) NOUN A buffalo is a wild animal like a large cow with horns that curve upward.

buf|fet /bʊfeɪ/ (**buffets**) NOUN A buffet is a meal that is arranged on a long table at a party or public occasion. Guests usually serve themselves. ❑ *After the event, there will be a buffet.*

bug /bʌg/ (**bugs**)
1 NOUN A bug is an insect. [INFORMAL]
2 NOUN A bug is an illness. [INFORMAL] ❑ *I think I have a stomach bug.*

B

3 **NOUN** TECHNOLOGY If there is a **bug** in a computer program, there is a mistake in it. ❑ *There is a bug in the software.*

build /bɪld/ (builds, building, built)
1 **VERB** If you **build** something, you make it by joining things together. ❑ *They are going to build a hotel here.* ❑ *The house was built in the early 19th century.*
2 **NONCOUNT NOUN** Someone's **build** is the shape of their body. ❑ *He's six feet tall and of medium build.*

build|er /bɪldər/ (builders) **NOUN** A **builder** is a person whose job is to build or repair houses and other buildings. ❑ *The builders have finished the roof.*

build|ing /bɪldɪŋ/ (buildings) **NOUN** A **building** is a structure that has a roof and walls. ❑ *They lived on the upper floor of the building.*
→ look at **city**

built /bɪlt/ **Built** is a form of the verb **build**.

bulb /bʌlb/ (bulbs)
1 **NOUN** A **bulb** is the glass part of a lamp that gives out light. ❑ *A single bulb hangs from the ceiling.*
2 **NOUN** SCIENCE A **bulb** is a root of a flower or plant. ❑ *...tulip bulbs.*

bulge /bʌldʒ/ (bulges, bulging, bulged)
1 **VERB** If something **bulges**, it sticks out. ❑ *His pockets were bulging with coins.*
2 **NOUN** **Bulges** are lumps that stick out. ❑ *The police officer notice a bulge under the man's coat.*

bulk /bʌlk/
1 The **bulk of** something is most of it. ❑ *The bulk of the money will go to the children's hospital in Dublin.*
2 If you buy or sell something **in bulk**, you buy or sell it in large amounts. ❑ *It is cheaper to buy supplies in bulk.*

bulky /bʌlki/ (bulkier, bulkiest) **ADJECTIVE** Something that is **bulky** is large and heavy. ❑ *The store can deliver bulky items like lawn mowers.*

bull /bʊl/ (bulls) **NOUN** A **bull** is a male animal of the cow family, and some other animals.

bull|dog /bʊldɔg/ (bulldogs) **NOUN** A **bulldog** is a short dog with a large square head.

bull|doz|er /bʊldoʊzər/ (bulldozers) **NOUN** A **bulldozer** is a large vehicle with a broad metal blade at the front that is used for moving large amounts of earth.

bul|let /bʊlɪt/ (bullets) **NOUN** A **bullet** is a small piece of metal that is shot out of a gun. ❑ *Police fired rubber bullets at the crowd.*

bul|letin /bʊlɪtɪn/ (bulletins) **NOUN** A **bulletin** is a short news report on the radio or television. ❑ *We heard the early morning news bulletin.*

bul|letin board (bulletin boards)
1 **NOUN** A **bulletin board** is a board on a wall for notices giving information. ❑ *Her telephone number was pinned to the bulletin board.*
2 **NOUN** TECHNOLOGY In computing, a **bulletin board** is a system that allows users to send and receive messages. ❑ *The Internet is the largest computer bulletin board in the world.*

bul|ly /bʊli/ (bullies, bullying, bullied)
1 **NOUN** A **bully** is someone who uses their strength or power to frighten other people. ❑ *He was the class bully.*
2 **VERB** If someone **bullies** you, they use their strength or power to frighten you. ❑ *I wasn't going to let him bully me.*

bumble|bee /bʌmbᵊlbi/ (bumblebees) also **bumble bee** **NOUN** A **bumblebee** is a large bee.

bump /bʌmp/ (bumps, bumping, bumped)
1 **VERB** If you **bump** into something or someone, you accidentally hit them while you are moving. ❑ *They stopped walking and I almost bumped into them.* ❑ *She bumped her head on a low branch.*
2 **NOUN** A **bump** is an injury that you get if you hit something or if something hits you. ❑ *She fell over and got a large bump on her head.*

bump|er /bʌmpər/ (bumpers) **NOUN** **Bumpers** are heavy bars at the front and back of a vehicle that protect the vehicle if it hits something. ❑ *I felt something hit the rear bumper of my car.*

bumpy /bʌmpi/ (bumpier, bumpiest) **ADJECTIVE** A **bumpy** road or path is not smooth or flat. ❑ *We rode our bicycles down the bumpy streets.*

bun /bʌn/ (buns)
1 **NOUN** A **bun** is bread in a small round shape. ❑ *He had a cinnamon bun and a glass of milk.*
2 **NOUN** If you have your hair in a **bun**, you have attached it tightly at the back of your head in the shape of a ball.
→ look at **bread**

b

bunch /bʌntʃ/ (**bunches**)
1. **NOUN** A **bunch of** people is a group of them. [INFORMAL] ❑ *They're a great bunch of kids.*
2. **NOUN** A **bunch of** flowers is a number of flowers with their stems held together. ❑ *He left a huge bunch of flowers in her hotel room.*
3. **NOUN** A **bunch of** bananas or grapes is a group of them growing together.
4. A **bunch of** things is a number of things. [INFORMAL] ❑ *We recorded a bunch of songs together.*

bun|dle /bʌndᵊl/ (**bundles**) **NOUN** A **bundle of** things is a number of things that are tied or wrapped together so that they can be carried or stored. ❑ *He left a bundle of papers on the floor.*

bunk /bʌŋk/ (**bunks**) **NOUN** A **bunk** is a narrow bed that is usually attached to a wall, especially in a ship. ❑ *Sally was lying on her narrow wooden bunk.*

bunk bed (**bunk beds**) **NOUN** Bunk beds are two single beds that are built one on top of the other. ❑ *The children slept in bunk beds.*

bun|ny /bʌni/ (**bunnies**) **NOUN** Bunny is a child's word for a rabbit. [INFORMAL]

buoy /bui/ (**buoys**) **NOUN** A **buoy** is an object floating in a lake or an ocean that shows ships and boats where they can go.

bur|den /bɜrdᵊn/ (**burdens**) **NOUN** A **burden** is something that causes people a lot of worry or hard work. ❑ *I don't want to become a burden on my family when I get old.*

bu|reau /byʊəroʊ/ (**bureaus**)
1. **NOUN** A **bureau** is an office, an organization, or a government department. ❑ *The Federal Bureau of Investigation has an office in Washington, D.C.*
2. **NOUN** A **bureau** is a piece of furniture with drawers in which you keep clothes or other things.

bu|reau|cra|cy /byʊrɒkrəsi/ (**bureaucracies**)
1. **NOUN** A **bureaucracy** is a management system controlled by a large number of officials. ❑ *It's hard for a bureaucracy to accept new ideas.*
2. **NONCOUNT NOUN** Bureaucracy means all the rules and procedures of government departments or other large organizations, especially when people think that these rules and procedures are complicated and cause long delays. ❑ *People complain about too much bureaucracy.*

burg|er /bɜrgər/ (**burgers**) **NOUN** A **burger** is meat that is cut into very small pieces and pressed into a flat round shape. Burgers are often eaten between two pieces of bread. **Burger** is short for **hamburger**. ❑ *I ordered a burger for lunch.*

bur|glar /bɜrglər/ (**burglars**) **NOUN** A **burglar** is someone who enters a building by force in order to steal things. ❑ *Dogs often help the police to catch burglars.*

bur|glar|ize /bɜrgləraɪz/ (**burglarizes, burglarizing, burglarized**) **VERB** If a building is **burglarized**, a thief enters it by force and steals things. ❑ *Her home was burglarized last week.*

bur|gla|ry /bɜrgləri/ (**burglaries**) **NOUN** If someone commits a **burglary**, they enter a building by force and steal things. ❑ *An 11-year-old boy committed a burglary.*

bur|ial /bɛriəl/ (**burials**) **NOUN** A **burial** is the act or ceremony of putting a dead body into a grave in the ground. ❑ *Charles and his two sons attended the burial.*

burn /bɜrn/ (**burns, burning, burned** or **burnt**)
1. **VERB** If you **burn** something, you destroy or damage it with fire. ❑ *She burned her old love letters.*
2. **VERB** If you **burn** part of your body, or **burn yourself**, you are injured by fire or by something very hot. ❑ *Take care not to burn your fingers.*
3. **NOUN** Burn is also a noun. ❑ *She suffered burns to her back.*
4. **VERB** If there is a fire somewhere, you say that a fire is **burning** there. ❑ *Forty forest fires were burning in Alberta yesterday.*
5. **VERB** If something **is burning**, it is on fire. ❑ *When I arrived, one of the vehicles was still burning.*
6. **VERB** To **burn** a CD means to copy something onto it. ❑ *I have the equipment to burn audio CDs.*
→ look at **greenhouse effect**

burnt /bɜrnt/ Burnt is a form of the verb **burn**.

burqa /bɜrkə/ (**burqas**) also **burka** **NOUN** A **burqa** is a long dress that covers the head and body and is traditionally worn by some women in Islamic countries.

B

burst /bɜrst/ (bursts, bursting, burst) **VERB**
If something **bursts**, it suddenly breaks open and the air or other substance inside it comes out. ❑ *The driver lost control of his car when a tire burst.*

▶ **burst out** If someone **bursts out** laughing, crying, or making another noise, they suddenly start making that noise. ❑ *The class burst out laughing.*

bury /bɛri/ (buries, burying, buried)
1 VERB To **bury** something means to put it into a hole in the ground and cover it up. ❑ *Some animals bury nuts and seeds.*
2 VERB To **bury** a dead person means to put their body into a grave and cover it with earth. ❑ *Soldiers helped to bury the dead.*

bus /bʌs/ (buses) **NOUN** A **bus** is a large motor vehicle that carries passengers. ❑ *He missed his last bus home.*
→ look at **route, transportation**

bush /bʊʃ/ (bushes)
1 NOUN The **bush** is an area in a hot country that is far from cities. Not many people live there. ❑ *...the Australian bush.*
2 NOUN A **bush** is a plant with leaves and branches that is smaller than a tree. ❑ *...a rose bush.*
→ look at **plant**

busily /bɪzɪli/ **ADVERB** If you do something **busily**, you do it in a very active way. ❑ *Workers were busily trying to repair the damage.*

business /bɪznɪs/ (businesses)
1 NONCOUNT NOUN **Business** is work that is related to producing, buying, and selling things. ❑ *He had a successful career in business.* ❑ *She attended Harvard Business School.*
2 NOUN A **business** is an organization that produces and sells goods or that provides a service. ❑ *The bakery is a family business.*

Word Partners	Use **business** with:
N.	business **decision**, business **expenses**, business **hours**, business **opportunity**, business **owner**, business **partner**, business **practices**, business **school** 1 2
ADJ.	**family** business, **online** business, **small** business 1 2
V.	**go out of** business, **run a** business 1 2

businessman /bɪznɪsmæn/ (businessmen)
NOUN A **businessman** is a man who works in business. ❑ *He's a rich businessman.*

businesswoman /bɪznɪswʊmən/ (businesswomen) **NOUN** A **businesswoman** is a woman who works in business. ❑ *She's a successful businesswoman who manages her own company.*

busy /bɪzi/ (busier, busiest)
1 ADJECTIVE When you are **busy**, you are working hard, so that you are not free to do anything else. ❑ *What is it? I'm busy.* ❑ *They are busy preparing for a party on Saturday.*
2 ADJECTIVE A **busy** place is full of people who are doing things. ❑ *We walked along a busy city street.*
3 ADJECTIVE When a telephone line is **busy**, you cannot make your call because the line is already being used by someone else. ❑ *I tried to reach him, but the line was busy.*
→ look at **calendar, day, factory, school**

but /bət, STRONG bʌt/
1 CONJUNCTION You use **but** to introduce something that is different than what you have just said. ❑ *I've enjoyed my vacation, but now it's time to get back to work.* ❑ *Heat the milk until it is very hot but not boiling.*
2 PREPOSITION **But** means "except." ❑ *You've done nothing but complain all day.*

butcher /bʊtʃər/ (butchers) **NOUN** A **butcher** is someone who cuts up and sells meat.
→ look at **meat**

butter /bʌtər/ (butters, buttering, buttered)
1 NONCOUNT NOUN **Butter** is a soft yellow food made from cream. You spread it on bread or use it in cooking. ❑ *The waitress brought us bread and butter.*
2 VERB If you **butter** bread or toast, you spread butter on it. ❑ *She put two pieces of bread on a plate and buttered them.*

butterfly /bʌtərflaɪ/ (butterflies) **NOUN** A **butterfly** is an insect with large colored wings. ❑ *Butterflies are attracted to the wild flowers.*

butterscotch /bʌtərskɒtʃ/ **NONCOUNT NOUN** **Butterscotch** is a type of hard brown candy made from butter and sugar.

button /bʌtᵊn/ (buttons, buttoning, buttoned)
1 NOUN **Buttons** are small hard objects that you push through holes (= buttonholes)

to fasten your clothes. ❑ *I bought a blue jacket with silver buttons.*

2 **VERB** If you **button** a shirt, a coat, or another piece of clothing, you fasten it by pushing its buttons through the buttonholes. ❑ *Ferguson stood up and buttoned his coat.*

3 **NOUN** A **button** is a small object on a piece of equipment that you press to operate it. ❑ *He put in a DVD and pressed the "play" button.*
→ look at **ATM**

Word Partners	Use **button** with:
V.	**sew on** a button **1**
	press a button, **push** a button **3**
N.	**shirt** button **1** **2**
PREP.	button **up** *something* **2**

buy /baɪ/ (**buys, buying, bought**) **VERB** If you **buy** something, you get it by paying money for it. ❑ *He could not afford to buy a house.* ❑ *Lizzie bought herself a bike.* ● **buy|er** (**buyers**) **NOUN** ❑ *Car buyers are more interested in safety than speed.*
→ look at **car, food, movie, shopping**

Word Partners	Use **buy** with:
V.	**afford to** buy, buy **and sell**
N.	buy **clothes**, buy **a condo**, buy **food**, buy **a house**, buy **tickets**
ADV.	buy **online**

buzz /bʌz/ (**buzzes, buzzing, buzzed**)
1 **VERB** If something **buzzes**, it makes a sound like a bee. ❑ *There was a fly buzzing around my head.*
2 **NOUN** Buzz is also a noun. ❑ *The annoying buzz of an insect kept us awake.*

by /baɪ/
1 **PREPOSITION** If something is done **by** a person or thing, that person or thing does it. ❑ *The dinner was served by his mother and sisters.* ❑ *She was woken by a loud noise in the street.*
2 **PREPOSITION** If a book or a painting is **by** a particular person, they wrote it or painted it. ❑ *Here's a painting by Van Gogh.*
3 **PREPOSITION** By is used to say how something is done. ❑ *We usually travel by car.*
4 If you are **by yourself**, you are alone. ❑ *A man was sitting by himself in a corner.*
5 If you do something **by yourself**, you do it without any help. ❑ *I can do it by myself.*
6 **PREPOSITION** Someone or something that is **by** something else is beside it. ❑ *Judith was sitting in a chair by the window.* ❑ *Jack stood by the door, ready to leave.*
7 **PREPOSITION** If a person or vehicle goes **by** you, they move past you without stopping. ❑ *A few cars passed close by me.*
8 **ADVERB** By is also an adverb. ❑ *People waved and smiled as she went by.*
9 **PREPOSITION** If something happens **by** a particular time, it happens at or before that time. ❑ *I'll be home by eight o'clock.*

bye /baɪ/ or **bye-bye** Bye and **bye-bye** are informal ways of saying goodbye. ❑ *Bye, Daddy.*

byte /baɪt/ (**bytes**) **NOUN** TECHNOLOGY In computing, a **byte** is a unit of information. ❑ *...two million bytes of data.*

Cc

cab /kæb/ (**cabs**) **NOUN** A **cab** is a car that you can hire with its driver, to take you where you want to go. ❑ *Can I call a cab?*

cab|bage /kæbɪdʒ/ (**cabbages**) **NOUN** A **cabbage** is a round vegetable with white, green, or purple leaves.

cab|in /kæbɪn/ (**cabins**)
1 **NOUN** A **cabin** is a small wooden house in the woods or mountains. ❑ *We stayed in a log cabin.*
2 **NOUN** A **cabin** is a small room on a boat. ❑ *He showed her to a small cabin.*
3 **NOUN** The **cabin** is the part of a plane where people sit. ❑ *He sat in the first-class cabin.*

cabi|net /kæbɪnɪt/ (**cabinets**)
1 **NOUN** A **cabinet** is a piece of furniture with shelves, used for storing things in. ❑ *I looked in the medicine cabinet.*
2 **NOUN** SOCIAL STUDIES The **cabinet** is a group of members of the government who give advice to the president, and who are responsible for its policies (= the plans and actions that they have agreed on).
→ look at **bathroom, kitchen**

ca|ble /keɪbəl/ (**cables**)
1 **NOUN** A **cable** is a very strong, thick rope, made of metal. ❑ *They used a cable made of steel wire.*
2 **NOUN** A **cable** is a thick wire that carries electricity. ❑ *The island gets its electricity from underground power cables.*
→ look at **computer**

ca|ble tele|vi|sion **NONCOUNT NOUN**
Cable television is a television system in which signals travel along wires. ❑ *We don't have cable television.*
→ look at **television**

cac|tus /kæktəs/ (**cacti** /kæktaɪ/) **NOUN** A **cactus** is a plant with lots of sharp points that grows in hot, dry places.

café /kæfeɪ/ (**cafés**) also **cafe** **NOUN** A **café** is a place where you can buy drinks and small meals.

caf|eteria /kæfɪtɪəriə/ (**cafeterias**) **NOUN** A **cafeteria** is a restaurant where you buy a meal and carry it to the table yourself. Places like hospitals, schools, and offices have **cafeterias**.

caf|feine /kæfin/ **NONCOUNT NOUN** **Caffeine** is a chemical in coffee and tea that makes you more active.

cage /keɪdʒ/ (**cages**) **NOUN** A **cage** is a structure made of metal bars where you keep birds or animals. ❑ *I hate to see birds in cages.*

cake /keɪk/ (**cakes**) **NOUN** A **cake** is a sweet food that you make from flour, eggs, sugar, and butter. ❑ *He ate a piece of chocolate cake.* ❑ *We made her a birthday cake.*

cal|cu|late /kælkyəleɪt/ (**calculates, calculating, calculated**) **VERB** MATH If you **calculate** an amount, you find it out by using numbers. ❑ *Have you calculated the cost of your trip?*
→ look at **geometry, math**

cal|cu|la|tion /kælkyəleɪʃⁿn/ (**calculations**) **NOUN** MATH You make a **calculation** when you find out a number or amount by using mathematics. ❑ *Ryan made a quick calculation in his head.*

cal|cu|la|tor /kælkyəleɪtər/ (**calculators**) **NOUN** A **calculator** is a small electronic machine that you use to calculate numbers. ❑ *He takes a pocket calculator to school.*
→ look at **office**

cal|en|dar /kælɪndər/ (**calendars**) **NOUN** A **calendar** is a list of days, weeks and months for a particular year. ❑ *There was a calendar on the wall.*
→ look at Word World: **calendar**
→ look at **season**

calf /kæf/ (**calves** /kævz/)
1 **NOUN** A **calf** is a young cow.

Word World calendar

middle day end date weekly

schedule month last next monthly

agenda year busy

weekend look at schedule check

weekday week

beginning holiday plan

Nouns / Adjectives / Verbs

2 **NOUN** Your **calf** is the thick part at the back of your leg, between your ankle and your knee.

call /kɔl/ (**calls, calling, called**)

1 **VERB** If you **call** someone a particular name, you give them that name. ❏ *I wanted to call the dog Mufty.* ❏ *Her daughter is called Charlotte.*

2 **VERB** If you **call** something, you say it in a loud voice. ❏ *Someone called his name.*

3 **VERB** If you **call** someone, you telephone them. ❏ *Would you call me as soon as you find out?* ❏ *I think we should call the doctor.*

4 **VERB** If you **call** somewhere, you make a short visit there. ❏ *A salesman called at the house.*

5 **NOUN** Call is also a noun. ❏ *The doctor was out on a call.*

6 **NOUN** When you make a telephone **call**, you telephone someone. ❏ *I made a phone call to my grandmother.*

→ look at **phone**

▶ **call back** If you **call** someone **back**, you telephone them in return for a call they made to you. ❏ *I'll call you back.*

▶ **call off** If you **call off** an event that has been planned, you cancel it. ❏ *He called off the trip.*

▶ **call on** If you **call on** someone, you visit them for a short time. ❏ *Sofia was intending to call on Miss Kitts.*

▶ **call up** If you **call** someone **up**, you telephone them. ❏ *When I'm in Pittsburgh, I'll call him up.*

Word Partners Use **call** with:

N. call **an ambulance**, call **a doctor**, call **the police** **3**
conference call, **emergency** call, **a number to** call, **phone** call, **telephone** call **6**

V. **get a** call, **make a** call, **return a** call, **take a** call, **wait for a** call **6**

call|er /kɔlər/ (**callers**) **NOUN** A **caller** is a person who is making a telephone call. ❏ *A caller told police what happened.*

→ look at **phone**

calm /kɑm/ (**calmer, calmest, calms, calming, calmed**)

1 **ADJECTIVE** A **calm** person is not worried, angry, or excited. ❏ *She is a calm, patient woman.* ❏ *Try to keep calm.* ● **calm|ly** **ADVERB** ❏ *Alan said calmly, "I don't believe you."*

2 **ADJECTIVE** If water is **calm**, it is not moving much. ❏ *The ocean was very calm and the stars were bright.*

3 **ADJECTIVE** If the weather is **calm**, there is not much wind. ❏ *It was a fine, calm day.*

→ look at **feeling, ocean, relax**

▶ **calm down** If you **calm down**, you become less upset or excited. ❏ *Calm down and listen to me.* ❏ *I'll try to calm him down.*

calo|rie /kæləri/ (**calories**) **NOUN** **SCIENCE** **Calories** are units that are used for measuring the amount of energy in food. ❏ *These sweet drinks have a lot of calories in them.*

came /keɪm/ **Came** is a form of the verb **come.**

cam|el /kæməl/ (**camels**) **NOUN** A **camel** is an animal with one or two large lumps on its back. **Camels** live in hot, dry places and are used for carrying people or things.

cam|era /kæmrə/ (**cameras**) **NOUN** A **camera** is a piece of equipment for taking photographs or making movies. ❏ *...a digital camera.*

cam|era phone (**camera phones**) **NOUN** **TECHNOLOGY** A **camera phone** is a cellphone that can take photographs.

camp /kæmp/ (**camps, camping, camped**)

1 **NOUN** A **camp** is a place where people live or stay in tents. ❏ *...an army camp.*

2 **NOUN** A **camp** is a place in the

C

countryside where care and activities are provided for children during the summer. ❑ *She's working with children on a summer camp.*

3 **VERB** If you **camp** somewhere, you stay there in a tent. ❑ *We camped near the beach.*

● **camp|ing** **NONCOUNT NOUN** ❑ *They went camping in Colorado.*

cam|paign /kæmpeɪn/ (**campaigns, campaigning, campaigned**)

1 **NOUN** A **campaign** is a number of things that you do over a period of time in order to get a particular result. ❑ *January marks the start of the election campaign.*

2 **VERB** If you **campaign**, you do certain things over a period of time in order to get a particular result. ❑ *We are campaigning for better health services.* ● **cam|paign|er** (**campaigners**) **NOUN** ❑ *...anti-war campaigners.*

→ look at **vote**

camp|er /kæmpər/ (**campers**) **NOUN** A **camper** is a person who is staying in a tent, for example on vacation. ❑ *The campers packed up their tents.*

camp|fire /kæmpfaɪər/ (**campfires**) **NOUN** A **campfire** is a fire that you light outdoors when you are camping.

camp|site /kæmpsaɪt/ (**campsites**) **NOUN** A **campsite** is a place where you can stay in a tent.

cam|pus /kæmpəs/ (**campuses**) **NOUN** A **campus** is an area of land that contains the main buildings of a university or college.

can
❶ MODAL USES
❷ CONTAINER

❶ **can** /kən, STRONG kæn/

LANGUAGE HELP
Use the form **cannot** in negative statements. When you are speaking, you can use the short form **can't**, pronounced /kænt/.

1 **MODAL VERB** If you **can** do something, you have the ability to do it. ❑ *I can take care of myself.* ❑ *Can you swim yet?*

2 **MODAL VERB** You use **can** to show that something is sometimes true. ❑ *Exercising alone can be boring.*

3 **MODAL VERB** You use **can** with words like "smell", "see," and "hear." ❑ *I can smell smoke.*

4 **MODAL VERB** If you **can** do something, you are allowed to do it. ❑ *Can I go to the party at the weekend?* ❑ *Sorry. We can't answer any questions.*

5 **MODAL VERB** You use **can** to make requests or offers. ❑ *Can I have a look at that book?* ❑ *Can I help you?*

❷ **can** /kæn/ (**cans**) **NOUN** A **can** is a metal container for food, drink, or paint. ❑ *...a can of tomato soup.*

→ look at **container**

ca|nal /kənæl/ (**canals**) **NOUN** GEOGRAPHY A **canal** is a long narrow path filled with water that boats travel along. ❑ *The Eerie Canal connects the Great Lakes with the Atlantic Ocean.*

can|cel /kæns³l/ (**cancels, canceling** or **cancelling, canceled** or **cancelled**) **VERB** If you **cancel** something that has been planned, you stop it from happening. ❑ *We canceled our trip to Washington.*

● **can|cel|la|tion** /kænsəleɪʃ³n/ (**cancellations**) **NOUN** ❑ *The cancellation of his visit upset many people.*

can|cer /kænsər/ (**cancers**) **NOUN** Cancer is a serious disease that makes groups of cells in the body grow when they should not. ❑ *Jane had cancer when she was 25.*

can|di|date /kændɪdeɪt/ (**candidates**) **NOUN** A **candidate** is someone who is trying to get a particular job, or trying to win a political position. ❑ *He is a candidate for governor of Illinois.*

→ look at **vote**

can|dle /kænd³l/ (**candles**) **NOUN** A **candle** is a long stick of wax with a piece of string through the middle, that you burn to give you light. ❑ *The only light in the bedroom came from a candle.*

candle|stick /kænd³lstɪk/ (**candlesticks**) **NOUN** A **candlestick** is a narrow object with a hole at the top that holds a candle.

can|dy /kændi/ (**candies**) **NOUN** Candy is sweet food such as chocolate or taffy. ❑ *I gave him a piece of candy.*

cane /keɪn/ (**canes**) **NOUN** A **cane** is a long stick that people use to help them walk. ❑ *He has used a cane for the last five years.*

→ look at **disability**

can|non /kænən/ (**cannons**) **NOUN** A **cannon** is a large heavy gun on wheels that was used in battles in the past. ❑ *The soldiers stood beside the cannons.*

can|not /kænɒt, kənɒt/ **Cannot** is the negative form of **can**.

ca|noe /kənu̱/ (canoes) **NOUN**
A **canoe** is a small, narrow boat that you move through the water using a short pole (= a paddle).

can't /kænt/ **Can't** is short for **cannot**.

can|vas /kænvəs/ (canvases)
1 **NONCOUNT NOUN** **Canvas** is a strong, heavy cloth that is used for making tents and bags. ❏ ...a canvas bag.
2 **NOUN** ARTS A **canvas** is a piece of this cloth that you paint on. ❏ ...an artist's canvas.

can|yon /kænyən/ (canyons) **NOUN** SCIENCE
A **canyon** is a long, narrow valley with very steep sides. ❏ ...the Grand Canyon.

cap /kæp/ (caps)
1 **NOUN** A **cap** is a soft, flat hat with a curved part at the front. ❏ He wore a dark blue baseball cap.
2 **NOUN** The **cap** of a bottle is its lid. ❏ She took the cap off her water bottle and drank while she waited for him.

ca|pable /ke̱ɪpəbəl/
1 **ADJECTIVE** If you are **capable of** doing something, you are able to do it. ❏ He was not even capable of standing up.
2 **ADJECTIVE** Someone who is **capable** is able to do something well. ❏ She's a very capable teacher.

ca|pac|ity /kəpæsɪti/ (capacities)
1 **NOUN** Your **capacity for** something is your ability to do it. ❏ Every human being has the capacity for love.
2 **NOUN** The **capacity** of something is the maximum amount that it can hold. ❏ The stadium has a capacity of 50,000.

cape /ke̱ɪp/ (capes)
1 **NOUN** SCIENCE A **cape** is a large piece of land that sticks out into the ocean. ❏ ...the Cape of Good Hope.
2 **NOUN** A **cape** is a long coat without sleeves, that covers your body and arms.

capi|tal /kæpɪtəl/ (capitals)
1 **NOUN** GEOGRAPHY The **capital** of a country is the city where its government meets. ❏ Berlin is the capital of Germany.
2 **NOUN** LANGUAGE ARTS A **capital** or a **capital letter** is the large letter that you use at the beginning of sentences and names. ❏ He wrote his name in capitals.
3 **NONCOUNT NOUN** **Capital** is money that you use to start a business. ❏ They provide capital for small businesses.

capi|tal|ism /kæpɪtəlɪzəm/ **NONCOUNT NOUN**
SOCIAL STUDIES **Capitalism** is an economic and political system in which property, business, and industry are privately owned and not owned by the state.

capi|tal|ist /kæpɪtəlɪst/ (capitalists)
1 **ADJECTIVE** SOCIAL STUDIES In a **capitalist** system, industry is owned by private companies rather than by the government. ❏ Banks plays an important part in the capitalist system.
2 **NOUN** SOCIAL STUDIES A **capitalist** is someone who believes in a system where industry is owned by private companies rather than by the government.

capi|tal pun|ish|ment **NONCOUNT NOUN**
Capital punishment is when a criminal is killed legally as a punishment. ❏ Capital punishment is not used in some countries.

capi|tol /kæpɪtəl/ (capitols) also **Capitol**
1 **NOUN** SOCIAL STUDIES A **capitol** is a building where a state's government meets. ❏ The state capitol was built in 1908.
2 **NOUN** SOCIAL STUDIES The **Capitol** is the government building in Washington, D.C., where the U.S. Congress meets. ❏ Thousands of people waited in front of the Capitol.

cap|sule /kæpsəl/ (capsules) **NOUN** A **capsule** is a very small closed tube with medicine inside it, that you swallow.

cap|tain /kæptɪn/ (captains)
1 **NOUN** In the army or navy, a **captain** is an officer of middle rank. ❏ He was a captain in the army.
2 **NOUN** SPORTS The **captain of** a sports team is its leader. ❏ Mickey Thomas is the captain of the tennis team.
3 **NOUN** The **captain** of an airplane or a ship is the person who is in charge of it. ❏ Who is the captain of this boat?

C

cap|tion /ˈkæpʃ°n/ (**captions**) **NOUN** A **caption** is a piece of writing next to a picture, that tells you something about the picture. ❏ *The photo had the caption "John, aged 6 years."*

cap|tive /ˈkæptɪv/ (**captives**)
1 **ADJECTIVE** A **captive** animal or person is being kept in a place and is not allowed to leave. ❏ *Scientists are studying the behavior of the captive birds.*
2 **NOUN** A **captive** is a prisoner.

cap|tiv|ity /kæpˈtɪvɪti/ **NONCOUNT NOUN**
Captivity is when you are kept in a place and you cannot leave. ❏ *The birds were kept in captivity.*

cap|ture /ˈkæptʃər/ (**captures, capturing, captured**) **VERB** If you **capture** someone or something, you catch them and keep them somewhere so that they cannot leave. ❏ *The enemy shot down the airplane and captured the pilot.*

car /kɑr/ (**cars**)
1 **NOUN** A **car** is a motor vehicle with space for about 5 people. ❏ *They arrived by car.*
2 **NOUN** A **car** is one of the long parts of a train. ❏ *He stood up and walked to the dining car.*
→ look at Word World: **car**
→ look at **transportation**

cara|mel /ˈkærəmɛl, -məl, ˈkɑrməl/
NONCOUNT NOUN **Caramel** is a type of sweet food made from burnt sugar, butter and milk.

car|bo|hy|drate /ˌkɑrboʊˈhaɪdreɪt/ (**carbohydrates**) **NOUN** **SCIENCE**
Carbohydrates are substances in foods that provide the body with energy. ❏ *You need to eat more carbohydrates such as bread, pasta, or potatoes.*

car|bon di|ox|ide /ˌkɑrbən daɪˈɒksaɪd/
NONCOUNT NOUN **SCIENCE** **Carbon dioxide** is a gas that animals and people produce when they breathe out.
→ look at **greenhouse effect**

car|bon mon|ox|ide /ˌkɑrbən məˈnɒksaɪd/
NONCOUNT NOUN **SCIENCE** **Carbon monoxide** is a poisonous gas that is produced by engines that use gasoline.

card /kɑrd/ (**cards**)
1 **NOUN** A **card** is a piece of stiff paper with a picture and a message, that you send to someone on a special occasion. ❏ *She sends me a card on my birthday.*
2 **NOUN** A **card** is a small piece of cardboard or plastic that has information about you written on it. ❏ *Please remember to bring your membership card.*
3 **NOUN** A **card** is a small piece of plastic that you use to pay for things. ❏ *He paid the bill with a credit card.*
4 **NOUN** **Cards** are pieces of stiff paper with numbers or pictures on them that you use for playing games. ❏ *They enjoy playing cards.*
→ look at **ATM, identification, play**

card|board /ˈkɑrdbɔrd/ **NONCOUNT NOUN**
Cardboard is thick, stiff paper that is used for making boxes. ❏ *...a cardboard box.*

car|di|gan /ˈkɑrdɪgən/ (**cardigans**) **NOUN** A **cardigan** is a sweater that opens at the front.

cardio- /ˈkɑrdioʊ/ **SCIENCE** When **cardio-** begins a word, it means something to do with the heart.

care /kɛər/ (**cares, caring, cared**)
1 **VERB** If you **care** about someone or something, you are interested in them, or you think they are very important. ❏ *We care about the environment.* ❏ *He still cared for me.*
2 **VERB** If you **care for** someone or something, you look after them. ❏ *A nurse cares for David in his home.*
3 **NONCOUNT NOUN** If you do something **with care**, you do it very carefully so that you do not make any mistakes. ❏ *He chose his words with care.*
4 If you **take care of** someone, you look

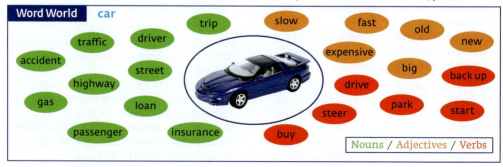

Word World   car

accident
traffic
driver
trip
highway
street
gas
loan
passenger
insurance

slow
fast
old
new
expensive
big
back up
drive
buy
steer
park
start

Nouns / Adjectives / Verbs

after them. ❏ *There was no one to take care of the children.*

ca|reer /kərɪər/ (**careers**) **NOUN** A **career** is a job, or the years of your life that you spend working. ❏ *She had a long career as a teacher.*
→ look at **job**

Word Builder **careful**

ful ≈ **filled with**

care + ful = careful
color + ful = colorful
help + ful = helpful
hope + ful = hopeful
stress + ful = stressful
use + ful = useful

---

care|ful /kɛərfəl/ **ADJECTIVE** If you are **careful**, you think a lot about what you are doing so that you do not make any mistakes. ❏ *Be very careful with this liquid, it can be dangerous.* ● **care|ful|ly** **ADVERB** ❏ *Have a nice time, and drive carefully.*

Word Partners Use **careful** with:

N.	careful **attention**, careful **planning**
V.	**be** careful
ADV.	**extremely** careful, **very** careful

---

care|giv|er /kɛərɡɪvər/ (**caregivers**) **NOUN** A **caregiver** is someone who takes care of a sick person or young children in their home. ❏ *We have employed the same caregiver for seventeen years.*

Word Builder **careless**

less ≈ **without**

care + less = careless
end + less = endless
help + less = helpless
home + less = homeless
use + less = useless
wire + less = wireless

---

care|less /kɛərlɪs/ **ADJECTIVE** If you are **careless**, you do not give enough attention to what you are doing, and so you make mistakes. ❏ *Some of my students were very careless with homework.*

care|tak|er /kɛərteɪkər/ (**caretakers**)
1 NOUN A **caretaker** is someone who looks after a building and the area around it.
2 NOUN Caretaker is another name for a **caregiver**.

car|go /kɑrɡoʊ/ (**cargoes**) **NOUN** The **cargo** of a ship or plane is the goods that it is carrying. ❏ *The ship was carrying a cargo of bananas.*

car|na|tion /kɑrneɪʃ°n/ (**carnations**) **NOUN** A **carnation** is a plant with white, pink, or red flowers.

car|ni|val /kɑrnɪv°l/ (**carnivals**) **NOUN** A **carnival** is a celebration in the street, with music and dancing.

car|ni|vore /kɑrnɪvɔr/ (**carnivores**) **NOUN** SCIENCE A **carnivore** is an animal that eats mainly meat. Compare with **herbivore** and **omnivore**.

car|ol /kærəl/ (**carols**) **NOUN** MUSIC **Carols** are religious songs that Christians sing usually at Christmas. ❏ *The children all sang carols as loudly as they could.*

car|pen|ter /kɑrpɪntər/ (**carpenters**) **NOUN** A **carpenter** is a person whose job is to make and repair wooden things.

car|pet /kɑrpɪt/ (**carpets**) **NOUN** A **carpet** is a thick, soft covering for the floor. ❏ *He picked up the clothes and vacuumed the carpets.*

car|pet|bag|ger /kɑrpɪtbæɡər/ (**carpetbaggers**) **NOUN** SOCIAL STUDIES A **carpetbagger** is someone who is trying to become a politician in an area that is not their home. ❏ *He was called a carpetbagger because he lived outside the district.*

car|rot /kærət/ (**carrots**) **NOUN** **Carrots** are long, thin, orange-colored vegetables. ❏ *We had chicken with potatoes, peas, and carrots.*
→ look at **vegetable**

car|ry /kæri/ (**carries, carrying, carried**)
1 VERB If you **carry** something, you hold it in your hand and take it with you. ❏ *He was carrying a briefcase.*
2 VERB If you **carry** something, you always have it with you. ❏ *You have to carry a passport.*
3 VERB To **carry** someone or something means to take them somewhere. ❏ *Trucks carrying food and medicine left the capital city yesterday.*
▶ **carry on** If you **carry on** doing something, you continue to do it. ❏ *The teacher carried on talking.*
▶ **carry out** If you **carry** something **out**, you do it. ❏ *They carried out tests in the laboratory.*

cart /kɑrt/ (**carts**)
1 NOUN A **cart** is an old-fashioned wooden vehicle that is usually pulled by a horse.
2 NOUN A **cart** or a **shopping cart** is a large plastic or metal basket on wheels that customers use in supermarkets.

C

C

car|ton /kɑrtᵊn/ (cartons) **NOUN** A **carton** is a plastic or cardboard container for food or drink. ❑ ...*a quart carton of milk.*
→ look at **container**

car|toon /kɑrtun/ (cartoons)
1 **NOUN** A **cartoon** is a funny drawing, often in a magazine or newspaper. ❑ ...*cartoon characters.*
2 **NOUN** A **cartoon** is a film that uses drawings for all the characters and scenes instead of real people or objects. ❑ *We watched children's cartoons on TV.*

car|tridge /kɑrtrɪdʒ/ (cartridges) **NOUN** A **cartridge** is a part of a machine you can easily remove when it is empty. ❑ *You need to change the ink cartridge in your printer.*

carve /kɑrv/ (carves, carving, carved)
1 **VERB** ARTS If you **carve** an object, you cut it out of wood or stone. ❑ *He carved the statue from one piece of rock.*
2 **VERB** If you **carve** meat, you cut slices from it. ❑ *Andrew began to carve the chicken.*

case /keɪs/ (cases)
1 **NOUN** A **case** is a particular situation, especially one that you are using as an example. ❑ *In some cases, it can be very difficult.*
2 **NOUN** A **case** is a crime that police are working on. ❑ ...*a murder case.*
3 **NOUN** A **case** is a container that is designed to hold or protect something. ❑ *He uses a black case for his glasses.*
4 You say **in any case** when you are adding another reason for something. ❑ *The concert was sold out, and in any case, most of us could not afford a ticket.*
5 If you do something **in case** a particular thing happens, you do it because that thing might happen. ❑ *I've brought some food in case we get hungry.*
6 **In that case** means if that is the situation. ❑ *"It's raining."—"Oh, in that case we'll have to stay in."*

cash /kæʃ/ (cashes, cashing, cashed)
1 **NONCOUNT NOUN** **Cash** is money in the form of bills and coins. ❑ ...*two thousand dollars in cash.*
2 **VERB** If you **cash** a check, you take it to a bank and get money for it.
→ look at **ATM, payment, shopping**

cash|ew /kæʃu, kæʃu/ (cashews) **NOUN** A **cashew** or a **cashew nut** is a curved nut that you can eat.

cash|ier /kæʃɪər/ (cashiers) **NOUN** A **cashier** is a person whose job is to take customers' money in stores or banks.

ca|si|no /kəsinoʊ/ (casinos) **NOUN** A **casino** is a place where people gamble (= risk money) by playing games.

cas|sette /kəsɛt/ (cassettes) **NOUN** A **cassette** is a small, flat plastic case containing tape that is used for recording and listening to sound.

cast /kæst/ (casts)
1 **NOUN** The **cast** of a play or a movie is all the people who act in it. ❑ *The show is very amusing and the cast is very good.*
2 **NOUN** A **cast** is a hard cover for protecting a broken arm or leg. ❑ *His arm is in a cast.*

cas|tle /kæsᵊl/ (castles) **NOUN** A **castle** is a large building with thick, high walls that was built in the

past to protect people during wars and battles.

cas|ual /kæʒuəl/
1 **ADJECTIVE** If you are **casual**, you are relaxed and not worried about what is happening. ❑ *She tried to sound casual, but she was frightened.* ● **casu|al|ly** **ADVERB** ❑ *"No need to hurry," Ben said casually.*
2 **ADJECTIVE** **Casual** clothes are clothes that you normally wear at home or on vacation, and not on formal occasions. ❑ *I also bought some casual clothes for the weekend.* ● **casu|al|ly** **ADVERB** ❑ *They were casually dressed.*
→ look at **wear**

casu|al|ty /kæʒuəlti/ (casualties) **NOUN** A **casualty** is a person who is injured or killed in a war or in an accident. ❑ *Helicopters bombed the town, causing many casualties.*

cat /kæt/ (cats) **NOUN** A **cat** is a small animal covered with fur that people often keep as a pet. ❑ *The cat sat on my lap, purring.*

cata|log /kætᵊlɒg/ (catalogs) also **catalogue** **NOUN** A **catalog** is a list of things you can buy from a particular company. ❑ *The website has an on-line catalog of products.*

ca|tas|tro|phe /kətǽstrəfi/ (**catastrophes**)
NOUN A **catastrophe** is an unexpected event that causes a lot of suffering or damage. ❑ *They learn how to deal with major catastrophes, including earthquakes.*

cata|stroph|ic /kætəstrɒfɪk/ **ADJECTIVE**
Catastrophic means extremely bad or serious, often causing a lot of damage. ❑ *A storm caused catastrophic damage to the houses.*

catch /kætʃ/ (**catches, catching, caught**)
1 VERB If you **catch** a person or animal, you find them and hold them. ❑ *Police say they are confident of catching the man.* ❑ *Where did you catch the fish?*
2 VERB SPORTS If you **catch** an object that is moving through the air, you take hold of it with your hands. ❑ *I jumped up to catch the ball.*
3 NOUN SPORTS **Catch** is also a noun. ❑ *That was a great catch.*
4 VERB If you **catch** part of your body somewhere, it accidentally gets stuck there. ❑ *I caught my finger in the car door.*
5 VERB When you **catch** a bus, train, or plane, you get on it in order to travel somewhere. ❑ *We caught the bus on the corner of the street.*
6 VERB If you **catch** someone doing something wrong, you see or find them doing it. ❑ *They caught him with $30,000 cash in a briefcase.*
7 VERB If you **catch** an illness, you become ill with it. ❑ *Keep warm, or you'll catch a cold.*
→ look at **health care**
▶ **catch up** **1** If you **catch up with** someone, you reach them by walking faster than they are walking. ❑ *I stopped and waited for her to catch up.*
2 To **catch up** means to reach the same level as someone else. ❑ *You'll have to work hard to catch up.*

Word Partners	Use **catch** with:
N.	catch a fish **1**
	catch a ball **2**
	catch a bus, catch a flight, catch a plane, catch a train **5**
	catch a thief **6**
PREP.	catch on *something* **4**

catch|er /kætʃər/ (**catchers**) **NOUN** In baseball, the **catcher** is the player who stands behind the batter (= the player who hits the ball).

cat|ego|rize /kætɪgəraɪz/ (**categorizes, categorizing, categorized**) **VERB** If you **categorize** people or things, you say which group or type they belong to. ❑ *Their music is usually categorized as jazz.*

cat|ego|ry /kætɪgɔri/ (**categories**) **NOUN** If people or things are divided into **categories**, they are divided into similar groups. ❑ *Their music falls into the category of "jazz."*

ca|ter /keɪtər/ (**caters, catering, catered**)
VERB If someone **caters for** a party, they provide the food for it. ❑ *We can cater for birthday parties of any size.*

cat|er|pil|lar /kætərpɪlər/ (**caterpillars**)
NOUN A **caterpillar** is a small animal with a long body that develops into a butterfly (= an insect with large colored wings).

ca|thedral /kəθidrəl/ (**cathedrals**) **NOUN**
A **cathedral** is a large and important church. ❑ *We visited some of the great cathedrals of Madrid.*

Catho|lic /kæθlɪk/ (**Catholics**)
1 ADJECTIVE The **Catholic** Church is a section of the Christian Church. ❑ *...a Catholic priest.*
2 NOUN A **Catholic** is a member of the Catholic Church. ❑ *His parents are Catholics.*

cat|sup /kætsəp/ **Catsup** is another word for **ketchup.** ❑ *...french fries with catsup.*

cat|tle /kætºl/ **PLURAL NOUN Cattle** are cows that are kept for their milk or meat.

caught /kɔt/ **Caught** is a form of the verb **catch.**

cau|li|flow|er /kɔliflaʊər/ (**cauliflowers**)
NOUN A **cauliflower** is a large, round, white vegetable surrounded by green leaves.
→ look at **vegetable**

cause /kɔz/ (**causes, causing, caused**)
1 NOUN The **cause of** an event is what makes it happen. ❑ *We still don't know the exact cause of the accident*
2 NOUN A **cause** is an aim that some people support or fight for. ❑ *A strong leader will help our cause.*
3 VERB To **cause** something means to make it happen. ❑ *Stress can cause headaches.*
→ look at **greenhouse effect, health care**

cau|tion /kɔʃºn/ **NONCOUNT NOUN Caution** is great care to avoid danger. ❑ *Always cross the street with caution.*

cau|tious /kɔʃəs/ **ADJECTIVE** A **cautious** person is very careful to try to avoid danger. ❑ *Doctors are cautious about using this new medication.* ● **cau|tious|ly ADVERB** ❑ *David* *moved cautiously forward and looked down into the water.*

cav|al|ry /kǽvəlri/ **NOUN** SOCIAL STUDIES
In the past, **the cavalry** was the group of soldiers in an army who rode horses. ❏ *He was a young cavalry officer.*

cave /keɪv/ (**caves**) **NOUN** SCIENCE A **cave** is a large hole in the side of a hill or under the ground.

cave|man /keɪvmæn/ (**cavemen**) **NOUN**
Cavemen were people in the past who lived mainly in caves.

cc /si si/ **cc** is used at the beginning of emails or at the end of a business letter to show that a copy is being sent to another person. ❏ *...cc j.jones@harpercollins.co.uk.*

CCTV /si si ti vi/ **NONCOUNT NOUN** CCTV is a short form for **closed-circuit television.** ❏ *We saw him on the CCTV camera.*

CD /si di/ (**CDs**) **NOUN** TECHNOLOGY A **CD** is a disk for storing music or computer information. **CD** is short for **compact disk.** ❏ *You can buy a CD of all her songs.*

CD burn|er /si di bɜrnər/ (**CD burners**) **NOUN** TECHNOLOGY A **CD burner** is a piece of computer equipment that you use for copying information or music from a computer onto a CD.

CD play|er (**CD players**) **NOUN** TECHNOLOGY A **CD player** is a machine that plays CDs.

CD-ROM /si di rɒm/ (**CD-ROMs**) **NOUN** TECHNOLOGY A **CD-ROM** is a CD that stores a very large amount of information that you can read using a computer.
→ look at **computer**

cease /sis/ (**ceases, ceasing, ceased**) **VERB**
When something **ceases,** it stops. [FORMAL] ❏ *At one o'clock the rain ceased.*

cease-fire /sisfaɪər/ (**cease-fires**) **NOUN** SOCIAL STUDIES A **cease-fire** is an agreement to stop fighting a war. ❏ *They have agreed to a ceasefire after three years of conflict.*

ceil|ing /silɪŋ/ (**ceilings**) **NOUN** A **ceiling** is the top inside part of a room. ❏ *The rooms all had high ceilings.*

cel|ebrate /sɛlɪbreɪt/ (**celebrates, celebrating, celebrated**) **VERB** If you **celebrate** something, you do something enjoyable for a special reason. ❏ *I passed my*

test and wanted to celebrate. ❏ *Dick celebrated his 60th birthday on Monday.* ● **cel|ebra|tion** /sɛlɪbreɪʃən/ (**celebrations**) **NOUN** ❏ *There was a celebration in our house that night.*

ce|leb|rity /sɪlɛbriti/ (**celebrities**) **NOUN**
A **celebrity** is someone who is famous. ❏ *Kylie Minogue will be our celebrity guest.*

cel|ery /sɛləri/ **NONCOUNT NOUN** Celery is a vegetable that consists of long, pale-green sticks. ❏ *Cut a stick of celery into small pieces.*

Sound Partners | cell, sell

cell /sɛl/ (**cells**)
1 **NOUN** SCIENCE A **cell** is the smallest part of an animal or plant. ❏ *We are studying blood cells.*
2 **NOUN** A **cell** is a small room with a lock in a prison or a police station. ❏ *How many prisoners were in the cell?*

cel|lar /sɛlər/ (**cellars**) **NOUN** A **cellar** is a large space under a building. ❏ *He kept the boxes in the cellar.*

cel|lo /tʃɛloʊ/ (**cellos**) **NOUN** MUSIC A **cello** is a musical instrument that is like a large violin. You sit behind it and rest it on the floor. ● **cel|list** /tʃɛlɪst/ (**cellists**) **NOUN** ❏ *He is a great cellist.*
→ look at **musical instrument**

cell|phone /sɛlfoʊn/ (**cellphones**) **NOUN** TECHNOLOGY A **cellphone** is a telephone that you can carry wherever you go. ❏ *The woman called the police on her cellphone.*
→ look at **phone**

Celsius /sɛlsiəs/ **ADJECTIVE** SCIENCE
Celsius is a way of measuring temperature. Water freezes at 0° Celsius and boils at 100° Celsius. ❏ *11° Celsius is 52° Fahrenheit.*
→ look at **measurement**

Usage | **Celsius**
Most of the world uses the **Celsius** or centigrade scale for temperature, but the U.S. uses the Fahrenheit scale.

ce|ment /sɪmɛnt/ **NONCOUNT NOUN** Cement is a gray powder that you mix with sand and water to make concrete.

cem|etery /sɛmətɛri/ (**cemeteries**) **NOUN**
A **cemetery** is a place where dead people are buried.

cen|sus /sɛnsəs/ (**censuses**) **NOUN** SOCIAL STUDIES A **census** is when a government counts all the people in a country. ❏ *That census counted a quarter of a billion Americans.*

cent /sɛnt/ (**cents**) **NOUN** A **cent** is a coin. There are one hundred cents in a dollar. ❏ *The book cost six dollars and fifty cents.*

cen|ter /sɛntər/ (**centers**)

1 **NOUN** The **center** of something is the middle of it. ❏ *We sat in the center of the room.*
2 **NOUN** A **center** is a place where people can take part in a particular activity, or get help. ❏ *The building is now a health center.*

cen|ti|li|ter /sɛntɪlitər/ (**centiliters**) **NOUN** A **centiliter** is ten milliliters or one-hundredth of a liter.

cen|ti|me|ter /sɛntɪmitər/ (**centimeters**) **NOUN** A **centimeter** is a unit for measuring length. There are ten millimeters in a centimeter. ❏ *This tiny plant is only a few centimeters high.*
→ look at **measurement**

cen|tral /sɛntrəl/ **ADJECTIVE** Something that is **central** is in the middle part of a place. ❏ *They live in Central America.*

cen|tral heat|ing **NONCOUNT NOUN** Central **heating** is a heating system that uses hot air or water to heat every part of a building.

cen|trifu|gal force /sɛntrɪfyəgᵊl fɔrs, -trɪfəgᵊl/ **NONCOUNT NOUN** SCIENCE **Centrifugal force** is the force that makes objects move away from the center when they are moving around a central point. ❏ *The juice is removed by centrifugal force.*

cen|tu|ry /sɛntʃəri/ (**centuries**) **NOUN** A **century** is one hundred years. ❏ *The story started a century ago.* ❏ *She was one of the most important painters of the nineteenth century.*

ce|ram|ic /sɪræmɪk/ (**ceramics**)

1 **NONCOUNT NOUN** ARTS **Ceramic** is clay (= a type of earth) that has been heated to a very high temperature so that it becomes hard. ❏ *The wall is covered with ceramic tiles.*
2 **PLURAL NOUN** ARTS **Ceramics** are ceramic objects. ❏ *The museum has a huge collection of Chinese ceramics.*

ce|real /sɪəriəl/ (**cereals**)

1 **NONCOUNT NOUN** **Cereal** is a food made from grain, that you can mix with milk and eat for breakfast. ❏ *I have a bowl of cereal every morning.*
2 **NOUN** **Cereals** are plants that produce grain for food. ❏ *Rice is similar to other cereal grains such as corn and wheat.*

cer|emo|nial /sɛrɪmoʊniəl/ **ADJECTIVE** Something that is **ceremonial** is used or done at a ceremony. ❏ *The children watched the ceremonial dances.*

cer|emo|ny /sɛrɪmoʊni/ (**ceremonies**) **NOUN** A **ceremony** is a formal event. ❏ *...a wedding ceremony.*

cer|tain /sɜrtᵊn/

1 **ADJECTIVE** If you are **certain** about something or if it is **certain**, you strongly believe it is true. ❏ *She's absolutely certain that she's going to recover.* ❏ *One thing is certain, both players are great sportsmen.*
2 If you know something **for certain**, you have no doubt at all about it. ❏ *She didn't know for certain if he was at home.*
3 If you **make certain that** something is the way you want it to be, you check it so that you are sure. ❏ *Parents should make certain that children do their homework.*

cer|tain|ly /sɜrtᵊnli/

1 **ADVERB** You use **certainly** to show that you are sure about what you are saying. ❏ *The meeting will almost certainly last an hour.*
2 **ADVERB** You use **certainly** when you are agreeing or disagreeing strongly with what someone has said. ❏ *"Are you still friends?"—"Certainly."* ❏ *"Perhaps I should go now."—"Certainly not!"*

cer|tain|ty /sɜrtᵊnti/ **NONCOUNT NOUN** **Certainty** is when you have no doubts at all about something. ❏ *I can tell you this with absolute certainty.*

cer|tifi|cate /sərtɪfɪkɪt/ (**certificates**) **NOUN** A **certificate** is an official document that proves that the facts on it are true. ❏ *You must show your birth certificate.* ❏ *I have a certificate signed by my teacher.*

cer|ti|fy /sɜrtɪfaɪ/ (**certifies, certifying, certified**) **VERB** If someone **certifies** something, they officially say that it is true. ❏ *The doctor certified that I was suffering from a chest infection.*

chain /tʃeɪn/ (**chains, chaining, chained**)

1 **NOUN** A **chain** is a line of metal rings that are connected together. ❏ *He wore a gold chain around his neck.*
2 **VERB** If a person or thing **is chained to** something, they are attached to it with a chain. ❏ *The dogs were chained to a fence.*

C

chair /tʃɛər/ (**chairs, chairing, chaired**)

1 **NOUN** A **chair** is a piece of furniture for one person to sit on, with a back and four legs. ❑ *He suddenly got up from his chair.*

2 **VERB** If you **chair** a meeting, you are the person who controls it. ❑ *They asked him to chair the committee meeting.*

→ look at **classroom, furniture**

chair|man /tʃɛərmən/ (**chairmen**) **NOUN**
The **chairman** of a meeting or organization is the person who controls it. ❑ *He is chairman of the committee that wrote the report.*

chair|person /tʃɛərpɜrsᵊn/ (**chairpersons**) **NOUN** The **chairperson** of a meeting or organization is the person who controls it. ❑ *She's the chairperson of the planning committee.*

chair|woman /tʃɛərwʊmən/ (**chairwomen**) **NOUN** The **chairwoman** of a meeting or organization is the woman who controls it. ❑ *The chairwoman welcomed us and opened the meeting.*

chalk /tʃɔk/

1 **NONCOUNT NOUN** Chalk is a soft white rock.

2 **NONCOUNT NOUN** ARTS Chalk is small sticks of chalk that you use for writing or drawing. ❑ *Now use a piece of colored chalk.*

→ look at **classroom**

chalk|board /tʃɔkbɔrd/ (**chalkboards**) **NOUN** A **chalkboard** is a dark-colored board that you write on with chalk.

→ look at **classroom**

chal|lenge /tʃælɪndʒ/ (**challenges, challenging, challenged**)

1 **NOUN** A challenge is something difficult to do. ❑ *His first challenge was learning the rules of the game.*

2 **VERB** If you **challenge** someone, you invite them to fight or play a game with you. ❑ *Jackson challenged O'Meara to another game.*

→ look at **school**

cham|pagne /ʃæmpeɪn/ **NONCOUNT NOUN** Champagne is an expensive French white wine with bubbles in it.

cham|pi|on /tʃæmpiən/ (**champions**) **NOUN** SPORTS A **champion** is the winner of a competition. ❑ *He was an Olympic champion twice.* ❑ *Kasparov became the world champion.*

Word Builder championship

ship ≈ **state of being**

champion + ship = champion**ship**
friend + ship = friend**ship**
leader + ship = leader**ship**
member + ship = member**ship**
owner + ship = owner**ship**
relation + ship = relation**ship**

cham|pi|on|ship /tʃæmpiənʃɪp/ (**championships**) **NOUN** SPORTS A **championship** is a competition to find the best player or team in a particular sport. ❑ *The world chess championship was on TV last night.*

chance /tʃæns/ (**chances**)

1 **NOUN** If there is a **chance** that something will happen, it is possible that it will happen. ❑ *There is a good chance that we can win the game against Australia.*

2 **NOUN** If you have a **chance to** do something, there is a time when you can do it. ❑ *Everyone gets a chance to vote.* ❑ *Millions of children never get the chance to go to school.*

3 Something that happens **by chance** was not planned by anyone. ❑ *He met Justin by chance in the street.*

Word Partners Use **chance** with:

ADJ.	**fair** chance, **good** chance, **slight** chance **1**
V.	**get a** chance, **give** *someone/something* a chance, **have a** chance, **miss a** chance **2**
N.	chance **of success**, chance **of winning 1** chance **meeting 3**

change /tʃeɪndʒ/ (**changes, changing, changed**)

1 **NOUN** If there is a **change**, something becomes different. ❑ *There will soon be some big changes in our company.*

2 **VERB** When something **changes** or when you **change** it, it becomes different. ❑ *The color of the sky changed from pink to blue.* ❑ *She changed into a happy woman.* ❑ *They should change the law.*

3 **VERB** To **change** something means to replace it with something new or different. ❑ *They decided to change the name of the band.* ❑ *He changed to a different medication.*

4 **VERB** When you **change** your clothes, you put on different ones. ❑ *Ben changed his shirt.* ❑ *They let her shower and change.*

5 **NONCOUNT NOUN** Your **change** is the

money that you get back when you pay with more money than something costs. ❑ *"There's your change."—"Thanks very much."*

6 **NONCOUNT NOUN** Change is coins. ❑ *"I need 36 cents. Do you have any change?"*

→ look at **climate, season, television, wear**

Word Partners	Use **change** with:
V.	**make a** change **1** **2**
ADJ.	**social** change, **sudden** change **1**
	loose change, **spare** change **5** **6**
N.	**change** direction **2**
	change **of address**, change **color**,
	change **the subject** **3**
	change **clothes** **4**

chan|nel /tʃænᵊl/ (**channels**)

1 **NOUN** A **channel** is a television station. ❑ *There is a huge number of television channels in America.*

2 **NOUN** GEOGRAPHY A **channel** is a narrow passage that water can flow along. ❑ *...a shipping channel.*

→ look at **television**

chant /tʃænt/ (**chants, chanting, chanted**)

1 **NOUN** A **chant** is a word or group of words that is repeated again and again. ❑ *Then the crowd started the chant of "U-S-A!"*

2 **VERB** If you **chant** something, you repeat the same words again and again. ❑ *The people chanted his name.* ❑ *The crowd chanted "We are with you."*

cha|os /keɪɒs/ **NONCOUNT NOUN** Chaos is when there is no order or organization. ❑ *The race ended in chaos.*

cha|ot|ic /keɪɒtɪk/ **ADJECTIVE** Something that is **chaotic** is completely confused and without order. ❑ *The city seemed to be a chaotic place to me.*

chap|el /tʃæpᵊl/ (**chapels**) **NOUN** A **chapel** is a room or part of a church that people pray in. ❑ *She went to the chapel on the hillside to pray.*

chap|ter /tʃæptər/ (**chapters**) **NOUN** LANGUAGE ARTS A **chapter** is a part of a book. ❑ *For more information, see Chapter 4.*

char|ac|ter /kærɪktər/ (**characters**)

1 **NOUN** The **character** of a person or place is all the things that make them different from other people or places. ❑ *It's difficult to understand the change in her character.*

2 **NOUN** LANGUAGE ARTS The **characters** in a story are the people in it. ❑ *Collard himself plays the main character.*

char|ac|ter|is|tic /kærɪktərɪstɪk/ (**characteristics**) **NOUN** A **characteristic** is a quality that is typical of someone or something. ❑ *The twins already had their own characteristics.*

char|coal /tʃɑrkoʊl/ **NONCOUNT NOUN** ARTS **Charcoal** is burnt wood that you can use for drawing. ❑ *We all did charcoal drawings of the building.*

charge /tʃɑrdʒ/ (**charges, charging, charged**)

1 **VERB** If you **charge** someone, you ask them to pay money for something. ❑ *The driver only charged us $2 each.* ❑ *How much do you charge for printing photos?*

2 **VERB** If you **charge** something you are buying to your credit card (= a plastic card that you use to buy things and pay for them later), you use a credit card to buy it. ❑ *I'll charge it to my Visa.*

3 **VERB** When the police **charge** someone, they formally tell them that they have done something wrong. ❑ *They have enough evidence to charge him.*

4 **VERB** SCIENCE To **charge** a battery means to put electricity into it. ❑ *Alex forgot to charge his cellphone.*

5 **NOUN** SCIENCE An electrical **charge** is the amount or type of electrical force that something has.

6 **NOUN** A **charge** is an amount of money that you have to pay for a service. ❑ *We can arrange this for a small charge.*

7 If you are **in charge of** someone or something, you are responsible for them. ❑ *Who is in charge here?*

→ look at **phone**

char|ity /tʃærɪti/ (**charities**) **NOUN** A **charity** is an organization that collects money for people who need help ❑ *Michael is working for a children's charity.*

Word Partners	Use **charity** with:
N.	**donation to** charity, charity **event**,
	money for charity, charity
	organization, charity **work**
V.	**collect for** charity, **donate to** charity,
	give to charity

charm /tʃɑrm/ **NONCOUNT NOUN** Charm is the quality of being pleasant and attractive. ❑ *This hotel has real charm.*

charm|ing /tʃɑrmɪŋ/ **ADJECTIVE** If someone is **charming**, they are very pleasant and attractive. ❑ *He seemed to be a charming young man.*

C

chart /tʃɑrt/ (**charts**) NOUN A **chart** is a diagram or graph that shows information. ❏ *See the chart on next page for more details.*

char|ter /tʃɑrtər/ (**charters**) NOUN SOCIAL STUDIES A **charter** is a formal document that describes the rights or principles of an organization. ❏ *...the United Nations Charter.*

chase /tʃeɪs/ (**chases, chasing, chased**)
1 VERB If you **chase** someone, you run after them in order to catch them. ❏ *She chased the boys for 100 yards.*
2 NOUN **Chase** is also a noun. ❏ *The chase ended at about 10:30 p.m. on Highway 522.*

chat /tʃæt/ (**chats, chatting, chatted**)
1 VERB When people **chat**, they talk in an informal, friendly way. ❏ *The women sit and chat at coffee time.* ❏ *I was chatting to him the other day.*
2 NOUN **Chat** is also a noun. ❏ *I had a chat with John.*

chat room (**chat rooms**) also **chatroom** NOUN TECHNOLOGY A **chat room** is a website where people can exchange messages.
→ look at **Internet**

chat|ter /tʃætər/ (**chatters, chattering, chattered**)
1 VERB If you **chatter**, you talk quickly about unimportant things. ❏ *Erica chattered about her grandchildren.*
2 NONCOUNT NOUN **Chatter** is also a noun. ❏ *The students stopped their noisy chatter.*
3 VERB If your teeth **chatter**, they keep knocking together because you are cold. ❏ *She was so cold her teeth chattered.*

chauf|feur /ʃoʊfər, ʃoʊfɜr/ (**chauffeurs**) NOUN A **chauffeur** is a person whose job is to drive for another person.

cheap /tʃip/ (**cheaper, cheapest**)
1 ADJECTIVE Goods or services that are **cheap** cost little money or less than you expected. ❏ *I'm going to rent a room if I can find somewhere cheap enough.* ❏ *People who own cars are calling for cheaper oil.* ● **cheap|ly** ADVERB ❏ *You can deliver more food more cheaply by ship.*
2 ADJECTIVE **Cheap** goods cost less money than similar products but their quality is often bad. ❏ *Don't buy any of those cheap watches.*
→ look at **shopping**

cheat /tʃit/ (**cheats, cheating, cheated**)
1 VERB If someone **cheats**, they do not obey the rules in a game or exam. ❏ *Students*

sometimes cheated in order to get into top schools.
2 NOUN **Cheat** is also a noun. ❏ *Are you calling me a cheat?.* ● **cheat|ing** NONCOUNT NOUN ❏ *The other players said he was cheating.*
→ look at **play**

Spelling Partners	check

check /tʃɛk/ (**checks, checking, checked**)
1 VERB If you **check** something, you make sure that it is correct. ❏ *Check the meanings of the words in a dictionary.* ❏ *I think there is an age limit, but I'll check.* ❏ *She checked whether she had a clean shirt.*
2 NOUN **Check** is also a noun. ❏ *We need to do some quick checks before the plane leaves.*
3 VERB If you **check** something that is written on a piece of paper, you put a mark like this ✔ next to it. ❏ *Please check the box below.*
4 VERB When you **check** your luggage at an airport, you give it to the airline so that it can go on your plane. ❏ *We checked our luggage early and walked around the airport.*
5 NOUN The **check** in a restaurant is a piece of paper with the cost of your meal on it.
6 NOUN A **check** is a printed form from a bank that you write on and use to pay for things. ❏ *He handed me a check for $1,500.*
→ look at **answer, calendar, payment**
▶ **check in** When you **check in** at an airport or a hotel, you tell the person at the desk that you have arrived. ❏ *He checked in at Amsterdam's Schiphol airport for a flight to Atlanta.*
▶ **check out** When you **check out of** a hotel, you pay the bill and leave. ❏ *They packed and checked out of the hotel.* ❏ *They checked out yesterday morning.*

Word Partners	Use **check** with:
N.	check **your bag**, check **your luggage** **4**
V.	**cash** a check, **deposit** a check, **pay with** a check, **write a** check **6**

checked /tʃɛkt/ ADJECTIVE Something that is **checked** has a pattern of small squares, usually of two colors. ❏ *The waiter had a checked shirt.*

check|ers /tʃɛkərz/ NONCOUNT NOUN **Checkers** is a game for two people, that you play with 24 round pieces on a board.
→ look at **play**

check-in (check-ins) **NOUN** At an airport, a **check-in** is the counter or desk where you check in.

check|ing ac|count (checking accounts) **NOUN** A **checking account** is a personal bank account that you can take money out of by writing a check (= a printed form that you write on and use to pay for things).

check mark (check marks) **NOUN** A **check mark** is a written mark like this ✔. You use it to show that something is correct or done.

check|out /tʃɛkaʊt/ (checkouts) **NOUN** In a supermarket or other store, a **checkout** is where you pay for the things you are buying.

check-up /tʃɛkʌp/ (check-ups) **NOUN** A **check-up** is an examination by your doctor or dentist.
→ look at **health care**

cheek /tʃik/ (cheeks) **NOUN** Your **cheeks** are the sides of your face below your eyes. ❑ *The tears started rolling down my cheeks.*
→ look at **face**

cheer /tʃɪər/ (cheers, cheering, cheered)
1 **VERB** When people **cheer**, they shout loudly to show they are pleased or to encourage someone. ❑ *We cheered as she went up the steps to the stage.*
2 **NOUN** **Cheer** is also a noun. ❑ *The audience gave him a loud cheer.*
▶ **cheer up** When you **cheer up** or **cheer** someone **up**, you become or make someone feel happier. ❑ *Cheer up. Life could be worse.* ❑ *Stop trying to cheer me up.*

cheer|ful /tʃɪərfəl/ **ADJECTIVE** Someone who is **cheerful** seems to be happy. ❑ *Paddy was always smiling and cheerful.* ● **cheer|ful|ly** **ADVERB** ❑ *"We've got good news," Pat said cheerfully.* ● **cheer|ful|ness** **NONCOUNT NOUN** ❑ *I liked his natural cheerfulness.*

cheer|leader /tʃɪərlidər/ (cheerleaders) **NOUN** **SPORTS** A **cheerleader** is one of a group of people who encourage the crowd to shout support for their team at a sports event.

cheese /tʃiz/ (cheeses) **NOUN** **Cheese** is a solid food made from milk. It is usually white or yellow. ❑ *We had bread and cheese for lunch.* ❑ *This shop sells delicious French cheeses.*

chef /ʃɛf/ (chefs) **NOUN** A **chef** is a cook in a restaurant.

chemi|cal /kɛmɪkəl/ (chemicals)
1 **ADJECTIVE** **SCIENCE** **Chemical** means relating to chemicals or chemistry. ❑ *Do you know what caused the chemical reaction?* ❑ *Almost all of the natural chemical elements are found in the ocean.*
2 **NOUN** **SCIENCE** **Chemicals** are substances that are used in a chemical process or made by a chemical process.
→ look at **pollution**

chem|ist /kɛmɪst/ (chemists) **NOUN** **SCIENCE** A **chemist** is a scientist who studies chemistry.

chem|is|try /kɛmɪstri/ **NONCOUNT NOUN** **SCIENCE** **Chemistry** is the science of gases, liquids, and solids, their structure, and how they change.
→ look at **science**

cher|ry /tʃɛri/ (cherries) **NOUN** **Cherries** are small, round fruit with red skins.

chess /tʃɛs/ **NONCOUNT NOUN** **Chess** is a game for two people, played on a board using different shaped pieces. ❑ *He was playing chess with his uncle.*
→ look at **play**

chest /tʃɛst/ (chests)
1 **NOUN** **SCIENCE** Your **chest** is the top part of the front of your body. ❑ *He folded his arms across his broad chest.* ❑ *He was shot in the chest.*
2 **NOUN** A **chest** is a large, strong box for storing things. ❑ *We know she has money locked in a chest somewhere.*
→ look at **body**

chew /tʃu/ (chews, chewing, chewed) **VERB** When you **chew** food, you break it up with your teeth in your mouth. ❑ *Always chew your food well.*
→ look at **eat**

chick /tʃɪk/ (chicks) **NOUN** A **chick** is a baby bird.

chick|en /tʃɪkɪn/ (chickens, chickening, chickened)
1 **NOUN** **Chickens** are birds that are kept on farms for their eggs and for their meat.
2 **NONCOUNT NOUN** **Chicken** is the meat of this bird. ❑ *We had chicken sandwiches.*
→ look at **bird, meat**
▶ **chicken out** If someone **chickens out**, they do not do something because they are afraid. [INFORMAL] ❑ *I wanted to ask Mom but I chickened out.*

chief /tʃif/ (chiefs)
1 **NOUN** The **chief** of a group is its leader. ❑ *The police chief has said very little.*

C

2 **ADJECTIVE** The **chief** thing is the most important one. ❑ *Sunburn is the chief cause of skin cancer.*

chief|ly /tʃiːfli/ **ADVERB** You use **chiefly** to mean not completely, but especially or mostly. ❑ *Rhodes is chiefly known for her fashion designs.*

child /tʃaɪld/ (**children**)
1 **NOUN** A **child** is a young boy or girl. ❑ *When I was a child I lived in a village.* ❑ *The show is free for children age 6 and under.*
2 **NOUN** Someone's **children** are their sons and daughters. ❑ *They have three young children.*
→ look at **age**

child|hood /tʃaɪldhʊd/ (**childhoods**) **NOUN** A person's **childhood** is when they are a child. ❑ *She had a happy childhood.*

child|ish /tʃaɪldɪʃ/ **ADJECTIVE** An adult who is **childish** behaves like a child. ❑ *Paco got up with a childish smile on his face.*

chil|dren /tʃɪldrən/ **Children** is the plural of **child**.

chili /tʃɪli/ (**chilies** or **chilis**) **NOUN** Chilies are small red or green peppers that taste very hot.

chill /tʃɪl/ (**chills, chilling, chilled**) **VERB** To **chill** something means to make it cold. ❑ *Chill the fruit salad in the fridge.*
▶ **chill out** To **chill out** means to relax. [INFORMAL] ❑ *After school, we chill out and watch TV.*

chil|ly /tʃɪli/ (**chillier, chilliest**) **ADJECTIVE** **Chilly** means rather cold. ❑ *It was a chilly afternoon.*

chim|ney /tʃɪmni/ (**chimneys**) **NOUN** A **chimney** is a pipe above a fire that lets the smoke travel up and out of the building. ❑ *Smoke from chimneys polluted the skies.*

chim|pan|zee /tʃɪmpænziː/ (**chimpanzees**) **NOUN** A **chimpanzee** is a type of small African ape (= the family of animals that is most similar to humans).

chin /tʃɪn/ (**chins**) **NOUN** Your **chin** is the part of your face below your mouth.

chi|na /tʃaɪnə/ **NONCOUNT NOUN** China is a hard white substance that is used for making expensive cups and plates. ❑ *He ate from a small bowl made of china.*

Spelling Partners **chip**

chip /tʃɪp/ (**chips, chipping, chipped**)
1 **NOUN** **Chips** or **potato chips** are very thin slices of fried potato. ❑ *My snack was a bag of potato chips.*
2 **NOUN** A **chip** is a very small part that controls a piece of electronic equipment. ❑ *...a computer chip.*
3 **NOUN** A **chip** is a small piece that has been broken off something. ❑ *It contains real chocolate chips.*
4 **VERB** If you **chip** something, you break a small piece off it. ❑ *The candy chipped the woman's tooth.* ● **chipped** **ADJECTIVE** ❑ *The paint on the door was badly chipped.*

choco|late /tʃɔːkəlɪt, tʃɔːklɪt/ (**chocolates**)
1 **NONCOUNT NOUN** Chocolate is a sweet brown food that you eat as a sweet, or that is used to give flavor to other food. ❑ *We shared a bar of chocolate.*
2 **NONCOUNT NOUN** Chocolate or **hot chocolate** is a hot drink made from chocolate. ❑ *The visitors can buy tea, coffee, and chocolate.*
3 **NOUN** Chocolates are small candies or nuts covered with chocolate. ❑ *The class gave the teacher a box of chocolates.*

choice /tʃɔɪs/ (**choices**)
1 **NOUN** If there is a **choice of** things, there are several of them and you can choose the one you want. ❑ *It comes in a choice of colors.* ❑ *There's a choice between meat or fish.*
2 **NOUN** Your **choice** is the thing or things that you choose. ❑ *Her husband didn't really agree with her choice.*
3 If you **have no choice**, you cannot choose to do something else. ❑ *We had to agree - we had no choice.*

choir /kwaɪər/ (**choirs**) **NOUN** MUSIC A **choir** is a group of people who sing together. ❑ *He sang in his church choir for years.*

choke /tʃoʊk/ (**chokes, choking, choked**) **VERB** If you **choke**, you cannot breathe because there is not enough air, or because something is blocking your throat. ❏ *A small child may choke on the toy.* ❏ *The smoke was choking her.*

cho|les|ter|ol /kəlɛstərɔl/ **NONCOUNT NOUN** SCIENCE **Cholesterol** is a substance that exists in your blood. Too much cholesterol in the blood can cause heart disease. ❏ *He has a dangerously high cholesterol level.*

choose /tʃuz/ (**chooses, choosing, chose, chosen**)

1 **VERB** If you **choose** someone or something, you decide to have that person or thing. ❏ *Each group will choose its own leader.* ❏ *You can choose from several different patterns.*

2 **VERB** If you **choose to** do something, you do it because you want to. ❏ *Many people choose to eat meat at dinner only.* ❏ *You can remain silent if you choose.*

→ look at **answer**

chop /tʃɒp/ (**chops, chopping, chopped**) **VERB** If you **chop** something, you cut it into pieces with a knife. ❏ *Chop the butter into small pieces.* ❏ *We started chopping wood for a fire.*

▶ **chop down** If you **chop down** a tree, you cut through its trunk (= the thick part that grows up from the ground). ❏ *Sometimes they chop down a tree for firewood.*

▶ **chop off** To **chop** something **off** means to cut it off. ❏ *Chop off the fish's heads and tails.*

chop|stick /tʃɒpstɪk/ (**chopsticks**) **NOUN** **Chopsticks** are thin sticks that people in East Asia use for eating food.

chord /kɔrd/ (**chords**) **NOUN** MUSIC A **chord** is a number of musical notes played or sung at the same time. ❏ *I can play a few chords on the guitar.*

chore /tʃɔr/ (**chores**) **NOUN** A **chore** is a job that you have to do, for example, cleaning the house. ❏ *After I finished my chores, I could go outside and play.*

→ look at Picture Dictionary: **chores**

cho|rus /kɔrəs/ (**choruses**)

1 **NOUN** MUSIC A **chorus** is the part of a song that you repeat several times. ❏ *Caroline sang two verses and the chorus of her song.*

2 **NOUN** MUSIC A **chorus** is a large group of people who sing together. ❏ *The Harvard*

orchestra and chorus performed Beethoven's Ninth Symphony.

chose /tʃoʊz/ **Chose** is a form of the verb **choose**.

cho|sen /tʃoʊzᵊn/ **Chosen** is a form of the verb **choose**.

chris|ten /krɪsᵊn/ (**christens, christening, christened**) **VERB** When a baby **is christened**, he or she is given a name during a Christian ceremony. ❏ *She was born in March and christened in June.*

chris|ten|ing /krɪsᵊnɪŋ/ (**christenings**) **NOUN** A **christening** is a ceremony in which members of a church welcome a baby and it is officially given its name. ❏ *I cried at my granddaughter's christening.*

Christian /krɪstʃən/ (**Christians**)

1 **NOUN** A **Christian** is someone who believes in Jesus Christ, and follows what he taught.

2 **ADJECTIVE** **Christian** means to do with Christians. ❏ *...the Christian Church.*

Chris|ti|an|ity /krɪstʃiænɪti/ **NONCOUNT NOUN** **Christianity** is a religion that believes in Jesus Christ and follows what he taught.

Christ|mas /krɪsməs/ (**Christmases**) **NOUN** **Christmas** is the period around the 25th of December, when Christians celebrate the birth of Jesus Christ. ❏ *"Merry Christmas!"* ❏ *We're staying at home for the Christmas holidays.*

chro|mo|some /kroʊməsoʊm/ (**chromosomes**) **NOUN** SCIENCE A **chromosome** is a part of a cell in an animal or a plant. ❏ *Each cell of our bodies contains 46 chromosomes.*

chub|by /tʃʌbi/ (**chubbier, chubbiest**) **ADJECTIVE** A **chubby** person is slightly fat. ❏ *Do you think I'm too chubby?*

chuck|le /tʃʌkᵊl/ (**chuckles, chuckling, chuckled**)

1 **VERB** When you **chuckle**, you laugh quietly. ❏ *He chuckled and said, "Of course not."*

2 **NOUN** **Chuckle** is also a noun. ❏ *He gave a little chuckle.*

chunk /tʃʌŋk/ (**chunks**) **NOUN** **Chunks of** something are thick, solid pieces of it. ❏ *Large chunks of ice floated past us.*

chunky /tʃʌŋki/ (**chunkier, chunkiest**) **ADJECTIVE** Something that is **chunky** is large and heavy. ❏ *She was wearing a chunky gold necklace.*

C

Picture Dictionary chores

mop

dust

wash

vacuum

sweep

iron

church /tʃɜrtʃ/ (churches) **NOUN** A church is a building where Christians go to pray. ❑ *We got married in Coburn United Methodist Church.* ❑ *The family has gone to church.*

ci|der /saɪdər/ **NONCOUNT NOUN** Cider is a drink made from apples. ❑ *He ordered a glass of cider.*

ci|gar /sɪgɑr/ (cigars) **NOUN** A cigar is a roll of dried tobacco leaves that some people smoke.

ciga|rette /sɪgərɛt/ (cigarettes) **NOUN** A **cigarette** is a small tube of paper containing dried leaves (= tobacco) that some people smoke.

cin|ema /sɪnɪmə/ (cinemas) **NOUN** A cinema is a building where people go to watch movies. ❑ *There is a mall with a multiplex cinema (= a cinema with several screens).*
→ look at **movie**

cin|na|mon /sɪnəmən/ **NONCOUNT NOUN** Cinnamon is a sweet spice used for adding flavor to food.

cir|cle /sɜrkᵊl/ (circles) **NOUN** MATH A circle is a round shape. ❑ *The Japanese flag is white, with a red circle in the center.* ❑ *She drew a mouth, a nose, and two circles for eyes.*
→ look at **answer**

cir|cuit /sɜrkɪt/ (circuits)
1 NOUN A circuit is a track that cars race around. ❑ *...the grand prix circuit.*
2 NOUN SCIENCE An electrical circuit is a complete path that electricity can flow around. ❑ *The electrical circuit was broken.*

cir|cu|lar /sɜrkyələr/ **ADJECTIVE** Something that is **circular** is shaped like a circle.

❑ *The house has a large garage and a circular driveway (= a piece of ground that leads from the road to the front of a building).*

cir|cu|late /sɜrkyəleɪt/ (circulates, circulating, circulated) **VERB** When something **circulates**, it moves easily and freely in a place. ❑ *The blood circulates through the body.* ● **cir|cu|la|tion NONCOUNT NOUN** ❑ *...the circulation of air.*

cir|cu|la|tion /sɜrkyəleɪʃᵊn/ **NONCOUNT NOUN** SCIENCE Your **circulation** is the movement of blood through your body. ❑ *Regular exercise is good for the circulation.*

cir|cum|fer|ence /sərkʌmfrəns/ **NONCOUNT NOUN** MATH The **circumference** of a circle is the distance around its edge. ❑ *Think of a way to calculate the Earth's circumference.*
→ look at **area**

cir|cum|navi|gate /sɜrkəmnævɪgeɪt/ (circumnavigates, circumnavigating, circumnavigated) **VERB** SOCIAL STUDIES If someone **circumnavigates** the world, they sail or fly all the way around it. [FORMAL] ❑ *Sir Francis Drake was the first Englishman to circumnavigate the world.*

cir|cum|stance /sɜrkəmstæns/ (circumstances) **NOUN** Circumstances are the facts about a particular situation. ❑ *You're doing really well, considering the circumstances.* ❑ *Under normal circumstances, this trip would only take about 20 minutes.*

cir|cus /sɜrkəs/ (circuses) **NOUN** A circus is a group of people and animals that travels around to different places and performs shows. ❑ *I always wanted to work as a clown in a circus.*

citi|zen /sɪtɪzᵊn/ (citizens)

1 **NOUN** **SOCIAL STUDIES** Someone who is a **citizen** of a particular country legally belongs to that country. ❑ *We are proud to be American citizens.*

2 **NOUN** The **citizens of** a town or city are the people who live there. ❑ *He traveled to Argentina to meet the citizens of Buenos Aires.*

cit|rus /sɪtrəs/ **ADJECTIVE** A **citrus** fruit is a juicy fruit with a sharp taste such as an orange or a lemon. ❑ *Citrus fruits are a good source of vitamin C.*

city /sɪti/ (cities) **NOUN** A **city** is a large town. ❑ *We visited the city of Los Angeles.*
→ look at Picture Dictionary: **city**

civ|il /sɪvᵊl/

1 **ADJECTIVE** You use **civil** to talk about the people of a country and their activities. ❑ *The American Civil War is also called the War Between the States.* ❑ *...civil rights.*

2 **ADJECTIVE** You use **civil** to talk about people or things that are connected with the state, and not with the army or the church. ❑ *We had a civil wedding in the town hall.*

3 **ADJECTIVE** Someone who is **civil** is polite, but not very friendly. [FORMAL] ❑ *Please try to be a little more civil to people.*

ci|vil|ian /sɪvɪlyən/ (civilians)

1 **NOUN** A **civilian** is a person who is not a member of a military organization. ❑ *The soldiers were not shooting at civilians.*

2 **ADJECTIVE** **Civilian** describes people or things that are not military. ❑ *The men were wearing civilian clothes.*

civi|li|za|tion /sɪvɪlɪzeɪʃᵊn/ (civilizations)
NOUN **SOCIAL STUDIES** A **civilization** is a group of people with their own social organization and culture. ❑ *We learned about the ancient civilizations of Greece.*
→ look at **history**

civi|lized /sɪvɪlaɪzd/

1 **ADJECTIVE** A **civilized** social group has a high level of organization. ❑ *Boxing should be illegal in a civilized society.*

2 **ADJECTIVE** A **civilized** person is polite and reasonable. ❑ *She was very civilized about it.*

civ|il rights **PLURAL NOUN** **SOCIAL STUDIES**
Civil rights are the legal rights that all people have to fair treatment. ❑ *She never stopped fighting for civil rights.*

civ|il war (civil wars) **NOUN** **SOCIAL STUDIES**
A **civil war** is a war between different groups of people who live in the same country. ❑ *When did the American Civil War begin?*

claim /kleɪm/ (claims, claiming, claimed)

1 **VERB** If someone **claims** something, they say that it is true. ❑ *She claimed that she was not responsible for the mistake.* ❑ *The man claimed to be very rich.*

2 **NOUN** A **claim** is something that someone says, which may or may not be true. ❑ *Most people just don't believe their claims.*

3 **VERB** If you **claim** something, you say that it belongs to you. ❑ *If nobody claims the money, you can keep it.*

4 **NOUN** A **claim** is something that you ask for because you think you should have it. ❑ *...an insurance claim.*

clam /klæm/ (clams) **NOUN** **Clams** are a type of shellfish.
→ look at **shellfish**

Picture Dictionary   city

hotel

restaurant

office building

State Bank

bank

HOTEL

My Diner

Museum

statue

ATM

STOP

park

crosswalk

museum

clamp /klæmp/ (clamps, clamping, clamped)
1 **NOUN** A **clamp** is a piece of equipment that holds two things together.
2 **VERB** When you **clamp** one thing **to** another, you fasten the two things together with a clamp. ❏ *Clamp the microphone to the stand.*

clap /klæp/ (claps, clapping, clapped) **VERB**
When you **clap**, you hit your hands together, usually to show that you like something. ❏ *The men danced and the women clapped.* ❏ *Margaret clapped her hands.*
→ look at **performance**

clarify /klærɪfaɪ/ (clarifies, clarifying, clarified) **VERB** To **clarify** something means to make it easier to understand, usually by explaining it. [FORMAL] ❏ *I would like to clarify those remarks I made.*

clarinet /klærɪnɛt/ (clarinets) **NOUN** MUSIC
A **clarinet** is a musical instrument that you blow. It is a long black wooden tube with keys on it that you press, and a single reed (= small flat part that moves and makes a sound when you blow).
→ look at **musical instrument**

clarity /klærɪti/ **NONCOUNT NOUN** **Clarity** is the quality of being clear and easy to understand. ❏ *This new law will bring some clarity to the situation.*

clash /klæʃ/ (clashes, clashing, clashed)
1 **VERB** When people **clash**, they fight or argue with each other. ❏ *He often clashed with his staff.*
2 **NOUN** **Clash** is also a noun. ❏ *There have been a number of clashes between police and students.*
3 **VERB** If one color **clashes with** another, they do not look nice together. ❏ *His pink shirt clashed with his red hair.*

clasp /klæsp/ (clasps, clasping, clasped)
1 **VERB** If you **clasp** someone or something, you hold them tightly. ❏ *She clasped the children to her.*
2 **NOUN** A **clasp** is a small object that fastens something. ❏ *Kathryn undid the metal clasp of her handbag.*

class /klæs/ (classes)
1 **NOUN** A **class** is a group of students who learn at school together. ❏ *He spent six months in a class with younger students.*
2 **NOUN** A **class** is a time when you learn something at school. ❏ *Classes start at 9 o'clock.* ❏ *We do lots of reading in class.*
3 **NOUN** A **class of** things is a group of them

that are the same in some way. ❏ *These vegetables all belong to the same class of plants.*
4 **NOUN** A **class** is one of the social groups into which people are divided. ❏ *These programs only help the middle class.*
→ look at **fitness**

classic /klæsɪk/ (classics)
1 **ADJECTIVE** A **classic** movie or piece of writing is very good, and has been popular for a long time. ❏ *Fleming directed the classic movie "The Wizard of Oz."*
2 **NOUN** **Classic** is also a noun. ❏ *"Jailhouse Rock" is one of the classics of modern popular music.*
3 **NONCOUNT NOUN** ARTS SOCIAL STUDIES
Classics is the study of the languages, literature, and cultures of ancient Greece and Rome.

classical /klæsɪkəl/ **ADJECTIVE** MUSIC
Classical describes music that is traditional in form, style, or content. ❏ *I like listening to classical music and reading.*
→ look at **history, music**

classify /klæsɪfaɪ/ (classifies, classifying, classified) **VERB** To **classify** things means to divide them into groups or types. ❏ *Vitamins can be classified into two categories.*

classmate /klæsmeɪt/ (classmates) **NOUN**
Your **classmates** are students who are in the same class as you at school.
→ look at **school**

classroom /klæsrum/ (classrooms) **NOUN**
A **classroom** is a room in a school where lessons take place.
→ look at Picture Dictionary: **classroom**
→ look at **school**

classy /klæsi/ (classier, classiest) **ADJECTIVE**
If someone or something is **classy**, they are fashionable and attractive, or of very good quality. [INFORMAL] ❏ *We had dinner at a classy restaurant.*

clause /klɔz/ (clauses) **NOUN** LANGUAGE ARTS
In grammar, a **clause** is a group of words that contains a verb.

claw /klɔ/ (claws) **NOUN**
The **claws** of a bird or animal are the thin, hard, pointed parts at the end of its feet. ❏ *Kittens have very sharp claws and teeth.*
→ look at **shellfish**

Picture Dictionary classroom

computer, screen, map, book, chalkboard, whiteboard, paper, pencil, eraser, pen, chalk, printer, desk, chair

---

clay /kleɪ/ **NONCOUNT NOUN** ARTS **Clay** is a type of earth that is soft when it is wet and hard when it is dry. Clay is used for making things such as pots and bricks. ❑ ...a clay pot.

clean /klin/ (cleaner, cleanest, cleans, cleaning, cleaned)
1 ADJECTIVE Something that is **clean** is not dirty. ❑ Make sure the children's hands are clean before they eat. ❑ This floor is easy to keep clean.
2 VERB If you **clean** something, you remove the dirt from it. ❑ He fell from a ladder while he was cleaning the windows.
→ look at **laundry, water**
▶ **clean up** **1** If you **clean up** a place, you clean it completely. ❑ Hundreds of workers are cleaning up the beaches.
2 If you **clean up** dirt, you remove it from a place. ❑ Who is going to clean up this mess?

Word Builder cleaner
er ≈ **something that does**
   clean + er = cleaner
   contain + er = container
   dry + er = dryer
   open + er = opener
   print + er = printer
   toast + er = toaster

clean|er /klinər/ (cleaners) **NOUN** A **cleaner** is a substance or a piece of equipment used for cleaning things. ❑ Wear gloves when you use oven cleaner.

clear /klɪər/ (clearer, clearest, clears, clearing, cleared)
1 ADJECTIVE Something that is **clear** is easy to understand, see, or hear. ❑ The instructions are clear and readable. ❑ It is clear that things will have to change. ❑ This camera takes very clear pictures. ● **clear|ly ADVERB** ❑ Clearly, the police cannot break the law.
2 ADJECTIVE If a substance is **clear**, it has no color and you can see through it. ❑ ...a clear plastic bag.
3 ADJECTIVE If a place is **clear**, it does not have anything blocking the way. ❑ The runway is clear—you can land.
4 ADJECTIVE If the sky is **clear**, there are no clouds. ❑ It was a beautiful day with a clear blue sky.
5 VERB When you **clear** a place, you remove things from it because you do not want or need them there. ❑ Can someone clear the table, please?
6 VERB When the sky **clears**, it stops raining. ❑ The sky cleared and the sun came out.
▶ **clear away** When you **clear** things **away**, you put away the things that you have been using. ❑ The waitress cleared away the plates.
▶ **clear out** If you **clear out** a closet or a place, you make it neat and throw away the things in it that you no longer want. ❑ I cleared out my desk before I left.
▶ **clear up** When you **clear up**, you make things neat and put them away. ❑ The children played while I cleared up.

clerk /klɜrk/ (clerks)
1 NOUN A **clerk** is a person whose job is to work with numbers or documents in an office. ❑ She works as a clerk in a travel agency.
2 NOUN A **clerk** is someone who sells things to customers in a store, or who works behind the main desk in a hotel. ❑ Thomas was working as a clerk in a shoe store.

clev|er /klɛvər/ (**cleverer, cleverest**)
ADJECTIVE Someone who is **clever** is intelligent and can think and understand quickly. ❑ *He's a very clever man.* ● **clev|er|ly** **ADVERB** ❑ *The garden has been cleverly designed.*

click /klɪk/ (**clicks, clicking, clicked**)
1 **VERB** If something **clicks** or if you **click** it, it makes a short, sharp sound. ❑ *Hundreds of cameras clicked as she stepped out of the car.*
2 **NOUN** **Click** is also a noun. ❑ *I heard a click and then her recorded voice.*
3 **VERB** TECHNOLOGY If you **click** on a part of a computer screen, you press one of the buttons on the mouse in order to make something happen on the screen. ❑ *I clicked on a link.*
4 **NOUN** TECHNOLOGY **Click** is also a noun. ❑ *You can check your email with a click of your mouse.*

cli|ent /klaɪənt/ (**clients**) **NOUN** A **client** is a person who pays someone for a service. ❑ *A lawyer and his client were sitting at the next table.*

cliff /klɪf/ (**cliffs**) **NOUN** SCIENCE A **cliff** is a high area of land with a very steep side. ❑ *The car rolled over the edge of a cliff.*
→ look at **landform**

cli|mate /klaɪmɪt/ **NONCOUNT NOUN** SCIENCE The **climate** of a place is the normal weather there. ❑ *She loves the hot and humid climate of Florida.*
→ look at Word World: **climate**
→ look at **greenhouse effect, season**

cli|max /klaɪmæks/ (**climaxes**) **NOUN** The **climax of** something is the most exciting or important moment, near the end. ❑ *The climax of the story is when Romeo and Juliet die.*

climb /klaɪm/ (**climbs, climbing, climbed**)
1 **VERB** If you **climb** or **climb up** something, you move toward the top of it. ❑ *Climbing the hill took half an hour.* ❑ *Climb up the steps onto the bridge.*
2 **NOUN** **Climb** is also a noun. ❑ *It was a hard climb to the top of the mountain.*
3 **VERB** If you **climb** somewhere, you move into or out of a small space. ❑ *The girls climbed into the car and drove off.* ❑ *He climbed out of his bed.*
4 **VERB** When something **climbs**, it increases in value or amount. ❑ *The price of gas has been climbing steadily.*
→ look at **tree**

Word Builder   **climber**

er ≈ someone who does
    climb + er = climber
    farm + er = farmer
    lead + er = leader
    own + er = owner
    play + er = player
    work + er = worker

---

climb|er /klaɪmər/ (**climbers**) **NOUN** SPORTS A **climber** is a person who climbs rocks or mountains. ❑ *A climber was rescued yesterday after falling 300 feet.*

climb|ing /klaɪmɪŋ/ **NONCOUNT NOUN** SPORTS **Climbing** is the activity of climbing rocks or mountains.

cling /klɪŋ/ (**clings, clinging, clung**) **VERB** If you **cling to** someone or something, you hold them tightly. ❑ *The man was rescued as he clung to the boat.*

clin|ic /klɪnɪk/ (**clinics**) **NOUN** A **clinic** is a place where people receive medical advice or treatment.

clini|cal /klɪnɪkᵊl/ **ADJECTIVE** **Clinical** means involving medical treatment or testing people for illnesses. ❑ *She received her clinical training in Chicago.*

clip /klɪp/ (**clips, clipping, clipped**)
1 **NOUN** A **clip** is a small object for holding things together. ❑ *She took the clip out of her hair.*

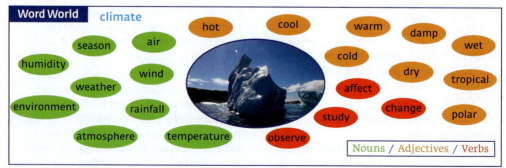

Word World   **climate**

hot   cool   warm   damp
season   air   wet
humidity   cold
wind   dry
weather   tropical
environment   affect
rainfall   change   polar
study
atmosphere   temperature   observe

Nouns / Adjectives / Verbs

2 NOUN A **clip** from a movie is a short piece of it that is broadcast separately. ❑ *They showed a film clip of the Apollo moon landing.*

3 VERB When you **clip** things together, you fasten them using a clip. ❑ *Clip the rope onto the ring.*

clock /klɒk/ (**clocks**)

1 NOUN A **clock** is a device that shows what time of day it is. ❑ *He could hear a clock ticking.*

2 If you do something **around the clock**, you do it all day and all night without stopping. ❑ *Firemen have been working around the clock.*

→ look at **time**

clock|wise /klɒkwaɪz/

1 ADVERB When something is moving **clockwise**, it is moving in a circle in the same direction as the hands on a clock. ❑ *The children started moving clockwise around the room.*

2 ADJECTIVE **Clockwise** is also an adjective. ❑ *Move your right arm around in a clockwise direction.*

Spelling Partners   close

close

❶ SHUTTING
❷ NEARNESS

❶ **close** /kloʊz/ (**closes, closing, closed**)

1 VERB When you **close** a door or a window, you shut it. ❑ *If you are cold, close the window.* ❑ *Zac closed the door quietly.*

2 VERB When a store **closes**, people cannot use it. ❑ *The store closes on public holidays.*

▶ **close down** If a business **closes down**, all work stops there, usually for ever. ❑ *That store closed down years ago.*

❷ **close** /kloʊs/ (**closer, closest**)

1 ADJECTIVE Something that is **close to** something else is near to it. ❑ *The apartment is close to the beach.* ❑ *The man moved closer.*

● **close|ly ADVERB** ❑ *They crowded closely around the fire.*

2 ADJECTIVE People who are **close** like each other very much and know each other well. ❑ *She was close to her sister, Gail.* ❑ *We were close friends at school.*

3 ADJECTIVE A **close** look at something is careful and complete. ❑ *Let's have a closer look.*

4 ADJECTIVE A **close** competition is won by only a small amount. ❑ *It was a close contest for a Senate seat.*

Word Partners   Use close with:

N. close **a door** ❶ **1**
    close **family**, close **friend**, close **relative** ❷ **2**
    close **attention** ❷ **3**

closed /kloʊzd/ **ADJECTIVE** When a store or business is **closed**, it is not open and you cannot buy or do anything there. ❑ *The supermarket was closed when we got there.*

clos|et /klɒzɪt/ (**closets**) **NOUN** A **closet** is a very small room for storing things, especially clothes. ❑ *My closet is full of clothes that I never wear.*

→ look at **house**

cloth /klɔθ/ (**cloths**)

1 NONCOUNT NOUN **Cloth** is material that is used for making clothing. ❑ *You need two yards of cloth.*

2 NOUN A **cloth** is a piece of cloth that you use for cleaning, drying, or protecting things. ❑ *Clean the surface with a damp cloth.*

clothes /kloʊz, kloʊðz/ **PLURAL NOUN** **Clothes** are the things that people wear, such as shirts, coats, pants, and dresses. ❑ *Milly went upstairs to change her clothes.*

→ look at **laundry**

cloth|ing /kloʊðɪŋ/ **NONCOUNT NOUN** **Clothing** is the things that people wear. ❑ *She works in a women's clothing store.*

→ look at Picture Dictionary: **clothing**

cloud /klaʊd/ (**clouds**)

1 NOUN A **cloud** is a white or gray mass in the sky that contains drops of water. ❑ *Clouds began to form in the sky.*

2 NOUN A **cloud of** smoke or dust is an amount of it floating in the air. ❑ *A cloud of black smoke spread across the sky.*

→ look at **weather**

cloudy /klaʊdi/ (**cloudier, cloudiest**) **ADJECTIVE** If it is **cloudy**, there are a lot of clouds in the sky. ❑ *It was a windy, cloudy day.*

clown /klaʊn/ (**clowns**) **NOUN** A **clown** is a performer who wears funny clothes and does silly things to make people laugh.

C

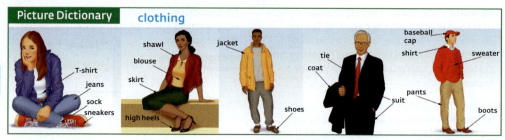

Picture Dictionary clothing

T-shirt, jeans, sock, sneakers, shawl, blouse, skirt, high heels, jacket, tie, coat, shoes, baseball cap, shirt, suit, pants, sweater, boots

club /klʌb/ (clubs)

1 **NOUN** A **club** is an organization of people who all like doing a particular activity. ❏ *He joined the local golf club.*

2 **NOUN** A **club** is a place where the members of a club meet. ❏ *I stopped at the club for a drink.*

3 **NOUN** A **club** is the same as a **nightclub**. ❏ *The streets are full of bars, clubs, and restaurants.* ❏ *It's a big dance hit in the clubs.*

4 **NOUN** A **club** is a long, thin, metal stick that you use to hit the ball in the game of golf.

5 **NOUN** A **club** is a thick, heavy stick that can be used as a weapon. ❏ *The men were carrying knives and clubs.*

cluck /klʌk/ (clucks, clucking, clucked) **VERB** When a chicken **clucks**, it makes short, low noises. ❏ *Several chickens clucked in the garden.*

clue /klu/ (clues) **NOUN** A **clue** is information that helps you to find an answer. ❏ *I'll give you a clue; the answer begins with the letter "p."*

clum|sy /klʌmzi/ (clumsier, clumsiest) **ADJECTIVE** A **clumsy** person does not move in a very easy way and often breaks things. ❏ *As a child she was very clumsy.* ❏ *Dad was rather clumsy on his skates.* ● **clum|si|ly** /klʌmzɪli/ **ADVERB** ❏ *He fell clumsily onto the bed.*

clung /klʌŋ/ **Clung** is a form of the verb **cling**.

clus|ter /klʌstər/ (clusters) **NOUN** A **cluster of** people or things is a small group of them close together. ❏ *There was a cluster of houses near the river.*

clutch /klʌtʃ/ (clutches, clutching, clutched)

1 **VERB** If you **clutch** something, you hold it very tightly. ❏ *Michelle clutched my arm.*

2 **NOUN** In a vehicle, the **clutch** is the part that you press with your foot before you change gears.

clut|ter /klʌtər/ (clutters, cluttering, cluttered)

1 **NONCOUNT NOUN** **Clutter** is a lot of things that you do not need in a messy state. ❏ *I'm a very tidy person, and I hate clutter.*

2 **VERB** If things or people **clutter** a place, they fill it in a messy way. ❏ *Empty cans clutter the desks.*

cm **cm** is short for **centimeter** or **centimeters**.

coach /koʊtʃ/ (coaches, coaching, coached)

1 **NOUN** SPORTS A **coach** is someone who is in charge of teaching a person or a sports team. ❏ *She's the women's soccer coach at Rowan University.*

2 **VERB** SPORTS If you **coach** someone, you help them to become better at a particular sport or skill. ❏ *She coached a golf team in San José.*

3 **NOUN** A **coach** is a vehicle with four wheels that is pulled by horses.

coal /koʊl/ **NONCOUNT NOUN** **Coal** is a hard black substance that comes from under the ground and is burned to give heat. ❏ *Put some more coal on the fire.*

coarse /kɔrs/ (coarser, coarsest) **ADJECTIVE** **Coarse** things feel dry and rough. ❏ *His skin was coarse and dry.*

coast /koʊst/ (coasts) **NOUN** SCIENCE GEOGRAPHY The **coast** is the land that is next to the ocean. ❏ *We stayed at a campsite on the coast.* ● **coast|al** /koʊstəl/ **ADJECTIVE** ❏ *Coastal areas have been flooded.*
→ look at **ocean**

coast|line /koʊstlaɪn/ (coastlines) **NOUN** SCIENCE GEOGRAPHY A country's **coastline** is the edge of its coast.

coat /koʊt/ (coats, coating, coated)

1 **NOUN** A **coat** is a piece of clothing with long sleeves that you wear over other clothes when you go outside. ❏ *He put on his coat and walked out.*

2 **NOUN** An animal's **coat** is its fur or hair.

3 **NOUN** A **coat of** paint is a thin layer of it. ❏ *The front door needs a new coat of paint.*

4 VERB If you **coat** something **with a** substance, you cover it with a thin layer of it. ❑ *Coat the fish with flour.*
→ look at **clothing**

cob|web /kɒbwɛb/ (**cobwebs**) **NOUN** A **cobweb** is the fine net that a spider makes for catching insects. ❑ *The windows are cracked and covered in cobwebs.*

cock|pit /kɒkpɪt/ (**cockpits**) **NOUN** In an airplane or racing car, the **cockpit** is the part where the pilot or driver sits.

cock|roach /kɒkroʊtʃ/ (**cockroaches**) **NOUN** A **cockroach** is a large brown insect that likes to live in places where food is kept.

co|coa /koʊkoʊ/
1 NONCOUNT NOUN Cocoa is a brown powder used for making chocolate.
2 NONCOUNT NOUN Cocoa is a hot drink made from cocoa powder and milk or water. ❑ *Let's have a cup of cocoa.*

co|co|nut /koʊkənʌt/ (**coconuts**)
1 NOUN A **coconut** is a very large nut with a hairy shell that grows on trees in warm countries.
2 NONCOUNT NOUN Coconut is the white flesh of a coconut. ❑ *Add two cups of grated coconut.*

co|coon /kəkun/ (**cocoons**) **NOUN** SCIENCE A **cocoon** is a case that some insects make around themselves before they grow into adults. ❑ *The butterfly slowly breaks out of its cocoon.*

cod /kɒd/ (**cod**)
1 NOUN A **cod** is a large ocean fish with white flesh.
2 NONCOUNT NOUN Cod is this fish eaten as food.

code /koʊd/ (**codes**)
1 NOUN A **code** is a set of rules for people to follow. ❑ *We keep a strict dress code (= people must wear particular clothes).*
2 NOUN A **code** is a secret way to replace the words in a message with other words or symbols, so that some people will not understand the message. ❑ *They sent messages using codes.*
3 NONCOUNT NOUN TECHNOLOGY Computer **code** is a set of instructions that a computer can understand.
4 NOUN A **code** is a group of numbers or letters that gives information about something. ❑ *The area code for western Pennsylvania is 412.*

cof|fee /kɔfi/
1 NONCOUNT NOUN Coffee is the beans (= seeds) of the coffee plant, made into a powder. ❑ *The island produces plenty of coffee.*
2 NONCOUNT NOUN Coffee is a drink made from boiling water and coffee beans. ❑ *Would you like some coffee?*

coffee|pot /kɔfipɒt/ (**coffeepots**) **NOUN** A **coffeepot** is a pot used for making and serving coffee.

cof|fin /kɔfɪn/ (**coffins**) **NOUN** A **coffin** is a box that you put a dead person in when you bury them.

coil /kɔɪl/ (**coils**) **NOUN** A **coil** is a piece of rope or wire that forms a series of rings. ❑ *He was carrying a coil of rope.*

coin /kɔɪn/ (**coins**) **NOUN** A **coin** is a small round piece of metal money. ❑ *She put the coins in her pocket.*
→ look at **payment**

co|in|ci|dence /koʊɪnsɪdəns/ (**coincidences**) **NOUN** A **coincidence** is when similar or related events happen at the same time without planning. ❑ *It is a coincidence that they arrived at the same time.* ❑ *We met by coincidence several years later.*

cold /koʊld/ (**colder, coldest, colds**)
1 ADJECTIVE If someone is **cold**, they feel uncomfortable because they are not warm enough. ❑ *I was freezing cold.* ❑ *Put on a sweater if you're cold.*
2 If something is **cold**, it does not have any warmth in it. ❑ *He washed his face with cold water.* ❑ *We went out into the cold, dark night.*
3 ADJECTIVE A **cold** person does not show emotion and is not friendly. ❑ *Her mother was an angry, cold woman.*
4 NOUN If you have a **cold**, you have an illness that makes liquid flow from your nose, and makes you cough. ❑ *I have a bad cold.*
5 If you **catch cold**, or **catch a cold**, you become ill with a cold. ❑ *Dry your hair so you don't catch cold.*
→ look at **climate, season, sick, water**

Word Partners	Use **cold** with:
N.	cold **air, dark and** cold, cold **night**, cold **rain**, cold **water**, cold **weather**, cold **wind 1**
ADV.	**bitterly** cold, **freezing** cold **1**
V.	**feel** cold, **get** cold **1**
	catch a cold, **get a** cold **4**

C

Cold War NOUN SOCIAL STUDIES The Cold War was the difficult relationship between the Soviet Union and the Western powers after the Second World War. ❑ *This was the first major crisis of the post-Cold War era.*

cole|slaw /koʊlslɔ/ NONCOUNT NOUN Coleslaw is a salad made from pieces of raw carrot and cabbage (= a round vegetable with white or green leaves), mixed with a special sauce (= mayonnaise).

col|lage /kəlɑʒ/ (collages) NOUN ARTS A **collage** is a picture that you make by sticking pieces of paper or cloth on a surface. ❑ *The children made a collage of words and pictures from magazines.*

col|lapse /kəlæps/ (collapses, collapsing, collapsed)
1 VERB If a structure or a person **collapses**, they fall very suddenly. ❑ *The bridge collapsed last October.* ❑ *He collapsed at his home last night.*
2 NONCOUNT NOUN Collapse is also a noun. ❑ *A few days after his collapse he was sitting up in bed.*

col|lar /kɒlər/ (collars)
1 NOUN The **collar** of a shirt or a coat is the part that goes around your neck. ❑ *He pulled up his jacket collar in the cold wind.*
2 NOUN A **collar** is a band of leather or plastic that you put around the neck of a dog or cat.

collar|bone /kɒlərboʊn/ (collarbones) NOUN SCIENCE Your **collarbones** are the two long bones between your throat and your shoulders. ❑ *Harold had a broken collarbone.*

col|league /kɒlig/ (colleagues) NOUN Your **colleagues** are the people you work with. ❑ *She's busy talking to a colleague.*
→ look at **job**

col|lect /kəlɛkt/ (collects, collecting, collected)
1 VERB If you **collect** things, you bring them together from several places or several people. ❑ *Two young girls collected wood for the fire.* ● **col|lec|tion** NONCOUNT NOUN ❑ *Computers can help with the collection of information.*
2 VERB If you **collect** things, you get them and save them over a period of time because you like them. ❑ *I collect stamps.*

col|lec|tion /kəlɛkʃⁿn/ (collections) NOUN A **collection of** things is a group of similar

or related things. ❑ *He has a large collection of paintings.*

col|lec|tor /kəlɛktər/ (collectors) NOUN A **collector** is someone who collects things that they like, such as stamps or old furniture. ❑ *Her parents were both art collectors.*

col|lege /kɒlɪdʒ/ (colleges) NOUN College is a place where students study after they leave high school. ❑ *I have one son in college.* ❑ *Joan is attending a local college.*

col|lide /kəlaɪd/ (collides, colliding, collided) VERB If people or vehicles **collide**, they crash into each other. ❑ *The two cars collided.* ❑ *He ran up the stairs and collided with Susan.*

col|lie /kɒli/ (collies) NOUN A **collie** or a **collie dog** is a dog with long hair and a long, narrow nose.

col|li|sion /kəlɪʒⁿn/ (collisions) NOUN A **collision** happens when two moving objects hit each other. ❑ *Many passengers were killed in the collision.*

co|lon /koʊlən/ (colons)
1 NOUN LANGUAGE ARTS A **colon** is a mark (:) that you can use to join parts of a sentence.
2 NOUN SCIENCE Your **colon** is the lower part of the tube that takes waste out of your body ❑ *...colon cancer.*
→ look at **punctuation**

colo|ny /kɒləni/ (colonies) NOUN SOCIAL STUDIES A **colony** is an area or a group of people that is controlled by another country. ❑ *Massachusetts was a British colony.*
→ look at **history**

col|or /kʌlər/ (colors, coloring, colored)
1 NOUN The **color** of something is the way it looks in the light. Red, blue, and green are colors. ❑ *"What color is the car?"—"It's red."* ❑ *Judy's favorite color is pink.*
2 ADJECTIVE A **color** television or photograph is one that shows things in all their colors, and not just in black, white, and gray. ❑ *The book is illustrated with color photos.*
3 VERB If you **color** something or **color** it **in**, you use pens or pencils to add color to a picture. ❑ *The children colored in their pictures.*
→ look at Picture Dictionary: **color**

col|ored /kʌlərd/ ADJECTIVE Colored means having a particular color or colors. ❑ *They wore brightly colored hats.*

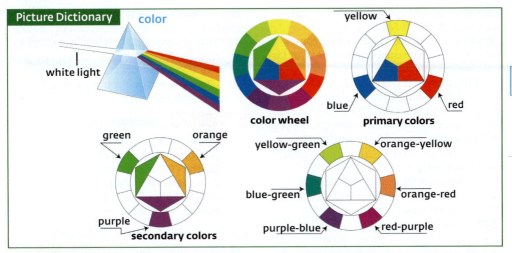

Picture Dictionary color

white light

color wheel

yellow
blue red
primary colors

green orange

purple
secondary colors

yellow-green orange-yellow
blue-green orange-red
purple-blue red-purple

C

Word Builder colorful

ful ≈ **filled with**

care + ful = careful
color + ful = colorful
help + ful = helpful
hope + ful = hopeful
stress + ful = stressful
use + ful = useful

col|or|ful /kʌlərfəl/ **ADJECTIVE** Something that is **colorful** has bright colors or a lot of different colors. ❑ *The people wore colorful clothes.*
→ look at **tree**

col|umn /kɒləm/ (**columns**)
1 NOUN A **column** is a tall, solid structure that supports part of a building. ❑ *The house has six white columns across the front.*
2 NOUN A **column** is a separate group of words that go straight up and down on a page. ❑ *The left column contains a list of names.*

coma /koʊmə/ (**comas**) **NOUN** If someone is in a **coma**, they are not conscious for a long time. ❑ *She was in a coma for seven weeks.*

comb /koʊm/ (**combs, combing, combed**)
1 NOUN A **comb** is a piece of plastic or metal with teeth (= narrow, pointed parts). You use a comb to make your hair neat.
2 VERB When you **comb** your hair, you make it neat using a comb. ❑ *He combed his hair carefully.*

com|bat (**combats, combating** or **combatting, combated** or **combatted**)

PRONUNCIATION HELP
Pronounce the noun /kɒmbæt/.
Pronounce the verb /kəmbæt/.

1 NONCOUNT NOUN Combat is fighting during a war. ❑ *More than 16 million men died in combat.*
2 VERB If people in authority try to **combat** something, they try to stop it from happening. ❑ *They've introduced new laws to combat crime.*

com|bi|na|tion /kɒmbɪneɪʃˠn/ (**combinations**) **NOUN** A **combination of** things is a mixture of them. ❑ *That is an interesting combination of colors.*

com|bine /kəmbaɪn/ (**combines, combining, combined**) **VERB** If you **combine** two or more things, or if they **combine**, they join or exist together. ❑ *Combine the flour with 3 tablespoons of water.* ❑ *Disease and hunger combine to kill thousands of people.*

come /kʌm/ (**comes, coming, came, come**)
1 VERB You use **come** to say that someone or something arrives somewhere, or moves toward you. ❑ *Two police officers came into the hall.* ❑ *He came to a door.* ❑ *Eleanor came to see her.* ❑ *Come here, Tom.*
2 VERB When an event or time **comes**, it happens. ❑ *The announcement came after a meeting at the White House.*
3 If something that you wish for or dream about **comes** true, it actually happens. ❑ *My life-long dream has just come true.*
4 VERB If someone or something **comes from** a particular place, that place is where they started. ❑ *Nearly half the students come*

from other countries. ❑ Most of Germany's oil comes from the North Sea.

5 VERB If someone or something **comes** first, next, or last, they are first, next, or last. ❑ I came last in the race.

▶ **come across** If you **come across** something or someone, you find them or meet them by chance. ❑ I came across a photo of my grandparents when I was looking for my diary.

▶ **come back** If someone **comes back** to a place, they return to it. ❑ He wants to come back to Washington.

▶ **come down** **1** If an amount **comes down**, it becomes less than it was before. ❑ Interest rates should come down.

2 If something **comes down**, it falls to the ground. ❑ The rain came down for hours.

▶ **come in** If someone **comes in**, they enter a place. ❑ Come in and sit down.

▶ **come off** If something **comes off**, it is removed. ❑ This lid won't come off.

▶ **come on** You say **"Come on"** to someone to encourage them to do something or to be quicker. ❑ Come on, or we'll be late.

▶ **come out** When the sun **comes out**, it appears in the sky because the clouds have moved away. ❑ Oh, look! The sun's coming out!

▶ **come to** If something **comes to** a particular amount, it adds up to it. ❑ Lunch came to $80.

▶ **come up** **1** If something **comes up** in a conversation, someone mentions it. ❑ The subject came up at work.

2 When the sun **comes up**, it rises. ❑ It will be so great watching the sun come up.

co|median /kəmiːdiən/ (**comedians**) **NOUN**
A **comedian** is a person whose job is to make people laugh. ❑ Who is your favorite comedian?

com|edy /kɒmədi/ (**comedies**) **NOUN**
LANGUAGE ARTS A **comedy** is a play, a movie, or a television program that is intended to make people laugh. ❑ The movie is a romantic comedy.

com|et /kɒmɪt/ (**comets**) **NOUN** SCIENCE
A **comet** is a bright object that has a long tail and travels around the sun.
→ look at **space**

com|fort /kʌmfərt/ (**comforts, comforting, comforted**)
1 NONCOUNT NOUN Comfort is being relaxed, and having no pain or worry. ❑ You can sit in comfort while you are watching the show.

2 NONCOUNT NOUN If you live in **comfort**, you have a pleasant life in which you have everything you need. ❑ He lived in comfort for the rest of his life.

3 VERB If you **comfort** someone, you make them feel less worried or unhappy. ❑ Ned tried to comfort her.

Word Builder	comfortable

able ≈ **able to be**

comfort + able = comfort**able**
depend + able = depend**able**
download + able = download**able**
enjoy + able = enjoy**able**
honor + able = honor**able**

com|fort|able /kʌmftəbəl, -fərtəbəl/
1 ADJECTIVE If furniture is **comfortable**, it makes you feel physically relaxed. ❑ This is a really comfortable chair. ❑ A home should be comfortable.

2 ADJECTIVE If a person is **comfortable**, they feel physically relaxed. ❑ Lie down on your bed and make yourself comfortable. ● **com|fort|ably**
ADVERB ❑ Are you sitting comfortably?
→ look at **wear**

com|ic /kɒmɪk/ **ADJECTIVE** A **comic** movie or actor makes you laugh. ❑ It is one of the greatest comic films.

comi|cal /kɒmɪkəl/ **ADJECTIVE** If something is **comical**, it makes you want to laugh because it is funny or silly. ❑ They had slightly comical smiles on their faces.

com|ic book /kɒmɪk bʊk/ (**comic books**)
NOUN A **comic book** is a magazine that contains stories told in drawings.

com|ma /kɒmə/ (**commas**) **NOUN**
LANGUAGE ARTS A **comma** is the punctuation mark (,).
→ look at **punctuation**

com|mand /kəmænd/ (**commands, commanding, commanded**)
1 NOUN A **command** is an official instruction to do something. ❑ He shouted a command at his soldiers. ❑ He obeyed the command.

2 NOUN TECHNOLOGY A **command** is an instruction that you give to a computer. ❑ The keyboard command "Ctrl+S" saves your document.

3 VERB If someone **commands** you to do something, they tell you that you must do it. ❑ He commanded his soldiers to attack.

com|mence /kəmɛns/ (**commences, commencing, commenced**) VERB When something **commences** or you **commence** it, it begins. [FORMAL] ❏ *The school year commences in the fall.*

com|ment /kɒmɛnt/ (**comments, commenting, commented**)

1 VERB If you **comment on** something, you give your opinion or say something about it. ❏ *Mr. Cooke has not commented on these reports.*

2 NOUN A **comment** is something that you say about a person or a situation. ❏ *It is difficult to make a comment about the situation.*

com|merce /kɒmɜrs/ NONCOUNT NOUN **Commerce** is the buying and selling of large amounts of goods. ❏ *There are rules for international commerce.*

com|mer|cial /kəmɜrʃəl/ (**commercials**)

1 ADJECTIVE **Commercial** means relating to the buying and selling of goods. ❏ *New York is a center of commercial activity.*

2 NOUN A **commercial** is an advertisement on television or radio. ❏ *There are too many commercials on TV these days.*

→ look at **television**

com|mit /kəmɪt/ (**commits, committing, committed**) VERB If someone **commits** a crime, they do something illegal. ❏ *I have never committed a crime.*

com|mit|ment /kəmɪtmənt/ (**commitments**)

1 NONCOUNT NOUN **Commitment** is when you work hard at something that you think is important. ❏ *They praised him for his commitment to peace.*

2 NOUN If you make a **commitment to** do something, you promise to do it. ❏ *We made a commitment to work together.*

com|mit|tee /kəmɪti/ (**committees**) NOUN A **committee** is a group of people who meet to make decisions or plans for a larger group. ❏ *I was on the tennis club committee for 20 years.*

com|mon /kɒmən/

1 ADJECTIVE If something is **common**, it is found in large numbers or it happens often. ❏ *Hansen is a common name in Norway.* ❏ *What is the most common cause of road accidents?*

● **com|mon|ly** ADVERB ❏ *Parsley is a commonly used herb.*

2 ADJECTIVE A **common** language, culture, or interest is shared by two or more people or groups. ❏ *The United States and Canada share a common language.*

3 If people or things have something **in common**, they have similar qualities or interests. ❏ *He had nothing in common with his sister.*

com|mon sense also **commonsense** NONCOUNT NOUN **Common sense** is the ability to make good judgments and to be sensible. ❏ *Use common sense: don't leave valuable items in your car.*

common|wealth /kɒmənwɛlθ/

1 NOUN SOCIAL STUDIES A **commonwealth** is a group of countries that have the same political or economic interests.

2 NOUN SOCIAL STUDIES **Commonwealth** is used in the official names of some countries and of several states in the US. ❏ *...the Commonwealth of Australia.* ❏ *...the Commonwealth of Massachusetts.*

com|mu|ni|cate /kəmyunɪkeɪt/ (**communicates, communicating, communicated**) VERB If you **communicate with** other people, you share information with them, for example by speaking or writing. ❏ *They communicate with their friends by cellphone.* ❏ *They use email to communicate with each other.* ● **com|mu|ni|ca|tion** /kəmyunɪkeɪʃ°n/ NONCOUNT NOUN ❏ *Good communication is important in business.*

Word World   **communication**

wireless · written · verbal · electronic · message · words · language · instant · good · talk · listening · speaking · tell · say · understand · information · gestures · email · speak · write · conversation · expressions · listen · listen

Nouns / Adjectives / Verbs

com|mu|ni|ca|tion /kəmyu̱nɪke̱ɪʃᵊn/ (communications) **PLURAL NOUN**
Communications are ways of sending or receiving information. ❑ ...a communications satellite.
→ look at Word World: **communication**
→ look at **Internet, language**

com|mun|ism /kɒ̱myənɪzəm/ also **Communism NONCOUNT NOUN**
SOCIAL STUDIES **Communism** is the political idea that people should not own private property and workers should control how things are produced. ❑ Walesa campaigned to end communism in his homeland, Poland.
● **com|mun|ist** also **Communist** /kɒ̱myənɪst/ (communists) **NOUN** ❑ He was a committed communist and an economics student at the University of Gdansk. ❑ She is a member of the Communist Party.

com|mu|ni|ty /kəmyu̱nɪti/ (communities)
1 NOUN A **community** is a group of people who live in a particular area. ❑ When you live in a small community, everyone knows you.
2 NOUN A **community** is a group of people who are similar in some way, or who have similar interests. ❑ The local community has asked for more police support.

com|mute /kəmyu̱t/ (commutes, commuting, commuted) **VERB** If you **commute**, you travel to work or school. ❑ Mike commutes to Miami every day.
● **com|mut|er** (commuters) **NOUN** ❑ In Tokyo, most commuters travel to work on trains.

com|pact /kəmpæ̱kt/ **ADJECTIVE** **Compact** things are small, or take up very little space. ❑ The garden is compact and easy to manage.

com|pact disc /kəmpæ̱kt dɪ̱sk/ (compact discs) **NOUN** TECHNOLOGY A **compact disc** is a small shiny disk that contains music or information. The short form **CD** is also used.

com|pan|ion /kəmpæ̱nyən/ (companions) **NOUN** A **companion** is someone who you spend time with or who you travel with. ❑ Her traveling companion was her father.

com|pa|ny /kʌ̱mpəni/ (companies)
1 NOUN A **company** is a business that sells goods or services. ❑ Her mother works for an insurance company.
2 NONCOUNT NOUN **Company** is having another person or other people with you. ❑ I always enjoy Nick's company.

3 If you **keep** someone **company**, you spend time with them and stop them from feeling lonely or bored. ❑ I'll stay here and keep Emma company.

com|pa|rable /kɒ̱mpərəbᵊl/ **ADJECTIVE** If two or more things are **comparable**, they are similar. ❑ House prices here are comparable to prices in Paris and Tokyo.

com|para|tive /kəmpæ̱rətɪv/ (comparatives) **NOUN** LANGUAGE ARTS
In grammar, the **comparative** is the form of an adjective or adverb that shows that one thing has more of a particular quality than something else has. For example, "bigger" is the comparative form of "big." Compare with **superlative**.

com|pare /kəmpɛ̱ər/ (compares, comparing, compared) **VERB** When you **compare** things, you consider how they are different and how they are similar. ❑ I use the Internet to compare prices.

com|pari|son /kəmpæ̱rɪsən/ (comparisons) **NOUN** When you make a **comparison**, you study the differences between two things. ❑ The information helps parents to make comparisons between schools.

com|part|ment /kəmpɑ̱rtmənt/ (compartments)
1 NOUN A **compartment** is a separate part inside a box or a bag where you keep things. ❑ The case has a separate compartment for camera accessories.
2 NOUN A **compartment** is one of the separate spaces of a railroad car. ❑ The family always sat in the first-class compartment.

com|pass /kʌ̱mpəs/ (compasses) **NOUN** GEOGRAPHY A **compass** is an instrument that people use for finding directions (north, south, east, and west). ❑ You'll need a map and a compass.

com|pat|ible /kəmpæ̱tɪbᵊl/
1 ADJECTIVE If things are **compatible**, they work well together. ❑ Is your MP3 player compatible with your computer?
2 ADJECTIVE If you are **compatible** with someone, you have a good relationship with them because you have similar opinions and interests. ❑ Hannah and I are very compatible.

com|pen|sa|tion /kɒ̱mpənse̱ɪʃᵊn/ **NONCOUNT NOUN** **Compensation** is money that someone who has had a bad experience claims from the person or organization who caused it. ❏ *He has to pay $5,960 compensation for the damage he caused.*

com|pete /kəmpit/ (**competes, competing, competed**) **VERB** If you **compete** in a contest or a game, you participate in it. ❏ *He will compete in the 10k road race again this year.*

com|pe|tence /kɒmpɪtəns/ **NONCOUNT NOUN** **Competence** is the ability to do something well. ❏ *No one doubts his competence.*

com|pe|tent /kɒmpɪtənt/ **ADJECTIVE** Someone who is **competent** is able to do something well. ❏ *He is a confident, competent driver.*

com|pe|ti|tion /kɒmpɪtɪʃ°n/ (**competitions**) **NOUN** A **competition** is an event in which people try to show that they are best at an activity. ❏ *The two boys entered a surfing competition.*

com|peti|tive /kəmpɛtɪtɪv/ **ADJECTIVE** A **competitive** person wants to be more successful than other people. ❏ *He has always been very competitive.*

com|peti|tor /kəmpɛtɪtər/ (**competitors**) **NOUN** A **competitor** is a person who takes part in a competition. ❏ *One of the oldest competitors won the silver medal.*

com|plain /kəmpleɪn/ (**complains, complaining, complained**)
1 VERB If you **complain**, you say that you are not satisfied with someone or something. ❏ *Voters complained about the election result.* ❏ *I shouldn't complain; I've got a good job.* ❏ *"Someone should do something about it," he complained.*
2 VERB If you **complain of** a pain or an illness, you say that you have it. ❏ *He went to the hospital, complaining of a sore neck.*

com|plaint /kəmpleɪnt/ (**complaints**) **NOUN** You make a **complaint** when you say that you are not satisfied. ❏ *The police received several complaints about the noise.*

com|plete /kəmplit/ (**completes, completing, completed**)
1 ADJECTIVE **Complete** means in every way. ❏ *His birthday party was a complete surprise.*
● **com|plete|ly ADVERB** ❏ *Thousands of homes have been completely destroyed.*
2 ADJECTIVE If a job is **complete**, it is finished. ❏ *The project is not yet complete.*

3 VERB If you **complete** a task, you finish it. ❏ *We hope to complete the project by January.*
4 VERB If you **complete** a form, you write the necessary information on it. ❏ *Complete the first part of the application form.*

com|plex (**complexes**)

> **PRONUNCIATION HELP**
> Pronounce the adjective /kəmplɛks/ or sometimes /kɒmplɛks/. Pronounce the noun /kɒmplɛks/.

1 ADJECTIVE Something that is **complex** has many parts and is difficult to understand. ❏ *Crime is a complex problem.*
2 NOUN A **complex** is a group of buildings used for a particular purpose. ❏ *The family moved to a new apartment complex.*

com|plex|ion /kəmplɛkʃ°n/ (**complexions**) **NOUN** Your **complexion** is the natural color of the skin on your face. ❏ *She had a pale complexion.*

com|pli|cate /kɒmplɪkeɪt/ (**complicates, complicating, complicated**) **VERB** To **complicate** something means to make it more difficult to understand or deal with. ❏ *Please don't complicate the situation.*

com|pli|cat|ed /kɒmplɪkeɪtɪd/ **ADJECTIVE** Something that is **complicated** has many parts, and is difficult to understand. ❏ *The situation is very complicated.*

com|pli|ca|tion /kɒmplɪkeɪʃ°n/ (**complications**) **NOUN** A **complication** is a problem or difficulty. ❏ *There were a number of complications.*

com|pli|ment (**compliments, complimenting, complimented**)

> **PRONUNCIATION HELP**
> Pronounce the verb /kɒmplɪmɛnt/. Pronounce the noun /kɒmplɪmənt/.

1 NOUN A **compliment** is something nice that you say to someone, for example about their appearance. ❏ *He was very nice to me and paid me several compliments.*
2 VERB If you **compliment** someone, you say something nice to them, for example about their appearance. ❏ *They complimented me on the way I looked.*

com|pose /kəmpoʊz/ (**composes, composing, composed**)
1 VERB The things that something **is composed of** are its parts or members. ❏ *Water is composed of oxygen and hydrogen.*

C

C

2 VERB MUSIC When someone **composes** a piece of music, a speech, or a letter, they write it. ❏ *Vivaldi composed a large number of concertos.*
→ look at **music**

com|pos|er /kəmpoʊzər/ (**composers**)
NOUN MUSIC A **composer** is a person who writes music. ❏ *Mozart and Beethoven were great composers.*

com|po|si|tion /kɒmpəzɪʃⁿn/ (**compositions**)
1 NOUN MUSIC A **composition** is a piece of music or writing.
2 NONCOUNT NOUN The **composition** of something is its parts or members. ❏ *They study the chemical composition of the food we eat.*

com|pound /kɒmpaʊnd/ (**compounds**)
1 NOUN SCIENCE In chemistry, a **compound** is a substance that is made from two or more elements. ❏ *Dioxins are chemical compounds that are produced when material is burned.*
2 ADJECTIVE LANGUAGE ARTS In grammar, a **compound** is a word that is made from two or more other words, for example "fire truck."

com|pre|hend /kɒmprɪhɛnd/ (**comprehends, comprehending, comprehended**) **VERB** If you do not **comprehend** something, you do not understand it. [FORMAL] ❏ *I don't think you fully comprehend what's happening.*

com|pre|hen|sion /kɒmprɪhɛnʃⁿn/ **NONCOUNT NOUN** **Comprehension** is the ability to understand something. [FORMAL] ❏ *...a reading comprehension test.*

com|pro|mise /kɒmprəmaɪz/ (**compromises**) **NOUN** A **compromise** is a situation in which people accept something slightly different from what they really want. ❏ *Try to reach a compromise between the demands of work and family life.*

com|pul|so|ry /kəmpʌlsəri/ **ADJECTIVE** If something is **compulsory**, you must do it. ❏ *In Australia, voting is compulsory.*

com|put|er /kəmpyutər/ (**computers**)
NOUN TECHNOLOGY A **computer** is an electronic machine that can store and deal with large amounts of information. ❏ *He watched the concert on his computer via the Internet.* ❏ *The company installed a $650,000 computer system.*
→ look at Picture Dictionary: **computer**
→ look at **classroom, Internet, office, school**

com|pu|ting /kəmpyutɪŋ/ **NONCOUNT NOUN** **Computing** is the activity of using a computer and writing programs for it. ❏ *They offer a course in business and computing.*

con|ceal /kənsil/ (**conceals, concealing, concealed**) **VERB** To **conceal** something means to hide it or keep it secret. ❏ *The hat concealed her hair.* ❏ *Robert could not conceal his happiness.*

con|ceive /kənsiv/ (**conceives, conceiving, conceived**)
1 VERB If you cannot **conceive of** something, you cannot imagine it or believe it. ❏ *I can't even conceive of that amount of money.*
2 VERB When a woman or a couple **conceives**, the woman becomes pregnant. ❏ *They have been trying to conceive for three years now.* ❏ *The baby was conceived naturally, and is due in October.*

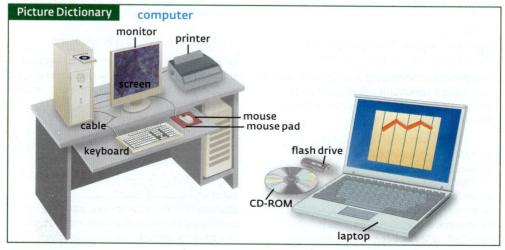

Picture Dictionary computer

monitor • printer • screen • mouse • mouse pad • cable • keyboard • flash drive • CD-ROM • laptop

con|cen|trate /kɒnsᵊntreɪt/ (concentrates, concentrating, concentrated) VERB You **concentrate on** something when you give it all your attention. ❏ *He should concentrate on his studies.* ❏ *She had to concentrate hard to win the race.*

con|cen|tra|tion /kɒnsᵊntreɪʃᵊn/ NONCOUNT NOUN Concentration on something means giving it all your attention. ❏ *At first there is greater concentration on speaking skills.*

con|cept /kɒnsɛpt/ (concepts) NOUN A **concept** is an idea about something. ❏ *Our laws are based on the concept of fairness.*

con|cern /kənsɜrn/ (concerns, concerning, concerned)
1 NONCOUNT NOUN Concern is worry about something. ❏ *She expressed concern about my grandfather's health.*
2 VERB If something **concerns** you, it worries you. ❏ *It concerns me that she hasn't telephoned.* ● **con|cerned** ADJECTIVE ❏ *I've been concerned about you lately.*
3 VERB If a book or a piece of information **concerns** a particular subject, it is about that subject. ❏ *The book concerns Sandy's two children.* ● **con|cerned** ADJECTIVE ❏ *Randolph's work is concerned with the effects of pollution.*

con|cern|ing /kənsɜrnɪŋ/ PREPOSITION You use **concerning** to show what a piece of information is about. [FORMAL] ❏ *Contact Mr. Coldwell for more information concerning the class.*

con|cert /kɒnsərt/ (concerts) NOUN MUSIC A **concert** is a performance of music. ❏ *We attended a concert by the great jazz pianist Harold Maburn.* ❏ *The weekend began with an outdoor rock concert.*
→ look at **performance**

con|clude /kənklud/ (concludes, concluding, concluded)
1 VERB If you **conclude** something, you make a decision after thinking about it carefully. ❏ *We've concluded that it's best to tell her the truth.* ❏ *So what can we conclude from this experiment?*
2 VERB When something **concludes**, it ends. [FORMAL] ❏ *The evening concluded with dinner and speeches.*

con|clu|sion /kənkluʒᵊn/ (conclusions)
1 NOUN A **conclusion** is a decision that you make after thinking carefully about something. ❏ *I've come to the conclusion that she's a great musician.*

2 NOUN LANGUAGE ARTS The **conclusion** of a story is its ending. ❏ *What do you understand from the conclusion of the story?*
→ look at **science**

con|crete /kɒnkrit/ NONCOUNT NOUN Concrete is a hard substance made by mixing a grey powder (= cement) with sand and water; it is used for building. ❏ *The hotel is constructed from steel and concrete.* ❏ *We sat on the concrete floor.*

con|demn /kəndɛm/ (condemns, condemning, condemned)
1 VERB If you **condemn** something, you say that it is not acceptable. ❏ *Police condemned the recent violence.*
2 VERB If someone **is condemned to** a punishment, they are given that punishment. ❏ *He was condemned to life in prison.*

con|di|tion /kəndɪʃᵊn/ (conditions)
1 NOUN The **condition** of someone or something is the state that they are in. ❏ *Doctors expect his condition to improve.* ❏ *The old house is in terrible condition.*
2 PLURAL NOUN The **conditions** in which people live or work are the things that affect their comfort and safety. ❏ *People are living in terrible conditions with little food or water.*
3 NOUN Someone who has a particular **condition** has a medical problem. ❏ *Doctors think he may have a heart condition.*

con|di|tion|al /kəndɪʃᵊnᵊl/ NOUN LANGUAGE ARTS In grammar, you use the **conditional** for talking about a situation that may exist or happen. Most conditionals begin with "if." For example "If you work hard, you'll pass your exams."

con|do|min|ium /kɒndəmɪniəm/ (condominiums)
1 NOUN A **condominium** is an apartment building in which each apartment is owned by the person who lives there.
2 NOUN A **condominium** is an apartment in a condominium.

con|duct (conducts, conducting, conducted)

> **PRONUNCIATION HELP**
> Pronounce the verb /kəndʌkt/. Pronounce the noun /kɒndʌkt/.

1 VERB When you **conduct** an activity or a task, you organize it and do it. ❏ *I decided to conduct an experiment.*

C

C

2 **VERB** If you **conduct** yourself in a particular way, you behave in that way. ❑ *The way he conducts himself embarrasses the family.*

3 **VERB** SCIENCE If something **conducts** heat or electricity, heat or electricity can pass through it.

4 **VERB** MUSIC When someone **conducts** musicians, they stand in front and direct the performance. ❑ *The new musical work was composed and conducted by Leonard Bernstein.*

5 **NONCOUNT NOUN** Someone's **conduct** is the way they behave. ❑ *She won a prize for good conduct in school.*

con|duc|tor /kənd∧ktər/ (**conductors**)

1 **NOUN** MUSIC A **conductor** is a person who stands in front of a group of musicians and directs their performance.

2 **NOUN** On a train, a **conductor** is a person whose job is to help passengers and check tickets.

cone /koʊn/ (**cones**)

1 **NOUN** MATH A **cone** is a solid shape with one flat round end and one pointed end. ❑ *Bright-orange traffic cones stop people from parking on the bridge.*

2 **NOUN** A **cone** is a thin cookie in the shape of a cone that you put ice cream into and eat. ❑ *...an ice-cream cone.*

3 **NOUN** A **cone** is the fruit of a tree such as a pine or a fir. ❑ *...a pine cone.*
→ look at **tree**

con|fer|ence /kɒnfərəns, -frəns/ (**conferences**) **NOUN** A **conference** is a long meeting about a particular subject. ❑ *We attended a conference on education last month.*

con|fess /kənfɛs/ (**confesses, confessing, confessed**) **VERB** When you **confess**, you admit that you did something wrong. ❑ *He confessed to seventeen murders.* ❑ *Ed confessed that he broke the window.*

con|fes|sion /kənfɛʃən/ (**confessions**) **NOUN** If you make a **confession**, you admit that you have done something wrong. ❑ *I have a confession to make. I lied about my age.*

con|fi|dence /kɒnfɪdəns/

1 **NONCOUNT NOUN** If you have **confidence** in someone, you feel that you can trust them. ❑ *I have great confidence in you.*

2 **NONCOUNT NOUN** If you have **confidence**, you feel sure about your own abilities and ideas. ❑ *The team is full of confidence.*

3 **NONCOUNT NOUN** If you tell someone something **in confidence**, you tell them a secret. ❑ *We told you all these things in confidence.*

con|fi|dent /kɒnfɪdənt/

1 **ADJECTIVE** If you are **confident** about something, you are certain that the result will be good. ❑ *I am confident that I'll get the job.*

2 **ADJECTIVE** People who are **confident** feel sure about their own abilities and ideas. ❑ *In time he became more confident and relaxed.*
● **con|fi|dent|ly** **ADVERB** ❑ *She walked confidently into the boss's office.*

con|fi|den|tial /kɒnfɪdɛnʃəl/ **ADJECTIVE** Information that is **confidential** must be kept secret. ❑ *After her death, some newspapers printed confidential information about her private life.* ● **con|fi|den|tial|ly** **ADVERB** ❑ *Any information they give will be treated confidentially.*

con|fine /kənfaɪn/ (**confines, confining, confined**) **VERB** If a person or an animal **is confined** in a particular place, they cannot leave it. ❑ *The animals are confined in tiny cages.*
● **con|fine|ment** /kənfaɪnmənt/ **NONCOUNT NOUN** ❑ *He read a lot during his two-year confinement in prison.*

con|firm /kənfɜrm/ (**confirms, confirming, confirmed**)

1 **VERB** When someone **confirms** something, they say that it is true. ❑ *The doctor confirmed that my nose was broken.*

2 **VERB** If you **confirm** a meeting or an arrangement, you say that it will definitely happen. ❑ *He called at seven to confirm our appointment.* ● **con|fir|ma|tion** **NONCOUNT NOUN** ❑ *You will receive confirmation of your order by email.*

con|flict (**conflicts, conflicting, conflicted**)

> **PRONUNCIATION HELP**
> Pronounce the noun /kɒnflɪkt/.
> Pronounce the verb /kənflɪkt/.

1 **NOUN** A **conflict** is a fight or an argument between people or countries. ❑ *The military conflict lasted many years.*

2 **VERB** If ideas or plans **conflict**, they are very different from each other. ❑ *His opinions usually conflicted with mine.*

con|form /kənfɔrm/ (**conforms, conforming, conformed**)

1 **VERB** If something **conforms to** a rule or a law, it follows it. ❑ *The lamp conforms to new safety standards.*

2 **VERB** If you **conform**, you behave in a way that most people think is correct or normal. ❑ *At her age, it is important to conform.*

con|fuse /kənfyuz/ (**confuses, confusing, confused**)

1 **VERB** If you **confuse** two things, you think one of them is the other one. ❑ *I always confuse my left with my right.* ● **con|fu|sion** /kənfyuʒ³n/ **NONCOUNT NOUN** ❑ *Use different colors to avoid confusion.*

2 **VERB** To **confuse** someone means to make it difficult for them to understand something. ❑ *My words confused him.*

con|fused /kənfyuzd/ **ADJECTIVE** If you are **confused**, you do not understand what is happening, or you do not know what to do. ❑ *People are confused about what's going to happen.*
→ look at **feeling**

con|fus|ing /kənfyuzɪŋ/ **ADJECTIVE** Something that is **confusing** is difficult to understand, and makes it difficult for people to know what to do. ❑ *The directions are really confusing.*

con|fu|sion /kənfyuʒ³n/

1 **NONCOUNT NOUN** If there is **confusion** about something, the facts are not clear. ❑ *There's still confusion about the number of students.*

2 **NONCOUNT NOUN** **Confusion** is a situation in which a lot of things are happening in a badly organized way. ❑ *People were pushing and shouting, and there was confusion everywhere.*

con|gratu|late /kəngrætʃəleɪt/ (**congratulates, congratulating, congratulated**) **VERB** If you **congratulate** someone, you express pleasure about something good that has happened to them. ❑ *She congratulated him on the birth of his son.* ● **con|gratu|la|tion** /kəngrætʃəleɪ³n/ **NONCOUNT NOUN** ❑ *We received several letters of congratulation.*

con|gratu|la|tions /kəngrætʃəleɪ³nz/ You say "**Congratulations**" to someone in order to congratulate them. ❑ *Congratulations on your new job.*

Con|gress /kɒŋgrɪs/ **NOUN** SOCIAL STUDIES **Congress** is the part of the government that makes laws in the United States. ❑ *Members of Congress are elected by the people.*

congress|man /kɒŋgrɪsmən/ (**congressmen**) **NOUN** SOCIAL STUDIES

A **congressman** is a male member of the U.S. Congress, especially of the House of Representatives.

congress|woman /kɒŋgrɪswʊmən/ (**congresswomen**) **NOUN** SOCIAL STUDIES A **congresswoman** is a female member of the U.S. Congress, especially of the House of Representatives.

con|junc|tion /kənd͡ʒʌŋkʃ³n/ (**conjunctions**) **NOUN** LANGUAGE ARTS A **conjunction** is a word that joins together parts of sentences. For example, "and" and "or" are conjunctions.

con|nect /kənɛkt/ (**connects, connecting, connected**)

1 **VERB** If you **connect** one thing **to** another, the two things are joined together. ❑ *Next, connect the printer to your computer.*

2 **VERB** If one train, plane, or boat **connects with** another, passengers can change to the other one and continue their trip. ❑ *The train connects with a plane to Ireland.*
→ look at **Internet**

con|nect|ed /kənɛktɪd/ **ADJECTIVE** If one thing is **connected with** another, there is a relationship between them. ❑ *She described the problems connected with a high-fat diet.*

con|nec|tion /kənɛkʃ³n/ (**connections**)

1 **NOUN** A **connection** is a relationship between two things, people, or groups. ❑ *I felt a strong connection between us.* ❑ *Children need to understand the connection between energy and the environment.*

2 **NOUN** A **connection** is a way of communicating using the telephone or a computer. ❑ *You'll need a fast Internet connection to view this site.*

3 **NOUN** A **connection** is a train, a bus, or a plane that allows you continue your trip by changing from one to another. ❑ *My flight was late and I missed the connection.*
→ look at **Internet**

con|quer /kɒŋkər/ (**conquers, conquering, conquered**)

1 **VERB** SOCIAL STUDIES If one country or group of people **conquers** another, they take complete control of their land. ❑ *Germany conquered France in 1940.*

2 **VERB** If you **conquer** a problem, you manage to deal with it. ❑ *I've conquered my fear of spiders.*

con|science /kɒnʃ°ns/ (consciences)

1 NOUN Your **conscience** is the part of your mind that tells you if what you are doing is wrong. ❑ *My conscience is clear about everything I have done (= I do not feel that I have done anything wrong).*

2 If you have a **guilty conscience**, you feel bad because you know you did something wrong. ❑ *She has a guilty conscience about downloading music from the Internet without paying.*

con|sci|en|tious /kɒnʃiɛnʃəs/ ADJECTIVE

Someone who is **conscientious** is careful to follow rules and do things correctly. ❑ *She is very conscientious about doing her homework.*

● **con|sci|en|tious|ly ADVERB** ❑ *He conscientiously exercised every night.*

con|scious /kɒnʃəs/

1 ADJECTIVE If you are **conscious of** something, you notice it. ❑ *She was conscious of Nick watching her across the room.*

2 ADJECTIVE If you are **conscious of** something, you think about it a lot because you think it is important. ❑ *I'm very conscious of my weight.*

3 ADJECTIVE Someone who is **conscious** is awake, and is not asleep or unconscious. ❑ *She was fully conscious soon after the operation.*

con|sent /kənsɛnt/ (consents, consenting, consented)

1 NONCOUNT NOUN If you give your **consent to** something, you allow someone to do it. [FORMAL] ❑ *Pollard finally gave his consent to the police search.*

2 VERB If you **consent to** something, you agree to do it or to allow it to happen. [FORMAL] ❑ *She consented to marry him.*

con|se|quence /kɒnsɪkwɛns, -kwəns/ (consequences) NOUN

Consequences are the results or effects of something that has happened. ❑ *She understood the consequences of her actions.*

con|se|quent|ly /kɒnsɪkwɛntli, -kwəntli/ ADVERB

You use **consequently** to talk about the result of something. [FORMAL] ❑ *He worked all night, and consequently he slept during the day.*

con|ser|va|tion /kɒnsərveɪʃ°n/ NONCOUNT NOUN SCIENCE

Conservation is taking care of the environment. ❑ *...wildlife conservation.*

→ look at Word World: **conservation**

con|serva|tive /kənsɜrvətɪv/ ADJECTIVE

Someone who is **conservative** does not like changes and new ideas. ❑ *People often become more conservative as they get older.*

con|serve /kənsɜrv/ (conserves, conserving, conserved)

1 VERB If you **conserve** energy or water, you use it carefully so that it lasts for a long time. ❑ *The factories have closed for the weekend to conserve energy.*

2 VERB If you **conserve** the environment, you take care of it. ❑ *World leaders agreed to work together to conserve forests.*

con|sid|er /kənsɪdər/ (considers, considering, considered)

1 VERB If you **consider** a person or a thing to be a particular way, that is your opinion of them. ❑ *The police consider him to be dangerous.*

2 VERB If you **consider** something, you think about it carefully. ❑ *The president says he's still considering the situation.* ❑ *You should consider the feelings of other people.*

● **con|sid|era|tion** /kənsɪdəreɪʃ°n/ **NONCOUNT NOUN** ❑ *After careful consideration, we've decided that a change is necessary.*

con|sid|er|able /kənsɪdərəb°l/ ADJECTIVE

Considerable means great or large. [FORMAL] ❑ *The land cost a considerable amount of money.*

● **con|sid|er|ably ADVERB** ❑ *The king's wife was considerably taller and larger than he was.*

Word World   **conservation**

wildlife · sustainable · recycled · extinct · nature · species · rare · habitat · forest · renewable · turn off · water · save · energy · land · prevent · reduce · environment · resources · protect

Nouns / Adjectives / Verbs

con|sid|er|ate /kənsɪdərɪt/ **ADJECTIVE**
Someone who is **considerate** thinks about and cares about the feelings of other people. ❏ *He's the most considerate man I know.*

con|sid|era|tion /kənsɪdəreɪʃᵊn/ **NONCOUNT NOUN** If you show **consideration**, you think about and care about the feelings of other people. ❏ *Show consideration for your neighbors.*

con|sist /kənsɪst/ (consists, consisting, consisted) **VERB** Something that **consists of** particular things or people is made up of them. ❏ *My diet consisted of cookies and milk.*

con|sist|ent /kənsɪstənt/ **ADJECTIVE**
Someone who is **consistent** always behaves in the same way. ❏ *Oakley is one of the team's most consistent players.* ● **con|sist|en|cy** **NONCOUNT NOUN** ❏ *She scores goals with great consistency.* ● **con|sist|ent|ly** **ADVERB** ❏ *The airline consistently wins awards for its service.*

con|sole (consoles, consoling, consoled)

> **PRONUNCIATION HELP**
> Pronounce the verb /kənsoʊl/. Pronounce the noun /kɒnsoʊl/.

1 **VERB** If you **console** someone who is unhappy, you try to make them feel more cheerful. ❏ *She started to cry and I tried to console her.*

2 **NOUN** A **console** is a part of a machine that has many switches and lights. You use these switches to operate the machine. ❏ *A light flashed on the console.*

con|so|nant /kɒnsənənt/ (consonants) **NOUN** LANGUAGE ARTS A **consonant** is one of the letters of the alphabet that is not a, e, i, o, or u. ❏ *The word "book" contains two consonants and two vowels.*
→ look at **language**

con|stant /kɒnstənt/ **ADJECTIVE** Something that is **constant** happens all the time or is always there. ❏ *Doctors say she is in constant pain.* ● **con|stant|ly** **ADVERB** ❏ *The direction of the wind is constantly changing.*

con|stitu|en|cy /kənstɪtʃuənsi/ (constituencies) **NOUN** SOCIAL STUDIES A **constituency** is an area, and the people who live in it. At an election, the people in the constituency choose one person for the government. ❏ *The two senators represent very different constituencies.*

con|stitu|ent /kənstɪtʃuənt/ (constituents) **NOUN** SOCIAL STUDIES A **constituent** is

someone who lives in a particular constituency (= an area that elects its own political representative). ❏ *He told his constituents that he would continue to support them.*

con|sti|tu|tion /kɒnstɪtuʃᵊn/ (constitutions) **NOUN** SOCIAL STUDIES The **constitution** is the laws of a country or of an organization. ❏ *The government has to write a new constitution this year.*

con|struct /kənstrʌkt/ (constructs, constructing, constructed) **VERB** If you **construct** something, you build it. ❏ *His company constructed an office building in Denver.*

con|struc|tion /kənstrʌkʃᵊn/ (constructions)
1 **NONCOUNT NOUN** **Construction** is building something. ❏ *He has started construction on a swimming pool.*
2 **NOUN** A **construction** is something that has been built. ❏ *The new theater is an impressive steel and glass construction.*

con|sult /kənsʌlt/ (consults, consulting, consulted) **VERB** If you **consult** someone you ask them for their advice. ❏ *Perhaps you should consult an attorney.* ● **con|sul|ta|tion** (consultations) **NOUN** ❏ *I had a consultation with a doctor.*

> **Word Builder** consultant
>
> *ant* ≈ **someone who does**
> account + ant = accountant
> assist + ant = assistant
> attend + ant = attendant
> consult + ant = consultant
> contest + ant = contestant

con|sult|ant /kənsʌltənt/ (consultants) **NOUN** A **consultant** is someone who gives expert advice on a subject. ❏ *Alex is a young management consultant from San Francisco.*

con|sume /kənsum/ (consumes, consuming, consumed)
1 **VERB** If you **consume** something, you eat or drink it. [FORMAL] ❏ *Martha consumed a box of cookies every day.*
2 **VERB** Something that **consumes** fuel, energy, or time, uses it. ❏ *Airlines consume huge amounts of fuel every day.*
→ look at **energy**

con|sum|er /kənsumər/ (consumers) **NOUN** A **consumer** is a person who buys something or uses a service. ❏ *What are my consumer rights?*

con|tact /kɒntækt/ (**contacts, contacting, contacted**)

1 **NONCOUNT NOUN** **Contact** is meeting or communicating with someone. ❑ *I don't have much contact with teenagers.* ❑ *Anita has not been in contact with us since last year.* ❑ *We are trying to make contact with the soldiers' families..*

2 **NONCOUNT NOUN** If people or things are in **contact**, they often meet or communicate by telephone or email. ❑ *I'm still in contact with my classmates from fifth grade.*

3 **VERB** If you **contact** someone, you telephone them or send them a message or a letter. ❑ *The girl's parents contacted the police.*

con|tact lens (**contact lenses**) **NOUN**
Contact lenses are small, very thin pieces of plastic that you put on your eyes to help you see better.

con|ta|gious /kənteɪdʒəs/ **ADJECTIVE** A **contagious** disease passes easily from one person to another. Compare with **infectious**. ❑ *The disease is highly contagious.*

con|tain /kənteɪn/ (**contains, containing, contained**) **VERB** If one thing **contains** other things, those things are inside it. ❑ *The envelope contained a Christmas card.*

Word Builder container

er ≈ **something that does**
> clean + er = cleaner
> contain + er = container
> dry + er = dryer
> open + er = opener
> print + er = printer
> toast + er = toaster

---

con|tain|er /kənteɪnər/ (**containers**) **NOUN**
A **container** is a box that is used for holding or storing things. ❑ *Store the food in a plastic container.*
→ look at Picture Dictionary: **containers**

con|tem|po|rary /kəntɛmpəreri/ (**contemporaries**)

1 **ADJECTIVE** **Contemporary** means existing now, or at the same time as someone else. ❑ *...contemporary art.*

2 **NOUN** Someone's **contemporary** is a person who is, or was, alive at the same time as them.

---

content
❶ NOUN USES
❷ ADJECTIVE USES

---

❶ **con|tent** /kɒntɛnt/ (**contents**)

1 **PLURAL NOUN** The **contents** of a container are the things inside it. ❑ *Empty the contents of the can into a bowl.*

2 **PLURAL NOUN** The **contents** of a book are its different chapters and sections. ❑ *There is no table of contents.*

❷ **con|tent** /kəntɛnt/ **ADJECTIVE** If you are **content**, you are happy or satisfied. ❑ *He says his daughter is quite content.*

con|tent|ed /kəntɛntɪd/ **ADJECTIVE** If you are **contented**, you are happy and satisfied. ❑ *Richard was a very contented baby.* ❑ *Whenever he comes home he is happy and contented.*

con|test /kɒntɛst/ (**contests**) **NOUN** A **contest** is a competition or a game. ❑ *It was an exciting contest.*

Picture Dictionary containers

bag

packet

carton

container

tube

package

bottle

jar

can

carton

Word Builder **contestant**

ant ≈ **someone who does**

account + ant = accountant
assist + ant = assistant
attend + ant = attendant
consult + ant = consultant
contest + ant = contestant

con|test|ant /kəntɛstənt/ (**contestants**)
NOUN A **contestant** is a person who takes part in a competition or a game. ❏ *Contestants on the TV show have to answer six questions correctly.*

con|text /kɒntɛkst/ (**contexts**)
1 NOUN The **context of** an event is the situation in which it happens. ❏ *Don't use this sort of language in a business context.*
2 NOUN The **context** of a word or a sentence is the words and sentences that come before and after it, that help you to understand its meaning.

con|ti|nent /kɒntɪnənt/ (**continents**) **NOUN**
GEOGRAPHY A **continent** is a very large area of land, such as Africa or Asia.
→ look at **earth, globe**

con|ti|nen|tal /kɒntɪnɛntəl/ **ADJECTIVE**
The **continental** United States is all the states that are on the main continent of North America, and not Hawaii or the Virgin Islands. ❏ *Pikes Peak is the highest mountain in the continental United States.*

con|tin|ual /kəntɪnyuəl/ **ADJECTIVE**
Something that is **continual** happens without stopping, or happens repeatedly. ❏ *The team has had almost continual success since last year.* ● **con|tinu|al|ly** **ADVERB** ❏ *Gemma cried almost continually when she was a baby.* ❏ *Malcolm was continually changing his mind.*

con|tinu|ation /kəntɪnyueɪʃən/ **NONCOUNT**
NOUN The **continuation of** something is the fact that it continues to happen or to exist. ❏ *We do not support the continuation of the war.*

con|tinue /kəntɪnyu/ (**continues, continuing, continued**)
1 VERB If something **continues**, it does not stop. ❏ *The war continued for another four years.*
2 VERB If you **continue to** do something, you do not stop doing it. ❏ *They continue to fight for justice.*
3 VERB If something **continues**, it starts again. ❏ *The trial continues today.*
4 VERB If you **continue** doing something,

you start doing it again. ❏ *She looked up for a minute and then continued drawing.*
5 VERB If you **continue** in a particular direction, you keep going in that direction. ❏ *He continued rapidly up the path.*

con|tinu|ous /kəntɪnyuəs/
1 ADJECTIVE A **continuous** event happens over a long time without stopping. ❏ *They heard continuous gunfire.* ● **con|tinu|ous|ly** **ADVERB** ❏ *The police are working continuously on the case.*
2 ADJECTIVE A **continuous** line has no spaces in it. ❏ *There was a continuous line of cars outside in the street.*
3 ADJECTIVE LANGUAGE ARTS In English grammar, the **continuous** form is made using the auxiliary "be" and the present participle of a verb, as in "I'm going on vacation."

con|tract /kɒntrækt/ (**contracts**) **NOUN**
A **contract** is an official agreement between two companies or two people. ❏ *He signed a contract to play for the team for two years.*

con|trac|tion /kəntrækʃən/ (**contractions**)
NOUN LANGUAGE ARTS A **contraction** is a short form of a word or words. ❏ *"It's" (with an apostrophe) can be used as a contraction for "it is."*

contra|dict /kɒntrədɪkt/ (**contradicts, contradicting, contradicted**) **VERB** If you **contradict** someone, you say that what they have just said is wrong. ❏ *She looked surprised, but she did not contradict him.*

con|tra|ry /kɒntrɛri/
1 ADJECTIVE **Contrary** ideas or opinions are completely different from each other. ❏ *Contrary to what people think, light exercise makes you less hungry.*
2 You use **on the contrary** when you disagree with something and you are going to say that the opposite is true. ❏ *"People just don't do things like that."—"On the contrary, they do them all the time."*

con|trast (**contrasts, contrasting, contrasted**)

PRONUNCIATION HELP
Pronounce the noun /kɒntræst/.
Pronounce the verb /kəntræst/.

1 NOUN A **contrast** is a clear difference between two or more people or things. ❏ *There is a clear contrast between the two men.*
2 VERB If you **contrast** things, you show

the differences between them. ❏ *In this section we contrast four different ideas.*

con|trib|ute /kəntrɪbyut/ (**contributes, contributing, contributed**) VERB If you **contribute** money **to** something, you help to pay for it. ❏ *The U.S. is contributing $4 billion to the project.* ● **con|tribu|tor** /kəntrɪbyətər/ (**contributors**) NOUN ❏ *The financial services industry is a major contributor to the economy.*

con|tri|bu|tion /kɒntrɪbyuʃⁿn/ (**contributions**) NOUN If you make a **contribution**, you give money to help to pay for something. ❏ *He made a $5,000 contribution to the charity.*

con|trol /kəntroʊl/ (**controls, controlling, controlled**)

1 NONCOUNT NOUN **Control of** something is the power to make all the important decisions about it. ❏ *He took control of every situation.*

2 If you are **in control of** something, you have the power to make all the important decisions about it. ❏ *She feels that she's in control of her life again.*

3 VERB If someone **controls** something, they have the power to make all the important decisions about it. ❏ *He controls the largest company in California.*

4 VERB If you **control** a person or a machine, you are able to make them do what you want them to do. ❏ *There was a computer system to control the gates.* ❏ *My parents couldn't control me.*

5 NONCOUNT NOUN **Control** is also a noun. ❏ *He lost control of his car.*

6 If something is **out of control**, people cannot deal with it. ❏ *The fire was out of control.*

7 If something is **under control**, people can deal with it. ❏ *The situation is under control.*

8 NOUN A **control** is a switch you use in order to operate a machine. ❏ *You operate the controls without looking at them.*

con|tro|ver|sial /kɒntrəvɜrʃⁿl/ ADJECTIVE A **controversial** subject is one that people argue about. ❏ *In business, I try to stay away from controversial subjects.*

con|tro|ver|sy /kɒntrəvɜrsi/ NONCOUNT NOUN **Controversy** is when people argue about something, or disapprove of it. ❏ *The TV show caused controversy when it was shown last year.*

con|veni|ence /kənvinyəns/ (**conveniences**)

1 NONCOUNT NOUN If something is done for your **convenience**, it is done in a way that is helpful for you. ❏ *We include an envelope for your convenience.*

2 NOUN **Conveniences** are pieces of equipment designed to make your life easier. ❏ *This apartment includes all the modern conveniences.*

con|veni|ent /kənvinyənt/

1 ADJECTIVE Something that is **convenient** is useful for a particular purpose. ❏ *This is a convenient place to get coffee before work.* ● **con|veni|ence** NONCOUNT NOUN ❏ *They may use a credit card for convenience.* ● **con|veni|ent|ly** ADVERB ❏ *The house is conveniently located close to the railroad station.*

2 ADJECTIVE A **convenient** time is a time when you are available to do something. ❏ *She will try to arrange a convenient time.*

con|ven|tion|al /kənvɛnʃənⁿl/

1 ADJECTIVE **Conventional** people behave in a way that is considered to be normal by most people. ❏ *I've always been quite conventional; I work hard and behave properly.*

2 ADJECTIVE A **conventional** method or product is one that is usually used. ❏ *In a conventional oven, bake at 350°F for 30 minutes.*

con|ver|sa|tion /kɒnvərseɪʃⁿn/ (**conversations**) NOUN If you have a **conversation with** someone, you talk to each other about something. ❏ *I had an interesting conversation with him.*

→ look at **communication, phone**

con|vert /kənvɜrt/ (**converts, converting, converted**) VERB To **convert** one thing **into** another means to change it into a different form. ❏ *The signal will be converted into electronic form.* ❏ *He wants to convert the building into a hotel.*

con|vict /kənvɪkt/ (**convicts, convicting, convicted**) VERB If someone **is convicted of** a crime, they are found guilty of it in a court of law. ❏ *He was convicted of murder.*

con|vince /kənvɪns/ (**convinces, convincing, convinced**)

1 VERB If someone or something **convinces** you **to** do something, they persuade you to do it. ❏ *He convinced her to marry Tom.*

2 VERB If someone or something **convinces** you **of** something, they make you believe that it is true or that it exists. ❏ *The new players have convinced me of their ability.*

● **con|vinced** /kənvɪnst/ **ADJECTIVE** ❑ *She was convinced that the diamonds were real.*

cook /kʊk/ (**cooks, cooking, cooked**)
1 **VERB** When you **cook** a meal, you prepare and heat food. ❑ *I have to go and cook dinner.* ❑ *Let the vegetables cook for about 10 minutes.*
2 **NOUN** A **cook** is a person who prepares and cooks food. ❑ *I'm a terrible cook.*
→ look at Picture Dictionary: **cook**
→ look at **food, meat**

cook|book /kʊkbʊk/ (**cookbooks**) **NOUN** A **cookbook** is a book that tells you how to prepare different meals.

cookie /kʊki/ (**cookies**) **NOUN** A **cookie** is a small, flat, sweet cake. ❑ *She brought us a plate of warm chocolate chip cookies.*

cook|ing /kʊkɪŋ/
1 **NONCOUNT NOUN** **Cooking** is the activity of preparing food. ❑ *He did the cooking and cleaning.*
2 **NONCOUNT NOUN** **Cooking** is food that is cooked in a particular way. ❑ *The restaurant specializes in Italian cooking.*

cool /kul/ (**cooler, coolest, cools, cooling, cooled**)
1 **ADJECTIVE** Something that is **cool** has a low temperature, but is not cold. ❑ *I felt the cool air on my neck.* ❑ *The water was cool.*
2 **ADJECTIVE** When you stay **cool** in a difficult situation, you remain calm. ❑ *You have to remain cool in very difficult situations.*
3 **ADJECTIVE** If a person or thing is **cool**, they are fashionable and interesting. [INFORMAL] ❑ *I met some really cool people last night.* ❑ *She had really cool boots.*
4 **VERB** When something **cools**, it becomes lower in temperature. ❑ *Drain the meat and allow it to cool.*

5 To **cool down** means the same as to **cool**. ❑ *Once it cools down, you'll be able to touch it.*
6 If someone **cools down**, they become less angry. ❑ *He has had time to cool down.*
→ look at **climate**

co|oper|ate /koʊɒpəreɪt/ (**cooperates, cooperating, cooperated**) **VERB** If you **cooperate with** someone, you work with them or help them. ❑ *He finally agreed to cooperate with the police.* ● **cooperative** /koʊɒpərətɪv/ **ADJECTIVE** ❑ *I made an effort to be cooperative.* ● **co|opera|tion** /koʊɒpəreɪʃ°n/ **NONCOUNT NOUN** ❑ *Thank you for your cooperation.*

co|or|di|nate /koʊɔrd°neɪt/ (**coordinates, coordinating, coordinated**)
1 **VERB** When you **coordinate** an activity, you organize it. ❑ *She coordinates the weekend activities.*
2 **VERB** If you **coordinate** the parts of your body, you make them work together well. ❑ *You need to coordinate legs, arms, and breathing.*
● **co|or|di|na|tion** **NONCOUNT NOUN** ❑ *You need great hand-eye coordination to hit the ball.*

cop /kɒp/ (**cops**) **NOUN** A **cop** is a policeman or policewoman. [INFORMAL] ❑ *The cops know where to find him.*

cope /koʊp/ (**copes, coping, coped**) **VERB** If you **cope with** a problem or task, you deal with it in a successful way. ❑ *The group has helped her cope with a serious illness.*

cop|per /kɒpər/ **NONCOUNT NOUN** **Copper** is a soft reddish-brown metal. ❑ *Chile produces much of the world's copper.*

copy /kɒpi/ (**copies, copying, copied**)
1 **NOUN** If you make a **copy of** something, you produce something that looks like the original thing. ❑ *I made a copy of Steve's letter.*

C

Picture Dictionary　**cook**

boil　　steam　　roast　　fry　　stir fry

bake　　microwave　　toast　　barbecue　　broil

C

2 NOUN A **copy of** a book or a newspaper is one of many that are exactly the same. ❑ *Did you get a copy of "USA Today?"*

3 VERB If you **copy** something, you make or write something that is exactly like the original thing. ❑ *Copy files from your old computer to your new one.*

4 VERB If you **copy** a person, you try to behave as they do. ❑ *Children try to copy the behavior of people they admire.*

→ look at **draw**

cor|al /kɔ̱rəl/ **NONCOUNT NOUN Coral** is a hard substance formed from the bones of very small ocean animals. ❑ *She was wearing a coral necklace.*

cord /kɔ̱rd/ (**cords**)

1 NONCOUNT NOUN Cord is strong, thick string. ❑ *She was carrying a package tied with heavy cord.*

2 NOUN A **cord** is an electrical wire covered in rubber or plastic. ❑ *Place all electrical cords out of children's reach.*

core /kɔ̱r/ (**cores**)

1 NOUN The **core** is the central part of a fruit that contains the seeds. ❑ *Annie put her apple core in the garbage.*

2 NOUN SCIENCE The Earth's **core** is its central part. ❑ *What is the temperature in the Earth's core?*

cork /kɔ̱rk/ (**corks**) **NOUN** A **cork** is an object that you push into the top of a bottle to close it. ❑ *He took the cork out of the bottle.*

cork|screw /kɔ̱rkskru/ (**corkscrews**) **NOUN** A **corkscrew** is a tool for pulling corks out of bottles.

corn /kɔ̱rn/ **NONCOUNT NOUN Corn** is a tall plant that produces long vegetables covered with yellow seeds, or the seeds of this plant. ❑ *...a can of sweetcorn.*

→ look at **vegetable**

cor|ner /kɔ̱rnər/ (**corners**) **NOUN** A **corner** is a point where two sides of something meet, or where a road meets another road. ❑ *There was a table in the corner of the room.* ❑ *He stood on the street corner, waiting for a taxi.*

cor|po|rate /kɔ̱rpərɪt, -prɪt/ **ADJECTIVE Corporate** means relating to large companies. ❑ *Our city apartments are popular with private and corporate customers.*

cor|po|ra|tion /kɔ̱rpəreɪʃ⁰n/ (**corporations**) **NOUN** A **corporation** is a large business or company. ❑ *Her father works for a big corporation.*

corpse /kɔ̱rps/ (**corpses**) **NOUN** A **corpse** is a dead body. ❑ *Police found the corpse in a nearby river.*

cor|rect /kərɛ̱kt/ (**corrects, correcting, corrected**)

1 ADJECTIVE Something is **correct** when it is right or true. ❑ *The correct answers can be found on page 8.* ● **cor|rect|ly ADVERB** ❑ *Did I pronounce your name correctly?*

2 VERB If you **correct** a problem or a mistake you make it right. ❑ *There is another way you can correct the problem.* ❑ *Students are given a chance to correct mistakes.* ● **cor|rec|tion** /kərɛ̱kʃ⁰n/ (**corrections**) **NOUN** ❑ *You may make corrections to your final test.*

→ look at **answer, grammar**

Word Partners Use **correct** with:
N. correct **answer**, correct **response** **1** correct **a mistake** **2**

cor|re|spond /kɔ̱rɪspɒnd/ (**corresponds, corresponding, corresponded**)

1 VERB If one thing **corresponds to** another, there is a close similarity or connection between them. ❑ *The rise in food prices corresponds closely to rises in oil prices.* ❑ *The two maps correspond closely.*

2 VERB If you **correspond with** someone, you write letters to them. ❑ *She still corresponds with her American friends.* ❑ *We corresponded regularly.*

cor|re|spond|ence /kɔ̱rɪspɒndəns/ **NONCOUNT NOUN** Someone's **correspondence** is the letters that they receive or send. ❑ *The website contains copies of Einstein's personal correspondence.*

cor|re|spond|ent /kɔ̱rɪspɒndənt/ (**correspondents**) **NOUN** A **correspondent** is a person who writes news reports. ❑ *He's the White House correspondent for The Times.*

cor|rupt /kərʌ̱pt/ (**corrupts, corrupting, corrupted**)

1 ADJECTIVE Someone who is **corrupt** behaves in a dishonest way in order to gain money or power. ❑ *We know that there are some officials who are corrupt.*

2 VERB TECHNOLOGY If a computer file or program **is corrupted**, it no longer works properly, and it may not be safe to use. ❑ *The files were corrupted by a virus.*

cos|met|ic /kɒzmɛtɪk/ (**cosmetics**) **NOUN**
Cosmetics are make-up products. ❑ *She wears nail polish and cosmetics.*

cost /kɔst/ (**costs, costing, cost**)
1 **NOUN** The **cost of** something is the amount of money you need in order to buy, do, or make it. ❑ *The cost of a loaf of bread has gone up.* ❑ *There will be an increase in the cost of mailing a letter.*
2 **VERB** If something **costs** an amount of money, you have to pay that amount in order to buy, do or make it. ❑ *This course costs $150 per person.* ❑ *It will cost us over $100,000 to buy new trucks.*

cost|ly /kɔstli/ (**costlier, costliest**) **ADJECTIVE**
Something that is **costly** is very expensive. ❑ *We must try to avoid such costly mistakes.*

cos|tume /kɒstum/ (**costumes**) **NOUN** ARTS
A **costume** is a set of clothes that someone wears in a performance. ❑ *The costumes and scenery were designed by Robert Rauschenberg.*
→ look at **performance**

cot /kɒt/ (**cots**) **NOUN** A **cot** is a narrow bed that you can fold and store in a small space.

cot|tage /kɒtɪdʒ/ (**cottages**) **NOUN** A **cottage** is a small house, usually in the country. ❑ *She lived in a little white cottage in the woods.*

cot|ton /kɒtᵊn/
1 **NONCOUNT NOUN** Cotton is cloth or thread that is made from the cotton plant. ❑ *He's wearing a cotton shirt.* ❑ *...a reel of cotton.*
2 **NONCOUNT NOUN** Cotton is a plant that is used for making cloth. ❑ *They own a large cotton plantation in Tennessee.*
3 **NONCOUNT NOUN** Cotton is a soft mass of this substance that you use for cleaning your skin. ❑ *Then take the cream off with cotton balls.*

couch /kaʊtʃ/ (**couches**) **NOUN** A **couch** is a long, comfortable seat for two or three people.
→ look at **furniture**

cough /kɔf/ (**coughs, coughing, coughed**)
1 **VERB** When you **cough**, you suddenly force air out of your throat with a noise. ❑ *James began to cough violently.*
2 **NOUN** Cough is also a noun. ❑ *Do you have any cough medicine?* ● **cough|ing** **NONCOUNT NOUN** ❑ *We could hear loud coughing in the background.*

3 **NOUN** A **cough** is an illness that makes you cough. ❑ *I had a cough for over a month.*
→ look at **sick**

could /kəd, STRONG kʊd/
1 **MODAL VERB** If you **could** do something, you were able to do it. ❑ *I could see that something was wrong.* ❑ *It was so dark that I couldn't see where I was going.*
2 **MODAL VERB** You use **could** to show that something is possibly true, or that it may possibly happen. ❑ *It could snow again tonight.* ❑ *"Where's Jack?"—"I'm not sure; he could be in the bathroom."*
3 **MODAL VERB** You use **could** in questions to make polite requests. ❑ *Could I stay tonight?* ❑ *He asked if he could have a cup of coffee.*

couldn't /kʊdᵊnt/ **Couldn't** is short for "could not."

could've /kʊdəv/ **Could've** is short for "could have."

coun|cil /kaʊnsᵊl/ (**councils**) **NOUN** A **council** is a group of people who are chosen to control a particular area. ❑ *The city council has decided to build a new school.*

coun|se|lor /kaʊnsələr/ (**counselors**)
1 **NOUN** A **counselor** is a young person who takes care of children at a summer camp. ❑ *Hicks worked as a camp counselor in the summer vacation.*
2 **NOUN** A **counselor** is someone whose job is to give people advice and help them with problems. ❑ *My husband and I went to see a marriage counselor.*

count /kaʊnt/ (**counts, counting, counted**)
1 **VERB** When you **count**, you say all the numbers in order. ❑ *Nancy counted slowly to five.*
2 **VERB** If you **count** all the things in a group, you see how many there are. ❑ *I counted the dollar bills.* ❑ *I counted 34 sheep on the hillside.*
3 **VERB** If someone or something **counts**, they are important. ❑ *Every penny counts if you want to be a millionaire.*
4 **ADJECTIVE** LANGUAGE ARTS A **count** noun is a noun that has a plural.
5 If you **keep count of** a number of things, you know how many have occurred. ❑ *Keep count of the number of hours you work.*
6 If you **lose count of** a number of things, you cannot remember how many there have been. ❑ *I lost count of the number of times she called.*

C

▶ **count on** If you **count on** someone or something, you feel sure they will help you. ❏ *You can count on us to keep your secret.* ❏ *Can we count on your support for Ms. Ryan?*

coun|ter /ka͟ʊntər/ (**counters**)

1 NOUN In a store or café, a **counter** is a long flat surface where customers are served. ❏ *That guy works behind the counter at the DVD rental store.*

2 NOUN A **counter** is a very small object that you use in board games. ❏ *Move your counter one square for each spot on the dice.*
→ look at **kitchen**

counter|clockwise /ka͟ʊntərklɒ͟kwaɪz/

1 ADVERB Something that moves **counterclockwise** moves in the opposite direction to the way the hands of a clock move. ❏ *Now turn the wheel counterclockwise.*

2 ADJECTIVE **Counterclockwise** is also an adjective. ❏ *Each group moves around the room in a counterclockwise direction.*

counter|feit /ka͟ʊntərfɪt/ ADJECTIVE

Counterfeit money, goods, or documents are not real, but they look exactly like real ones. ❏ *He admitted using counterfeit bills.*

count noun (**count nouns**) NOUN

LANGUAGE ARTS A **count noun** is a noun such as "bird," "chair," or "year" that has a singular and a plural form.

coun|try /ka͟ʌntri/ (**countries**)

1 NOUN SOCIAL STUDIES GEOGRAPHY A **country** is an area of the world with its own government and people. ❏ *This is the greatest country in the world.* ❏ *We crossed the border between the two countries.*

2 NOUN The **country** is land that is away from cities and towns. ❏ *You can live a healthy life in the country.* ❏ *She was cycling along a country road.* ❏ *She lived alone in a small house in the country.*

3 NONCOUNT NOUN **Country** music is a style of popular music from the southern United States. ❏ *I always wanted to play country music.*

country|side /ka͟ʌntrisaɪd/ NONCOUNT NOUN

The **countryside** is land that is away from cities and towns. ❏ *I've always loved the English countryside.*

coun|ty /ka͟ʊnti/ (**counties**) NOUN A **county** is a part of a state or country. ❏ *...Palm Beach County.*

cou|ple /ka͟ʌpəl/ (**couples**)

1 A **couple of** people or things means two or

around two of them. ❏ *There are a couple of police officers outside.* ❏ *Things should get better in a couple of days.*

2 PRONOUN **Couple** is also a pronoun. ❏ *Out of 750 customers, there may be a couple that are unhappy.*

3 NOUN A **couple** is two people who are married or who are having a romantic relationship. ❏ *The couple have no children.*

cou|pon /ku͟ːpɒn, kyu͟ː-/ (**coupons**) NOUN

A **coupon** is a piece of paper that allows you to pay less money than usual for a product, or to get it free. ❏ *Cut out the coupon on page 2 and take it to your local supermarket.*

cour|age /kɜ͟rɪdʒ/ NONCOUNT NOUN **Courage** is the quality someone shows when they are not afraid. ❏ *The girl had the courage to tell the police.*

cou|ra|geous /kəre͟ɪdʒəs/ ADJECTIVE

Someone who is **courageous** shows courage. ❏ *The courageous girl saved her baby sister from a house fire.*

course /kɔ͟rs/ (**courses**)

1 NOUN A **course** is a series of lessons on a particular subject. ❏ *I'm taking a course in business administration.*

2 NOUN A **course** is one part of a meal. ❏ *Lunch was excellent, especially the first course.*

3 NOUN SPORTS In sports, a **course** is an area of land for racing, or for playing golf. ❏ *The hotel complex has a swimming pool, tennis courts, and a golf course.*

4 Someone or something **changes course** when they start going in a different direction. ❏ *The pilot changed course to land in Chicago.*

court /kɔ͟rt/ (**courts**)

1 NOUN A **court** is a place where a judge and a group of people (= a jury) decide if someone has done something wrong. ❏ *The man will appear in court later this month.*

2 NOUN SPORTS A **court** is an area for playing a game such as tennis. ❏ *The hotel has several tennis courts.*

cour|teous /kɜ͟rtiəs/ ADJECTIVE Someone who is **courteous** is polite. ❏ *He was a kind and courteous man.* ● **cour|teous|ly** ADVERB ❏ *He nodded courteously to me.*

cour|tesy /kɜ͟rtɪsi/ NONCOUNT NOUN

Courtesy is polite behavior that shows that you consider other people's feelings. [FORMAL] ❏ *Showing courtesy to other drivers costs nothing.*

court|yard /kɔrtyard/ (**courtyards**) NOUN
A **courtyard** is an open area that is surrounded
by buildings or walls. ❑ *The second bedroom
overlooked the courtyard.*

cous|in /kʌzᵊn/ (**cousins**) NOUN Your **cousin**
is the child of your uncle or your aunt. ❑ *Do
you know my cousin Alex?*

cov|er /kʌvər/ (**covers, covering, covered**)
1 VERB If you **cover** something, you put
something over it to protect it. ❑ *Cover the
dish with a heavy lid.*
2 VERB If one thing **covers** another, it
forms a layer over its surface. ❑ *Snow covered
the city.* ❑ *The desk was covered with papers.*
3 NOUN A **cover** is something that is put
over an object to protect it. ❑ *Keep a plastic
cover on your computer when you are not using it.*
4 NOUN The **cover** of a book or a magazine
is the outside part of it. ❑ *She appeared on the
cover of last week's "Zoo" magazine.*

cow /kaʊ/ (**cows**) NOUN A **cow** is a large
female animal that is kept on farms for its
milk. ❑ *Dad went out to milk the cows.*
→ look at **farm**

cow|ard /kaʊərd/ (**cowards**) NOUN A
coward is someone who has no courage.
❑ *They called him a coward because he refused to fight.*

cow|ard|ly /kaʊərdli/ ADJECTIVE A **cowardly**
person is not brave and is easily frightened.
❑ *I was too cowardly to complain.*

cow|boy /kaʊbɔɪ/ (**cowboys**) NOUN A **cowboy**
is a man who rides a horse and takes care of
cows in North America.

cozy /koʊzi/ (**cozier, coziest**) ADJECTIVE
A **cozy** place is comfortable and warm.
❑ *You can relax in the cozy hotel lounge.*

crab /kræb/ (**crabs**)
1 NOUN A **crab** is an ocean animal with a
shell and five pairs of legs. Crabs usually
move sideways.
2 NONCOUNT NOUN **Crab** is the meat of this
animal. ❑ *I'll have the crab salad, please.*
→ look at **shellfish**

crack /kræk/ (**cracks, cracking, cracked**)
1 VERB If something hard **cracks**, it
becomes slightly broken, with lines
appearing on its surface. ❑ *The plane's
windshield cracked.* ❑ *...a cracked mirror.*
2 NOUN A **crack** is a very narrow gap
between two things. ❑ *Kathryn saw him
through a crack in the curtains.*

3 NOUN A **crack** is a line that appears on
the surface when it is slightly broken.
❑ *The plate had a crack in it.*
4 NOUN A **crack** is a sharp sound, like the
sound of a piece of wood breaking.
❑ *Suddenly there was a loud crack.*

crack|er /krækər/ (**crackers**) NOUN A
cracker is a thin, hard piece of baked bread
that people sometimes eat with cheese.

crack|le /krækᵊl/ (**crackles, crackling,
crackled**) VERB Something that **crackles**
makes a lot of short, sharp noises. ❑ *The radio
crackled again.*

cra|dle /kreɪdᵊl/
(**cradles**) NOUN
A **cradle** is a
baby's bed that
you can move
from side to side.

craft /kræft/ (**crafts**) NOUN A **craft** is an
activity that involves making things
skillfully with your hands. ❑ *We want to teach
our children about native crafts and culture.*

crafty /kræfti/ (**craftier, craftiest**) ADJECTIVE
Someone who is **crafty** gets what they want
in a clever way, perhaps by being dishonest.
❑ *She was so crafty, nobody ever suspected her.*

cramp /kræmp/ (**cramps**) NOUN A **cramp** is
a sudden strong pain in a muscle. ❑ *Mike was
complaining of stomach cramps.*

cran|berry /krænberi/ (**cranberries**) NOUN
Cranberries are small red fruits with a sour
taste, that are often used for making a sauce
that you eat with meat.

crane /kreɪn/ (**cranes**)
1 NOUN A **crane** is a large machine with a
long arm that can lift very heavy things.
2 NOUN A **crane** is a large water bird with
a long neck and long legs.

crash /kræʃ/ (**crashes, crashing, crashed**)
1 NOUN A **crash** is an accident in which a
vehicle hits something. ❑ *His son was killed in
a car crash.*
2 NOUN A **crash** is a sudden loud noise.
❑ *People said they heard a loud crash at about 1:30 a.m.*
3 VERB If a vehicle **crashes into** something,
it hits it. ❑ *The plane crashed into a nearby field.*
❑ *Her car crashed into the back of a truck.*
4 VERB TECHNOLOGY If a computer or a
computer program **crashes**, it suddenly

stops working. ❏ *My computer crashed for the second time that day.*

crate /kreɪt/ (crates) NOUN A **crate** is a large box for moving or storing things. ❏ *The pictures are packed in wooden crates.*

cra|ter /kreɪtər/ (craters) NOUN SCIENCE A **crater** is a very large hole in the top of a volcano (= a mountain that forces hot gas and rocks into the air). ❏ *Rocks shot up three miles from the volcano's crater.*

crawl /krɔl/ (crawls, crawling, crawled)
1 VERB When you **crawl**, you move on your hands and knees. ❏ *I began to crawl toward the door.*
2 NONCOUNT NOUN SPORTS **Crawl** is a way of swimming in which you lie on your front and move one arm over your head, and then the other, while kicking your legs. ❏ *Neil is learning to swim crawl.*

cray|on /kreɪɒn/ (crayons) NOUN A **crayon** is a small colored stick that you use for drawing.

cra|zy /kreɪzi/ (crazier, craziest)
1 ADJECTIVE Someone who is **crazy** is very strange or not at all sensible. [INFORMAL] ❏ *People obviously thought we were crazy.* ● **cra|zi|ly** ADVERB ❏ *He ran crazily around in circles.*
2 ADJECTIVE Someone who is going **crazy** is extremely bored or upset, or feels they cannot wait for something any longer. [INFORMAL] ❏ *Annie thought she might go crazy if she didn't find out soon.*
3 ADJECTIVE If you are **crazy about** someone or something, you like them very much. [INFORMAL] ❏ *He's still crazy about his job.* ❏ *We're crazy about each other.*

creak /krik/ (creaks, creaking, creaked)
1 VERB If something **creaks**, it makes a short, high sound when you move it. ❏ *The stairs creaked under his feet.* ❏ *The door creaked open.*
2 NOUN **Creak** is also a noun. ❏ *The door opened with a creak.*

cream /krim/ (creams)
1 NONCOUNT NOUN **Cream** is a thick liquid that is made from milk. ❏ *She went to the store to buy some cream.*
2 NOUN A **cream** is a substance that you rub into your skin. ❏ *...hand cream.*
3 ADJECTIVE Something that is **cream** is yellowish-white in color. ❏ *She wore a cream silk shirt.*

4 NOUN **Cream** is also a noun. ❏ *Many women say they can't wear cream.*

creamy /krimi/ (creamier, creamiest)
1 ADJECTIVE Food or drink that is **creamy** has a lot of cream or milk in it. ❏ *I like rich, creamy coffee.*
2 ADJECTIVE Food that is **creamy** is soft and smooth. ❏ *We had pasta in a rich, creamy sauce.*

crease /kris/ (creases, creasing, creased)
1 NOUN **Creases** are the lines that appear in cloth or paper when it has been folded. ❏ *Dad always wears pants with sharp creases.*
2 VERB If cloth **creases**, lines form in it when it is pressed or folded. ❏ *Most clothes crease a bit when you are traveling.* ● **creased** ADJECTIVE ❏ *His clothes were terribly creased.*

cre|ate /krieɪt/ (creates, creating, created)
VERB To **create** something means to make it happen or exist. ❏ *It's great for a group of schoolchildren to create a show like this.* ❏ *Could this solution create problems for us in the future?* ● **crea|tor** /krieɪtər/ (creators) NOUN ❏ *...Matt Groening, creator of The Simpsons.*

crea|tion /krieɪʃ°n/ (creations) NOUN You can call something that someone has made a **creation**. ❏ *The new bathroom is my own creation.*

crea|tive /krieɪtɪv/
1 ADJECTIVE A **creative** person is good at having new ideas. ❏ *When you don't have much money, you have to be creative.*
2 ADJECTIVE If you use something in a **creative** way, you use it in a new way. ❏ *He is famous for his creative use of words.*

crea|ture /kritʃər/ (creatures) NOUN A **creature** is a living thing that is not a plant. ❏ *Like all living creatures, birds need plenty of water.*

cred|it /krɛdɪt/ (credits)
1 NONCOUNT NOUN If you buy something **on credit**, you are allowed to have it and pay for it later. ❏ *We buy everything on credit.*
2 NONCOUNT NOUN If you get **the credit for** something, people praise you because they think you are responsible for it. ❏ *I can't take all the credit myself.*
3 NOUN A **credit** is one part of a course at a school or a college. ❏ *He doesn't have enough credits to graduate.*
4 PLURAL NOUN The **credits** is the list of all the people who made a movie or a television program. ❏ *It was great to see my name in the credits.*

cred|it card (credit cards) NOUN A credit card is a card that you use to buy something and pay for it later. ❑ *Call this number to order by credit card.*
→ look at **payment, shopping**

creek /kriːk/ (creeks) NOUN A creek is a stream or a small river. ❑ *The road follows Austin Creek for a few miles.*

creep /kriːp/ (creeps, creeping, crept) VERB If you **creep** somewhere, you move there quietly and slowly. ❑ *He crept up the stairs.*

creepy /kriːpi/ (creepier, creepiest) ADJECTIVE Something or someone that is **creepy** makes you feel nervous or frightened. [INFORMAL] ❑ *This place is really creepy at night.*

crept /krɛpt/ **Crept** is a form of the verb **creep**.

cres|cent /krɛsənt/ (crescents) NOUN A **crescent** is a curved shape like the shape of a new moon.

crew /kruː/ (crews) NOUN The **crew** of a ship or aircraft is the people who work on it. ❑ *He was new on the crew of the space shuttle.* ❑ *These ships carry small crews of about twenty men.*

crib /krɪb/ (cribs) NOUN A **crib** is a bed with high sides for a baby.
→ look at **furniture**

crime /kraɪm/ (crimes) NOUN A **crime** is an illegal act. ❑ *The police are searching the scene of the crime.*

crimi|nal /krɪmɪnəl/ (criminals) NOUN A **criminal** is a person who does something illegal. ❑ *We want to protect ourselves against dangerous criminals.*

crip|ple /krɪpəl/ (cripples, crippling, crippled) VERB Someone who **is crippled** by an injury can never move their body normally again. ❑ *Mr. Easton was crippled in an accident.*

cri|sis /kraɪsɪs/ (crises /kraɪsiz/) NOUN A **crisis** is a situation that is very serious or dangerous. ❑ *This is a worldwide crisis that affects us all.*

crisp /krɪsp/ (crisper, crispest) ADJECTIVE Food that is **crisp** is pleasantly hard. ❑ *Bake the potatoes for 15 minutes, until they're nice and crisp.* ❑ *...crisp bacon.*

crit|ic /krɪtɪk/ (critics) NOUN A **critic** is a person who writes and gives their opinion about books, movies, music, or art. ❑ *Mather was a film critic for many years.*

criti|cal /krɪtɪkəl/
1 ADJECTIVE A **critical** situation is very serious and dangerous. ❑ *The economic situation may soon become critical.* ● **criti|cal|ly** ADVERB ❑ *Food supplies are critically low.*
2 ADJECTIVE To be **critical** means to criticize a person or a thing. ❑ *His report is critical of the judges.* ● **criti|cal|ly** ADVERB ❑ *She spoke critically about Lara.*

criti|cism /krɪtɪsɪzəm/ (criticisms)
1 NONCOUNT NOUN **Criticism** is when someone expresses disapproval of someone or something. ❑ *The president faced strong criticism for his remarks.*
2 NOUN A **criticism** is a statement that expresses disapproval. ❑ *Teachers should say something positive before making a criticism.*

criti|cize /krɪtɪsaɪz/ (criticizes, criticizing, criticized) VERB If you **criticize** someone or something, you express your disapproval of them. ❑ *His mother rarely criticized him.*

croco|dile /krɒkədaɪl/ (crocodiles) NOUN A **crocodile** is a large animal with a long body, a long mouth and sharp teeth. Crocodiles live in rivers.

crook /krʊk/ (crooks) NOUN A **crook** is a dishonest person or a criminal. [INFORMAL] ❑ *The man is a crook and a liar.*

crook|ed /krʊkɪd/ ADJECTIVE Something that is **crooked** is not straight. ❑ *I looked at his crooked broken nose.*

crop /krɒp/ (crops) NOUN **Crops** are plants that people grow for food. ❑ *Rice farmers here still plant their crops by hand.*
→ look at **plant**

---
cross
❶ MOVING ACROSS
❷ ANGRY
---

❶ **cross** /krɒs/ (crosses, crossing, crossed)
1 VERB If you **cross** a place, you move to the other side of it. ❑ *She crossed the road without looking.*
2 VERB SPORTS In sports, if you **cross** the ball, you hit it or kick it from one side of the field to a person on the other side. ❑ *Ronaldinho crossed the ball into the penalty area.*
3 NOUN SPORTS In sports, a **cross** is the act of hitting or kicking the ball from one side of the field to a person on the other side.
4 VERB If you **cross** your arms, legs, or fingers, you put one of them on top of the

other. ❑ *Jill crossed her legs.*

5 NOUN A **cross** is a shape like †. It is the most important Christian symbol. ❑ *She wore a cross around her neck.*

6 NOUN A **cross** is a written mark in the shape of an X. ❑ *Put a cross next to those activities you like.*

▶ **cross out** If you **cross out** words, you draw a line through them. ❑ *He crossed out her name and added his own.*

→ look at **answer**

❷ cross /krɔs/ (**crosser, crossest**) **ADJECTIVE** Someone who is **cross** is angry. ❑ *I'm terribly cross with him.* ● **cross|ly ADVERB** ❑ *"No, no, no," Morris said crossly.*

cross|roads /krɔsroʊdz/ (**crossroads**) **NOUN** A **crossroads** is a place where two roads cross each other. ❑ *Turn right at the first crossroads.*

cross|walk /krɔswɔk/ (**crosswalks**) **NOUN**

A **crosswalk** is a place where drivers must stop to let people walk across a street.
→ look at **city**

cross|word /krɔswɜrd/ (**crosswords**) **NOUN** A **crossword** or a **crossword puzzle** is a printed word game that consists of a pattern of black and white squares. You write the answers down or across on the white squares. ❑ *He could do the New York Times crossword puzzle in 15 minutes.*

crouch /kraʊtʃ/ (**crouches, crouching, crouched**) **VERB** If you **crouch**, you bend your legs so that you are close to the ground. ❑ *We crouched in the bushes to hide.*

crow /kroʊ/ (**crows, crowing, crowed**)
1 NOUN A **crow** is a large black bird that makes a loud noise.
2 VERB When a rooster (= male chicken) **crows**, it makes a loud sound, often early in the morning. ❑ *We had to get up when the rooster crowed.*

crowd /kraʊd/ (**crowds, crowding, crowded**)
1 NOUN A **crowd** is a large group of people who have gathered together. ❑ *A huge crowd gathered in the town square.*
2 VERB When people **crowd around** someone or something, they move closely

together around them. ❑ *The children crowded around him.*

3 VERB If a lot of people **crowd into** a place, they enter it so that it becomes very full. ❑ *Thousands of people crowded into the city center to see the president.*

crowd|ed /kraʊdɪd/ **ADJECTIVE** A **crowded** place is full of people. ❑ *He looked slowly around the small crowded room.* ❑ *This is a crowded city of 2 million.*

crown /kraʊn/ (**crowns, crowning, crowned**)
1 NOUN A **crown** is a gold or silver circle that a king or a queen wears on their head.

2 VERB
SOCIAL STUDIES When a king or a queen **is crowned**, they officially become king or queen, and a crown is put on their head. ❑ *Two days later, Juan Carlos was crowned king.*

crude /kruːd/ (**cruder, crudest**)
1 ADJECTIVE Something that is **crude** is simple and rough. ❑ *We sat on crude wooden boxes.* ● **crude|ly ADVERB** ❑ *Someone has crudely painted over the original sign.*
2 ADJECTIVE A **crude** person or joke is rude or offensive. ❑ *The boys sang loudly and told crude jokes.* ❑ *Please don't be so crude.*
● **crude|ly ADVERB** ❑ *He hated it when she spoke so crudely.*

cru|el /kruːəl/ (**crueler, cruelest**) **ADJECTIVE** Someone who is **cruel** deliberately makes people suffer. ❑ *Children can be very cruel.*
● **cru|el|ly ADVERB** ❑ *Douglas was often treated cruelly by his sisters.* ● **cru|el|ty** /kruːəlti/ **NONCOUNT NOUN** ❑ *There are laws against cruelty to animals.*

cruise /kruːz/ (**cruises, cruising, cruised**)
1 NOUN A **cruise** is a vacation that you spend on a ship or boat. ❑ *He and his wife went on a world cruise.*
2 VERB If a car, a ship, or an aircraft **cruises** somewhere, it moves at a steady comfortable speed. ❑ *A black and white police car cruised past.*

crumb /krʌm/ (**crumbs**) **NOUN** **Crumbs** are small pieces that fall from bread when you break it. ❑ *I stood up, brushing crumbs from my pants.*

crum|ble /krʌmbəl/ (crumbles, crumbling, crumbled)

1 **VERB** If a building or a wall is **crumbling**, pieces are breaking off it. ❑ *The stone wall was crumbling away in places.*

2 **VERB** If you **crumble** something, you break it into a lot of small pieces. ❑ *Crumble the goat cheese into a salad bowl.*

crum|ple /krʌmpəl/ (crumples, crumpling, crumpled) **VERB** If you **crumple** paper or cloth, you press it, making a lot of lines and folds in it. ❑ *She crumpled the paper in her hand.* **Crumple up** means the same as **crumple**. ❑ *She crumpled up the note.* ● **crum|pled** **ADJECTIVE** ❑ *His uniform was crumpled and dirty.*

crunch /krʌntʃ/ (crunches, crunching, crunched)

1 **VERB** When a lot of small stones **crunch**, they make a loud noise when you walk or drive over them. ❑ *The gravel crunched under his boots.*

2 **NOUN** Crunch is also a noun. ❑ *We heard the crunch of tires on the road up to the house.*

3 **VERB** If you **crunch** something, you noisily break it into small pieces between your teeth. ❑ *She crunched an ice cube loudly.*

crunchy /krʌntʃi/ (crunchier, crunchiest) **ADJECTIVE** Food that is **crunchy** is pleasantly hard, so that it makes a noise when you eat it. ❑ *We enjoyed the fresh, crunchy vegetables.*

crush /krʌʃ/ (crushes, crushing, crushed) **VERB** If you **crush** something, you press it very hard so that it breaks or loses its shape. ❑ *Andrew crushed his empty can.* ❑ *The drinks were full of crushed ice.*

crust /krʌst/ (crusts)

1 **NOUN** The **crust** on a loaf of bread is the hard outer part. ❑ *Cut the crusts off the bread.*

2 **NOUN** The Earth's **crust** is its outer layer. ❑ *Earthquakes damage the Earth's crust.*

crutch /krʌtʃ/ (crutches) **NOUN** A **crutch** is a long stick that you use to support yourself when you walk. ❑ *I can walk without crutches now.*

cry /kraɪ/ (cries, crying, cried)

1 **VERB** When you **cry**, tears come from your eyes. ❑ *I hung up the phone and started to cry.*

2 **VERB** If you **cry** something, you say it very loudly. ❑ *"Nancy Drew," she cried, "you're under arrest!"*

3 **Cry out** means the same as **cry**. ❑ *"You're wrong, you're all wrong!" Henry cried out.*

4 **NOUN** A **cry** is a loud, high sound that you make when you feel a strong emotion. ❑ *She saw the spider and let out a cry of horror.*

5 **NOUN** A bird's or an animal's **cry** is the loud, high sound that it makes. ❑ *The cry of a strange bird sounded like a whistle.*

→ look at **feeling**

crys|tal /krɪstəl/ (crystals)

1 **NOUN** A **crystal** is a small, hard piece of a natural substance such as salt or ice. ❑ *...salt crystals.* ❑ *...ice crystals.*

2 **NONCOUNT NOUN** SCIENCE **Crystal** is a transparent rock used in jewelry. ❑ *Liza wore a crystal necklace at her wedding.*

3 **NONCOUNT NOUN** **Crystal** is high-quality glass. ❑ *Their drinking glasses were made from crystal.*

cub /kʌb/ (cubs) **NOUN** A **cub** is a young wild animal such as a bear. ❑ *...young lion cubs.*

cube /kyub/ (cubes) **NOUN** MATH A **cube** is a solid object with six square surfaces. ❑ *She took a tray of ice cubes from the freezer.* ❑ *He dropped two sugar cubes into his coffee.*

cu|bic /kyubɪk/ **ADJECTIVE** MATH You use **cubic** to talk about units of volume. ❑ *They moved 3 billion cubic meters of earth.*

cuckoo /kuku, kuku/ (cuckoos) **NOUN** A **cuckoo** is a bird that has a call that sounds like "cuck-oo", and lays its eggs in other birds' nests.

cu|cum|ber /kyukʌmbər/ (cucumbers) **NOUN** A **cucumber** is a long dark-green vegetable that you eat raw. ❑ *We had cheese and cucumber sandwiches for lunch.*

→ look at **vegetable**

cud|dle /kʌdəl/ (cuddles, cuddling, cuddled)

1 **VERB** If you **cuddle** someone, you put your arms around them and hold them close. ❑ *Everybody wanted to cuddle the baby.*

2 **NOUN** Cuddle is also a noun. ❑ *I just wanted to give him a cuddle.*

cud|dly /kʌdli/ (cuddlier, cuddliest) **ADJECTIVE** A **cuddly** person or animal looks soft and pleasant, and makes you want to put your arms around them. ❑ *...a big, cuddly teddy bear.*

cue /kyu/ (cues)

1 **NOUN** A **cue** is an action or a statement that tells someone that they should do something. ❑ *The church bell struck eleven. That was my cue to leave.*

2 NOUN A **cue** is a long, thin wooden stick that you use to hit the ball across the table in some games.

cuff /kʌf/ (**cuffs**)

1 NOUN The **cuffs** of a shirt are the ends of the sleeves. ❑ *He was wearing a blue shirt with a white collar and white cuffs.*

2 NOUN The **cuffs** on a pair of pants are the ends of the legs that are folded up.

cul|ti|vate /kʌltɪveɪt/ (**cultivates, cultivating, cultivated**) **VERB** If you **cultivate** land, you grow plants on it. ❑ *She cultivated a small garden of her own.*

cul|tur|al /kʌltʃərəl/ **ADJECTIVE Cultural** means relating to the arts. ❑ *We've organized a range of sports and cultural events.*

cul|ture /kʌltʃər/ (**cultures**)

1 NONCOUNT NOUN ARTS **Culture** is activities such as art, music, literature, and theater. ❑ *Movies are part of our popular culture.*

2 NOUN SOCIAL STUDIES A **culture** is the way of life, the traditions and beliefs of a particular group of people. ❑ *I live in the city among people from different cultures.*

→ look at **history**

cun|ning /kʌnɪŋ/ **ADJECTIVE** A **cunning** person is clever and possibly dishonest. ❑ *Police described the man as cunning and dangerous.*

cup /kʌp/ (**cups**)

1 NOUN A **cup** is a small round container that you drink from. ❑ *Let's have a cup of coffee.*

2 NOUN A **cup** is a measure of 16 tablespoons or 8 fluid ounces. ❑ *Gradually add 1 cup of milk.* ❑ *Add half a cup of sugar, and mix.*

3 NOUN A **cup** is a large round metal container that is given as a prize to the winner of a competition. ❑ *I think New Zealand will win the cup.*

4 NOUN Cup is used in the names of some competitions that have a cup as a prize. ❑ *...the Ryder Cup.*

cup|board /kʌbərd/ (**cupboards**) **NOUN** A **cupboard** is a piece of furniture with doors, and shelves for storing food or dishes. ❑ *The kitchen cupboard was full of cans of soup.*

cup|cake /kʌpkeɪk/ (**cupcakes**) **NOUN** Cupcakes are small cakes for one person.

cu|pid /kyupɪd/ Someone who **is playing cupid** is trying to bring two people together to start a romantic relationship.

curb /kɜrb/ (**curbs**) **NOUN** The **curb** is the edge of a sidewalk next to the road. ❑ *I pulled over to the curb.*

cure /kyʊər/ (**cures, curing, cured**)

1 VERB If a doctor or a treatment **cures** someone or their illness, the person becomes well again. ❑ *The new medicine cured her headaches.* ❑ *Almost overnight I was cured.*

2 NOUN A **cure for** an illness is a treatment that makes the person well again. ❑ *There is still no cure for a cold.*

→ look at **health care**

cu|ri|os|ity /kyʊərɪɒsɪti/ **NONCOUNT NOUN Curiosity** is a desire to know about something. ❑ *The children show a lot of curiosity about the past.*

cu|ri|ous /kyʊəriəs/ **ADJECTIVE** If you are **curious about** something, you want to know more about it. ❑ *Steve was curious about the place I came from.* ● **cu|ri|ous|ly ADVERB** ❑ *The woman in the shop looked at them curiously.*

curl /kɜrl/ (**curls, curling, curled**)

1 NOUN If you have **curls**, your hair is shaped in curves. ❑ *She was talking to a little girl with blonde curls.*

2 VERB If your hair **curls**, it forms curved shapes. ❑ *Her hair curled around her shoulders.* ❑ *Maria curled her hair for the party.*

▶ **curl up** If you **curl up**, you move your head, arms, and legs close to your body. ❑ *She curled up next to him.*

curly /kɜrli/ (**curlier, curliest**) **ADJECTIVE Curly** hair is shaped in curves. ❑ *I've got naturally curly hair.*

→ look at **hair**

cur|ren|cy /kɜrənsi/ (**currencies**) **NOUN** SOCIAL STUDIES The money that is used in a particular country is its **currency**. ❑ *The plans were for a single European currency.*

cur|rent /kɜrənt/ (**currents**)

1 NOUN SCIENCE A **current** is a steady flow of water, air, or energy. ❑ *The fish move with the ocean currents.* ❑ *I felt a current of cool air.* ❑ *The wires carry a powerful electric current.*

2 ADJECTIVE Current events are happening now. ❑ *The current situation is different than the one in 1990.* ● **cur|rent|ly ADVERB** ❑ *He is currently unmarried.*

→ look at **ocean**

cur|ricu|lum /kərɪkyələm/ (**curriculums** or **curricula** /kərɪkyələ/) **NOUN** A **curriculum** is all the courses of study that are taught in a school or a college. ❏ *Business skills should be part of the school curriculum.*

cur|ry /kɜri/ **NONCOUNT NOUN Curry** is a dish, originally from Asia, that is cooked with hot spices. ❏ *Our favorite dish is the vegetable curry.*

curse /kɜrs/ (**curses, cursing, cursed**)
1 **VERB** If you **curse**, you use very rude or offensive language. [FORMAL] ❏ *Jake nodded, but he was cursing silently.*
2 **NOUN Curse** is also a noun. ❏ *Shouts and curses came from all directions.*
3 **NOUN** A **curse** is a strange power that seems to cause unpleasant things to happen to someone. ❏ *He believed that an evil spirit put a curse on his business.*

cur|sor /kɜrsər/ (**cursors**) **NOUN** TECHNOLOGY On a computer screen, the **cursor** is a small line that shows where you are working. ❏ *He moved the cursor and clicked the mouse.*

cur|tain /kɜrtᵊn/ (**curtains**)
1 **NOUN Curtains** are pieces of material that hang from the top of a window. ❏ *She closed her bedroom curtains.*
2 **NOUN** In a theater, **the curtain** is the large piece of material that hangs at the front of the stage until a performance begins. ❏ *The curtain fell, and the audience stood and applauded.*
→ look at **bathroom, furniture**

curve /kɜrv/ (**curves, curving, curved**)
1 **NOUN** A **curve** is a smooth, bent line. ❏ *She carefully drew the curve of his lips.*
2 **VERB** If something **curves**, it has the shape of a curve or moves in a curve. ❏ *Her spine curved forward.* ❏ *The ball curved through the air.* ● **curved ADJECTIVE** ❏ *...curved lines.*

cush|ion /kuʃᵊn/ (**cushions**) **NOUN** A **cushion** is a bag of soft material that you put on a seat to make it more comfortable. ❏ *The cat lay on a velvet cushion.*

cus|tard /kʌstərd/ **NONCOUNT NOUN Custard** is a sweet yellow dish made of milk, eggs, and sugar. ❏ *We had frozen custard for dessert.*

cus|to|dian /kʌstoʊdiən/ (**custodians**) **NOUN** The **custodian** of an office or a school is the person whose job is to take care of the building and the ground around it. ❏ *He worked as a school custodian for 20 years.*

cus|tom /kʌstəm/ (**customs**) **NOUN** A **custom** is something that is usual or

traditional among a particular group of people. ❏ *This is an ancient Japanese custom.* ❏ *It was the custom to give presents.*

cus|tom|er /kʌstəmər/ (**customers**) **NOUN** A **customer** is someone who buys something. ❏ *I was a very satisfied customer.*
→ look at **restaurant, shopping**

cus|toms /kʌstəmz/ **NONCOUNT NOUN Customs** is the place at an airport, for example, where people have to show certain goods that they have bought abroad. ❏ *He walked through customs.*

cut /kʌt/ (**cuts, cutting, cut**)
1 **VERB** If you **cut** something, you use something sharp to remove part of it, or to break it. ❏ *Mrs. Haines cut the ribbon.* ❏ *Cut the tomatoes in half.* ❏ *You had your hair cut, it looks great.*
2 **NOUN Cut** is also a noun. ❏ *Carefully make a cut in the fabric.*
3 **VERB** If you **cut yourself**, you accidentally injure yourself on a sharp object so that you bleed. ❏ *I started to cry because I cut my finger.*
4 **NOUN Cut** is also a noun. ❏ *He had a cut on his left eyebrow.*
5 **VERB** If you **cut** something, you reduce it. ❏ *We need to cut costs.*
6 **NOUN Cut** is also a noun. ❏ *The government announced a 2% cut in interest rates.*
▶ **cut down 1** If you **cut down on** something, you use or do less of it. ❏ *He cut down on coffee.*
2 If you **cut down** a tree, you cut through it so that it falls to the ground. ❏ *They cut down several trees.*
▶ **cut off** If you **cut** something **off**, you remove it using scissors or a knife. ❏ *Mrs. Johnson cut off a large piece of meat.*
▶ **cut out** If you **cut** something **out**, you remove it using scissors or a knife. ❏ *I cut the picture out and stuck it on my wall.*
▶ **cut up** If you **cut** something **up**, you cut it into several pieces. ❏ *Cut up the tomatoes.*

cut and paste (**cuts and pastes, cutting and pasting, cut and pasted**) **VERB** TECHNOLOGY When you **cut and paste** words or pictures on a computer, you remove them from one place and copy them to another place. ❏ *You can cut and paste words, phrases, sentences, or even paragraphs from one part of your document to another.*

cute /kyut/ (**cuter, cutest**) **ADJECTIVE** A **cute** person or thing is pretty or attractive.

C

[INFORMAL] ❏ *Oh, look at that dog! He's so cute.* ❏ *I thought that girl was really cute.*

cut|lery /kʌtləri/ **NONCOUNT NOUN** Cutlery is knives, forks, and spoons. ❏ *We had to eat our breakfast with plastic cutlery.*

cy|ber|space /saɪbərspeɪs/ **NONCOUNT NOUN** TECHNOLOGY Cyberspace is the imaginary place where electronic communications take place. ❏ *Our cyberspace communications started in an Internet chat room.*

cy|cle /saɪkᵊl/ (cycles, cycling, cycled)
1 NOUN SCIENCE A **cycle** is a process that is repeated again and again. ❏ *We are studying the life cycle of the plant.*
2 VERB SPORTS If you **cycle**, you ride a bicycle. ❏ *He cycles to school every day.*
● **cy|cling** NONCOUNT NOUN ❏ *The quiet country roads are ideal for cycling.*

cy|clist /saɪklɪst/ (cyclists) **NOUN** SPORTS A **cyclist** is someone who rides a bicycle. ❏ *We must have better protection for cyclists.*

cyl|in|der /sɪlɪndər/ (cylinders) **NOUN** MATH A **cylinder** is a shape or a container with circular ends and long straight sides. ❏ *Never store or change gas cylinders near a flame.*

cym|bal /sɪmbᵊl/ (cymbals) **NOUN** MUSIC A **cymbal** is a flat, round, metal musical instrument that makes a loud noise when you hit it, or when you hit two of them together.

cyni|cal /sɪnɪkᵊl/ **ADJECTIVE** A **cynical** person believes that people are usually bad or dishonest. ❏ *He has a cynical view of the world.* ● **cyni|cal|ly** ADVERB ❏ *He laughed cynically.*

C

Dd

dad /dæd/ (dads) **NOUN** Your **dad** is your father. [INFORMAL] ❑ *Don't tell my mom and dad about this!*

dad|dy /dædi/ (daddies) **NOUN** Children often call their father **daddy**. [INFORMAL] ❑ *Look at me, Daddy!* ❑ *My daddy always reads me stories and helps me with my homework.*

daf|fo|dil /dæfədɪl/ (daffodils) **NOUN** A **daffodil** is a yellow flower with a long stem that appears in spring.

dai|ly /deɪli/
1 **ADVERB** Something that happens **daily**, happens every day. ❑ *The students use this dictionary almost daily.*
2 **ADJECTIVE** **Daily** is also an adjective. ❑ *The French daily newspaper "Le Monde" was first to report the story.*
→ look at **day, news**

dain|ty /deɪnti/ (daintier, daintiest) **ADJECTIVE** A **dainty** movement, person, or object is small, delicate, and pretty. ❑ *Did she walk here in her dainty little shoes?.* ● **dain|ti|ly** **ADVERB** ❑ *She walked daintily down the steps.*

dairy /dɛəri/ (dairies)
1 **NOUN** A **dairy** is a place where milk, and food made from milk, such as butter, cream, and cheese are produced.
2 **ADJECTIVE** **Dairy** is used for talking about foods such as butter and cheese that are made from milk. ❑ *He can't eat dairy products.*

dai|sy /deɪzi/ (daisies) **NOUN** A **daisy** is a small wild flower with a yellow center and white petals.

dam /dæm/ (dams) **NOUN** A **dam** is a wall that is built across a river in order to make a lake. ❑ *Before the dam was built, the Campbell River often flooded.*

dam|age /dæmɪdʒ/ (damages, damaging, damaged)
1 **VERB** To **damage** something means to break it or harm it. ❑ *He damaged a car with a baseball bat.* ❑ *The new tax will badly damage Australian industries.* ● **dam|ag|ing** **ADJECTIVE** ❑ *We can see the damaging effects of pollution in cities.*
2 **NONCOUNT NOUN** **Damage** is physical harm that happens to an object. ❑ *The explosion caused a lot of damage to the house.*

damp /dæmp/ (damper, dampest) **ADJECTIVE** Something that is **damp** is slightly wet. ❑ *Her hair was still damp.* ❑ *We went out into the damp, cold air.*
→ look at **climate**

dance /dæns/ (dances, dancing, danced)
1 **VERB** ARTS When you **dance**, you move your body to music. ❑ *She turned on the radio and danced around the room.* ❑ *Shall we dance?* ● **danc|ing** **NONCOUNT NOUN** ❑ *Let's go dancing tonight.*
2 **NOUN** A **dance** is a particular series of movements that you usually do in time to music. ❑ *...a traditional Scottish dance.*
3 **NOUN** A **dance** is a party where people dance with each other. ❑ *At the school dance he talked to her all evening.*

Word Partners	Use **dance** with:
v.	let's dance **1** **2**
	choreograph a dance, **learn to** dance **2**
N.	dance **class**, dance **moves**, dance **music**, dance **partner** **2**

danc|er /dænsər/ (dancers) **NOUN** ARTS A **dancer** is a person who earns money by dancing, or a person who is dancing. ❑ *She's a dancer with the New York City Ballet.*
→ look at **performance**

dan|de|lion /dændɪlaɪən/ (dandelions) **NOUN** A **dandelion** is a wild plant with yellow flowers that turn into balls of soft white seeds.

dan|ger /deɪndʒər/ (dangers)
1 **NONCOUNT NOUN** If you are **in danger**, it is possible that something unpleasant will happen, or that you may be harmed or killed. ❑ *I'm worried. I think Mary's in danger.*

D

2 NOUN A **danger** is something or someone that can hurt or harm you. ❑ *They warned us about the dangers of driving too fast.*

dan|ger|ous /deɪndʒərəs, deɪndʒrəs/
ADJECTIVE If something is **dangerous**, it may harm you. ❑ *We are in a very dangerous situation.* ❑ *He owns a dangerous dog.* ● **dan|ger|ous|ly ADVERB** ❑ *He is dangerously ill.*
→ look at **greenhouse effect, pollution**

dare /dɛər/ (**dares, daring, dared**)
1 VERB If you **dare to** do something, you are brave enough to do it. ❑ *Most people don't dare to disagree with Harry.*
2 MODAL VERB **Dare** is also a modal verb. ❑ *She dare not leave the house.*
3 VERB If you **dare** someone **to** do something, you ask them if they will do it in order to see if they are brave enough. ❑ *His friends dared him to ask Mr. Roberts for the money.*
4 You say "**how dare you**" to someone when you are very angry about something that they have done. ❑ *How dare you say that about my mother!*

dar|ing /dɛərɪŋ/ **ADJECTIVE** A **daring** person is willing to do things that might be dangerous or shocking. ❑ *He made a daring escape from the island in a small boat.*

dark /dɑrk/ (**darker, darkest**)
1 ADJECTIVE When it is **dark**, there is not much light. ❑ *It was too dark to see much.*
● **dark|ness NONCOUNT NOUN** ❑ *The light went out, and we were in total darkness.* ● **dark|ly ADVERB** ❑ *...a darkly lit hall.*
2 ADJECTIVE When it gets **dark**, night comes. ❑ *People shut the curtains when it gets dark.*
3 ADJECTIVE Something **dark** is black or a color close to black. ❑ *He wore a dark suit.* ❑ *...a dark blue dress.* ● **dark|ly ADVERB** ❑ *His skin was darkly tanned.*
4 ADJECTIVE If someone has **dark** hair, eyes, or skin, they have brown or black hair, eyes, or skin. ❑ *He had dark, curly hair.*
5 NOUN The **dark** is the lack of light in a place. ❑ *Children are often afraid of the dark.*

dar|ling /dɑrlɪŋ/ (**darlings**)
1 NOUN You call someone **darling** if you love them or like them very much. ❑ *Thank you, darling.*
2 ADJECTIVE **Darling** describes someone or something that you like very much. [INFORMAL] ❑ *They have a darling baby boy.*

dart /dɑrt/ (**darts, darting, darted**)
1 VERB If a person or animal **darts** somewhere, they move there suddenly and quickly. ❑ *Ingrid darted across the street.*
2 NOUN A **dart** is a small, narrow object with a sharp point that you can throw or shoot.
3 NONCOUNT NOUN SPORTS **Darts** is a game in which you throw darts (= small pointed objects) at a round board that has numbers on it. ❑ *I enjoy playing darts.*

dash /dæʃ/ (**dashes, dashing, dashed**)
1 VERB If you **dash** somewhere, you go there quickly and suddenly. ❑ *She dashed downstairs when the doorbell rang.*
2 NOUN If you **make** a **dash** for a place, you go there quickly and suddenly. ❑ *She screamed and made a dash for the door.*
3 NOUN LANGUAGE ARTS A **dash** is a short, straight, horizontal line that you use in writing. ❑ *Sometimes people use a dash (—) where they could use a colon (:).*

dash|board /dæʃbɔrd/ (**dashboards**) **NOUN** The **dashboard** in a car is the area in front of the driver where most of the controls are. ❑ *The clock on the dashboard showed two o'clock.*

da|ta /deɪtə, dætə/
1 PLURAL NOUN You can talk about information as **data**, especially when it is in the form of facts or numbers. ❑ *Government data shows that unemployment is going up.*
2 NONCOUNT NOUN TECHNOLOGY **Data** is information that can be used by a computer program. ❑ *A CD-ROM can hold huge amounts of data.*

data|base /deɪtəbeɪs, dætə-/ (**databases**) also **data base NOUN** TECHNOLOGY A **database** is a collection of data that is stored in a computer and that can easily be used and added to. ❑ *There is a database of names of people who are allowed to vote.*

date /deɪt/ (**dates, dating, dated**)
1 NOUN A **date** is a particular day and month or a particular year. ❑ *"What's the date today?" "July 23."*
2 NOUN A **date** is an arrangement to meet a boyfriend or a girlfriend. ❑ *I have a date with Bob tonight.*
3 VERB If you **are dating** someone, you go out with them regularly because you are having a romantic relationship with them. ❑ *I dated a woman who was a teacher.*
4 NOUN A **date** is a small, dark-brown,

sticky fruit with a stone inside.
→ look at **calendar**

daugh|ter /dɔtər/ (**daughters**) NOUN
Someone's **daughter** is their female child. ❏ We met Flora and her daughter Catherine. ❏ She's the daughter of a university professor.

daughter-in-law (**daughters-in-law**) NOUN
Someone's **daughter-in-law** is the wife of their son.

dawn /dɔn/ (**dawns**) NOUN Dawn is the time of day when the sky becomes light in the morning. ❏ Nancy woke at dawn.

day /deɪ/ (**days**)
1 NOUN A **day** is one period of twenty-four hours. There are seven days in a week. ❏ They'll be back in three days. ❏ It snowed every day last week.
2 NOUN The **day** is the time when it is light outside. ❏ We spent the day watching tennis. ❏ The streets are busy during the day.
3 One **day** or **some day** means at some time in the future. ❏ I dream of living in Dallas some day. ❏ I hope one day you will find someone who will make you happy.
→ look at Word World: **day**
→ look at **calendar**

day|dream /deɪdrim/ (**daydreams, daydreaming, daydreamed**)
1 VERB If you **daydream**, you think about pleasant things for a period of time. ❏ I was daydreaming about a job in France.
2 NOUN A **daydream** is a series of pleasant thoughts, usually about things that you would like to happen. ❏ She was looking out the window in a daydream.
→ look at **relax**

day|light /deɪlaɪt/ NONCOUNT NOUN
Daylight is the natural light that there is during the day. ❏ A little daylight came through a crack in the wall.

day|time /deɪtaɪm/ NOUN The **daytime** is the part of a day between the time when it gets light and the time when it gets dark. ❏ He rarely went anywhere in the daytime; he was always out at night.

dead /dɛd/
1 ADJECTIVE A person, animal, or plant that is **dead** has stopped living. ❏ She told me her husband was dead. ❏ They put the dead body into the ambulance.
2 PLURAL NOUN The **dead** are people who have died. ❏ Two soldiers were among the dead.
3 ADJECTIVE A piece of electrical equipment that is **dead** has stopped working. ❏ I answered the phone and the line went dead.

dead|line /dɛdlaɪn/ (**deadlines**) NOUN
A **deadline** is a time or date before which a piece of work must be finished. ❏ We missed the deadline because of several problems.

dead|ly /dɛdli/ (**deadlier, deadliest**)
ADJECTIVE If something is **deadly**, it can kill a person or animal. ❏ This disease killed 70 people in Malaysia last year.

deaf /dɛf/ (**deafer, deafest**)
1 ADJECTIVE Someone who is **deaf** is unable to hear anything, or is unable to hear very well. ❏ She is now totally deaf.
2 PLURAL NOUN The **deaf** are people who are deaf. ❏ Marianne works as a part-time teacher for the deaf.
→ look at **disability**

deaf|en /dɛfən/ (**deafens, deafening, deafened**) VERB If a noise **deafens** you, it is so loud that you cannot hear anything else. ❏ The noise of the engine deafened her.

deaf|en|ing /dɛfənɪŋ/ ADJECTIVE A **deafening** noise is a very loud noise. ❏ All we could hear was the deafening sound of gunfire.

deal /dil/ (**deals, dealing, dealt**)
1 NOUN If you **make** a **deal**, you make an

d

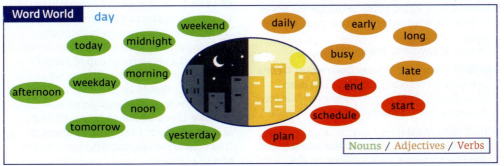

agreement with someone, especially in business. ❑ *They made a deal to share the money between them.*

2 **VERB** If a company **deals in** a type of goods, it buys or sells those goods. ❑ *They deal in antiques.* ●**deal|er** (**dealers**) **NOUN** ❑ *...an antique dealer.*

3 **VERB** If you **deal** playing cards, you give them out to the players in a game of cards. ❑ *She dealt each player a card.*

4 **Deal out** means the same as **deal**. ❑ *Dalton dealt out five cards to each player.*

5 If you have **a great deal of** a particular thing, you have a lot of it. ❑ *You can earn a great deal of money in this job.*

▸ **deal with** When you **deal with** something or someone, you give your attention to them. ❑ *Could you deal with this customer, please?*

Sound Partners	dear, deer

dear /dɪər/ (**dearer, dearest**)

1 **ADJECTIVE** **Dear** describes someone that you love. ❑ *Mrs. Cavendish is a dear friend of mine.*

2 **ADJECTIVE** You write **Dear** at the beginning of a letter or an email, followed by the name of the person you are writing to. ❑ *Dear Peter, How are you?* ❑ *Dear Sir or Madam...*

death /dɛθ/ (**deaths**) **NOUN** **Death** is the end of the life of a person or animal. ❑ *1.5 million people are in danger of death from hunger.* ❑ *It's the thirtieth anniversary of her death.*

de|bate /dɪbeɪt/ (**debates, debating, debated**)

1 **NOUN** A **debate** is a long discussion or argument. ❑ *The debate will continue until they vote on Thursday.* ❑ *There has been a lot of debate among teachers about this subject.*

2 **VERB** If people **debate** a topic, they discuss it. ❑ *The committee will debate the issue today.* ❑ *They were debating which team would win.*

deb|it card /dɛbɪt kɑrd/ (**debit cards**) **NOUN** A **debit card** is a bank card that you can use to pay for things.

→ look at **payment, shopping**

de|bris /dəbri, deɪ-/ **NONCOUNT NOUN** **Debris** is pieces from something that has been destroyed. ❑ *Debris from the plane was found over an area the size of a soccer field.*

debt /dɛt/ (**debts**)

1 **NOUN** A **debt** is an amount of money that you owe someone. ❑ *He is still paying off his debts.*

2 If you are **in debt**, or if you get **into debt**, you owe money. ❑ *Many students get into debt.*

dec|ade /dɛkeɪd/ (**decades**) **NOUN** A **decade** is a period of ten years. ❑ *She spent a decade studying in San Francisco.*

de|cay /dɪkeɪ/ (**decays, decaying, decayed**)

1 **VERB** When something **decays**, it is gradually destroyed by a natural process. ❑ *The bodies slowly decayed.*

2 **NONCOUNT NOUN** **Decay** is also a noun. ❑ *Eating too much candy causes tooth decay.*

de|ceive /dɪsiv/ (**deceives, deceiving, deceived**) **VERB** If you **deceive** someone, you make them believe something that is not true. ❑ *She accused the government of trying to deceive the public.*

De|cem|ber /dɪsɛmbər/ **NOUN** **December** is the twelfth and last month of the year. ❑ *I arrived on a bright morning in December.*

de|cent /disənt/

1 **ADJECTIVE** **Decent** describes something that is acceptable or good enough. ❑ *He didn't get a decent explanation.* ●**de|cent|ly** **ADVERB** ❑ *They treated their prisoners decently.*

2 **ADJECTIVE** **Decent** describes something that is morally right or polite. ❑ *It was very decent of him to call and explain.*

de|cep|tion /dɪsɛpʃən/ **NONCOUNT NOUN** **Deception** is when someone deliberately makes you believe something that is not true. ❑ *Lies and deception are not a good way to start a marriage.*

de|cep|tive /dɪsɛptɪv/ **ADJECTIVE** If something is **deceptive**, it makes you believe something that is not true. ❑ *The ocean looked warm, but appearances can be deceptive.* ●**de|cep|tive|ly** **ADVERB** ❑ *The atmosphere in the hall was deceptively peaceful.*

de|cide /dɪsaɪd/ (**decides, deciding, decided**)

1 **VERB** If you **decide** to do something, you choose to do it after thinking about it. ❑ *She decided to take a course in philosophy.* ❑ *Think about it very carefully before you decide.*

2 **VERB** If a person or group of people **decides** something, they choose what something should be like. ❑ *Schools need to decide the best way of testing students.*

3 **VERB** If you **decide** that something is true, you form that opinion about it. ❑ *He decided Franklin was suffering from a bad cold.*

deci|mal /dɛsɪməl/ (decimals)

1 **NOUN** MATH A **decimal** is part of a number that is written in the form of a dot followed by one or more numbers. ❑ *The interest rate is shown as a decimal, such as 0.10, which means 10%.*

2 **ADJECTIVE** MATH A **decimal** system involves counting in units of ten. ❑ *The mathematics of ancient Egypt used a decimal system.*
→ look at **fraction**

deci|mal point (decimal points) **NOUN** MATH A **decimal point** is the dot that you use when you write a number as a decimal. ❑ *A waiter forgot to put the decimal point in the $13.09 bill.*
→ look at **math**

de|ci|sion /dɪsɪʒən/ (decisions) **NOUN** When you make a **decision**, you choose what to do. ❑ *I don't want to make the wrong decision and regret it later.*

Word Partners	Use **decision** with:
ADJ.	**difficult** decision, **important** decision, **right** decision, **wise** decision, **wrong** decision
V.	**make a** decision, **reach a** decision

Spelling Partners deck

deck /dɛk/ (decks)

1 **NOUN** A **deck** on a vehicle such as a bus or ship is a lower or upper level in it. ❑ *We went on a luxury ship with five passenger decks.*

2 **NOUN** A **deck** is a flat wooden area attached to a house, where people can sit. ❑ *A deck leads into the main room of the home.*

3 **NOUN** A **deck** of cards is a complete set of playing cards. ❑ *Matt picked up the cards and shuffled the deck.*

dec|la|ra|tion /dɛkləreɪʃən/ (declarations) **NOUN** A **declaration** is something that is said officially. ❑ *We consider these attacks to be a declaration of war.*

Dec|la|ra|tion of In|de|pend|ence **NOUN** SOCIAL STUDIES The **Declaration of Independence** is the official document of July 4, 1776, that stated that thirteen American colonies (= areas where British people went to live) were no longer ruled by Great Britain.

de|clare /dɪklɛər/ (declares, declaring, declared)

1 **VERB** If you **declare** that something is true, you say that it is true in a firm, clear way. ❑ *Melinda declared that she was leaving home.*

2 **VERB** If you **declare** something, you officially state that it is the case. ❑ *The president finally declared an end to the war.* ❑ *The judges declared Mr. Stevens innocent.*

3 **VERB** If you **declare** goods that you have bought in another country, you say how much you have bought so that you can pay tax on it. ❑ *Please declare all food, plants and animal products.*

de|cline /dɪklaɪn/ (declines, declining, declined)

1 **VERB** If something **declines**, it becomes less in amount, importance, or strength. ❑ *The local population is declining.*

2 **VERB** If you **decline** something, you politely refuse to accept it. [FORMAL] ❑ *He declined their invitation.*

de|cor /deɪkɔr/ **NONCOUNT NOUN** The **decor** of a house or room is the style of its furniture and the way it is decorated. ❑ *The decor is simple—white walls.*

deco|rate /dɛkəreɪt/ (decorates, decorating, decorated)

1 **VERB** If you **decorate** something, you make it more attractive by adding things to it. ❑ *He decorated his room with pictures of sports stars.*

2 **VERB** If you **decorate** a room or the inside of a building, you put new paint or paper on the walls and the ceiling. ❑ *They were decorating Jemma's bedroom.* ● **deco|rat|ing** **NONCOUNT NOUN** ❑ *I did a lot of the decorating myself.*

deco|ra|tion /dɛkəreɪʃən/ (decorations)

1 **NOUN** **Decorations** are things that are used for making something look more attractive. ❑ *Colorful paper decorations were hanging from the ceiling.*

2 **NONCOUNT NOUN** The **decoration** of a room is its furniture and the paint or paper on the walls. ❑ *The decoration was practical for a family home.*

deco|ra|tive /dɛkərətɪv, -əreɪtɪv/ **ADJECTIVE** Something **decorative** is intended to look pretty or attractive. ❑ *The drapes are only decorative – they do not open or close.*

d

D

de|crease (decreases, decreasing, decreased)

> **PRONUNCIATION HELP**
> Pronounce the verb /dɪkriːs/. Pronounce
> the noun /dɪkriːs/ or /dɪkriːs/.

1 **VERB** When something **decreases**, it
becomes less in amount, size, or strength.
❑ *The average price decreased from $134,000 to
$126,000.* ❑ *Property may start to decrease in value.*
2 **NOUN** A **decrease in** the amount, size, or
strength of something is when it becomes
less. ❑ *There has been a decrease in the number of
people without a job.*

dedi|cate /dɛdɪkeɪt/ (dedicates, dedicating,
dedicated) **VERB** If someone **dedicates** a
book, a play, or a piece of music **to** you, they
say on the first page that they have written
it for you. ❑ *She dedicated her first book to her
sons.* ● **dedi|ca|tion** (dedications) **NOUN**
❑ *I read the dedication at the beginning of the book.*

de|duct /dɪdʌkt/ (deducts, deducting,
deducted) **VERB** When you **deduct** an
amount from a total, you make the total
smaller by that amount. ❑ *The company
deducted the money from his wages.*

deed /diːd/ (deeds) **NOUN** A **deed** is
something that is done, especially something
that is very good or very bad. ❑ *The people who
did this evil deed must be punished.*

deep /diːp/ (deeper, deepest)
1 **ADJECTIVE** If something is **deep**, it goes
down a long way. ❑ *The water is very deep.*
❑ *The kids dug a deep hole in the center of the garden.*
2 **ADVERB** Deep is also an adverb. ❑ *She put
her hands deep into her pockets.*
3 **ADJECTIVE** You use **deep** to emphasize
the seriousness or strength of something.
❑ *He expressed his deep sympathy to the family.*
● **deep|ly** **ADVERB** ❑ *He loved his brother deeply.*
4 **ADJECTIVE** A **deep** sound is low and
usually strong. ❑ *He spoke in a deep, warm voice.*
5 **ADJECTIVE** Deep describes colors that are
strong and dark. ❑ *The sky was deep blue and
starry.*
6 **ADJECTIVE** If you are in a **deep** sleep, it is
difficult for someone to wake you. ❑ *Una fell
into a deep sleep.* ● **deep|ly** **ADVERB** ❑ *She slept
deeply, but woke early.*
7 **ADJECTIVE** A **deep** breath fills the whole of
your lungs. ❑ *Cal took a long, deep breath, as he
tried to control his emotions.* ● **deep|ly** **ADVERB**
❑ *She sighed deeply.*
→ look at **ocean**

deep|en /diːpən/ (deepens, deepening,
deepened) **VERB** If a situation or emotion
deepens, it becomes stronger. ❑ *These
friendships will probably deepen in your teenage years.*

> **Sound Partners** deer, dear

deer /dɪər/ (deer) **NOUN** A **deer** is a large
wild animal that eats grass and leaves. A
male deer usually has large horns that are
like branches.

de|fault /dɪfɔːlt/ **NONCOUNT NOUN** The
default is the way that something will be
done if you do not give any other
instruction. ❑ *The default setting on the printer is
for color.*

de|feat /dɪfiːt/ (defeats, defeating, defeated)
1 **VERB** If you **defeat** someone, you beat
them in a battle, a game, or a competition.
❑ *They defeated the French army in 1954.*
2 **NOUN** Defeat is the experience of being
beaten in a battle, a game, or a competition.
❑ *He didn't want to accept defeat.* ❑ *I remember the
team's defeat at Sacramento.*

de|fec|tive /dɪfɛktɪv/ **ADJECTIVE** If
something is **defective**, it does not work
properly. ❑ *We returned the defective equipment.*

de|fend /dɪfɛnd/ (defends, defending,
defended)
1 **VERB** If you **defend** someone or
something, you take action in order to
protect them. ❑ *The army must be able to defend
its own country against attack.*
2 **VERB** **SPORTS** In sports, if you are
defending, you are trying to stop the other
team from getting points.
3 **VERB** If you **defend** a decision, you argue
in support of it. ❑ *The president defended his
decision to go to war.*
4 **VERB** When a lawyer **defends** a person in
a court, they argue that the person is not
guilty of a particular crime. ❑ *He has hired a
lawyer to defend him in court.*

de|fend|er /dɪfɛndər/ (defenders) **NOUN**
SPORTS A **defender** in a game is a player
whose main task is to try and stop the other
side from scoring. ❑ *Lewis was the team's top
defender.*

de|fense /dɪfɛns/

> **LANGUAGE HELP**
> Pronounce **defense** /diːfɛns/ in meaning
> **3**.

1 **NONCOUNT NOUN** Defense is action to protect someone or something against attack. ❏ *The land was flat, which made defense difficult.*

2 **NONCOUNT NOUN** Defense is the organization of a country's armies and weapons, and their use to protect the country. ❏ *Twenty-eight percent of the country's money is spent on defense.* ❏ *...the U.S. Defense Secretary.*

3 **NOUN** SPORTS In games such as soccer or hockey, the **defense** is the group of players in a team who try to stop the opposing players from scoring a goal or a point. ❏ *Their defense was weak and allowed in 12 goals.*

de|fen|sive /dɪfɛnsɪv/ **ADJECTIVE** SPORTS In games such as soccer or hockey, **defensive** describes the way that the players defend the goal. ❏ *The team is known for its strong defensive play.*

de|fi|ant /dɪfaɪənt/ **ADJECTIVE** A **defiant** person refuses to obey someone. ❏ *She stood looking at her father with a defiant expression on her face.* ● **de|fi|ant|ly** **ADVERB** ❏ *They defiantly refused to accept the plan.*

defi|cit /dɛfəsɪt/ (**deficits**) **NOUN** A **deficit** is the amount by which something is less than the amount that is needed. ❏ *The state budget showed a deficit of five billion dollars.*

de|fine /dɪfaɪn/ (**defines, defining, defined**) **VERB** If you **define** something, you say clearly what it is and what it means. ❏ *The government defines a household as "a group of people who live in the same house."*
→ look at **dictionary**

defi|nite /dɛfɪnɪt/
1 **ADJECTIVE** A **definite** decision or arrangement is firm and clear, and will probably not be changed. ❏ *I need a definite answer soon.* ❏ *I want to make some definite plans for the future.*
2 **ADJECTIVE** Definite information is true, rather than being an opinion or a guess. ❏ *We didn't have any definite proof.*

defi|nite ar|ti|cle (**definite articles**) **NOUN** LANGUAGE ARTS The **definite article** is the word "the." ❏ *Placenames often have a definite article, as in "The Alps."*

defi|nite|ly /dɛfɪnɪtli/ **ADVERB** You use **definitely** to show that you are certain about something. ❏ *The extra money will definitely help.*

defi|ni|tion /dɛfɪnɪʃᵊn/ (**definitions**) **NOUN** LANGUAGE ARTS A **definition** gives the meaning of a word or an expression, especially in a dictionary. ❏ *The definition of marriage has changed over time.*
→ look at **dictionary**

de|form /dɪfɔrm/ (**deforms, deforming, deformed**) **VERB** If something **deforms** a person's body, it causes it to have an unnatural shape. ❏ *The disease deforms the arms and the legs.* ● **de|formed** **ADJECTIVE** ❏ *He had a deformed right leg.*

defy /dɪfaɪ/ (**defies, defying, defied**) **VERB** If you **defy** someone or something, you refuse to obey them. ❏ *This was the first time I defied my mother.*

de|gree /dɪgri/ (**degrees**)
1 **NOUN** SCIENCE A **degree** is a unit for measuring temperatures. It is often written as °, for example, 70°. ❏ *It's over 80 degrees outside.*
2 **NOUN** MATH A **degree** is a unit for measuring angles. It is often written as °, for example, 90°. ❏ *It was pointing outward at an angle of 45 degrees.*
3 **NOUN** A **degree** is a qualification that you receive when you have successfully completed a course of study at a college or university. ❏ *He has an engineering degree.*
→ look at **geometry**

de|lay /dɪleɪ/ (**delays, delaying, delayed**)
1 **VERB** If you **delay** doing something, you do not do it immediately or at the planned time, but you leave it until later. ❏ *Many women delay motherhood because they want to have a career.*
2 **VERB** To **delay** someone or something means to make them late. ❏ *Passengers were delayed at the airport for five hours.*
3 **NOUN** If there is a **delay**, something does not happen until later than planned. ❏ *He apologized for the delay.*

del|egate /dɛlɪgɪt/ (**delegates**) **NOUN** SOCIAL STUDIES A **delegate** is a person who represents a group of other people at a meeting, for example. ❏ *About 750 delegates attended the conference.*

de|lete /dɪlit/ (**deletes, deleting, deleted**) **VERB** TECHNOLOGY If you **delete** something that has been written down or stored in a computer, you put a line through it or remove it. ❏ *He deleted files from the computer.*
→ look at **email**

d

de|lib|er|ate /dɪlɪ́bərɪt/ **ADJECTIVE** A **deliberate** action is one that you intended. ❑ *They told deliberate lies in order to sell newspapers.* ● **de|lib|er|ate|ly** **ADVERB** ❑ *He started the fire deliberately.*

deli|cate /dɛ́lɪkɪt/
1 **ADJECTIVE** Something that is **delicate** can break or become damaged easily. ❑ *The machine even washes delicate glassware.* ❑ *Do not rub the delicate skin around the eyes.*
2 **ADJECTIVE** A **delicate** color, taste, or smell is pleasant and light. ❑ *The beans have a delicate flavor.*

deli|ca|tes|sen /dɛ́lɪkətɛ̀sᵊn/ (**delicatessens**) **NOUN** A **delicatessen** is a store that sells food such as cold meats and cheeses.

de|li|cious /dɪlɪ́ʃəs/ **ADJECTIVE** Food that is **delicious** tastes very good. ❑ *There was a wide choice of delicious meals.* ● **de|li|cious|ly** **ADVERB** ❑ *This yogurt has a deliciously creamy flavor.*
→ look at **food**

de|light /dɪláɪt/ **NONCOUNT NOUN** Delight is a feeling of great pleasure. ❑ *He expressed delight at the news.* ❑ *Andrew laughed with delight.*

de|light|ed /dɪláɪtɪd/ **ADJECTIVE** If you are **delighted**, you are extremely pleased about something. ❑ *Frank was delighted to see her.*

de|liv|er /dɪlɪ́vər/ (**delivers, delivering, delivered**) **VERB** If you **deliver** something somewhere, you take it there. ❑ *Only 90% of first-class mail is delivered on time.* ❑ *The Canadians plan to deliver more food to Somalia.*

de|liv|ery /dɪlɪ́vəri/ (**deliveries**)
1 **NONCOUNT NOUN** Delivery is when someone brings letters, packages, or other goods to an arranged place. ❑ *Please allow 28 days for delivery.*
2 **NOUN** A **delivery** of something is the goods that are delivered. ❑ *I got a delivery of fresh eggs this morning.*

de|luxe /dɪlʌ́ks/ **ADJECTIVE** Deluxe goods or services are better and more expensive than ordinary ones. ❑ *She only stays in deluxe hotel suites.*

de|mand /dɪmǽnd/ (**demands, demanding, demanded**)
1 **VERB** If you **demand** information or action, you ask for it in a very firm way. ❑ *The victim's family is demanding an investigation*

into the shooting. ❑ *He demanded that I give him an answer.*
2 **NOUN** A **demand** is a firm request for something. ❑ *There were demands for better services.*
3 If someone or something is **in demand** or **in great demand**, they are very popular and a lot of people want them. ❑ *Math teachers are always in demand.*

de|moc|ra|cy /dɪmɒ́krəsi/ (**democracies**)
1 **NONCOUNT NOUN** SOCIAL STUDIES **Democracy** is a system of government in which people choose their leaders by voting for them in elections. ❑ *We're studying democracy in Eastern Europe.*
2 **NOUN** SOCIAL STUDIES A **democracy** is a country in which the people choose their government by voting for it. ❑ *...the new democracies of Eastern Europe.*
→ look at **vote**

demo|crat /dɛ́məkræt/ (**democrats**)
1 **NOUN** SOCIAL STUDIES A **Democrat** is a supporter of a political party that has the word "democrat" or "democratic" in its title, for example, the Democratic Party in the United States. ❑ *Democrats voted against the plan.*
2 **NOUN** SOCIAL STUDIES A **democrat** is a person who believes in and wants democracy. ❑ *This is the time for democrats and not dictators.*

demo|crat|ic /dɛ̀məkrǽtɪk/
1 **ADJECTIVE** SOCIAL STUDIES A **democratic** country, government, or political system has leaders who are elected by the people that they govern. ❑ *Bolivia returned to democratic rule in 1982.*
2 **ADJECTIVE** SOCIAL STUDIES Something that is **democratic** is based on the idea that everyone has equal rights and should be involved in making important decisions. ❑ *Education is the basis of a democratic society.*
→ look at **vote**

de|mol|ish /dɪmɒ́lɪʃ/ (**demolishes, demolishing, demolished**) **VERB** To demolish a building means to destroy it completely. ❑ *The storm demolished buildings and flooded streets.* ● **demo|li|tion** /dɛ̀məlɪ́ʃᵊn/ **NONCOUNT NOUN** ❑ *The bomb caused the total demolition of the old bridge.*

dem|on|strate /dɛ́mənstreɪt/ (**demonstrates, demonstrating, demonstrated**)

1 **VERB** If you **demonstrate** something, you show people how it works or how to do it. ❏ *Several companies were demonstrating their new products.* ● **dem|on|stra|tion** (**demonstrations**) **NOUN** ❏ *We watched a cooking demonstration.*

2 **VERB** When people **demonstrate**, they march or gather somewhere to show that they oppose or support something. ❏ *200,000 people demonstrated against the war.* ● **dem|on|stra|tion** (**demonstrations**) **NOUN** ❏ *Soldiers broke up an anti-government demonstration.* ● **de|mon|stra|tor** (**demonstrators**) **NOUN** ❏ *Police were dealing with a crowd of demonstrators.*

den /dɛn/ (**dens**)
1 **NOUN** A **den** is the home of some types of wild animal.
2 **NOUN** Your **den** is a quiet room in your house where you can go to study, work, or relax.

de|ni|al /dɪnaɪəl/ (**denials**) **NOUN** A **denial** of something is when you say that it is not true, or that it does not exist. ❏ *There have been many official denials of the government's involvement.*

den|im /dɛnɪm/ **NONCOUNT NOUN** **Denim** is a thick cotton cloth, usually blue, which is used for making clothes. ❏ *...a denim jacket.*

dense /dɛns/ (**denser, densest**)
1 **ADJECTIVE** Something that is **dense** contains a lot of things or people in a small area. ❏ *The road runs through a dense forest.*
● **dense|ly** **ADVERB** ❏ *Java is a densely populated island.*
2 **ADJECTIVE** **Dense** fog (= cloud that is close to the ground) or smoke is very thick. ❏ *The planes came close to each other in dense fog.*
3 **ADJECTIVE** **SCIENCE** In science, a **dense** substance is very heavy for its size. ❏ *Ice is less dense than water, and so it floats.*

den|sity /dɛnsɪti/ (**densities**) **NOUN** **SCIENCE** In science, the **density** of a substance or object is how heavy it is for its size. ❏ *Jupiter's moon Io has a density of 3.5 grams per cubic centimeter.*

dent /dɛnt/ (**dents, denting, dented**)
1 **VERB** If you **dent** the surface of something, you make a hollow area in it by hitting it. ❏ *The stone dented the car's fender.*
2 **NOUN** A **dent** is a hollow in the surface of something that has been hit or pressed too hard. ❏ *There was a dent in the car door.*

den|tal /dɛntᵊl/ **ADJECTIVE** **SCIENCE** **Dental** means relating to teeth. ❏ *Regular dental care is important.*

den|tist /dɛntɪst/ (**dentists**)
1 **NOUN** A **dentist** is a person whose job is to examine and treat people's teeth. ❏ *Visit your dentist twice a year for a checkup.*
2 **NOUN** The **dentist** or the **dentist's** is the place where a dentist works. ❏ *I'm going to the dentist's after school.*

deny /dɪnaɪ/ (**denies, denying, denied**) **VERB** When you **deny** something, you state that it is not true. ❏ *Robby denied stealing the bike.* ❏ *He denied that he was involved in the crime.*

de|odor|ant /dioʊdərənt/ (**deodorants**) **NONCOUNT NOUN** **Deodorant** is a substance that you can put on your skin to hide or prevent bad smells.

de|part /dɪpɑrt/ (**departs, departing, departed**) **VERB** When something or someone **departs**, they leave. ❏ *Flight 43 will depart from Denver at 11:45 a.m.* ❏ *In the morning, Mr. McDonald departed for Sydney.*

de|part|ment /dɪpɑrtmənt/ (**departments**)
1 **NOUN** A **department** is one of the sections in an organization such as a government, a business, or a university. ❏ *She works for the U.S. Department of Health and Human Services.*
2 **NOUN** A **department** is one of the sections in a large store. ❏ *He works in the shoe department.*

de|part|ment store (**department stores**) **NOUN** A **department store** is a large store that sells many different types of goods.
→ look at **shopping**

de|par|ture /dɪpɑrtʃər/ (**departures**) **NOUN** **Departure** is the act of going away from somewhere. ❏ *Illness delayed the president's departure for Helsinki.*

de|par|tures /dɪpɑrtərz/ **NOUN** In an airport, **departures** is the place where passengers wait before they get onto their plane.

de|pend /dɪpɛnd/ (**depends, depending, depended**)
1 **VERB** If one thing **depends on** another, the first thing will be affected by the second thing. ❏ *The cooking time depends on the size of the potato.*
2 **VERB** If you **depend on** someone or something, you need them in order to do something. ❏ *He depended on his writing for his income.*

d

D

3 **VERB** If you can **depend on** someone or something, you know that they will support you or help you when you need them. ❑ *"You can depend on me," I assured him.*

Word Builder **dependable**

able ≈ able to be

comfort + able = comfort**able**
depend + able = depend**able**
download + able = download**able**
enjoy + able = enjoy**able**
honor + able = honor**able**

---

de|pend|able /dɪpɛndəbᵊl/ **ADJECTIVE** You say that someone is **dependable** when you feel that they will always be helpful and sensible. ❑ *He was a dependable friend.*

de|pend|ent /dɪpɛndənt/ (**dependents**) also **dependant**
1 **ADJECTIVE** If you are **dependent on** something or someone, you need them in order to succeed or to be able to survive. ❑ *The young gorillas are completely dependent on their mothers.* ● **de|pend|ence** **NONCOUNT NOUN** ❑ *We discussed the city's dependence on tourism.*
2 **NOUN** Your **dependents** are the people you support financially, such as your children. ❑ *He's a single man with no dependents.*

de|pos|it /dɪpɒzɪt/ (**deposits**)
1 **NOUN** A **deposit** is a sum of money that is part of the full price of something, and that you pay when you agree to buy it. ❑ *He paid a $500 deposit for the car.*
2 **NOUN** A **deposit** is an amount of a substance that has been left somewhere as a result of a chemical or geological process. ❑ *...underground deposits of gold.*
3 **NOUN** A **deposit** is an amount of money that you put into a bank account. ❑ *I made a deposit every week.*
→ look at **ATM**

de|pot /dipoʊ/ (**depots**) **NOUN** A **depot** is a place where goods or vehicles are kept until they are needed. ❑ *The food is stored in a depot at the airport.* ❑ *...a bus depot.*

de|press /dɪprɛs/ (**depresses, depressing, depressed**) **VERB** If someone or something **depresses** you, they make you feel sad. ❑ *This time of year always depresses me.*

de|pressed /dɪprɛst/ **ADJECTIVE** If you are **depressed**, you are sad, and you feel that you cannot enjoy anything. ❑ *She was very depressed after her husband died.*

de|press|ing /dɪprɛsɪŋ/ **ADJECTIVE** Something that is **depressing** makes you feel sad. ❑ *The view from the window was gray and depressing.*

de|pres|sion /dɪprɛʃᵊn/ (**depressions**)
1 **NONCOUNT NOUN** **Depression** is a state of mind in which you are sad and you feel that you cannot enjoy anything. ❑ *Mr. Thomas was suffering from depression.*
2 **NOUN** **SOCIAL STUDIES** A **depression** is a time when there is very little economic activity, which causes a lot of unemployment and social problems.
3 **NOUN** **SOCIAL STUDIES** **The Depression** or **The Great Depression** was a period in the U.S. during the 1920s and 1930s when there were very few jobs because the economy was in a bad state. ❑ *...the Great Depression of the 1930s.*

de|prive /dɪpraɪv/ (**deprives, depriving, deprived**) **VERB** If you **deprive** someone **of** something, you take it away from them, or you prevent them from having it. ❑ *They were deprived of fuel to heat their homes.* ● **dep|ri|va|tion** /dɛprɪveɪʃᵊn/ **NONCOUNT NOUN** ❑ *Many new mothers were suffering from sleep deprivation.* ● **de|prived** **ADJECTIVE** ❑ *These are some of the most deprived children in the country.*

depth /dɛpθ/ (**depths**)
1 **NOUN** The **depth** of something is how deep it is. ❑ *The average depth of the ocean is 4000 meters.* ❑ *The lake is fourteen feet in depth.*
2 If you deal with a subject **in depth**, you deal with it in a very detailed way. ❑ *We will discuss these three areas in depth.*

depu|ty /dɛpyəti/ (**deputies**)
1 **NOUN** A **deputy** is the second most important person in an organization. ❑ *Dr. Thomas is a former deputy director of NASA's astronaut office.*
2 **NOUN** A **deputy** is a police officer. ❑ *Robyn asked the deputy if she could speak with Sheriff Adkins.*

de|scend /dɪsɛnd/ (**descends, descending, descended**) **VERB** If you **descend**, you move down from a higher level to a lower level. [FORMAL] ❑ *We descended to the basement.*

de|scend|ant /dɪsɛndənt/ (**descendants**) **NOUN** **SOCIAL STUDIES** Someone's **descendants** are their children, their grandchildren and all their family that live after them. ❑ *He says that he is a descendant of King David.*

de|scribe /dɪskraɪb/ (describes, describing, described) **VERB** If you **describe** something , you say what it is like. ❑ *She described what she did in her spare time.* ❑ *The poem describes their life together.*

→ look at **science**

de|scrip|tion /dɪskrɪpʃ°n/ (descriptions) **NOUN** A **description** is an explanation of what someone looks like, or what something is. ❑ *Police have given a description of the man.* ❑ *He gave a detailed description of how the new system will work.*

des|ert (deserts, deserting, deserted)

> **PRONUNCIATION HELP**
> Pronounce the noun /dɛzərt/. Pronounce the verb /dɪzɜrt/.

1 NOUN SCIENCE GEOGRAPHY A **desert** is a large area of land where there is almost no water, trees, or plants. ❑ *They traveled through the Sahara Desert.*
2 VERB If people **desert** a place, they leave it and it becomes empty. ❑ *Poor farmers are deserting their fields and coming to the cities to find jobs.* ● **de|sert|ed** **ADJECTIVE** ❑ *She led them into a deserted street.*
3 VERB If someone **deserts** you, they go away and leave you, and no longer help or support you. ❑ *Sadly, most of her friends have deserted her.*

de|serve /dɪzɜrv/ (deserves, deserving, deserved) **VERB** If a person or thing **deserves** something, they should receive it because of their actions or qualities. ❑ *These people deserve to get more money.*

de|sign /dɪzaɪn/ (designs, designing, designed)
1 VERB When you **design** something new, you plan what it should be like. ❑ *They wanted to design a machine that was both attractive and practical.*
2 NONCOUNT NOUN ARTS **Design** is the process of planning and drawing things. ❑ *He had a talent for design.*
3 NOUN ARTS A **design** is a drawing that shows how something should be built or made. ❑ *They drew the design for the house.*
4 NOUN ARTS A **design** is a pattern of lines, flowers, or shapes that is used for decorating something. ❑ *The tablecloths come in three different designs.*

de|sign|er /dɪzaɪnər/ (designers) **NOUN** ARTS A **designer** is a person whose job is to design

things by making drawings of them. ❑ *Carolyne is a fashion designer.*

de|sir|able /dɪzaɪərəb°l/ **ADJECTIVE** If something is **desirable**, you want to have it or do it because it is useful or attractive. ❑ *The house is in a desirable neighborhood, close to schools.*

de|sire /dɪzaɪər/ (desires, desiring, desired)
1 NOUN A **desire** is a strong wish to do or have something. ❑ *I had a strong desire to help people.*
2 VERB If you **desire** something, you want it. [FORMAL] ❑ *This house is ideal for someone who desires a bit of peace.* ● **de|sired** **ADJECTIVE** ❑ *This will produce the desired effect.*

desk /dɛsk/ (desks)
1 NOUN A **desk** is a table that you sit at to write or work.
2 NOUN A **desk** is a place in a public building where you can get information. ❑ *They asked for Miss Minton at the reception desk.*
→ look at **classroom, furniture, office**

desk|top /dɛsktɒp/ (desktops) also **desk-top**
1 ADJECTIVE TECHNOLOGY **Desktop** computers are a convenient size for using on a desk or a table.
2 NOUN TECHNOLOGY The **desktop** of a computer is the images that you see on the screen when the computer is ready to use. ❑ *You can rearrange the icons on the desktop.*

des|pair /dɪspɛər/ (despairs, despairing, despaired)
1 NONCOUNT NOUN **Despair** is the feeling that everything is wrong and that nothing will improve. ❑ *I looked at my wife in despair.*
2 VERB If you **despair**, you feel that everything is wrong and that nothing will improve. ❑ *"Oh, I despair sometimes," she said, looking at the mess.*

des|per|ate /dɛspərɪt/
1 ADJECTIVE If you are **desperate**, you are willing to try anything to change your situation. ❑ *He was desperate to get back to the city.* ❑ *There were hundreds of patients desperate for his help.* ● **des|per|ate|ly** **ADVERB** ❑ *Thousands of people are desperately trying to leave the country.*
2 ADJECTIVE A **desperate** situation is very difficult, serious, or dangerous. ❑ *Conditions in the hospitals are desperate.*

des|pera|tion /dɛspəreɪʃ°n/ **NONCOUNT NOUN** **Desperation** is the feeling that you

D

have when you are in such a bad situation that you will try anything to change it. ❏ *There was a look of desperation in her eyes.*

des|pise /dɪspaɪz/ (**despises, despising, despised**) VERB If you **despise** something or someone, you dislike them very much. ❏ *She despises dishonesty, and she hated lying to Dave.*

de|spite /dɪspaɪt/ PREPOSITION You use **despite** to introduce a fact that makes something surprising. ❏ *The event was a success, despite the rain.*

des|sert /dɪzɜrt/ (**desserts**) NOUN Dessert is something sweet that you eat at the end of a meal. ❏ *She had ice cream for dessert.*
→ look at **eat**

dessert|spoon /dɪzɜrtspun/ (**dessertspoons**) NOUN A **dessertspoon** is a fairly large spoon that you use for eating desserts.

des|ti|na|tion /dɛstɪneɪʃ°n/ (**destinations**) NOUN Your **destination** is the place you are going to. ❏ *He wanted to arrive at his destination before dark.* ❏ *Ellis Island is one of America's most popular tourist destinations.*

des|ti|ny /dɛstɪni/ (**destinies**) NOUN A person's **destiny** is everything that happens to them during their life, including what will happen in the future. ❏ *Do we control our own destiny?*

de|stroy /dɪstrɔɪ/ (**destroys, destroying, destroyed**) VERB To **destroy** something means to cause so much damage to it that it cannot be used any longer, or it does not exist any longer. ❏ *The original house was destroyed by fire.* ● **de|struc|tion** /dɪstrʌkʃ°n/ NONCOUNT NOUN ❏ *We must stop the destruction of our forests.*

de|struc|tive /dɪstrʌktɪv/ ADJECTIVE Something that is **destructive** can cause great damage. ❏ *...a destructive storm.*

de|tach /dɪtætʃ/ (**detaches, detaching, detached**) VERB If you **detach** something, you remove it. [FORMAL] ❏ *Detach the card and mail it to this address.*

de|tached /dɪtætʃt/ ADJECTIVE A **detached** building is one that is not joined to any other building. ❏ *We have a house with a detached garage.*

de|tail /dɪteɪl/ (**details**)
1 NOUN The **details of** something are its

small, individual parts. ❏ *We discussed the details of the letter.*
2 PLURAL NOUN **Details** about someone or something are facts about them. ❏ *See the bottom of this page for details of how to apply for this offer.*
3 If you discuss a situation or examine something **in detail**, you talk about many different facts or parts of it. ❏ *Examine the contract in detail before signing it.*

de|tailed /dɪteɪld/ ADJECTIVE A **detailed** report or plan contains a lot of details. ❏ *She gave us a detailed description of the man.*

de|tect /dɪtɛkt/ (**detects, detecting, detected**) VERB If you **detect** something, you find it or notice it. ❏ *One of the hotel guests detected the smell of smoke.* ❏ *Arnold could detect a sadness in the old man's face.* ● **de|tec|tion** NONCOUNT NOUN ❏ *The process is used in the detection of cancer.*

de|tec|tive /dɪtɛktɪv/ (**detectives**) NOUN A **detective** is someone whose job is to discover what has happened in a crime, and to find the people who did it. ❏ *Detectives are still searching for the four men.*

de|ter|gent /dɪtɜrdʒ°nt/ (**detergents**) NOUN **Detergent** is a chemical substance that is used for washing things such as clothes or dishes. ❏ *Hand-wash the gloves in warm water, using a mild detergent.*
→ look at **laundry**

de|terio|rate /dɪtɪəriəreɪt/ (**deteriorates, deteriorating, deteriorated**) VERB If something **deteriorates**, it becomes worse. ❏ *Her eyesight is rapidly deteriorating.* ● **de|terio|ra|tion** /dɪtɪəriəreɪʃ°n/ NOUN ❏ *Too little sleep can cause a deterioration in your health.*

de|ter|mi|na|tion /dɪtɜrmɪneɪʃ°n/ NONCOUNT NOUN **Determination** is the feeling you have when you have firmly decided to do something. ❏ *Everyone behaved with courage and determination.*

de|ter|mine /dɪtɜrmɪn/ (**determines, determining, determined**)
1 VERB If something **determines** what will happen, it controls it. [FORMAL] ❏ *The size of the chicken pieces will determine the cooking time.*
2 VERB To **determine** a fact means to discover it. [FORMAL] ❏ *The investigation will determine what really happened.*

de|ter|mined /dɪtɜrmɪnd/ **ADJECTIVE** If you are **determined to** do something, you have made a firm decision to do it. ❑ *He is determined to win gold at the Olympics.*

de|test /dɪtɛst/ (**detests, detesting, detested**) **VERB** If you **detest** someone or something, you dislike them very much. ❑ *You are probably aware that I detest smoking.*

dev|as|tate /dɛvəsteɪt/ (**devastates, devastating, devastated**) **VERB** If something **devastates** an area or a place, it damages it very badly or destroys it completely. ❑ *The earthquake devastated parts of Indonesia.* ● **dev|as|ta|tion** /dɛvəsteɪʃ°n/ **NONCOUNT NOUN** ❑ *The war brought massive devastation to the area.*

de|vel|op /dɪvɛləp/ (**develops, developing, developed**)

1 **VERB** When something **develops**, it grows or changes over a period of time. ❑ *Children need time to develop.* ❑ *By 1992, their friendship had developed into love.* ● **de|vel|oped** **ADJECTIVE** ❑ *Their bodies were well developed and very fit.* ● **de|vel|op|ment** **NONCOUNT NOUN** ❑ *We've been studying the development of language.*

2 **VERB** If a problem or difficulty **develops**, it begins to occur. ❑ *A problem developed aboard the space shuttle.*

3 **VERB** If someone **develops** a new product, they design it and produce it. ❑ *Scientists have developed a car paint that changes color.*

de|vel|op|ment /dɪvɛləpmənt/ (**developments**)

1 **NONCOUNT NOUN** **Development** is the growth of a business or an industry. ❑ *Our business is the development of new technology.*

2 **NOUN** A **development** is an event or incident that has recently happened and has an effect on an existing situation. ❑ *Police say this is an important development in the investigation.*

de|vice /dɪvaɪs/ (**devices**) **NOUN** A **device** is an object that has been invented for a particular purpose. ❑ *He used an electronic device to measure the rooms.*

dev|il /dɛv°l/ **NOUN** Some people believe that **the devil** is an evil spirit that makes bad things happen.

de|vise /dɪvaɪz/ (**devises, devising, devised**) **VERB** If you **devise** a plan, you have the idea for it. ❑ *We devised a plan to help him.*

de|vote /dɪvoʊt/ (**devotes, devoting, devoted**) **VERB** If you **devote** yourself, your time, or your energy **to** something, you spend all or most of your time or energy on it. ❑ *He devoted the rest of his life to science.*

de|vot|ed /dɪvoʊtɪd/ **ADJECTIVE** Someone who is **devoted to** a person loves that person very much. ❑ *He was devoted to his wife.*

Sound Partners dew, do, due

dew /du/ **NONCOUNT NOUN** **Dew** is small drops of water that form on the ground during the night. ❑ *The dew formed on the leaves.*

dia|be|tes /daɪəbitɪs, -tiz/ **NONCOUNT NOUN** **Diabetes** is a medical condition in which someone has too much sugar in their blood.

di|ag|nose /daɪəgnoʊs/ (**diagnoses, diagnosing, diagnosed**) **VERB** If someone **is diagnosed as** having a particular illness, a doctor discovers what is wrong with them. ❑ *His wife was diagnosed with diabetes.*

di|ag|no|sis /daɪəgnoʊsɪs/ (**diagnoses**) **NOUN** **Diagnosis** is when a doctor discovers what is wrong with someone who is ill. ❑ *I had a second test to confirm the diagnosis.*

di|ago|nal /daɪægən°l, -ægn°l/ **ADJECTIVE** MATH A **diagonal** line goes from one corner of a square across to the opposite corner. ❑ *The screen showed a pattern of diagonal lines.* ● **di|ago|nal|ly** **ADVERB** ❑ *He ran diagonally across the field.*

dia|gram /daɪəgræm/ (**diagrams**) **NOUN** A **diagram** is a simple drawing of lines and is used, for example, to explain how a machine works. ❑ *He showed us a diagram of the inside of a computer.*

dial /daɪəl/ (**dials, dialing, dialed**)

1 **NOUN** A **dial** is the part of a machine or a piece of equipment that shows you the time or a measurement. ❑ *The dial on the clock showed five minutes to seven.*

2 **NOUN** A **dial** is a small wheel on a piece of equipment that you can move in order to control the way it works. ❑ *He turned the dial on the radio.*

3 **VERB** If you **dial** or if you **dial** a number, you press the buttons on a telephone in order to call someone. ❑ *Dial the number, followed by the "#" sign.*

→ look at **phone**

dia|lect /daɪəlɛkt/ (**dialects**) **NOUN** A **dialect** is a form of a language that people speak in a particular area. ❏ *They were speaking in the local dialect.*

dia|log box /daɪəlɔg bɒks/ (**dialog boxes**) NOUN TECHNOLOGY A **dialog box** is a small area that appears on a computer screen, containing information or questions. ❏ *Clicking here brings up another dialog box.*

dia|logue /daɪəlɔg/ (**dialogues**) also **dialog** NOUN LANGUAGE ARTS A **dialogue** is a conversation between two people in a book, a movie, or a play. ❏ *He writes great dialogues.* ❏ *The movie contains some very funny dialogue.*

dial-up ADJECTIVE TECHNOLOGY A **dial-up** connection to the Internet uses a normal telephone line. ❏ *This website takes a few minutes to load over a dial-up connection.*

di|am|eter /daɪæmɪtər/ (**diameters**) NOUN MATH The **diameter** of a round object is the length of a straight line that can be drawn across it, passing through the middle of it. ❏ *The tube is much smaller than the diameter of a human hair.*
→ look at **area, geometry**

dia|mond /daɪmənd, daɪə-/ (**diamonds**)
1 NOUN A **diamond** is a hard, clear, stone that is very expensive, and is used for making jewelry. ❏ *...a pair of diamond earrings.*
2 NOUN A **diamond** is the shape ♦. ❏ *A baseball field is in the shape of a diamond.*

dia|per /daɪpər, daɪə-/ (**diapers**) NOUN A **diaper** is a piece of soft cloth or paper that you fasten around a baby's bottom and between its legs. ❏ *She fed the baby and changed its diaper.*
→ look at **bag**

di|ar|rhea /daɪəriə/ NONCOUNT NOUN If someone has **diarrhea**, all the waste products come out of their body as liquid because they are sick. ❏ *Many team members suffered from diarrhea.*

dia|ry /daɪəri/ (**diaries**) NOUN A **diary** is a book that has a separate space for each day of the year. You use a diary to write down things that you plan to do, or to record what happens in your life. ❏ *I read the entry from his diary for July 10, 1940.*

dice /daɪs/ (**dice**) NOUN A **dice** is a small block of wood or plastic with spots on its sides, used for playing games. ❏ *I threw both dice and got a double 6.*

dic|tate /dɪkteɪt, dɪkteɪt/ (**dictates, dictating, dictated**)
1 VERB If you **dictate** something, you say it or record it onto a machine, so that someone else can write it down. ❏ *He dictated his life story into a tape recorder while he was in prison.*
2 VERB If you **dictate to** someone, you tell them what they must do. ❏ *Why should they dictate to us what we should eat?*

dic|ta|tion /dɪkteɪʃən/ NONCOUNT NOUN **Dictation** is when one person speaks and someone else writes down what they are saying. ❏ *She was taking dictation from the dean of the graduate school.*

dic|ta|tor /dɪkteɪtər/ (**dictators**) NOUN SOCIAL STUDIES A **dictator** is a ruler who has complete power in a country. ❏ *The country was ruled by a dictator for more than twenty years.*

dic|tion|ary /dɪkʃəneri/ (**dictionaries**) NOUN LANGUAGE ARTS A **dictionary** is a book in which the words and phrases of a language are listed, together with their meanings. ❏ *We checked the spelling in the dictionary.*
→ look at Word World: **dictionary**

did /dɪd/ **Did** is a form of the verb **do**.

didn't /dɪdənt/ **Didn't** is short for "did not."

die /daɪ/ (**dies, dying, died**)
1 VERB When people, animals, and plants **die**, they stop living. ❏ *My dog died last week.* ❏ *Sadly, my mother died of cancer.*

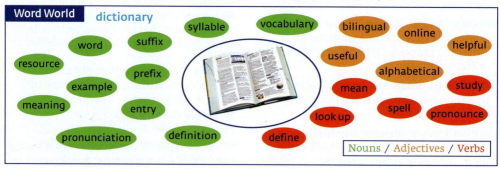

Word World — dictionary

Nouns / Adjectives / Verbs

2 **VERB** You can say that you **are dying for** something if you want it very much. [INFORMAL] ❑ *I'm dying for some fresh air.*

3 **VERB** You can say that you **are dying to** do something if you want to do it very much. [INFORMAL] ❑ *I was dying to read the news.*

4 **VERB** When something **dies**, it gradually becomes weaker, until it no longer exists. ❑ *My love for you will never die.*

die|sel /dizᵊl/ **NONCOUNT NOUN** Diesel or **diesel oil** is a fuel that is used in some vehicles' engines.

diet /daɪɪt/ (diets, dieting, dieted)

1 **NOUN** Your **diet** is the type of food that you regularly eat. ❑ *It's never too late to improve your diet.*

2 **NOUN** If you are on a **diet**, you eat special types of food, or you eat less food than usual. ❑ *Have you been on a diet? You've lost a lot of weight.*

3 **VERB** If you **are dieting**, you eat special types of food or you eat less food than usual. ❑ *I've been dieting since the birth of my child.*
→ look at **eat**

Word Partners	Use **diet** with:
ADJ.	**balanced** diet, **healthy** diet, **proper** diet, **vegetarian** diet **1** **strict** diet **3**
N.	diet and exercise **1** **2**
PREP.	**on a** diet **2**

dif|fer /dɪfər/ (differs, differing, differed) **VERB** If two or more things **differ**, they are different from each other. ❑ *The story he told police differed from the one he told his mother.*

dif|fer|ence /dɪfərəns, dɪfrəns/ (differences)

1 **NOUN** The **difference** between two things is the way in which they are different from each other. ❑ *The main difference between the two computers is the price.*

2 **NOUN** A **difference** between two quantities is the amount by which one quantity is more or less than the other. ❑ *The difference between 8532 and 8522 is 10.*

3 If something **makes** a **difference** or **makes** a lot of **difference**, it has an important effect on you. ❑ *Where you live makes such a difference to the way you feel.* If something **makes** no **difference**, it does not have any effect on what you are doing. ❑ *The weather makes no difference to me in my job.*

dif|fer|ent /dɪfərənt, dɪfrənt/

1 **ADJECTIVE** If two people or things are **different**, they are not like each other. ❑ *London was different from most European capital cities.* ● **dif|fer|ent|ly** **ADVERB** ❑ *Every person learns differently.*

2 **ADJECTIVE** You use **different** to show that you are talking about two or more separate things of the same type. ❑ *Different countries export different products.*

3 **ADJECTIVE** You say something is **different** when it is unusual. ❑ *Her taste in clothes is interesting and different.*

dif|fi|cult /dɪfɪkʌlt, -kəlt/

1 **ADJECTIVE** Something that is **difficult** is not easy to do, understand, or deal with. ❑ *The homework was too difficult for us.* ❑ *It was a very difficult decision to make.*

2 **ADJECTIVE** Someone who is **difficult** behaves in a way that is not reasonable or helpful. ❑ *My son is 10 years old and a very difficult child.*
→ look at **language, math**

dif|fi|cul|ty /dɪfɪkʌlti, -kəlti/ (difficulties)

1 **NOUN** A **difficulty** is a problem. ❑ *There's always the difficulty of getting information.*

2 **NONCOUNT NOUN** If you have **difficulty** doing something, you are not able to do it easily. ❑ *Do you have difficulty walking?*

dig /dɪg/ (digs, digging, dug) **VERB** If people or animals **dig**, they make a hole in the ground. ❑ *I grabbed the shovel and started digging.* ❑ *First, dig a large hole in the ground.*

di|gest (digests, digesting, digested) **VERB** **SCIENCE** When you **digest** food, it passes through your body to your stomach. ❑ *Do not swim for an hour after a meal to allow time to digest your food.*

● **di|ges|tion** /daɪdʒɛstʃən/ **NONCOUNT NOUN** ❑ *Peppermint helps digestion.*

dig|it /dɪdʒɪt/ (digits) **NOUN** **MATH** A **digit** is a written symbol for any of the ten numbers from 0 to 9. ❑ *Her telephone number differs from mine by one digit.*

digi|tal /dɪdʒɪtᵊl/

1 **ADJECTIVE** **TECHNOLOGY** **Digital** systems record or send information in the form of thousands of very small signals. ❑ *Most people now have digital television.*

d

2 ADJECTIVE TECHNOLOGY Digital equipment gives information in the form of numbers. Compare with **analog**. ❑ *I've got a new digital watch.*
→ look at **Internet, time**

dig|ni|fied /dɪgnɪfaɪd/ **ADJECTIVE** Someone or something that is **dignified** is calm, serious, and deserves respect. ❑ *He was a very dignified and charming man.*

dig|nity /dɪgnɪti/ **NONCOUNT NOUN** If someone behaves or moves with **dignity**, they are serious, calm, and controlled. ❑ *She received the news with quiet dignity.*

di|lem|ma /dɪlɛmə/ (**dilemmas**) **NOUN** A **dilemma** is a difficult situation in which you have to make a choice between two things. ❑ *He was facing a dilemma: should he return to his country or stay in Europe?*

dili|gent /dɪlɪdʒənt/ **ADJECTIVE** Someone who is **diligent** works hard in a careful and thorough way. ❑ *She's a diligent student.*
● **dili|gence** /dɪlɪdʒəns/ **NONCOUNT NOUN** ❑ *He performed his duties with diligence.*
● **dili|gent|ly ADVERB** ❑ *He was diligently searching the house.*

di|lute /daɪlut/ (**dilutes, diluting, diluted**) **VERB** SCIENCE If you **dilute** a liquid, you add water or another liquid to it. ❑ *This juice is quite strong, but you can dilute it with water.* ❑ *The liquid is then diluted.*

dim /dɪm/ (**dimmer, dimmest, dims, dimming, dimmed**)
1 ADJECTIVE Dim light is not bright. ❑ *She waited in the dim light.* ● **dim|ly ADVERB** ❑ *Two lamps burned dimly.*
2 VERB If you **dim** a light, it becomes less bright. ❑ *Could someone dim the lights, please?*

dime /daɪm/ (**dimes**) **NOUN** A **dime** is a U.S. coin worth ten cents.

di|men|sion /dɪmɛnʃᵊn, daɪ-/ (**dimensions**) **PLURAL NOUN** MATH The **dimensions** of something are its measurements. ❑ *We do not yet know the exact dimensions of the room.*

dine /daɪn/ (**dines, dining, dined**) **VERB** When you **dine**, you have dinner. [FORMAL] ❑ *He drives a nice car and dines at the best restaurants.*

din|er /daɪnər/ (**diners**) **NOUN** A **diner** is a small cheap restaurant that is often open all day. ❑ *...an all-night diner.*

din|ing room (**dining rooms**) **NOUN** A dining room is a room where people eat their meals.
→ look at **house**

din|ner /dɪnər/ (**dinners**)
1 NOUN Dinner is the main meal of the day, usually served in the evening. ❑ *She invited us for dinner.* ❑ *Would you like to stay and have dinner?*
2 NOUN A **dinner** is a formal social event in the evening at which a meal is served. ❑ *...a series of official dinners.*
→ look at **eat**

din|ner|time /dɪnərtaɪm/ also **dinner time** **NONCOUNT NOUN** Dinnertime is the time of the day when most people have their dinner. ❑ *The telephone call came just before dinnertime.*

di|no|saur /daɪnəsɔr/ (**dinosaurs**) **NOUN** Dinosaurs were large animals that lived millions of years ago.

dip /dɪp/ (**dips, dipping, dipped**)
1 VERB If you **dip** something in a liquid, you put it in and then quickly take it out again. ❑ *Dip each apple in the syrup.*
2 NOUN A **dip** is a thick sauce that you dip pieces of food into before eating them. ❑ *We sat and watched the Super Bowl with a huge plate of chips and dips.*

di|plo|ma /dɪploʊmə/ (**diplomas**) **NOUN** A **diploma** is a qualification that a student who has completed a course of study may receive. ❑ *He was awarded a diploma in social work.*

di|plo|ma|cy /dɪploʊməsi/ **NONCOUNT NOUN** Diplomacy is the activity or profession of managing relations between the governments of different countries. ❑ *If diplomacy fails, there could be a war.*

dip|lo|mat /dɪpləmæt/ (**diplomats**) **NOUN** A **diplomat** is a senior official whose job is to discuss international affairs with officials from other countries. ❑ *Sir Harold is a Western diplomat with experience in Asia.*

dip|lo|mat|ic /dɪpləmætɪk/
1 ADJECTIVE Diplomatic means relating to diplomacy and diplomats. ❑ *The two countries enjoy good diplomatic relations.*
● **dip|lo|mati|cal|ly** /dɪpləmætɪkli/ **ADVERB** ❑ *The conflict was resolved diplomatically.*
2 ADJECTIVE Someone who is **diplomatic** is careful to say or do things without

offending people. ❑ *She is very direct, but I prefer a more diplomatic approach.* ● **dip|lo|mati|cal|ly** ADVERB ❑ *"Of course," agreed Sloan diplomatically.*

di|rect /dɪrɛkt, daɪ-/ (**directs, directing, directed**)

1 ADJECTIVE **Direct** means moving toward a place or an object, without changing direction and without stopping. ❑ *They took a direct flight to Athens.*

2 ADVERB **Direct** is also an adverb. ❑ *You can fly direct from Seattle to London.* ● **di|rect|ly** ADVERB ❑ *On arriving in New York, Dylan went directly to Greenwich Village.*

3 ADJECTIVE **Direct** means with nothing else in between. ❑ *Protect your plants from direct sunlight .*

4 ADVERB **Direct** is also an adverb. ❑ *More farms are selling direct to consumers.* ● **di|rect|ly** ADVERB ❑ *Never look directly at the sun.*

5 ADJECTIVE Someone whose behavior is **direct** is honest and open, and says exactly what they mean. ❑ *He avoided giving a direct answer.* ● **di|rect|ly** ADVERB ❑ *Explain simply and directly what you hope to achieve.*

● **di|rect|ness** NONCOUNT NOUN ❑ *He spoke with rare directness.*

6 VERB When someone **directs** a project or a group of people, they are responsible for organizing them. ❑ *Christopher will direct everyday operations.* ● **di|rec|tion** /dɪrɛkʃᵊn, daɪ-/ NONCOUNT NOUN ❑ *Organizations need clear direction.*

7 VERB When someone **directs** a movie, play, or television program, they are responsible for the way in which it is performed. ❑ *Branagh himself will direct the movie.*

→ look at **route**

di|rec|tion /dɪrɛkʃᵊn, daɪ-/ (**directions**)

1 NOUN A **direction** is the general line that someone or something is moving or pointing in. ❑ *The nearest town was ten miles in the opposite direction.* ❑ *He started walking in the direction of Larry's shop.*

2 PLURAL NOUN **Directions** are instructions that tell you what to do, how to do something, or how to get somewhere. ❑ *She stopped the car to ask for directions.*

→ look at **route**

di|rect|ly /dɪrɛktli, daɪ-/ ADVERB If one thing is **directly** above, below, or in front of another thing, there is nothing between them. ❑ *They live in the apartment directly above us.*

di|rect ob|ject (**direct objects**) NOUN In grammar, the **direct object** of a verb is the noun or pronoun that is directly affected by the action of the subject. For example, in "I saw him yesterday," "him" is the direct object. Compare **indirect object**.

di|rec|tor /dɪrɛktər, daɪ-/ (**directors**)

1 NOUN The **directors** of a company or an organization are the people who control it. ❑ *We wrote to the directors of the bank.*

2 NOUN ARTS The **director** of a play, movie, or television program is the person who tells the actors and technical staff what to do.

di|rec|tory /dɪrɛktəri, daɪ-/ (**directories**) NOUN A **directory** is a book containing lists of people's names, addresses, and telephone numbers. ❑ *You'll find our number in the telephone directory.*

dirt /dɜrt/

1 NONCOUNT NOUN If there is **dirt** on something, there is dust or mud on it. ❑ *I started to clean the dirt off my hands.*

2 NONCOUNT NOUN You can call the earth on the ground **dirt**. ❑ *They all sat on the dirt under a tree.*

dirty /dɜrti/ (**dirtier, dirtiest**) ADJECTIVE If something is **dirty**, it needs to be cleaned. ❑ *She collected the dirty plates from the table.*

→ look at **laundry, pollution**

dis|abil|ity /dɪsəbɪlɪti/ (**disabilities**) NOUN A **disability** is a permanent injury or condition that makes it difficult for someone to work or live normally. ❑ *We're building a new classroom for people with disabilities.*

→ look at Word World: **disability**

dis|abled /dɪseɪbᵊld/ ADJECTIVE Someone who is **disabled** has an injury or condition that makes it difficult for them to move around. ❑ *...parents of disabled children.*

dis|ad|vant|age /dɪsədvæntɪdʒ/ (**disadvantages**)

1 NOUN A **disadvantage** is something that makes things more difficult for you. ❑ *The big disadvantage of this computer is its size.*

2 If you are **at a disadvantage**, you have a difficulty that many other people do not have. ❑ *Children from poor families were at a disadvantage.*

d

Word World   disability

deaf · unable · able · accessible · cane · active · blind · independent · ability · ramp · have · participate · needs · wheelchair · aid · need · use · do · Seeing Eye dog · assistance · access

Nouns / Adjectives / Verbs

Word Builder   disagree

dis ≈ **not**

dis + agree = disagree
dis + appear = disappear
dis + connect = disconnect
dis + honest = dishonest
dis + obey = disobey
dis + organized = disorganized

dis|agree /dɪsəgriː/ (**disagrees, disagreeing, disagreed**)

1 **VERB** If you **disagree with** someone, you have a different opinion from theirs. ❑ *I really have to disagree with you here.* ❑ *O'Brien disagreed with the suggestion that his team played badly.*
2 **VERB** If you **disagree with** an action or decision, you disapprove of it. ❑ *I respect the president but I disagree with his decision.*

dis|agree|ment /dɪsəgriːmənt/ **NOUN** **Disagreement** is when people do not agree with something. ❑ *Britain and France have expressed disagreement with the plan.*

Word Builder   disappear

dis ≈ **not**

dis + agree = disagree
dis + appear = disappear
dis + connect = disconnect
dis + honest = dishonest
dis + obey = disobey
dis + organized = disorganized

dis|ap|pear /dɪsəpɪər/ (**disappears, disappearing, disappeared**) **VERB** If someone or something **disappears**, they go away and you cannot see them.
❑ *His daughter disappeared thirteen years ago.*
❑ *The sun disappeared and it started raining again.*
● **dis|ap|pear|ance** (**disappearances**) **NOUN**
❑ *Her disappearance is a mystery.*

dis|ap|point /dɪsəpɔɪnt/ (**disappoints, disappointing, disappointed**) **VERB**

If something **disappoints** you, it is not as good as you hoped. ❑ *The team did not disappoint the crowd.* ● **dis|ap|point|ing** **ADJECTIVE** ❑ *The restaurant looked great, but the food was disappointing.*

dis|ap|point|ed /dɪsəpɔɪntɪd/ **ADJECTIVE** If you are **disappointed**, you are sad because something has not happened or because something is not as good as you hoped.
❑ *I was disappointed that John was not there.*

dis|ap|point|ment /dɪsəpɔɪntmənt/ (**disappointments**)

1 **NONCOUNT NOUN** **Disappointment** is the feeling you have when you are disappointed. ❑ *She couldn't hide the disappointment in her voice.*
2 **NOUN** Something or someone that is a **disappointment** is not as good as you hoped. ❑ *The loss was a huge disappointment for the fans.*

dis|ap|prov|al /dɪsəpruːvəl/ **NONCOUNT NOUN** If you show **disapproval**, you show that you do not approve of someone or something. ❑ *He stared at Marina with disapproval.*

dis|ap|prove /dɪsəpruːv/ (**disapproves, disapproving, disapproved**) **VERB** If you **disapprove of** something or someone, you do not like them, or do not approve of them. ❑ *Most people disapprove of violence.*

dis|as|ter /dɪzæstər/ (**disasters**)

1 **NOUN** A **disaster** is a very bad accident or event that may hurt many people. ❑ *It was the second air disaster (= plane crash) that month.*
2 **NOUN** If something is a **disaster**, it is not at all successful. ❑ *The concert was a total disaster.*

→ look at Picture Dictionary: **natural disasters**

dis|as|trous /dɪzæstrəs/ **ADJECTIVE** A **disastrous** event causes a lot of problems for many people. ❑ *The country suffered a disastrous earthquake in July.*

D

Picture Dictionary natural disasters

blizzard

drought

earthquake

flood

hurricane

volcano eruption

dis|be|lief /dɪsbɪlíf/ **NONCOUNT NOUN**
Disbelief is when you do not believe that
something is true or real. ❑ *She looked at him
in disbelief.*

dis|card /dɪskɑrd/ (discards, discarding,
discarded) **VERB** If you **discard**
something, you get rid of it. ❑ *Do not
discard your receipt.*

dis|ci|pline /dɪsɪplɪn/
1 NONCOUNT NOUN Discipline is the
practice of making people obey rules.
❑ *Children need discipline in order to feel secure
and safe.*
2 NONCOUNT NOUN Discipline is the quality
of being able to obey particular rules and
standards. ❑ *He was impressed by the team's
speed and discipline.*

disc jock|ey /dɪsk dʒɒki/ (disc jockeys)
also **disk jockey NOUN** A **disc jockey** is
someone whose job is to play music and
talk on the radio.

dis|close /dɪsklóʊz/ (discloses, disclosing,
disclosed) **VERB** If you **disclose** information,
you tell people about it. ❑ *They refused to
disclose details of the deal.*

dis|co /dɪskoʊ/ (discos) **NOUN** A **disco** is a
place or an event where people dance to
pop music. ❑ *Fridays and Saturdays are regular
disco nights.*

dis|com|fort /dɪskʌmfərt/ **NONCOUNT NOUN**
Discomfort is an unpleasant feeling in part
of your body. ❑ *Steve had some discomfort, but no
real pain.*

Word Builder disconnect

dis ≈ **not**

dis + agree = disagree
dis + appear = disappear
dis + connect = disconnect
dis + honest = dishonest
dis + obey = disobey
dis + organized = disorganized

dis|con|nect /dɪskənɛ́kt/ (disconnects,
disconnecting, disconnected) **VERB** If you
disconnect a piece of equipment, you stop
electricity or water from going into it.
❑ *Try disconnecting the telephone for a while.*

dis|count /dɪskaʊnt/ (discounts) **NOUN**
A **discount** is a reduction in the usual price
of something. ❑ *All staff get a 20% discount.*
→ look at **shopping**

dis|cour|age /dɪskɜ́rɪdʒ/ (discourages,
discouraging, discouraged) **VERB** If someone
or something **discourages** you, you do not
want to do a particular activity any more.
❑ *Learning a language may be difficult at first.
Don't let this discourage you.* ● **dis|cour|aged**
ADJECTIVE ❑ *He felt discouraged by his lack of progress.*

dis|cov|er /dɪskʌ́vər/ (discovers,
discovering, discovered)
1 VERB If you **discover** something that you
did not know about before, you become
aware of it. ❑ *She discovered that her daughter
was earning $40 a day.*
2 VERB If something **is discovered**,
someone finds it. ❑ *The car was discovered on
a roadside outside the city.*
3 VERB When someone **discovers** a new
place, substance, or method, they are the

D

first person to find it or use it. ❏ *Who was the first European to discover America?*
→ look at **history**

dis|cov|ery /dɪskʌvəri/ (**discoveries**)
1 NOUN If someone makes a **discovery**, they become aware of something that they did not know about before. ❏ *I made a surprising discovery.*
2 NOUN If someone makes a **discovery**, they are the first person to find or become aware of something that no one knew about before. ❏ *In that year, two important discoveries were made.*

dis|creet /dɪskriːt/ ADJECTIVE If you are **discreet**, you are polite and careful in what you do or say. ❏ *He was a real gentleman, and he was always very discreet.*

dis|crimi|nate /dɪskrɪmɪneɪt/ (**discriminates, discriminating, discriminated**) VERB SOCIAL STUDIES To **discriminate against** a group of people means to treat them unfairly. ❏ *They believe the law discriminates against women.*

dis|crimi|na|tion /dɪskrɪmɪneɪʃ³n/ NONCOUNT NOUN SOCIAL STUDIES **Discrimination** is the practice of treating one person or group unfairly. ❏ *Many companies are breaking age discrimination laws.*

dis|cus /dɪskəs/ (**discuses**) NOUN SPORTS The **discus** is the sport of throwing a heavy round object. ❏ *He won the discus at the Montreal Olympics.*

dis|cuss /dɪskʌs/ (**discusses, discussing, discussed**) VERB If people **discuss** something, they talk about it. ❏ *We are meeting next week to discuss plans for the future.*

dis|cus|sion /dɪskʌʃ³n/ (**discussions**) NOUN A **discussion** is a conversation about a subject. ❏ *Managers are having informal discussions later today.*

dis|ease /dɪziːz/ (**diseases**) NOUN A **disease** is an illness that affects people, animals, or plants. ❏ *There are no drugs available to treat this disease.* ❏ *...heart disease.*

dis|grace /dɪsgreɪs/ NOUN If something is **a disgrace**, it is very bad or wrong. ❏ *His behavior was a disgrace.*

dis|grace|ful /dɪsgreɪsfəl/ ADJECTIVE If you say that something is **disgraceful**, you strongly disapprove of it. ❏ *The way they treated him was disgraceful.*

● **dis|grace|ful|ly** ADVERB ❏ *His brother behaved disgracefully.*

dis|guise /dɪsgaɪz/ (**disguises, disguising, disguised**)
1 NOUN If you are **in disguise**, you have changed the way you look so that people will not recognize you. ❏ *He traveled in disguise.*
2 VERB To **disguise** something means to hide it or make it appear different so that people will not recognize it. ❏ *I tried to disguise the fact that I was ill.* ● **dis|guised** ADJECTIVE ❏ *The robber was disguised as a medical worker.*

dis|gust /dɪsgʌst/ NONCOUNT NOUN **Disgust** is a feeling of very strong dislike or disapproval. ❏ *George watched in disgust.*

dis|gust|ed /dɪsgʌstɪd/ ADJECTIVE If you are **disgusted**, you feel a strong sense of dislike and disapproval. ❏ *I'm disgusted by the way that he was treated.*

dis|gust|ing /dɪsgʌstɪŋ/ ADJECTIVE If something is **disgusting**, it is extremely unpleasant or unacceptable. ❏ *The food tasted disgusting.*

dish /dɪʃ/ (**dishes**)
1 NOUN A **dish** is a shallow container for cooking or serving food. ❏ *Pour the mixture into a square glass dish.*
2 NOUN A **dish** is food that is prepared in a particular way. ❏ *There are plenty of delicious dishes to choose from.*
→ look at **kitchen**

Word Builder	**dishonest**
dis ≈ **not**	

dis + agree = **dis**agree
dis + appear = **dis**appear
dis + connect = **dis**connect
dis + honest = **dis**honest
dis + obey = **dis**obey
dis + organized = **dis**organized

---

dis|hon|est /dɪsɒnɪst/ ADJECTIVE If someone is **dishonest**, they are not honest, and you cannot trust them. ❏ *I admit that I was dishonest with him.*

dis|hon|es|ty /dɪsɒnɪsti/ NONCOUNT NOUN **Dishonesty** is dishonest behavior. ❏ *She accused the government of dishonesty.*

dish|washer /dɪʃwɒʃər/ (**dishwashers**) NOUN A **dishwasher** is a machine that washes and dries dishes.
→ look at **kitchen**

dish|washing liq|uid /dɪʃwɒʃɪŋ lɪkwɪd/
NOUN Dishwashing liquid is liquid soap that you add to hot water to clean dirty dishes.

dis|in|fect /dɪsɪnfɛkt/ (**disinfects, disinfecting, disinfected**) **VERB** If you **disinfect** something, you clean it using a substance that kills bacteria. ❑ *Chlorine is used for disinfecting water.*

dis|in|fect|ant /dɪsɪnfɛktənt/ (**disinfectants**) **NOUN** Disinfectant is a substance that kills bacteria. ❑ *They washed their hands with disinfectant.*

disk /dɪsk/ (**disks**) also **disc**
1 **NOUN** A **disk** is a flat, circular object. ❑ *The food processor has three slicing disks.*
2 **NOUN** TECHNOLOGY In a computer, the **disk** is the part where information is stored. ❑ *The program uses 2.5 megabytes of disk space.*

disk drive (**disk drives**) **NOUN** TECHNOLOGY The **disk drive** on a computer is the part that holds a disk.

dis|like /dɪslaɪk/ (**dislikes, disliking, disliked**)
1 **VERB** If you **dislike** someone or something, you think they are unpleasant and you do not like them. ❑ *Many children dislike the taste of green vegetables.*
2 **NOUN** Your **dislikes** are the things that you do not like. ❑ *Make a list of your likes and dislikes about your job.*

dis|may /dɪsmeɪ/ **NONCOUNT NOUN** Dismay is a strong feeling of fear, worry, or sadness. [FORMAL] ❑ *Local people reacted with dismay.*
● **dis|mayed** **ADJECTIVE** ❑ *Glen was shocked and dismayed at her reaction.*

dis|miss /dɪsmɪs/ (**dismisses, dismissing, dismissed**)
1 **VERB** If you **dismiss** something, you say that it is not important enough for you to consider. ❑ *Perry dismissed the suggestion as nonsense.*
2 **VERB** If you **are dismissed** by someone in authority, they tell you that you can leave. ❑ *Two more witnesses were heard, and dismissed.*

Word Builder   **disobey**

dis ≈ **not**

    dis + agree = **dis**agree
    dis + appear = **dis**appear
    dis + connect = **dis**connect
    dis + honest = **dis**honest
    dis + obey = **dis**obey
    dis + organized = **dis**organized

dis|obey /dɪsəbeɪ/ (**disobeys, disobeying, disobeyed**) **VERB** When someone **disobeys** a person or an order, they do not do what they have been told to do. ❑ *He often disobeyed his mother and father.*

Word Builder   **disorganized**

dis ≈ **not**

    dis + agree = **dis**agree
    dis + appear = **dis**appear
    dis + connect = **dis**connect
    dis + honest = **dis**honest
    dis + obey = **dis**obey
    dis + organized = **dis**organized

dis|or|gan|ized /dɪsɔrgənaɪzd/
1 **ADJECTIVE** Something that is **disorganized** is badly arranged, planned or managed. ❑ *He walked into the large, disorganized office.*
2 **ADJECTIVE** Someone who is **disorganized** is very bad at organizing things in their life. ❑ *My boss is completely disorganized.*

dis|pens|er /dɪspɛnsər/ (**dispensers**) **NOUN** A **dispenser** is a machine or a container from which you can get something. ❑ *...a soap dispenser.*
→ look at **ATM**

dis|play /dɪspleɪ/ (**displays, displaying, displayed**)
1 **VERB** If you **display** something, you put it in a place where people can see it. ❑ *Old soldiers proudly displayed their medals.*
2 **NONCOUNT NOUN** Display is also a noun. ❑ *The artist's work is on display in New York next month.*
3 **NOUN** A **display** is an arrangement of things that have been put in a particular place, so that people can see them easily. ❑ *In the second gallery, there was a display of World War II aircraft.*

dis|pos|able /dɪspoʊzəbəl/ **ADJECTIVE** A **disposable** product is designed to be thrown away after it has been used. ❑ *...disposable diapers.*

dis|pos|al /dɪspoʊzəl/ **NONCOUNT NOUN** Disposal is when you get rid of something that you no longer want or need. ❑ *...waste disposal.*

dis|pose /dɪspoʊz/ (**disposes, disposing, disposed**)
▶ **dispose of** If you **dispose of** something, you get rid of it. ❑ *How do they dispose of nuclear waste?*

dis|pute /dɪspyut/ (**disputes**) NOUN A **dispute** happens when two people or groups cannot agree about something. ❏ *The government had to do something to end the dispute.*

dis|quali|fy /dɪskwɒlɪfaɪ/ (**disqualifies, disqualifying, disqualified**) VERB When someone **is disqualified**, they are stopped from taking part in a competition. ❏ *Thomson was disqualified from the race.*

dis|rupt /dɪsrʌpt/ (**disrupts, disrupting, disrupted**) VERB If someone or something **disrupts** an event, they cause difficulties that prevent it from continuing. ❏ *Several injuries disrupted preparations this week.*
● **dis|rup|tion** (**disruptions**) NOUN ❏ *The bad weather caused disruption at many airports.*

dis|rup|tive /dɪsrʌptɪv/ ADJECTIVE If someone is **disruptive**, they prevent something from continuing in a normal way. ❏ *We have a lot of difficult, disruptive children.*

dis|sat|is|fied /dɪssætɪsfaɪd/ ADJECTIVE If you are **dissatisfied**, you are not happy about something. ❏ *Thousands of dissatisfied customers called the company to complain.*

dis|sect /dɪsɛkt, daɪ-/ (**dissects, dissecting, dissected**) VERB SCIENCE If someone **dissects** a dead body, they cut it open in order to examine it. ❏ *We dissected a frog in biology class.*
● **dis|sec|tion** /dɪsɛkʃ°n, daɪ-/ (**dissections**) NOUN ❏ *The dissection of the tiny insect took place under a microscope.*

dis|solve /dɪzɒlv/ (**dissolves, dissolving, dissolved**) VERB SCIENCE If a substance **dissolves** in liquid, it becomes mixed with the liquid and disappears. ❏ *Heat the mixture gently until the sugar dissolves.*

dis|tance /dɪstəns/ (**distances**)
1 NOUN The **distance between** two places is the amount of space between them. ❏ *Measure the distance between the wall and the table.*
2 Something that is **in the distance** is a long way away from you. ❏ *We had a beautiful view of the countryside with the mountains in the distance.*
3 If you see something **from a distance**, you see it from a long way away. ❏ *From a distance, the lake looked beautiful.*

dis|tant /dɪstənt/
1 ADJECTIVE **Distant** means very far away. ❏ *The mountains were on the distant horizon.*

2 ADJECTIVE A **distant** relative is one who you are not closely related to. ❏ *I received a letter from a distant cousin.*

dis|tinct /dɪstɪŋkt/
1 ADJECTIVE If something is **distinct from** something else, it is different from it. ❏ *Quebec is quite distinct from the rest of Canada.*
2 ADJECTIVE If something is **distinct**, you can hear, see, or taste it clearly. ❏ *Each vegetable has its own distinct flavor.*

dis|tinc|tion /dɪstɪŋkʃ°n/ (**distinctions**) If you **draw a distinction** or **make a distinction**, you say that two things are different. ❏ *He makes a distinction between art and culture.*

dis|tin|guish /dɪstɪŋgwɪʃ/ (**distinguishes, distinguishing, distinguished**) VERB If you can **distinguish between** two things, you can see or understand how they are different. ❏ *When do babies learn to distinguish between men and women?*

dis|tin|guished /dɪstɪŋgwɪʃt/ ADJECTIVE Someone who is **distinguished** is very successful and has a good reputation. ❏ *He came from a distinguished academic family.*

dis|tract /dɪstrækt/ (**distracts, distracting, distracted**) VERB If something **distracts** you, it takes your attention away from what you are doing. ❏ *I'm easily distracted by noise.*

dis|trac|tion /dɪstrækʃ°n/ (**distractions**) NOUN A **distraction** is something that turns your attention away from something you want to concentrate on. ❏ *DVD players in cars are a dangerous distraction for drivers.*

dis|tress /dɪstrɛs/ NONCOUNT NOUN **Distress** is a strong feeling of sadness or pain. ❏ *The condition can cause great distress in young people.*
● **dis|tress|ing** ADJECTIVE ❏ *It is very distressing when your baby is sick.*

dis|trib|ute /dɪstrɪbyut/ (**distributes, distributing, distributed**) VERB If you **distribute** things, you give them to a number of people. ❏ *They distributed free tickets to young people.* ● **dis|tri|bu|tion** /dɪstrɪbyuʃ°n/ NONCOUNT NOUN ❏ *They are trying to stop the illegal distribution of music over the Internet.*

dis|trict /dɪstrɪkt/ (**districts**) NOUN A **district** is a particular area of a city or country. ❏ *I drove around the business district.*

dis|turb /dɪstɜrb/ (**disturbs, disturbing, disturbed**)

1 **VERB** If you **disturb** someone, you interrupt and upset them. ❏ *Sorry, am I disturbing you?*
2 **VERB** If something **disturbs** you, it makes you feel upset or worried. ❏ *He was disturbed by the news of the attack.*

dis|turb|ance /dɪstɜrbəns/ (**disturbances**)
NOUN A **disturbance** is an event in which people behave violently in public. ❏ *During the disturbance, three men were hurt.*

dis|turb|ing /dɪstɜrbɪŋ/ **ADJECTIVE**
Something that is **disturbing** makes you feel worried or upset. ❏ *We've received some disturbing news.*

dis|used /dɪsyuzd/ **ADJECTIVE** A **disused** place or building is empty and is no longer used. ❏ *...a disused gas station.*

ditch /dɪtʃ/ (**ditches**) **NOUN** A **ditch** is a deep, long, narrow hole that carries water away from a road or a field. ❏ *Both vehicles landed in a ditch.*

dive /daɪv/ (**dives, diving, dived** or **dove, dived**)
1 **VERB** **SPORTS** If you **dive into** water, you jump in so that your arms and your head go in first. ❏ *Ben dove into a river.*
2 **NOUN** **SPORTS** **Dive** is also a noun. ❏ *Pam walked out and did another perfect dive.* ● **div|ing** **NONCOUNT NOUN** ❏ *Shaun won medals in diving and swimming.*
3 **VERB** **SPORTS** If you **dive**, you go under the surface of the ocean or a lake, using special equipment for breathing. ❏ *We were diving to look at fish.*
4 **NOUN** **SPORTS** **Dive** is also a noun. ❏ *He is already planning the next dive.* ● **div|er** (**divers**) **NOUN** ❏ *...a deep-sea diver.* ● **div|ing** **NONCOUNT NOUN** ❏ *...equipment for diving.*

di|verse /dɪvɜrs, daɪ-/ **ADJECTIVE** If a group of people or things is **diverse**, it is made up of many different people or things. ❏ *We have a very diverse group of students this year.*

di|ver|sion /dɪvɜrʒ³n, daɪ-/ (**diversions**)
NOUN A **diversion** is an activity that takes your attention away from what you are doing. ❏ *The trip was a welcome diversion from their troubles at home.*

di|vert /dɪvɜrt, daɪ-/ (**diverts, diverting, diverted**) **VERB** To **divert** vehicles or travelers means to make them go a different route. ❏ *The plane was diverted to Boston's Logan International Airport.*

di|vide /dɪvaɪd/ (**divides, dividing, divided**)
1 **VERB** When people or things **are divided** or **divide into** smaller groups or parts, they become separated into smaller parts.
❏ *Divide the pastry in half.* ❏ *The class was divided into two groups of six.*
2 **VERB** **MATH** If you **divide** one number **by** another number, you find out how many times the second number can fit into the first number. ❏ *Measure the floor area and divide it by six.*
3 **VERB** If a line **divides** two areas, it makes the two areas separate. ❏ *A 1969-mile border divides Mexico from the United States.*
4 **VERB** If something **divides** people, they cannot agree about it. ❏ *Several major issues divided the country.*
→ look at **math**
▶ **divide up** If you **divide** something **up**, you separate it into smaller or more useful groups. ❏ *They divided the country up into four areas.*

div|ing board (**diving boards**) **NOUN** **SPORTS**

A **diving board** is a board at the edge of a swimming pool from which people can jump into the water.

di|vi|sion /dɪvɪʒ³n/ (**divisions**)
1 **NONCOUNT NOUN** The **division of** something is when someone or something separates it into parts. ❏ *...the division of land after the war.*
2 **NONCOUNT NOUN** **MATH** **Division** is the process of dividing one number by another number. ❏ *I taught my daughter how to do division.*
3 **NOUN** In a large organization, a **division** is a group of departments with similar tasks. ❏ *She manages the bank's Latin American division.*
→ look at **math**

di|vorce /dɪvɔrs/ (**divorces, divorcing, divorced**)
1 **NOUN** A **divorce** is the legal ending of a marriage. ❏ *Many marriages end in divorce.*
2 **VERB** If a man and woman **get divorced** or if one of them **divorces** the other, their marriage is legally ended. ❏ *Jack and Lillian got divorced in 2006.* ❏ *He divorced me and married my friend.*

di|vorced /dɪvɔrst/ **ADJECTIVE** Someone who is **divorced** from their former husband or wife is no longer legally married to them. ❑ *He is divorced, with a young son.*

DIY /dˌi aɪ wˌaɪ/ **NONCOUNT NOUN** DIY is the activity of making or repairing things yourself, especially in your home. **DIY** is short for **do-it-yourself.** ❑ ...*a DIY project.*

diz|zy /dˌɪzi/ (**dizzier, dizziest**) **ADJECTIVE** If you feel **dizzy**, you feel that you are losing your balance and that you are going to fall. ❑ *Her head hurt, and she felt slightly dizzy.*

● **diz|zi|ness NONCOUNT NOUN** ❑ *His head injury caused dizziness.*

→ look at **sick**

DJ /dˌi dʒeɪ/ (**DJs**) also **D.J.**, **dj NOUN** A DJ is the same as a **disc jockey.**

---

do

❶ AUXILIARY VERB USES
❷ OTHER VERB USES

Sound Partners   do, dew, due

❶ **do** /də, STRONG duː/ (**does, doing, did, done**)

> **LANGUAGE HELP**
> When you are speaking, you can use the negative short forms **don't** for **do not** and **didn't** for **did not.**

1 VERB **Do** is used with "not" to form the negative of main verbs. ❑ *They don't work very hard.* ❑ *I did not know Jamie had a car.*

2 VERB **Do** is used with another verb to form questions. ❑ *Do you like music?* ❑ *What did he say?*

3 VERB You use **do** instead of repeating a verb when you are answering a question. ❑ *"Do you think he is telling the truth?"—"Yes, I do."*

❷ **do** /duː/ (**does, doing, did, done**)

1 VERB When you **do** something, you take some action or perform an activity or task. ❑ *I was trying to do some work.* ❑ *After lunch Elizabeth and I did the dishes.*

2 VERB If you ask someone what they **do**, you want to know what their job is. ❑ *"What does your father do?"—"He's a doctor."*

3 VERB If something **will do**, it is good enough. ❑ *It doesn't matter what you wear— anything warm will do.*

4 If one thing **has** or **is** something **to do with** another thing, the two things are connected. ❑ *Clarke insists all this has nothing to do with him.*

→ look at **disability**

▶ **do up** If you **do** something **up**, you fasten it. ❑ *Mari did up the buttons.*

▶ **do without** If you **do without** something, you are able to continue, although you do not have it. ❑ *We can do without their help.*

dock /dɒk/ (**docks, docking, docked**)

1 NOUN A dock is an area of water beside land where ships go so that people can get on or off them.

2 VERB When a ship **docks**, it is brought into a dock. ❑ *The crash happened as the ferry tried to dock on Staten Island.*

doc|tor /dɒktər/ (**doctors**)

1 NOUN A **doctor** is a person whose job is to treat people who are sick or injured. ❑ *Be sure to speak to your doctor before planning your trip.*

2 NOUN A **doctor** is someone who has been awarded the highest academic degree by a university. ❑ *He is a doctor of philosophy.*

→ look at **health care**

docu|ment /dɒkyəmənt/ (**documents**)

1 NOUN A **document** is an official piece of paper with important information on it. ❑ *Always read legal documents carefully before you sign them.*

2 NOUN TECHNOLOGY A **document** is a piece of text that is stored on a computer. ❑ *Remember to save your document before you send it.*

docu|men|tary /dɒkyəmɛntəri, -tri/ (**documentaries**) **NOUN** A **documentary** is a television program or a movie that provides information about a particular subject. ❑ *Did you see that documentary on TV last night?*

dodge /dɒdʒ/ (**dodges, dodging, dodged**)

1 VERB If you **dodge**, you move suddenly, especially to avoid something. ❑ *I dodged back behind the tree and waited.*

2 VERB If you **dodge** something, you avoid it by moving. ❑ *He dodged a speeding car.*

does /dəz, STRONG dʌz/ **Does** is a form of the verb **do.**

doesn't /dʌzᵊnt/ **Doesn't** is short for "does not."

dog /dɔg/ (**dogs**) **NOUN** A **dog** is an animal that is often kept by people as a pet. ❑ *He was walking his dog.*

→ look at **animal**

dog|gie /dɔgi/ (**doggies**) also **doggy NOUN** Doggie is a child's word for a dog.

doll /dɒl/ (**dolls**) **NOUN** A **doll** is a child's toy that looks like a small person or baby.

dol|lar /dɒlər/ (**dollars**) **NOUN** The **dollar** ($) is the unit of money that is used in the U.S., Canada, and some other countries. There are 100 **cents** in a **dollar**. ❑ *She earns seven dollars an hour.*

dol|phin /dɒlfɪn/ (**dolphins**) **NOUN** A **dolphin** is a large, gray or black and white intelligent animal that lives in the ocean.

do|main name /doʊmeɪn neɪm/ (**domain names**) **NOUN** TECHNOLOGY A **domain name** is the main part of a website address that tells you who the website belongs to. ❑ *I've just bought the domain name "AdamWilson.com"*

dome /doʊm/ (**domes**) **NOUN** A **dome** is a round roof. ❑ *Kiev is known as "the city of golden domes."*

do|mes|tic /dəmɛstɪk/
1 **ADJECTIVE** **Domestic** means happening or existing within one particular country. ❑ *The airline offers over 100 domestic flights a day.*
2 **ADJECTIVE** **Domestic** means relating to the home and family. ❑ *We eat together and share domestic chores.*

domi|nate /dɒmɪneɪt/ (**dominates, dominating, dominated**) **VERB** If one country or person **dominates** another, they have power over them. ❑ *Women are no longer dominated by men.*

domi|no /dɒmɪnoʊ/ (**dominoes**) **NOUN** **Dominoes** is a game that uses small rectangular blocks, called dominoes, that are marked with spots.

do|nate /doʊneɪt, doʊneɪt/ (**donates, donating, donated**)
1 **VERB** If you **donate** something **to** an organization, you give it to them. ❑ *He often donates large amounts of money to charity.*
● **do|na|tion** /doʊneɪʃᵊn/ (**donations**) **NOUN** ❑ *Employees make regular donations to charity.*
2 **VERB** If you **donate** your blood or a part of your body, you allow doctors to use it to help someone who is sick. ❑ *If you are able to donate blood, you should do it.*

done /dʌn/ **Done** is a form of the verb **do**.

don|key /dɒŋki/ (**donkeys**) **NOUN** A **donkey** is an animal like a small horse with long ears.

do|nor /doʊnər/ (**donors**) **NOUN** A **donor** is a person who gives a part of their body or some of their blood so that doctors can use them to help someone who is sick. ❑ *...a blood donor.*

don't /doʊnt/ **Don't** is short for "do not."

door /dɔr/ (**doors**)
1 **NOUN** A **door** is a piece of wood, glass, or metal that fills an entrance. ❑ *I knocked at the front door, but there was no answer.*
2 **NOUN** A **door** is the space in a wall when a door is open. ❑ *She looked through the door of the kitchen.*
3 When you **answer the door**, you open a door because someone has knocked on it or rung the bell. ❑ *Carol answered the door as soon as I knocked.*
4 If someone goes **door to door**, they go along a street stopping at each house. ❑ *They are going from door to door collecting money.*

door|bell /dɔrbɛl/ (**doorbells**) **NOUN** A **doorbell** is a bell next to a door that you can ring to tell the people inside that you are there.

door|knob /dɔrnɒb/ (**doorknobs**) **NOUN** A **doorknob** is a round handle on a door.

door|step /dɔrstɛp/ (**doorsteps**) **NOUN** A **doorstep** is a step in front of a door outside a building. ❑ *I went and sat on the doorstep.*

door|way /dɔrweɪ/ (**doorways**) **NOUN** A **doorway** is a space in a wall where a door opens and closes. ❑ *David was standing in the doorway.*

dorm /dɔrm/ (**dorms**) **NOUN** A **dorm** is a **dormitory.** [INFORMAL] ❑ *...a university dorm.*

dor|mi|tory /dɔrmɪtɔri/ (**dormitories**) **NOUN** A **dormitory** is a building at a school or a university where students live. ❑ *She lived in a college dormitory.*

dose /doʊs/ (**doses**) **NOUN** A **dose of** medicine or a drug is an amount you take at one time. ❑ *You can treat the infection with one big dose of antibiotics.*

d

dot /dɒt/ (**dots**) **NOUN** A **dot** is a very small round mark, like the one on the letter "i," or in the names of websites. ❑ *He makes paintings with little tiny dots of color.*

> **Usage**   **dot**
>
> When you tell someone an email or website address say the . or period as **dot**. For example, the website elt.heinle.com sounds like: elt **dot** heinle **dot** com.

dot|ted /dɒtɪd/ **ADJECTIVE** A **dotted** line is a line made of a row of dots. ❑ *Cut along the dotted line.*

dou|ble /dʌbᵊl/ (**doubles, doubling, doubled**)
1 ADJECTIVE You use **double** to show that something has two parts. ❑ *This room has double doors opening on to a balcony.*
2 ADJECTIVE **Double** means twice the normal size. ❑ *I gave him a double portion of ice cream.*
3 ADJECTIVE A **double** room or bed is intended for two people, usually a couple. ❑ *The hotel charges $180 for a double room.* ❑ *One of the bedrooms has a double bed.*
4 VERB When something **doubles**, it becomes twice as big. ❑ *The number of students has doubled from 50 to 100.*

dou|ble bass /dʌbᵊl beɪs/ (**double basses**)
NOUN MUSIC A **double bass** is a very big wooden musical instrument with four strings.

double-click (**double-clicks, double-clicking, double-clicked**) **VERB** TECHNOLOGY
If you **double-click on** an area of a computer screen, you press one of the buttons on the mouse (= the part that you move around with your hand) twice quickly in order to make something happen. ❑ *Double-click on a file to start the application.*

doubt /daʊt/ (**doubts, doubting, doubted**)
1 NOUN If you have a **doubt** or **doubts** about something, you do not feel certain about it. ❑ *Rendell had doubts about the plan.* ❑ *There is no doubt that the Earth's climate is changing.*
2 VERB If you **doubt** something, you think that it is probably not true. ❑ *I doubt if I'll learn anything new from this lesson.*
3 VERB If you **doubt** someone, you think that they may be saying something that is not true. ❑ *No one doubted him.*
4 If you are **in doubt** about something, you are not sure about it. ❑ *He is in no doubt about what to do.*

5 You use **no doubt** to show that you feel certain about something. ❑ *She will no doubt be here soon.*

doubt|ful /daʊtfəl/
1 ADJECTIVE If it is **doubtful that** something will happen, it seems that it will probably not happen. ❑ *It is doubtful that he will marry again.*
2 ADJECTIVE If you are **doubtful about** something, you do not feel sure about it. ❑ *Sophie sounded doubtful about the idea.*

dough /doʊ/ **NONCOUNT NOUN** **Dough** is a mixture of flour, water, and other things that can be cooked to make bread and cakes. ❑ *Leave the cookie dough in a cool place overnight.*

dough|nut /doʊnʌt, -nət/ (**doughnuts**) also **donut** **NOUN** A **doughnut** is a sweet round cake with a hole in the middle.

dove /dʌv/ (**doves**) **NOUN** A **dove** is a bird that is used as a symbol of peace.

down /daʊn/
1 PREPOSITION **Down** means toward a lower level, or in a lower place. ❑ *A man came down the stairs to meet them.* ❑ *He was halfway down the hill.* ❑ *She was looking down at her papers.*
2 ADVERB **Down** is also an adverb. ❑ *She went down to the kitchen.*
3 PREPOSITION If you go **down** a road or a river, you go along it. ❑ *They walked quickly down the street.*
4 ADVERB If you put something **down**, you put it onto a surface. ❑ *Danny put down his glass.*
5 ADVERB If an amount goes **down**, it decreases. ❑ *Prices went down today.*
6 ADJECTIVE If you are feeling **down**, you are feeling unhappy or depressed. [INFORMAL] ❑ *The man sounded really down.*
7 ADJECTIVE TECHNOLOGY If a computer system is **down**, it is not working. ❑ *The computer's down again.*

> **Word Builder**   **downhill**
>
> *down* ≈ **below, lower**
>   down + hill = **down**hill
>   down + load = **down**load
>   down + stairs = **down**stairs
>   sun + down = sun**down**

down|hill /daʊnhɪl/
1 ADVERB If something or someone is moving **downhill**, they are moving down a slope. ❑ *He walked downhill toward the river.*
2 ADJECTIVE **Downhill** is also an adjective. ❑ *...downhill ski runs.*

Word Builder	**download**

down ≈ below, lower

down + hill = downhill
down + load = download
down + stairs = downstairs
sun + down = sundown

---

down|load /daʊnloʊd/ (**downloads, downloading, downloaded**) VERB
TECHNOLOGY If you **download** information, you move it to your computer from a bigger computer or network. ❑ *You can download the software from the Internet.*
→ look at **email, Internet**

Word Builder	**downloadable**

able ≈ able to be

comfort + able = comfortable
depend + able = dependable
download + able = downloadable
enjoy + able = enjoyable
honor + able = honorable

---

down|load|able /daʊnloʊdəbəl/ ADJECTIVE
TECHNOLOGY If a computer file is **downloadable**, you can copy it to another computer. ❑ *More information is available in the downloadable files below.*

down|pour /daʊnpɔr/ (**downpours**) NOUN
A **downpour** is a sudden heavy fall of rain. ❑ *The heavy downpours caused problems for motorists last night.*

Word Builder	**downstairs**

down ≈ below, lower

down + hill = downhill
down + load = download
down + stairs = downstairs
sun + down = sundown

---

down|stairs /daʊnstɛərz/
1 ADVERB If you go **downstairs** in a building, you walk down the stairs toward the ground floor. ❑ *Denise went downstairs and made some tea.*
2 ADVERB If someone or something is **downstairs** in a building, they are on a lower floor than you. ❑ *The telephone was downstairs in the kitchen.*
3 ADJECTIVE **Downstairs** rooms are on the first floor of a building. ❑ *She painted the downstairs rooms.*

down|town /daʊntaʊn/
1 ADJECTIVE The **downtown** part of a city is where the large stores and businesses are.

❑ *He works in an office in downtown Chicago.*
2 ADVERB **Downtown** is also an adverb. ❑ *He worked downtown for an insurance firm.*

down|ward /daʊnwərd/
1 ADJECTIVE A **downward** movement or look goes to a lower place or a lower level. ❑ *John waved his hand in a downward motion.*
2 ADVERB If you move or look **downward**, you move or look toward the ground or a lower level. ❑ *Ben pointed downward with his stick.*
3 ADVERB If an amount or rate moves **downward**, it decreases. ❑ *Inflation is moving downward.*

doze /doʊz/ (**dozes, dozing, dozed**) VERB
When you **doze**, you sleep lightly or for a short period. ❑ *She dozed for a while in the cabin.*
▶ **doze off** If you **doze off**, you fall into a light sleep. ❑ *I closed my eyes and dozed off.*

doz|en /dʌzən/ (**dozens**)

> LANGUAGE HELP
> The plural form is **dozen** after a number.

1 A **dozen** means twelve. ❑ *Will you buy a loaf of bread and a dozen eggs please?*
2 **Dozens of** things or people means a lot of them. ❑ *The storm destroyed dozens of buildings.*

Dr. (**Drs.**) **Dr.** is short for **Doctor.** ❑ *...Dr. John Hardy of Vanderbilt Hospital.*

drab /dræb/ (**drabber, drabbest**) ADJECTIVE
Something that is **drab** is dull and boring. ❑ *He was living in a small, drab apartment in Tokyo.*

draft /dræft/ (**drafts**)
1 NOUN LANGUAGE ARTS A **draft** is a piece of writing that you have not finished working on. ❑ *I emailed a first draft of the article to him.*
2 NOUN A **draft** is cold air that comes into a room. ❑ *Block drafts around doors and windows.*
→ look at **email, writing**

drag /dræg/ (**drags, dragging, dragged**)
1 VERB If you **drag** something, you pull it along the ground. ❑ *He dragged his chair toward the table.*
2 VERB If you **drag** a computer image, you use the mouse to move it on the screen. ❑ *Simply drag and drop the file into the desired folder.*
3 VERB If a period of time or an event **drags**, it seems to last a long time. ❑ *The minutes dragged past.*

drag and drop (**drags and drops, dragging and dropping, dragged and dropped**) also
drag-and-drop
1 VERB TECHNOLOGY If you **drag and drop**

D

computer files or images, you move them from one place to another on the computer screen. ❏ *Drag and drop the folder to the hard drive.* **2** **NONCOUNT NOUN** **Drag and drop** is also a noun. ❏ *Copying software onto an iPod is as easy as drag and drop.*

drag|on /drǽgən/ (**dragons**) **NOUN** In stories, a **dragon** is an animal with rough skin that has wings and breathes out fire.

drain /dreɪn/ (**drains, draining, drained**)
1 **VERB** If you **drain** a liquid, you remove it by making it flow somewhere else. ❏ *They built the tunnel to drain water out of the mines.*
2 **VERB** If you **drain** food, you remove the liquid that it has been in. ❏ *Drain the pasta well.*
3 **NOUN** A **drain** is a pipe or an opening that carries a liquid away from a place. ❏ *A piece of soap was clogging the drain.*
→ look at **bathroom**

dra|ma /drάmə, drǽmə/ (**dramas**)
1 **NOUN** ARTS LANGUAGE ARTS A **drama** is a serious play or movie. ❏ *The movie is a drama about a woman searching for her children.*
2 **NOUN** A real situation that is exciting can be called a **drama**. ❏ *This novel is full of drama.*

dra|mat|ic /drəmǽtɪk/ **ADJECTIVE** A **dramatic** change or event is a big change that happens suddenly. ❏ *There's been a dramatic change in the way we shop.*
● **dra|mati|cal|ly** /drəmǽtɪkli/ **ADVERB** ❏ *The climate has changed dramatically.*

drank /drǽŋk/ **Drank** is a form of the verb **drink**.

drape /dreɪp/ (**drapes, draping, draped**)
1 **VERB** If you **drape** a piece of cloth somewhere, you put it there so that it hangs down. ❏ *He draped the damp towel over a chair.*
2 **NOUN** **Drapes** are pieces of heavy fabric that you hang from the top of a window. ❏ *He pulled the drapes shut.*

dras|tic /drǽstɪk/ **ADJECTIVE** A **drastic** action has a very big effect. ❏ *Drastic measures are needed to improve the situation.*

draw /drɔ/ (**draws, drawing, drew, drawn**)
1 **VERB** ARTS When you **draw**, you use a pencil or pen to make a picture. ❏ *She was drawing with a pencil.* ❏ *I've drawn a picture of you.*
● **draw|ing** **NONCOUNT NOUN** ❏ *I like dancing, singing, and drawing.*
2 **VERB** If a vehicle **draws** somewhere, it moves there. ❏ *The taxi was drawing away.* ❏ *The train was drawing into the station.*
3 **VERB** If you **draw** something or someone somewhere, you move them there. ❏ *He drew his chair nearer the fire.* ❏ *He drew Caroline close to him.*
4 **VERB** When you **draw** the drapes (= long pieces of cloth that cover a window), you pull them across a window. ❏ *He went to the window and drew the drapes.*
5 **VERB** If you **draw** money out of a bank account, you get it from the account so that you can use it. ❏ *A few months ago he drew out nearly all his savings.*
→ look at Picture Dictionary: **draw**
→ look at **geometry**
▶ **draw up** If you **draw up** a list or a plan, you write it or type it. ❏ *They drew up a formal agreement.*

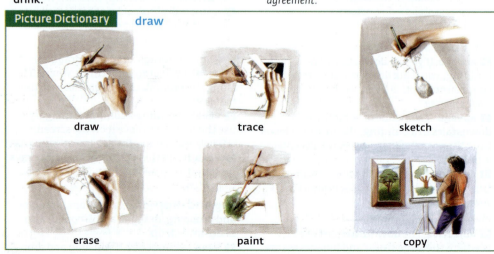

Picture Dictionary **draw**

draw

trace

sketch

erase

paint

copy

draw|back /drɔbæk/ (drawbacks) NOUN
A **drawback** is a part of something that makes it less useful than you would like. ❑ *The apartment's only drawback was that it was too small.*

drawer /drɔr/ (drawers) NOUN A **drawer** is part of a desk, for example, that you can pull out and put things in. ❑ *She opened her desk drawer and took out the book.*
→ look at **kitchen**

draw|ing /drɔɪŋ/ (drawings) NOUN ARTS
A **drawing** is a picture made with a pencil or pen. ❑ *She did a drawing of me.*

drawn /drɔn/ **Drawn** is a form of the verb **draw**.

dread /drɛd/ (dreads, dreading, dreaded)
VERB If you **dread** something, you feel very anxious because you think it will be unpleasant or upsetting. ❑ *I've been dreading this moment for a long time.*

dread|ful /drɛdfəl/ ADJECTIVE **Dreadful** means very unpleasant, or very poor in quality. ❑ *They told us the dreadful news.* ❑ *I didn't enjoy the movie; the acting was dreadful.*

dream /drim/ (dreams, dreaming, dreamed or dreamt)
1 NOUN A **dream** is a series of events that you see in your mind while you are asleep. ❑ *He had a dream about Claire.*
2 NOUN A **dream** is something that you often think about because you would like it to happen. ❑ *After all these years, my dream has finally come true.*
3 VERB When you **dream**, you see events in your mind while you are asleep. ❑ *Richard dreamed that he was on a bus.* ❑ *She dreamed about her baby.*
4 VERB If you often think about something that you would like, you can say that you **dream of** it. ❑ *She dreamed of becoming an actress.*
→ look at **relax**

dress /drɛs/ (dresses, dressing, dressed)
1 NOUN A **dress** is a piece of woman's or girl's clothing that covers the body and part of the legs. ❑ *She was wearing a short black dress.*
2 NONCOUNT NOUN Particular types of clothing are sometimes called **dress**. ❑ *He wore formal evening dress.*

3 VERB When you **dress** or **dress yourself**, you put on clothes. ❑ *Sarah waited while he dressed.*
→ look at **wear**
▶ **dress up** **1** If you **dress up**, you put on formal clothes. ❑ *You do not need to dress up for dinner.*
2 If you **dress up**, you put on clothes that make you look like someone else for fun. ❑ *He was dressed up like a cowboy.*

dressed /drɛst/ ADJECTIVE If you are **dressed**, you are wearing clothes. ❑ *He threw her into a swimming pool, fully dressed.*

dress|er /drɛsər/ (dressers) NOUN A **dresser** is a piece of furniture with several drawers in it, usually for holding clothes.
→ look at **furniture**

drew /dru/ **Drew** is a form of the verb **draw**.

drib|ble /drɪbəl/ (dribbles, dribbling, dribbled)
1 VERB If a liquid **dribbles** somewhere, it flows there in a thin stream. ❑ *Blood dribbled down Harry's face.*
2 VERB When players **dribble** the ball in a game, they keep it moving by using their hand or foot. ❑ *Owen dribbled the ball toward Ferris.*

dried /draɪd/ ADJECTIVE **Dried** food has had all the water removed from it so that it will last for a long time. ❑ *...dried herbs.*
→ look at **meat**

dri|er /draɪər/ → look up **dry, dryer**

drift /drɪft/ (drifts, drifting, drifted) VERB When something **drifts** somewhere, it is carried there by wind or water. ❑ *We drifted up the river.*
▶ **drift off** If you **drift off** to sleep, you gradually fall asleep. ❑ *He finally drifted off to sleep.*

drill /drɪl/ (drills, drilling, drilled)
1 NOUN A **drill** is a tool for making holes. ❑ *...an electric drill.*
2 VERB When you **drill** a hole in something, you make a hole in it using a drill. ❑ *You'll need to drill a hole in the wall.*

drink /drɪŋk/ (drinks, drinking, drank, drunk)
1 VERB When you **drink** a liquid, you take it into your mouth and swallow it. ❑ *He drank his cup of coffee.* ● **drink|er** (drinkers) NOUN ❑ *We're all coffee drinkers.*
2 VERB To **drink** means to drink alcohol. ❑ *He drinks too much.* ● **drink|er** (drinkers) NOUN ❑ *I'm not a heavy drinker.*

d

3 **NOUN** A **drink** is an amount of a liquid that you drink. ❏ *I'll get you a drink of water.*
→ look at **eat**

drip /drɪp/ (**drips, dripping, dripped**)
1 **VERB** When liquid **drips** somewhere, it falls in drops. ❏ *The rain dripped down my face.*
2 **VERB** When something that contains a liquid **drips**, drops of liquid escape from it. ❏ *A faucet in the kitchen was dripping.*

drive /draɪv/ (**drives, driving, drove, driven**)
1 **VERB** When you **drive**, you control the movement and direction of a car or other vehicle. ❏ *I drove into town.* ❏ *She never learned to drive.* ❏ *We drove the car to Richmond.*
● **driv|ing** **NONCOUNT NOUN** ❏ *...a driving instructor.*
2 **VERB** If you **drive** someone somewhere, you take them there in a car. ❏ *She drove him to the train station.*
3 **NOUN** A **drive** is a trip in a car. ❏ *Let's go for a drive on Sunday.*
4 **NOUN** The **drive** is the part of a computer that reads and stores information. ❏ *Save your work on drive C.*
→ look at **route**

driv|er /draɪvər/ (**drivers**) **NOUN** A **driver** is a person who drives a bus, a car, or a train, for example. ❏ *The driver got out of his truck.* ❏ *...a taxi driver.*
→ look at **car**

driv|er's li|cense (**driver's licenses**) **NOUN** A **driver's license** is a card that shows that you have passed a driving test and that you are allowed to drive.
→ look at **identification**

drive-through (**drive-throughs**) also **drive-thru** **NOUN** A **drive-through** is a place with a window at a bank, restaurant or store where you can be served without leaving your car. ❏ *...a fast-food drive-through.*

drive|way /draɪvweɪ/ (**driveways**) **NOUN** A **driveway** is a small road that leads from the street to the front of a building. ❏ *There is a driveway and garage at the front of the house.*

droop /druːp/ (**droops, drooping, drooped**) **VERB** If something **droops**, it hangs or leans downward. ❏ *His eyelids drooped and he yawned.*

drop /drɒp/ (**drops, dropping, dropped**)
1 **VERB** If a level or an amount **drops**, it quickly becomes less. ❏ *Temperatures can drop to freezing at night.*
2 **NOUN** **Drop** is also a noun. ❏ *There was a sudden drop in the number of visitors to the site.*
3 **VERB** If you **drop** something, you let it fall. ❏ *I dropped my glasses and broke them.*
4 **VERB** If you **drop** someone somewhere, you take them there in a car and leave them there. ❏ *He dropped me outside the hotel.*
5 **Drop off** means the same as **drop.**
❏ *Dad dropped me off at school on his way to work.*
6 **NOUN** A **drop of** a liquid is a very small amount of it shaped like a little ball. ❏ *...a drop of water.*
→ look at **water**
▶ **drop by** If you **drop by**, you visit someone informally. ❏ *She will drop by later.*
▶ **drop in** If you **drop in**, or **drop in on** someone, you visit them informally. ❏ *Why not drop in for a chat?*
▶ **drop off** If you **drop off** to sleep, you go to sleep. [INFORMAL] ❏ *I lay on the bed and dropped off to sleep.*
▶ **drop out** If someone **drops out of** school or a race, for example, they leave it without finishing. ❏ *He dropped out of high school at the age of 16.*

drop-down me|nu (**drop-down menus**)
NOUN TECHNOLOGY On a computer screen, a **drop-down menu** is a list of choices that appears, usually when you click on a small arrow. ❏ *If you click on the search box, a drop-down menu appears.*

drought /draʊt/ (**droughts**) **NOUN** A **drought** is a long period of time with no rain. ❏ *The drought has killed all their crops.*
→ look at **disaster**

drove /droʊv/ **Drove** is a form of the verb **drive.**

drown /draʊn/ (**drowns, drowning, drowned**) **VERB** When someone **drowns**, they die under water because they cannot breathe. ❏ *A child can drown in only a few inches of water.*

drowsy /draʊzi/ (**drowsier, drowsiest**) **ADJECTIVE** If you feel **drowsy**, you feel tired and you cannot think clearly. ❏ *He felt pleasantly drowsy.*

drug /drʌg/ (**drugs**)
1 **NOUN** SCIENCE A **drug** is a chemical that is used as a medicine. ❏ *The new drug is too expensive for most African countries.*

2 **NOUN** Drugs are illegal substances that some people take because they enjoy their effects. ❑ *She was sure Leo was taking drugs.*

drug ad|dict (drug addicts) **NOUN** A drug addict is someone who cannot stop using illegal drugs.

drug|store /drʌgstɔr/ (drugstores) **NOUN** A **drugstore** is a store where medicines, make-up, and some other things are sold.

drum /drʌm/ (drums) **NOUN** MUSIC A **drum** is a simple musical instrument that you hit with sticks or with your hands. ● **drum|mer** (drummers) **NOUN** ❑ *He was a drummer in a band.* → look at **musical instrument**

drunk /drʌŋk/
1 **ADJECTIVE** Someone who is **drunk** has drunk too much alcohol. ❑ *He got drunk and fell down the stairs.*
2 **Drunk** is a form of the verb **drink**.

dry /draɪ/ (drier or dryer, driest, dries, drying, dried)
1 **ADJECTIVE** If something is **dry**, there is no water on it or in it. ❑ *Clean the metal with a soft dry cloth.*
2 **ADJECTIVE** If the weather is **dry**, there is no rain. ❑ *The Sahara is one of the driest places in Africa.*
3 **VERB** When something **dries**, it becomes dry. ❑ *Let your hair dry naturally if possible.*
4 **VERB** When you **dry** something, you remove the water from it. ❑ *Mrs. Madrigal picked up a towel and began drying dishes.*
→ look at **climate, laundry, season**
▶ **dry up** If something **dries up**, it becomes completely dry. ❑ *The river dried up.*

dry-clean (dry-cleans, dry-cleaning, dry-cleaned) **VERB** When clothes are **dry-cleaned**, they are cleaned with a chemical rather than with water. ❑ *The suit must be dry-cleaned.*

Word Builder   **dryer**

er ≈ **something that does**
    clean + er = cleaner
    contain + er = container
    dry + er = dryer
    open + er = opener
    print + er = printer
    toast + er = toaster

---

dry|er /draɪər/ (dryers) also **drier** **NOUN** A **dryer** is a machine for drying things. ❑ *Put the clothes in the dryer for a few minutes.*
→ look at **laundry**

duck /dʌk/ (ducks, ducking, ducked)
1 **NOUN** A **duck** is a bird that lives near water. ❑ *A few ducks were swimming around in the shallow water.*
2 **NONCOUNT NOUN** **Duck** is meat from this bird. ❑ *...roasted duck.*
3 **VERB** If you **duck**, you move your head quickly downward so that something does not hit you, or so that someone does not see you. ❑ *There was a loud noise and I ducked.*
→ look at **bird**

dude /dud/ (dudes) **NOUN** A **dude** is a man. **Dude** is sometimes used as an informal greeting for a man. [INFORMAL] ❑ *He's a real cool dude.* ❑ *Hey, dude, how're you doing?*

Sound Partners   due, dew, do

due /du/
1 If a situation is **due to** something, it exists as a result of that thing. ❑ *She couldn't do the job, due to pain in her hands.*
2 **ADJECTIVE** If something is **due** at a particular time, it is expected to happen or arrive at that time. ❑ *The results are due at the end of the month.*
3 **ADJECTIVE** Money that is **due** is owed to someone. ❑ *When is the next payment due?*

duet /duɛt/ (duets) **NOUN** MUSIC A **duet** is a piece of music performed by two people. ❑ *She sang a duet with Maurice Gibb.*

dug /dʌg/ **Dug** is a form of the verb **dig**.

duke /duk/ (dukes) **NOUN** A **duke** is a man with a very high social rank in some countries. ❑ *...the Duke of Edinburgh.*

dull /dʌl/ (duller, dullest)
1 **ADJECTIVE** **Dull** means not interesting or exciting. ❑ *I thought he was boring and dull.*
2 **ADJECTIVE** A **dull** color or light is not bright. ❑ *...the dull gray sky of London.*

dumb /dʌm/ (dumber, dumbest)
1 **ADJECTIVE** Someone who is **dumb** is completely unable to speak. ❑ *He was born deaf and dumb.*
2 **ADJECTIVE** If you call a person **dumb**, you mean that they are stupid. [INFORMAL] ❑ *He was a brilliant guy. He made me feel dumb.*
3 **ADJECTIVE** If something is **dumb**, it is silly and annoying. [INFORMAL] ❑ *He had this dumb idea.*

dum|my /dʌmi/ (dummies)
1 **NOUN** A **dummy** is a model of a person, often used in safety tests. ❑ *...a crash-test dummy.*

d

2 NOUN If you call a person a **dummy**, you are rudely saying that they are stupid. [INFORMAL]

dump /dʌmp/ (**dumps, dumping, dumped**)
1 VERB If you **dump** something somewhere, you leave it there quickly and without being careful. [INFORMAL] ❑ *We dumped our bags at the hotel and went to the market.*
2 VERB If something **is dumped** somewhere, it is put or left there because it is no longer wanted. [INFORMAL] ❑ *The robbers' car was dumped near the freeway.*
3 VERB If someone **dumps** their girlfriend or boyfriend, they end their relationship. [INFORMAL] ❑ *My boyfriend dumped me last night.*
4 NOUN A **dump** is a place where you can take garbage. ❑ *He took his trash to the dump.*
5 NOUN If a place is a **dump**, it is ugly and unpleasant. [INFORMAL] ❑ *"What a dump!" Christabel said, looking at the house.*
→ look at **pollution**

dump|ster /dʌmpstər/ (**dumpsters**) NOUN
A **dumpster** is a large metal container for holding garbage. [TRADEMARK]

dune /dun/ (**dunes**) NOUN SCIENCE A **dune** is a hill of sand near the ocean or in a desert. ❑ *Behind the beach is an area of sand dunes and grass.*
→ look at **beach**

duo /duoʊ/ (**duos**) NOUN MUSIC A **duo** is a pair of musicians, singers, or other performers. ❑ *...a famous singing duo.*

du|rable /dʊərəbəl/ ADJECTIVE Something that is **durable** is strong and lasts a long time. ❑ *It's one of the most durable tennis shoes on the market.*

dur|ing /dʊərɪŋ/ PREPOSITION If something happens **during** a period of time, it happens between the beginning and the end of that period. ❑ *Storms are common during the winter.* ❑ *I fell asleep during the performance.*

dusk /dʌsk/ NONCOUNT NOUN Dusk is the time just before night when it is not completely dark. ❑ *We arrived home at dusk.*

dust /dʌst/ (**dusts, dusting, dusted**)
1 NONCOUNT NOUN Dust is a fine powder of dry earth or dirt. ❑ *I could see a thick layer of dust on the stairs.*
2 VERB When you **dust** furniture, you remove dust from it with a cloth. ❑ *I dusted and polished the furniture in the living room.* ❑ *I was dusting in his study.*
→ look at **chore**

dusty /dʌsti/ (**dustier, dustiest**) ADJECTIVE If something is **dusty**, it is covered with dust. ❑ *...a dusty room.*

duty /duti/ (**duties**)
1 NOUN A **duty** is work that you have to do. ❑ *I did my duties without complaining.*
2 NOUN If something is your **duty**, you feel that you have to do it. ❑ *I consider it my duty to warn you of the dangers.*
3 If someone is **off duty**, they are not working. If someone is **on duty**, they are working. ❑ *The two police officers were off duty when the accident happened.*

duty-free ADJECTIVE Duty-free goods are sold at airports or on airplanes at a cheaper price than usual. ❑ *...duty-free perfume.*

DVD /di vi di/ (**DVDs**) NOUN TECHNOLOGY A **DVD** is a disk on which a movie or music is recorded. **DVD** is short for "digital video disk." ❑ *...a DVD player.*
→ look at **movie**

DVD burn|er /di vi di bɜrnər/ (**DVD burners**) or **DVD writer** NOUN TECHNOLOGY A **DVD burner** is a piece of computer equipment that you use for putting information onto a DVD.

DVD play|er (**DVD players**) NOUN TECHNOLOGY A **DVD player** is a machine for showing movies that are stored on a DVD. ❑ *We got a portable DVD player for the kids to watch in the car.*

dwarf /dwɔrf/ (**dwarves, dwarfs**)
1 NOUN A **dwarf** is a very short person with short arms and legs.
2 NOUN In children's stories, a **dwarf** is a small man who sometimes has magical powers.

dye /daɪ/ (**dyes, dyeing, dyed**)
1 VERB If you **dye** something, you change its color by putting it in a special liquid. ❑ *He had to dye his hair for the movie.*
2 NOUN Dye is a substance that is used for changing the color of cloth or hair. ❑ *...a bottle of hair dye.*

dy|nam|ic /daɪnæmɪk/ ADJECTIVE Someone who is **dynamic** is full of energy, or has new and exciting ideas. ❑ *He was a dynamic and energetic leader.*

dys|lexia /dɪslɛksiə/ NONCOUNT NOUN **Dyslexia** is a condition that affects the brain, making it difficult for someone to read and write.

Ee

each /itʃ/

1 **ADJECTIVE** **Each** person or thing is every person or thing. ❑ *Each book is beautifully illustrated.* ❑ *The library buys 2,000 new books each year.*

2 **PRONOUN** **Each** is also a pronoun. ❑ *We each have different needs and interests.*

3 **ADVERB** **Each** is also an adverb. ❑ *Tickets are six dollars each.*

4 **Each of** means every one of. ❑ *He gave each of them a book.* ❑ *Each of these exercises takes one or two minutes to do.*

5 **PRONOUN** You use **each other** to show that each member of a group does something to or for the other members. ❑ *We looked at each other in silence.*

> **Usage** **each**
> Sentences that begin with **each** take a singular verb. ***Each** student **has** the book.*

eager /igər/ **ADJECTIVE** If you are **eager to** do something, you want to do it very much. ❑ *The children are all very eager to learn.*

● **eager|ly** **ADVERB** ❑ *"So what do you think will happen?" he asked eagerly.*

eagle /igəl/ (**eagles**) **NOUN** An **eagle** is a large bird that eats small animals.

ear /ɪər/ (**ears**) **NOUN** Your **ears** are the two parts of your body that you hear sounds with. ❑ *He whispered something in her ear.*
→ look at **face**, **sense**

ear|ache /ɪəreɪk/ **NONCOUNT NOUN** If you have **earache**, you have a pain inside your ear. ❑ *I woke up in the morning with terrible earache.*

ear|drum /ɪərdrʌm/ (**eardrums**) also **ear drum** **NOUN** **SCIENCE** Your **eardrums** are the parts inside your ears that react when sound waves reach them. ❑ *The explosion burst Ollie Williams' eardrum.*

ear|ly /ɜrli/ (**earlier, earliest**)

1 **ADVERB** **Early** means before the usual time. ❑ *I had to get up early this morning.* ❑ *She arrived early to get a place at the front.*

2 **ADJECTIVE** **Early** is also an adjective. ❑ *I want to get an early start in the morning.*
→ look at **day**

earn /ɜrn/ (**earns, earning, earned**)

1 **VERB** If you **earn** money, you receive money for work that you do. ❑ *She earns $37,000 a year.*

2 **VERB** If you **earn** something, you get it because you deserve it. ❑ *A good manager earns the respect of his team.*

ear|phone /ɪərfoʊn/ (**earphones**) **NOUN** **Earphones** are things that you wear on or in your ears so that you can listen to music or the radio without anyone else hearing.

ear|ring /ɪərɪŋ/ (**earrings**) **NOUN** **Earrings** are jewelry that you wear on your ears. ❑ *The woman wore large, gold earrings.*

earth /ɜrθ/

1 **NOUN** **GEOGRAPHY** **Earth** or **the Earth** is the planet that we live on. ❑ *The space shuttle Atlantis returned safely to Earth today.*

2 **NOUN** **SCIENCE** **Earth** is the substance in which plants grow. ❑ *...a huge pile of earth.*

3 You use **on earth** in questions that begin with "how," "why," "what," or "where," to show that you are very surprised. ❑ *How on earth did that happen?*
→ look at Word World: **earth**
→ look at **greenhouse effect**

earth|quake /ɜrθkweɪk/ (**earthquakes**) **NOUN** **SCIENCE** An **earthquake** is when the ground shakes because the Earth's surface is moving. ❑ *...the San Francisco earthquake of 1906.*
→ look at **disaster**

ease /iz/

1 If you do something **with ease**, you do it without difficulty or effort. ❑ *Anne passed her exams with ease.*

2 If you are **at ease**, you are feeling confident and relaxed. ❑ *It is important that you feel at ease with your doctor.*

Word World   **earth**

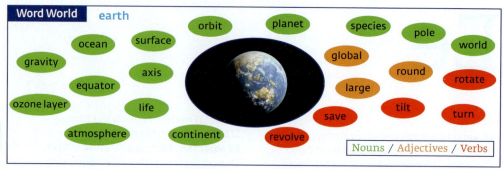

Nouns / Adjectives / Verbs

easel /iz^əl/ (easels) **NOUN** ARTS
An **easel** is a stand that supports a picture while an artist is working on it.

east /ist/ also **East**

1 **NONCOUNT NOUN** GEOGRAPHY The **east** is the direction that is in front of you when you look at the sun in the morning. ❑ *The city lies to the east of the river.*

2 **ADJECTIVE** GEOGRAPHY **East** is also an adjective. ❑ *There is a line of hills along the east coast.*

3 **ADVERB** If you go **east**, you travel toward the east. ❑ *Go east on Route 9.*

4 **ADJECTIVE** An **east** wind is a wind that blows from the east. ❑ *A cold east wind was blowing.*

5 **NOUN** GEOGRAPHY The **East** is the southern and eastern part of Asia, including India, China, and Japan.
→ look at **globe**

east|er|ly /istərli/

1 **ADJECTIVE** GEOGRAPHY **Easterly** means to the east or toward the east. ❑ *We sailed slowly along the coast in an easterly direction.*

2 **ADJECTIVE** An **easterly** wind is a wind that blows from the east. ❑ *It was a beautiful September day, with cool easterly winds.*

east|ern /istərn/

1 **ADJECTIVE** GEOGRAPHY **Eastern** means in or from the east of a place. ❑ *...Eastern Europe.*

2 **ADJECTIVE** SOCIAL STUDIES **Eastern** describes things or ideas that come from the countries of the East, such as India, China, or Japan. ❑ *Exports to Eastern countries have gone down.*

easy /izi/ (easier, easiest)

1 **ADJECTIVE** If a task is **easy**, you can do it without difficulty. ❑ *Losing weight is not an easy task.* ❑ *The software is easy to use.* ● **easi|ly** **ADVERB** ❑ *Most students were easily able to find jobs at the end of the course.*

2 If someone tells you to **take it easy**, they mean that you should relax and that you should not worry. [INFORMAL] ❑ *I suggest you take it easy for a week or two.*
→ look at **language, math, play, relax**

eat /it/ (eats, eating, ate, eaten) **VERB** When you **eat** something, you put it into your mouth and swallow it. ❑ *What did you eat last night?* ❑ *I ate slowly and without speaking.*
→ look at Word World: **eat**
→ look at **food, meat**

ec|cen|tric /ɪksɛntrɪk/ **ADJECTIVE** Someone who is **eccentric** is unusual, and has habits that are different from those of most people. ❑ *He is an eccentric character who likes wearing unusual clothes.*

Word World   **eat**

Nouns / Adjectives / Verbs

echo /ɛkoʊ/ (**echoes, echoing, echoed**)
1 NOUN SCIENCE An **echo** is a sound that you hear again because it hits a surface and then comes back. ❑ *I heard the echo of someone laughing across the hall.*
2 VERB If a sound **echoes**, you hear it again because it hits a surface and then comes back. ❑ *His feet echoed on the stone floor.*

eclipse /ɪklɪps/ (**eclipses**) NOUN SCIENCE
An **eclipse** happens when the light from the sun or the moon is blocked for a short time because of the position of the sun, the moon, and the Earth. ❑ *The last total solar eclipse was in November.*

eco-friendly ADJECTIVE **Eco-friendly** products or services are less harmful to the environment than other similar products or services. ❑ *...eco-friendly laundry detergent.*

ecol|ogy /ɪkɒlədʒi/ NONCOUNT NOUN
SCIENCE **Ecology** is the study of the relationships between living things and their environment. ❑ *He is professor of ecology at the university.* ● **ecolo|gist** (**ecologists**)
NOUN ❑ *Ecologists are concerned that these chemicals will pollute lakes.* ● **eco|logi|cal** /ɛkəlɒdʒɪkəl, ik-/ ADJECTIVE ❑ *How can we save the Earth from ecological disaster?.*

eco|nom|ic /ɛkənɒmɪk, ik-/ ADJECTIVE
Economic means connected with the organization of the money and industry of a country. ❑ *The economic situation is very bad.*

eco|nomi|cal /ɛkənɒmɪkəl, ik-/ ADJECTIVE
Something that is **economical** does not need a lot of money to make it work. ❑ *People are driving smaller and more economical cars.*
● **eco|nomi|cal|ly** ADVERB ❑ *Services could be operated more economically.*

eco|nom|ics /ɛkənɒmɪks, ik-/ NONCOUNT
NOUN SOCIAL STUDIES **Economics** is the study of the way in which money and industry are organized in a society. ❑ *His sister is studying economics.*

econo|mist /ɪkɒnəmɪst/ (**economists**)
NOUN SOCIAL STUDIES An **economist** is a person who studies economics.

econo|my /ɪkɒnəmi/ (**economies**) NOUN
SOCIAL STUDIES An **economy** is the system for organizing the money and industry of the world, a country, or local government. ❑ *The Indian economy is changing fast.*

eco|sys|tem /ɛkoʊsɪstəm, ik-/
(**ecosystems**) NOUN SCIENCE An **ecosystem** is the relationship between all the living things in a particular area together. ❑ *These industries are destroying whole ecosystems.*

edge /ɛdʒ/ (**edges**)
1 NOUN The **edge** of something is the part of it that is farthest from the middle. ❑ *We lived in an apartment block on the edge of town.* ❑ *She was standing at the water's edge.*

2 NOUN The **edge** of a knife is its sharp side. ❑ *His hand touched the edge of the sword.*

ed|ible /ɛdɪbəl/ ADJECTIVE If something is **edible**, it is safe to eat. ❑ *The flowers are edible, and they look wonderful in salads.*

edit /ɛdɪt/ (**edits, editing, edited**) VERB If you **edit** a text, you check it and correct the mistakes in it. ❑ *She helped him edit his paper.*
→ look at **writing**

edi|tion /ɪdɪʃən/ (**editions**) NOUN An **edition** is one of a number of books, magazines, or newspapers that is printed at one time. ❑ *The second edition was published in Canada.*

edi|tor /ɛdɪtər/ (**editors**) NOUN An **editor** is a person who checks and corrects texts. ❑ *He works as an editor of children's books.*

edu|cate /ɛdʒʊkeɪt/ (**educates, educating, educated**)
1 VERB When someone **is educated**, he or she is taught at a school or college. ❑ *He was educated at Yale and Stanford.*
2 VERB To **educate** people means to teach them better ways of doing something. ❑ *We want to educate people about healthy eating.*

edu|cat|ed /ɛdʒʊkeɪtɪd/ ADJECTIVE Someone who is **educated** has a lot of knowledge. ❑ *He was an educated and honest man.*

edu|ca|tion /ɛdʒʊkeɪʃən/ NONCOUNT NOUN
Education involves teaching and learning. ❑ *My children's education is important to me.* ❑ *We need better health education.*
● **edu|ca|tion|al** /ɛdʒʊkeɪʃənəl/ ADJECTIVE
❑ *...the American educational system.*
→ look at **school, television**

eel /il/ (**eels**) NOUN An **eel** is a long, thin fish that looks like a snake.

ef|fect /ɪfɛkt/ (**effects**) NOUN An **effect** is a change or a reaction that is the result of something. ❑ *Parents worry about the effect of junk food on their child's health.*

e

E

ef|fec|tive /ɪfɛktɪv/ **ADJECTIVE** Something that is **effective** produces the results that you wanted. ❏ *No drugs are effective against this disease.* ● **ef|fec|tive|ly** **ADVERB** ❏ *We need to use water more effectively.*

ef|fi|cient /ɪfɪʃⁿnt/ **ADJECTIVE** If something or someone is **efficient**, they are able to do tasks successfully, without wasting time or energy. ❏ *The engine is efficient and powerful.* ● **ef|fi|cien|cy** /ɪfɪʃ°nsi/ **NONCOUNT NOUN** ❏ *We must think of ways to improve efficiency.* ● **ef|fi|cient|ly** **ADVERB** ❏ *We want people to use energy more efficiently.*
→ look at **factory**

ef|fort /ɛfərt/ (**efforts**) **NOUN** If you make an **effort to** do something, you try very hard to do it. ❏ *You should make an effort to speak the local language when you go abroad.*

e.g. /i dʒi/ **e.g.** means "for example." ❏ *We need professionals of all types, e.g., teachers, lawyers.*

egg /ɛg/ (**eggs**)
1 **NOUN** An **egg** is a round object that is produced by a female bird and contains a baby bird. Other animals such as insects and fish also lay eggs.
2 **NOUN** In many countries, an **egg** means a hen's egg, that people eat as food. ❏ *Break the eggs into a bowl.*
→ look at **bird**

egg|plant /ɛgplænt/ (**eggplants**) **NOUN** An **eggplant** is a vegetable with a smooth, dark purple skin.
→ look at **vegetable**

| **Sound Partners** | eight, ate |

eight /eɪt/ **MATH** **Eight** is the number 8.
→ look at **number**

Word Builder **eighteen**

teen ≈ plus ten, from 13-19
eight + teen = eighteen
four + teen = fourteen
nine + teen = nineteen
seven + teen = seventeen
six + teen = sixteen
teen + age = teenage

eight|een /eɪtin/ **MATH** **Eighteen** is the number 18.

eighth /eɪtθ/ (**eighths**)
1 **ADJECTIVE, ADVERB** **MATH** The **eighth** item in a series is the one that you count as

number eight. ❏ *Shekhar was the eighth prime minister of India.*
2 **NOUN** **MATH** An **eighth** is one of eight equal parts of something (⅛). ❏ *The ring was an eighth of an inch thick.*
→ look at **number**

eighty /eɪti/ **MATH** **Eighty** is the number 80.

either /iðər, aɪðər/
1 You use **either...or...** to show that there are two possibilities to choose from. ❏ *Either she goes or I go.* ❏ *I will either walk or take the bus.* ❏ *You can contact him either by phone or by email.*
2 **PRONOUN** **Either** is also a pronoun. ❏ *She wants a husband and children. I don't want either.*
3 **ADJECTIVE** **Either** means each. ❏ *The teams waited at either end of the gym.* ❏ *He couldn't remember either man's name.*
4 **Either of** means each of. ❏ *There are no simple answers to either of those questions.*
5 **ADJECTIVE** **Either** means one of two things or people. ❏ *You can choose either date.*
6 **ADVERB** You use **either** in negative sentences to mean also. ❏ *He said nothing, and she did not speak either.*

eject /ɪdʒɛkt/ (**ejects, ejecting, ejected**) **VERB** To **eject** something means to remove it or push it out. ❏ *You can eject the disc from the camera and insert it into a DVD player.*

elas|tic /ɪlæstɪk/ **NONCOUNT NOUN** **Elastic** is a rubber material that stretches when you pull it, and returns to its original size and shape when you let it go. ❏ *The hat has a piece of elastic that goes under the chin.*

el|bow /ɛlboʊ/ (**elbows**) **NOUN** Your **elbow** is the part in the middle of your arm where it bends. ❏ *She leaned forward, with her elbows on the table.*
→ look at **body**

el|der|ly /ɛldərli/
1 **ADJECTIVE** You use **elderly** as a polite way of saying that someone is old. ❏ *An elderly couple lived in the house next door.*
2 **PLURAL NOUN** The **elderly** are people who are old. ❏ *It's a lovely home for the elderly.*
→ look at **age**

elect /ɪlɛkt/ (**elects, electing, elected**) **VERB** **SOCIAL STUDIES** When people **elect** someone, they choose that person to represent them, by voting for them. ❏ *The people have elected a new president.*
→ look at **vote**

elec|tion /ɪlɛkʃ°n/ (elections) NOUN
SOCIAL STUDIES An **election** is a process in which people vote to choose a person who will hold an official position. ❑ *She won her first election in 2000.*
→ look at **vote**

Elec|toral College /ɪlɛktərəl kɒlɪdʒ/ NOUN
SOCIAL STUDIES In the United States, the **Electoral College** consists of the representatives in each state who elect the president of the United States. ❑ *He won enough Electoral College votes to win the election.*
→ look at **vote**

elec|toral vote /ɪlɛktərəl voʊt/ NOUN
SOCIAL STUDIES In the United States, the **electoral vote** is the number of votes that each state has that its representatives can use to elect a new president. ❑ *California's 55 electoral votes are the most of any state.*

elec|tric /ɪlɛktrɪk/
1 ADJECTIVE SCIENCE An **electric** machine or piece of equipment works using electricity. ❑ *Kelly loves to play the electric guitar.*
2 ADJECTIVE **Electric** power lines carry electricity.

elec|tri|cal /ɪlɛktrɪk°l/ ADJECTIVE **Electrical** equipment works using electricity.

elec|tri|cian /ɪlɛktrɪʃ°n, ilɛk-/ (electricians) NOUN An **electrician** is a person whose job is to repair electrical equipment.

elec|tric|ity /ɪlɛktrɪsiti, ilɛk-/ NONCOUNT
NOUN SCIENCE **Electricity** is energy that is used for heating and lighting, and to provide power for machines.
→ look at **energy**

elec|tric shock (electric shocks) NOUN
If you get an **electric shock**, you get a sudden painful feeling when electricity goes through your body.

elec|tron|ic /ɪlɛktrɒnɪk, i-/ ADJECTIVE
Electronic equipment has small electrical parts that make it work. ❑ *Please do not use electronic equipment on the plane.*
● **elec|troni|cal|ly** ADVERB ❑ *The gates are operated electronically.*
→ look at **communication**

el|egant /ɛlɪgənt/ ADJECTIVE An **elegant** person or thing is beautiful in a simple way. ❑ *Our room was elegant, with high ceilings and tall, narrow windows.*

el|ement /ɛlɪmənt/ (elements)
1 NOUN The different **elements** of

something are the different parts of it. ❑ *Good health is an important element in our lives.*
2 NOUN SCIENCE An **element** is a basic chemical substance such as gold, oxygen, or carbon.

el|emen|ta|ry /ɛlɪmɛntəri, -tri/ ADJECTIVE
Something that is **elementary** is very easy and basic. ❑ *It's a simple system that uses elementary mathematics.*

el|emen|ta|ry school (elementary schools)
NOUN An **elementary school** is a school where children go from the ages of six to eleven.

el|ephant /ɛlɪfənt/ (elephants) NOUN An **elephant** is a very large animal with a long nose called a trunk.

el|eva|tor /ɛlɪveɪtər/ (elevators) NOUN An **elevator** is a machine that carries people or things up and down inside tall buildings. ❑ *We took the elevator to the fourteenth floor.*

elev|en /ɪlɛv°n/ MATH **Eleven** is the number 11.
→ look at **number**

elf /ɛlf/ (elves) NOUN In children's stories, **elves** are small magical creatures that play tricks on people.

eli|gible /ɛlɪdʒɪb°l/ ADJECTIVE Someone who is **eligible to** do something is allowed to do it. ❑ *Almost half the population are eligible to vote.*

elimi|nate /ɪlɪmɪneɪt/ (eliminates, eliminating, eliminated) VERB To **eliminate** something means to remove it completely.
[FORMAL] ❑ *The touch screen eliminates the need for a keyboard.*

else /ɛls/ ADJECTIVE You use **else** after words such as "someone," and "everyone," and after question words like "what" to talk about another person, place, or thing. ❑ *She is much taller than everyone else.* ❑ *What else did you get for your birthday?*

else|where /ɛlswɛər/ ADVERB **Elsewhere** means in other places or to another place. ❑ *80 percent of the state's residents were born elsewhere.*

email /imeɪl/ (emails, emailing, emailed)
also **e-mail**
1 NOUN TECHNOLOGY **Email** is a system of sending written messages from one computer to another. **Email** is short for **electronic mail**. ❑ *You can contact us by email.*

e

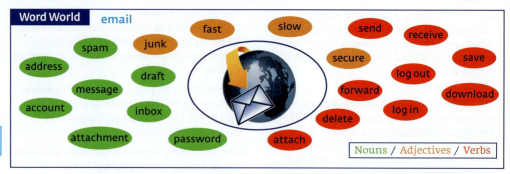

Word World email

fast slow send receive

spam junk secure save

address draft log out

message forward download

account inbox log in

delete

attachment password attach

Nouns / Adjectives / Verbs

2 **VERB** If you **email** someone, you send them an email. ❑ *Jamie emailed me to say he couldn't come.*
→ look at Word World: **email**
→ look at **communication, Internet**

eman|ci|pa|tion /ɪmænsɪpeɪʃᵊn/
NONCOUNT NOUN SOCIAL STUDIES
Emancipation is the process of giving people freedom and rights. ❑ *...the emancipation of women in the 20th century.*

em|bar|rass /ɪmbærəs/ (**embarrasses, embarrassing, embarrassed**) **VERB** If something or someone **embarrasses** you, they make you feel shy or ashamed. ❑ *His mother's behavior embarrassed him.*
● **em|bar|rass|ing** **ADJECTIVE** ❑ *He always found Judith a bit embarrassing.*

em|bar|rassed /ɪmbærəst/ **ADJECTIVE**
A person who is **embarrassed** feels shy, ashamed, or guilty about something. ❑ *He looked a bit embarrassed when he noticed his mistake.*
→ look at **feeling**

em|bar|rass|ment /ɪmbærəsmənt/
NONCOUNT NOUN **Embarrassment** is the feeling you have when you are embarrassed. ❑ *I feel no embarrassment at making mistakes or failing.*

em|bas|sy /ɛmbəsi/ (**embassies**) **NOUN** An **embassy** is a group of people who represent their government in a foreign country. The building in which they work is also called an **embassy**. ❑ *The embassy advised British nationals to leave the country immediately.* ❑ *The embassy was surrounded by the FBI.*

em|brace /ɪmbreɪs/ (**embraces, embracing, embraced**) **VERB** If you **embrace** someone, you put your arms around them to show that you love or like them. ❑ *Penelope came forward and embraced her sister.* ❑ *People were crying with joy and embracing.*

em|broi|der /ɪmbrɔɪdər/ (**embroiders, embroidering, embroidered**) **VERB** If clothing or cloth **is embroidered with** a design, the design is sewn on it. ❑ *The dress was embroidered with small red flowers.*

em|broi|dery /ɪmbrɔɪdəri/ **NONCOUNT NOUN**
Embroidery is a pattern of threads that is sewn onto cloth. ❑ *The shorts had blue embroidery over the pockets.*

em|bryo /ɛmbrioʊ/ (**embryos**) **NOUN**
SCIENCE An **embryo** is an animal or a human in the very early stages of development before it is born.

em|er|ald /ɛmərəld, ɛmrəld/ (**emeralds**)
NOUN An **emerald** is a bright green stone that is used in jewelry.

emerge /ɪmɜrdʒ/ (**emerges, emerging, emerged**) **VERB** To **emerge** means to come out from a place. ❑ *Richard was waiting outside the door as she emerged from her house.*

emer|gen|cy /ɪmɜrdʒᵊnsi/ (**emergencies**)
1 **NOUN** An **emergency** is a serious situation, such as an accident, when people need help quickly. ❑ *Come quickly. This is an emergency!*
2 **ADJECTIVE** An **emergency** action is one that is done or arranged quickly, because an emergency has happened. ❑ *The board held an emergency meeting.*
→ look at **phone**

emer|gen|cy room (**emergency rooms**)
NOUN The **emergency room** is the part of a hospital where people who have serious injuries or sudden illnesses can get treatment. The abbreviation **ER** is often used.

emi|grate /ɛmɪgreɪt/ (**emigrates, emigrating, emigrated**) **VERB** If you **emigrate**, you leave your own country and go to live in another country. ❑ *His parents emigrated to the U.S. in 1954.*

emo|tion /ɪmoʊʃⁿn/ (emotions) NOUN An **emotion** is a feeling such as joy or love. ❑ *Andrew never shows his emotions in public.* ❑ *Jill's voice was full of emotion.*
→ look at **feeling**

emo|tion|al /ɪmoʊʃənᵊl/
1 ADJECTIVE **Emotional** means concerned with feelings. ❑ *After my wife's death, I needed some emotional support.* ● **emo|tion|al|ly** ADVERB ❑ *By the end of the show, I was physically and emotionally exhausted.*
2 ADJECTIVE If someone is **emotional**, they often show their feelings, especially when they are upset. ❑ *He is a very emotional man.*

em|per|or /ɛmpərər/ (emperors) NOUN SOCIAL STUDIES An **emperor** is a man who rules a group of countries (= an empire). ❑ *...the emperor of Japan.*

em|pha|sis /ɛmfəsɪs/ (emphases /ɛmfəsiz/)
1 NOUN **Emphasis** is special importance that is given to something. ❑ *Schools should place more emphasis on health education.*
2 NOUN LANGUAGE ARTS **Emphasis** is extra force that you put on a word or part of a word when you are speaking. ❑ *The emphasis is on the first syllable of the word "elephant."*

em|pha|size /ɛmfəsaɪz/ (emphasizes, emphasizing, emphasized) VERB To **emphasize** something means to show that it is especially important. ❑ *He emphasizes the importance of reading to young children.*

em|pire /ɛmpaɪər/ (empires) NOUN SOCIAL STUDIES An **empire** is a number of separate nations that are all controlled by the ruler of one particular country. ❑ *...the Roman Empire.*

em|ploy /ɪmplɔɪ/ (employs, employing, employed) VERB If a person or a company **employs** you, they pay you to work for them. ❑ *The company employs 18 workers.*

em|ployee /ɪmplɔɪi/ (employees) NOUN An **employee** is a person who is paid to work for another person or a company. ❑ *The police believe that airport employees were involved.*
→ look at **job**

em|ploy|er /ɪmplɔɪər/ (employers) NOUN Your **employer** is the person or the company that you work for. ❑ *Your employer should agree to pay you for this work.*

em|ploy|ment /ɪmplɔɪmənt/ NONCOUNT NOUN **Employment** is work that you are paid for. ❑ *She was unable to find employment.*

emp|ty /ɛmpti/ (emptier, emptiest, empties, emptying, emptied)
1 ADJECTIVE An **empty** place or container has no people or things in it. ❑ *The room was cold and empty.* ❑ *There were empty beer cans all over the floor.*
2 VERB If you **empty** a container, you remove its contents. ❑ *I emptied the garbage can.* ❑ *Empty the noodles into a bowl.*

Word Partners	Use **empty** with:
N.	empty **bottle**, empty **box**, empty **building**, empty **room**, empty **seat**, empty **space**, empty **stomach 1** empty **the trash 2**

Word Builder   **enable**
en ≈ in, into, on
   en + able = **en**able
   en + joy = **en**joy
   en + large = **en**large
   en + sure = **en**sure

en|able /ɪneɪbᵊl/ (enables, enabling, enabled) VERB If someone or something **enables** you **to** do something, they make it possible for you to do it. ❑ *The new test will enable doctors to treat the disease early.*

en|close /ɪnkloʊz/ (encloses, enclosing, enclosed)
1 VERB If a place or an object **is enclosed** by something, the place or object is completely surrounded by it. ❑ *The park is enclosed by a wooden fence.*
2 VERB If you **enclose** something with a letter, you put it in the same envelope as the letter. ❑ *I have enclosed a check for $100.*

en|core /ɒŋkɔr, -kɔr/ (encores) NOUN An **encore** is a short extra performance at the end of a show that a musician gives because the audience has asked for it. ❑ *Lang's final encore last night was "Barefoot."*

en|coun|ter /ɪnkaʊntər/ (encounters, encountering, encountered)
1 VERB If you **encounter** problems or difficulties, you experience them. ❑ *Every day of our lives we encounter stress.*
2 VERB If you **encounter** someone, you meet them, usually unexpectedly. [FORMAL] ❑ *Did you encounter anyone in the building?*
3 NOUN **Encounter** is also a noun. ❑ *Rachel had a romantic encounter with a guy called Richard.*

e

en|cour|age /ɪnkɜrɪdʒ/ (**encourages, encouraging, encouraged**)

1 **VERB** If you **encourage** someone, you give them hope or confidence. ❑ *When things aren't going well, he encourages me.*

2 **VERB** If you **encourage** someone **to** do something, you try to persuade them to do it. ❑ *We want to encourage people to take more exercise.*

en|cour|age|ment /ɪnkɜrɪdʒmənt/ **NONCOUNT NOUN** **Encouragement** is the act of encouraging someone. ❑ *Friends gave me a lot of encouragement.*

en|cour|ag|ing /ɪnkɜrɪdʒɪŋ/ **ADJECTIVE** Something that is **encouraging** gives people hope or confidence. ❑ *The results have been encouraging.*

en|cy|clo|pedia /ɪnsaɪkləpidiə/ (**encyclopedias**) also **encyclopaedia** **NOUN** An **encyclopedia** is a book or a CD-ROM containing facts about many different subjects.

end /ɛnd/ (**ends, ending, ended**)

1 **NOUN** The **end of** a period of time or a story is the final point in it. ❑ *Work will start before the end of the year.* ❑ *Don't tell me the end of the story!*

2 **NOUN** The **end of** a long object is the farthest part of it. ❑ *Both ends of the tunnel were blocked.*

3 **VERB** When an activity **ends**, it reaches its final point and stops. ❑ *The meeting quickly ended.*

4 If you cannot **make ends meet**, you do not have enough money for the things you need. ❑ *With Betty's salary they couldn't make ends meet.*

5 When something happens for hours, days, weeks, or years **on end**, it happens continuously and without stopping for that amount of time. ❑ *We can talk for hours on end.*

→ look at **calendar, day, season**

▶ **end up** If you **end up** in a particular place, you are in that place after a series of events. ❑ *We ended up back at the house again.*

en|dan|gered spe|cies /ɪndeɪndʒərd spiʃiz/ (**endangered species**) **NOUN** **SCIENCE** An **endangered species** is a type of animal that may soon disappear from the world. ❑ *These African beetles are on the list of endangered species.*

end|ing /ɛndɪŋ/ (**endings**) **NOUN** You can call the last part of a book or a movie the **ending**. ❑ *The film has a happy ending.*

Word Builder	**endless**

less ≈ **without**

    care + **less** = care**less**
    end + **less** = end**less**
    help + **less** = help**less**
    home + **less** = home**less**
    use + **less** = use**less**
    wire + **less** = wire**less**

end|less /ɛndlɪs/ **ADJECTIVE** Something that is **endless** lasts for a very long time. ❑ *The morning classes seemed endless.* ● **end|less|ly** **ADVERB** ❑ *They talk about it endlessly.*

en|dur|ance /ɪnduərəns/ **NONCOUNT NOUN** **Endurance** is the ability to continue with a difficult activity over a long period of time. ❑ *The exercise will improve strength and endurance.*

en|dure /ɪnduər/ (**endures, enduring, endured**) **VERB** If a person or an organization **endures** a difficult situation, they experience it. ❑ *The company endured heavy financial losses.*

en|emy /ɛnəmi/ (**enemies**)

1 **NOUN** If someone is your **enemy**, they hate you, and want to harm you. ❑ *His enemies hated and feared him.*

2 **NOUN** The **enemy** is an army that is fighting against you in a war. ❑ *We are going to attack the enemy tomorrow morning.*

en|er|get|ic /ɛnərdʒɛtɪk/ **ADJECTIVE** An **energetic** person has a lot of energy. ❑ *Young children are very energetic.*

en|er|gy /ɛnərdʒi/

1 **NONCOUNT NOUN** **Energy** is the ability and strength to do active physical things. ❑ *He's saving his energy for next week's race.*

2 **NONCOUNT NOUN** **SCIENCE** **Energy** is the power from electricity or the sun, for example, that makes machines work or provides heat. ❑ *These machines are powered with energy from the sun.*

→ look at Word World: **energy**
→ look at **conservation**

en|gage /ɪngeɪdʒ/ (**engages, engaging, engaged**)

1 **VERB** If you **engage in** an activity, you do it. [FORMAL] ❑ *Many of these young people engage in criminal activities.*

2 **VERB** If something **engages** you, it keeps you interested in it. ❑ *He has an amazing ability to engage an audience.*

Word World   energy

power   oil   nuclear   renewable

heat   source   natural   waste

gas   fuel   solar   use

resource   consume

light   wind   save   supply

electricity   fossil fuel   reduce

produce

Nouns / Adjectives / Verbs

e

en|gaged /ɪnɡeɪdʒd/ **ADJECTIVE** When two people are **engaged**, they have agreed to marry each other. ❑ *We got engaged on my 26th birthday.*

en|gage|ment /ɪnɡeɪdʒmənt/ (**engagements**) **NOUN** An **engagement** is an agreement that two people have made with each other to get married. ❑ *We announced our engagement in November.*

en|gine /ɛndʒɪn/ (**engines**)
1 NOUN The **engine** of a car is the part that produces the power to make it move. ❑ *He got into the driving seat and started the engine.*
2 NOUN An **engine** is the front part of a train that pulls it. ❑ *In 1941, trains were pulled by steam engines.*

en|gi|neer /ɛndʒɪnɪər/ (**engineers**)
1 NOUN An **engineer** is a person who designs, builds, and repairs machines, or structures such as roads, railroads, and bridges.
2 NOUN An **engineer** is a person who repairs mechanical or electrical machines. ❑ *They sent an engineer to fix the computer.*

en|gi|neer|ing /ɛndʒɪnɪərɪŋ/ **NONCOUNT NOUN** Engineering is the work of designing and constructing machines or structures such as roads and bridges. ❑ *She studies science and engineering at college.*

Eng|lish /ɪŋɡlɪʃ/
1 NONCOUNT NOUN LANGUAGE ARTS **English** is the language spoken by people who live in Great Britain and Ireland, the United States, Canada, Australia, and many other countries. ❑ *Do you speak English?*
2 ADJECTIVE English means belonging to or relating to England. ❑ *He began to enjoy the English way of life.*

en|hance /ɪnhæns/ (**enhances, enhancing, enhanced**) **VERB** To **enhance** something means to improve its quality. ❑ *A little sugar enhances the natural sweet flavor of the peas.*

Word Builder   enjoy
en ≈ in, into, on
en + able = enable
en + joy = enjoy
en + large = enlarge
en + sure = ensure

en|joy /ɪndʒɔɪ/ (**enjoys, enjoying, enjoyed**)
1 VERB If you **enjoy** something, you like doing it. ❑ *I enjoyed playing basketball.*
2 VERB If you **enjoy yourself**, you have a good time doing something. ❑ *I am really enjoying myself at the moment.*
→ look at **relax**

Word Builder   enjoyable
able ≈ able to be
comfort + able = comfortable
depend + able = dependable
download + able = downloadable
enjoy + able = enjoyable
honor + able = honorable

en|joy|able /ɪndʒɔɪəbəl/ **ADJECTIVE** Something that is **enjoyable** gives you pleasure. ❑ *The movie was much more enjoyable than I expected.*

en|joy|ment /ɪndʒɔɪmənt/ **NONCOUNT NOUN** Enjoyment is the feeling of pleasure that you have when you do something that you like. ❑ *We get a lot of enjoyment from our garden.*

Word Builder   enlarge
en ≈ in, into, on
en + able = enable
en + joy = enjoy
en + large = enlarge
en + sure = ensure

en|large /ɪnlɑrdʒ/ (**enlarges, enlarging, enlarged**) **VERB** When you **enlarge**

something, you make it bigger. ❑ *You can enlarge these photographs.*

enor|mous /ɪnɔrməs/ **ADJECTIVE** Something that is **enormous** is extremely large in size. ❑ *The main bedroom is enormous.* ❑ *It was an enormous disappointment.* ● **enor|mous|ly ADVERB** ❑ *I admired him enormously.*

enough /ɪnʌf/
1 ADJECTIVE **Enough** means as much as you need. ❑ *They had enough cash for a one-way ticket.*
2 ADVERB **Enough** is also an adverb. ❑ *I was old enough to work and earn money.*
3 PRONOUN **Enough** is also a pronoun. ❑ *They are not doing enough.*

en|roll /ɪnroʊl/ (**enrolls, enrolling, enrolled**) **VERB** If you **enroll** in a class, you officially join it. ❑ *He has already enrolled at medical college.* ❑ *Already, 46 students are enrolled in the two classes.*

Word Builder ensure

en ≈ in, into, on
en + able = enable
en + joy = enjoy
en + large = enlarge
en + sure = ensure

---

en|sure /ɪnʃʊər/ (**ensures, ensuring, ensured**) **VERB** To **ensure** something means to make sure that it happens. [FORMAL] ❑ *The school ensures the safety of all students.* ❑ *We will work hard to ensure that this doesn't happen again.*

en|ter /ɛntər/ (**enters, entering, entered**)
1 VERB When you **enter** a place such as a room or a building, you go into it. [FORMAL] ❑ *He entered the room and stood near the door.*
2 VERB If you **enter** a competition or a race, you state that you will be a part of it. ❑ *To enter the competition, simply go to our website and fill in the details.*
3 VERB If you **enter** information, you write or type it in a form or a book, or into a computer. ❑ *They enter the addresses into the computer.*
→ look at **ATM**

en|ter|prise /ɛntərpraɪz/ (**enterprises**) **NOUN** An **enterprise** is a company or a business. ❑ *We provide help for small and medium-sized enterprises.*

en|ter|tain /ɛntərteɪn/ (**entertains, entertaining, entertained**)
1 VERB If you **entertain** people, you do something that amuses or interests them.

❑ *They were entertained by singers and dancers.*
● **en|ter|tain|ing ADJECTIVE** ❑ *His show is entertaining, intelligent, and funny.*
2 VERB If you **entertain** guests, you invite them to your home and give them food and drink. ❑ *This is the season for entertaining outdoors.*

en|ter|tain|er /ɛntərteɪnər/ (**entertainers**) **NOUN** An **entertainer** is a person whose job is to entertain audiences, for example, by telling jokes, singing, or dancing. ❑ *Chaplin was possibly the greatest entertainer of the twentieth century.*

en|ter|tain|ment /ɛntərteɪnmənt/ **NONCOUNT NOUN** **Entertainment** is performances of plays and movies, and activities such as reading and watching television, that give people pleasure. ❑ *At the party, there was children's entertainment and a swimming competition.*

en|thu|si|asm /ɪnθuziæzəm/ **NONCOUNT NOUN** **Enthusiasm** is the feeling that you have when you really enjoy something or want to do something. ❑ *Does your girlfriend share your enthusiasm for sports?*

en|thu|si|ast /ɪnθuziæst/ (**enthusiasts**) **NOUN** An **enthusiast** is a person who is very interested in a particular activity, and who spends a lot of time on it. ❑ *Ryan is a sports car enthusiast.*

en|thu|si|as|tic /ɪnθuziæstɪk/ **ADJECTIVE** If you are **enthusiastic about** something, you show how much you like it or enjoy it. ❑ *Tom was not very enthusiastic about the idea.*

en|tire /ɪntaɪər/ **ADJECTIVE** You use **entire** when you want to make it clear that you are talking about all of something. ❑ *He spent his entire life in China.*

en|tire|ly /ɪntaɪərli/ **ADVERB** **Entirely** means completely and not just partly. ❑ *I agree entirely.* ❑ *I'm not entirely sure what I'm supposed to do.*

en|ti|tle /ɪntaɪtəl/ (**entitles, entitling, entitled**) **VERB** If you **are entitled to** something, you are allowed to have it or do it. ❑ *They are entitled to first class travel.*

en|trance /ɛntrəns/ (**entrances**)
1 NOUN The **entrance to** a place is the door or gate where you go into it. ❑ *He came out of a side entrance.*

2 NOUN Someone's **entrance** is when they arrive in a room. ❑ *She didn't notice her father's entrance.*

3 NONCOUNT NOUN If you gain **entrance to** a place, you are allowed to go into it. ❑ *We tried to go in, but we were refused entrance.*

en|tre|pre|neur /ɒntrəprənɜr, -nʊər/ (**entrepreneurs**) **NOUN** An **entrepreneur** is a person who starts a business.

en|try /ɛntri/

1 NONCOUNT NOUN **Entry to** a particular place is when you go into it. ❑ *Entry to the museum is free.*

2 No Entry is used on signs to show that you are not allowed to go into a particular area.

→ look at **dictionary**

en|velope /ɛnvəloʊp, ɒn-/ (**envelopes**) **NOUN** An **envelope** is the paper cover in which you put a letter before you send it to someone. ❑ *She put the letter back into the envelope and handed it to me.*

→ look at **office**

en|vi|ous /ɛnviəs/ **ADJECTIVE** If you are **envious of** someone, you want something that they have. ❑ *I'm not envious of your success.*
● **en|vi|ous|ly** **ADVERB** ❑ *People talked enviously about his good luck.*

en|vi|ron|ment /ɪnvaɪrənmənt, -vaɪərn-/ (**environments**)

1 NOUN Someone's **environment** is the conditions in which they live or work. ❑ *The children are taught in a safe and happy environment.*

2 NOUN SCIENCE The **environment** is the natural world of land, the oceans, the air, plants, and animals. ❑ *Please respect the environment by recycling.* ● **en|vi|ron|men|tal** /ɪnvaɪrənmɛntᵊl, -vaɪərn-/ **ADJECTIVE** ❑ *Environmental groups protested loudly during the conference.* ● **en|vi|ron|men|tal|ly** **ADVERB** ❑ *...environmentally friendly cleaning products.*

→ look at **climate, conservation, pollution**

Word Partners	Use **environment** with:
ADJ.	**safe** environment, **supportive** environment, **unhealthy** environment **1** **natural** environment **2**
V.	**damage the** environment, **protect the** environment **2**

envy /ɛnvi/ (**envies, envying, envied**)

1 VERB If you **envy** someone, you wish that you had the same things that they have. ❑ *I don't envy young people these days.*

2 NONCOUNT NOUN **Envy** is also a noun. ❑ *She was full of envy when she heard their news.*

epic /ɛpɪk/ (**epics**)

1 NOUN LANGUAGE ARTS An **epic** is a long book, poem, or movie about important events. ❑ *We read Homer's epics about the Trojan war.*

2 ADJECTIVE **Epic** is also an adjective. ❑ *This is an epic story of love and war.*

epi|dem|ic /ɛpɪdɛmɪk/ (**epidemics**) **NOUN** If there is an **epidemic of** a particular disease, it affects a large number of people. ❑ *...a flu epidemic.*

epi|logue /ɛpɪlɔg/ (**epilogues**) also **epilog** **NOUN** LANGUAGE ARTS An **epilogue** is an extra part that is added at the end of a piece of writing.

epi|sode /ɛpɪsoʊd/ (**episodes**) **NOUN** An **episode** is one of the parts of a story on television or radio. ❑ *The final episode will be shown next Sunday.*

equal /ikwəl/ (**equals, equaling, equaled**)

1 ADJECTIVE If two things are **equal**, they are the same in size, number, or value. ❑ *There are equal numbers of men and women.*
● **equal|ly** **ADVERB** ❑ *The money will be divided equally among his three children.*

2 ADJECTIVE If different groups of people are given **equal** treatment, they have the same rights or are treated in the same way. ❑ *We want equal rights at work.* ● **equal|ly** **ADVERB** ❑ *The system should treat everyone equally.*

3 NOUN Someone who is your **equal** has the same ability or rights as you have. ❑ *You and I are equals.*

4 VERB MATH If something **equals** a particular number or amount, it is the same as that amount. ❑ *9 minus 7 equals 2.*

→ look at **math**

equal|ity /ikwɒlɪti/ **NONCOUNT NOUN** **Equality** is the fair treatment of all the people in a group. ❑ *Few people really believed in racial equality in the 1800s.*

equal op|por|tu|nity **NONCOUNT NOUN** **Equal opportunity** means giving everyone the same opportunities for employment and pay. ❑ *We believe in equal opportunity for women.*

e

E

equal sign (equal signs) NOUN MATH An **equal sign** is the sign =, which is used in mathematics to show that two numbers are equal.

equa|tion /ɪkweɪʒⁿn/ (equations) NOUN MATH An **equation** is a mathematical statement that two amounts or values are the same.

equa|tor /ɪkweɪtər/ NOUN GEOGRAPHY The **equator** is a line that is shown on maps around the middle of the world.
→ look at **earth, globe**

equa|to|rial /ˌikwətɔriəl, ˌɛk-/ ADJECTIVE GEOGRAPHY **Equatorial** regions are at or near the equator (= the imaginary line around the middle of the Earth). ❑ The cassava plant grows in most equatorial regions.

equip /ɪkwɪp/ (equips, equipping, equipped) VERB If a person or thing **is equipped with** something, they have the things that they need to do a particular job. ❑ The army is equipped with 5,000 tanks. ❑ The phone is equipped with a camera.

equip|ment /ɪkwɪpmənt/ NONCOUNT NOUN **Equipment** is all the things that are used for a particular purpose. ❑ ...tractors and other farm equipment.

equiva|lent /ɪkwɪvələnt/ (equivalents)
1 NOUN If one thing is the **equivalent of** another, they are the same, or they are used in the same way. ❑ His pay is the equivalent of about $2,000 a month. ❑ The Internet has become the modern equivalent of the phone.
2 ADJECTIVE **Equivalent** is also an adjective. ❑ ...an equivalent amount.

ER /i ɑr/ (ERs) NOUN The **ER** is the part of a hospital where people go when they have seriously hurt themselves or when they suddenly become sick. **ER** is short for **emergency room**.

era /ɪərə/ (eras) NOUN An **era** is a period of time that is considered as a single unit. ❑ Their leader promised them a new era of peace.

erase /ɪreɪs/ (erases, erasing, erased) VERB If you **erase** writing or a mark, you remove it. ❑ She erased his name from her address book.
→ look at **draw**

eras|er /ɪreɪsər/ (erasers) NOUN An **eraser** is an object that is used for removing marks that have been written using a pencil.
→ look at **classroom**

erect /ɪrɛkt/ (erects, erecting, erected)
1 VERB If people **erect** a building or a bridge, they build it. [FORMAL] ❑ The building was erected in 1900.
2 ADJECTIVE People or things that are **erect** are straight and upright. ❑ Stand erect, with your arms hanging naturally.

erode /ɪroʊd/ (erodes, eroding, eroded) VERB If the weather, the sea, or the wind **erodes** rock or soil, they gradually destroy it. ❑ The sea is gradually eroding the coastline. ● **ero|sion** /ɪroʊʒⁿn/ NOUN ❑ The storms caused soil erosion and flooding.

er|rand /ɛrənd/ (errands) NOUN An **errand** is a short trip to do a job, for example, when you go to a store to buy something. ❑ We ran errands and took her meals when she was sick.

er|ror /ɛrər/ (errors) NOUN An **error** is a mistake. ❑ You should check your work for errors in grammar or spelling.

erupt /ɪrʌpt/ (erupts, erupting, erupted) VERB SCIENCE When a volcano **erupts**, it throws out a lot of hot, melted rock (= lava). ❑ Krakatoa erupted in 1883. ● **erup|tion** /ɪrʌpʃⁿn/ (eruptions) NOUN ❑ The country's last volcanic eruption was 600 years ago.
→ look at **disaster**

es|ca|late /ɛskəleɪt/ (escalates, escalating, escalated) VERB If a bad situation **escalates**, it becomes worse. ❑ Nobody wants the situation to escalate.

es|ca|la|tor /ɛskəleɪtər/ (escalators) NOUN An **escalator** is a set of moving stairs. ❑ Take the escalator to the third floor.

es|cape /ɪskeɪp/ (escapes, escaping, escaped)
1 VERB If you **escape from** a place, you manage to get away from it. ❑ A prisoner has escaped from a jail in northern Texas.
2 NOUN **Escape** is also a noun. ❑ He made his escape at night.
3 VERB You **escape** when you avoid an accident. ❑ The man's girlfriend escaped unhurt. ❑ The two officers escaped serious injury.
4 NOUN **Escape** is also a noun. ❑ I had a narrow escape on the bridge.

esopha|gus /ɪsɒfəgəs/ (esophaguses) NOUN SCIENCE Your **esophagus** is the tube in your body that carries the food from your throat to your stomach. ❑ He has cancer of the esophagus.

es|pe|cial|ly /ɪspɛʃˀli/ **ADVERB** You use **especially** to show that something you are mentioning is more important or true. ❑ *Millions of wild flowers grow in the valleys, especially in April and May.*

es|say /ɛseɪ/ (**essays**) **NOUN** LANGUAGE ARTS An **essay** is a short piece of writing on a subject. ❑ *We asked Jason to write an essay about his hometown.*
→ look at **writing**

es|sen|tial /ɪsɛnʃˀl/ **ADJECTIVE** Something that is **essential** is necessary. ❑ *Play is an essential part of a child's development.*

es|tab|lish /ɪstæblɪʃ/ (**establishes, establishing, established**)
1 **VERB** If someone **establishes** an organization, they create it. ❑ *He established the business in 1990.*
2 **VERB** If you **establish** contact with someone, you start to have contact with them. [FORMAL] ❑ *He wants to establish contact with his family.*
3 **VERB** If you **establish that** something is true, you discover facts that show that it is true. [FORMAL] ❑ *Medical tests established that she had a heart defect.*

es|tab|lish|ment /ɪstæblɪʃmənt/ (**establishments**)
1 **NOUN** An **establishment** is an organization in a building in a particular place. [FORMAL] ❑ *...an educational establishment.*
2 **NOUN** The **establishment** is the people who have power in a country. ❑ *...the American establishment.*

es|tate /ɪsteɪt/ (**estates**) **NOUN** An **estate** is a large house in a large area of land in the country, owned by a person or an organization. ❑ *He spent the holidays at his aunt's 300-acre estate.*

es|ti|mate (**estimates, estimating, estimated**)

> **PRONUNCIATION HELP**
> Pronounce the verb /ɛstɪmeɪt/. Pronounce the noun /ɛstɪmɪt/.

1 **VERB** If you **estimate** an amount or a value, you say how much you think there is of it. ❑ *It's difficult to estimate how much money is involved.*
2 **NOUN** **Estimate** is also a noun. ❑ *She made an estimate of the truck's speed.*

etc. /ɛt sɛtərə, -sɛtrə/ **etc.** is used at the end of a list to show that you have not given a full list. **etc.** is short for "etcetera." ❑ *She knew all about my schoolwork, my hospital work, etc.*

et|cet|era /ɛtsɛtərə, -sɛtrə/ also **et cetera**
→ look up **etc.**

eter|nal /ɪtɜrnˀl/ **ADJECTIVE** Something that is **eternal** lasts forever. ❑ *What's the secret of eternal happiness?*

ethi|cal /ɛθɪkˀl/
1 **ADJECTIVE** **Ethical** means relating to beliefs about right and wrong. ❑ *Heather is now a vegetarian for ethical reasons.*
2 **ADJECTIVE** If something is **ethical**, it is morally right or morally acceptable. ❑ *...ethical business practices.*

eth|nic /ɛθnɪk/ **ADJECTIVE** SOCIAL STUDIES **Ethnic** means relating to groups of people that have the same culture or belong to the same race. ❑ *Most of their friends come from other ethnic groups.*

euro /yʊəroʊ/ (**euros**) **NOUN** The **euro** is a unit of money that is used by many countries in the European Union (= an organization that encourages trade).

Euro|pean /yʊərəpiən/ (**Europeans**)
1 **ADJECTIVE** SOCIAL STUDIES **European** means belonging to or coming from Europe. ❑ *...European countries.*
2 **NOUN** SOCIAL STUDIES A **European** is a person who comes from Europe.

evacu|ate /ɪvækyueɪt/ (**evacuates, evacuating, evacuated**) **VERB** If people are **evacuated from** a place, they move out of it because it is dangerous. ❑ *Families were evacuated from the area because of the fighting.*

evalu|ate /ɪvælyueɪt/ (**evaluates, evaluating, evaluated**) **VERB** If you **evaluate** something or someone, you consider them in order to decide how good or bad they are. ❑ *We need to evaluate the situation very carefully.*
● **evalu|ation** /ɪvælyueɪʃˀn/ (**evaluations**) **NOUN** ❑ *The program includes an evaluation of students' writing skills.*

evapo|rate /ɪvæpəreɪt/ (**evaporates, evaporating, evaporated**) **VERB** SCIENCE When a liquid **evaporates**, it changes into a gas. ❑ *Boil the sauce until most of the liquid evaporates.*

eve /iv/ (**eves**) **NOUN** The **eve of** a particular event or occasion is the day before it, or the period of time just before it. ❑ *The story begins on the eve of her birthday.*

even /ˈivən/

1 **ADJECTIVE** MATH An **even** number can be divided exactly by two.

2 **ADJECTIVE** An **even** surface is smooth and flat. ❑ *You will need a table with an even surface.*

3 **ADJECTIVE** An **even** competition is equally balanced between the two sides. ❑ *It was an even game.*

4 **ADVERB** You use **even** to say that something is rather surprising. ❑ *Rob still seems happy, even after the bad news.*

5 **ADVERB** You use **even** to make another word stronger. ❑ *Our car is big, but theirs is even bigger.*

6 You use **even if** or **even though** to show that a particular fact does not change anything. ❑ *Cynthia is never embarrassed, even if she makes a mistake.* ❑ *She wasn't embarrassed, even though she made a mistake.*

7 You use **even so** to add a surprising fact. ❑ *The bus was nearly empty. Even so, the man sat down next to her.*

Usage   **even**

Even is used for emphasis or to say that something is surprising. *The wind was so strong it* ***even*** *blew down trees. I can't* ***even*** *believe it!*

---

eve|ning /ˈivnɪŋ/ (**evenings**) **NOUN** The **evening** is the part of each day between the end of the afternoon and midnight. ❑ *That evening he went to see a movie.* ❑ *We usually have dinner at seven in the evening.*
→ look at **time**

event /ɪˈvɛnt/ (**events**)

1 **NOUN** An **event** is something that happens. ❑ *This terrible event caused death and injury to many.*

2 **NOUN** An **event** is an organized activity or celebration. ❑ *Several cultural and sports events were canceled.*
→ look at **history**

even|tual /ɪˈvɛntʃuəl/ **ADJECTIVE** The **eventual** result of something is what happens at the end of it. ❑ *The eventual winner will receive $200,000.*

even|tu|al|ly /ɪˈvɛntʃuəli/ **ADVERB** **Eventually** means at some later time, especially after a lot of delays or problems. ❑ *They eventually married in 1996.* ❑ *Eventually your child will leave home.*

ever /ˈɛvər/ **ADVERB** **Ever** means at any time. It is usually used in questions and negative

sentences. ❑ *I don't think I'll ever trust people again.* ❑ *Have you ever seen anything like it?* ❑ *Japan is more powerful than ever before.*

every /ˈɛvri/

1 **ADJECTIVE** You use **every** to show that you are talking about all the members of a group. ❑ *Every room has a window facing the ocean.* ❑ *Every child gets a free piece of fruit.*

2 **ADJECTIVE** You use **every** to say how often something happens. ❑ *We had to attend meetings every day.* ❑ *He saw his family once every two weeks.*

3 If something happens **every other day**, it happens one day, then it does not happen the next day, and continues in this way. ❑ *I called my mother every other day.*

every|body /ˈɛvribɒdi, -bʌdi/ **Everybody** means the same as **everyone**.

every|day /ˈɛvrideɪ/ **ADJECTIVE** **Everyday** describes something that is a regular part of your life. ❑ *They were doing everyday activities around the house.* ❑ *Computers are a central part of everyday life.*

every|one /ˈɛvriwʌn/ **PRONOUN** **Everyone** or **everybody** means all people, or all the people in a particular group. ❑ *Everyone on the street was shocked when they heard the news.* ❑ *Not everyone thinks that the government is acting fairly.*

every|thing /ˈɛvriθɪŋ/

1 **PRONOUN** You use **everything** when you are talking about all the objects, actions, or facts in a situation. ❑ *Everything in his life has changed.* ❑ *Susan and I do everything together.*

2 **PRONOUN** You use **everything** when you are talking about all the important things in your life. ❑ *Is everything all right?*

every|where /ˈɛvriwɛər/ or **everyplace** **ADVERB** You use **everywhere** when you are talking about a whole area or all the places in a particular area. ❑ *People everywhere want the same things.* ❑ *We went everywhere together.*

evi|dence /ˈɛvɪdəns/ **NONCOUNT NOUN** **Evidence** is an object or a piece of information that makes you believe that something is true or has really happened. ❑ *There is no evidence that he stole the money.* ❑ *Evidence shows that most of us are happy with our lives.*

evi|dent /ˈɛvɪdənt/ **ADJECTIVE** If something is **evident**, you notice it easily. ❑ *Changes are* evident across the country. ❑ It was evident that she was not feeling well.

evi|dent|ly /ɛvɪdəntli, -dɛnt-/ **ADVERB**
You use **evidently** to say that something is clearly true. ❑ The two men evidently knew each other.

evil /iːvəl/ **ADJECTIVE** If an act or a person is **evil**, they are morally very bad. ❑ Who's the most evil person in all of history?

evo|lu|tion /ɛvəluːʃən, iːv-/
1 **NONCOUNT NOUN** SCIENCE **Evolution** is a process in which animals or plants slowly change over many years. ❑ The evolution of mammals involved many changes in the body.
2 **NONCOUNT NOUN** **Evolution** is a process of gradual development in a particular situation or thing over a period of time. [FORMAL] ❑ This was an important period in the evolution of modern science.

evolve /ɪvɒlv/ (**evolves, evolving, evolved**)
1 **VERB** SCIENCE When animals or plants **evolve**, they gradually change and develop into different forms. ❑ The theory is that humans evolved from apes.
2 **VERB** If something **evolves**, it gradually develops over a period of time into something different. ❑ Popular music evolved from folk songs.

ex|act /ɪgzækt/ **ADJECTIVE** **Exact** means correct and complete in every way. ❑ I don't remember the exact words. ❑ Can you tell me the exact date of the incident?

ex|act|ly /ɪgzæktli/
1 **ADVERB** If you give facts or amounts **exactly**, you give them correctly and completely. ❑ The tower was exactly a hundred meters in height.
2 **ADVERB** **Exactly** means in every way, or with all the details. ❑ Both drugs will be exactly the same.
3 **ADVERB** You can say "**exactly**" when you are agreeing with someone. ❑ Eve nodded. "Exactly."

ex|ag|ger|ate /ɪgzædʒəreɪt/ (**exaggerates, exaggerating, exaggerated**) **VERB** If you **exaggerate**, you say that something is bigger, worse, or more important than it really is. ❑ He thinks I'm exaggerating. ❑ Try not to exaggerate the risks of traveling alone.
● **ex|ag|gera|tion** /ɪgzædʒəreɪʃən/ (**exaggerations**) **NOUN** ❑ It's not an exaggeration, it's a fact.

exam /ɪgzæm/ (**exams**) **NOUN** An **exam** is a formal test that you take to show your knowledge of a subject. ❑ I don't want to take any more exams.

ex|ami|na|tion /ɪgzæmɪneɪʃən/ (**examinations**)
1 **NOUN** An **examination** is the same as an **exam**. [FORMAL]
2 **NOUN** If you have a medical **examination**, a doctor looks at your body in order to check how healthy you are. ❑ She is waiting for the results of a medical examination.

ex|am|ine /ɪgzæmɪn/ (**examines, examining, examined**) **VERB** If you **examine** something or someone, you look at them carefully. ❑ He examined her documents. ❑ A doctor examined her and could find nothing wrong.
● **ex|ami|na|tion** /ɪgzæmɪneɪʃən/ (**examinations**) **NOUN** ❑ The government said the plan needed careful examination.

ex|am|ple /ɪgzæmpəl/ (**examples**)
1 **NOUN** An **example** is something that shows what other things in a particular group are like. ❑ The building is a fine example of 19th-century architecture.
2 You use **for example** to introduce an example of something. ❑ The technique can be used for treating diseases like cancer, for example.
→ look at **dictionary**

ex|ceed /ɪksiːd/ (**exceeds, exceeding, exceeded**) **VERB** If something **exceeds** a particular amount, it is greater than that amount. [FORMAL] ❑ The cost of a new boat exceeded $100,000.

ex|cel|lence /ɛksələns/ **NONCOUNT NOUN** **Excellence** is the quality of being extremely good in some way. ❑ She won an award for excellence in teaching.

ex|cel|lent /ɛksələnt/ **ADJECTIVE** Something that is **excellent** is extremely good. ❑ The printing quality is excellent.

ex|cept /ɪksɛpt/
1 **PREPOSITION** You use **except** or **except for** to show that you are not including a particular thing or person. ❑ The shops are open every day except Sunday. ❑ The room was empty except for a television.
2 **CONJUNCTION** **Except** is also a conjunction. ❑ I'm much better now, except that I still have a headache.

ex|cep|tion /ɪksɛpʃən/ (**exceptions**) **NOUN** An **exception** is a particular thing, person,

e

or situation that is not included in what you say. ❏ *Not many musicians can sing well and play well, but Eddie is an exception.*

ex|cep|tion|al /ɪksɛpʃənᵊl/ **ADJECTIVE**
Exceptional describes someone or something that is better than others in some way. ❏ *He is a player with exceptional ability.* ● **ex|cep|tion|al|ly ADVERB** ❏ *She's an exceptionally talented dancer.*

ex|cess /ɛksɛs/ **ADJECTIVE** Excess amounts are more than is usual or ncessary. ❏ *After cooking the fish, pour out any excess fat.*

ex|ces|sive /ɪksɛsɪv/ **ADJECTIVE** If the amount or level of something is **excessive**, it is more than is necessary. ❏ *Their spending on clothes is excessive.*

ex|change /ɪkstʃeɪndʒ/ (**exchanges, exchanging, exchanged**)
1 VERB If two or more people **exchange** things, they give them to each other at the same time. ❏ *We exchanged addresses.*
2 NOUN Exchange is also a noun. ❏ *There will be a meal, followed by the exchange of gifts.*
3 VERB If you **exchange** something, you take it back to a store and get a different thing. ❏ *If you are unhappy with the product, we will exchange it.*
→ look at **shopping**

ex|change rate (**exchange rates**) **NOUN**
The **exchange rate** of one country's money is the amount of another country's money that you can buy with it. ❏ *The exchange rate is around 3.7 pesos to the dollar.*

ex|cite /ɪksaɪt/ (**excites, exciting, excited**)
VERB If something **excites** you, it makes you feel very happy or enthusiastic. ❏ *Scientists are excited by the discovery of a new type of whale.*

ex|cit|ed /ɪksaɪtɪd/ **ADJECTIVE** If you are **excited**, you are very happy or enthusiastic. ❏ *I was excited about playing football again.*
→ look at **feeling**

ex|cite|ment /ɪksaɪtmənt/ **NONCOUNT NOUN** Excitement is the feeling you have when you are excited. ❏ *He shouted with excitement.*

ex|cit|ing /ɪksaɪtɪŋ/ **ADJECTIVE** If something is **exciting**, it makes you feel very happy or enthusiastic. ❏ *The movie is exciting, and also very scary.*

ex|cla|ma|tion /ɛksklǝmeɪʃᵊn/
(**exclamations**) **NOUN** An **exclamation** is

something that you say suddenly and loudly, showing that you are excited or angry. ❏ *Sue gave an exclamation when she saw the house.*

ex|cla|ma|tion point (**exclamation points**) or **exclamation mark NOUN** LANGUAGE ARTS
An **exclamation point** is the sign ! that is used in writing to show that a word or a sentence is an exclamation (= something that someone says loudly and suddenly).
→ look at **punctuation**

ex|clude /ɪksklud/ (**excludes, excluding, excluded**)
1 VERB If you **exclude** someone **from** a place or an activity, you prevent them from entering it or doing it. ❏ *The public was excluded from both meetings.*
2 VERB If you **exclude** something, you deliberately do not use it or consider it. ❏ *The price excludes taxes.*

ex|clu|sive /ɪksklusɪv/ **ADJECTIVE**
Something that is **exclusive** is available only to people who are rich or powerful. ❏ *It was a private, exclusive club.*

ex|clu|sive|ly /ɪksklusɪvli/ **ADVERB**
Exclusively is used for talking about situations that involve only the place or thing mentioned, and nothing else. ❏ *This perfume is available exclusively from selected David Jones stores.*

ex|cuse (**excuses, excusing, excused**)

> **PRONUNCIATION HELP**
> Pronounce the noun /ɪkskyus/. Pronounce the verb /ɪkskyuz/.

1 NOUN An **excuse** is a reason that you give in order to explain why you did something. ❏ *They are trying to find excuses for their failure.*
2 VERB If you **excuse** someone **for** doing something, you forgive them for it. ❏ *I'm not excusing him for what he did.*
3 You say "**Excuse me**" when you want to politely get someone's attention. ❏ *Excuse me, but are you Mr. Hess?*

ex|ecute /ɛksɪkyut/ (**executes, executing, executed**) **VERB** To **execute** someone means to kill them as a punishment. ❏ *These soldiers were executed by the army in World War I.*
● **ex|ecu|tion** /ɛksɪkyuʃᵊn/ (**executions**)
NOUN ❏ *He wrote the story a week before his execution for murder.*

ex|ecu|tive /ɪgzɛkyǝtɪv/ (**executives**) **NOUN**
An **executive** is someone who has an

important job at a company. ❑ *She loved her job as an advertising executive.*

exec|utive branch (**executive branches**) NOUN SOCIAL STUDIES The **executive branch** of a government is all the people and departments that run the country. ❑ *The president is the head of the executive branch of our government.*

ex|empt /ɪgzɛmpt/ ADJECTIVE If someone is **exempt from** a rule or a duty, they do not have to obey it or perform it. ❑ *Men in college were exempt from military service.*

ex|er|cise /ɛksərsaɪz/ (**exercises, exercising, exercised**)

1 PLURAL NOUN SPORTS **Exercises** are a series of movements that you do in order to stay healthy and strong. ❑ *I do special neck and shoulder exercises every morning.*

2 NOUN An **exercise** is an activity that you do in order to practice a skill. ❑ *Dennis said that the writing exercise was very useful.*

3 VERB SPORTS When you **exercise**, you move your body in order to stay healthy and strong. ❑ *You should exercise at least two or three times a week.*

4 NONCOUNT NOUN **Exercise** is also a noun. ❑ *Lack of exercise can cause sleep problems.*
→ look at **fitness**

ex|hale /ɛksheɪl/ (**exhales, exhaling, exhaled**) VERB When you **exhale**, you breathe air out of your body. [FORMAL] ❑ *Hold your breath for a moment and then exhale.*

ex|haust /ɪgzɔst/ (**exhausts, exhausting, exhausted**)

1 VERB If something **exhausts** you, it makes you very tired. ❑ *We were worried that the trip would exhaust him.* ● **ex|haust|ed** ADJECTIVE ❑ *She was too exhausted to talk.* ● **ex|haust|ing** ADJECTIVE ❑ *It was an exhausting climb to the top of the hill.* ● **ex|haus|tion** /ɪgzɔstʃ°n/ NONCOUNT NOUN ❑ *He fainted from exhaustion.*

2 NONCOUNT NOUN **Exhaust** is the gas or steam that the engine of a vehicle produces. ❑ *The vehicle's exhaust fumes began to fill the yard.*
→ look at **pollution**

ex|hib|it /ɪgzɪbɪt/ (**exhibits, exhibiting, exhibited**)

1 VERB ARTS When an object **is exhibited**, it is put in a public place such as a museum so that people can come to look at it. ❑ *The paintings were exhibited in Paris in 1874.*

2 NOUN ARTS An **exhibit** is a public display of art or interesting objects. ❑ *These objects are part of an exhibit at the Museum of Modern Art.*

ex|hi|bi|tion /ɛksɪbɪʃ°n/ (**exhibitions**) NOUN ARTS An **exhibition** is a public event where art or interesting objects are shown. ❑ *The Museum of the City of New York has an exhibition of photographs.*

ex|ist /ɪgzɪst/ (**exists, existing, existed**) VERB If something **exists**, it is a real thing or situation. ❑ *It is clear that a serious problem exists.*

ex|ist|ence /ɪgzɪstəns/ NONCOUNT NOUN The **existence** of something is the fact that it is a real thing or situation. ❑ *We can understand the existence of stars and planets.* ❑ *The club is still in existence.*

ex|ist|ing /ɪgzɪstɪŋ/ ADJECTIVE **Existing** describes something that is in this world or available now. ❑ *There is a need to improve existing products.*

exit /ɛgzɪt, ɛksɪt/ (**exits, exiting, exited**)

1 NOUN The **exit** is the door that you use to leave a public building. ❑ *He walked toward the exit.*

2 VERB If you **exit** a place, you leave it. ❑ *Exit the freeway at 128th Street Southwest.*

ex|ot|ic /ɪgzɒtɪk/ ADJECTIVE Something that is **exotic** is unusual and interesting, usually because it comes from another country. ❑ *The house has a garden with exotic plants.*

ex|pand /ɪkspænd/ (**expands, expanding, expanded**) VERB If something **expands**, it becomes larger. ❑ *The industry expanded in the 19th century.* ❑ *We want to expand children's knowledge of the world.* ● **ex|pan|sion** /ɪkspænʃ°n/ NONCOUNT NOUN ❑ *Local people are against the expansion of the airport.*

ex|pect /ɪkspɛkt/ (**expects, expecting, expected**)

1 VERB If you **expect** something **to** happen, you believe that it will happen. ❑ *He expects to lose his job.* ❑ *We expect the price of bananas to rise.*

2 VERB If you **are expecting** something or someone, you believe that they will arrive soon. ❑ *I wasn't expecting a visitor.*

3 VERB If you **expect** a person **to** do something, you believe that it is the person's duty to do it. ❑ *I expect you to help around the house.*

e

4 **VERB** If a woman **is expecting** a baby, she has a baby growing inside her. ❑ *She announced that she was expecting another child.*

ex|pec|ta|tion /ɛkspɛkteɪʃᵊn/ (**expectations**) **NOUN** A person's **expectations** are beliefs they have about how something should happen. ❑ *Young people have high expectations for the future.*

ex|pel /ɪkspɛl/ (**expels, expelling, expelled**) **VERB** If someone **is expelled from** a school or an organization, they are officially told to leave. ❑ *Two students were expelled for cheating.*

ex|pense /ɪkspɛns/ (**expenses**)
1 **NONCOUNT NOUN** Expense is the cost or price of something. ❑ *He bought a big television at great expense.*
2 **PLURAL NOUN** Expenses are amounts of money that you spend on things. ❑ *Her hotel expenses were paid by the company.*

ex|pen|sive /ɪkspɛnsɪv/ **ADJECTIVE** If something is **expensive**, it costs a lot of money. ❑ *People thought that healthy food was more expensive than fast food.*
→ look at **car, shopping**

ex|peri|ence /ɪkspɪəriəns/ (**experiences, experiencing, experienced**)
1 **NONCOUNT NOUN** Experience is knowledge or skill in a job or an activity that you have done for a long time. ❑ *No teaching experience is necessary.* ● **ex|pe|ri|enced** **ADJECTIVE** ❑ *He is an experienced pilot.*
2 **NOUN** An **experience** is something important that happens to you. ❑ *What has been your most enjoyable experience?*
3 **VERB** If you **experience** something, it happens to you. ❑ *I have never experienced true love.*

ex|peri|ment (**experiments, experimenting, experimented**)

> **PRONUNCIATION HELP**
> Pronounce the noun /ɪkspɛrɪmənt/.
> Pronounce the verb /ɪkspɛrɪmɛnt/.

1 **NOUN** SCIENCE An **experiment** is a scientific test that you do in order to discover what happens to something. ❑ *Laboratory experiments show that vitamin D slows cancer growth.*
2 **VERB** SCIENCE If you **experiment with** something or **experiment on** it, you do a scientific test on it. ❑ *The scientists have experimented on mice.*

3 **NOUN** An **experiment** is when you test a new idea or method. ❑ *They started the magazine as an experiment.*
4 **VERB** To **experiment** means to test a new idea or method. ❑ *I like cooking, and I have the time to experiment.*
→ look at **science**

Word Partners	Use **experiment** with:
ADJ.	**scientific** experiment **1** **simple** experiment **1** **3**
V.	**conduct an** experiment, **perform an** experiment, **try an** experiment **1** **3**

ex|peri|men|tal /ɪkspɛrɪmɛntᵊl/ **ADJECTIVE** Something that is **experimental** is new, or uses new ideas or methods. ❑ *...an experimental musician.*

ex|pert /ɛkspɜrt/ (**experts**) **NOUN** An **expert** is a person who knows a lot about a particular subject. ❑ *His brother is a computer expert.*

ex|per|tise /ɛkspɜrtiz/ **NONCOUNT NOUN** Expertise is special skill or knowledge. ❑ *We're looking for someone with expertise in foreign languages.*

ex|pire /ɪkspaɪər/ (**expires, expiring, expired**) **VERB** When a document **expires**, it cannot be used any more. ❑ *My contract expires in July.*

ex|plain /ɪkspleɪn/ (**explains, explaining, explained**)
1 **VERB** If you **explain** something to someone, you describe it so that they can understand it. ❑ *He explained the law in simple language.* ❑ *Professor Griffiths explained how the drug works.*
2 **VERB** If you **explain** something that happened, you give reasons for it. ❑ *She left a note explaining her actions.* ❑ *Can you explain why you didn't telephone?*

ex|pla|na|tion /ɛkspləneɪʃᵊn/ (**explanations**) **NOUN** An **explanation** is information that you give someone to help them to understand something. ❑ *There was no explanation for the car accident.*

ex|plic|it /ɪksplɪsɪt/ **ADJECTIVE** Something that is **explicit** is expressed or shown clearly, without hiding anything. ❑ *Many parents worry about explicit violence on television.*

ex|plode /ɪksploʊd/ (**explodes, exploding, exploded**) **VERB** If an object such as a bomb **explodes**, it bursts with great force. ❑ *A second bomb exploded in the capital yesterday.*

ex|ploit /ɪksplɔɪt/ (exploits, exploiting, exploited) **VERB** If someone **exploits** you, they treat you unfairly by using your work or ideas. ❑ *They said that he exploited other musicians.*

ex|plore /ɪksplɔr/ (explores, exploring, explored) **VERB** If you **explore** a place, you travel around it to find out what it is like. ❑ *The best way to explore the area is in a boat.*
● **ex|plo|ra|tion** /ɛkspləreɪʃ°n/ (explorations) **NOUN** ❑ *He led the first English exploration of North America.* ● **ex|plor|er** (explorers) **NOUN** ❑ *Who was the US explorer who discovered the Titanic shipwreck?*
→ look at **history**

ex|plo|sion /ɪksploʊʒ°n/ (explosions) **NOUN** An **explosion** is when something suddenly bursts with a loud sound. ❑ *Six soldiers were injured in the explosion.*

ex|plo|sive /ɪksploʊsɪv/ (explosives)
1 **NOUN** An **explosive** is a substance or an object that can cause an explosion. ❑ *The 400 pounds of explosives were packaged in yellow bags.*
2 **ADJECTIVE** **Explosive** is also an adjective. ❑ *No explosive device was found.*

Word Builder export

port ≈ **carry**

air + port = air**port**
ex + port = ex**port**
im + port = im**port**
port + able = **port**able
trans + port = trans**port**

---

ex|port (exports, exporting, exported)

> **PRONUNCIATION HELP**
> Pronounce the verb /ɪkspɔrt/. Pronounce the noun /ɛkspɔrt/.

1 **VERB** SOCIAL STUDIES To **export** products means to sell them to another country. ❑ *They also export beef.* ❑ *The company now exports to Japan.*
2 **NONCOUNT NOUN** **Export** is also a noun. ❑ *A lot of our land is used for growing crops for export.* ● **ex|port|er** /ɛkspɔrtər, ɪkspɔrtər/ (exporters) **NOUN** ❑ *Brazil is a big exporter of coffee.*
3 **NOUN** **Exports** are goods that one country sells to another country. ❑ *Spain's main export is oil.*

ex|pose /ɪkspoʊz/ (exposes, exposing, exposed) **VERB** To **expose** something means to show it so that people can see it. ❑ *Vitamin D is made when the skin is exposed to sunlight.*

ex|press /ɪksprɛs/ (expresses, expressing, expressed)
1 **VERB** When you **express** an idea or feeling, you show what you think or feel. ❑ *Only one company expressed an interest in his plan.*
2 **ADJECTIVE** You use an **express** service when you want to send or receive things faster than usual. ❑ *An express mail service is available.*
3 **NOUN** An **express** or an **express train** is a fast train that stops at only a few stations. ❑ *The express to Kuala Lumpur has just left Singapore station.*

ex|pres|sion /ɪksprɛʃ°n/ (expressions)
1 **NOUN** Your **expression** is the way that your face looks at a particular moment. ❑ *There was an expression of sadness on his face.*
2 **NOUN** An **expression** is a word or phrase. ❑ *Try to learn a few words and expressions in the language.*
→ look at **communication**

ex|pres|sive /ɪksprɛsɪv/ **ADJECTIVE** Something that is **expressive** clearly shows a person's feelings. ❑ *He has a very expressive little face, so you always know what he's thinking.*

ex|press|way /ɪksprɛsweɪ/ (expressways) **NOUN** An **expressway** is a wide road that allows cars to travel very fast over a long distance. ❑ *The E11 expressway connects Paris and Barcelona.*

ex|tend /ɪkstɛnd/ (extends, extending, extended) **VERB** If you **extend** something, you make it longer. ❑ *These treatments have extended the lives of people with cancer.*

ex|ten|sion /ɪkstɛnʃ°n/ (extensions)
1 **NOUN** An **extension** is an extra period of time for which something lasts. ❑ *He was given a six-month extension to his visa.*
2 **NOUN** An **extension** is a telephone that connects to the main telephone line in a building. ❑ *She can talk to me on extension 308.*

ex|ten|sive /ɪkstɛnsɪv/ **ADJECTIVE** If something is **extensive**, it covers a wide area. ❑ *It is a four-bedroom house with extensive gardens.*

ex|tent /ɪkstɛnt/ **NOUN** When you talk about **the extent of** a situation, you are talking about how important or serious it is. ❑ *The government has information on the extent of industrial pollution.* ❑ *He soon discovered the extent of the damage.*

e

ex|te|ri|or /ɪkstɪəriər/ (**exteriors**)
1 **NOUN** The **exterior** of something is its outside surface. ❑ *They are going to paint the exterior of the building.*
2 **ADJECTIVE** You use **exterior** to talk about the outside parts of something. ❑ *...exterior walls.*

ex|ter|nal /ɪkstɜrnᵊl/ **ADJECTIVE** Something that is **external** happens or exists outside a place, a person, or an area. ❑ *You lose a lot of heat through external walls.*

ex|tinct /ɪkstɪŋkt/ **ADJECTIVE** SCIENCE A type of animal or plant that is **extinct** does not exist any more. ❑ *Many animals could become extinct in less than 10 years.*
→ look at **conservation**

ex|tinc|tion /ɪkstɪŋkʃᵊn/ **NONCOUNT NOUN** The **extinction** of a species of animal or plant is the death of all its living members. ❑ *We are trying to save these animals from extinction.*

ex|tin|guish /ɪkstɪŋgwɪʃ/ (**extinguishes, extinguishing, extinguished**) **VERB** If you **extinguish** a fire, you stop it from burning. [FORMAL] ❑ *It took about 50 minutes to extinguish the fire.*

ex|tra /ɛkstrə/
1 **ADJECTIVE** An **extra** amount, person, or thing is another one or amount that is added. ❑ *He used the extra time to check his work.*
2 **ADVERB** Extra is also an adverb. ❑ *You may be charged $10 extra for this service.*

ex|tract /ɪkstrækt/ (**extracts, extracting, extracted**) **VERB** If you **extract** something, you take it out or pull it out. ❑ *A dentist may decide to extract the tooth.*

extraor|di|nary /ɪkstrɔrdᵊnɛri/
1 **ADJECTIVE** If something or someone is **extraordinary**, they have an extremely good or special quality. ❑ *He's an extraordinary musician.*
2 **ADJECTIVE** If something is **extraordinary**, it is very unusual or surprising. ❑ *An extraordinary thing just happened.*

ex|trava|gant /ɪkstrævəgənt/
1 **ADJECTIVE** Someone who is **extravagant** spends too much money. ❑ *He was extravagant in all things – his clothing and his partying.*

2 **ADJECTIVE** Something that is **extravagant** costs too much money. ❑ *He came home with extravagant gifts for everyone.*

ex|treme /ɪkstrim/ **ADJECTIVE** Extreme means very great in degree. ❑ *You should use any drug with extreme care.* ● **ex|treme|ly** **ADVERB** ❑ *My cellphone is extremely useful when I am away from home.*

eye /aɪ/ (**eyes**)
1 **NOUN** Your **eyes** are the parts of your body with which you see. ❑ *I opened my eyes and looked.* ❑ *Mrs. Brooke was a tall lady with dark brown eyes.*
2 If something **catches** your **eye**, you suddenly notice it. ❑ *A movement across the garden caught her eye.*
3 If you **catch** someone's **eye**, you do something to attract their attention, so that you can speak to them. ❑ *He tried to catch Annie's eye.*
4 If you **have** your **eye on** something, you want to have it. [INFORMAL] ❑ *I've had my eye on that dress for a while now.*
→ look at **face, sense**

eye|ball /aɪbɔl/ (**eyeballs**) **NOUN** SCIENCE Your **eyeballs** are the parts of your eyes that are like white balls.

eye|brow /aɪbraʊ/ (**eyebrows**) **NOUN** Your **eyebrows** are the lines of hair that grow above your eyes.
→ look at **face**

eye|glasses /aɪglæsɪz/ **PLURAL NOUN** Eyeglasses are two pieces of glass or plastic (= lenses) in a frame, that some people wear in front of their eyes to help them to see better. ❑ *...a pair of eyeglasses.*

eye|lash /aɪlæʃ/ (**eyelashes**) **NOUN** Your **eyelashes** are the hairs that grow on the edges of your eyes.
→ look at **face**

eye|lid /aɪlɪd/ (**eyelids**) **NOUN** Your **eyelids** are the pieces of skin that cover your eyes when they are closed.
→ look at **face**

eye|sight /aɪsaɪt/ **NONCOUNT NOUN** Your **eyesight** is your ability to see. ❑ *He cannot get a driver's license because he has poor eyesight.*

Ff

fa|ble /feɪbᵊl/ (fables) **NOUN** LANGUAGE ARTS
A **fable** is a type of story, usually about
animals, that teaches a lesson about human
behavior. ❑ *Here is a children's fable about love
and honesty.*

fab|ric /fæbrɪk/ (fabrics) **NOUN** Fabric is
cloth that you use for making things like
clothes and bags. ❑ *The shirt is made from
beautiful soft fabric.*

fabu|lous /fæbyələs/ **ADJECTIVE** Something
that is **fabulous** is very good. [INFORMAL]
❑ *The apartment offers fabulous views of the city.*

face /feɪs/ (faces, facing, faced)
1 **NOUN** Your **face** is the front part of your
head. ❑ *She had a beautiful face.*
2 **NOUN** The **face** of something is the front
or a vertical side of it. ❑ *...the south face of
Mount Everest.* ❑ *...a clock face.*
3 **VERB** To **face** a particular direction
means to look in that direction. ❑ *They stood
facing each other.* ❑ *Our house faces south.*
4 **VERB** If you **face** something unpleasant,
you have to deal with it. ❑ *Williams faces life in
prison.* ❑ *I can't face telling my girlfriend.*
5 If you are **face to face** with someone, you
can look at them directly. ❑ *I got off the bus
and came face to face with my teacher.*
6 If you **make a face**, you change your face

into an ugly expression. ❑ *She made a face at
the horrible smell.*
→ look at Picture Dictionary: **face**

fa|cili|tate /fəsɪlɪteɪt/ (facilitates, facilitating,
facilitated) **VERB** If you **facilitate** an action, you
help it to happen. [FORMAL] ❑ *The discussion
will be facilitated by two professional counselors.*

fa|cil|ity /fəsɪlɪti/ (facilities) **NOUN** Facilities
are rooms, buildings, or pieces of equipment
that are used for a particular purpose. ❑ *The
hotel has excellent sports facilities, including a golf
course.*

fact /fækt/ (facts)
1 **NOUN** A **fact** is something that you know is
true. ❑ *He doesn't hide the fact that he wants to win.*
2 You use **in fact** when you are giving more
information about something that you have
just said. ❑ *I don't watch television; in fact, I no
longer own a TV.*
→ look at **history**

fac|tor /fæktər/ (factors) **NOUN** A **factor** is
something that helps to produce a result.
❑ *Exercise is an important factor in a healthy lifestyle.*

fac|to|ry /fæktəri, -tri/ (factories) **NOUN**
A **factory** is a large building where people
use machines to make goods.
→ look at Word World: **factory**

f

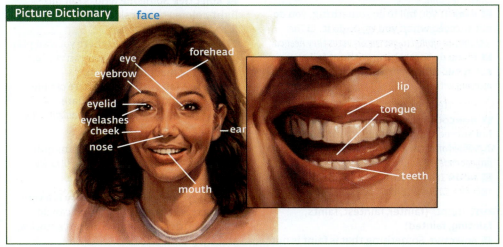

Picture Dictionary face

forehead
eye
eyebrow
eyelid
eyelashes
cheek
nose
ear
mouth

lip
tongue
teeth

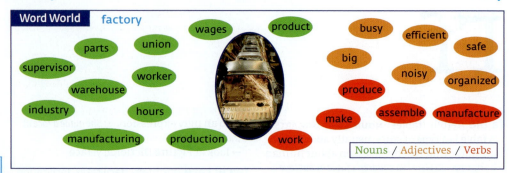

Word World **factory**

wages · product · busy · efficient · safe
parts · union · big · noisy · organized
supervisor · worker · produce
warehouse · make · assemble · manufacture
industry · hours
manufacturing · production · work

Nouns / Adjectives / Verbs

fac|ul|ty /fǽkəlti/ (**faculties**) **NOUN** Faculty is all the teaching staff of a university or a college, or of one department. ❑ *The new program creates more work for faculty.*

fade /feɪd/ (**fades, fading, faded**) **VERB** When something **fades**, it becomes lighter in color. ❑ *The color suddenly faded from her cheeks.* ❑ *Sunlight has faded the carpets and curtains.* ● **fad|ed ADJECTIVE** ❑ *Michael was wearing faded jeans and a green cotton shirt.*

Fahr|en|heit /fǽrənhaɪt/ **ADJECTIVE** SCIENCE Fahrenheit is a way of measuring how hot something is. It is shown by the symbol °F. Water freezes at 32 °F (0 °C) and boils at 212 °F (100 °C). ❑ *The temperature was above 100 °F.*

> **Usage** **Fahrenheit**
>
> The Fahrenheit scale is usually used for temperature in the U.S. You can write it as the degree symbol °**F**. *Today it is 75°F and sunny.*

fail /feɪl/ (**fails, failing, failed**)
1 VERB If you **fail** an exam or a test, you do not pass it. ❑ *75 percent of high school students failed the exam.*
2 VERB If you **fail** to do something, you do not succeed when you try to do it. ❑ *The Republicans failed to get the 60 votes they needed.*
3 If you do something **without fail**, you always do it. ❑ *Andrew attended every board meeting without fail.*

fail|ure /feɪlyər/ (**failures**)
1 NONCOUNT NOUN Failure is when you do not succeed in doing something. ❑ *Brian was depressed after the failure of his marriage.* ❑ *The project ended in failure in late 2001.*
2 NOUN If something is **a failure**, it is not a success. ❑ *His first novel was a failure.*

faint /feɪnt/ (**fainter, faintest, faints, fainting, fainted**)
1 ADJECTIVE Something that is **faint** is not strong or clear. ❑ *I could hear the faint sound of traffic far in the distance.* ❑ *There was still the faint hope that Kimberly might return.* ● **faint|ly ADVERB** ❑ *The room smelled faintly of paint.*
2 ADJECTIVE Someone who is **faint** feels that they are going to fall, usually because they are sick or very tired. ❑ *Ryan was unsteady on his feet and felt faint.*
3 VERB If you **faint**, you become unconscious for a short time. ❑ *She suddenly fell forward and fainted.*
→ look at **sick**

fair /fɛər/ (**fairer, fairest, fairs**)
1 ADJECTIVE Something or someone that is **fair** treats everyone in the same way. ❑ *It's not fair; she's got more than me!* ❑ *I wanted everyone to get fair treatment.* ● **fair|ly ADVERB** ❑ *We solved the problem quickly and fairly.*
● **fair|ness NONCOUNT NOUN** ❑ *There were concerns about the fairness of the election campaign.*
2 ADJECTIVE If something is **fair**, it is not bad, but it is not very good. ❑ *"What did you think of the movie?"—"Hmm. Fair."*
3 ADJECTIVE Someone who is **fair** has light-colored hair or skin. ❑ *My mother is very fair.* ❑ *Eric had thick fair hair.*
4 NOUN A **fair** is a place where you can play games to win prizes, and you can ride on special, big machines for fun.
5 NOUN A **fair** is an event where people show, buy, and sell goods, or share information. ❑ *US Airways is organizing a job fair to hire new workers.*

fair|ly /fɛərli/ **ADVERB** Fairly means quite. ❑ *The team have been playing fairly well lately.* ❑ *She's fairly good at math and science.*

fairy /fɛəri/ (**fairies**) **NOUN** A fairy is a very small creature with wings, that can do magic. Fairies appear in children's stories, and they are not real.

fairy tale (fairy tales) also **fairytale** NOUN
LANGUAGE ARTS A **fairy tale** is a story for
children about magic and fairies.

faith /feɪθ/ (faiths)

1 NONCOUNT NOUN If you have **faith in**
someone or something, you feel sure that
they are able to do something, or that they
will behave honestly. ❏ I have faith in the
honesty of my employees.

2 NOUN A **faith** is a particular religion.
❏ The children will learn about a variety of faiths
such as Islam and Judaism.

faith|ful /feɪθfəl/ ADJECTIVE If you are
faithful, you always support your family and
friends. ❏ Help your brothers and sisters, and be
faithful to your friends. ● **faith|ful|ly** ADVERB
❏ Mary has worked faithfully for the company for
many years.

fake /feɪk/ (fakes)

1 ADJECTIVE A **fake** thing is a copy of
something, especially of something that is
valuable. ❏ The men used fake passports to get
into the country.

2 NOUN A **fake** is something that is fake.
❏ Art experts think that the painting is a fake.

fall /fɔl/ (falls, falling, fell, fallen)

1 VERB If someone or something **falls**, they
move quickly toward the ground by
accident. ❏ Tyler fell from his horse and broke his
arm. ❏ Jacob lost his balance and fell backwards.
❏ There was a huge crash as a large painting fell off
the wall.

2 NOUN A **fall** is when you fall to the
ground. ❏ Grandpa broke his right leg in a bad fall.

3 **Fall down** means the same as **fall**. ❏ The
wind hit Chris so hard, he fell down.

4 VERB When rain or snow **falls**, it comes
down from the sky. ❏ More than 30 inches of
rain fell in 6 days.

5 NOUN **Fall** is the season between summer
and winter, when the leaves start to fall off
the trees. ❏ They got married in the fall of 1991.

6 VERB If something **falls**, it becomes less
or lower. ❏ Unemployment fell to 4.6 percent in
May. ❏ Here, temperatures at night can fall below
freezing.

7 NOUN A **fall** is when something becomes
less or lower. ❏ There has been a sharp fall in the
value of the dollar.

8 VERB If you **fall** asleep or if you **fall** ill, you
start to sleep or you become ill. ❏ Emily
suddenly fell ill and was rushed to hospital.
→ look at **season**

▶ **fall apart** If something **falls apart**, it
breaks into pieces. ❏ Gradually, the old building
fell apart.

▶ **fall behind** If you **fall behind**, you do not
make progress or move forward as fast as
other people. ❏ Some of the students fell behind
in their work.

▶ **fall off** If something **falls off**, it comes
away from the thing it was fixed to. ❏ An
engine fell off the wing of the airplane.

▶ **fall out** **1** If your hair or your tooth **falls
out**, it comes out.
2 If you **fall out** with someone, you have an
argument and stop being friendly with
them. ❏ Ashley has fallen out with her boyfriend.

fall|en /fɔlən/ **Fallen** is a form of the verb **fall**.

false /fɔls/

1 ADJECTIVE If something is **false**, it is
wrong or not true. ❏ The president received false
information from his advisers. ● **false|ly** ADVERB
❏ She was falsely accused of stealing.

2 ADJECTIVE **False** objects are not real or not
natural. ❏ My grandma has false teeth.

fame /feɪm/ NONCOUNT NOUN **Fame** is when
you are very well known by a lot of people.
❏ Connery gained fame as Agent 007 in the Bond
movies.

fa|mili|ar /fəmɪlyər/ ADJECTIVE If someone
or something is **familiar**, you have seem
them or heard of them before. ❏ That boy's
face looks familiar. ❏ Her name sounds familiar to me.

fami|ly /fæmɪli, fæmli/ (families) NOUN
A **family** is a group of people who are related
to each other, usually parents and their
children. ❏ William and his family live in Hawaii.
❏ A ticket for a family of four costs $68.
→ look at Picture Dictionary: **family**

fam|ine /fæmɪn/ (famines) NOUN A **famine**
is a time when there is not enough food for
people to eat, and many people die. ❏ Their
country is suffering from famine and war.

fa|mous /feɪməs/ ADJECTIVE Someone or
something that is **famous** is very well
known. ❏ Edvard Munch's painting "The Scream"
is one of the world's most famous paintings.

fan /fæn/ (fans, fanning,
fanned)

1 NOUN If you are a **fan** of
someone or something, you
like them very much.
❏ If you're a Johnny Depp fan,
you'll love this movie.

F

Picture Dictionary   family

grandfather   grandmother

uncle   aunt   father   mother   father-in-law   mother-in-law

brother-in-law   sister   sister-in-law   brother   husband

wife

2   **NOUN** A **fan** is a piece of equipment that moves the air around a room to make you cooler.

3   **NOUN** A **fan** is a flat object that you move backward and forward in front of your face to make you cooler.

4   **VERB** If you **fan** yourself when you are hot, you move a fan or another flat object around in front of yourself, to make yourself feel cooler. ❑ *Jessica fanned herself with a newspaper.*

fa|nat|ic /fənætɪk/ (fanatics) **NOUN** A **fanatic** is someone whose behavior or opinions are very extreme. ❑ *I am not a religious fanatic but I am a Christian.*

fan|cy /fænsi/ (fancier, fanciest) **ADJECTIVE** Something that is **fancy** is not simple or ordinary. ❑ *...fancy jewelry.*

fan|tas|tic /fæntæstɪk/ **ADJECTIVE** If something is **fantastic**, it is very good. [INFORMAL] ❑ *Sarah has a fantastic social life—she's always out.*

fan|ta|sy /fæntəsi/ (fantasies) **NOUN** A **fantasy** is an imaginary story or thought that is very different from real life. ❑ *Everyone has had a fantasy about winning the lottery.* ❑ *...a fantasy novel.*

FAQ /fæk/ (FAQs) **NOUN** TECHNOLOGY You often see **FAQ** written on websites. **FAQ** means questions about a particular subject, and it is short for "frequently asked questions."

far /fɑr/ (farther or further)
1   **ADVERB** If one place, thing, or person is **far** away from another, there is a great distance between them. ❑ *We've gone too far to go back now.* ❑ *My sister moved even farther away from home.*

2   **ADVERB** You use **far** in questions and statements about distances. ❑ *How far is it to San Francisco?*

3   **So far** means up until now. ❑ *So far, they have failed.*

4   **ADVERB** **Far** means "very much" when you are comparing things. ❑ *Your essay is far better than mine.*

5   You use **by far** to say that someone or something is the biggest, the best, or the most important. ❑ *Unemployment is by far the most important issue.*

6   **Far from** means not at all. ❑ *What they said was far from the truth.*

fare /fɛər/ (fares) **NOUN** A **fare** is the money that you pay for a trip in a bus, a train, an airplane, or a taxi. ❑ *The fare is $11 one way.* ❑ *He could not afford the fare.*

fare|well /fɛərwɛl/ (farewells)
1   **NOUN** If you **say farewell** to someone, or **say your farewells**, you say goodbye to them. ❑ *We said our farewells and got in the car.* ❑ *They said farewell at the café.*

2   **ADJECTIVE** You organize a **farewell** event in order to say goodbye to people. ❑ *Before she left, she organized a farewell party for family and friends.*

farm /fɑrm/ (farms) **NOUN** A **farm** is a piece of land where people grow crops and keep animals, and the buildings on it. ❑ *Both boys like to work on the farm.*
→ look at Picture Dictionary: **farm**

Picture Dictionary farm

hay

barn

horse

orchard

greenhouse

tractor plow

cow

sheep

pig

Word Builder **farmer**

er ≈ **someone who does**

climb + **er** = climb**er**
farm + **er** = farm**er**
lead + **er** = lead**er**
own + **er** = own**er**
play + **er** = play**er**
work + **er** = work**er**

farm|er /fɑrmər/ (**farmers**) **NOUN** A **farmer** is a person who owns or works on a farm.

farm|house /fɑrmhaʊs/ (**farmhouses**) **NOUN** A **farmhouse** is the house on a farm where the farmer lives.

farm|ing /fɑrmɪŋ/ **NONCOUNT NOUN** **Farming** is the job of growing crops or keeping animals on a farm.

far|ther /fɑrðər/ **Farther** means the same as **further**.

far|thest /fɑrðɪst/ **Farthest** means the same as **furthest**.

fas|ci|nate /fæsɪneɪt/ (**fascinates, fascinating, fascinated**) **VERB** If something **fascinates** you, you find it extremely interesting. ❑ *American history fascinates me.*

fas|ci|nat|ed /fæsɪneɪtɪd/ **ADJECTIVE** If you are **fascinated by** something, you think it is very interesting. ❑ *My brother is fascinated by racing cars.*

fas|ci|nat|ing /fæsɪneɪtɪŋ/ **ADJECTIVE** If something is **fascinating**, it is very interesting. ❑ *Madagascar is a fascinating place.*
→ look at **science**

fash|ion /fæʃ⁰n/ (**fashions**)
1 **NOUN** **Fashion** is the activity or business that involves styles of clothing and appearance. ❑ *The magazine contains 20 full-color pages of fashion.*
2 A **fashion** is a style of clothing that is popular at a particular time. ❑ *Long dresses were the fashion when I was a child.*
3 If something is **in fashion**, it is popular at a particular time. If it is **out of fashion**, it is not popular. ❑ *Long dresses were in fashion back then.*

fash|ion|able /fæʃənəb⁰l/
1 **ADJECTIVE** Something or someone that is **fashionable** is popular at a particular time. ❑ *Long dresses will be very fashionable this year.*
2 **ADJECTIVE** Someone who is **fashionable** wears fashionable clothes. ● **fash|ion|ably** **ADVERB** ❑ *Brianna is always fashionably dressed.*

fast /fæst/ (**faster, fastest, fasts, fasting, fasted**)
1 **ADJECTIVE** Something or someone that is **fast** is quick. ❑ *Jane has always loved fast cars.* ❑ *I'm a fast reader.* ❑ *The subway is the fastest way to get around New York.*
2 **ADVERB** If something moves **fast**, it moves quickly. ❑ *James drives too fast.* ❑ *Can't you run any faster?*
3 **ADVERB** If something happens **fast**, it happens without any delay. ❑ *You need to see a doctor—fast!*
4 **VERB** If you **fast**, you do not eat any food for a period of time.
5 **NOUN** A **fast** is when you do not eat food for a period of time. ❑ *The fast ends at sunset.*
6 Someone who is **fast asleep** is deeply

asleep. ❑ *Anna climbed into bed and five minutes later she was fast asleep.*
→ look at **car, email, food, route**

fas|ten /fæsᵊn/ (**fastens, fastening, fastened**)
1 **VERB** When you **fasten** something, you join the two sides of it together so that it is closed. ❑ *Heather got quickly into her car and fastened the seat-belt.*
2 **VERB** If you **fasten** one thing **to** another, you attach the first thing to the second. ❑ *There was a notice fastened to the gate.*

fast food **NONCOUNT NOUN** Fast food is hot food that is served quickly in a restaurant. ❑ *He likes fast food like hamburgers, pizzas, and hot dogs.*
→ look at **eat**

fat /fæt/ (**fatter, fattest**)
1 **ADJECTIVE** A **fat** person weighs too much. ❑ *I ate too much and I began to get fat.*
2 **ADJECTIVE** A **fat** object is very thick or wide. ❑ *Emily picked up a fat book and handed it to me.*
3 **NONCOUNT NOUN** Fat is a substance containing oil that is found in some foods. ❑ *Cream contains a lot of fat.*
4 **NONCOUNT NOUN** Fat is the soft substance that people and animals have under their skin.
→ look at **meat**

fa|tal /feɪtᵊl/
1 **ADJECTIVE** A **fatal** action has very bad results. ❑ *Justin made the fatal mistake of lending her some money.*
2 **ADJECTIVE** A **fatal** accident or illness causes someone's death. ❑ *The TV star was attacked in a fatal stabbing.* ● **fa|tal|ly** **ADVERB** ❑ *The soldier was fatally wounded in the chest.*

fa|tal|ity /fətæliti/ (**fatalities**) **NOUN** A **fatality** is a death that is caused by an accident or by violence. [FORMAL] ❑ *Yesterday's fatality is the 36th this year.*

fate /feɪt/ (**fates**)
1 **NONCOUNT NOUN** Fate is a power that some people believe controls everything that happens in the world. ❑ *I think it was fate that Andy and I met.*
2 **NOUN** Someone's or something's **fate** is what happens to them. ❑ *Frank was never seen again, and we never knew his fate.*

fa|ther /fɑðər/ (**fathers**) **NOUN** Your **father** is your male parent. ❑ *His father was an artist.*
→ look at **family**

father-in-law (**fathers-in-law**) **NOUN** Someone's **father-in-law** is the father of their husband or wife.
→ look at **family**

fa|tigue /fətig/ **NONCOUNT NOUN** Fatigue is a feeling of being extremely tired. ❑ *He was taken to hospital suffering from extreme fatigue.*

fau|cet /fɔsɪt/ (**faucets**) **NOUN** A **faucet** is an object that controls the flow of a liquid or a gas from a pipe. Sinks and baths have faucets. ❑ *Tina turned off the faucet and dried her hands.*
→ look at **bathroom**

fault /fɔlt/ (**faults**)
1 **NOUN** If something bad is your **fault**, you made it happen. ❑ *The accident was my fault.*
2 **NOUN** A **fault** in someone or something is a weakness in them. ❑ *Brandon's worst fault is his temper.*
3 **NOUN** SCIENCE A **fault** is a large crack in the surface of the Earth. ❑ *The San Andreas Fault is in the San Francisco area.*

faulty /fɔlti/ **ADJECTIVE** Faulty equipment is not working well. ❑ *The car had worn tires and faulty brakes.*

fa|vor /feɪvər/ (**favors**)
1 **NOUN** If you **do** someone **a favor**, you do something to help them. ❑ *Please would you do me a favor and give David a message for me?*
2 If you are **in favor of** something, you think that it is a good thing. ❑ *I'm in favor of income tax cuts.*

fa|vor|able /feɪvərəbᵊl/
1 **ADJECTIVE** If your opinion of something is **favorable**, you think that it is right or good. ❑ *The president's speech received favorable reviews.*
2 **ADJECTIVE** Favorable conditions are good. ❑ *We hope that the weather will be favorable.*

fa|vor|ite /feɪvərɪt, feɪvrɪt/ (**favorites**)
1 **ADJECTIVE** Your **favorite** thing or person is the one that you like more than all the others. ❑ *What is your favorite movie?*
2 **NOUN** Your **favorite** is the person or thing that you like more than all the others. ❑ *Of all the seasons, fall is my favorite.*
→ look at **food, movie, season**

fax /fæks/ (**faxes, faxing, faxed**)
1 **NOUN** A **fax** or a **fax machine** is a special machine that is joined to a telephone line. You use a **fax** to send and receive documents.

F

2 **NOUN** A **fax** is a copy of a document that you send or receive using a fax machine. ❑ *I sent Daniel a long fax this morning.*

3 **VERB** If you **fax** a document to someone, you send it to their fax machine. ❑ *I faxed a copy of the letter to my boss.*

fear /fɪər/ (**fears, fearing, feared**)
1 **NONCOUNT NOUN** **Fear** is the unpleasant feeling you have when you think that you are in danger. ❑ *My whole body was shaking with fear.*
2 **NOUN** A **fear** is a thought that something unpleasant might happen. ❑ *Sara has a fear of spiders.*
3 **VERB** If you **fear** someone or something, you are very afraid of them. ❑ *Many people fear flying.*

fear|ful /fɪərfəl/ **ADJECTIVE** If you are **fearful** of something, you are afraid of it. [FORMAL] ❑ *They were all fearful of losing their jobs.*

fear|less /fɪərlɪs/ **ADJECTIVE** If someone is **fearless**, they are not afraid of anything. ❑ *He was brave and fearless—a true hero.*

feast /fist/ (**feasts**) **NOUN** A **feast** is a large and special meal for a lot of people. ❑ *On Friday night, they had a wedding feast for 1,000 guests.*

feat /fit/ (**feats**) **NOUN** A **feat** is a very brave or difficult act. ❑ *The men performed feats of physical bravery.*

feath|er /fɛðər/ (**feathers**) **NOUN** A bird's **feathers** are the light soft things that cover its body. ❑ *...peacock feathers.*

fea|ture /fitʃər/ (**features**)
1 **NOUN** A **feature of** something is an important part of it. ❑ *The house has many attractive features, including a swimming pool.*
2 **NOUN** A **feature** is a special story in a newspaper or magazine. ❑ *There was a feature on Tom Cruise in the New York Times.*
3 **PLURAL NOUN** Your **features** are your eyes, nose, mouth, and other parts of your face. ❑ *Emily's best feature is her dark eyes.*

Feb|ru|ary /fɛbyuɛri, fɛbru-/ **NOUN** **February** is the second month of the year. ❑ *The band's U.S. tour starts on February 7.*

fed /fɛd/ **Fed** is a form of the verb **feed**.

fed|er|al /fɛdərəl/
1 **ADJECTIVE** SOCIAL STUDIES In a **federal** country or system, a group of states is controlled by a central government.

2 **ADJECTIVE** SOCIAL STUDIES **Federal** means relating to the national government of a federal country. ❑ *The federal government moved to Washington in the fall of 1800.*

fed|er|al govern|ment (**federal governments**) **NOUN** SOCIAL STUDIES A **federal government** controls all the states of a country as a group.

fed|er|al|ism /fɛdərəlɪzəm/ **NONCOUNT NOUN** SOCIAL STUDIES **Federalism** is a political system in which a central government controls separate states. ❑ *The basic principle of American federalism is fixed in the tenth amendment.*

fed up **ADJECTIVE** If you are **fed up**, you are unhappy or bored. [INFORMAL] ❑ *My brother soon became fed up with city life.*

fee /fi/ (**fees**)
1 **NOUN** A **fee** is the money that you pay to be allowed to do something. ❑ *We paid the small entrance fee and drove inside.*
2 **NOUN** A **fee** is the money that you pay a person or an organization for advice or for a service. ❑ *We had to pay the lawyer fees ourselves.*

fee|ble /fibəl/ (**feebler, feeblest**) **ADJECTIVE** If someone or something is **feeble**, they are weak. ❑ *My uncle was old and feeble, and was not able to walk far.* ● **fee|bly** **ADVERB** ❑ *Her left hand moved feebly at her side.*

feed /fid/ (**feeds, feeding, fed**) **VERB** If you **feed** a person or an animal, you give them food. ❑ *It's time to feed the baby.* ❑ *It's usually best to feed a small dog twice a day.*

feed|back /fidbæk/ **NONCOUNT NOUN** If you get **feedback on** your work, someone tells you how well or badly you are doing. ❑ *Ask your teacher for feedback on your work.*

feel /fil/ (**feels, feeling, felt**)
1 **VERB** If you **feel** a particular emotion or a physical feeling, you experience it. ❑ *I am feeling really happy today.* ❑ *I felt a sharp pain in my shoulder.* ❑ *How do you feel?*
2 **VERB** The way that something **feels** is the way it seems when you touch it or experience it. ❑ *The blanket feels soft.* ❑ *The sun felt hot on my back.* ❑ *The room felt rather cold.*
3 **VERB** If you **feel** something, you touch it with your hand, so that you can find out what it is like. ❑ *The doctor felt my pulse.* ❑ *Feel how soft this leather is.*
4 **VERB** If you can **feel** something, you are

f

aware of it because you touch it or it touches you. ❑ *Anna felt something touching her face.*

5 **VERB** If you talk about how you **feel**, you tell someone your opinion about it. ❑ *We feel that this decision is fair.* ❑ *She felt guilty about spending so much money on clothes.*

6 **VERB** If you **feel like** doing something, you want to do it. ❑ *"I just don't feel like going out tonight," Rose said quietly.*

→ look at **feeling, sense, sick**

▶ **feel for** **1** If you **feel for** something, you try to find it using your hands and not your eyes. ❑ *I felt for my keys in my pocket.*

2 If you **feel for** someone, you have sympathy for them. ❑ *Nicole was crying, and I really felt for her.*

feel|ing /fíliŋ/ (**feelings**)

1 **NOUN** A **feeling** is something that you feel in your mind or your body. ❑ *I had feelings of sadness and loneliness.*

2 **NOUN** If you have **a feeling that** something is going to happen, you think that it is probably going to happen. ❑ *I have a feeling that everything will be all right.*

3 **PLURAL NOUN** Your **feelings** about something are what you think and feel about it. ❑ *They have strong feelings about politics.*

4 **PLURAL NOUN** If you **hurt someone's feelings**, you say or do something that makes them upset. ❑ *I'm really sorry if I hurt your feelings.*

5 **NONCOUNT NOUN** **Feeling** in part of your body is the ability to feel things there. ❑ *After the accident, Jason had no feeling in his legs.*

→ look at Word World: **feeling**

feet /fít/ **Feet** is the plural of **foot**.

fell /fɛl/ **Fell** is a form of the verb **fall**.

fel|low /fɛloʊ/ (**fellows**)

1 **NOUN** A **fellow** is a man. ❑ *Chris was a cheerful fellow.*

2 **ADJECTIVE** **Fellow** describes people who are like you or from the same place as you. ❑ *Richard was just 18 when he married fellow student Barbara.*

felo|ny /fɛləni/ (**felonies**) **NOUN** A **felony** is a very serious crime. ❑ *The judge found him guilty of six felonies.*

felt /fɛlt/

1 **Felt** is a form of the verb **feel**.

2 **NONCOUNT NOUN** **Felt** is a type of soft thick cloth. ❑ *Amy was wearing an old felt hat.*

fe|male /fíimeɪl/ (**females**)

1 **NOUN** SCIENCE A **female** is any animal, including humans, that can give birth to babies or lay eggs. ❑ *Each female will lay just one egg.*

2 **ADJECTIVE** SCIENCE **Female** is also an adjective. ❑ *...female gorillas.*

3 **NOUN** A **female** is a woman or a girl. ❑ *This disease affects males more than females.*

4 **ADJECTIVE** **Female** is also an adjective. ❑ *Who is your favorite female singer?*

Usage   **female**

In everyday conversation, you should avoid saying **female** to refer to women, because that may offend people. **Female** as a noun is mainly used in scientific or medical language. *The leader of the herd of elephants is usually the oldest female.* Say **woman** or **women** when you are talking about people. *My boss is a woman.*

femi|nine /fɛmɪnɪn/

1 **ADJECTIVE** **Feminine** qualities and things are considered to be typical of women. ❑ *I love feminine clothes, so I wear skirts a lot.* ❑ *His voice was strangely feminine.*

2 **ADJECTIVE** LANGUAGE ARTS In some languages, a **feminine** noun, pronoun, or adjective has a different form from other forms (such as "masculine" forms). Compare with **masculine**

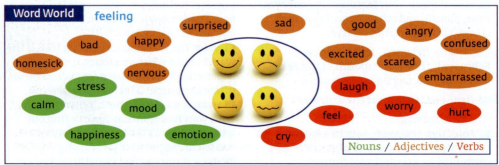

Word World: feeling

Nouns / Adjectives / Verbs

femi|nism /fɛmɪnɪzəm/ **NONCOUNT NOUN**
SOCIAL STUDIES **Feminism** is the belief that
women should have the same rights and
opportunities as men.

femi|nist /fɛmɪnɪst/ (**feminists**)
1 **NOUN** SOCIAL STUDIES A **feminist** is a
person who believes in feminism.
❏ *Feminists argue that women should not have to
choose between children and a career.*
2 **ADJECTIVE** **Feminist** groups, ideas, and
activities are involved in feminism.
❏ *...feminist writer Simone de Beauvoir.*

fence /fɛns/ (**fences**) **NOUN** A **fence** is a
wooden or metal wall around a piece of
land.

fend|er /fɛndər/ (**fenders**) **NOUN** The **fender**
of a car is the area above the wheels.

fern /fɜrn/ (**ferns**) **NOUN** A **fern** is a plant
that has long stems with leaves that look
like feathers.

fer|ry /fɛri/ (**ferries**) **NOUN** A **ferry** is a boat
that takes people or things a short distance
across water. ❏ *They crossed the River Gambia
by ferry.*
→ look at **transportation**

fer|tile /fɜrtˑl/
1 **ADJECTIVE** SCIENCE If land or soil is **fertile**,
plants grow very well in it.
2 **ADJECTIVE** SCIENCE A person who is **fertile**
is able to have babies. ● **fer|til|ity** **NONCOUNT
NOUN** ❏ *Smoking and drinking alcohol affect
fertility.*

fer|ti|liz|er /fɜrtˑlaɪzər/ (**fertilizers**)
NONCOUNT NOUN **Fertilizer** is a substance
that you put on soil to make plants grow
better.

fes|ti|val /fɛstɪvˑl/ (**festivals**)
1 **NOUN** ARTS A **festival** is a series of special
events such as concerts or plays. ❏ *The actress
was in Rome for the city's film festival.*
2 **NOUN** A **festival** is a time when people
celebrate a special event. ❏ *Shavuot is a
two-day festival for Jews.*

fetch /fɛtʃ/ (**fetches, fetching, fetched**) **VERB**
If you **fetch** something or someone, you go
somewhere and bring them back. ❏ *Sylvia
fetched a towel from the bathroom.* ❏ *Please could
you fetch me a glass of water?*

fe|tus /fitəs/ (**fetuses**) **NOUN** SCIENCE A **fetus**
is an animal or a human being before it is
born.

fe|ver /fivər/ (**fevers**) **NOUN** If you have a
fever when you are sick, your body is too hot.
❏ *Jim had a high fever.*
→ look at **sick**

fe|ver|ish /fivərɪʃ/ **ADJECTIVE** If you are
feverish, you have a fever. ❏ *Joshua was
feverish and wouldn't eat anything.*

few /fyu/ (**fewer, fewest**)
1 **ADJECTIVE** A **few** means some, but not
many. ❏ *I'm having a dinner party for a few close
friends.* ❏ *Here are a few ideas that might help you.*
PRONOUN A **few** is also a pronoun. ❏ *Most
were Americans but a few were British.*
2 A **few of** means some, but not many.
❏ *I met a few of her friends at the party.*
3 **ADJECTIVE** **Few** means not many. ❏ *She had
few friends.*
4 **PRONOUN** **Few** is also a pronoun. ❏ *Few can
survive more than a week without water.*
5 **Few of** means not many. ❏ *Few of the
houses still had lights on.*

fi|an|cé /fiɑnseɪ, fiɑnseɪ/ (**fiancés**) **NOUN**
A woman's **fiancé** is the man that she is
going to marry.

fi|an|cée /fiɑnseɪ, fiɑnseɪ/ (**fiancées**) **NOUN**
A man's **fiancée** is the woman that he is
going to marry.

fi|ber /faɪbər/ (**fibers**)
1 **NOUN** A **fiber** is a thin thread that is used
for making cloth or rope. ❏ *We only sell
clothing made from natural fibers.*
2 **NONCOUNT NOUN** **Fiber** is the part of a
fruit or a vegetable that helps all the food
you eat to move through your body. ❏ *Most
vegetables contain fiber.*

fic|tion /fɪkʃˑn/ **NONCOUNT NOUN**
LANGUAGE ARTS **Fiction** is books and stories
about people and events that are not real.
● **fictional** **ADJECTIVE** ❏ *...Harry Potter, the
fictional hero of J.K. Rowling's books.*

fidg|et /fɪdʒɪt/ (**fidgets, fidgeting, fidgeted**)
VERB If you **fidget**, you keep moving slightly,
because you are nervous or bored. ❏ *Brenda
fidgeted in her seat.*

field /fild/ (**fields**)
1 **NOUN** A **field** is a piece of land where
crops are grown, or where animals are kept.
❏ *We drove past fields of sunflowers.*
2 **NOUN** SPORTS A sports **field** is a piece of
land where sports are played. ❏ *...a baseball
field.*

f

3 **VERB** SPORTS In a game of baseball, the team that **is fielding** is trying to catch the ball, while the other team is trying to hit it. ❏ *The Tigers were pitching and fielding superbly.*

4 **NOUN** A **field** is a subject that someone knows a lot about. ❏ *Professor Greenwood is an expert in the field of international law.*

field|er /fíldər/ (**fielders**) **NOUN** A **fielder** is a player in some sports who has to pick up or catch the ball after a player from the other team has hit it. ❏ *He hit 10 home runs and he's also a good fielder.*

fierce /fíərs/ (**fiercer, fiercest**)

1 **ADJECTIVE** A **fierce** animal or person is very angry and is likely to attack you.
● **fierce|ly** **ADVERB** ❏ *"Go away!" she said fiercely.*
2 **ADJECTIVE** **Fierce** feelings or actions are very strong or enthusiastic. ❏ *There's fierce competition for places in the team.* ● **fierce|ly** **ADVERB** ❏ *Amanda is fiercely ambitious.*

fif|teen /fíftín/ MATH **Fifteen** is the number 15.

fifth /fífθ/ (**fifths**)

1 **ADJECTIVE, ADVERB** MATH The **fifth** item in a series is the one that you count as number five. ❏ *This is his fifth trip to Australia.*
2 **NOUN** MATH A **fifth** is one of five equal parts of something (⅕). ❏ *The machine allows us to do the job in a fifth of the usual time.*
→ look at **number**

fif|ty /fífti/ MATH **Fifty** is the number 50.

fig /fíg/ (**figs**) **NOUN** A **fig** is a soft sweet fruit full of tiny seeds. Figs grow on trees in hot countries.
→ look at **fruit**

fight /fáɪt/ (**fights, fighting, fought**)

1 **VERB** When people **fight**, they try to hurt each other with words or by using physical force. ❏ *"Stop fighting!" Mom shouted.* ❏ *Susan fought a lot with her younger sister.*
3 **NOUN** If people have a **fight**, they try to hurt each other. ❏ *I had a fight with Simon at the party last night.*
4 **VERB** If you **fight** something unpleasant, you try very hard to stop it. ❏ *It is very hard to fight forest fires.*
5 **VERB** If you **fight** for something, you try very hard to get it. ❏ *Lee had to fight hard for his place on the team.*
6 **VERB** When people **fight**, they argue. [INFORMAL] ❏ *Robert's parents fight all the time.*

fight|er /fáɪtər/ (**fighters**) **NOUN** A **fighter** is a person who fights another person, especially as a sport. ❏ *He was a professional fighter for 17 years.*

fig|ure /fígyər/ (**figures, figuring, figured**)

1 **NOUN** MATH A **figure** is one of the symbols from 0 to 9 that you use to write numbers. ❏ *They've put the figures in the wrong column.* ❏ *John earns a seven-figure salary—$1,000,000 at least.*
2 **NOUN** MATH A **figure** is an amount expressed as a number. ❏ *Can I see your latest sales figures?*
3 **NOUN** A **figure** is the shape of a person you cannot see clearly. ❏ *Two figures moved behind the thin curtain.*
4 **NOUN** Your **figure** is the shape of your body. ❏ *Lauren has a very good figure.*
▶ **figure out** If you **figure out** a solution to a problem, you succeed in solving it. [INFORMAL] ❏ *We couldn't figure out how to use the equipment.*
→ look at **geometry**

file /fáɪl/ (**files, filing, filed**)

1 **NOUN** A **file** is a box or a type of envelope that you keep papers in. ❏ *The file contained letters and reports.*
2 **NOUN** TECHNOLOGY A **file** is a collection of information that you keep on your computer. ❏ *I deleted the files by mistake.*
3 **NOUN** A **file** is a tool that you use for rubbing rough objects to make them smooth. ❏ *...a nail file.*
4 **VERB** If you **file** a document, you put it in the correct envelope. ❏ *The letters are all filed alphabetically.*
5 **VERB** If you **file** something, you make it smooth. ❏ *Mom was filing her nails.*
6 **VERB** If people **file** somewhere, they walk there in a line, one behind the other. ❏ *More than 10,000 people filed past the dead woman's coffin.*
7 A group of people who are walking or standing **in single file** are in a line, one behind the other.

file|name /fáɪlneɪm/ (**filenames**) **NOUN** TECHNOLOGY A **filename** is the name that you give to a particular computer file.

file-sharing also **file sharing** **NONCOUNT** **NOUN** TECHNOLOGY **File-sharing** is a way of sharing computer files among a large number of users.

fill /fíl/ (**fills, filling, filled**)

1 **VERB** If you **fill** a container with

something, it becomes full of it. ❑ *Rachel went to the bathroom and filled a glass with water.*
2 If a place **fills up**, it become full. ❑ *The theater was filling up quickly.*
3 **VERB** If something **fills** a space, the space is full of it. ❑ *Rows of desks filled the office.*
4 **Fill up** means the same as **fill**. ❑ *Filling up your car's gas tank these days is very expensive.*
● **filled** **ADJECTIVE** ❑ *The museum is filled with historical objects.*
5 **VERB** If you **fill** a hole, you put a substance into it to make the surface smooth again. ❑ *Fill the cracks between walls and window frames.*
6 **Fill in** means the same as **fill**. ❑ *Start by filling in any cracks.*
▶ **fill in** If you **fill in** or **fill out** a form, you write information in the spaces. ❑ *When you have filled in the form, send it to your employer.*
→ look at **answer**

fill|ing /fɪlɪŋ/ (**fillings**)
1 **NOUN** A **filling** is a small amount of metal that fills a hole in a tooth. ❑ *The dentist said I needed two fillings.*
2 **NOUN** The **filling** in a cake, a pie, or a sandwich is what is inside it. ❑ *Next, make the pie filling.*

film /fɪlm/ (**films, filming, filmed**)
1 **NOUN** **ARTS** A **film** is a movie. ❑ *I'm going to see a film tonight.*
2 **VERB** **ARTS** If you **film** something, you use a camera to take moving pictures of it. ❑ *He filmed her life story.*
3 **NOUN** A **film** is the roll of plastic that is used for taking photographs in some older cameras. ❑ *Emily put a new roll of film into the camera.*
→ look at **movie**

fil|ter /fɪltər/ (**filters, filtering, filtered**)
1 **NOUN** **SCIENCE** A **filter** is an object that only allows liquid or air to pass through it, and that holds back solid parts such as dirt or dust. ❑ *The water filters are available in different styles, colors, and designs.*
2 **VERB** **SCIENCE** If you **filter** a liquid or air, you clean it by passing it through a filter. ❑ *The device cleans and filters the air.*

filthy /fɪlθi/ (**filthier, filthiest**) **ADJECTIVE** Something that is **filthy** is very dirty. ❑ *He always wore a filthy old jacket.*

fin /fɪn/ (**fins**) **NOUN** A fish's **fins** are the flat parts like wings that help it to swim.

fi|nal /faɪnᵊl/ (**finals**)
1 **ADJECTIVE** In a series of things, the **final** one is the last one. ❑ *The team's final game of the season will be tomorrow.*
2 **ADJECTIVE** If a decision is **final**, it cannot be changed. ❑ *The judges' decision is final.*
3 **NOUN** **SPORTS** The **final** is the last game or race in a series, that decides who is the winner. ❑ *Williams played in the final of the US Open in 1997.*
4 **PLURAL NOUN** When you take your **finals** or your **final exams**, you take the last and most important exams in a class. ❑ *Anna took her finals in the summer.* ❑ *I'm studying for my final exams.*

fi|nal|ist /faɪnᵊlɪst/ (**finalists**) **NOUN** A **finalist** is someone who reaches the final of a competition. ❑ *Thompson was an Olympic finalist in 1996.*

fi|nal|ly /faɪnᵊli/
1 **ADVERB** If something **finally** happens, it happens after a long time. ❑ *The letter finally arrived at the end of last week.*
2 **ADVERB** You use **finally** before you say the last thing in a list. ❑ *Combine the flour and the cheese, and finally, add the cream.*

fi|nance /faɪnæns, fɪnæns/ (**finances, financing, financed**)
1 **VERB** When someone **finances** something, they provide the money to pay for it. ❑ *The government used the money to finance the war.*
2 **Finance** is when people manage large amounts of money. ❑ *Professor Buckley teaches finance and law at Princeton University.*
3 **PLURAL NOUN** Your **finances** are the money that you have. ❑ *Take control of your finances now and save thousands of dollars.*

fi|nan|cial /faɪnænʃᵊl, fɪn-/ **ADJECTIVE** **Financial** means relating to money. ❑ *The company is in financial difficulties.*

find /faɪnd/ (**finds, finding, found**)
1 **VERB** If you **find** something, you see it after you have been looking for it. ❑ *The police searched the house and found a gun.* ❑ *David has finally found a job.*
2 **VERB** If you **find** something, you see something by chance. ❑ *If you find my purse, can you let me know?*
3 **VERB** When a court **finds** someone guilty or not guilty, it says that they are guilty or not guilty of a crime. ❑ *The woman was found guilty of murdering her husband.*

4 VERB You can use **find** to express your opinion about something. ❑ *I find his behavior extremely rude.* ❑ *We all found the movie very funny.*

5 If you **find** your **way** somewhere, you get there by choosing the right way to go. ❑ *We lost our dog, but he found his way home.*

→ look at **job**

▶ **find out** If you **find** something **out**, you learn the facts about it. ❑ *I'll watch the next episode to find out what happens.*

fine /faɪn/ (**fines, fining, fined, finer, finest**)

1 ADJECTIVE Something that is **fine** is very good. ❑ *There is a fine view of the countryside.*

2 ADJECTIVE If you are **fine**, you are well or happy. ❑ *Lina is fine and sends you her love.*

3 ADJECTIVE If something is **fine**, it is satisfactory or acceptable. ❑ *Everything is going to be just fine.*

4 ADJECTIVE Something that is **fine** is very thin. ❑ *...fine hairs.*

5 ADJECTIVE When the weather is **fine**, the sun is shining.

6 NOUN A **fine** is money that someone has to pay because they have done something wrong.

7 VERB If someone **is fined**, they have to pay some money because they have done something wrong. ❑ *She was fined $300 for driving dangerously.*

fine art (**fine arts**) **NONCOUNT NOUN** ARTS **Fine art** is the paintings and objects that artists produce for other people's pleasure, rather than for a particular use. ❑ *...the Santa Fe Museum of Fine Arts.*

fin|ger /fɪŋgər/ (**fingers**)

1 NOUN Your **fingers** are the long thin parts at the end of each hand. ❑ *Amber had a huge diamond ring on her finger.*

2 If you **cross** your **fingers**, you put one finger on top of another and hope for good luck.

→ look at **hand**

finger|nail /fɪŋgərneɪl/ (**fingernails**) **NOUN** Your **fingernails** are the thin hard parts at the end of each of your fingers.

→ look at **hand**

finger|print /fɪŋgərprɪnt/ (**fingerprints**) **NOUN** **Fingerprints** are the marks that your fingers make when they touch something. ❑ *His fingerprints were found on the gun.*

finger|tip /fɪŋgərtɪp/ (**fingertips**) also **finger-tip NOUN** Your **fingertips** are the

ends of your fingers. ❑ *He plays the drum very lightly with his fingertips.*

fin|ish /fɪnɪʃ/ (**finishes, finishing, finished**)

1 VERB When you **finish** doing something, you stop doing it. ❑ *Dad finished eating, and left the room.*

2 **Finish up** means the same as **finish**. ❑ *We waited outside while Nick finished up his meeting.*

3 VERB When something **finishes**, it ends. ❑ *The concert finished just after midnight.*

4 NOUN The **finish** of something is the end of it or the last part of it. ❑ *There was an exciting finish to the women's 800-meter race.*

Word Partners	Use **finish** with:
N.	finish **a conversation**, finish **school**, finish **work** **1**
	finish **a job**, **time to** finish **1** **2**

fin|ished /fɪnɪʃt/ **ADJECTIVE** Someone who is **finished with** something is no longer using it. ❑ *When you have finished with the book, please give it back to your teacher.*

fir /fɜr/ (**firs**) **NOUN** SCIENCE A **fir** or a **fir tree** is a tall tree with thin leaves (= needles) that do not fall in winter.

→ look at **plant**

fire /faɪər/ (**fires, firing, fired**)

1 NONCOUNT NOUN **Fire** is the hot, bright flames that come from things that are burning. ❑ *We learned how to make fire and hunt for fish.*

2 NOUN **Fire** or a **fire** is flames that destroy buildings or forests. ❑ *87 people died in a fire at the theater.* ❑ *...a forest fire.*

3 NOUN A **fire** is a burning pile of wood or coal that you make. ❑ *There was a fire in the fireplace.*

4 VERB If someone **fires** a gun or a bullet, they shoot it. ❑ *Have you ever fired a gun before?*

5 VERB If an employer **fires** you, he or she tells you to leave your job. ❑ *She was fired from that job in August.*

6 If something **catches fire**, it starts burning. ❑ *Several buildings caught fire in the explosion.*

7 If something is **on fire**, it is burning and being damaged by a fire. ❑ *Quick! My car's on fire!*

8 If you **set fire to** something or if you **set** it **on fire**, you make it start to burn.

fire alarm (**fire alarms**) **NOUN** A **fire alarm** is a piece of equipment that makes a loud noise to warn people when there is a fire.

fire|arm /ˈfaɪərɑrm/ (firearms) NOUN
Firearms are guns. [FORMAL] ❑ *The guards were carrying firearms.*

fire|cracker /ˈfaɪərkrækər/ (firecrackers)
NOUN A **firecracker** is an object that explodes with several loud noises when you light it.

fire de|part|ment (fire departments) NOUN
The **fire department** is the organization whose job is to stop fires.

fire en|gine (fire engines) NOUN A **fire engine** is a large vehicle that carries people and equipment for putting out fires.

fire ex|tin|guish|er /ˈfaɪər ɪkstɪŋɡwɪʃər/
(fire extinguishers) NOUN A **fire extinguisher** is a metal container with water or chemicals inside for stopping fires.

fire|fight|er /ˈfaɪərfaɪtər/ (firefighters)
NOUN A **firefighter** is a person whose job is to put out fires.

fire|place /ˈfaɪərpleɪs/ (fireplaces) NOUN In a room, the **fireplace** is the place made out of brick or stone where you can light a fire.

fire|work /ˈfaɪərwɜrk/ (fireworks) NOUN
Fireworks are things that fly up into the air and explode, making bright colors in the sky. ❑ *We watched the fireworks from the balcony.*

firm /fɜrm/ (firms, firmer, firmest)
1 NOUN A **firm** is a group of people who work together. ❑ *Kevin works for a Chicago law firm.*
2 ADJECTIVE If something is **firm**, it is not soft. ❑ *When you buy fruit, make sure it is firm.*
3 ADJECTIVE A **firm** physical action is strong. ❑ *His handshake was firm.* ● **firm|ly** ADVERB ❑ *She held me firmly by the elbow.*
4 ADJECTIVE A **firm** person does not change their mind. ❑ *She was firm with him. "I don't want to see you again."* ● **firm|ly** ADVERB ❑ *"You must go to bed now, kids," he said firmly.*

first /fɜrst/
1 ADJECTIVE, ADVERB The **first** thing or person is the one that comes before all the others. ❑ *January is the first month of the year.* ❑ *Aaron and Steve came first in the junior competition.*
2 ADVERB If you do something **first**, you do it before you do anything else. ❑ *First I went to the police and told them what happened.*
3 ADVERB If you do something **first**, you do it before anyone else. ❑ *The people who lived nearby arrived first.*

4 You use **first of all** to introduce the first thing that you want to say. ❑ *First of all, I'd like to thank you for coming.*
5 You use **at first** when you are talking about what happened at the beginning of an event. ❑ *At first, he seemed surprised by my questions.*
→ look at **number**

first aid NONCOUNT NOUN First aid is simple medical treatment that you give to a sick or injured person. ❑ *Each group leader must do a course in basic first aid.*

first-class also **first class**
1 ADJECTIVE **First-class** describes something that people consider to be of the highest standard. ❑ *The Altea is a newly built first-class hotel.*
2 ADJECTIVE **First-class** seats on a train or an airplane are the best and most expensive seats. ❑ *He won two first-class tickets to fly to Dublin.*
3 ADVERB **First class** is also an adverb. ❑ *We never fly first class.*
4 ADJECTIVE **First-class** mail is used for sending letters and cards. ❑ *...a first-class letter.*

first floor (first floors) NOUN The **first floor** of a building is the floor that is on the same level as the ground.

First Lady (First Ladies) NOUN
SOCIAL STUDIES The **First Lady** in a country or a state is the wife of the president or the governor.

first name (first names) NOUN Your **first name** is the name that comes before your family name. ❑ *"What's Dr. Garcia's first name?" "It's Maria. Maria Garcia."*

fish /fɪʃ/ (fish or fishes, fishes, fishing, fished)
1 NOUN A **fish** is an animal that lives and swims in water, that people eat as food. ❑ *Dave caught a 3-pound fish this morning.* ❑ *This fish is delicious.*
2 VERB If you **fish**, you try to catch fish. ❑ *Brian learned to fish in the Colorado River.*
→ look at **ocean**

fisher|man /ˈfɪʃərmən/ (fishermen) NOUN
A **fisherman** is a person who catches fish as a job or for sport.

fish|ing /ˈfɪʃɪŋ/ NONCOUNT NOUN SPORTS
Fishing is the sport or business of catching fish.

fish|ing rod (**fishing rods**) **NOUN** SPORTS A **fishing rod** is a long thin pole with a thread and a hook, that is used for catching fish.

fist /fɪst/ (**fists**) **NOUN** Your **fist** is your hand with your fingers closed tightly together.
❑ *Steve stood up and shook an angry fist at Patrick.*

---

fit

❶ BEING RIGHT OR GOING IN THE RIGHT PLACE
❷ HEALTHY
❸ UNCONTROLLABLE MOVEMENTS

---

❶ **fit** /fɪt/ (**fits, fitting, fitted** or **fit**)
1 **VERB** If something **fits**, it is the right size for someone or something. ❑ *The costume fit the child perfectly.* ❑ *The game is small enough to fit into your pocket.*
2 **VERB** If you **fit** something somewhere, you attach it there. ❑ *He fits locks on the doors.*
3 **ADJECTIVE** If something is **fit** for a particular purpose, it is good enough for that purpose. ❑ *Only two of the bicycles were fit for the road.*
→ look at **wear**
▶ **fit in** If you manage to **fit** someone or something **in**, you find time or space for them. ❑ *The dentist can fit you in just after lunch.* ❑ *We can't fit any more children in the car.*

❷ **fit** /fɪt/ (**fitter, fittest**) **ADJECTIVE** Someone who is **fit** is healthy and strong. ❑ *You're looking very fit. I can tell you exercise regularly.*
● **fit|ness** **NONCOUNT NOUN** ❑ *Sophie is a fitness instructor.*
→ look at Word World: **fitness**

❸ **fit** /fɪt/ (**fits**)
1 **NOUN** If you have a **fit of** coughing or laughter, you suddenly start coughing or laughing. ❑ *I suddenly had a fit of coughing.*
2 **NOUN** If someone has a **fit** they suddenly become unconscious and their body makes violent movements.

five /faɪv/ MATH **Five** is the number 5.
→ look at **number**

fix /fɪks/ (**fixes, fixing, fixed**)
1 **VERB** If you **fix** something, you repair it. ❑ *This morning, a man came to fix my washing machine.*
2 **VERB** If you **fix** a meal, you prepare it. ❑ *Everyone helped to fix dinner.*
3 **VERB** If you **fix** a problem, you find a way of dealing with it. ❑ *Getting married does not fix problems.*

flag /flæg/ (**flags**) **NOUN** A **flag** is a piece of colored cloth with a pattern on it that is used as a symbol for a country or an organization. ❑ *The crowd was shouting and waving American flags.*

flake /fleɪk/ (**flakes, flaking, flaked**)
1 **NOUN** A **flake** is a small thin piece of something. ❑ *Large flakes of snow began to fall.*
2 **VERB** If paint **flakes** or **flakes off**, small thin pieces of it come off.

flame /fleɪm/ (**flames**)
1 **NOUN** A **flame** is the bright burning gas that comes from a fire. ❑ *The flames almost burned her fingers.*
2 If something **bursts into flames**, it suddenly starts burning strongly. ❑ *The plane crashed and burst into flames.*
3 Something that is **in flames** is burning. ❑ *When we arrived, the house was in flames.*

flam|mable /flæməbᵊl/ **ADJECTIVE** **Flammable** things burn easily. ❑ *Always store paint and flammable liquids away from the house.*

flap /flæp/ (**flaps, flapping, flapped**)
1 **VERB** If something **flaps**, it moves quickly up and down or from side to side. ❑ *Sheets flapped on the clothes line.*

Word World   **fitness**

physical   healthy   sweaty   important   flexible   bike   yoga   sport   strong   fun   exercise   weight   workout   run   class   stretch   walk   strength   play   aerobics   swim

Nouns / Adjectives / Verbs

2 **VERB** If a bird **flaps** its wings, it moves its wings up and down quickly. ❑ *The birds flapped their wings and flew across the lake.*

3 **NOUN** A **flap** of something is a flat piece that can move up and down or from side to side. ❑ *I opened the flap of the envelope and took out the letter.*

flash /flæʃ/ (flashes, flashing, flashed)
1 **NOUN** A **flash** is a sudden bright light. ❑ *There was a flash of lightning.*
2 **VERB** If a light **flashes**, it shines on and off very quickly. ❑ *They could see a lighthouse flashing through the fog.*

flash drive (flash drives) **NOUN** TECHNOLOGY A **flash drive** is a small object for storing computer information that you can carry with you and use in different computers.
→ look at **computer**

flash|light /flæʃlaɪt/ (flashlights) **NOUN** A **flashlight** is a small electric light that you can carry in your hand. ❑ *Adam shone a flashlight into the backyard but he couldn't see anyone.*

flat /flæt/ (flatter, flattest)
1 **ADJECTIVE** Something that is **flat** is level or smooth. ❑ *Tiles can be fixed to any flat surface.* ❑ *...a flat roof.*
2 **ADJECTIVE** A **flat** tire or ball does not have enough air in it.
3 **ADJECTIVE** MUSIC A B **flat** or an E **flat**, for example, is a note that is slightly lower than B or E. Compare with **sharp**.

flat|ten /flætᵊn/ (flattens, flattening, flattened) **VERB** If you **flatten** something, you make it flat. ❑ *Flatten the bread dough with your hands.*

flat|ter /flætər/ (flatters, flattering, flattered) **VERB** If you **flatter** someone, you say nice things to them because you want them to like you. ❑ *Everyone likes to be flattered, to be told that they're beautiful.*

flat|ter|ing /flætərɪŋ/ **ADJECTIVE** Something that is **flattering** makes you look or seem attractive or important. ❑ *It was a very flattering photograph—he looked like a movie star.*

fla|vor /fleɪvər/ (flavors, flavoring, flavored)
1 **NOUN** The **flavor** of a food or drink is its taste. ❑ *I added some pepper for extra flavor.*
2 **VERB** If you **flavor** food or drink, you add something to it to give it a particular taste. ❑ *Flavor your favorite dishes with herbs and spices.*
→ look at **food**

fla|vor|ing /fleɪvərɪŋ/ (flavorings) **NOUN** **Flavorings** are substances that you add to food or drink to give it a particular taste.

flaw /flɔ/ (flaws) **NOUN** A **flaw** in something is something that is wrong with it. ❑ *There are a number of flaws in his theory.*

flea /fli/ (fleas) **NOUN** A **flea** is a very small insect that jumps. Fleas live on the bodies of humans or animals, and drink their blood as food. ❑ *Our dog has fleas.*

fled /flɛd/ **Fled** is a form of the verb **flee**.

flee /fli/ (flees, fleeing, fled) **VERB** If you **flee** from something or someone, you run away from them. [FORMAL] ❑ *He slammed the door behind him and fled.*

fleece /flis/ (fleeces)
1 **NOUN** A sheep's **fleece** is the coat of wool that covers it.
2 **NOUN** A **fleece** is a jacket or a sweater made from a soft warm cloth (= fleece). ❑ *He was wearing track pants and a dark blue fleece.*

fleet /flit/ (fleets) **NOUN** A **fleet** is a large group of boats, aircraft, or cars. ❑ *The fleet sailed out to the ocean.*

flesh /flɛʃ/
1 **NONCOUNT NOUN** **Flesh** is the soft part of your body that is between your bones and your skin. ❑ *The bullet went straight through the flesh of his arm.*
2 **NONCOUNT NOUN** The **flesh** of a fruit or a vegetable is the soft part that is inside it.

flew /flu/ **Flew** is a form of the verb **fly**.

flex|ible /flɛksɪbᵊl/
1 **ADJECTIVE** If something is **flexible**, it bends easily without breaking. ❑ *These children's books have flexible plastic covers.*
2 **ADJECTIVE** If something or someone is **flexible**, they are able to change easily. ❑ *I'm very lucky to have flexible working hours.*
● **flexi|bil|ity** **NONCOUNT NOUN** ❑ *It's possible to go there by bus, but a car gives more flexibility.*
→ look at **fitness**

flick /flɪk/ (flicks, flicking, flicked)
1 **NOUN** A **flick** is a quick, sharp movement. ❑ *The pony gave a quick flick of its tail.*
2 **VERB** If you **flick** something, you move it using a quick, sharp movement. ❑ *He shook his head to flick hair out of his eyes.*

flick|er /flɪkər/ (flickers, flickering, flickered)
1 **VERB** If a light or a flame **flickers**, it

f

shines in a way that is not steady. ❑ *The lights flickered, and suddenly it was dark.*

2 NOUN A **flicker** is an unsteady flame. ❑ *He could see the flicker of flames.*

flight /flaɪt/ (**flights**)

1 NOUN A **flight** is a trip in an aircraft. ❑ *The flight to New York will take four hours.* ❑ *Our flight was two hours late.*

2 NOUN A **flight of** stairs is a set of stairs that go from one level to another. ❑ *Ashley walked up the short flight of steps.*

3 NONCOUNT NOUN **Flight** is the action of flying. ❑ *The photograph showed an eagle in flight.*

fling /flɪŋ/ (**flings, flinging, flung**) VERB If you **fling** something somewhere, you throw it there using a lot of force. ❑ *She flung down the magazine and ran from the room.*

flip /flɪp/ (**flips, flipping, flipped**)

1 VERB If you **flip** through the pages of a book, you turn the pages quickly. ❑ *He was flipping through a magazine in the living room.*

2 VERB If something **flips** over, it turns over quickly so that it is on its other side. ❑ *The car flipped over and burst into flames.*

flip|per /flɪpər/ (**flippers**) NOUN **Flippers** are long, flat rubber shoes that you wear to help you to swim faster.

flirt /flɜrt/ (**flirts, flirting, flirted**)

1 VERB If you **flirt**, you behave toward someone in a way that shows that you think they are attractive. ❑ *My brother was flirting with all the girls.*

2 NOUN Someone who is a **flirt** likes to flirt a lot. ❑ *I'm not a flirt. I'm only interested in my boyfriend.*

float /floʊt/ (**floats, floating, floated**)

1 VERB If something **floats**, it stays on the surface of a liquid, and does not sink. ❑ *A plastic bottle was floating in the water.*

2 VERB If something **floats** in the air, it moves slowly and gently through it. ❑ *A yellow balloon floated past.*

3 NOUN A **float** is an object that stays on the surface of the water and supports your body while you are learning to swim.

flock /flɒk/ (**flocks**) NOUN A **flock of** birds, sheep, or goats is a group of them. ❑ *A flock of birds flew overhead.*

flood /flʌd/ (**floods, flooding, flooded**)

1 NOUN If there is a **flood**, a lot of water

covers land that is usually dry. ❑ *More than 70 people died in the floods.*

2 VERB If water **floods** an area, the area becomes covered with water. ❑ *The water tank burst and flooded the house.* ● **flood|ing** NONCOUNT NOUN ❑ *The flooding is the worst in sixty-five years.*

→ look at **disaster**

flood|light /flʌdlaɪt/ (**floodlights**) NOUN **Floodlights** are very powerful lights that are used outside for lighting public buildings and sports grounds at night.

floor /flɔr/ (**floors**)

1 NOUN The **floor** of a room is the part of it that you walk on. ❑ *There were no seats, so we sat on the floor.*

2 NOUN A **floor** of a building is all the rooms that are on a particular level. ❑ *The café was on the seventh floor.*

flop /flɒp/ (**flops, flopping, flopped**) VERB If you **flop** down, you sit down suddenly and heavily because you are so tired. ❑ *Ben flopped down on the bed and fell asleep at once.*

flop|py /flɒpi/ (**floppier, floppiest**) ADJECTIVE **Floppy** things are loose, and hang down. ❑ *Stephanie was wearing a blue floppy hat.*

flop|py disk (**floppy disks**) NOUN TECHNOLOGY A **floppy disk** is a small plastic computer disk that is used for storing information.

flo|rist /flɔrɪst/ (**florists**)

1 NOUN A **florist** is a person who works in a store that sells flowers.

2 NOUN A **florist** or a **florist's** is a store where you can buy flowers.

floss /flɔs/ (**flosses, flossing, flossed**) VERB When you **floss**, you use a special type of strong string to clean between your teeth. ❑ *Brush your teeth after each meal and floss every day.*

Sound Partners	flour, flower

flour /flaʊər/ NONCOUNT NOUN **Flour** is a fine powder that is used for making bread, cakes, and pastry.

flour|ish /flɜrɪʃ/ (**flourishes, flourishing, flourished**) VERB If something **flourishes**, it grows or develops very well. ❑ *This plant flourishes in warm climates.* ❑ *Heckart's career really flourished in the 1950s.*

flow /floʊ/ (**flows, flowing, flowed**)

1 VERB If something **flows** somewhere, it

moves there in a steady and continuous way. ❏ *A stream flowed gently down into the valley.*

2 NONCOUNT NOUN A **flow** is a steady, continuous movement in a particular direction. ❏ *Vicky tried to stop the flow of blood.* ❏ *The new tunnel will speed up traffic flow.*
→ look at **water**

Sound Partners flower, flour

---

flow|er /fla͟ʊər/ (**flowers, flowering, flowered**)
1 NOUN A **flower** is the brightly colored part of a plant. ❏ *Dad gave Mom a huge bunch of flowers.*
2 VERB When a plant or a tree **flowers**, its flowers appear. ❏ *These plants will flower soon.*
→ look at **plant**

flown /flo͟ʊn/ **Flown** is a form of the verb **fly**.

flu /flu͟/ **NONCOUNT NOUN Flu** is an illness that is like a very bad cold. **Flu** is short for "influenza." ❏ *I've got the flu and I ache all over.*
→ look at **sick**

flu|ent /flu͟ənt/ **ADJECTIVE** If you are **fluent in** a particular language, you can speak it easily and correctly. ❏ *Jose is fluent in Spanish and English.* ● **flu|ent|ly ADVERB** ❏ *He spoke three languages fluently.*

fluffy /flʌ͟fi/ (**fluffier, fluffiest**) **ADJECTIVE** If something is **fluffy**, it is very soft. ❏ *I dried myself with a big fluffy towel.*

flu|id /flu͟ɪd/ (**fluids**) **NOUN** A **fluid** is a liquid. [FORMAL] ❏ *Make sure that you drink plenty of fluids.*

flung /flʌ͟ŋ/ **Flung** is a form of the verb **fling**.

flunk /flʌ͟ŋk/ (**flunks, flunking, flunked**) **VERB** If you **flunk** an exam or a course, you do not pass it. [INFORMAL] ❏ *Three of the students flunked the math test.*

flush /flʌ͟ʃ/ (**flushes, flushing, flushed**)
1 VERB If you **flush**, your face becomes red because you are hot, ill, embarrassed, or angry. ● **flushed ADJECTIVE** ❏ *Amanda was flushed with embarrassment.*
2 VERB If you **flush** something, you clean it with water. ❏ *I heard someone flushing the toilet.*

flute /flu͟t/ (**flutes**) **NOUN** MUSIC A **flute** is a musical instrument that you play by blowing. You hold it sideways to your mouth.
→ look at **musical instrument**

flut|ter /flʌ͟tər/ (**flutters, fluttering, fluttered**) **VERB** If something **flutters**, it makes a lot of quick, light movements. ❏ *The butterfly fluttered its wings.*

fly /fla͟ɪ/ (**flies, flying, flew, flown**)
1 NOUN A **fly** is a small insect with two wings.
2 VERB When something **flies**, it moves through the air. ❏ *The planes flew through the clouds.*
3 VERB If you **fly** somewhere, you travel there in an aircraft. ❏ *Jerry flew to Los Angeles this morning.*
4 VERB When someone **flies** an aircraft, they make it move through the air. ❏ *He flew a small plane to Cuba.* ❏ *I learned to fly in Vietnam.*

fly|er /fla͟ɪər/ (**flyers**) also **flier NOUN** A **flyer** is a small printed notice that advertises something. ❏ *A tall girl gave us a flyer for the concert.*

foam /fo͟ʊm/ **NONCOUNT NOUN Foam** is the mass of small bubbles that you sometimes see on the surface of a liquid. ❏ *He drank his cappuccino, and wiped the foam off his mustache.*

fo|cus /fo͟ʊkəs/ (**focuses, focusing, focused**)
1 VERB If you **focus on** something, you give all your attention to it. ❏ *Voters' attention is now focused on the war.*
2 VERB If you **focus** a camera, you make changes to it so that you can see clearly through it. ❏ *The camera was focused on his terrified face.*
3 NOUN The **focus** of something is the thing that receives most attention. ❏ *Wherever she goes, she's the focus of attention.*

fog /fɒ͟g/ **NONCOUNT NOUN Fog** is thick cloud that is close to the ground. ❏ *The car crash happened in thick fog.*
→ look at **weather**

fog|gy /fɒ͟gi/ (**foggier, foggiest**) **ADJECTIVE** When it is **foggy**, there is fog.

foil /fɔ͟ɪl/ **NONCOUNT NOUN Foil** is very thin metal sheets that you use for wrapping food in. ❏ *Cover the turkey with foil and cook it for another 20 minutes.*

fold /fo͟ʊld/ (**folds, folding, folded**)
1 VERB If you **fold** a piece of paper or cloth, you bend it so that one part covers another part. ❏ *He folded the paper carefully.* ❏ *I folded the towels and put them in the closet.*
2 VERB If a piece of furniture **folds**, you can make it smaller by bending or closing parts of it. ❏ *The car has folding rear seats.*
3 Fold up means the same as **fold**. ❏ *When you don't need to use it, the table folds up.*
4 VERB When you **fold** your arms, you put one arm under the other and hold them over your chest.

f

F

5 **NOUN** A **fold** in a piece of paper or cloth is a bend that you make in it when you put one part of it over another part and press the edge. ❑ *Make another fold down the middle of the paper.*
→ look at **laundry**

fold|er /foʊldər/ (**folders**)
1 **NOUN** A **folder** is a folded piece of cardboard or plastic that you keep papers in. ❑ *Liz carried her work folders into the study.*
2 **NOUN** TECHNOLOGY A **folder** is a group of files that are stored together on a computer. ❑ *I deleted the folder by mistake.*
→ look at **office**

folk /foʊk/ (**folks**)

> **LANGUAGE HELP**
> **Folk** can also be the plural for meaning **1**.

1 **PLURAL NOUN** You can call people **folk** or **folks**. ❑ *Most folks around here think she's a bit crazy.*
2 **PLURAL NOUN** Your **folks** are your mother and father. [INFORMAL] ❑ *I'll introduce you to my folks.*
3 **ADJECTIVE** ARTS **Folk** art, customs, and music belong to a particular group of people or country. ❑ *This is a collection of traditional folk music from nearly 30 countries.*

folk music /foʊk myuzɪk/ **NONCOUNT NOUN** MUSIC **Folk music** or **folk** is music that is traditional or typical of a particular community or nation. ❑ *I listen to a variety of music including classical and folk.*

fol|low /fɒloʊ/ (**follows, following, followed**)
1 **VERB** If you **follow** someone, you move along behind them. ❑ *We followed him up the steps.* ❑ *Please follow me, madam.* ❑ *She realized that the car was following her.*
2 **VERB** If you **follow** a path, you go somewhere using the path to direct you. ❑ *All we had to do was follow the road.*

3 **VERB** If you **follow** an instruction, you do something in the way that it says. ❑ *Follow the instructions carefully.*
4 **VERB** If you are able to **follow** an explanation or a movie, you understand it. ❑ *Can you follow the story so far?* ❑ *I'm sorry, I don't follow.*
5 You use **as follows** to introduce a list or an explanation. ❑ *The winners are as follows: E. Walker; R. Foster; R. Gates.*
→ look at **route**

> **Word Partners** Use **follow** with:
> ADV. **closely** follow **1** – **4**
> N. follow **a road**, follow **signs**, follow **a trail 2**
> follow **advice**, follow **directions**, follow **instructions**, follow **orders**, follow **rules 3**
> follow **a story 4**

fol|low|ing /fɒloʊɪŋ/ **ADJECTIVE** The **following** day, week, or year is the day, week, or year after the one you have just mentioned. ❑ *We had dinner together on Friday and then met for lunch the following day.*

fond /fɒnd/ (**fonder, fondest**) **ADJECTIVE** If you are **fond of** someone or something, you like them very much. ❑ *I am very fond of Michael.* ❑ *Dad's fond of singing.* ❑ *Mrs. Johnson was very fond of cats.*

font /fɒnt/ (**fonts**) **NOUN** In printing, a **font** is a set of letters of the same style and size. ❑ *You can change the font so that it's easier to read.*

food /fud/ **NONCOUNT NOUN** **Food** is what people and animals eat. ❑ *The waitress brought our meal and said, "Enjoy your food!"* ❑ *The people were starving—there was no food to eat.*
→ look at Word World: **food**
→ look at **eat**

food chain (**food chains**) **NOUN** SCIENCE The **food chain** is the natural process by

Word World food

delicious · favorite · hungry · fresh · frozen · organic · salty · healthy · fast · meat · seafood · fruit · sweet · taste · flavor · cook · eat · wash · supermarket · vegetable · prepare · buy

Nouns / Adjectives / Verbs

Picture Dictionary   foot

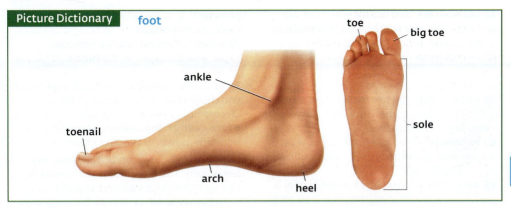

- toe
- big toe
- ankle
- sole
- toenail
- arch
- heel

which one living thing is eaten by another, which is then eaten by another, and so on.

fool /ful/ (fools, fooling, fooled)

1 **NOUN** A **fool** is a stupid or silly person. ❑ I didn't understand anything. I felt like a fool.

2 **VERB** If you **fool** someone, you make them believe something that is not true. ❑ Harris fooled people into believing she was a doctor.

3 If you **make a fool of** someone, you make them seem silly by telling people about something stupid that they have done, or by tricking them. ❑ Your brother is making a fool of you.

▶ **fool around** If you **fool around**, you behave in a silly way. ❑ They fool around and get into trouble at school.

fool|ish /fulɪʃ/ **ADJECTIVE** Foolish behavior is stupid or silly. ❑ It would be foolish to ignore the risks. ● **fool|ish|ly** **ADVERB** ❑ He knows that he acted foolishly.

Spelling Partners   foot

foot /fut/ (feet)

1 **NOUN** Your **feet** are the parts of your body that are at the ends of your legs, and that you stand on. ❑ We danced until our feet were sore. ❑ He's suffering from a foot injury.

2 **NOUN** A **foot** is a unit for measuring length. A foot is equal to 30.48 centimeters. There are 12 inches in a foot. The plural form is **feet** or **foot**. ❑ We were six thousand feet above sea level. ❑ The room is 10 foot long and 6 foot wide.

3 **NOUN** The **foot of** something is the part that is farthest from its top. ❑ He was waiting at the foot of the stairs.

4 If you go somewhere **on foot**, you walk

there. ❑ We explored the island on foot.

5 If you are **on** your **feet**, you are standing up. ❑ Everyone was on their feet shouting and clapping.

6 If you **put** your **feet up**, you have a rest. ❑ I'll do the chores, so you can put your feet up.

→ look at Picture Dictionary: **foot**

→ look at **body, measurement**

foot|ball /futbɔl/ (footballs)

1 **NONCOUNT NOUN** SPORTS Football is a game for two teams of eleven players. Each team tries to win points by kicking, carrying, or throwing the ball into an area at the other end of the field. ❑ Paul loves playing football.

2 **NOUN** SPORTS A **football** is a ball that is used for playing football. ❑ Antonio kicked the football off the field.

foot|print /futprɪnt/ (footprints) **NOUN** Your **footprint** is the mark that your foot makes on the ground.

foot|step /futstɛp/ (footsteps) **NOUN** A **footstep** is the sound that you make each time your foot touches the ground when you are walking. ❑ I heard footsteps outside.

Sound Partners   for, four

for /fər, STRONG fɔr/

1 **PREPOSITION** If something is **for** someone, they will have it or use it. ❑ These flowers are for you. ❑ I reserved a table for two at the restaurant.

2 **PREPOSITION** If you work **for** a person or a company, they employ you. ❑ He works for a bank.

3 **PREPOSITION** If someone does something **for** you, they do it so that you do not have to do it. ❑ I held the door open for the next person.

4 **PREPOSITION** A word **for** something, is a word that has that meaning. ❑ In French, the word for "love" is "amour."

5 PREPOSITION You use **for** when you are talking about the way in which something is used. ❏ This knife is for slicing bread.

6 PREPOSITION A bus, train, plane, or boat **for** a place is going there. ❏ They took the train for Rio early the next morning.

7 PREPOSITION You use **for** when you are saying how long something lasts. ❏ We talked for about half an hour.

8 PREPOSITION You use **for** to say how far someone or something goes. ❏ We continued to drive for a few miles.

9 PREPOSITION If you buy something **for** a particular amount of money, that is its price. ❏ The Martins sold their house for 1.4 million dollars.

10 PREPOSITION If you are **for** someone or something, you agree with them or support them. ❏ Well, are you for us or against us?

11 PREPOSITION If you play **for** a particular team, you are in that team. ❏ Kristy plays hockey for the high-school team.

> **Usage** for
> You can use **for** to describe a length of time. Gabriela studied English **for** three years. Luis lived in Texas **for** two years. Mei wants to travel in Australia **for** two months.

for|bid /fərbɪd, fɔr-/ (forbids, forbidding, forbade, forbidden) VERB If you **forbid** someone **to** do something, you tell them that they must not do it. ❏ My parents have forbidden me to see my boyfriend.

for|bid|den /fərbɪdᵊn, fɔr-/ ADJECTIVE If something is **forbidden**, you are not allowed to do it. ❏ Smoking is forbidden here.

force /fɔrs/ (forces, forcing, forced)
1 VERB If someone **forces** you **to** do something, they make you do it when you do not want to. ❏ They forced him to give them the money.
2 VERB If someone **forces** a lock, a door, or a window, they break the lock. ❏ Police forced the door of the apartment and arrested Mr. Roberts.
3 NONCOUNT NOUN If someone uses **force** to do something, they use their strength to do it. ❏ Police used force to break up the fight.
4 NONCOUNT NOUN SCIENCE **Force** is the power or strength that something has. ❏ The force of the explosion destroyed the building.
5 NOUN **Forces** are groups of people, for example soldiers or police officers, who do a particular job. ❏ Russian forces entered the region in 1994.

fore|cast /fɔrkæst/ (forecasts, forecasting, forecast, forecasted)
1 NOUN A **forecast** is what someone expects will happen in the future. ❏ Did you see the weather forecast?
2 VERB If you **forecast** events, you say what you think is going to happen in the future. ❏ Economists were forecasting higher oil prices.
● **fore|cast|er** (forecasters) NOUN ❏ David worked for 34 years as a weather forecaster.

fore|ground /fɔrgraʊnd/ (foregrounds) NOUN ARTS The **foreground** of a picture is the part that seems nearest to you. Compare with **background**. ❏ There are five people and a dog in the foreground of the painting.

fore|head /fɔrhɛd, fɔrɪd/ (foreheads) NOUN Your **forehead** is the front part of your head between your eyebrows and your hair. → look at **face**

for|eign /fɔrɪn/ ADJECTIVE Someone or something that is **foreign** comes from a country that is not your own. ❏ It's good to learn a foreign language. → look at **language, movie**

for|eign|er /fɔrɪnər/ (foreigners) NOUN A **foreigner** is someone who comes from a different country.

fore|see /fɔrsi/ (foresees, foreseeing, foresaw, foreseen) VERB If you **foresee** something, you expect and believe that it will happen. ❏ He did not foresee any problems.

for|est /fɔrɪst/ (forests) NOUN GEOGRAPHY A **forest** is a large area where trees grow close together. ❏ ...a forest fire. → look at **conservation, tree**

for|ever /fɔrɛvər, fər-/
1 ADVERB Something that will continue **forever** will always continue. ❏ I think that we will live together forever.
2 ADVERB Something that has gone or changed **forever** will never come back or return to the way it was. ❏ His pain was gone forever.

fore|word /fɔrwɜrd/ (forewords) NOUN LANGUAGE ARTS A **foreword** is an introduction to a book. ❏ She has written the foreword to a cookbook.

for|gave /fərgeɪv/ **Forgave** is a form of the verb **forgive**.

forge /fɔrdʒ/ (forges, forging, forged) VERB If someone **forges** paper money, a document, or a painting, they make illegal copies of it in order to cheat people. ❑ *He admitted to forging passports.* ❑ *They used forged documents to leave the country.* ● **forg|er** (**forgers**) **NOUN** ❑ *He's an expert art forger.*

for|gery /fˈɔrdʒəri/ (**forgeries**)

1 NOUN A **forgery** is something that has been forged. ❑ *The letter was a forgery.*

2 NONCOUNT NOUN **Forgery** is the crime of forging money, documents, or paintings.

for|get /fərgˈɛt/ (**forgets, forgetting, forgot, forgotten**)

1 VERB If you **forget** something, you cannot think of it, although you knew it in the past. ❑ *She forgot where she left the car.*

2 VERB If you **forget** something, you do not remember it. ❑ *He never forgets his dad's birthday.* ❑ *I forgot to lock the door.*

Word Partners	Use **forget** with:
ADJ.	**easy to** forget, **hard to** forget **1 2**
ADV.	**never** forget, **quickly** forget, **soon** forget **1 2**

for|get|ful /fərgˈɛtfəl/ **ADJECTIVE** Someone who is **forgetful** often does not remember things. ❑ *My mother became very forgetful and confused when she got old.*

for|give /fərgˈɪv/ (**forgives, forgiving, forgave, forgiven**) **VERB** If you **forgive** someone who has done something bad or wrong, you stop being angry with them. ❑ *Hopefully Jane will understand and forgive you.* ❑ *Irene forgave Terry for stealing her money.*

for|got /fərgˈɒt/ **Forgot** is a form of the verb **forget.**

for|got|ten /fərgˈɒtⁿn/ **Forgotten** is a form of the verb **forget.**

fork /fˈɔrk/ (**forks, forking, forked**)

1 NOUN A **fork** is a tool with long metal points, used for eating food. ❑ *Please use your knife and fork.*

2 NOUN A **fork** in a road, path, or river is where it divides into two parts and forms a "Y" shape. ❑ *We arrived at a fork in the road.*

3 VERB If a road, path, or river **forks**, it divides into two.

→ look at **restaurant**

form /fˈɔrm/ (**forms, forming, formed**)

1 NOUN A **form of** something is a type of it. ❑ *She has a rare form of the disease.* ❑ *I am against violence in any form.*

2 NOUN The **form** of something is its shape or the way it appears. ❑ *The dress fits the form of the body exactly.*

3 NOUN A **form** is a piece of paper with questions on it and spaces where you should write the answers. ❑ *Please fill in this form and sign it at the bottom.*

4 VERB When you **form** a particular shape, you make it. ❑ *Form a diamond shape with your legs.*

5 VERB Things or people **form** something when they are all parts of it. ❑ *These articles formed the basis of Randolph's book.*

6 VERB If you **form** an organization, you start it. ❑ *They tried to form a study group on human rights.*

7 NOUN LANGUAGE ARTS In grammar, the **form** of a noun or a verb is the way that it is spelled or spoken when it is used to talk about the plural, the past, or the present, for example.

for|mal /fˈɔrməl/ **ADJECTIVE** **Formal** speech or behavior is very correct and serious rather than relaxed and friendly. ❑ *We received a very formal letter of apology.* ● **for|mal|ly** **ADVERB** ❑ *He spoke formally, and without expression.* ● **for|mal|ity** **NONCOUNT NOUN** ❑ *Lilly's formality and seriousness amused him.*

→ look at **grammar, writing**

for|mat /fˈɔrmæt/ (**formats, formatting, formatted**)

1 NOUN TECHNOLOGY The **format** of a computer document is the way in which the text is arranged. ❑ *You can change the format of your document from two columns to three.*

2 VERB TECHNOLOGY You **format** a document when you arrange the design of the text in it. ❑ *The software can automatically format the text in a document as you type it.*

for|ma|tion /fɔrmˈeɪʃⁿn/ (**formations**)

1 NONCOUNT NOUN The **formation of** something is the beginning of its existence. ❑ *The vitamin is essential for the formation of red blood cells.*

2 NOUN SCIENCE A rock or cloud **formation** is rock or cloud of a particular shape or structure.

for|mer /fˈɔrmər/

1 ADJECTIVE You use **former** when you are talking about someone's or something's position in the past. ❑ *There was an interview with the former president, Richard Nixon.*

2 PRONOUN When two people or things have just been mentioned, you can talk about the first of them as **the former.**

f

❏ *Both the seeds and the leaves are useful—the former for soups, and the latter for salads.*

for|mer|ly /fɔrmərli/ **ADVERB** If something happened **formerly**, it happened in the past. ❏ *He was formerly in the navy.*

for|mi|dable /fɔrmɪdəbᵊl, fərmɪd-/ **ADJECTIVE** Something or someone that is **formidable** makes you feel slightly frightened. ❏ *We have a formidable task ahead of us.*

for|mu|la /fɔrmyələ/ (**formulae** /fɔrmyəli/ or **formulas**)

1 **NOUN** MATH A **formula** is a group of letters, numbers, or other symbols that represents a scientific rule. ❏ *This mathematical formula describes the distances of the planets from the Sun.*

2 **NOUN** SCIENCE The **formula** for a substance is a description of the chemical elements that it contains. ❏ *Glucose and fructose have the same chemical formula.*
→ look at **science**

for|mu|late /fɔrmyəleɪt/ (**formulates, formulating, formulated**) **VERB** If you **formulate** a plan, you invent it, thinking about the details carefully. ❏ *Little by little, he formulated his plan for escape.*

fort /fɔrt/ (**forts**) **NOUN** A **fort** is a strong building that is used as a military base.

for|tress /fɔrtrɪs/ (**fortresses**) **NOUN** A **fortress** is a castle or other large strong building that is difficult for enemies to enter.

for|tu|nate /fɔrtʃənɪt/ **ADJECTIVE** If someone or something is **fortunate**, they are lucky. ❏ *He was extremely fortunate to survive.* ❏ *She is in the fortunate position of having plenty of choice.*

for|tu|nate|ly /fɔrtʃənɪtli/ **ADVERB** You can say **fortunately** when you start to talk about an event or a situation that is good. ❏ *Fortunately, the weather last winter was good.*

for|tune /fɔrtʃən/ (**fortunes**)

1 **NOUN** A **fortune** is a very large amount of money. ❏ *He made a fortune buying and selling houses.*

2 **NONCOUNT NOUN** **Fortune** or good **fortune** is good luck. ❏ *Patrick still can't believe his good fortune.*

for|ty /fɔrti/ (**forties**)

1 MATH **Forty** is the number 40.

2 **PLURAL NOUN** The **forties** is the decade between 1940 and 1949. ❏ *They met in London in the Forties.*

for|ty-niner /fɔrti naɪnər/ (**forty-niners**) **NOUN** SOCIAL STUDIES A **forty-niner** was a person who tried to find gold in California in 1849.

for|ward /fɔrwərd/ (**forwards, forwarding, forwarded**)

1 **ADVERB** If you move or look **forward**, you move or look in a direction that is in front of you. ❏ *He came forward and asked for help.* ❏ *She fell forward on to her face.*

2 **ADVERB** **Forward** means in a position near the front of something. ❏ *Try to get a seat as far forward as possible.*

3 **VERB** If you **forward** a letter or an email **to** someone, you send it to them after you have received it. ❏ *He asks each person to forward the email to 10 other people.*
→ look at **email**

for|ward slash (**forward slashes**) **NOUN** TECHNOLOGY A **forward slash** is the sloping line / that separates letters, words, or numbers.

fos|sil /fɒsᵊl/ (**fossils**) **NOUN** SCIENCE A **fossil** is the part of a plant or an animal that died a long time ago and has turned into rock.

fos|sil fuel (**fossil fuels**) **NOUN** SCIENCE A **fossil fuel** is a substance such as coal or oil that is found in the ground and used for producing power. ❏ *When we burn fossil fuels, we use oxygen and produce carbon dioxide.*
→ look at **energy**

fos|ter /fɒstər/ **ADJECTIVE** **Foster** parents are people who are paid by the government to take care of someone else's child for a period of time.

fought /fɔt/ **Fought** is a form of the verb **fight**.

foul /faʊl/ (**fouler, foulest, fouls**)

1 **ADJECTIVE** Something that is **foul** is dirty, and smells or tastes unpleasant. ❏ *...foul, polluted water.*

2 **ADJECTIVE** **Foul** language is offensive and contains rude words.

3 **NOUN** SPORTS In a game or a sport, a **foul** is a move that is not allowed according to the rules. ❏ *Why did the referee not call a foul?*

found /faʊnd/ (**founds, founding, founded**)

1 **Found** is a form of the verb **find**.

2 **VERB** When an organization **is founded** by someone, that person starts it. ❏ *The New*

York Free-Loan Society was founded in 1892.

● **found|er** (**founders**) NOUN ❏ *He was one of the founders of the United Nations.*

foun|da|tion /faʊndeɪʃⁿn/ (**foundations**)

1 PLURAL NOUN The **foundations** of a building are the bricks, stones, or concrete that it is built on. ❏ *Are the foundations of the house strong enough?*

2 NOUN A **foundation** is an organization that provides money for a special purpose. ❏ *We applied for support from the National Foundation for Educational Research.*

foun|tain /faʊntɪn/ (**fountains**)

1 NOUN A **fountain** is a structure in a pool or a lake where water is forced up into the air and falls down again.

2 NOUN A **fountain** is a piece of equipment that you can drink water from in a public place.

Sound Partners   four, for

---

four /fɔr/ MATH **Four** is the number 4.

→ look at **number**

Word Builder   **fourteen**

teen ≈ plus ten, from 13-19

   eight + **teen** = eigh**teen**
   four + **teen** = four**teen**
   nine + **teen** = nine**teen**
   seven + **teen** = seven**teen**
   six + **teen** = six**teen**
   teen + age = **teen**age

---

four|teen /fɔrtin/ MATH **Fourteen** is the number 14.

fourth /fɔrθ/ (**fourths**)

1 ADJECTIVE, ADVERB MATH The **fourth** item in a series is the one that you count as

number four. ❏ *Last year's winner is in fourth place in today's race.*

2 NOUN MATH A **fourth** is one of four equal parts of something (¼). ❏ *A fourth of the public want a national vote on the new tax.*

→ look at **number**

fowl /faʊl/ (**fowl**) NOUN **Fowl** are birds that can be eaten as food, such as a chickens.

fox /fɒks/ (**foxes**) NOUN A **fox** is a wild animal that looks like a dog, has red fur and a thick tail.

frac|tion /frækʃⁿn/ (**fractions**)

1 NOUN MATH A **fraction** is a part of a whole number. For example, ½ and ⅓ are both fractions.

2 NOUN A **fraction of** something is a very small amount of it. ❏ *She hesitated for a fraction of a second.*

→ look at Picture Dictionary: **fractions**

→ look at **math**

frac|ture /fræktʃər/ (**fractures, fracturing, fractured**)

1 NOUN A **fracture** is a break in something, especially a bone. ❏ *She suffered a hip fracture.*

2 VERB If a bone **is fractured**, it has a crack or a break in it. ❏ *Several of his ribs were fractured in the fall.*

frag|ile /frædʒəl/ ADJECTIVE Something that is **fragile** is easily broken or damaged. ❏ *His fragile bones are the result of a bad diet.*

frag|ment /frægmənt/ (**fragments**) NOUN A **fragment of** something is a small piece of it. ❏ *We tried to pick up the tiny fragments of glass.*

fra|grance /freɪgrəns/ (**fragrances**) NOUN A **fragrance** is a pleasant or sweet smell. ❏ *The cream is easy to apply and has a pleasant fragrance.*

f

Picture Dictionary   **fractions**

fraction	decimal	percentage
$\frac{1}{4}$	0.25	25%

fraction	decimal	percentage
$\frac{1}{3}$	0.33	33%

fraction	decimal	percentage
$\frac{1}{2}$	0.50	50%

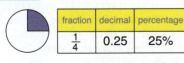

adding fractions

problem: solution:

$1\frac{1}{4}$ $1\frac{1}{4}$

$+2\frac{1}{2}$ $+2\frac{2}{4}$

? $3\frac{3}{4}$

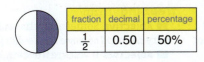

subtracting fractions

problem: solution:

$5\frac{2}{3}$ $5\frac{4}{6}$

$-1\frac{1}{6}$ $-1\frac{1}{6}$

? $4\frac{3}{6} = 4\frac{1}{2}$

F

frail /freɪl/ (frailer, frailest) **ADJECTIVE**
Someone who is **frail** is not very strong or
healthy. ❏ *He looked very frail in his hospital bed.*

frame /freɪm/ (frames, framing, framed)
1 NOUN The **frame** of a picture is the wood,
metal, or plastic around it. ❏ *She had a
photograph of her mother in a silver frame.*
2 VERB When a picture **is framed**, it is put
in a frame. ❏ *The picture has already been framed
and hung on the wall.*

frame|work /freɪmwɜrk/ (frameworks)
NOUN A **framework** is a structure that forms
a support for something. ❏ *The wooden shelves
sit on a steel framework.*

frank /fræŋk/ (franks, franker, frankest)
1 ADJECTIVE Someone who is **frank** says
things in an open and honest way. ❏ *My
husband has not been frank with me.* ● **frank|ly**
ADVERB ❏ *You can talk frankly to me.*
2 NOUN A **frank** is a long thin piece of hot
cooked meat (= a sausage). ❏ *I really enjoy
eating franks and beans.*

frank|ly /fræŋkli/ **ADVERB** You use **frankly**
when you are going to say something that
may be surprising or direct. ❏ *Frankly, this
whole thing is getting boring.*

fran|tic /fræntɪk/ **ADJECTIVE** A person who is
frantic is very frightened or worried, and
does not know what to do. ❏ *They became
frantic when their 4-year-old son did not return.*
● **fran|ti|cal|ly** /fræntɪkli/ **ADVERB** ❏ *Two
people were waving frantically from the boat.*

fraud /frɔd/ **NONCOUNT NOUN** **Fraud** is the
crime of getting money by not telling the
truth. ❏ *He was jailed for two years for fraud.*

freak /frik/ (freaks)
1 ADJECTIVE A **freak** event or action is one
that is very unusual. ❏ *James broke his leg in a
freak accident playing golf.*
2 NOUN People are sometimes called **freaks**
when their behavior or appearance is very
different or unusual. ❏ *I'm not a freak—I'm just
like you guys.*

freck|le /frɛkᵊl/ (freckles) **NOUN** **Freckles** are
small light brown spots on your skin,
especially on your face. ❏ *He had short red hair
and freckles.*

free /fri/ (freer, freest, frees, freeing, freed)
1 ADJECTIVE If something is **free**, you do not
have to pay for it. ❏ *The classes are free, with
lunch provided.*

2 ADJECTIVE Someone or something that is
free is not controlled by rules or other
people. ❏ *They are free to bring their friends home
at any time.* ● **free|ly** **ADVERB** ❏ *They all express
their opinions freely in class.*
3 ADJECTIVE Someone who is **free** is not a
prisoner. ❏ *He walked from the court house a
free man.*
4 ADJECTIVE **Free** time is time when you do
not have any work to do. ❏ *She spent her free
time shopping.*
5 ADJECTIVE If a seat is **free**, it is not being
used by anyone.
6 VERB If you **free** someone or something,
you help them to get out of a place. ❏ *Rescue
workers freed him by cutting away part of the car.*

free|dom /fridəm/ **NONCOUNT NOUN**
Freedom is the state of being allowed to do
what you want to do. ❏ *They enjoy the freedom
to spend their money as they wish.* ❏ *We are
fighting for freedom of choice.*
→ look at **history**

Word Partners	Use **freedom** with:
N.	freedom **of choice**, **feeling of** freedom, freedom **of the press**, **sense of** freedom, freedom **of speech**

free|way /friweɪ/ (freeways) **NOUN** A **freeway**
is a main road that has been specially built
for fast travel over long distances.
→ look at **route**

freeze /friz/ (freezes, freezing, froze, frozen)
1 VERB SCIENCE If a liquid **freezes**, it
becomes solid because the temperature is
low. ❏ *If the temperature drops below 32 °F, water
freezes.* ❏ *The ground froze solid.* ● **freez|ing**
NONCOUNT NOUN ❏ *The damage was caused by
freezing and thawing.*
2 VERB If you **freeze** food or drink, you
make it very cold in order to preserve it.
3 VERB If you **freeze**, you stand completely
still. ❏ *"Freeze," shouted the police officer.*
→ look at **meat, water**

freez|er /frizər/ (freezers) **NOUN** A **freezer** is
a large container or part of a refrigerator
used for freezing food.
→ look at **kitchen**

freez|ing /frizɪŋ/
1 ADJECTIVE Something that is **freezing** is
very cold. ❏ *The movie theater was freezing.*
2 ADJECTIVE If you are **freezing**, you feel
very cold. ❏ *"You must be freezing," she said.*

freight /freɪt/ **NONCOUNT NOUN** Freight is goods that are moved by trucks, trains, ships, or airplanes. ❑ *...a freight train.*

French fries /frɛntʃ fraɪz/ **PLURAL NOUN** French fries are long, thin pieces of potato that are fried (= cooked in hot oil).

French horn /frɛntʃ hɔrn/ (**French horns**) **NOUN** MUSIC A **French horn** is a musical instrument shaped like a long round metal tube with one wide end, that is played by blowing into it.

fre|quen|cy /frikwənsi/ (**frequencies**)
1 **NONCOUNT NOUN** The **frequency** of an event is the number of times it happens. ❑ *The frequency of Kara's phone calls increased.*
2 **NOUN** SCIENCE The **frequency** of a sound wave or a radio wave is the number of times it vibrates (= moves quickly up and down) within a period of time. ❑ *You can't hear waves of such a high frequency.*

fre|quent /frikwənt/ **ADJECTIVE** If something is **frequent**, it happens often. ❑ *Bordeaux is on the main Paris-Madrid line so there are frequent trains.* ● **fre|quent|ly** **ADVERB** ❑ *He was frequently unhappy.*

fresh /frɛʃ/ (**fresher, freshest**)
1 **ADJECTIVE** Fresh food has been picked or produced recently. ❑ *We only sell fresh fish that has been caught locally.*
2 **ADJECTIVE** Something that is **fresh** has been done, made, or experienced recently. ❑ *There were fresh car tracks in the snow.* ● **fresh|ly** **ADVERB** ❑ *We bought some freshly-baked bread.*
3 **ADJECTIVE** Something that smells, tastes, or feels **fresh**, is clean or cool. ❑ *The air was fresh and she immediately felt better.*
4 **ADJECTIVE** A **fresh** thing or amount replaces or is added to an existing thing or amount. ❑ *The waiter placed a fresh glass on the table.*
→ look at **food, meat**

fresh|man /frɛʃmən/ (**freshmen**) **NOUN** In the United States, a **freshman** is a student who is in their first year at a high school or college.

Fri|day /fraɪdeɪ, -di/ (**Fridays**) **NOUN** Friday is the day after Thursday and before Saturday. ❑ *He is going home on Friday.* ❑ *...Friday November 6.*

fridge /frɪdʒ/ (**fridges**) **NOUN** A **fridge** is the same as a **refrigerator**. [INFORMAL]

friend /frɛnd/ (**friends**)
1 **NOUN** A **friend** is someone who you like and know well. ❑ *She's my best friend.* ❑ *She was never a close friend of mine.*
2 **PLURAL NOUN** If you are **friends with** someone, you are their friend and they are yours. ❑ *I still wanted to be friends with Alison.* ❑ *We remained good friends.*
3 If you **make friends with** someone, you meet them and become their friend. ❑ *He has made friends with the kids on the street.* ❑ *Dennis made friends easily.*

Word Partners	Use **friend** with:
ADJ.	**best** friend, **close** friend, **dear** friend, **faithful** friend, **former** friend, **good** friend, **loyal** friend, **mutual** friend, **old** friend, **personal** friend, **trusted** friend **1**
N.	**childhood** friend, friend **of the family**, friend **or relative** **1**
V.	**tell a** friend **1** **make a** friend **3**

friend|ly /frɛndli/ (**friendlier, friendliest**)
ADJECTIVE If someone is **friendly**, they behave in a pleasant, kind way. ❑ *Godfrey was friendly to me.* ❑ *The man had a pleasant, friendly face.*

Word Builder	friendship
ship ≈ state of being	

champion + **ship** = champion**ship**
friend + **ship** = friend**ship**
leader + **ship** = leader**ship**
member + **ship** = member**ship**
owner + **ship** = owner**ship**
relation + **ship** = relation**ship**

friend|ship /frɛndʃɪp/ (**friendships**) **NOUN** A **friendship** is a relationship between two or more friends. ❑ *Their friendship has lasted more than sixty years.*

fries /fraɪz/ **PLURAL NOUN** Fries are the same as **French fries**.

fright /fraɪt/ (**frights**)
1 **NONCOUNT NOUN** Fright is a sudden feeling of fear. ❑ *There was a loud noise, and Franklin jumped with fright.*
2 **NOUN** A **fright** is an experience that makes you suddenly afraid. ❑ *The snake raised its head, which gave everyone a fright.*

fright|en /fraɪtᵊn/ (**frightens, frightening, frightened**) **VERB** Something or someone that **frightens** you makes you suddenly feel afraid, anxious, or nervous. ❑ *He knew that Soli was trying to frighten him.*

fright|ened /fraɪtᵊnd/ **ADJECTIVE** A **frightened** person or animal is anxious or afraid. ❏ *She was frightened of making a mistake.*

fright|en|ing /fraɪtᵊnɪŋ/ **ADJECTIVE** If something is **frightening**, it makes you feel afraid, anxious, or nervous. ❏ *It was a very frightening experience.*

frill /frɪl/ (**frills**) **NOUN** A **frill** is a long narrow strip of cloth or paper with a lot of folds in it, used as a decoration. ❏ *She loves party dresses with ribbons and frills.*

fringe /frɪndʒ/ (**fringes**) **NOUN** A **fringe** is a row of hanging threads that is used for decorating a piece of cloth. ❏ *The jacket had leather fringes on the sleeves.*

frog /frɒg/ (**frogs**) **NOUN** A **frog** is a small animal with smooth skin, big eyes, and long back legs that it uses for jumping.
→ look at **animal**

from /frəm, STRONG frʌm/

1 **PREPOSITION** If something comes **from** a person, they give it to you or send it to you. ❏ *I received a letter from Mary yesterday.* ❏ *The watch was a present from his wife.*

2 **PREPOSITION** Someone who comes **from** a particular place lives there or was born there. ❏ *I come from New Zealand.*

3 **PREPOSITION** If someone or something moves **from** a place, they leave it. ❏ *Everyone watched as she ran from the room.* ❏ *Mr. Baker traveled from Washington to London for the meeting.*

4 **PREPOSITION** You can use **from** when you are talking about how far away something is. ❏ *The park is only a hundred yards from the center of town.* ❏ *How far is the hotel from here?*

5 **PREPOSITION** You use **from** to say what was used to make something. ❏ *This bread is made from white flour.* ❏ *The cans are made from steel.*

6 **PREPOSITION** If something changes **from** one thing **to** another, it stops being the first thing and becomes the second thing. ❏ *Unemployment fell from 7.5 to 7.2%.*

7 **PREPOSITION** You can use **from** to talk about the beginning of a period of time. ❏ *Breakfast is available from 6 a.m.*

front /frʌnt/ (**fronts**)

1 **NOUN** The **front of** something is the part of it that faces you, or that faces forward. ❏ *Stand at the front of the line.*

2 A person or thing that is **in front** is ahead of others in a moving group. ❏ *Don't drive too close to the car in front.*

3 Someone who is **in front** in a competition is winning. ❏ *Richard Dunwoody is in front in the race.*

4 Someone or something that is **in front of** a particular thing is facing it, ahead of it, or close to the front part of it. ❏ *She sat down in front of her mirror.* ❏ *A child ran in front of my car.*

5 If you do or say something **in front of** someone else, you do or say it when they are present. ❏ *They never argued in front of their children.*

fron|tier /frʌntɪər, frɒn-/ (**frontiers**)

1 **NOUN** A **frontier** is an area of land where people are just starting to live. ❏ *...a frontier town.*

2 **NOUN** SOCIAL STUDIES In the western part of America before the twentieth century, the **frontier** was the part that Europeans had reached. ❏ *The family moved west to the frontier, and took up land in Dixon County.*

frost /frɒst/ (**frosts, frosting, frosted**)

1 **NONCOUNT NOUN** **Frost** is ice like white powder that forms outside when the weather is very cold. ❏ *There was frost on my windshield this morning.*

2 **VERB** If you **frost** a cake, you cover and decorate it with **frosting**.

frost|ing /frɒstɪŋ/ **NONCOUNT NOUN** **Frosting** is a sweet substance that is used for decorating cakes.

frown /fraʊn/ (**frowns, frowning, frowned**)

1 **VERB** When someone **frowns**, their eyebrows move together because they are annoyed, worried, or confused, or because they are concentrating. ❏ *Nancy shook her head, frowning.* ❏ *He frowned at her anxiously.*

2 **NOUN** **Frown** is also a noun. ❏ *There was a deep frown on the boy's face.*

froze /froʊz/ **Froze** is a form of the verb **freeze**.

fro|zen /froʊzᵊn/

1 **Frozen** is a form of the verb **freeze**.

2 **ADJECTIVE** If the ground is **frozen** it has become hard because the weather is very cold. ❏ *It was extremely cold and the ground was frozen hard.*

3 **ADJECTIVE** **Frozen** food has been stored at a very low temperature. ❏ *Frozen fish is a healthy convenience food.*

4 **ADJECTIVE** If you are **frozen**, you are very cold. ❏ *I'm frozen out here.*
→ look at **food, meat**

F

Picture Dictionary   fruit

peel — apple — banana — lemon — figs — kiwi fruit — skin — grapes — seeds — orange — segment — pear — pineapple — watermelon

fruit /fru̱t/ (fruit)

NOUN Fruit is the part of a tree that contains seeds, covered with a substance that you can eat. ❑ *Fresh fruit and vegetables provide fiber and vitamins.* ❑ *We grow bananas and other tropical fruits here.*
→ look at Picture Dictionary: **fruit**
→ look at **food, tree**

frus|trate /frʌ̱streɪt/ (frustrates, frustrating, frustrated) **VERB** If a problem **frustrates** you, it upsets or makes you angry because you cannot do anything about it. ❑ *His lack of ambition frustrated me.*
● **frus|trat|ed ADJECTIVE** ❑ *Roberta felt frustrated and angry.* ● **frus|trat|ing ADJECTIVE** ❑ *This situation is very frustrating for us.*
● **frus|tra|tion** /frʌ̱streɪʃ³n/ **NONCOUNT NOUN** ❑ *The team was beginning to show signs of frustration.*

fry /fra̱ɪ/ (fries, frying, fried)
1 VERB When you **fry** food, you cook it in hot fat or oil. ❑ *Fry the onions until brown.*
2 PLURAL NOUN Fries are the same as **French fries.**
→ look at **cook, meat**

fudge /fʌ̱dʒ/ **NONCOUNT NOUN** Fudge is soft candy made from butter, sugar, and milk, and sometimes chocolate. ❑ *For dessert, we had coffee served with home-made fudge. It was delicious.*

fuel /fyu̱əl/ **NONCOUNT NOUN** Fuel is a substance such as coal or oil that is burned to provide heat or power. ❑ *They bought some fuel on the freeway.*
→ look at **energy**

ful|fill /fʊlfɪ̱l/ (fulfills, fulfilling, fulfilled) **VERB** If you **fulfill** a promise or a dream, you manage to do what you said or hoped you would do. ❑ *She fulfilled her dream of starting law school.*

full /fʊ̱l/ (fuller, fullest)
1 ADJECTIVE If a container is **full**, it contains as much liquid or as many people or things as it can. ❑ *The gas tank was full.* ❑ *Her case was full of clothes.* ❑ *Sorry. The bus is full.*
2 ADJECTIVE If you feel **full**, you do not want any more food. ❑ *You should stop eating when you're full.*
3 ADJECTIVE Your **full** name is your first name, other names that you may have, and your family name. ❑ *"May I have your full name?"—"Yes, it's Patricia Mary White."*
4 ADJECTIVE A **full** description is complete, with nothing missing. ❑ *For full details of the event, visit our website.*
5 ADJECTIVE You use **full** when you are saying that something is as big, loud, strong, fast, etc. as possible. ❑ *The car crashed into the wall at full speed.*
6 ADJECTIVE When there is a **full** moon, the moon is a bright, complete circle.
7 If you do something **in full**, you do it completely, giving every detail. ❑ *Mr. Thompson signed his name in full.*
→ look at **eat**

full-time also **full time**
1 ADJECTIVE Full-time work or study involves working or studying for all of each

normal working week. ❑ *I'm looking for a full-time job.*

2 ADVERB **Full-time** is also an adverb. ❑ *Deirdre works full-time.*

→ look at **job**

ful|ly /fʊli/

1 ADVERB **Fully** means completely. ❑ *We are fully aware of the problem.*

2 ADVERB If you deal with something **fully**, you deal with every detail of it. ❑ *He promised to answer fully and truthfully.*

fun /fʌn/

1 NONCOUNT NOUN **Fun** is pleasure and enjoyment. ❑ *It's interesting and it's also fun.* ❑ *It could be fun to watch them.*

2 NONCOUNT NOUN Someone who is **fun** is interesting or amusing. ❑ *Liz was always so much fun.*

3 If you do something **for fun**, you do it as a joke, without wanting to cause any harm. ❑ *Don't say such things, even for fun.*

4 If you **make fun of** someone or something, you laugh at them or make jokes about them. ❑ *Don't make fun of me.*

→ look at **fitness, play, relax**

func|tion /fʌŋkʃ°n/ (**functions, functioning, functioned**)

1 NOUN The **function** of something or someone is the useful thing that they do. ❑ *One of the main functions of the skin is protection.*

2 NOUN A **function** is a large formal dinner or party. ❑ *He attended a private function hosted by one of his students.*

3 VERB If a machine or a system **is functioning**, it is working well. ❑ *Your heart is functioning normally.*

func|tion|al /fʌŋkʃən°l/

1 ADJECTIVE **Functional** things are useful rather than decorative. ❑ *I like modern, functional furniture.*

2 ADJECTIVE **Functional** equipment works in the way that it is supposed to. ❑ *We have fully functional smoke alarms on all staircases.*

fund /fʌnd/ (**funds, funding, funded**)

1 PLURAL NOUN **Funds** are amounts of money that are available to be spent. ❑ *We're having a concert to raise funds for cancer research.*

2 NOUN A **fund** is an amount of money that people save for a particular purpose. ❑ *There is a scholarship fund for engineering students.*

3 VERB When a person or an organization **funds** something, they provide money for it. ❑ *The Foundation has funded a variety of programs.*

fun|da|men|tal /fʌndəmɛnt°l/ **ADJECTIVE** **Fundamental** things are very important and necessary. ❑ *I'll give you five fundamental steps for a healthy lifestyle.* ❑ *We all have a fundamental right to protect ourselves.* ● **fun|da|men|tal|ly** **ADVERB** ❑ *He is fundamentally a good man.*

fund|ing /fʌndɪŋ/ **NONCOUNT NOUN** **Funding** is money that a government or organization provides for a particular purpose. ❑ *They are hoping to get government funding for the program.*

fund-raising also **fundraising** **NONCOUNT NOUN** **Fund-raising** is the activity of collecting money for a particular use.

fu|ner|al /fyunərəl/ (**funerals**) **NOUN** A **funeral** is a ceremony that takes place when the body of someone who has died is buried or cremated (= burned). ❑ *The funeral will be in Joplin, Missouri.*

fun|gus /fʌŋgəs/ (**fungi** /fʌndʒaɪ, -ŋgaɪ/ or **funguses**) **NOUN** SCIENCE A **fungus** is a plant that has no flowers, leaves, or green color, and grows in wet places. ❑ *This fungus likes living in warm, wet places.* ❑ *There were mushrooms and other fungi growing out of the wall.*

fun|nel /fʌn°l/ (**funnels**)

1 NOUN A **funnel** is a tube with a wide, round top, used for pouring liquids into a container such as a bottle.

2 NOUN A **funnel** is a tube on the top of a ship or railroad engine where steam can escape.

fun|ny /fʌni/ (**funnier, funniest**)

1 ADJECTIVE Someone or something that is **funny** is amusing and likely to make you smile or laugh. ❑ *I'll tell you a funny story.*

2 ADJECTIVE A **funny** thing or person is strange, surprising, or confusing. ❑ *Children get some very funny ideas sometimes!* ❑ *There's something funny about him.*

3 ADJECTIVE If you feel **funny**, you feel slightly ill. [INFORMAL] ❑ *My head began to ache and my stomach felt funny.*

→ look at **movie**

fur /fɜr/ **NONCOUNT NOUN** **Fur** is the thick hair that grows on the bodies of many animals. ❑ *This creature's fur is short, dense, and silky.*

fu|ri|ous /fyʊəriəs/ **ADJECTIVE** Someone who is **furious** is extremely angry. ❑ *He is furious at the way he has been treated.*

fur|nace /fɜrnɪs/ (**furnaces**) **NOUN** A **furnace** is a container with a very hot fire inside it. ❑ *The iron bars glow in the red hot furnace.*

Picture Dictionary — furniture

- curtains
- picture
- bookcase
- chair
- lamp
- bed
- crib
- mirror
- armchair
- desk
- dresser
- couch / sofa
- table
- rug

f

fur|ni|ture /fɜ́rnɪtʃər/ **NONCOUNT NOUN**
Furniture is large objects such as tables,
chairs, or beds. ❏ *Each piece of furniture
matched the style of the house.*
→ look at Picture Dictionary: **furniture**

fur|ry /fɜ́ri/ (**furrier, furriest**)
1 **ADJECTIVE** A **furry** animal is covered with
thick, soft hair.
2 **ADJECTIVE** Something that is **furry** feels
similar to fur. ❏ *The leaves are soft and furry.*

fury /fyʊ́əri/ **NONCOUNT NOUN** Fury is violent
or very strong anger. ❏ *Her eyes were full of fury.*

fuse /fyuz/ (**fuses**) **NOUN** A **fuse** is a small
wire in a piece of electrical equipment that
melts when too much electricity passes
through it. ❏ *The fuse blew as he pressed the
button to start the motor.*

fuss /fʌs/ (**fusses, fussing, fussed**)
1 **NOUN** Fuss is anxious or excited behavior
that is not useful. ❏ *I don't know what all the
fuss is about.*
2 **VERB** If you **fuss**, you worry or behave in a
nervous, anxious way about things that are
not important. ❏ *Carol fussed about getting me
a drink.*
3 **VERB** If you **fuss over** someone, you pay
them a lot of attention and do things to
make them happy or comfortable. ❏ *Aunt
Laura fussed over him all afternoon.*

fussy /fʌ́si/ (**fussier, fussiest**) **ADJECTIVE**
Someone who is **fussy** is very difficult to
please and is interested in small details.
❏ *She is very fussy about her food.*

fu|ture /fyútʃər/ (**futures**)
1 **NOUN** The **future** is the time that will
come after now. ❏ *He was making plans for the
future.*
2 **ADJECTIVE** Future things will happen or
exist after the present time. ❏ *The lives of
future generations will be affected by our decisions.*
3 **NOUN** Someone's **future** is what will
happen to them after the present time.
❏ *His future depends on the result of the election.*
4 You say **in the future** when you are
talking about what will happen after now.
❏ *I asked her to be more careful in the future.*
→ look at **grammar**

Word Partners	Use **future** with:
ADJ.	**bright** future, **distant** future, **near** future, **uncertain** future **1**
V.	**have a** future, **plan for the** future, **predict the** future **1**
N.	future **date**, future **events**, future **generations**, future **plans**, **for** future **reference** **2**

future tense (**future tenses**) **NOUN**
LANGUAGE ARTS In grammar, **the future tense**
is the form that is used for talking about the
time that will come after the present.

Gg

gadg|et /ɡædʒɪt/ (gadgets) NOUN A **gadget** is a small machine or useful object. ❑ *The store sells computers and other electronic gadgets.*

gain /ɡeɪn/ (gains, gaining, gained)
1 VERB If you **gain** something, you get it. ❑ *You can gain access to the website for $14 a month.* ❑ *Students can gain valuable experience by working during their vacations.*
2 VERB To **gain** something means to have more of it. ❑ *Some women gain weight after they have a baby.* ❑ *The car was gaining speed as it came toward us.*
3 NOUN **Gain** is also a noun. ❑ *Sales showed a gain of nearly 8% last month.*

gal|axy /ɡæləksi/ (galaxies) also **Galaxy** NOUN SCIENCE A **galaxy** is a very large group of stars and planets. ❑ *Astronomers have discovered a distant galaxy.*
→ look at **space**

gale /ɡeɪl/ (gales) NOUN A **gale** is a very strong wind. ❑ *A strong gale was blowing.*

gal|lery /ɡæləri/ (galleries) NOUN ARTS A **gallery** is a place where people go to look at art. ❑ *We visited an art gallery.*

gal|lon /ɡælən/ (gallons) NOUN MATH A **gallon** is a unit for measuring liquids. A **gallon** is equal to 3.785 liters. There are eight pints in a gallon. ❑ *The tank holds 1,000 gallons of water.*
→ look at **measurement**

gal|lop /ɡæləp/ (gallops, galloping, galloped) VERB When a horse **gallops**, it runs very fast. ❑ *The horses galloped away.*

gam|ble /ɡæmbᵊl/ (gambles, gambling, gambled)
1 NOUN A **gamble** is a risk that you take because you hope that something good will happen. ❑ *She took a gamble and started up her own business.*
2 VERB If you **gamble on** something, you take a risk because you hope that something good will happen. ❑ *Companies sometimes have to gamble on new products.*
3 VERB If you **gamble**, you risk money in a game or on the result of a race or competition. ❑ *John gambled heavily on horse racing.*

gam|bler /ɡæmblər/ (gamblers) NOUN A **gambler** is someone who risks money regularly, for example in card games or horse racing. ❑ *Her husband was a heavy gambler.*

gam|bling /ɡæmblɪŋ/ NONCOUNT NOUN **Gambling** is the act or activity of risking money, for example in card games or horse racing. ❑ *The gambling laws are quite tough.*

game /ɡeɪm/ (games)
1 NOUN SPORTS A **game** is an activity or a sport in which you try to win against someone. ❑ *Football is a popular game.* ❑ *We played a game of cards.*
2 NOUN SPORTS A **game** is one particular occasion when you play a game. ❑ *It was the first game of the season.*
→ look at **play, relax**

game con|sole (game consoles) or **games console** NOUN TECHNOLOGY A **game console** is a piece of electronic equipment that is used for playing computer games on a television screen. ❑ *More than half of six- to ten-year-olds have a game console.*
→ look at **play**

gang /ɡæŋ/ (gangs)
1 NOUN A **gang** is a group of people, especially young people, who go around together and often deliberately cause trouble. ❑ *They had a fight with another gang.*
2 NOUN A **gang** is an organized group of criminals. ❑ *Police are hunting for a gang that has stolen several cars.*

gap /ɡæp/ (gaps)
1 NOUN A **gap** is a space between two things. ❑ *There was a narrow gap between the curtains.*
2 NOUN A **gap** is a hole in something. ❑ *His horse escaped through a gap in the fence.*

gar|age /ɡərɑʒ/ (garages)
1 NOUN A **garage** is a building where you keep a car. ❑ *The house has a large garage.*

2 **NOUN** A **garage** is a place where you can have your car repaired. ❏ *Nancy took her car to a local garage.*

gar|age sale (**garage sales**) **NOUN** If you have a **garage sale**, you sell clothes and toys and things that you do not want, usually in your garage.

gar|bage /gɑrbɪdʒ/
1 **NONCOUNT NOUN** **Garbage** is things such as old papers, empty cans, and old food that you do not want anymore. ❏ *They took the trash to a garbage dump.*
2 **NONCOUNT NOUN** If you say that an idea or opinion is **garbage**, you mean that you think it is not true or not important. [INFORMAL] ❏ *I think this theory is garbage.*
→ look at **pollution**

gar|bage can (**garbage cans**) **NOUN** A **garbage can** is a container for garbage.

gar|bage man (**garbage men**) **NOUN** A **garbage man** is a person whose job is to take people's garbage away.

gar|den /gɑrdᵊn/ (**gardens, gardening, gardened**)
1 **NOUN** A **garden** is the part of a yard where you grow flowers and vegetables. ❏ *She had a beautiful garden.*
2 **VERB** If you **garden**, you do work in your garden. ❏ *Jim gardened on weekends.*
● **gar|den|ing** **NONCOUNT NOUN** ❏ *My favorite hobby is gardening.*
3 **PLURAL NOUN** **Gardens** are places with plants, trees, and grass, that people can visit. ❏ *The gardens are open from 10:30 a.m. until 5:00 p.m.*

gar|den|er /gɑrdᵊnər/ (**gardeners**) **NOUN** A **gardener** is a person who works in a garden. ❏ *She employed a gardener.*

gar|lic /gɑrlɪk/ **NONCOUNT NOUN** **Garlic** is a plant like a small onion with a strong flavor, which you use in cooking. ❏ *When the oil is hot, add a clove of garlic.*

gar|ment /gɑrmənt/ (**garments**) **NOUN** A **garment** is a piece of clothing. ❏ *Exports of garments to the U.S. fell 3%.*

gas /gæs/ (**gases**)
1 **NOUN** SCIENCE A **gas** is any substance that is not a liquid or a solid. ❏ *Hydrogen is a gas, not a metal.*
2 **NONCOUNT NOUN** **Gas** is a liquid that you put into a car or other vehicle to make it

work. **Gas** is short for **gasoline**. ❏ *The car had a full tank of gas.*
→ look at **car, energy, water**

gaso|line /gæsəlin/ **NONCOUNT NOUN** **Gasoline** is a liquid that you put into a car or other vehicle to make it work.

gasp /gæsp/ (**gasps, gasping, gasped**)
1 **NOUN** A **gasp** is a short, quick breath of air that you take in through your mouth. ❏ *There was a gasp from the crowd as he scored the goal.*
2 **VERB** When you **gasp**, you take a short, quick breath through your mouth. ❏ *She gasped for air.*

gas sta|tion (**gas stations**) **NOUN** A **gas station** is a place where you can buy gas for your car.

gate /geɪt/ (**gates**)
1 **NOUN** A **gate** is a structure like a door that you use to enter a field, or the area around a building. ❏ *He opened the gate and walked up to the house.*

2 **NOUN** In an airport, a **gate** is a place where passengers leave the airport and get on an airplane. ❏ *Please go to gate 15.*

gath|er /gæðər/ (**gathers, gathering, gathered**)
1 **VERB** If people **gather** somewhere, they come together in a group. ❏ *We gathered around the fireplace and talked.*
2 **VERB** If you **gather** things, you collect them together so that you can use them. ❏ *They gathered enough firewood to make a fire.* ❏ *He used a hidden tape recorder to gather information.*

gath|er|ing /gæðərɪŋ/ (**gatherings**) **NOUN** A **gathering** is a group of people meeting together for a particular purpose. ❏ *They held a large family gathering.*

gauge /geɪdʒ/ (**gauges, gauging, gauged**)
1 **VERB** If you **gauge** something, you measure it or judge it. ❏ *She found it hard to gauge his mood.*
2 **NOUN** A **gauge** is a piece of equipment that measures the amount or level of something. ❏ *The temperature gauge showed that the water was boiling.*

g

gave /geɪv/ **Gave** is a form of the verb **give**.

gay /geɪ/ **ADJECTIVE** A **gay** man or woman is attracted to people of the same sex. ❏ *The quality of life for gay men has improved.*

gaze /geɪz/ (**gazes, gazing, gazed**) **VERB** If you **gaze at** someone or something, you look steadily at them for a long time. ❏ *She was gazing at herself in the mirror.* ❏ *He gazed into the fire.*

gear /gɪər/ (**gears**)
1 **NOUN** **Gears** are the part of an engine that changes engine power into movement. ❏ *On a hill, use low gears.* ❏ *The car was in fourth gear.*
2 **NONCOUNT NOUN** The **gear** involved in a particular activity is the equipment or special clothing that you use. ❏ *He took his fishing gear with him.* ❏ *...camping gear.*

gear|shift /gɪərʃɪft/ (**gearshifts**) **NOUN** The **gearshift** is the handle that you use to change gear in a car or other vehicle.

GED /dʒi i di/ **NOUN** The **GED** is a test in basic subject areas such as math and English for adults who did not finish high school. The test shows that they have the same academic skills as a high school graduate (= someone who finished high school). **GED** is short for **General Educational Development**. ❏ *We help students who did not complete high school to obtain their GED certificate.* ❏ *...the GED Test.*

gee /dʒi/ **EXCLAMATION** People sometimes say **gee** to make a comment stronger. [INFORMAL] ❏ *Gee, it's hot.*

geese /gis/ **Geese** is the plural of **goose**.

gel /dʒɛl/ **NONCOUNT NOUN** **Gel** is a thick substance like jelly, especially one that you use to keep your hair in a particular style.

gem /dʒɛm/ (**gems**) **NOUN** A **gem** is a valuable stone that is used in jewelry. ❏ *...precious gems.*

gen|der /dʒɛndər/ (**genders**) **NOUN** A person's **gender** is the fact that they are male or female. ❏ *We do not know the children's ages and genders.*

gene /dʒin/ (**genes**) **NOUN** SCIENCE A **gene** is the part of a cell that controls a person's, animal's, or plant's physical characteristics, growth, and development. ❏ *He carries the gene for red hair.*

gen|er|al /dʒɛnərəl/ (**generals**)
1 **ADJECTIVE** **General** describes something that involves most people and things. ❏ *There is not enough general understanding of this problem.*
2 You use **in general** to talk about something as a whole, rather than part of it. ❏ *We need to improve our educational system in general.*
3 **NOUN** A **general** is an officer with a high rank in the army. ❏ *The troops received a visit from the general.*

gen|er|al elec|tion (**general elections**) **NOUN** SOCIAL STUDIES A **general election** is a time when people choose a new government. Compare with **primary**.

gen|er|al|ize /dʒɛnrəlaɪz/ (**generalizes, generalizing, generalized**) **VERB** If you **generalize**, you say something that is usually, but not always, true. ❏ *You shouldn't generalize and say that all men are the same.*

gen|er|al|ly /dʒɛnrəli/
1 **ADVERB** **Generally** describes something without giving any particular details. ❏ *He was generally a good man.*
2 **ADVERB** You use **generally** to say that something usually happens, but not always. ❏ *It is generally true that darker fruits contain more iron.*

gen|er|ate /dʒɛnəreɪt/ (**generates, generating, generated**)
1 **VERB** To **generate** something means to cause it to exist. ❏ *The reforms will generate new jobs.*
2 **VERB** To **generate** a form of energy or power means to produce it. ❏ *We use oil to generate electricity.*

gen|era|tion /dʒɛnəreɪʃ°n/ (**generations**) **NOUN** A **generation** is all the people in a group or country who are of a similar age. ❏ *The current generation of teens are the richest in history.*

gen|era|tor /dʒɛnəreɪtər/ (**generators**) **NOUN** A **generator** is a machine that produces electricity. ❏ *The house has its own power generators.*

gen|er|ous /dʒɛnərəs/ **ADJECTIVE** A **generous** person gives you more than you expect of something. ❏ *He is generous with his money.* ● **gen|er|os|ity** /dʒɛnərɒsiti/ **NONCOUNT NOUN** ❏ *Diana was surprised by his kindness and generosity.* ● **gen|er|ous|ly** **ADVERB** ❏ *We would like to thank everyone who generously gave their time.*

G

ge|net|ic /dʒɪnɛtɪk/ **ADJECTIVE** SCIENCE
Genetic describes something that is related
to genetics or genes. ❑ *...a rare genetic disease.*

ge|neti|cal|ly modi|fied /dʒɪnɛtɪkli
mɒdɪfaɪd/ **ADJECTIVE** SCIENCE Genetically
modified plants and animals have had their
genetic structure (= pattern of chemicals in
cells) changed in order to make them more
suitable for a particular purpose. The short
form **GM** is also used.

ge|net|ics /dʒɪnɛtɪks/ **NONCOUNT NOUN**
SCIENCE Genetics is the study of how
qualities are passed on from parents to
children. ❑ *Genetics is changing our
understanding of cancer.*

ge|ni|us /dʒinyəs/ (**geniuses**) **NOUN** A
genius is a very skilled or intelligent person.
❑ *Chaplin was a comic genius.*

gen|tle /dʒɛntəl/ (**gentler, gentlest**)
1 **ADJECTIVE** Someone who is **gentle** is kind,
mild, and calm. ❑ *My husband was a quiet and
gentle man.* ● **gen|tly** **ADVERB** ❑ *She smiled
gently at him.*
2 **ADJECTIVE** Gentle actions or movements
are calm, slow, or soft. ❑ *Rest and gentle
exercise will make you feel better.* ● **gen|tly**
ADVERB ❑ *Patrick took her gently by the arm.*

gentle|man /dʒɛntəlmən/ (**gentlemen**)
1 **NOUN** A **gentleman** is a man who is
polite, educated, and kind to other people.
❑ *He was always such a gentleman.*
2 **PLURAL NOUN** You can use **gentlemen** to
talk to men or to talk about them in a polite
way. ❑ *This way, please, ladies and gentlemen.*

genu|ine /dʒɛnyuɪn/ **ADJECTIVE** If a person
or thing is **genuine**, they are true and real.
❑ *He's a genuine American hero.* ❑ *We have a
genuine friendship.*

ge|nus /dʒinəs/ (**genera** /dʒɛnərə/) **NOUN**
SCIENCE A **genus** is a type of animal or plant.
❑ *...a genus of plants called "Lonas."*

ge|og|ra|phy /dʒiɒgrəfi/ **NONCOUNT NOUN**
GEOGRAPHY **Geography** is the study of the
countries of the world and things such as
the land, oceans, weather, towns, and
population.

ge|ol|ogy /dʒiɒlədʒi/ **NONCOUNT NOUN**
SCIENCE **Geology** is the study of the Earth's
structure, surface, and origins. ❑ *He was
professor of geology at the University of Georgia.*
● **ge|olo|gist** (**geologists**) **NOUN** ❑ *Geologists
have studied the way that heat flows from the Earth.*

ge|om|etry /dʒiɒmɪtri/ **NONCOUNT NOUN**
MATH **Geometry** is the branch of
mathematics relating to lines, angles,
curves, and shapes. ❑ *They're studying basic
geometry.*
→ look at Word World: **geometry**
→ look at **math**

germ /dʒɜrm/ (**germs**) **NOUN** A **germ** is a
very small living thing that can cause
disease or illness. ❑ *This chemical is used for
killing germs.*

ges|ture /dʒɛstʃər/ (**gestures, gesturing,
gestured**)
1 **NOUN** A **gesture** is a movement that you
make with a part of your body, especially
your hands, to express emotion or
information. ❑ *Sarah made a gesture with her
fist.*
2 **VERB** If you **gesture**, you use movements
of your hands or head to tell someone
something. ❑ *I gestured toward the house.*
→ look at **communication**

get /gɛt/ (**gets, getting, got, gotten** or **got**)
1 **VERB** You use **get** with adjectives to mean
"become." ❑ *The boys were getting bored.*
❑ *Don't worry. Things will get better.*
2 **VERB** If you **get** someone **to** do
something, you make them do it. ❑ *They got
him to give them a lift in his car.*
3 **VERB** If you **get** something done,

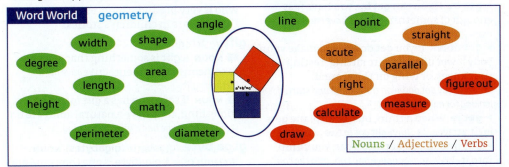

someone does it for you. ❑ *Why don't you get your car fixed?*

4 **VERB** If you **get** somewhere, you arrive there. ❑ *He got home at 4 a.m.* ❑ *How do I get to your place from here?*

5 **VERB** You sometimes use **get** with another verb when you are talking about something that happens to someone. [INFORMAL] ❑ *He got arrested for possession of drugs.*

6 **VERB** If you **get** something, you buy it or obtain it. ❑ *Dad needs to get a birthday present for Mom.* ❑ *I got a job at the store.*

7 **VERB** If you **get** something, you receive it. ❑ *I'm getting a bike for my birthday.* ❑ *He gets a lot of letters from fans.*

8 **VERB** If you **get** someone or something, you go and bring them to a particular place. ❑ *I went downstairs to get the mail.* ❑ *It's time to get the kids from school.*

9 **VERB** If you **get** a joke, you understand it. ❑ *Dad laughed, but I didn't get the joke.*

10 **VERB** If you **get** an illness or a disease, you become sick with it. ❑ *I've got flu.*

11 **VERB** When you **get** a train, bus, airplane, or boat, you leave a place on a particular train, bus, airplane, or boat. ❑ *I got the train home at 10.45 p.m.*

▶ **get along** If you **get along with** someone, you have a friendly relationship with them. You can also say that two people **get along**. ❑ *He's always complaining. I can't get along with him.* ❑ *We all get along well.*

▶ **get away** When someone or something **gets away**, they escape. ❑ *The thieves got away through an upstairs window.*

▶ **get away with** If you **get away with** doing something wrong, you are not punished for it. ❑ *Criminals know how to steal and get away with it.*

▶ **get back** If you **get back** somewhere, you return there. ❑ *I'll call you when we get back from Scotland.*

▶ **get by** If you can **get by**, you have just enough of something. ❑ *We have enough money to get by.*

▶ **get down** If you **get down**, you make your body lower until you are sitting, resting on your knees, or lying on the ground. ❑ *Everybody got down on the ground and started looking for my earring.*

▶ **get in** When a train, bus, or airplane **gets in**, it arrives. ❑ *Our flight got in two hours late.*

▶ **get into** If you **get into** a car, you climb into it. ❑ *We said goodbye and I got into the cab.*

▶ **get off** If you **get off** a bus, train, or bicycle, you leave it. ❑ *He got off the train at Central Station.*

▶ **get on** If you **get on with** something, you continue doing it or start doing it. ❑ *Jane got on with her work.*

▶ **get out** **1** If you **get out**, you leave a place because you want to escape from it. ❑ *They got out of the country just in time.*

2 If you **get out** of a car, you leave it. ❑ *A man got out of the van and ran away.*

▶ **get over** If you **get over** an unhappy experience or an illness, you become happy or well again. ❑ *It took me a long time to get over her death.*

▶ **get through** If you **get through** a task or an amount of work, you complete it. ❑ *We got through plenty of work today.*

▶ **get together** When people **get together**, they meet in order to talk about something or to spend time together. ❑ *Thanksgiving is a time for families to get together.*

▶ **get up** **1** When someone who is sitting or lying down **gets up**, they move their body so that they are standing. ❑ *I got up and walked over to the window.*

2 When you **get up**, you get out of bed. ❑ *They have to get up early in the morning.*

ghet|to /gɛtoʊ/ (**ghettos** or **ghettoes**) NOUN A **ghetto** is a part of a city where many poor people live. ❑ *They came from the inner-city ghettos.*

ghost /goʊst/ (**ghosts**) NOUN A **ghost** is the spirit of a dead person that someone believes they can see or feel. ❑ *He saw the ghost of a dead man.*

gi|ant /dʒaɪənt/ (**giants**)

1 **ADJECTIVE** Something that is **giant** is very large or important. ❑ *America's giant car makers are located in Detroit.* ❑ *They watched the concert on a giant TV screen.*

2 **NOUN** A **giant** is an imaginary person who is very big and strong, especially one that appears in children's stories.

gift /gɪft/ (**gifts**)

1 **NOUN** A **gift** is something that you give to someone as a present. ❑ *We gave her a birthday gift.*

2 **NOUN** If someone has a **gift for** doing something, they have a natural ability to do it. ❑ *He found he had a gift for teaching.*

gi|ga|byte /gɪgəbaɪt/ (**gigabytes**) NOUN TECHNOLOGY A **gigabyte** is one thousand and twenty-four megabytes (= a unit for measuring the size of a computer's memory).

gi|gan|tic /dʒaɪgæntɪk/ **ADJECTIVE** If something is **gigantic**, it is extremely large. ❑ *There are gigantic rocks along the roadside.*

gig|gle /gɪgəl/ (**giggles, giggling, giggled**)
1 VERB If you **giggle**, you laugh in a silly way, like a child. ❑ *The girls began to giggle.*
2 NOUN Giggle is also a noun. ❑ *He gave a little giggle.*

gin|ger /dʒɪndʒər/ **NONCOUNT NOUN** Ginger is a plant with a sweet, spicy flavor that you use in cooking.

gi|raffe /dʒɪræf/ (**giraffes**) **NOUN** A **giraffe** is a large animal with a very long neck, long legs, and dark spots on its body.

girl /gɜrl/ (**girls**) **NOUN** A **girl** is a female child. ❑ *They have two girls and a boy.*

> **Usage** **girl**
> It is important not to talk about an adult female as a **girl**. This may cause offense. Use **woman** instead. *I'm studying with Diana. She's a **woman** from my English class.*

girl|friend /gɜrlfrɛnd/ (**girlfriends**)
1 NOUN A **girlfriend** is a girl or woman who someone is having a romantic relationship with. ❑ *Does he have a girlfriend?*
2 NOUN A **girlfriend** is a female friend. ❑ *I had lunch with my girlfriends.*

Girl Scout (**Girl Scouts**)
1 NOUN The **Girl Scouts** is an organization that teaches girls practical skills, and encourages them to help other people. ❑ *I joined the Girl Scouts at age 10.*
2 NOUN A **Girl Scout** is a member of the Girl Scouts. ❑ *If you are aged between five and seventeen, you can become a Girl Scout.*

give /gɪv/ (**gives, giving, gave, given**)
1 VERB If you **give** someone something, you let them have it. ❑ *My parents gave me a watch for my birthday.* ❑ *They gave him the job.* ❑ *I gave him my phone number.*
2 VERB If you **give** someone an object, you pass it to them, so that they can take it. ❑ *Give me that pencil.* ❑ *Please give me your bag to carry.*
3 VERB You can use **give** with nouns when you are talking about physical actions. For

example, "She gave a smile" means "She smiled." ❑ *She gave me a big kiss.* ❑ *He gave her a friendly smile.*
4 VERB If you **give** a party, you organize it. ❑ *I gave a dinner party for a few friends.*
→ look at **identification**
▶ **give away** If you **give away** something that you own, you give it to someone. ❑ *She likes to give away plants from her garden.*
▶ **give back** If you **give** something **back**, you return it to the person who gave it to you. ❑ *I gave the book back to him.* ❑ *Give me back my camera.*
▶ **give in** If you **give in**, you agree to do something although you do not really want to do it. ❑ *After saying "no" a hundred times, I finally gave in and said "yes."*
▶ **give out** If you **give out** a number of things, you give one to each person in a group of people. ❑ *Our teacher gave out papers, pencils, and calculators for the math test.*
▶ **give up 1** If you **give up** something, you stop doing it or having it. ❑ *We gave up hope of finding the fishermen.*
2 If you **give up**, you decide that you cannot do something and you stop trying to do it. ❑ *I give up. I'll never understand this.*

giv|en /gɪvən/ **Given** is a form of the verb **give**.

glaci|er /gleɪʃər/ (**glaciers**) **NOUN** SCIENCE A **glacier** is a very large amount of ice that moves very slowly, usually down a mountain.

glad /glæd/ **ADJECTIVE** If you are **glad** about something, you are happy and pleased about it. ❑ *They seemed glad to see me.* ❑ *I'm glad you like the present.* ● **glad|ly** **ADVERB** ❑ *Malcolm gladly accepted the invitation.*

glam|or|ous /glæmərəs/ **ADJECTIVE** If someone or something is **glamorous**, they are very attractive, exciting, or interesting. ❑ *She looked glamorous in a white dress.*

glance /glæns/ (**glances, glancing, glanced**)
1 VERB If you **glance at** something or someone, you look at them very quickly. ❑ *He glanced at his watch.*
2 NOUN A **glance** is a quick look at someone or something. ❑ *Trevor and I exchanged a glance.*

glare /glɛər/ (**glares, glaring, glared**)
1 VERB If you **glare at** someone, you look at them with an angry expression on your

face. ❑ *The old woman glared at him.*

2 **NOUN** A **glare** is an angry look. ❑ *She gave him a furious glare.*

3 **VERB** If the sun or a light **glares**, it shines with a very bright light. ❑ *The sun glared down on us.*

4 **NONCOUNT NOUN** Glare is very bright light that is difficult to look at. ❑ *...the glare from a car's lights.*

Spelling Partners **glass**

glass /glɑs, glæs/ (**glasses**)

1 **NONCOUNT NOUN** Glass is a hard, transparent substance that is used for making things such as windows and bottles. ❑ *He served the salad in a glass bowl.*

2 **NOUN** A **glass** is a container made from glass, which you can drink from. ❑ *He picked up his glass and drank.* ❑ *I drink a glass of milk every day.*

3 **PLURAL NOUN** Glasses are two pieces of glass or plastic (= lenses) in a frame, that some people wear in front of their eyes to help them to see better. ❑ *He took off his glasses.*
→ look at **kitchen, restaurant, wear**

gleam /glim/ (**gleams, gleaming, gleamed**) **VERB** If an object or a surface **gleams**, it shines with a soft light. ❑ *His black hair gleamed in the sun.*

glide /glaɪd/ (**glides, gliding, glided**)

1 **VERB** If you **glide** somewhere, you move quietly and easily. ❑ *Waiters glide between the tables carrying trays.*

2 **VERB** When birds or airplanes **glide**, they move along by floating in the air. ❑ *Geese glide over the lake.*

glim|mer /glɪmər/ (**glimmers, glimmering, glimmered**)

1 **VERB** If something **glimmers**, it shines with a weak light. ❑ *The moon glimmered through the mist.*

2 **NOUN** A **glimmer** is a weak light. ❑ *In the east there was a glimmer of light.*

3 **NOUN** A **glimmer of** something is a small sign of it. ❑ *The new drug offers a glimmer of hope for patients.*

glimpse /glɪmps/ (**glimpses, glimpsing, glimpsed**)

1 **NOUN** If you get a **glimpse of** someone or something, you see them for a very short amount of time. ❑ *Fans waited outside the hotel to catch a glimpse of the star.*

2 **VERB** If you **glimpse** someone or something, you see them for a very short amount of time. ❑ *She glimpsed a poster through the car window.*

glis|ten /glɪsᵊn/ (**glistens, glistening, glistened**) **VERB** If something **glistens**, it shines, usually because it is wet. ❑ *The ocean glistened in the sunlight.* ❑ *David's face was glistening with sweat.*

glit|ter /glɪtər/ (**glitters, glittering, glittered**) **VERB** If something **glitters**, small flashes of light shine from different parts of it. ❑ *The ring glittered on Andrea's finger.*

glob|al /gloʊbᵊl/ **ADJECTIVE** Global means relating to the whole world. ❑ *American businesses compete in a global economy.*

● **glob|al|ly** **ADVERB** ❑ *The company employs 5,800 people globally, including 2,000 in Colorado.*
→ look at **earth, Internet**

glob|al econo|my **NOUN** SOCIAL STUDIES The **global economy** is the way in which the nations of the world work together through international trade and financial matters. ❑ *We will soon see the effect of rising oil prices on the global economy.*

glo|bal|ization /gloʊbᵊlaɪzeɪʃᵊn/ **NONCOUNT NOUN** SOCIAL STUDIES Globalization is the idea that the world is developing a single economy as a result of improved technology and communications. ❑ *The report focuses on the globalization of business activities around the world.*

glob|al warm|ing **NONCOUNT NOUN** SCIENCE Global warming is the gradual rise in the Earth's temperature caused by high levels of certain gases. ❑ *If we use less energy we can help to reduce global warming.*
→ look at **greenhouse effect**

globe /gloʊb/ (**globes**)

1 **NOUN** GEOGRAPHY A **globe** is an object shaped like a ball with a map of the world on it. ❑ *A large globe stood on his desk.*

2 **NOUN** You can call the world **the globe** when you want to say how big it is or that something happens in many different parts of it. ❑ *Thousands of people across the globe took part in the survey.*
→ look at Picture Dictionary: **globe**

G

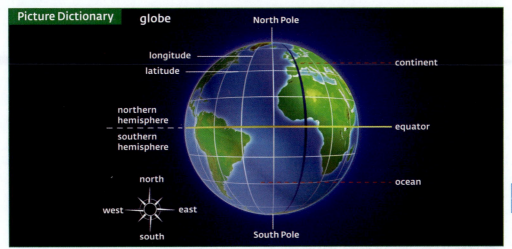

Picture Dictionary   globe

North Pole

longitude — continent

latitude

northern hemisphere

southern hemisphere — equator

north

west — east

ocean

south

South Pole

g

gloomy /glumi/ (**gloomier, gloomiest**)
   1 **ADJECTIVE** If a place is **gloomy**, it is almost dark so that you cannot see very well.
   ❑ *Inside it's gloomy after all that sunshine.*
   2 **ADJECTIVE** If people are **gloomy**, they are unhappy and they do not think that the situation will get better. ❑ *He is gloomy about the future of the country.*
   3 **ADJECTIVE** If a situation is **gloomy**, it does not give you much hope of success or happiness. ❑ *The economic prospects for next year are gloomy.*

glo|ri|ous /glɔriəs/
   1 **ADJECTIVE** Something that is **glorious** is very beautiful. ❑ *We saw a glorious rainbow.*
   ● **glo|ri|ous|ly** **ADVERB** ❑ *The trees are gloriously colored in the fall.*
   2 **ADJECTIVE** If something is **glorious**, it makes you feel very happy. ❑ *He has glorious memories of his days as a champion.*
   ● **glo|ri|ous|ly** **ADVERB** ❑ *It was a gloriously sunny morning.*
   3 **ADJECTIVE** A **glorious** experience or occasion involves great fame or success.
   ❑ *He had a glorious career as a broadcaster and writer.* ● **glo|ri|ous|ly** **ADVERB** ❑ *The mission was gloriously successful.*

glo|ry /glɔri/ **NONCOUNT NOUN** Glory is the fame and admiration from other people that you gain by doing something great. ❑ *He had his moment of glory when he won the cycling race.*

glos|sa|ry /glɔsəri/ (**glossaries**) **NOUN**
   LANGUAGE ARTS A **glossary** is a list of difficult words that are used in a book or special subject, with explanations of their meanings.

glossy /glɔsi/ (**glossier, glossiest**) **ADJECTIVE**
   Glossy means smooth and shiny. ❑ *She had glossy black hair.*

glove /glʌv/ (**gloves**) **NOUN** Gloves are pieces of clothing that you wear on your hands, with a separate part for each finger.
   ❑ *He put his gloves in his pocket.*

glow /gloʊ/ (**glows, glowing, glowed**)
   1 **NOUN** A **glow** is a soft, steady light, for example the light from a fire when there are no flames. ❑ *She saw the red glow of a fire.*
   2 **VERB** If something **glows**, it makes a soft, steady light. ❑ *The lantern glowed softly in the darkness.*

glue /glu/ (**glues, glueing** or **gluing, glued**)
   1 **NONCOUNT NOUN** Glue is a sticky substance used for joining things together.
   ❑ *You will need scissors and a tube of glue.*
   2 **VERB** If you **glue** one object to another, you stick them together with glue. ❑ *She glued the pieces of newspaper together.*

GM /dʒi ɛm/ **ADJECTIVE** GM crops have had one or more genes changed to make them stronger or to help them grow. **GM** is short for **genetically modified**. ❑ *They are growing large-scale GM food crops, like soybeans.*

go /goʊ/ (**goes, going, went, gone**)
   1 **VERB** When you **go** somewhere, you move or travel there. ❑ *We went to Rome on vacation.* ❑ *I went home for the weekend.* ❑ *It took an hour to go three miles.*
   2 **VERB** When you **go**, you leave the place where you are. ❑ *It's time for me to go.*
   3 **VERB** You use **go** to say that you leave a place in order to do something. ❑ *We went*

swimming early this morning. ❑ They've gone shopping. ❑ He went for a walk. ❑ I'll go and make breakfast.

4 **VERB** If you **go to** school, work, or church, you visit it regularly. ❑ Does your daughter go to school yet?

5 **VERB** When you say where a road or path **goes**, you are saying where it leads to. ❑ This road goes from Blairstown to Millbrook Village.

6 **VERB** If something **goes** in a particular place, that is the place where you normally keep it. ❑ The shoes go on the shoe shelf.

7 **VERB** **Go** means become. ❑ I'm going crazy. ❑ The meat has gone bad.

8 **VERB** You use **go** to talk about the way that something happens. ❑ How's your job going? ❑ Everything is going wrong.

9 **VERB** If a machine **is going**, it is working. ❑ Can you get my car going again?

10 **VERB** If something **goes with** something else, or if two things **go together**, they look or taste good together. ❑ Those pants would go with my blue shirt. ❑ Cheese and tomato go together well.

11 If someone **is making a go of** something, they are trying to have some success with it. ❑ She's determined to make a go of her music career.

12 If someone is always **on the go**, they are always busy and active. [INFORMAL] ❑ In my job I am on the go all the time.

13 In a restaurant, you ask for food **to go** when you want to take it with you and eat it somewhere else. ❑ She ordered coffee to go.
→ look at **movie, route, school, season**

▸ **go ahead** If an event **goes ahead**, it takes place. ❑ The wedding went ahead as planned, about 14 hours after the accident.

▸ **go away** **1** If you **go away**, you leave a place or a person. ❑ Just go away and leave me alone!

2 If you **go away**, you leave a place and spend time somewhere else, especially as a vacation. ❑ Why don't we go away this weekend?

▸ **go back** If you **go back** somewhere, you return there. ❑ He'll be going back to college soon.

▸ **go by** When time **goes by**, it passes. ❑ The week went by so quickly.

▸ **go down** **1** If an amount **goes down**, it becomes less. ❑ House prices went down last month.

2 When the sun **goes down**, it goes below the line between the land and the sky. ❑ It gets cold after the sun goes down.

▸ **go off** **1** If a bomb **goes off**, it explodes.

❑ A bomb went off, destroying the vehicle.

2 If food **goes off**, it is no longer good to eat or drink. ❑ This fish has gone off.

▸ **go on** **1** If you **go on** doing something, you continue to do it. ❑ She just went on laughing.

2 If something **is going on**, it is happening. ❑ While this conversation was going on, I just listened.

▸ **go out** **1** If you **go out**, you leave your home to do something enjoyable. ❑ I'm going out tonight.

2 If you **go out with** someone, you have a romantic relationship with them. ❑ I've been going out with my girlfriend for three months.

3 If a light **goes out**, it stops shining. ❑ The bedroom light went out after a moment.

4 If a fire **goes out**, it stops burning. ❑ The fire went out and the room became cold.

▸ **go over** If you **go over** something, you look at it or think about it very carefully. ❑ We went over the details again.

▸ **go through** If you **go through** a difficult experience, you experience it. ❑ He went through a difficult time when his wife died.

▸ **go up** If an amount **goes up**, it becomes greater. ❑ The cost of calls went up to $1.95 a minute.

goal /goʊl/ (**goals**)

1 **NOUN** SPORTS In games such as soccer, the **goal** is the place where the players try to get the ball in order to win a point for their team. ❑ The ball went straight into the goal.

2 **NOUN** SPORTS In games such as soccer, a **goal** is a point that is scored when the ball goes into the goal. ❑ He scored five goals in one playoff game.

3 **NOUN** Your **goal** is the aim or purpose that you have when you do something. ❑ Our goal is to make patients comfortable.

Word Partners	Use **goal** with:
V.	**score a goal, shoot at a goal** **1** **2**
	accomplish a goal, **share a** goal **3**
ADJ.	**winning** goal **1** **2**
	attainable goal, **main** goal **3**

goal|keeper /goʊlkipər/ (**goalkeepers**)
NOUN SPORTS A **goalkeeper** is the player on a sports team whose job is to guard the goal.

goal|less /goʊllɪs/ **ADJECTIVE** SPORTS In soccer, a **goalless** game ends with no goals scored. ❑ Goalkeeper Antonin Kinsky played his first goalless game this season.

goal|post /ɡoʊlpoʊst/ (**goalposts**) NOUN
SPORTS A **goalpost** is one of the two wooden posts that form the goal in games such as soccer.

goat /ɡoʊt/ (**goats**) NOUN A **goat** is an animal that is about the size of a sheep. Goats have horns, and hairs on their chin that look like a beard.

gob|ble /ɡɒbəl/ (**gobbles, gobbling, gobbled**) VERB If you **gobble** food, or **gobble** it **up**, you eat it very quickly. ❑ *Pete hungrily gobbled up the rest of the sandwiches.*

god /ɡɒd/ (**gods**)
1 NOUN In many religions, **God** is the name given to the spirit that people believe created the world. ❑ *He believes in God.*
2 NOUN In many religions, **gods** are spirits that people believe have power over a particular part of the world or nature. ❑ *Poseidon was the Greek god of the sea.*

god|dess /ɡɒdɪs/ (**goddesses**) NOUN In many religions, a **goddess** is a female spirit that people believe to have power over a particular part of the world or nature. ❑ *There was a statue of a goddess in the temple.*

gog|gles /ɡɒɡəlz/ PLURAL NOUN Goggles are large glasses that fit closely to your face around your eyes to protect them. ❑ *...a pair of swimming goggles.*

going /ɡoʊɪŋ/
1 If something **is going to** happen, it will happen in the future. ❑ *I think it's going to be successful.* ❑ *You're going to enjoy this.*
2 You say that you **are going to** do something when you intend to do it. ❑ *I'm going to go to bed.* ❑ *He announced that he's going to resign.*

gold /ɡoʊld/
1 NONCOUNT NOUN **Gold** is a valuable, yellow-colored metal that is used for making jewelry, ornaments, and coins. ❑ *...a ring made of gold.* ❑ *The price of gold was going up.*
2 NONCOUNT NOUN **Gold** is jewelry and other things that are made of gold. ❑ *We handed over all our gold and money.*
3 ADJECTIVE Something that is **gold** is bright-yellow in color, and is often shiny. ❑ *He wore a black and gold shirt.*

gold|en /ɡoʊldən/
1 ADJECTIVE Something that is **golden** has a bright yellow color. ❑ *She combed her golden hair.*
2 ADJECTIVE **Golden** things are made of gold. ❑ *He wore a golden chain.*

gold|fish /ɡoʊldfɪʃ/ (**goldfish**) NOUN
Goldfish are small orange fish that people often keep as pets.

gold med|al (**gold medals**) NOUN A **gold medal** is an award made of gold metal that you get as first prize in a competition. ❑ *Her dream is to win a gold medal at the Winter Olympics.*

golf /ɡɒlf/ NONCOUNT NOUN SPORTS **Golf** is a game in which you use long sticks (= golf clubs) to hit a small, hard ball into holes. ❑ *Do you play golf?* ● **golf|er** (**golfers**) NOUN ❑ *He is one of the world's best golfers.* ● **golf|ing** NONCOUNT NOUN ❑ *You can play tennis or go golfing.*

golf club (**golf clubs**) NOUN SPORTS A **golf club** is a long, thin, metal stick with a piece of wood or metal at one end that you use to hit the ball when you play golf.

golf course (**golf courses**) NOUN SPORTS A **golf course** is a large area of grass where people play golf.

gone /ɡɔn/
1 **Gone** is a form of the verb **go**.
2 ADJECTIVE When someone is **gone**, they have left the place where you are and are no longer there. ❑ *Things were hard for her while he was gone.* ❑ *He's already been gone four hours!*

good /ɡʊd/ (**better, best**)
1 ADJECTIVE **Good** means pleasant or enjoyable. ❑ *We had a really good time.* ❑ *These people want a better life for their children.*
2 ADJECTIVE **Good** means of a high quality or level. ❑ *Good food is important for your health.* ❑ *Our customers want the best possible quality at a low price.*
3 ADJECTIVE A **good** place or time for an activity is a suitable place or time for it. ❑ *This room is a good place for relaxing and reading.*
4 ADJECTIVE A **good** idea, reason, or decision is a sensible one. ❑ *It's a good idea to keep your desk neat.* ❑ *There was a good reason for his strange behavior.*
5 ADJECTIVE If you are **good at** something, you are skillful at doing it. ❑ *I'm not very good at singing.*

g

6 **ADJECTIVE** A child who is **good** behaves well. ❑ *The children were very good.*

7 **ADJECTIVE** Someone who is **good** is kind and thoughtful. ❑ *You are good to me.*

8 **NOUN** Good is what people consider to be morally right. ❑ *They should know the difference between good and bad, right and wrong.*

9 **NOUN** If something is **no good**, it will not bring any success. ❑ *I asked her to repeat the question, but it was no good–I couldn't understand her.* ❑ *It's no good worrying about it now.*

10 If something disappears **for good**, it never comes back. ❑ *These forests may be gone for good.*

→ look at **communication, feeling, job, movie, news, play, sense**

good after|noon You say "Good afternoon" when you see or speak to someone in the afternoon. [FORMAL]

good|bye /gʊdbaɪ/ (**goodbyes**) also **good-bye** You say "Goodbye" to someone when you or they are leaving a place, or at the end of a telephone conversation.

good eve|ning You say "Good evening" the first time you see or speak to someone in the evening. [FORMAL]

good guy (**good guys**) **NOUN** You can call the good characters in a movie or story the **good guys**. You can also talk about the **good guys** in a situation in real life. [INFORMAL] ❑ *We're the good guys in this situation.*

good-looking (**better-looking, best-looking**) **ADJECTIVE** Someone who is **good-looking** has an attractive face. ❑ *Katy noticed him because he was good-looking.*

good morn|ing You say "Good morning" the first time you see or speak to someone in the morning. [FORMAL]

good|ness /gʊdnɪs/ **NONCOUNT NOUN** Goodness is the quality of being kind, helpful, and honest. ❑ *He believes in human goodness.*

good night You say "Good night" to someone late in the evening before you go home or go to bed.

goods /gʊdz/ **PLURAL NOUN** Goods are things that you can buy or sell. ❑ *Companies sell goods or services.*

goof /guf/ (**goofs, goofing, goofed**) **NOUN** A **goof** is a small mistake. [INFORMAL] ❑ *There were a few minor technical goofs.*

▶ **goof off** If someone **goofs off**, they waste time and do nothing. [INFORMAL] ❑ *I goofed off all day.*

Google /guɡəl/ (**Googles, Googling, Googled**) **1** **NONCOUNT NOUN** TECHNOLOGY **Google** is a computer program that you can use to search for information on the Internet. [TRADEMARK] ❑ *Why don't you look him up on Google?* **2** **VERB** TECHNOLOGY If you **Google** information, you search for it on the Internet using Google. [TRADEMARK] ❑ *We googled her name, and found her website.*

goose /gus/ (**geese**) **NOUN** A **goose** is a large bird that has a long neck. ❑ *The Canada Goose is a beautiful bird.*

gor|geous /gɔrdʒəs/ **ADJECTIVE** Someone or something that is **gorgeous** is very pleasant or attractive. [INFORMAL] ❑ *It's a gorgeous day.* ❑ *You look gorgeous.*

go|ril|la /gərɪlə/ (**gorillas**) **NOUN** A **gorilla** is a very large animal with long arms, black fur, and a black face.

gos|pel /gɒspəl/ **NONCOUNT NOUN** MUSIC **Gospel** or **gospel music** is a style of religious music. ❑ *I used to sing gospel.*

gos|sip /gɒsɪp/ (**gossips, gossiping, gossiped**) **1** **NONCOUNT NOUN** Gossip is informal conversation about other people. ❑ *There has been gossip about the reasons for his absence.* **2** **VERB** If you **gossip**, you talk in an informal way, especially about other people or local events. ❑ *They sat at the kitchen table gossiping.*

got /gɒt/ **1** Got is a form of the verb **get**. **2** You use **have got** to say that you have a particular thing. ❑ *I've got a coat just like this.* **3** You use **have got to** when you are saying that something must happen. ❑ *I'm not happy with the situation, but I've got to accept it.*

got|ten /gɒtən/ **Gotten** is a form of the verb **get**.

gov|ern /gʌvərn/ (**governs, governing, governed**) **VERB** SOCIAL STUDIES To **govern** a country means to officially control and organize it. ❑ *The people choose who they want to govern their country.*

gov|ern|ment /gʌvərnmənt/ (**governments**) **NOUN** SOCIAL STUDIES The **government** is the group of people who control and organize a country, a state, or a

city. ❏ *The government has decided to make changes.* ● **gov|ern|men|tal** /gʌvərnmɛntᵊl/ **ADJECTIVE** **Governmental** means relating to a particular government. ❏ *She works for a governmental agency.*
→ look at **vote**

gov|er|nor /gʌvərnər/ (**governors**) **NOUN** SOCIAL STUDIES A **governor** is a person who is in charge of part of a country. ❏ *He was governor of Iowa.*
→ look at **vote**

gown /gaʊn/ (**gowns**)
1 **NOUN** A **gown** is a long dress that women wear on formal occasions. ❏ *She was wearing a ball gown.*
2 **NOUN** A **gown** is a loose black piece of clothing that students wear at their graduation ceremony (= the ceremony where they receive their degree). ❏ *He was wearing a university graduation gown.*

GPA /dʒi pi eɪ/ (**GPAs**) **NOUN** **GPA** is short for **grade point average**. ❏ *You need a good GPA to get into graduate school.*

grab /græb/ (**grabs, grabbing, grabbed**) **VERB** If you **grab** something, you take something suddenly and roughly. ❏ *I grabbed her hand.*

grace|ful /greɪsfəl/ **ADJECTIVE** Someone or something that is **graceful** moves in a smooth and attractive way. ❏ *His movements were smooth and graceful.* ● **grace|ful|ly** **ADVERB** ❏ *She stepped gracefully onto the stage.*

grad /græd/ (**grads**) **NOUN** A **grad** is a **graduate**. [INFORMAL]

grade /greɪd/ (**grades, grading, graded**)
1 **NOUN** A **grade** is a group of classes in a school where all the children are a similar age. ❏ *Mr. White teaches first grade.*
2 **NOUN** Your **grade** is the mark that a teacher gives you to show how good your work is. ❏ *The best grade you can get is an A.*
3 **VERB** If you **grade** something, you judge its quality. ❏ *Restaurants are graded according to the quality of the food and service.* ❏ *Teachers grade the students' work from A to F.*
4 **NOUN** The **grade** of a product is its level of quality. ❏ *The price of all grades of gasoline has gone up.*

grade point av|er|age (**grade point averages**) also **grade-point average** **NOUN** A student's **grade point average** is a measure of how good their work is, based on

an average of all the grades they receive. ❏ *She had the highest grade point average in the class.*

grad|ual /grædʒuəl/ **ADJECTIVE** A **gradual** change or process happens slowly, over a long period of time. ❏ *Losing weight is a gradual process.* ● **gradu|al|ly** /grædʒuəli/ **ADVERB** ❏ *We are gradually learning to use the new computer system.*

gradu|ate (**graduates, graduating, graduated**)

> **PRONUNCIATION HELP**
> Pronounce the noun /grædʒuɪt/.
> Pronounce the verb /grædʒueɪt/.

1 **NOUN** A **graduate** is a student who has completed a course at a high school, college, or university. ❏ *His parents are both college graduates.*
2 **VERB** When a student **graduates,** they complete their studies at school or university. ❏ *Her son just graduated from high school.*
→ look at **school**

gradua|tion /grædʒueɪʃᵊn/ (**graduations**) **NOUN** A **graduation** is a special ceremony for students when they have completed their studies at a university, college, or school. ❏ *Her parents came to her graduation.*

graf|fi|ti /grəfiti/ **NONCOUNT NOUN** **Graffiti** is words or pictures that people write or draw on walls or in public places. ❏ *There was graffiti all over the walls.*

grain /greɪn/ (**grains**)
1 **NOUN** A **grain of** a particular crop is a single seed from it. ❏ *He was grateful for every single grain of rice.*
2 **NOUN** A **grain of** sand or salt is a tiny, hard piece of it. ❏ *How many grains of sand are there in the desert?*

gram /græm/ (**grams**) **NOUN** MATH SCIENCE A **gram** is a unit of weight. There are one thousand grams in a kilogram. ❏ *A soccer ball weighs about 400 grams.*

gram|mar /græmər/ **NONCOUNT NOUN** LANGUAGE ARTS **Grammar** is a set of rules for a language that describes how words go together to form sentences. ❏ *You need to know the basic rules of grammar.*
→ look at Word World: **grammar**
→ look at **language**

g

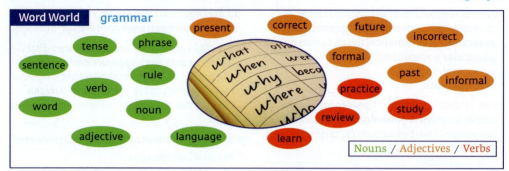

Word World grammar

present correct future incorrect

tense phrase formal

sentence rule past informal

verb practice

word noun study

adjective language review

learn

what other were becom where who

Nouns / Adjectives / Verbs

G

gram|mati|cal /grəmætɪkᵊl/
1 ADJECTIVE LANGUAGE ARTS **Grammatical** describes something that relates to grammar. ❏ *He studied a book of grammatical rules.*
2 ADJECTIVE LANGUAGE ARTS If language is **grammatical**, it is correct because it obeys the rules of grammar. ❏ *We want to see if students can write grammatical English.*

grand /grænd/ (**grander, grandest**)
ADJECTIVE If a building or a place is **grand**, its size or appearance is very impressive. ❏ *The courthouse is a grand building in the center of town.*

grand|child /græntʃaɪld/ (**grandchildren**)
NOUN Someone's **grandchild** is the child of their son or daughter. ❏ *You're grandma's favorite grandchild.*

grand|daughter /grændɔtər/
(**granddaughters**) **NOUN** Someone's **granddaughter** is the daughter of their son or daughter. ❏ *This is my granddaughter, Amelia.*

grand|father /grænfɑðər/ (**grandfathers**)
NOUN Your **grandfather** is the father of your father or mother. ❏ *His grandfather was a professor.*
→ look at **family**

grand|ma /grænmɑ/ (**grandmas**) **NOUN**
Your **grandma** is your grandmother.
[INFORMAL] ❏ *Grandma was from Scotland.*

grand|mother /grænmʌðər/
(**grandmothers**) **NOUN** Your **grandmother** is the mother of your father or mother. ❏ *My grandmothers were both teachers.*
→ look at **family**

grand|pa /grænpɑ/ (**grandpas**) **NOUN** Your **grandpa** is your grandfather. [INFORMAL]
❏ *Grandpa was sitting in the yard.*

grand|parent /grænpɛərənt, -pær-/
(**grandparents**) **NOUN** Your **grandparents** are the parents of your father or mother.
❏ *Tammy lives with her grandparents.*

grand|son /grænsʌn/ (**grandsons**) **NOUN**
Someone's **grandson** is the son of their son or daughter. ❏ *My grandson's birthday was on Tuesday.*

gran|ny /græni/ (**grannies**) **NOUN** Granny
is an informal word for grandmother.
[INFORMAL] ❏ *I hugged my granny.*

gra|no|la /grənoʊlə/ **NONCOUNT NOUN**
Granola is a breakfast food that contains fruit and nuts. ❏ *I usually have granola for breakfast.*

grant /grænt/ (**grants, granting, granted**)
1 NOUN A **grant** is an amount of money that a government gives to a person or to an organization for a special purpose. ❏ *They got a grant to research the disease.*
2 VERB If someone **grants** you something, you are allowed to have it. [FORMAL] ❏ *France granted him political asylum.*
3 If someone **takes** you **for granted**, they do not show that they are grateful for anything that you do. ❏ *She feels that her family take her for granted.*

grape /greɪp/ (**grapes**) **NOUN** Grapes are
small green or purple fruit that grow in bunches. ❏ *I bought six oranges and a small bunch of grapes.*
→ look at **fruit**

grape|fruit /greɪpfrut/ (**grapefruit**)

> **LANGUAGE HELP**
> The plural can also be **grapefruits**.

NOUN A **grapefruit** is a large, round, yellow fruit that has a slightly sour taste.

graph /græf/ (**graphs**) **NOUN** MATH A **graph**
is a picture that shows the relationship

between sets of numbers or measurements. ❑ *The graph shows that prices went up about 20 percent last year.*

graph|ics /grǽfɪks/ **PLURAL NOUN** ARTS TECHNOLOGY **Graphics** are drawings, pictures, or symbols, especially when they are produced by a computer. ❑ *The game's graphics are very good, so you can see things clearly.*

grasp /grǽsp/ (**grasps, grasping, grasped**)
1 **VERB** If you **grasp** something, you take it in your hand and hold it very firmly. ❑ *He grasped both my hands.*
2 **NOUN** A **grasp** is a very firm hold or grip. ❑ *He took her hand in a firm grasp.*
3 **VERB** If you **grasp** something that is complicated, you understand it. ❑ *I don't think you have grasped how serious this problem is.*
4 **NOUN** A **grasp of** a subject is an understanding of it. ❑ *She has a good grasp of geometry.*

grass /grǽs/ **NONCOUNT NOUN** **Grass** is a plant with thin, green leaves that cover the surface of the ground. ❑ *We sat on the grass and ate our picnic.*
→ look at **plant**

grass|hopper /grǽshɒpər/ (**grasshoppers**) **NOUN** A **grasshopper** is an insect that jumps high into the air and makes a sound with its long back legs.

grassy /grǽsi/ (**grassier, grassiest**) **ADJECTIVE** A **grassy** area of land is covered in grass. ❑ *...a grassy hillside.*

grate|ful /greɪtfəl/ **ADJECTIVE** If you are **grateful for** something that someone gives you or does for you, you feel glad and you want to thank them. ❑ *She was grateful to him for being so helpful.* ● **grate|ful|ly** **ADVERB** ❑ *He said that any help would be gratefully received.*

grati|tude /grǽtɪtud/ **NONCOUNT NOUN** **Gratitude** is the feeling you have when you want to thank someone. ❑ *He expressed gratitude to everyone for their help.*

grave /greɪv/ (**graves, graver, gravest**)
1 **NOUN** A **grave** is a place where a dead person is buried. ❑ *They visit her grave twice a year.*
2 **ADJECTIVE** A **grave** event or situation is very serious and important. ❑ *These weapons are a grave danger to the world.*

grave|yard /greɪvyɑrd/ (**graveyards**) **NOUN** A **graveyard** is an area of land where dead

people are buried. ❑ *They went to the graveyard to put flowers on her grave.*

grav|ity /grǽvɪti/ **NONCOUNT NOUN** SCIENCE **Gravity** is the force that makes things fall to the ground. ❑ *The force of gravity pulls everything down.*
→ look at **earth**

gra|vy /greɪvi/ **NONCOUNT NOUN** **Gravy** is a sauce made from the juices that come from meat when it cooks.

gray /greɪ/ (**grayer, grayest**)
1 **ADJECTIVE** Something that is **gray** is a mixture of black and white, like the color of clouds on a rainy day. ❑ *...a gray suit.*
2 **NOUN** **Gray** is also a noun. ❑ *Expect to see more grays and browns this fall.*
→ look at **hair**

grease /gris/
1 **NONCOUNT NOUN** **Grease** is a thick substance like oil. ❑ *His hands were covered in grease.*
2 **NONCOUNT NOUN** **Grease** is animal fat that is produced when you cook meat. ❑ *I could smell bacon grease.*

greasy /grisi, -zi/ (**greasier, greasiest**) **ADJECTIVE** Something that is **greasy** has grease on it or in it. ❑ *He wiped the greasy counter.*

great /greɪt/ (**greater, greatest**)
1 **ADJECTIVE** **Great** or **great big** describes something that is very large. ❑ *She had a great big smile on her face.*
2 **ADJECTIVE** **Great** means large in amount or degree. ❑ *She lived to a great age.* ● **great|ly** **ADVERB** [FORMAL] ❑ *He will be greatly missed.*
3 **ADJECTIVE** **Great** describes someone or something that is important, famous, or exciting. ❑ *They made great scientific discoveries.* ❑ *He has the ability to be a great player.*
● **great|ness** **NONCOUNT NOUN** ❑ *She dreamed of achieving greatness.*
4 **EXCLAMATION** If something is **great**, it is very good. ❑ *I thought it was a great idea.* ❑ *Oh great! You made a cake.*

greed /grid/ **NONCOUNT NOUN** **Greed** is the feeling that you want to have more of something than you need. ❑ *People say that the world economy is based on greed.*

greedy /gridi/ (**greedier, greediest**) **ADJECTIVE** If someone is **greedy**, they want to have more of something than they need.

g

❑ *They still want more money? I think that's a bit greedy.* ● **greedi|ly** ADVERB ❑ *He raised the bottle to his lips and drank greedily.*

green /griːn/ (**greener, greenest, greens**)

1 ADJECTIVE Something that is **green** is the color of grass or leaves. ❑ *She wore a green dress.*

2 NOUN **Green** is also a noun. ❑ *I've never looked good in green.*

3 ADJECTIVE **Green** ideas and organizations relate to the protection of the environment. ❑ *...the Green Party.*

→ look at **color, tree**

green|house /griːnhaʊs/ (**greenhouses**)

NOUN A **greenhouse** is a glass building where you grow plants to protect them from bad weather.

→ look at **farm**

green|house ef|fect NOUN SCIENCE The **greenhouse effect** is the problem of the Earth's temperature getting higher because of the gases that go into the air. ❑ *Carbon dioxide is one of the gases that contribute to the greenhouse effect.*

→ look at Word World: **greenhouse effect**

green|house gas (**greenhouse gases**)

NOUN SCIENCE **Greenhouse gases** are the gases that cause a gradual rise in the Earth's temperature. The main greenhouse gas is carbon dioxide. ❑ *They signed an international agreement to limit greenhouse gases.*

→ look at **greenhouse effect**

greet /griːt/ (**greets, greeting, greeted**) VERB When you **greet** someone, you say "Hello" or shake hands with them. ❑ *She greeted him when he came in from school.*

greet|ing /griːtɪŋ/ (**greetings**) NOUN A **greeting** is something friendly that you say or do when you meet someone. ❑ *We exchanged friendly greetings.*

grew /gruː/ **Grew** is a form of the verb **grow**.

grid /grɪd/ (**grids**) NOUN A **grid** is a pattern of straight lines that cross over each other to make squares. On maps, you can use the grid to help you find a particular thing or place. ❑ *The number puzzle uses a grid of nine squares.*

grief /griːf/ NONCOUNT NOUN **Grief** is a feeling of great sadness. ❑ *We all experience grief at some point in our lives.*

grieve /griːv/ (**grieves, grieving, grieved**) VERB If you **grieve over** something, especially someone's death, you feel very sad about it. ❑ *He's grieving over his dead wife.*

grill /grɪl/ (**grills, grilling, grilled**)

1 NOUN A **grill** is a flat frame of metal bars that you can use to cook food over a fire. ❑ *We cooked the fish on a grill over the fire.*

2 VERB When you **grill** food, or when it **grills**, you cook it on metal bars above a fire or barbecue. ❑ *Grill the steaks for about 5 minutes each side.*

→ look at **cook, meat**

grin /grɪn/ (**grins, grinning, grinned**)

1 VERB When you **grin**, you have a big smile on your face. ❑ *He grinned with pleasure.* ❑ *Phillip grinned at her.*

2 NOUN A **grin** is a broad smile. ❑ *She had a big grin on her face.*

grind /graɪnd/ (**grinds, grinding, ground**) VERB If you **grind** a substance, you rub it against something hard until it becomes a fine powder. ❑ *Grind some pepper into the sauce.*

grip /grɪp/ (**grips, gripping, gripped**)

1 VERB If you **grip** something, you take it with your hand and hold it firmly. ❑ *She gripped the rope.*

2 NOUN A **grip** is a firm, strong hold on something. ❑ *Keep a tight grip on your purse.*

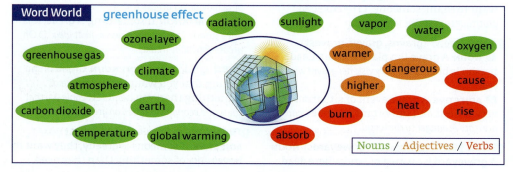

Word World — greenhouse effect

radiation, sunlight, vapor, water, ozone layer, greenhouse gas, climate, atmosphere, carbon dioxide, earth, temperature, global warming, warmer, higher, dangerous, oxygen, cause, burn, heat, rise, absorb

Nouns / Adjectives / Verbs

groan /groʊn/ (**groans, groaning, groaned**)
 1 **VERB** If you **groan**, you make a long, low sound because you are feeling pain, or because you are unhappy about something. ❑ *He began to groan with pain.* ❑ *The man on the floor was groaning.*
 2 **NOUN** **Groan** is also a noun. ❑ *I heard a groan from the crowd.*

gro|cery /groʊsəri, groʊsri/ (**groceries**)
 1 **NOUN** A **grocery** or a **grocery store** is a store that sells food. ❑ *I went to the grocery store to buy some milk.*
 2 **PLURAL NOUN** **Groceries** are the things that you buy at a grocery or at a supermarket. ❑ *...a small bag of groceries.*

groom /grum/ (**grooms, grooming, groomed**)
 1 **NOUN** A **groom** is a person whose job is to look after horses.
 2 **VERB** If you **groom** an animal, you clean its fur, usually by brushing it. ❑ *She groomed the horses regularly.*

groove /gruv/ (**grooves**) **NOUN** A **groove** is a deep line that is cut into a surface. ❑ *He used a knife to cut a groove in the stick.*

gross /groʊs/ (**grosser, grossest**) **ADJECTIVE** Someone or something that is **gross** is very unpleasant. [INFORMAL] ❑ *Some scenes in the movie were really gross.*

gross na|tion|al prod|uct (**gross national products**) **NOUN** SOCIAL STUDIES A country's **gross national product** is the total value of all its income in a particular year.

grouch /graʊtʃ/ (**grouches**) **NOUN** A **grouch** is someone who is always complaining. [INFORMAL] ❑ *Sorry to be such a grouch.*

ground /graʊnd/
 1 **NOUN** The **ground** is the surface of the Earth or the floor of a room. ❑ *They are sitting on the ground.* ❑ *Jack fell to the ground.*
 2 **PLURAL NOUN** The **grounds** of a large building are the area of land that surrounds it. ❑ *... the palace grounds.*

ground|hog /graʊndhɔg/ (**groundhogs**) **NOUN** A **groundhog** is a small animal with red or brown fur that is found in North America.

group /grup/ (**groups**)
 1 **NOUN** A **group of** people or things is a number of them that are together. ❑ *A small group of people stood on the street corner.*
 2 **NOUN** A **group** is a number of people who play music together. ❑ *He played guitar in a rock group.*

grow /groʊ/ (**grows, growing, grew, grown**)
 1 **VERB** When someone or something **grows**, they gradually become bigger. ❑ *All children grow at different rates.*
 2 **VERB** If a plant or tree **grows** in a particular place, it lives there. ❑ *There were roses growing by the side of the door.*
 3 **VERB** If you **grow** a particular type of plant, you put seeds or young plants in the ground and take care of them. ❑ *I always grow a few red onions.* ● **grow|er** (**growers**) **NOUN** ❑ *...apple growers.*
 4 **VERB** When your hair or nails **grow**, they gradually become longer. ❑ *My hair grows really fast.*
 → look at **tree**
 ▶ **grow out of** **1** If you **grow out of** a type of behavior, you stop behaving in that way as you get older. ❑ *Most children who bite their nails grow out of it.*
 2 When a child **grows out of** a piece of clothing, they become too big to wear it. ❑ *You've grown out of your shoes again.*
 ▶ **grow up** When someone **grows up**, they gradually change from being a child into being an adult. ❑ *She grew up in Tokyo.*

growl /graʊl/ (**growls, growling, growled**)
 1 **VERB** When a dog or other animal **growls**, it makes a low noise in its throat, usually because it is angry. ❑ *The dog was growling and showing its teeth.*
 2 **NOUN** **Growl** is also a noun. ❑ *The animal gave a growl.*

grown /groʊn/ **ADJECTIVE** A **grown** man or woman is one who is fully developed. ❑ *Why do grown men love games so much?*

grown-up also **grownup** (**grown-ups**)
 1 **NOUN** **Grown-up** is a child's word for an adult ❑ *Jan's almost a grown-up now.*
 2 **ADJECTIVE** Someone who is **grown-up** is an adult and no longer depends on their parents or another adult. ❑ *She has two grown-up children who both live nearby.*

growth /groʊθ/
 1 **NONCOUNT NOUN** The **growth of** something is its development. ❑ *The city's population growth slowed to 1.6% last year.* ❑ *The government expects strong economic growth.*
 2 **NONCOUNT NOUN** The **growth** of a person, animal, or plant is the process of getting bigger. ❑ *Milk is important for a baby's growth and development.*

g

grudge /grʌdʒ/ (**grudges**) **NOUN** If you have a **grudge against** someone, you feel angry with them because of something they did in the past. ❏ *He seems to have a grudge against me.*

grum|ble /grʌmbᵊl/ (**grumbles, grumbling, grumbled**)

1 **VERB** If someone **grumbles**, they complain about something. ❏ *They grumble about how hard they have to work.* ❏ *Dad grumbled that we never cleaned our rooms.*

2 **NOUN** Grumble is also a noun. ❏ *The high prices have brought grumbles from some customers.*

grumpy /grʌmpi/ (**grumpier, grumpiest**) **ADJECTIVE** If someone is **grumpy**, they are a little angry. ❏ *He's getting grumpy and depressed.* ● **grumpi|ly** **ADVERB** ❏ *"Go away, I'm busy," said Ken grumpily.*

grunt /grʌnt/ (**grunts, grunting, grunted**)

1 **VERB** If you **grunt**, you make a low sound, especially because you are annoyed or not interested in something. ❏ *When I said hello he just grunted.* ❏ *"Huh," he grunted.*

2 **NOUN** Grunt is also a noun. ❏ *Barbara replied with a grunt.*

guar|an|tee /gærənti/ (**guarantees, guaranteeing, guaranteed**)

1 **VERB** If you **guarantee** something, you promise that it will happen. ❏ *We guarantee the safety of our products.* ❏ *I guarantee that you will enjoy this movie.*

2 **NOUN** Guarantee is also a noun. ❏ *He gave me a guarantee he would finish the job.*

3 **NOUN** A **guarantee** is a written promise by a company to repair a product or give you a new one if it has anything wrong with it. ❏ *Keep the guarantee in case something goes wrong.*

4 **VERB** If a company **guarantees** its product or work, they provide a guarantee for it. ❏ *All our computers are guaranteed for 12 months.*

guard /gɑrd/ (**guards, guarding, guarded**)

1 **VERB** If you **guard** a place, person, or object, you stand near them to watch and protect them. ❏ *Armed police guarded the court.*

2 **VERB** If you **guard** someone, you watch them and keep them in a particular place to stop them from escaping. ❏ *Marines with rifles guarded them.*

3 **NOUN** A **guard** is a soldier, or a police officer, who is guarding a particular place or person. ❏ *The prisoners attacked their guards.*

guard|ian /gɑrdiən/ (**guardians**) **NOUN** A **guardian** is someone who is legally responsible for another person, often a child. ❏ *Diana's grandmother was her legal guardian.*

guer|ril|la /gərɪlə/ (**guerrillas**) also **guerilla** **NOUN** A **guerrilla** is a person who fights for a military group that does not form part of the regular military. ❏ *Five soldiers were killed in a guerrilla attack.*

guess /gɛs/ (**guesses, guessing, guessed**)

1 **VERB** If you **guess** something, you give an answer or provide an opinion when you do not know if it is true. ❏ *Yvonne guessed that he was around 40 years old.* ❏ *Guess what I just did!*

2 **NOUN** A **guess** is an attempt to give an answer or provide an opinion when you do not know if it is true. ❏ *He made a guess at her age.* ❏ *If you don't know, just have a guess.*

guest /gɛst/ (**guests**)

1 **NOUN** A **guest** is someone who you invite to your home or to an event. ❏ *She was a guest at the wedding.*

2 **NOUN** A **guest** is someone who is staying in a hotel. ❏ *A few guests were having breakfast.*

guid|ance /gaɪdᵊns/ **NONCOUNT NOUN** **Guidance** is help and advice. ❏ *My tennis game improved under his guidance.*

guide /gaɪd/ (**guides, guiding, guided**)

1 **NOUN** A **guide** is a book or website that gives you information to help you do or understand something. ❏ *He found a step-by-step guide to building your own home.*

2 **NOUN** A **guide** is a book or website that gives tourists information about a town, area, or country. ❏ *The guide to Paris lists hotel rooms for as little as $35 a night.*

3 **NOUN** A **guide** is someone who shows tourists around places such as museums or cities. ❏ *A guide will take you on a tour of the city.*

4 **VERB** If you **guide** someone somewhere, you go there with them to show them the way. ❏ *He took her by the arm and guided her toward the door.*

guilt /gɪlt/

1 **NONCOUNT NOUN** **Guilt** is an unhappy feeling that you have when you think that you have done something wrong. ❏ *She felt a lot of guilt about her children's unhappiness.*

2 **NONCOUNT NOUN** **Guilt** is the fact that you have done something wrong or illegal. ❏ *The jury was convinced of his guilt.*

guilty /gɪlti/ (**guiltier, guiltiest**)

1 **ADJECTIVE** If you feel **guilty**, you feel unhappy because you think that you have done something wrong. ❏ *I feel so guilty,*

leaving all this work to you. ● **guilti|ly** ADVERB
❏ *He looked up guiltily when I walked in.*
2 ADJECTIVE If someone is **guilty of** a crime or offense, they have done it. ❏ *They were found guilty of murder.*

guinea pig /gɪni pɪg/ (**guinea pigs**)
1 NOUN A **guinea pig** is a person who is used in an experiment. ❏ *The doctor used himself as a guinea pig in his research.*
2 NOUN A **guinea pig** is a small animal with fur and no tail. People often keep guinea pigs as pets.

gui|tar /gɪtɑr/ (**guitars**) NOUN MUSIC A **guitar** is a musical instrument with strings.
→ look at **musical instrument**

Word Builder | **guitarist**

ist ≈ **person who does this**
    art + ist = artist
    guitar + ist = guitarist
    journal + ist = journalist
    novel + ist = novelist

---

gui|tar|ist /gɪtɑrɪst/ (**guitarists**) NOUN
MUSIC A **guitarist** is a person who plays the guitar. ❏ *He's one of the world's best jazz guitarists.*

gulf /gʌlf/ (**gulfs**) NOUN GEOGRAPHY A **gulf** is a large area of ocean that has land almost all the way around it. ❏ *A storm is crossing the Gulf of Mexico.*

gulp /gʌlp/ (**gulps, gulping, gulped**)
1 VERB If you **gulp** something, you eat or drink it very quickly. ❏ *She gulped her soda.*
2 NOUN A **gulp of** air, food, or drink is a large amount of it that you swallow. ❏ *She took a gulp of fresh air.*

gum /gʌm/ (**gums**)
1 NONCOUNT NOUN **Gum** is a sweet sticky substance that you keep in your mouth for a long time but do not swallow. ❏ *I do not chew gum in public.*
2 NOUN SCIENCE Your **gums** are the areas of firm, pink flesh inside your mouth, where your teeth grow. ❏ *Gently brush your teeth and gums.*

gun /gʌn/ (**guns**) NOUN A **gun** is a weapon that shoots bullets. ❏ *He pointed the gun at the police officer.*

gun|fire /gʌnfaɪr/ NONCOUNT NOUN **Gunfire** is the repeated shooting of guns. ❏ *We heard the sound of gunfire.*

gun|man /gʌnmən/ (**gunmen**) NOUN A **gunman** is a criminal who uses a gun.
❏ *A gunman fired at police.*

gush /gʌʃ/ (**gushes, gushing, gushed**)
1 VERB When liquid **gushes**, it flows very quickly and strongly. ❏ *Gallons of water gushed out of the tank.*
2 NOUN A **gush of** liquid is an amount of it that suddenly flows out of a place. ❏ *I heard a gush of water.*

gust /gʌst/ (**gusts**) NOUN A **gust** is a short, strong, sudden rush of wind. ❏ *A gust of wind came down the valley.*

gut /gʌt/ (**guts**)
1 NOUN SCIENCE The **gut** is the tube inside the body of a person or animal that food passes through after it has been in the stomach. ❏ *The food then passes into the gut.*
2 NOUN If you have the **guts** to do something that is difficult or unpleasant, you have the courage to do it. [INFORMAL]
❏ *She has the guts to say what she thinks.*

gut|ter /gʌtər/ (**gutters**)
1 NOUN The **gutter** is the edge of a road, where water collects and flows away when it rains. ❏ *His hat fell into the gutter.*
2 NOUN A **gutter** is a pipe under the edge of a roof that carries water away when it rains. ❏ *We need to fix the gutters.*

guy /gaɪ/ (**guys**) NOUN A **guy** is a man.
[INFORMAL] ❏ *I was working with a guy from Milwaukee.*

gym /dʒɪm/ (**gyms**) NOUN SPORTS A **gym** is a club, a building, or a large room with equipment for doing physical exercises.
❏ *I go to the gym twice a week.*
→ look at **bag**

gym|na|sium /dʒɪmneɪziəm/ (**gymnasiums** or **gymnasia** /dʒɪmneɪziə/) NOUN SPORTS
A **gymnasium** is the same as a **gym**. [FORMAL]

gym|nas|tics /dʒɪmnæstɪks/ NONCOUNT
NOUN SPORTS **Gymnastics** is a sport that consists of physical exercises that develop your strength and your ability to move easily. ❏ *The women's gymnastics team won a silver medal.*

Hh

ha /hɑ/ **EXCLAMATION** People say "**ha**" to show that they are surprised, annoyed, or pleased. ❑ *"Ha!" said James. "Did you really believe me?"*

hab|it /hæbɪt/ (**habits**)
  1 **NOUN** A **habit** is something that you do often or regularly. ❑ *He has many bad habits, such as biting his nails.*
  2 If you **are in the habit of** doing something, you do it regularly. ❑ *They were in the habit of watching TV every night.*

habi|tat /hæbɪtæt/ (**habitats**) **NOUN**
SCIENCE The **habitat** of an animal or a plant is the environment in which it lives or grows. ❑ *In its natural habitat, the plant will grow up to 25 feet.*
→ look at **conservation**

had /hæd/ **Had** is a form of the verb **have**.

hadn't /hædᵊnt/ **Hadn't** is short for "had not."

ha ha **EXCLAMATION** You write **ha ha** to show the sound that people make when they laugh. ❑ *"Ha ha!" he laughed.*

hail /heɪl/ **NONCOUNT NOUN** **SCIENCE** **Hail** is small balls of ice that fall like rain from the sky. ❑ *There will be storms with heavy rain and hail.*

hair /hɛər/ (**hairs**)
  1 **NONCOUNT NOUN** Your **hair** is the fine threads that grow on your head. ❑ *I wash my hair every night.*

2 **NOUN** **Hair** is the short threads that grow on the bodies of humans and animals. ❑ *Most men have hair on their chest.* ❑ *There were dog hairs all over the sofa.*
→ look at Picture Dictionary: **hair**

Word Partners	Use **hair** with:
ADJ.	**black** hair, **blonde** hair, **brown** hair, **curly** hair, **gray** hair, **straight** hair, **wavy** hair **1**
V.	**bleach** *your* hair, **brush** *your* hair, **comb** *your* hair, **color** *your* hair, **cut** *your* hair, **do** *your* hair, **dry** *your* hair, **fix** *your* hair, **lose** *your* hair, **pull** *someone's* hair, **wash** *your* hair **1**

hair|cut /hɛərkʌt/ (**haircuts**) **NOUN** If you get a **haircut**, someone cuts your hair for you. ❑ *You need a haircut.*

hair|dresser /hɛərdrɛsər/ (**hairdressers**)
NOUN A **hairdresser** is a person whose job is to cut and style people's hair. ❑ *She works as a hairdresser.*

hair|style /hɛərstaɪl/ (**hairstyles**) **NOUN**
Your **hairstyle** is the style in which your hair has been cut or arranged. ❑ *I think her new hairstyle looks great.*

hairy /hɛəri/ (**hairier, hairiest**) **ADJECTIVE**
Someone or something that is **hairy** is covered with hairs. ❑ *He was wearing shorts that showed his hairy legs.*

Picture Dictionary   hair

beard   braid   pigtails   ponytail   bangs   straight hair   curly hair   wavy hair

short hair   long hair   blonde   brown   black   red   gray

H

half /hæf/ (halves /hævz/)

1 MATH **Half of** a number, an amount, or an object is one of two equal parts. ❑ *More than half of all U.S. houses are heated with gas.*

2 MATH You use **half a**, **half an**, or **half the** to talk about one of two equal parts of the thing mentioned. ❑ *We sat and talked for half an hour.* ❑ *They only received half the money.*

3 ADJECTIVE **Half** is also an adjective. ❑ *I'll stay with you for the first half hour.*

4 ADVERB You use **half** to say that something is only partly in the state that you are describing. ❑ *The glass was half empty.*

half-hour (half-hours) NOUN A half-hour is a period of thirty minutes. ❑ *The talk was followed by a half-hour of discussion.*

half|time /hæftaɪm/ NONCOUNT NOUN

SPORTS **Halftime** is the period between the two parts of a sports event, when the players take a short rest. ❑ *We bought something to eat during halftime.*

half|way /hæfweɪ/

1 ADVERB **Halfway** means in the middle of a place or between two points. ❑ *He was halfway up the ladder.*

2 ADVERB **Halfway** means in the middle of an event or period of time. ❑ *We were more than halfway through our tour.*

hall /hɔl/ (halls)

1 NOUN The **hall** in a house or an apartment is the area that connects one room to another. ❑ *The hall leads to a large living room.*

2 NOUN A **hall** is a large room or a building that is used for public events such as concerts and meetings. ❑ *We went into the dance hall.*
→ look at **house**

Hal|low|een /hæloʊwin/ also Hallowe'en

NONCOUNT NOUN **Halloween** is the night of October 31st when children wear special clothes, and walk from house to house asking for candy.

hall|way /hɔlweɪ/ (hallways) NOUN A **hallway** in a building is an area with doors that lead into other rooms. ❑ *They walked along the quiet hallway.*

halt /hɔlt/ (halts, halting, halted)

1 VERB When someone **halts** something, they stop it. ❑ *Officials halted the race at 5:30 p.m. yesterday.*

2 If someone or something **comes to a halt**, they stop moving. ❑ *The elevator came to a halt at the first floor.*

halves /hævz/ **Halves** is the plural of **half**.

ham /hæm/ NONCOUNT NOUN **Ham** is meat from a pig that has been prepared with salt and spices. ❑ *We had ham sandwiches for lunch.*

ham|burg|er /hæmbɜrgər/ (hamburgers)

NOUN A **hamburger** is a type of food made from small pieces of meat that have been shaped into a flat circle. Hamburgers are fried or grilled and are often eaten in a round piece of bread (called a roll).
→ look at **meat**

ham|mer /hæmər/ (hammers, hammering, hammered)

1 NOUN A **hammer** is a tool that is made from a heavy piece of metal attached to the end of a handle. It is used for hitting nails into wood. ❑ *She got a hammer and a nail and two pieces of wood.*

2 VERB If you **hammer** an object such as a nail, you hit it with a hammer. ❑ *She hammered a nail into the window frame.*

ham|per /hæmpər/ (hampers, hampering, hampered)

1 NOUN A **hamper** is a large container with a cover for dirty clothes. ❑ *He threw the dirty sheets into the hamper.*

2 VERB If someone or something **hampers** you, they make it difficult for you to do what you are trying to do. ❑ *The bad weather hampered the rescue operation.*

ham|ster /hæmstər/ (hamsters) NOUN

A **hamster** is a small animal that is similar to a mouse, that is often kept as a pet.

hand /hænd/ (hands, handing, handed)

1 NOUN Your **hands** are the parts of your body at the end of your arms that you use for holding things. ❑ *I put my hand into my pocket and took out the letter.*

2 NOUN If you ask someone for **a hand** with something, you are asking them to help you. ❑ *Come and give me a hand in the kitchen.*

3 NOUN The **hands** of a clock or a watch are the long thin parts that move to show the time.

4 VERB If you **hand** something **to** someone, you put it into their hand. ❑ *He handed me a piece of paper.*

5 If you make something **by hand**, you do it using your hands rather than a machine. ❑ *The dress was made by hand.*

h

Picture Dictionary   hand

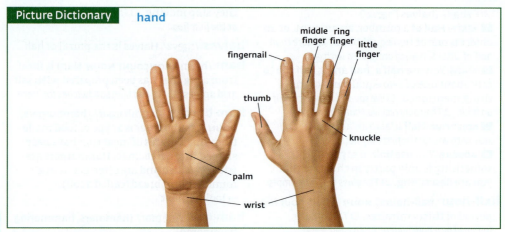

6 If two people are **walking hand in hand**, they are holding each other by the hand. ❑ *They go everywhere hand in hand.*

7 If someone or something is **on hand**, they are near and ready to be used. ❑ *There are experts on hand to give you all the help you need.*

8 You use **on the one hand** to talk about the first of two different ways of looking at something. ❑ *On the one hand, the body cannot survive without fat. On the other hand, if the body has too much fat, our health starts to suffer.*

9 You use **on the other hand** to introduce the second of two opposite ways of looking at something. ❑ *The movie lost money. Reviews, on the other hand, were mostly favorable.*

10 If a person or a situation **gets out of hand**, you are no longer able to control them. ❑ *The argument got out of hand when her boyfriend hit her.*

→ look at Picture Dictionary: **hand**

→ look at **body, time**

▶ **hand in** If you **hand in** something, you take it to someone and give it to them. ❑ *I need to hand in my homework today.* ❑ *They found $7,500 in cash on the street and handed it in to police.*

▶ **hand out** If you **hand** things **out**, you give one to each person in a group. ❑ *My job was to hand out the prizes.*

hand|bag /hændbæg/ (**handbags**) **NOUN** A **handbag** is a small bag that a woman uses for carrying things such as money and keys.

→ look at **bag**

hand|book /hændbʊk/ (**handbooks**) **NOUN** A **handbook** is a book that gives you advice and instructions about a particular subject. ❑ *The staff handbook says we get two weeks of vacation.*

hand|cuff /hændkʌf/ (**handcuffs, handcuffing, handcuffed**)

1 **PLURAL NOUN** **Handcuffs** are two connected metal rings that can be locked around someone's wrists. ❑ *He was taken to prison in handcuffs.*

2 **VERB** If you **handcuff** someone, you put handcuffs around their wrists. ❑ *Police tried to handcuff him but he ran away.*

hand|ful /hændfʊl/ (**handfuls**)

1 **NOUN** A **handful of** people or things is a small number of them. ❑ *Only a handful of people knew his secret.*

2 **NOUN** A **handful of** something is the amount that you can hold in your hand. ❑ *She threw a handful of sand into the water.*

handi|capped /hændikæpt/ **ADJECTIVE** Someone who is **handicapped** has a physical or mental condition that makes them unable to do certain things. ❑ *She works with handicapped children.*

→ look at **disability**

hand|ker|chief /hæŋkərtʃɪf/ (**handkerchiefs**) **NOUN** A **handkerchief** is a small square piece of cloth that you use for blowing your nose.

han|dle /hænd³l/ (**handles, handling, handled**)

1 **NOUN** A **handle** is an object that is attached to a door or drawer, used for opening and closing it. ❑ *I turned the handle and the door opened.*

2 **NOUN** A **handle** is the part of a tool, a bag, or a cup, that you hold. ❑ *I held the knife handle tightly.*

3 **VERB** If you **handle** a situation, you deal with it. ❑ *I think I handled the meeting very badly.*

4 **VERB** When you **handle** something, you hold it or move it with your hands. ❏ *Wash your hands before handling food.*

hand|made /hǽndmeɪd/ also **hand-made**
ADJECTIVE **Handmade** objects have been made by someone without using machines. ❏ *The store sells beautiful handmade jewelry.*

hand|out /hǽndaʊt/ (**handouts**) **NOUN**
A **handout** is a piece of paper containing information that is given to people in a meeting or a class. ❏ *The instructions are all written in the handout.*

hand|shake /hǽndʃeɪk/ (**handshakes**)
NOUN If you give someone a **handshake**, you take their right hand with your own right hand and move it up and down as a way of greeting them or showing that you have agreed about something. ❏ *He has a strong handshake.*

hand|some /hǽnsəm/ **ADJECTIVE** A **handsome** man has an attractive face. ❏ *The photo showed a tall, handsome soldier.*

hand|writing /hǽndraɪtɪŋ/ **NONCOUNT**
NOUN Your **handwriting** is your style of writing with a pen or a pencil. ❏ *The address was in Anna's handwriting.*

handy /hǽndi/ (**handier, handiest**)
1 **ADJECTIVE** Something that is **handy** is useful. ❏ *The book gives handy ideas on growing plants.*
2 **ADJECTIVE** A thing or place that is **handy** is nearby and easy to reach. ❏ *Make sure you have a pencil and paper handy.*

hang /hǽŋ/ (**hangs, hanging, hung** or **hanged**)

> **LANGUAGE HELP**
> Use **hangs, hanging, hanged** for meaning **3**.

1 **VERB** If something **hangs** somewhere, it is attached there so that it does not touch the ground. ❏ *Flags hang at every entrance.*
2 **VERB** If you **hang** something somewhere, you attach it there so that it does not touch the ground. ❏ *She hung her clothes outside to dry.*
3 **VERB** If someone **is hanged**, they are killed by having a rope tied around their neck. ❏ *The five men were hanged on Tuesday.*
▶ **hang on** **1** If you ask someone to **hang on**, you want them to wait. [INFORMAL] ❏ *Can you hang on for a minute?*
2 If you **hang on to** or **hang onto** something, you hold it very tightly.

❏ *He hung on to the rail as he went downstairs.*
→ look at **wear**
▶ **hang out** If you **hang out** in a particular place or area, you spend a lot of time there. [INFORMAL] ❏ *I often hang out at the mall.*
▶ **hang up** If you **hang up**, you end a phone call. ❏ *Don't hang up on me!*

hap|pen /hǽpən/ (**happens, happening, happened**)
1 **VERB** Something that **happens** takes place without being planned. ❏ *We don't know what will happen.*
2 **VERB** When something **happens to** you, it takes place and affects you. ❏ *What's the worst thing that has ever happened to you?*
3 **VERB** If you **happen to** do something, you do it by chance. ❏ *I happened to be at the library at the same time as Jim.*

hap|pi|ly /hǽpɪli/ **ADVERB** If you add **happily** to something you say, it shows that you are glad that something happened. ❏ *Happily, this situation will soon get much easier.*

hap|py /hǽpi/ (**happier, happiest**)
1 **ADJECTIVE** Someone who is **happy** feels pleased and satisfied. ❏ *Marina was a happy child.* ● **hap|pi|ly** **ADVERB** ❏ *The children played happily together all day.* ● **hap|pi|ness**
NONCOUNT NOUN ❏ *I think she was looking for happiness.*
2 **ADJECTIVE** A **happy** time, place, or relationship is full of happy feelings and pleasant experiences. ❏ *She had a very happy childhood.* ❏ *Grandma's house was always a happy place.*
3 **ADJECTIVE** If you are **happy to** do something, you are very willing to do it. ❏ *I'm happy to answer any questions.*
4 **ADJECTIVE** **Happy** is used in some expressions to say that you hope someone will enjoy a special occasion. ❏ *Happy Birthday!*
→ look at **feeling, relax**

har|bor /hɑ́rbər/ (**harbors**) **NOUN** A **harbor** is an area of water next to the land where boats can safely stay. ❏ *The fishing boats left the harbor and went out to sea.*

hard /hɑ́rd/ (**harder, hardest**)
1 **ADJECTIVE** Something that is **hard** feels very firm, and is not easily bent, cut, or broken. ❏ *The glass hit the hard wooden floor.*
2 **ADJECTIVE** Something that is **hard** is very difficult to do or deal with. ❏ *That's a very hard question.* ❏ *She's had a hard life.*

h

3 ADVERB If you work **hard**, you work with a lot of effort. ❏ *If I work hard, I'll finish the job tomorrow.*

4 ADJECTIVE **Hard** is also an adjective. ❏ *I admire him because he's a hard worker.*
→ look at **play**

hard disk (hard disks) **NOUN** TECHNOLOGY
A computer's **hard disk** is the part inside it where information and programs are stored.

hard drive (hard drives) **NOUN** TECHNOLOGY
The **hard drive** on a computer is the part that contains the computer's hard disk. ❏ *You can download music to your hard drive.*

hard|ly /hɑrdli/
1 ADVERB You use **hardly** to say that something is almost, or only just true. ❏ *I hardly know you.* ❏ *I've hardly slept for three days.*
2 ADVERB You use **hardly** in expressions such as **hardly ever** and **hardly any** to mean almost never or almost none. ❏ *We hardly ever eat fish.* ❏ *They hire young workers with hardly any experience.*

hard|ware /hɑrdwɛər/
1 NONCOUNT NOUN TECHNOLOGY In computer systems, **hardware** is things such as the computer, the keyboard, and the screen, rather than the software programs that tell the computer what to do. Compare with **software**. ❏ *The hardware costs about $200.*
2 NONCOUNT NOUN **Hardware** is tools and equipment that are used in the home and garden. ❏ *He bought a hammer and some nails at a hardware store.*

harm /hɑrm/ (harms, harming, harmed)
1 VERB To **harm** someone or something means to injure or damage them. ❏ *The boys didn't mean to harm anyone.* ❏ *This product may harm the environment.*
2 NONCOUNT NOUN **Harm** is injury or damage to a person or thing. ❏ *Don't worry. He won't do you any harm.*

harm|ful /hɑrmfəl/ **ADJECTIVE** Something that is **harmful** has a bad effect on someone or something. ❏ *People should know about the harmful effects of the sun.*
→ look at **pollution**

harm|less /hɑrmlɪs/ **ADJECTIVE** Something that is **harmless** does not have any bad effects. ❏ *These insects are harmless.*

har|mo|ny /hɑrməni/ (harmonies)
1 NONCOUNT NOUN If people are living in **harmony**, they are living together without harming anyone or anything. ❏ *People have lived in harmony with nature for centuries.*
2 NOUN MUSIC **Harmony** is the pleasant combination of different notes of music played at the same time. ❏ *The children were singing in harmony.*
→ look at **music**

harp /hɑrp/ (harps) **NOUN** MUSIC A **harp** is a large musical instrument that has strings stretched from the top to the bottom of a frame. You play the harp with your fingers.

harsh /hɑrʃ/ (harsher, harshest)
1 ADJECTIVE If something is **harsh**, it is hard and unpleasant. ❏ *We met during the first harsh winter after the war.*
2 ADJECTIVE **Harsh** actions or speech are unkind. ❏ *She said many harsh things about her brother.* ● **harsh|ly** **ADVERB** ❏ *He was harshly treated in prison.*
3 ADJECTIVE Something that is **harsh** is unpleasant because it is too hard, bright, or rough. ❏ *The leaves can burn badly in harsh sunlight.*

har|vest /hɑrvɪst/ (harvests, harvesting, harvested)
1 NOUN The **harvest** is the gathering of a farm crop. ❏ *Wheat harvests were poor in both Europe and America last year.*
2 VERB When you **harvest** a crop, you gather it in. ❏ *Farmers here still plant and harvest their crops by hand.*

has /hæz/ **Has** is a form of the verb **have**.

hasn't /hæzənt/ **Hasn't** is short for "has not."

haste /heɪst/ **NONCOUNT NOUN** **Haste** is when you do things too quickly. ❏ *He almost fell down the stairs in his haste to get to the phone.*

has|ty /heɪsti/ (hastier, hastiest) **ADJECTIVE** A **hasty** action is done suddenly or quickly. ❏ *Perhaps I was too hasty when I said she couldn't come.* ● **hasti|ly** /heɪstɪli/ **ADVERB** ❏ *A meeting was hastily arranged to discuss the problem.*

hat /hæt/ (hats) **NOUN** A **hat** is a thing that you wear on your head. ❏ *Look for a woman in a red hat.*

hatch /hætʃ/ (hatches, hatching, hatched)
VERB When a baby bird, an insect, or another animal **hatches**, it comes out of its egg by breaking the shell. You can also say that an egg **hatches**. ❏ *The young birds died soon after they hatched.* ❏ *The eggs hatch after a week.*

H

hate /heɪt/ (hates, hating, hated)
1 **VERB** If you **hate** someone or something, you have a strong feeling of dislike for them. ❑ *She thinks that everyone hates her.* ❑ *He hates losing.*
2 **NONCOUNT NOUN** Hate is also a noun. ❑ *He spoke of the hate that he felt for some people.*

haul /hɔl/ (hauls, hauling, hauled) **VERB** If you **haul** something somewhere, you move it using a lot of effort. ❑ *They hauled the car out of the water.*

haunt|ed /hɔntɪd/ **ADJECTIVE** A **haunted** building is a place where people believe ghosts (= spirits of dead people) appear. ❑ *Tracy said the house was haunted.*

---
have
① AUXILIARY VERB USES
② USED WITH NOUNS DESCRIBING ACTIONS
③ OTHER VERB USES AND PHRASES
④ MODAL PHRASES
---

① have /hv, həv, STRONG hæv/ (has, having, had)

> **LANGUAGE HELP**
> When you are speaking, you can use the short forms **I've** for **I have** and **hasn't** for **has not.**

VERB You use **have** and **has** with another verb to form the present perfect. ❑ *Alex hasn't left yet.* ❑ *What have you found?* ❑ *Frankie hasn't been feeling well today.*

② have /hæv/ (has, having, had) **VERB** You can use **have** with a noun to talk about an action or an event. ❑ *Come and have a look at this!* ❑ *We had a long talk last night.* ❑ *Come and have a meal with us tonight.* ❑ *We are having a meeting to decide what to do.* ❑ *I had an accident and broke my wrist.*

③ have /hæv/ (has, having, had)
1 **VERB** You use **have** to say that someone or something owns something. ❑ *Billy has a new bicycle.*
2 **VERB** You use **have** to talk about people's relationships. ❑ *Do you have any brothers or sisters?*
3 **VERB** You use **have** when you are talking about a person's appearance or character. ❑ *You have beautiful eyes.* ❑ *George has a terrible temper.*
4 **VERB** If you **have** something in a

particular position or state, it is in that position or state. ❑ *Mary had her eyes closed.*
5 **VERB** If you **have** something done, someone does it for you. ❑ *He had his hair cut yesterday.*
→ look at **disability, job**

④ have /hæv, hæf/ (has, having, had) You use **have to** when you are saying that someone must do something, or that something must happen. If you do not **have to** do something, it is not necessary for you to do it. ❑ *I have to go home soon.* ❑ *You have to tell me the truth.* ❑ *"You don't have to explain."*

haven't /hævᵊnt/ **Haven't** is short for "have not."

hawk /hɔk/ (hawks) **NOUN** A **hawk** is a large bird that catches and eats small birds and animals.

hay /heɪ/ **NONCOUNT NOUN** Hay is grass that has been cut and dried so that it can be used for feeding animals.
→ look at **farm**

haz|ard /hæzərd/ (hazards) **NOUN** A **hazard** is something that could be dangerous. ❑ *Too much salt may be a health hazard.*
→ look at **pollution**

HDTV /eɪtʃ di ti vi/ **NONCOUNT NOUN** **TECHNOLOGY** HDTV is a television system that provides a very clear image. **HDTV** is short for "high-definition television." ❑ *The quality of digital TV is better, especially HDTV.*

he /hi, i, STRONG hi/ **PRONOUN** You use **he** to talk about a man, a boy, or a male animal. ❑ *John was my boss, but he couldn't remember my name.*

head /hɛd/ (heads, heading, headed)
1 **NOUN** Your **head** is the top part of your body that has your eyes, mouth, and brain in it. ❑ *The ball came down and hit him on the head.*
2 **NOUN** Your **head** is your mind. ❑ *I just said the first thing that came into my head.*
3 **NOUN** The **head** of a company or organization is the person who is in charge of it. ❑ *I spoke to the head of the department.*
4 **NOUN** The **head** of something is the top, the start, or the most important end of it. ❑ *She sat at the head of the table.*
5 **VERB** If you **head** a department, a company,

or an organization, you are the person who is in charge of it. ❑ *Michael Williams heads the department's Office of Civil Rights.*

6 **VERB** If you **are heading** for a particular place, you are going toward that place. ❑ *We're heading back to Washington tomorrow.*

7 The cost or amount **a head** or **per head** is the cost or amount for one person. ❑ *This simple meal costs less than $3 a head.*

→ look at **body**

head|ache /hɛdeɪk/ (**headaches**) **NOUN** If you have a **headache**, you have a pain in your head. ❑ *I have a terrible headache.*

→ look at **sick**

head|first /hɛdfɜrst/ also **head-first**

ADVERB If you fall or jump **headfirst**, your head is in front of your body when you are moving. ❑ *He fell headfirst down the stairs.*

head|ing /hɛdɪŋ/ (**headings**) **NOUN** A **heading** is a title that is written at the top of a page. ❑ *When you read the book, notice the chapter headings.*

head|light /hɛdlaɪt/ (**headlights**) **NOUN** A vehicle's **headlights** are the large lights at the front. ❑ *He turned on the car's headlights when the rain started.*

head|line /hɛdlaɪn/ (**headlines**)

1 **NOUN** A **headline** is the title of a newspaper story, printed in large letters. ❑ *The headline said: "New Government Plans."*

2 **PLURAL NOUN** The **headlines** are the important parts of the news that you hear first on radio or television news reports. ❑ *Claudia Polley read the news headlines.*

→ look at **news**

head of state (**heads of state**) **NOUN**

SOCIAL STUDIES A **head of state** is the leader of a country, for example a president, a king, or a queen. ❑ *More than 200 heads of state attended the meeting.*

head|phones
/hɛdfoʊnz/
PLURAL NOUN
Headphones
are things that
you wear on
your ears so
that you can listen to music or the radio
without anyone else hearing. ❑ *I listened to the program on headphones.*

head|quarters /hɛdkwɔrtərz/ **NOUN** The **headquarters** of an organization are its main offices. ❑ *The news broadcast came from Chicago's police headquarters.*

Sound Partners	heal, heel

heal /hil/ (**heals, healing, healed**) **VERB** When a broken bone or other injury **heals**, it becomes healthy again. ❑ *It took six months for her injuries to heal.*

→ look at **health care**

health /hɛlθ/ **NONCOUNT NOUN** A person's **health** is the condition of their body. ❑ *Too much fatty food is bad for your health.*

health care also **healthcare** **NONCOUNT NOUN** Health care is services for preventing and treating illnesses and injuries. ❑ *Nobody wants to pay more money for health care.*

→ look at Word World: **health care**

healthy /hɛlθi/ (**healthier, healthiest**)

1 **ADJECTIVE** Someone who is **healthy** is well and is not often sick. ❑ *People need to exercise to be healthy.*

2 **ADJECTIVE** Something that is **healthy** is good for your health. ❑ *Try to eat a healthy diet.*

→ look at **eat, fitness, food, health care**

Word Partners	Use **healthy** with:
N.	healthy **baby** **1** healthy **appetite**, healthy **diet**, healthy **food**, healthy **lifestyle**, healthy **skin** **2**

Word World   health care

medicine · serious · healthy · unhealthy · cure · check-up · sick · doctor · treat · recover · hospital · cure · symptoms · patient · heal · prevent · cause · prescription · treatment · catch

Nouns / Adjectives / Verbs

heap /hip/ (**heaps, heaping, heaped**)

1 **NOUN** A **heap of** things is a messy pile of them. ❏ *There was a heap of clothes in the corner of the room.*

2 **VERB** If you **heap** things in a pile, you put them in a large pile. ❏ *His mother heaped more carrots onto Michael's plate.*

Sound Partners	hear, here

hear /hɪər/ (**hears, hearing, heard** /hɜrd/)

1 **VERB** When you **hear** a sound, you become aware of it through your ears. ❏ *She could hear music in the distance.* ❏ *I heard him say, "Thanks."*

2 **VERB** If you **hear from** someone, you receive a letter, an email or a telephone call from them. ❏ *It's always great to hear from you.*

3 **VERB** If you **hear** information about something, you find out about it by someone telling you, or from the radio or television. ❏ *My mother heard about the school from Karen.* ❏ *I hear that Bruce Springsteen is playing at Madison Square Garden tomorrow evening.*

4 **VERB** If you **have heard of** something or someone, you know about them. ❏ *I've heard of him, but I've never met him.*

→ look at **music, news, sense**

hear|ing /hɪərɪŋ/ **NONCOUNT NOUN** Hearing is the sense that makes it possible for you to be aware of sounds. ❏ *His hearing was excellent.*

→ look at **sense**

hear|ing aid (**hearing aids**) **NOUN** A **hearing aid** is a small piece of equipment that people wear in their ear to help them to hear better.

heart /hɑrt/ (**hearts**)

1 **NOUN** **SCIENCE** Your **heart** is the part inside your chest that makes the blood move around your body. ❏ *His heart was beating fast.*

2 **NOUN** Your **heart** is your deep feelings. ❏ *Anne's words filled her heart with joy.*

3 **NOUN** The **heart of** a place is the middle part of it. ❏ *They own a busy hotel in the heart of the city.*

4 **NOUN** A **heart** is the shape ♥.

5 If someone **breaks** your **heart**, they make you very unhappy. ❏ *I fell in love on vacation but the girl broke my heart.*

6 If you know a poem or a song **by heart**, you can remember every word of it. ❏ *Mike knew this song by heart.*

heart at|tack (**heart attacks**) **NOUN** If someone has a **heart attack**, they suddenly have a lot of pain in their chest and their heart stops working. ❏ *He died of a heart attack.*

heart|beat /hɑrtbit/ (**heartbeats**) **NOUN** **SCIENCE** Your **heartbeat** is the regular movement of your heart as it pushes blood through your body. ❏ *The doctor listened to her heartbeat.*

heat /hit/ (**heats, heating, heated**)

1 **VERB** When you **heat** something, you make it hot. ❏ *Heat the tomatoes and oil in a pan.*

2 **NONCOUNT NOUN** Heat is the feeling of being hot. ❏ *Our clothes dried quickly in the heat of the sun.*

→ look at **energy, greenhouse effect**

heat|er /hitər/ (**heaters**) **NOUN** A **heater** is a piece of equipment that is used for making a room warm. ❏ *There's an electric heater in the bedroom.*

heav|en /hɛvən/ (**heavens**) **NONCOUNT NOUN** Heaven is the place where some people believe good people go when they die. ❏ *I believe that when I die I will go to heaven.*

heavy /hɛvi/ (**heavier, heaviest**)

1 **ADJECTIVE** Something that is **heavy** weighs a lot. ❏ *This bag is very heavy. What's in it?*

2 **ADJECTIVE** You use **heavy** to talk about how much someone or something weighs. ❏ *How heavy is your suitcase?*

3 **ADJECTIVE** Heavy means great in amount. ❏ *We drove through heavy traffic for two hours.*

● **heavi|ly** **ADVERB** ❏ *It rained heavily all day.*

hec|tic /hɛktɪk/ **ADJECTIVE** A **hectic** situation is very busy and involves a lot of activity. ❏ *Ben had a hectic work schedule.*

he'd /hid, id, STRONG hid/

1 **He'd** is short for "he had." ❏ *He'd seen her before.*

2 **He'd** is short for "he would." ❏ *He'd like to come with us.*

Sound Partners	heel, heal

heel /hil/ (**heels**)

1 **NOUN** Your **heel** is the back part of your foot, just below your ankle. ❏ *I have a big blister on my heel.*

2 **NOUN** The **heel** of a shoe is the raised part on the bottom at the back. ❏ *She always wears shoes with high heels.*

→ look at **clothes, foot**

height /haɪt/ (**heights**)

1 **NOUN** The **height** of a person or thing is their size from the bottom to the top. ❏ *Her*

h

weight is normal for her height. ❏ I am five feet six inches in height.

2 **NOUN** A particular **height** is the distance that something is above the ground. ❏ You can change the height of the seat.

→ look at **area, geometry**

heir /ɛər/ (**heirs**) **NOUN** An **heir** is someone who will receive a person's money or property when that person dies. ❏ Elizabeth was her father's heir.

held /hɛld/ **Held** is a form of the verb **hold**.

heli|cop|ter
/hɛlikɒptər/
(**helicopters**)
NOUN A
helicopter is an
aircraft with

long blades on top that go around very fast. It is able to stay still in the air and to move straight upward or downward.

he|lium /hiliəm/ **NONCOUNT NOUN** SCIENCE **Helium** is a very light gas that has no color or smell, that is often used for filling balloons (= small rubber bags filled with air or gas).

hell /hɛl/ **NONCOUNT NOUN** **Hell** is the place where people believe bad people go when they die. ❏ My mother says I'll go to hell if I lie.

he'll /hil, il, STRONG hil/ **He'll** is short for "he will." ❏ He'll be very successful, I'm sure.

hel|lo /hɛloʊ/ also **hullo**

1 You say "**Hello**" to someone when you meet them. ❏ Hello, Trish. How are you?

2 You say "**Hello**" when you answer the phone. ❏ Cohen picked up the phone and said, "Hello?"

hel|met
/hɛlmɪt/
(**helmets**) **NOUN**
A helmet is a
hat made of a
hard material,
which you

wear to protect your head.

help /hɛlp/ (**helps, helping, helped**)

1 **VERB** If you **help** someone, you make it easier for them to do something. ❏ Can somebody help me, please? ❏ You can help by giving them some money.

2 **NONCOUNT NOUN** **Help** is also a noun. ❏ Thanks very much for your help.

3 **VERB** If something **helps**, it improves a situation. ❏ Thanks for your advice. That helps.

4 **VERB** If you **help yourself to** something, you take what you want. ❏ There's bread on the table. Help yourself.

5 If you **can't help** the way you feel or behave, you cannot stop it from happening. ❏ I couldn't help laughing when I saw her face.

Word Builder	helpful

ful ≈ **filled with**

    care + ful = careful
    color + ful = colorful
    help + ful = helpful
    hope + ful = hopeful
    stress + ful = stressful
    use + ful = useful

help|ful /hɛlpfəl/ **ADJECTIVE** If someone is **helpful**, they help you by being useful or willing to work for you. ❏ The staff in the hotel are very helpful.

→ look at **dictionary**

Word Builder	helpless

less ≈ **without**

    care + less = careless
    end + less = endless
    help + less = helpless
    home + less = homeless
    use + less = useless
    wire + less = wireless

help|less /hɛlpləs/ **ADJECTIVE** If you are **helpless**, you do not have the strength or ability to do anything useful. ❏ Parents often feel helpless when their children are sick.

● **help|less|ly** **ADVERB** ❏ They watched helplessly as the house burned to the ground.

hemi|sphere /hɛmɪsfɪər/ (**hemispheres**)

1 **NOUN** GEOGRAPHY A **hemisphere** is one half of the Earth.

2 **NOUN** MATH A **hemisphere** is one half of a sphere (= an object that is shaped like a ball).

→ look at **globe**

hen /hɛn/ (**hens**) **NOUN** A **hen** is a female chicken.

her /hər, ər, STRONG hɜr/

1 **PRONOUN** You use **her** to talk about a woman, a girl, or a female animal. ❏ I told her that dinner was ready.

2 **ADJECTIVE** You use **her** to show that something belongs to or relates to a girl or a woman. ❏ She took her coat off and sat down. ❏ She traveled around the world with her husband.

herb /ɜrb/ (**herbs**) **NOUN** An **herb** is a plant whose leaves are used in cooking to add flavor to food, or as a medicine. ❏ *Fry the mushrooms in a little olive oil and add the chopped herbs.* ● **herb|al** ADJECTIVE ❏ *Do you know any herbal remedies for colds?*

her|bi|vore /hɜrbɪvɔr, ɜr-/ (**herbivores**)
NOUN SCIENCE A **herbivore** is an animal that eats only plants. Compare **carnivore** and **omnivore**.

herd /hɜrd/ (**herds**) NOUN A **herd** is a large group of one type of animal that lives together. ❏ *Herds of elephants crossed the river each day.*

Sound Partners	here, hear

here /hɪər/
1 ADVERB You use **here** when you are talking about the place where you are. ❏ *I can't stay here all day.* ❏ *Come and sit here.*
2 ADVERB You use **here** when you are offering or giving something to someone. ❏ *Here's your coffee.*

here's /hɪərz/ **Here's** is short for "here is." ❏ *I know you don't have much money, so here's some cash.*

hero /hɪəroʊ/ (**heroes**)
1 NOUN LANGUAGE ARTS The **hero** of a story is the main male character. ❏ *The actor Daniel Radcliffe plays the hero in the Harry Potter movies.*
2 NOUN A **hero** is someone who has done something brave or good. ❏ *Mr. Mandela is a hero who has inspired millions.*

he|ro|ic /hɪroʊɪk/ ADJECTIVE If a person or their actions are **heroic**, you admire them because they have been very brave. ❏ *He made a heroic effort to save the boy from the fire.*

hero|in /hɛroʊɪn/ NONCOUNT NOUN Heroin is a strong illegal drug.

hero|ine /hɛroʊɪn/ (**heroines**)
1 NOUN LANGUAGE ARTS The **heroine** of a story is the main female character. ❏ *The heroine of the book is a young doctor.*
2 NOUN A **heroine** is a woman who has done something brave or good. ❏ *China's first gold medal winner became a national heroine.*

hers /hɜrz/ PRONOUN You use **hers** to show that something belongs to a woman, a girl, or a female animal. ❏ *She admitted that the bag was hers.*

her|self /hərsɛlf/
1 PRONOUN You use **herself** to talk about a woman, a girl, or a female animal that you have just mentioned. ❏ *She looked at herself in*

the mirror. ❏ *If she's not careful, she'll hurt herself.*
2 PRONOUN If a woman or a girl does something **herself**, she, and not anyone else, does it. ❏ *She doesn't go to the hairdresser's. She cuts it herself.*

he's /hiz, iz, STRONG hiz/ **He's** is short for "he is" or "he has." ❏ *He's coming home tomorrow.*

hesi|tate /hɛzɪteɪt/ (**hesitates, hesitating, hesitated**) VERB If you **hesitate**, you do not act quickly, usually because you are not sure about what to say or do. ❏ *Catherine hesitated before answering.* ● **hesi|ta|tion** /hɛzɪteɪʃ°n/ (**hesitations**) NOUN ❏ *After some hesitation, she replied, "I'll have to think about that."*

hexa|gon /hɛksəgɒn/ (**hexagons**) NOUN MATH A **hexagon** is a shape with six straight sides.

hey /heɪ/
1 In informal situations, you say or shout "**hey**" to attract someone's attention. ❏ *"Hey! Be careful!" shouted Patty.*
2 In informal situations, you can say "**hey**" to greet someone. ❏ *He smiled and said "Hey, Kate."*

hi /haɪ/ In informal situations, you say "**hi**" to greet someone. ❏ *"Hi, Liz," she said.*

hi|ber|na|tion /haɪbərneɪʃ°n/ NONCOUNT NOUN SCIENCE **Hibernation** is when some animals sleep through the winter. ❏ *The animals consume three times more calories to prepare for hibernation.*

hic|cup /hɪkʌp/ (**hiccups, hiccuping** or **hiccupping, hiccuped** or **hiccupped**)
1 NOUN When you have **hiccups**, you make repeated short sounds in your throat, often because you have been eating or drinking too quickly. ❏ *Do you know how to cure hiccups?*
2 VERB When you **hiccup**, you make repeated short sounds in your throat. ❏ *He laughed so hard he started hiccuping.*

hid /hɪd/ **Hid** is a form of the verb **hide**.

hid|den /hɪd°n/
1 **Hidden** is a form of the verb **hide**.
2 ADJECTIVE **Hidden** things are not easy to see or know about. ❏ *There are hidden dangers on the beach.*

hide /haɪd/ (**hides, hiding, hid, hidden**)
1 VERB If you **hide** something or someone, you put them in a place where they cannot

h

easily be seen or found. ❑ *He hid the bicycle behind the wall.*

2 VERB If you **hide**, you go somewhere where people cannot easily find you. ❑ *The little boy hid in the closet.*

3 VERB To **hide** something means to cover it so that people cannot see it. ❑ *She hid her face in her hands.*

4 VERB If you **hide** what you feel or know, you do not let people know about it. ❑ *Lee tried to hide his excitement.*

hid|eous /hɪdiəs/ **ADJECTIVE** If someone or something is **hideous**, they are very ugly or unpleasant. ❑ *She saw a hideous face at the window.* ❑ *He was injured in a hideous knife attack.*
● **hid|eous|ly ADVERB** ❑ *I was convinced that I was hideously ugly.*

high /haɪ/ (**higher, highest**)

1 ADJECTIVE Something that is **high** extends a long way from the bottom to the top. ❑ *They lived in a house with a high wall around it.* ❑ *Mount Marcy is the highest mountain in the Adirondacks.*

2 ADJECTIVE You use **high** to talk or ask about how much something measures from the bottom to the top. ❑ *The grass in the yard was a foot high.*

3 ADJECTIVE If something is **high**, it is a long way above the ground. ❑ *I looked down from the high window.* ❑ *The sun was high in the sky.*

4 ADVERB High is also an adverb. ❑ *She can jump higher than other people.*

5 ADJECTIVE High means great in amount, or strength. ❑ *High winds destroyed many trees and buildings.* ❑ *The number of people injured was high.*

6 ADJECTIVE A **high** sound or voice is not deep. ❑ *She spoke in a high voice.*
→ look at **greenhouse effect**

high jump NOUN SPORTS The **high jump** is a sports event that involves jumping over a bar that can be raised higher after each jump.

high|light /haɪlaɪt/ (**highlights, highlighting, highlighted**)

1 VERB If someone or something **highlights** a point or problem, they show that it is important. ❑ *Her talk highlighted the problems of homeless people.*

2 NOUN The **highlights of** an event are the most interesting parts of it. ❑ *That tennis game was one of the highlights of the tournament.*

high|ly /haɪli/

1 ADVERB Highly is used before some adjectives to mean "very." ❑ *Mr. Singh was a highly successful salesman.*

2 ADVERB If you think **highly** of something or someone, you think they are very good. ❑ *Michael thought highly of the school.*

high school (**high schools**) **NOUN** A high **school** is a school for children usually aged between fourteen and eighteen. ❑ *My daughter has just started high school.*

high-tech /haɪ tɛk/ also **high tech, hi tech ADJECTIVE TECHNOLOGY High-tech** equipment uses modern methods and computers. ❑ *...high-tech camera equipment.*

high|way /haɪweɪ/ (**highways**) **NOUN** A **highway** is a main road that connects towns or cities. ❑ *The accident happened on the highway between Chicago and Madison.*
→ look at **car, route**

hi|jack /haɪdʒæk/ (**hijacks, hijacking, hijacked**)

1 VERB If someone **hijacks** a plane or other vehicle, they illegally take control of it while it is traveling from one place to another. ❑ *Two men hijacked the plane.*

2 NOUN Hijack is also a noun. ❑ *Finally, six months after the hijack, he was arrested.*

hike /haɪk/ (**hikes, hiking, hiked**)

1 NOUN A **hike** is a long walk, especially outside of a city. ❑ *We went for a hike up Mount Desmond.*

2 VERB If you **hike**, you go for a long walk. ❑ *We hiked through the Fish River Canyon.* ● **hik|er** (**hikers**) **NOUN** ❑ *The hikers spent the night in the mountains.* ● **hik|ing NONCOUNT NOUN** ❑ *I love hiking in the mountains.*

hi|lari|ous /hɪlɛəriəs/ **ADJECTIVE** If something is **hilarious**, it is very funny. ❑ *He told me a hilarious story.*

hill /hɪl/ (**hills**) **NOUN SCIENCE GEOGRAPHY** A **hill** is an area of land that is higher than the land around it. ❑ *The castle is on a hill above the old town.*

hill|side /hɪlsaɪd/ (**hillsides**) **NOUN** A **hillside** is the slope of a hill.

hilly /hɪli/ (**hillier, hilliest**) **ADJECTIVE** A **hilly** area has a lot of hills. ❑ *The countryside in this area is quite hilly.*

him /hɪm/ **PRONOUN** You use **him** to talk about a man, a boy, or a male animal.

❏ *Elaine met him at the railroad station.* ❏ *Is Sam there? Let me talk to him.*

him|self /hɪmsɛlf/

1 **PRONOUN** You use **himself** to talk about a man, a boy, or a male animal that you have just mentioned. ❏ *He poured himself a cup of coffee.* ❏ *He was talking to himself.*

2 **PRONOUN** If a man or a boy does something **himself**, he, and not anyone else, does it. ❏ *He made your card himself.* ❏ *He'll probably tell you about it himself.*

Hin|du /hɪndu/ (**Hindus**)

1 **NOUN** A **Hindu** is a person who believes in Hinduism.

2 **ADJECTIVE** **Hindu** describes things that belong or relate to Hinduism. ❏ *We visited a Hindu temple.*

Hin|du|ism /hɪnduɪzəm/ **NONCOUNT NOUN**
Hinduism is an Indian religion. It has many gods and teaches that people have another life on Earth after they die.

hinge /hɪndʒ/ (**hinges**) **NOUN** A **hinge** is a piece of metal that is used for joining two pieces of wood together so that they open and shut. ❏ *The hinge is broken and the door won't shut.*

hint /hɪnt/ (**hints, hinting, hinted**)

1 **NOUN** A **hint** is a suggestion that is not made directly. ❏ *Has he given you any hints about what he wants for his birthday?*

2 **VERB** If you **hint at** something, you suggest it in a way that is not direct. ❏ *She has hinted at the possibility of having a baby.*

3 **NOUN** A **hint** is a helpful piece of advice. ❏ *Here are some helpful hints to make your trip easier.*

hip /hɪp/ (**hips**) **NOUN** Your **hips** are the two areas or bones at the sides of your body between the tops of your legs and your waist. ❏ *Tracey put her hands on her hips and laughed.*

hip-hop **NONCOUNT NOUN** MUSIC Hip-hop is a type of music and dance that developed among African-American people in the United States in the 1970s and 1980s.

hip|po /hɪpoʊ/ (**hippos**) **NOUN** A **hippo** is a hippopotamus. [INFORMAL]

hippo|pota|mus /hɪpəpɒtəməs/ (**hippopotamuses**) **NOUN** A **hippopotamus** is a very large animal with short legs and thick skin that lives in and near rivers.

hire /haɪər/ (**hires, hiring, hired**) **VERB** If you **hire** someone, you pay them to do a job for you. ❏ *He just hired a new secretary.*

his

> **PRONUNCIATION HELP**
> Pronounce the adjective /hɪz/. Pronounce the pronoun /hɪz/.

1 **ADJECTIVE** You use **his** to show that something belongs or relates to a man, a boy, or a male animal. ❏ *He spent part of his career in Hollywood.* ❏ *He went to the party with his girlfriend.*

2 **PRONOUN** **His** is also a pronoun. ❏ *Henry said the decision was his.*

hiss /hɪs/ (**hisses, hissing, hissed**)

1 **VERB** To **hiss** means to make a sound like a long "s." ❏ *My cat hisses when I step on its tail.*

2 **NOUN** **Hiss** is also a noun. ❏ *The hiss of steam came from the kitchen.*

his|to|ry /hɪstəri, -tri/

1 **NONCOUNT NOUN** SOCIAL STUDIES History is events that happened in the past. ❏ *The film showed great moments in football history.*

2 **NONCOUNT NOUN** SOCIAL STUDIES History is the study of events that happened in the past. ❏ *He studied history at Indiana University.*
→ look at Word World: **history**

hit /hɪt/ (**hits, hitting, hit**)

1 **VERB** If you **hit** someone or something,

Word World   history

events, classical, ancient, modern, people, facts, past, American, timeline, culture, natural, freedom, research, world, war, colony, study, civilization, independence, explore, discover

Nouns / Adjectives / Verbs

you touch them with a lot of force. ❏ *She hit the ball hard.*

2 **VERB** When one thing **hits** another, it touches it with a lot of force. ❏ *The car hit a traffic sign.*

3 **NOUN** Hit is also a noun. ❏ *The building took a direct hit from the bomb.*

4 **VERB** If something **hits** a person, a place, or a thing, it affects them very badly. ❏ *The earthquake hit northern Peru.*

5 **NOUN** If a CD, a movie, or a play is a **hit**, it is very popular and successful. ❏ *The song was a big hit in Japan.*

6 **NOUN** A **hit** is a single visit to a web page. ❏ *The company has had 78,000 hits on its website.*

7 **NOUN** If someone who is searching for information on the Internet gets a **hit**, they find a website that contains that information.

hitch|hike /hɪtʃhaɪk/ (**hitchhikes, hitchhiking, hitchhiked**) **VERB** If you **hitchhike**, you travel by getting rides from passing vehicles without paying. ❏ *Neil hitchhiked to New York during his vacation.*

● **hitch|hiker** (**hitchhikers**) **NOUN** ❏ *On my way to Vancouver I picked up a hitchhiker.*

HIV /eɪtʃ aɪ viː/

1 **NONCOUNT NOUN** HIV is a virus (= a harmful thing that can make you sick) that reduces the ability of people's bodies to fight illness and that can cause **AIDS**.

2 If someone is **HIV positive**, they are infected with the HIV virus, and may develop AIDS. If someone is **HIV negative**, they are not infected with the virus.

hive /haɪv/ (**hives**) **NOUN** A **hive** is a structure in which bees live.

ho /hoʊ/ **EXCLAMATION** Ho is a word that you can use to call someone to get their attention.

hoax /hoʊks/ (**hoaxes**) **NOUN** A **hoax** is when someone says that something bad is going to happen, when this is not true. ❏ *Police say that the bomb alert was a hoax.*

hob|by /hɒbi/ (**hobbies**) **NOUN** A **hobby** is an activity that you enjoy doing in your free time. ❏ *My hobbies are music and tennis.*

hock|ey /hɒki/ **NONCOUNT NOUN** SPORTS Hockey is a game that is played on ice between two teams who try to score goals using long curved sticks to hit a small rubber disk. ❏ *The Australian men's hockey team finished second.*

hock|ey stick (**hockey sticks**) **NOUN** SPORTS A **hockey stick** is a long curved stick that is used for hitting a small rubber disk in the game of hockey. ❏ *The Australian men's hockey team finished second.*

hold /hoʊld/ (**holds, holding, held**)

1 **VERB** When you **hold** something, you have it in your hands or your arms. ❏ *She held his hand tightly.* ❏ *I held the baby in my arms.*

2 **NOUN** Hold is also a noun. ❏ *Cooper took hold of the rope and pulled on it.*

3 **VERB** When you **hold** something in a particular position, you put it into that position and keep it there. ❏ *Hold your hands up.* ❏ *Try to hold the camera steady.*

4 **NOUN** In a ship or an airplane, the **hold** is the place where goods or luggage are stored.

5 **VERB** If something **holds** a particular amount of something, it can contain that amount. ❏ *One CD-ROM disk can hold over 100,000 pages of text.*

6 **VERB** You can use **hold** with nouns such as "party," and "meeting," to talk about particular activities that people are organizing. ❏ *The country will hold elections within a year.*

7 **VERB** If someone asks you to **hold**, or to **hold the line**, when you are making a telephone call, they are asking you to wait for a short time. ❏ *Please can you hold, sir?*

8 If you **get hold of** something, you find it, usually after some difficulty. ❏ *It is hard to get hold of medicines in some areas of the country.*

9 If you **get hold of** someone, you succeed in speaking to them. ❏ *I've called him several times but I can't get hold of him.*

▶ **hold back** When you **hold** someone or something **back**, you stop them from moving forwards or from doing something. ❏ *The police held back the crowd.*

▶ **hold on** or **hold onto** If you **hold on** or **hold onto** something, you keep your hand on it or around it. ❏ *The thief pulled me to the ground but I held onto my purse.*

▶ **hold up** If someone or something **holds** you **up**, they make you late. ❏ *I won't hold you up—I just have one quick question.*

holdup /hoʊldʌp/ (**holdups**) also **hold-up** **NOUN** A **holdup** is when someone uses a weapon to make someone give them money or other valuable things. ❏ *Police are looking for a man after a hold-up in a local bank.*

H

Sound Partners   hole, whole

hole /hoʊl/ (holes) NOUN A **hole** is an opening or an empty space in something. ❑ *He dug a hole 45 feet wide and 15 feet deep.* ❑ *I've got a hole in my jeans.*

holi|day /hɒlɪdeɪ/ (holidays) NOUN A **holiday** is a day when people do not go to work or school because of a religious or national celebration. ❑ *...the Jewish holiday of Passover.* → look at **calendar, relax**

hol|ler /hɒlər/ (hollers, hollering, hollered) VERB If you **holler**, you shout loudly. [INFORMAL] ❑ *"Watch out!" he hollered.*

hol|low /hɒloʊ/ ADJECTIVE Something that is **hollow** has an empty space inside it. ❑ *...a hollow tree.*

hol|ly /hɒli/ NOUN **Holly** is a plant that has hard, shiny leaves with sharp points, and red berries (= small round fruit) in winter.

holo|caust /hɒləkɔst, hoʊlə-/ NOUN SOCIAL STUDIES The **Holocaust** is the organized killing by the Nazis of millions of Jews during the Second World War.

holy /hoʊli/ (holier, holiest) ADJECTIVE Something that is **holy** is connected with God or a particular religion. ❑ *This is a holy place.*

home /hoʊm/ (homes)
1 NOUN Someone's **home** is the house or apartment where they live. ❑ *He died from a fall at his home in London.* ❑ *Hi, Mom, I'm home!*
2 ADVERB **Home** means to or at the place where you live. ❑ *She wasn't feeling well and she wanted to go home.*
3 NOUN A **home** is a building where people who cannot care for themselves live and are cared for. ❑ *It's a home for elderly people.*
4 ADV When a sports team plays **at home**, it plays on its own ground. Compare with **away**. ❑ *The Red Sox are playing at home tonight.* ADJ **Home** is also an adjective. ❑ *Nolan may return for Saturday's home game against the New York Rangers.*

Word Partners   Use **home** with:
v.	**build a** home, **buy a** home, **call** home, **come** home, **drive** home, **feel at** home, **fly** home, **get** home, **go** home, **leave** home, **phone** home, **return** home, **sit** *at* home, **stay** *at* home, **walk** home **1** **2**
ADJ.	**close to** home, **new** home **1** **2**

Word Builder   homeless
less ≈ **without**
care + less = careless
end + less = endless
help + less = helpless
home + less = homeless
use + less = useless
wire + less = wireless

home|less /hoʊmlɪs/
1 ADJECTIVE **Homeless** people have nowhere to live. ❑ *There are a lot of homeless families in the city.*
2 PLURAL NOUN The **homeless** are people who are homeless. ❑ *We're collecting money for the homeless.*

home|ly /hoʊmli/ ADJECTIVE If someone is **homely**, they are not very attractive. ❑ *John was homely and overweight.*

home|made /hoʊmmeɪd/ ADJECTIVE Something that is **homemade** has been made in someone's home, rather than in a store or factory. ❑ *I miss my mother's homemade bread.*

home page (home pages) NOUN TECHNOLOGY On the Internet, a person's or an organization's **home page** is the main page of their website. ❑ *The company offers a number of services on its home page.*

home|sick /hoʊmsɪk/ ADJECTIVE If you are **homesick**, you feel unhappy because you are away from home and you are missing your family and friends. ❑ *He was homesick for his family.* → look at **feeling**

home|work /hoʊmwɜrk/ NONCOUNT NOUN **Homework** is schoolwork that teachers give to students to do at home in the evening or on the weekend. ❑ *Have you done your homework, Gemma?* → look at **school**

homo|sex|ual /hoʊmoʊsɛkʃuəl/ (homosexuals)
1 ADJECTIVE Someone who is **homosexual** is sexually attracted to people of the same sex. ❑ *The study found that 4 to 10 percent of American men are homosexual.*
2 NOUN **Homosexual** is also a noun. ❑ *The organization wants equal treatment for homosexuals.*

hon|est /ɒnɪst/
1 ADJECTIVE If someone is **honest**, they always tell the truth and they do not steal or cheat. ❑ *She's honest, and I trust her.*

h

● **hon|est|ly** ADVERB ❏ *Please try to answer these questions honestly.*

2 ADVERB You say "**honest**" before or after a statement to show that you want people to believe you. [INFORMAL] ❏ *I'm not sure, honest.*

● **hon|est|ly** ADVERB ❏ *Honestly, I don't know anything about it.*

hon|es|ty /ɒnɪsti/ NONCOUNT NOUN **Honesty** is the quality of being honest. ❏ *I admire his courage and honesty.*

hon|ey /hʌni/ (**honeys**)
1 NONCOUNT NOUN **Honey** is a sweet, sticky food that is made by bees (= black and yellow insects).
2 NOUN You call someone **honey** as a sign of affection. ❏ *Honey, I don't think that's a good idea.*

honey|moon /hʌnimun/ (**honeymoons**) NOUN A **honeymoon** is a vacation taken by a man and a woman who have just gotten married. ❏ *We went to Florida on our honeymoon.*

hon|or /ɒnər/ (**honors, honoring, honored**)
1 NOUN An **honor** is a special award that is given to someone. ❏ *He won many honors—among them an award for his movie performance.*
2 VERB If someone **is honored**, they are given public praise for something they have done. ❏ *Maradona was honored with an award from Argentina's soccer association.*

Word Builder honorable

able ≈ **able to be**

comfort + able = comfortable
depend + able = dependable
download + able = downloadable
enjoy + able = enjoyable
honor + able = honorable

---

hon|or|able /ɒnərəbəl/ ADJECTIVE If people or actions are **honorable**, they are good, and the person has a right to be respected. ❏ *I'm sure his intentions were perfectly honorable.*

Spelling Partners hood

---

hood /hʊd/ (**hoods**)
1 NOUN A **hood** is the part of a coat that you can pull up to cover your head. ❏ *Put up your hood—it's starting to rain.*
2 NOUN The **hood** of a car is the metal cover over the engine. ❏ *Dad raised the hood of the truck.*

hoof /hʊf, huf/ (**hoofs** or **hooves**) NOUN **Hooves** are the hard parts of the feet of horses, cows and some other animals. ❏ *He heard the sound of horses' hooves behind him.*

hook /hʊk/ (**hooks**)
1 NOUN A **hook** is a curved piece of metal or plastic that you use for hanging things on. ❏ *His jacket hung from a hook.*
2 NOUN A **hook** is a curved piece of metal with a sharp point that you tie to the end of a fishing line to catch fish with. ❏ *Mr. Kruger removed the hook from the fish's mouth.*

hoop /hup/ (**hoops**)
1 NOUN A **hoop** is a ring made of wood, metal, or plastic. ❏ *Jessica was wearing jeans, sneakers and gold hoop earrings.*
2 NOUN A basketball **hoop** is the ring that players try to throw the ball into in order to score points for their team.

hoot /hut/ (**hoots, hooting, hooted**)
1 VERB If an owl **hoots**, it makes a loud noise. ❏ *An owl hooted in the distance.*
2 NOUN **Hoot** is also a noun. ❏ *Suddenly, he heard the loud hoot of a train.*

hooves /huvz/ **Hooves** is a plural of **hoof**.

hop /hɒp/ (**hops, hopping, hopped**)
1 VERB If you **hop**, you move by jumping on one foot.
2 VERB When birds and animals **hop**, they move by jumping on both of their feet or all four of their feet together. ❏ *A small brown bird hopped in front of them.*
3 NOUN A **hop** is a short jump.
4 VERB If you **hop** somewhere, you move there quickly or suddenly. [INFORMAL] ❏ *We hopped on the train.*

hope /hoʊp/ (**hopes, hoping, hoped**)
1 VERB If you **hope** that something is true, or that something will happen, you want it to be true or you want it to happen. ❏ *The team are hoping to win a medal at the Olympic Games.* ❏ *I hope that you get better soon.* ❏ *We're all hoping for some good weather.* ❏ *"I hope we'll meet again soon." "I hope so, too."*
2 NOUN **Hope** is the feeling of wanting something good to happen, and believing that it will happen. ❏ *What are your hopes for the future?* ❏ *This medicine will give new hope to millions of people around the world.* ❏ *As time passes, the police are losing hope of finding the men alive.*

Word Builder   *hopeful*

ful ≈ **filled with**

    care + ful = care**ful**
    color + ful = color**ful**
    help + ful = help**ful**
    hope + ful = hope**ful**
    stress + ful = stress**ful**
    use + ful = use**ful**

---

hope|ful /hoʊpfəl/ **ADJECTIVE** If you are **hopeful**, you think that something that you want will probably happen. ❑ *The doctors are hopeful that Grandma will get better soon.*

hope|ful|ly /hoʊpfəli/
1 **ADVERB** You say **hopefully** when you are talking about something that you hope will happen. ❑ *Hopefully, you won't have any more problems.*
2 **ADVERB** If you do something **hopefully**, you do it hoping that something good will happen. ❑ *David looked hopefully at the coffee pot.*

hope|less /hoʊplɪs/
1 **ADJECTIVE** Someone or something that is **hopeless** has no chance of success. ❑ *I don't believe the situation is hopeless.*
2 **ADJECTIVE** If someone or something is **hopeless**, they are very bad. ❑ *I'm hopeless at sport.* ● **hope|less|ly** **ADVERB** ❑ *Harry realized that he was hopelessly lost.*

ho|ri|zon /həraɪzᵊn/ (**horizons**) **NOUN** The **horizon** is the line that appears between the sky and the land or the ocean. ❑ *A small boat appeared on the horizon.*

hori|zon|tal /hɔrɪzɒntᵊl/ **ADJECTIVE** Something that is **horizontal** is flat and level with the ground. ❑ *She was wearing a gray sweater with black horizontal stripes.*

hor|mone /hɔrmoʊn/ (**hormones**) **NOUN** SCIENCE A **hormone** is a chemical substance in your body that affects the way your body works. ❑ *This hormone is present in both sexes.*

Spelling Partners   **horn**

---

horn /hɔrn/ (**horns**)
1 **NOUN** An animal's **horns** are the hard pointed things that grow from its head.
2 **NOUN** A **horn** is an object in a car or another vehicle that makes a loud noise, and that you use as a warning of danger. ❑ *I could hear the sound of a car horn outside.*
3 **NOUN** MUSIC A **horn** is a musical instrument with a long metal tube that you play by blowing into it. ❑ *Joshua started playing the horn when he was eight.*

horo|scope /hɔrəskoʊp/ (**horoscopes**) **NOUN** Your **horoscope** is what some people believe will happen to you in the future, using the position of the stars when you were born. ❑ *I always read my horoscope in the newspaper.*

hor|ri|ble /hɔrɪbᵊl, hɒr-/ **ADJECTIVE** If someone or something is **horrible**, they are very unpleasant. [INFORMAL] ❑ *The smell was horrible.* ❑ *It was a horrible experience.* ❑ *Stop being horrible to me!* ● **hor|ri|bly** /hɔrɪbli, hɒr-/ **ADVERB** ❑ *Sam was feeling horribly ill.*

hor|ri|fy /hɔrɪfaɪ, hɒr-/ (**horrifies, horrifying, horrified**) **VERB** If someone **is horrified**, they are very shocked. ❑ *His family was horrified by the news.* ● **hor|ri|fy|ing** **ADJECTIVE** ❑ *It was a horrifying sight.*

hor|ror /hɔrər, hɒr-/
1 **NONCOUNT NOUN** **Horror** is a feeling of great shock and fear when you see or experience something very unpleasant. ❑ *I felt sick with horror.*
2 **ADJECTIVE** A **horror** movie is a very frightening movie that you watch for entertainment. ❑ *I'm not a fan of horror movies.*

horse /hɔrs/ (**horses**) **NOUN** A **horse** is a large animal that people can ride. ❑ *Have you ever ridden a horse?*
→ look at **farm**

horse|back rid|ing /hɔrsbæk raɪdɪŋ/ **NONCOUNT NOUN** SPORTS **Horseback riding** is the activity of riding a horse.

horse rac|ing **NONCOUNT NOUN** SPORTS **Horse racing** is a sport in which people ride horses in races.

horse|shoe /hɔrsʃu/ (**horseshoes**) **NOUN** A **horseshoe** is a piece of metal in the shape of a U, that is fixed to a horse's foot. People sometimes hang a **horseshoe** on the wall as a sign of good luck.

hose /hoʊz/ (**hoses**) **NOUN** A **hose** is a long rubber or plastic pipe that you use to put water on plants or on a fire.

hos|pi|tal /hɒspɪtᵊl/ (**hospitals**) **NOUN** A **hospital** is a place where doctors and

h

nurses care for people who are sick or injured. ❑ *The two men were taken to the hospital after the car crash.*
→ look at **health care**

host /hoʊst/ (**hosts**) **NOUN** The **host** at a party is the person who has invited the guests. ❑ *I didn't know anyone at the party, except the host.*

hos|tage /hɒstɪdʒ/ (**hostages**)
1 **NOUN** A **hostage** is someone who is kept as a prisoner by people until the people get what they want. ❑ *The two hostages were freed yesterday.*
2 If someone **is taken hostage**, they are taken and kept as a hostage. ❑ *He was taken hostage on his first trip to the country.*

host|ess /hoʊstɪs/ (**hostesses**) **NOUN** The **hostess** at a party is the woman who has invited the guests. ❑ *She's the perfect hostess, making sure that all her guests are relaxed and happy.*

hos|tile /hɒstᵊl/ **ADJECTIVE** A **hostile** person or group of people is very unfriendly. ❑ *A large, hostile crowd surrounded him.*

hot /hɒt/ (**hotter, hottest**)
1 **ADJECTIVE** Someone or something that is **hot** has a high temperature. ❑ *When the oil is hot, add the sliced onion.* ❑ *Have some hot coffee. That will warm you up.* ❑ *I was too hot and tired to eat.*
2 **ADJECTIVE** **Hot** describes the weather when the temperature is high. ❑ *It's too hot to play tennis.*
3 **ADJECTIVE** **Hot** food has a strong, burning taste. ❑ *I love eating hot curries.*
→ look at **climate, water**

hot dog (**hot dogs**) **NOUN** A **hot dog** is a long piece of bread with a hot sausage (= a long thin piece of hot cooked meat) inside it. ❑ *The children ate hot dogs and ice cream at Melissa's birthday party.*

ho|tel /hoʊtɛl/ (**hotels**) **NOUN** A **hotel** is a building where people pay to sleep and eat meals. ❑ *Janet stayed the night in a small hotel near the harbor.*
→ look at **city**

Sound Partners hour, our

hour /aʊər/ (**hours**) **NOUN** An **hour** is a period of sixty minutes. ❑ *They waited for about two hours.* ❑ *I only slept about half an hour last night.*
→ look at **factory, time**

hour|ly /aʊərli/
1 **ADJECTIVE** An **hourly** event happens once every hour. ❑ *He listened to the hourly news program on the radio.*
2 **ADVERB** Something that happens **hourly**, happens once every hour. ❑ *The buses run hourly between the two cities.*

house /haʊs/ (**houses**)
1 **NOUN** A **house** is a building where people live. ❑ *Amy's invited me to her house for dinner.* ❑ *Grandma has moved to a small house in the country.*
2 **NOUN** SOCIAL STUDIES You can call one of the two parts of the U.S. Congress a **House**. The House of Representatives is sometimes called **the House**. ❑ *Some members of the House and Senate worked all day yesterday.*
→ look at Picture Dictionary: **house**

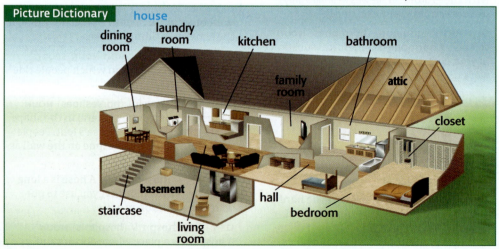

Picture Dictionary house

dining room — laundry room — kitchen — bathroom — family room — attic — closet — staircase — basement — hall — bedroom — living room

H

Word Partners	Use **house** with:
v.	**build** a house, **buy** a house, **live in** a house, **own** a house, **rent** a house, **sell** a house **1**
ADJ.	**empty** house, **expensive** house, **little** house, **new** house, **old** house **1**

house|hold /haʊshoʊld/ (households)
NOUN A **household** is all the people who live together in a house. ❑ *I grew up in a large household, with three brothers and three sisters.*

house|wife /haʊswaɪf/ (housewives) **NOUN**
A **housewife** is a woman who does not have a paid job, but spends most of her time looking after her house and family. ❑ *Sarah's a housewife and mother of four children.*

house|work /haʊswɜrk/ **NONCOUNT NOUN**
Housework is the work that you do to keep a house clean and neat. ❑ *Men are doing more housework nowadays.*

hov|er /hʌvər/ (hovers, hovering, hovered)
VERB If something **hovers**, it stays in one place in the air, and does not move forward or backward. ❑ *Helicopters hovered over the scene of the accident.*

how /haʊ/
1 **ADVERB** You use **how** to ask about the way that something happens or is done. ❑ *How do you spell his name? ❑ "How do you get to work?" "By bus." ❑ How does a cellphone work?*
2 **ADVERB** You use **how** to ask questions about time, or the amount or age of something. ❑ *How much money do you have? ❑ How many people will be at the dinner? ❑ How long will you stay? ❑ How old is your son?*
3 **ADVERB** You use **how** when you are asking someone whether something was good. ❑ *How was your trip to Orlando?*
4 **ADVERB** You use **how** to ask if someone is well. ❑ *Hi! How are you doing? ❑ How's Rosie?*
5 **ADVERB** You say "**How about...**" when you are suggesting something to someone. ❑ *How about a cup of coffee? ❑ How about meeting tonight?*
6 It is polite to say "**How do you do?**" when you meet someone for the first time. They answer by saying "**How do you do?**" also.

how|ever /haʊɛvər/
1 **ADVERB** You use **however** when you are saying something that is not expected because of what you have just said ❑ *The apartment is rather small. It is, however, much nicer than our old apartment.*

2 **CONJUNCTION** You use **however** when you want to say that it makes no difference how something is done. ❑ *Wear your hair however you want.*

howl /haʊl/ (howls, howling, howled)
1 **VERB** If a person or animal **howls**, they make a long, loud, crying sound. ❑ *A dog suddenly howled. ❑ Daniel fell to the ground, howling with pain.*
2 **NOUN** **Howl** is also a noun. ❑ *The dog gave a long howl.*

HTML /eɪtʃ ti ɛm ɛl/ **NONCOUNT NOUN**
TECHNOLOGY **HTML** is the standard way of preparing documents so that people can read them on the Internet. **HTML** is short for "hypertext markup language." ❑ *I'm teaching myself HTML.*

hub /hʌb/ (hubs) **NOUN** If a place is the **hub of** an activity, it is a very important center for that activity. ❑ *They say that New York is the hub of the art world.*

hug /hʌg/ (hugs, hugging, hugged)
1 **VERB** When you **hug** someone, you put your arms around them and hold them tightly, to show your love or friendship. ❑ *Crystal hugged him and invited him to dinner the next day.*
2 **NOUN** **Hug** is also a noun. ❑ *She gave him a hug and said "Well done."*

huge /hyudʒ/ (huger, hugest) **ADJECTIVE**
Something or someone that is **huge** is very large. ❑ *Emily was wearing huge dark sunglasses.*
● **huge|ly** **ADVERB** ❑ *This hotel is hugely popular.*

hum /hʌm/ (hums, humming, hummed)
1 **VERB** If something or someone **hums**, they make a low continuous noise. ❑ *The birds sang and the bees hummed.*
2 **NOUN** **Hum** is also a noun. ❑ *I could hear the distant hum of traffic.*
3 **VERB** When you **hum** a tune, you sing a tune with your lips closed. ❑ *Barbara began humming a song.*

hu|man /hyumən/ (humans)
1 **ADJECTIVE** **Human** means relating to people, and not animals or machines. ❑ *What is the smallest bone in the human body?*
2 **NOUN** A **human** is a person, rather than an animal or a machine. ❑ *Humans are capable of some terrible crimes.*

hu|man be|ing (human beings) **NOUN**
SCIENCE A **human being** is a man, a woman, or a child. ❑ *Every human being has the right to freedom.*

h

hu|man|ity /hyumǽnɪti/
1 NONCOUNT NOUN Humanity is all the people in the world. ❑ Can humanity survive the future?
2 NONCOUNT NOUN Humanity is the quality of being kind and thoughtful. ❑ Her speech showed great humanity.

hu|man na|ture NONCOUNT NOUN Human nature is the way that most people behave. ❑ It is human nature to worry about your children.

hu|man race NOUN The human race means all the people living in the world. ❑ Some people believe that the human race is destroying the Earth.

hu|man rights PLURAL NOUN SOCIAL STUDIES Human rights are basic rights that all people should have. ❑ Both armies promised to respect human rights.

hum|ble /hʌ́mbəl/ (humbler, humblest)
1 ADJECTIVE A humble person does not believe that they are better than other people. ❑ He remains humble about his achievements.
2 ADJECTIVE A humble person or thing is ordinary and not special in any way. ❑ Ms. Cruz comes from a humble background.

hu|mid /hyúmɪd/ ADJECTIVE Humid weather is wet and warm. ❑ Tomorrow, we can expect hot and humid conditions.

hu|mid|ity /hyumɪ́diti/ NONCOUNT NOUN Humidity is the amount of water in the air. ❑ The humidity is relatively low at the moment.
→ look at **climate**

hu|mor /hyúmər/ NONCOUNT NOUN Humor is the quality of being funny. ❑ I laughed when I saw the humor of the situation.

hu|mor|ous /hyúmərəs/ ADJECTIVE If someone or something is humorous, they make you laugh or smile. ❑ He usually likes to write humorous poems. ● **hu|mor|ous|ly** ADVERB ❑ Mr. Stevenson smiled humorously.

hump /hʌ́mp/ (humps)
1 NOUN A hump is a small hill or raised area.
2 NOUN A camel's hump is the large lump on its back. ❑ Camels store water in their hump.

hun|dred /hʌ́ndrɪd/ (hundreds)

> **LANGUAGE HELP**
> The plural form is **hundred** after a number.

1 MATH A hundred or one hundred is the number 100. ❑ More than a hundred people were there.

2 Hundreds of things or people means a lot of them. ❑ He received hundreds of letters.

hung /hʌ́ŋ/ Hung is a form of the verb **hang**.

hun|ger /hʌ́ŋgər/ NONCOUNT NOUN Hunger is the feeling that you get when you need something to eat. ❑ Hunger is the body's signal that you need to eat.

hun|gry /hʌ́ŋgri/ (hungrier, hungriest) ADJECTIVE When you are hungry, you want to eat. ❑ My friend was hungry, so we drove to a shopping mall to get some food. ● **hun|gri|ly** /hʌ́ŋgrɪli/ ADVERB ❑ James ate hungrily.
→ look at **eat, food**

hunt /hʌ́nt/ (hunts, hunting, hunted)
1 VERB When people or animals hunt, they chase and kill wild animals for food or as a sport. ❑ I learned to hunt and fish when I was a child.
2 NOUN A hunt is when people chase and kill wild animals for food or as a sport. ❑ Dad went on a moose hunt last year. ● **hunt|ing** NONCOUNT NOUN ❑ He went deer hunting with his cousins.
3 VERB If you hunt for something or someone, you try to find them by searching carefully. ❑ Police are still hunting for clues at the victim's apartment.
4 NOUN A hunt is a careful search for something. ❑ Many people helped in the hunt for the missing children. ● **hunt|ing** NONCOUNT NOUN ❑ Job hunting is not easy.

hunt|er /hʌ́ntər/ (hunters) NOUN A hunter is a person who hunts wild animals for food or as a sport. ❑ Hundreds of deer hunters will visit the area this season.

hur|dle /hɜ́rdəl/ (hurdles)
1 NOUN A hurdle is a difficulty that may stop you from doing something. ❑ Writing a résumé is the first hurdle in a job search.
2 NOUN SPORTS Hurdles is a race in which people have to jump over a series of frames. ❑ Davis won the 400 meter hurdles.

hur|ri|cane /hɜ́rɪkeɪn, hʌ́r-/ (hurricanes) NOUN SCIENCE A hurricane is a storm with very strong winds and rain.
→ look at **disaster**

hur|ry /hɜ́ri, hʌ́r-/ (hurries, hurrying, hurried)
1 VERB If you hurry, you move or do something as quickly as you can. ❑ Claire hurried along the road. ❑ Everyone hurried to find a seat.

2 NOUN If you are **in a hurry**, you need or want to do something quickly. ❏ *I'm sorry, I'm in a hurry and I have to go!*

▶ **hurry up** If you tell someone to **hurry up**, you are telling them to do something more quickly. ❏ *Hurry up and get ready, or you'll miss the school bus!*

hurt /hɜrt/ (**hurts, hurting, hurt**)

1 VERB If you **hurt** someone or something, you make them feel pain. ❏ *Yasin hurt himself while he was playing baseball.* ❏ *I fell over and hurt my leg yesterday.*

2 VERB If a part of your body **hurts**, you feel pain there. ❏ *His arm hurt.*

3 ADJECTIVE If you are **hurt**, you have been injured. ❏ *How badly are you hurt?*

4 VERB If you **hurt** someone, you say or do something that makes them unhappy. ❏ *I'm really sorry if I hurt your feelings.*

5 ADJECTIVE If you are **hurt**, you are upset because of something that someone has said or done. ❏ *She was deeply hurt by what Smith said.*

→ look at **feeling, sick**

hus|band /hʌzbənd/ (**husbands**) NOUN
A woman's **husband** is the man she is married to. ❏ *Eva married her husband in 1957.*
→ look at **family**

hush /hʌʃ/

1 You say "**Hush!**" when you are telling someone to be quiet. ❏ *Hush! The teacher's talking.*

2 NOUN There is a **hush** in a place when everything is quiet. ❏ *There was a sudden hush in the room.*

hut /hʌt/ (**huts**) NOUN A **hut** is a small simple building, especially one made of wood.

hy|brid /haɪbrɪd/ (**hybrids**)

1 NOUN SCIENCE A **hybrid** is an animal or a plant that is made from two different types of animal or plant. ❏ *A mule is a hybrid of a horse and a donkey.*

2 ADJECTIVE **Hybrid** is also an adjective. ❏ *The hybrid seed produces larger flowers.*

3 NOUN TECHNOLOGY A **hybrid** or a **hybrid car** is a car that can use either gasoline or electricity as its power. ❏ *Hybrid cars can go almost 600 miles between refueling.*

hy|giene /haɪdʒin/ NONCOUNT NOUN
Hygiene is the practice of keeping yourself and the things you use clean. ❏ *The key to*

good hygiene is washing your hands before touching food. ● **hy|gien|ic** /haɪdʒɛnɪk/ ADJECTIVE ❏ *This kitchen is easy to keep clean and hygienic.*

hymn /hɪm/ (**hymns**) NOUN MUSIC A **hymn** is a religious song that Christians (= people who believe in Jesus Christ) sing in church. ❏ *I like singing hymns.*

hyper|link /haɪpərlɪŋk/ (**hyperlinks**) NOUN TECHNOLOGY In a document on a computer, a **hyperlink** is a link to another part of the document or to another document. ❏ *Web pages are full of hyperlinks.*

hy|phen /haɪfən/ (**hyphens**) NOUN LANGUAGE ARTS A **hyphen** is the punctuation sign (-) that you use to join two words together, as in "left-handed." You also use a hyphen to show that a word continues on the next line.
→ look at **punctuation**

hyp|no|sis /hɪpnoʊsɪs/ NONCOUNT NOUN
Hypnosis is when someone is in a sort of deep sleep, but they can still see, hear, and speak. ❏ *Ms. Chorley uses hypnosis to help her clients relax.*

hyp|no|tize /hɪpnətaɪz/ (**hypnotizes, hypnotizing, hypnotized**) VERB If someone **hypnotizes** you, they put you into a sort of deep sleep, but you can still see, hear, or speak to them. ● **hyp|no|tism** /hɪpnətɪzəm/ NONCOUNT NOUN ❏ *The doctor used hypnotism to help her deal with her fear of flying.* ● **hyp|no|tist** (**hypnotists**) NOUN ❏ *My sister-in-law makes regular visits to a hypnotist.*

hys|teri|cal /hɪstɛrɪkəl/

1 ADJECTIVE If you are **hysterical**, you are so excited or upset that you cannot control your feelings. ❏ *Calm down. Don't get hysterical.* ● **hys|teri|cal|ly** /hɪstɛrɪkli/ ADVERB ❏ *One young girl screamed hysterically and fell to the ground.*

2 ADJECTIVE **Hysterical** laughter is loud and cannot be controlled. [INFORMAL] ❏ *We could hear hysterical laughter coming from the kitchen.* ● **hys|teri|cal|ly** ADVERB ❏ *Everyone was laughing hysterically.*

3 ADJECTIVE If something or someone is **hysterical**, they are very funny. [INFORMAL] ❏ *Robert's stories are always hysterical.* ● **hys|teri|cal|ly** ADVERB ❏ *His new movie is hysterically funny.*

h

Ii

I /aɪ/ **PRONOUN** You use **I** to talk about yourself. You use **I** as the subject of a verb. ❑ *I live in Arizona.* ❑ *Jim and I are getting married.*

ice /aɪs/ **NONCOUNT NOUN** Ice is frozen water. ❑ *The ground was covered with ice.* ❑ *Do you want ice in your soda?*

ice|berg /aɪsbɜrg/ (**icebergs**) **NOUN** SCIENCE An **iceberg** is a very large piece of ice that floats in the ocean.

ice cream (**ice creams**)
1 **NONCOUNT NOUN** Ice cream is a very cold sweet food that is made from frozen cream. ❑ *Serve the pie warm with vanilla ice cream.*
2 **NOUN** An **ice cream** is a portion of ice cream. ❑ *Do you want an ice cream?*

ice hock|ey **NONCOUNT NOUN** SPORTS **Ice hockey** is a game that is played on ice by two teams. They use long curved sticks to try to hit a small rubber disk (= a puck) into a goal.

ici|cle /aɪsɪkəl/ (**icicles**) **NOUN** An **icicle** is a long pointed piece of ice that hangs down from a surface.

icon /aɪkɒn/ (**icons**) **NOUN** TECHNOLOGY An **icon** is a picture on a computer screen that you can choose using a mouse, in order to open a particular program. ❑ *Kate clicked on the mail icon on her computer screen.*

icy /aɪsi/ (**icier, iciest**)
1 **ADJECTIVE** Something that is **icy** is extremely cold. ❑ *An icy wind was blowing.*
2 **ADJECTIVE** An **icy** road has ice on it.

ID /aɪ di/ **NONCOUNT NOUN** If you have **ID**, you are carrying a document that shows who you are. ❑ *I had no ID so I couldn't prove that it was my car.*

I'd /aɪd/
1 **I'd** is short for "I had." ❑ *I was sure I'd seen her before.*
2 **I'd** is short for "I would." ❑ *There are some questions I'd like to ask.*

idea /aɪdiə/ (**ideas**)
1 **NOUN** An **idea** is a thought, especially a new one. ❑ *These people have a lot of great ideas.* ❑ *"Let's have something to eat."—"Good idea."*
2 **NOUN** If you have an **idea** of something, you know something about it. ❑ *We had no idea what was happening.*
3 **NOUN** The **idea** of something is its aim or purpose. ❑ *The idea is to have fun.*
→ look at **writing**

Word Partners	Use **idea** with:
ADJ.	**bad** idea, **bright** idea, **brilliant** idea, **crazy** idea, **different** idea, **dumb** idea, **great** idea, **interesting** idea, **new** idea, **original** idea **1** **the main** idea, **the whole** idea **3**

ideal /aɪdiəl/ (**ideals**)
1 **ADJECTIVE** The **ideal** person or thing for a particular purpose is the best possible person or thing for it. ❑ *You are the ideal person to do the job.*
2 **ADJECTIVE** An **ideal** situation is a perfect one. ❑ *Imagine for a moment that you're living in an ideal world.*
3 **NOUN** An **ideal** is a principle or idea that people try to achieve. ❑ *We must defend the ideals of liberty and freedom.*

iden|ti|cal /aɪdɛntɪkəl/ **ADJECTIVE** Things that are **identical** are exactly the same. ❑ *The houses were almost identical.*

iden|ti|fi|ca|tion /aɪdɛntɪfɪkeɪʃən/ **NONCOUNT NOUN** If someone asks you for some **identification**, they want to see a document that proves who you are. ❑ *The police asked him to show some identification.*
→ look at Word World: **identification**

iden|ti|fy /aɪdɛntɪfaɪ/ (**identifies, identifying, identified**) **VERB** If you can **identify** someone or something, you are able to say who or what they are. ❑ *Now we have identified the problem, we must decide how to fix it.* ❑ *The handbook tells you how to identify the different birds.* ● **iden|ti|fi|ca|tion** /aɪdɛntɪfɪkeɪʃən/ **NONCOUNT NOUN** ❑ *Early identification of the disease is important.*

Word World

identification

card / passport / driver's license / name / identity / information / proof / birthday / photograph

private / necessary / legal / personal / important / protect / show / need / give / verify

Nouns / Adjectives / Verbs

iden|tity /aɪdɛntɪti/ (**identities**) **NOUN** Your **identity** is who you are. ❑ *He uses the name Abu to hide his identity.*
→ look at **identification**

iden|tity theft **NONCOUNT NOUN** Identity **theft** is the crime of stealing someone's personal information, making it possible to use their bank account. ❑ *Cases of criminal identity theft are going to increase.*

idi|om /ɪdiəm/ (**idioms**) **NOUN**
LANGUAGE ARTS An **idiom** is a group of words that have a particular meaning when you use them together. For example, "to hit the roof" is an idiom that means to become very angry.

id|iot /ɪdiət/ (**idiots**) **NOUN** An **idiot** is someone who is very stupid. ❑ *I felt like an idiot.*

idol /aɪdᵊl/ (**idols**) **NOUN** An **idol** is a famous person who is greatly admired or loved. ❑ *The crowd cheered when their idol waved to the cameras.*

if /ɪf/
1 **CONJUNCTION** You use **if** to talk about things that might happen. ❑ *You can go if you want.* ❑ *He might win—if he's lucky.*
2 **CONJUNCTION** You use **if** when you are talking about a question that someone has asked. ❑ *He asked if I wanted some water.*
3 You use **if only** to express a strong wish. ❑ *If only I had a car.*
4 You use **as if** to compare one thing with another. ❑ *He moved his hand as if he was writing something.*

ig|no|rant /ɪgnərənt/ **ADJECTIVE** An **ignorant** person does not know things. ❑ *People don't want to appear ignorant.* ❑ *Most people are ignorant of these facts.* ● **ig|no|rance** /ɪgnərəns/ **NONCOUNT NOUN** ❑ *I feel embarrassed by my ignorance of world history.*

ig|nore /ɪgnɔr/ (**ignores, ignoring, ignored**) **VERB** If you **ignore** someone or something, you do not pay any attention to them. ❑ *Her husband ignored her.*

ill /ɪl/ **ADJECTIVE** Someone who is **ill** is not in good health. ❑ *He is seriously ill with cancer.*

I'll /aɪl/ **I'll** is short for "I will" or "I shall." ❑ *I'll go there tomorrow.*

il|legal /ɪligᵊl/ **ADJECTIVE** If something is **illegal**, it is not allowed by law. ❑ *It is illegal for the interviewer to ask your age.* ❑ *I have done nothing illegal.* ● **il|legal|ly** **ADVERB** ❑ *He received a fine for parking illegally.*

ill|ness /ɪlnɪs/ (**illnesses**)
1 **NOUN** An **illness** is a particular disease or a period of bad health. ❑ *She is recovering from a serious illness.*
2 **NONCOUNT NOUN** **Illness** is the fact or experience of being ill. ❑ *He was away from school because of illness.*

il|lu|sion /ɪluʒᵊn/ (**illusions**)
1 **NOUN** An **illusion** is a false idea or belief. ❑ *He's under the illusion that money makes people happy.*
2 **NOUN** An **illusion** is something that seems to exist. ❑ *Large windows can give the illusion of more space.*

il|lus|trate /ɪləstreɪt/ (**illustrates, illustrating, illustrated**) **VERB** If you **illustrate** a book, you put pictures into it. ❑ *She illustrates children's books.* ● **il|lus|tra|tion** (**illustrations**) **NOUN** ❑ *It's a book with beautiful illustrations.*

IM /aɪ ɛm/ **NOUN** TECHNOLOGY **IM** is short for **instant messaging**. ❑ *The device lets you chat via IM.*

I'm /aɪm/ **I'm** is short for "I am." ❑ *I'm sorry.*

im|age /ɪmɪdʒ/ (**images**)
1 **NOUN** An **image** is a picture of someone or something. [FORMAL] ❑ *The image on screen changes every 10 seconds.*
2 **NOUN** If you have an **image** of something or someone, you have a picture or idea of them in your mind. ❑ *If you talk about California, people have an image of sunny blue skies.*

i

3 **NOUN** The **image** of a person, a group, or an organization is the way that they appear to other people. ❏ *The government does not have a good public image.*

im|agi|nary /ɪmˈædʒɪnɛri/ **ADJECTIVE** An **imaginary** person, place, or thing exists only in your mind or in a story, and not in real life. ❏ *Lots of children have imaginary friends.*

im|agi|na|tion /ɪmˌædʒɪˈneɪʃ³n/ (**imaginations**) **NOUN** Your **imagination** is your ability to invent pictures or ideas in your mind. ❏ *You must use your imagination to find an answer to this problem.*

im|ag|ine /ɪˈmædʒɪn/ (**imagines, imagining, imagined**)

1 **VERB** If you **imagine** something, you form a picture or idea of it in your mind. ❏ *He could not imagine a more peaceful scene.*

2 **VERB** If you **imagine** something, you think that you have seen, heard, or experienced that thing, but in fact you have not. ❏ *I realize that I imagined the whole thing.*

imi|tate /ˈɪmɪteɪt/ (**imitates, imitating, imitated**) **VERB** If you **imitate** someone, you copy what they do or produce. ❏ *I didn't like the way he imitated my voice.*

imi|ta|tion /ˌɪmɪˈteɪʃ³n/ (**imitations**)

1 **NOUN** An **imitation** of something is a copy of it. ❏ *He tried to do an imitation of an English accent.* ❏ *Make sure you get the real thing—don't buy an imitation.*

2 **ADJECTIVE** **Imitation** things are made to look like other, more expensive products. ❏ *The books are covered in imitation leather.*

Word Builder   **immature**

im ≈ **not**

    im + mature = immature
    im + patient = impatient
    im + perfect = imperfect
    im + possible = impossible

---

im|ma|ture /ˌɪmətˈʃʊər, -tʊər/ **ADJECTIVE** Someone who is **immature** behaves in a silly way that is more typical of young people. ❏ *His parents thought he was too immature to get married.*

im|medi|ate /ɪˈmidiɪt/ **ADJECTIVE** Something that is **immediate** happens next or very soon. ❏ *There is no immediate solution to the problem.*

im|medi|ate|ly /ɪˈmidiɪtli/ **ADVERB** Something that happens **immediately**, happens without any delay. ❏ *"Call the police immediately!" she shouted.*

im|mense /ɪˈmɛns/ **ADJECTIVE** Something that is **immense** is extremely large. ❏ *We still need to do an immense amount of work.*

im|mense|ly /ɪˈmɛnsli/ **ADVERB** Immensely means very much. ❏ *I enjoyed the movie immensely.*

im|mi|grant /ˈɪmɪgrənt/ (**immigrants**) **NOUN** SOCIAL STUDIES An **immigrant** is a person who comes to live in a country from another country. ❏ *The company employs several immigrant workers.*

im|mi|gra|tion /ˌɪmɪˈgreɪʃ³n/ **NONCOUNT** **NOUN** Immigration is when people come into a country to live and work there. ❏ *The government is changing the immigration laws.*

im|mor|al /ɪˈmɔrəl/ **ADJECTIVE** Someone or something that is **immoral** is bad or wrong. ❏ *Some people think that it's immoral to earn a lot of money.*

im|mor|tal /ɪˈmɔrtəl/ **ADJECTIVE** Someone or something that is **immortal** will live or last forever. ❏ *They prayed to their immortal gods.* ❏ *When you're young, you think you're immortal.*

im|mune /ɪˈmyun/ **ADJECTIVE** If you are **immune to** a particular disease, it cannot affect you. ❏ *Some people are naturally immune to measles.*

im|pact /ˈɪmpækt/ (**impacts**)

1 **NOUN** If something has an **impact**, it has a strong effect. ❏ *The experience had a huge impact on her.*

2 **NOUN** An **impact** is the action of one object hitting another. ❏ *The impact of the crash turned the truck over.*

Word Builder   **impatient**

im ≈ **not**

    im + mature = immature
    im + patient = impatient
    im + perfect = imperfect
    im + possible = impossible

---

im|pa|tient /ɪmˈpeɪʃ³nt/

1 **ADJECTIVE** If you are **impatient**, you are annoyed because you have to wait too long for something. ❏ *People are impatient for the war to be over.* ● **im|pa|tient|ly** **ADVERB** ❏ *She waited impatiently for the mail to arrive.*

2 **ADJECTIVE** If you are **impatient**, things or people annoy you very quickly. ❏ *Try not to be impatient with your kids.* ● **im|pa|tience** **NONCOUNT NOUN** ❏ *She tried to hide her growing impatience with him.*

im|peach /ɪmpitʃ/ (**impeaches, impeaching, impeached**) **VERB** SOCIAL STUDIES If an official body **impeaches** a president or a government official, it decides that the president or the official has committed a serious crime. ❑ *The Republicans wanted to impeach the president.*

im|pera|tive /ɪmpɛrətɪv/ **NOUN** LANGUAGE ARTS In grammar, **the imperative** consists of the base form of a verb and usually has no subject. The imperative is used for telling someone to do something. Examples are "Go away" and "Please be careful."

Word Builder **imperfect**

im ≈ **not**
    im + mature = **im**mature
    im + patient = **im**patient
    im + perfect = **im**perfect
    im + possible = **im**possible

---

im|per|fect /ɪmpɜrfɪkt/ **ADJECTIVE** Something that is **imperfect** has faults. [FORMAL] ❑ *We live in an imperfect world.*

im|peri|al|ism /ɪmpɪəriəlɪzəm/ **NONCOUNT NOUN** SOCIAL STUDIES **Imperialism** is a system in which a powerful country controls other countries. ❑ *These nations are victims of imperialism.* ● **im|peri|al|ist** (**imperialists**) **NOUN** ❑ *She accused me of being a Western imperialist.*

Word Builder **import**

port ≈ **carry**
    air + port = **air**port
    ex + port = **ex**port
    im + port = **im**port
    port + able = **port**able
    trans + port = **trans**port

---

im|port (**imports, importing, imported**)

> **PRONUNCIATION HELP**
> Pronounce the verb /ɪmpɔrt/ or /ɪmpɔrt/. Pronounce the noun /ɪmpɔrt/.

1 VERB SOCIAL STUDIES To **import** goods means to buy them from another country for use in your own country. ❑ *The U.S. imports over half of its oil.*
2 NOUN **Import** is also a noun. ❑ *Cheap imports are adding to the problems of our farmers.* ● **im|port|er** (**importers**) **NOUN** ❑ *Japan is the biggest importer of U.S. beef.*

im|por|tant /ɪmpɔrtᵊnt/
1 ADJECTIVE If something is **important** to

you, you feel that you must do, have, or think about it. ❑ *The most important thing in my life is my career.* ❑ *It's important to answer her questions honestly.* ● **im|por|tance** **NONCOUNT NOUN** ❑ *The teacher stressed the importance of doing our homework.* ● **im|por|tant|ly** **ADVERB** ❑ *I was hungry, and, more importantly, my children were hungry.*
2 ADJECTIVE Someone who is **important** has influence or power. ❑ *She's an important person in the world of television.*
→ look at **fitness, identification, news**

Word Builder **impossible**

im ≈ **not**
    im + mature = **im**mature
    im + patient = **im**patient
    im + perfect = **im**perfect
    im + possible = **im**possible

---

im|pos|sible /ɪmpɒsɪbᵊl/ **ADJECTIVE** Something that is **impossible** cannot be done or cannot happen. ❑ *It is impossible for me to get another job at my age.* ❑ *The snow made it impossible to play the game.*

im|prac|ti|cal /ɪmpræktɪkᵊl/ **ADJECTIVE** Something that is **impractical** is not sensible or realistic. ❑ *She was wearing impractical high-heeled shoes.*

im|press /ɪmprɛs/ (**impresses, impressing, impressed**) **VERB** If something **impresses** you, you feel great admiration for it. ❑ *Their speed impressed everyone.* ● **im|pressed** **ADJECTIVE** ❑ *I was very impressed by his lecture.*

im|pres|sion /ɪmprɛʃᵊn/ (**impressions**)
1 NOUN Your **impression** of a person or thing is what you feel or think about them. ❑ *What were your first impressions of college?*
2 If someone or something **makes an impression**, they have a strong effect on you. ❑ *It's her first day at work and she has already made an impression.*
3 If you are **under the impression that** something is true, you believe that it is true. ❑ *I was under the impression that you were moving to New York.*

im|pres|sive /ɪmprɛsɪv/ **ADJECTIVE** Something that is **impressive** makes you feel strong admiration. ❑ *They collected an impressive amount of cash: $390.8 million.*

im|prove /ɪmpruv/ (**improves, improving, improved**) **VERB** If something **improves**, it gets better. ❑ *Your general health will improve if* you drink more water. ❏ Their French improved during their trip to Paris. ❏ We are trying to improve our services to customers. ● **im|prove|ment** /ɪmpruːvmənt/ (**improvements**) NOUN ❏ There have been some great improvements in technology in recent years.

im|pulse /ɪmpʌls/ (**impulses**)
1 NOUN An **impulse** is a sudden feeling that you must do something. ❏ I felt a sudden impulse to tell her that I loved her.
2 If you do something **on impulse**, you suddenly decide to do it. ❏ Sean usually acts on impulse.

im|pul|sive /ɪmpʌlsɪv/ ADJECTIVE An **impulsive** person does things suddenly, without thinking about them carefully first. ❏ He is too impulsive to be a good leader.

in

> **PRONUNCIATION HELP**
> Pronounce the preposition /ɪn/.
> Pronounce the adverb /ɪn/.

1 PREPOSITION You use **in** when you are saying where someone or something is. ❏ My brother was playing in the backyard. ❏ Mark now lives in Singapore. ❏ Are you still in bed? It's almost lunchtime!
2 ADVERB If you **are in**, you are at your home or the place where you work. ❏ Maria isn't in just now.
3 PREPOSITION If you are dressed **in** a piece of clothing, you are wearing it. ❏ Who is the woman in the red dress?
4 PREPOSITION You use **in** when you are talking about the job that someone does. ❏ John's son is in the navy. ❏ Dad works in the music industry.
5 PREPOSITION If something happens **in** a particular period of time, it happens during that time. ❏ He was born in 1996. ❏ Sales improved in April.
6 PREPOSITION If you do something **in** a particular period of time, that is how long it takes. ❏ He walked two hundred miles in eight days.
7 PREPOSITION You use **in** to talk about a state or situation. ❏ Dave was in a hurry to get back to work. ❏ The kitchen's in a mess.
8 PREPOSITION You use **in** to talk about the way that something is done or said. ❏ Please do not write in pencil—use a pen. ❏ The men were speaking in Russian. ❏ She always talks in a loud voice.
9 ADJECTIVE SPORTS In games such as tennis or basketball, a ball that is **in** is inside the area of play. Compare with **out**.

❏ The line judge signalled that the ball was in. → look at **location**

in|abil|ity /ɪnəbɪlɪti/ NONCOUNT NOUN Someone's **inability to** do something is the fact that they cannot do it. ❏ Her inability to concentrate could cause an accident.

in|ac|cu|rate /ɪnækyərɪt/ ADJECTIVE Information that is **inaccurate** is not completely correct. ❏ Her comments are inaccurate and untrue.

in|ad|equate /ɪnædɪkwɪt/ ADJECTIVE If something is **inadequate**, there is not enough of it, or it is not good enough. ❏ Inadequate sleep was the cause of his headaches.

in|ap|pro|pri|ate /ɪnəproupriːt/ ADJECTIVE Something that is **inappropriate** is wrong or bad in a particular situation. ❏ The movie is inappropriate for young children.

in|augu|rate /ɪnɔːgyʊreɪt/ (**inaugurates, inaugurating, inaugurated**) VERB SOCIAL STUDIES When a new leader is **inaugurated**, they are given their new position at an official ceremony. ❏ The new president will be inaugurated on January 20th.
● **in|augu|ra|tion** /ɪnɔːgyʊreɪʃⁿn/ (**inaugurations**) NOUN ❏ ...the inauguration of the new governor.

> **Word Builder** **inbox**
> *in* ≈ **in**
> in + box = **in**box
> in + doors = **in**doors
> in + land = **in**land
> in + put = **in**put
> in + side = **in**side

in|box /ɪnbɒks/ (**inboxes**) also **in-box** NOUN TECHNOLOGY Your **inbox** is where your computer stores emails that have arrived for you. ❏ I went home and checked my inbox. → look at **email**

Inc. **Inc.** is short for "Incorporated" when it is used after a company's name. ❏ ...BP America Inc.

in|ca|pable /ɪnkeɪpəbⁿl/ ADJECTIVE Someone who is **incapable of** doing something is unable to do it. ❏ She is incapable of making sensible decisions.

in|cen|tive /ɪnsɛntɪv/ (**incentives**) NOUN An **incentive** is something that makes you want to do something. ❏ We want to give our employees an incentive to work hard.

inch /ɪntʃ/ (inches) **NOUN** **MATH** An **inch** is a unit for measuring length. There are 2.54 centimeters in an inch. There are twelve inches in a foot. ❑ *Dig a hole 18 inches deep.*
→ look at **measurement**

in|ci|dent /ɪnsɪdənt/ (incidents) **NOUN** An **incident** is something unpleasant that happens. [FORMAL] ❑ *The incident happened in the early hours of Sunday morning.*

in|clined /ɪnklaɪnd/ **ADJECTIVE** If you say that you are **inclined to** have a particular opinion, you mean that you have this opinion, but you do not feel strongly about it. ❑ *I am inclined to agree with Alan.*

in|clude /ɪnklud/ (includes, including, included) **VERB** If something **includes** another thing, it has that thing as one of its parts. ❑ *The trip will include a day at the beach.*

in|clud|ing /ɪnkludɪŋ/ **PREPOSITION** You use **including** to talk about people or things that are part of a particular group of people or things. ❑ *Thousands were killed, including many women and children.*

in|come /ɪnkʌm/ (incomes) **NOUN** A person's **income** is the money that they earn or receive. ❑ *Many of the families here are on low incomes.*

in|come tax (income taxes) **NOUN** Income **tax** is a part of your income that you have to pay regularly to the government. ❑ *You pay income tax every month.*

in|com|pe|tent /ɪnkɒmpɪtənt/ **ADJECTIVE** Someone who is **incompetent** is unable to do a job properly. ❑ *He always fires incompetent employees.*

Word Builder **incomplete**

in ≈ **not**

in + complete = **in**complete
in + correct = **in**correct
in + dependent = **in**dependent
in + direct = **in**direct
in + secure = **in**secure
in + visible = **in**visible

---

in|com|plete /ɪnkəmplit/ **ADJECTIVE** Something that is **incomplete** is not yet finished, or does not have all the parts that it needs. ❑ *The data we have is incomplete.*

in|con|sid|er|ate /ɪnkənsɪdərɪt/ **ADJECTIVE** Someone who is **inconsiderate** does not think enough about how their behavior will affect other people. ❑ *It was inconsiderate of her to come without calling.*

in|con|ven|ient /ɪnkənvinyənt/ **ADJECTIVE** Something that is **inconvenient** causes difficulties for someone. ❑ *I know it's inconvenient, but I have to see you now.*

Word Builder **incorrect**

in ≈ **not**

in + complete = **in**complete
in + correct = **in**correct
in + dependent = **in**dependent
in + direct = **in**direct
in + secure = **in**secure
in + visible = **in**visible

---

in|cor|rect /ɪnkərɛkt/ **ADJECTIVE** Something that is **incorrect** is wrong or untrue. ❑ *The answer he gave was incorrect.* ● **in|cor|rect|ly** **ADVERB** ❑ *The article suggested, incorrectly, that he was sick.*
→ look at **grammar**

in|crease (increases, increasing, increased)

PRONUNCIATION HELP
Pronounce the verb /ɪnkris/. Pronounce the noun /ɪnkris/.

---

1 **VERB** If something **increases**, it gets bigger in some way. ❑ *The population continues to increase.* ❑ *Japanese exports increased by 2% last year.*
2 **NOUN** If there is an **increase in** the number, level, or amount of something, it becomes greater. ❑ *There was a sudden increase in the cost of oil.*

in|creas|ing|ly /ɪnkrisɪŋli/ **ADVERB** You can use **increasingly** to talk about a situation that is happening more and more. ❑ *He was finding it increasingly difficult to make decisions.*

in|cred|ible /ɪnkrɛdɪbəl/
1 **ADJECTIVE** You use **incredible** to say how good something is, or to make what you are saying stronger. ❑ *The food was incredible.* ❑ *I work an incredible number of hours.* ● **in|cred|ibly** **ADVERB** ❑ *It was incredibly hard work.*
2 **ADJECTIVE** If you say that something is **incredible**, you mean that you cannot believe it is really true. ❑ *It seems incredible that nobody saw the danger.*

in|deed /ɪndid/
1 **ADVERB** You use **indeed** to make something you have said stronger. ❑ *He admitted that he had indeed paid him.*
2 **ADVERB** You use **indeed** to make the word "very" stronger. ❑ *The results were very strange indeed.*

i

in|defi|nite /ɪndɛfɪnɪt/ **ADJECTIVE** If a situation or period is **indefinite**, people have not decided when it will end. ❑ *He was sent to jail for an indefinite period.* ● **in|defi|nite|ly ADVERB** ❑ *We cannot allow this situation to continue indefinitely.*

in|defi|nite ar|ti|cle (indefinite articles) **NOUN** LANGUAGE ARTS The words "a" and "an" are sometimes called **the indefinite article**.

in|den|tured serv|ant /ɪndɛntʃərd sɜrvənt/ (indentured servants) **NOUN** SOCIAL STUDIES In the past, an **indentured servant** was a worker who had to serve another person in exchange for things such as food, clothes and a place to sleep, for a period of time that was agreed in a contract.

in|de|pend|ence /ɪndɪpɛndəns/
1 **NONCOUNT NOUN** SOCIAL STUDIES If a country has **independence**, it is not ruled by another country. ❑ *In 1816, Argentina declared its independence from Spain.*
2 **NONCOUNT NOUN** Someone's **independence** is the fact that they do not need help from other people. ❑ *He was afraid of losing his independence.*
→ look at **history**

Word Builder   **independent**

in ≈ **not**
  in + complete = incomplete
  in + correct = incorrect
  in + dependent = independent
  in + direct = indirect
  in + secure = insecure
  in + visible = invisible
---

in|de|pend|ent /ɪndɪpɛndənt/
1 **ADJECTIVE** If things or people are **independent**, they are not affected by, or do not need help from, other people. ❑ *We need an independent review.* ● **in|de|pen|dent|ly ADVERB** ❑ *We have groups of people working independently in different parts of the world.*
2 **ADJECTIVE** If someone is **independent**, they can take care of themselves without needing help or money from anyone else. ❑ *Children become more independent as they grow.* ● **in|de|pen|dent|ly ADVERB** ❑ *We want to help disabled students to live independently.*
3 **ADJECTIVE** **Independent** countries and states are not ruled by other countries, but have their own government. ❑ *Papua New Guinea became independent from Australia in 1975.* ● **in|de|pend|ence NONCOUNT NOUN**

❑ *Argentina declared its independence from Spain in 1816.*
→ look at **disability**

in|dex /ɪndɛks/ (indexes) **NOUN** LANGUAGE ARTS An **index** is a list printed at the back of a book that tells you what is included in it and on which pages you can find each item. ❑ *There's a subject index at the back of the book.*

In|dian /ɪndiən/ (Indians) **NOUN** SOCIAL STUDIES **Indians** are the people who lived in America before Europeans arrived. Now, people prefer to call them **Native Americans**.

in|di|cate /ɪndɪkeɪt/ (indicates, indicating, indicated)
1 **VERB** One thing **indicates** another when the first thing shows that the second is true. ❑ *The report indicates that most people agree.*
2 **VERB** If you **indicate** something to someone, you show them where it is. [FORMAL] ❑ *He indicated a chair. "Sit down."*

in|di|ca|tion /ɪndɪkeɪʃən/ (indications) **NOUN** An **indication** is a sign that suggests something. ❑ *This statement is a strong indication that the government is changing its mind.*

in|dif|fer|ent /ɪndɪfərənt/ **ADJECTIVE** Someone who is **indifferent to** something is not at all interested in it. ❑ *We have become indifferent to the suffering of other people.*

in|di|ges|tion /ɪndɪdʒɛstʃən, -daɪ-/ **NONCOUNT NOUN** If you have **indigestion**, you have pains in your stomach because of something that you have eaten.

Word Builder   **indirect**

in ≈ **not**
  in + complete = incomplete
  in + correct = incorrect
  in + dependent = independent
  in + direct = indirect
  in + secure = insecure
  in + visible = invisible
---

in|di|rect /ɪndaɪrɛkt, -dɪr-/
1 **ADJECTIVE** An **indirect** result or effect is not caused directly by the person or thing mentioned, but it does happen because of them. ❑ *Millions could die of hunger as an indirect result of the war.* ● **in|di|rect|ly ADVERB** ❑ *The government is indirectly responsible for the violence.*
2 **ADJECTIVE** An **indirect** route or journey is not the shortest route between two places. ❑ *He took an indirect route back home.*

3 **ADJECTIVE** **Indirect** remarks suggest something, without stating it clearly. ❑ *It was an indirect criticism of the president.* ● **in|di|rect|ly** **ADVERB** ❑ *She indirectly suggested that he should leave.*

in|di|rect ob|ject (indirect objects) **NOUN** LANGUAGE ARTS In a sentence, an **indirect object** is the thing or person that something is done to. For example, in "She gave him her address," "him" is the indirect object. Compare with **direct object**.

in|di|vid|ual /ɪndɪvɪdʒuəl/ (individuals)
1 **ADJECTIVE** **Individual** means relating to one person or thing, rather than to a large group. ❑ *We ask each individual customer for suggestions.* ● **in|di|vid|ual|ly** **ADVERB** ❑ *You can remove each seat individually.*
2 **NOUN** An **individual** is a person. ❑ *We want to reward individuals who do good things.*

in|door /ɪndɔr/ **ADJECTIVE** **Indoor** activities happen inside a building and not outside. ❑ *The hotel has an indoor pool.*

Word Builder **indoors**

in ≈ **in**

in + box = **in**box
in + doors = **in**doors
in + land = **in**land
in + put = **in**put
in + side = **in**side

---

in|doors /ɪndɔrz/ **ADVERB** If something happens **indoors**, it happens inside a building. ❑ *They warned us to close the windows and stay indoors.*

in|dus|trial /ɪndʌstriəl/
1 **ADJECTIVE** SOCIAL STUDIES **Industrial** describes things that relate to industry. ❑ *The company sells industrial machinery and equipment.*
2 **ADJECTIVE** SOCIAL STUDIES An **industrial** city or country is one in which industry is very important. ❑ *...Western industrial countries.*

in|dus|try /ɪndəstri/ (industries)
1 **NONCOUNT NOUN** SOCIAL STUDIES **Industry** is the work of making things in factories. ❑ *The meeting was for leaders in banking and industry.*
2 **NOUN** SOCIAL STUDIES A particular **industry** consists of all the people and activities involved in making a particular product or providing a particular service. ❑ *The country depends on its tourism industry.*
→ look at **factory**

in|ef|fi|cient /ɪnɪfɪʃənt/ **ADJECTIVE** Someone or something that is **inefficient**, does not use time or energy in the best way. ❑ *...inefficient work methods.*

in|equal|ity /ɪnɪkwɒliti/ **NONCOUNT NOUN** **Inequality** is when people do not have the same social position, wealth, or chances. ❑ *Now there is even greater inequality between the rich and the poor.*

in|evi|table /ɪnɛvɪtəbəl/ **ADJECTIVE** Something that is **inevitable** cannot be prevented or avoided. ❑ *Suffering is an inevitable part of life.* ● **in|evi|tably** /ɪnɛvɪtəbli/ **ADVERB** ❑ *Advances in technology will inevitably lead to unemployment.*

in|ex|pe|ri|enced /ɪnɪkspɪəriənst/ **ADJECTIVE** If you are **inexperienced**, you have little knowledge or experience of a particular subject. ❑ *She was treated by an inexperienced young doctor.*

in|fant /ɪnfənt/ (infants) **NOUN** An **infant** is a baby or very young child. [FORMAL] ❑ *He held the infant in his arms.*
→ look at **age**

in|fect /ɪnfɛkt/ (infects, infecting, infected) **VERB** To **infect** people or animals means to give them a disease or an illness. ❑ *A single mosquito can infect a large number of people.*
● **in|fec|tion** /ɪnfɛkʃən/ **NONCOUNT NOUN** ❑ *Even a small cut can lead to infection.*

in|fec|tion /ɪnfɛkʃən/ (infections) **NOUN** An **infection** is an illness that is caused by bacteria. ❑ *Ear infections are common in young children.*
→ look at **sick**

in|fec|tious /ɪnfɛkʃəs/ **ADJECTIVE** A disease that is **infectious** can be passed easily from one person to another. Compare with **contagious**. ❑ *The disease is highly infectious.*

in|fe|ri|or /ɪnfɪəriər/ **ADJECTIVE** Something that is **inferior** is not as good as something else. ❑ *If you buy it somewhere else, you'll get an inferior product.*

in|fer|tile /ɪnfɜrtəl/
1 **ADJECTIVE** A person or animal that is **infertile** is unable to produce babies. ❑ *Ten percent of couples are infertile.*
2 **ADJECTIVE** **Infertile** soil is of poor quality. ❑ *Nothing grew on the land, which was poor and infertile.*

in|fi|nite /ˈɪnfɪnɪt/ **ADJECTIVE** Something that is **infinite** has no limit, end, or edge. ❑ *There is an infinite number of stars.*

in|fini|tive /ɪnˈfɪnɪtɪv/ (**infinitives**) **NOUN** LANGUAGE ARTS The **infinitive** of a verb is the basic form, for example, "do," "be," "take," and "eat." The infinitive is often used with "to" in front of it.

in|flat|able /ɪnˈfleɪtəbəl/ **ADJECTIVE** An **inflatable** object needs to be filled with air when you want to use it. ❑ *The children were playing on the inflatable castle.*

in|flate /ɪnˈfleɪt/ **VERB** If you **inflate** something, you fill it with air. ❑ *You should inflate tires to the level recommended by the manufacturer.*

in|fla|tion /ɪnˈfleɪʃən/ **NONCOUNT NOUN** **Inflation** is a general increase in the prices of goods and services in a country. ❑ *The whole world is suffering from rising inflation.*

in|flu|ence /ˈɪnfluəns/ (**influences, influencing, influenced**)

1 **NONCOUNT NOUN** **Influence** is the power to make other people agree with you or do what you want. ❑ *He used his influence to get his son into medical school.*

2 **VERB** If you **influence** someone, you use your power to make them agree with you or do what you want. ❑ *The newspapers tried to influence public opinion.*

3 **NOUN** To have an **influence on** people or situations means to affect what they do or what happens. ❑ *Alan had a big influence on my career.*

in|flu|en|tial /ˌɪnfluˈɛnʃəl/ **ADJECTIVE** Someone or something that is **influential** has a lot of influence over people or events. ❑ *He was influential in changing the law.*

info /ˈɪnfoʊ/ **NONCOUNT NOUN** **Info** is information. [INFORMAL] ❑ *For more info call 414-3935.*

in|form /ɪnˈfɔrm/ (**informs, informing, informed**) **VERB** If you **inform** someone **of** something, you tell them about it. ❑ *We will inform you of any changes.* ❑ *My daughter informed me that she was leaving home.*

in|for|mal /ɪnˈfɔrməl/ **ADJECTIVE** **Informal** means relaxed and friendly, rather than serious or official. ❑ *Her style of writing is very informal.* ❑ *The house has an informal atmosphere.*

● **in|for|mal|ly** **ADVERB** ❑ *She was chatting informally to the children.*
→ look at **grammar, writing**

in|for|ma|tion /ˌɪnfərˈmeɪʃən/

1 **NONCOUNT NOUN** **Information** about someone or something is facts about them. ❑ *Pat did not give her any information about Sarah.* ❑ *We can provide information on training.*

2 **NONCOUNT NOUN** **Information** is a service that you can telephone to find out someone's telephone number. ❑ *He called information, and they gave him the number.*
→ look at **communication, identification**

Word Partners	Use **information** with:
ADJ.	**background** information, **important** information, **new** information, **personal** information **1**
V.	**find** information, **get** information, **have** information, **need** information, **provide** information, **want** information **1**

in|for|ma|tion tech|nol|ogy **NONCOUNT NOUN** TECHNOLOGY **Information technology** is the theory and practice of using computers. The short form **I.T.** is often used. ❑ *He works in the information technology industry.*

in|forma|tive /ɪnˈfɔrmətɪv/ **ADJECTIVE** Something that is **informative** gives you useful information. ❑ *The meeting was friendly and informative.*

in|gre|di|ent /ɪnˈɡridiənt/ (**ingredients**) **NOUN** **Ingredients** are the things that you use to make something, especially when you are cooking. ❑ *Mix together all the ingredients.*

in|hab|it /ɪnˈhæbɪt/ (**inhabits, inhabiting, inhabited**) **VERB** If a place **is inhabited** by a group of people, those people live there. ❑ *The people who inhabit these islands do not use money.*

in|hab|it|ant /ɪnˈhæbɪtənt/ (**inhabitants**) **NOUN** The **inhabitants** of a place are the people who live there. ❑ *The inhabitants of the town wrote a letter to the president.*

in|hale /ɪnˈheɪl/ (**inhales, inhaling, inhaled**) **VERB** When you **inhale**, you breathe in. ❑ *He took a long slow breath, inhaling deeply.* ❑ *The men inhaled the poisonous gas and began to feel sick.*

in|her|it /ɪnˈhɛrɪt/ (**inherits, inheriting, inherited**)

1 **VERB** If you **inherit** money or property,

you receive it from someone who has died. ❏ *He has no child to inherit his house.*

2 **VERB** If you **inherit** a personal quality, you are born with it because other members of your family had it. ❏ *Her children have inherited her love of sports.*

in|her|it|ance /ɪnhɛrɪtᵊns/ (**inheritances**)
NOUN An **inheritance** is money or property that you receive from someone who has died. ❏ *She used her inheritance to buy a house.*

ini|tial /ɪnɪʃᵊl/ (**initials**)
1 **ADJECTIVE** **Initial** means happening at the beginning of a process. ❏ *The initial reaction has been excellent.*
2 **NOUN** **Initials** are the capital letters that begin each word of a name. ❏ *She drove a silver car with her initials on the side.*

ini|tial|ly /ɪnɪʃəli/ **ADVERB** **Initially** means near the beginning of a process or situation. ❏ *The list initially included 11 players.*

in|ject /ɪndʒɛkt/ (**injects, injecting, injected**)
VERB To **inject** a substance into someone means to put it into their body using a special type of needle. ❏ *The drug was injected into patients four times a week.*

in|jec|tion /ɪndʒɛkʃn/ (**injections**) **NOUN** If you have an **injection**, someone puts medicine into your body using a special type of needle. ❏ *They gave me an injection to help me sleep.*

in|jure /ɪndʒər/ (**injures, injuring, injured**)
VERB If you **injure** a person or animal, you damage part of their body. ❏ *The bomb seriously injured five people.*

in|jured /ɪndʒərd/
1 **ADJECTIVE** An **injured** person or animal has suffered damage to part of their body. ❏ *Nurses helped the injured man.*
2 **PLURAL NOUN** The **injured** are people who are injured. ❏ *Army helicopters moved the injured.*

in|ju|ry /ɪndʒəri/ (**injuries**) **NOUN** An **injury** is damage to a person's or an animal's body. ❏ *He was suffering from serious head injuries.*

in|jus|tice /ɪndʒʌstɪs/ **NONCOUNT NOUN**
Injustice is when a situation is not fair or right. ❏ *They have fought injustice all their lives.*

ink /ɪŋk/ **NONCOUNT NOUN** **Ink** is the colored liquid that you use for writing or printing. ❏ *The letter was written in blue ink.*

Word Builder **inland**

in ≈ **in**

in + box = **in**box
in + doors = **in**doors
in + land = **in**land
in + put = **in**put
in + side = **in**side

in|land

PRONUNCIATION HELP
Pronounce the adverb /ɪnlænd, -lənd/.
Pronounce the adjective /ɪnlənd/.

1 **ADVERB** **Inland** means not beside the ocean, and in or near the middle of a country. ❏ *Most of the population lives inland.* ❏ *The town is about 15 minutes' drive inland from Pensacola.*
2 **ADJECTIVE** **Inland** places are not beside the ocean, but are in or near the middle of a country. ❏ *...inland lakes.*

in-laws **PLURAL NOUN** Your **in-laws** are the parents of your husband or wife. ❏ *At Christmas, we had lunch with my in-laws.*

in|ner /ɪnər/ **ADJECTIVE** The **inner** parts of something are the parts inside it, or the parts closest to the center. ❏ *James has an infection of the inner ear.*

in|ner city (**inner cities**) **NOUN** The **inner city** is the poor areas near the center of a big city. ❏ *Samuel grew up in an inner-city neighborhood in Houston.*

in|no|cence /ɪnəsəns/
1 **NONCOUNT NOUN** **Innocence** is the quality of having no experience or knowledge of the more difficult aspects of life. ❏ *Ah! The sweet innocence of youth!*
2 **NONCOUNT NOUN** If someone proves their **innocence**, they prove that they are not guilty of a crime. ❏ *This information could prove your brother's innocence.*

in|no|cent /ɪnəsənt/
1 **ADJECTIVE** If you are **innocent**, you are not guilty of a crime. ❏ *The jury found him innocent of murder.*
2 **ADJECTIVE** If someone is **innocent**, they have no experience or knowledge of the more difficult aspects of life. ❏ *They seemed so young and innocent.*

in|no|va|tion /ɪnəveɪʃn/ (**innovations**)
NOUN An **innovation** is a new thing or a new way of doing something. ❏ *They showed us some of their latest technological innovations.*

in|no|va|tive /ɪnəveɪtɪv/

1 **ADJECTIVE** Something that is **innovative** is new and different. ❑ *The company produces innovative car designs.*

2 **ADJECTIVE** An **innovative** person has new ideas and does different things. ❑ *He is one of America's most innovative film-makers.*

Word Builder   **input**

in ≈ **in**

     in + box = inbox
     in + doors = indoors
     in + land = inland
     in + put = input
     in + side = inside

---

in|put /ɪnpʊt/ (**inputs, inputting, input**)

1 **NONCOUNT NOUN** **Input** is the help, information, or advice that one person gives to another person. ❑ *There has been a lot of hard work and input from the public.*

2 **NONCOUNT NOUN** **Input** is information that you type into a computer. ❑ *Who is responsible for data input here?*

3 **VERB** If you **input** information into a computer, you type it using a keyboard. ❑ *We need more staff to input the data.*

in|quire /ɪnkwaɪər/ (**inquires, inquiring, inquired**) **VERB** If you **inquire** about something, you ask for information about it. [FORMAL] ❑ *"What are you doing here?" she inquired.* ❑ *He called the company to inquire about a job.*

in|quiry /ɪnkwaɪəri, ɪŋkwɪri/ (**inquiries**)

1 **NOUN** If you make an **inquiry**, you ask a question in order to get some information. ❑ *Dad made some inquiries and found her address.*

2 **NOUN** An **inquiry** takes place when people officially try to find out the truth about something. ❑ *Pike is leading the inquiry into the shooting.*

in|quisi|tive /ɪnkwɪzɪtɪv/ **ADJECTIVE** An **inquisitive** person likes finding out about things. ❑ *Amy was very inquisitive, always wanting to know how things worked.*

in|sane /ɪnseɪn/

1 **ADJECTIVE** Someone who is **insane** is seriously mentally ill. ❑ *For a while, I thought I was going insane.*

2 **ADJECTIVE** If an idea or an action is **insane**, it is very foolish. ❑ *I thought the idea was completely insane.*

in|sect /ɪnsɛkt/ (**insects**) **NOUN** An **insect** is a very small animal that has six legs. Most insects have wings.

Word Builder   **insecure**

in ≈ **not**

     in + complete = incomplete
     in + correct = incorrect
     in + dependent = independent
     in + direct = indirect
     in + secure = insecure
     in + visible = invisible

---

in|secure /ɪnsɪkyʊər/

1 **ADJECTIVE** If you are **insecure**, you think that you are not good enough. ❑ *Most people are a little insecure about their looks.*

● **in|secu|rity** /ɪnsɪkyʊərɪti/ **NONCOUNT NOUN** ❑ *Both men and women can have feelings of shyness and insecurity.*

2 **ADJECTIVE** Something that is **insecure** is not safe, or is not firm and steady. ❑ *Don't take risks with an insecure ladder.*

in|sen|si|tive /ɪnsɛnsɪtɪv/ **ADJECTIVE** If someone is **insensitive**, they do not think about or care about other people's feelings. ❑ *My husband is very insensitive to my problem.*

● **in|sen|si|tiv|ity** /ɪnsɛnsɪtɪvɪti/ **NONCOUNT NOUN** ❑ *I'm sorry about my insensitivity toward her.*

in|sert /ɪnsɜrt/ (**inserts, inserting, inserted**) **VERB** If you **insert** an object **into** something, you put the object inside it. ❑ *Mike took a key from his pocket and inserted it into the lock.*
→ look at **ATM**

Word Builder   **inside**

in ≈ **in**

     in + box = inbox
     in + doors = indoors
     in + land = inland
     in + put = input
     in + side = inside

---

in|side /ɪnsaɪd/

PRONUNCIATION HELP
Pronounce the preposition /ɪnsaɪd/.

1 **PREPOSITION** Something or someone that is **inside** or **inside of** something, is in it. ❑ *Inside the envelope was a photograph.*

2 **ADJECTIVE** **Inside** is also an adjective. ❑ *Josh took his cellphone from the inside pocket of his jacket.*

3 **ADVERB** If you go **inside**, you go into a building. ❑ *The couple chatted on the doorstep before going inside.*

4 **NOUN** The **inside** of something is the inner part of it. ❑ *I've painted the inside of the house.*

5 If a piece of clothing is **inside out**, the part

that is normally inside is on the outside. ❏ *I didn't realize that my shirt was inside out.*

in|sight /ɪnsaɪt/ (**insights**) NOUN An **insight into** something is a good understanding of it. ❏ *This book provides fascinating insights into the way the mind works.*

in|sig|nifi|cant /ɪnsɪgnɪfɪkənt/ ADJECTIVE Something that is **insignificant** is not important. ❏ *In 1949, Bonn was a small, insignificant city.*

in|sist /ɪnsɪst/ (**insists, insisting, insisted**)
1 VERB If you **insist**, you say firmly that something must happen. ❏ *Rob insisted on driving them to the station.* ❏ *He insisted that I stay for dinner.*
2 VERB If you **insist** that something is true, you say so very firmly. ❏ *Clarke insisted that he was telling the truth.*

in|spect /ɪnspɛkt/ (**inspects, inspecting, inspected**) VERB If you **inspect** something, you look at it very carefully. ❏ *Dad inspected the car carefully before he bought it.*
● **in|spec|tion** /ɪnspɛkʃ°n/ (**inspections**) NOUN ❏ *Dixon still makes weekly inspections of all his stores.*

in|spec|tor /ɪnspɛktər/ (**inspectors**)
1 NOUN An **inspector** is a person whose job is to check that people do things correctly. ❏ *...a fire inspector.*
2 NOUN An **inspector** is an officer in the police. ❏ *...Police Inspector John Taylor.*

in|spi|ra|tion /ɪnspɪreɪʃ°n/ NONCOUNT NOUN **Inspiration** is a feeling of enthusiasm and new ideas that you get from someone or something. ❏ *My inspiration as a writer comes from poets like Walt Whitman.*

in|spire /ɪnspaɪər/ (**inspires, inspiring, inspired**)
1 VERB If someone or something **inspires** you, they give you new ideas and a strong feeling of enthusiasm. ❏ *Singer and songwriter Bob Dylan inspired a generation of young people.*
● **in|spir|ing** ADJECTIVE ❏ *She was one of the most inspiring people I ever met.*
2 VERB If someone or something **inspires** a particular feeling in people, it makes them feel that way. ❏ *A teacher has to inspire confidence in the students.*

in|stall /ɪnstɔl/ (**installs, installing, installed**) VERB If you **install** something, you put it somewhere so that it is ready to be used.

❏ *They installed a new telephone line in the apartment.* ● **in|stal|la|tion** NONCOUNT NOUN ❏ *The installation of smoke alarms could save hundreds of lives.*

in|stall|ment /ɪnstɔlmənt/ (**installments**)
1 NOUN If you pay for something in **installments**, you make small regular payments for it over a period of time. ❏ *She is repaying the loan in monthly installments of $300.*
2 NOUN An **installment** is one part of a story in a magazine, or on TV or radio. ❏ *Charles Dickens' fourth novel, The Old Curiosity Shop, was published in 1840-41, in weekly installments.*

in|stance /ɪnstəns/ You say **for instance** when you are giving an example of what you are talking about. ❏ *I want to talk about environmental issues, for instance, global warming.*

in|stant /ɪnstənt/ (**instants**)
1 NOUN An **instant** is a very short period of time. ❏ *For an instant, I wanted to cry.*
2 ADJECTIVE **Instant** means immediate. ❏ *Her book was an instant success.* ● **in|stant|ly** ADVERB ❏ *The man was killed instantly.*
3 ADJECTIVE **Instant** food or drink can be prepared very quickly and easily. ❏ *He stirred instant coffee into a mug of hot water.*
→ look at **communication**

in|stant mes|sag|ing NONCOUNT NOUN TECHNOLOGY **Instant messaging** is the activity of sending written messages from one computer to another. The message appears immediately on the screen of the computer you send it to if this computer is also using the service. ❏ *Instant messaging is my favorite way to communicate with friends.*
→ look at **Internet**

in|stead /ɪnstɛd/
1 If you do one thing **instead of** another, you do the first thing and not the second thing. ❏ *Why don't you walk to work, instead of driving?*
2 ADVERB If you do not do something, but do something else **instead**, you do the second thing and not the first thing. ❏ *Robert didn't want to go bowling. He went to the movies instead.*

in|stinct /ɪnstɪŋkt/ (**instincts**) NOUN **Instinct** is the natural way that a person or animal behaves or reacts. ❏ *My first instinct was to laugh.*

in|stinc|tive /ɪnstɪŋktɪv/ ADJECTIVE An **instinctive** feeling or action is one that you

i

have or do without stopping to think first. ❏ *Smiling is instinctive to all human beings.*
● **in|stinc|tive|ly** ADVERB ❏ *When the phone rang, Jane instinctively knew something was wrong.*

in|sti|tute /ˈɪnstɪtut/ (**institutes**) NOUN An **institute** is an organization or a place where people study a particular subject in detail in order to discover new facts. ❏ *My uncle works at the National Cancer Institute.*

in|sti|tu|tion /ˌɪnstɪˈtuʃⁿn/ (**institutions**) NOUN An **institution** is a large organization such as a school, a bank, or a church. ❏ *Most financial institutions offer interest-only loans for home-buyers.*

in|struct /ɪnˈstrʌkt/ (**instructs, instructing, instructed**)
1 VERB If you **instruct** someone **to** do something, you formally tell them to do it. [FORMAL] ❏ *Grandpa's doctor instructed him to get more fresh air.*
2 VERB If you **instruct** someone **in** a subject, you teach it to them. ❏ *Our teachers instruct the children in music, dance, and physical education.*

in|struc|tion /ɪnˈstrʌkʃⁿn/ (**instructions**)
1 NOUN An **instruction** is something that someone tells you to do. ❏ *We had instructions from our teacher not to leave the building.*
2 PLURAL NOUN **Instructions** are information on how to do something. ❏ *The cook book uses simple instructions and photographs.*

in|struc|tor /ɪnˈstrʌktər/ (**instructors**) NOUN An **instructor** is someone whose job is to teach a skill or an activity. ❏ *Rachel is a swimming instructor.*

in|stru|ment /ˈɪnstrəmənt/ (**instruments**)
1 NOUN An **instrument** is a tool that you use for doing a particular job. ❏ *...scientific instruments.*
2 NOUN MUSIC A musical **instrument** is an object that you use for making music. ❏ *Tim plays four musical instruments, including piano and guitar.*
→ look at **music**

in|stru|men|tal /ˌɪnstrəˈmɛntⁿl/
1 ADJECTIVE Someone or something that is **instrumental in** something helps to make it happen. ❏ *Mr. Johnson was instrumental in the company's success.*
2 ADJECTIVE MUSIC **Instrumental** music is for musical instruments only, and not for voices. ❏ *We welcomed the visitors with traditional dance and instrumental music.*

in|su|late /ˈɪnsəleɪt/ (**insulates, insulating, insulated**) VERB SCIENCE If a piece of equipment **is insulated**, it is covered with rubber or plastic to prevent electricity from passing through it. ❏ *...insulated wire.*

in|sult (**insults, insulting, insulted**)

> **PRONUNCIATION HELP**
> Pronounce the verb /ɪnˈsʌlt/. Pronounce the noun /ˈɪnsʌlt/.

1 VERB If someone **insults** you, they say or do something to you that is rude or offensive. ❏ *I'm sorry. I didn't mean to insult you.*
● **in|sult|ed** ADJECTIVE ❏ *I was really insulted by the way he spoke to me.* ● **in|sult|ing** ADJECTIVE ❏ *Don't use insulting language.*
2 NOUN An **insult** is something rude that a person says or does. ❏ *The boys shouted insults at each other.*

in|sur|ance /ɪnˈʃʊərəns/ NONCOUNT NOUN **Insurance** is an agreement that you make with a company in which you pay money to them regularly, and they pay you if something bad happens to you or to your property. ❏ *I pay about $100 per month for auto insurance.*
→ look at **car**

in|sure /ɪnˈʃʊər/ (**insures, insuring, insured**) VERB If you **insure** yourself or your property, you pay money regularly to a company so that, if you become ill, or if your property is damaged or stolen, the company will pay you an amount of money. ❏ *It costs a lot of money to insure your car.*

in|tel|lec|tual /ˌɪntɪˈlɛktʃuəl/ ADJECTIVE **Intellectual** means involving a person's ability to think and to understand ideas and information. ❏ *Dr. Miller is an expert on the intellectual development of children.*

in|tel|li|gence /ɪnˈtɛlɪdʒⁿns/
1 NONCOUNT NOUN **Intelligence** is the ability to understand and learn things quickly and well. ❏ *Stephanie's a woman of great intelligence.*
2 NONCOUNT NOUN **Intelligence** is information that is collected by the government or the army about other countries' activities. ❏ *There is a need for better military intelligence.*

in|tel|li|gent /ɪnˈtɛlɪdʒⁿnt/ ADJECTIVE An **intelligent** person or animal is able to think, understand, and learn things quickly and well. ❏ *Susan's a very intelligent woman.*

● **in|tel|li|gent|ly** ADVERB ❑ *William can talk intelligently on many different subjects.*

in|tend /ɪntɛnd/ (**intends, intending, intended**)

1 VERB If you **intend** to do something, you have decided to do it. ❑ *We're intending to stay in Philadelphia for four years.* ❑ *What do you intend to do when you leave college?*

2 VERB If something **is intended** for a particular purpose or person, it has been planned or made for that purpose. ❑ *This money is intended for schools.* ❑ *The big windows were intended to make the room brighter.*

in|tense /ɪntɛns/ ADJECTIVE Something that is **intense** is very great or strong. ❑ *The intense heat made him sweat.* ● **in|tense|ly** ADVERB ❑ *The fast-food business is intensely competitive.*

in|ten|sive /ɪntɛnsɪv/ ADJECTIVE Intensive activities involve a lot of effort or many people. ❑ *The program begins with sixteen weeks of intensive training.* ● **in|ten|sive|ly** ADVERB ❑ *Dan is working intensively on his new book.*

in|ten|tion /ɪntɛnʃ³n/ (**intentions**) NOUN An **intention** is something that you plan to do. ❑ *It is my intention to retire later this year.* ❑ *Karen has no intention of getting married again.*

in|ten|tion|al /ɪntɛnʃən³l/ ADJECTIVE If something is **intentional**, you do it on purpose, and not by mistake. ❑ *I'm sorry if I hurt him—it wasn't intentional.*

● **in|ten|tion|al|ly** ADVERB ❑ *He intentionally crashed his car to collect insurance money.*

in|ter|ac|tive /ɪntəræktɪv/ ADJECTIVE An **interactive** piece of equipment allows direct communication between itself and the user. ❑ *Press the red button on your interactive TV to vote for your favorite singer.*

in|ter|est /ɪntrɪst, -tərɪst/ (**interests, interesting, interested**)

1 NOUN If you have an **interest in** something, you want to know more about it. ❑ *There is a lot of interest in making the book into a film.* ❑ *She liked Jason at first, but she soon lost interest in him.*

2 NOUN Your **interests** are the things that you like doing. ❑ *"What are your interests?" "I enjoy riding horses and I also play tennis."*

3 VERB If something **interests** you, you want to know more about it. ❑ *Fashion does not interest her.*

4 NONCOUNT NOUN **Interest** is the extra money that you pay if you have borrowed money, or the extra money that you receive if you have money in some types of bank account. ❑ *Do you earn interest on your checking account?* ❑ *How much interest do you have to pay on the loan?*

in|ter|est|ed /ɪntərɛstɪd, -trɪstɪd/ ADJECTIVE If you are **interested in** something, you want to know more about it. ❑ *I thought you might be interested in this article in the newspaper.*

in|ter|est|ing /ɪntərɛstɪŋ, -trɪstɪŋ/ ADJECTIVE If you find something **interesting**, you want to know more about it. ❑ *It was interesting to be in a new town.*

● **in|ter|est|ing|ly** /ɪntərɛstɪŋli, -trɪstɪŋli/ ADVERB ❑ *Interestingly, there are no British writers on the list.*

→ look at **school, science, television**

in|ter|fere /ɪntərfɪər/ (**interferes, interfering, interfered**)

1 VERB If you **interfere**, you get involved in a situation when other people do not want you to. ❑ *I wish everyone would stop interfering and just leave me alone.* ● **inter|fer|ence** /ɪntərfɪərəns/ NONCOUNT NOUN ❑ *She didn't appreciate her mother's interference in her life.*

2 VERB Something that **interferes with** an activity stops it from going well. ❑ *Cellphones can interfere with aircraft equipment.*

in|te|ri|or /ɪntɪəriər/ (**interiors**) NOUN The **interior** of something is the inside part of it. ❑ *The interior of the house was dark and old-fashioned.* ● **interior** ADJECTIVE ❑ *They painted the interior walls of the house white.*

inter|medi|ate /ɪntərmidiɪt/ ADJECTIVE An **intermediate** level is in the middle level, between two other levels. ❑ *We teach beginner, intermediate, and advanced level students.*

in|ter|nal /ɪntɜrn³l/ ADJECTIVE Something **internal** exists or happens on the inside of something. ❑ *After the accident, Aaron suffered internal bleeding.*

inter|na|tion|al /ɪntərnæʃən³l/ ADJECTIVE **International** events or situations involve different countries. ❑ *The best way to end poverty is through international trade.*

● **inter|na|tion|al|ly** ADVERB ❑ *Bruce Lee is an internationally famous movie star.*

→ look at **news, phone**

In|ter|net /ɪntərnɛt/ also **internet** NOUN TECHNOLOGY The **Internet** is the network that allows computer users to connect with

Word World   Internet

computer   connection   URL   World Wide Web   remote   vast

communication   email   global   secure

browser   digital   download

chat room   network   connect to

instant messaging   browse   search   access

Nouns / Adjectives / Verbs

computers all over the world, and that carries email. ❑ *Do you have Internet access at home?*
→ look at Word World: **Internet**

in|ter|pret /ɪntɜrprɪt/ (**interprets, interpreting, interpreted**)
1 **VERB** If you **interpret** something in a particular way, you decide what it means. ❑ *You can interpret the data in different ways.*
2 **VERB** If you **interpret** what someone is saying, you put the words that they are saying into another language.
● **in|ter|pret|er** /ɪntɜrprɪtər/ (**interpreters**) **NOUN** ❑ *Speaking through an interpreter, he said that he was very happy to be in the United States.*

in|ter|ro|gate /ɪntɛrəgeɪt/ (**interrogates, interrogating, interrogated**) **VERB** If a police officer **interrogates** someone, they ask them questions for a long time in order to get some information from them. ❑ *Mr. Wright was interrogated by police for eight hours on Thursday night.* ● **in|ter|ro|ga|tion** /ɪntɛrəgeɪʃⁿn/ (**interrogations**) **NOUN** ❑ *He confessed during an interrogation by police.*

in|ter|rupt /ɪntərʌpt/ (**interrupts, interrupting, interrupted**)
1 **VERB** If you **interrupt** someone, you say or do something that causes them to stop what they are doing. ❑ *Don't interrupt the teacher when she's speaking.* ❑ *I'm sorry to interrupt, but there's a phone call for you.* ● **in|ter|rup|tion** /ɪntərʌpʃⁿn/ (**interruptions**) **NOUN** ❑ *I can't concentrate on my work—there are too many interruptions.*
2 **VERB** If someone or something **interrupts** an activity, they cause it to stop for a period of time. ❑ *Rain interrupted the tennis match for two hours.* ● **in|ter|rup|tion** **NOUN** ❑ *The meeting continued with no more interruptions.*

in|ter|val /ɪntərvⁿl/ (**intervals**) **NOUN** An **interval** is the period of time between two events. ❑ *We met again after an interval of 12 years.*

inter|view /ɪntərvyu/ (**interviews, interviewing, interviewed**)
1 **NOUN** An **interview** is a formal meeting in which someone asks you questions to find out if you are the right person for a job.
2 **VERB** If you **are interviewed** for a particular job, someone asks you questions about yourself to find out if you are the right person for it. ❑ *Anna was interviewed for a job at The New York Times yesterday.* ● **inter|view|er** (**interviewers**) **NOUN** ❑ *The interviewer asked me why I wanted the job.*
→ look at **job**

in|tes|tine /ɪntɛstɪn/ (**intestines**) **NOUN** Your **intestines** are the tubes in your body that food passes through when it has left your stomach.

in|ti|mate /ɪntɪmɪt/ **ADJECTIVE** If you have an **intimate** friendship with someone, you know them very well and you like them a lot. ❑ *I told my intimate friends I wanted to have a baby.* ● **in|ti|mate|ly** **ADVERB** ❑ *He knows the family fairly well, but not intimately.*

in|timi|date /ɪntɪmɪdeɪt/ (**intimidates, intimidating, intimidated**) **VERB** If you **intimidate** someone, you frighten them, in order to make them do what you want. ❑ *Many people feel intimidated by these teenage gangs.*
● **in|timi|da|tion** /ɪntɪmɪdeɪʃⁿn/ **NONCOUNT NOUN** ❑ *Witnesses are often afraid of intimidation.*

into /ɪntu/
1 **PREPOSITION** If you put one thing **into** another thing, you put the first thing inside the second thing. ❑ *Put the apples into a dish.*
2 **PREPOSITION** If you go **into** a place or a vehicle, you move from being outside it to being inside it. ❑ *Mom got into the car and started the engine.*
3 **PREPOSITION** If you crash **into** something, you hit it accidentally. ❑ *A train crashed into the barrier at the end of the track.*

4 **PREPOSITION** When you change **into** a piece of clothing, you put it on. ❑ *I'm cold—I'll change into some warmer clothes.*

5 **PREPOSITION** If something changes **into** something else, it changes so that it has a new form. ❑ *The book has been made into a movie.*

6 **PREPOSITION** You use **into** when you are talking about how something is divided. ❑ *I cut the cake into 12 slices.*

7 **PREPOSITION** You use **into** when you are dividing one number by another number. ❑ *5 into 15 is 3.*

in|tol|er|ant /ɪntɒlərənt/ **ADJECTIVE** If you are **intolerant**, you do not accept people who behave and think differently to you. ❑ *They are intolerant of the opinions of others.*

● **in|tol|er|ance** **NONCOUNT NOUN** ❑ *They worry about people's intolerance toward foreigners.*

in|tra|net /ɪntrənɛt/ (**intranets**) **NOUN** TECHNOLOGY An **intranet** is a network of computers in a particular organization.

in|tran|si|tive /ɪntrænsɪtɪv/ **ADJECTIVE** LANGUAGE ARTS An **intransitive** verb does not have an object.

intro|duce /ɪntrədus/ (**introduces, introducing, introduced**)

1 **VERB** If you **introduce** people, you tell them each other's names so that they can get to know each other. If you **introduce yourself** to someone, you tell them your name. ❑ *Tim, may I introduce you to my wife, Jennifer?* ❑ *Before the meeting, we all introduced ourselves.* ● **intro|duc|tion** /ɪntrədʌkʃ°n/ (**introductions**) **NOUN** ❑ *Elaine, the hostess, made the introductions.*

2 **VERB** If you introduce something new, you bring it to a place or make it exist for the first time. ❑ *The airline introduced a new direct service from Houston last month.*

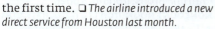

● **intro|duc|tion** /ɪntrədʌkʃ°n/ **NONCOUNT NOUN** ❑ *Did the introduction of the euro affect prices?*

intro|duc|tion /ɪntrədʌkʃ°n/ (**introductions**) **NOUN** LANGUAGE ARTS The **introduction to** a book is the part at the beginning that tells you what the book is about. ❑ *J.D. Salinger wrote the introduction to the book.*

in|trud|er /ɪntrudər/ (**intruders**) **NOUN** An **intruder** is a person who goes into a place without permission. ❑ *Mrs. Baker called 911 when an intruder entered her home.*

in|tui|tion /ɪntuɪʃ°n/ **NONCOUNT NOUN** **Intuition** is an ability to know or understand something through your feelings. ❑ *My intuition told me that I could trust him.*

in|vade /ɪnveɪd/ (**invades, invading, invaded**) **VERB** If an army **invades** a country, it attacks and enters it. ❑ *In 1944 the Allies invaded the Italian mainland.*

in|va|lid (**invalids**)

> **PRONUNCIATION HELP**
> Pronounce the noun /ɪnvəlɪd/. Pronounce the adjective /ɪnvælɪd/.

1 **NOUN** An **invalid** is someone who needs to be cared for by another person because they are very sick or badly injured. ❑ *Both of Mary's parents were invalids.*

2 **ADJECTIVE** If a document is **invalid**, it cannot be accepted, because it breaks an official rule. ❑ *He was trying to board a flight for the Philippines with an invalid passport.*

in|va|sion /ɪnveɪʒ°n/ (**invasions**) **NOUN** If there is an **invasion** of a country, an army enters it and attacks it. ❑ *Cyprus has been divided since an invasion in 1974.*

in|vent /ɪnvɛnt/ (**invents, inventing, invented**)

1 **VERB** If you **invent** something, you are the first person to think of it or make it. ❑ *The ballpoint pen was invented by the Hungarian, Laszlo Biro.* ● **in|ven|tor** (**inventors**) **NOUN** ❑ *Alexander Graham Bell was the inventor of the telephone.*

2 **VERB** If you **invent** a story or an excuse, you try to make other people believe that it is true when it is not. ❑ *Heather invented an excuse not to attend Ryan's birthday party.*

in|ven|tion /ɪnvɛnʃ°n/ (**inventions**)

1 **NOUN** An **invention** is something that has been invented by someone. ❑ *Paper was a Chinese invention.*

2 **NONCOUNT NOUN** **Invention** is when something that has never been made or used before is invented. ❑ *The invention of the telescope led to the discovery of Uranus in 1781.*

in|ver|te|brate /ɪnvɜrtɪbrɪt/ (**invertebrates**)

1 **NOUN** SCIENCE An **invertebrate** is an animal that does not have a spine (= bones in its back). Compare with **vertebrate**.

i

ADJECTIVE Invertebrate is also an adjective. ❑ *Ponds contain many invertebrate species.*

in|vest /ɪnvɛst/ (**invests, investing, invested**) **VERB** If you **invest** your money, you put it into a business or a bank, to try to make a profit from it. ❑ *He invested millions of dollars in the business.*

in|ves|ti|gate /ɪnvɛstɪgeɪt/ (**investigates, investigating, investigated**) **VERB** If you **investigate** something, you try to find out what happened. ❑ *Police are investigating how the accident happened.* ● **in|ves|ti|ga|tion** /ɪnvɛstɪgeɪʃ°n/ (**investigations**) **NOUN** ❑ *We have begun an investigation into the man's death.*

in|ves|ti|ga|tor /ɪnvɛstɪgeɪtər/ (**investigators**) **NOUN** An **investigator** is someone whose job it is to find out about something. ❑ *Investigators have been questioning the survivors.*

in|vest|ment /ɪnvɛstmənt/ (**investments**)
1 **NONCOUNT NOUN Investment** is the activity of investing money. ❑ *John's an investment advisor in Chicago.*
2 **NOUN** An **investment** is an amount of money that you invest, or the thing that you invest it in. ❑ *Anthony made a $1 million investment in the company.*

Word Builder **invisible**

in ≈ **not**

   in + complete = incomplete
   in + correct = incorrect
   in + dependent = independent
   in + direct = indirect
   in + secure = insecure
   in + visible = invisible

---

in|vis|ible /ɪnvɪzɪb°l/ **ADJECTIVE** If something is **invisible**, you cannot see it. ❑ *In the story, Matilda becomes invisible after eating blue candy.*

in|vi|ta|tion /ɪnvɪteɪʃ°n/ (**invitations**) **NOUN** If you have an **invitation** to an event, someone has asked you to go to it. ❑ *I accepted Sarah's invitation to her birthday party.*

in|vite /ɪnvaɪt/ (**invites, inviting, invited**) **VERB** If you **invite** someone to an event, you ask them to come to it. ❑ *She invited him to her 26th birthday party.*

in|voice /ɪnvɔɪs/ (**invoices, invoicing, invoiced**)
1 **NOUN** An **invoice** is a document that shows how much money you must pay for goods you have ordered or the work that someone has done for you. ❑ *We sent them an invoice for $11,000 four months ago.*
2 **VERB** If you **invoice** someone, you send them a bill for the goods you have sent them or the work you have done for them. ❑ *You will not be invoiced for the work until January.*

in|volve /ɪnvɒlv/ (**involves, involving, involved**)
1 **VERB** If an activity **involves** something, that thing is a necessary part of it. ❑ *Running a household involves lots of different skills.*
2 **VERB** If an activity **involves** someone, they are taking part in it. ❑ *The scandal involved a former senator.*
3 **VERB** If you **involve** someone **in** something, you get them to take part in it. ❑ *We involve the children in everything we do.*

in|volved /ɪnvɒlvd/ **ADJECTIVE** If you are **involved in** something, you take part in it. ❑ *All of their children are involved in the family business.*

in|volve|ment /ɪnvɒlvmənt/ **NONCOUNT NOUN** If you have an **involvement in** something, you take part in it. ❑ *Edwards has always denied any involvement in the crime.*

iPod /aɪpɒd/ (**iPods**) **NOUN** TECHNOLOGY An **iPod** is a small piece of electronic equipment that you can carry with you. It stores music, photos, and movies. [TRADEMARK]

iris /aɪrɪs/ (**irises**) **NOUN** SCIENCE The **iris** is the round colored part of a person's eye.

Spelling Partners **iron**

---

iron /aɪrɒn/ (**irons, ironing, ironed**)
1 **NONCOUNT NOUN Iron** is a hard, dark gray metal. ❑ *We waited for the iron gates to open.*
2 **NOUN** An **iron** is a piece of electrical equipment with a flat metal base that you heat and move over clothes to make them smooth.
3 **VERB** If you **iron** clothes, you make them smooth using an iron. ❑ *I began to iron some shirts.* ● **iron|ing** **NONCOUNT NOUN** ❑ *I was doing the ironing when she called.*
→ look at **chore, laundry, wear**

iron|ic /aɪrɒnɪk/ or **ironical** /aɪrɒnɪkᵊl/
ADJECTIVE An **ironic** fact or situation is
strange or funny because it is very different
from what people expect. ❑ *It is ironic that we
lie in the sun to make our skin look more attractive.*
● **ironi|cal|ly** /aɪrɒnɪkli/ **ADVERB** ❑ *His
enormous dog is ironically called "Tiny."*

iro|ny /aɪrəni, aɪər-/ **NONCOUNT NOUN**
LANGUAGE ARTS **Irony** is a type of humor
where you say the opposite of what you
really mean. ❑ *"You're early!" he said, as we
arrived two hours late, his voice full of irony.*

Word Builder   **irrational**

ir ≈ **not**

     ir + rational = **ir**rational
     ir + regular = **ir**regular
     ir + relevant = **ir**relevant
     ir + responsible = **ir**responsible
---

ir|ra|tion|al /ɪræʃənᵊl/ **ADJECTIVE** Irrational
behavior is not based on sensible, clear
thinking. ❑ *I think hatred is often irrational.*
● **ir|ra|tion|al|ly** **ADVERB** ❑ *My husband is
irrationally jealous of my ex-boyfriends.*

Word Builder   **irregular**

ir ≈ **not**

     ir + rational = **ir**rational
     ir + regular = **ir**regular
     ir + relevant = **ir**relevant
     ir + responsible = **ir**responsible
---

ir|regu|lar /ɪrɛgyələr/
 1 **ADJECTIVE** If something is **irregular**, the
periods of time between it happening are of
different lengths. ❑ *The tests showed that his
heartbeat was irregular.* ● **ir|regu|lar|ly** **ADVERB**
❑ *He was eating irregularly and losing weight.*
 2 **ADJECTIVE** LANGUAGE ARTS An **irregular** noun
or verb does not follow the usual rules of
grammar. For example, "run" is an irregular
verb, because the past form is "ran" (and not
"runned.") Compare with **regular**.

Word Builder   **irrelevant**

ir ≈ **not**

     ir + rational = **ir**rational
     ir + regular = **ir**regular
     ir + relevant = **ir**relevant
     ir + responsible = **ir**responsible
---

ir|rel|evant /ɪrɛlɪvᵊnt/ **ADJECTIVE** If
something is **irrelevant**, it is not connected
with what you are talking about or doing.
❑ *Remove any irrelevant details from your essay.*

Word Builder   **irresponsible**

ir ≈ **not**

     ir + rational = **ir**rational
     ir + regular = **ir**regular
     ir + relevant = **ir**relevant
     ir + responsible = **ir**responsible
---

ir|re|spon|sible /ɪrɪspɒnsɪbᵊl/ **ADJECTIVE**
Someone who is **irresponsible** does not
think about the possible results of their
actions. ❑ *There are still too many irresponsible
drivers who use their cellphones while driving.*

ir|ri|table /ɪrɪtəbᵊl/ **ADJECTIVE** If you are
irritable, you become angry very easily.
❑ *After waiting for him for over an hour, Amber was
feeling irritable.* ● **ir|ri|tably** /ɪrɪtəbli/ **ADVERB**
❑ *"Why are you talking so loudly?" he asked irritably.*

ir|ri|tate /ɪrɪteɪt/ (**irritates, irritating,
irritated**)
 1 **VERB** If something **irritates** you, it keeps
annoying you. ❑ *His voice really irritates me.*
● **ir|ri|tat|ed** **ADJECTIVE** ❑ *He has become
increasingly irritated by questions about his retirement.*
● **ir|ri|tat|ing** **ADJECTIVE** ❑ *The children have an
irritating habit of leaving the door open.*
 2 **VERB** If something **irritates** a part of your
body, it makes it slightly painful. ❑ *The smoke
from the fire irritated his eyes, nose and throat.*

ir|ri|ta|tion /ɪrɪteɪʃᵊn/ (**irritations**)
 1 **NONCOUNT NOUN** Irritation is the feeling
you have when you are annoyed. ❑ *David
tried not to show his irritation.*
 2 **NOUN** Irritation is a feeling of slight pain
in a part of your body. ❑ *These oils may cause
irritation to sensitive skins.*

is /ɪz/ **Is** is a form of the verb **be**.

Is|lam /ɪslɑm/ **NONCOUNT NOUN** Islam is the
religion that was started by Muhammed.
❑ *Michael converted to Islam at the age of 16.*
● **Is|lam|ic** /ɪslæmɪk, -lɑ-/ **ADJECTIVE** ❑ *He's
an expert in Islamic law.*

is|land /aɪlənd/ (**islands**) **NOUN** SCIENCE
GEOGRAPHY An **island** is a piece of land that is
completely
surrounded by
water. ❑ *They
live on the
Caribbean island
of Barbados.*
→ look at
landform

isle /aɪl/ (**isles**) **NOUN** An **isle** is an island.
❑ *Ireland is sometimes called "the emerald isle."*

isn't /ˈɪzᵊnt/ **Isn't** is short for "is not."

iso|late /ˈaɪsəleɪt/ (**isolates, isolating, isolated**) **VERB** If you **isolate** someone, you keep them away from other people. ❏ *Julie was quickly isolated from other patients in the hospital.*

iso|lat|ed /ˈaɪsəleɪtɪd/ **ADJECTIVE** An **isolated** place is far away from other places. ❏ *Mark and his girlfriend have bought an isolated farmhouse in Spain.*

ISP /ˌaɪ ɛs ˈpi/ (**ISPs**) **NOUN** TECHNOLOGY An **ISP** is a company that provides Internet and email services. **ISP** is short for "Internet service provider."

is|sue /ˈɪʃu/ (**issues, issuing, issued**)
   1 **NOUN** An **issue** is an important subject that people are talking about. ❏ *Climate change is a major environmental issue.*
   2 **NOUN** An **issue** of a magazine or a newspaper is the copy of it that is published in a particular month or on a particular day. ❏ *Have you read the latest issue of the "Scientific American?"*
   3 **VERB** If you **issue** something, you officially say it or give it. ❏ *The government issued a warning of possible attacks.* ❏ *The embassy has stopped issuing visas to journalists.*

I.T. /ˌaɪ ˈti/ TECHNOLOGY **I.T.** is short for **information technology**. ❏ *The company needs people with I.T. skills.*

it /ɪt/
   1 **PRONOUN** You use **it** when you are talking about an object, an animal, a thing, or a situation that you have already mentioned. ❏ *They live in a beautiful cottage. Here's a photo of it.* ❏ *She has a problem but she's too embarrassed to talk about it.*
   2 **PRONOUN** You use **it** before certain nouns, adjectives, and verbs to talk about your feelings. ❏ *It was nice to see Steve again.* ❏ *It's a pity you can't come to the party, Sarah.*
   3 **PRONOUN** You use **it** when you are talking about the time, the date, the weather, or the distance to a place. ❏ *It's three o'clock.* ❏ *It was Saturday, so she was at home.* ❏ *It was snowing yesterday.* ❏ *It's ten miles to the next gas station.*
   4 **PRONOUN** You use **it** when you are saying who someone is. ❏ *"Who's that on the phone?"—"It's Mrs. Williams."*

ital|ic /ɪˈtælɪk/ (**italics**)
   1 **PLURAL NOUN** **Italics** are letters that slope to the right. The examples in this dictionary are printed in italics.
   2 **ADJECTIVE** **Italic** letters slope to the right.

itch /ɪtʃ/ (**itches, itching, itched**)
   1 **VERB** When a part of your body **itches**, you have an unpleasant feeling on your skin that makes you want to scratch it. ❏ *Her perfume made my eyes itch.*
   2 **NOUN** **Itch** is also a noun. ❏ *Can you scratch my back? I've got an itch.* ● **itchy** **ADJECTIVE** ❏ *My eyes feel itchy and sore.*
   → look at **sick**

it'd /ˈɪtəd/
   1 **It'd** is short for "it would." ❏ *It'd be better to keep quiet.*
   2 **It'd** is short for "it had." ❏ *Marcie was watching a movie. It'd just started.*

item /ˈaɪtəm/ (**items**)
   1 **NOUN** An **item** is one thing in a list or a group of things. ❏ *The most valuable item in the sale was a Picasso drawing.*
   2 **NOUN** An **item** is a piece of news in a newspaper or magazine, or on television or radio. ❏ *There was an item in the paper about him.*

it'll /ˈɪtᵊl/ **It'll** is short for "it will." ❏ *It'll be nice to see them next weekend.*

its /ɪts/ **ADJECTIVE** You use **its** to show that something belongs or relates to a thing, a place, or an animal that has just been mentioned. ❏ *He held the knife by its handle.*

it's /ɪts/ **It's** is short for "it is" or "it has."

it|self /ɪtˈsɛlf/
   1 **PRONOUN** You use **itself** as the object of a verb or preposition when an animal or thing is both the subject and the object of the verb. ❏ *The kitten washed itself, then lay down by the fire.*
   2 **PRONOUN** You use **itself** to make a word stronger. ❏ *There are lots of good restaurants on the road to Wilmington, and in Wilmington itself.*
   3 **PRONOUN** If an animal or a thing does something **by itself**, it does it without any help. ❏ *The company are working on a car that can drive by itself.*

I've /aɪv/ **I've** is short for "I have." ❏ *I've been invited to a party.*

ivy /ˈaɪvi/ **NOUN** **Ivy** is a dark-green plant that grows up walls or along the ground.

Jj

jack /dʒæk/ (jacks) **NOUN** A jack is a tool for lifting a car slightly. ❏ *You'll find the jack under the spare tire in the trunk.*

jack|et /dʒækɪt/ (jackets) **NOUN** A jacket is a short coat with long sleeves. ❏ *He wore a black leather jacket.*
→ look at **clothing**

jack|pot /dʒækpɒt/ (jackpots) **NOUN** The **jackpot** is a large sum of money that is the most valuable prize in a game. ❏ *She won the jackpot of $5 million.*

jag|ged /dʒægɪd/ **ADJECTIVE** Something that is **jagged** has a rough shape or edge with lots of sharp points. ❏ *There were sharp jagged rocks just below the surface of the water.*

jail /dʒeɪl/ (jails) **NOUN** A jail is a place where criminals have to stay as a punishment. ❏ *He went to jail for 15 years.* ❏ *Three prisoners escaped from a jail.*

 Spelling Partners   **jam**

jam /dʒæm/ (jams, jamming, jammed)
1 **VERB** If you **jam** something into a place, you push it there hard. ❏ *He jammed the key in the lock.*
2 **NONCOUNT NOUN** Jam is a sweet food that contains soft fruit and sugar. ❏ *Kate spread the strawberry jam on her toast.*
3 **NOUN** If there is a traffic **jam** on a road, there are so many vehicles there that they cannot move. ❏ *The trucks sat in a traffic jam for ten hours.*

jani|tor /dʒænɪtər/ (janitors) **NOUN** A janitor is a person whose job is to clean and take care of a building. ❏ *The janitor finished cleaning the classrooms, and locked the school for the night.*

Janu|ary /dʒænyuɛri/ **NOUN** January is the first month of the year. ❏ *We always have snow in January.*

jar /dʒɑr/ (jars) **NOUN** A jar is a glass container with a lid that is used for storing food. ❏ *There were several glass jars filled with candy.*
→ look at **container**

jave|lin /dʒævlɪn/ (javelins) **NOUN** SPORTS A **javelin** is a long pointed stick that is thrown in sports competitions.

jaw /dʒɔ/ (jaws) **NOUN** SCIENCE A person's or animal's **jaws** are the top and bottom bones of their mouth. ❏ *Andrew broke his jaw.*

jay /dʒeɪ/ (jays) **NOUN** A jay is a noisy bird with blue or gray feathers.
→ look at **bird**

jazz /dʒæz/ **NONCOUNT NOUN** MUSIC Jazz is a style of music that has strong rhythms. ❏ *The club plays live jazz on Sundays.*

jeal|ous /dʒɛləs/
1 **ADJECTIVE** If someone is **jealous**, they feel angry because they think that another person is trying to take away someone or something that they love. ❏ *He got jealous and there was a fight.*
2 **ADJECTIVE** If you are **jealous of** another person's possessions or qualities, you feel angry because you do not have them. ❏ *She was jealous of her sister's success.* ● **jeal|ous|ly** **ADVERB** ❏ *Gloria looked jealously at his new car.*

jeal|ousy /dʒɛləsi/ **NONCOUNT NOUN** **Jealousy** is the feeling of anger that someone has when they think that another person is trying to take away someone or something that they love. ❏ *He could not control his jealousy when he saw her new husband.*

jeans /dʒinz/ **PLURAL NOUN** Jeans are pants that are made of strong cotton cloth. ❏ *We saw a young man in jeans and a T-shirt.*
→ look at **clothing**

Jeep /dʒip/ (Jeeps) **NOUN** A Jeep is a type of car that can travel over rough ground. [TRADEMARK] ❏ *...a U.S. Army Jeep.*

Jell-O **NONCOUNT NOUN** Jell-O is a soft sweet food made from fruit juice and sugar that moves from side to side when you touch it. [TRADEMARK] ❑ *After dinner, we always had red Jell-O with ice cream.*

jel|ly /dʒɛli/ **NONCOUNT NOUN** Jelly is a sweet food made by cooking fruit with a large amount of sugar. **Jelly** is usually spread on bread. ❑ *She loved peanut butter and jelly sandwiches.*

jerk /dʒɜrk/ (jerks, jerking, jerked)
1 VERB If you **jerk** something, you move it a short distance very suddenly and quickly. ❑ *Sam jerked his head in my direction.*
2 NOUN Jerk is also a noun. ❑ *He gave a jerk of his head to the other two men.*
3 NOUN If you call someone a **jerk**, you are rudely saying that they annoy you. [INFORMAL]

jerky /dʒɜrki/ (jerkier, jerkiest) **ADJECTIVE** Jerky movements are very sudden and quick. ❑ *Avoid any sudden or jerky movements.*

jer|sey /dʒɜrzi/ (jerseys) **NOUN** A **jersey** is a piece of clothing with sleeves that you wear on the top part of your body ❑ *The boys wore baseball caps and sports jerseys.*

jet /dʒɛt/ (jets)
1 NOUN A **jet** is an aircraft that is powered by jet engines. ❑ *He arrived from Key West by jet.*

2 NOUN A **jet** of liquid or gas is a strong, fast, thin stream of it. ❑ *A jet of water poured through the windows.*

jet lag /dʒɛt læg/ **NONCOUNT NOUN** If you have **jet lag**, you feel tired after a long trip by airplane. ❑ *We were tired because we still had jet lag.*

Jew /dʒu/ (Jews) **NOUN** A **Jew** is a person who practices the religion of Judaism.

jew|el /dʒuəl/ (jewels) **NOUN** A **jewel** is a valuable stone, such as a diamond. ❑ *The box was filled with precious jewels and gold.*

jew|el|ry /dʒuəlri/ **NONCOUNT NOUN** Jewelry is decorations that you wear on your body, such as a ring that you wear on your finger. ❑ *He sold his wife's gold jewelry.*

Jew|ish /dʒuɪʃ/
1 ADJECTIVE If something is **Jewish** it belongs or relates to the religion of Judaism. ❑ *We celebrated the Jewish festival of Passover.*

2 ADJECTIVE A **Jewish** person believes in and practices the religion of Judaism. ❑ *She was from a traditional Jewish family.*

jig|saw /dʒɪgsɔ/ (jigsaws)
NOUN A **jigsaw** or **jigsaw puzzle** is a picture on cardboard or wood that has been cut up into different shapes that you have to put back together again. ❑ *The children put the last pieces in the jigsaw puzzle.*

jin|gle /dʒɪŋgəl/ (jingles, jingling, jingled)
VERB When something **jingles**, it makes a gentle sound like small bells. ❑ *Her bracelets jingled on her thin wrist.* ❑ *Brian put his hands in his pockets and jingled some coins.*

job /dʒɒb/ (jobs)
1 NOUN A **job** is the work that someone does to earn money. ❑ *I want to get a job.* ❑ *Terry was looking for a new job.*
2 NOUN A **job** is a particular task. ❑ *I have some jobs to do in the house today.*
3 NOUN If someone is doing a good **job**, they are doing something well. ❑ *Most of our teachers are doing a good job in the classroom.*
→ look at Word World: **job**

job|less /dʒɒbləs/ **ADJECTIVE** Someone who is **jobless** does not have a job. ❑ *The number of jobless people went up last month.*

jock|ey /dʒɒki/ (jockeys) **NOUN** SPORTS A **jockey** is someone who rides a horse in a race.

jog /dʒɒg/ (jogs, jogging, jogged)
1 VERB SPORTS If you **jog**, you run slowly, often as a form of exercise. ❑ *They went jogging every morning.*
2 NOUN SPORTS Jog is also a noun. ❑ *He went for an early morning jog.* ●**jog|ger** (joggers) **NOUN** ❑ *The park was full of joggers.* ●**jog|ging** **NONCOUNT NOUN** ❑ *The jogging helped him to lose weight.*

join /dʒɔɪn/ (joins, joining, joined)
1 VERB If you **join** an organization, you become a member of it. ❑ *He joined the Army five years ago.*
2 VERB If you **join** a line, you stand at the end of it so that you are part of it. ❑ *He joined the line of people waiting to get on the bus.*
3 VERB To **join** two things means to attach or fasten them together. ❑ *"And" is often used for joining two sentences.* ❑ *Join the two squares of fabric to make a bag.*

J

Word World job

Nouns / Adjectives / Verbs

---

joint /dʒɔɪnt/ (**joints**)

1 NOUN SCIENCE A **joint** is a part of your body such as your elbow or knee where two bones meet and are able to move together. ❏ *Her joints ache if she exercises.*

2 ADJECTIVE **Joint** means shared by two or more people. ❏ *We opened a joint bank account.*

● **joint|ly** ADVERB ❏ *They jointly write and direct every film themselves.*

joke /dʒoʊk/ (**jokes, joking, joked**)

1 NOUN A **joke** is something that someone says to make you laugh. ❏ *He made a joke about it.*

2 VERB If you **joke**, you say amusing things, or say something that is not true for fun. ❏ *She often joked about her big feet.* ❏ *I was only joking!*

jol|ly /dʒɒli/ (**jollier, jolliest**) ADJECTIVE Someone who is **jolly** is happy and cheerful. ❏ *She was a jolly, kind woman.*

jolt /dʒoʊlt/ (**jolts, jolting, jolted**)

1 VERB If something **jolts**, it moves suddenly and quite violently. ❏ *An earthquake jolted the Philippines early Wednesday.* ❏ *The train jolted again.*

2 NOUN **Jolt** is also a noun. ❏ *The plane hit the runway with a jolt.*

jot /dʒɒt/ (**jots, jotting, jotted**) VERB If you **jot** something **down**, you write it down. ❏ *David jotted down the address on a notepad.* ❏ *Could you jot his name on this piece of paper?*

jour|nal /dʒɜrnəl/ (**journals**)

1 NOUN LANGUAGE ARTS A **journal** is a magazine or newspaper that deals with a special subject. ❏ *The results were published in scientific journals.*

2 NOUN LANGUAGE ARTS A **journal** is a notebook or diary. ❏ *Sara wrote her private thoughts in her journal.*

Word Builder journalist

ist ≈ **person who does this**

art + ist = artist
guitar + ist = guitarist
journal + ist = journalist
novel + ist = novelist

---

jour|nal|ist /dʒɜrnəlɪst/ (**journalists**) NOUN A **journalist** is a person whose job is to collect news stories and write about them for newspapers, magazines, television, or radio. ❏ *The president spoke to an audience of two hundred journalists.* ● **jour|nal|ism** NONCOUNT NOUN ❏ *He began a career in journalism.*

jour|ney /dʒɜrni/ (**journeys**) NOUN When you make a **journey**, you travel from one place to another. ❏ *Their journey took them from New York to San Francisco.*

joy /dʒɔɪ/ NONCOUNT NOUN **Joy** is a feeling of great happiness. ❏ *She shouted with joy.*

joy|ful /dʒɔɪfəl/ ADJECTIVE Something that is **joyful** causes happiness and pleasure. [FORMAL] ❏ *A wedding is a joyful occasion.*

● **joy|ful|ly** ADVERB ❏ *The children cheered joyfully.*

Ju|da|ism /dʒudiɪzəm, -deɪ-/ NONCOUNT NOUN **Judaism** is the religion of the Jewish people.

judge /dʒʌdʒ/ (**judges, judging, judged**)

1 NOUN A **judge** is the person in a court of law who decides how criminals should be punished. ❏ *The judge sent him to jail for 100 days.*

2 NOUN A **judge** is a person who decides who will be the winner of a competition. ❏ *A panel of judges will choose the winner.*

3 VERB If you **judge** a competition, you decide who is the winner. ❏ *He will judge the contest and award the prize.*

4 VERB If you **judge** something or someone, you form an opinion about them. ❏ *People should wait, and judge the movie when they see it.*

j

judg|ment /dʒʌdʒmənt/ (**judgments**)
1 NONCOUNT NOUN **Judgment** is the ability to make sensible decisions about what to do. ❑ *I respect his judgment, and I'll follow his advice.*
2 NOUN A **judgment** is a decision made by a judge or by a court of law. ❑ *We are waiting for a judgment from the Supreme Court.*

ju|di|cial branch /dʒudɪʃəl bræntʃ/ NOUN SOCIAL STUDIES The **judicial branch** is the part of the government of the United States that applies laws.

judo /dʒudoʊ/ NONCOUNT NOUN SPORTS **Judo** is a sport in which two people fight without weapons. ❑ *He was also a black belt in judo.*

jug /dʒʌg/ (**jugs**) NOUN A **jug** is a container with a handle used for holding and pouring liquids.

jug|gle /dʒʌgəl/ (**juggles, juggling, juggled**)
VERB If you **juggle**, you throw and catch several things repeatedly and try to keep them in the air. ❑ *She was juggling five balls.* ● **jug|gler** (**jugglers**) NOUN ❑ *He was a professional juggler.* ● **jug|gl|ing** NONCOUNT NOUN ❑ *It's a children's show, with juggling and comedy.*

juice /dʒus/ (**juices**)
1 NONCOUNT NOUN **Juice** is the liquid from a fruit or vegetable. ❑ *He had a large glass of fresh orange juice.*
2 PLURAL NOUN The **juices** of a piece of meat are the liquid that comes out of it when you cook it. ❑ *Pour off the juices and put the meat in a frying pan.*

juicy /dʒusi/ (**juicier, juiciest**) ADJECTIVE If food is **juicy**, it has a lot of juice in it and is very enjoyable to eat. ❑ *The waiter brought a thick, juicy steak to the table.*

July /dʒʊlaɪ/ NOUN **July** is the seventh month of the year. ❑ *In July 1969, Neil Armstrong walked on the moon.*

jum|bo /dʒʌmboʊ/ (**jumbos**)
1 ADJECTIVE **Jumbo** means very large. ❑ *The jumbo shrimp were fresh and juicy.*
2 NOUN A **jumbo** or a **jumbo jet** is a very large aircraft.

jump /dʒʌmp/ (**jumps, jumping, jumped**)
1 VERB If you **jump**, you bend your knees, push against the ground with your feet, and move quickly upward into the air. ❑ *I jumped over the fence.*

2 NOUN **Jump** is also a noun. ❑ *She set a world record for the longest jump by a woman.*
3 VERB If you **jump** somewhere, you move there quickly and suddenly. ❑ *Adam jumped up when he heard the doorbell.*
4 VERB If something **makes** you **jump**, it makes you move suddenly because you are frightened or surprised. ❑ *The phone rang and made her jump.*
5 VERB If you **jump at** an offer or an opportunity, you accept it quickly and with enthusiasm. ❑ *She jumped at the chance to be on TV.*

June /dʒun/ NOUN **June** is the sixth month of the year. ❑ *He spent two weeks with us in June 2006.*

jun|gle /dʒʌŋgəl/ (**jungles**) NOUN A **jungle** is a forest in a tropical country where large numbers of tall trees and plants grow very close together. ❑ *The trail led them deeper into the jungle.*

jun|ior /dʒunyər/ (**juniors**)
1 NOUN A **junior** is a student in the third year of high school or college. ❑ *Her son is a junior in high school.*
2 ADJECTIVE A **junior** official or employee has a low position in an organization.

jun|ior high school (**junior high schools**) or **junior high** NOUN A **junior high school** or a **junior high** is a school for students from grade seven through grades nine or ten. ❑ *I teach junior high school and I love it.* ❑ *She attended Benjamin Franklin Junior High.*

junk /dʒʌŋk/ NONCOUNT NOUN **Junk** is old and useless things that you do not want or need. [INFORMAL] ❑ *What are you going to do with all that junk, Larry?*
→ look at **email**

jury /dʒʊəri/ (**juries**) NOUN In a court of law, the **jury** is a group of people who listen to the facts about a crime and decide if a person is guilty or not. ❑ *The jury decided she was not guilty of murder.*

just
1 ADVERB USES
2 ADJECTIVE USE

1 just /dʒʌst/
1 ADVERB If something **just happened**, it happened a very short time ago. ❑ *I just had the most awful dream.*
2 ADVERB If you are **just** doing something, you are doing it now. ❑ *I'm just making some coffee.*

3 **ADVERB** **Just** means only. ❑ *It costs just a few dollars.*

4 **ADVERB** You use **just** to make the word that follows it stronger. ❑ *Just stop talking and listen to me!*

5 **ADVERB** **Just** means exactly. ❑ *They are just like the rest of us.*

6 **Just about** means almost. ❑ *All our money is just about gone.*

7 You say **just a minute, just a moment,** or **just a second** when you are asking someone to wait for a short time. ❑ *Just a moment. What did you say?*

❷ **just** /dʒʌst/ **ADJECTIVE** A situation that is **just** is fair or right. [FORMAL] ❑ *I think he got his just punishment.*

jus|tice /dʒʌstɪs/ (**justices**)
   1 **NONCOUNT NOUN** **Justice** is the fair treatment of people. ❑ *We want freedom, justice and equality.*
   2 **NOUN** A **justice** is a judge. ❑ *He is a justice on the Supreme Court.*

jus|ti|fied /dʒʌstɪfaɪd/ **ADJECTIVE** A decision, action, or idea that is **justified** is reasonable and acceptable. ❑ *In my opinion, the decision was justified.* ❑ *I work very hard, so I feel justified in asking for more money.*

jus|ti|fy /dʒʌstɪfaɪ/ (**justifies, justifying, justified**) **VERB** To **justify** a decision or an action means to show that it is reasonable or necessary. ❑ *Is there anything that can justify a war?*

j

Kk

kan|ga|roo /kǽŋgərú/
(kangaroos) **NOUN** A kangaroo
is a large Australian animal.
Female kangaroos carry
their babies in a pocket
on their stomach.

ka|ra|te /kərɑ́ti/ **NONCOUNT NOUN** SPORTS
Karate is a Japanese sport in which people
fight using their hands and feet.

KB or **K** TECHNOLOGY **KB** or **K** is short for
kilobyte or **kilobytes**.

keen /kín/ (keener, keenest)
1 **ADJECTIVE** If you are **keen**, you want to do
something or you are very interested in it.
❑ *Charles was keen to show his family the photos.*
❑ *Father was always a keen golfer.*
2 **ADJECTIVE** If you have a **keen** sense of
something, you are very interested in it or
good at it. ❑ *For this job, you need to have a keen
sense of adventure.*

keep /kíp/ (keeps, keeping, kept)
1 **VERB** If someone **keeps** in a particular
state or place, they remain in it. ❑ *Keep
away from the doors while the train is moving.*
❑ *We burned wood to keep warm.* ❑ *"Keep
still!"*
2 **VERB** If someone or something **keeps** a
person or thing in a particular state or place,
they make them stay in it. ❑ *The noise of the
traffic kept him awake.* ❑ *He kept his head down,
hiding his face.*
3 **VERB** If you **keep** doing something,
you do it many times or you continue to
do it. ❑ *I keep forgetting the password for my
computer.* ❑ *She kept running although she was
exhausted.*
4 **VERB** If you **keep** something, you
continue to have it. If you **keep** it
somewhere, you store it there. ❑ *I want to
keep these clothes, and I want to give these away.*
❑ *She kept her money under the bed.*
5 **VERB** When you **keep** a promise, you do
what you said you would do. ❑ *He kept his
promise to come to my birthday party.*
▶ **keep up** **1** If you **keep up with** someone

or something, you move as fast as they do so
that you are moving together. ❑ *Sam walked
faster to keep up with his father.*
2 If you **keep** something **up**, you continue
to do it. ❑ *I could not keep the diet up for longer
than a month.*

ken|nel /kɛ́nˀl/ (kennels) **NOUN** A kennel is
a place where you can leave your dog when
you go away somewhere. ❑ *The dogs will stay
at the kennel until tomorrow.*

kept /kɛ́pt/ **Kept** is a form of the verb **keep**.

ker|chief /kɜ́rtʃɪf/ (kerchiefs) **NOUN** A
kerchief is a piece of cloth that you wear
on your head or around your neck.

ket|chup /kɛ́tʃʌp/ **NONCOUNT NOUN**
Ketchup is a thick, red sauce made from
tomatoes. ❑ *He was eating a burger with
ketchup.*

ket|tle /kɛ́tˀl/ (kettles) **NOUN** A kettle is a
metal container with a lid and a handle,
that you use for boiling water. ❑ *I'll put the
kettle on and make us some tea.*

Spelling Partners   **key**

---

key /kí/ (keys)
1 **NOUN** A **key** is a specially shaped piece of
metal that opens or closes a lock. ❑ *They put
the key in the door and entered.*
2 **NOUN** TECHNOLOGY The **keys** on a
computer keyboard are the buttons that you
press in order to operate it. ❑ *Now press the
"Delete" key.*
3 **NOUN** MUSIC The **keys** of a piano are the
white and black bars that you press in order
to play it.
4 **NOUN** MUSIC In music, a **key** is a
particular scale of musical notes. ❑ *...the key
of A minor.*
5 **ADJECTIVE** The **key** person or thing in a
group is the most important one. ❑ *He's a key
player on the team.*

key|board /kíbɔrd/ (**keyboards**)
1 **NOUN** TECHNOLOGY The **keyboard** of a computer is the set of keys that you press in order to operate it.
2 **NOUN** MUSIC The **keyboard** of a piano or organ is the set of black and white keys that you press when you play it.
→ look at **computer**

key|hole /kíːhoʊl/ (**keyholes**) **NOUN** A **keyhole** is the part of a lock where you put a key. ❑ *I looked through the keyhole, but I couldn't see anything inside.*

key ring (**key rings**) **NOUN** A **key ring** is a metal ring on which you keep keys. ❑ *He pulled his key ring from his pocket.*

key|word /kíwɜrd/ (**keywords**) also **key word** **NOUN** TECHNOLOGY A **keyword** is a word or phrase that you can use when you are searching for a particular document in an Internet search. ❑ *Users can search by title, by author, by subject, and by keyword.*

kg MATH SCIENCE **kg** is short for **kilogram** or **kilograms**.

kha|ki /kǽki/ **ADJECTIVE** Something that is **khaki** is greenish-brown or yellowish-brown in color. ❑ *He was dressed in khaki trousers.*

kHz SCIENCE In writing, **kHz** is short for **kilohertz**.

kick /kík/ (**kicks, kicking, kicked**)
1 **VERB** If you **kick** someone or something, you hit them with your foot. ❑ *He kicked the door hard.* ❑ *He kicked the ball away.*
2 **NOUN** Kick is also a noun. ❑ *Johnson scored in the fifth minute with a free kick.*
3 **VERB** If you **kick**, you move your legs up and down quickly. ❑ *Abby was taken away, kicking and screaming.* ❑ *The baby smiled and kicked her legs.*
4 **NOUN** A **kick** is a feeling of pleasure or excitement. [INFORMAL] ❑ *I love acting. I get a big kick out of it.*

kid /kíd/ (**kids, kidding, kidded**)
1 **NOUN** A **kid** is a child. [INFORMAL] ❑ *They have three kids.*
2 **VERB** If you **are kidding**, you are saying something that is not really true, as a joke. [INFORMAL] ❑ *I thought he was kidding but he was serious.* ❑ *I'm just kidding.*

kid|nap /kídnæp/ (**kidnaps, kidnapping** or **kidnaping, kidnapped** or **kidnaped**) **VERB** If someone **is kidnapped**, they are taken away by force and kept as a prisoner often until their friends or family pay a large amount of money. ❑ *The tourists were kidnapped by a group of men with guns.* ● **kid|nap|per** (**kidnappers**) **NOUN** ❑ *His kidnappers have threatened to kill him.* ● **kid|nap|ping** (**kidnappings**) **NOUN** ❑ *Williams was jailed for eight years for the kidnapping.*

kid|ney /kídni/ (**kidneys**) **NOUN** SCIENCE Your **kidneys** are the two organs in your body that remove waste liquid from your blood. ❑ *She urgently needs a kidney transplant.*

kill /kíl/ (**kills, killing, killed**) **VERB** If a person, an animal, or another living thing **is killed**, something or someone makes them die. ❑ *More than 1,000 people have been killed by the armed forces.* ❑ *Drugs can kill.* ● **kill|ing** **NONCOUNT NOUN** ❑ *The TV news reported the killing of seven people.*

kill|er /kílər/ (**killers**)
1 **NOUN** A **killer** is a person who has killed someone. ❑ *The police are searching for the killers.*
2 **NOUN** You can talk about something that causes death as a **killer**. ❑ *Heart disease is the biggest killer of men in some countries.*

kilo /kíloʊ/ (**kilos**) **NOUN** MATH SCIENCE A **kilo** is the same as a **kilogram**. ❑ *He's lost ten kilos in weight.*

kilo|byte /kíləbaɪt/ (**kilobytes**) **NOUN** TECHNOLOGY In computing, a **kilobyte** is a unit for measuring information. There are 1,024 bytes in a kilobyte.

kilo|gram /kíləgræm/ (**kilograms**) **NOUN** MATH SCIENCE A **kilogram** is a unit for measuring weight. One kilogram is equal to 2.2 pounds, and there are one thousand grams in a kilogram. ❑ *The box weighs 4.5 kilograms.*

kilo|hertz /kíləhɜrts/ (**kilohertz**) **NOUN** SCIENCE A **kilohertz** is a unit for measuring radio waves. ❑ *The frequency of the radio waves slowly increased to 4 kilohertz.*

kilo|meter /kíləmɪtər, kɪlɒmɪtər/ (**kilometers**) **NOUN** MATH A **kilometer** is a unit for measuring distance. One kilometer is equal to 0.62 miles, and there are one thousand meters in a kilometer. ❑ *We're now only one kilometer from the border.*
→ look at **measurement**

k

kilo|watt /kɪləwɒt/ (kilowatts) **NOUN**
SCIENCE A **kilowatt** is a unit of electrical power. ❏ *The system produces 25 kilowatts of power.*

---
kind
❶ NOUN USE AND PHRASE
❷ ADJECTIVE USE
---

❶ **kind** /kaɪnd/ (kinds)
1 **NOUN** A particular **kind of** thing is a type of that thing. ❏ *What kind of car do you drive?* ❏ *He travels a lot, and sees all kinds of interesting things.*
2 **Kind of** means "a little" or "in some way." [INFORMAL] ❏ *When I was new at school, some girls were kind of mean to me.*

❷ **kind** /kaɪnd/ (kinder, kindest) **ADJECTIVE**
Someone who is **kind** is friendly and helpful. ❏ *Thank you for being so kind to me.* ● **kind|ly** **ADVERB** ❏ *The woman smiled kindly at her.* ● **kind|ness** **NONCOUNT NOUN** ❏ *I'll never forget his generosity and kindness.*

kin|der|gar|ten /kɪndərgɑrtᵊn/ **NONCOUNT NOUN** Kindergarten is a class for children aged 4 to 6 years old. ❏ *She's in kindergarten now.*

kind|ly /kaɪndli/ **ADJECTIVE** Kindly means kind and caring. ❏ *He gave her a kindly smile.*

king /kɪŋ/ (kings) **NOUN** SOCIAL STUDIES
A **king** is a man from a royal family, who is the head of state of that country. ❏ *...the king and queen of Spain.*

king|dom /kɪŋdəm/ (kingdoms) **NOUN**
SOCIAL STUDIES A **kingdom** is a country that is ruled by a king or a queen. ❏ *...the Kingdom of Denmark.*

ki|osk /kiɒsk/ (kiosks) **NOUN** A **kiosk** is a small building with a window where people can buy things like newspapers. ❏ *I was getting a newspaper at the kiosk.*

kiss /kɪs/ (kisses, kissing, kissed)
1 **VERB** If you **kiss** someone, you touch them with your lips to show love, or to greet them. ❏ *She smiled and kissed him on the cheek.* ❏ *The woman gently kissed her baby.* ❏ *We kissed goodbye at the airport.*
2 **NOUN** Kiss is also a noun. ❏ *I put my arms around her and gave her a kiss.*

kit /kɪt/ (kits)
1 **NOUN** A **kit** is a group of items that are kept and used together for a particular purpose. ❏ *...a first aid kit.* ❏ *She just got her first drum kit.*
2 **NOUN** A **kit** is a set of parts that you can put together in order to make something. ❏ *...a model airplane kit.*

kitch|en /kɪtʃᵊn/ (kitchens) **NOUN** A **kitchen** is a room that is used for cooking.
→ look at Picture Dictionary: **kitchen**
→ look at **house**

kite /kaɪt/ (kites) **NOUN**
A **kite** is a toy that you fly in the wind at the end of a long string. ❏ *We went to the beach to fly kites.*

kit|ten /kɪtᵊn/ (kittens) **NOUN** A **kitten** is a very young cat.

kiwi fruit /kiwi frut/ (kiwi fruits)

LANGUAGE HELP
The plural can also be **kiwi fruit**.

K

Picture Dictionary — kitchen

freezer — dishes — cabinet
glasses
coffee pot — microwave — counter
sink — stove
drawer
refrigerator
dishwasher
oven

NOUN A **kiwi fruit** is a small fruit with brown skin, black seeds, and bright green flesh.
→ look at **fruit**

km (**kms**) MATH **km** is short for **kilometer**.

knead /nid/ (**kneads, kneading, kneaded**)
VERB When you **knead** a mixture for making bread, you press and stretch it with your hands to make it smooth. ❑ *Knead the dough for a few minutes.*

knee /ni/ (**knees**) **NOUN** Your **knee** is the part in the middle of your leg where it bends. ❑ *Lie down and bring your knees up toward your chest.*
→ look at **body**

kneel /nil/ (**kneels, kneeling, kneeled** or **knelt**)
1 **VERB** When you **kneel**, you bend your legs and rest with one or both of your knees on the ground. ❑ *She knelt by the bed and prayed.* ❑ *Other people were kneeling, but she just sat.*
2 **Kneel down** means the same as **kneel**. ❑ *She kneeled down beside him.*

knew /nu/ **Knew** is a form of the verb **know**.

knife /naɪf/ (**knives**) **NOUN** A **knife** is a sharp flat piece of metal with a handle, that you can use to cut things or as a weapon. ❑ *I stopped eating and put down my knife and fork.*
→ look at **restaurant**

knight /naɪt/ (**knights**) **NOUN** SOCIAL STUDIES In the past, a **knight** was a special type of soldier who rode a horse. ❑ *...King Arthur's knights.*

knit /nɪt/ (**knits, knitting, knitted**) **VERB** If you **knit** a piece of clothing, you make it from wool by using two long needles (= sticks). ❑ *I had many hours to knit and sew.* ❑ *I have already started knitting baby clothes.*
● **knit|ting** **NONCOUNT NOUN** ❑ *My favorite hobbies are knitting and reading.*

knives /naɪvz/ **Knives** is the plural of **knife**.

knob /nɒb/ (**knobs**) **NOUN** A **knob** is a round handle or switch. ❑ *He turned the knob and pushed the door.* ❑ *...a volume knob.*

knock /nɒk/ (**knocks, knocking, knocked**)
1 **VERB** If you **knock on** something, you hit it in order to make a noise. ❑ *She went to Simon's apartment and knocked on the door.*
2 **NOUN** **Knock** is also a noun. ❑ *They heard a knock at the front door.* ● **knock|ing** **NONCOUNT NOUN** ❑ *There was a loud knocking at the door.*
3 **VERB** If you **knock** something, you touch

or hit it roughly. ❑ *She accidentally knocked the glass and it fell off the shelf.*
4 To **knock** someone or something **over** means to hit them so that they fall over. ❑ *The third wave was so strong it knocked me over.* ❑ *She stood up suddenly, knocking over a glass of milk.*
▶ **knock down** To **knock down** a building or part of a building means to destroy it. ❑ *We're knocking down the wall between the kitchen and the dining room.*
▶ **knock out** To **knock** someone **out** means to hit them hard on the head so that they fall and cannot get up again. ❑ *He was knocked out in a fight.*

knot /nɒt/ (**knots, knotting, knotted**)
1 **VERB** If you **knot** two pieces of string or rope, you tie them together. ❑ *He knotted the laces securely together.*
2 **NOUN** **Knot** is also a noun. ❑ *Tony wore a bright red scarf tied in a knot around his neck.*

Sound Partners   know, no

know /noʊ/ (**knows, knowing, knew, known**)
1 **VERB** If you **know** a fact or an answer, you have that information in your mind. ❑ *You should know the answer to that question.* ❑ *I don't know his name.* ❑ *"How old is he?"—"I don't know."*
2 **VERB** If you **know** a person or a place, you are familiar with them. ❑ *I've known him for nine years.* ❑ *I know Chicago well. I used to live there.*
3 **VERB** If you **know about** something, you understand it. ❑ *My mother knows a lot about antiques.* ❑ *I know how you feel.*
4 You say "**I know**" when you are agreeing with what someone has just said. ❑ *"The weather is awful."—"I know."*
5 You use **you know** when you want someone to listen to what you are saying. [INFORMAL] ❑ *I'm doing this for you, you know.*

knowl|edge /nɒlɪdʒ/ **NONCOUNT NOUN** **Knowledge** is information and understanding about a subject. ❑ *He has a wide knowledge of sports.* ❑ *Scientists have very little knowledge of the disease.*

knowl|edge|able /nɒlɪdʒəbᵊl/ also **knowledgable** **ADJECTIVE** Someone who is **knowledgeable** knows a lot about a particular subject. ❑ *Our staff are all extremely knowledgeable about our products.*

k

known /n<u>ou</u>n/

1 **Known** is a form of the verb **know**.

2 **ADJECTIVE** Someone or something that is **known** is familiar to a particular group of people. ❏ *Hawaii is known for its beautiful beaches.*

knuck|le /n<u>ʌ</u>kəl/ (**knuckles**) **NOUN** Your **knuckles** are the parts where your fingers join your hands, and where your fingers bend. ❏ *She tapped on the door with her knuckles.*

→ look at **hand**

Ko|ran /kɔr<u>a</u>n, -r<u>æ</u>n/ **NOUN** The **Koran** is the most important book in the religion of Islam.

kW SCIENCE In writing, **kW** is short for **kilowatt**.

Ll

lab /læb/ (labs) NOUN SCIENCE A **lab** is the same as a **laboratory**.

la|bel /leɪbᵊl/ (labels, labeling, labeled)

1 NOUN A **label** is a piece of paper or plastic that is attached to an object to give information about it. ❑ *Always read the label on the bottle.*

2 VERB If something **is labeled**, it has a label on it. ❑ *All foods must be clearly labeled.*

la|bor /leɪbər/

1 NONCOUNT NOUN **Labor** is very hard work, usually physical work. ❑ *The punishment for refusing to fight was a year's hard labor.*

2 NONCOUNT NOUN SOCIAL STUDIES **Labor** is the workers of a country or an industry. ❑ *Employers want cheap labor.*

la|bora|tory /læbrətɔri/ (laboratories)

NOUN SCIENCE A **laboratory** is a building or a room where scientific work is done. ❑ *He works in a research laboratory at Columbia University.*

→ look at **science**

Word Partners	Use **laboratory** with:
N.	laboratory **conditions**, laboratory **equipment**, laboratory **experiment**, **research** laboratory, laboratory **technician**, laboratory **test**

lace /leɪs/ (laces, lacing, laced)

1 NONCOUNT NOUN **Lace** is a delicate cloth with a design made of fine threads. ❑ *She wore a blue dress with a lace collar.*

2 NOUN **Laces** are thin pieces of material that are used for fastening shoes. ❑ *Barry put on his shoes and tied the laces.*

3 VERB If you **lace** a pair of shoes, you pull the laces through the holes and tie them together. ❑ *I laced my shoes tightly.*

lack /læk/ (lacks, lacking, lacked)

1 NONCOUNT NOUN If there is a **lack of** something, there is not enough of it or it does not exist. ❑ *I was tired from lack of sleep.*

2 VERB If someone or something **lacks** a particular quality, they do not have that quality or they do not have enough of it. ❑ *The meat lacked flavor.*

lad|der /lædər/ (ladders)

NOUN A **ladder** is a piece of equipment used for reaching high places. It is made of two long pieces of wood or metal with short steps between them. ❑ *He climbed the ladder so he could see over the wall.*

lady /leɪdi/ (ladies) NOUN You can use **lady** when you are talking about a woman in a polite way. ❑ *She's a very sweet old lady.*

lady|bug /leɪdibʌg/ (ladybugs) NOUN A **ladybug** is a small round insect that is red or yellow with black spots.

laid /leɪd/ **Laid** is a form of the verb **lay**.

laid-back ADJECTIVE If someone is **laid-back**, they behave in a calm, relaxed way. [INFORMAL] ❑ *Everyone here is really laid-back.*

lain /leɪn/ **Lain** is a form of the verb **lie**.

lake /leɪk/ (lakes) NOUN SCIENCE GEOGRAPHY A **lake** is a large area of water with land around it. ❑ *They went fishing in the lake.*

→ look at **landform, river, water**

lamb /læm/ (lambs)

1 NOUN A **lamb** is a young sheep.

2 NONCOUNT NOUN **Lamb** is the flesh of a lamb eaten as food. ❑ *For supper she served lamb and vegetables.*

→ look at **meat**

lame /leɪm/ (lamer, lamest)

1 ADJECTIVE A **lame** animal or person cannot walk very well. ❑ *The horses were lame and the men were tired.*

2 ADJECTIVE A **lame** excuse is not a very good excuse. ❑ *He gave me some lame excuse about being too busy to call me.*

lamp /læmp/ (lamps) NOUN A **lamp** is a light that works using electricity or by burning

oil or gas. ❑ *She switched on the lamp by her bed.*
→ look at **furniture**

land /lænd/ (**lands, landing, landed**)
1 **NONCOUNT NOUN** GEOGRAPHY **Land** is an
area of ground, especially one that is used
for a particular purpose such as farming or
building. ❑ *There is not enough good farm land.*
2 **VERB** When someone or something **lands**,
they come down to the ground after moving
through the air. ❑ *The ball landed 20 feet away.*
3 **VERB** When a plane or a ship **lands**, it
arrives somewhere. ❑ *The plane landed just
after 10 pm.* ● **land|ing** (**landings**) **NOUN** ❑ *The
pilot made an emergency landing into the ocean.*
→ look at **conservation**

Word Partners	Use **land** with:
N.	**acres of** land, **area of** land, **desert** land, **piece of** land, **plot of** land **1**
V.	**buy** land, **own** land, **sell** land **1**
ADJ.	**fertile** land, **flat** land, **private** land, **public** land, **vacant** land, **vast** land **1**

land|form /lændfɔrm/ (**landforms**) also
land form **NOUN** GEOGRAPHY SCIENCE
A **landform** is a natural feature of the Earth's
surface, such as a hill, a lake, or a beach.
❑ *This small country has a wide variety of landforms.*
→ look at Picture Dictionary: **landforms**

land|ing /lændɪŋ/ (**landings**) **NOUN** In a
house or other building, a **landing** is the flat
area at the top of the stairs.

land|lady /lændleɪdi/ (**landladies**) **NOUN**
A **landlady** is a woman who owns a building
and allows people to live there in return for
rent. ❑ *There was a note under the door from my
landlady.*

land|lord /lændlɔrd/ (**landlords**) **NOUN** A
landlord is a man who owns a building and
allows people to live there in return for rent.
❑ *His landlord doubled the rent.*

land|mark /lændmɑrk/ (**landmarks**) **NOUN**
A **landmark** is a building or other object that
helps people to know where they are. ❑ *The
Empire State Building is a New York landmark.*

land|scape /lændskeɪp/ (**landscapes**)
1 **NOUN** The **landscape** is everything you
can see when you look across an area of
land. ❑ *We traveled through the beautiful
landscape of eastern Idaho*
2 **NOUN** ARTS A **landscape** is a painting that
shows a scene in the countryside. ❑ *She
paints landscapes of hills and river valleys.*

lane /leɪn/ (**lanes**)
1 **NOUN** A **lane** is a narrow road, especially
in the countryside. ❑ *Our house was on a quiet
country lane.*
2 **NOUN** A **lane** is a part of a road that is
marked by a painted line. ❑ *The truck was
traveling at 20 mph in the slow lane.*

lan|guage /læŋgwɪdʒ/ (**languages**)
1 **NOUN** LANGUAGE ARTS A **language** is a
system of sounds and written symbols that
people of a particular country or region use
in talking or writing. ❑ *The English language
has over 500,000 words.* ❑ *Students must learn to
speak a second language.*
2 **NONCOUNT NOUN** LANGUAGE ARTS
Language is the use of a system of
communication that has a set of sounds or
written symbols. ❑ *Some children develop
language more quickly than others.*
→ look at Word World: **language**
→ look at **communication, grammar**

L

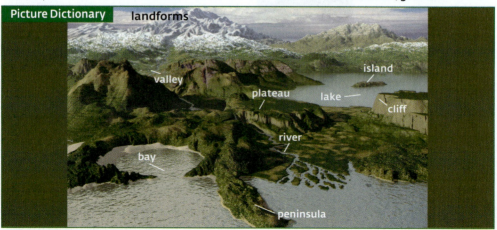

Picture Dictionary landforms

valley
island
plateau
lake
cliff
river
bay
peninsula

Word World language

vowel

difficult

foreign

native

communication

syllable

speak

easy

sounds

write

translate

grammar

read

consonant

learner

pronounce

study

vocabulary

alphabet

listen

learn

Nouns / Adjectives / Verbs

lan|tern /ˈlæntərn/ (lanterns) **NOUN** A **lantern** is a light in a metal frame with glass sides.

lap /læp/ (laps, lapping, lapped)
1 **NOUN** Your **lap** is the flat area formed by the tops of your legs when you are sitting down. ❑ Anthony was sitting on his dad's lap.
2 **NOUN** SPORTS In a race, someone completes a **lap** when they have gone around a course once. ❑ He was not able to run the last lap of the race.
3 **VERB** When an animal **laps** a drink, it uses short quick movements of its tongue to take liquid up into its mouth. ❑ The cat lapped milk from a dish.

la|pel /ləˈpɛl/ (lapels) **NOUN** The **lapels** of a jacket or a coat are the folds on the front. ❑ He wore a flower in his lapel.

lap|top /ˈlæptɒp/ (laptops) **NOUN** TECHNOLOGY A **laptop** is a small computer that you can carry with you. ❑ She was working at her laptop.
→ look at **bag, computer**

large /lɑrdʒ/ (larger, largest)
1 **ADJECTIVE** A **large** thing or person is greater in size than most other things of the same type. ❑ This fish lives mainly in large rivers and lakes. ❑ In the largest room a few people were sitting on the floor.
2 **ADJECTIVE** A **large** amount or number is more than the average amount or number. ❑ The robbers got away with a large amount of cash. ❑ A large number of people are still looking for jobs.
→ look at **earth, shopping**

large|ly /ˈlɑrdʒli/ **ADVERB** You use **largely** to say that something is mostly true. ❑ The program is largely paid for by taxes. ❑ The government is largely to blame for this.

la|ser /ˈleɪzər/ (lasers) **NOUN** SCIENCE A **laser** is a strong light that is produced by a special machine. ❑ Doctors are trying new laser technology to help patients.

la|ser print|er (laser printers) **NOUN** TECHNOLOGY A **laser printer** is a computer printer that produces clear words and pictures on paper using laser beams (= strong lines of light).

last /læst/ (lasts, lasting, lasted)
1 **ADJECTIVE** You use **last** to talk about the most recent day, night, or year. ❑ I got married last July. ❑ He didn't come home last night.
2 **ADJECTIVE** The **last** event, person, or thing is the most recent one. ❑ A lot has changed since my last visit.
3 **ADJECTIVE** The **last** thing, person, event, or period of time is the one that happens or comes after all the others of the same type. ❑ I read the last three pages of the chapter.
4 **ADVERB** If you do something **last**, you do it at the end, or after everyone else. ❑ I arrived home last.
5 **PRONOUN** If you are **the last to** do something, everyone else does it before you. ❑ Rosa was the last to go to bed.
6 **ADJECTIVE** The **last** thing or person is the only one that is left. ❑ Can I have the last piece of pizza?
7 **VERB** If a situation **lasts** for a particular length of time, it continues to exist for that length of time. ❑ The marriage lasted for less than two years.
8 **VERB** If something **lasts** for a particular length of time, it can be used for that time. ❑ One tube of glue lasts for a long time.
9 If something happens **at last**, it happens after you have been hoping for it for a long time. ❑ I'm so glad that we've found you at last!
→ look at **calendar**

last|ing /ˈlæstɪŋ/ **ADJECTIVE** **Lasting** describes something that continues to exist for a very long time. ❑ Everyone wants lasting peace.

last|ly /ˈlæstli/ **ADVERB** You use **lastly** when you want to mention a final item. ❑ Lastly, can I ask about your future plans?

last name (last names) **NOUN** Your **last name** is the name of your family. In English, your **last** name comes after all your other names. ❑ *"What is your last name?"—"Garcia."*

latch /lætʃ/ (latches) **NOUN** A **latch** is a metal bar that you use to fasten a door or a gate. You lift the bar to open the door or gate. ❑ *She lifted the latch and pushed the door open.*

late /leɪt/ (later, latest)
1 **ADVERB** **Late** means near the end of a period of time. ❑ *It was late in the afternoon.* ❑ *He married late in life.*
2 **ADJECTIVE** **Late** is also an adjective. ❑ *He was in his late 20s.*
3 **ADJECTIVE** If it is **late**, it is near the end of the day. ❑ *It was very late and the streets were empty.*
4 **ADVERB** **Late** means after the time that something should start or happen. ❑ *Steve arrived late for his class.*
5 **ADJECTIVE** **Late** is also an adjective. ❑ *The train was 40 minutes late.*
→ look at **day**

late|ly /leɪtli/ **ADVERB** You use **lately** to talk about events that happened recently. ❑ *Dad's health hasn't been good lately.*

lat|er /leɪtər/
1 **Later** is a form of the adjective **late**.
2 **ADVERB** You use **later** to talk about a time that is after the one that you have been talking about ❑ *He joined the company in 1990 and left his job ten years later.*

lat|est /leɪtɪst/
1 **Latest** is a form of the adjective **late**.
2 **ADJECTIVE** **Latest** describes something that is the most recent thing of its type. ❑ *I really liked her latest book.*
3 **ADJECTIVE** **Latest** describes something that is new and modern. ❑ *That store sells only the latest fashions.*
→ look at **news**

lati|tude /lætɪtud/ (latitudes) **NOUN** GEOGRAPHY The **latitude** of a place is its distance from the equator (= the line around the middle of the Earth). Compare with **longitude**. ❑ *The evenings are already long at this northern latitude.*
→ look at **globe**

lat|ter /lætər/
1 **PRONOUN** When two people or things have just been mentioned, you can call the second one **the latter**. You can call the first

of them **the former**. ❑ *He found his cousin and uncle. The latter was sick.*
2 **ADJECTIVE** **Latter** is also an adjective. ❑ *Some people like speaking in public and some don't. Mike belongs in the latter group.*

laugh /læf/ (laughs, laughing, laughed)
1 **VERB** When you **laugh**, you make a sound while smiling to show that you think something is funny. ❑ *When I saw what he was wearing, I started to laugh.* ❑ *Some of the boys laughed at his jokes.*
2 **NOUN** **Laugh** is also a noun. ❑ *Len gave a loud laugh.*
3 **VERB** If people **laugh at** someone or something, they make jokes about them. ❑ *People used to laugh at me because I was so small.*
→ look at **feeling**

laugh|ter /læftər/ **NONCOUNT NOUN** **Laughter** is the sound of people laughing. ❑ *Their laughter filled the room.*

launch /lɔntʃ/ (launches, launching, launched)
1 **VERB** To **launch** a spacecraft (= a vehicle that goes into space) means to send it away from Earth. To launch a ship or a boat means to put it into water. ❑ *NASA plans to launch a new satellite.* ❑ *The Titanic was launched in 1911.*
2 **VERB** To **launch** a large and important activity means to start it. ❑ *The police have launched a search for the missing girl.*

laun|dro|mat /lɔndrəmæt/ (laundromats) **NOUN** A **laundromat** is a place where people pay to use machines to wash and dry their clothes.
→ look at **laundry**

laun|dry /lɔndri/ (laundries)
1 **NONCOUNT NOUN** **Laundry** is clothes and other things that are going to be washed. ❑ *I'll do your laundry.*
2 **NOUN** A **laundry** is a business that washes and irons clothes and other things for people. ❑ *He takes his shirts to the laundry.*
→ look at Word World: **laundry**
→ look at **house**

lava /lɑvə, lævə/ **NONCOUNT NOUN** SCIENCE **Lava** is the very hot liquid rock that comes out of a volcano (= a mountain with a hole at the top that throws out hot substances). ❑ *Lava poured from the volcano.*

lava|tory /lævətɔri/ (lavatories) **NOUN** A **lavatory** is a room with toilets and sinks

L

Word World laundry

washing machine — clothes — dryer — soap — wet — clean

stained — wrinkled — wash

bleach — stain — bleach — dirty — iron — fold

ironing — basket — dry

laundromat — detergent — bleach

Nouns / Adjectives / Verbs

in a public building. ❑ *The ladies' lavatory is over there, on the left.*

law /lɔ/ (**laws**)

1 **NONCOUNT NOUN** **The law** is a system of rules that a society or a government develops to deal with things like crime. ❑ *Driving too fast is against the law.* ❑ *These companies are breaking the law.*

2 **NOUN** A **law** is one of the rules in a system of law. ❑ *The government has introduced a new law to protect young people.*

law|ful /lɔfəl/ **ADJECTIVE** If an activity is **lawful**, it is allowed by law. [FORMAL] ❑ *We want fair and lawful treatment of prisoners.* ● **law|ful|ly** **ADVERB** ❑ *Did the police act lawfully in shooting him?*

lawn /lɔn/ (**lawns**) **NOUN** A **lawn** is an area of short grass around a house or another building. ❑ *They were sitting on the lawn, eating their lunch.*

lawn|mow|er /lɔnmoʊər/ (**lawnmowers**) **NOUN** A **lawnmower** is a machine for cutting grass.

law|suit /lɔsut/ (**lawsuits**) **NOUN** A **lawsuit** is a case that a court of law deals with. [FORMAL] ❑ *The lawsuit accuses him of theft and kidnapping.*

law|yer /lɔɪər, lɔyər/ (**lawyers**) **NOUN** A **lawyer** is a person who advises people about the law and represents them in court. ❑ *His lawyers say that he is not guilty.*

lay /leɪ/ (**lays, laying, laid**)

LANGUAGE HELP
Lay is a form of the verb **lie**.

1 **VERB** If you **lay** something somewhere, you put it there carefully. ❑ *He laid the newspaper on the desk.* ❑ *She gently laid the baby in her crib.*

2 **VERB** When a female bird **lays** an egg, it pushes an egg out of its body.

lay|er /leɪər/ (**layers**) **NOUN** A **layer** is a substance or a material that covers a surface, or that lies between two other things. ❑ *A fresh layer of snow covered the street.*

lay|out /leɪaʊt/ (**layouts**) **NOUN** The **layout** of a place is the way the parts of it are arranged. ❑ *He tried to remember the layout of the farmhouse.*

lazy /leɪzi/ (**lazier, laziest**) **ADJECTIVE** If someone is **lazy**, they do not want to work. ❑ *I'm not lazy; I like to be busy.* ● **la|zi|ness** **NONCOUNT NOUN** ❑ *Too much TV encourages laziness.*

lb.

LANGUAGE HELP
The plural is **lbs.** or **lb.**

MATH **lb.** is short for **pound**, when you are talking about weight. ❑ *The baby weighed 8 lbs. 5 oz.*

lead

1 BEING AHEAD OR TAKING SOMEONE SOMEWHERE
2 SUBSTANCES

1 lead /lid/ (**leads, leading, led**)

1 **VERB** If you **lead** a group of people, you go in front of them. ❑ *A jazz band led the parade.*

2 **VERB** If you **lead** someone to a place, you take them there. ❑ *I took his hand and led him into the house.*

3 **VERB** If a road or a path **leads** somewhere, it goes there. ❑ *This path leads down to the beach.*

4 **VERB** If you **are leading** in a race or a competition, you are winning. ❑ *The Eagles led by three points at half-time.*

5 **NOUN** If you are **in the lead** in a race or a competition, you are winning. ❑ *Harvard were already in the lead after ten minutes.*

6 **VERB** If you **lead** a group of people, you are in control of them. ❑ *Chris leads a large team of salespeople.*

I

7 **VERB** You can use **lead** when you are describing someone's life. ❑ *She led a normal, happy life.*

8 **VERB** If something **leads to** a situation, it causes that situation. ❑ *Every time we talk about money it leads to an argument.*

❷ lead /lɛd/ (**leads**)

1 **NONCOUNT NOUN** **Lead** is a soft, gray, heavy metal. ❑ *In the past, most water pipes were made of lead.*

2 **NOUN** The **lead** in a pencil is the gray part in the middle of it that makes a mark on paper. ❑ *He started writing, but his pencil lead immediately broke.*

Word Builder   **leader**

er ≈ someone who does

    climb + **er** = climb**er**
    farm + **er** = farm**er**
    lead + **er** = lead**er**
    own + **er** = own**er**
    play + **er** = play**er**
    work + **er** = work**er**

---

lead|er /lidər/ (**leaders**)

1 **NOUN** The **leader** of a group of people or an organization is the person who is in charge of it. ❑ *Members today will elect a new leader.*

2 **NOUN** The **leader** in a race or a competition is the person who is in front of all the others, or who is winning. ❑ *The leader came in two minutes before the other runners.*

Word Builder   **leadership**

ship ≈ state of being

    champion + **ship** = champion**ship**
    friend + **ship** = friend**ship**
    leader + **ship** = leader**ship**
    member + **ship** = member**ship**
    owner + **ship** = owner**ship**
    relation + **ship** = relation**ship**

---

lead|er|ship /lidərʃɪp/

1 **NONCOUNT NOUN** You call people who are in control of a group or organization the **leadership** ❑ *He attended a meeting with the Croatian leadership.*

2 **NONCOUNT NOUN** Someone's **leadership** is their position of being in control of a group of people. ❑ *The company doubled in size under her leadership.*

lead|ing /lidɪŋ/

1 **ADJECTIVE** A **leading** person or thing in a particular area is the most important or successful one. ❑ *...a leading violin player.*

2 **ADJECTIVE** In a race or a competition, the **leading** person or team is the one who is winning. ❑ *It always feels good to be in the leading team.*

leaf /lif/ (**leaves** or **leafs**) **NOUN** The **leaves** of a tree or a plant are the parts that are flat, thin, and usually green. ❑ *A brown, dry oak leaf fell into the water.*

→ look at **tree**

leaf|let /liflɪt/ (**leaflets**) **NOUN** A **leaflet** is a piece of paper containing information about a particular subject. ❑ *My doctor gave me a leaflet about healthy eating.*

league /lig/ (**leagues**)

1 **NOUN** A **league** is a group of people, clubs, or countries that have joined together for a particular purpose. ❑ *The League of Nations was formed after World War I.*

2 **NOUN** **SPORTS** A **league** is a group of teams that play against each other. ❑ *The Boston Red Sox won the American League series.*

leak /lik/ (**leaks, leaking, leaked**)

1 **VERB** If a container **leaks**, there is a hole in it that lets liquid or gas escape. ❑ *The roof leaks every time it rains.*

2 If liquid or gas **leaks** from a container, it escapes through a hole in it. ❑ *The water is leaking out from the bottom of the bucket.*

3 **NOUN** **Leak** is also a noun. ❑ *A gas leak caused the explosion.*

lean /lin/ (**leans, leaning, leaned, leaner, leanest**)

1 **VERB** When you **lean**, you bend your body from your waist in a particular direction. ❑ *The driver leaned across and opened the passenger door.*

2 **VERB** If you **lean on** or **against** someone or something, you rest on them. ❑ *She was feeling tired and leaned against him.*

3 **ADJECTIVE** If meat is **lean**, it does not have very much fat.

4 **ADJECTIVE** If a person is **lean**, they are thin, and they look fit and healthy. ❑ *He was lean and strong.*

→ look at **meat**

leap /lip/ (**leaps, leaping, leaped** or **leapt**)

1 **VERB** If you **leap**, you jump high in the air or you jump a long distance. ❑ *He leaped in the air and waved his hands.*

2 **NOUN** Leap is also a noun. ❑ *Powell won the long jump with a leap of 8 meters 95 centimeters.*

3 **VERB** To **leap** somewhere means to move there suddenly and quickly. ❑ *The two men leaped into the car and drove away.*

learn /lɜrn/ (**learns, learning, learned** or **learnt**) **VERB** If you **learn** something, you get knowledge or a skill by studying, training, or through experience. ❑ *Where did you learn English?* ❑ *He is learning to play the piano.*

● **learn|er** (**learners**) **NOUN** ❑ *Clint is a quick learner; he's one of my smarter students.*

→ look at **grammar, language, school**

Word Partners	Use **learn** with:
N.	**children** learn, learn **from experience**, learn **a language**, learn **a lesson**, learn **from mistakes**, **opportunity to** learn, **people** learn, learn **in school**, learn **a skill**, **students** learn
V.	learn **to drive**, **have to** learn, **need to** learn, learn **to read**, learn **to speak**, learn **to swim**, **try to** learn, **want to** learn, learn **to write**

lease /lis/ (**leases, leasing, leased**)

1 **NOUN** A **lease** is a legal agreement that allows someone to pay money so that they can use something for a particular period of time. ❑ *She signed a one-year lease on the apartment.*

2 **VERB** If you **lease** something **from** someone, you pay them, and they allow you to use it. ❑ *He leased an apartment in Toronto.*

3 **VERB** If someone **leases** something **to** you, you pay them, and they allow you to use it. ❑ *She's going to lease the building to students.*

leash /liʃ/ (**leashes**) **NOUN** A **leash** is a long thin piece of leather or a chain, that you use to control a dog. ❑ *All dogs in public places should be on a leash.*

least /list/

1 **At least** means not less than a particular number or amount. ❑ *Drink at least half a pint of milk each day.*

2 **ADJECTIVE** You use **the least** to mean a smaller amount than anyone or anything else, or the smallest amount possible. ❑ *He wants to spend the least amount of money possible on a car.*

3 **PRONOUN** Least is also a pronoun. ❑ *The report found that teenage girls exercised the least.*

4 **ADVERB** Least is also an adverb. ❑ *He is one of the least friendly people I have ever met.*

leath|er /lɛðər/ **NONCOUNT NOUN** Leather is animal skin that is used for making shoes, clothes, bags, and furniture. ❑ *She bought a leather jacket.*

leave /liv/ (**leaves, leaving, left**)

1 **VERB** If you **leave** a place or a person, you go away from them. ❑ *He left the country yesterday.* ❑ *My flight leaves in less than an hour.*

2 **VERB** If you **leave** something in a particular place, you do not bring it with you. ❑ *I left my bags in the car.*

3 **VERB** If you **leave** part of something, you do not use it all. ❑ *Please leave some cake for me!*

4 **VERB** If you **leave** something **to** someone, you give it to them when you die. ❑ *He left everything to his wife when he died.*

5 **VERB** If you **leave** something in a place, you forget to bring it with you. ❑ *I left my purse in the gas station.*

6 If you **leave** someone **alone**, you do not speak to them or annoy them. ❑ *Please just leave me alone!*

7 If you **leave** something **alone**, you do not touch it. ❑ *Leave my purse alone!*

8 **NONCOUNT NOUN** Leave is a period of time when you are away from work. ❑ *Why don't you take a few days' leave?*

9 **NONCOUNT NOUN** If you are **on leave**, you are not working at your job. ❑ *She has gone on leave for a week.*

▶ **leave out** If you **leave** someone or something **out**, you do not include them. ❑ *Why did they leave her out of the team?*

leaves /livz/ **Leaves** is the plural form of **leaf**, and a form of the verb **leave**.

lec|ture /lɛktʃər/ (**lectures, lecturing, lectured**)

1 **NOUN** A **lecture** is a talk that someone gives in order to teach people about a particular subject. ❑ *We attended a lecture by Professor Eric Robinson.*

2 **VERB** If you **lecture on** a particular subject, you give a lecture about it. ❑ *She invited him to Atlanta to lecture on the history of art.*

led /lɛd/ **Led** is a form of the verb **lead**.

ledge /lɛdʒ/ (**ledges**)

1 **NOUN** A **ledge** is a narrow shelf of rock on the side of a mountain.

2 NOUN A **ledge** is a narrow shelf along the bottom edge of a window. ❑ ...a window ledge.

leek /lik/ (**leeks**) **NOUN Leeks** are long, thin vegetables that are white at one end and have long green leaves.

---

left
1 REMAINING
2 DIRECTION AND POLITICAL GROUPINGS

---

1 left /lɛft/
1 Left is a form of the verb **leave**.
2 ADJECTIVE If there is a certain amount of something **left**, it is still there after everything else has gone or been used. ❑ Is there any milk left?

2 left /lɛft/
1 NOUN You use the **left** to talk about the side or direction that is the same side as your heart. ❑ The bank is on the left at the end of the road. ❑ There is a high brick wall to the left of the building.
2 ADVERB Left is also an adverb. ❑ Turn left at the corner.
3 ADJECTIVE Your **left** arm, hand, or leg is the one that is opposite the side that most people write with. ❑ I've broken my left leg.

left-handed ADJECTIVE Someone who is **left-handed** uses their left hand rather than their right hand for activities such as writing and sports. ❑ A left-handed tennis player won the tournament.

left|over /lɛftoʊvər/ (**leftovers**)
1 PLURAL NOUN You can call food that has not been eaten after a meal **leftovers**. ❑ Put any leftovers in the refrigerator.
2 ADJECTIVE Leftover describes an amount of something that remains after the rest of it has been used or eaten. ❑ If you have any leftover chicken, use it to make this delicious pie.

leg /lɛg/ (**legs**)
1 NOUN A person's or animal's **legs** are the long parts of their body that they use for walking and standing. ❑ He broke his right leg in a motorcycle accident.
2 NOUN The **legs** of a pair of pants are the parts that cover your legs. ❑ Anthony dried his hands on the legs of his jeans.
3 NOUN The **legs** of a table or a chair are the long parts that it stands on. ❑ ...a broken chair leg.
→ look at **body, shellfish**

le|gal /liɡəl/
1 ADJECTIVE Legal describes things that relate to the law. ❑ He promised to take legal action. ❑ ...the legal system.
2 ADJECTIVE An action or a situation that is **legal** is allowed by law. ❑ My actions were completely legal.
→ look at **identification**

le|gal|ize /liɡəlaɪz/ (**legalizes, legalizing, legalized**) **VERB** If something **is legalized**, a law is passed that makes it legal. ❑ Divorce was legalized in 1981.

leg|end /lɛdʒənd/ (**legends**) **NOUN** LANGUAGE ARTS A **legend** is a very old and popular story. ❑ The play is based on an ancient Greek legend.

leg|is|la|tive branch /lɛdʒɪsleɪtɪv bræntʃ/ **NONCOUNT NOUN** SOCIAL STUDIES The **legislative branch** is the part of the government of the United States that makes and changes laws.

leg|is|la|ture /lɛdʒɪsleɪtʃər/ (**legislatures**) **NOUN** SOCIAL STUDIES The **legislature** of a country is the group of people who have the power to make laws. [FORMAL] ❑ State legislature passed a law forbidding this practice.

lei|sure /liʒər, lɛʒ-/ **NONCOUNT NOUN Leisure** is the time when you are not working, when you can relax and do things that you enjoy. ❑ They spend their leisure time painting or drawing.
→ look at **relax**

lei|sure|ly /liʒərli, lɛʒ-/
1 ADJECTIVE A **leisurely** activity is done in a relaxed way. ❑ Lunch was a leisurely meal.
2 ADVERB Leisurely is also an adverb. ❑ We walked leisurely into the hotel.

lem|on /lɛmən/ (**lemons**) **NOUN** A **lemon** is a yellow fruit with very sour juice. ❑ I like a slice of lemon in my tea.
→ look at **fruit**

lem|on|ade /lɛməneɪd/ **NONCOUNT NOUN Lemonade** is a drink that is made from lemons, sugar, and water. ❑ They ordered two glasses of lemonade.

lend /lɛnd/ (**lends, lending, lent**)
1 VERB When a person or an organization such as a bank **lends** you money, they give it to you and you agree to pay it back later. ❑ The government will lend you money at very good rates.
2 VERB If you **lend** something that you own, you allow someone to use it for a period of time. ❑ Will you lend me your pen?

L

length /lɛŋθ/ (lengths)

1 **NOUN** The **length** of something is its measurement from one end to the other. ❑ *The table is about a meter in length.*

2 **NOUN** The **length** of an event is how long it lasts. ❑ *The average length of a patient's stay in the hospital is about 48 hours.*

3 If someone does something **at length**, they do it for a long time or in great detail. ❑ *They spoke at length about their families.*

→ look at **geometry**

length|en /lɛŋθən/ (lengthens, lengthening, lengthened)

1 **VERB** When you **lengthen** something, you make it longer. ❑ *This exercise will lengthen the muscles in your legs.*

2 When something lengthens, it becomes longer. ❑ *The sun went down and the shadows lengthened.*

lengthy /lɛŋθi/ (lengthier, lengthiest)

1 **ADJECTIVE** **Lengthy** describes an event or a process that lasts for a long time. ❑ *There was a lengthy meeting to decide the company's future.*

2 **ADJECTIVE** A **lengthy** piece of writing contains a lot of words. ❑ *The United Nations produced a lengthy report on the subject.*

lens /lɛnz/ (lenses) **NOUN** SCIENCE A **lens** is a thin, curved piece of glass or plastic that is used in things such as cameras and glasses. A lens makes things look larger, smaller, or clearer. ❑ *I bought a powerful lens for my camera.*

lent /lɛnt/ **Lent** is a form of the verb **lend**.

len|til /lɛntɪl, -tᵊl/ (lentils) **NOUN** Lentils are small, round, dried seeds that you use in cooking, for example to make soups.

leop|ard /lɛpərd/ (leopards) **NOUN** A leopard is a large, wild cat. Leopards have yellow fur with black spots, and live in Africa and Asia.

les|bian /lɛzbiən/ (lesbians)

1 **NOUN** A lesbian is a woman who is sexually attracted to other women. ❑ *The main character in the novel is a lesbian.*

2 **ADJECTIVE** **Lesbian** is also an adjective. ❑ *The organization supports lesbian and gay members.*

less /lɛs/

1 **ADJECTIVE** You use **less** to show that there is a smaller amount of something than before or than is usual. ❑ *People should eat less fat.* ❑ *He earns less money than his brother.*

2 **PRONOUN** Less is also a pronoun. ❑ *He thinks people should spend less and save more.*

3 You use **less than** to talk about a smaller amount of something than the amount mentioned. ❑ *The population of the country is less than 12 million.*

less|en /lɛsᵊn/ (lessens, lessening, lessened) **VERB** If something **lessens** or you **lessen** it, it becomes smaller. ❑ *A change in diet might lessen your risk of heart disease.*

les|son /lɛsᵊn/ (lessons) **NOUN** A **lesson** is a time when you learn about a particular subject. ❑ *Johanna has started taking piano lessons.*

let /lɛt/ (lets, letting, let)

1 **VERB** If you **let** something happen, you do not try to stop it. ❑ *I just let him sleep.*

2 **VERB** If you **let** someone do something, you give them your permission to do it. ❑ *I love candy but Mom doesn't let me eat it very often.*

3 **VERB** If you **let** someone into or out of a place, you allow them to enter or leave. ❑ *I went down and let them into the building.*

4 **VERB** If you **let** an apartment to someone, they pay you, and you allow them to live in it. ❑ *When I moved to London, I let my apartment in New York.*

5 **VERB** You use **let me** when you are offering to do something. ❑ *Let me hang up your coat.*

6 **VERB** You say **let's** (short for **let us**) when you are making a suggestion. ❑ *I'm bored. Let's go home.*

7 If you **let go of** someone or something, you stop holding them. ❑ *She let go of Mona's hand.*

8 If you **let** someone **know** something, you tell them about it. ❑ *I want to let them know that I'm safe.*

▶ **let off** If you **let** someone **off**, you give them a lighter punishment than they expect or no punishment at all. ❑ *He thought that if he said he was sorry, the judge would let him off.*

le|thal /liθᵊl/ **ADJECTIVE** A substance that is **lethal** can kill people or animals. ❑ *She swallowed a lethal dose of sleeping pills.*

let's /lɛts/ **Let's** is short for "let us."

Spelling Partners **letter**

let|ter /lɛtər/ (letters)

1 **NOUN** If you write a **letter** to someone, you write a message on paper and send it to them. ❑ *I received a letter from a friend.*

❏ *Mrs. Franklin sent a letter offering me the job.*
2 **NOUN** LANGUAGE ARTS **Letters** are written symbols that represent the sounds in a language. ❏ *The children practiced writing the letters of the alphabet.*

let|ter|ing /lɛtərɪŋ/ **NONCOUNT NOUN**
Lettering is writing or printing. ❏ *On the door was a small blue sign with white lettering.*

let|tuce /lɛtɪs/ (**lettuces**) **NOUN** A **lettuce** is a plant with large green leaves that is eaten mainly in salads.

lev|el /lɛvəl/ (**levels**)
1 **NOUN** A high or low **level** describes the amount or quality of something. ❏ *We have the lowest level of inflation since 1986.*
2 **NOUN** The **level** of something is its height. ❏ *The water level is 6.5 feet below normal.*
3 **ADJECTIVE** If one thing is **level with** another thing, it is at the same height as it. ❏ *He sat down so his face was level with the boy's.*
4 **ADJECTIVE** When something is **level**, it is completely flat. ❏ *Make sure the ground is level before you start building.*

lev|er /livər, lɛv-/ (**levers**)
1 **NOUN** A **lever** is a handle that you push or pull to operate a machine. ❏ *Push the lever to switch the machine on.*
2 **NOUN** A **lever** is a bar that you use to lift something heavy. You put one end of it under the heavy object, and then push down on the other end. ❏ *Joseph found a stick to use as a lever and lifted up the stone.*

lia|ble /laɪəbəl/ If something **is liable to** happen, it is very likely to happen. ❏ *Some of this old equipment is liable to break down.*

liar /laɪər/ (**liars**) **NOUN** A **liar** is someone who tells lies. ❏ *He's a liar and a cheat.*

lib|er|al /lɪbərəl, lɪbrəl/ **ADJECTIVE** Someone who has **liberal** ideas understands and accepts that other people have different ideas and beliefs, and may behave differently than them. ❏ *My parents are very liberal and relaxed.*

lib|er|ty /lɪbərti/ **NONCOUNT NOUN** **Liberty** is the freedom to live in the way that you want to. ❏ *We must do all we can to defend liberty and justice.*

li|brar|ian /laɪbrɛəriən/ (**librarians**) **NOUN** A **librarian** is a person who works in a library.

li|brary /laɪbrɛri/ (**libraries**) **NOUN** A public **library** is a building where books, newspapers, DVDs, and music are kept for people to use or borrow. ❏ *I found the book I needed at the local library.*
→ look at **school**

lice /laɪs/ **PLURAL NOUN** **Lice** are small insects that live on the bodies of people or animals.

li|cense /laɪsᵊns/ (**licenses**) **NOUN** A **license** is an official document that gives you permission to do, use, or own something. ❏ *You need a license to drive a car.*

li|cense plate (**license plates**) **NOUN** A **license plate** is a metal sign on the back of a vehicle that shows its official number. ❏ *She drives a car with California license plates.*

lick /lɪk/ (**licks, licking, licked**)
1 **VERB** When you **lick** something, you move your tongue across its surface. ❏ *She licked the stamp and pressed it onto the envelope.*
2 **NOUN** **Lick** is also a noun. ❏ *Can I have a lick of your ice cream?*

lico|rice /lɪkərɪʃ, -ɪs/ **NONCOUNT NOUN**
Licorice is a firm black substance with a strong taste that is used for making a type of candy.

lid /lɪd/ (**lids**) **NOUN** A **lid** is the top of a container that can be removed. ❏ *She lifted the lid of the box.*

lie
1 POSITION OR SITUATION
2 THINGS THAT ARE NOT TRUE

1 lie /laɪ/ (**lies, lying, lay, lain**)
1 **VERB** If you **are lying** somewhere, your body is flat, and you are not standing or sitting. ❏ *There was a man lying on the ground.*
2 **VERB** If an object **lies** in a particular place, it is in a flat position there. ❏ *His clothes were lying on the floor by the bed.*
▶ **lie down** When you **lie down**, you move your body so that it is flat on something, usually when you want to rest or sleep. ❏ *Why don't you go upstairs and lie down?*

2 lie /laɪ/ (**lies, lying, lied**)
1 **NOUN** A **lie** is something that someone says or writes that they know is not true. ❏ *You told me a lie!* ❏ *"How old are you?"— "Eighteen."—"That's a lie."*
2 **VERB** If someone **is lying**, they are saying something that they know is not true. ❏ *I know he's lying.* ❏ *Never lie to me again.*

L

Word Partners	Use **lie** with:
ADJ.	lie **awake** ❶ **1** lie **flat** ❶ **2**
N.	lie **on** *your* **back**, lie **on the beach**, lie **in a bed**, lie **on a couch**, lie **on a sofa** ❶ **1** lie **on the floor**, lie **on the ground** ❶ **2**
V.	**tell** a **lie** ❷ **1**

lieu|ten|ant /lutɛnənt/ (**lieutenants**) **NOUN**
A **lieutenant** is an officer in the military or in the U.S. police force. ❏ *Lieutenant Campbell ordered the man to stop.*

life /laɪf/ (**lives** /laɪvz/)
1 **NOUN** Someone's **life** is their state of being alive, or the period of time when they are alive. ❏ *Your life is in danger.* ❏ *A nurse tried to save his life.* ❏ *He spent the last fourteen years of his life in France.*
2 **NONCOUNT NOUN** Someone or something that is full of **life** is interesting and full of energy. ❏ *The town was full of life.*
→ look at **earth**

life|boat /laɪfboʊt/ (**lifeboats**) **NOUN** A **lifeboat** is a boat that is used for saving people who are in danger on the ocean.

life cy|cle (**life cycles**) **NOUN** SCIENCE The **life cycle** of an animal or a plant is the series of changes that happen to it from the beginning of its life until its death. ❏ *This plant completes its life cycle in a single season.*

life|guard /laɪfgɑrd/ (**lifeguards**) **NOUN**
A **lifeguard** is a person who works at a beach or a swimming pool and helps people when they are in danger.

life pre|serv|er /laɪf prɪzɜrvər/ (**life preservers**) **NOUN** A **life preserver** is a ring or a jacket that helps you float if you fall into deep water.

life|style /laɪfstaɪl/ (**lifestyles**) also **life-style, life style** **NOUN** The **lifestyle** of a particular person or group is the way they have chosen to live and behave. ❏ *She talked about the benefits of leading a healthier lifestyle.*

life|time /laɪftaɪm/ (**lifetimes**) **NOUN**
A **lifetime** is the length of time that someone is alive. ❏ *He traveled a lot during his lifetime.*

lift /lɪft/ (**lifts, lifting, lifted**)
1 **VERB** If you **lift** something, you take it and move it upward. ❏ *He lifted the bag onto his shoulder.*
2 **Lift up** means the same as **lift**. ❏ *She lifted the baby up and gave him to me.*

3 **NOUN** If you give someone a **lift** somewhere, you take them there in your car. ❏ *He often gave me a lift home.*

Spelling Partners light

light
❶ BRIGHTNESS
❷ NOT GREAT IN WEIGHT OR AMOUNT

❶ **light** /laɪt/ (**lights, lighting, lit** or **lighted, lighter, lightest**)
1 **NONCOUNT NOUN** SCIENCE **Light** is the energy that comes from the sun, that lets you see things. ❏ *He opened the curtains, and suddenly the room was filled with light.*
2 **NOUN** A **light** is an electric lamp that produces light. ❏ *Remember to turn the lights out when you leave.*
3 **VERB** If a place or an object **is lit** by something, it has light shining on it. ❏ *The room was lit by only one light.*
4 **ADJECTIVE** If it is **light**, the sun is providing light during the day. ❏ *Here it gets light at about 6 a.m.*
5 **VERB** If you **light** a candle or a fire, it starts burning. ❏ *Stephen took a match and lit the candle.*
→ look at **energy**

❷ **light** /laɪt/ (**lighter, lightest**)
1 **ADJECTIVE** Something that is **light** is not heavy, and is easy to lift or move. ❏ *The printer is quite light, so it's easy to move around.*
2 **ADJECTIVE** Something that is **light** is not very great in amount or power. ❏ *She had a light lunch of salad and fruit.* ❏ *There was a light wind that day.*
3 **ADJECTIVE** Something that is **light** is pale in color. ❏ *He was wearing jeans and a light-blue T-shirt.*
→ look at **color**

light bulb (**light bulbs**) **NOUN** A **light bulb** is the glass part that you put in an electric light to produce light.

light|en /laɪtᵊn/ (**lightens, lightening, lightened**) **VERB** When you **lighten** something, you make it less dark. ❏ *She lightened her hair with a special cream.*
▶ **lighten up** If you say that someone should **lighten up**, you mean that they

I

should be more relaxed or less serious. ❑ *You should lighten up and enjoy yourself a bit more.*

light|er /laɪtər/ (**lighters**) **NOUN** A **lighter** is a small object that produces a flame. It is used for lighting things such as candles or fires.

light|house /laɪthaʊs/ (**lighthouses**) **NOUN** A **lighthouse** is a tower that is built near or in the ocean. It has a flashing lamp that warns ships of danger.
→ look at **beach**

light|ing /laɪtɪŋ/ **NONCOUNT NOUN** The **lighting** in a place is the way that it is lit. ❑ *The kitchen had bright overhead lighting.*

light|ning /laɪtnɪŋ/ **NONCOUNT NOUN** SCIENCE **Lightning** is the very bright flashes of light in the sky that happen during a storm. ❑ *One man died when he was struck by lightning.* ❑ *Another flash of lightning lit up the house.*

lik|able /laɪkəbᵊl/ also **likeable** **ADJECTIVE** Someone or something that is **likable** is pleasant and easy to be with. ❑ *He was a clever and likable guy.*

---

like

❶ PREPOSITION USES
❷ VERB USES

---

❶ **like** /laɪk, laɪk/
1 **PREPOSITION** If one person or thing is **like** another, they are similar to that person or thing. ❑ *He looks like my uncle.* ❑ *His house is just like yours.*
2 **PREPOSITION** If you say what something or someone is **like**, you are talking about how they seem to you. ❑ *What does Maria look like?* ❑ *"What was the party like?"—"Great!"*
3 **PREPOSITION** You can use **like** to give an example. ❑ *...large cities like New York and Chicago.*

❷ **like** /laɪk/ (**likes, liking, liked**)
1 **VERB** If you **like** something or someone, you think they are interesting, enjoyable, or attractive. ❑ *He likes baseball.* ❑ *Do you like swimming?*
2 **VERB** If you say that you **would like** something, you are saying politely that you want it. ❑ *Would you like some coffee?* ❑ *I'd like to ask you a few questions.*
3 You say **if you like** when you are suggesting something to someone, in an informal way. ❑ *You can stay here if you like.*

like|able /laɪkəbᵊl/ → look up **likable**

like|li|hood /laɪklihʊd/ **NONCOUNT NOUN** The **likelihood of** something happening is how probable it is. ❑ *The likelihood of getting the disease is small.*

like|ly /laɪkli/ (**likelier, likeliest**)
1 **ADJECTIVE** You use **likely** to say that something is probably true in a particular situation. ❑ *A gas leak was the most likely cause of the explosion.*
2 **ADJECTIVE** If someone or something is **likely to** do a particular thing, they will probably do it. ❑ *Eric is a bright young man who is likely to succeed in life.*

like|ness /laɪknɪs/ (**likenesses**) **NOUN** If a picture of someone is a good **likeness**, it looks just like them. ❑ *The artist's drawing is an excellent likeness of my sister.*

like|wise /laɪkwaɪz/ **ADVERB** If you do something and someone else does **likewise**, you both do the same thing. ❑ *He gave money to charity and encouraged others to do likewise.*

lik|ing /laɪkɪŋ/ If something is **to** your **liking**, it suits you. ❑ *London was more to his liking than Rome.*

li|lac /laɪlək/ (**lilacs**)
1 **NONCOUNT NOUN** **Lilac** is a purple, pink, or white flower that grows on a small tree. ❑ *Lilac grew against the garden wall.*
2 **ADJECTIVE** Something that is **lilac** is pale purple in color. ❑ *The bride wore a lilac dress.*
3 **NOUN** **Lilac** is also a noun. ❑ *Would you prefer lilac or yellow for your bedroom?*

lily /lɪli/ (**lilies**) **NOUN** A **lily** is a plant with large sweet-smelling flowers.

limb /lɪm/ (**limbs**) **NOUN** Your **limbs** are your arms and legs. ❑ *She stretched out her aching limbs.*
→ look at **tree**

lime /laɪm/ (**limes**) **NOUN** A **lime** is a round, green fruit that tastes like a lemon. ❑ *Use fresh lime juice and fresh herbs in modern Asian cooking.*

lim|it /lɪmɪt/ (**limits, limiting, limited**)
1 **NOUN** A **limit** is the greatest amount or degree of something. ❑ *There is no limit to how much fresh fruit you should eat in a day.*
2 **NOUN** A **limit** is the largest or smallest amount of something that is allowed. ❑ *He was driving 40 miles per hour over the speed limit.*
3 **VERB** If you **limit** something, you stop it from becoming greater than a particular amount. ❑ *Try to limit the amount of time you spend on the Internet.*

L

lim|ou|sine /lɪməzin/ (limousines) NOUN A limousine is a large and very comfortable car. **Limo** is an informal word for **limousine**. ❑ *As the president's limousine approached, the crowd began to cheer.*

limp /lɪmp/ (limps, limping, limped, limper, limpest)

1 VERB If a person or animal **limps**, they walk with difficulty because they have hurt one of their legs or feet. ❑ *James limps because of a hip injury.*

2 NOUN Limp is also a noun. ❑ *Anne walks with a limp.*

3 ADJECTIVE If something is **limp**, it is soft or weak. ❑ *Her body was limp and she was too weak to move.*

Spelling Partners   line

---

line /laɪn/ (lines, lining, lined)

1 NOUN A line is a long, thin mark on something. ❑ *Draw a line at the bottom of the page.*

2 NOUN A **line** of people or vehicles is a number of them that are waiting one behind the other. ❑ *There was a line of people waiting to go into the movie theater.*

3 NOUN A **line** is a long piece of string or rope that you use for a particular purpose. ❑ *Melissa was outside, hanging the clothes on the line.*

4 NOUN A **line** is a route that trains move along. ❑ *We stayed on the train to the end of the line.*

5 NOUN A **line** is a very long wire for telephones or electricity. ❑ *Suddenly the telephone line went dead.*

6 VERB If people or things **line** a road, they stand in lines along it. ❑ *Thousands of local people lined the streets to welcome the president.*

7 VERB If you **line** a container, you cover the inside of it with something. ❑ *Line the box with newspaper.*

8 When people **stand in line** or **wait in line**, they stand one behind the other in a line, waiting for something. ❑ *For the homeless, standing in line for meals is part of the daily routine.*
→ look at **geometry**

lin|en /lɪnɪn/ NONCOUNT NOUN Linen is a type of strong cloth. ❑ *She wore a white linen suit.*

lin|er /laɪnər/ (liners) NOUN A liner is a large ship in which people travel long distances, especially on vacation. ❑ *...a luxury ocean liner.*

lin|gerie /lɑnʒərei, læn-/ NONCOUNT NOUN Lingerie is women's underwear. ❑ *The store sells expensive designer lingerie.*

lin|ing /laɪnɪŋ/ (linings) NOUN A lining is a piece of cloth that is attached to the inside of a piece of clothing or a curtain. ❑ *She wore a black jacket with a red lining.*

link /lɪŋk/ (links, linking, linked)

1 NOUN If there is a **link between** two things, there is a connection between them, often because one of them causes the other. ❑ *Scientists believe there is a link between poor diet and cancer.*

2 VERB Link is also a verb. ❑ *Studies have linked television violence with aggressive behavior.*

3 NOUN In computing, a **link** is an area on the screen that allows you to move from one web page or website to another. ❑ *The website has links to other tourism sites.*

4 NOUN A **link** is one of the rings in a chain. ❑ *She was wearing a chain of heavy gold links.*

lion /laɪən/ (lions) NOUN A lion is a large wild cat that lives in Africa. Lions have yellow fur, and male lions have long hair on their head and neck (= a mane).
→ look at **animal**

lip /lɪp/ (lips) NOUN Your lips are the two outer parts of the edge of your mouth. ❑ *He kissed her gently on the lips.*
→ look at **face**

lip|stick /lɪpstɪk/ (lipsticks) NOUN Lipstick is a colored substance that women sometimes put on their lips. ❑ *She was wearing red lipstick.*

liq|uid /lɪkwɪd/ (liquids) NOUN SCIENCE A **liquid** is a substance that is not a solid or a gas. **Liquids** flow and can be poured. Water and oil are **liquids**. ❑ *She took out a small bottle of clear liquid.* ❑ *Drink plenty of liquids while flying and after you land.*
→ look at **water**

liq|uor /lɪkər/ NONCOUNT NOUN Liquor is strong alcoholic drink. ❑ *She never drinks liquor.*

list /lɪst/ (lists, listing, listed)

1 NOUN A list is a set of names or other things that are written or printed one below the other. ❑ *I added coffee to my shopping list.* ❑ *There were six names on the list.*

2 **VERB** If you **list** names or other things, you write or say them one after another. ❑ *The students listed the sports they liked best.*

lis|ten /lɪsᵊn/ (**listens, listening, listened**)
1 **VERB** If you **listen to** something or someone, you give your attention to a sound, or to what someone is saying. ❑ *He spends his time listening to the radio.*
2 You say **listen** when you want someone to pay attention to you because you are going to say something. ❑ *Listen, there's something I should warn you about.*
→ look at **communication, language, music, news**

lis|ten|er /lɪsənər, lɪsnər/ (**listeners**) **NOUN**
A **listener** is someone who is listening to a speaker. ❑ *When he finished talking, his listeners applauded loudly.*

lit /lɪt/ **Lit** is a form of the verb **light.**

li|ter /litər/ (**liters**) **NOUN** MATH SCIENCE
A **liter** is a unit for measuring liquid. There are 1,000 milliliters in a liter. ❑ *Adults should drink about two liters of water each day.*
→ look at **measurement**

lit|era|cy /lɪtərəsi/ **NONCOUNT NOUN**
Literacy is the ability to read and write. ❑ *The library's adult literacy program helps about 2,000 people a year.*

lit|er|al|ly /lɪtərəli/
1 **ADVERB** If you translate something from another language **literally**, you say what each word means in another language. ❑ *Volkswagen literally means "people's car."*
2 **ADVERB** Some people use **literally** to emphasize what they are saying. ❑ *The view is literally breathtaking.*

lit|era|ture /lɪtərətʃər, -tʃʊər/ **NONCOUNT NOUN** LANGUAGE ARTS **Literature** is books, plays, and poetry that most people consider to be of high quality. ❑ *Chris is studying English literature at Columbia University.*

lit|ter /lɪtər/ (**litters, littering, littered**)
1 **NONCOUNT NOUN** **Litter** is paper or garbage that people leave lying on the ground in public places. ❑ *I hate it when I see people dropping litter.*
2 **VERB** If things **litter** a place, they are lying around it or over it in a messy way. ❑ *Broken glass littered the sidewalk.*
●**lit|tered** **ADJECTIVE** ❑ *The room was littered with toys.*

3 **NOUN** A **litter** is all the babies that are born to an animal at the same time. ❑ *Our cat has just given birth to a litter of three kittens.*

little
❶ ADJECTIVE, PRONOUN, AND ADVERB USES
❷ ADJECTIVE USES

❶ **lit|tle** /lɪtᵊl/
1 **ADJECTIVE** You use **little** to show that there is only a very small amount of something. ❑ *I have little money and little free time.* ❑ *I get very little sleep these days.*
2 **PRONOUN** **Little** is also a pronoun. ❑ *He ate little, and drank less.*
3 **ADVERB** **Little** means not very often or not very much. ❑ *They spoke very little.*
4 **A little** is a small amount of something. ❑ *I need a little help sometimes.* ❑ *They get paid for it. Not much. Just a little.*
5 **ADVERB** **A little** or **a little bit** means rather, or to a small degree. ❑ *He was a little bit afraid of the dog.*

❷ **lit|tle** /lɪtᵊl/ (**littler, littlest**)
1 **ADJECTIVE** **Little** things are small. ❑ *We all sat at a little table.*
2 **ADJECTIVE** A **little** distance or period of time is short. ❑ *Go down the road a little way and then turn left.* ❑ *We waited for a little while, and then we went home.*

live
❶ VERB USES
❷ ADJECTIVE AND ADVERB USES

❶ **live** /lɪv/ (**lives, living, lived**)
1 **VERB** If you **live** in a particular place, your home is there. ❑ *She lived in New York for 10 years.* ❑ *Where do you live?*
2 **VERB** If someone **lives** in a particular way, they have that type of life. ❑ *Nash lives a quiet life in Princeton.*
3 **VERB** To **live** means to be alive. ❑ *We all need water to live.*
4 **VERB** If someone **lives to** a particular age, they stay alive until they are that age. ❑ *He lived to 103.*
▶ **live on** If an animal **lives on** a particular food, it eats this type of food. ❑ *Sheep live mainly on grass.*

❷ **live** /laɪv/
1 **ADJECTIVE** SCIENCE **Live** animals or plants are not dead. ❑ *The local market sells live animals.*
2 **ADJECTIVE** A **live** television or radio

L

program is one that you watch at the same time that it happens. ❑ *They watch all the live football games on TV.*

3 **ADVERB** Live is also an adverb. ❑ *The president's speech was broadcast live.*
→ look at **television**

live|ly /laɪvli/ (livelier, liveliest) **ADJECTIVE** If you are **lively**, you are cheerful and you have a lot of energy. ❑ *Amy is a lively, sociable little girl.*

liv|er /lɪvər/ (livers)
1 **NOUN** SCIENCE Your **liver** is the large organ in your body that cleans your blood. ❑ *...liver disease.*
2 **NOUN** Liver is the liver of some animals that you can cook and eat. ❑ *They ate lamb's liver for dinner.*

lives

> **PRONUNCIATION HELP**
> Pronounce meaning **1** /laɪvz/. Pronounce meaning **2** /lɪvz/.

1 Lives is the plural of **life**.
2 Lives is a form of the verb **live**.

liv|ing /lɪvɪŋ/
1 **ADJECTIVE** A **living** person or animal is alive, and not dead. ❑ *He is perhaps the world's most famous living artist.* ❑ *He has no living relatives.*
2 **NOUN** The work that you do for a **living** is the work that you do to earn money. ❑ *What does she do for a living?* ❑ *Scott earns a living as a lawyer.*
3 **NONCOUNT NOUN** You use **living** when you are talking about the way that people live. ❑ *Mom believes in healthy living.*

liv|ing room (living rooms) also **living-room** **NOUN** The **living room** in a house is the room where people sit together and talk or watch television. ❑ *We were sitting in the living room watching TV.*
→ look at **house**

liz|ard /lɪzərd/ (lizards) **NOUN** A **lizard** is a small animal with a long tail and rough skin.

load /loʊd/ (loads, loading, loaded)
1 **VERB** If you **load** a vehicle or a container, you put a large amount of things into it. ❑ *The men finished loading the truck.*

2 **NOUN** A **load** is something heavy that is being carried. ❑ *This car can take a big load.*

loaf /loʊf/ (loaves) **NOUN** A **loaf** of bread is bread that has been shaped and baked in one piece. ❑ *He bought a loaf of bread and some ham and cheese.*
→ look at **bread**

Loaf|er /loʊfər/ (Loafers) **NOUN** Loafers are low leather shoes that you can put on quickly and easily. [TRADEMARK]

loan /loʊn/ (loans, loaning, loaned)
1 **NOUN** A **loan** is an amount of money that you borrow. ❑ *Right now it's very difficult to get a loan from a bank.*
2 **VERB** If you **loan** something to someone, you lend it to them. ❑ *Brandon loaned his girlfriend $6,000.*
→ look at **car**

loathe /loʊð/ (loathes, loathing, loathed) **VERB** If you **loathe** something or someone, you dislike them very much. [FORMAL] ❑ *The two men loathe each other.*

loaves /loʊvz/ Loaves is the plural of **loaf**.

lob|by /lɒbi/ (lobbies) **NOUN** The **lobby** is the area inside the entrance to a big building. ❑ *I met her in the hotel lobby.*

lob|ster /lɒbstər/ (lobsters) **NOUN** A **lobster** is an ocean animal that has a hard shell and eight legs. ❑ *She sold me two live lobsters.*
→ look at **shellfish**

lo|cal /loʊkəl/ **ADJECTIVE** Something that is **local** is in, or relates to, the area where you live. ❑ *Susan put an advertisement in the local paper.* ● **lo|cal|ly** **ADVERB** ❑ *I prefer to shop locally.*
→ look at **news, phone**

lo|cated /loʊkeɪtɪd/ **ADJECTIVE** If something is **located** somewhere, it is in that place. ❑ *The gym and beauty salon are located on the second floor.*

lo|ca|tion /loʊkeɪʃən/ (locations) **NOUN** A **location** is the place where something is. ❑ *For dates and locations of the meetings, call this number.*
→ look at Picture Dictionary: **location**

lock /lɒk/ (locks, locking, locked)
1 **VERB** When you **lock** a door or a container, you close it with a key. ❑ *Are you sure you locked the front door?*
2 **NOUN** The **lock** on a door or a container is the part that you use to keep it shut and to

l

Picture Dictionary **location**

The squirrel is in the tree.

The squirrel is above/over the bench.

The squirrel is on the bench.

The squirrel is between the bench and the tree.

The squirrel is behind the bench.

The squirrel is under/underneath the bench.

The squirrel is in front of the bench.

L

make sure that no-one can open it. You can open a lock with a key. ❑ *She turned the key in the lock and opened the door.*

3 **VERB** If you **lock** something or someone in a place, you put them there and close the door or the lid with a key. ❑ *She locked the case in the closet.*

▶ **lock away** If you **lock** something **away** in a place, you put it there and close it with a key. ❑ *She cleaned her jewelry and locked it away in a case.*

▶ **lock up** If you **lock up**, you lock all the windows and doors of a house or a car. ❑ *Don't forget to lock up before you leave.*

lock|er /lɒkər/ (**lockers**) **NOUN** A **locker** is a small cupboard with a lock, that you keep things in at a school or at a sports club.

lo|co|mo|tive /loʊkəmoʊtɪv/ (**locomotives**) **NOUN** A **locomotive** is a large vehicle that pulls a train. [FORMAL]

lodge /lɒdʒ/ (**lodges, lodging, lodged**)
1 **NOUN** A **lodge** is a small house in the countryside or in the mountains where people stay on vacation. ❑ *We stayed in a lodge about 17 miles north of Paonia, Colorado.*
2 **VERB** If you **lodge** a complaint or a claim, you officially make it. ❑ *The children's parents lodged a formal complaint against the school.*

loft /lɒft/ (**lofts**)
1 **NOUN** A **loft** is the space directly under the roof of a building. ❑ *The loft was filled with boxes of old photos.*
2 **NOUN** A **loft** is an apartment in the upper part of an old factory or a similar building. ❑ *Jack lives in a luxury loft in New York.*

log /lɒg/ (**logs, logging, logged**)
1 **NOUN** A **log** is a thick piece of wood that has been cut from a tree.
❑ *...a log fire.*

2 **NOUN** A **log** is a written record of the things that happen each day.
❑ *They examined the three men's telephone logs.*
3 **VERB** If you **log** something that happens, you write it down as a record of the event. ❑ *They log everything that comes in and out of the warehouse.*

▶ **log in** or **log on** TECHNOLOGY If you **log in** or **log on**, you type a special secret word so that you can start using a computer or a website. ❑ *She turned on her computer and logged in.*
→ look at **email**

▶ **log out** or **log off** TECHNOLOGY If you **log out** or **log off**, you stop using a computer or a website by clicking on an instruction. ❑ *I logged off and went out for a walk.*
→ look at **email**

log|ic /lɒdʒɪk/ **NONCOUNT NOUN** Logic is a way of working things out, by saying that one fact must be true if another fact is true. ❑ *The students study philosophy and logic.*

logi|cal /lɒdʒɪkᵊl/ **ADJECTIVE** If something is **logical**, it seems reasonable or sensible. ❑ *There must be a logical explanation for his behavior.*

logo /loʊgoʊ/ (**logos**) **NOUN** The **logo** of an organization is the special design that it puts on all its products or advertisements. ❑ *The company's logo is a penguin.*

LOL   LOL is short for "laughing out loud" or "lots of love," and is often used in email and text messages.

lol|li|pop /lɒlipɒp/ (lollipops) **NOUN**
A **lollipop** is a hard candy on the end of a stick. ❏ *What's your favorite flavor of lollipop?*

lone|ly /loʊnli/ (lonelier, loneliest)
1 **ADJECTIVE** If you are **lonely**, you are unhappy because you are alone. ❏ *Mr. Garcia has been lonely since his wife died.* ● **lone|li|ness NONCOUNT NOUN** ❏ *I have a fear of loneliness.*
2 **ADJECTIVE** A **lonely** place is a place where very few people go. ❏ *Her car broke down on a lonely country road.*

lone|some /loʊnsəm/ **ADJECTIVE** If you are **lonesome**, you are unhappy because you are alone. ❏ *Her favorite song is "Are You Lonesome Tonight?" by Elvis Presley.*

long
1 TIME AND DISTANCE USES
2 VERB USE

1 long /lɔŋ/ (longer /lɔŋɡər/, longest /lɔŋɡɪst/)
1 **ADVERB** **Long** means a lot of time. ❏ *Cleaning up didn't take too long.* ❏ *Have you been waiting long?*
2 **ADJECTIVE** A **long** event lasts for a lot of time. ❏ *We had a long meeting.* ❏ *She is planning a long vacation in Europe.* ❏ *"How long is the movie?"—"About two hours."*
3 **ADJECTIVE** Something that is **long** measures a great distance from one end to the other. ❏ *There was a long table in the middle of the kitchen.* ❏ *Lucy had long dark hair.*
4 **ADJECTIVE** A **long** distance is a great distance. ❏ *The long trip made him tired.*
5 **As long as** or **so long as** means "if." ❏ *They can do what they want as long as they are not breaking the law.*
→ look at **day, hair, writing**

2 long /lɔŋ/ (longs, longing, longed) **VERB**
If you **long for** something, you want it very much. ❏ *I'm longing to meet her.* ● **long|ing NONCOUNT NOUN** ❏ *She still feels a longing for her own home and country.*

long-distance **ADJECTIVE** You use **long-distance** to talk about travel or communication between places that are a long way from each other. ❏ *Long-distance travel can be very tiring.* ❏ *Stacey makes a lot of long-distance calls on her cellphone.*
→ look at **phone**

lon|gi|tude /lɒndʒɪtud/ (longitudes) **NOUN**
GEOGRAPHY The **longitude** of a place is how far it is to the west or east of an imaginary line that goes from the North Pole to the South Pole. Compare with **latitude**.
→ look at **globe**

long jump **NONCOUNT NOUN** **SPORTS** The **long jump** is a sports event that involves jumping as far as you can.

look /lʊk/ (looks, looking, looked)
1 **VERB** If you **look** in a particular direction, you turn your eyes so that you can see what is there. ❏ *I looked out of the window.* ❏ *If you look, you'll see a lake.*
2 **NOUN** **Look** is also a noun. ❏ *Lucille took a last look in the mirror.*
3 **VERB** If you **look for** something or someone, you try to find them. ❏ *I'm looking for a child.* ❏ *I looked everywhere for my purse.*
4 You say **look** when you want someone to pay attention to you. ❏ *Look, I'm sorry. I didn't mean it.*
5 **EXCLAMATION** If you say or shout "**look out!**" to someone, you are warning them that they are in danger. ❏ *"Look out!" somebody shouted, as the truck started to move toward us.*
6 **VERB** You use **look** when you are describing the way that a person seems to be. ❏ *"You look lovely, Marcia!"* ❏ *Sheila was looking sad.*
7 **NOUN** If someone or something has a particular **look**, they have a particular appearance or expression. ❏ *He saw the look of surprise on her face.* ❏ *Be very careful. I don't like the look of those guys.*
→ look at **calendar**
▶ **look after** If you **look after** someone or something, you take care of them. ❏ *Maria looks after the kids while I'm at work.*
▶ **look forward to** If you **look forward to** something that is going to happen, you want it to happen because you think you will enjoy it. ❏ *She's looking forward to her vacation in Hawaii.*
▶ **look out for** If you **look out for** someone or something, you pay attention so that you see it if it happens. ❏ *Officers are looking out for the stolen vehicle.*
▶ **look up** If you **look up** a fact or a piece of information, you find it by looking in a book or on a computer. ❏ *I looked up your number in my address book.*
→ look at **dictionary**

loom /lum/ (looms, looming, loomed)

1 VERB If an unpleasant event **is looming**, it will probably happen soon. ❑ *Another economic crisis is looming.*

2 NOUN A **loom** is a machine that is used for making cloth.

loop /lup/ (loops) **NOUN** A **loop** is a shape like a circle in a piece of string or rope. ❑ *On the ground beside them was a loop of rope.*

loose /lus/ (looser, loosest)

1 ADJECTIVE Something that is **loose** is not firmly fixed to something else. ❑ *One of Hannah's top front teeth is loose.* ● **loose|ly ADVERB** ❑ *He held the gun loosely in his hand.*

2 ADJECTIVE If people or animals break **loose**, they escape from the place where they are held. ❑ *Our dog got loose and ran away yesterday.*

3 ADJECTIVE Loose clothes do not fit closely. ❑ *Wear loose, comfortable clothing when exercising.* ● **loose|ly ADVERB** ❑ *A scarf hung loosely around his neck.*

→ look at **wear**

loose-leaf ADJECTIVE A **loose-leaf** hard cover contains pages that you can remove or add easily. ❑ *...a loose-leaf binder.*

loos|en /lusᵊn/ (loosens, loosening, loosened) **VERB** If you **loosen** something, you make it less tight. ❑ *He loosened his tie around his neck.*

lord /lord/ (lords)

1 NOUN A **lord** is a man with a high position in society. ❑ *Kathleen Kennedy married Lord Cavendish in 1944.*

2 NOUN In some religions, people call God and Jesus Christ, the **Lord**. ❑ *She prayed now. "Lord, help me to find courage."*

lose /luz/ (loses, losing, lost)

1 VERB If you **lose** a game, you do not win it. ❑ *Our team lost the game by one point.* ❑ *No one likes to lose.*

2 VERB If you **lose** something, you do not know where it is. ❑ *I've lost my keys.*

3 VERB If you **lose** something, you do not have it anymore because someone has taken it away from you. ❑ *I lost my job when the company shut down.*

4 VERB If you **lose** weight, you become less heavy. ❑ *His doctor told him to lose weight.*

5 VERB If a business **loses** money, it earns less money than it spends. ❑ *The company has been losing money for the last three years.*

→ look at **play, vote**

los|er /luzər/ (losers)

1 NOUN The **losers** of a game are the people who do not win. ❑ *In any game, there's always a winner and a loser.*

2 If you are a **good loser**, you accept that you have lost a game without complaining. If you are a **bad loser**, you do not like losing, and you complain about it. ❑ *I try to be a good loser.*

loss /los/ (losses)

1 NONCOUNT NOUN Loss is when you do not have something that you used to have, or when you have less of it than before. ❑ *The first symptoms are a slight fever and a loss of appetite.*

2 NONCOUNT NOUN The **loss** of a relative or a friend is their death. ❑ *He is mourning the loss of his wife and child.*

3 NOUN If a business makes a **loss**, it earns less money than it spends. ❑ *The company made a loss again last year.*

lost /lost/

1 Lost is a form of the verb **lose**.

2 ADJECTIVE If you are **lost**, you do not know where you are, and you are unable to find your way. ❑ *I realized I was lost.*

3 ADJECTIVE If something is **lost**, you cannot find it. ❑ *We complained to the airline about our lost luggage.*

lost and found

1 NOUN Lost and found is the area in a public place where they keep things that people have lost.

2 ADJECTIVE Lost-and-found things are things that someone has lost and that someone else has found.

lot /lot/ (lots)

1 A lot of something or **lots of** it is a large amount of it. ❑ *A lot of our land is used to grow crops.* ❑ *He drank lots of milk.*

2 PRONOUN Lot is also a pronoun. ❑ *I learned a lot from him.*

3 ADVERB A lot means very much or often. ❑ *Matthew goes out quite a lot.* ❑ *I like you a lot.*

lo|tion /louʃᵊn/ (lotions) **NOUN** A **lotion** is a liquid that you use to clean or protect your skin. ❑ *Remember to put on some suntan lotion.*

lot|tery /lotəri/ (lotteries) **NOUN** A **lottery** is a type of game where people buy tickets with numbers on them. If the numbers on your ticket are chosen, you win a prize. ❑ *She has won the national lottery twice.*

loud /laʊd/ (louder, loudest)

1 **ADJECTIVE** If a noise is **loud**, the level of sound is very high. ❑ *The music was so loud that I couldn't hear what she was saying.* ● **loud|ly** **ADVERB** ❑ *The cat rolled onto its back, purring loudly.*

2 If you say something **out loud**, you say it so that other people can hear it. ❑ *Parts of the book made me laugh out loud.*

→ look at **music, sense**

lounge /laʊndʒ/ (lounges) NOUN

A **lounge** is a room in a hotel or an airport where people can sit. ❑ *...an airport lounge.*

louse /laʊs/ (lice) NOUN

A **louse** is a small insect that lives on people's and animal's bodies.

lousy /laʊzi/ (lousier, lousiest) ADJECTIVE

If something or someone is **lousy**, they are very bad. [INFORMAL] ❑ *The weather was lousy all weekend.* ❑ *I was a lousy secretary.*

lov|able /lʌvəbªl/ ADJECTIVE

If someone is **lovable**, they are easy to love. ❑ *He is a sweet, lovable dog.*

love /lʌv/ (loves, loving, loved)

1 **VERB** If you **love** someone, you care very much about them, or you have strong romantic feelings for them. ❑ *Oh, Amy, I love you.* ❑ *You will love your baby from the moment she is born.*

2 **NONCOUNT NOUN** **Love** is the very strong warm feeling that you have when you care very much about someone, or you have strong romantic feelings for them. ❑ *In the four years since we married, our love has grown stronger.* ❑ *...a love story.*

3 **VERB** If you **love** something, you like it very much. ❑ *I love food, I love cooking and I love eating.* ❑ *Sophie loves to play the piano.*

4 You can write **love**, **love from**, and **all my love**, before your name, at the end of a letter to a friend or a relative. ❑ *The letter ended, "With lots of love from Anna."*

5 If you **fall in love with** someone, you start to love them in a romantic way. ❑ *Maria fell in love with Danny as soon as she met him.*

love|ly /lʌvli/ (lovelier, loveliest) ADJECTIVE

If someone or something is **lovely**, they are beautiful, very nice, or very enjoyable. ❑ *You look lovely, Marcia.* ❑ *Sam has a lovely voice.* ❑ *"Thank you for a lovely evening!"*

lov|er /lʌvər/ (lovers)

1 **NOUN** People who are **lovers** are having a sexual relationship but they are not married. ❑ *Every Thursday she met her lover Leon.*

2 **NOUN** If you are a **lover** of something, you like it very much. ❑ *The website is for music lovers.*

lov|ing /lʌvɪŋ/ ADJECTIVE

If you are **loving**, you feel or show love for other people. ❑ *My parents had a loving relationship.* ● **lov|ing|ly** **ADVERB** ❑ *Brian looked lovingly at Mary.*

low /loʊ/ (lower, lowest)

1 **ADJECTIVE** If something is **low**, it is close to the ground. ❑ *It was late afternoon and the sun was low in the sky.* ● **low** **ADVERB** ❑ *An airplane flew low over the beach.*

2 **ADJECTIVE** If something is **low**, it is small in amount. ❑ *House prices are still very low.*

3 **ADJECTIVE** If the quality of something is **low**, it is very bad. ❑ *The hospital was criticized for its low standards of care.*

4 **ADJECTIVE** A **low** sound or noise is deep and quiet. ❑ *His voice was so low she couldn't hear him.*

low|er /loʊər/ (lowers, lowering, lowered)

1 **ADJECTIVE** The **lower** of two things is the bottom one. ❑ *Emily bit her lower lip nervously.*

2 **VERB** If you **lower** something, you move it down. ❑ *They lowered the coffin into the grave.*

3 **VERB** If you **lower** something, you make it less. ❑ *The Central Bank lowered interest rates yesterday.*

low|er case NONCOUNT NOUN LANGUAGE ARTS

If you write or type something **in lower case**, you write or type it using small letters, not capital letters. Compare with **upper case**. ❑ *Type your user name and password in lower case.*

loy|al /lɔɪəl/ ADJECTIVE

If you are **loyal**, you keep your friends or your beliefs, even in difficult times. ❑ *They have always stayed loyal to the Republican party.* ● **loy|al|ly** **ADVERB** ❑ *The staff loyally supported their boss.*

loy|al|ty /lɔɪəlti/ NONCOUNT NOUN

Loyalty is when you continue to be someone's friend, or to believe in something, even in difficult times. ❑ *I believe in family loyalty.*

luck /lʌk/

1 **NONCOUNT NOUN** **Luck** or **good luck** is the good things that happen to you, that have not been caused by yourself or other people. ❑ *Before the game, we shook hands and wished each other luck.*

2 **NONCOUNT NOUN** **Bad luck** is the bad things that happen to you, that have not been caused by yourself or other people. ❑ *We had a lot of bad luck during the first half of this season.*

3 If you say "**Good luck**" to someone, you are telling them that you hope they will be successful in something they are trying to do. [INFORMAL]

lucki|ly /lʌkɪli/ **ADVERB** You use **luckily** when you want to say that it is good that something happened. ❑ *Luckily, nobody was seriously injured in the accident.*

lucky /lʌki/ (**luckier, luckiest**)
1 **ADJECTIVE** You say that someone is **lucky** when they have good luck. ❑ *I am luckier than most people here. I have a job.* ❑ *Rob is very lucky to be alive after that accident.*
2 **ADJECTIVE** A **lucky** object is something that people believe brings them good luck. ❑ *I'm wearing my lucky shirt. How can I lose?*

lug|gage /lʌgɪdʒ/ **NONCOUNT NOUN** Luggage is the bags that you take with you when you travel. ❑ *"Do you have any luggage?"—"Just my briefcase."*

lug|gage rack (**luggage racks**) **NOUN** A **luggage rack** is a shelf for putting luggage on in a train or a bus.

luke|warm /lukwɔrm/ **ADJECTIVE** If a liquid is **lukewarm**, it is only slightly warm. ❑ *Freddy drank the lukewarm coffee.*

lulla|by /lʌləbaɪ/ (**lullabies**) **NOUN** A **lullaby** is a quiet song that is sung to babies to help them to go to sleep.

lump /lʌmp/ (**lumps**)
1 **NOUN** A **lump** is a solid piece of something. ❑ *...a lump of coal.*
2 **NOUN** A **lump** on or in your body is a small, hard part. ❑ *I've got a painful lump in my mouth.*

lunch /lʌntʃ/ (**lunches**) **NOUN** Lunch is the meal that you have in the middle of the day.

❑ *Are you free for lunch?* ❑ *Dad doesn't enjoy business lunches.*
→ look at **eat**

lunch|room /lʌntʃrum/ (**lunchrooms**) **NOUN** A **lunchroom** is the room in a school or at work where you buy or eat your lunch. ❑ *They sat together in the lunchroom, that was full of students.*

lunch|time /lʌntʃtaɪm/ **NONCOUNT NOUN** Lunchtime is the time of the day when people have their lunch. ❑ *Could we meet at lunchtime?*

lung /lʌŋ/ (**lungs**) **NOUN** SCIENCE Your **lungs** are the two large organs inside your chest that you use for breathing. ❑ *Her father died of lung cancer last year.*

lush /lʌʃ/ (**lusher, lushest**) **ADJECTIVE** Lush fields or gardens have a lot of very healthy grass or plants. ❑ *The lawn was lush and green.*

luxu|ri|ous /lʌgʒʊəriəs/ **ADJECTIVE** If something is **luxurious**, it is very comfortable and expensive. ❑ *My aunt and uncle stayed in a luxurious hotel in Paris.*

luxu|ry /lʌkʃəri, lʌgʒə-/ (**luxuries**)
1 **NONCOUNT NOUN** Luxury is a way of living when you are able to buy all the beautiful and expensive things that you want. ❑ *He leads a life of luxury.*
2 **NOUN** A **luxury** is something pleasant and expensive that people want but do not really need. ❑ *Having a vacation is a luxury they can no longer afford.*

ly|ing /laɪɪŋ/ **Lying** is a form of the verb **lie**.

lyr|ics /lɪrɪks/ **PLURAL NOUN** MUSIC The **lyrics** of a song are its words. ❑ *The music is great, and the lyrics are so funny.*

L

Mm

ma /mɑː/ (**mas**) NOUN Some people call their mother **ma**. [INFORMAL] ❑ *Ma was still at work when I got back.*

ma'am /mæm/ NOUN People sometimes say **ma'am** as a polite way of talking to a woman. ❑ *Would you repeat that please, ma'am?*

maca|ro|ni /mækərouni/ NONCOUNT NOUN **Macaroni** is a type of pasta made in the shape of short, hollow tubes.

ma|chine /məʃiːn/ (**machines**) NOUN A **machine** is a piece of equipment that uses electricity or an engine to do a particular job. ❑ *I put the coin in the coffee machine.*

ma|chine gun (**machine guns**) NOUN A **machine gun** is a gun that shoots a lot of bullets very quickly. ❑ *Attackers fired machine guns at the car.*

ma|chin|ery /məʃiːnəri/ NONCOUNT NOUN **Machinery** means large pieces of electrical equipment that do a particular job. ❑ *We need to invest in new machinery for our factories.*

mad /mæd/ (**madder, maddest**)
1 ADJECTIVE If someone is **mad**, they are very angry. [INFORMAL] ❑ *You're just mad at me because I'm late.*
2 ADJECTIVE Someone who is **mad** has a medical condition that makes them behave in a strange way. [INFORMAL] ❑ *She was afraid of going mad.*
3 ADJECTIVE If you are **mad about** something or someone, you like them very much. [INFORMAL] ❑ *I'm mad about sports.* ❑ *He's mad about you.*
4 ADJECTIVE **Mad** behavior is not controlled. ❑ *There was a mad rush to get out of the building.*
● **mad|ly** ADVERB ❑ *People on the streets were waving madly.*

mad|am /mædəm/ also **Madam** NOUN **Madam** is a polite way of talking to a woman. ❑ *Good morning, madam.*

made /meɪd/
1 **Made** is a form of the verb **make**.
2 ADJECTIVE If something is **made of** a particular substance, that substance was used to make it. ❑ *The top of the table is made of glass.*

mad|ly /mædli/ ADVERB You can use **madly** to show that one person loves another person very much. ❑ *She is madly in love with him.*

maga|zine /mægəziːn, -zin/ (**magazines**) NOUN A **magazine** is a thin book with stories and pictures that you can buy every week or every month. ❑ *...a fashion magazine.*
→ look at **news**

mag|ic /mædʒɪk/
1 NONCOUNT NOUN **Magic** is a special power that seems to make impossible things happen. ❑ *Most children believe in magic.*
2 NONCOUNT NOUN **Magic** is tricks that a person performs in order to entertain people. ❑ *His stage act combines magic, music, and humor.*

magi|cal /mædʒɪkəl/ ADJECTIVE Something that is **magical** seems to use magic. ❑ *I loved the story of a little boy who has magical powers.*

ma|gi|cian /mədʒɪʃən/ (**magicians**) NOUN A **magician** is a person who entertains people by doing magic tricks.

mag|net /mægnɪt/ (**magnets**) NOUN SCIENCE A **magnet** is a piece of special metal that attracts iron toward it. ❑ *The children used a magnet to find objects made of iron.*

mag|net|ic /mægnɛtɪk/
1 ADJECTIVE SCIENCE If something is **magnetic**, it acts like a magnet. ❑ *Because steel is made from iron, it is magnetic.*
2 ADJECTIVE TECHNOLOGY **Magnetic** describes objects that use a magnetic substance to hold information that can be read by computers. ❑ *The bank sent him an ID card with a magnetic strip.*

mag|nifi|cent /mægnɪfɪsənt/ ADJECTIVE Something or someone that is **magnificent** is extremely good or beautiful. ❑ *They bought a magnificent country house.*

mag|ni|fy /mǽgnɪfaɪ/
(**magnifies, magnifying, magnified**) **VERB** If you **magnify** something, you make it look larger than it really is. ❑ *This telescope magnifies objects 11 times.*

maid /meɪd/ (**maids**)
NOUN A **maid** is a woman whose job is to clean rooms in a hotel or a private house. ❑ *A maid comes every morning to clean the hotel room.*

mail /meɪl/ (**mails, mailing, mailed**)
1 NONCOUNT NOUN The **mail** is the system that you use for sending and receiving letters and packages. ❑ *Your check is in the mail.*
2 NONCOUNT NOUN Mail is the letters and packages or email that you receive. ❑ *There was no mail this morning.*
3 VERB If you **mail** something to someone, you send it to them by mail. ❑ *He mailed the information to a French newspaper.* ❑ *He mailed me the contract.*
4 NONCOUNT NOUN Mail is email. ❑ *With web-based email, you can check your mail from anywhere.*

mail|box /meɪlbɒks/ (**mailboxes**)
1 NOUN A **mailbox** is a box outside your home where your letters are delivered. ❑ *The next day there was a letter in her mailbox.*
2 NOUN A **mailbox** is a box in a public place where you put letters that you want to send. ❑ *He dropped the letters into the mailbox.*
3 NOUN TECHNOLOGY On a computer, your **mailbox** is the file where your email is stored. ❑ *There were 30 new messages in his mailbox.*
→ look at **email**

mail carrier /meɪl kæriər/ (**mail carriers**)
NOUN A **mail carrier** is a person whose job is to collect and deliver letters and packages that you send by mail.

mail|man /meɪlmæn/ (**mailmen**) **NOUN**
A **mailman** is a **mail carrier**.

mail or|der **NONCOUNT NOUN** Mail order is a system of buying goods, in which you order things from a website or a special book (called a catalog), and the company sends them to you by mail. ❑ *The toys are available by mail order.*

main /meɪn/ **ADJECTIVE** The **main** thing is the most important one of several similar things. ❑ *The main reason I came today was to say sorry.*

main clause (**main clauses**) **NOUN**
LANGUAGE ARTS A **main clause** is a part of a sentence that can stand alone as a complete sentence.

main|land /meɪnlænd/ **NONCOUNT NOUN**
You can use **the mainland** to talk about the largest piece of land in a country, not including any smaller islands. ❑ *The island's teenagers go to school on the mainland.*

main|ly /meɪnli/ **ADVERB** You use **mainly** to say that a statement is mostly true. ❑ *The African people living here are mainly from Senegal.*

main|tain /meɪnteɪn/ (**maintains, maintaining, maintained**)
1 VERB If you **maintain** something, you make it continue at the same level. ❑ *The army is trying to maintain order in the country.*
2 VERB If you **maintain** a road, a building, a vehicle, or a machine, you keep it in good condition. ❑ *The house costs a lot to maintain.*

main|te|nance /meɪntɪnəns/ **NONCOUNT NOUN** The **maintenance** of something is the process of keeping it in good condition. ❑ *Maintenance work on the building starts next week.*

ma|jes|tic /mədʒɛstɪk/ **ADJECTIVE** If something or someone is **majestic**, they are very beautiful and grand. ❑ *We will miss the majestic mountains and the emerald green ocean.*

maj|es|ty /mædʒɪsti/ (**majesties**)
1 NOUN People use **Your Majesty** when they are talking to a king or a queen, or **Her Majesty** or **His Majesty** when they are talking about a king or a queen. ❑ *His Majesty would like to see you now.*
2 NONCOUNT NOUN Majesty is the quality of being beautiful and grand. ❑ *The poem describes the majesty of the mountains.*

ma|jor /meɪdʒər/ (**majors, majoring, majored**)
1 ADJECTIVE Major describes something that is more important than other things. ❑ *Homelessness is a major problem in some cities.*
2 NOUN At a university or a college, a student's **major** is the main subject that they are studying. ❑ *"What's your major?"—"Chemistry."*
3 VERB If a student at a university or a college **majors in** a particular subject, that subject is the main one they study. ❑ *He majored in finance at Claremont College.*
4 NOUN A **major** is an officer of high rank in the army. ❑ *...Major Wayne Rollings.*

M

5 MUSIC In music, **major** is used for talking about a scale (= a series of musical notes) with half steps in sound between the third and fourth and the seventh and eighth notes. Compare with **minor**. ❑ *A C major scale uses only the white keys on a piano.*

ma|jor|ity /mədʒɔrɪti/ (**majorities**) NOUN The **majority** of people or things in a group is more than half of them. ❑ *The majority of my patients are women.*

ma|jor leagues PLURAL NOUN SPORTS The **major leagues** are groups of top baseball teams that play against each other. ❑ *At 47, he was the oldest player in the major leagues last season.*

make /meɪk/ (**makes, making, made**)
1 VERB If you **make** something, you produce it, build it, or create it. ❑ *She makes all her own clothes.* ❑ *All our furniture is made from solid wood.*
2 VERB You can use **make** with nouns to show that someone does or says something. ❑ *I'd just like to make a comment.* ❑ *I made a few phone calls.*
3 VERB If something **makes** you do or feel something, it causes you to do or feel it. ❑ *The smoke made him cough.* ❑ *My boss's behavior makes me so angry!*
4 VERB If you **make** someone do something, you force them to do it. ❑ *Mom made me apologize to him.*
5 VERB If you **make** something **into** something else, you change it. ❑ *They made their apartment into a beautiful home.*
6 VERB If you **make** money, you earn it. ❑ *He's good-looking, smart, and makes lots of money.*
7 NOUN The **make** of something is the name of the company that made it. ❑ *What make of car do you drive?*
8 VERB You can use **make** to say what two numbers add up to. ❑ *Four twos make eight.*
→ look at **factory, news**
▶ **make out** If you **make** something **out**, you can see, hear or understand it. ❑ *I could just make out a tall figure of a man.* ❑ *I couldn't make out what he was saying.*
▶ **make up** **1** If you **make up** a story or excuse, you invent it. ❑ *It was all lies. I made it all up.*
2 If two people **make up** after an argument, they become friends again. ❑ *You two are always fighting and then making up again.*

mak|er /meɪkər/ (**makers**) NOUN The **maker** of something is the person or company that makes it. ❑ *Japan's two largest car makers reported increased sales last month.*

make|up /meɪkʌp/ NONCOUNT NOUN **Makeup** is the creams and powders that people put on their face to make themselves look more attractive. Actors also wear makeup. ❑ *She doesn't usually wear much makeup.*

ma|laria /məlɛəriə/ NONCOUNT NOUN **Malaria** is a serious disease that mosquitoes (= small flying insects) carry.

male /meɪl/ (**males**)
1 NOUN SCIENCE A **male** is a person or an animal that belongs to the sex that does not have babies. ❑ *Two 17-year-old males were arrested at their high school on Tuesday.*
2 ADJECTIVE **Male** is also an adjective. ❑ *She reported the unacceptable behavior of her male colleagues.* ❑ *Two male cats were fighting in the street.*
3 ADJECTIVE **Male** means relating to men rather than women. ❑ *The rate of male unemployment has gone up.*

mall /mɔl/ (**malls**) NOUN A **mall** is a large shopping area.
→ look at **shopping**

mama /mɑmə, məmɑ/ (**mamas**) also **mamma** NOUN **Mama** means the same as **mother**. [INFORMAL]

mam|mal /mæməl/ (**mammals**) NOUN SCIENCE **Mammals** are animals that feed their babies with milk.

mammy /mæmi/ (**mammies**) NOUN **Mammy** is a child's word for "mother."

man /mæn/ (**men**)
1 NOUN A **man** is an adult male human. ❑ *A handsome man walked into the room.* ❑ *Both men and women will enjoy this movie.*
2 NOUN People sometimes use **Man** and **men** to talk about all humans, including both males and females. Some people dislike this use, and prefer to say **human beings** or **people**. ❑ *Man first arrived in the Americas thousands of years ago.*
→ look at **age**

man|age /mænɪdʒ/ (**manages, managing, managed**)
1 VERB If you **manage** a business, you control it. ❑ *Two years after starting the job, he was managing the store.*

m

2 VERB If you **manage to** do something, especially something difficult, you succeed in doing it. ❏ *Three girls managed to escape the fire.*

man|age|ment /mænɪdʒmənt/
1 NONCOUNT NOUN Management is the control of a business or another organization. ❏ *The zoo needed better management, not more money.*
2 NONCOUNT NOUN The people who control a business or other organization are the **management**. ❏ *The management is trying hard to keep employees happy.*

man|ag|er /mænɪdʒər/ (**managers**) **NOUN**
A **manager** is a person who controls all or part of a business or an organization. ❏ *Each department manager is responsible for staff training.*

mane /meɪn/ (**manes**) **NOUN** The **mane** on some animals is the long, thick hair that grows from its neck. ❏ *You can wash the horse's mane at the same time as its body.*

ma|neu|ver /mənuvər/ (**maneuvers, maneuvering, maneuvered**)
1 VERB If you **maneuver** something into or out of a difficult position, you skillfully move it there. ❏ *He maneuvered the car through the narrow gate.*
2 NOUN Maneuver is also a noun. ❏ *The airplanes performed some difficult maneuvers.*

man|go /mæŋgoʊ/ (**mangoes** or **mangos**) **NOUN** A **mango** is a large, sweet, yellow or red fruit that grows on trees in hot countries.

man|hole /mænhoʊl/ (**manholes**) **NOUN** A **manhole** is a hole in a road, covered by a metal lid, that workers use when they want to examine the pipes under the road.

mani|cure /mænɪkyʊər/ (**manicures, manicuring, manicured**)
1 VERB If you **manicure** your hands or nails, you care for them by rubbing cream into your skin and cleaning and cutting your nails. ❏ *She carefully manicured her long nails.*
2 NOUN Manicure is also a noun. ❏ *I have an appointment for a manicure this afternoon.*

ma|nipu|late /mənɪpyəleɪt/ (**manipulates, manipulating, manipulated**) **VERB** If you **manipulate** people or events, you control them for your own benefit. ❏ *The government is trying to manipulate public opinion.*

man|kind /mænkaɪnd/ **NONCOUNT NOUN** You can call all humans **mankind** when you

are considering them as a group. Some people dislike this use. ❏ *We hope for a better future for all mankind.*

man-made also **manmade ADJECTIVE**
Man-made things are made by people. ❏ *Some of the world's problems are man-made.* ❏ *When the dam was built, three man-made lakes were created.*

manned /mænd/ **ADJECTIVE** A **manned** vehicle has people in it who are operating its controls. ❏ *The United States have sent a manned spacecraft into space.*

man|ner /mænər/ (**manners**)
1 NOUN The **manner** in which you do something is the way that you do it. ❏ *She smiled in a friendly manner.*
2 PLURAL NOUN Your **manners** are how polite you are when you are with other people. ❏ *He dressed well and had perfect manners.* ❏ *Is it bad manners to talk on a cellphone on the train?*

man|sion /mænʃən/ (**mansions**) **NOUN**
A **mansion** is a very large, expensive house. ❏ *He bought an eighteenth-century mansion in New Hampshire.*

manu|al /mænyuəl/ (**manuals**)
1 ADJECTIVE Manual work is work in which you use your hands or your physical strength. ❏ *He began his career as a manual worker.*
2 ADJECTIVE Manual means operated by hand, rather than by electricity or a motor. ❏ *We used a manual pump to get the water out of the hole.*
3 NOUN A **manual** is a book that tells you how to do something. ❏ *He advised me to read the instruction manual first.*

manu|fac|ture /mænyəfæktʃər/ (**manufactures, manufacturing, manufactured**)
1 VERB To **manufacture** something means to make it in a factory. ❏ *The company manufactures plastics.*
2 NONCOUNT NOUN Manufacture is also a noun. ❏ *Coal is used in the manufacture of steel.*
→ look at **factory**

manu|fac|tur|er /mænyəfæktʃərər/ (**manufacturers**) **NOUN** A **manufacturer** is a company that makes large amounts of things. ❏ *He works for the world's largest doll manufacturer.*

manu|fac|turing /mˈænjəfæktʃərɪŋ/

NONCOUNT NOUN Manufacturing is the business of making things in factories. ❑ *During the 1980s, 300,000 workers in the manufacturing industry lost their jobs.*

→ look at **factory**

many /mˈɛni/

1 ADJECTIVE You use **many** to talk about a large number of people or things. ❑ *Many people would disagree with that opinion.* ❑ *Not many stores are open on Sunday.*

2 PRONOUN Many is also a pronoun. ❑ *He made a list of his friends. There weren't many.*

3 You use **many of** for talking about a large number of people or things. ❑ *Why do many of us feel that we need to get married?*

4 ADVERB You use **many** when you are asking or replying to questions about numbers of things or people. ❑ *"How many of their songs were hits?"—"Not very many."*

> **Usage**   **many**
>
> Use **many** with count nouns. Here are some examples. *Many cafés have tables outside. How many pairs of shoes do you have?*

map /mˈæp/ (**maps**) **NOUN** GEOGRAPHY A **map** is a drawing of a particular area such as a city or a country, that shows things like mountains, rivers, and roads. ❑ *The detailed map helps tourists find their way around the city.*

→ look at **classroom, route**

ma|ple /mˈeɪpəl/ (**maples**)

1 NOUN A **maple** or a **maple tree** is a tree with leaves that turn a bright red or gold color in the fall.

2 NONCOUNT NOUN Maple is the wood of this tree. ❑ *Next to the sofa was a solid maple table.*

→ look at **tree**

mara|thon /mˈærəθɒn/ (**marathons**) **NOUN** SPORTS A **marathon** is a race in which people run a distance of 26 miles, which is about 42 km. ❑ *He is running in his first marathon next weekend.*

mar|ble /mˈɑrbəl/

1 NONCOUNT NOUN ARTS Marble is a type of very hard rock that people use to make parts of buildings or statues (= models of people).

2 NONCOUNT NOUN Marbles is a children's game that you play with small balls made of colored glass (called marbles). ❑ *Two boys were playing marbles.*

march /mˈɑrtʃ/ (**marches, marching, marched**)

1 VERB When soldiers **march** somewhere, they walk there with regular steps, as a group. ❑ *Some soldiers were marching down the street.*

2 NOUN March is also a noun. ❑ *After a short march, the soldiers entered the village.*

3 VERB When a large group of people **march**, they walk through the streets together in order to show that they disagree with something. ❑ *Thousands of people marched through the city to protest against the war.*

4 NOUN March is also a noun. ❑ *Organizers expect 300,000 protesters to join the march.*

5 VERB If someone **marches** somewhere, they walk there quickly, often because they are angry. ❑ *He marched into the kitchen without knocking.*

March /mˈɑrtʃ/ **NOUN** March is the third month of the year. ❑ *I flew to Milwaukee in March.* ❑ *She was born on March 6, 1920.*

mar|ga|rine /mˈɑrdʒərɪn/ (**margarines**)

NONCOUNT NOUN Margarine is a yellow substance that is made from vegetable oil, and is similar to butter.

mar|gin /mˈɑrdʒɪn/ (**margins**)

1 NOUN A **margin** is the difference between two amounts. ❑ *The team won with a 5-point margin.*

2 NOUN The **margin** of a page is the empty space down the side. ❑ *She wrote comments in the margin.*

ma|rine /mərˈin/ (**marines**)

1 NOUN A **marine** is a soldier who is specially trained to fight at sea as well as on land. ❑ *A few Marines were wounded.*

2 ADJECTIVE Marine describes things relating to the ocean. ❑ *The film shows the colorful marine life in the Indian Ocean.*

mari|tal /mˈærɪtəl/ **ADJECTIVE** Marital means relating to marriage. ❑ *When I was thirteen, my parents started having marital problems.*

mark /mˈɑrk/ (**marks, marking, marked**)

1 NOUN A **mark** is a small area of dirt that has accidentally gotten onto a surface or a piece of clothing. ❑ *There was a red paint mark on the wall.*

2 NOUN A **mark** is a written or printed symbol. ❑ *...a question mark.*

3 VERB If you **mark** something with a particular word, you write that word on it. ❑ *She marked the bill "paid."*

m

4 **VERB** When a teacher **marks** a student's work, the teacher writes a number or a letter on it to show how good it is. ❑ *The teacher was marking essays after class.*

5 **VERB** If something **marks** a place, it shows where a particular thing is. ❑ *A big hole in the road marks the place where the bomb landed.*

mar|ket /mɑrkɪt/ (**markets, marketing, marketed**)

1 **NOUN** A **market** is a place where people buy and sell products. ❑ *They usually buy their fruit and vegetables at the market.*

2 **NOUN** The **market** for a particular product is the people who want to buy it. ❑ *The market for organic wines is growing.*

3 **VERB** If you **market** a product you advertise it and sell it. ❑ *The products were marketed under a different brand name in Europe.*

● **mar|ket|ing** **NONCOUNT NOUN** ❑ *She works in the marketing department of a large company.*

mar|ma|lade /mɑrməleɪd/ **NONCOUNT NOUN** Marmalade is a food like jelly that is usually made from oranges.

mar|riage /mærɪdʒ/ (**marriages**)

1 **NOUN** A **marriage** is the relationship between a husband and a wife. ❑ *In a good marriage, both husband and wife are happy.*

2 **NOUN** A **marriage** is the time when two people get married. ❑ *...a marriage ceremony.*

mar|ried /mærid/ **ADJECTIVE** If you are **married**, you have a husband or a wife. ❑ *We have been married for 14 years.* ❑ *She is married to an Englishman.*

mar|ry /mæri/ (**marries, marrying, married**)
VERB When two people **get married** or **marry**, they legally become husband and wife in a special ceremony. ❑ *I thought he would change after we got married.* ❑ *They married a month after they met.* ❑ *He wants to marry her.*

marsh /mɑrʃ/ (**marshes**) **NOUN** **SCIENCE** A **marsh** is a soft, wet area of land.

marsh|mal|low /mɑrʃmɛloʊ, -mæloʊ/ (**marshmallows**) **NOUN** Marshmallows are soft pink or white candies.

mar|vel|ous /mɑrvələs/ **ADJECTIVE** If someone or something is **marvelous**, they are very good. ❑ *It's a marvelous piece of music.*

mas|cu|line /mæskyəlɪn/
1 **ADJECTIVE** Masculine qualities are typical of men. ❑ *She has a deep, rather masculine voice.*

2 **ADJECTIVE** **LANGUAGE ARTS** In some languages, a **masculine** noun, pronoun, or adjective has a different form from other forms (such as "feminine" forms). Compare with **feminine**.

mash /mæʃ/ (**mashes, mashing, mashed**) **VERB** If you **mash** food, you press it to make it soft. ❑ *Mash the bananas with a fork.*

mask /mæsk/ (**masks**)
NOUN A **mask** is something that you wear over your face to protect it or to hide it. ❑ *A man wearing a mask entered the restaurant at about 1:40 p.m. and took out a gun.* ❑ *Wear a mask to protect yourself from the smoke.*

masked /mæskt/
ADJECTIVE If someone is **masked**, they are wearing a mask. ❑ *Two masked men came through the doors carrying guns.*

mass /mæs/ (**masses**)
1 **NOUN** A **mass of** something is a large amount of it. ❑ *She had a mass of black hair.*

2 **Masses of** something is a large amount of it. [INFORMAL] ❑ *I have masses of work to do.*

3 **SCIENCE** **Mass** is the amount of physical matter that something contains. ❑ *Pluto and Triton have nearly the same size, mass, and density.*

4 **NONCOUNT NOUN** Mass is a Christian church ceremony, especially in a Roman Catholic church. ❑ *She went to Mass each day.*

mas|sa|cre /mæsəkər/ (**massacres, massacring, massacred**)
1 **NOUN** A **massacre** happens when a large number of people are killed at the same time in a violent and cruel way. ❑ *Her mother died in the massacre.*

2 **VERB** If people **are massacred**, a large number of them are killed in a violent and cruel way. ❑ *Three hundred people were massacred by the soldiers.*

mas|sage /məsɑʒ/ (**massages, massaging, massaged**)
1 **NOUN** Massage is the activity of rubbing someone's body to make them relax or to reduce their pain. ❑ *Alex asked me if I wanted a massage.*

2 **VERB** If you **massage** a part of someone's body, you rub it in order to make them relax or reduce their pain. ❑ *She continued massaging her right foot.*

M

mas|sive /mǽsɪv/ **ADJECTIVE** Something that is **massive** is very large. ❑ *They borrowed massive amounts of money.*

mass-produce (mass-produces, mass-producing, mass-produced) **VERB** To **mass-produce** something means to make it in large amounts, usually by machine. ❑ *Most of the food we eat is mass-produced in large factories.* ● **mass-produced** **ADJECTIVE** ❑ *It was cheaper to buy mass-produced food.*

mast /mǽst/ (masts) **NOUN** The **masts** of a boat are the tall poles that support its sails.

mas|ter /mǽstər/ (masters, mastering, mastered)
1 **NOUN** A person's or an animal's **master** is the man who controls that person or animal. ❑ *The dog was listening to its master's voice.*
2 **NOUN** If someone is a **master** of a particular activity, they are extremely skilled at it. ❑ *She was a master of the English language.*
3 **VERB** If you **master** something, you learn how to do it well. ❑ *David soon mastered the skills of baseball.*

master|piece /mǽstərpis/ (masterpieces) **NOUN** ARTS A **masterpiece** is an extremely good painting, novel, movie, or other work of art. ❑ *His book is a masterpiece.*

mas|ter's de|gree (master's degrees) **NOUN** A **master's degree** is a university qualification that is of a higher level than an ordinary degree.

mat /mǽt/ (mats)
1 **NOUN** A **mat** is a small piece of cloth, wood, or plastic that you put on a table to protect it. ❑ *...a set of red and white check place mats.*
2 **NOUN** A **mat** is a small piece of thick material that you put on the floor. ❑ *There was a letter on the doormat.*

match /mǽtʃ/ (matches, matching, matched)
1 **NOUN** A **match** is a small wooden or paper stick that produces a flame when you move it along a rough surface. ❑ *Kate lit a match and held it up to the candle.*
2 **NOUN** SPORTS A **match** is an organized game of tennis (= a game for two or four players, who try to hit a ball across a net

between them). ❑ *He was watching a tennis match.*
3 **VERB** If something **matches** another thing, they have the same color or design, or they look good together. ❑ *Do these shoes match my dress?* ● **match|ing** **ADJECTIVE** ❑ *She wore a hat and a matching scarf.*

mate /méɪt/ (mates, mating, mated)
1 **NOUN** SCIENCE An animal's **mate** is its sexual partner. ❑ *The male bird shows its brightly colored feathers to attract a mate.*
2 **VERB** SCIENCE When animals **mate**, a male and a female have sex in order to produce babies. ❑ *After mating, the female does not eat.*

ma|terial /mətɪ́əriəl/ (materials)
1 **NONCOUNT NOUN** **Material** is cloth. ❑ *The thick material of her skirt was too warm for summer.*
2 **PLURAL NOUN** **Materials** are the things that you need for a particular activity. ❑ *...building materials.*

ma|ter|nal /mətɜ́rnəl/ **ADJECTIVE** **Maternal** describes feelings or actions that are typical of a mother toward her child. ❑ *No love is stronger than maternal love.*

math /mǽθ/ **NONCOUNT NOUN** MATH **Math** is the same as **mathematics**. ❑ *He studied math in college.*
→ look at Word World: **math**
→ look at **geometry**

math|emati|cal /mǽθəmǽtɪkəl/ **ADJECTIVE** MATH Something that is **mathematical** involves numbers and calculating. ❑ *He made some quick mathematical calculations.*
→ look at **math**

math|emat|ics /mǽθəmǽtɪks/ **NONCOUNT NOUN** MATH **Mathematics** is the study of numbers, quantities, or shapes. ❑ *Dr. Lewis is a professor of mathematics at Boston College.*

mati|nee /mǽtəneɪ/ (matinees) **NOUN** A **matinee** is a performance of a play or a showing of a movie in the afternoon.

mat|ter /mǽtər/ (matters, mattering, mattered)
1 **NOUN** A **matter** is something that you must talk about or do. ❑ *She wanted to discuss a private matter with me.*
2 **PLURAL NOUN** You use **matters** to talk about a situation that someone is involved in. ❑ *If it would make matters easier, I will come to New York.*

m

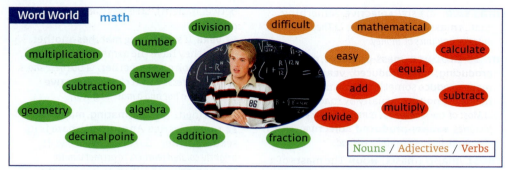

Word World | **math**

division · number · difficult · mathematical · multiplication · easy · calculate · answer · equal · subtraction · add · subtract · geometry · algebra · multiply · divide · decimal point · addition · fraction

Nouns / Adjectives / Verbs

3 **NOUN** You say "What's the matter?" when you think that someone has a problem and you want to know what it is. ❏ *Carol, what's the matter? You don't seem happy.*
4 **VERB** If you say that something does not **matter**, you mean that it is not important to you. ❏ *A lot of the food goes on the floor but that doesn't matter.*
5 **NONCOUNT NOUN** Matter is a type of substance. ❏ *There was a strong smell of rotting vegetable matter.*

mat|tress /mǽtrɪs/ (**mattresses**) **NOUN** On a bed, the **mattress** is the thick, soft part that you lie on.

ma|ture /mətyʊ́ər, -tʊ́ər, -tʃʊ́ər/ (**matures, maturing, matured, maturer, maturest**)
1 **VERB** When a child or a young animal **matures**, it becomes an adult. ❏ *The children will face many challenges as they mature into adulthood.*
2 **ADJECTIVE** A **mature** person or animal is fully grown.
3 **ADJECTIVE** If someone is **mature**, their behavior is responsible and sensible. ❏ *Fiona was mature for her age.* ● **ma|tur|ity** **NONCOUNT NOUN** ❏ *Her speech showed great maturity.*

maxi|mum /mǽksɪməm/
1 **ADJECTIVE** You use **maximum** to describe the largest amount possible. ❏ *Today's maximum temperature in the city will be 80 degrees.*
2 **NOUN** Maximum is also a noun. ❏ *Brett faces a maximum of two years in prison.*

may /meɪ/
1 **MODAL VERB** You use **may** to show that there is a possibility that something will happen or that something is true. ❏ *We may have some rain today.* ❏ *I may be back next year.*
2 **MODAL VERB** You use **may** to say that someone is allowed to do something. ❏ *You may send a check or pay by credit card.* ❏ *May we come in?*

May /meɪ/ **NOUN** May is the fifth month of the year. ❏ *We went to Canada on vacation in May.*

may|be /méɪbi/
1 **ADVERB** You use **maybe** when you are uncertain about something. ❏ *Maybe she is in love.* ❏ *I do think about having children, maybe when I'm 40.*
2 **ADVERB** You use **maybe** when you are making suggestions or giving advice. ❏ *Maybe we can go to the movies or something.* ❏ *Maybe you should see a doctor.* ❏ *Maybe you should go there and look at it.*

may|on|naise /méɪəneɪz/ **NONCOUNT NOUN** Mayonnaise is a cold, thick sauce made from eggs and oil.

mayor /méɪər, mέər/ (**mayors**) **NOUN** SOCIAL STUDIES The **mayor** of a city or a town is the person who is responsible for its government. ❏ *The mayor of New York made a speech.*

maze /meɪz/ (**mazes**) **NOUN** A **maze** is a place that is difficult to find your way through. ❏ *Only the local people know their way through the town's maze of streets.*

me /mi, STRONG mi/ **PRONOUN** A speaker uses **me** when talking about himself or herself. ❏ *He asked me to go to California with him.*

mead|ow /mέdoʊ/ (**meadows**) **NOUN** A **meadow** is a field that has grass and flowers growing in it.

meal /mil/ (**meals**)
1 **NOUN** A **meal** is an occasion when people sit down and eat. ❏ *She sat next to him during the meal.*
2 **NOUN** A **meal** is the food you eat during a meal. ❏ *Logan finished his meal in silence.*
→ look at **eat**

M

Word Partners	Use **meal** with:
V.	**enjoy a** meal, **miss a** meal, **skip a** meal **1 2** **cook a** meal, **eat a** meal, **have a** meal, **order a** meal, **prepare a** meal, **serve a** meal **2**
ADJ.	**balanced** meal, **big** meal, **delicious** meal, **good** meal, **hot** meal, **large** meal, **simple** meal **2**

---
mean
---
❶ VERB USES
❷ ADJECTIVE USE
❸ NOUN USE

❶ **mean** /mi̱n/ (means, meaning, meant)
1 **VERB** If something **means** something, it has that meaning. ❑ *"Unable" means "not able."* ❑ *What does "software" mean?*

2 **VERB** If something **means** a lot **to** you, it is very important to you. ❑ *Be careful with the photos. They mean a lot to me.*

3 **VERB** If one thing **means** another, the second thing will happen because of the first thing. ❑ *The new factory means more jobs for people.*

4 **VERB** If you **mean** what you are saying, you are serious about it. ❑ *He said he loves her, and I think he meant it.*

5 **VERB** If someone **meant to** do something, they did it deliberately. ❑ *I'm so sorry. I didn't mean to hurt you.*
→ look at **dictionary**

❷ **mean** /mi̱n/ (meaner, meanest)
ADJECTIVE If someone is **mean**, they are unkind, or cruel. ❑ *Don't be mean to your brother!*

❸ **mean** /mi̱n/ (means) **NOUN** **MATH**
In math, the **mean** is the amount that you get if you add a set of numbers together and divide them by the number of things that you originally added together. For example, the mean of 1, 3, 5, and 7 is 4 (1+3+5+7=16; 16÷4=4).

mean|ing /mi̱nɪŋ/ (meanings) **NOUN** The **meaning** of a word or an expression is the idea that it represents. ❑ *Do you know the meaning of the words you're singing?*
→ look at **dictionary**

mean|ing|less /mi̱nɪŋlɪs/ **ADJECTIVE**
Something that is **meaningless** has no meaning or purpose. ❑ *After her death, he felt that his life was meaningless.*

means /mi̱nz/ **NOUN** A **means** of doing something is a way to do it. **Means** is both the singular and the plural form for this use. ❑ *He searched for a door or some other means of escape.*

meant /me̱nt/
1 **Meant** is a form of the verb **mean**.
2 **ADJECTIVE** You use **meant to** to say that something or someone was intended to be or do a particular thing. ❑ *I can't say any more, it's meant to be a big secret.* ❑ *He was meant to arrive an hour ago.*

mean|time /mi̱ntaɪm/ You use **in the meantime** or **meantime** to talk about the period of time between two events. ❑ *Elizabeth wants to go to college but in the meantime she has to work.*

mean|while /mi̱nwaɪl/ **ADVERB** You use **meanwhile** to talk about the period of time

m

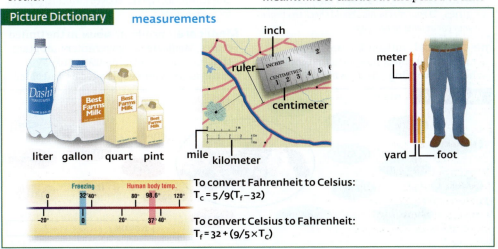

Picture Dictionary   **measurements**

inch

Dashi

Best Farms Milk

ruler

INCHES 1   2

CENTIMETRES
1 2 3 4 5

centimeter

meter

liter   gallon   quart   pint   mile   kilometer

yard   foot

Freezing   Human body temp.
0   32° 40°   80° 98.6° 120°
−20°   0   20°   37° 40°

To convert Fahrenheit to Celsius:
$T_c = 5/9(T_f - 32)$

To convert Celsius to Fahrenheit:
$T_f = 32 + (9/5 \times T_c)$

between two events or what happens while another thing is happening. ❏ *I'll be ready to meet them tomorrow. Meanwhile, I'm going to talk to Karen.* ❏ *We stayed up late into the night. Meanwhile, the snow was still falling outside.*

mea|sles /mˈiːzᵊlz/ **NONCOUNT NOUN** Measles is an illness that gives you a high fever and red spots on your skin.

meas|ure /mˈɛʒər/ (**measures, measuring, measured**)

1 **VERB** If you **measure** something, you find out its size. ❏ *Measure the length of the table.*
2 **VERB** If something **measures** a particular length or amount, that is its size. ❏ *The football field measures 400 feet.*
3 **NOUN** When someone takes **measures** to do something, they act in a particular way to try to do it. [FORMAL] ❏ *The police are taking measures to deal with the problem.*
→ look at **geometry, science**

meas|ure|ment /mˈɛʒərmənt/ (**measurements**) **NOUN** A **measurement** is the number that you get when you measure something. ❏ *You'll need to take the measurements of the room when you go to buy the furniture.*
→ look at Picture Dictionary: **measurements**

| **M** |

| **Sound Partners** | meat, meet |

meat /mˈiːt/ **NONCOUNT NOUN** Meat is the part of an animal that people cook and eat. ❏ *I don't eat meat or fish.*
→ look at Word World: **meat**
→ look at **food**

me|chan|ic /mɪkˈænɪk/ (**mechanics**) **NOUN** A **mechanic** is a person whose job is to repair machines and engines, especially car engines. ❏ *Your mechanic should check the brakes on your car at least once a year.*

me|chani|cal /mɪkˈænɪkᵊl/ **ADJECTIVE** A **mechanical** object has parts that move when it is working. ❏ *...a mechanical clock.*

mecha|nism /mˈɛkənɪzəm/ (**mechanisms**) **NOUN** A **mechanism** is a part of a machine. ❏ *The locking mechanism on the car door was broken.*

med|al /mˈɛdᵊl/ (**medals**) **NOUN** A **medal** is a small metal disk that you receive as a prize for doing something very good. ❏ *He won the Olympic gold medal.*

me|dia /mˈiːdiə/
1 **NOUN** **ARTS** You can call television, radio, newspapers, and magazines **the media**.
❏ *A lot of people in the media have asked me that question.* ❏ *They told their story to the news media.*
2 **ARTS** **Media** is a plural of **medium**.
→ look at **news**

median /mˈiːdiən/ (**medians**) **NOUN** **MATH** In math, the **median** is the number that is in the middle of a set of numbers when they are arranged in order. For example, in the numbers 1, 2, 3, 4, 5, the median is 3.

med|ic /mˈɛdɪk/ (**medics**) **NOUN** A **medic** is a doctor who works with the military. ❏ *Jack is an army medic.*

Medi|caid /mˈɛdɪkeɪd/ **NOUN** In the United States, **Medicaid** is a government program that helps to pay medical costs for people who cannot pay them.

medi|cal /mˈɛdɪkᵊl/ (**medicals**) **ADJECTIVE** **Medical** means relating to illness and injuries and how to treat or prevent them. ❏ *Several police officers received medical treatment for their injuries.*

Medi|care /mˈɛdɪkɛər/ **NOUN** In the United States, **Medicare** is a government program that provides health insurance to pay medical costs for people aged 65 and older.

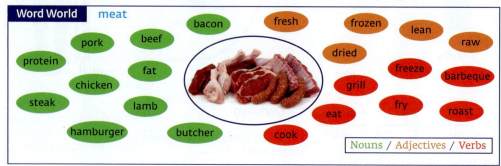

Word World   **meat**

bacon · pork · beef · protein · fat · chicken · steak · lamb · hamburger · butcher

fresh · frozen · lean · raw · dried · freeze · grill · barbeque · fry · roast · eat · cook

Nouns / Adjectives / Verbs

medi|ca|tion /mɛdɪkeɪʃˀn/ **NONCOUNT NOUN**
Medication is medicine that is used for
treating and curing illness. ❑ *Are you taking
any medication?*

medi|cine /mɛdɪsɪn/ (**medicines**)
1 **NONCOUNT NOUN** Medicine is the
treatment of illness and injuries by doctors
and nurses. ❑ *He decided on a career in medicine.*
2 **NOUN** Medicine is a substance that you
use to treat or cure an illness. ❑ *The medicine
saved his life.*
→ look at **health care**

me|di|eval /mɪdiivˀl, mɪdivˀl/ **ADJECTIVE**
SOCIAL STUDIES Something that is **medieval**
relates to the period of European history
between A.D. 476 and about A.D. 1500.
❑ *On our trip we visited a medieval castle.*

me|dium /midiəm/ (**mediums** or **media**)
1 **ADJECTIVE** If something is of **medium** size,
it is neither large nor small. ❑ *Mix the cream
and eggs in a medium bowl.* ❑ *For this recipe, you
will need one medium-sized onion.*
2 **NOUN** **ARTS** A **medium** is a substance or
material such as paint, wood, or stone that
an artist uses. ❑ *Hyatt uses the medium of oil
paint.*
→ look at **shopping**

Sound Partners	meet, meat

meet /mit/ (**meets, meeting, met**)
1 **VERB** If you **meet** someone who you
know, you see them by chance and you
speak to them. ❑ *I met Shona in town today.*
2 **VERB** If you **meet** someone who you do
not know, you see them and speak to them
for the first time. ❑ *I have just met an amazing
man.*
3 **VERB** If two or more people **meet**, they go
somewhere because they have planned to be
there together. ❑ *We could meet for a game of
tennis after work.*
4 **VERB** If you **meet** someone at a place, you
go there and wait for them to arrive. ❑ *Mom
met me at the station.*
5 **VERB** The place where two lines **meet** is
the place where they join together. ❑ *This is
the point where the two rivers meet.*
6 **NOUN** **SPORTS** A **meet** is a sports
competition. ❑ *He never misses swim meets or
baseball games.*

meet|ing /mitɪŋ/ (**meetings**) **NOUN**
A **meeting** is an event in which a group of
people come together to discuss things or to

make decisions. ❑ *Can we have a meeting to
discuss that?*

mega|byte /mɛgəbaɪt/ (**megabytes**) **NOUN**
TECHNOLOGY In computing, a **megabyte** is a
unit for measuring information. There are
one million bytes in a megabyte. ❑ *The hard
drive has 256 megabytes of memory.*

melo|dy /mɛlədi/ (**melodies**) **NOUN** **MUSIC**
A **melody** is a group of musical notes that
sound pleasant together. ❑ *He could sing a
melody before he could talk.*
→ look at **music**

mel|on /mɛlən/ (**melons**) **NOUN** A **melon** is a
large fruit with soft, sweet flesh and a hard
green or yellow skin. ❑ *For dessert, there were
grapes and juicy slices of melon.*

melt /mɛlt/ (**melts, melting, melted**) **VERB**
When a solid substance **melts**, it changes to
a liquid because it has become warm. ❑ *The
snow melted.* ❑ *Melt the chocolate in a bowl.*

melt|ing point (**melting points**) **NOUN**
SCIENCE The **melting point** of a substance is
the temperature at which it melts when you
heat it.

mem|ber /mɛmbər/ (**members**) **NOUN**
A **member** of a group or an organization is
someone or something that belongs to that
group or organization. ❑ *Joe is a member of the
Democratic party.* ❑ *A member of the team saw the
accident.*

Word Builder	membership

ship ≈ **state of being**
    champion + **ship** = champion**ship**
    friend + **ship** = friend**ship**
    leader + **ship** = leader**ship**
    member + **ship** = member**ship**
    owner + **ship** = owner**ship**
    relation + **ship** = relation**ship**

mem|ber|ship /mɛmbərʃɪp/ (**memberships**)
1 **NONCOUNT NOUN** Membership in an
organization means being a member of it.
❑ *Employees have free membership at the gym.*
2 **NOUN** The **membership** of an
organization is the people who belong to it.
❑ *By 2008, the organization had a membership of
409,000.*

memo /mɛmoʊ/ (**memos**) **NOUN** A **memo** is
a short note that you send to a person who
works with you. ❑ *He sent a memo to everyone in
his department.*

m

memo|rable /mɛmərəbəl/ **ADJECTIVE**
Something that is **memorable** is easy to
remember because it is special or very
enjoyable. ❑ *Our wedding was a very
memorable day.*

me|mo|rial /mɪmɔriəl/ (memorials) **NOUN**
A **memorial** is something that you build in
order to remind people of a famous person
or event. ❑ *He wanted to build a memorial to
Columbus.*

memo|rize /mɛməraɪz/ (memorizes,
memorizing, memorized) **VERB** If you
memorize something, you learn it so that
you can remember it exactly. ❑ *He tried to
memorize the way to Rose's street.*

memo|ry /mɛməri/ (memories)
1 NOUN Your **memory** is your ability to
remember things. ❑ *All the details of the
meeting are clear in my memory.* ❑ *He has a good
memory for faces.*
2 NOUN A **memory** is something that you
remember from the past. ❑ *She has happy
memories of her childhood.*
3 NOUN TECHNOLOGY A computer's
memory is the part where it stores
information. ❑ *The data is stored in the
computer's memory.*

> **Word Partners** Use **memory** with:
>
> ADJ. bad memory, **good** memory, **long-term**
> memory, **short-term** memory, **poor**
> memory, **in recent** memory **1**
> bad memory, **good** memory **1 2**
> **happy** memory, **painful** memory, **sad**
> memory **2**

memo|ry card (memory cards) **NOUN**
TECHNOLOGY A **memory card** is a small part
that stores information inside a piece of
electronic equipment such as a camera.

memo|ry stick (memory sticks) **NOUN**
TECHNOLOGY A **memory stick** is a small
object for storing computer information
that you can carry with you and use in
different computers.

men /mɛn/ **Men** is the plural of **man**.

mend /mɛnd/ (mends, mending, mended)
VERB If you **mend** a hole in a piece of
clothing, you repair it by sewing it. ❑ *He
earns money by mending clothes.*

men's room (men's rooms) **NOUN** The men's
room is a bathroom for men in a public
building.

mens|wear /mɛnzwɛər/ **NONCOUNT NOUN**
Menswear is clothing for men. ❑ *Charlton
bought the menswear store in 2005.*

men|tal /mɛntəl/ **ADJECTIVE** Mental means
relating to the mind. ❑ *...mental illness.*
● **men|tal|ly** **ADVERB** ❑ *The exam made him
mentally tired.*

men|tion /mɛnʃən/ (mentions, mentioning,
mentioned) **VERB** If you **mention**
something, you say something about it,
without giving much information.
❑ *She mentioned her mother but not her father.*
❑ *I mentioned that I didn't really like pop music.*

menu /mɛnyu/ (menus)
1 NOUN In a restaurant, the **menu** is a list
of the food and drink that you can have
there. ❑ *A waiter offered him the menu.*
2 NOUN TECHNOLOGY On a computer
screen, a **menu** is a list of choices, showing
things that you can do using a particular
program. ❑ *Press F7 to show the print menu.*
→ look at **restaurant**

meow /miaʊ/ (meows, meowing, meowed)
1 NOUN Meow is the sound that a cat
makes. ❑ *We could hear the meow of a cat.*
2 VERB Meow is also a verb. ❑ *The cat meowed
for her food.*

mer|chan|dise /mɜrtʃəndaɪz, -daɪs/
NONCOUNT NOUN Merchandise is products
that you can buy. [FORMAL] ❑ *The company's
annual soccer merchandise sales are about $1.5 billion.*

mer|cu|ry /mɜrkyəri/ **NONCOUNT NOUN**
SCIENCE Mercury is a silver-colored liquid
metal that is used in thermometers.

mer|cy /mɜrsi/ **NONCOUNT NOUN** If someone
shows **mercy**, they choose not to harm or
punish someone. ❑ *His life was now at the
mercy of a judge.*

mere /mɪər/ **ADJECTIVE** You use **mere** to say
that something is small or not important.
❑ *A mere five percent of school principals are women.*

mere|ly /mɪərli/ **ADVERB** You use **merely** to
emphasize that something is only the thing
you are describing and nothing more.
❑ *She said this was merely her own opinion.*
❑ *Dieter merely looked at him, saying nothing.*

merge /mɜrdʒ/ (merges, merging, merged)
VERB If two things **merge**, they join
together to make one new thing. ❑ *His
company has merged with the advertising firm
Saatchi & Saatchi.*

M

mer|it /mɛrɪt/ (**merits**)

1 NONCOUNT NOUN If something has **merit**, it has good qualities. ❑ The drawings have great artistic merit.

2 PLURAL NOUN The **merits** of something are its good points. ❑ We will consider the merits of all candidates before making our decision.

mer|maid /mɜrmeɪd/ (**mermaids**) **NOUN**
In stories, a **mermaid** is a woman who has a fish's tail and lives in the ocean.

mer|ry /mɛri/ (**merrier, merriest**) **ADJECTIVE**
Merry means happy and cheerful. ❑ She sang a merry little tune. ❑ Merry Christmas, everyone!

mess /mɛs/ (**messes, messing, messed**)

1 NOUN If something is **a mess**, it is not neat. ❑ After the party, the house was a mess.

2 NOUN If a situation is **a mess**, it is full of problems. ❑ I've made such a mess of my life. ❑ Those are the reasons why the economy is in such a mess.

▶ **mess around** If you **mess around**, you spend time doing things for fun, or for no particular reason. ❑ We were just messing around playing with paint.

▶ **mess up 1** If you **mess** something **up**, you make something go wrong. [INFORMAL] ❑ This has messed up our plans.

2 If you **mess up** a place or a thing, you make it dirty or not neat. [INFORMAL] ❑ He didn't want to mess up his neat hair.

mes|sage /mɛsɪdʒ/ (**messages, messaging, messaged**)

1 NOUN A **message** is a piece of information that you send to someone. ❑ I'm getting emails and messages from friends all over the world.

2 VERB TECHNOLOGY If you **message** someone, you send them an electronic message using a computer. ❑ I messaged her yesterday but she didn't reply.
→ look at **communication, email, phone**

mes|sage board (**message boards**) **NOUN**
TECHNOLOGY A **message board** is a system that allows users to send and receive messages on the Internet.

mes|sen|ger /mɛsɪndʒər/ (**messengers**)
NOUN A **messenger** is a person whose job is to take messages or packages to people. ❑ A messenger delivered a large envelope to his office.
→ look at **bag**

messy /mɛsi/ (**messier, messiest**)

1 ADJECTIVE A **messy** person or activity makes things dirty or not neat. ❑ She's a terribly messy cook.

2 ADJECTIVE Something that is **messy** is not neat. ❑ His writing is rather messy.

met /mɛt/ **Met** is a form of the verb **meet**.

met|al /mɛtᵊl/ (**metals**) **NOUN** Metal is a hard substance such as iron, steel, or gold. ❑ All of the houses had metal roofs.

me|tal|lic /mətælɪk/ **ADJECTIVE Metallic** things look or sound like metal. ❑ The car has heated seats, metallic paint and a sun roof.

meta|phor /mɛtəfɔr/ (**metaphors**) **NOUN**
LANGUAGE ARTS A **metaphor** is a way of describing someone or something by showing their similarity with something else. For example, the metaphor "a shining light" describes a person who is very skilful or intelligent. ❑ She uses a lot of religious metaphors in her writing.

me|teor /mitiər/ (**meteors**) **NOUN** SCIENCE
A **meteor** is a piece of rock from space that burns very brightly when it falls to Earth.

me|ter /mitər/ (**meters**)

1 NOUN MATH A **meter** is an instrument that measures and records something. ❑ A man came to read the electricity meter.

2 NOUN MATH A **meter** is a unit for measuring length. There are 100 centimeters in a meter. ❑ She's running the 1,500 meter race.
→ look at **measurement**

meth|od /mɛθəd/ (**methods**) **NOUN**
A **method** is a particular way of doing something. ❑ Teachers are allowed to try out different teaching methods.

met|ric /mɛtrɪk/ **ADJECTIVE** MATH SCIENCE
A **metric** measurement is given in meters, grams, or liters. ❑ A gram is a unit of weight in the metric system.

met|ric ton (**metric tons**) **NOUN** SCIENCE
A **metric ton** is 1,000 kilograms. ❑ The Wall Street Journal uses 220,000 metric tons of paper each year.

mg MATH SCIENCE **mg** is short for **milligram** or **milligrams**. ❑ ...300 mg of calcium.

mice /maɪs/ **Mice** is the plural of **mouse**.

mi|crobe /maɪkroʊb/ (**microbes**) **NOUN**
SCIENCE A **microbe** is a very small living thing that you cannot see without special equipment. ❑ We have to kill the microbes that cause food poisoning.

m

micro|chip /ˈmaɪkroʊtʃɪp/ (microchips)
NOUN TECHNOLOGY A **microchip** is a very small part inside a computer that makes it work.

micro|phone /ˈmaɪkrəfoʊn/ (microphones)
NOUN A **microphone** is a piece of electronic equipment that you use to make sounds louder or to record them onto a machine.

micro|scope /ˈmaɪkrəskoʊp/ (microscopes)
NOUN SCIENCE A **microscope** is a scientific instrument that makes very small objects look bigger.

micro|wave /ˈmaɪkroʊweɪv/ (microwaves)
NOUN A **microwave** or a **microwave oven** is an oven that cooks food very quickly using electric waves.
→ look at **cook, kitchen**

mid|day /ˈmɪddeɪ/ **NONCOUNT NOUN** Midday is twelve o'clock in the middle of the day.
❏ At midday everyone had lunch.

mid|dle /ˈmɪdəl/ (middles)
1 **NOUN** The **middle of** something is the part of it that is farthest from its edges.
❏ Howard stood in the middle of the room.
2 **ADJECTIVE** The **middle** object in a row of objects is the one that has an equal number of objects on each side. ❏ The middle button of his uniform jacket was missing.
3 **NOUN** The **middle of** a period of time is the part between the beginning and the end. ❏ I woke up in the middle of the night and heard a noise outside.
4 If you are **in the middle of** doing something, you are busy doing it. ❏ I'm in the middle of cooking dinner.
→ look at **calendar, day**

mid|dle age **NONCOUNT NOUN** Middle age is the time in your life when you are between the ages of about 40 and 65. ❏ Men often gain weight in middle age.

middle-aged **ADJECTIVE** A **middle-aged** person is between the ages of about 40 and 65.
❏ Most of the men were middle-aged, married businessmen.
→ look at **age**

Mid|dle Ages **PLURAL NOUN** SOCIAL STUDIES In European history, **the Middle Ages** was the period of time between the end of the Roman Empire in 476 AD and about 1500 AD.

mid|dle class (middle classes)
1 **NOUN** SOCIAL STUDIES The **middle class** or **middle classes** are the people in a society who are not very rich and not very poor, for example business people, doctors, and teachers.
❏ Most writers come from the middle class.
2 **ADJECTIVE** Middle class is also an adjective. ❏ They live in a very middle class area.

middle school (middle schools) **NOUN**
A **middle school** is a school for children between the ages of 10 and 13. ❏ ...Harlem Park Middle School.

mid|night /ˈmɪdnaɪt/ **NONCOUNT NOUN**
Midnight is twelve o'clock in the middle of the night. ❏ It was well after midnight.
→ look at **day, time**

mid|way /ˈmɪdweɪ/
1 **ADVERB** If something is **midway between** two places, it is the same distance from each of them. ❏ The studio is midway between his office and his home.
2 **ADJECTIVE** Midway is also an adjective.
❏ Fresno is close to the midway point between Los Angeles and San Francisco.
3 **ADVERB** If something happens **midway through** a period of time, it happens during the middle part of it. ❏ He crashed midway through the race.

---

might

1 MODAL USE
2 NOUN USE

---

1 might /maɪt/ **MODAL VERB** You use **might** when something is possible. ❏ I might go to study in England. ❏ They still hope that he might be alive.

2 might /maɪt/ **NONCOUNT NOUN** Might is power or strength. ❏ I pulled with all my might.

mightn't /ˈmaɪtənt/ **Mightn't** is short for "might not."

might've /ˈmaɪtəv/ **Might've** is short for "might have."

mighty /ˈmaɪti/ (mightier, mightiest)
ADJECTIVE Mighty describes something that is very large or powerful. ❏ There was a mighty roar from the crowd as the band came on stage.

mi|graine /ˈmaɪgreɪn/ (migraines) **NOUN**
A **migraine** is a severe pain in your head that makes you feel very ill. ❏ Her mother suffered from migraines.

M

mi|grant /maɪgrənt/ (**migrants**) **NOUN**
SOCIAL STUDIES A **migrant** is a person who
moves from one place to another, especially
in order to find work. ❏ *Most of his workers
were migrants from the South.*

mi|grate /maɪgreɪt/ (**migrates, migrating,
migrated**)
1 **VERB** SOCIAL STUDIES If people **migrate**,
they move from one place to another,
usually in order to find work. ❏ *People migrate
to cities like Jakarta searching for work.*
● **mi|gra|tion** /maɪgreɪʃ°n/ (**migrations**)
NOUN ❏ *There was a large migration of people to
the city.*
2 **VERB** When birds, fish, or animals
migrate, they move from one part of the
world to another at the same time every
year. ❏ *Most birds have to fly long distances to
migrate.* ● **mi|gra|tion** **NOUN** ❏ *Scientists are
tracking the migration of bears.*

mike /maɪk/ (**mikes**) **NOUN** A **mike** is the
same as a **microphone**. [INFORMAL]

mild /maɪld/ (**milder, mildest**)
1 **ADJECTIVE** **Mild** describes something that
is not very strong. ❏ *This cheese has a soft, mild
flavor.*
2 **ADJECTIVE** **Mild** weather is pleasant
because it is not too hot and not too cold.
❏ *We like the area because it has very mild winters.*

mile /maɪl/ (**miles**) **NOUN** MATH A **mile** is a
unit for measuring distance. A **mile** is equal
to 1.6 kilometers. There are 5,280 feet in a
mile. ❏ *They drove 600 miles across the desert.*
→ look at **measurement**

mile|age /maɪlɪdʒ/ (**mileages**) **NONCOUNT**
NOUN **Mileage** is the distance that you have
traveled, measured in miles. ❏ *The car has a
low mileage.*

mili|tary /mɪlɪtɛri/
1 **ADJECTIVE** **Military** means relating to the
armed forces of a country. ❏ *Military action
may become necessary.* ❏ *The president attended a
meeting of military leaders.*
2 **NONCOUNT NOUN** **The military** are the
armed forces of a country. ❏ *The military have
said very little about the attacks.*

milk /mɪlk/ (**milks, milking, milked**)
1 **NONCOUNT NOUN** SCIENCE **Milk** is the
white liquid that cows, and some other
animals produce, which people drink.
❏ *He went out to buy a quart of milk.*
2 **VERB** If someone **milks** a cow or another

animal, they take milk from it. ❏ *Farm
workers milks the cows in the morning.*
3 **NONCOUNT NOUN** SCIENCE **Milk** is the
white liquid that a mother makes in her
body to feed her baby. ❏ *Milk from the mother's
breast is a perfect food for the human baby.*

milky /mɪlki/ (**milkier, milkiest**) **ADJECTIVE**
Drinks or food that are **milky** contain a lot of
milk. ❏ *I want a big cup of milky coffee.*

mill /mɪl/ (**mills**)
1 **NOUN** A **mill** is a building in which flour
is made from grain. ❏ *The old mill is now
a restaurant.*
2 **NOUN** A **mill** is a factory where materials
such as steel, wool, or cotton are made.
❏ *He started work in a cotton mill at the age of ten.*

mil|len|nium /mɪlɛniəm/ (**millenniums** or
millennia) **NOUN** A **millennium** is a period of
one thousand years. [FORMAL] ❏ *The year 2000
was the beginning of a new millennium.*

mil|li|gram /mɪlɪgræm/ (**milligrams**) **NOUN**
MATH SCIENCE A **milligram** is a unit for
measuring weight. There are one thousand
milligrams in a gram. ❏ *He added 0.5 milligrams
of sodium.*

mil|li|li|ter /mɪlɪlitər/ (**milliliters**) **NOUN**
MATH A **milliliter** is a unit for measuring
volume for liquids and gases. There are one
thousand milliliters in a liter. ❏ *The nurse
measured 100 milliliters of blood.*

mil|li|meter /mɪlɪmitər/ (**millimeters**)
NOUN MATH A **millimeter** is a unit for
measuring length. There are ten
millimeters in a centimeter. ❏ *The creature is
tiny, just 10 millimeters long.*

mil|lion /mɪlyən/ (**millions**)

> **LANGUAGE HELP**
> The plural form is **million** after a number.

1 MATH A **million** or one **million** is the
number 1,000,000. ❏ *Five million people visit
the county each year.*
2 **Millions of** people or things means a very
large number of them. ❏ *The program was
watched on television in millions of homes.*

mil|lion|aire /mɪlyənɛər/ (**millionaires**)
NOUN A **millionaire** is a person who has
more than a million dollars. ❏ *By the time he
died, he was a millionaire.*

mime /maɪm/ (**mimes, miming, mimed**)
1 **NONCOUNT NOUN** ARTS **Mime** is a way of
telling a story using your face, hands, and

m

body, but without using speech. ❏ *The story is told through music and mime.*

2 **VERB** If you **mime** something, you describe it using movements rather than speech. ❏ *He mimed the act of hammering a nail into a piece of wood.*

mim|ic /mɪmɪk/ (**mimics, mimicking, mimicked**) **VERB** If you **mimic** the way someone moves or speaks, you copy them in an amusing way. ❏ *He could mimic anybody, and often made Olivia laugh.*

mind /maɪnd/ (**minds, minding, minded**)

1 **NOUN** Your **mind** is all your thoughts and the way that you think about things. ❏ *She is a bit deaf, but her mind is still sharp.*

2 If you **change** your **mind**, you change a decision or an opinion. ❏ *I was going to vote for him, but I changed my mind.*

3 If you **make up** your **mind**, you decide something. ❏ *He made up his mind to call Kathy.*

4 If something is **on** your **mind**, you are worried about it and you think about it a lot. ❏ *I don't sleep well. I've got a lot on my mind.*

5 If someone is **out of their mind**, they are crazy. [INFORMAL] ❏ *What are you doing? Are you out of your mind?*

6 If something **takes** your **mind off** a problem, it helps you to stop thinking about it for a while. ❏ *A movie might take your mind off your problems.*

7 **VERB** If you do not **mind** something, you do not feel annoyed or angry about it. ❏ *"Mr. Hernandez, would you mind waiting here a moment?"* ❏ *It was hard work but she didn't mind.*

8 **VERB** If you have a choice, and you say that you do not **mind**, you mean that you are happy to do or have either of them. ❏ *"Would you rather play tennis or baseball?"—"I don't mind."*

9 You say **never mind** when something is not important. ❏ *"He's going to be late."— "Oh, never mind, we'll start eating without him."*

10 If you **wouldn't mind** something, you would like it. ❏ *I wouldn't mind a cup of coffee.*

> **mine**
> ❶ PRONOUN USE
> ❷ NOUN AND VERB USES

❶ mine /maɪn/ **PRONOUN** **Mine** means belonging to me. ❏ *Her right hand was close to mine.* ❏ *That isn't your bag, it's mine.*

❷ mine /maɪn/ (**mines, mining, mined**)

1 **NOUN** A **mine** is a deep hole in the ground from which people dig coal, diamonds, or gold. ❏ *The company owns gold and silver mines.*

2 **VERB** When people **mine**, they dig deep holes and tunnels into the ground to remove coal, diamonds, or gold. ❏ *Diamonds are mined in South Africa.* ● **min|er** (**miners**) **NOUN** ❏ *My father was a miner.*

3 **NOUN** A **mine** is a bomb that is hidden under the ground.

min|er|al /mɪnərəl/ (**minerals**) **NOUN** SCIENCE A **mineral** is a natural substance such as gold, salt, or coal that comes from the ground.

min|er|al wa|ter **NONCOUNT NOUN** **Mineral water** is water that comes from the ground that contains substances that are good for your health.

minia|ture /mɪniətʃər, -tʃʊər/ **ADJECTIVE** **Miniature** things are very small, or much smaller than usual. ❏ *The toy house was filled with miniature chairs and tables.*

mini|mal /mɪnɪməl/ **ADJECTIVE** If an effect is **minimal**, it is very small. ❏ *The health risk is minimal, so there's no need to worry.*

mini|mize /mɪnɪmaɪz/ (**minimizes, minimizing, minimized**) **VERB** If you **minimize** something, you make it as small as possible. ❏ *We have done everything possible to minimize the risk of accidents.*

mini|mum /mɪnɪməm/

1 **ADJECTIVE** You use **minimum** to talk about the smallest amount that is possible. ❏ *Pupils remain at school at least until the minimum age of 16.* ❏ *Many people in the country are still working for less than the minimum wage.*

2 **NOUN** **Minimum** is also a noun. ❏ *Dr. Rayman runs a minimum of three miles every day.*

min|is|ter /mɪnɪstər/ (**ministers**)

1 **NOUN** A **minister** is a religious leader in some types of church. ❏ *Thirty priests, ministers, and rabbis attended the meeting.*

2 **NOUN** In some countries, a **minister** is a senior person in a government. ❏ *Clark became finance minister in 1991.*

min|is|try /mɪnɪstri/ (**ministries**) **NOUN** In some countries, a **ministry** is a government department that deals with one particular thing. ❏ *He has worked for both the ministry of education and the ministry of the interior.*

mi|nor /maɪnər/

1 **ADJECTIVE** If something is **minor**, it is not very important or serious. ❏ *The soldier suffered only minor injuries.* ❏ *They both have minor roles in the movie.*

2 MUSIC In music, **minor** is used for talking about a scale (= a series of musical notes) in which the third note is one half step lower that the related major scale. Compare with **major**. ❑ *...an A minor scale.*

mi|nor|ity /mɪnɔrɪti, maɪ-/ (**minorities**)
NOUN A **minority** of people or things is fewer than half of them. ❑ *Only a minority of mothers in this neighborhood go out to work.*

mint /mɪnt/ (**mints**)
1 NONCOUNT NOUN **Mint** is a plant that has leaves with a fresh, strong taste and smell. ❑ *The waiter brought us two glasses of mint tea.*
2 NOUN A **mint** is a candy with this flavor. ❑ *Sam offered me a mint.*

mi|nus /maɪnəs/ (**minuses**)
1 CONJUNCTION MATH You use **minus** when you are taking one number away from another number. ❑ *One minus one is zero.*
2 ADJECTIVE MATH You use **minus** before a number or an amount to show that it is less than zero. ❑ *The temperature dropped to minus 20 degrees F.*

> Usage   **minus**
>
> In math the minus sign is a short line - between two numbers, 24 - 2 = 20. In words, this equation is *twenty-four* **minus** *two equals twenty.*

minute
❶ NOUN USES
❷ ADJECTIVE USE

❶ mi|nute /mɪnɪt/ (**minutes**)
1 NOUN A **minute** is a unit for measuring time. There are sixty seconds in one minute, and there are sixty minutes in one hour. ❑ *The pizza will take twenty minutes to cook.*
2 If something will happen **in a minute**, it will happen very soon. ❑ *The doctor will be with you in a minute.*
3 If you ask someone to do something **this minute**, you want them to do it immediately. ❑ *You come back here this minute!*
4 You say **just a minute** or **wait a minute** when you want someone to wait for a short period of time. ❑ *Wait a minute, something is wrong here.*
→ look at **time**

❷ mi|nute /maɪnut/ ADJECTIVE Something that is **minute** is very small. ❑ *You only need to use a minute amount of glue.*

Minute|man /mɪnɪtmæn/ (**Minutemen**)
NOUN SOCIAL STUDIES In the American Revolution, a **Minuteman** was a soldier who promised to be ready to fight in one minute, if he was needed.

mira|cle /mɪrəkᵊl/ (**miracles**) NOUN
A **miracle** is a surprising and lucky event that you cannot explain. ❑ *It's a miracle that Chris survived the accident.*

mir|ror /mɪrər/ (**mirrors**)
NOUN A **mirror** is a flat piece of special glass that you can see yourself in. ❑ *Dan looked at himself in the mirror.*
→ look at **furniture**

> **Word Builder**   **misbehavior**
>
> *mis* ≈ **wrong**
>   mis + behavior = **mis**behavior
>   mis + fortune = **mis**fortune
>   mis + lead   = **mis**lead
>   mis + spell   = **mis**spell
>   mis + trust   = **mis**trust
>   mis + understand = **mis**understand

mis|be|hav|ior /mɪsbɪheɪvyər/ NONCOUNT NOUN **Misbehavior** is bad behavior. [FORMAL] ❑ *Our teachers will not tolerate misbehavior.* ❑ *They could not tell what was causing their son's misbehavior.*

mis|chief /mɪstʃɪf/ NONCOUNT NOUN **Mischief** is bad or silly behavior that is annoying but not too serious. ❑ *Jacob's a typical little boy—full of mischief.*

mis|chie|vous /mɪstʃɪvəs/ ADJECTIVE
A **mischievous** person likes to play tricks on people and behave in a silly, but not very bad way. ❑ *Megan gave me a mischievous smile.* ❑ *She behaves like a mischievous child sometimes.*
● **mis|chie|vous|ly** ADVERB ❑ *Thomas grinned mischievously at Anna.*

mis|er|able /mɪzərəbᵊl/
1 ADJECTIVE If you are **miserable**, you are very unhappy. ❑ *My job was making me miserable.* ● **mis|er|ably** /mɪzərəbli/ ADVERB ❑ *"I feel so guilty," Diane said miserably.*
2 ADJECTIVE If something is **miserable**, it makes you feel unhappy. ❑ *It was a gray, wet, miserable day.*

mis|ery /mɪzəri/ NONCOUNT NOUN **Misery** is great unhappiness. ❑ *People never forget the misery of war.* ❑ *All that money brought them nothing but sadness and misery.*

m

Word Builder	misfortune

mis ≈ **wrong**

mis + behavior = misbehavior
mis + fortune = misfortune
mis + lead = mislead
mis + spell = misspell
mis + trust = mistrust
mis + understand = misunderstand

mis|for|tune /mɪsfɔrtʃən/ (**misfortunes**)
NOUN A **misfortune** is something unpleasant or unlucky that happens to you. ❏ *She seems to enjoy other people's misfortunes.*

Word Builder	mislead

mis ≈ **wrong**

mis + behavior = misbehavior
mis + fortune = misfortune
mis + lead = mislead
mis + spell = misspell
mis + trust = mistrust
mis + understand = misunderstand

mis|lead /mɪslid/ (**misleads, misleading, misled**) **VERB** If you **mislead** someone, you make them believe something that is not true. ❏ *The administration has misled the public about this issue.*

mis|lead|ing /mɪslidɪŋ/ **ADJECTIVE** If a message is **misleading**, it makes you believe something that is not true. ❏ *Companies must make sure that their advertisements are not misleading.*

mis|led /mɪslɛd/ **Misled** is a form of the verb **mislead**.

miss

❶ AS PART OF A WOMAN'S NAME
❷ VERB USES

❶ **Miss** /mɪs/ (**Misses**) **NOUN** You use **Miss** in front of the name of a girl or a woman who is not married. [FORMAL] ❏ *It was nice talking to you, Miss Ellis.*

❷ **miss** /mɪs/ (**misses, missing, missed**)
1 VERB If you **miss** something that you are trying to hit or catch, you do not manage to hit it or catch it. ❏ *His first shot missed the goal completely.* ❏ *Morrison just missed the ball.*
2 VERB If you **miss** something, you do not notice it. ❏ *What did he say? I missed it.*
3 VERB If you **miss** someone who is not with you, you feel sad that they are not there. ❏ *I miss my family terribly.*

4 VERB If you **miss** something, you feel sad because you no longer have it. ❏ *I love my new apartment, but I miss my garden.*
5 VERB If you **miss** an airplane or a train, you arrive too late to get on it. ❏ *He missed the last bus home.*
6 VERB If you **miss** a meeting or an activity, you do not take part in it. ❏ *He missed the party because he had to work.*
▶ **miss out** If you **miss out** on something, you do not have the chance take part in it. ❏ *You missed out on all the fun yesterday.*

mis|sile /mɪsᵊl/ (**missiles**)
1 NOUN A **missile** is a weapon that flies through the air and explodes when it hits something. ❏ *The army fired missiles at the building.*
2 NOUN A **missile** is anything that you can throw as a weapon. ❏ *The youths were throwing missiles at the police.*

miss|ing /mɪsɪŋ/ **ADJECTIVE** If someone or something is **missing**, they are not in their usual place, and you cannot find them. ❏ *I discovered that my cellphone was missing.* ❏ *Police are hunting for the missing girl.*

mis|sion /mɪʃᵊn/ (**missions**) **NOUN** A **mission** is an important job that someone has to do, especially one that involves traveling. ❏ *His government sent him on a mission to North America.*

Word Builder	misspell

mis ≈ **wrong**

mis + behavior = misbehavior
mis + fortune = misfortune
mis + lead = mislead
mis + spell = misspell
mis + trust = mistrust
mis + understand = misunderstand

mis|spell /mɪsspɛl/ (**misspells, misspelling, misspelled**) **VERB** If someone **misspells** a word, they do not spell it correctly. ❏ *Sorry I misspelled your last name.*

mist /mɪst/ **NONCOUNT NOUN** Mist is a lot of tiny drops of water in the air, that make it difficult to see. ❏ *The mist did not lift until midday.* ● **misty** **ADJECTIVE** ❏ *Charlie looked across the misty valley.*

mis|take /mɪsteɪk/ (**mistakes, mistaking, mistook, mistaken**)
1 NOUN A **mistake** is something that is not correct. ❏ *Tony made three spelling mistakes in the letter.*

M

2 If you do something **by mistake**, you do something that you did not want or plan to do. ❑ *I was in a hurry and called the wrong number by mistake.*

3 **VERB** If you **mistake** one person **for** another person, you wrongly think that they are the other person. ❑ *People are always mistaking Lauren for her sister because they are so alike.*

Word Partners   Use **mistake** with:

V.	**admit a** mistake, **correct a** mistake, **fix a** mistake, **make a** mistake **1**
ADJ.	**big** mistake, **common** mistake, **costly** mistake, **honest** mistake, **huge** mistake, **serious** mistake, **terrible** mistake **1**

---

mis|tak|en /mɪsteɪkən/ **ADJECTIVE** If you are **mistaken about** something, you are wrong about it. ❑ *I think that you must be mistaken—Jackie wouldn't do a thing like that.*
● **mis|tak|en|ly** **ADVERB** ❑ *The thieves mistakenly believed there was no one in the house.*

mis|took /mɪstʊk/ **Mistook** is a form of the verb **mistake.**

Word Builder   mistrust

mis ≈ **wrong**

   mis + behavior = misbehavior
   mis + fortune = misfortune
   mis + lead = mislead
   mis + spell = misspell
   mis + trust = mistrust
   mis + understand = misunderstand

---

mis|trust /mɪstrʌst/ (**mistrusts, mistrusting, mistrusted**)
1 **NONCOUNT NOUN** **Mistrust** is the feeling that you have when you do not trust someone. ❑ *There is a deep mistrust of the police around here.*
2 **VERB** If you **mistrust** someone, you do not trust them. ❑ *He mistrusts all journalists.*

Word Builder   misunderstand

mis ≈ **wrong**

   mis + behavior = misbehavior
   mis + fortune = misfortune
   mis + lead = mislead
   mis + spell = misspell
   mis + trust = mistrust
   mis + understand = misunderstand

---

mis|under|stand /mɪsʌndərstænd/ (**misunderstands, misunderstanding, misunderstood**) **VERB** If you **misunderstand** someone or something, you do not understand them correctly. ❑ *I think you've misunderstood me.*

mis|under|stand|ing /mɪsʌndərstændɪŋ/ (**misunderstandings**) **NOUN** A **misunderstanding** is a situation where someone does not understand something correctly. ❑ *Make your plans clear to avoid misunderstandings.*

mis|under|stood /mɪsʌndərstʊd/ **Misunderstood** is a form of the verb **misunderstand.**

mit|ten /mɪtən/ (**mittens**) **NOUN** **Mittens** are gloves that have one part that covers your thumb and another part that covers your four fingers together. ❑ *...a pair of mittens.*

mix /mɪks/ (**mixes, mixing, mixed**)
1 **VERB** If you **mix** things, you put different things together so that they make something new. ❑ *Mix the sugar with the butter.*
2 **VERB** If two substances **mix**, they join together and make something new. ❑ *Oil and water don't mix.* **SCIENCE**
▶ **mix up** If you **mix up** two things or people, you think that one of them is the other one. ❑ *People often mix me up with my brother.* ❑ *Children often mix up their words.*

mixed /mɪkst/ **ADJECTIVE** If something is **mixed**, it includes different types of things or people. ❑ *There was a very mixed group of people at the party.* ❑ *For lunch we had pasta and a mixed salad.*

mix|er /mɪksər/ (**mixers**) **NOUN** A **mixer** is a machine that you use for mixing things together. ❑ *Beat the egg yolks and sugar with an electric mixer.*

mix|ture /mɪkstʃər/ (**mixtures**) **NOUN** A **mixture** is a substance that you make by mixing different substances together. ❑ *The sauce is a mixture of chocolate and cream.*

ml **MATH** **SCIENCE** **ml** is short for **milliliter** or **milliliters.** ❑ *Boil the sugar and 100 ml of water.*

mm **MATH** **mm** is short for **millimeter** or **millimeters.** ❑ *...a 135 mm lens.*

m

moan /moʊn/ (moans, moaning, moaned)
1 VERB If you **moan**, you make a low sound because you are unhappy or in pain. ❑ *The wounded soldier was moaning in pain.*
2 NOUN Moan is also a noun. ❑ *She gave a soft moan of discomfort.*

mo|bile /moʊbəl/ **ADJECTIVE** Someone or something that is **mobile** can easily move or be moved from place to place. ❑ *The family live in a three-bedroom mobile home near Las Cruces in New Mexico.* ❑ *Grandpa's eighty but he's still very mobile.*

mock /mɒk/ (mocks, mocking, mocked)
VERB If you **mock** someone, you laugh at them and try to make them feel foolish. ❑ *My friends mocked me because I didn't have a girlfriend.*

mod|al /moʊdəl/ (modals) **NOUN**
LANGUAGE ARTS In grammar, a **modal** or a **modal auxiliary** is a word such as "can" or "would" that you use with another verb to express ideas such as possibility, intention, or necessity.

mod|el /mɒdəl/ (models, modeling, modeled)
1 NOUN ARTS A **model** is a small copy of something. ❑ *At school, the children are making a model of the solar system.* ❑ *I made the model using paper and glue.*
2 ADJECTIVE Model is also an adjective. ❑ *I spent my childhood building model aircraft.*
3 NOUN A **model** of a vehicle or a machine is a particular design of it. ❑ *You don't need an expensive computer, just a basic model.*
4 NOUN ARTS An artist's **model** is a person who sits or stands in front of an artist so that they can draw or paint them. ❑ *The model for his painting was his sister.*
5 NOUN A **model** is a person whose job is to wear and show new clothes in photographs and at fashion shows, so that people can see them and buy them. ❑ *Kim dreams of becoming a fashion model.*
6 VERB If you **model**, you wear clothes as a model. ❑ *Nicole began modeling at age 15.*

mo|dem /moʊdəm, -dɛm/ (modems) **NOUN**
TECHNOLOGY A **modem** is a piece of equipment that uses a telephone line to connect computers. ❑ *…a cellphone with a built-in modem.*

mod|er|ate /mɒdərɪt/ **ADJECTIVE** If something is **moderate**, it is not too much

or too little. ❑ *Temperatures are moderate between October and March.* ● **mod|er|ate|ly ADVERB** ❑ *Heat the oil until it is moderately hot.*

mod|ern /mɒdərn/ **ADJECTIVE** If something is **modern**, it is new, or it relates to the present time. ❑ *I like antiques, but my husband prefers modern furniture.* ❑ *… modern society.*
→ look at **history**

mod|ern|ize /mɒdərnaɪz/ (modernizes, modernizing, modernized) **VERB** To **modernize** a system or a factory means to change it by introducing new equipment, methods, or ideas. ❑ *We need to modernize our schools.*

mod|est /mɒdɪst/ **ADJECTIVE** If you are **modest**, you do not talk much about your abilities, skills, or successes. ❑ *He's modest, as well as being a great player.* ● **mod|est|ly ADVERB** ❑ *"I was just lucky," Hughes said modestly.*

mod|es|ty /mɒdɪsti/ **NONCOUNT NOUN**
If you show **modesty**, you do not talk much about your abilities, skills or successes. ❑ *His humor and gentle modesty won affection and friendships everywhere.*

modi|fy /mɒdɪfaɪ/ (modifies, modifying, modified) **VERB** If you **modify** something, you change it slightly, usually in order to improve it. ❑ *Helen and her husband modified the design of the house to suit their family's needs.*
● **modi|fi|ca|tion** /mɒdɪfɪkeɪʃən/ (modifications) **NOUN** ❑ *They made a few small modifications to the plan.*

moist /mɔɪst/ (moister, moistest) **ADJECTIVE** If something is **moist**, it is slightly wet. ❑ *The soil was moist after the rain.*

mois|ture /mɔɪstʃər/ **NONCOUNT NOUN**
Moisture is small drops of water in the air, on a surface, or in the ground. ❑ *Keep the food covered so that it doesn't lose moisture.*

mold /moʊld/ (molds, molding, molded)
1 NOUN A **mold** is a hollow container that you pour liquid into. When the liquid becomes solid, it takes the same shape as the mold. ❑ *Pour the mixture into molds and place them in the refrigerator.*
2 VERB If you **mold** a soft substance, you make it into a particular shape. ❑ *The mixture is heated then molded.*
3 NONCOUNT NOUN **Mold** is a soft gray, green, or blue substance that grows on old food or on damp surfaces. ❑ *Hannah discovered mold growing in her bedroom closet.*

Spelling Partners   mole

mole /moʊl/ (moles)

1 **NOUN** A **mole** is a natural dark spot on your skin. ❏ *Rebecca has a mole on the side of her nose.*

2 **NOUN** A **mole** is a small animal with black fur that lives under the ground.

mol|ecule /mɒlɪkyul/ (molecules) **NOUN**
SCIENCE A **molecule** is the smallest amount of a chemical substance that can exist by itself. ❏ *When hydrogen and oxygen molecules combine, the reaction produces heat and water.*

mom /mɒm/ (moms) **NOUN** Your **mom** is your mother. [INFORMAL] ❏ *We waited for my mom and dad to get home.* ❏ *Bye, Mom. Love you.*

mo|ment /moʊmənt/ (moments)

1 **NOUN** A **moment** is a very short period of time. ❏ *In a moment he was gone.*

2 **NOUN** A particular **moment** is the time when something happens. ❏ *At that moment a car stopped at the house.*

3 If something is happening **at the moment**, it is happening at or around the time when you are speaking. ❏ *At the moment, the team is playing very well.*

4 If something is true **for the moment**, it is true now, but it may not be true in the future. ❏ *For the moment, everything is fine.*

5 If something is going to happen **in a moment**, it is going to happen very soon. ❏ *"Please take a seat. Mr. Garcia will see you in a moment."*

mom|ma /mɒmə/ (mommas) **NOUN** Young children call their mothers **Momma**. [INFORMAL] ❏ *I loved Momma's perfume and her soft shining hair.*

mom|my /mɒmi/ (mommies) **NOUN** Young children call their mother **Mommy**. [INFORMAL] ❏ *Please can I have a cookie, Mommy?*

mon|ar|chy /mɒnərki/ (monarchies) **NOUN**
SOCIAL STUDIES A **monarchy** is a system in which a country has a king or a queen. ❏ *Greece abolished the monarchy in 1974.*

Mon|day /mʌndeɪ, -di/ (Mondays) **NOUN**
Monday is the day after Sunday and before Tuesday. ❏ *I went back to work on Monday.* ❏ *The first meeting was last Monday.*

mon|ey /mʌni/ **NONCOUNT NOUN** **Money** is the coins or bills that you use to buy things. ❏ *Cars cost a lot of money.* ❏ *She spends too much money on clothes and shoes.*
→ look at **ATM, payment**

moni|tor /mɒnɪtər/ (monitors, monitoring, monitored) **VERB** If you **monitor** something, you watch how it develops or progresses over a period of time. ❏ *Doctors closely monitored her progress.*
→ look at **computer**

monk /mʌŋk/ (monks) **NOUN** A **monk** is a member of a group of religious men who live together in a special building.

mon|key /mʌŋki/ (monkeys) **NOUN** A **monkey** is an animal that has a long tail and can climb trees.

mo|nopo|ly /mənɒpəli/ (monopolies)

1 **NOUN** **SOCIAL STUDIES** If a company or a person has a **monopoly on** an industry, they have complete control over it. ❏ *The East India Company had a monopoly on all trade to Britain from the East.*

2 **NOUN** **SOCIAL STUDIES** A **monopoly** is the only company that provides a particular product. ❏ *The company is a state-owned monopoly.*

mo|noto|nous /mənɒtᵊnəs/ **ADJECTIVE** If something is **monotonous**, it is very boring because it never changes. ❏ *It's monotonous work, like most factory jobs.*

mon|soon /mɒnsun/ (monsoons) **NOUN**
SCIENCE In Southern Asia, the **monsoon** is the season when there is a lot of very heavy rain. ❏ *The monsoon season lasts for about four months each year.*

mon|ster /mɒnstər/ (monsters) **NOUN**
In stories, a **monster** is a big, ugly, and frightening creature. ❏ *The movie is about a monster in the bedroom closet.*

month /mʌnθ/ (months) **NOUN** A **month** is one of the twelve parts that a year is divided into. ❏ *September is the ninth month of the year.* ❏ *We go on vacation next month.*
→ look at **calendar, season**

month|ly /mʌnθli/

1 **ADJECTIVE** A **monthly** event happens every month. ❏ *The monthly rent for his apartment is $1,000.*

2 **ADVERB** **Monthly** is also an adverb. ❏ *The magazine is published monthly.*
→ look at **calendar**

m

monu|ment /mɒnyəmənt/ (**monuments**) **NOUN**
SOCIAL STUDIES A **monument** is something that you build to help people remember an important event or person. ❑ *This monument was built in memory of the soldiers who died in the war.*

moo /mu/ (**moos, mooing, mooed**) **VERB** When cows **moo**, they make a long, low sound. ❑ *We could hear the cows mooing.*

mood /mud/ (**moods**) **NOUN** Your **mood** is the way you are feeling at a particular time. ❑ *Dad is in a very good mood today.* ❑ *I had an argument with my girlfriend, so I was in a bad mood.*
→ look at **feeling**

moody /mudi/ (**moodier, moodiest**) **ADJECTIVE** If you are **moody**, you often become sad or angry without any warning. ❑ *David's mother is very moody.*

moon /mun/ (**moons**) **NOUN** SCIENCE The **moon** is the large object that shines in the sky at night. ❑ *The first man on the moon was an American, Neil Armstrong.*
→ look at **space**

moon|light /munlaɪt/ **NONCOUNT NOUN** **Moonlight** is the light that comes from the moon at night. ❑ *They walked along the road in the moonlight.*

moose /mus/ (**moose**) **NOUN** A **moose** is the largest member of the deer family. (A **deer** = a large wild animal with horns that are like branches). ❑ *In the fall, they hunt moose and deer.*

mop /mɒp/ (**mops, mopping, mopped**)
1 **NOUN** A **mop** is a long stick with a lot of thick pieces of string at one end. You use it for washing floors.
2 **VERB** If you **mop** a floor, you clean it with a mop. ❑ *I could see a woman mopping the stairs.*
→ look at **chore**

mor|al /mɔrᵊl/ (**morals**)
1 **PLURAL NOUN** Your **morals** are your ideas and beliefs about right and wrong behavior. ❑ *Amy has strong morals and high standards.*
2 **ADJECTIVE** Something **moral** relates to people's beliefs about what is right or wrong. ❑ *We all have a moral duty to stop racism.*
● **mor|al|ly** **ADVERB** ❑ *It is morally wrong to kill a person.*

3 **NOUN** LANGUAGE ARTS The **moral** of a story or event is what you learn from it about how you should or should not behave. ❑ *The moral of this sad story is "do not trust anyone."*

more /mɔr/
1 **ADJECTIVE** You use **more** to talk about a greater amount of something. ❑ *More people are surviving heart attacks than ever before.* ❑ *I need more time to think about what to do.*
2 **PRONOUN** **More** is also a pronoun. ❑ *As they worked harder, they ate more.* ❑ *We should be doing more to help these people.*
3 **ADVERB** **More** shows that something continues to happen. ❑ *You should talk about your problems more.*
4 **More of** something means a greater amount of it than before, or than usual. ❑ *They're doing more of their own work.*
5 You use **more than** to talk about a greater amount of something than the amount mentioned. ❑ *The airport had been closed for more than a year.*
6 You can use **more and more** to show that something is becoming greater all the time. ❑ *She began eating more and more.*

more|over /mɔroʊvər/ **ADVERB** You use **moreover** when you are adding more information about something. [FORMAL] ❑ *She saw that there was a man behind her. Moreover, he was staring at her.*

morn|ing /mɔrnɪŋ/ (**mornings**)
1 **NOUN** The **morning** is the part of each day between the time that people usually wake up and noon. ❑ *Tomorrow morning we will take a walk around the city.* ❑ *On Sunday morning the telephone woke Bill.*
2 If you say that something will happen **in the morning**, you mean that it will happen during the morning of the following day. ❑ *I'm flying to St. Louis in the morning.*
→ look at **day, time**

mort|gage /mɔrgɪdʒ/ (**mortgages**) **NOUN** A **mortgage** is a loan of money that you get from a bank in order to buy a house. ❑ *I had to sell my home because I couldn't afford the mortgage payments.*

mo|sa|ic /moʊzeɪɪk/ (**mosaics**) **NOUN** ARTS A **mosaic** is a surface that is made of small pieces of colored glass or stone. ❑ *...a Roman house with a beautiful mosaic floor.*

Mos|lem /mʌzlɪm, mʊs-/ → look up **Muslim**

mosque /mɒsk/ (**mosques**) **NOUN** A **mosque** is a building where Muslims go to pray.

M

mos|qui|to /məskitoʊ/ (**mosquitoes** or **mosquitos**) **NOUN** Mosquitos are small flying insects that bite people and animals.

moss /mɔs/ **NONCOUNT NOUN** Moss is a very small, soft, green plant that grows on wet soil, or on wood or stone. ❏ *The ground was covered with moss.*

most /moʊst/

1 You use **most of** to talk about the largest quantity of people or things. ❏ *Most of the houses here are very old.* ❏ *I was away from home most of the time.*

2 ADJECTIVE You use **most** to talk about the largest amount of people or things. ❏ *Most people think he is a great actor.*

3 PRONOUN Most is also a pronoun. ❏ *Seventeen people were hurt. Most were students.*

4 ADVERB You use **most** to show that something is true or happens more than anything else. ❏ *What do you like most about your job?*

5 If you **make the most of** something, you use it in the best possible way. ❏ *You should make the most of what you have if you want to be happy.*

most|ly /moʊstli/ **ADVERB** If something is **mostly** true, it is almost always true. ❏ *My friends are mostly students.* ❏ *Cars are made mostly of metal.*

mo|tel /moʊtɛl/ (**motels**) **NOUN** A **motel** is a hotel for people who are traveling by car.

moth /mɔθ/ (**moths**) **NOUN** A **moth** is an insect that has large wings and is attracted by lights at night.

moth|er /mʌðər/ (**mothers**) **NOUN** Your **mother** is your female parent. ❏ *She's a mother of two children.*
→ look at **family**

moth|er|hood /mʌðərhʊd/ **NONCOUNT NOUN** Motherhood is the state of being a mother. ❏ *I love motherhood. It's just the most extraordinary thing.*

mother-in-law (**mothers-in-law**) **NOUN** Someone's **mother-in-law** is the mother of their husband or wife.
→ look at **family**

mo|tion /moʊʃ°n/ **NONCOUNT NOUN** Motion is movement. ❏ *The doors will not open when the elevator is in motion.*

mo|tion|less /moʊʃ°nlɪs/ **ADJECTIVE** If someone or something is **motionless**, they are not moving at all. ❏ *They stood motionless, staring at each other.*

mo|ti|vate /moʊtɪveɪt/ (**motivates, motivating, motivated**) **VERB** If someone **motivates** you to do something, they make you feel determined to do it. ❏ *How do you motivate people to work hard?* ● **mo|ti|vat|ed ADJECTIVE** ❏ *We are looking for a highly motivated and hard-working professional.* ● **mo|ti|va|tion** /moʊtɪveɪʃ°n/ **NONCOUNT NOUN** ❏ *His poor performance is caused by lack of motivation.*

mo|tive /moʊtɪv/ (**motives**) **NOUN** Your **motive** for doing something is your reason for doing it. ❏ *Police do not think robbery was a motive for the killing.*

mo|tor /moʊtər/ (**motors**) **NOUN** The **motor** in a machine is the part that makes it move or work. ❏ *She got in the boat and started the motor.*

motor|cycle /moʊtərsaɪk°l/ (**motorcycles**) **NOUN** A **motorcycle** is a vehicle with two wheels and an engine.
→ look at **transportation**

motor|cyclist /moʊtərsaɪklɪst/ (**motorcyclists**) **NOUN** A **motorcyclist** is a person who rides a motorcycle.

mo|tor|ist /moʊtərɪst/ (**motorists**) **NOUN** A **motorist** is a person who drives a car. ❏ *Motorists should take extra care on the roads when it is raining.*

mot|to /mɒtoʊ/ (**mottoes** or **mottos**) **NOUN** A **motto** is a short sentence or phrase that gives a rule for sensible behavior. ❏ *My motto is "Don't start what you can't finish."*

mound /maʊnd/ (**mounds**)

1 NOUN A **mound** of something is a large, round pile of it. ❏ *...huge mounds of dirt.*

2 NOUN In baseball, the **mound** is the raised area where the pitcher (= the person who throws the ball) stands to throw the ball. ❏ *He went to the mound to talk with the pitcher.*

moun|tain /maʊnt°n/ (**mountains**)

1 NOUN SCIENCE GEOGRAPHY A **mountain** is a very high area of land with steep sides. ❏ *Mt. McKinley is the highest mountain in North America.*

2 A **mountain of** something is a very large amount of it. [INFORMAL] ❏ *He has a mountain of homework.*
→ look at **landform**

m

moun|tain bike (mountain bikes) **NOUN**
SPORTS A **mountain bike** is a bicycle with
a strong frame and thick tires.

moun|tain|eer /maʊntᵊnɪər/
(mountaineers) **NOUN** A **mountaineer** is a
person who is skillful at climbing the steep
sides of mountains.

moun|tain|ous /maʊntᵊnəs/ **ADJECTIVE**
A **mountainous** place has a lot of
mountains. ❏ *There were some beautiful shots
of the country's mountainous landscape.*

mourn /mɔrn/ (mourns, mourning,
mourned) **VERB** If you **mourn for** someone
who has died, you show your deep sadness
in the way that you behave. ❏ *He mourned for
his dead son.* ● **mourning NONCOUNT NOUN**
❏ *He is still in mourning for his fiancee.*

mourn|er /mɔrnər/ (mourners) **NOUN**
A **mourner** is a person who goes to a
funeral. ❏ *Crowds of mourners gathered outside
the church.*

mouse /maʊs/ (mice)
1 NOUN A **mouse** is a small animal with a
long tail. ❏ *My little sister has three pet mice.*
2 NOUN TECHNOLOGY A **mouse** is an object
that you use to do things on a computer
without using the keyboard. ❏ *I clicked the
mouse and the message appeared on the screen.*
→ look at **animal**, **computer**

mouse pad (mouse pads) also **mousepad**
NOUN TECHNOLOGY A **mouse pad** is a flat
piece of soft material that you move the
mouse on when you use a computer.
→ look at **computer**

mousse /mus/
NONCOUNT NOUN Mousse
is a sweet, light food
made from eggs and
cream. ❏ *His favorite
dessert is chocolate mousse.*

mouth /maʊθ/ (mouths)
1 NOUN SCIENCE Your **mouth** is the part of
your face that you use for eating or
speaking. ❏ *When you cough, please cover your
mouth.*
2 NOUN SCIENCE The **mouth** of a cave or a
bottle is its entrance or opening. ❏ *He
stopped at the mouth of the tunnel.*
3 NOUN GEOGRAPHY The **mouth** of a river is
the place where it goes into the ocean.
→ look at **face**

mouth|ful /maʊθfʊl/ (mouthfuls) **NOUN**
A **mouthful of** drink or food is the amount
that you can put in your mouth at one time.
❏ *She drank a mouthful of coffee.*

move /muv/ (moves, moving, moved)
1 VERB When you **move** something, you
put it in a different place. ❏ *A police officer
asked him to move his car.*
2 VERB When someone or something
moves, they change their position or go to
a different place. ❏ *The train began to move.*
❏ *She waited for him to get up, but he didn't move.*
3 NOUN Move is also a noun. ❏ *The doctor
made a move toward the door.*
4 NOUN A **move** is something you do in
order to achieve something. ❏ *Leaving my job
was a good move.*
5 VERB If you **move**, you go to live in a
different place. ❏ *She's moving to Seattle next
month.*
6 NOUN Move is also a noun. ❏ *After his move
to New York, he got a job as an actor.*
7 VERB If something **moves** you, it makes
you have strong feelings for another person.
❏ *The story surprised and moved me.* ● **moved
ADJECTIVE** ❏ *We felt quite moved when we heard
his story.*
▶ **move in** When you **move in** somewhere,
you begin to live there. ❏ *A new family has
moved in next door.*
▶ **move out** If you **move out**, you stop
living in a particular place. ❏ *I wasn't happy
living there, so I decided to move out.*

move|ment /muvmənt/ (movements)
1 NOUN Movement means changing
position, or going from one place to another.
❏ *Brian was injured and now has limited movement
in his left arm.*
2 NOUN A **movement** is a group of people
who have the same beliefs or ideas. ❏ *It was
one of the biggest political movements in the
country.*

mov|er /muvər/ (movers) **NOUN** Movers are
people whose job is to move furniture or
equipment from one building to another.

movie /muvi/ (movies)
1 NOUN A **movie** is a story that is shown in
a series of moving pictures. ❏ *Matton made
a movie about the Dutch painter Rembrandt.*
2 PLURAL NOUN If you go to **the movies**, you
go to see a movie in a movie theater. ❏ *Sam
took her to the movies last week.*
→ look at Word World: **movie**

M

Word World   **movie**

scary   good   funny   foreign

star   actor   bad

theater   DVD   favorite   romantic

ticket   rent

TV   film   see   watch

go

animation   cinema   buy

Nouns / Adjectives / Verbs

movie star (movie stars) **NOUN** A **movie star** is a famous actor or actress who acts in movies.

movie thea|ter (movie theaters) **NOUN** A **movie theater** is a place where people go to watch movies.

mov|ing /muːvɪŋ/ **ADJECTIVE** If something is **moving**, it makes you feel a strong emotion such as sadness, pity, or sympathy. ❏ *This is a moving story of the love between a master and his loyal dog.*

mow /moʊ/ (mows, mowing, mowed, mown) **VERB** If you **mow** an area of grass, you cut it using a machine (called a mower). ❏ *Connor was in the backyard, mowing the lawn.*

mower /moʊər/ **NOUN** A **mower** is a machine that you use to cut grass. ❏ *Clean the mower before and after cutting your lawn.*

moz|za|rel|la /mɑːtsərɛlə, moʊt-/ **NONCOUNT NOUN** **Mozzarella** is a type of white Italian cheese. ❏ *Maria made a delicious pizza topped with tomato and mozzarella.*

MP3 /ɛm pi θriː/ (MP3s) **NOUN** TECHNOLOGY An **MP3** is a type of computer file that contains music.

MP3 play|er (MP3 players) **NOUN** TECHNOLOGY An **MP3 player** is a small machine for listening to music that is stored on computer files.

mph also **m.p.h.** MATH **mph** shows the speed of a vehicle. **mph** is short for "miles per hour." ❏ *On this road, you must not drive faster than 20 mph.*

Mr. /mɪstər/ **NOUN** You use **Mr.** before a man's name when you want to be polite or formal. ❏ *Could I please speak to Mr. Johnson?* ❏ *Our teacher this semester is called Mr. Becker.*

Mrs. /mɪsɪz/ **NOUN** You use **Mrs.** before the name of a married woman when you want

to be polite or formal. ❏ *Hello, Mrs. Morley. How are you?* ❏ *Excuse me, does Mrs. Anne Pritchard live here?*

Ms. /mɪz/ **NOUN** You can use **Ms.**, especially in written English, before a woman's name, instead of **Mrs** or **Miss**. ❏ *Ms. Kennedy refused to speak to reporters after the meeting.*

much /mʌtʃ/

1 **ADJECTIVE** You use **much** to talk about the large amount of something. ❏ *I ate too much food.* ❏ *These plants do not need much water.* ❏ *I don't have much free time these days.*

2 **PRONOUN** **Much** is also a pronoun. ❏ *I ate too much.*

3 **ADVERB** If something does not happen **much**, it does not happen very often. ❏ *Gwen did not see her father very much.*

4 **ADVERB** **Much** means a lot. ❏ *His car is much bigger than mine.* ❏ *Thank you very much.* ❏ *He doesn't like jazz much.*

5 **ADJECTIVE** You use **how much** to ask questions about amounts. ❏ *How much money did you spend?*

> **Usage**   **much**
>
> Use **much** with noncount nouns. Here are some examples. *My dog doesn't drink **much** water. Carlos has too **much** work to do.*

mud /mʌd/ **NONCOUNT NOUN** **Mud** is a sticky mixture of earth and water. ❏ *Andy's clothes were covered with mud.*

mud|dy /mʌdi/ (muddier, muddiest) **ADJECTIVE** If something is **muddy**, it is covered in mud. ❏ *Philip left his muddy boots at the kitchen door.*

muf|fin /mʌfɪn/ (muffins) **NOUN** **Muffins** are small, round, sweet cakes that often have fruit inside. People usually eat muffins for breakfast. ❏ *Mrs. Williams handed her a blueberry muffin.*

m

mug /mʌg/ (mugs, mugging, mugged)
1 **NOUN** A **mug** is a deep cup with straight sides. ❏ *He poured tea into the mugs.*
2 **VERB** If someone **mugs** you, they attack you and steal your money. ❏ *I was walking to my car when this guy tried to mug me.* ● **mug|ging** (muggings) **NOUN** ❏ *Muggings are unusual in this neighborhood.* ● **mug|ger** (muggers) **NOUN** ❏ *When the mugger grabbed her purse, Ms. Jones fell to the ground.*

multi|col|ored /mʌltikʌlərd/ **ADJECTIVE** A **multicolored** object has many different colors. ❏ *Diego was wearing a new, multicolored shirt.*

multi|media /mʌltimidiə/ **NONCOUNT NOUN** **ARTS** **Multimedia** computer programs have sound, pictures, and film, as well as text. ❏ *Most of his teachers use multimedia in the classroom.*

multi|na|tion|al /mʌltinæʃənᵊl/ (multinationals)
1 **ADJECTIVE** A **multinational** company has offices or businesses in many different countries.
2 **NOUN** **Multinational** is also a noun. ❏ *Large multinationals control the industry.*
3 **ADJECTIVE** **Multinational** organizations involve people from several different countries. ❏ *The U.S. troops will be part of a multinational force.*

multi|ple /mʌltɪpᵊl/ **ADJECTIVE** You use **multiple** to talk about things that consist of many parts, involve many people, or have many uses. ❏ *He died of multiple injuries.*

multi|ply /mʌltɪplaɪ/ (multiplies, multiplying, multiplied) **VERB** **MATH** If you **multiply** a number, you add it to itself a certain number of times. ❏ *What do you get if you multiply six by nine?* ● **multi|pli|ca|tion** **NONCOUNT NOUN** ❏ *...a multiplication sum.*
→ look at **math**

multi|story /mʌltistɔri/ also **multistoried** **ADJECTIVE** A **multistory** building has several floors at different levels above the ground. ❏ *The store is in a big multistory building.*

mum|ble /mʌmbᵊl/ (mumbles, mumbling, mumbled)
1 **VERB** If you **mumble**, you speak quietly and not clearly. ❏ *The boy blushed and mumbled a few words.*
2 **NOUN** **Mumble** is also a noun. ❏ *His voice fell to a low mumble.*

mum|my /mʌmi/ (mummies) **NOUN** A **mummy** is a dead body that was preserved long ago by being rubbed with special oils and wrapped in cloth. ❏ *...an Ancient Egyptian mummy.*

mu|nici|pal /myunɪsɪpᵊl/ **ADJECTIVE** **SOCIAL STUDIES** **Municipal** means relating to a city or a town and its local government. ❏ *Her office was in a new municipal building in Flemington, New Jersey.*

mur|der /mɜrdər/ (murders, murdering, murdered)
1 **NOUN** **Murder** is the crime of deliberately killing a person. ❏ *The jury found him guilty of murder.* ❏ *The detective has worked on hundreds of murder cases.*
2 **VERB** If someone **murders** another person, they commit the crime of killing them deliberately. ❏ *The movie is about a woman who murders her husband.* ● **mur|der|er** /mɜrdərər/ (murderers) **NOUN** ❏ *One of these men is the murderer.*

mur|mur /mɜrmər/ (murmurs, murmuring, murmured)
1 **VERB** If you **murmur** something, you say it very quietly. ❏ *He turned and murmured something to Karen.* ❏ *"It's lovely," she murmured.*
2 **NOUN** A **murmur** is the low, soft sound of a voice or voices. ❏ *They spoke in low murmurs.*

mus|cle /mʌsᵊl/ (muscles) **NOUN** **SCIENCE** Your **muscles** are the parts inside your body that connect your bones, and that help you to move. ❏ *Exercise helps to keep your muscles strong.*

mus|cu|lar /mʌskyələr/ **ADJECTIVE** If you are **muscular**, you have strong, firm muscles. ❏ *Jordan was tall and muscular.*

mu|seum /myuziəm/ (museums) **NOUN** **ARTS** A **museum** is a building where you can look at interesting and valuable objects. ❏ *Hundreds of people came to the museum to see the exhibition.*
→ look at **city**

mush|room /mʌʃrum/ (mushrooms) **NOUN** A **mushroom** is a plant with a short stem and a round top that you can eat. ❏ *There are many types of wild mushrooms, and some of them are poisonous.*

mu|sic /myuzɪk/
1 **NONCOUNT NOUN** **MUSIC** **Music** is the pleasant sound that you make when you

Word World　**music**

note
loud
beautiful
song
singer
soft
classical
sound
melody
compose
rhythm
hear
musician
beat
listen to
write
play
instruments
harmony
sing

Nouns / Adjectives / Verbs

sing or play instruments. ❏ *Diane is studying classical music.* ❏ *What's your favorite music?*
2 **NONCOUNT NOUN** MUSIC **Music** is the symbols that you write on paper to tell people what to sing or play. ❏ *He can't read music.*
→ look at Word World: **music**

mu|si|cal /myuˈzɪkəl/ (**musicals**)
1 **ADJECTIVE** MUSIC **Musical** means relating to playing or studying music. ❏ *Many of the kids have real musical talent.*
2 **NOUN** MUSIC A **musical** is a play or a movie that uses singing and dancing in the story. ❏ *Have you seen the musical, "Miss Saigon?"*
3 **ADJECTIVE** MUSIC If you are **musical**, you have a natural ability and interest in music. ❏ *I come from a musical family.*

mu|si|cal in|stru|ment (**musical instruments**) **NOUN** MUSIC A **musical instrument** is an object such as a piano, a guitar, or a violin that you play in order to produce music. ❏ *The drum is one of the oldest musical instruments.*
→ look at Picture Dictionary: **musical instruments**

mu|si|cian /myuˈzɪʃən/ (**musicians**) **NOUN** MUSIC A **musician** is a person who plays a musical instrument as their job or hobby. ❏ *Michael is a brilliant musician.*
→ look at **music, performance**

Mus|lim /ˈmʌzlɪm, ˈmʊzlɪm/ (**Muslims**)
1 **NOUN** A **Muslim** is someone who believes in the religion of Islam and lives according to its rules.
2 **ADJECTIVE** **Muslim** means relating to Islam or Muslims. ❏ *...an ancient Muslim mosque.*

must /məst, STRONG mʌst/
1 **MODAL VERB** You use **must** to show that you think something is very important or necessary. ❏ *Your clothes must fit well.* ❏ *You must tell me everything you know.*
2 **MODAL VERB** You use **must** to show that you are almost sure that something is true. ❏ *Claire's car isn't there, so she must be at work.*

mus|tache /ˈmʌstæʃ/ (**mustaches**) **NOUN**
A man's **mustache** is the hair that grows on his upper lip. ❏ *David has a black mustache and beard.*

m

Picture Dictionary　**musical instruments**

xylophone　　trumpet　　flute　　clarinet　　cello

piano　　guitar　　violin　　saxophone　　drum

mus|tard /mʌstərd/

NONCOUNT NOUN
Mustard is a spicy yellow or brown sauce that you eat with meat. ❑ *I had a roast beef and mustard sandwich for lunch.*

mustn't /mʌsᵊnt/ **Mustn't** is short for "must not."

must've /mʌstəv/ **Must've** is short for "must have."

mut|ter /mʌtər/ (**mutters, muttering, muttered**) **VERB** If you **mutter**, you speak in a very quiet voice that is difficult to hear, often when you are angry about something. ❑ *"He's crazy," she muttered.*

mu|tu|al /myutʃuəl/ **ADJECTIVE** If a feeling or an action is **mutual**, it is felt or done by two people or groups. ❑ *It was a mutual decision by Dean and me.* ❑ *Nick didn't like me, and the feeling was mutual.*

my /maɪ/ **ADJECTIVE** You use **my** to show that something belongs or relates to yourself. ❑ *We can eat at my apartment tonight.*

my|self /maɪsɛlf/
1 **PRONOUN** You use **myself** when the person speaking or writing is both the subject and the object of the verb. ❑ *I asked myself what I should do.*
2 **PRONOUN** You use **myself** to say that you do something alone without help from anyone else. ❑ *"Where did you get that dress?"—"I made it myself".*

mys|teri|ous /mɪstɪəriəs/ **ADJECTIVE** If someone or something is **mysterious**, they are strange, and you do not know about them or understand them. ❑ *A mysterious illness made him sick.* ● **mys|teri|ous|ly** **ADVERB** ❑ *The evidence mysteriously disappeared.*

mys|tery /mɪstəri, mɪstri/ (**mysteries**)
1 **NOUN** A **mystery** is something that you cannot explain or understand. ❑ *Why he behaved in this way is a mystery.*
2 **NOUN** **LANGUAGE ARTS** A **mystery** is a story or a movie about a crime or strange events that are only explained at the end. ❑ *I was alone at home watching a murder mystery on TV.*

myth /mɪθ/ (**myths**)
1 **NOUN** **LANGUAGE ARTS** A **myth** is an ancient story about gods and magic. ❑ *...the famous Greek myth of Medusa, the snake-haired monster.*
2 **NOUN** If a belief or an explanation is a **myth**, it is not true. ❑ *This story is a myth.*

M

Nn

nag /næg/ (nags, nagging, nagged) **VERB**
If someone **nags** you, they keep asking you
to do something. ❑ *My mom's always nagging
me about getting a good job.*

nail /neɪl/ (nails, nailing, nailed)
1 **NOUN** A **nail** is a thin piece of metal
with one pointed end and one flat
end. You hit the flat end with a
hammer in order to push
the nail into a wall.
❑ *A mirror hung on a nail above the sink.*
2 **VERB** If you **nail** something somewhere,
you fasten it there using one or more nails.
❑ *The sign was nailed to a tree.*
3 **NOUN** Your **nails** are the thin hard parts
that grow at the ends of your fingers and
toes. ❑ *Try to keep your nails short.*

na|ive /naɪiv/ also **naïve** **ADJECTIVE** If
someone is **naive**, they do not have a lot of
experience, and they expect things to be
easy. ❑ *I was naive to think they would agree.*

na|ked /neɪkɪd/ **ADJECTIVE** Someone who is
naked is not wearing any clothes. ❑ *She held
the naked baby in her arms.*

name /neɪm/ (names, naming, named)
1 **NOUN** A person's **name** is the word or
words that you use to talk to them, or to talk
about them. ❑ *"What's his name?"—"Peter."*
2 **NOUN** The **name** of a place or a thing is
the word or words that you use to talk about
them. ❑ *They changed the name of the street.*
3 **VERB** When you **name** someone or
something, you give them a name. ❑ *He
named his first child Christopher after his brother.*
4 If someone **calls** you **names**, they say
unpleasant things to you. ❑ *At my last school
they called me names because I looked different than
everyone else.*
→ look at **identification**

nan|ny /næni/ (nannies) **NOUN** A **nanny** is a
person whose job is to take care of children.

nap /næp/ (naps) **NOUN** A **nap** is a short sleep
that you have, usually during the day. ❑ *We
had a nap after lunch.*

nap|kin /næpkɪn/ (napkins) **NOUN** A **napkin**
is a square of cloth or paper that you use
when you are eating to protect your clothes,
or to wipe your mouth or hands. ❑ *I ate the
sandwich and wiped my face with a paper napkin.*
→ look at **restaurant**

nar|ra|tor /næreɪtər/ (narrators) **NOUN**
LANGUAGE ARTS A **narrator** is the person who
tells the story in a book or a film. ❑ *The story's
narrator is a famous actress.*

nar|row /næroʊ/ (narrower, narrowest)
ADJECTIVE Something that is **narrow** is a
small distance from one side to the other.
❑ *We walked through the town's narrow streets.*

nas|ty /næsti/ (nastier, nastiest)
1 **ADJECTIVE** Something that is **nasty** is very
unpleasant. ❑ *The tax increase was a nasty
surprise for businesses.*
2 **ADJECTIVE** A **nasty** person is unkind or
unpleasant. ❑ *If anyone is nasty to you, you
should tell the teacher.*

na|tion /neɪʃən/ (nations) **NOUN**
SOCIAL STUDIES A **nation** is an individual
country, its people, and its social and political
structures. ❑ *...the United States and other nations.*

na|tion|al /næʃənəl/
1 **ADJECTIVE** **National** means relating to the
whole of a country or a nation. ❑ *He plays for
the Canadian national team.* ❑ *The ad appeared in
the national newspapers.*
2 **ADJECTIVE** **National** means typical of the
people or traditions of a particular country
or nation. ❑ *Baseball is the national pastime.*

na|tion|al holi|day (national holidays)
NOUN A **national holiday** is a day when
people do not go to work or to school, in
order to celebrate a special event. ❑ *Today is
a national holiday in Japan.*

na|tion|al|ism /næʃənəlɪzəm/
1 **NONCOUNT NOUN** SOCIAL STUDIES
Nationalism is a person's strong love for
their nation and their feeling that it is
better than any other nation. ❑ *Extreme
nationalism is common during wars.*

2 **NONCOUNT NOUN** SOCIAL STUDIES
Nationalism is a group's desire to become a separate country. ❑ *He gave support to Serbian nationalism.*

na|tion|al|ity /næʃənælɪti/ (**nationalities**)
NOUN SOCIAL STUDIES If you have the **nationality** of a particular country, you are a legal citizen of that country. ❑ *I'm not sure of her nationality, but I think she's Canadian.*

nation|wide /neɪʃ°nwaɪd/
1 **ADJECTIVE** **Nationwide** activities or situations happen or exist in all parts of a country. ❑ *Car crime is a nationwide problem.*
2 **ADVERB** **Nationwide** is also an adverb. ❑ *Unemployment fell nationwide last month.*

na|tive /neɪtɪv/ (**natives**)
1 **ADJECTIVE** Your **native** country, region or, town is where you were born. ❑ *It was his first visit to his native country since 1948.* ❑ *Joshua Halpern is a native Northern Californian.*
2 **NOUN** A **native of** a particular country, region, or town is someone who was born there. ❑ *Dr. Aubin is a native of St. Louis.*
3 **ADJECTIVE** Your **native** language is the first language that you learned to speak when you were a child. ❑ *Her native language was Swedish.*
→ look at **language**

Na|tive Ameri|can (**Native Americans**)
1 **NOUN** SOCIAL STUDIES **Native Americans** are people from any of the groups who were living in North America before people arrived from Europe. ❑ *Native Americans comprise about 1% of the population of the United States.*
2 **ADJECTIVE** **Native American** is also an adjective. ❑ *We want to gain a better understanding of Native American culture.*

natu|ral /nætʃərəl, nætʃrəl/
1 **ADJECTIVE** If something is **natural**, it is normal. ❑ *It is natural for young people to want excitement.*
2 **ADJECTIVE** **Natural** things exist in nature and were not created by people. ❑ *I love the natural beauty of the landscape.* ● **natu|ral|ly** **ADVERB** ❑ *Allow your hair to dry naturally in the sun.*
→ look at **energy, history, science**

natu|rali|za|tion /nætʃərəlɪzeɪʃ°n, nætʃrəl-/
NONCOUNT NOUN SOCIAL STUDIES
Naturalization is the process by which a person from one country can officially become a citizen (= member) of another

nation. ❑ *They promised to be loyal to the U.S. and they received their naturalization papers.*

natu|ral|ly /nætʃərəli, nætʃrəli/ **ADVERB**
You use **naturally** to show that something is very obvious and not surprising. ❑ *When things go wrong, we naturally feel disappointed.*

na|ture /neɪtʃər/
1 **NONCOUNT NOUN** SCIENCE **Nature** is all the animals, plants, and other things in the world that are not made by people. ❑ *The essay discusses the relationship between humans and nature.*
2 **NOUN** Someone's **nature** is their character, which they show by the way they behave. ❑ *People called her "Sunny" because of her friendly nature.*
→ look at **conservation, science**

naugh|ty /nɔti/ (**naughtier, naughtiest**)
ADJECTIVE A **naughty** child behaves badly or does not do what someone tells them to do. ❑ *When I'm very naughty, my mom sends me to bed early.*

nau|sea /nɔziə, -ʒə, -siə, -ʃə/ **NONCOUNT**
NOUN **Nausea** is a feeling that you are going to vomit. ❑ *The symptoms include headaches and nausea.*
→ look at **sick**

na|val /neɪvəl/ **ADJECTIVE** **Naval** means relating to a country's navy. ❑ *He was a senior naval officer.*

navi|gate /nævɪgeɪt/ (**navigates, navigating, navigated**)
1 **VERB** You **navigate** when you find the direction that you need to travel in, using a map or the sun, for example. ❑ *We navigated using the sun by day and the stars by night.*
2 **VERB** TECHNOLOGY If you **navigate** a website, you find the information that you need by clicking on particular words or images (= links) that take you from one web page to another. ❑ *A home page gives users information and helps them to navigate the site.*
● **navi|ga|tion** /nævɪgeɪʃ°n/ **NONCOUNT**
NOUN ❑ *The planes had their navigation lights on.*

navy /neɪvi/ (**navies**) **NOUN** A country's **navy** is the military force that can fight at sea, and the ships they use. ❑ *Her son is in the navy.*

navy blue
1 **ADJECTIVE** Something that is **navy blue** is very dark blue. ❑ *I wore navy-blue pants.*

N

2 NOUN **Navy blue** is also a noun. ❏ *She was dressed in navy blue.*

near /nɪər/ (**nearer, nearest**)
1 PREPOSITION If something is **near** a place, a thing, or a person, it is a short distance from them. ❏ *Don't come near me!* ❏ *The café is near the station in Edmonton.*
2 If something will happen **in the near future**, it will happen very soon. ❏ *I hope I'll be able to meet her sometime in the near future.*

near|by /nɪərbaɪ/
1 ADVERB If something is **nearby**, it is only a short distance away. ❏ *Her sister lives nearby.*
2 ADJECTIVE **Nearby** is also an adjective. ❏ *He sat at a nearby table.*

near|ly /nɪərli/
1 ADVERB If something is **nearly** a particular amount, it is very close to that amount but is a little less than it. ❏ *He has worked for the company for nearly 20 years.*
2 ADVERB If something is **nearly** a certain state, it is very close to that state but has not reached it. ❏ *"What time is it?"—"Nearly five o'clock."* ❏ *I've nearly finished.*

near-sighted ADJECTIVE Someone who is **near-sighted** cannot clearly see things that are far away. ❏ *She was near-sighted, so she had to wear glasses.*

neat /nit/ (**neater, neatest**)
1 ADJECTIVE A **neat** place, thing, or person is organized and clean, and has everything in the correct place. ❏ *She made sure that the apartment was clean and neat before she left.*
● **neat|ly** ADVERB ❏ *He folded his newspaper neatly and put it in his bag.*
2 ADJECTIVE If you say that someone or something is **neat**, you mean that you like them a lot. [INFORMAL] ❏ *He thought Mike was a really neat guy.*

nec|es|sary /nɛsɪsɛri/ ADJECTIVE Something that is **necessary** is needed to make something happen. ❏ *Experience is necessary for this job.* ❏ *I'm sure I've got the necessary skills for this job.*
→ look at **identification**

ne|ces|sity /nɪsɛsɪti/ (**necessities**) NOUN **Necessities** are things that you must have to live. ❏ *Water is a basic necessity of life.*

neck /nɛk/ (**necks**)
1 NOUN Your **neck** is the part of your body between your head and the rest of your body.

❏ *He was wearing a red scarf around his neck.*
2 NOUN The **neck** of a shirt or a dress is the part that surrounds your neck. ❏ *She wore a dress with a low neck.*
→ look at **body**

neck|lace /nɛklɪs/ (**necklaces**) NOUN A **necklace** is a piece of jewelry that you wear around your neck. ❏ *She was wearing a diamond necklace.*

nec|tar|ine /nɛktərin/ (**nectarines**) NOUN A **nectarine** is a red and yellow fruit with a smooth skin.

need /nid/ (**needs, needing, needed**)
1 VERB If you **need** something, you must have it. ❏ *He desperately needed money.*
2 VERB If you **need to** do something, you must do it. ❏ *I need to make a phone call.*
3 NOUN If there is a **need for** something, it is necessary to have or to do that thing. ❏ *There is a need for more schools in the area.*
4 NOUN Your **needs** are the things that are necessary for you to live or to succeed in life. ❏ *Parents have to look after their child's physical and emotional needs.*
→ look at **disability, identification, job**

nee|dle /nid³l/ (**needles**)
1 NOUN A **needle** is a small, thin metal tool with a sharp point that you use for sewing. ❏ *If you get me a needle and thread, I'll sew the button on.*
2 NOUN A **needle** is a thin hollow metal tube with a sharp point that is used for putting a drug into someone's body. ❏ *Dirty needles spread disease.*
3 NOUN On an instrument that measures speed or weight, the **needle** is the long strip of metal or plastic that moves backward and forward, showing the measurement. ❏ *The needle on the boiler is pointing to 200 degrees.*
4 NOUN **Needles** are the thin, hard, pointed parts of some trees that stay green all year. ❏ *There was a thick layer of pine needles on the ground.*

need|less /nidlɪs/ ADJECTIVE Something that is **needless** is not necessary or can be avoided. ❏ *His death was so needless.*
● **need|less|ly** ADVERB ❏ *Children are dying needlessly.*

needy /nídi/ (needier, neediest)

1 ADJECTIVE **Needy** people do not have enough food, medicine, or clothing. ❑ *They provide housing for needy families.*

2 PLURAL NOUN **The needy** are people who are needy. ❑ *We are trying to get food to the needy.*

nega|tive /nέgətɪv/

1 ADJECTIVE A **negative** situation or experience is unpleasant or harmful. ❑ *Patients talked about their negative childhood experiences.*

2 ADJECTIVE If someone is **negative** they consider only the bad aspects of a situation. ❑ *When someone asks for your opinion, don't be negative.* ● **nega|tive|ly** ADVERB ❑ *Why do so many people think negatively?*

3 ADJECTIVE A **negative** reply or decision is the answer "no." ❑ *Dr. Velayati gave a negative response.* ● **nega|tive|ly** ADVERB ❑ *Sixty percent of people answered negatively.*

4 ADJECTIVE MATH A **negative** number is less than zero. Compare with **positive**.

5 ADJECTIVE LANGUAGE ARTS In grammar, a **negative** form or word expresses the meaning "no" or "not." For example, "don't" and "haven't" are negative forms.

ne|glect /nɪglέkt/ (neglects, neglecting, neglected)

1 VERB If you **neglect** someone or something, you do not take care of them. ❑ *The neighbors claim that she is neglecting her children.*

2 NONCOUNT NOUN **Neglect** is also a noun. ❑ *The house is being repaired after years of neglect.*

neg|li|gence /nέglɪdʒ³ns/ NONCOUNT NOUN **Negligence** is when someone does not do something that they should do. ❑ *His negligence caused the accident.* ● **neg|li|gent** ADJECTIVE ❑ *The jury decided that the airline was negligent.* ● **neg|li|gent|ly** ADVERB ❑ *I believe that the physician acted negligently.*

ne|go|ti|ate /nɪgóʊʃieɪt/ (negotiates, negotiating, negotiated) VERB If people **negotiate with** each other, they talk about a problem or a situation in order to reach an agreement. ❑ *The president is willing to negotiate with the Democrats.*

ne|go|tia|tion /nɪgóʊʃieɪ³n/ (negotiations) NOUN **Negotiations** are discussions between people, during which they try to reach an agreement. ❑ *The negotiations were successful.*

neigh|bor /néɪbər/ (neighbors) NOUN Your **neighbor** is someone who lives near you. ❑ *Sometimes we invite the neighbors over for dinner.*

neigh|bor|hood /néɪbərhʊd/ (neighborhoods) NOUN A **neighborhood** is one of the parts of a town where people live. ❑ *He's from a rich Los Angeles neighborhood.*

nei|ther /níðər, náɪ-/

1 ADJECTIVE **Neither** means not one or the other of two things or people. ❑ *At first, neither man could speak.*

2 **Neither of** means not one or the other of two things or people. ❑ *Neither of us felt like going out.*

3 You use **neither...nor...** when you are talking about two or more things that are not true or that do not happen. ❑ *Professor Hisamatsu spoke neither English nor German.*

4 ADVERB **Neither** means also not. ❑ *I never learned to swim and neither did they.*

neon /níɒn/ ADJECTIVE **Neon** lights or signs are made from glass tubes filled with a special gas (= neon) that produces a bright electric light. ❑ *In the city streets the neon lights flashed.*

neph|ew /nέfyu/ (nephews) NOUN Someone's **nephew** is the son of their sister or their brother. ❑ *I am planning a birthday party for my nephew.*

nerve /nɜ́rv/ (nerves)

1 NOUN SCIENCE **Nerves** are long thin threads in your body that send messages between your brain and other parts of your body. ❑ *...pain from a damaged nerve.*

2 PLURAL NOUN Someone's **nerves** are their feelings of worry or fear. ❑ *He plays the piano to calm his nerves and relax.*

3 NONCOUNT NOUN **Nerve** is the courage that you need to do something difficult or dangerous. ❑ *I don't know why he lost his nerve.*

4 If someone or something **gets on** your **nerves**, they annoy you. [INFORMAL] ❑ *The children's noisy games were getting on his nerves.*

nerv|ous /nɜ́rvəs/ ADJECTIVE If you are **nervous**, you are frightened or worried. ❑ *I was very nervous during the job interview.* ● **nerv|ous|ly** ADVERB ❑ *Beth stood up nervously when the men came into the room.* ● **nerv|ous|ness** NONCOUNT NOUN ❑ *I smiled warmly so he wouldn't see my nervousness.*

→ look at **feeling**

N

nest /nɛst/ (nests, nesting, nested)

1 NOUN A nest is the place where a bird, a small animal, or an insect keeps its eggs or its babies.  ❑ *The cuckoo leaves its eggs in the nests of other birds.*

2 VERB When a bird **nests** somewhere, it builds a nest and lays its eggs there. ❑ *There are birds nesting on the cliffs.*
→ look at **bird**

net /nɛt/ (nets)

1 NONCOUNT NOUN Net is a material made of threads or wire with spaces in between. ❑ *There was a basketball net hanging from the garage.*

2 NOUN A net is a piece of net that you use for a particular purpose. ❑ *...a fishing net.*

3 NONCOUNT NOUN TECHNOLOGY The Net is the same as the **Internet**. ❑ *We've been on the Net since 1993.*

4 NOUN SPORTS In basketball, the net is the loose material that hangs down from the metal ring that you put the ball through.

5 NOUN SPORTS In tennis, the net is the object that you hit the ball over.

net|work /nɛtwɜrk/ (networks)

1 NOUN A radio or a television **network** is a company that broadcasts radio or television programs in a particular area. ❑ *He was a sports presenter on a local TV network.*

2 NOUN TECHNOLOGY A **network of** people or things is a large number of them that have a connection with each other and that work together. ❑ *She has a strong network of friends and family to help her.* ❑ *Their computers are connected on a wireless network.*
→ look at **Internet, phone**

neu|tral /nutrəl/

1 ADJECTIVE SOCIAL STUDIES A **neutral** person or country does not support either side in an argument or a war. ❑ *Let's meet on neutral territory.*

2 ADJECTIVE If you have a **neutral** expression or a **neutral** voice, you do not show what you are thinking or feeling. ❑ *Isabel said in a neutral voice, "You're very late, darling."*

3 NONCOUNT NOUN Neutral is the position between the gears of a vehicle, in which the gears are not connected to the engine. ❑ *She put the truck in neutral and started it again.*

nev|er /nɛvər/ ADVERB Never means at no time in the past, the present, or the future. ❑ *I have never been abroad before.* ❑ *That was a mistake. I'll never do it again.* ❑ *Never look directly at the sun.*

never|the|less /nɛvərðəlɛs/ ADVERB **Nevertheless** means "although something is true." [FORMAL] ❑ *Leon had problems, but nevertheless managed to finish his most famous painting.*

new /nu/ (newer, newest)

1 ADJECTIVE Something that is **new** has been recently created or invented. ❑ *They've just opened a new hotel.* ❑ *These ideas are not new.*

2 ADJECTIVE Something that is **new** has not been used or owned by anyone. ❑ *That afternoon she went out and bought a new dress.* ❑ *There are many boats, new and used, for sale.*

3 ADJECTIVE New describes someone or something that has replaced another person or thing. ❑ *I had to find somewhere new to live.* ❑ *Rachel has a new boyfriend.*
→ look at **car, job, shopping, wear**

new|born /nuborn/ ADJECTIVE A **newborn** baby or animal is one that has just been born. ❑ *...a mother and her newborn child.*

new|comer /nukʌmər/ (newcomers) NOUN A **newcomer** is a person who has recently arrived in a place. ❑ *She's a newcomer to Salt Lake City.*

new|ly /nuli/ ADVERB You can use **newly** to show that an action or a situation is very recent. ❑ *She was young at the time, and newly married.*

news /nuz/

1 NONCOUNT NOUN News is information about recent events. ❑ *We waited and waited for news of him.* ❑ *I've just had some bad news.*

2 NONCOUNT NOUN News is information about recent events that is reported in newspapers, or on the radio, television, or Internet. ❑ *Here are some of the top stories in the news.*

n

Word World　**news**

local　daily　good　international

media　important　bad　latest　listen to

newspaper　radio　read

website　podcast　magazine　make　see　watch

headline　television　hear

Nouns / Adjectives / Verbs

3 NOUN **The news** is a television or radio program that gives information about recent events. ❑ *I heard all about the bombs on the news.*
→ look at Word World: **news**
→ look at **television**

N

news\letter /núzlɛtər/ (**newsletters**) NOUN
A **newsletter** is a report giving information about an organization that is sent regularly to its members. ❑ *All members receive a free monthly newsletter.*

news\paper /núzpeɪpər, nús-/ (**newspapers**) NOUN A **newspaper** is a number of large sheets of folded paper, with news, advertisements, and other information printed on them. ❑ *They read about it in the newspaper.*
→ look at **news**

New Year's Day NONCOUNT NOUN
New Year's Day is the time when people celebrate the start of a year.

next /nɛkst/
1 ADJECTIVE The **next** thing is the one that comes immediately after this one or after the previous one. ❑ *I got up early the next morning.* ❑ *I took the next available flight.* ❑ *Who will be the next mayor?*
2 ADJECTIVE You use **next** to talk about the first day, week, or year that comes after this one or the previous one. ❑ *Let's go see a movie next week.* ❑ *He retires next January.*

3 ADJECTIVE The **next** place is the one that is nearest to you. ❑ *There was a party going on in the next room.*
4 ADVERB The thing that happens **next** is the thing that happens immediately after something else. ❑ *I don't know what to do next.*
5 If one thing is **next to** another, it is at the side of it. ❑ *She sat down next to him on the sofa.*
→ look at **calendar**

nib\ble /níbəl/ (**nibbles, nibbling, nibbled**)
VERB If you **nibble** food, you eat it by biting very small pieces of it. ❑ *She nibbled at a piece of bread.*

nice /naɪs/ (**nicer, nicest**)
1 ADJECTIVE If something is **nice**, it is attractive, pleasant, or enjoyable. ❑ *The chocolate-chip cookies were nice.* ❑ *It's nice to be here together again.* ● **nice\ly** ADVERB ❑ *The book is nicely illustrated.*
2 ADJECTIVE If someone is **nice**, they are friendly and pleasant. ❑ *I've met your father and he's very nice.* ❑ *They were extremely nice to me.* ● **nice\ly** ADVERB ❑ *He treated you nicely.*

nick\el /níkəl/ (**nickels**)
1 NONCOUNT NOUN **Nickel** is a hard, silver-colored metal.
2 NOUN In the United States and Canada, a **nickel** is a coin that is worth five cents. ❑ *The large glass jar was filled with nickels, dimes, and quarters.*

nick\name /níkneɪm/ (**nicknames, nicknaming, nicknamed**)
1 NOUN A **nickname** is an informal name

for someone or something. ❑ *Red got his nickname for his red hair.*

2 **VERB** If you **nickname** someone or something, you give them an informal name. ❑ *The children nicknamed him "The Giraffe" because he was so tall.*

niece /ni̱s/ (**nieces**) **NOUN** Someone's **niece** is the daughter of their sister or their brother. ❑ *He bought a present for his niece.*

night /na̱ɪt/ (**nights**)

1 **NOUN** The **night** is the time when it is dark outside, and most people sleep. ❑ *The rain continued all night.* ❑ *It was a dark, cold night.* ❑ *It's eleven o'clock at night in Moscow.*

2 **NOUN** The **night** is the period of time between the end of the afternoon and the time that you go to bed. ❑ *Did you go to Kelly's party last night?*

→ look at **time**

night|gown /na̱ɪtgaʊn/ (**nightgowns**) **NOUN** A **nightgown** is a loose dress that a woman or a girl wears in bed.

night|ly /na̱ɪtli/

1 **ADJECTIVE** A **nightly** event happens every night. ❑ *We watched the nightly news.*

2 **ADVERB** **Nightly** is also an adverb. ❑ *She appears nightly on the television news.*

night|mare /na̱ɪtmɛər/ (**nightmares**)

1 **NOUN** A **nightmare** is a very frightening dream. ❑ *She had nightmares for weeks after seeing that movie.*

2 **NOUN** If a situation is a **nightmare**, it is very unpleasant. ❑ *New York traffic is a nightmare.*

nine /na̱ɪn/ **MATH** **Nine** is the number 9.
→ look at **number**

nine-eleven /na̱ɪn ɪle̱vᵊn/ or **nine eleven, 9/11** **NOUN** You can use **9/11** or **nine-eleven** to talk about the attacks that took place in the United States on September 11, 2001. ❑ *Everything changed after nine-eleven.*

Word Builder   **nineteen**

teen ≈ **plus ten, from 13-19**

     eight + teen = eighteen
     four + teen = fourteen
     nine + teen = nineteen
     seven + teen = seventeen
     six + teen = sixteen
     teen + age = teenage

---

nine|teen /na̱ɪnti̱n/ **MATH** **Nineteen** is the number 19.

nine|ty /na̱ɪnti/ **MATH** **Ninety** is the number 90.

ninth /na̱ɪnθ/ (**ninths**)

1 **ADJECTIVE, ADVERB** **MATH** The **ninth** item in a series is the one that you count as number nine. ❑ *...January the ninth.* ❑ *...students in the ninth grade.*

2 **NOUN** **MATH** A **ninth** is one of nine equal parts of something (⅑). ❑ *The area covers one-ninth of the Earth's surface.*

→ look at **number**

Sound Partners   no, know

---

no /no̱ʊ/

1 You use **no** to give a negative response to a question. ❑ *"Are you having any problems?"—"No, I'm O.K." ❑ "Here, have mine."—"No, thanks; this is fine." ❑ "Can I have another cookie?"—"No; you've had enough."*

2 **EXCLAMATION** You use **no** when you are shocked or disappointed about something. ❑ *Oh no, not again.*

3 **ADJECTIVE** **No** means not any or not one person or thing. ❑ *He had no intention of paying.* ❑ *In this game, there are no rules.*

4 **ADJECTIVE** **No** is used in notices to say that something is not allowed. ❑ *...no parking.* ❑ *...NO ENTRY.*

No. (**Nos**) **No.** is short for **number**. ❑ *He was named the nation's No.1 college football star.*

no|body /no̱ʊbɒdi, -bʌdi/ **PRONOUN** **Nobody** means not a single person. ❑ *For a long time nobody spoke.*

nod /nɒ̱d/ (**nods, nodding, nodded**)

1 **VERB** If you **nod**, you move your head downward and upward to show that you are answering "yes" to a question, or to show that you agree. ❑ *"Are you okay?" I asked. She nodded and smiled.*

2 **NOUN** **Nod** is also a noun. ❑ *She gave a nod and said, "I see."*

noise /nɔ̱ɪz/ (**noises**)

1 **NONCOUNT NOUN** **Noise** is a loud sound. ❑ *I'll never forget the noise from the crowd at the end of the game.*

2 **NOUN** A **noise** is a sound that someone or something makes. ❑ *Suddenly there was a noise like thunder.*

noisy /nɔ̱ɪzi/ (**noisier, noisiest**)

1 **ADJECTIVE** A **noisy** person or thing makes a lot of loud or unpleasant noise. ❑ *It was a car with a particularly noisy engine.* ● **noisi|ly** **ADVERB** ❑ *The students cheered noisily.*

n

2 **ADJECTIVE** A **noisy** place is full of a lot of loud or unpleasant noise. ❑ *The airport was crowded and noisy.*
→ look at **factory**

nomi|nate /nɒmɪneɪt/ (**nominates, nominating, nominated**) **VERB** If you **nominate** someone, you formally suggest their name for a job, a position, or a prize. ❑ *He was nominated by the Democratic Party for the presidency of the United States.*

nomi|na|tion /nɒmɪneɪʃⁿn/ (**nominations**) **NOUN** A **nomination** is an official suggestion that someone should be considered for a job, a position, or a prize. ❑ *He'll probably get a nomination for best actor.*

non|count noun /nɒnkaʊnt naʊn/ (**noncount nouns**) **NOUN** LANGUAGE ARTS A **noncount noun** is a noun that has only one form and that you cannot use with "a" or "one." ❑ *A noncount noun, such as "baggage," "silver," or "advice," does not form a plural.*

none /nʌn/
1 **None of** something means not one or not any. ❑ *None of us knew her.*
2 **PRONOUN None** is also a pronoun. ❑ *I searched the Internet for information, but found none.*

none|the|less /nʌnðələs/ **ADVERB**
Nonetheless means "although something is true." [FORMAL] ❑ *There is still a long way to go. Nonetheless, some progress has been made.*

Word Builder	nonfat
non ≈ **not**	
non + fat = nonfat	
non + fiction = nonfiction	
non + sense = nonsense	
non + stop = nonstop	

non|fat /nɒnfæt/ **ADJECTIVE Nonfat** food and drinks have very little or no fat in them. ❑ *A glass of nonfat milk contains about 80 calories.*

Word Builder	nonfiction
non ≈ **not**	
non + fat = nonfat	
non + fiction = nonfiction	
non + sense = nonsense	
non + stop = nonstop	

non|fic|tion /nɒnfɪkʃⁿn/ **NONCOUNT NOUN** LANGUAGE ARTS **Nonfiction** is writing that is about real people and events rather than imaginary ones. ❑ *The school library contains both fiction and nonfiction.*

Word Builder	nonsense
non ≈ **not**	
non + fat = nonfat	
non + fiction = nonfiction	
non + sense = nonsense	
non + stop = nonstop	

non|sense /nɒnsɛns, -səns/ **NONCOUNT NOUN** If something is **nonsense**, it is not true or it is silly. ❑ *Most doctors say that this idea is complete nonsense.* ❑ *Peter said I was talking nonsense.*

Word Builder	nonstop
non ≈ **not**	
non + fat = nonfat	
non + fiction = nonfiction	
non + sense = nonsense	
non + stop = nonstop	

non|stop /nɒnstɒp/
1 **ADJECTIVE** Something that is **nonstop** continues without stopping. ❑ *A nonstop flight from London takes you straight to Antigua.*
2 **ADVERB Nonstop** is also an adverb. ❑ *We drove nonstop from New York to Miami.*

noo|dle /nuːdⁿl/ (**noodles**) **NOUN** Noodles are long, thin strips of pasta (= a type of food made from eggs, flour and water). They are used especially in Chinese and Italian cooking.

noon /nuːn/ **NONCOUNT NOUN** Noon is twelve o'clock in the middle of the day. ❑ *The meeting started at noon.*
→ look at **day, time**

no one **PRONOUN** No one means not a single person, or not a single member of a particular group or set. ❑ *We asked everyone in the room, but no one wanted to help.*

noon|time /nuːntaɪm/ **NONCOUNT NOUN** **Noontime** is the middle part of the day. ❑ *He always came home for a hot meal at noontime.*

nor /nɔr/ **CONJUNCTION** You use **nor** after "neither" to introduce the second of two negative things. ❑ *Neither his friends nor his family knew how old he was.*

norm /nɔrm/ **NOUN** If a situation is **the norm**, it is usual and expected. ❑ *Families of six or seven are the norm in here.*

nor|mal /nɔrmⁿl/ **ADJECTIVE** Something that is **normal** is usual and ordinary. ❑ *Her height and weight are normal for her age.*

N

nor|mal|ly /nɔrməli/

1 ADVERB If something **normally** happens, it usually happens. ❑ *Normally the bill is less than $30 a month.* ❑ *I normally get up at 7 a.m. for work.*

2 ADVERB If you do something **normally**, you do it in the usual or ordinary way. ❑ *She's getting better and beginning to eat normally again.*

north /nɔrθ/ also **North**

1 NONCOUNT NOUN GEOGRAPHY The **north** is the direction that is on your left when you are looking at the sun in the morning. ❑ *In the north, snow and ice cover the ground.* ❑ *He lives in the north of Canada.*

2 ADVERB GEOGRAPHY If you go **north**, you travel toward the north. ❑ *Anita drove north up Pacific Highway.*

3 ADJECTIVE The **north** part of a place is the part that is toward the north. ❑ *...North America.*

4 ADJECTIVE A **north** wind is a wind that blows from the north. ❑ *A cold north wind was blowing.*

→ look at **globe**

north|east /nɔrθist/

1 NONCOUNT NOUN GEOGRAPHY The **northeast** is the direction that is between north and east. ❑ *They live in Jerusalem, more than 250 miles to the northeast.*

2 ADJECTIVE GEOGRAPHY **Northeast** means in or from the northeast. ❑ *...northeast Louisiana.*

north|eastern /nɔrθistərn/ ADJECTIVE GEOGRAPHY **Northeastern** means in or from the northeast part of a place. ❑ *Ian comes from northeastern England.*

nor|ther|ly /nɔrðərli/

1 ADJECTIVE GEOGRAPHY **Northerly** means to the north or toward the north. ❑ *The storm is moving in a northerly direction.*

2 ADJECTIVE A **northerly** wind blows from the north. ❑ *...a cold northerly wind.*

north|ern /nɔrðərn/ also **Northern**

ADJECTIVE GEOGRAPHY **Northern** means in or from the north of a place. ❑ *...Northern Ireland.*

north|west /nɔrθwɛst/

1 NONCOUNT NOUN GEOGRAPHY The **northwest** is the direction that is between north and west.

2 ADJECTIVE GEOGRAPHY **Northwest** means in or from the northwest.

north|western /nɔrθwɛstərn/ ADJECTIVE GEOGRAPHY **Northwestern** means in or from the northwest part of a place.

nose /noʊz/ (**noses**) NOUN Your **nose** is the part of your face that sticks out above your mouth. You use it for smelling and for breathing. ❑ *She wiped her nose with a tissue.*

→ look at **face, sense**

no-show (**no-shows**) NOUN A **no-show** is someone who is expected to be at a place, but who does not arrive. ❑ *Williams was a no-show at last week's game in Milwaukee.*

nos|tril /nɒstrɪl/ (**nostrils**) NOUN SCIENCE Your **nostrils** are the two holes at the end of your nose. ❑ *Keeping your mouth closed, breathe in through your nostrils.*

not /nɒt/

> **LANGUAGE HELP**
>
> Use the short form **n't** when you are speaking English. For example, "didn't" is short for "did not."

ADVERB You use **not** to form negative sentences. ❑ *Their plan was not working.* ❑ *I don't trust Peter anymore.* **Not at all** is a strong way of saying "No" or of agreeing that the answer to a question is "No." ❑ *"Sorry, am I bothering you?"—"No. Not at all."*

note /noʊt/ (**notes**)

1 NOUN A **note** is a short letter. ❑ *Steven wrote her a note and left it on the table.*

2 NOUN A **note** is something that you write down to remind yourself of something. ❑ *She didn't take notes on the lecture.*

3 NOUN In a book or an article, a **note** is a short piece of extra information. ❑ *See Note 16 on p. 223.*

4 NOUN MUSIC A **note** is one particular sound, or a symbol that represents this sound. ❑ *She has a deep voice and can't sing high notes.*

→ look at **music**

> **Word Partners** Use **note** with:
>
> v.   leave a note, send a note **1**
>   find a note, read a note, scribble a note, write a note **1** **2**
>   make a note **2**

note|book /noʊtbʊk/ (**notebooks**)

1 NOUN A **notebook** is a small book for writing notes in. ❑ *He took a notebook and pen from his pocket.*

2 NOUN TECHNOLOGY A **notebook** computer is a small personal computer

n

that you can carry with you. ❏ *She watched the DVD on her notebook computer.*
→ look at **office**

noth|ing /nʌθɪŋ/ **PRONOUN** Nothing means not a single thing, or not a single part of something. ❏ *There is nothing wrong with the car.* ❏ *There was nothing in the refrigerator except some butter.*

no|tice /noʊtɪs/ (**notices, noticing, noticed**)
1 **VERB** If you **notice** something or someone, you become aware of them. ❏ *Did you notice anything unusual about him?* ❏ *She noticed he was acting strangely.* ❏ *Luckily, I noticed where you left the car.*
2 **NOUN** A **notice** is a piece of writing in a place where everyone can read it. ❏ *She posted a notice on the bulletin board.* ❏ *The notice said "Please close the door."*
3 **NONCOUNT NOUN** If you give **notice** about something that is going to happen, you give a warning in advance that it is going to happen. ❏ *They moved her to a different office without notice.* ❏ *You must give 30 days' notice if you want to cancel the contract.*

no|tice|able /noʊtɪsəbəl/ **ADJECTIVE** Something that is **noticeable** is easy to see, hear, or recognize. ❏ *This hotel is slightly more expensive, but the difference is noticeable.*

no|ti|fy /noʊtɪfaɪ/ (**notifies, notifying, notified**) **VERB** If you **notify** someone of something, you officially tell them about it. [FORMAL] ❏ *We have notified the police.*

noun /naʊn/ (**nouns**) **NOUN** LANGUAGE ARTS A **noun** is a word such as "car," "love," or "Anne" that is used for talking about a person or a thing.
→ look at **grammar**

nour|ish /nɜrɪʃ/ (**nourishes, nourishing, nourished**) **VERB** To **nourish** a person, an animal, or a plant means to give them the food that they need to live, grow, and be healthy. ❏ *The food she eats nourishes both her and the baby.* ● **nour|ish|ing** **ADJECTIVE** ❏ *...nourishing home-cooked food.*
● **nour|ish|ment** **NONCOUNT NOUN** ❏ *These delicious drinks will provide sick children with the nourishment they need to recover.*

nov|el /nɒvəl/ (**novels**) **NOUN** LANGUAGE ARTS A **novel** is a long written story about imaginary people and events. ❏ *He's reading a novel by Herman Hesse.*

Word Builder **novelist**
ist ≈ **person who does this**
art + ist = artist
guitar + ist = guitarist
journal + ist = journalist
novel + ist = novelist

nov|el|ist /nɒvəlɪst/ (**novelists**) **NOUN** LANGUAGE ARTS A **novelist** is a person who writes novels (= long written stories about imaginary people and events). ❏ *He was one of America's great novelists.*

nov|el|ty /nɒvəlti/ (**novelties**) **NOUN** A **novelty** is something that is new and interesting. ❏ *Tourists are still a novelty on the island.*

No|vem|ber /noʊvɛmbər/ **NOUN** November is the eleventh month of the year. ❏ *He came to New York in November 1939.*

now /naʊ/
1 **ADVERB** You use **now** to talk about the present time. ❏ *I must go now.* ❏ *She should know that by now.*
2 **PRONOUN** Now is also a pronoun. ❏ *Now is your chance to talk to him.*
3 **CONJUNCTION** You use **now** or **now that** to show that something has happened, and as a result something else will happen. ❏ *Now that our children are older, I have time to help other people.*
4 If something happens **now and then** or **every now and again**, it happens sometimes but not very often or regularly. ❏ *Now and then they heard the sound of a heavy truck outside.*

nowa|days /naʊədeɪz/ **ADVERB** Nowadays means now generally, and not in the past. ❏ *Nowadays almost all children spend some time playing electronic and computer games.*

no|where /noʊwɛər/ **ADVERB** You use **nowhere** to mean "not in any place" or "not to any place." ❏ *Nowhere is the problem worse than in Asia.* ❏ *I have nowhere else to go.*

nu|clear /nukliər/ **ADJECTIVE** SCIENCE Nuclear describes the energy that is released when the central parts (= nuclei) of atoms are split or combined. ❏ *We're building a nuclear power station.* ❏ *They don't have any nuclear weapons.*
→ look at **energy**

nu|cleus /nukliəs/ (**nuclei** /nukliaɪ/) **NOUN** SCIENCE The **nucleus** of an atom or cell is the central part of it.

nude /nud/ (nudes)
1 **ADJECTIVE** A **nude** person is not wearing any clothes. ❏ *She came into the room, almost completely nude.*
2 **NOUN** ARTS A **nude** is a painting or a piece of art that shows someone who is not wearing any clothes.

nudge /nʌdʒ/ (nudges, nudging, nudged)
1 **VERB** If you **nudge** someone, you push them gently, usually with your elbow. ❏ *I nudged Stan and pointed again.*
2 **NOUN** **Nudge** is also a noun. ❏ *She gave him a nudge.*

nui|sance /nusᵊns/ (nuisances) **NOUN**
If someone or something is a **nuisance**, they annoy you. ❏ *He can be a bit of a nuisance sometimes.*

numb /nʌm/ (number, numbest) **ADJECTIVE**
If a part of your body is **numb**, you cannot feel anything there. ❏ *It was so cold that his fingers were numb.*

num|ber /nʌmbər/ (numbers, numbering, numbered)
1 **NOUN** MATH A **number** is a word such as "two," "nine," or "twelve," or a symbol such as 1, 3, or 47 that is used in counting. ❏ *I don't know my room number.* ❏ *What's your phone number?*
2 **NOUN** You use **number** with words such as "large" or "small" to say approximately how many things or people there are.
❏ *I received a large number of emails on the subject.*
3 **VERB** If you **number** something, you mark it with a number, usually starting at 1. ❏ *He cut the paper up into tiny squares, and he numbered each one.*
→ look at Picture Dictionary: **numbers**
→ look at **ATM, math, phone**

nu|mer|al /numərəl/ (numerals) **NOUN**
MATH **Numerals** are written symbols that represent numbers. ❏ *The Roman numeral for 7 is VII.*

nu|mer|ous /numərəs/ **ADJECTIVE** If people or things are **numerous**, they exist in large numbers. ❏ *He made numerous attempts to lose weight.*

nun /nʌn/ (nuns) **NOUN** A **nun** is a member of a group of religious women who often live together in a special building. ❏ *When I was seventeen, I decided to become a nun.*

nurse /nɜrs/ (nurses, nursing, nursed)
1 **NOUN** A **nurse** is a person whose job is to care for people who are sick. ❏ *She thanked the nurses who cared for her.*
2 **VERB** If you **nurse** someone, you care for them when they are sick. ❏ *My mother has nursed him for the last ten years.*

nurse|ry /nɜrsəri/ (nurseries)
1 **NOUN** A **nursery** is a place where people grow and sell plants. ❏ *Buy your plants at the local nursery.*
2 **NOUN** A **nursery** is a room in a family home in which the young children of the family sleep or play. ❏ *We painted bright pictures on the walls in the children's nursery.*

nurse|ry rhyme (nursery rhymes) **NOUN**
A **nursery rhyme** is a poem or a song for young children.

nurs|ing home (nursing homes) **NOUN**
A **nursing home** is a place where old or sick people live. ❏ *He died in a nursing home in Florida at the age of 87.*

nut /nʌt/ (nuts)

1 **NOUN** A **nut** is a dry fruit with a hard shell.
❏ *Nuts and seeds are very good for you.*
2 **NOUN** A **nut** is a thick metal ring that you put onto a bolt (= a long piece of metal). Nuts and bolts are used for holding heavy things together.
❏ *If you want to repair the wheels, you must remove the four nuts.*

n

Picture Dictionary			numbers			
1	one	1st	first	7	seven	7th	seventh
2	two	2nd	second	8	eight	8th	eighth
3	three	3rd	third	9	nine	9th	ninth
4	four	4th	fourth	10	ten	10th	tenth
5	five	5th	fifth	11	eleven	11th	eleventh
6	six	6th	sixth	12	twelve	12th	twelfth

3 NOUN If someone is a baseball **nut** or a health **nut**, for example, they are very enthusiastic about that activity. [INFORMAL] ❑ *It is possible to stay healthy without being a health nut.*

4 ADJECTIVE If you are **nuts about** something or someone, you like them very much. [INFORMAL] ❑ *She's nuts about you and you're in love with her.*

5 ADJECTIVE If someone is **nuts**, they are crazy. [INFORMAL] ❑ *You guys are nuts.*

nu|tri|ent /n<u>u</u>triənt/ (nutrients) NOUN SCIENCE **Nutrients** are substances that help plants and animals to grow and stay healthy. ❑ *The juice contains vitamins, minerals, and other essential nutrients.*

nu|tri|tion /nutr<u>ɪ</u>ʃ°n/ NONCOUNT NOUN **Nutrition** is the way that the body uses the food that it needs to grow and stay healthy. ❑ *He talked to the children about the importance of good nutrition and exercise.*
→ look at **eat**

ny|lon /n<u>aɪ</u>lɒn/ NONCOUNT NOUN **Nylon** is a strong, artificial cloth. ❑ *I packed a sleeping bag, a pocket knife, and some strong nylon rope.*

N

Oo

oak /oʊk/ (oaks)
1 **NOUN** An **oak** or an **oak tree** is a type of large tree.
2 **NONCOUNT NOUN** Oak is the wood of this tree. ❑ *He sat down at the oak table.*
→ look at **tree**

oar /ɔr/ (oars) **NOUN**
Oars are long poles with one flat end that you use for rowing a boat.

oasis /oʊeɪsɪs/ (oases /oʊeɪsiz/) **NOUN**
GEOGRAPHY An **oasis** is a small area in a desert where you find water and plants.

oat|meal /oʊtmil/ **NONCOUNT NOUN**
Oatmeal is a hot, thick food that people eat for breakfast. It is made from oats cooked in water or milk.

oats /oʊts/ **PLURAL NOUN** Oats are a type of grain that is used in foods.

obedi|ent /oʊbidiənt/ **ADJECTIVE** A person or an animal that is **obedient** does what they are told to do. ❑ *As a child, Charlotte was an obedient daughter.* ● **obedi|ence** /oʊbidiəns/
NONCOUNT NOUN ❑ *He expected complete obedience from his sons.* ● **obedi|ent|ly** **ADVERB**
❑ *The dog sat beside him obediently.*

obese /oʊbis/ **ADJECTIVE** If someone is **obese**, they are very fat, in a way that is not healthy. ❑ *Obese people often have more health problems than thinner people.*

obey /oʊbeɪ/ (obeys, obeying, obeyed) **VERB**
If you **obey** a person or a command, you do what you are told to do. ❑ *Most people obey the law.*

ob|ject (objects, objecting, objected)

> **PRONUNCIATION HELP**
> Pronounce the noun /ɒbdʒɪkt/. Pronounce the verb /əbdʒɛkt/.

1 **NOUN** An **object** is a thing that has a shape, and that is not alive. ❑ *I have to wear glasses because I can't see distant objects clearly.*

❑ *We could hear someone throwing small, hard objects on to the roof.*
2 **NOUN** The **object** of what someone is doing is their purpose. ❑ *The object of the event is to raise money.*
3 **NOUN** LANGUAGE ARTS In grammar, the **object** of a verb is the person or thing that is affected by the action.
4 **VERB** If you **object** to something, you say that you do not agree with it, or that you do not like it. ❑ *A lot of people objected to the book.*

ob|jec|tion /əbdʒɛkʃən/ (objections) **NOUN**
If you state an **objection**, you say that you do not like or agree with something. ❑ *I don't have any objection to people making money.*

ob|jec|tive /əbdʒɛktɪv/ (objectives) **NOUN**
Your **objective** is what you are trying to achieve. ❑ *Our main objective was to find the child.*

ob|li|ga|tion /ɒblɪgeɪʃən/ (obligations)
NOUN If you have an **obligation to** do something, you should do it. ❑ *The judge has an obligation to find out the truth.*

ob|liga|tory /əblɪgətɔri/ **ADJECTIVE** If something is **obligatory**, you must do it because of a rule or a law. ❑ *These medical tests are not obligatory.*

oblige /əblaɪdʒ/ (obliges, obliging, obliged)
VERB If you **are obliged to** do something, a situation or law makes it necessary for you to do it. ❑ *My family needed the money so I was obliged to work.*

ob|long /ɒblɔŋ/ (oblongs) **NOUN** MATH
An **oblong** is a shape that has two long sides and two short sides. ❑ *Ten people sat around a large oblong table.*

oboe /oʊboʊ/ (oboes) **NOUN** MUSIC An **oboe** is a musical instrument that you blow. It is a long black wooden tube with keys on it that you press, and a double reed (= small flat part that moves and makes a sound when you blow).

ob|scene /əbsin/ **ADJECTIVE** Something that is **obscene** offends you because it relates to sex or violence in an unpleasant and shocking way. ❑ *...obscene photographs.*

ob|serve /əbzɜrv/ (**observes, observing, observed**) **VERB** If you **observe** a person or thing, you watch them carefully in order to learn something about them. ❑ *Olson observed the behavior of babies.*
→ look at **climate, science**

ob|ses|sion /əbsɛʃ°n/ (**obsessions**) **NOUN** If someone has an **obsession** with a person or thing, they spend too much time thinking about them. ❑ *She tried to forget her obsession with Christopher.*

ob|sta|cle /ɒbstək°l/ (**obstacles**) **NOUN** An **obstacle** is something that makes it difficult for you to do what you want to do. ❑ *We had to overcome two major obstacles.*

ob|sti|nate /ɒbstɪnɪt/ **ADJECTIVE** An **obstinate** person is determined to do what they want, and you cannot persuade them to do something else. ❑ *When she says "no," nothing can make her change, and she can be very obstinate.*

ob|struct /əbstrʌkt/ (**obstructs, obstructing, obstructed**) **VERB** If someone or something **obstructs** a place, they block it, making it difficult for you to get past. ❑ *A group of cars obstructed the road.*

ob|struc|tion /əbstrʌkʃ°n/ (**obstructions**) **NOUN** An **obstruction** is something that blocks a road or path. ❑ *The cars outside his house were causing an obstruction.*

ob|tain /əbteɪn/ (**obtains, obtaining, obtained**) **VERB** To **obtain** something means to get it. [FORMAL] ❑ *Evans tried to obtain a false passport.*

ob|vi|ous /ɒbviəs/ **ADJECTIVE** If something is **obvious**, it is easy to see or understand. ❑ *It's obvious that he's worried about us.*

Word Partners	Use **obvious** with:
N.	obvious **answer**, obvious **choice**, obvious **differences**, obvious **example**, obvious **question**, obvious **reasons**, obvious **solution**

ob|vi|ous|ly /ɒbviəsli/ **ADVERB** You use **obviously** to show that something is easily noticed, seen, or recognized. ❑ *He obviously likes you very much.*

oc|ca|sion /əkeɪʒ°n/ (**occasions**)
1 **NOUN** An **occasion** is a time when something happens. ❑ *I gave her money on several occasions.*
2 **NOUN** An **occasion** is an important event, ceremony, or celebration. ❑ *The wedding was a happy occasion.*

oc|ca|sion|al /əkeɪʒən°l/ **ADJECTIVE** **Occasional** means happening sometimes, but not often. ❑ *I get occasional headaches.*
● **oc|ca|sion|al|ly** **ADVERB** ❑ *He misbehaves occasionally.*

oc|cu|pant /ɒkyəpənt/ (**occupants**) **NOUN** The **occupants** of a building or a room are the people who live or work there. ❑ *Most of the occupants left the building before the fire spread.*

oc|cu|pa|tion /ɒkyəpeɪʃ°n/ (**occupations**)
1 **NOUN** Your **occupation** is your job. ❑ *Please write down your name and occupation.*
2 **NOUN** An **occupation** is something that you spend time doing, either for fun or because it needs to be done. ❑ *Cooking was his favorite occupation.*
3 **NONCOUNT NOUN** The **occupation** of a country happens when a foreign army enters it and controls it. ❑ *She lived in France during Nazi Germany's occupation.*

oc|cu|py /ɒkyəpaɪ/ (**occupies, occupying, occupied**)
1 **VERB** The people who **occupy** a place are the people who live or work there. ❑ *The company occupies the top floor of the building.*
2 **VERB** If a room or a seat **is occupied**, someone is using it. ❑ *The chair was occupied by his wife.*
3 **VERB** If an army **occupies** a place, they move into it and use force to control it. ❑ *U.S. forces occupy a part of the country.*
4 **VERB** If something **occupies** you or your mind, you are busy doing it or thinking about it. ❑ *Her career occupies all of her time.*
● **oc|cu|pied** **ADJECTIVE** ❑ *Don't get bored. Keep your brain occupied.*

oc|cur /əkɜr/ (**occurs, occurring, occurred**)
1 **VERB** When something **occurs**, it happens. ❑ *The car crash occurred at night.*
2 **VERB** If a thought or an idea **occurs to** you, you suddenly think of it. ❑ *Suddenly it occurred to her that the door might be open.*

oc|cur|rence /əkɜrəns/ (**occurrences**) **NOUN** An **occurrence** is something that happens. [FORMAL] ❑ *Complaints against the company were an everyday occurrence.*

Word World ocean

fish whale wave

ship deep

calm

water beach stormy

tide blue salty

shore coast swim

sail

seaweed current

fish

Nouns / Adjectives / Verbs

---

ocean /ouʃⁿn/ (**oceans**)

1 **NOUN** GEOGRAPHY **The ocean** is the salty water that covers much of the Earth's surface. ❑ *The house is on a cliff overlooking the ocean.*

2 **NOUN** GEOGRAPHY An **ocean** is one of the five very large areas of salt water on the Earth's surface. ❑ *...the Pacific Ocean.*

→ look at Word World: **ocean**

→ look at **beach, earth, globe, river**

o'clock /əklɒk/ **ADVERB** You use **o'clock** after numbers from one to twelve to say what time it is. ❑ *I went to bed at ten o'clock last night.*

> **Usage** **o'clock**
>
> Use **o'clock** for times that are exactly on the hour. *"Is it four o'clock yet?" "Not yet, it's three forty-five."*

oc|tave /ɒktɪv/ (**octaves**) **NOUN** MUSIC An **octave** is a series of eight notes in music, or the difference between the first and last notes in the series.

Oc|to|ber /ɒktoubər/ **NOUN** October is the tenth month of the year. ❑ *...in early October.* ❑ *They left on October 2.*

oc|to|pus /ɒktəpəs/ (**octopuses**) **NOUN** An **octopus** is a soft ocean animal with eight long arms.

odd /ɒd/ (**odder, oddest**)

1 **ADJECTIVE** If someone or something is **odd**, they are strange or unusual. ❑ *His behavior was odd.* ● **odd|ly** **ADVERB** ❑ *He dresses rather oddly.*

2 **ADJECTIVE** MATH **Odd** numbers, such as 3 and 17, are numbers that cannot be divided exactly by the number two.

3 **ADJECTIVE** You say that two things are **odd** when they do not belong to the same set or pair. ❑ *I'm wearing odd socks.*

odds /ɒdz/ **PLURAL NOUN** The **odds** that something will happen are how likely it is to happen. ❑ *What are the odds of finding a parking space right outside the door?*

odor /oudər/ (**odors**) **NOUN** An **odor** is a smell. ❑ *A bad egg will have an unpleasant odor when you break open the shell.*

of /əv, STRONG ʌv/

1 **PREPOSITION** You use **of** to say what someone or something is connected with. ❑ *Police searched the homes of the criminals.* ❑ *...the mayor of Los Angeles.*

2 **PREPOSITION** You use **of** to say what something relates to. ❑ *He was trying to hide his feelings of anger.*

3 **PREPOSITION** You use **of** to talk about someone or something else who is involved in an action. ❑ *He was dreaming of her.*

4 **PREPOSITION** You use **of** to show that someone or something is part of a larger group. ❑ *She is the youngest child of three.*

5 **PREPOSITION** You use **of** to talk about amounts or contents. ❑ *The boy was drinking a glass of milk.*

6 **PREPOSITION** You use **of** to say what caused a person's or an animal's death. ❑ *He died of a heart attack.*

7 **PREPOSITION** **Of** describes someone's behavior. ❑ *It's very kind of you to help.* ❑ *It was rude of him to interrupt you.*

of course

1 **ADVERB** You say **of course** to suggest that something is not surprising. ❑ *Of course there were lots of interesting things to see.*

2 You use **of course** as a polite way of giving permission. ❑ *"Can I ask you something?"* *—"Yes, of course."*

off /ɔf/

1 **PREPOSITION** If you take something **off** another thing, it is no longer on it. ❑ *He took his feet off the desk.*

o

2 ADVERB Off is also an adverb. ❏ *I broke off a piece of chocolate and ate it.*

3 PREPOSITION When you get **off** a bus, a train, or an airplane, you come out of it. ❏ *Don't get off a moving train!*

4 ADVERB Off is also an adverb. ❏ *At the next station, the man got off.*

5 PREPOSITION If you keep **off** a piece of land, you do not go there. ❏ *The police told visitors to keep off the beach.*

6 ADVERB If you go **off**, you go away. ❏ *He was just about to drive off.*

7 ADVERB If you have time **off**, you do not go to work or school. ❏ *She had the day off.* ❏ *I'm off tomorrow.*

8 ADVERB If something is a long time **off**, it will not happen for a long time. ❏ *An agreement is still a long way off.*

9 ADVERB If an event is **off**, it is canceled. ❏ *The wedding is off.*

10 ADVERB When a piece of electrical equipment is **off**, it is not being used. ❏ *Her bedroom light was off.*

of|fend /əfɛnd/ (**offends, offending, offended**) **VERB** If you **offend** someone, you say or do something that upsets them. ❏ *I'm sorry if I offended you.*

of|fense /əfɛns/ (**offenses**)

> **PRONUNCIATION HELP**
> Pronounce /ɔfɛns/ for meaning **3**.

1 NOUN An **offense** is a crime that breaks a law. ❏ *There is a fine of $1,000 for a first offense.*

2 NONCOUNT NOUN Offense is behavior that upsets people. ❏ *He didn't mean to cause offense.*

3 NOUN In sports such as football or basketball, **the offense** is the team that has the ball and is trying to score.

4 If you **take offense**, you are upset by something that someone says or does. ❏ *Many people took offense at his sexist jokes.*

of|fen|sive /əfɛnsɪv/ **ADJECTIVE** Something that is **offensive** upsets people because it is rude or insulting. ❏ *...an offensive remark.*

of|fer /ɔfər/ (**offers, offering, offered**)

1 VERB If you **offer** something to someone, you ask them if they would like to have it. ❏ *He offered his seat to the young woman.* ❏ *She offered him a cup of coffee.*

2 VERB If you **offer to** do something, you say that you are willing to do it. ❏ *Peter offered to teach me to drive.*

3 NOUN An **offer** is something that someone says they will give you or do for you. ❏ *I hope you will accept my offer of help.*

of|fice /ɔfɪs/ (**offices**)

1 NOUN An **office** is a place where people work sitting at a desk. ❏ *I work in an office with about 25 people.*

2 NOUN An **office** is a department of an organization, especially the government. ❏ *...the Congressional Budget Office.*

3 NOUN An **office** is a small building or room where people can go for information or tickets. ❏ *...a tourist office.*

4 NOUN A doctor's **office** is a place where a doctor sees patients.

5 NONCOUNT NOUN If someone holds **office** in a government, they have an important job. ❏ *The events marked the president's four years in office.*
→ look at Picture Dictionary: **office**
→ look at **city**

of|fic|er /ɔfɪsər/ (**officers**)

1 NOUN In the armed forces, an **officer** is a person who is in charge of other people. ❏ *...an army officer.*

Picture Dictionary   **office**

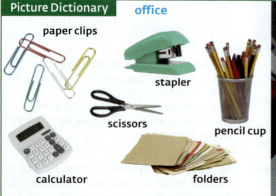

- paper clips
- stapler
- scissors
- pencil cup
- calculator
- folders

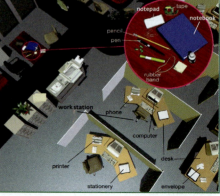

- notepad
- tape
- notebook
- pencil
- pen
- rubber band
- work station
- phone
- computer
- desk
- printer
- stationery
- envelope

2 NOUN Members of the police force can be called **officers**. ❑ *The officer saw no sign of a robbery.* ❑ *Officer Montoya was the first on the scene.*

3 NOUN An **officer** is a person who has a responsible position in a government organization. ❑ *She's the chief executive officer of the company.*

of|fi|cial /əfɪʃ°l/ (**officials**)
1 ADJECTIVE **Official** means approved by the government or by someone in power. ❑ *They destroyed all the official documents.* ● **of|fi|cial|ly ADVERB** ❑ *The results have not been officially announced.*

2 ADJECTIVE **Official** activities are carried out by a person in power as part of their job. ❑ *The president is in Brazil for an official visit.*

3 NOUN An **official** is a person who holds a position of power in an organization. ❑ *White House officials said that they discussed the matter this morning.*

off|line /ɔflaɪn/
1 ADJECTIVE TECHNOLOGY If you are **offline**, your computer is not connected to the Internet. Compare with **online**. ❑ *Test your website offline before you put it on the Web.*
2 ADVERB TECHNOLOGY **Offline** is also an adverb. ❑ *Most software programs allow you to write emails offline.*

of|ten /ɔf°n/
1 ADVERB If something **often** happens, it happens many times or much of the time. ❑ *They often spend the weekend together.* ❑ *That doesn't happen very often.*

2 ADVERB You use **how often** to ask questions about frequency. ❑ *How often do you brush your teeth?*

3 If something happens **every so often**, it happens sometimes, but not very often. ❑ *She visited every so often.*

oh /oʊ/ **EXCLAMATION** You use **oh** to express a feeling such as surprise, pain, annoyance, or happiness. ❑ *"Oh!" Kenny said. "Has everyone gone?"*

oil /ɔɪl/ (**oils, oiling, oiled**)
1 NONCOUNT NOUN **Oil** is a smooth, thick liquid that is used for making machines work. Oil is found underground. ❑ *The company buys and sells 600,000 barrels of oil a day.*
2 VERB If you **oil** something, you put oil onto or into it to make it work smoothly or to protect it. ❑ *He oiled the lock on the door.*
3 NOUN **Oil** is a smooth, thick liquid made

from plants, that is often used for cooking. ❑ *...olive oil.*
→ look at **energy**

oil paint|ing (**oil paintings**) **NOUN ARTS**
An **oil painting** is a picture that is painted using oil paints.

oily /ɔɪli/ (**oilier, oiliest**) **ADJECTIVE**
Something that is **oily** looks, feels, or tastes like oil. ❑ *He wiped his hands on an oily rag.* ❑ *Paul thought the sauce was too oily.*

oint|ment /ɔɪntmənt/ (**ointments**) **NOUN**
An **ointment** is a smooth, thick substance that you put on sore or damaged skin. ❑ *Ointments are available for the treatment of skin problems.*

okay /oʊkeɪ/ also **OK, O.K., ok**
1 ADJECTIVE If something is **okay**, it is acceptable. [INFORMAL] ❑ *Is it okay if I go by myself?*
2 ADVERB **Okay** is also an adverb. ❑ *We seemed to manage okay.*
3 ADJECTIVE If someone is **okay**, they are safe and well. [INFORMAL] ❑ *Check that the baby's okay.*
4 You can say "**Okay**" to show that you agree to something. [INFORMAL] ❑ *"Just tell him I would like to talk to him."—"OK."*
5 You can say "**Okay?**" to check whether the person you are talking to understands what you have said and accepts it. [INFORMAL] ❑ *We'll meet next week, OK?*

old /oʊld/ (**older, oldest**)
1 ADJECTIVE Someone who is **old** has lived for many years and is not young. ❑ *Mr. Kaufmann was a small old man with a beard.*
2 ADJECTIVE You use **old** to talk or ask about the age of someone or something. ❑ *He is three months old.* ❑ *Her car is less than three years old.*
3 ADJECTIVE Something that is **old** has existed for a long time. ❑ *We live in a beautiful old house.* ❑ *These books look very old.*
4 ADJECTIVE You use **old** to talk about something that used to be part of your life. ❑ *I still remember my old school.*
5 ADJECTIVE An **old** friend is someone who has been your friend for a long time. ❑ *I called my old friend John Horner.*
→ look at **car, tree, wear**

old age **NONCOUNT NOUN** Your **old age** is the part of your life when you are old. ❑ *They didn't have much money in their old age.*

o

old-fashioned ADJECTIVE Something that is **old-fashioned** is no longer used, done, or believed by most people. ❑ *The kitchen was old-fashioned and in bad condition.*

ol|ive /ɒlɪv/ (olives) NOUN **Olives** are small green or black fruits with a bitter taste.

ol|ive oil (olive oils) NOUN **Olive oil** is a type of oil that is used in cooking.

Olym|pic Games /əlɪmpɪk geɪmz/ NOUN **The Olympic Games** is an international sports competition that takes place every four years, each time in a different country.

ome|let /ɒmlɪt, ɒmələt/ (omelets) also **omelette** NOUN An **omelet** is a type of food made by beating eggs and cooking them in a frying pan. ❑ *She made a cheese omelet.*

omit /oʊmɪt/ (omits, omitting, omitted) VERB If you **omit** something, you do not include it. ❑ *Omit the salt in this recipe.*

om|ni|vore /ɒmnɪvɔr/ (omnivores) NOUN SCIENCE An **omnivore** is an animal that eats both meat and plants. Compare with **carnivore** and **herbivore**.

on /ɒn/

1 PREPOSITION If someone or something is **on** a surface, they are resting on it. ❑ *He was sitting on the sofa.* ❑ *There was a large box on the table.*

2 PREPOSITION If something is **on** a surface, it is attached to it. ❑ *We hung some paintings on the walls.* ❑ *You've got dirt on your face.*

3 ADVERB When you **put a piece of clothing on**, you put it on a part of your body. If you **have** it **on**, you are wearing it. ❑ *He put his coat on.* ❑ *I can't go out. I don't have any shoes on.*

4 PREPOSITION If you get **on** a bus, train, or airplane, you go into it. If you are **on** it, you are traveling in it. ❑ *We got on the plane.*

5 PREPOSITION If you do something **on** an instrument or a machine, you do it using that instrument or machine. ❑ *I played these songs on the piano.* ❑ *My dad called me on his cellphone.*

6 PREPOSITION If you do something **on** a piece of equipment, you do it using that piece of equipment. ❑ *She spends most of the day on the computer.* ❑ *My dad called me on my cellphone.* ❑ *Let's look it up on the Internet.*

7 PREPOSITION If a television or radio program is being broadcast, you can say that it is **on** television or **on** the radio. ❑ *What's on TV tonight?*

8 PREPOSITION If something happens **on** a particular day or date, that is when it happens. ❑ *This year's event will be on June 19th.* ❑ *We'll see you on Tuesday.*

9 ADVERB You use **on** to say that someone is continuing to do something. ❑ *They walked on for a while.*

10 PREPOSITION Books or ideas **on** a particular subject are about that subject. ❑ *He wrote a book on the history of Russian ballet.*

11 ADVERB When a machine or an electric light is **on**, it is being used. ❑ *The lights were on, but nobody was at home.*

→ look at **location**

once /wʌns/

1 ADVERB If something happens **once**, it happens one time only. ❑ *I met Miquela once, at a party.* ❑ *The baby hasn't once slept through the night.*

2 ADVERB If something was **once** true, it was true at some time in the past, but is no longer true. ❑ *Her parents once owned a store.*

3 CONJUNCTION If something happens **once** another thing has happened, it happens immediately afterward. ❑ *The decision was easy once he read the letter.*

4 If you do something **at once**, you do it immediately. ❑ *I have to go at once.*

5 **For once** is used for emphasizing that something happens on this particular occasion only. ❑ *For once, Dad is not complaining.*

Sound Partners	one, won

one /wʌn/ (ones)

1 MATH **One** is the number 1. ❑ *They have one daughter.*

2 PRONOUN You can use **one** instead of the name of a person or thing. ❑ *"Which dress do you prefer?"—"I like the red one."* ❑ *Cut up the large potatoes, but leave the small ones, please.*

3 ADJECTIVE You can use **one** when you are talking about a time in the past or in the future. ❑ *Would you like to go out one night?*

4 PRONOUN **One** means people in general. [FORMAL] ❑ *One can get very tired on these long flights.*

5 **One or two** means a few. ❑ *We made one or two changes.*

→ look at **number**

one's /wʌnz/

1 **ADJECTIVE** You use **one's** to show that something belongs to or relates to people in general. [FORMAL] ❑ *It is natural to want to care for one's family and children.*

2 **One's** is a spoken form of "one is" or "one has." ❑ *No one's going to hurt you.* ❑ *This one's been broken too.*

one|self /wʌnsɛlf/

1 **PRONOUN** Speakers or writers use **oneself** to make statements about themselves and people in general. [FORMAL] ❑ *To work, one must have time to oneself.*

2 **By oneself** means alone. [FORMAL] ❑ *Traveling by oneself can be an enjoyable experience.*

one-way

1 **ADJECTIVE** On **one-way** streets, traffic can only move in one direction.

2 **ADJECTIVE** A **one-way** ticket is for a trip from one place to another, but not back again. ❑ *She used the money to buy a one-way ticket to New Zealand.*

on|ion /ʌnyən/ (**onions**) **NOUN** An **onion** is a round vegetable with many layers. It has a strong, sharp smell and taste.

→ look at **vegetable**

on|line /ɒnlaɪn/

1 **ADJECTIVE** An **online** company makes its goods and services available on the Internet. ❑ *...an online bookstore.*

2 **ADJECTIVE** TECHNOLOGY If you are **online**, your computer is connected to the Internet. Compare with **offline**. ❑ *You can chat to other people who are online.*

3 **ADVERB** TECHNOLOGY **Online** is also an adverb. ❑ *I buy most of my clothes and shoes online.*

→ look at **dictionary, shopping**

on|looker /ɒnlʊkər/ (**onlookers**) **NOUN** An **onlooker** is someone who watches an event but does not take part in it. ❑ *A group of onlookers stood and watched the fight.*

only /oʊnli/

1 **ADVERB** **Only** means "and nobody or nothing else." ❑ *Only one person knew the answer.* ❑ *We have only twelve students in our class.*

2 **ADJECTIVE** The **only** person or thing is the one person or thing of a particular type. ❑ *She's the only girl in the class.*

3 **ADJECTIVE** An **only** child is a child who has no brothers or sisters. ❑ *I'm an only child, and I like it.*

4 **ADVERB** You use **only** when you are saying how small or short something is. ❑ *Their house is only a few miles from here.*

5 **CONJUNCTION** **Only** means "but." [INFORMAL] ❑ *It's like my house, only it's nicer.*

onto /ɒntu/

1 **PREPOSITION** If something moves **onto** a surface, it moves to a position on that surface. ❑ *The cat climbed onto her lap.*

2 **PREPOSITION** When you get **onto** a bus, train, or plane, you enter it. ❑ *He got onto the plane.*

ooh /u/ also **oo** **EXCLAMATION** People say "**ooh**" when they are surprised or excited, or when they think something is pleasant or unpleasant. [INFORMAL] ❑ *"Ooh, that hurts."*

oops /ʊps/ **EXCLAMATION** You say **oops!** when a small mistake or accident has happened. ❑ *Oops! Sorry. Are you all right?*

ooze /uz/ (**oozes, oozing, oozed**) **VERB** When a thick liquid **oozes**, it flows out of something slowly and in small amounts. ❑ *They drank the liquid that oozed from the fruit.*

open /oʊpən/ (**opens, opening, opened**)

1 **VERB** If you **open** something, you move it so that it is no longer covered or closed. ❑ *He opened the window.* ❑ *After a few seconds, I opened my eyes.*

2 **ADJECTIVE** **Open** is also an adjective. ❑ *His eyes were open and he was smiling.*

3 **VERB** If you **open** a container, you remove part of it so that you can take out what is inside. ❑ *Nicole opened the silver box on the table.*

4 **VERB** If you **open** a book, you move the covers so that you can see the pages inside. ❑ *He opened the book and started to read.*

5 **VERB** If you **open** a computer file, you give the computer an instruction to show it on the screen. ❑ *To open a file, go to the File menu.*

6 **VERB** When a store, office, or public building **opens**, people can go into it. ❑ *The banks will open again on Monday morning.*

7 **ADJECTIVE** **Open** is also an adjective. ❑ *The store is open Monday through Friday, 9 a.m. to 6 p.m.*

8 **ADJECTIVE** If a person is **open**, they are honest about their thoughts and feelings. ❑ *He was always open with her.*

9 **ADJECTIVE** If you are **open to** suggestions or ideas, you are ready and willing to consider or accept them. ❑ *We are always open to suggestions.*

o

Word Builder   opener

er ≈ **something that does**

clean + er = clean**er**
contain + er = contain**er**
dry + er = dry**er**
open + er = open**er**
print + er = print**er**
toast + er = toast**er**

open|er /oupənər/ (**openers**) **NOUN** An **opener** is a tool that is used for opening cans or bottles. ❑ *...a can opener.*

open|ing /oupənɪŋ/ (**openings**)
1 **ADJECTIVE** The **opening** event, day, or week in a series is the first one. ❑ *The team lost the opening game.*
2 **NOUN** An **opening** is a hole or an empty space that things or people can pass through. ❑ *He managed to get through a narrow opening in the fence.*

open-minded **ADJECTIVE** An **open-minded** person is willing to listen to other people's ideas. ❑ *He says that he is open-minded about tomorrow's talks.*

op|era /ɒpərə, ɒprə/ (**operas**) **NOUN** **MUSIC** An **opera** is a play with music in which all the words are sung. ❑ *...an opera singer.*
● **op|er|at|ic** /ɒpərætɪk/ **ADJECTIVE** ❑ *He was famous for his operatic voice.*

op|er|ate /ɒpəreɪt/ (**operates, operating, operated**)
1 **VERB** If an organization **operates**, it does the work it is supposed to. ❑ *The organization has been operating in the area for some time.*
2 **VERB** When you **operate** a machine, you make it work. ❑ *Weston showed him how to operate the machine.*
3 **VERB** When doctors **operate on** a patient, they cut open the patient's body in order to remove or repair a part. ❑ *Surgeons operated on Max to remove a brain tumor.*

op|er|at|ing sys|tem (**operating systems**) **NOUN** **TECHNOLOGY** The **operating system** of a computer is the main program that controls all the other programs. ❑ *Which operating system do you use?*

op|era|tion /ɒpəreɪʃən/ (**operations**)
1 **NOUN** An **operation** is an organized activity that involves many people doing different things. ❑ *The rescue operation began on Friday.*

2 **NOUN** When a patient has an **operation**, a doctor cuts open their body in order to remove, replace, or repair a part. ❑ *Charles had an operation on his arm.*

op|era|tor /ɒpəreɪtər/ (**operators**)
1 **NOUN** An **operator** is a person who connects telephone calls in a place such as an office or hotel. ❑ *He called the operator.*
2 **NOUN** An **operator** is a person who is employed to operate or control a machine. ❑ *...a crane operator.*
3 **NOUN** An **operator** is a person or a company that operates a business. ❑ *Several tour operators offer day trips to lakes and castles around the city.*

opin|ion /əpɪnyən/ (**opinions**)
1 **NOUN** Your **opinion** about something is what you think about it. ❑ *I didn't ask for your opinion.*
2 **NOUN** Your **opinion of** someone is what you think about their character or ability. ❑ *I don't have a very high opinion of Thomas.*

op|po|nent /əpounənt/ (**opponents**) **NOUN** **SPORTS** In a fight or a sports competition, your **opponent** is the person who is against you. ❑ *She'll face six opponents in today's race.*

op|por|tu|nity /ɒpərtunɪti/ (**opportunities**) **NOUN** An **opportunity** is a situation in which it is possible for you to do something that you want to do. ❑ *I had an opportunity to go to New York and study.*

Word Partners   Use **opportunity** with:

ADJ.	**economic** opportunity, **educational** opportunity, **equal** opportunity, **great** opportunity, **lost** opportunity, **rare** opportunity, **unique** opportunity
V.	**have an** opportunity, **miss an** opportunity, **see an** opportunity, opportunity **to speak**, **take advantage of an** opportunity

op|pose /əpouz/ (**opposes, opposing, opposed**) **VERB** If you **oppose** something, you disagree with what someone wants to do, and you try to stop them from doing it. ❑ *He said that he would oppose any tax increase.*

op|posed /əpouzd/ **ADJECTIVE** If you **are opposed to** something, you disagree with it. ❑ *I am opposed to any form of terrorism.*

op|po|site /ɒpəzɪt/ (**opposites**)
1 **PREPOSITION** If one person or thing is **opposite** another, it is across from them. ❑ *Jennie sat opposite Sam at breakfast.*

O

2 **ADVERB** Opposite is also an adverb. ❑ *He looked at the buildings opposite.*

3 **ADJECTIVE** Opposite describes similar things that are completely different in a particular way. ❑ *We watched the cars driving in the opposite direction.*

4 **NOUN** The opposite of someone or something is the person or thing that is most different from them. ❑ *Whatever he says, he's probably thinking the opposite.*

op|po|si|tion /ɒpəzɪʃᵊn/ **NONCOUNT NOUN** Opposition is strong disagreement. ❑ *There is strong opposition to the plan from local people.*

op|ti|cian /ɒptɪʃᵊn/ (**opticians**) **NOUN** An **optician** is a person whose job is to make and sell glasses.

op|ti|mism /ɒptɪmɪzəm/ **NONCOUNT NOUN** Optimism is a feeling of hope about the success of something. ❑ *There is optimism about the possibility of peace.* ● **op|ti|mist** (**optimists**) **NOUN** ❑ *He is an optimist about the country's future.*

op|ti|mis|tic /ɒptɪmɪstɪk/ **ADJECTIVE** Someone who is **optimistic** has hope about the success of something. ❑ *She is optimistic that they can reach an agreement.*

op|tion /ɒpʃᵊn/ (**options**) **NOUN** An **option** is a choice between two or more things. ❑ *We will consider all options before making a decision.*

op|tion|al /ɒpʃənᵊl/ **ADJECTIVE** If something is **optional**, you can choose whether or not you do it or have it. ❑ *All students have to study math, but history and geography are optional.*

or /ər, STRONG ɔr/

1 **CONJUNCTION** You use **or** to show choices or possibilities. ❑ *"Do you want tea or coffee?" John asked.* ❑ *Either you change your behavior, or you will have to leave.*

2 **CONJUNCTION** You use **or** between two numbers to show that you are giving an approximate amount. ❑ *You should only drink one or two cups of coffee a day.*

3 **CONJUNCTION** You use **or** to introduce a warning that something bad could happen. ❑ *She has to have the operation, or she will die.*

oral /ɔrəl/

1 **ADJECTIVE** Oral communication is spoken rather than written. ❑ *The English test includes written and oral examinations.*

2 **ADJECTIVE** Oral means relating to your mouth. ❑ *...good oral hygiene.*

or|ange /ɔrɪndʒ/ (**oranges**)

1 **ADJECTIVE** Something that is **orange** is of a color between red and yellow.

2 **NOUN** Orange is also a noun. ❑ *His supporters were dressed in orange.*

3 **NOUN** An **orange** is a round, juicy fruit with a thick, orange-colored skin. → look at **color, fruit**

or|bit /ɔrbɪt/ (**orbits, orbiting, orbited**)

1 **NOUN** SCIENCE An **orbit** is the curved path of an object that goes around a planet, a moon, or the sun. ❑ *The Earth has an orbit that changes.*

2 **VERB** SCIENCE If something **orbits** a planet, a moon, or the sun, it moves around it in a curved path. ❑ *The moon orbits the Earth.* → look at **earth**

or|chard /ɔrtʃərd/ (**orchards**) **NOUN** An **orchard** is an area of land where fruit trees grow. → look at **farm, tree**

or|ches|tra /ɔrkɪstrə/ (**orchestras**) **NOUN** MUSIC An **orchestra** is a large group of musicians who play different instruments together. ❑ *The orchestra began to play.*

or|deal /ɔrdil/ (**ordeals**) **NOUN** An **ordeal** is a difficult and very unpleasant experience. ❑ *The attack was a terrifying ordeal for both victims.*

order
❶ IN ORDER TO
❷ COMMANDS AND REQUESTS
❸ THE WAY THINGS ARE ARRANGED

❶ or|der /ɔrdər/ If you do something **in order to** achieve something, you do it because you want to achieve that thing. ❑ *The operation was necessary in order to save the baby's life*

❷ or|der /ɔrdər/ (**orders, ordering, ordered**)

1 **VERB** If you **order** someone **to** do something, you tell them to do it. ❑ *Williams ordered him to leave.*

2 **NOUN** If someone gives you an **order**, they tell you to do something. ❑ *The commander gave his men orders to move out of the camp.*

3 **VERB** When you **order** something from a company, you ask for it to be sent to you. ❑ *They ordered a new washing machine on the Internet.*

4 **VERB** When you **order** food and drinks in

a restaurant, you ask for them to be brought to you. ❏ *The waitress asked, "Are you ready to order?"*

5 **NOUN** Someone's **order** is what they have asked for in return for money. ❏ *He's just placed an order for a new car.* ❏ *The waiter returned with their order.*

→ look at **payment**

❸ **or|der** /ɔrdər/

1 **NONCOUNT NOUN** If you arrange things **in** a particular **order**, you put one thing first, another thing second, another thing third, and so on. ❏ *The books are all arranged in alphabetical order.*

2 **NONCOUNT NOUN** **Order** is the situation that exists when everything is in the correct place, or happens at the correct time. ❏ *I love rules, and I love order.* ❏ *Everything on the desk is in order.*

3 **NONCOUNT NOUN** **Order** is the situation that exists when people obey the law and do not fight or riot. ❏ *The army went to the islands to restore order.*

4 A machine or piece of equipment that is **in working order** is working properly. ❏ *His old car is still in perfect working order.*

5 A machine or piece of equipment that is **out of order** does not work. ❏ *Their phone's out of order.*

or|der|ly /ɔrdərli/ **ADJECTIVE** Something that is **orderly** is neat and has everything in the correct place. ❏ *It's a beautiful, clean, and orderly city.*

or|di|nary /ɔrdəneri/

1 **ADJECTIVE** **Ordinary** people or things are normal and not special or different. ❏ *These are just ordinary people living ordinary lives.*

2 Something that is **out of the ordinary** is unusual or different. ❏ *The police asked people to report anything out of the ordinary.*

or|gan /ɔrgən/ (**organs**)

1 **NOUN** SCIENCE An **organ** is a part of your body that has a particular purpose. ❏ *The brain is the most powerful organ in the body.*

2 **NOUN** MUSIC An **organ** is a large musical instrument that is like a piano. ❏ *...a church organ.*

or|gan|ic /ɔrgænɪk/ **ADJECTIVE** SCIENCE **Organic** food is grown without using chemicals. ❏ *We buy only organic fruits and vegetables.*

→ look at **food**

or|gan|ism /ɔrgənɪzəm/ (**organisms**) **NOUN** SCIENCE An **organism** is a living thing. ❏ *We study very small organisms such as bacteria.*

or|gani|za|tion /ɔrgənɪzeɪʃən/ (**organizations**)

1 **NOUN** An **organization** is an official group of people such as a business or a club. ❏ *She worked for the same organization for six years.*

2 **NONCOUNT NOUN** If you help in the **organization** of an activity, you help to plan or arrange it. ❏ *I helped in the organization of the concert.*

or|gan|ize /ɔrgənaɪz/ (**organizes, organizing, organized**)

1 **VERB** If you **organize** an activity, you plan or arrange it. ❏ *We decided to organize a concert.*

● **or|gan|iz|er** (**organizers**) **NOUN** ❏ *Organizers are hoping to raise $65,000 from the concert.*

2 **VERB** If you **organize** things, you plan or arrange them in a neat and effective way. ❏ *He began to organize his papers.*

or|gan|ized /ɔrgənaɪzd/ **ADJECTIVE** Someone who is **organized** plans their work and activities carefully. ❏ *Managers need to be very organized.*

→ look at **factory**

ori|en|tal /ɔrient̬əl/ **ADJECTIVE** You use **oriental** to talk about things that come from places in eastern Asia. **Oriental** should not be used for talking about people. ❏ *He was an expert in oriental art.*

ori|gin /ɔrɪdʒɪn/ (**origins**) **NOUN** The **origin** of a thing or a person is the way they started. ❏ *Scientists study the origin of life on Earth.* ❏ *...Americans of Hispanic origin.*

origi|nal /ərɪdʒɪnəl/ (**originals**)

1 **ADJECTIVE** You use **original** when you are talking about something that existed at the beginning. ❏ *The original plan was to go by bus.*

● **origi|nal|ly** **ADVERB** ❏ *Wright lives in London but he is originally from Melbourne.*

2 **NOUN** If something is an **original**, it is not a copy. ❏ *Make a copy of the document and send the original to your employer.*

3 **ADJECTIVE** **Original** work shows that the person who did it has imagination and new ideas. ❏ *He is the most original painter of the past 100 years.*

or|na|ment /ɔrnəmənt/ (**ornaments**) **NOUN** An **ornament** is an attractive object that you use to decorate your home. ❏ *There were a few ornaments on the shelf.*

or|phan /ˈɔrfən/ (orphans) **NOUN** An orphan is a child whose parents are dead.

or|phan|age /ˈɔrfənɪdʒ/ (orphanages) **NOUN** An orphanage is a place where orphans live.

OS /ˌou ˈɛs/ (OS's) **NOUN** OS is short for operating system.

os|trich /ˈɔstrɪtʃ/ (ostriches) **NOUN** An ostrich is a very large bird that cannot fly.

oth|er /ˈʌðər/ (others)
1 **ADJECTIVE** You use other when you are talking about more things or people that are like the thing or person you have mentioned. ❏ *Mr. Johnson and the other teachers are very worried.*
2 **PRONOUN** Other is also a pronoun. ❏ *He had a pen in one hand and a book in the other.*
3 **ADJECTIVE** You use other when you are talking about a thing or a person that is different from the thing or person you have mentioned. ❏ *He will have to accept it; there is no other way.*
4 **ADJECTIVE** You use the other to talk about the second of two things or people. ❏ *William was at the other end of the room.*
5 **ADJECTIVE** You use the other day when you are talking about a recent day. ❏ *I called her the other day.*

other|wise /ˈʌðərwaɪz/
1 **ADVERB** You use otherwise to say what the result would be if the situation was different. ❏ *I really enjoy this job, otherwise I would not be here.*
2 **ADVERB** You use otherwise when you mention a different condition or way. ❏ *He was very tired but otherwise happy.* ❏ *Take one pill three times a day, unless you are told otherwise by a doctor.*

ouch /aʊtʃ/ **EXCLAMATION** People say ouch! when they suddenly feel pain. ❏ *The stones cut her feet. "Ouch, ouch!" she cried.*

ought /ɔt/
1 If someone ought to do something, it is the right thing to do. ❏ *You ought to read this book.*
2 You use ought to when you think something will be true or will happen. ❏ *"This party ought to be fun," he told Alex.*

oughtn't /ˈɔtᵊnt/ Oughtn't is short for "ought not."

ounce /aʊns/ (ounces) **NOUN** MATH An ounce is a unit for measuring weight. There are sixteen ounces in a pound and one ounce is equal to 28.35 grams.

| **Sound Partners** | our, hour |

our /aʊər/ **ADJECTIVE** You use our to show that something belongs or relates both to you and to one or more other people. ❏ *We're expecting our first baby.*

ours /aʊərz/ **PRONOUN** You use ours when you are talking about something that belongs to you and one or more other people. ❏ *That car is ours.*

our|selves /aʊərsˈɛlvz/
1 **PRONOUN** You use ourselves when you are talking about yourself and one or more other people. ❏ *We sat by the fire to keep ourselves warm.*
2 **PRONOUN** "We did it ourselves" means that you and one or more other people did it, rather than anyone else. ❏ *We built the house ourselves.*

out /aʊt/
1 **ADVERB** When you take something out, you remove it from a place. ❏ *He took out his notebook.*
2 **ADVERB** If you are out, you are not at home. ❏ *I called you yesterday, but you were out.*
3 **ADJECTIVE** If a light is out, it is no longer shining. ❏ *All the lights were out in the house.*
4 **ADJECTIVE** If a fire goes out, it is no longer burning. ❏ *Please don't let the fire go out.*
5 **ADJECTIVE** If something is out, it is in stores and people can buy it. ❏ *Their new CD is out now.*
6 **ADVERB** Out is also an adverb. ❏ *The book came out in 2006.*
7 **ADJECTIVE** In games such as tennis or basketball, a ball that is out is outside the area of play. Compare with in. ❏ *The referee agreed that the ball was out.*
8 If you go out of a place, you leave it. ❏ *She ran out of the house.*
9 If you take something out of a container, you remove it. ❏ *I took the key out of my purse.*
10 If you are out of something, you no longer have any of it. ❏ *We're out of milk. Can you get some at the supermarket?*
11 If something is made out of a particular material, it has been produced from it. ❏ *The house is made out of wood.*
12 You use out of when you are talking about a smaller group that is part of a larger

o

group. ❏ *Three out of four people say there's too much violence on TV.*

out|break /aʊtbreɪk/ (**outbreaks**) **NOUN** If there is an **outbreak of** violence or a disease, it suddenly starts to happen. ❏ *This is the worst ever outbreak of the disease.*

out|come /aʊtkʌm/ (**outcomes**) **NOUN** The **outcome** of an activity is the situation that exists at the end of it. ❏ *It's too early to know the outcome of the election.*

out|door /aʊtdɔr/ **ADJECTIVE** Outdoor activities happen outside and not in a building. ❏ *If you enjoy outdoor activities, you should try rock climbing.*

out|doors /aʊtdɔrz/ **ADVERB** If something happens **outdoors**, it happens outside rather than in a building. ❏ *It was warm enough to play outdoors all afternoon.*

out|er /aʊtər/ **ADJECTIVE** The **outer** parts of something are the parts that cover the other parts. ❏ *This material forms the hard outer surface of the tooth.*

out|fit /aʊtfɪt/ (**outfits**) **NOUN** An **outfit** is a set of clothes. ❏ *I need a new outfit for the wedding.*
→ look at **wear**

out|ing /aʊtɪŋ/ (**outings**) **NOUN** An **outing** is a short trip, usually with a group of people. ❏ *We went on an outing to the local movie theater.*

out|let /aʊtlɛt, -lɪt/ (**outlets**)
1 **NOUN** An **outlet** is a store that sells the goods made by a particular manufacturer at a low price. The goods often come straight from the factory. ❏ *...a factory outlet.*
2 **NOUN** If someone has an **outlet for** their feelings or ideas, they have a way to express them. ❏ *He found another outlet for his anger.*
3 **NOUN** An **outlet** is a place in a wall where you can connect electrical equipment to the electricity supply. ❏ *Plug the device into an electric outlet.*

out|line /aʊtlaɪn/ (**outlines, outlining, outlined**)
1 **NOUN** An **outline** is a general explanation or description of something. ❏ *We are sending you an outline of the plan.*
2 **VERB** Outline is also a verb. ❏ *The report outlined some possible changes to the rules.*
3 **NOUN** An **outline** of an object or person is its general shape. ❏ *He could only see the dark outline of the man.*
→ look at **writing**

out|look /aʊtlʊk/ (**outlooks**)
1 **NOUN** The **outlook** for something is whether it is going to be successful. ❏ *The economic outlook is not good.*
2 **NOUN** Your **outlook** is your general feeling about life. ❏ *He had a positive outlook on life.*

out of date also **out-of-date ADJECTIVE** Something that is **out of date** is old-fashioned and no longer useful. ❏ *The rules are out of date.* ❏ *They were using an out-of-date map.*

out|rage (**outrages, outraging, outraged**)

> **PRONUNCIATION HELP**
> Pronounce the verb /aʊtreɪdʒ/. Pronounce the noun /aʊtreɪdʒ/.

1 **VERB** If you **are outraged** by something, it shocks you or makes you very angry. ❏ *Many people were outraged by his comments.*
2 **NONCOUNT NOUN** Outrage is an intense feeling of anger and shock. ❏ *Several teachers wrote to the newspapers to express their outrage.*

out|ra|geous /aʊtreɪdʒəs/ **ADJECTIVE** Something that is **outrageous** shocks you or makes you very angry. ❏ *It was outrageous behavior.*

out|side /aʊtsaɪd/ (**outsides**)
1 **NOUN** The **outside** of something is the part that surrounds or covers the rest of it. ❏ *The outside of the building was recently painted.*
2 **ADJECTIVE** Outside is also an adjective. ❏ *The outside wall is painted white.*
3 **ADVERB** If you are **outside**, you are not in a building, but you are very close to it. ❏ *She went outside to look for Sam.*
4 **PREPOSITION** Outside is also a preposition. ❏ *She found him standing outside the classroom.*

> **Word Partners** Use **outside** with:
> N.   outside **a building**, outside **a car**, outside **a room**, outside **a store** **1** **3**
> V.   **gather** outside, **go** outside, **park** outside, **sit** outside, **stand** outside, **step** outside, **wait** outside **3**

out|skirts /aʊtskɜrts/ **PLURAL NOUN** The **outskirts of** a city or a town are the parts of it that are farthest away from its center. ❏ *I live on the outskirts of the city.*

out|smart /aʊtsmɑrt/ (**outsmarts, outsmarting, outsmarted**) **VERB** If you **outsmart** someone, you find a clever way to be better or more successful than them. ❏ *They love games that allow them to outsmart other people.*

O

out|stand|ing /aʊtstændɪŋ/ **ADJECTIVE** An **outstanding** person or thing is much better than others of a similar type. ❑ *She is an outstanding athlete.*

oval /oʊvᵊl/ **ADJECTIVE** **Oval** things have a shape like an egg. ❑ *She had an oval face with large, dark eyes.*

oven /ʌvᵊn/ (**ovens**) **NOUN** An **oven** is a piece of equipment for cooking that is like a large metal box with a door.
→ look at **kitchen**

over /oʊvər/

1 **PREPOSITION** If one thing is **over** another thing, the first thing is directly above or higher than the second thing. ❑ *There was a gold mirror over the fireplace.* ❑ *I heard some planes flying over the house.*

2 **PREPOSITION** If one thing is **over** another thing, it covers part or all of it. ❑ *He lay down and pulled the blanket over himself.* ❑ *Pour the sauce over the mushrooms.*

3 **PREPOSITION** If someone or something goes **over** something, they get to the other side of it by going across it to the other side. ❑ *They jumped over the wall.*

4 **ADVERB** You can use **over** when you are talking about a short distance. ❑ *Come over here!* ❑ *The café is just over there.*

5 **ADVERB** If something turns **over**, its position changes so that the part that was facing up is now facing down. ❑ *His car rolled over on an icy road.*

6 **PREPOSITION** If something is **over** an amount, it is more than that amount. ❑ *The house cost over $1 million.*

7 **ADVERB** If you do something **over**, you do it again. ❑ *If you don't like it, you can just do it over.*

8 **ADJECTIVE** If an activity is **over**, it is completely finished. ❑ *The war is over.* ❑ *I am glad it's all over.*
→ look at **location**

over|all (**overalls**)

1 **ADJECTIVE** /oʊvərɔl/ You use **overall** when you are talking about a situation in general or about the whole thing. ❑ *We are very happy with the company's overall performance.*

2 **PLURAL NOUN** /oʊvərɔlz/ **Overalls** are pants with a piece of cloth that covers your chest.

over|came /oʊvərkeɪm/ **Overcame** is a form of the verb **overcome**.

over|cast /oʊvərkæst/ **ADJECTIVE** If the sky is **overcast**, it is completely covered with cloud. ❑ *He looked up at the gray, overcast sky.*

over|come /oʊvərkʌm/ (**overcomes, overcoming, overcame, overcome**)

1 **VERB** If you **overcome** a problem or a feeling, you successfully deal with it and control it. ❑ *Molly finally overcame her fear of flying.*

2 **VERB** If you **are overcome by** a feeling, you feel it very strongly. ❑ *The night before the test I was overcome by fear.*

Word Builder	overcrowded
over ≈ **too much**	
over + crowded = over**crowded**	
over + due = over**due**	
over + flow = over**flow**	
over + heat = over**heat**	
over + sleep = over**sleep**	
over + weight = over**weight**	

over|crowd|ed /oʊvərkraʊdɪd/ **ADJECTIVE** An **overcrowded** place has too many people in it. ❑ *We sat on the overcrowded beach.*

Word Builder	overdue
over ≈ **too much**	
over + crowded = over**crowded**	
over + due = over**due**	
over + flow = over**flow**	
over + heat = over**heat**	
over + sleep = over**sleep**	
over + weight = over**weight**	

over|due /oʊvərdu/ **ADJECTIVE** If something is **overdue**, it should have happened or arrived before now. ❑ *Your tax payment is overdue.* ❑ *Mr. Giuliano said the changes were long overdue.*

Word Builder	overflow
over ≈ **too much**	
over + crowded = over**crowded**	
over + due = over**due**	
over + flow = over**flow**	
over + heat = over**heat**	
over + sleep = over**sleep**	
over + weight = over**weight**	

over|flow /oʊvərfloʊ/ (**overflows, overflowing, overflowed**)

o

1 VERB If a container **overflows**, the liquid that is in it flows over the edges. ❏ *The sink overflowed.*

2 VERB If a liquid or a river **overflows**, it flows over the edges of the place it is in. ❏ *During the heavy rains, the river overflowed.*

over|head

PRONUNCIATION HELP
Pronounce the adjective /ouvərhɛd/.
Pronounce the adverb /ouvərhɛd/.

1 ADJECTIVE Something that is **overhead** is above you. ❏ *She turned on the overhead light.*
2 ADVERB **Overhead** is also an adverb.
❏ *Planes passed overhead.*

over|hear /ouvərhɪər/ (overhears, overhearing, overheard) VERB If you **overhear** someone, you hear what they are saying when they are not talking to you.
❏ *I overheard two doctors discussing me.*

Word Builder **overheat**

over ≈ **too much**

over + crowded = over**crowded**
over + due = over**due**
over + flow = over**flow**
over + heat = over**heat**
over + sleep = over**sleep**
over + weight = over**weight**

over|heat /ouvərhit/ (overheats, overheating, overheated) VERB If something **overheats**, it becomes too hot. ❏ *The car's engine was overheating.*

over|lap /ouvərlæp/ (overlaps, overlapping, overlapped) VERB If two things **overlap**, a part of the first thing covers a part of the other. ❏ *The two circles overlap.*

over|look /ouvərlʊk/ (overlooks, overlooking, overlooked)
1 VERB If you **overlook** a fact or a problem, you do not notice it. ❏ *We cannot overlook this important fact.*
2 VERB If a building or window **overlooks** a place, you can see the place clearly from the building or window. ❏ *The hotel's rooms overlook a beautiful garden.*

over|night /ouvərnaɪt/
1 ADVERB Something that happens **overnight** happens through the whole night or at some point during the night.
❏ *The decision was made overnight.*

2 ADJECTIVE **Overnight** is also an adjective.
❏ *He decided to take an overnight fishing trip.*

over|seas /ouvərsiz/
1 ADJECTIVE **Overseas** describes things or people that are in or that come from foreign countries across the ocean. ❏ *He enjoyed his overseas trip.*
2 ADVERB **Overseas** is also an adverb. ❏ *He's now working overseas.*

Word Builder **oversleep**

over ≈ **too much**

over + crowded = over**crowded**
over + due = over**due**
over + flow = over**flow**
over + heat = over**heat**
over + sleep = over**sleep**
over + weight = over**weight**

over|sleep /ouvərslip/ (oversleeps, oversleeping, overslept) VERB If you **oversleep**, you sleep longer than you should. ❏ *I forgot to set my alarm and I overslept.*

over|time /ouvərtaɪm/ NONCOUNT NOUN **Overtime** is extra time that you spend doing your job. ❏ *He worked overtime to finish the job.*

Word Builder **overweight**

over ≈ **too much**

over + crowded = over**crowded**
over + due = over**due**
over + flow = over**flow**
over + heat = over**heat**
over + sleep = over**sleep**
over + weight = over**weight**

over|weight /ouvərweɪt/ ADJECTIVE Someone who is **overweight** weighs more than is considered healthy or attractive.

over|whelm|ing /ouvərwɛlmɪŋ/ ADJECTIVE An **overwhelming** feeling affects you very strongly. ❏ *She had an overwhelming feeling of guilt.*

owe /ou/ (owes, owing, owed)
1 VERB If you **owe** money **to** someone, you have to pay money to them. ❏ *The company owes money to more than 60 banks.* ❏ *Blake owed him $50.*
2 VERB If you **owe** someone something, you want to do something for them because you are grateful. ❏ *She thought Will owed her a favor.*

owl /au̯l/ (owls) **NOUN** An **owl** is a bird with large eyes that is active at night.
→ look at **bird**

own /ou̯n/ (owns, owning, owned)
1 **ADJECTIVE** You use **own** to say that something belongs to or is done by a particular person or thing. ❏ *I wanted to have my own business.* ❏ *They prefer to make their own decisions.*
2 **PRONOUN** **Own** is also a pronoun. ❏ *The man's face was a few inches from my own.*
3 **ADJECTIVE** You use **own** to say that something is used by only one person or thing. ❏ *Jennifer wanted her own room.*
4 **VERB** If you **own** something, it belongs to you. ❏ *His father owns a local computer store.*
5 When you are **on** your **own**, you are alone. ❏ *He lives on his own.*
6 If you do something **on** your **own**, you do it without any help. ❏ *I work best on my own.*

Word Builder   owner

er ≈ **someone who does**
> climb + er = climber
> farm + er = farmer
> lead + er = leader
> own + er = owner
> play + er = player
> work + er = worker

---

own|er /ou̯nər/ (owners) **NOUN** If you are the **owner** of something, it belongs to you. ❏ *My brother is the owner of the store.*

Word Builder   ownership

ship ≈ **state of being**
> champion + ship = championship
> friend + ship = friendship
> leader + ship = leadership
> member + ship = membership
> owner + ship = ownership
> relation + ship = relationship

---

own|er|ship /ou̯nərʃɪp/ **NONCOUNT NOUN** **Ownership** of something is when you own it. ❏ *There has been an increase in home ownership.*

oxy|gen /ɒksɪdʒən/ **NONCOUNT NOUN** SCIENCE **Oxygen** is a gas in the air that is needed by all plants and animals.
→ look at **greenhouse effect**

oys|ter /ɔɪstər/ (oysters) **NOUN** An **oyster** is a small flat ocean animal that has a hard shell and is eaten as food. Oysters can produce pearls (= small round white objects used for making jewelry)

oz. MATH **Oz.** is short for **ounce**. ❏ *...1 oz. of butter.*

ozone lay|er /ou̯zou̯n le͟ɪər/ **NOUN** SCIENCE The **ozone layer** is the area high above the Earth's surface that protects living things from the harmful effects of the sun. ❏ *Scientists discovered another hole in the ozone layer last month.*
→ look at **earth, greenhouse effect**

O

Pp

pace /peɪs/ (paces, pacing, paced)
1 **NOUN** The **pace** of something is the speed at which it happens. ❑ *Since her illness, she is taking life at a slower pace.*
2 **NOUN** A **pace** is the distance that you move when you take one step. ❑ *Peter walked a few paces behind me.*
3 **VERB** If you **pace** a small area, you keep walking around in it because you are worried. ❑ *As they waited, Kravis paced the room nervously.*

paci|fi|er /pæsɪfaɪər/ (pacifiers) **NOUN** A **pacifier** is an object that you put in a baby's mouth to stop it from crying.

pack /pæk/ (packs, packing, packed)
1 **VERB** When you **pack** a bag, you put clothes and other things into it, because you are going away. ❑ *When I was 17, I packed my bags and left home.* ❑ *I began to pack for the trip.*
2 **NOUN** A **pack of** things is a collection of them together in a container. ❑ *...a pack of playing cards.* ❑ *...a pack of gum.*
3 **NOUN** A **pack of** wild dogs or similar animals is a group of them.

pack|age /pækɪdʒ/ (packages) **NOUN** A **package** is something wrapped in paper, or in a box or an envelope. ❑ *I tore open the package.*
→ look at **container**

pack|ag|ing /pækɪdʒɪŋ/ **NONCOUNT NOUN** **Packaging** is the paper or plastic that something is in when you buy it. ❑ *Avoid buying food with plastic packaging.*

pack|et /pækɪt/ (packets)
1 **NOUN** A **packet** is a set of information about a particular subject. ❑ *Call us for a free information packet.*
2 **NOUN** A **packet** is a small box, bag, or envelope in which an amount of something is sold. ❑ *He bought a packet of cookies.*
→ look at **container**

pad /pæd/ (pads)
1 **NOUN** A **pad** is a thick, flat piece of soft material, used for cleaning things or for protection. ❑ *Please wear a helmet and elbow pads.* ❑ *Have you tried using an oven-cleaning pad?*
2 **NOUN** A **pad of** paper is a number of pieces of paper attached together along one side. ❑ *Have a pad ready and write down the information.*

pad|ded /pædɪd/ **ADJECTIVE** Something that is **padded** has soft material in it that makes it softer or warmer, or that protects it. ❑ *...a padded jacket.* ❑ *...a padded envelope.*

pad|ding /pædɪŋ/ **NONCOUNT NOUN** **Padding** is soft material in something that makes it softer or warmer, or that protects it. ❑ *These headphones have foam rubber padding.* ❑ *Players must wear padding to protect them from injury.*

pad|dle /pædəl/ (paddles, paddling, paddled)
1 **NOUN** SPORTS A **paddle** is a short pole with a wide flat part at the end, that you use to move a small boat through water.
2 **VERB** **Paddle** is also a verb. ❑ *He paddled a canoe across the Congo river.*
3 **NOUN** A **paddle** is a specially shaped bat that is used for hitting the ball in the game of ping pong (= a game in which two players hit a light ball over a small net across a table).

pad|lock /pædlɒk/ (padlocks) **NOUN** A **padlock** is a metal lock that is used for fastening two things together. ❑ *They put a padlock on the door of his house.*

page /peɪdʒ/ (pages) **NOUN** A **page** is one side of a piece of paper in a book, a magazine, or a newspaper. ❑ *Turn to page 4.* ❑ *The story was on the front page of USA Today.*

paid /peɪd/
1 **Paid** is a form of the verb **pay**.
2 **ADJECTIVE** A **paid** worker receives money in exchange for working for an employer. ❑ *A small team of paid staff manages the company.* ❑ *His wife is a well-paid accountant.*

pail /peɪl/ (pails) **NOUN** A **pail** is a round container with a handle for carrying water.

pain /peɪn/ (pains)
1 **NOUN** **Pain** is the feeling that you have in a part of your body, because of illness or an injury. ❑ *I felt a sharp pain in my lower back.*

P

2 NONCOUNT NOUN Pain is the sadness that you feel when something upsets you. ❑ *I could see that my words caused him great pain.*

3 If you call someone or something **a pain** or **a pain in the neck**, you mean that they are very annoying. [INFORMAL] ❑ *I like her work, but she can be a pain in the neck.*

4 If you are **in pain**, you feel pain. ❑ *My legs are sore and I'm in pain all the time.*

pain|ful /peɪnfəl/
1 ADJECTIVE If a part of your body is **painful**, it hurts. ❑ *Her toe was swollen and painful.*
● **pain|ful|ly** ADVERB ❑ *Matt banged his head painfully as he climbed out of the window.*
2 ADJECTIVE **Painful** experiences and memories make you feel sad and upset. ❑ *His unkind remarks brought back painful memories.*

pain|killer /peɪnkɪlər/ (**painkillers**) NOUN A **painkiller** is a drug that reduces or stops physical pain.

pain|less /peɪnlɪs/ ADJECTIVE If a treatment is **painless** it causes no physical pain. ❑ *The operation is a quick, painless procedure.*

paint /peɪnt/ (**paints, painting, painted**)
1 NONCOUNT NOUN ARTS **Paint** is a colored liquid that you put onto a surface with a brush. ❑ *We'll need about three cans of red paint.*
2 VERB If you **paint** a wall or an object, you cover it with paint. ❑ *They started to paint the walls.*
3 VERB ARTS If you **paint** something or **paint** a picture of it, you produce a picture of it using paint. ❑ *He is very good at painting flowers.* ❑ *Monet painted hundreds of pictures of water lilies.*
→ look at **draw**

paint|brush /peɪntbrʌʃ/ (**paintbrushes**) NOUN A **paintbrush** is a brush that you use for painting.

paint|er /peɪntər/ (**painters**)
1 NOUN ARTS A **painter** is an artist who paints pictures. ❑ *The movie is about the Dutch painter, Vincent van Gogh.*
2 NOUN A **painter** is a person whose job is to paint walls, doors, or other parts of buildings. ❑ *I worked as a house painter for about five years.*

paint|ing /peɪntɪŋ/ (**paintings**)
1 NOUN ARTS A **painting** is a picture that someone has painted. ❑ *She hung a large painting on the wall.*

2 NONCOUNT NOUN ARTS **Painting** is the activity of painting pictures or covering surfaces with paint. ❑ *She really enjoys painting and gardening.*

pair /pɛər/ (**pairs**)
1 NOUN A **pair of** things is two things of the same size and shape that are used together. ❑ *She wore a pair of plain black shoes.* ❑ *...a pair of earrings.*
2 NOUN You can call some objects that have two main parts of the same size and shape a **pair**. ❑ *He was wearing a pair of old jeans.* ❑ *She took a pair of scissors out of her purse.*
3 A **pair** is two people who are in a romantic relationship together. ❑ *The pair met five years ago at university, and are planning to marry next year.*
4 NOUN You can call two people a **pair** when they are standing or walking together. ❑ *...a pair of teenage boys.*

pa|jam|as /pədʒɑməz, -dʒæm-/ PLURAL NOUN **Pajamas** are loose pants and a top that people wear in bed. ❑ *I don't usually get out of my pajamas on Saturday mornings.*
→ look at **wear**

pal /pæl/ (**pals**) NOUN Your **pals** are your friends. [INFORMAL] ❑ *They talked like old pals.*

pal|ace /pælɪs/ (**palaces**) NOUN A **palace** is a very large impressive house where a king, a queen, or a president lives. ❑ *We visited Buckingham Palace.*

pale /peɪl/ (**paler, palest**)
1 ADJECTIVE A **pale** color is not strong or bright. ❑ *She's wearing a pale blue dress.*
2 ADJECTIVE If someone looks **pale**, their face is a lighter color than usual. ❑ *She looked pale and tired.*

palm /pɑm/ (**palms**)
1 NOUN A **palm** or a **palm tree** is a tree that grows in hot countries. It has long leaves at the top, and no branches. ❑ *...white sand and palm trees.*
2 NOUN The **palm of** your hand is the inside part of your hand, between your fingers and your wrist. ❑ *Dornberg hit the table with the palm of his hand.*
→ look at **hand**

pam|phlet /pæmflɪt/ (**pamphlets**) NOUN A **pamphlet** is a very thin book with a paper cover that gives information about something. ❑ *They gave me a pamphlet about parenting.*

P

pan /pæn/ (pans) NOUN A **pan** is a round metal container with a long handle, that you use for cooking things in. ❑ *Heat the butter and oil in a large pan.*

pan|cake /pænkeɪk/ (pancakes) NOUN A **pancake** is a thin, flat, round cooked food made from milk, flour, and eggs. People often eat pancakes for breakfast, with butter and syrup.

pan|da /pændə/ (pandas) NOUN A **panda** is a large animal with black and white fur.
→ look at **animal**

pane /peɪn/ (panes) NOUN A **pane** of glass is a flat sheet of glass in a window or a door.

pan|el /pænəl/ (panels)
1 NOUN A **panel** is a small group of people who discuss something in public or who make a decision. ❑ *The government will take advice from a panel of experts.*
2 NOUN A **panel** is a flat piece of wood or other material that forms part of a larger object such as a door. ❑ *There was a glass panel in the center of the door.*
3 NOUN A control **panel** is a board with switches and controls on it. ❑ *You can switch the lights on or off using a control panel.*

pan|ic /pænɪk/ (panics, panicking, panicked)
1 NOUN **Panic** is a strong feeling of worry or fear that makes you act without thinking carefully. ❑ *An earthquake caused panic among the population.*
2 VERB If you **panic**, you suddenly feel worried or afraid, and act without thinking carefully. ❑ *Guests panicked and screamed when the bomb exploded.*

pant /pænt/ (pants, panting, panted) VERB If a person or an animal **pants**, they breathe quickly and loudly, because they have been running or because they are very hot. ❑ *Dogs lose body heat by panting and sweating.*

panties /pæntiz/ PLURAL NOUN **Panties** are underwear for women or girls that covers the lower part of the body, but not the legs.

pants /pænts/ PLURAL NOUN **Pants** are a piece of clothing that covers the lower part of your body and each leg. ❑ *He wore brown corduroy pants and a white cotton shirt.*
→ look at **clothing**

pant|suit /pæntsut/ (pantsuits) also **pants suit** NOUN A **pantsuit** is a woman's pants and jacket, made from the same material. ❑ *She wore a white blouse and a gray pantsuit.*

pan|ty|hose /pæntihoʊz/ also **panty hose** PLURAL NOUN **Pantyhose** are a piece of thin clothing worn by women, that covers the body from the waist down to the feet.

papa /pɑpə/ (papas) NOUN Some people call their father **papa**. ❑ *Uncle Maurice was older than my papa.*

pa|per /peɪpər/ (papers)
1 NONCOUNT NOUN **Paper** is a material that you write on or wrap things with. ❑ *He wrote his name down on a piece of paper.* ❑ *He carried the groceries in a paper bag.*
2 NOUN A **paper** is a newspaper. ❑ *I might get a paper when I go downtown.*
3 PLURAL NOUN **Papers** are sheets of paper with information on them. ❑ *The briefcase also contained important official papers.*
→ look at **bag, classroom**

Word Partners	Use **paper** with:
ADJ.	**blank** paper, **brown** paper, **colored** paper, **recycled** paper **1** **daily** paper **2**
V.	**fold** paper **1** **read the** paper **2**
N.	**morning** paper **2**

paper|back /peɪpərbæk/ (paperbacks) NOUN A **paperback** is a book with a thin cardboard or paper cover. ❑ *I'll buy the book when it comes out in paperback.*

paper|boy /peɪpərbɔɪ/ (paperboys) NOUN A **paperboy** is a boy who delivers newspapers to people's homes.

paper|work /peɪpərwɜrk/ NONCOUNT NOUN **Paperwork** is work that involves dealing with letters, reports, and records. ❑ *There will be paperwork—forms to fill in, letters to write.*

para|chute /pærəʃut/ (parachutes) NOUN A **parachute** is a large piece of thin cloth that a person attaches to their body when they jump from an aircraft to help them float safely to the ground. ❑ *They fell 41,000 feet before opening their parachutes.*

P

pa|rade /pəreɪd/ (parades) NOUN A **parade** is a line of people or vehicles moving through a public place in order to celebrate an important event. ❑ *A military parade marched down Pennsylvania Avenue.*

para|dise /pærədaɪs/ (paradises)
1 NOUN In some religions, **paradise** is a beautiful place where good people go after they die.
2 NOUN You can call a beautiful or perfect place **paradise** or **a paradise**. ❑ *The island really is a tropical paradise.*

para|graph /pærəgræf/ (paragraphs) NOUN
LANGUAGE ARTS A **paragraph** is a section of a piece of writing. ❑ *The essay begins with a short introductory paragraph.*
→ look at **writing**

par|al|lel /pærəlɛl/ ADJECTIVE MATH If two lines are **parallel**, they are the same distance apart along their whole length. ❑ *Remsen Street is parallel with Montague Street.*
→ look at **geometry**

para|lyze /pærəlaɪz/ (paralyzes, paralyzing, paralyzed) VERB If someone **is paralyzed** by an accident or an illness, they are unable to move all or part of their body ❑ *She is paralyzed from the waist down.*

par|cel /pɑrsəl/ (parcels) NOUN A **parcel** is something that is wrapped in paper so that it can be sent by mail. ❑ *They sent parcels of food and clothing.*

par|don /pɑrdən/
1 You say "**Pardon?,**" "**I beg your pardon?,**" or "**Pardon me?**" when you want someone to repeat what they have just said. ❑ *"Will you let me open it?"—"Pardon?"—"Can I open it?"*
2 You say "**I beg your pardon**" as a way of apologizing for making a small mistake. ❑ *I beg your pardon. I thought you were someone else.*

par|ent /pɛərənt, pær-/ (parents) NOUN Your **parents** are your mother and father. ❑ *Children need their parents.* ● **pa|ren|tal** /pərɛntəl/ ADJECTIVE ❑ *Children must have parental permission to attend the party.*

par|ent|hood /pɛərənthʊd, pær-/
NONCOUNT NOUN **Parenthood** is the state of being a parent. ❑ *They had to deal with the responsibilities of parenthood.*

park /pɑrk/ (parks, parking, parked)
1 NOUN A **park** is a public area of land with grass and trees, usually in a town, where people go to relax and enjoy themselves. ❑ *...Central Park.* ❑ *I took a walk with the dog around the park.*

2 NOUN A **park** is a place where people play baseball. ❑ *We played baseball in that park every summer.*
3 VERB When you **park** somewhere, you drive a vehicle into a position and you leave it there. ❑ *They parked in the street outside the house.* ❑ *He found a place to park the car.*
● **parking** NONCOUNT NOUN ❑ *Parking is allowed only on one side of the street.*
→ look at **city, car**

park|ing lot (parking lots) NOUN A **parking lot** is an area of ground where people can leave their cars. ❑ *I found a parking lot one block up the street.*

park|way /pɑrkweɪ/ (parkways) NOUN A **parkway** is a wide road with trees and grass on both sides.

par|lia|ment /pɑrləmənt/ (parliaments) also **Parliament** NOUN SOCIAL STUDIES The **parliament** of some countries is the group of people who make or change its laws. ❑ *The German Parliament today approved the policy.*

paro|dy /pærədi/ (parodies) NOUN
LANGUAGE ARTS A **parody** is a piece of writing, drama, or music that copies something in an amusing way. ❑ *The school show was a parody of the "Star Wars" movies.*

pa|role /pəroʊl/ NONCOUNT NOUN A prisoner who is given **parole** may leave prison early if he or she promises to behave well. ❑ *He will soon be able to apply for parole.*

par|rot /pærət/ (parrots) NOUN A **parrot** is a tropical bird with a curved beak and very bright or gray feathers.

pars|ley /pɑrsli/ NONCOUNT NOUN **Parsley** is a type of plant (= a herb) with small green leaves that you use in cooking.

P

part /pɑrt/ (parts, parting, parted)

1 NOUN **Part of** something is a piece of it. ❑ *This was a part of Paris he loved.* ❑ *Perry spent part of his childhood in Canada.*

2 NOUN A **part** is a piece of a machine. ❑ *The company makes small parts for airplanes.*

3 NOUN A **part** in a play or movie is one character's words and actions. ❑ *He played the part of Hamlet.*

4 If you **take part in** an activity, you do it together with other people. ❑ *Thousands of students took part in the demonstrations.*
→ look at **factory**

▶ **part with** If you **part with** something that you would prefer to keep, you give it or sell it to someone else. ❑ *Think carefully before parting with money.*

par|tial /pɑrʃ°l/ ADJECTIVE You use **partial** to talk about something that is not complete. ❑ *These plants prefer to grow in partial shade.*
● **par|tial|ly** ADVERB ❑ *Lisa is partially blind.*

par|tici|pant /pɑrtɪsɪpənt/ (participants) NOUN The **participants** in an activity are the people who take part in it. ❑ *Participants in the course will learn techniques to improve their memory.*

par|tici|pate /pɑrtɪsɪpeɪt/ (participates, participating, participated) VERB If you **participate in** an activity, you take part in it. ❑ *Some of the children participated in sports, or other physical activities.* ● **par|tici|pa|tion** /pɑrtɪsɪpeɪʃ°n/ NONCOUNT NOUN ❑ *Doctors recommend exercise or participation in sport at least two times a week.*
→ look at **disability**

par|ti|ci|ple /pɑrtɪsɪp°l/ (participles) NOUN LANGUAGE ARTS In grammar, a **participle** is a form of the verb that usually ends in "-ed" or "-ing."

par|ticu|lar /pərtɪkyələr/

1 ADJECTIVE You use **particular** to show that you are talking about one thing or one type of thing rather than other similar ones. ❑ *Where did you hear that particular story?* ❑ *I have to know exactly why I'm doing a particular job.*

2 ADJECTIVE You can use **particular** to show that something is greater or stronger than usual. ❑ *We place particular importance on language training.*

3 ADJECTIVE Someone who is **particular** chooses and does things very carefully. ❑ *Ted is very particular about the clothes he wears.*

par|ticu|lar|ly /pərtɪkyələrli/ ADVERB **Particularly** means more than others. ❑ *Keep your office space looking good, particularly your desk.* ❑ *I particularly liked the wooden chairs.*

part|ly /pɑrtli/ ADVERB **Partly** means not completely, but a little. ❑ *It's partly my fault.*

part|ner /pɑrtnər/ (partners)

1 NOUN Your **partner** is your husband or wife, or your boyfriend or girlfriend. ❑ *Len's partner died four years ago.*

2 NOUN Your **partner** in an activity such as a game or a dance is the person you are playing or dancing with. ❑ *She needed a new partner for the doubles game.*

3 NOUN The **partners** in a firm or a business are the people who own it. ❑ *He's a partner in a Chicago law firm.*

part|ner|ship /pɑrtnərʃɪp/ (partnerships) NOUN A **partnership** is a relationship in which two or more people or groups work together. ❑ *We want to develop a closer partnership between the government and the auto industry.*

part of speech (parts of speech) NOUN LANGUAGE ARTS In grammar, a **part of speech** is a particular class of word such as noun, adjective, or verb.

part-time

> **LANGUAGE HELP**
> The adverb is spelled **part time**.

1 ADJECTIVE If someone is a **part-time** worker or has a **part-time** job, they work for only part of each day or week. ❑ *She is trying to get a part-time job in an office.*

2 ADVERB **Part time** is also an adverb. ❑ *I want to work part time.*
→ look at **job**

par|ty /pɑrti/ (parties)

1 NOUN A **party** is a social event at which people enjoy themselves doing things like eating or dancing. ❑ *The couple met at a party.* ❑ *We organized a huge birthday party.*

2 NOUN A **party** is a political organization whose members have similar aims and beliefs. ❑ *He is a member of the Republican Party.*

3 NOUN A **party of** people is a group of them doing something together. ❑ *We passed by a party of tourists.*

pass /pæs/ (passes, passing, passed)

1 VERB When you **pass** someone or something, you go past them. ❑ *When she passed the library door, the telephone began to ring.* ❑ *Jane stood aside to let her pass.*

P

2 VERB When someone or something **passes** in a particular direction, they move in that direction. ❑ *He passed through the doorway into the kitchen.* ❑ *A helicopter passed overhead.*

3 VERB If you **pass** an object **to** someone, you give it to them. ❑ *Pam passed the books to Dr. Wong.*

4 VERB In sport, if you **pass** the ball **to** someone, you kick or throw it to them. ❑ *Hawkins passed the ball to Payton.*

5 NOUN In sport, a **pass** is an act of throwing or kicking the ball to someone on your team. ❑ *Bryan Randall threw a short pass to Ernest Wilford.*

6 VERB If you **pass** something **on to** someone, you give them some information. ❑ *Mary Hayes passed on the news to McEvoy.*

7 VERB When time **passes**, it goes by. ❑ *Time passes quickly when you are enjoying yourself.*

8 VERB If you **pass** time in a particular way, you spend it in that way. ❑ *The children passed the time watching TV.*

9 VERB If you **pass** an examination, you succeed in it. ❑ *Tina passed her driving test last week.*

10 VERB SOCIAL STUDIES When a government **passes** a new law, they formally agree to it. ❑ *Congress passed a law that allowed banks to sell insurance.*

→ look at **school, season**

▶ **pass away** If someone **passes away**, they die. [FORMAL] ❑ *She passed away last year.*

▶ **pass out** If you **pass out**, you suddenly become unconscious. ❑ *He felt sick and then passed out.*

pas|sage /pæsɪdʒ/ (**passages**)

1 NOUN A **passage** is a long narrow space that connects one place or room with another. ❑ *A dark narrow passage led to the kitchen.*

2 NOUN LANGUAGE ARTS A **passage** is a short part of a book. ❑ *He read a passage to her from one of Max's books.*

pas|sen|ger /pæsɪndʒər/ (**passengers**)

NOUN A **passenger** in a vehicle such as a bus, a boat, or a plane is a person who is traveling in it, but who is not driving it. ❑ *Mr. Smith was a passenger in the car when it crashed.*

→ look at **car**

pass|ing grade **NOUN** A **passing grade** is the grade you must get in order to pass a test or examination. ❑ *The passing grade on this exam is seventy.*

pas|sion /pæʃ°n/ (**passions**)

1 NONCOUNT NOUN Passion is a very strong feeling about something or a strong belief in something. ❑ *He spoke with great passion.*

2 NOUN If you have a **passion for** something, you have a very strong interest in it and you like it very much. ❑ *She has a passion for music.*

pas|sion|ate /pæʃənɪt/ **ADJECTIVE** If you are **passionate about** something, you have very strong feelings about it or a strong belief in it. ❑ *He is very passionate about the project.*

pas|sive /pæsɪv/

1 ADJECTIVE A **passive** person allows things to happen without taking action. ❑ *I disliked his passive attitude.* ● **pas|sive|ly** **ADVERB** ❑ *He sat there passively, waiting for me to say something.*

2 NOUN LANGUAGE ARTS In grammar, **the passive** is the form of a verb that you use to show that the subject does not perform the action but is affected by it. For example, in "He's been murdered," the verb **murder** is in the passive. Compare with **active**.

Pass|over /pæsoʊvər/ **NONCOUNT NOUN** Passover is a Jewish festival that begins in March or April and lasts for seven or eight days.

pass|port /pæspɔrt/ (**passports**) **NOUN** Your **passport** is an official document that you have to show when you enter or leave a country. ❑ *You should take your passport with you when you change your money.*

→ look at **identification**

pass|word /pæswɜrd/ (**passwords**) **NOUN** TECHNOLOGY A **password** is a secret word or phrase that allows you to enter a place or to use a computer system. ❑ *Please contact us for a username and password.*

→ look at **email**

past /pæst/

1 NOUN The **past** is the time before the present, and the things that happened then. ❑ *In the past, most babies with the disease died.*

2 PREPOSITION You use **past** to talk about a time that is thirty minutes or less after a particular hour. ❑ *It's ten past eleven.*

3 PREPOSITION If you go **past** someone or something, you pass them. ❑ *I walked past him.*

4 ADVERB Past is also an adverb. ❑ *An ambulance drove past.*

→ look at **grammar, history**

P

pasta

pas|ta /pɑstə/ **NONCOUNT NOUN** Pasta is a type of food made from a mixture of flour, eggs, and water that is made into different shapes and then boiled. ❑ *Italian pizzas and pasta are the restaurant's specialty.*

paste /peɪst/ (**pastes, pasting, pasted**)

1 VERB If you **paste** something onto a surface, you put glue on it and stick it on. ❑ *He pasted labels onto the bottles.*

2 VERB If you **paste** text or images into a computer document, you copy or move them into it from another part of the document, or from another document. ❑ *The text can be copied and pasted into your email program.*

pas|tel /pæstɛl/ (**pastels**)

1 ADJECTIVE Pastel colors are pale rather than dark or bright. ❑ *Mother always chooses clothes in delicate pastel shades.* ❑ *...pastel pink, blue, and green.*

2 NOUN ARTS Pastels are sticks of color made of a substance like chalk, and used by artists for drawing. ❑ *This paper is ideal for use with paints, crayons, and pastels.*

pas|tor /pæstər/ (**pastors**) **NOUN** A **pastor** is a religious leader in some churches.

pas|try /peɪstri/ (**pastries**)

1 NONCOUNT NOUN Pastry is a food made from flour, fat, and water that is often used for making pies (= a dish of meat, vegetables or fruit with a cover made of pastry).

2 NOUN A **pastry** is a small cake made with sweet pastry. ❑ *The bakery sells delicious cakes and pastries.*

past tense (**past tenses**) **NOUN**
LANGUAGE ARTS In grammar, **the past tense** is the form that is used for talking about the time that came before the present. For example, the past tense of the verb "see" is "saw."

pat /pæt/ (**pats, patting, patted**)

1 VERB If you **pat** something or someone, you touch them lightly with your flat hand. ❑ *"Don't you worry," she said, patting me on the knee.* ❑ *The lady patted her hair nervously.*

2 NOUN Pat is also a noun. ❑ *He gave her a friendly pat on the shoulder.*

patch /pætʃ/ (**patches**)

1 NOUN A **patch** on a surface is a part that is different in appearance from the area around it. ❑ *She noticed the bald patch on the top of his head.* ❑ *There was a small patch of blue in the gray clouds.*

2 NOUN A **patch** is a piece of cloth that you use to cover a hole in a piece of clothing. ❑ *Brad was wearing an old jacket with leather patches on the elbows.*

path /pæθ/ (**paths**) **NOUN** A **path** is a long, narrow piece of ground that people walk along. ❑ *We followed the path along the cliff.*

pa|thet|ic /pəθɛtɪk/ **ADJECTIVE** If someone or something is **pathetic**, they are weak or not very good. ❑ *What a pathetic attempt to hide the truth.*

pa|tience /peɪʃəns/ **NONCOUNT NOUN** If you have **patience**, you are able to stay calm and not get annoyed, for example, when something takes a long time. ❑ *He doesn't have the patience to wait.*

pa|tient /peɪʃənt/ (**patients**)

1 NOUN A **patient** is a person who receives medical treatment from a doctor. ❑ *The patient was suffering from heart problems.*

2 ADJECTIVE If you are **patient**, you stay calm and you do not get annoyed, for example, when something takes a long time. ❑ *Please be patient—your check will arrive soon.* ● **pa|tient|ly ADVERB** ❑ *She waited patiently for Frances to finish talking.*
→ look at **health care**

pa|tio /pætioʊ/ (**patios**) **NOUN** A **patio** is a flat area next to a house, where people can sit and relax or eat.

pa|tri|ot /peɪtriət/ (**patriots**)

1 NOUN A **patriot** is a person who loves their country and feels very loyal toward it. ❑ *He was a true patriot, supporting the government's war effort.*

2 NOUN SOCIAL STUDIES In America in the 18th century, the **Patriots** were the people who came from Britain, who rejected British rule and fought in the American Revolution. ❑ *The leaders of the Patriots are now called "The Founding Fathers of the United States."*

pat|ri|ot|ic /peɪtriɒtɪk/ **ADJECTIVE** Someone who is **patriotic** loves their country and feels very loyal toward it. ❑ *They are very patriotic guys who give everything for their country.*

P

pa|trol /pətroʊl/ (patrols, patrolling, patrolled)

1 **VERB** When soldiers, police, or guards **patrol** an area, they move around it to make sure that there is no trouble there. ❏ *Prison officers continued to patrol the grounds.*

2 **NOUN** Patrol is also a noun. ❏ *The army is now on patrol.*

3 **NOUN** A **patrol** is a group of soldiers or vehicles that move around an area in order to make sure that there is no trouble there. ❏ *The three men attacked a border patrol last night.*

pat|tern /pætərn/ (patterns)

1 **NOUN** A **pattern** is the repeated or regular way in which something happens or is done. ❏ *All three attacks followed the same pattern.*

2 **NOUN** ARTS A **pattern** is an arrangement of lines or shapes that form a design. ❏ *The carpet had a pattern of light and dark stripes.*

pause /pɔz/ (pauses, pausing, paused)

1 **VERB** If you **pause** while you are doing something, you stop for a short time and then continue. ❏ *"It's rather embarrassing," he began, and paused.* ❏ *She started speaking when I paused for breath.*

2 **NOUN** A **pause** is a short period of time when you stop doing something. ❏ *After a pause Al said: "I'm sorry if I upset you."*

pave|ment /peɪvmənt/ (pavements) **NOUN** The **pavement** is the hard surface of a road. ❏ *It was difficult to control the car on the wet pavement.*

paw /pɔ/ (paws) **NOUN** The **paws** of an animal such as a cat, dog, or bear are its feet. ❏ *The kitten was black with white front paws.*

pay /peɪ/ (pays, paying, paid)

1 **VERB** When you **pay for** something, you give someone an amount of money for it. ❏ *Can I pay for my ticket with a credit card?*

2 **VERB** When you **pay** a bill or a debt, you give someone an amount of money for it. ❏ *She paid the hotel bill before she left.* ❏ *The company was fined and ordered to pay court costs.*

3 **VERB** When you **are paid**, you get your salary from your employer. ❏ *The lawyer was paid a huge salary.* ❏ *I get paid monthly.*

4 **NONCOUNT NOUN** Pay is also a noun. ❏ *They complained about their pay and working conditions.*

→ look at **shopping**

▶ **pay back** If you **pay back** money that you have borrowed from someone, you give them an equal amount at a later time. ❏ *He promised to pay the money back as soon as he could.*

pay|check /peɪtʃɛk/ (paychecks) **NOUN** Your **paycheck** is the money that your employer gives you for the work that you have done . ❏ *I get a small paycheck every month.*

→ look at **job**

pay|ment /peɪmənt/ (payments)

1 **NOUN** A **payment** is an amount of money that is paid to someone. ❏ *You will receive 13 monthly payments.*

2 **NONCOUNT NOUN** Payment is the act of paying money or of being paid. ❏ *Players now expect payment for interviews.*

→ look at Picture Dictionary: **payments**

P

Picture Dictionary   payments

credit card

debit card

money / cash — bills / coins

check

money order

PC /pi si/ (**PCs**) **NOUN** **TECHNOLOGY** A **PC** is a computer that people use at school, at home, or in an office. **PC** is short for **personal computer**. ❏ *The price of PCs is falling.*

PDF /pi di ɛf/ **NONCOUNT NOUN** **TECHNOLOGY** **PDF** files are computer documents that look exactly like the original documents. **PDF** is short for "Portable Document Format."

pea /pi/ (**peas**) **NOUN** **Peas** are very small, round, green vegetables.

| Sound Partners | peace, piece |
---

peace /pis/
1 **NONCOUNT NOUN** When there is **peace** in a country, there is not a war. ❏ *The new rulers brought peace to the country.* ❏ *The two countries signed a peace agreement.*
2 **NONCOUNT NOUN** **Peace** is the state of being quiet and calm. ❏ *I just want some peace and quiet.*

peace|ful /pisfəl/
1 **ADJECTIVE** **Peaceful** means not involving war or violence. ❏ *He has attempted to find a peaceful solution to the conflict.* ● **peace|ful|ly** **ADVERB** ❏ *The governor asked the protestors to leave peacefully.*
2 **ADJECTIVE** A **peaceful** place or time is quiet and calm. ❏ *The backyard looked so peaceful.*
→ look at **relax**

peach /pitʃ/ (**peaches**)
1 **NOUN** A **peach** is a round fruit with a soft red and orange skin.
2 **ADJECTIVE** Something that is **peach** is of a pale color between pink and orange. ❏ *...a peach silk blouse.*
3 **NOUN** **Peach** is also a noun. ❏ *The room was decorated in peach.*

peak /pik/ (**peaks**)
1 **NOUN** The **peak** of a process or an activity is the point at which it is at its strongest. ❏ *His career was at its peak when he died.*
2 **NOUN** A **peak** is a mountain or the top of a mountain. ❏ *They could see the snowy peaks of the Canadian Rockies.*

pea|nut /pinʌt, -nət/ (**peanuts**) **NOUN** **Peanuts** are small nuts that you can eat.

pear /pɛər/ (**pears**) **NOUN** A **pear** is a juicy fruit that is narrow at the top and wider at the bottom. Pears have white flesh and green, yellow, or brown skin.
→ look at **fruit**

pearl /pɜrl/ (**pearls**) **NOUN** A **pearl** is a hard, white, shiny, round object that grows inside the shell of an oyster (= a water creature). **Pearls** are used for making jewelry. ❏ *She wore a string of pearls.*

peas|ant /pɛzᵊnt/ (**peasants**) **NOUN** People call small farmers or farm workers in poor countries **peasants**. ❏ *The film describes the customs and habits of peasants in Peru.*

peb|ble /pɛbᵊl/ (**pebbles**) **NOUN** A **pebble** is a small, smooth stone.

pe|cu|liar /pɪkyulyər/ **ADJECTIVE** A **peculiar** person or thing is strange or unusual. ❏ *Mr. Kennet has a rather peculiar sense of humor.*

ped|al /pɛdᵊl/ (**pedals, pedaling, pedaled**)
1 **NOUN** The **pedals** on a bicycle are the two parts that you push with your feet to make the bicycle move.
2 **VERB** When you **pedal** a bicycle, you push the pedals around with your feet to make it move. ❏ *We pedaled slowly through the city streets.*
3 **NOUN** A **pedal** in a car or on a machine is a part that you press with your foot in order to control it. ❏ *...the brake pedal.*

pe|des|trian /pɪdɛstriən/ (**pedestrians**) **NOUN** A **pedestrian** is a person who is walking, especially in a town or city. ❏ *The city's sidewalks were busy with pedestrians.*

pe|dom|eter /pɪdɒmɪtər/ (**pedometers**) **NOUN** A **pedometer** is a piece of equipment that measures the distance that someone has walked.

peek /pik/ (**peeks, peeking, peeked**)
1 **VERB** If you **peek at** something or someone, you look at them quickly and often secretly. ❏ *She peeked at him through a crack in the wall.*
2 **NOUN** **Peek** is also a noun. ❏ *I had a peek at his computer screen.*

peel /pil/ (**peels, peeling, peeled**)
1 **NONCOUNT NOUN** The **peel** of a fruit such as a lemon or an apple is its skin. ❏ *Add in the grated lemon peel.*
2 **VERB** When you **peel** fruit or vegetables, you remove their skins. ❏ *She began peeling potatoes.*

3 VERB If something **peels off** a surface, it comes away from it. ❑ *Paint was peeling off the walls.* ❑ *It took me two days to peel off the labels.*
→ look at **fruit**

peep /pip/ (**peeps, peeping, peeped**)
1 VERB If you **peep at** something, you take a quick look at it. ❑ *A small child was peeping through the window at him.*
2 NOUN Peep is also a noun. ❑ *She lifted the lid and took a quick peep inside.*

peer /pɪər/ (**peers, peering, peered**) VERB If you **peer at** something, you look at it very closely, usually because it is difficult to see clearly. ❑ *He found her peering at a computer print-out.*

peer press|ure NONCOUNT NOUN If someone does something because of **peer pressure**, they do it because other people in their social group do it. ❑ *I don't let peer pressure affect me. I think for myself.*

peg /pɛg/ (**pegs**)
1 NOUN A **peg** is a small piece of wood or metal that you use for attaching one thing to another thing. ❑ *He builds furniture using wooden pegs instead of nails.*
2 NOUN A **peg** is a small hook on a wall that you hang things on. ❑ *His work jacket hung on the peg in the kitchen.*

pel|vis /pɛlvɪs/ (**pelvises**) NOUN SCIENCE Your **pelvis** is the wide, curved group of bones between your back and your legs.

pen /pɛn/ (**pens**) NOUN A **pen** is a long thin object that you use for writing with ink (= a colored liquid).
→ look at **classroom, office**

pen|al|ty /pɛnəlti/ (**penalties**)
1 NOUN A **penalty** is a punishment for doing something that is against a law or rule. ❑ *The maximum penalty for dangerous driving is five years in prison.*
2 NOUN SPORTS In sports such as football and hockey, a **penalty** is a punishment for the team that breaks a rule, and an advantage for the other team. ❑ *His first goal came on a penalty kick in the fifty-second minute.*

pen|cil /pɛnsəl/ (**pencils**) NOUN ARTS A **pencil** is a thin piece of wood with a black or colored substance through the middle that you use to write or draw with. ❑ *She used a pencil and some blank paper to draw the picture.*
→ look at **classroom, office**

pen|etrate /pɛnɪtreɪt/ (**penetrates, penetrating, penetrated**) VERB If something **penetrates** an object, it gets into it or passes through it. ❑ *X-rays can penetrate many objects.*

pen|guin /pɛŋgwɪn/ (**penguins**) NOUN A **penguin** is a black and white bird that lives in very cold places. Penguins can swim but they cannot fly.
→ look at **animal**

pen|in|su|la /pənɪnsələ, -nɪnsyə-/ (**peninsulas**) NOUN GEOGRAPHY A **peninsula** is a long narrow piece of land that sticks out from a larger piece of land and is almost completely surrounded by water. ❑ *...the Alaskan peninsula.*
→ look at **landform**

pe|nis /pinɪs/ (**penises**) NOUN A man's **penis** is the part of his body that he uses when he gets rid of waste liquid (= urine) and when he has sex.

pen|ny /pɛni/ (**pennies**) NOUN A **penny** is one cent, or a coin worth one cent. [INFORMAL] ❑ *The price of gasoline rose by more than a penny a gallon.*

pen|sion /pɛnʃən/ (**pensions**) NOUN A **pension** is money that you regularly receive from a business or the government after you stop working because of your age. ❑ *He gets a $35,000 a year pension.*

pen|ta|gon /pɛntəgɑːn/ (**pentagons**) NOUN MATH A **pentagon** is a shape with five straight sides.

pent|house /pɛnthaʊs/ (**penthouses**) NOUN A **penthouse** is an expensive apartment at the top of a tall building. ❑ *She lives in an elegant Manhattan penthouse.*

peo|ple /pipəl/ PLURAL NOUN People are men, women, and children. ❑ *Millions of people have lost their homes.* ❑ *He's reading a book about the people of Angola.*
→ look at **history**

pep|per /pɛpər/ (**peppers**)
1 NONCOUNT NOUN Pepper is a spice with a hot taste that you put on food. ❑ *Season with salt and pepper.*
2 NOUN A **pepper** is a hollow green, red, or yellow vegetable with seeds inside it. ❑ *Thinly slice two red or green peppers.*
→ look at **vegetable**

pepper|mint /pɛpərmɪnt/ (**peppermints**)
1 NONCOUNT NOUN Peppermint is a strong,

P

sharp flavor from the peppermint plant.
2 **NOUN** A **peppermint** is a piece of candy with a peppermint flavor.

per /pər, STRONG pɜr/ **PREPOSITION** You use **per** to talk about each one of something. For example, if a vehicle is traveling at 40 miles **per** hour, it travels 40 miles each hour. ❑ *They spend $200 per week on groceries.*

per|an|num /pər ænəm/ **ADVERB** A particular amount **per annum** means that amount each year. ❑ *They must pay a fee of $3000 per annum.*

per|ceive /pərsiv/ (**perceives, perceiving, perceived**)
1 **VERB** If you **perceive** something, you notice, or realize it, especially when it is not obvious. ❑ *A great artist teaches us to perceive reality in a different way.*
2 **VERB** If you **perceive** something **as** a particular thing, it is your opinion that it is that thing. ❑ *Stress is widely perceived as a cause of heart disease.*

percent /pərsɛnt/ (**percent**) **NOUN** MATH
You use **percent** to talk about amounts as parts of a hundred. One hundred percent (100%) is all of something, and 50 percent (50%) is half. ❑ *Only ten percent of our customers live in this city.*

per|cent|age /pərsɛntɪdʒ/ (**percentages**)
NOUN MATH A **percentage** is an amount of something. ❑ *He regularly eats foods with a high percentage of protein.*
→ look at **fraction**

perch /pɜrtʃ/ (**perches, perching, perched**)
1 **VERB** If you **perch on** something, you sit on the edge of it. ❑ *He perched on the corner of the desk.*
2 **VERB** When a bird **perches on** a branch or a wall, it lands on it and stands there. ❑ *Two doves perched on a nearby fence.*

per|cus|sion /pərkʌʃ°n/ **NONCOUNT NOUN**
MUSIC **Percussion** instruments are musical instruments that you hit, such as drums. ❑ *This is a piece for the orchestra's powerful percussion section.*

per|fect /pɜrfɪkt/ **ADJECTIVE** Something that is **perfect** is as good as it could possibly be. ❑ *He spoke perfect English.* ❑ *Nobody is perfect.*
● **per|fect|ly** **ADVERB** ❑ *The system worked perfectly.*

per|fec|tion /pərfɛkʃ°n/ **NONCOUNT NOUN**
Perfection is the quality of being as good as possible. ❑ *The meat was cooked to perfection.*

perfect tense (**perfect tenses**) **NOUN**
LANGUAGE ARTS In grammar, **the perfect tense** is the form that is used for talking about an action that has been completed before the present time. For example, in the sentence: "I have never seen that movie," the verb "see" is in the perfect tense.

per|form /pərfɔrm/ (**performs, performing, performed**)
1 **VERB** When you **perform** a task or an action, you do it. ❑ *You must perform this exercise correctly to avoid back pain.*
2 **VERB** If you **perform** a play, a piece of music, or a dance, you do it in front of an audience. ❑ *They will be performing works by Bach and Scarlatti.* ● **per|form|er** (**performers**)
NOUN ❑ *She was one of the top jazz performers in New York City.*
3 **VERB** If someone or something **performs well**, they work well or achieve a good result. ❑ *He has not performed well on his exams.* ❑ *The industry has performed poorly this year.*
→ look at **performance**

per|for|mance /pərfɔrm.əns/ (**performances**)
1 **NOUN** If you give a **performance**, you entertain an audience by singing, dancing, or acting. ❑ *They were giving a performance of Bizet's "Carmen."*

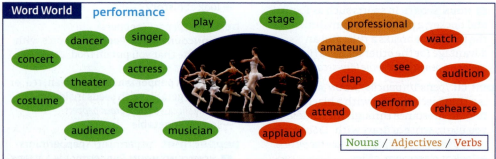

Word World — performance

play · stage · professional · watch · dancer · singer · amateur · see · concert · actress · clap · audition · theater · costume · actor · attend · perform · rehearse · audience · musician · applaud

Nouns / Adjectives / Verbs

2 NOUN Someone's or something's **performance** is how successful they are or how well they do something. ❑ *The study looked at the performance of 18 surgeons.* ❑ *He spoke about the poor performance of the economy.*

→ look at Word World: **performance**

per|fume /pɜrfyum, pərfyum/ (**perfumes**) **NOUN** Perfume is a liquid with a pleasant smell that you put on your skin. ❑ *The hall smelled of her mother's perfume.*

per|haps /pərhæps, præps/ **ADVERB** You use **perhaps** to show that you are not sure whether something is true, possible, or likely. ❑ *In the end they lost millions, perhaps billions.* ❑ *Perhaps, in time, they will understand.*

pe|rim|eter /pərɪmɪtər/ (**perimeters**) **NOUN** **MATH** The **perimeter** of a flat shape is the total distance around its edge. ❑ *To work out the perimeter of a rectangle, you need to know its length and width.*

→ look at **area, geometry**

pe|ri|od /pɪəriəd/ (**periods**)
1 NOUN A **period** is a length of time. ❑ *He couldn't work for a long period of time.*
2 NOUN LANGUAGE ARTS A **period** is the punctuation mark (.) that you use at the end of a sentence.
3 NOUN A woman's **period** is the time when she loses blood from her body each month.
→ look at **punctuation**

per|ma|nent /pɜrmənənt/ **ADJECTIVE** If something is **permanent** it continues forever or for a very long time. ❑ *Some ear infections can cause permanent damage.* ❑ *He's never had a permanent job.*
● **per|ma|nent|ly** **ADVERB** ❑ *His confidence has been permanently affected.*

per|mis|sion /pərmɪʃ⁰n/ **NONCOUNT NOUN** If you give someone **permission to** do something, you allow them to do it. ❑ *He asked permission to leave the room.* ❑ *They cannot leave the country without permission.*

per|mit (**permits, permitting, permitted**)

> **PRONUNCIATION HELP**
> Pronounce the verb /pərmɪt/. Pronounce the noun /pɜrmɪt/.

1 VERB If someone **permits** you **to** do something, they allow you to do it. [FORMAL] ❑ *The guards permitted me to bring my camera.*
2 NOUN A **permit** is an official document

that allows you to do something. ❑ *She hasn't got a work permit.*

per|se|vere /pɜrsɪvɪər/ (**perseveres, persevering, persevered**) **VERB** If you **persevere with** something difficult, you continue to do it. ❑ *Berman ignored their criticisms, and persevered with his plan.*

per|son /pɜrs⁰n/ (**people** or **persons**)
1 NOUN A **person** is a man, a woman, or a child. ❑ *At least one person died and several others were injured.* ❑ *They were both lovely, friendly people.*
2 If you meet or see someone **in person**, you are in the same place as them, and not speaking to them on the telephone or writing to them. ❑ *She saw him in person for the first time last night.*

per|son|al /pɜrsən⁰l/
1 ADJECTIVE A **personal** opinion or experience relates to a particular person. ❑ *The story is based on his own personal experience.* ❑ *That's my personal opinion.*
2 ADJECTIVE **Personal** matters relate to your feelings, relationships, and health. ❑ *Did he mention that he has any personal problems?*
→ look at **identification**

per|son|al com|put|er (**personal computers**) **NOUN** TECHNOLOGY A **personal computer** is a computer that you use at work, school, or home. The short form **PC** is also used.

per|son|al|ity /pɜrsənælɪti/ (**personalities**) **NOUN** Your **personality** is the qualities that make you different from other people. ❑ *She has such a kind, friendly personality.*

per|son|al|ly /pɜrsənəli/
1 ADVERB You use **personally** to emphasize that you are giving your own opinion. ❑ *Personally I think it's a waste of time.*
2 ADVERB If you do something **personally**, you do it yourself rather than letting someone else do it. ❑ *He wrote to them personally to explain the situation.*

per|son|nel /pɜrsənɛl/ **PLURAL NOUN** The **personnel** of an organization are the people who work for it. ❑ *The president will give a speech to military personnel at the army base.*

per|spec|tive /pərspɛktɪv/ (**perspectives**)
1 NOUN A particular **perspective** is a way of thinking about something. ❑ *The death of his father has given him a new perspective on life.*
2 NOUN ARTS In art, **perspective** is a way of

p

making some objects or people in a picture seem further away than others.

per|spi|ra|tion /pɜrspɪreɪʃ°n/ **NONCOUNT NOUN** Perspiration is the liquid that appears on your skin when you are hot. [FORMAL] ❑ *His hands were wet with perspiration.*

per|suade /pərsweɪd/ (**persuades, persuading, persuaded**) **VERB** If you **persuade** someone **to** do something, you make them do it by talking to them. ❑ *My husband persuaded me to come.*

per|sua|sion /pərsweɪʒ°n/ **NONCOUNT NOUN** Persuasion is the process of making someone do or think something. ❑ *After much persuasion from Ellis, she agreed to perform.*

pes|si|mism /pɛsɪmɪzəm/ **NONCOUNT NOUN** Pessimism is the belief that bad things are going to happen. ❑ *There was a general pessimism about the economy.* ● **pes|si|mist** (**pessimists**) **NOUN** ❑ *I'm a natural pessimist, so I usually expect the worst.* ● **pes|si|mis|tic** /pɛsɪmɪstɪk/ **ADJECTIVE** ❑ *She is so pessimistic about the future.*

pest /pɛst/ (**pests**)
1 NOUN Pests are insects or small animals that damage crops or food. ❑ *They use chemicals to fight pests and diseases.*
2 NOUN If someone, especially a child, is a **pest**, they are annoying you. [INFORMAL] ❑ *He climbed on the table, pulled my hair, and was generally a pest.*

pet /pɛt/ (**pets**) **NOUN** A **pet** is an animal that you keep in your home. ❑ *He loved his pet dog.* ❑ *You should not keep wild animals as pets.*

pet|al /pɛt°l/ (**petals**) **NOUN** The **petals** of a flower are the thin colored parts that form the flower. ❑ *Her perfume smelled of rose petals.*

pe|ti|tion /pətɪʃ°n/ (**petitions**) **NOUN** SOCIAL STUDIES A **petition** is a document that contains the signatures of a group of people who are asking a government or other official group to do a particular thing. ❑ *The government received a petition signed by 4,500 people.*

phar|ma|cist /fɑrməsɪst/ (**pharmacists**) **NOUN** A **pharmacist** is a person whose job is to prepare and sell medicines. ❑ *Ask your pharmacist for advice.*

phar|ma|cy /fɑrməsi/ (**pharmacies**) **NOUN** A **pharmacy** is a place where you can buy medicines. ❑ *Pick up the medicine from the pharmacy.*

phase /feɪz/ (**phases**) **NOUN** A **phase** is a particular stage in a process. ❑ *6000 women will take part in the first phase of the project.*

phi|loso|pher /fɪlɒsəfər/ (**philosophers**) **NOUN** A **philosopher** is a person who studies or writes about philosophy. ❑ *He admired the Greek philosopher Plato.*

phi|loso|phy /fɪlɒsəfi/ (**philosophies**)
1 NONCOUNT NOUN Philosophy is the study of ideas about the meaning of life. ❑ *She is studying traditional Chinese philosophy.*
● **philo|sophi|cal** /fɪləsɒfɪk°l/ **ADJECTIVE** ❑ *They often had philosophical discussions.*
2 NOUN A **philosophy** is a particular theory or belief. ❑ *The best philosophy is to change to a low-sugar diet.*

phone /foʊn/ (**phones, phoning, phoned**)
1 NOUN A **phone** is a piece of equipment that you use to talk to someone else in another place. ❑ *Two minutes later the phone rang.*
2 VERB When you **phone** someone, you contact them and speak to them by telephone. ❑ *He phoned Laura to see if she was better.* ❑ *"Did anybody phone?" asked Alberg.*
3 If someone is **on the phone**, they are speaking to someone by telephone. ❑ *She's always on the phone.*
→ look at Word World: **phone**
→ look at **office**

Word World | phone

local — international — long-distance
conversation
network — number — emergency — text
cellphone — use
message — caller — dial — ring — talk
service — telephone — charge — call

Nouns / Adjectives / Verbs

phone call (phone calls) **NOUN** If you make a **phone call**, you enter a number into a telephone and speak to someone who is in another place. ❑ *I have to make a phone call.*

pho|ny /foʊni/ (phonier, phoniest, phonies) also **phoney**
1 **ADJECTIVE** Something that is **phony** is not real. [INFORMAL] ❑ *He made some phony excuse.* ❑ *I answered my phone in a phony British accent.*
2 **ADJECTIVE** Someone who is **phony** is pretending to be better or nicer than they really are. [INFORMAL] ❑ *The people there are so phony.*
3 **NOUN** Phony is also a noun. ❑ *He's such a phony.*

pho|to /foʊtoʊ/ (photos) **NOUN** A **photo** is the same as a **photograph**.

photo|copi|er /foʊtəkɒpiər/ (photocopiers) **NOUN** A **photocopier** is a machine that copies documents by photographing them.

photo|copy /foʊtəkɒpi/ (photocopies, photocopying, photocopied)
1 **NOUN** A **photocopy** is a copy of a document that you make using a special machine (= a photocopier). ❑ *He gave me a photocopy of the letter.*
2 **VERB** If you **photocopy** a document, you make a copy of it using a photocopier. ❑ *He photocopied the documents before sending them off.*

photo|graph /foʊtəgræf/ (photographs, photographing, photographed)
1 **NOUN** ARTS A **photograph** is a picture that you take with a camera. ❑ *He wants to take some photographs of the house.*
2 **VERB** ARTS When you **photograph** someone or something, you use a camera to take a picture of them. [FORMAL] ❑ *She photographed the children.*
→ look at **identification**

pho|tog|ra|pher /fətɒgrəfər/ (photographers) **NOUN** A **photographer** is someone who takes photographs as a job or a hobby. ❑ *He's a professional photographer.*

pho|tog|ra|phy /fətɒgrəfi/ **NONCOUNT NOUN** ARTS Photography is the skill or process of producing photographs. ❑ *Photography is one of her hobbies.*

photo|syn|the|sis /foʊtoʊsɪnθəsɪs/ **NONCOUNT NOUN** SCIENCE Photosynthesis is the way that green plants make their food using the light of the sun.

phras|al verb /freɪzəl vɜrb/ (phrasal verbs) **NOUN** LANGUAGE ARTS A **phrasal verb** is a combination of a verb and an adverb or preposition, for example, "get over" or "give up," which together have a particular meaning.

phrase /freɪz/ (phrases) **NOUN** LANGUAGE ARTS A **phrase** is a group of words that you use together as part of a sentence, for example, "in the morning." ❑ *At the end of the book, there is a glossary of useful words and phrases.*
→ look at **grammar, writing**

phys ed /fɪz ɛd/ **NONCOUNT NOUN** Phys ed is the same as **physical education**. [INFORMAL] ❑ *Don teaches phys ed at a junior high school.*

physi|cal /fɪzɪkəl/ **ADJECTIVE** Physical means connected with a person's body, rather than with their mind. ❑ *Physical activity promotes good health.* ● **physi|cal|ly** **ADVERB** ❑ *Kerry is physically active and in excellent health.*
→ look at **fitness, science**

physi|cal edu|ca|tion **NONCOUNT NOUN** SPORTS Physical education is the school subject in which students do physical exercises or take part in physical games and sports.

phy|si|cian /fɪzɪʃən/ (physicians) **NOUN** A **physician** is a medical doctor. [FORMAL] ❑ *Ask your family physician for advice.*

physi|cist /fɪzɪsɪst/ (physicists) **NOUN** A **physicist** is a person who studies physics. ❑ *He was one of the best nuclear physicists in the country.*

phys|ics /fɪzɪks/ **NONCOUNT NOUN** SCIENCE Physics is the scientific study of things such as heat, light, and sound. ❑ *His favorite school subjects were chemistry and physics.*
→ look at **science**

pia|nist /piænɪst, piənɪst/ (pianists) **NOUN** MUSIC A **pianist** is a person who plays the piano. ❑ *She wants to be a concert pianist.*

pi|ano /piænoʊ, pyænoʊ/ (pianos) **NOUN** MUSIC A **piano** is a large musical instrument that you play by pressing black and white bars (= keys). ❑ *I taught myself how to play the piano.*
→ look at **musical instrument**

pic|co|lo /pɪkəloʊ/ (piccolos) **NOUN** MUSIC A **piccolo** is a musical instrument that is like a small flute (= a pipe that you put across your lips and blow).

P

pick /pɪk/ (picks, picking, picked)

1 **VERB** If you **pick** a particular person or thing, you choose that one. ❑ *Mr. Nowell picked ten people to interview.*

2 **VERB** When you **pick** flowers, fruit, or leaves, you take them from a plant or tree. ❑ *I've picked some flowers from the garden.*

▶ **pick on** If someone **picks on** you, they repeatedly criticize you or treat you unkindly. [INFORMAL] ❑ *Bullies often pick on younger children.*

▶ **pick out** **1** If you **pick out** someone or something, you recognize them when it is difficult to see them. ❑ *I had trouble picking out the words, even with my glasses on.*

2 If you **pick** someone or something **out**, you choose them from a group of people or things. ❑ *They picked me out to represent the whole team.*

▶ **pick up** **1** When you **pick** something **up**, you lift it up. ❑ *He picked his cap up from the floor.*

2 When you **pick up** someone or something, you collect them from a place, often in a car. ❑ *Please could you will pick me up at 5pm?* ❑ *She went to her parents' house to pick up some clean clothes.*

3 If you **pick up** a skill or an idea, you learn it without really trying over a period of time. [INFORMAL] ❑ *Her children have picked up English really quickly.*

pick|le /pɪkᵊl/ (pickles) **PLURAL NOUN** Pickles are small cucumbers (= long green vegetables) that are kept in liquid for a long time to give them a strong, sharp taste. ❑ *We had hamburgers with pickles, ketchup, and mustard.*

pic|nic /pɪknɪk/ (picnics, picnicking, picnicked)

1 **NOUN** When people have a **picnic**, they eat a meal outdoors, usually in a park or a forest, or at the beach. ❑ *We're going on a picnic tomorrow.*

2 **VERB** When people **picnic** somewhere, they have a picnic. ❑ *Afterward, we picnicked by the river.*

pic|ture /pɪktʃər/ (pictures, picturing, pictured)

1 **NOUN** ARTS A **picture** is a drawing or painting. ❑ *She drew a picture with colored chalk.*

2 **NOUN** A **picture** is a photograph. ❑ *I love taking pictures of animals.*

3 **VERB** If you **picture** something you think of it and see it in your mind. ❑ *He pictured her with long black hair.*

pie /paɪ/ (pies) **NOUN** A **pie** is a dish of fruit, meat, or vegetables that is covered with pastry (= a mixture of flour, butter, and water) and baked. ❑ *We each had a slice of apple pie.*

Sound Partners	piece, peace

piece /piːs/ (pieces)

1 **NOUN** A **piece of** something is a part of it. ❑ *You must only take one piece of cake.* ❑ *Cut the chicken into pieces.*

2 **NOUN** A **piece of** something is an amount of it. ❑ *That's an interesting piece of information.* ❑ *This is his finest piece of work yet.* ❑ *He has composed 1500 pieces of music for TV.*

3 If something is **in pieces**, it is broken. ❑ *The china vase was in pieces on the floor.*

pier /pɪər/ (piers) **NOUN** A **pier** is a long, flat structure that is built out from the land at the edge of an area of water so that people can get into and out of boats easily. ❑ *The ship was tied up at Chicago's Navy Pier.*

pierce /pɪərs/ (pierces, piercing, pierced)

1 **VERB** If you **pierce** something, you make a hole in it with a sharp object. ❑ *Pierce the chicken with a sharp knife to check that it is cooked.*

2 **VERB** If you have your ears **pierced**, small holes are made through them so that you can wear earrings (= jewelry for the ears) in them. ❑ *I'm having my ears pierced on Saturday.*

pierc|ing /pɪərsɪŋ/ **ADJECTIVE** A **piercing** sound is high, and clear in a sharp and unpleasant way. ❑ *She let out a piercing scream.*

pig /pɪg/ (pigs)

1 **NOUN** A **pig** is a farm animal with a fat body and short legs, that is kept for its meat. ❑ *Kids can help feed the pigs.*

2 **NOUN** **Pig** is a rude way of talking about someone who is unkind or who eats too much. [INFORMAL] ❑ *You've eaten my toast, you greedy pig!*

→ look at **farm**

pi|geon /pɪdʒɪn/ (pigeons) **NOUN** A **pigeon** is a large gray bird that is often seen in cities.

→ look at **bird**

pig|tail /pɪgteɪl/ (pigtails) NOUN A **pigtail** is a length of hair hanging loose in a bunch, or twisted and tied at the end. ❑ *Her hair was tied back in pigtails.*
→ look at **hair**

Pilates /pɪlɑtiz/ NONCOUNT NOUN SPORTS **Pilates** is a type of exercise that helps you to bend more easily, and develops the muscles in your back and abdomen (= the part of your body below your chest). ❑ *I do Pilates every day before breakfast.*

pile /paɪl/ (piles, piling, piled)
1 NOUN A **pile of** things is several of them lying on top of each other. ❑ *We searched through the pile of boxes.* ❑ *There was a huge pile of shoes by the door.*
2 VERB If you **pile** things somewhere, you put them there so that they form a pile. ❑ *He was piling clothes into the suitcase.*
▶ **pile up** If you **pile** things **up**, you put one on top of another to form a pile. ❑ *They piled up rocks to build a wall.*

pil|grim /pɪlgrɪm/ (pilgrims) NOUN SOCIAL STUDIES The **Pilgrims** were the people who left England and went to live in America in the early seventeenth century.

pill /pɪl/ (pills) NOUN **Pills** are small solid round pieces of medicine that you swallow. ❑ *Why do I have to take all these pills?*

pil|lar /pɪlər/ (pillars) NOUN A **pillar** is a tall solid structure that usually supports part of a building. ❑ *There were eight huge pillars supporting the roof.*

pil|low /pɪloʊ/ (pillows) NOUN A **pillow** is a soft object that you rest your head on when you are in bed.

pillow|case /pɪloʊkeɪs/ (pillowcases) NOUN A **pillowcase** is a cloth cover for a pillow (= the soft object that you put your head on in bed).

pi|lot /paɪlət/ (pilots) NOUN A **pilot** is a person who controls an aircraft. ❑ *He spent seventeen years as an airline pilot.*

pin /pɪn/ (pins, pinning, pinned)
1 NOUN A **pin** is a very small thin piece of metal with a point at one end. ❑ *She looked in her box of needles and pins.*
2 VERB If you **pin** something **on** or **to** something, you fix it there with a pin. ❑ *They pinned a notice to the door.*
3 VERB If someone **pins** you in a particular position, they press you against a surface so

that you cannot move. ❑ *I pinned him down until the police arrived.*
4 NOUN A **pin** is a decorative object that you wear on your clothing that is fastened with a pointed piece of metal. ❑ *We sell all kinds of necklaces, bracelets, and pins.*

pinch /pɪntʃ/ (pinches, pinching, pinched)
1 VERB If you **pinch** someone, you press their skin between your thumb and first finger. ❑ *She pinched his arm as hard as she could.*
2 NOUN **Pinch** is also a noun. ❑ *She gave him a little pinch.*
3 NOUN A **pinch of** salt, pepper, or other powder is the amount of it that you can hold between your thumb and your first finger. ❑ *Add a pinch of cinnamon to the apples.*

pine /paɪn/ (pines)
1 NOUN A **pine** is a tall tree with long thin leaves that it keeps all year. ❑ *The high mountains are covered in pine trees.*
2 NONCOUNT NOUN **Pine** is the wood of this tree. ❑ *There's a big pine table in the kitchen.*

pine|apple /paɪnæpəl/ (pineapples) NOUN A **pineapple** is a large fruit with sweet yellow flesh and thick brown skin.
→ look at **fruit**

Ping-Pong NONCOUNT NOUN SPORTS **Ping-Pong** is a game in which one or two players on either side of a table hit a small light ball across a low net across the table. [TRADEMARK]

pink /pɪŋk/ (pinks, pinker, pinkest)
1 ADJECTIVE Something that is **pink** is of the color between red and white. ❑ *She wore pink lipstick.*
2 NOUN **Pink** is also a noun. ❑ *I prefer pale pinks and blues.*

pint /paɪnt/ (pints) NOUN A **pint** is a unit for measuring liquids that is equal to 0.57 liters. ❑ *Each carton contains a pint of ice cream.*
→ look at **measurement**

pio|neer /paɪənɪər/ (pioneers, pioneering, pioneered)
1 NOUN A **pioneer** in a particular activity is one of the first people to be involved in it. ❑ *He was one of the leading pioneers of the Internet.*
2 VERB Someone who **pioneers** a new activity, invention, or process is one of the first people to do it. ❑ *Professor Alec Jeffreys pioneered DNA tests.*
3 NOUN SOCIAL STUDIES **Pioneers** are people who leave their own country and go and live in a place that has not been lived in before.

P

pipe /paɪp/ (pipes)

1 **NOUN** A **pipe** is a long tube through which a liquid or a gas can flow. ❑ *They are going to replace the old water pipes.*

2 **NOUN** A **pipe** is an object that is used for smoking tobacco (= the dried leaves that are used for making cigarettes). ❑ *Do you smoke a pipe?*

pipe|line /paɪplaɪn/ (pipelines) **NOUN**

A **pipeline** is a large pipe that carries oil, gas, or water over a long distance. ❑ *The pipeline provides water for people living in the valley.*

pi|rate /paɪrɪt/ (pirates, pirating, pirated)

1 **NOUN** **Pirates** are people who attack ships and steal property from them. ❑ *The hero must find the pirates and the hidden gold.*

2 **VERB** Someone who **pirates** CDs, DVDs, books, or computer programs copies them and sells them illegally. ❑ *Computer crimes include stealing data and pirating software.*

pis|tol /pɪstᵊl/ (pistols) **NOUN** A **pistol** is a small gun.

pit /pɪt/ (pits)

1 **NOUN** A **pit** is a large hole that is dug in the ground. ❑ *The bodies were buried together in a single pit.*

2 **NOUN** A **pit** is the part of a coal mine that is under the ground.

3 **NOUN** A **pit** is the large hard seed of a fruit. ❑ *I don't always remove the cherry pits.*

pitch /pɪtʃ/ (pitches, pitching, pitched)

1 **VERB** If you **pitch** something somewhere, you throw it. ❑ *We spent long, hot afternoons pitching a baseball.*

2 **NONCOUNT NOUN** The **pitch** of a sound is how high or low it is. ❑ *The pitch of a voice falls at the end of a sentence.*

Spelling Partners	pitcher

pitch|er /pɪtʃər/ (pitchers)

1 **NOUN** A **pitcher** is a container with a handle, that is used for holding and pouring liquids. ❑ *We asked for a pitcher of iced water.*

2 **NOUN** **SPORTS** In baseball, the **pitcher** is the person who throws the ball to the batter (= the person who tries to hit it).

pity /pɪti/ (pities, pitying, pitied)

1 **VERB** If you **pity** someone, you feel very

sorry for them. ❑ *I don't know whether to hate or pity him.*

2 **NONCOUNT NOUN** **Pity** is also a noun. ❑ *He felt a sudden tender pity for her.*

3 **NOUN** If you say that it is **a pity** that something is true, you mean that you feel disappointed about it. ❑ *It's a pity you arrived so late.*

piz|za /pitsə/ (pizzas) **NOUN** A **pizza** is a flat,

round piece of bread that is covered with tomatoes, cheese, and sometimes other foods, and then baked in an oven. ❑ *I ordered a thin-crust pizza.*

pjs /pidʒeɪz/ also pj's **PLURAL NOUN** **Pjs** are

the same as **pajamas**. [INFORMAL] ❑ *I work from home and live in my pjs most of the time.*

place /pleɪs/ (places, placing, placed)

1 **NOUN** A **place** is a particular building, area, town, or country. ❑ *Keep your dog on a leash in public places.* ❑ *Please state your time and place of birth.*

2 **NOUN** The right or usual position for something is its **place**. ❑ *He returned the photo to its place on the shelf.*

3 **NOUN** A **place** is a seat for one person. ❑ *This girl was sitting in my place.*

4 **NOUN** Your **place** in a race or competition is your position. ❑ *Victoria is in third place with 22 points.*

5 **NOUN** Your **place** is your home. [INFORMAL] ❑ *Let's all go back to my place!*

6 **VERB** If you **place** something somewhere, you put it there. ❑ *Brand placed the letter in his pocket.*

7 **VERB** If you **place an order**, you ask for someone to bring something to you. ❑ *It is a good idea to place your order early.*

8 If something is **in place**, it is in the correct position. ❑ *A wide band held her hair in place.*

9 You use **in place of** to mean instead of. ❑ *Try using herbs and spices in place of salt.*

10 When something **takes place**, it happens. ❑ *The discussions took place in Paris.*

plain /pleɪn/ (plainer, plainest, plains)

1 **ADJECTIVE** Something that is **plain** is all the same color and has no pattern or writing on it. ❑ *A plain carpet makes a room look bigger.* ❑ *He placed the paper in a plain envelope.*

2 **ADJECTIVE** Something that is **plain** is very simple in style. ❑ *It was a plain, gray stone house.*

3 **ADJECTIVE** If a fact or a situation is **plain**, it is easy to recognize or understand. ❑ *It was plain to him what he had to do.*

4 **ADJECTIVE** Someone who is **plain** looks ordinary and not at all beautiful. ❑ *She was a shy, rather plain girl.*

5 **NOUN** A **plain** is a large flat area of land with very few trees on it. ❑ *She stood alone on the grassy plain.*

plain|ly /pleɪnli/ **ADVERB** You use **plainly** when something can easily be seen, noticed, or recognized. ❑ *I could plainly see him turning his head.*

plan /plæn/ (**plans, planning, planned**)
1 **NOUN** A **plan** is a method for doing something that you think about in advance. ❑ *They are meeting to discuss the peace plan.* ❑ *She says that everything is going according to plan.*
2 **VERB** If you **plan** what you are going to do, you decide in detail what you are going to do. ❑ *Plan what you're going to eat.* ❑ *He plans to leave Baghdad on Monday.* ❑ *They came together to plan for the future.*
3 **PLURAL NOUN** If you have **plans**, you are intending to do something. ❑ *We have plans to build a new kitchen at the back of the house.*
4 **NOUN** A **plan of** something is a detailed drawing of it. ❑ *Draw a plan of the garden before you start planting.*
→ look at **calendar, day, route**

plane /pleɪn/ (**planes**) **NOUN** A **plane** is a vehicle with wings and engines that can fly. ❑ *He had plenty of time to catch his plane.*

plan|et /plænɪt/ (**planets**) **NOUN** SCIENCE A **planet** is a large, round object in space that moves around a star. The Earth is a planet. ❑ *We study the planets in the solar system.*
→ look at **earth, space**

plan|ner /plænər/ (**planners**) **NOUN** Planners are people whose job is to make decisions about what is going to be done in the future.

plan|ning /plænɪŋ/ **NONCOUNT NOUN** Planning is the process of deciding in detail how to do something. ❑ *The trip needs careful planning.*

plant /plænt/ (**plants, planting, planted**)
1 **NOUN** SCIENCE A **plant** is a living thing that grows in the earth and has a stem, leaves, and roots. ❑ *Water each plant daily.*
2 **VERB** When you **plant** something, you put it into the ground so that it will grow. ❑ *He plans to plant fruit trees.*
3 **NOUN** A **plant** is a factory, or a place where power is produced. ❑ *We visited one of Ford's car assembly plants.*
→ look at Picture Dictionary: **plants**
→ look at **tree**

plan|ta|tion /plænteɪʃ°n/ (**plantations**) **NOUN** A **plantation** is a large piece of land where crops such as rubber, tea, or sugar are grown. ❑ *The fruit comes from the banana plantations in Costa Rica.*

plas|ma screen /plæzmə skrin/ (**plasma screens**) or **plasma display** **NOUN** TECHNOLOGY A **plasma screen** is a type of thin television screen or computer screen with good quality images.

plas|ter /plæstər/ (**plasters, plastering, plastered**)
1 **NONCOUNT NOUN** Plaster is a substance

P

Picture Dictionary   **plants**

fir tree

flowers

grass   crop

tree

weed

bush/shrub

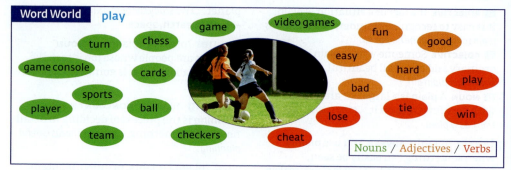

Word World play

turn · chess · game · video games · fun · good · game console · easy · hard · cards · sports · bad · play · player · ball · tie · win · lose · team · checkers · cheat

Nouns / Adjectives / Verbs

---

that is used for making a smooth surface on the inside of walls and ceilings. ❑ *There were huge cracks in the plaster.*

2 VERB If you **plaster** a wall or a ceiling, you cover it with a layer of plaster. ❑ *He has just plastered the ceiling.*

plas|tic /plǽstɪk/ **NONCOUNT NOUN** Plastic is a light but strong material that is produced by a chemical process. ❑ *The windows are made from sheets of plastic.* ❑ *...a plastic bottle.* ❑ *...a plastic bag.*
→ look at **bag**

plas|tic sur|gery **NONCOUNT NOUN** Plastic surgery is an operation to repair damaged skin, or to improve someone's appearance. ❑ *She had plastic surgery to change the shape of her nose.*

plate /pleɪt/ (**plates**) **NOUN** A **plate** is a flat dish that is used for holding food. ❑ *Anita pushed her plate away.* ❑ *He ate a huge plate of bacon and eggs.*
→ look at **restaurant**

plat|eau /plætoʊ/ (**plateaus** or **plateaux**) **NOUN** **GEOGRAPHY** A **plateau** is a large area of high and fairly flat land. ❑ *The house is on a wide grassy plateau.*
→ look at **landform**

plat|form /plǽtfɔrm/ (**platforms**)
1 NOUN A **platform** is a flat raised structure on which someone or something can stand. ❑ *He walked toward the platform to begin his speech.*
2 NOUN A **platform** in a train station is the area where you wait for a train. ❑ *...a subway platform.*

plati|num /plǽtɪnəm, plǽtnəm/
NONCOUNT NOUN Platinum is a very valuable metal that looks like silver.

play /pleɪ/ (**plays, playing, played**)
1 VERB When children or animals **play**,

they spend time using toys and taking part in games. ❑ *Polly was playing with her dolls.*
2 NONCOUNT NOUN Play is also a noun. ❑ *Children learn mainly through play.*
3 VERB SPORTS When you **play** a game or a sport, you take part in it. ❑ *The twins played cards.* ❑ *I used to play basketball.*
4 VERB SPORTS When one person or team **plays** another, they compete against them in a sport or a game. ❑ *Dallas will play Green Bay today.*
5 VERB If you **play** a joke or a trick on someone, you deceive them or give them a surprise for fun. ❑ *She wanted to play a trick on her friends.*
6 NOUN ARTS A **play** is a piece of writing performed in a theater, on the radio, or on television. ❑ *"Hamlet" is my favorite play.*
7 VERB ARTS If an actor **plays** a character in a play or movie, he or she performs the part of that character. ❑ *He played Mr. Hyde in the movie.*
8 VERB MUSIC If you **play** a musical instrument, you produce music from it. ❑ *Nina was playing the piano.* ❑ *He played for me.*
9 VERB If you **play** a CD, you put it into a machine and listen to it. ❑ *She played her CDs too loudly.*
→ look at Word World: **play**
→ look at **fitness, music, performance, play**

Word Builder player

er ≈ **someone who does**

climb + er = climber
farm + er = farmer
lead + er = leader
own + er = owner
play + er = player
work + er = worker

play|er /pleɪər/ (**players**)
1 NOUN SPORTS A **player** is a person who takes part in a sport or game. ❑ *She was a good*

P

tennis player. ❑ *The game is for three players.*
2 **NOUN** MUSIC You can use **player** for a musician. ❑ *He's a professional trumpet player.*
→ look at **play**

play|ful /pleɪfəl/ **ADJECTIVE** A **playful** person or action is not very serious. ❑ *She gave him a playful kiss.*

play|ground /pleɪgraʊnd/ (**playgrounds**) **NOUN** A **playground** is a piece of land where children can play. ❑ *The park has playground equipment made of wood.*

play|group /pleɪgrup/ (**playgroups**) also **play group** **NOUN** A **playgroup** is an informal school for very young children.

play|ing card (**playing cards**) **NOUN** Playing **cards** are thin pieces of cardboard with numbers or pictures printed on them that are used for playing games. ❑ *He started to shuffle a deck of playing cards.*

play|ing field (**playing fields**) **NOUN** A **playing field** is a large area of grass where people play sports. ❑ *The town has three grass playing fields and 18 football teams.*

play|mate /pleɪmeɪt/ (**playmates**) **NOUN** A child's **playmate** is another child who plays with them. ❑ *It's normal for young children to invent imaginary playmates.*

play|pen /pleɪpɛn/ (**playpens**) **NOUN** A **playpen** is a small structure with bars or a net around the sides, where young children can play safely.

play|room /pleɪrum/ (**playrooms**) **NOUN** A **playroom** is a room in a house for children to play in.

play|wright /pleɪraɪt/ (**playwrights**) **NOUN** LANGUAGE ARTS A **playwright** is a person who writes plays.

pla|za /plɑzə, plæzə/ (**plazas**)
1 **NOUN** A **plaza** is an open square in a city. ❑ *Across the busy plaza, street sellers sell hot dogs.*
2 **NOUN** A **plaza** is a group of stores or buildings that are joined together or share common areas. ❑ *...a shopping plaza.*

plea /pli/ (**pleas**) **NOUN** A **plea** is an emotional request for something. ❑ *Their president made a desperate plea for international help.* ❑ *...an emotional plea for help.*

plead /plid/ (**pleads, pleading, pleaded, pled**)
1 **VERB** If you **plead with** someone to do something, you ask them in an emotional

way to do it. ❑ *The lady pleaded with her daughter to come back home.*
2 **VERB** When someone **pleads guilty** or **not guilty** in a court of law, they officially say that they are guilty or not guilty of the crime. ❑ *Morris pleaded guilty to robbery.*

pleas|ant /plɛzənt/
1 **ADJECTIVE** Something that is **pleasant** is enjoyable or attractive. ❑ *It was a very pleasant surprise to receive a free ticket.* ❑ *I have many pleasant memories of this place.*
2 **ADJECTIVE** Someone who is **pleasant** is nice and friendly. ❑ *The doctor was a handsome, pleasant young man.*

please /pliz/ (**pleases, pleasing, pleased**)
1 **ADVERB** You say **please** when you are politely asking someone to do something. ❑ *Can you help us, please?* ❑ *Please come in.* ❑ *Can we have the bill, please?*
2 **ADVERB** You say **please** when you are accepting something politely. ❑ *"Tea?"—"Yes, please."*
3 **VERB** If someone or something **pleases** you, they make you feel happy and satisfied. ❑ *I just want to please you.* ❑ *He always tried to please her.*

pleased /plizd/
1 **ADJECTIVE** If you are **pleased**, you are happy about something or satisfied with something. ❑ *I'm so pleased that we solved the problem.* ❑ *I'm pleased with the way things have been going.* ❑ *I am very pleased about the result.*
2 "**Pleased to meet you**" is a polite way of saying hello to someone that you are meeting for the first time.

pleas|ing /plizɪŋ/ **ADJECTIVE** Something that is **pleasing** gives you pleasure and satisfaction. ❑ *The pleasing smell of fresh coffee came from the kitchen.*

pleas|ure /plɛʒər/ (**pleasures**)
1 **NONCOUNT NOUN** Something that gives you **pleasure** makes you feel happy and satisfied. ❑ *Watching sports gave him great pleasure.* ❑ *Everybody takes pleasure in eating.*
2 **NOUN** A **pleasure** is an activity or an experience that you find enjoyable. ❑ *Watching TV is our only pleasure.* ❑ *It was a pleasure to see her smiling face.*
3 You can say "**It's a pleasure**" as a polite way of answering someone who thanks you for doing something. ❑ *"Thanks very much for waiting for me."—"It's a pleasure."*
→ look at **relax**

P

plen|ty /plɛnti/
1 If there is **plenty of** something, there is a large amount of it. ❑ *Don't worry. There's still plenty of time.* ❑ *Most businesses face plenty of competition.*
2 **PRONOUN** Plenty is also a pronoun. ❑ *I don't like long interviews. Fifteen minutes is plenty.*

pli|ers /plaɪərz/ **PLURAL NOUN** Pliers are a tool with two handles at one end and two hard, flat, metal parts at the other that are used for holding or pulling things. ❑ *Hold the nail at its base with narrow pointed pliers.*

plop /plɒp/ (**plops, plopping, plopped**)
1 **NOUN** A **plop** is the soft sound of something dropping into water. ❑ *Another drop of water fell with a soft plop.*
2 **VERB** If something soft **plops** somewhere, it drops there with a gentle sound. ❑ *The ice cream plopped to the ground.*

plot /plɒt/ (**plots, plotting, plotted**)
1 **VERB** If people **plot to** do something, they plan secretly to do it. ❑ *They plotted to overthrow the government.*
2 **NOUN** Plot is also a noun. ❑ *We have uncovered a plot to kill the president.*
3 **NOUN** LANGUAGE ARTS The **plot** of a movie or a book is a series of events that make up the story. ❑ *He told me the plot of his new book.*
4 **NOUN** A **plot** is a small piece of land, especially one that is intended for a particular purpose. ❑ *I bought a small plot of land and built a house on it.*

plow /plaʊ/ (**plows, plowing, plowed**)
1 **NOUN** A **plow** is a large farming tool that is pulled across the soil to turn it over, usually before seeds are planted.
2 **VERB** When someone **plows** an area of land, they turn over the soil using a plow. ❑ *They were using horses to plow their fields.*
3 **VERB** If a vehicle **plows into** a person or thing, it hits it with great force. ❑ *The speeding vehicle plowed into a crowd of people.*
→ look at **farm**

pluck /plʌk/ (**plucks, plucking, plucked**)
VERB If you **pluck** a musical instrument, you pull the strings with your fingers, so that they make a sound. ❑ *Nell was plucking a harp.*

plug /plʌg/ (**plugs, plugging, plugged**)
1 **NOUN** A **plug** on a piece of electrical equipment is the plastic object with metal pins that connects it to the electricity supply. ❑ *Remove the power plug when you have finished.*
2 **NOUN** A **plug** is a round object that you use to block the hole in a bathtub or a sink. ❑ *She put in the plug and filled the sink with cold water.*
3 **VERB** If you **plug** a hole, you block it with something. ❑ *We are working to plug a major oil leak.*
▶ **plug in** If you **plug** a piece of electrical equipment **in**, you connect it to the electricity supply. ❑ *I had a TV, but there was no place to plug it in.*

plum /plʌm/ (**plums**) **NOUN** A **plum** is a small, sweet fruit with a smooth purple, red, or yellow skin and a large seed (= a pit) in the middle.

plumb|er /plʌmər/ (**plumbers**) **NOUN** A **plumber** is a person whose job is to put in and repair water and gas pipes.

plump /plʌmp/ (**plumper, plumpest**)
ADJECTIVE A **plump** person is round and rather heavy. ❑ *Maria was small and plump.*

plunge /plʌndʒ/ (**plunges, plunging, plunged**)
1 **VERB** If something or someone **plunges** into water, they fall or throw themselves into it. ❑ *The bus plunged into a river.*
2 **VERB** If you **plunge** an object **into** something, you push it violently into it. ❑ *He plunged a fork into his dinner.*

plu|ral /plʊərəl/ (**plurals**)
1 **NOUN** LANGUAGE ARTS The **plural** of a noun is the form of it that is used for talking about more than one person or thing. ❑ *"People" is the plural of "person."*
2 **ADJECTIVE** Plural is also an adjective. ❑ *"Men" is the plural form of "man."*

plus /plʌs/ (**pluses**) **CONJUNCTION** MATH You say **plus** to show that one number is being added to another. ❑ *Two plus two equals four.*

Usage **plus**

In math the plus sign is a small symbol + between two numbers, 42 + 7 = 49. In words, this equation is *forty-two **plus** seven equals forty-nine.*

p.m. /pi ɛm/ also **pm** **ADVERB** You use **p.m.** after a number when you are talking about a particular time between 12 noon and 12 midnight. Compare with **a.m.** ❑ *The pool is open from 7:00 a.m. to 9:00 p.m. every day.*

P

pneu|mo|nia /nʊmoʊnyə, -moʊniə/
NONCOUNT NOUN Pneumonia is a serious disease that affects the lungs. ❑ *She nearly died of pneumonia.*

pock|et /pɒkɪt/ (**pockets**)
1 **NOUN** A **pocket** is a small bag that forms part of a piece of clothing. ❑ *He put the key in his jacket pocket.*
2 **ADJECTIVE** Pocket describes something that is small enough to fit into a pocket. ❑ *...a pocket calculator.*

pocket|book /pɒkɪtbʊk/ (**pocketbooks**)
NOUN A **pocketbook** is a small bag in which a woman carries small things such as her money and keys.

pock|et knife (**pocket knives**) **NOUN** A **pocket knife** is a small knife with a blade that folds into the handle.

pod /pɒd/ (**pods**) **NOUN** A **pod** is a seed container that grows on some plants. ❑ *We bought fresh peas in their pods.*

pod|cast /pɒdkæst/ (**podcasts**) **NOUN** TECHNOLOGY A **podcast** is a file containing a radio show or something similar, that you can listen to on a computer or an MP3 player (= a small piece of electrical equipment for listening to music). ❑ *There are thousands of new podcasts available every day.*
→ look at **news**

poem /poʊəm/ (**poems**) **NOUN** LANGUAGE ARTS A **poem** is a piece of writing in which the words are chosen for their beauty and sound, and are carefully arranged, often in short lines. ❑ *He read to her from a book of love poems.*

poet /poʊɪt/ (**poets**) **NOUN** LANGUAGE ARTS A **poet** is a person who writes poems. ❑ *He was a painter and a poet.*

po|et|ry /poʊɪtri/ **NONCOUNT NOUN** LANGUAGE ARTS **Poetry** is the form of literature that consists of poems. ❑ *We studied Russian poetry last semester.*
→ look at **writing**

point /pɔɪnt/ (**points, pointing, pointed**)
1 **NOUN** A **point** is an idea or a fact. ❑ *We disagreed with every point she made.*
2 **NOUN** The **point of** something is the purpose of it. ❑ *What is the point of worrying?* ❑ *There's no point in fighting.*

3 **NOUN** A **point** is a particular position or time. ❑ *We're all going to die at some point.*
4 **NOUN** The **point** of a knife is the thin, sharp end of it. ❑ *Griego felt the cold sharp point of a knife against his neck.*
5 **NOUN** A **point** is the small dot that separates whole numbers from parts of numbers. ❑ *The highest temperature today was 98.5˚ (ninety-eight point five degrees).*
6 **NOUN** A **point** is a mark that you win in a game or a sport. ❑ *Chamberlain scored 50 points.*
7 **VERB** If you **point at** a person or a thing, you use your finger to show where they are. ❑ *I pointed at the boy sitting near me.*
8 **VERB** If you **point** something **at** someone, you hold it toward them. ❑ *She smiled when Laura pointed a camera at her.*
9 If you are **on the point of** doing something, you are about to do it. ❑ *He was on the point of answering when the phone rang.*
10 Your **point of view** is your opinion about something. ❑ *We would like to hear your point of view.*
→ look at **geometry**
▶ **point out** If you **point out** a fact, you tell someone about it or show it to them. ❑ *He pointed out the errors in the book.*

point|ed /pɔɪntɪd/ **ADJECTIVE** Something that is **pointed** has a point at one end. ❑ *William was uncomfortable in his new pointed shoes.*

point|less /pɔɪntlɪs/ **ADJECTIVE** Something that is **pointless** has no sense or purpose. ❑ *Without an audience the performance is pointless.*

point of view (**points of view**) **NOUN** Your **point of view** is your opinion on a particular subject. ❑ *Thanks for your point of view, John.*

poi|son /pɔɪzᵊn/ (**poisons, poisoning, poisoned**)
1 **NOUN** Poison is a substance that harms or kills people or animals if they swallow or touch it. ❑ *Poison from the factory is causing the fish to die.*
2 **VERB** To **poison** someone or something means to harm them by giving them poison. ❑ *They say that she poisoned her husband.*
→ look at **pollution**

poi|son|ous /pɔɪzᵊnəs/
1 **ADJECTIVE** Something that is **poisonous** will kill you or harm you if you swallow or touch it. ❑ *All parts of this tree are poisonous.*
2 **ADJECTIVE** An animal that is **poisonous** produces a substance that will kill you or

P

make you sick if it bites you. ❑ *The zoo keeps a selection of poisonous spiders and snakes.*
→ look at **pollution**

poke /pouk/ (pokes, poking, poked)

1 VERB If you **poke** someone or something, you quickly push them with your finger or with a sharp object. ❑ *Lindy poked him in the ribs.*

2 NOUN Poke is also a noun. ❑ *John gave Richard a playful poke.*

3 VERB If you **poke** one thing **into** another, you push the first thing into the second thing. ❑ *He poked his finger into the hole.*

pok|er /poukər/ **NONCOUNT NOUN** Poker is a card game, usually played in order to win money. ❑ *Lon and I play in the same weekly poker game.*

po|lar /poulər/ **ADJECTIVE** GEOGRAPHY Polar means near the North Pole or South Pole. ❑ *We watched a program about life in the polar regions.*
→ look at **climate**

pole /poul/ (poles)

1 NOUN A **pole** is a long thin piece of wood or metal, used especially for supporting things. ❑ *The car went off the road, knocking down a telephone pole.*

2 NOUN GEOGRAPHY The Earth's **poles** are its two opposite ends, which are its most northern and southern points. ❑ *For six months of the year, there is very little light at the poles.*
→ look at **earth, globe**

po|lice /pəlis/

1 PLURAL NOUN The **police** is the organization that is responsible for making sure that people obey the law. ❑ *The police are looking for the car.* ❑ *Police say they have arrested twenty people.*

2 PLURAL NOUN Police are men and women who are members of the police. ❑ *More than one hundred police are in the area.*

po|lice de|part|ment (police departments) **NOUN** A **police department** is an organization that is responsible for making sure that people obey the law. ❑ *They have called in the Los Angeles Police Department.*

police|man /pəlismən/ (policemen) **NOUN** A **policeman** is a man who is a member of the police force.

po|lice of|fic|er (police officers) **NOUN** A **police officer** is a member of the police. ❑ *...a senior police officer.*

po|lice sta|tion (police stations) **NOUN** A **police station** is the local office of the police in a particular area. ❑ *Two police officers arrested him and took him to the police station.*

police|woman /pəliswumən/ (policewomen) **NOUN** A **policewoman** is a woman who is a member of the police.

poli|cy /pɒlɪsi/ (policies) **NOUN** SOCIAL STUDIES A **policy** is a set of ideas or plans about a particular subject, especially in politics, economics, or business. ❑ *There will be some important changes in foreign policy.*

pol|ish /pɒlɪʃ/ (polishes, polishing, polished)

1 NONCOUNT NOUN Polish is a substance that you put on a surface in order to clean it and make it shine. ❑ *Furniture polish will clean and protect your table.*

2 VERB If you **polish** something, you rub it to make it shine. ❑ *He polished his shoes.*

po|lite /pəlaɪt/ **ADJECTIVE** A **polite** person behaves with respect toward other people. ❑ *He seemed a quiet and very polite young man.* ● **po|lite|ly ADVERB** ❑ *"Your home is beautiful," I said politely.* ● **po|lite|ness NONCOUNT NOUN** ❑ *She listened to him, but only out of politeness.*

po|liti|cal /pəlɪtɪkəl/ **ADJECTIVE** SOCIAL STUDIES Political means relating to politics or the government. ❑ *I am not a member of any political party.* ● **po|liti|cal|ly** /pəlɪtɪkli/ **ADVERB** ❑ *Politically, this is a very risky move.*
→ look at **vote**

po|liti|cal par|ty (political parties) **NOUN** SOCIAL STUDIES A **political party** is an organization whose members share similar ideas and beliefs about politics. ❑ *Some members of the main political parties gave interviews to reporters.*
→ look at **vote**

poli|ti|cian /pɒlɪtɪʃən/ (politicians) **NOUN** A **politician** is a person who works in politics, especially a member of a government. ❑ *They have arrested a number of politicians.*
→ look at **vote**

poli|tics /pɒlɪtɪks/

1 NONCOUNT NOUN SOCIAL STUDIES Politics is the activities and ideas that are concerned with government. ❑ *He was involved in local politics.*

2 PLURAL NOUN Your **politics** are your beliefs about how a country should be governed. ❑ *His politics are extreme and often confused.*

poll /poʊl/ (polls)

1 **NOUN** A **poll** is a way of discovering what people think about something by asking them questions. ❑ *The polls are showing that women are very involved in this campaign.*

2 **PLURAL NOUN** People **go to the polls** when they vote in an election. ❑ *Voters go to the polls on Sunday to elect a new president.*

→ look at **vote**

pol|len /pɒlən/ **NONCOUNT NOUN** SCIENCE **Pollen** is a powder that is produced by flowers. ❑ *The male bee carries the pollen from one flower to another.*

pol|lute /pəlut/ (pollutes, polluting, polluted) **VERB** To **pollute** water, air, or land means to make it dirty. ❑ *Industry pollutes our rivers with chemicals.* ● **pol|lut|ed** **ADJECTIVE** ❑ *Fish are dying in the polluted rivers.*

→ look at **pollution, water**

pol|lu|tion /pəluʃᵊn/

1 **NONCOUNT NOUN** **Pollution** is the process of making water, air, or land dirty and dangerous. ❑ *The government announced plans for reducing pollution of the air, sea, rivers, and soil.*

2 **NONCOUNT NOUN** **Pollution** is poisonous substances that pollute water, air, or land. ❑ *The level of pollution in the river was falling.*

→ look at Word World: **pollution**

poly|es|ter /pɒliɛstər/ **NONCOUNT NOUN** **Polyester** is a type of artificial cloth that is mainly used for making clothes. ❑ *He wore a green polyester shirt.*

pond /pɒnd/ (ponds) **NOUN** A **pond** is a small area of water. ❑ *We sat on a bench beside the duck pond.*

pony /poʊni/ (ponies) **NOUN** A **pony** is a small or young horse.

pony|tail /poʊniteɪl/ (ponytails) **NOUN** A **ponytail** is a hairstyle in which your hair is tied up at the back of your head and hangs down like a horse's tail. ❑ *Her long, fine hair was tied back in a ponytail.*

→ look at **hair**

pool /pul/ (pools)

1 **NOUN** A **pool** is the same as a **swimming pool**. ❑ *Does the hotel have a heated indoor pool?*

2 **NONCOUNT NOUN** **Pool** is a game that is played on a special table. Players use a long stick to hit a white ball so that it knocks colored balls into six holes around the edge of the table.

Sound Partners   poor, pour

poor /pʊər/ (poorer, poorest)

1 **ADJECTIVE** Someone who is **poor** has very little money and few possessions. ❑ *"We were very poor in those days," he says.*

2 **PLURAL NOUN** **The poor** are people who are poor. ❑ *There are huge differences between the rich and the poor.*

3 **ADJECTIVE** You use **poor** to show that you are sorry for someone. ❑ *I feel sorry for that poor child.* ❑ *Poor Mike. Does he feel better now?*

4 **ADJECTIVE** Something that is **poor** is bad. ❑ *The illegal copies are of very poor quality.* ❑ *The actors gave a poor performance.* ● **poor|ly** **ADVERB** ❑ *"We played poorly in the first game,"* Mendez said.

pop /pɒp/ (pops, popping, popped)

1 **NONCOUNT NOUN** **Pop** is modern music that usually has a strong rhythm and uses electronic equipment. ❑ *Their music is a combination of Caribbean rhythms and European pop.* ❑ *Her room is covered with posters of pop stars.*

2 **VERB** If something **pops**, it makes a short sharp sound. ❑ *He heard a balloon pop behind his head.*

3 **NOUN** **Pop** is also a noun. ❑ *Each piece of corn will make a loud pop when it is cooked.*

4 **NOUN** Some people call their father **Pop**. [INFORMAL] ❑ *I looked at Pop and he had big tears in his eyes.*

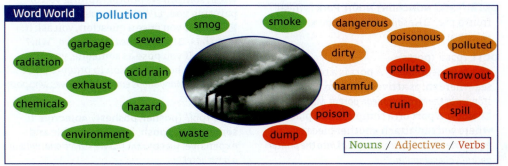

Word World   **pollution**

smog   smoke   dangerous   poisonous   polluted
garbage   sewer   dirty   pollute
radiation   acid rain   harmful   throw out
exhaust
chemicals   hazard   poison   ruin   spill
environment   waste   dump

Nouns / Adjectives / Verbs

P

pop|corn /pɒpkɔrn/ **NONCOUNT NOUN**
Popcorn is a type of food that consists of grains of corn that have been heated until they have burst and become large and light.

pope /poup/ (**popes**) **NOUN** The pope is the leader of the Roman Catholic Church. ❏ *The pope prayed for peace.*

popu|lar /pɒpyələr/
1 **ADJECTIVE** Something or someone that is **popular** is liked by a lot of people. ❏ *He was the most popular politician in Arkansas.* ❏ *Chocolate sauce is always popular with kids.*
● **popu|lar|ity** /pɒpyəlærɪti/ **NONCOUNT NOUN** ❏ *The singer's popularity grew even more with his successful 1999 album.*
2 **ADJECTIVE** Popular ideas or opinions are held by most people. ❏ *There is a popular belief that unemployment causes crime.*

Word Partners	Use **popular** with:
N.	popular **culture**, popular **magazine**, popular **movie**, popular **music**, popular **novel**, popular **restaurant**, popular **song**, popular **TV show** **1**
ADV.	**extremely** popular, **more** popular, **most** popular, **very** popular **1**

popu|la|tion /pɒpyəleɪʃᵊn/ (**populations**)
NOUN SOCIAL STUDIES The **population** of a country or an area is all the people who live in it. ❏ *Bangladesh now has a population of about 150 million.*

porch /pɔrtʃ/ (**porches**) **NOUN** A **porch** is a raised structure that is built along the outside wall of a house and is often covered with a roof. ❏ *He stood on the porch, waving as we drove away.*

pore /pɔr/ (**pores**) **NOUN** Your **pores** are the very small holes in your skin. ❏ *Use hot water to clear blocked pores.*

pork /pɔrk/ **NONCOUNT NOUN** Pork is meat from a pig. ❏ *He said he didn't eat pork.*
→ look at **meat**

port /pɔrt/ (**ports**)
1 **NOUN** GEOGRAPHY A **port** is a town by the sea where ships arrive and leave. ❏ *We stopped at the Mediterranean port of Marseilles.*
2 **NOUN** A **port** on a computer is a place where you can attach another piece of equipment. ❏ *The scanner plugs into the printer port of your computer.*

Word Builder	portable
port ≈ **carry**	
	air + port = air**port**
	ex + port = ex**port**
	im + port = im**port**
	port + able = **port**able
	trans + port = trans**port**

port|able /pɔrtəbᵊl/ **ADJECTIVE** Something that is **portable** is designed to be carried or moved around. ❏ *The iPod can be used as a portable storage device for all types of files.*

por|ter /pɔrtər/ (**porters**) **NOUN** A **porter** is a person whose job is to carry things, for example, people's baggage. ❏ *Our taxi arrived at the station and a porter came to the door.*

por|tion /pɔrʃᵊn/ (**portions**)
1 **NOUN** A **portion of** something is a part of it. ❏ *Only a small portion of the castle was damaged.* ❏ *I have spent a large portion of my life here.*
2 **NOUN** A **portion** is the amount of food that is given to one person at a meal. ❏ *The portions were huge.*
→ look at **eat**

por|trait /pɔrtrɪt, -treɪt/ (**portraits**) **NOUN** A **portrait** is a painting, a drawing, or a photograph of a particular person. ❏ *The wall was covered with family portraits.*

por|tray /pɔrtreɪ/ (**portrays, portraying, portrayed**) **VERB** To **portray** someone or something means to represent them, for example in a book or a movie. ❏ *The film portrays a group of young people who live in lower Manhattan.*

pose /pouz/ (**poses, posing, posed**)
1 **VERB** If you **pose for** a photograph or a painting, you stay in one position so that someone can photograph you or paint you. ❏ *The six foreign ministers posed for photographs.*
2 **NOUN** A **pose** is a position that you stay in when someone is photographing you or painting you. ❏ *We tried various poses.*
3 **VERB** If you **pose** a question, you ask it. [FORMAL] ❏ *I finally posed the question, "Why?"*
4 **VERB** If you **pose as** someone, you pretend to be that person in order to trick people. ❏ *Many shops employ detectives who pose as customers.*

posh /pɒʃ/ (**posher, poshest**) **ADJECTIVE** If something is **posh**, it is fashionable and expensive. [INFORMAL] ❏ *We stayed one night in a posh hotel.*

po|si|tion /pəzɪʃᵊn/ (positions)

1 **NOUN** The **position** of someone or something is the place where they are. ❏ *Measure and mark the position of the handle on the door.*

2 **NOUN** Your **position** is the way you are sitting, lying, or standing. ❏ *Mr. Dambar raised himself to a sitting position.*

3 **NOUN** A **position** in a company or organization is a job. [FORMAL] ❏ *He left a career in teaching to take a position with IBM.*

4 **NOUN** Your **position** at a particular time is the situation you are in. ❏ *He's going to be in a very difficult position if things go badly.* ❏ *The club's financial position is still uncertain.*

posi|tive /pɒzɪtɪv/

1 **ADJECTIVE** If you are **positive**, you are hopeful and confident. ❏ *Be positive about your future.* ● **posi|tive|ly** **ADVERB** ❏ *You really must try to start thinking positively.*

2 **ADJECTIVE** A **positive** experience is pleasant and helpful. ❏ *I want to have a positive effect on my children's lives.*

3 **ADJECTIVE** If you are **positive** about something, you are completely sure about it. ❏ *"Judith's never late. Are you sure she said eight?"—"Positive."*

4 **ADJECTIVE** If a medical or scientific test is **positive**, it shows that something has happened or is present. ❏ *If the test is positive, treatment will start immediately.*

5 **ADJECTIVE** MATH A **positive** number is higher than zero. Compare with **negative**.

pos|sess /pəzɛs/ (possesses, possessing, possessed) **VERB** If you **possess** something, you have it or own it. ❏ *They sold everything they possessed to raise the money.*

pos|ses|sion /pəzɛʃᵊn/ (possessions)

1 **NONCOUNT NOUN** If you are **in possession of** something, you have it. [FORMAL] ❏ *Those documents are now in the possession of the Washington Post.*

2 **NOUN** Your **possessions** are the things that you own or have with you at a particular time. ❏ *People have lost their homes and all their possessions.*

pos|ses|sive /pəzɛsɪv/ **ADJECTIVE**

LANGUAGE ARTS In grammar, a **possessive** word is a word such as "my" or "his" that shows who or what something belongs to.

pos|sibil|ity /pɒsɪbɪlɪti/ (possibilities) **NOUN**

If there is a **possibility that** something will happen, it might happen. ❏ *There is a possibility that they jailed the wrong man.*

pos|sible /pɒsɪbᵊl/

1 **ADJECTIVE** If it is **possible** to do something, that thing can be done. ❏ *If it is possible to find out where your brother is, we will.* ❏ *Anything is possible if you want it enough.*

2 **ADJECTIVE** If it is **possible that** something is true, it might be true, although you do not know for sure. ❏ *It is possible that he's telling the truth.*

3 **ADJECTIVE** If you do something **as** soon **as possible**, you do it as soon as you can. ❏ *Please make your decision as soon as possible.*

pos|sibly /pɒsɪbli/

1 **ADVERB** You use **possibly** when you are not sure if something is true or if it will happen. ❏ *Exercise will possibly protect against heart attacks.*

2 **ADVERB** You use **possibly** to say that something is possible. ❏ *They've done everything they can possibly think of.* ❏ *I can't possibly answer that!*

post /poʊst/ (posts, posting, posted)

1 **VERB** If you **post** signs on a wall, you put them there so that everyone can see them. ❏ *Officials began posting warning notices.*

2 **VERB** TECHNOLOGY If you **post** information on the Internet, you put it on a website so that other people can see it. ❏ *The statement was posted on the Internet.*

3 **NOUN** A **post** is an important job in an organization. [FORMAL] ❏ *She accepted the post of the director's assistant.*

4 **NOUN** A **post** is a strong piece of wood or metal that is set into in the ground. ❏ *The car went through a red light and hit a fence post.*

post|age /poʊstɪdʒ/ **NONCOUNT NOUN**

Postage is the money that you pay for sending mail. ❏ *All prices include postage.*

post|card /poʊstkɑrd/ (postcards) also post card **NOUN** A **postcard** is a thin card, often with a picture on one side, that you can write on and mail to someone without using an envelope.

post|er /poʊstər/ (posters) **NOUN** A **poster** is a large notice or picture that you stick on a wall. ❏ *I saw a poster for the jazz festival in Monterey.*

Post-it (Post-its) **NOUN** **Post-its** or **Post-it notes** are small pieces of paper for writing notes that are sticky on one side. [TRADEMARK] ❏ *Mark the important pages with Post-it notes.*

p

post of|fice (post offices)

1 **NOUN** A **post office** is a building where you can buy stamps and send mail. ❑ *She needed to get to the post office before it closed.*

2 **NOUN** You can use **the post office** to talk about the U.S. Postal Service.

post|pone /poʊstpoʊn, poʊspoʊn/ (postpones, postponing, postponed) **VERB** If you **postpone** an event, you arrange for it to happen at a later time. ❑ *He decided to postpone the trip until the following day.*

pos|ture /pɒstʃər/ **NOUN** Your **posture** is the position in which you stand or sit. ❑ *You can make your stomach look flatter by improving your posture.*

pot /pɒt/ (pots)

1 **NOUN** A **pot** is a deep round container used for cooking food. ❑ *The shelf is full of metal cooking pots.*

2 **NOUN** A **pot** is a round container that is used for a particular purpose. ❑ *She asked him to pass the coffee pot.* ❑ *...a pot of paint.*

→ look at **kitchen**

po|ta|to /pəteɪtoʊ/ (potatoes) **NOUN** **Potatoes** are hard round white vegetables with brown or red skins. They grow under the ground.

→ look at **vegetable**

po|ta|to chip (potato chips) **NOUN** **Potato chips** are very thin slices of potato that have been cooked until they are hard, dry, and crisp.

po|ten|tial /pətɛnʃəl/

1 **ADJECTIVE** You use **potential** to say that someone or something could become a particular type of person or thing. ❑ *The company has identified 60 potential customers.* ❑ *We are aware of the potential problems.*

● **po|ten|tial|ly** **ADVERB** ❑ *This is a potentially dangerous situation.*

2 **NONCOUNT NOUN** If someone or something has **potential**, they could become successful or useful in the future. ❑ *The boy has great potential.*

pot|tery /pɒtəri/ **NONCOUNT NOUN** ARTS **Pottery** is pots, dishes, and other objects made from a special type of earth (= clay). ❑ *The store sells a fine range of pottery.*

poul|try /poʊltri/ **PLURAL NOUN** You can use **poultry** to talk about birds that you keep for their eggs and meat, such as chickens.

pounce /paʊns/ (pounces, pouncing, pounced) **VERB** If a person or an animal **pounces on** someone or something, they suddenly jump on them. ❑ *He pounced on the photographer and knocked him to the ground.*

pound /paʊnd/ (pounds)

1 **NOUN** A **pound** is a unit of weight that is used in the U.S., Britain, and some other countries. One pound is equal to 0.454 kilograms. ❑ *Her weight was under ninety pounds.* ❑ *...a pound of cheese.*

2 **NOUN** The **pound** (£) is the unit of money that is used in Britain.

Sound Partners	pour, poor

pour /pɔr/ (pours, pouring, poured)

1 **VERB** If you **pour** a liquid or other substance, you make it flow out of a container. ❑ *She poured some water into a bowl.*

2 **VERB** If you **pour** someone a drink, you put some of the drink in a cup or a glass for them. ❑ *She asked Tillie to pour her a cup of coffee.*

3 **VERB** When a liquid **pours** somewhere, it flows there quickly and in large amounts. ❑ *Blood was pouring from his broken nose.* ❑ *Tears poured down our faces.*

4 **VERB** When it rains very heavily, you can say that **it is pouring**. ❑ *It was still pouring outside.*

→ look at **water**

pov|er|ty /pɒvərti/ **NONCOUNT NOUN** **Poverty** is the state of being very poor. ❑ *Many of these people are living in poverty.*

pow|der /paʊdər/ **NONCOUNT NOUN** **Powder** is a fine dry dust. ❑ *Put a small amount of the powder into a container and mix with water.* ❑ *...cocoa powder.*

pow|er /paʊər/ (powers)

1 **NONCOUNT NOUN** If someone has **power**, they have control over people. ❑ *When children are young, parents still have a lot of power.*

2 **NONCOUNT NOUN** Your **power to** do something is your ability to do it. ❑ *She has the power to charm anyone.*

P

3 **NONCOUNT NOUN** If someone in authority has the **power** to do something, they have the legal right to do it. ❑ *The police have the power to arrest people who carry knives.*

4 **NONCOUNT NOUN** If a group of people are **in power**, they are in charge of a country or an organization. ❑ *Idi Amin was in power for eight years.*

5 **NONCOUNT NOUN** SCIENCE The **power** of something is its physical strength or the ability that it has to affect things. ❑ *This vehicle has more power and better brakes.*

6 **NONCOUNT NOUN** **Power** is energy that can be used for making electricity or for making machines work. ❑ *Nuclear power is cleaner than coal.* ❑ *The storm left a million homes without electrical power.*

7 **NOUN** MATH In math, **power** is used for talking about the number of times that you multiply a number by itself. For example, "5 to the power of 5" means "5x5x5x5x5."
→ look at **energy**

pow|er|ful /paʊərfəl/

1 **ADJECTIVE** A **powerful** person or organization is able to control people and events. ❑ *You're a powerful man—people will listen to you.* ❑ *Russia and India are two large, powerful countries.*

2 **ADJECTIVE** Someone's body is **powerful** if it is physically strong. ❑ *He lifts weights to maintain his powerful muscles.*

3 **ADJECTIVE** A **powerful** machine or substance is very strong. ❑ *We need more and more powerful computer systems.*

4 **ADJECTIVE** A **powerful** smell is very strong. ❑ *There was a powerful smell of gasoline in the car.*

5 **ADJECTIVE** A **powerful** voice is loud. ❑ *Mrs. Jones's powerful voice interrupted them.*

pow|er|less /paʊrlɪs/ **ADJECTIVE** Someone who is **powerless** is unable to do anything to control a situation. ❑ *If you don't have money, you're powerless.* ❑ *Security guards were powerless to stop the crowd.*

pow|er line (power lines) **NOUN** A **power line** is a cable, especially above ground, along which electricity travels to an area or building.

prac|ti|cal /præktɪkəl/

1 **ADJECTIVE** **Practical** means involving real situations and events, rather than ideas and theories. ❑ *Our system is the most practical way of preventing crime.*

2 **ADJECTIVE** If someone is **practical**, they make sensible decisions and deal effectively

with problems. ❑ *We need a practical person to take care of the details.* ❑ *You were always so practical, Maria.*

3 **ADJECTIVE** **Practical** clothes are useful rather than just being fashionable or attractive. ❑ *We'll need plenty of lightweight, practical clothes.*

prac|ti|cal|ly /præktɪkli/ **ADVERB** **Practically** means almost. ❑ *He's known the old man practically all his life.*

prac|tice /præktɪs/ (practices, practicing, practiced)

1 **NOUN** A **practice** is something that people do regularly. ❑ *They campaign against the practice of using animals for experiments.*

2 **NONCOUNT NOUN** **Practice** is the act of doing something regularly in order to be able to do it better. ❑ *It takes a lot of practice to become a good musician.*

3 **VERB** If you **practice** something, you do it regularly in order to do it better. ❑ *She practiced the piano in the school basement.* ❑ *Keep practicing, and maybe next time you'll do better*
→ look at **grammar**

prai|rie /prɛəri/ (prairies) **NOUN** GEOGRAPHY A **prairie** is a large area of flat land in North America where very few trees grow.

praise /preɪz/ (praises, praising, praised)

1 **VERB** If you **praise** someone or something, you say that you admire or respect them for something they have done. ❑ *The passengers praised John for saving their lives.*

2 **NONCOUNT NOUN** **Praise** is also a noun. ❑ *The ladies are full of praise for the staff.*

pray /preɪ/ (prays, praying, prayed)

1 **VERB** When people **pray**, they speak to God or a god. ❑ *We pray that Billy's family will now find peace.*

2 **VERB** If you **are praying** that something will happen, you are hoping for it very much. ❑ *I'm praying for good weather.* ❑ *I'm praying that someone will do something before it's too late.*

prayer /prɛər/ (prayers)

1 **NOUN** A **prayer** is the words that a person says when they speak to God or a god. ❑ *They should say a prayer for the people on both sides.*

2 **NONCOUNT NOUN** **Prayer** is the activity of speaking to God or a god. ❑ *The monks give their lives to prayer.*

pre|cau|tion /prɪkɔʃən/ (precautions) **NOUN** A **precaution** is an action that is intended to prevent something bad from happening.

P

❏ *Just as a precaution, he should move to a place of safety.*

pre|cede /prɪsi̱d/ (**precedes, preceding, preceded**) **VERB** If one event or period of time **precedes** another, it happens before it. [FORMAL] ❏ *Adjectives usually precede the noun they describe.*

pre|cious /pre̱ʃəs/
1 **ADJECTIVE** **Precious** objects are worth a lot of money because they are rare. ❏ *The company mines precious metals throughout North America.*
2 **ADJECTIVE** If something is **precious** to you, it is important to you, and you do not want to lose it. ❏ *Her family's support is particularly precious to Josie.*

pre|cise /prɪsa̱ɪs/ **ADJECTIVE** Something that is **precise** is exact and accurate in all its details. ❏ *I can remember the precise moment when I heard the news.*

pre|cise|ly /prɪsa̱ɪsli/ **ADVERB** Precisely means accurately and exactly. ❏ *Nobody knows precisely how many people are still living there.*

pre|ci|sion /prɪsɪ̱ʒ°n/ **NONCOUNT NOUN** If you do something **with precision**, you do it exactly as it should be done. ❏ *He hits the ball with precision.*

preda|tor /pre̱dətər/ (**predators**) **NOUN**
SCIENCE A **predator** is an animal that kills and eats other animals. ❏ *With no natural predators on the island, the animals lived happily.*

pre|dict /prɪdɪ̱kt/ (**predicts, predicting, predicted**) **VERB** If you **predict** an event, you say that it will happen. ❏ *The old man correctly predicted the results of fifteen matches.*
→ look at **science**

pre|dict|able /prɪdɪ̱ktəb°l/ **ADJECTIVE** If an event is **predictable**, it is obvious in advance that it will happen. ❏ *This was a predictable reaction.*

pre|dic|tion /prɪdɪ̱kʃ°n/ (**predictions**) **NOUN** If you make a **prediction**, you say what you think will happen. ❏ *My prediction is that the process will take about 5 years.*

pref|ace /pre̱fɪs/ (**prefaces**) **NOUN**
LANGUAGE ARTS A **preface** is an introduction at the beginning of a book. ❏ *Have you read the preface to Kelman's novel?*

pre|fer /prɪfɜ̱r/ (**prefers, preferring, preferred**) **VERB** If you **prefer** someone or something, you like that person or thing better than

another. ❏ *Does he prefer a particular sort of music?* ❏ *I preferred books and people to politics.* ❏ *He would prefer to be in Philadelphia.*

pref|er|able /pre̱fərəb°l, pre̱frə-, prɪfɜ̱rə-/ **ADJECTIVE** When one thing is **preferable to** another, it is better or more suitable. ❏ *For me, a trip to the supermarket is preferable to buying food on the Internet.* ● **pref|er|ably** /pre̱fərəbli, pre̱frə-, prɪfɜ̱rə-/ **ADVERB** ❏ *Get exercise, preferably in the fresh air.*

pref|er|ence /pre̱fərəns/ (**preferences**) **NOUN** If you have a **preference for** something, you would like to have or do that thing rather than something else. ❏ *Customers have shown a preference for salty snacks.*

pre|fix /pri̱fɪks/ (**prefixes**) **NOUN**
LANGUAGE ARTS A **prefix** is a letter or group of letters that is added to the beginning of a word in order to form a different word. For example, the prefix "un-" is added to "happy" to form "unhappy." Compare with **suffix**.
→ look at **dictionary**

preg|nant /pre̱gnənt/ **ADJECTIVE** If a woman or a female animal is **pregnant**, she has a baby or babies developing in her body. ❏ *I'm seven months pregnant.* ● **preg|nan|cy** /pre̱gnənsi/ (**pregnancies**) **NOUN** ❏ *We keep a record of your weight gain during pregnancy.*

preju|dice /pre̱dʒədɪs/ (**prejudices**) **NOUN**
SOCIAL STUDIES **Prejudice** is an unreasonable dislike of a particular group of people or things. ❏ *These people have always suffered from racial prejudice.* ❏ *There seems to be some prejudice against workers over 45.*

preju|diced /pre̱dʒədɪst/ **ADJECTIVE** A person who is **prejudiced** against someone from a different group has an unreasonable dislike of them. ❏ *They complained that the police were racially prejudiced.*

pre|limi|nary /prɪlɪ̱mɪneri/ **ADJECTIVE** **Preliminary** activities or discussions take place at the beginning of an event, often as a form of preparation. ❏ *Preliminary results show the Republican Party with 11 percent of the vote.*

prema|ture /pri̱mətʃʊər/
1 **ADJECTIVE** Something that is **premature** happens earlier than people expect. ❏ *Heart disease is a common cause of premature death.*
2 **ADJECTIVE** A **premature** baby is one that was born before the date when it was expected

to be born. ❏ *Even very young premature babies respond to their mother's presence.*

prem|ier /prɪmɪər/ (**premiers**) **NOUN**
A country's **premier** is its leader. ❏ *He will meet the Australian premier John Howard.*

prepa|ra|tion /prɛpəreɪʃ°n/ (**preparations**)
1 **NONCOUNT NOUN** Preparation is the process of getting something ready for use. ❏ *Todd put the papers in his briefcase in preparation for the meeting.*
2 **PLURAL NOUN** Preparations are all the arrangements that are made for a future event. ❏ *We were making preparations for our wedding.*

pre|pare /prɪpɛər/ (**prepares, preparing, prepared**)
1 **VERB** If you **prepare** something, you make it ready. ❏ *We will need several weeks to prepare the report for publication.*
2 **VERB** If you **prepare for** an event, you get ready for it. ❏ *You should begin to prepare for the cost of your child's education.*
3 **VERB** When you **prepare** food, you get it ready to be eaten. ❏ *She started preparing dinner.*
→ look at **food**

Word Partners	Use **prepare** with:
N.	prepare **a list**, prepare **a plan**, prepare **a report** **1** prepare **dinner**, prepare **food**, prepare **a meal** **3**

pre|pared /prɪpɛərd/
1 **ADJECTIVE** If you are **prepared to** do something, you are willing to do it if necessary. ❏ *Are you prepared to help if we need you?*
2 **ADJECTIVE** If you are **prepared for** something that you think is going to happen, you are ready for it. ❏ *Police are prepared for large crowds.*

prepo|si|tion /prɛpəzɪʃ°n/ (**prepositions**)
NOUN LANGUAGE ARTS A **preposition** is a word such as "by," "for," "into," or "with" that usually comes before a noun.

pre|scribe /prɪskraɪb/ (**prescribes, prescribing, prescribed**) **VERB** If a doctor **prescribes** medicine or treatment for you, he or she tells you what medicine or treatment to have. ❏ *The physician examines the patient and prescribes medication.*

pre|scrip|tion /prɪskrɪpʃ°n/ (**prescriptions**)
NOUN A **prescription** is a piece of paper on which a doctor writes an order for medicine.

❏ *He gave me a prescription for some cream.*
→ look at **health care**

pres|ence /prɛz°ns/ (**presences**)
1 **NOUN** Someone's **presence** in a place is the fact that they are there. ❏ *His presence always causes trouble.*
2 If you are **in** someone's **presence**, you are in the same place as that person. ❏ *Children should do their homework in the presence of their parents.*

present
① ADJECTIVE AND NOUN USES   **②** VERB USE

① pres|ent /prɛz°nt/ (**presents**)
1 **ADJECTIVE** You use **present** to talk about things and people that exist now. ❏ *The present situation is very difficult for us.*
2 A situation that exists **at present** exists now. ❏ *At present, we do not know the cause of the disease.*
3 **ADJECTIVE** If someone is **present at** an event, they are there. ❏ *Nearly 85 percent of men are present at the birth of their children.*
4 **NOUN** A **present** is something that you give to someone, for example, on their birthday. ❏ *She bought a birthday present for her mother.*
→ look at **grammar**

② pres|ent /prɪzɛnt/ (**presents, presenting, presented**) **VERB** If you **present** something, you formally give it to someone. ❏ *The mayor presented him with a gold medal.* ❏ *Betty will present the prizes to the winners.*
● **pres|en|ta|tion** **NONCOUNT NOUN** ❏ *The evening began with the presentation of awards.*

pres|en|ta|tion /prɪzɛnteɪʃ°n/ (**presentations**)
1 **NOUN** A **presentation** is an event at which someone is given an award. ❏ *He received his award at a presentation in Kansas City.*
2 **NOUN** When someone gives a **presentation**, they show or explain something to a group of people. ❏ *Philip and I gave a short presentation.*

pres|ent con|tin|uous **NOUN** LANGUAGE ARTS
In English grammar, the **present continuous** is the structure that uses "be" and the "-ing" form of a verb. An example of the present continuous is "He is walking down the road."

pres|ent per|fect **NOUN** LANGUAGE ARTS
In grammar, the **present perfect** is the form of a verb that you use to talk about things that began in the past and are still

P

happening or still important in the present. It is formed with the verb "have" and a past participle (= a verb form that ends in "-ed" for regular verbs). An example of the present perfect is "She has promised to come."

pre|sent tense (present tenses) NOUN
LANGUAGE ARTS In grammar, **the present tense** is the form that is used for talking about things that exist, things that are happening now, or things that happen regularly.

pre|serva|tive /prɪzɜrvətɪv/ (preservatives) NOUN A **preservative** is a chemical that keeps something in good condition. ❑ *The list shows all the preservatives used in food processing.*

pre|serve /prɪzɜrv/ (preserves, preserving, preserved)
1 VERB If you **preserve** something, you take action to save it or protect it. ❑ *We need to preserve the forest.* ● **pres|er|va|tion** NONCOUNT NOUN ❑ *We're collecting money for the preservation of our historic buildings.*
2 VERB If you **preserve** food, you treat it in order to make it last longer. ❑ *Use only enough sugar to preserve the plums.*

pre|side /prɪzaɪd/ (presides, presiding, presided) VERB If you **preside over** a meeting, you are in charge. ❑ *He presided over the weekly meetings of the organization.*

presi|den|cy /prɛzɪdənsi/ (presidencies) NOUN The **presidency** of a country or organization is the position of being the president. ❑ *He was offered the presidency of the University of Saskatchewan.*

presi|dent /prɛzɪdənt/ (presidents)
1 NOUN SOCIAL STUDIES The **president** of a country that has no king or queen is the person who is in charge of that country. ❑ *The president must act quickly.*
2 NOUN The **president** of an organization is the person who has the highest position in it. ❑ *He is the national president of the Screen Actors Guild.*
→ look at **vote**

presi|den|tial /prɛzɪdɛnʃºl/ ADJECTIVE
Presidential activities or things relate or belong to a president. ❑ *He is reporting on Peru's presidential election.*

press /prɛs/ (presses, pressing, pressed)
1 VERB If you **press** something somewhere, you push it firmly against something else.

❑ *He pressed his back against the door.*
2 VERB If you **press** a button or a switch, you push it with your finger in order to make a machine work. ❑ *David pressed a button and the door closed.*
3 VERB If you **press** something, you push hard against it with your foot or hand. ❑ *He pressed the gas pedal hard.*
4 VERB If you **press** clothes, you iron them. ❑ *Vera pressed his shirt.*
5 NOUN The **press** consists of newspapers and magazines, and the people who write for them. ❑ *She gave several interviews to the local press.*

pres|sure /prɛʃər/
1 NONCOUNT NOUN **Pressure** is force that you produce when you press hard on something. ❑ *The pressure of his fingers on her arm relaxed.*
2 NONCOUNT NOUN SCIENCE The **pressure** in a place or a container is the force produced by the gas or liquid in it. ❑ *If the pressure falls in the cabin, an oxygen mask will drop in front of you.*
3 NONCOUNT NOUN If you are experiencing **pressure**, you feel that you must do a lot of things or make an important decision in very little time. ❑ *Can you work under pressure?*

pre|sum|ably /prɪzuməbli/ ADVERB
Something that is **presumably** true is probably true. ❑ *He's not going this year, presumably because of his age.*

pre|sume /prɪzum/ (presumes, presuming, presumed) VERB If you **presume that** something is true, you think that it is true, although you are not sure. ❑ *I presume that you're here on business.* ❑ *"Has he been home all week?"—"I presume so."*

pre|tend /prɪtɛnd/ (pretends, pretending, pretended)
1 VERB If you **pretend that** something is true, you try to make people believe that it is true, although in fact it is not. ❑ *I pretend that things are really okay when they're not.* ❑ *He pretended to be asleep.*
2 VERB If you **pretend that** you are doing something, you imagine that you are doing it, for example, as part of a game. ❑ *She can sunbathe and pretend she's in Cancun.*

pret|ty /prɪti/ (prettier, prettiest)
1 ADJECTIVE Someone, especially a girl, who is **pretty**, looks nice and is attractive in a delicate way. ❑ *She's a very charming and very pretty girl.*

2 **ADJECTIVE** A place or a thing that is **pretty** is attractive and pleasant. ❏ *We stayed in a very pretty little town.*

3 **ADVERB** You can use **pretty** before an adjective or adverb to mean "fairly." [INFORMAL] ❏ *I had a pretty good idea what she was going to do.*

pret|zel /pr**ɛ**ts**ə**l/ (pretzels) **NOUN** A **pretzel** is a type of small, shiny biscuit with salt on the outside.

pre|vent /pr**ɪ**v**ɛ**nt/ (prevents, preventing, prevented) **VERB** To **prevent** something means to make sure that it does not happen. ❏ *The best way to prevent injury is to wear a seat belt.* ❏ *The disease can prevent you from walking properly.* ● **pre|ven|tion** **NONCOUNT NOUN** ❏ *Scientists are still learning about the prevention of heart disease.*
→ look at **conservation, health care**

prey /pr**eɪ**/ **NONCOUNT NOUN** SCIENCE An animal's **prey** is the birds or other animals that it hunts and eats in order to live. ❏ *These animals can hunt prey in the water or in trees.*

price /pr**aɪ**s/ (prices)
1 **NOUN** The **price** of something is the amount of money that you have to pay in order to buy it. ❏ *We have seen huge changes in the price of gas.* ❏ *They expect house prices to rise.*
2 If you want something **at any price**, you are determined to get it. ❏ *They wanted fame at any price.*

price|less /pr**aɪ**sl**ɪ**s/
1 **ADJECTIVE** Something that is **priceless** is worth a very large amount of money. ❏ *Several priceless treasures were stolen from the Palace Museum last night.*
2 **ADJECTIVE** **Priceless** means extremely useful or valuable. ❏ *Our national parks are priceless treasures.*

pricey /pr**aɪ**si/ (pricier, priciest) also **pricy** **ADJECTIVE** If something is **pricey**, it is expensive. [INFORMAL] ❏ *Medical insurance is very pricey.*

prick /pr**ɪ**k/ (pricks, pricking, pricked)
1 **VERB** If you **prick** something, you make small holes in it with a sharp object. ❏ *Prick the potatoes and rub the skins with salt.*
2 **VERB** If something sharp **pricks** you, it presses into your skin and hurts you. ❏ *It felt like a needle pricking me in the foot.*

pride /pr**aɪ**d/
1 **NONCOUNT NOUN** **Pride** is a feeling of satisfaction that you have because you have done something well. ❏ *We all felt the sense of pride when we finished early.* ❏ *We take pride in offering you the highest standards.*
2 **NONCOUNT NOUN** **Pride** is a sense of dignity and self-respect. ❏ *His pride wouldn't allow him to ask for help.*

priest /pr**i**st/ (priests) **NOUN** A **priest** is a person who has religious duties in a place where people worship. ❏ *He trained to be a Catholic priest.*

pri|mari|ly /pra**ɪ**m**ɛ**r**ɪ**li/ **ADVERB** You use **primarily** to say what is mainly true in a particular situation. ❏ *These reports come primarily from passengers on the plane.*

pri|ma|ry /pr**aɪ**m**ɛ**ri, -m**ə**ri/ (primaries)
1 **ADJECTIVE** **Primary** describes something that is most important for someone or something. [FORMAL] ❏ *Language difficulties were the primary cause of his problems.*
2 **ADJECTIVE** **Primary** education is the first few years of formal education for children. ❏ *Most primary students now have experience with computers.*
3 **NOUN** SOCIAL STUDIES A **primary** or a **primary election** is an election in a state in the U.S. in which people vote for someone to represent a political party. Compare with **general election**. ❏ *He won the 1968 New Hampshire primary.*

pri|ma|ry col|or (primary colors) **NOUN** ARTS **Primary colors** are the three colors (red, yellow, and blue) that can be mixed together to produce other colors. ❏ *The toys come in bright primary colors that kids will love.*
→ look at **color**

prime min|is|ter /pr**aɪ**m m**ɪ**n**ɪ**st**ə**r/ (prime ministers) **NOUN** SOCIAL STUDIES The leader of the government in some countries is called the **prime minister**. ❏ *Vaughan Lewis is the former prime minister of St. Lucia.*

primi|tive /pr**ɪ**m**ɪ**t**ɪ**v/
1 **ADJECTIVE** **Primitive** means belonging to a society in which people live in a very simple way, usually without industries or a writing system. ❏ *He has traveled the world, visiting many primitive societies.*
2 **ADJECTIVE** **Primitive** means belonging to a very early period in the development of an animal or plant. ❏ *...primitive man.*

P

3 **ADJECTIVE** If something is **primitive**, it is very simple in style. ❑ *The conditions in the camp are primitive.*

prince /prɪns/ (**princes**) **NOUN** A **prince** is a male member of a royal family, especially the son of the king or queen.

prin|cess /prɪnsɪs, -sɛs/ (**princesses**) **NOUN** A **princess** is a female member of a royal family, usually the daughter of a king or queen or the wife of a prince.

prin|ci|pal /prɪnsɪpəl/ (**principals**)
1 **ADJECTIVE** **Principal** means first in order of importance. ❑ *Money was not the principal reason for his action.* ❑ *Newspapers were the principal source of information.*
2 **NOUN** The **principal** of a school is the person in charge of the school. ❑ *Donald King is the principal of Dartmouth High School.*

prin|ci|ple /prɪnsɪpəl/ (**principles**)
1 **NOUN** Your **principles** are the rules and ideas that you have about how you should behave. ❑ *It's against my principles to be dishonest.*
2 **NOUN** A **principle** is a rule about how something works or happens. ❑ *The first principle of democracy is that people should have the right to vote.*

print /prɪnt/ (**prints, printing, printed**)
1 **VERB** If you **print** something, you use a machine to put words or pictures on paper. ❑ *The publishers have printed 40,000 copies of the novel.*
2 **NONCOUNT NOUN** **Print** is all the letters and numbers in a printed document. ❑ *I can't read this—the print is too small.*
3 **VERB** If you **print** words, you write in letters that are not joined together. ❑ *Please sign here, then print your name and address.*
▶ **print out** If you **print** a computer file **out**, you use a machine to produce a copy of it on paper. ❑ *I printed out a copy of the letter and put it on Mr. Miller's desk.*
→ look at **writing**

Word Builder	printer

er ≈ **something that does**
> clean + er = cleaner
> contain + er = container
> dry + er = dryer
> open + er = opener
> print + er = printer
> toast + er = toaster

print|er /prɪntər/ (**printers**)
1 **NOUN** A **printer** is a machine for printing copies of computer documents on paper.
2 **NOUN** A **printer** is a person or a company whose job is printing things such as books. ❑ *Franklin was a printer, a publisher, and a diplomat.*
→ look at **classroom, computer, office**

print|out /prɪntaʊt/ (**printouts**) also **print-out** **NOUN** A **printout** is a piece of paper with information from a computer printed on it. ❑ *Maria gave me a printout of the email.*

pri|or /praɪər/ If something happens **prior to** a particular time or event, it happens before that time or event. [FORMAL] ❑ *Prior to his trip to Japan, Steven was in New York.*

pri|or|ity /praɪɔrɪti/ (**priorities**)
1 **NOUN** If something is a **priority**, it is the most important thing, and you have to deal with it before everything else. ❑ *Her children are her first priority.* ❑ *The government's priority is to build more schools.*
2 If you **give priority to** something or someone, you treat them as more important than anything else. ❑ *The government should give priority to environmental issues.*
3 If something **takes priority over** other things, it is more important than other things. ❑ *The needs of the poor must take priority over the desires of the rich.*

pris|on /prɪzən/ (**prisons**) **NOUN** A **prison** is a building where criminals are kept as punishment. ❑ *He was sent to prison for five years.*

pris|on|er /prɪzənər/ (**prisoners**) **NOUN** A **prisoner** is a person who is not free, usually because they are in prison. ❑ *A prisoner escaped from Arrowhead Correctional Center early Monday.* ❑ *More than 30,000 Australians were taken prisoner in World War II.*

pri|va|cy /praɪvəsi/ **NONCOUNT NOUN** **Privacy** is the freedom to do things without people knowing what you are doing. ❑ *What I do in the privacy of my own home is not your business.* ❑ *We have changed the names to protect the privacy of those involved.*

pri|vate /praɪvɪt/
1 **ADJECTIVE** **Private** companies are not owned by the government. ❑ *...a private hospital.* ❑ *Their children go to a private school.*
2 **ADJECTIVE** If something is **private**, it is only for one particular person or group, and

P

not for everyone. ❑ *The door was marked "Private."* ❑ *It was a private conversation, so I'm not going to talk about it to anyone else.* ● **pri|vate|ly ADVERB** ❑ *We need to talk privately.*

3 ADJECTIVE Your **private life** is the part of your life that concerns your personal relationships and activities, and not your job. ❑ *I've always kept my private and professional life separate.*

4 ADJECTIVE A **private** place is quiet, and you can be alone there without being disturbed. ❑ *It was the only private place they could find.*

5 If you do something **in private**, you do it without other people being there. ❑ *Mark asked to talk to his boss in private.*
→ look at **identification**

privi|lege /prɪvɪlɪdʒ, prɪvlɪdʒ/ (**privileges**) **NOUN** A **privilege** is a special advantage that only one person or group has. ❑ *We are not asking for special privileges, we simply want equal opportunity.*

privi|leged /prɪvɪlɪdʒd, prɪvlɪdʒd/ **ADJECTIVE** If you are **privileged**, you have an advantage that most other people do not have, often because you are rich. ❑ *They had a privileged childhood.*

prize /praɪz/ (**prizes**) **NOUN** A **prize** is money or a special object that you give to the person who wins a game, a race, or a competition. ❑ *He won first prize in the golf tournament.*

prob|abil|ity /prɒbəbɪlɪti/ **NONCOUNT NOUN** MATH The **probability of** something happening is how likely it is to happen. ❑ *We believe there is a high probability of success.*

prob|able /prɒbəbəl/ **ADJECTIVE** If something is **probable**, it is likely to be true or likely to happen. ❑ *Jess is a great player, and it's highly probable that she will win.*

prob|ably /prɒbəbli/ **ADVERB** Something that is **probably** true is likely to be true, although you are not sure. ❑ *I will probably go home on Tuesday.* ❑ *Van Gogh is probably the best-known painter in the world.*

prob|lem /prɒbləm/ (**problems**)
1 NOUN A **problem** is something or someone that causes difficulties, or that makes you worry. ❑ *Pollution is a problem in this city.* ❑ *The government has failed to solve the problem of unemployment.*

2 NOUN A **problem** is a special type of question that you have to think hard about

in order to answer. ❑ *...a math problem.*
→ look at **fraction**

pro|cedure /prəsidʒər/ (**procedures**) **NOUN** A **procedure** is the usual or correct way of doing something. ❑ *If your car is stolen, the correct procedure is to report the theft to the local police.*

pro|ceed /prəsid/ (**proceeds, proceeding, proceeded**)
1 VERB If you **proceed to** do something, you do it after doing something else. ❑ *He picked up a book, which he proceeded to read.*
2 VERB If something **proceeds**, it continues. [FORMAL] ❑ *The building work is proceeding very slowly.*

pro|cess /prɒsɛs/ (**processes**) **NOUN** A **process** is a series of actions that have a particular result. ❑ *After the war, the population began the long process of returning to normal life.*

Word Partners	Use **process** with:
N.	**application** process, **learning** process, **planning** process
V.	**begin a** process, **complete a** process, **describe a** process, **start a** process
ADJ.	**complicated** process, **difficult** process, **long** process, **normal** process, **slow** process, **whole** process

pro|ces|sion /prəsɛʃən/ (**processions**) **NOUN** A **procession** is a line of people or vehicles that follow one another as part of a ceremony. ❑ *Sam watched the procession pass him slowly on its way to Fourth Avenue.*

pro|ces|sor /prɒsɛsər/ (**processors**) **NOUN** A **processor** is the part of a computer that performs the tasks that the user has requested.

pro|duce (**produces, producing, produced**)

> **PRONUNCIATION HELP**
> Pronounce the verb /prədus/. Pronounce the noun /prɒdus/ or /proudus/.

1 VERB If you **produce** something, you make it or grow it. ❑ *The company produces about 2.3 million tons of steel a year.* ● **pro|duc|er** (**producers**) **NOUN** ❑ *Saudi Arabia is the world's leading oil producer.*

2 VERB If one thing **produces** another thing, it causes the second thing to happen. ❑ *The talks failed to produce results.*

3 VERB If you **produce** a play or a movie, you organize it and decide how it should be made. ❑ *The movie was produced and directed by Johnny White.* ● **pro|duc|er** (**producers**) **NOUN**

P

❑ *The movie was created by producer Alison Millar.* **4** **NONCOUNT NOUN** Produce is fruit and vegetables that are grown to be sold. ❑ *The restaurant uses as much local produce as possible.*
→ look at **energy, factory, tree**

prod|uct /prɒdʌkt/ (**products**) **NOUN** A **product** is something that you make or grow, in order to sell it. ❑ *This cellphone is one of the company's most successful products.*
→ look at **factory**

pro|duc|tion /prədʌkʃən/ (**productions**)
1 **NONCOUNT NOUN** Production is the process of making or growing something in large amounts, or the amount of goods that you make or grow. ❑ *This car went into production last year.* ❑ *The factory needs to increase production.*
2 **NOUN** A **production** is a play or other show that is performed in a theater.
❑ *Tonight our class is going to see a production of "Othello."*
→ look at **factory**

pro|duc|tive /prədʌktɪv/ **ADJECTIVE** If someone or something is **productive**, they produce or do a lot. ❑ *Training makes workers more productive.*

pro|fes|sion /prəfɛʃən/ (**professions**) **NOUN** A **profession** is a type of job for which you need special education or training. ❑ *Ava was a doctor by profession.*

pro|fes|sion|al /prəfɛʃənəl/ (**professionals**)
1 **ADJECTIVE** Professional means relating to a person's work, especially work that requires special training. ❑ *Get professional advice from your accountant first.*
2 **ADJECTIVE** Professional describes people who do a particular activity for money rather than as a hobby. ❑ *My parents were professional musicians.*
3 **NOUN** Professional is also a noun. ❑ *The competition is open to both professionals and amateurs.* ● **pro|fes|sion|al|ly** **ADVERB** ❑ *I've been singing professionally for 10 years.*
→ look at **performance**

pro|fes|sor /prəfɛsər/ (**professors**) **NOUN** A **professor** is a teacher at a university or a college. ❑ *Kate is a professor of history at George Washington University.*

pro|file /proʊfaɪl/ (**profiles**) **NOUN** Your **profile** is the shape of your face when people see it from the side. ❑ *He was slim, with black hair and a handsome profile.*

prof|it /prɒfɪt/ (**profits**) **NOUN** A **profit** is the amount of money that you gain when you sell something for more than you paid for it. ❑ *When he sold the house, Chris made a profit of about $50,000.*

prof|it|able /prɒfɪtəbəl/ **ADJECTIVE** If something is **profitable**, it makes a profit. ❑ *The business started to be profitable in its second year.*

pro|gram /proʊgræm, -grəm/ (**programs, programming, programmed**)
1 **NOUN** A **program** is a plan of things to do. ❑ *The art gallery's education program includes art classes for all ages.*
2 **NOUN** A **program** is a television or radio show. ❑ *...a network television program.*
3 **NOUN** A theater or concert **program** is a small book or sheet of paper that tells you about the play or concert. ❑ *When you go to concerts, it's helpful to read the program.*
4 **NOUN** **TECHNOLOGY** A **program** is a set of instructions that a computer uses to do a particular task. ❑ *Ada Lovelace wrote the world's first computer program in 1842.*
5 **VERB** **TECHNOLOGY** When you **program** a computer or a machine, you give it a set of instructions so that it can do a particular task. ❑ *They can teach you how to program a computer in two weeks.* ● **pro|gram|ming** **NONCOUNT NOUN** ❑ *Java is a popular programming language.* ● **pro|gram|mer** (**programmers**) **NOUN** ❑ *Greg works as a computer programmer.*
→ look at **television**

pro|gress (**progresses, progressing, progressed**)

> **PRONUNCIATION HELP**
> Pronounce the noun /prɒgrɛs/. Pronounce the verb /prəgrɛs/.

1 **NONCOUNT NOUN** Progress is the process of gradually improving or getting nearer to achieving something. ❑ *We are making progress in the fight against cancer.*
2 **VERB** If you **progress**, you improve or become more advanced or successful. ❑ *All our students are progressing well.*
3 **VERB** If events **progress**, they continue to happen over a period of time. ❑ *As the evening progressed, Leila grew tired.*
4 If something is **in progress**, it has started and is still happening. ❑ *The game was already in progress when we arrived.*

P

pro|hib|it /prouhɪbɪt/ (**prohibits, prohibiting, prohibited**) **VERB** If a rule or a law **prohibits** something, it makes it illegal. [FORMAL] ❏ Smoking is prohibited here.

pro|hi|bi|tion /prouɪbɪʃᵊn/ (**prohibitions**)
1 NOUN A **prohibition** is a law that says you must not do something. ❏ The government intends to remove the prohibition on exporting live horses.
2 NONCOUNT NOUN SOCIAL STUDIES In the United States, **Prohibition** was the period between 1920 and 1933 when it was illegal to make or sell alcoholic drinks.

proj|ect /prɒdʒɛkt/ (**projects**)
1 NOUN A **project** is a plan that takes a lot of time and effort. ❏ The charity is funding a housing project in India.
2 NOUN When a student does a **project** on a subject, they find out a lot of information about the subject and then they write about it. ❏ Our class has just finished a project on ancient Greece.

pro|jec|tor /prədʒɛktər/ (**projectors**) **NOUN** A **projector** is a machine that shows movies or pictures on a screen or wall.

pro|logue /proulɒg/ (**prologues**) also **prolog**
NOUN LANGUAGE ARTS A **prologue** is a part of a play, book, or movie that introduces the story. ❏ She first appears in the prologue to the novel.

pro|long /prəlɔŋ/ (**prolongs, prolonging, prolonged**) **VERB** If you **prolong** something, you make it last longer. ❏ I did not wish to prolong the conversation.

prom /prɒm/ (**proms**) **NOUN** A **prom** is a formal dance for high school students to celebrate the end of the school year. ❏ She accepted his invitation to the senior prom.

promi|nent /prɒmɪnənt/
1 ADJECTIVE A **prominent** person is important and well-known. ❏ Michelle is married to a prominent lawyer in Portland.
2 ADJECTIVE If something is **prominent**, it is big, and you can see it very easily. ❏ ...a prominent nose.

prom|ise /prɒmɪs/ (**promises, promising, promised**)
1 VERB If you **promise that** you will do something, you say that you will certainly do it. ❏ She promised to write to me soon. ❏ I promise that I'll help you all I can. ❏ Promise me you'll come to the party.

2 NOUN Promise is also a noun. ❏ If you make a promise, you should keep it. ❏ James broke every promise he made.

pro|mote /prəmoʊt/ (**promotes, promoting, promoted**)
1 VERB If you **promote** something, you help to make it successful. ❏ There will be a new TV campaign to promote the products.
2 VERB If someone **is promoted**, they are given a more important job in the organization that they work for. ❏ Richard has just been promoted to general manager.
● **pro|mo|tion** **NOUN** ❏ We went out for dinner to celebrate Dad's promotion.

prompt /prɒmpt/ **ADJECTIVE** A **prompt** action is done without waiting. ❏ These questions require prompt answers from the government.

prompt|ly /prɒmptli/
1 ADVERB If you do something **promptly**, you do it immediately. ❏ Grandma sat down, and promptly fell asleep.
2 ADVERB If you do something **promptly at** a particular time, you do it at exactly that time. ❏ Promptly at seven o'clock, we left the hotel.

pro|noun /prounaʊn/ (**pronouns**) **NOUN** LANGUAGE ARTS A **pronoun** is a word that you use instead of a noun when you are talking about someone or something. "It," "she," "something," and "myself" are pronouns.

pro|nounce /prənaʊns/ (**pronounces, pronouncing, pronounced**) **VERB** When you **pronounce** a word, you make its sound. ❏ Have I pronounced your name correctly?
→ look at **dictionary, language**

pro|nun|cia|tion /prənʌnsieɪʃᵊn/ (**pronunciations**) **NOUN** LANGUAGE ARTS The **pronunciation** of a word is the way that you say it. ❏ We are learning about the differences between Canadian and American pronunciation.
→ look at **dictionary**

proof /pruf/ **NONCOUNT NOUN Proof** is something that shows that something else is true or exists. ❏ The scientists hope to find proof that there is water on Mars.
→ look at **identification**

propa|gan|da /prɒpəgændə/ **NONCOUNT NOUN** SOCIAL STUDIES **Propaganda** is information that a political organization uses in order to influence people. ❏ The state media began a huge propaganda campaign.

P

pro|pel|ler /prəpɛlər/ (**propellers**) **NOUN**
A **propeller** is a part of a boat or an aircraft that turns around very fast and makes the boat or the aircraft move. ❑ *One of the ship's propellers was damaged in the accident.*

prop|er /prɒpər/ **ADJECTIVE** The **proper** thing or way is the one that is correct or most suitable. ❑ *The book is intended as a guide to proper behavior.*

prop|er name (**proper names**) **NOUN**
A **proper name** is the name of a particular person, place, organization, or thing. **Proper names** begin with a capital letter.

prop|er noun (**proper nouns**) **NOUN**
LANGUAGE ARTS A **proper noun** is the name of a particular person, place, organization, or thing. Proper nouns begin with a capital letter.

prop|er|ty /prɒpərti/ (**properties**)
1 **NONCOUNT NOUN** Your **property** is anything that belongs to you. [FORMAL] ❑ *"That's my property. You can't just take it."*
2 **NOUN** A **property** is a building and the land around it. [FORMAL] ❑ *Get out of here—this is a private property!*

proph|et /prɒfɪt/ (**prophets**) **NOUN** In some religions, a **prophet** is a person who is sent by God to lead people and to teach them about the religion. ❑ *Muhammad is the Holy Prophet of Islam.*

pro|por|tion /prəpɔrʃᵊn/ (**proportions**)
1 **NOUN** A **proportion of** an amount is a part of it. [FORMAL] ❑ *A large proportion of the fish in that area have died.*
2 **NOUN** The **proportion of** one type of person or thing in a group is the number of them compared to the total number of people or things in the group. ❑ *The proportion of the population using cellphones is 80-85%.*
3 **NONCOUNT NOUN** ARTS **Proportion** is the correct relationship between the size of objects in a piece of art. ❑ *...the symmetry and proportion of classical Greek and Roman architecture.*

pro|po|sal /prəpouzᵊl/ (**proposals**)
1 **NOUN** A **proposal** is a suggestion or a plan. ❑ *The president has announced new proposals for a peace agreement.*
2 **NOUN** A **proposal** is the act of asking someone to marry you. ❑ *Pam accepted Randy's proposal of marriage.*

pro|pose /prəpouz/ (**proposes, proposing, proposed**)
1 **VERB** If you **propose** a plan or an idea, you suggest it. ❑ *The minister has proposed a change in the law.*
2 **VERB** If you **propose to** someone, you ask them to marry you. ❑ *David proposed to his girlfriend when they were on vacation in Paris.*

prose /prouz/ **NONCOUNT NOUN** LANGUAGE ARTS **Prose** is ordinary written language, not poetry. ❑ *Hannah writes both poetry and prose.*

pros|ecute /prɒsɪkyut/ (**prosecutes, prosecuting, prosecuted**) **VERB** If the police **prosecute** a person, they say formally in a law court that the person has committed a crime. ❑ *The man was prosecuted for a killing at a gas station in Virginia.* ● **pros|ecu|tion** (**prosecutions**) **NOUN** ❑ *This evidence led to the prosecution of the former leader.*

proslav|ery /prouslɛɪvəri/ **ADJECTIVE** SOCIAL STUDIES **Proslavery** ideas support the belief that people can be owned and forced to work with little or no pay.

pro|tect /prətɛkt/ (**protects, protecting, protected**) **VERB** If you **protect** someone or something, you keep them safe from harm or damage. ❑ *Make sure you protect your children from the sun's harmful rays.*
→ look at **conservation, identification**

pro|tec|tion /prətɛkʃᵊn/ (**protections**)
NONCOUNT NOUN If something gives you **protection** against something unpleasant, it stops you from being harmed or damaged by it. ❑ *Long-sleeved t-shirts offer greater protection against the sun.*

pro|tec|tive /prətɛktɪv/
1 **ADJECTIVE** **Protective** things are intended to protect you from injury or harm. ❑ *You should wear protective gloves when you are gardening.*
2 **ADJECTIVE** If someone is **protective toward** you, they look after you and try to keep you safe. ❑ *Ben is very protective toward his mother.*

pro|tein /proutin/ (**proteins**) **NOUN** **Protein** is a substance that the body needs. It is found in meat, eggs, fish, and milk. ❑ *Fish is a major source of protein.*
→ look at **meat**

pro|test (**protests, protesting, protested**)

> **PRONUNCIATION HELP**
> Pronounce the verb /prətɛst/ and /proutɛst/. Pronounce the noun /proutɛst/.

P

1 VERB If you **protest**, you say or show publicly that you do not approve of something. ❑ *The students were protesting against the arrest of one of their teachers.*
● **pro|test|er** also **protestor** NOUN (**protesters**) ❑ *The protesters say that the government is corrupt.*
2 NOUN A **protest** is the act of showing publicly that you do not approve of something. ❑ *I took part in a protest against the war.*

Prot|es|tant /prɒtɪstənt/ (**Protestants**) NOUN A **Protestant** is a Christian (= a person who believes that Jesus Christ is the son of God) who is not a Catholic (= a member of the part of the Christian church whose leader is known as the Pope).

proud /praʊd/ (**prouder, proudest**)
1 ADJECTIVE If you feel **proud**, you feel pleased and satisfied about something good that you or other people close to you have done. ❑ *The college principal was very proud of her students' sucess.* ● **proud|ly** ADVERB ❑ *Nick wears his police uniform proudly.*
2 ADJECTIVE If you are **proud**, you think that you are better or more important than other people. ❑ *He described his boss as "proud and selfish."*

prove /pruv/ (**proves, proving, proved**) VERB If you **prove** something, you show that it is true. ❑ *Everyone knows that there is a link between diet and health.* ❑ *These results prove that we were right.*

prov|erb /prɒvɜrb/ (**proverbs**) NOUN A **proverb** is a short sentence that people often say, because it gives advice or tells you something about life. ❑ *An old Arab proverb says, "The enemy of my enemy is my friend."*

pro|vide /prəvaɪd/ (**provides, providing, provided**) VERB If you **provide** something that someone needs or wants, you give it to them. ❑ *The company's website provides lots of useful information.* ❑ *The refugees were provided with food and accommodation.*

pro|vid|ed /prəvaɪdɪd/ CONJUNCTION If something will happen **provided** or **providing** that something else happens, the first thing will happen only if the second thing also happens. ❑ *He can go running at his age, provided that he is sensible.*

pro|vid|ing /prəvaɪdɪŋ/ CONJUNCTION → look up **provided**

prov|ince /prɒvɪns/ (**provinces**) NOUN A **province** is a large part of a country that has its own local government. ❑ *...the Canadian province of British Columbia.*

pro|vin|cial /prəvɪnʃəl/ ADJECTIVE Provincial means relating to a province. ❑ *Victoria is the provincial capital of British Columbia.*

pro|vi|sion /prəvɪʒən/ NONCOUNT NOUN The **provision of** something is the act of giving it to people who need or want it. ❑ *This department is responsible for the provision of legal services.*

pro|vi|sion|al /prəvɪʒənəl/ ADJECTIVE Something that is **provisional** has been arranged or exists now, but it may be changed in the future. ❑ *Your provisional driver's license is valid for 18 months.*
● **pro|vi|sion|al|ly** ADVERB ❑ *She provisionally accepted the job offer.*

pro|voke /prəvoʊk/ (**provokes, provoking, provoked**) VERB If you **provoke** someone, you deliberately annoy them and try to make them angry. ❑ *The demonstrators did not provoke the police and everyone remained calm.*

prowl /praʊl/ (**prowls, prowling, prowled**) VERB If an animal or a person **prowls around**, they move around quietly, waiting to do something. ❑ *Gangs of youths prowled the area.*

prune /prun/ (**prunes**) NOUN A **prune** is a dried plum.

P.S. /pi ɛs/ also **PS** You write **P.S.** when you add at something at the end of a letter after you have signed it. ❑ *P.S. Please show your friends this letter.*

psy|chi|a|trist /sɪkaɪətrɪst/ (**psychiatrists**) NOUN A **psychiatrist** is a doctor who takes care of people who have illnesses of the mind. ❑ *When Sarah was 16, a psychiatrist treated her for depression.*

psycho|logi|cal /saɪkəlɒdʒɪkəl/ ADJECTIVE **Psychological** means concerned with a person's mind and thoughts. ❑ *Guilt can lead to psychological illness.*

psy|chol|ogy /saɪkɒlədʒi/ NONCOUNT NOUN SCIENCE **Psychology** is the study of the human mind and the reasons for people's behavior. ❑ *Scott is a professor of educational psychology at the University of Connecticut.*
● **psy|cholo|gist** (**psychologists**) NOUN ❑ *Amy is seeing a psychologist.*

P

pub|lic /pʌblɪk/
1 **NOUN** The public is people in general, or everyone. ❏ *The exhibition is open to the public from tomorrow.*
2 **ADJECTIVE** Public means relating to all the people in a country or a community. ❏ *The government's policies still have strong public support.*
3 **ADJECTIVE** Public buildings and services are for everyone to use. ❏ *The New York Public Library was built in 1911.* ❏ *...public transportation.*
4 If you say or do something **in public**, you say or do it when other people are there. ❏ *He hasn't performed in public in more than 40 years.*

pub|li|ca|tion /pʌblɪkeɪʃⁿn/ (**publications**)
1 **NONCOUNT NOUN** The **publication** of a book or a magazine is the act of printing it and sending it to stores to be sold. ❏ *The store stayed open late to celebrate the book's publication.*
2 **NOUN** A **publication** is a book or a magazine. ❏ *My uncle has written for several publications.*

pub|lic|ity /pʌblɪsɪti/ **NONCOUNT NOUN**
Publicity means providing people with information about a person, or a product. ❏ *A lot of publicity was given to the talks.* ❏ *We are planning a publicity campaign against racism.*

pub|li|cize /pʌblɪsaɪz/ (**publicizes, publicizing, publicized**) **VERB** If you **publicize** something, you let people know about it. ❏ *The author appeared on television to publicize her latest book.*

pub|lic of|fice **NONCOUNT NOUN**
SOCIAL STUDIES Someone who is in **public office** has been elected by the public to do a job. ❏ *He held public office for twenty years.*

pub|lish /pʌblɪʃ/ (**publishes, publishing, published**) **VERB** When a company **publishes** a book, a magazine, or a newspaper, it prepares and prints copies of it. ❏ *Harper Collins will publish his new novel on March 4.*

pub|lish|er /pʌblɪʃər/ (**publishers**) **NOUN**
A **publisher** is a person or a company that publishes books, newspapers, or magazines. ❏ *She sent the book to a publisher and got a positive response.*

pud|ding /pʊdɪŋ/ (**puddings**) **NOUN** Pudding is a soft, sweet dessert made from eggs and milk. ❏ *For dessert, there was chocolate pudding.*

pud|dle /pʌdᵊl/ (**puddles**) **NOUN** A puddle is a small pool of water on the ground. ❏ *Young children love splashing in puddles.*

puff /pʌf/ (**puffs, puffing, puffed**)
1 **NOUN** A **puff of** air or smoke is a small amount of it that is blown from somewhere. ❏ *Puffs of steam rose into the air and vanished.*
2 **VERB** If you **are puffing**, you are breathing loudly and quickly, usually because you have been running. ❏ *He puffs and pants if he has to walk up a flight of stairs.*

pull /pʊl/ (**pulls, pulling, pulled**)
1 **VERB** When you **pull** something, you hold it firmly and use force to move it. ❏ *The dentist had to pull out all Grandpa's teeth.* ❏ *I helped to pull the boy out of the water.*

❏ *Someone pulled her hair.*
2 **NOUN** Pull is also a noun. ❏ *He felt a pull on the fishing line.*
▸ **pull away** When a vehicle or a driver **pulls away**, the vehicle starts moving forward. ❏ *I watched the car back out of the driveway and pull away.*
▸ **pull down** If you **pull down** a building, you deliberately destroy it. ❏ *They pulled the offices down, leaving a large open space.*
▸ **pull in** If a vehicle or a driver **pulls in** somewhere, the vehicle stops there. ❏ *The bus pulled in at the side of the road.*
▸ **pull into** When a vehicle or driver **pulls into** a place, the vehicle moves into the place and stops there. ❏ *David pulled into the driveway in front of her garage.*
▸ **pull out** When a vehicle or a driver **pulls out**, the vehicle moves out into the road or nearer the center of the road. ❏ *I looked in the rear mirror, and pulled out into the street.*
▸ **pull over** When a vehicle or driver **pulls over**, the vehicle moves closer to the side of the road and stops there. ❏ *I pulled over to let the police car pass.*
▸ **pull yourself together** If someone tells you to **pull yourself together**, they are telling you to control your feelings and be calm again. ❏ *"Now stop crying and pull yourself together!"*
▸ **pull up** When a vehicle or driver **pulls up**, the vehicle slows down and stops. ❏ *The cab pulled up and the driver jumped out.*

pull|over /pʊloʊvər/ (**pullovers**) **NOUN** A **pullover** is a warm piece of clothing that covers the upper part of your body and your arms.

Picture Dictionary   punctuation

A: I want to learn to drive; however, cars scare me.
              semicolon   period

B: Why not take a driver-training course?
               hyphen   question mark

A: I'm not ready.
   apostrophe

B: I know! If you want, I'll teach you to drive.
     exclamation point   comma

A: OK, but remember this: it was your idea, not mine.
                  colon

pulse /pʌls/ (pulses) **NOUN** SCIENCE Your
pulse is the regular beat of your heart that
you can feel when you touch your wrist and
other parts of your body. ❏ *Dr. Garcia checked
her pulse and breathing.*

pump /pʌmp/ (pumps, pumping, pumped)
1 **NOUN** A **pump** is a machine that makes a
liquid or gas flow in a particular direction.
❏ *A pump brings water directly from the well.*
❏ *There are three water pumps in the village.*
2 **VERB** If something **pumps** a liquid or a
gas in a particular direction, it makes it flow
in that direction using a pump. ❏ *The heart
pumps blood around the body.*

pump|kin /pʌmpkɪn/ (pumpkins) **NOUN** A
pumpkin is a large, round, orange vegetable
with a thick skin. ❏ *...pumpkin pie.*

pun /pʌn/ (puns) **NOUN** A **pun** is a clever and
amusing use of a word or phrase that has
two meanings. For example: "Where do
peas have their eyes tested?"—"In an iPod."
(= in an "eye pod.").

punch /pʌntʃ/ (punches, punching,
punched)
1 **VERB** If you **punch** someone or
something, you hit them hard with your
fist (= your hand, when your fingers are all
closed tightly). ❏ *During a concert, the singer
punched a photographer.*
2 **NOUN** **Punch** is also a noun. ❏ *My brother
gave me a punch in the nose.*
3 **VERB** If you **punch** holes in something,
you make holes in it by pushing or pressing
it with something sharp. ❏ *I took a pen and
punched a hole in the box.*

punc|tu|al /pʌŋktʃuəl/ **ADJECTIVE** If you are
punctual, you arrive somewhere at the right
time. ❏ *He's always very punctual.*
● **punc|tu|al|ly** **ADVERB** ❏ *The guests all arrived
punctually, at eight o'clock.*

punc|tua|tion /pʌŋktʃueɪʃªn/ **NONCOUNT**
NOUN LANGUAGE ARTS **Punctuation** is signs
such as ( ), !, or ? that you use to divide writing
into sentences and phrases. ❏ *You have to give
more attention to punctuation and grammar.*
→ look at Picture Dictionary: **punctuation**
→ look at **writing**

punc|tua|tion mark (punctuation marks)
NOUN LANGUAGE ARTS A **punctuation mark** is
a symbol such as ( ), !, or ?.

punc|ture /pʌŋktʃər/ (punctures,
puncturing, punctured)
1 **NOUN** A **puncture** is a small hole that has
been made by a sharp object. ❏ *I repaired the
puncture in my front tire.*
2 **VERB** If a sharp object **punctures**
something, it makes a hole in it. ❏ *The bullet
punctured his left lung.*

pun|ish /pʌnɪʃ/ (punishes, punishing,
punished) **VERB** If you **punish** someone, you
make them suffer in some way because they
have done something wrong. ❏ *His parents
punished him for being rude.*

pun|ish|ment /pʌnɪʃmənt/ (punishments)
NOUN A **punishment** is a particular way of
punishing someone. ❏ *There will be tougher
punishments for violent crimes.*

pup /pʌp/ (pups)
1 **NOUN** A **pup** is a young dog. ❏ *We've had
Pongo since he was a pup.*
2 **NOUN** The babies of some other animals
are called **pups**. ❏ *...gray seal pups.*

pu|pil /pyupɪl/ (pupils)
1 **NOUN** The **pupils** of an elementary school
are the children who go to it. ❏ *Around 270
pupils attend this school.*
2 **NOUN** The **pupils** of your eyes are the
small, round, black holes in the center of
them. ❏ *In low light the pupils are wide open to
allow light into the eye.*

p

pup|pet /pʌpɪt/ (puppets) NOUN A **puppet** is a small model of a person or animal that you can move.

pup|py /pʌpi/ (puppies) NOUN A **puppy** is a young dog.

pur|chase /pɜrtʃɪs/ (purchases, purchasing, purchased)

1 VERB If you **purchase** something, you buy it. [FORMAL] ❏ *He purchased a ticket for the concert.*

2 NONCOUNT NOUN The **purchase** of something is the act of buying it. [FORMAL] ❏ *The Canadian company announced the purchase of 1,663 stores in the U.S.*

3 NOUN A **purchase** is something that you buy. [FORMAL] ❏ *Her latest purchase is a shiny, black motorcycle.*

pure /pyʊər/ (purer, purest)

1 ADJECTIVE A **pure** substance is not mixed with anything else. ❏ *I bought a carton of pure orange juice.*

2 ADJECTIVE If something is **pure**, it is clean and does not contain any harmful substances. ❏ *The water is so pure that we drink it from the stream.*

3 ADJECTIVE **Pure** means complete and total. ❏ *There was a look of pure surprise on his face.*

pure|ly /pyʊərli/ ADVERB **Purely** means only or completely. ❏ *This car is designed purely for speed.*

Pu|ri|tan /pyʊərɪtᵊn/ (Puritans) NOUN SOCIAL STUDIES The **Puritans** were a group of English religious people in the 16th and 17th centuries, who lived in a very strict way. Many of these people moved to the United States.

pur|ple /pɜrpᵊl/ (purples)

1 ADJECTIVE Something that is **purple** is a red-blue color. ❏ *She wore a purple dress.*

2 NOUN **Purple** is also a noun. ❏ *I love the purples and grays of the Scottish mountains.*
→ look at **color**

pur|pose /pɜrpəs/ (purposes)

1 NOUN The **purpose** of something is the reason why you do it. ❏ *The purpose of the occasion was to raise money for charity.*

2 If you do something **on purpose**, you do it deliberately. ❏ *I'm sure that Pedro hit me on purpose.*

purr /pɜr/ (purrs, purring, purred) VERB When a cat **purrs**, it makes a low sound with its throat. ❏ *The little, black kitten purred and rubbed against my leg.*

purse /pɜrs/ (purses) NOUN A **purse** is a small bag that women use to carry money and other things. ❏ *Lauren reached in her purse for her keys.*
→ look at **bag**

pur|sue /pərsu/ (pursues, pursuing, pursued) VERB If you **pursue** someone or something, you follow them because you want to catch them. [FORMAL] ❏ *Police pursued the driver for two miles.*

pur|suit /pərsut/ NONCOUNT NOUN If you are **in pursuit of** something, you are trying to get it. ❏ *He has traveled the world in pursuit of his dream.*

push /pʊʃ/ (pushes, pushing, pushed)

1 VERB If you **push** something, you use force to make it move forward or away from you. ❏ *I pushed back my chair and stood up.* ❏ *The men pushed him into the car and locked the door.* ❏ *Justin put both hands on the door and pushed hard.*

2 NOUN **Push** is also a noun. ❏ *Laura gave me a sharp push and I fell to the ground.*

3 VERB If you **push** a button on a machine, you press it with your finger. ❏ *Christina got inside the elevator and pushed the button for the third floor.*

push-up (push-ups) NOUN SPORTS **Push-ups** are exercises to make your upper body stronger. You do them by lying on your front and pushing your body up with your hands until your arms are straight.

put /pʊt/ (puts, putting, put)

1 VERB If you **put** something in a particular place or position, you move it into that place or position. ❏ *Steven put the photograph on the desk.* ❏ *She put her hand on Grace's arm.* ❏ *Now, where did I put my purse?*

2 VERB If you **put** someone or something in a particular state or situation, you cause them to be in that state or situation. ❏ *Your carelessness put the children in danger.*

▶ **put away** If you **put** something **away**, you put it back in the place where it is usually kept. ❏ *Kyle put the milk away in the refrigerator.*

▶ **put down** If you **put** something **down** somewhere, you stop holding it and place it on a surface. ❏ *The woman put down her newspaper and looked at me.*

▶ **put off** If you **put** something **off**, you delay doing it. ❏ *Tony always puts off making difficult decisions.*

▶ **put on** **1** If you **put on** clothing or make-up, you place it on your body in order to wear it. ❏ *Grandma put her coat on and went out.* ❏ *She put on lipstick and combed her hair.*
2 If you **put on** weight, you become heavier. ❏ *I'm lucky—I never put on weight.*
3 If you **put on** a piece of electrical equipment, you make it start working. ❏ *Maria sat up in bed and put on the light.*
4 If you **put** a CD **on**, you place it in a CD player and listen to it.
→ look at **wear**

▶ **put out** If you **put out** a fire, you make it stop burning. ❏ *All day, firefighters have been trying to put out the blaze.*

▶ **put up** **1** If you **put up** a wall or a building, you build it. ❏ *The Smiths have put up electric fences on their farm.*
2 If you **put up** a poster or a notice, you attach it to a wall or board. ❏ *They're putting new street signs up.*

▶ **put up with** If you **put up with** someone or something unpleasant, you accept them without complaining. ❏ *I won't put up with your bad behavior any longer.* ❏ *It was a very bad injury, and he's put up with a lot of pain.*

puz|zle /pʌzᵊl/ (**puzzles, puzzling, puzzled**)
1 **VERB** If something **puzzles** you, you do not understand it and you feel confused. ❏ *My sister's behavior puzzles me.* ● **puz|zled** /pʌzᵊld/ **ADJECTIVE** ❏ *Joshua was puzzled by her reaction to the news.* ● **puz|zling** **ADJECTIVE** ❏ *Michael's comments are very puzzling.*
2 **NOUN** A **puzzle** is a question, a game, or a toy that is difficult to answer correctly, or to put together properly. ❏ *Mom loves doing word puzzles.*
3 **NOUN** Someone or something that is hard to understand is **a puzzle**. ❏ *The rise in the number of accidents on the highway remains a puzzle.*

pyra|mid /pɪrəmɪd/ (**pyramids**) **NOUN** MATH
A **pyramid** is a solid shape with a flat base and flat sides that form a point where they meet at the top. ❏ *...the Egyptian Pyramids.*

py|thon /paɪθɒn, -θən/ (**pythons**) **NOUN**
A **python** is a type of large snake.

P

Qq

qt. MATH qt. is short for **quart**.

Q-tip /kyu̱ tɪp/ (**Q-tips**) NOUN A Q-tip is a small stick with a piece of cotton at each end, that you can use for cleaning your ears. [TRADEMARK]

quack /kwæk/ (**quacks, quacking, quacked**)
1 VERB When a duck **quacks**, it makes its usual sound. ❏ *There were ducks quacking on the lawn.*
2 NOUN Quack is also a noun. ❏ *Suddenly he heard a quack.*

quali|fi|ca|tion /kwɒlɪfɪkeɪʃᵊn/ (**qualifications**) NOUN Qualifications are the examination results or the skills that you need to be able to do something. ❏ *I believe I have all the qualifications to be a good teacher.* ❏ *All our workers have professional qualifications in engineering or electronics.*

quali|fied /kwɒlɪfaɪd/ ADJECTIVE Someone who is **qualified** has the right skills or special training in a particular subject. ❏ *Blake is qualified in both UK and US law.*

quali|fy /kwɒlɪfaɪ/ (**qualifies, qualifying, qualified**)
1 VERB If you **qualify** in a competition, you are successful in one part of it and you can go on to the next stage. ❏ *We qualified for the final by beating Stanford.* ● **quali|fi|er** (**qualifiers**) NOUN ❏ *Robert was the fastest qualifier for the 800 meters final.*
2 VERB If you **qualify** for something, you have the right to do it or have it. ❏ *This course does not qualify you for a job in sales.*
3 VERB When someone **qualifies**, they finish their training for a particular job. ❏ *I qualified, and started teaching last year.*

qual|ity /kwɒlɪti/ (**qualities**)
1 NONCOUNT NOUN The **quality** of something is how good or bad it is. ❏ *The quality of the food here is excellent.*
2 NOUN A **quality** is a particular characteristic of a person or thing. ❏ *He has a childlike quality.*

quan|tity /kwɒntɪti/ (**quantities**) NOUN A **quantity** is an amount. ❏ *Pour a small quantity of water into a pan.*

quar|rel /kwɒrəl/ (**quarrels, quarreling, quarreled**)
1 NOUN A **quarrel** is an angry argument between two or more people. ❏ *I had a terrible quarrel with my brothers.*
2 VERB When two or more people **quarrel**, they have an angry argument. ❏ *Yes, we quarreled over something silly.*

quar|ry /kwɒri/ (**quarries**) NOUN A **quarry** is an area that is dug out from a piece of land in order to get stone or minerals from it.

quart /kwɔrt/ (**quarts**) NOUN MATH A **quart** is a unit for measuring liquid that is equal to two pints. ❏ *Use a quart of milk.*
→ look at **measurement**

quar|ter /kwɔrtər/ (**quarters**)
1 NOUN MATH A **quarter** is one of four equal parts of something. ❏ *A quarter of the residents are over 55 years old.* ❏ *I'll be with you in a quarter of an hour.*
2 NOUN A **quarter** is an American or Canadian coin that is worth 25 cents.
3 NOUN A **quarter** is a fixed period of three months. ❏ *We will send you a bill every quarter.*
4 NONCOUNT NOUN When you are telling the time, you use **quarter** to talk about the fifteen minutes before or after an hour. ❏ *He came over at quarter after eight in the morning.* ❏ *We arrived at quarter of nine that night.*

quarter|back /kwɔrtərbæk/ (**quarterbacks**) NOUN In football, a **quarterback** is the player on the attacking team who begins each play, and who decides which play to use.

quar|tet /kwɔrtɛt/ (**quartets**)
1 NOUN MUSIC A **quartet** is a group of four people who play musical instruments or sing together.
2 NOUN MUSIC A **quartet** is a piece of music for four instruments or four singers.

quartz /kwɔrts/ NONCOUNT NOUN Quartz is a hard, shiny mineral that is used in making electronic equipment and very accurate watches and clocks.

queen /kwin/ (queens) NOUN

SOCIAL STUDIES A **queen** is a woman who rules a country. ❑ ...*Queen Elizabeth.*

ques|tion /kwɛstʃˀn/ (questions, questioning, questioned)

1 NOUN A **question** is something that you say or write in order to ask a person about something. ❑ *They asked a lot of questions about her health.*

2 VERB If you **question** someone, you ask them a lot of questions about something. ❑ *The doctor questioned Jim about his parents.*

● **ques|tion|ing** NONCOUNT NOUN ❑ *The police want thirty-two people for questioning.*

3 VERB If you **question** something, you express doubts about it. ❑ *They never question the doctor's decisions.*

4 NOUN If there is no **question** about something, there is no doubt about it. ❑ *There's no question about their success.*

5 NOUN A **question** is a problem or a subject that needs to be considered. ❑ *The question of nuclear energy is complex.*

6 NOUN The **questions** on an examination are the problems that test your knowledge. ❑ *Please answer all six questions.*

7 Something that is **out of the question** is completely impossible. ❑ *An expensive vacation is out of the question for him.*

Word Partners	Use **question** with:
V.	**answer a** question, **ask a** question **1**
N.	**answer to a** question, **response to a** question **1**
ADJ.	**difficult** question, **good** question, **important** question **1**

ques|tion mark (question marks) NOUN

LANGUAGE ARTS A **question mark** is the mark (?) that is used in writing at the end of a question.

→ look at **punctuation**

quick /kwɪk/ (quicker, quickest)

1 ADJECTIVE Someone or something that is **quick** moves or does things with great speed. ❑ *You'll have to be quick.* ● **quick|ly** ADVERB ❑ *Cussane worked quickly.*

2 ADJECTIVE Something that is **quick** takes or lasts only a short time. ❑ *He took a quick look around the room.* ● **quick|ly** ADVERB ❑ *You can get fit quite quickly if you exercise.*

3 ADJECTIVE **Quick** means happening with very little delay. ❑ *We are hoping for a quick end to the strike.* ● **quick|ly** ADVERB ❑ *We need to get the money back as quickly as possible.*

qui|et /kwaɪɪt/ (quieter, quietest)

1 ADJECTIVE Someone or something that is **quiet** makes only a small amount of noise. ❑ *The car has an extremely quiet engine.*

● **qui|et|ly** ADVERB ❑ *She spoke so quietly that we couldn't understand what she said.*

2 ADJECTIVE If a place is **quiet**, there is no activity or trouble there. ❑ *It's a quiet little village.*

3 ADJECTIVE If you are **quiet**, you are not saying anything. ❑ *Be quiet and go to sleep.*

● **qui|et|ly** ADVERB ❑ *Amy stood quietly in the doorway.*

→ look at **relax**

Word Partners	Use **quiet** with:
N.	quiet **day**, quiet **evening**, quiet **night**, quiet **life** **1**
	quiet **neighborhood**, **peace and** quiet, quiet **place**, quiet **spot**, quiet **street** **2**
ADV.	**real** quiet, **relatively** quiet, **too** quiet, **very** quiet **1** – **3**
V.	**be** quiet, **keep** quiet **3**

quilt /kwɪlt/ (quilts) NOUN

A **quilt** is a bed cover made by sewing pieces of colored cloth together. ❑ *An old quilt was on the bed.*

quit /kwɪt/ (quits, quitting, quit)

1 VERB If you **quit**, you choose to stop doing an activity. [INFORMAL] ❑ *Christina quit her job last year.* ❑ *That's enough! I quit!*

2 VERB If you **quit** doing something, you stop doing it. ❑ *Quit talking now and do some work.*

→ look at **job**

quite /kwaɪt/

1 ADVERB **Quite** means very but not extremely. ❑ *I felt quite bad about it at the time.* ❑ *I knew her mother quite well.* ❑ *Our house is quite a long way from the city.*

2 ADVERB **Quite** means completely. ❑ *I've not quite finished my project.* ❑ *My position is quite different.*

3 You use **quite a** or **quite an** before a noun to say that a person or thing is very impressive or unusual. ❑ *He's quite a character.*

quiz /kwɪz/ (quizzes)

1 NOUN A **quiz** is a game or a competition in which someone tests your knowledge by asking you questions. ❑ *We'll have a quiz after we visit the museum.*

q

2 **NOUN** A **quiz** is a short test that a teacher gives to a class. ❏ *We had a vocabulary quiz today in English class.*

quo|ta|tion /kwoʊteɪʃ°n/ (**quotations**)
NOUN LANGUAGE ARTS A **quotation** is a sentence or a phrase from a book, a poem, a speech, or a play. ❏ *He used quotations from Martin Luther King Jr. in his lecture.*

quo|ta|tion mark (**quotation marks**) **NOUN** LANGUAGE ARTS **Quotation marks** are marks that are used in writing to show where speech begins and ends. They are usually written or printed as "...".

quote /kwoʊt/ (**quotes, quoting, quoted**)
1 **VERB** If you **quote** someone, or **quote** from something, you repeat what someone has written or said. ❏ *I gave the letter to the reporter and he quoted from it.*

2 **NOUN** A **quote from** a book, a poem, a play, or a speech is a section from it. ❏ *He finished with a quote from one of his favorite poems.*

3 **PLURAL NOUN** **Quotes** are the same as **quotation marks.** [INFORMAL] ❏ *The word "remembered" is in quotes here.*

Q

Rr

rab|bi /ˈræbaɪ/ (**rabbis**) NOUN A **rabbi** is a
Jewish religious leader.

rab|bit /ˈræbɪt/ (**rabbits**) NOUN A **rabbit** is a
small animal that has long ears and lives in
a hole in the ground.
→ look at **animal**

rac|coon /ræˈkun/ (**raccoons**)
NOUN A **raccoon** is a small
animal from North and Central
America, that has dark fur,
with white stripes on its face
and on its long tail.

race /reɪs/ (**races, racing, raced**)
■ NOUN SPORTS A **race** is a competition to
see who is the fastest. ❑ *Mark easily won the
race.* ❑ *...a horse race.*
■ VERB If you **race**, you take part in a race.
❑ *Leo started racing in the early 1950s.* ❑ *We raced
them to the top of the hill.*
■ NOUN A **race** is one of the major groups
that humans can be divided into according
to their physical features, such as the color
of their skin. ❑ *The college welcomes students of
all races.*
■ VERB If you **race** somewhere, you go there
as quickly as possible. ❑ *He raced across town
to the hospital.*

race|track /ˈreɪstræk/ (**racetracks**) also **race
track** NOUN SOCIAL STUDIES A **racetrack** is
a track for races between runners, horses,
dogs, cars, or motorcycles. ❑ *...a horse
racetrack.*

ra|cial /ˈreɪʃ³l/ ADJECTIVE **Racial** describes
things relating to people's race. ❑ *The new
law promotes racial equality.* ● **ra|cial|ly** ADVERB
❑ *...a racially mixed school.*

rac|ing /ˈreɪsɪŋ/ NONCOUNT NOUN **Racing** is
the sport of competing in races. ❑ *...a racing
car.*

rac|ism /ˈreɪsɪzəm/ NONCOUNT NOUN
SOCIAL STUDIES **Racism** is the belief that
people of some races are not as good as
others. ❑ *Many of these children experienced
racism in their daily lives.*

rac|ist /ˈreɪsɪst/ (**racists**)
■ ADJECTIVE **Racist** people, things,
opinions, or behavior are influenced by
the belief that some people are better than
others because they belong to a particular
race. ❑ *We live in a racist society.*
■ NOUN A **racist** is someone who is racist.
❑ *He was attacked by a gang of white racists.*

rack /ræk/ (**racks**) NOUN A **rack** is a frame
or shelf, usually with bars, that is used for
holding things. ❑ *Put all your bags in the
luggage rack.*

rack|et /ˈrækɪt/ (**rackets**)
■ NOUN SPORTS A **racket** is a bat with
strings across it, that is used in some ball
games. ❑ *I got a tennis racket for my birthday.*
■ NOUN A **racket** is a loud, unpleasant
noise. ❑ *The children were making a racket
upstairs.*

ra|dar /ˈreɪdɑr/ NONCOUNT NOUN SCIENCE
Radar is a way of discovering the position of
objects when they cannot be seen, by using
radio signals. ❑ *They saw the submarine on the
ship's radar screen.*

ra|dia|tion /ˌreɪdiˈeɪʃ³n/ NONCOUNT NOUN
SCIENCE **Radiation** is a type of energy that
comes from some substances. Too much
radiation is harmful to living things.
❑ *The gas protects the Earth against radiation
from the sun.*
→ look at **greenhouse effect, pollution**

ra|dia|tor /ˈreɪdieɪtər/ (**radiators**)
■ NOUN A **radiator** is a metal object that is
full of hot water or steam, and is used for
heating a room.
■ NOUN The **radiator** in a car is the part of
the engine that is filled with water in order
to cool the engine.

ra|dio /ˈreɪdioʊ/ (**radios, radioing, radioed**)
■ NOUN A **radio** is a piece of equipment that
you use in order to listen to radio programs.
❑ *He turned on the radio.*
■ NONCOUNT NOUN **Radio** is a system of
sending and receiving sound using

electronic signals. ❏ *They are in radio contact with the leader.*

3 **NOUN** A **radio** is a piece of equipment that is used for sending and receiving spoken messages. ❏ *The police officer called for extra help on his radio.*

4 **VERB** If you **radio** someone, you send a spoken message to them by radio. ❏ *The officer radioed for advice.*

→ look at **news**

radio|ac|tive /reɪdioʊæktɪv/ **ADJECTIVE**
Something that is **radioactive** contains a substance that produces a type of energy that can be harmful to living things. ❏ *Germany forbids the import of radioactive waste products.*

ra|dio wave (radio waves) **NOUN** SCIENCE
Radio waves are the form in which radio signals travel.

ra|dius /reɪdiəs/ (radii /reɪdiaɪ/) **NOUN** MATH
The **radius** of a circle is the distance from its center to its outside edge. ❏ *We offer free delivery within a 5-mile radius of our store.*

→ look at **area**

raf|fle /ræfəl/ (raffles) **NOUN** A **raffle** is a competition in which you buy tickets with numbers on them. If your number is chosen, you win a prize. ❏ *...raffle tickets.*

raft /ræft/ (rafts) **NOUN** A **raft** is a floating structure that is made from large pieces of wood that are tied together.

rag /ræg/ (rags)
1 **NOUN** A **rag** is a piece of old cloth. ❏ *He was wiping his hands on an oily rag.*
2 **PLURAL NOUN** **Rags** are old torn clothes. ❏ *The streets were full of children dressed in rags.*

rage /reɪdʒ/ **NONCOUNT NOUN** **Rage** is strong anger that is difficult to control. ❏ *His face was red with rage.*

rag|ged /rægɪd/
1 **ADJECTIVE** Someone who is **ragged** is wearing clothes that are old and torn. ❏ *A thin ragged man sat on the park bench.*
2 **ADJECTIVE** **Ragged** clothes are old and torn.

raid /reɪd/ (raids, raiding, raided)
1 **VERB** If police officers or soldiers **raid** a building, they enter it suddenly in order to look for someone or something. ❏ *Police raided the company's offices.*
2 **NOUN** **Raid** is also a noun. ❏ *They were arrested after a raid on a house by police.*

rail /reɪl/ (rails)
1 **NOUN** A **rail** is a horizontal bar that you hold for support. ❏ *She held the hand rail tightly.*
2 **NOUN** A **rail** is a horizontal bar that you hang things on. ❏ *...a curtain rail.*
3 **NOUN** **Rails** are the steel bars that trains run on. ❏ *The train left the rails.*
4 **NONCOUNT NOUN** If you travel **by rail**, you travel on a train. ❏ *The president arrived by rail.*

rail|ing /reɪlɪŋ/ (railings) **NOUN** A **railing** is a fence that is made from metal bars. ❏ *He jumped over the railing to shake hands with the fans.*

rail|road /reɪlroʊd/ (railroads)
1 **NOUN** A **railroad** is a route between two places that trains travel along on metal rails. ❏ *...railroad tracks.*
2 **NOUN** A **railroad** is a company or an organization that operates railroad routes. ❏ *They send goods on the Chicago and Northwestern Railroad.*

rain /reɪn/ (rains, raining, rained)
1 **NONCOUNT NOUN** SCIENCE **Rain** is water that falls from the clouds in small drops. ❏ *We got very wet in the rain.*
2 **VERB** When rain falls, you can say that **it is raining**. ❏ *It was raining hard.*

→ look at **water, weather**

rain|bow /reɪnboʊ/ (rainbows) **NOUN**
A **rainbow** is a half circle of different colors that you can sometimes see in the sky when it rains.

rain|coat /reɪnkoʊt/ (raincoats) **NOUN**
A **raincoat** is a coat that you can wear to keep dry when it rains.

rain|drop /reɪndrɒp/ (raindrops) **NOUN**
A **raindrop** is a single drop of rain.

rain|fall /reɪnfɔl/ **NONCOUNT NOUN** SCIENCE
Rainfall is the amount of rain that falls in a place during a particular period. ❏ *This month we have recorded below average rainfall.*

→ look at **climate**

rain|for|est /reɪnfɔrɪst/ (rainforests) **NOUN**
GEOGRAPHY A **rainforest** is a thick forest of tall trees that grows in tropical areas where there is a lot of rain. ❏ *We watched a program about the destruction of the Amazon Rainforest.*

R

rainy /ˈreɪni/ (rainier, rainiest) ADJECTIVE
If it is **rainy**, it is raining a lot. ❏ *Here are some fun things to do on a rainy day.*
→ look at **season**

raise /reɪz/ (raises, raising, raised)
1 VERB If you **raise** something, you move it upward. ❏ *He raised his hand to wave.* ❏ *Milton raised the glass to his lips.*
2 VERB If you **raise** the rate or level of something, you increase it. ❏ *Many stores have raised their prices.*
3 VERB If you **raise** your **voice**, you speak more loudly.
4 NOUN A **raise** is an increase in the amount of money that you are paid for your work. ❏ *Kelly got a raise of $100.*
5 VERB If you **raise** money **for** a particular purpose, you ask people for money for it. ❏ *The event is to raise money for the school.*
6 VERB If you **raise** a subject, you start to talk about it. ❏ *The matter will be raised at our annual meeting.*
7 VERB To **raise** children means to take care of them until they are grown up. ❏ *She raised four children on her own.*

rai|sin /ˈreɪzᵊn/ (raisins) NOUN Raisins are dried grapes (= small green or purple fruits).

rake /reɪk/ (rakes, raking, raked)
1 NOUN A **rake** is a garden tool with a long handle, used for collecting loose grass or leaves.
2 VERB If you **rake** leaves, you move them using a rake. ❏ *We raked the leaves into piles.*

ral|ly /ˈræli/ (rallies) NOUN A **rally** is a large public meeting that is held in order to show support for something. ❏ *They organized a rally to demand better working conditions.*

ram /ræm/ (rams, ramming, rammed)
1 VERB If a vehicle **rams** something, it crashes into it. ❏ *The truck rammed a car.*
2 NOUN A **ram** is an adult male sheep.

RAM /ræm/ NONCOUNT NOUN TECHNOLOGY
RAM is the part of a computer where information is stored while you are using it. RAM is short for "Random Access Memory." ❏ *...a PC with 512 MB RAM.*

ramp /ræmp/ (ramps) NOUN A **ramp** is a surface with a slope between two places that are at different levels. ❏ *There's a wheelchair ramp at the front entrance of the school.*
→ look at **disability**

ran /ræn/ **Ran** is a form of the verb **run**.

ranch /ræntʃ/ (ranches) NOUN A **ranch** is a large farm used for keeping animals. ❏ *He owns a cattle ranch in Texas.*

ran|dom /ˈrændəm/
1 ADJECTIVE A **random** process is one in which all the people or things involved have an equal chance of being chosen. ❏ *The survey used a random sample of two thousand people.*
2 ADJECTIVE If events are **random**, they do not follow a plan or pattern. ❏ *We have seen random violence against innocent victims.*
3 If something happens **at random**, it happens without a plan or pattern. ❏ *The gunman fired at random.*

rang /ræŋ/ **Rang** is a form of the verb **ring**.

range /reɪndʒ/ (ranges, ranging, ranged)
1 NOUN A **range of** things is a number of different things of the same type. ❏ *These products come in a wide range of colors.*
2 NOUN A **range** is the complete group that is included between two points on a scale. ❏ *The average age range is between 35 and 55.*
3 NOUN The **range of** something is the largest area in which it can reach things. ❏ *This electric car has a range of 100 miles.*
4 VERB If things **range between** two points on a scale, they are between these two fixed points. ❏ *The children range in age from five to fourteen.*
5 NOUN A **range** of mountains or hills is a group of them. ❏ *...snowy mountain ranges.*

rang|er /ˈreɪndʒər/ (rangers) NOUN A **ranger** is a person whose job is to take care of a forest or a large park. ❏ *He's a park ranger at the National Park.*

rank /ræŋk/ (ranks) NOUN Someone's **rank** is the position that they have in an organization. ❏ *He holds the rank of colonel in the U.S. Army.*

ran|som /ˈrænsəm/ (ransoms) NOUN A **ransom** is the money that has to be paid to someone so that they will set a person free. ❏ *Her kidnapper asked for a $250,000 ransom.*

rap /ræp/ (raps, rapping, rapped)
1 NONCOUNT NOUN MUSIC **Rap** is a type of modern music in which the words are spoken. ❏ *He performs with a rap group.*
● **rap|per** (rappers) NOUN ❏ *He's a singer and a talented rapper.*

2 **VERB** MUSIC Someone who **raps** performs rap music.

rape /reɪp/ (**rapes, raping, raped**)

1 **VERB** If someone **is raped**, they are forced to have sex when they do not want to. ❑ *Many women were raped during the war.* ● **rapist** (**rapists**) **NOUN** ❑ *The information led to the rapist's arrest.*

2 **NOUN** Rape is the crime of forcing someone to have sex.

rap|id /ræpɪd/

1 **ADJECTIVE** A **rapid** change happens very quickly. ❑ *This is the end of the country's rapid economic growth.* ● **rap|id|ly** **ADVERB** ❑ *The firm continues to grow rapidly.*

2 **ADJECTIVE** A **rapid** movement is very fast. ❑ *He walked at a rapid pace.* ● **rap|id|ly** **ADVERB** ❑ *He was moving rapidly around the room.*

rare /reər/ (**rarer, rarest**)

1 **ADJECTIVE** Something that is **rare** is not seen or heard very often. ❑ *This is one of the rarest birds in the world.*

2 **ADJECTIVE** An event or situation that is **rare** does not happen very often. ❑ *They have dinner together on the rare occasions when they are both at home.*

3 **ADJECTIVE** Meat that is **rare** is cooked very lightly so that the inside is still red.
→ look at **conservation**

rare|ly /reərli/ **ADVERB** If something **rarely** happens, it does not happen very often.

rash /ræʃ/ (**rashes**)

1 **ADJECTIVE** If someone is **rash**, they act without thinking carefully first. ❑ *Don't make any rash decisions.*

2 **NOUN** A **rash** is an area of red spots that appears on your skin. ❑ *I always get a rash when I eat nuts.*

rasp|berry /ræzbɛri/ (**raspberries**) **NOUN** Raspberries are small, soft, red fruits that grow on bushes.

rat /ræt/ (**rats**) **NOUN** A **rat** is an animal that has a long tail and looks like a large mouse.

rate /reɪt/ (**rates**)

1 **NOUN** The **rate** at which something happens is how fast or how often it happens. ❑ *An adult's heart rate is about 72 beats per minute.* ❑ *Spain has the lowest birth rate in Europe.*

2 **NOUN** A **rate** is the amount of money that goods or services cost. ❑ *The hotel offers a special weekend rate.*

3 **At any rate** means "anyway". ❑ *His friends liked her—well, most of them at any rate.*

Word Partners	Use **rate** with:
ADJ.	**average** rate, **faster** rate, **slow** rate, **steady** rate **1**
N.	**birth** rate, rate **of change**, **crime** rate, **heart** rate, **pulse** rate, **unemployment** rate **1**

ra|ther /ræðər/

1 You use **rather than** to mention a thing or situation that is not done. ❑ *I use the bike when I can rather than the car.*

2 **CONJUNCTION** **Rather than** is also a conjunction. ❑ *Use glass bottles again rather than throw them away.*

3 If you **would rather** do something, you would prefer to do it. ❑ *Kids would rather play than study.*

4 **ADVERB** You use **rather** to mean "more than a little." ❑ *I thought the movie was rather boring.*

rat|ing /reɪtɪŋ/ (**ratings**) **NOUN** A **rating** is a measurement of how good or popular something is. ❑ *The president's popularity rating is at its lowest point.*

ra|tio /reɪʃoʊ, -ʃioʊ/ (**ratios**) **NOUN** MATH A **ratio** is a relationship between two things when it is expressed in numbers or amounts. ❑ *The adult to child ratio is one to six.*

ra|tion /ræʃ°n, reɪ-/ (**rations, rationing, rationed**)

1 **NOUN** Your **ration** of something is a small amount that you are allowed to have when there is not much of it. ❑ *The meat ration was 250 grams per month.*

2 **VERB** When something **is rationed**, you are only allowed to have a small amount of it. ❑ *Food such as bread and rice was rationed.*

3 **PLURAL NOUN** Rations are the food that is given to soldiers or to people who do not have enough food.

ra|tion|al /ræʃən°l/ **ADJECTIVE** Rational decisions and thoughts are based on reason rather than on emotion. ❑ *They discussed it in a rational manner.* ● **ra|tion|al|ly** **ADVERB** ❑ *It is difficult to think rationally when you're worried.*

rat|tle /ræt°l/ (**rattles, rattling, rattled**)

1 **VERB** When something **rattles**, it makes short, sharp, knocking sounds because it is hitting against something hard. ❑ *The windows rattled in the wind.*

R

2 **NOUN** **Rattle** is also a noun. ❏ *I heard the rattle of the door handle.*

3 **NOUN** A **rattle** is a baby's toy with small, loose objects inside that make a noise when the baby shakes it.

rattle|snake /ˈrætˠlsneɪk/ (rattlesnakes)
NOUN A **rattlesnake** is a snake that lives in America. When it is afraid or angry, it shakes the hard skin at the end of its body and makes a rattling (= short, sharp, knocking) sound. **Rattlesnakes** are dangerous because their bite contains a strong poison.

rave /reɪv/ (raves, raving, raved) **VERB**
If you **rave about** something, you speak or write about it with great enthusiasm. ❏ *Rachel raved about the movie.*

raw /rɔ/ (rawer, rawest)
1 **ADJECTIVE** **Raw** materials or substances are in their natural state. ❏ *...raw sugar.*
2 **ADJECTIVE** **Raw** food has not been cooked. ❏ *This is a Japanese dish made of raw fish.*
→ look at **meat**

ray /reɪ/ (rays) **NOUN** **SCIENCE**
A **ray** of light is a narrow line of light. ❏ *Protect your eyes against the sun's rays.*

ra|zor /ˈreɪzər/ (razors)
NOUN A **razor** is a tool that people use for shaving.

reach /ritʃ/ (reaches, reaching, reached)
1 **VERB** When someone or something **reaches** a place, they arrive there. ❏ *He did not stop until he reached the door.*
2 **VERB** If someone or something has **reached** a certain level or amount, they are at that level or amount. ❏ *The number of unemployed could reach 3 million next year.*
3 **VERB** If you **reach** somewhere, you move your arm and hand to take or touch something. ❏ *Judy reached into her bag.*
4 **VERB** If you can **reach** something, you are able to touch it by stretching out your arm or leg. ❏ *Can you reach your toes with your fingertips?*
5 **VERB** If you try to **reach** someone, you try to contact them, usually by telephone. ❏ *You can reach me at this phone number.*

re|act /riˈækt/ (reacts, reacting, reacted)
1 **VERB** When you **react to** something that has happened, you behave in a particular way because of it. ❏ *They reacted violently to the news.*

2 **VERB** When one chemical substance **reacts with** another, or when two chemical substances **react**, they combine chemically to form another substance. ❏ *Calcium reacts with water.*

re|ac|tion /riˈækʃˠn/ (reactions)
1 **NOUN** Your **reaction to** something is what you feel, say, or do because of it. ❏ *He showed no reaction when I told him the result.*
2 **NOUN** A chemical **reaction** is a process in which two substances combine together chemically to form another substance. ❏ *...a chemical reaction between oxygen and hydrogen.*

read (reads, reading, read)

> **PRONUNCIATION HELP**
> Pronounce the present tense /rid/.
> Pronounce the past tense and the past participle /rɛd/.

1 **VERB** **LANGUAGE ARTS** When you **read** a book or a story, you look at the written words and understand them. ❏ *Have you read this book?* ❏ *I read about it in the paper.* ❏ *She spends all her time reading.*
2 **VERB** When you **read** words that you can see, you say them. ❏ *Kevin always read a story to the twins when he got home.*
3 **VERB** If someone **reads** your mind or thoughts, he or she knows exactly what you are thinking.
→ look at **language, news, relax**

Word Partners	Use **read** with:
ADV.	read **carefully**, read **silently** **1**
N.	read **a book**, read **a magazine**, read **a newspaper**, read **a sign** **1** **2**
V.	**able to** read, **like to** read, **learn to** read, **want to** read **1** **2**
	listen to *someone* read **2**

read|er /ˈridər/ (readers) **NOUN**
LANGUAGE ARTS The **readers** of a newspaper, a magazine, or a book are the people who read it. ❏ *The article gives readers an interesting view of life in Spain.*

read|ily /ˈrɛdɪli/ **ADVERB**
If you do something **readily**, you do it in a way that shows that you are very willing to do it. ❏ *I asked her to help, and she readily agreed.*

read|ing /ˈridɪŋ/ **NONCOUNT NOUN**
Reading is the activity of reading books. ❏ *I love reading.*

r

ready /rɛdi/ (**readier, readiest**)

1 **ADJECTIVE** If someone is **ready**, they are completely prepared for something. ❑ *It takes her a long time to get ready for school.*

2 **ADJECTIVE** If something is **ready**, it has been prepared and is now able to be used. ❑ *Go and tell your sister that lunch is ready.*

3 **ADJECTIVE** If you are **ready to** do something, you are willing to do it. ❑ *They were ready to help.*

real /ril/

1 **ADJECTIVE** Something that is **real** actually exists. ❑ *No, it wasn't a dream. It was real.*

2 **ADJECTIVE** A material or an object that is **real** is natural, and not a copy. ❑ *I love the smell of real leather.*

3 **ADJECTIVE** Someone's **real** reason or intention is their true reason or intention. ❑ *This was the real reason for her call.*

4 **ADVERB** You can use **real** to mean very. [INFORMAL] ❑ *He is finding prison life real tough.*

real es|tate **NONCOUNT NOUN** **Real estate** is property in the form of land and buildings. ❑ *We are thinking of investing in real estate.*

re|al|is|tic /riəlɪstɪk/

1 **ADJECTIVE** If you are **realistic** about a situation, you recognize and accept its true nature. ❑ *Police must be realistic about violent crime.*

2 **ADJECTIVE** You say that a picture, a story, or a movie is **realistic** when the people and things in it are like people and things in real life.

re|al|ity /riæliti/ (**realities**)

1 **NONCOUNT NOUN** You use **reality** to talk about real things rather than imagined or invented ideas. ❑ *Her dream ended and she had to return to reality.*

2 **NOUN** The **reality of** a situation is the truth about it, especially when it is unpleasant. ❑ *Politicians do not understand the realities of war.*

re|al|ize /riəlaɪz/ (**realizes, realizing, realized**) **VERB** If you **realize** that something is true, you become aware of that fact or you understand it. ❑ *As soon as we realized that something was wrong, we rushed to help.* ❑ *People don't realize how serious the situation is.*

● **re|a|li|za|tion** **NOUN** ❑ *The realization suddenly came to me; I was going to die.*

re|al|ly /riəli/

1 **ADVERB** You can use **really** to give a sentence a stronger meaning. ❑ *I'm very sorry. I really am.*

2 **ADVERB** You use **really** when you are discussing the real facts about something. ❑ *You're not really leaving, are you?*

3 You can say **"really?"** to express surprise at what someone has said. ❑ *"I once met the president."—"Really?"*

re|appear /riəpɪər/ (**reappears, reappearing, reappeared**) **VERB** When people or things **reappear**, they return again after they have been away or out of sight.

rear /rɪər/ (**rears, rearing, reared**)

1 **NOUN** The **rear** of something is the back part of it. ❑ *Mr. Forbes was sitting in the rear of the vehicle.* ❑ *The car hit the rear of the truck.*

2 **ADJECTIVE** **Rear** is also an adjective. ❑ *You must fasten all rear seat belts.*

3 **VERB** If you **rear** children, you take care of them until they are old enough to take care of themselves. ❑ *I was reared in Texas.*

4 **VERB** If you **rear** a young animal, you keep and take care of it until it is old enough to be used for work or food. ❑ *She spends a lot of time rearing animals.*

5 **VERB** When a horse **rears**, it moves the front part of its body upward, so that it is standing on its back legs. ❑ *The horse reared and threw off its rider.*

re|arrange /riəreɪndʒ/ (**rearranges, rearranging, rearranged**) **VERB** If you **rearrange** things, you change the way that they are organized. ❑ *Malcolm rearranged all the furniture.*

rea|son /rizᵊn/ (**reasons**)

1 **NOUN** The **reason for** something is a fact or situation that explains why it happens. ❑ *There is a reason for every important thing that happens.*

2 **NONCOUNT NOUN** **Reason** is the ability that people have to think and to make sensible judgments. ❑ *He was more interested in emotion than reason.*

Word Partners	Use **reason** with:
ADJ.	**good** reason, **main** reason, **major** reason, **obvious** reason, **only** reason, **real** reason, **same** reason, **simple** reason **1**

rea|son|able /rizənəbᵊl/

1 **ADJECTIVE** A **reasonable** person is someone who is fair and sensible. ❑ *She seems to be a reasonable person.*

2 **ADJECTIVE** If a decision or an action is **reasonable**, it is fair and sensible. ❑ *That's a perfectly reasonable decision.*

R

3 **ADJECTIVE** If something is **reasonable**, it is fairly good, but not very good. ❏ *The boy spoke reasonable French.* ● **rea|son|ably** **ADVERB** ❏ *I can dance reasonably well.*

re|assure /riəʃʊər/ (reassures, reassuring, reassured) **VERB** If you **reassure** someone, you say or do things to make them stop worrying about something. ● **re|assur|ance** **NONCOUNT NOUN** ❏ *He needed reassurance that she loved him.*

re|assur|ing /riəʃʊərɪŋ/ **ADJECTIVE** If someone is **reassuring**, they make you feel less worried about something. ❏ *It was reassuring to hear Jane's voice.*

re|bel (rebels, rebelling, rebelled)

> **PRONUNCIATION HELP**
> Pronounce the noun /rɛbəl/. Pronounce the verb /rɪbɛl/.

1 **NOUN** **Rebels** are people who are fighting against the people who are in charge somewhere, for example the government. ❏ *There is still heavy fighting between rebels and government forces.*
2 **VERB** When someone **rebels**, they fight against the people who are in charge. ❏ *Teenagers often rebel against their parents.*

re|bel|lion /rɪbɛlyən/ (rebellions) **NOUN** SOCIAL STUDIES A **rebellion** is when a large group of people fight against the people who are in charge, for example, the government. ❏ *We are awaiting the government's response to the rebellion.*

re|boot /ribut/ (reboots, rebooting, rebooted) **VERB** TECHNOLOGY If you **reboot** a computer, you turn it off and start it again. ❏ *When you reboot your computer, the software is ready to use.*

re|call /rɪkɔl/ (recalls, recalling, recalled) **VERB** When you **recall** something, you remember it. ❏ *He recalled meeting Pollard during a business trip.*

re|ceipt /rɪsit/ (receipts) **NOUN** A **receipt** is a piece of paper that you get from someone to show that they have received something from you. ❏ *I gave her a receipt for the money.*
→ look at **ATM**

re|ceive /rɪsiv/ (receives, receiving, received) **VERB** When you **receive** something, you get it after someone gives it to you or sends it to you. ❏ *They received their awards at a ceremony in San Francisco.*
→ look at **email**

re|ceiv|er /rɪsivər/ (receivers) **NOUN** A telephone's **receiver** is the part that you hold near to your ear and speak into. ❏ *She picked up the receiver and started to dial.*

re|cent /risənt/ **ADJECTIVE** A **recent** event or period of time happened only a short while ago. ❏ *Brad broke his leg on a recent trip to Hawaii.*

re|cent|ly /risəntli/ **ADVERB** If something happened **recently**, it happened only a short time ago. ❏ *The bank recently opened a branch in Miami.*

re|cep|tion /rɪsɛpʃən/ (receptions)
1 **NOUN** A **reception** is a formal party that is given to welcome someone, or to celebrate a special event. ❏ *We were invited to their wedding reception.*
2 **NONCOUNT NOUN** **Reception** in a hotel or a large building is the desk that you go to when you first arrive. ❏ *She was waiting at reception.*

re|cep|tion|ist /rɪsɛpʃənɪst/ (receptionists) **NOUN** A **receptionist** in a hotel or other large building is a person whose job is to answer the telephone and deal with visitors.

re|cess /rɪsɛs, risɛs/ **NONCOUNT NOUN** In a school, **recess** is the period of time between classes when the children are allowed to play. ❏ *She visited the school library during recess.*

re|ces|sion /rɪsɛʃən/ (recessions) **NOUN** A **recession** is a period when the economy of a country is not performing well. ❏ *The oil price increases sent Europe into recession.*

reci|pe /rɛsɪpi/ (recipes) **NOUN** A **recipe** is a list of food and a set of instructions telling you how to cook something. ❏ *Do you have a recipe for chocolate cake?*

re|cite /rɪsaɪt/ (recites, reciting, recited) **VERB** When someone **recites** a poem or other piece of writing, they say it aloud after they have learned it. ❏ *We each had to recite a poem in front of the class.*

reck|less /rɛklɪs/ **ADJECTIVE** A **reckless** person does not care about danger, or the results of his or her actions. ❏ *He was stopped for reckless driving.*

rec|og|ni|tion /rɛkəgnɪʃən/ **NONCOUNT NOUN** **Recognition** is the act of knowing who a person is or what something is when you see them. ❏ *There was no sign of recognition on her face.*

rec|og|nize /rɛkəgnaɪz/ (**recognizes, recognizing, recognized**) VERB If you **recognize** someone or something, you know who or what they are because you have seen or heard them before. ❑ *She recognized him immediately.*

rec|ol|lec|tion /rɛkəlɛkʃən/ (**recollections**) NOUN If you have a **recollection of** something, you remember it. ❑ *Pat has few recollections of the trip.*

rec|om|mend /rɛkəmɛnd/ (**recommends, recommending, recommended**)

1 VERB If someone **recommends** a person or thing to you, they suggest that you would find that person or thing good or useful. ❑ *I recommend Barbados as a place for a vacation.* ❑ *I'll recommend you for the job.*

● **rec|om|men|da|tion** (**recommendations**) NOUN ❑ *The best way of finding a dentist is to get someone else's recommendation.*

2 VERB If you **recommend** that something is done, you suggest that it should be done. ❑ *The doctor recommended that I lose some weight.*

● **recommendation** NOUN ❑ *We listened to the committee's recommendations.*

Re|con|struc|tion /rikənstrʌksən/ NONCOUNT NOUN SOCIAL STUDIES **Reconstruction** was the period between 1865 and 1877 when northern and southern American states joined together again after the American Civil War.

rec|ord (**records, recording, recorded**)

> PRONUNCIATION HELP
> Pronounce the noun /rɛkərd/. Pronounce the verb /rɪkɔrd/.

1 NOUN If you keep a **record of** something, you keep a written account or photographs of it so that it can be looked at later. ❑ *Keep a record of all the payments.*

2 VERB If you **record** a piece of information or an event, you write it down or photograph it so that in the future people can look at it. ❑ *Her letters record the details of her life in China.*

3 VERB If you **record** a speech or a performance, you store it in a computer file or on a disk so that it can be heard or seen again later. ❑ *Viewers can record the films.*

4 NOUN A **record** is a round, flat piece of black plastic on which sound, especially music, is stored, and that can be played on a record player.

5 NOUN A **record** is the best result ever in a particular sport or activity. ❑ *He set the world record of 12.92 seconds.*

→ look at **history, television**

re|cord|er /rɪkɔrdər/ (**recorders**) NOUN MUSIC A **recorder** is a wooden or plastic musical instrument in the shape of a pipe. You play it by blowing down one end and covering holes with your fingers.

re|cord|ing /rɪkɔrdɪŋ/ (**recordings**)

1 NOUN A **recording of** moving pictures and sounds is a computer file or a disk on which they are stored. ❑ *There is a video recording of his police interview.*

2 NONCOUNT NOUN **Recording** is the process of storing moving pictures and sounds on digital files or disks. ❑ *This has been a bad time for the recording industry.*

re|count /rɪkaʊnt/ (**recounts, recounting, recounted**) VERB If you **recount** a story or an event, you tell or describe it to people. [FORMAL] ❑ *He recounted the story of his first day at work.*

re|cov|er /rɪkʌvər/ (**recovers, recovering, recovered**)

1 VERB When you **recover from** an illness or an injury, you become well again. ❑ *He is recovering from a knee injury.*

2 VERB If you **recover** something that has been lost or stolen, you find it or get it back. ❑ *Police searched houses and finally recovered stolen goods.*

→ look at **health care**

re|cov|ery /rɪkʌvəri/ (**recoveries**) NOUN If a sick person makes a **recovery**, he or she becomes well again. ❑ *Natalie is making an excellent recovery from a serious knee injury.*

rec|rea|tion /rɛkrieɪʃən/ NONCOUNT NOUN **Recreation** is things that you do in your spare time to relax. ❑ *Saturday afternoon is for recreation.*

→ look at **relax**

re|cruit /rɪkrut/ (**recruits, recruiting, recruited**)

1 VERB If you **recruit** people for an organization, you ask them to join it. ❑ *We need to recruit and train more teachers.*

● **re|cruit|ment** NONCOUNT NOUN ❑ *There has been a drop in the recruitment of soldiers.*

2 NOUN A **recruit** is a person who has recently joined an organization or an army. ❑ *He's a new recruit to the police department.*

rec|tan|gle /rɛktæŋgəl/ (**rectangles**)
NOUN MATH A **rectangle** is a shape with four straight sides. ● **rec|tan|gu|lar** /rɛktæŋgyələr/ **ADJECTIVE** ❏ *The room contains a rectangular table.*

re|cur /rɪkɜr/ (**recurs, recurring, recurred**)
VERB Something that **recurs** happens more than once. ❏ *I have a recurring dream about being late for an important meeting.*

Word Builder   recycle

re ≈ again

    re + cycle = recycle
    re + fresh = refresh
    re + think = rethink
    re + view = review
    re + write = rewrite

---

re|cy|cle /risaɪkəl/ (**recycles, recycling, recycled**) **VERB** If you **recycle** things such as paper or bottles that have already been used, you put them through a process so that they can be used again.
→ look at **conservation**

red /rɛd/ (**reds, redder, reddest**)
1 **ADJECTIVE** Something that is **red** is the color of blood or of a tomato. ❏ *...a bunch of red roses.*
2 **NOUN** Red is also a noun. ❏ *She was dressed in red.*
3 **ADJECTIVE** Red hair is between red and brown in color.
→ look at **color, hair**

re|duce /rɪdus/ (**reduces, reducing, reduced**)
VERB If you **reduce** something, you make it smaller. ❏ *Exercise reduces the risks of heart disease.*
→ look at **conservation, energy**

re|duc|tion /rɪdʌkʃən/ (**reductions**) **NOUN** When there is a **reduction in** something, it is made smaller. ❏ *We have noticed a sudden reduction in prices.*

reed /rid/ (**reeds**) **NOUN** Reeds are tall plants that grow in large groups in shallow water or on wet ground.

reef /rif/ (**reefs**) **NOUN** SCIENCE A **reef** is a long line of rocks or sand in the ocean. ❏ *The ship hit coral reefs off the north-eastern coast of Australia.*

re|fer /rɪfɜr/ (**refers, referring, referred**)
1 **VERB** If you **refer to** a particular subject or person, you mention them. ❏ *He referred to his trip to Canada.* ● **ref|er|ence** /rɛfərəns, rɛfrəns/ (**references**) **NOUN** ❏ *He made no reference to any agreement.*
2 **VERB** If a word **refers to** a particular thing, it describes it. ❏ *The word "man" refers to an adult male.*
3 **VERB** If you **refer to** a book or to the Internet for information, you look there in order to find something out. ❏ *He referred briefly to his notebook.* ● **ref|er|ence** NONCOUNT NOUN ❏ *Keep this book in a safe place for reference.*

ref|eree /rɛfəri/ (**referees, refereeing, refereed**)
1 **NOUN** SPORTS The **referee** is the person who controls a sports event such as a football game or a boxing match.
2 **VERB** SPORTS When someone **referees** a sports event, they act as referee. ❏ *Vautrot refereed in two soccer games.*

ref|er|ence /rɛfərəns, rɛfrəns/ (**references**)
1 **ADJECTIVE** Reference books are books that you look at when you need information or facts about a subject.
2 **NOUN** A **reference** is a letter that is written by someone who knows you, describing your character and your abilities. ❏ *My boss gave me a good reference.*
3 You use **with reference to** or **in reference to** in order to say what something is about. ❏ *I am writing in reference to your advertisement for a personal assistant.*

re|flect /rɪflɛkt/ (**reflects, reflecting, reflected**)
1 **VERB** If something **reflects** an opinion or a situation, it shows that it exists. ❏ *The report reflects the views of both students and teachers.*
2 **VERB** When light or heat **reflects** off a surface, it is sent back from the surface. ❏ *The sun reflected off the snow-covered mountains.*
3 **VERB** When something **is reflected** in a mirror or in water, you can see its image there. ❏ *His face was reflected in the mirror.*

re|flec|tion /rɪflɛkʃən/ (**reflections**)
1 **NOUN** A **reflection** is an image that you can see in a mirror or in glass or water. ❏ *Meg stared at her reflection in the mirror.*

r

2 **NOUN** If something is a **reflection of** a person's opinion or **of** a situation, it shows that that opinion or situation exists. ❏ *His drawings are a reflection of his own unhappiness.*

re|flex|ive pro|noun /rɪflɛksɪv proʊnaʊn/ (reflexive pronouns) **NOUN** LANGUAGE ARTS A **reflexive pronoun** is a word such as "myself" that you use to talk about the subject of a sentence.

re|flex|ive verb /rɪflɛksɪv vɜrb/ (reflexive verbs) **NOUN** LANGUAGE ARTS A **reflexive verb** is a verb whose subject and object always refer to the same person or thing. An example is "to enjoy yourself."

re|form /rɪfɔrm/ (reforms, reforming, reformed)
1 **NONCOUNT NOUN** SOCIAL STUDIES **Reform** consists of changes and improvements to a law or a social system. ❏ *We will introduce a program of economic reform.*
2 **NOUN** A **reform** is a change that is intended to be an improvement. ❏ *The government promised tax reforms.*
3 **VERB** SOCIAL STUDIES Someone who **reforms** a law or a social system changes or improves it. ❏ *He has plans to reform the country's economy.*
4 **VERB** When someone **reforms**, they start behaving well. ❏ *After his time in prison, James promised to reform.*

Word Builder | **refresh**

re ≈ **again**

re + cycle = recycle
re + fresh = refresh
re + think = rethink
re + view = review
re + write = rewrite

---

re|fresh /rɪfrɛʃ/ (refreshes, refreshing, refreshed) **VERB** If something **refreshes** you when you are hot, tired, or thirsty, it makes you feel better. ❏ *The water refreshed them.*
● **re|freshed** **ADJECTIVE** ❏ *He awoke feeling completely refreshed.*

re|fresh|ing /rɪfrɛʃɪŋ/
1 **ADJECTIVE** If something is **refreshing**, it makes you feel less hot, tired, or thirsty. ❏ *They serve refreshing drinks at the poolside.*
2 **ADJECTIVE** You say that something is **refreshing** when it is unusual in a pleasant way. ❏ *It's refreshing to hear someone speaking so honestly.*

re|fresh|ment /rɪfrɛʃmənt/ (refreshments) **PLURAL NOUN** **Refreshments** are drinks and small amounts of food that are provided, for example, during a meeting or a trip. ❏ *Refreshments will be provided.*

re|frig|era|tor /rɪfrɪdʒəreɪtər/ (refrigerators) **NOUN** A **refrigerator** is a large electric container that is used for keeping food cool.
→ look at **kitchen**

ref|uge /rɛfyudʒ/ (refuges)
1 **NONCOUNT NOUN** If you take **refuge** somewhere, you go there to try to protect yourself from harm. ❏ *They took refuge in a shelter.*
2 **NOUN** A **refuge** is a place where you go for safety and protection. ❏ *He works in a refuge for homeless people.*

refu|gee /rɛfyudʒi/ (refugees) **NOUN** **Refugees** are people who have been forced to leave their homes or their country, because it is too dangerous for them there. ❏ *She grew up in a refugee camp in Pakistan.*

re|fund (refunds, refunding, refunded)

PRONUNCIATION HELP
Pronounce the noun /rifʌnd/. Pronounce the verb /rɪfʌnd/.

1 **NOUN** A **refund** is money that is returned to you because you have paid too much, or because you have returned goods to a store. ❏ *He took the boots back to the store and asked for a refund.*
2 **VERB** If someone **refunds** your money, they return what you have paid them. ❏ *We will refund your delivery costs if the items arrive later than 12 noon.*

re|fus|al /rɪfyuzəl/ (refusals) **NOUN** A **refusal to** do something is when someone says that they will not do it, allow it, or accept it. ❏ *The workers have repeated their refusal to take part in the program.*

re|fuse /rɪfyuz/ (refuses, refusing, refused)
1 **VERB** If you **refuse to** do something, you say strongly that you will not do it. ❏ *He refused to comment.*
2 **VERB** If someone **refuses** you something, they say that they will not give it to you. ❏ *The United States has refused him a visa.*
3 **VERB** If you **refuse** something that is offered to you, you do not accept it. ❏ *The patient has the right to refuse treatment.*

R

v. refuse **to answer**, refuse **to cooperate**, refuse **to go**, refuse **to participate**, refuse **to pay** **1**
refuse **to allow**, refuse **to give** **2**
refuse **to accept** **3**

re|gard /rɪgɑrd/ (**regards, regarding, regarded**)
1 **VERB** If you **regard** someone or something **as** being a particular thing, you believe that they are that thing. ❑ *He was regarded as the most successful president of modern times.*
2 **NONCOUNT NOUN** If you have **regard** for someone or something, you respect them. ❑ *I have a very high regard for him and his achievements.*

re|gard|ing /rɪgɑrdɪŋ/ **PREPOSITION** You can use **regarding** to say what subject is being talked or written about. ❑ *He refused to give any information regarding the man's financial situation.*

re|gard|less /rɪgɑrdlɪs/ If something happens **regardless of** something else, the first thing is not affected or influenced at all by the second thing. ❑ *The organization helps anyone regardless of their age.*

reg|gae /rɛgeɪ/ **NONCOUNT NOUN** MUSIC **Reggae** is a type of West Indian popular music with a very strong beat.

regi|ment /rɛdʒɪmənt/ (**regiments**) **NOUN** A **regiment** is a part of an army.

re|gion /ridʒən/ (**regions**) **NOUN** GEOGRAPHY A **region** is an area of a country or of the world. ❑ *Do you have a map of the coastal region of South Carolina?* ● **re|gion|al** **ADJECTIVE** ❑ *...Hawaiian regional cooking.*

reg|is|ter /rɛdʒɪstər/ (**registers, registering, registered**)
1 **NOUN** A **register** is an official list of people or things. ❑ *We'll check the register of births, deaths, and marriages.*
2 **VERB** If you **register** to do something, you put your name on an official list, in order to be able to do that thing. ❑ *Thousands of people registered to vote.* ● **regi|stra|tion** /rɛdʒɪstreɪʃən/ **NONCOUNT NOUN** ❑ *The website is free, but it asks for registration from users.*
3 **VERB** When something **registers on** a scale or a measuring instrument, it shows a particular value. ❑ *The earthquake registered 5.7 on the Richter scale.*

re|gret /rɪgrɛt/ (**regrets, regretting, regretted**)
1 **VERB** If you **regret** something that you did, you feel sorry that you did it. ❑ *I regret my decision to leave my job.* ❑ *I regret breaking up with my boyfriend.*
2 **NOUN** **Regret** is a feeling of sadness or disappointment, caused by something that you have done or not done. ❑ *He had no regrets about leaving.*

regu|lar /rɛgyələr/
1 **ADJECTIVE** **Regular** events have equal amounts of time between them, so that they happen, for example, at the same time each day or each week. ❑ *Get regular exercise.*
2 **ADJECTIVE** **Regular** events happen often. ❑ *We meet on a regular basis.* ● **regu|lar|ly** **ADVERB** ❑ *He writes regularly for the magazine.*
3 **ADJECTIVE** If you are a **regular** customer at a store or a **regular** visitor to a place, you go there often. ❑ *She was a regular visitor to the museum.*
4 **ADJECTIVE** **Regular** means normal or ordinary. ❑ *Fred is just a regular guy.*
5 **ADJECTIVE** If something has a **regular** shape, both halves are the same and it has straight or smooth edges. ❑ *He's a man of average height with regular features.*
6 **ADJECTIVE** LANGUAGE ARTS A **regular** noun or verb follows the usual rules of grammar. For example, "work" is a regular verb, because the past is formed with "-ed." Compare with **irregular**. ❑ *The past tense of English regular verbs ends in -ed.*

N. regular **basis**, regular **checkups**, regular **exercise**, regular **meetings**, regular **schedule**, regular **visits** **1** **2**
regular **customer**, regular **visitor** **3**
regular **coffee**, regular **guy**, regular **hours**, regular **mail**, regular **season** **4**
regular **verbs** **6**

regu|late /rɛgyəleɪt/ (**regulates, regulating, regulated**) **VERB** SOCIAL STUDIES To **regulate** an activity means to control it with rules. ❑ *The government introduced new laws to regulate the food industry.*

regu|la|tion /rɛgyəleɪʃən/ (**regulations**) **NOUN** **Regulations** are rules for controlling the way something is done or the way people behave. ❑ *Here are the new safety regulations.*

r

re|hears|al /rɪhɜrsᵊl/ (rehearsals) NOUN
ARTS A **rehearsal** of a performance is a
practice of it. ❏ *Tomorrow we start rehearsals for
the concert.*

re|hearse /rɪhɜrs/ (rehearses, rehearsing,
rehearsed) VERB ARTS When people
rehearse a play, a dance, or a piece of music,
they practice it. ❏ *The actors are rehearsing a
play.* ❏ *Thousands of people are rehearsing for the
ceremony.*
→ look at **performance**

reign /reɪn/ (reigns, reigning, reigned)
1 VERB SOCIAL STUDIES When a king or
queen **reigns**, he or she rules a country.
❏ *Henry II reigned in England from 1154 to 1189.*
2 NOUN **Reign** is also a noun. ❏ *...Queen
Victoria's reign.*

rein /reɪn/ (reins) PLURAL NOUN **Reins** are
the long thin pieces of leather that fit
around a horse's neck, and that are used
for controling the horse. ❏ *She held
the reins while the horse pulled.*

rein|deer /reɪndɪər/ (reindeer)
NOUN A **reindeer** is a big animal
with large horns that lives in
northern areas of Europe, Asia,
and America.

re|ject /rɪdʒɛkt/ (rejects, rejecting,
rejected)
1 VERB If you **reject** something, you do not
accept it or agree to it. ❏ *The president rejected
the offer.*
2 VERB If someone **is rejected** for a job or
a course of study, it is not offered to them.
❏ *He was rejected by several universities.*
● **re|jec|tion** (rejections) NOUN ❏ *Be prepared
for lots of rejections before you get a job.*

re|joice /rɪdʒɔɪs/ (rejoices, rejoicing,
rejoiced) VERB If you **rejoice**, you are very
happy about something and you show this
in the way that you behave. ❏ *We rejoiced in
the victory.* ● **re|joic|ing** NONCOUNT NOUN
❏ *There was much rejoicing at the news.*

re|late /rɪleɪt/ (relates, relating, related)
1 VERB If something **relates to** a particular
subject, it is about that subject. ❏ *We are
collecting all the information relating to the crime.*
2 VERB The way that two things **relate**, or
the way that one thing **relates to** another,
is the connection that exists between them.
❏ *There is new thinking about how the two sciences
relate.*

re|lat|ed /rɪleɪtɪd/
1 ADJECTIVE If two things are **related**, they
are connected in some way. ❏ *Crime and
poverty are closely related.*
2 ADJECTIVE People who are **related** belong
to the same family. ❏ *The boys have the same
last name but they are not related.*

re|la|tion /rɪleɪʃᵊn/ (relations)
1 PLURAL NOUN **Relations** between people,
groups, or countries are the way in which
they behave toward each other. ❏ *The country
has good relations with Israel.*
2 NOUN The **relation of** one thing **to**
another is the connection between them.
❏ *He has spent years studying the relation between
exercise and health.*
3 NOUN Your **relations** are the members of
your family. ❏ *We make frequent visits to friends
and relations.*

Word Builder | **relationship**

ship ≈ **state of being**
    champion + ship = champion**ship**
    friend + ship = friend**ship**
    leader + ship = leader**ship**
    member + ship = member**ship**
    owner + ship = owner**ship**
    relation + ship = relation**ship**

---

re|la|tion|ship /rɪleɪʃᵊnʃɪp/ (relationships)
1 NOUN The **relationship** between two
people or groups is the way in which they
feel and behave toward each other. ❏ *The
ministers want to maintain the friendly relationship
between the two countries.*
2 NOUN A **relationship** is a close friendship
between two people, especially involving
romantic or sexual feelings. ❏ *She could not
accept that their relationship was over.*
3 NOUN The **relationship** between two
things is the way in which they are
connected. ❏ *Is there a relationship between diet
and cancer?*

rela|tive /rɛlətɪv/ (relatives) NOUN Your
relatives are the members of your family.
❏ *Ask a relative to look after the children.*

re|lax /rɪlæks/ (relaxes, relaxing, relaxed)
1 VERB If you **relax**, you feel more calm and
less worried. ❏ *You should relax and stop
worrying.* ● **re|laxa|tion** /rɪlækseɪʃᵊn/
NONCOUNT NOUN ❏ *Try learning some relaxation
techniques.* ● **re|laxed** ADJECTIVE ❏ *The
atmosphere at lunch was relaxed.* ● **re|lax|ing**
ADJECTIVE ❏ *I find cooking very relaxing.*

R

Word World   **relax**

time · easy · peaceful · happy · leisure · games · calm · quiet · holiday · yoga · daydream · pleasure · dream · enjoy · vacation · fun · read · rest · recreation · weekend · sleep

Nouns / Adjectives / Verbs

2 VERB When you **relax** a part of your body, it becomes less stiff or tight. ❏ *Have a massage to relax your muscles.*

re|lay /rɪleɪ/ (relays) **NOUN** SPORTS A **relay** or a **relay race** is a race between two or more teams in which each member of the team runs or swims one section of the race. ❏ *Britain's chances of winning the relay are good.*

re|lease /rɪliːs/ (releases, releasing, released)
1 VERB If a person or an animal **is released**, they are allowed to go free. ❏ *He was released from prison the next day.*
2 VERB If you **release** someone or something, you stop holding them. [FORMAL] ❏ *He released her hand.*
3 VERB When an entertainer or a company **releases** a new CD, DVD, or movie, it becomes available so that people can buy it or see it. ❏ *He is releasing a CD of love songs.*
4 NOUN A new **release** is a new CD, DVD, or movie that has just become available for people to buy or see.

rel|evant /rɛləvənt/ **ADJECTIVE** Something that is **relevant to** a situation or person is important in that situation or to that person. ❏ *They are trying to make politics more relevant to younger people.*

re|li|able /rɪlaɪəbəl/
1 ADJECTIVE People or things that are **reliable** can be trusted to work well. ❏ *She was efficient and reliable.*
2 ADJECTIVE Information that is **reliable** is probably correct. ❏ *There is no reliable information about how many people have died.*
● **re|li|ably ADVERB** ❏ *We are reliably informed that he is here.* ● **re|li|a|bi|li|ty NONCOUNT NOUN** ❏ *We have serious doubts about the reliability of this information.*

re|lief /rɪliːf/ (reliefs)
1 NONCOUNT NOUN If you feel **relief**, you feel happy because something unpleasant has

not happened or is no longer happening. ❏ *I breathed a sigh of relief.*
2 NONCOUNT NOUN Relief from pain or worry is when it stops. ❏ *These drugs will give relief from pain.*
3 NONCOUNT NOUN Relief is money, food, or clothing that is provided for people who suddenly need it. ❏ *Relief agencies are hoping to provide food and shelter in the flooded area.*
4 NOUN ARTS A **relief** is a piece of art that consists of a raised surface on a flat background.

re|lieved /rɪliːvd/ **ADJECTIVE** If you are **relieved**, you feel happy because something unpleasant has not happened or is no longer happening. ❏ *We are relieved to be back home.*

re|li|gion /rɪlɪdʒən/ (religions)
1 NONCOUNT NOUN Religion is belief in a god or gods and the activities that are connected with this belief. ❏ *There's little interest in organized religion.*
2 NOUN A **religion** is a particular system of belief in a god or gods and the activities that are connected with this system. ❏ *...the Christian religion.*

re|li|gious /rɪlɪdʒəs/
1 ADJECTIVE Religious means connected with religion. ❏ *Religious groups are able to meet quite freely.*
2 ADJECTIVE Someone who is **religious** has a strong belief in a god or gods.

re|li|gious free|dom NONCOUNT NOUN SOCIAL STUDIES People who have **religious freedom** may choose to follow any religion that they wish. ❏ *We believe that religious freedom should be treated as a human right.*

re|luc|tant /rɪlʌktənt/ **ADJECTIVE** If you are **reluctant to** do something, you are unwilling to do it. ❏ *Mr. Spero was reluctant to ask for help.* ● **re|luc|tant|ly ADVERB** ❏ *We have reluctantly agreed to let him go.*

r

● **re|luc|tance** NONCOUNT NOUN ❑ *Frank boarded his train with great reluctance.*

rely /rɪlaɪ/ (relies, relying, relied)

1 VERB If you **rely on** someone or something, you need them in order to live or work properly. ❑ *They relied heavily on our advice.*

2 VERB If you can **rely on** someone to work well or to behave as you want them to, you can trust them to do this. ❑ *I know I can rely on you to deal with the problem.*

re|main /rɪmeɪn/ (remains, remaining, remained)

1 VERB To **remain** in a particular state or condition means to stay in that state or condition. ❑ *The men remained silent.* ❑ *The government remained in control.*

2 VERB If you **remain** in a place, you stay there and do not move away. ❑ *Police asked people to remain in their homes.*

3 PLURAL NOUN The **remains of** something are the parts of it that are left after most of it has been taken away or destroyed. ❑ *They were cleaning up the remains of their picnic.*

re|main|der /rɪmeɪndər/ NOUN The **remainder of** something is the part that is still there after the first part has gone. ❑ *He drank the remainder of his coffee.*

re|main|ing /rɪmeɪnɪŋ/ ADJECTIVE The **remaining** things or people out of a group are the things or people that still exist, or that are still present. ❑ *He spoke to his few remaining supporters.*

re|mark /rɪmɑrk/ (remarks, remarking, remarked)

1 VERB If you **remark** that something is true, you say that it is true. ❑ *He remarked that it was very cold.* ❑ *She remarked on how tired I looked.*

2 NOUN If you make a **remark** about something, you say something about it. ❑ *She made rude remarks about his weight.*

re|mark|able /rɪmɑrkəbəl/ ADJECTIVE Someone or something that is **remarkable** is very unusual or surprising in a good way. ❑ *He was a remarkable man.* ● **re|mark|ably** /rɪmɑrkəbli/ ADVERB ❑ *The book was remarkably successful.*

rem|edy /rɛmədi/ (remedies)

1 NOUN A **remedy** is a successful way of dealing with a problem. ❑ *The government's remedy involved tax increases.*

2 NOUN A **remedy** is something that is intended to cure you when you are ill. ❑ *...natural remedies for infections.*

re|mem|ber /rɪmɛmbər/ (remembers, remembering, remembered)

1 VERB If you **remember** people or events from the past, you still have an idea of them in your mind. ❑ *I remember the first time I met him.* ❑ *I remember that we went to his wedding.* ❑ *The weather was terrible; do you remember?*

2 VERB If you **remember** that something is true, you become aware of it again after a time when you did not think about it. ❑ *She remembered that she was going to the club that evening.*

3 VERB If you **remember to** do something, you do it when you intend to. ❑ *Please remember to mail the letter.*

Word Partners	Use **remember** with:
ADV.	**always** remember, **still** remember **1**
CONJ.	remember **what**, remember **when**, remember **where**, remember **why** **1**
ADJ.	**easy to** remember, **important to** remember **1** – **3**

re|mind /rɪmaɪnd/ (reminds, reminding, reminded)

1 VERB If someone **reminds** you **of** a fact or event that you already know about, they say something that makes you think about it. ❑ *She reminded Tim of the last time they met.*

2 VERB If someone **reminds** you **to** do a particular thing, they say something that makes you remember to do it. ❑ *Can you remind me to buy some milk?*

3 VERB If someone or something **reminds** you **of** another person or thing, they are similar to them and they make you think about them. ❑ *She reminds me of your sister.*

re|mind|er /rɪmaɪndər/ (reminders) NOUN A **reminder of** something makes you think about it again. ❑ *The scar on her hand was a constant reminder of the accident.*

re|morse /rɪmɔrs/ NONCOUNT NOUN **Remorse** is a strong feeling of sadness and regret about something wrong that you have done. ❑ *He was filled with remorse.*

re|mote /rɪmoʊt/ (remoter, remotest) ADJECTIVE **Remote** areas are far away from cities and places where most people live. ❑ *They came from distant villages in remote areas.*
→ look at **Internet**

re|mote con|trol (remote controls) NOUN
The **remote control** for a television or other piece of equipment is the piece of equipment that you use to control the machine from a distance. ❑ *Rachel picked up the remote control and turned on the television.*
→ look at **television**

re|mote|ly /rɪmoʊtli/ ADVERB You use **remotely** to emphasize the negative meaning of a sentence. ❑ *He wasn't remotely interested in her.*

re|mov|al /rɪmu̯vᵊl/ NONCOUNT NOUN The **removal** of something is the act of removing it. ❑ *She had surgery for the removal of a tumor.*

re|move /rɪmuv/ (removes, removing, removed)
1 VERB If you **remove** something from a place, you take it away. [FORMAL] ❑ *Remove the cake from the oven when it is cooked.*
2 VERB If you **remove** clothing, you take it off. [FORMAL] ❑ *He removed his jacket.*

re|new /rɪnu̯/ (renews, renewing, renewed) VERB When you **renew** something, you get a new one to replace the old one, or you arrange for the old one to continue. ❑ *Larry's landlord refused to renew his lease.*

re|new|able /rɪnu̯ᵊbᵊl/ ADJECTIVE **Renewable** resources are natural ones such as wind, water, and sunlight that are always available. ❑ *...renewable energy sources.*
→ look at **conservation, energy**

rent /rɛnt/ (rents, renting, rented)
1 VERB If you **rent** something, you pay its owner in order to be able to use it yourself. ❑ *She rents a house with three other women.*
2 VERB If you **rent** something **to** someone, you let them have it and use it in exchange for money. ❑ *She rented rooms to university students.*
3 If you **rent** something **out**, you let someone have it and use it in exchange for money. ❑ *Last summer Brian rented out his house and went camping.*
4 NONCOUNT NOUN **Rent** is the amount of money that you pay to use something that belongs to someone else. ❑ *She worked hard to pay the rent on the apartment.*
→ look at **movie**

re|pair /rɪpɛ̯ər/ (repairs, repairing, repaired)
1 VERB If you **repair** something that has been damaged or is not working properly, you fix it. ❑ *Goldman has repaired the roof.*

2 NOUN A **repair** is something that you do to fix something that has been damaged or that is not working properly. ❑ *Repairs were made to the roof.*

re|pair|man /rɪpɛ̯ərmæn/ (repairmen) NOUN A **repairman** is a man whose job is to fix broken machines.

re|pay /rɪpeɪ̯/ (repays, repaying, repaid) VERB If you **repay** a debt, you pay back the money that you borrowed from someone.

re|pay|ment /rɪpeɪ̯mənt/ (repayments)
1 NONCOUNT NOUN The **repayment of** money is the act or process of paying it back to the person you borrowed it from. ❑ *The bank will expect the repayment of the $114 million loan.*
2 NOUN A **repayment** is money that you pay back to the person you borrowed it from. ❑ *He took a loan with small, frequent repayments.*

re|peat /rɪpit/ (repeats, repeating, repeated)
1 VERB If you **repeat** something, you say it or write it again. ❑ *She repeated her request for more money.* ❑ *He repeated that he was innocent.*
2 VERB If you **repeat** something that someone else has said or written, you say or write the same thing. ❑ *She had a habit of repeating everything I said to her.*
3 VERB If you **repeat** an action, you do it again. ❑ *Repeat this exercise five times a week.*
4 NOUN A **repeat** is a television or radio program that has been shown before.

re|peat|ed /rɪpitɪd/ ADJECTIVE **Repeated** actions are ones that happen many times. ❑ *He did not return the money, despite repeated reminders.* ● **re|peat|ed|ly** ADVERB ❑ *I asked him repeatedly to help me.*

rep|eti|tion /rɛpɪtɪʃᵊn/ (repetitions) NOUN If there is a **repetition of** an event, it happens again. ❑ *The city government wants to prevent a repetition of last year's violence.*

re|peti|tive /rɪpɛtɪtɪv/ ADJECTIVE Something that is **repetitive** involves repeating an action many times. ❑ *They are factory workers who do repetitive jobs.*

re|place /rɪpleɪs/ (replaces, replacing, replaced)
1 VERB If one person or thing **replaces** another, they do the job of the other person or thing. ❑ *During the war, many women replaced male workers.*

2 VERB If you **replace** something that is damaged or lost, you get a new one. ❑ *The shower broke so we have to replace it.*

3 VERB If you **replace** something, you put it back where it was before. ❑ *Replace the caps on the bottles.*

re|place|ment /rɪpleɪsmənt/ (**replacements**) **NOUN** You can call a person or thing that replaces another a **replacement**. ❑ *It won't be easy to find a replacement for Grace.*

re|play /rɪpleɪ/ (**replays**) **NOUN** A **replay** of an action on television is when it is broadcast again. ❑ *We watched the replay of the game.*

re|ply /rɪplaɪ/ (**replies, replying, replied**)
1 VERB When you **reply to** something that someone says or writes to you, you say or write an answer to them. ❑ *"That's a nice dress," said Michael. "Thanks," she replied.* ❑ *He replied that this was impossible.* ❑ *He never replied to my letters.*
2 NOUN A **reply** is something that you say or write when you answer someone. ❑ *I called his name, but there was no reply.*

re|port /rɪpɔrt/ (**reports, reporting, reported**)
1 VERB If you **report** something that happened, you tell people about it. ❑ *I reported the crime to the police.* ❑ *Officials reported that four people were killed.*
2 NOUN A **report** is a newspaper article or a broadcast that gives information about something that happened. ❑ *According to a newspaper report, they are getting married.*
3 NOUN A **report** is a piece of work that a student writes on a particular subject. ❑ *We had to do a book report on "Huckleberry Finn."*
4 VERB If someone **reports** you **to** an official person or organization, they tell them about something wrong that you have done. ❑ *His boss reported him to the police.*

re|port card (**report cards**) **NOUN** A **report card** is an official document that shows how well or how badly a student worked in school. ❑ *I got all "A"s on my report card.*

re|port|er /rɪpɔrtər/ (**reporters**) **NOUN** A **reporter** is someone who writes newspaper articles or broadcasts the news. ❑ *My dad is a TV reporter.*

rep|re|sent /rɛprɪzɛnt/ (**represents, representing, represented**)
1 VERB If a lawyer or a politician **represents** a person or a group, they act or make

decisions for them. ❑ *We vote for politicians to represent us.*
2 VERB If a sign **represents** something, it means that thing. ❑ *The red line on the map represents a wall.*

rep|re|sen|ta|tion /rɛprɪzɛnteɪʃⁿn/
NONCOUNT NOUN SOCIAL STUDIES If you have **representation** on a committee, someone on the committee supports you. ❑ *These people have no representation in Congress.*

rep|re|senta|tive /rɛprɪzɛntətɪv/ (**representatives**) **NOUN** SOCIAL STUDIES A **representative** is a person who acts or makes decisions for another person or group. ❑ *Michael is our class representative.*
→ look at **vote**

rep|re|senta|tive gov|ern|ment
NONCOUNT NOUN SOCIAL STUDIES **Representative government** is a system in which the people of a country elect particular people to represent them in their government.

re|pro|duce /riprədus/ (**reproduces, reproducing, reproduced**)
1 VERB If you try to **reproduce** something, you copy it. ❑ *The effect was hard to reproduce.*
2 VERB SCIENCE When people, animals, or plants **reproduce**, they produce babies, eggs, or seeds. ● **re|pro|duc|tion** /riprədʌkʃⁿn/ **NONCOUNT NOUN** ❑ *...human reproduction.*

rep|tile /rɛptaɪl, -tɪl/ (**reptiles**) **NOUN** **Reptiles** are a group of animals that lay eggs and have cold blood. Snakes are reptiles.

re|pub|lic /rɪpʌblɪk/ (**republics**) **NOUN** SOCIAL STUDIES A **republic** is a country where the people choose their government. ❑ *In 1918, Austria became a republic.*

Re|pub|li|can /rɪpʌblɪkən/ (**Republicans**)
1 ADJECTIVE SOCIAL STUDIES **Republican** is used for talking about people who belong to or support the Republican Party (= one of the two main political parties in the U.S.). ❑ *Lower taxes made Republican voters happy.*
2 NOUN A **Republican** is someone who belongs to or supports the Republican Party. ❑ *What made you decide to become a Republican?*
→ look at **vote**

re|pul|sive /rɪpʌlsɪv/ **ADJECTIVE** If a person or a thing is **repulsive**, they are so unpleasant that people do not want to see them. ❑ *Some people found the movie repulsive.*

R

repu|ta|tion /ˌrɛpyəˈteɪʃ°n/ (reputations)
NOUN Your **reputation** is the opinion that people have about you. ❑ *This college has a good reputation.* ❑ *He has a reputation for honesty.*

re|quest /rɪˈkwɛst/ (requests, requesting, requested)
1 VERB If you **request** something, you ask for it politely or formally. [FORMAL] ❑ *To request more information, please check this box.*
2 NOUN If you **make** a **request**, you politely or formally ask someone to do something. ❑ *They agreed to his request for more money.*

re|quire /rɪˈkwaɪər/ (requires, requiring, required)
1 VERB If you **require** something, you need it. [FORMAL] ❑ *If you require more information, please write to this address.*
2 VERB If a law or a rule **requires** you **to** do something, you have to do it. [FORMAL] ❑ *The rules require employers to provide safety training.*

re|quire|ment /rɪˈkwaɪərmənt/ (requirements) **NOUN** A **requirement** is something that you must have. ❑ *Our products meet all legal requirements.*

res|cue /ˈrɛskyu/ (rescues, rescuing, rescued)
1 VERB If you **rescue** someone, you save them from a dangerous situation. ❑ *They rescued 20 people from the roof of the building.*
2 NOUN A **rescue** is an attempt to save someone from a dangerous situation. ❑ *He helped in the rescue of a bus driver from the river.* ❑ *...a big rescue operation.*
3 If someone **comes to** your **rescue**, they help you when you are in danger. ❑ *A neighbor came to her rescue.*

re|search /rɪˈsɜrtʃ, ˈrisɜrtʃ/ (researches, researching, researched)
1 NONCOUNT NOUN **Research** involves studying something and trying to discover facts about it. ❑ *My brother does scientific research.*
2 VERB If you **research** something, you try to discover facts about it. ❑ *She spent two years researching the subject.*
→ look at **history, science, writing**

re|sem|blance /rɪˈzɛmbləns/ (resemblances) **NOUN** If there is a **resemblance** between two people or things, they are similar to each other. ❑ *There was a strong resemblance between the two girls.*

re|sem|ble /rɪˈzɛmbəl/ (resembles, resembling, resembled) **VERB** If one person

or thing **resembles** another, they look similar to each other. ❑ *She resembles her mother.*

re|sent /rɪˈzɛnt/ (resents, resenting, resented) **VERB** If you **resent** something, you feel angry about it because you think it is not fair. ❑ *Certain people resented my success.*

re|sent|ment /rɪˈzɛntmənt/ **NONCOUNT NOUN** **Resentment** is anger that someone feels about something because they think it is not fair. ❑ *Too many rules can cause resentment.*

res|er|va|tion /ˌrɛzərˈveɪʃ°n/ (reservations) **NOUN** If you **make** a **reservation**, you ask a hotel or a restaurant to keep a room or a table for you. ❑ *Have you canceled our reservation?*

re|serve /rɪˈzɜrv/ (reserves, reserving, reserved)
1 VERB If something **is reserved for** a particular person or purpose, it is kept for them. ❑ *A room was reserved for him.*
2 NOUN A **reserve** is a supply of something that you can use when you need it. ❑ *Saudi Arabia has the world's largest oil reserves.*
3 If you have something **in reserve**, you have a supply of it that you can use when you need it. ❑ *I always try to keep a little money in reserve.*

re|served /rɪˈzɜrvd/ **ADJECTIVE** Someone who is **reserved** hides their feelings. ❑ *He was quiet and reserved.*

res|er|voir /ˈrɛzərvwɑr/ (reservoirs) **NOUN** GEOGRAPHY A **reservoir** is a lake that is used for storing water before people use it. ❑ *The reservoir provides drinking water for the city of Utica, NY.*

resi|dence /ˈrɛzɪdəns/ (residences)
1 NOUN A **residence** is a large house where an important person lives. [FORMAL] ❑ *...the president's official residence.*
2 NONCOUNT NOUN Your place of **residence** is the place where you live. [FORMAL]

resi|dent /ˈrɛzɪdənt/ (residents) **NOUN** The **residents** of a house or an area are the people who live there. ❑ *Local residents complained that the road was dangerous.*

resi|den|tial /ˌrɛzɪˈdɛnʃ°l/ **ADJECTIVE** A **residential** area contains houses rather than offices or stores. ❑ *We drove through a residential area of Maryland.*

r

re|sign /rɪzaɪn/ (**resigns, resigning, resigned**)

1 **VERB** If you **resign** from a job, you tell your employer that you are leaving it. ❑ *He was forced to resign.*

2 **VERB** If you **resign yourself to** an unpleasant situation, you accept it because you cannot change it. ❑ *We resigned ourselves to another summer without a boat.*

res|ig|na|tion /rɛzɪgneɪʃ°n/ (**resignations**) **NOUN** Your **resignation** is when you tell your employer that you are leaving your job. ❑ *Barbara offered her resignation this morning.*

re|sist /rɪzɪst/ (**resists, resisting, resisted**)

1 **VERB** If you **resist** a force or a change, you fight against it. ❑ *There are people in the organization who resist change.*

2 **VERB** If you **resist** a feeling that you want to do something, you stop yourself from doing it although you would like to do it. ❑ *Resist the temptation to help your child too much.*

re|sist|ance /rɪzɪstəns/ **NONCOUNT NOUN** **Resistance** to a force or a change is when you fight back against it. ❑ *I am aware of his resistance to anything new.* ❑ *The soldiers are facing strong resistance.*

reso|lu|tion /rɛzəluʃ°n/ (**resolutions**) **NOUN** If you make a **resolution**, you decide to try very hard to do something. ❑ *They made a resolution to get more exercise.*

re|solve /rɪzɒlv/ (**resolves, resolving, resolved**)

1 **VERB** If you **resolve** a problem, an argument, or a difficulty, you find a solution to it. [FORMAL] ❑ *We must resolve these problems.*

2 **VERB** If you **resolve to** do something, you make a decision to do it. [FORMAL] ❑ *Judy resolved to be a better friend.*

re|sort /rɪzɔrt/ (**resorts**)

1 **NOUN** A **resort** is a place that provides activities for people who stay there during their vacation. ❑ *The ski resorts are busy.*

2 If you do something **as a last resort**, you do it because you can find no other solution to a problem. ❑ *As a last resort, we hired an expert.*

re|source /risɔrs/ (**resources**) **NOUN** The **resources** of a country, an organization, or a person are the money and other things that they have and can use. ❑ *We must protect the country's natural resources, including water.*

→ look at **conservation, dictionary, energy, water**

re|spect /rɪspɛkt/ (**respects, respecting, respected**)

1 **VERB** If you **respect** someone, you have a good opinion of them. ❑ *I want people to respect me for my work.*

2 **NONCOUNT NOUN** If you have **respect for** someone or something, you have a good opinion of them, and you consider them to be important. ❑ *I have great respect for Tom.* ❑ *You should show respect for people's rights.*

re|spect|able /rɪspɛktəb°l/ **ADJECTIVE** If someone or something is **respectable**, people have a good opinion of them, and think they are morally correct. ❑ *He comes from a respectable family.*

re|spect|ful /rɪspɛktfəl/ **ADJECTIVE** If you are **respectful**, you are polite to people. ❑ *The children were always respectful to older people.*

res|pi|ra|tion /rɛspɪreɪʃ°n/ **NONCOUNT NOUN** SCIENCE In humans and animals, **respiration** is the process of breathing.

re|spond /rɪspɒnd/ (**responds, responding, responded**) **VERB** When you **respond** to something that someone does or says, you react to it by doing or saying something. ❑ *They responded to the president's request for financial help.* ❑ *The army responded with bombs.*

re|sponse /rɪspɒns/ (**responses**) **NOUN** Your **response** to something that someone does or says is your reply or your reaction to it. ❑ *There was no response to his remarks.*

re|spon|sibil|ity /rɪspɒnsɪbɪlɪti/ (**responsibilities**)

1 **NONCOUNT NOUN** If you have **responsibility** for something or someone, it is your job to deal with them. ❑ *Each manager had responsibility for ten people.*

2 **NONCOUNT NOUN** If you accept **responsibility for** something that happened, you agree that it was your fault. ❑ *No one admitted responsibility for the attacks.*

3 **PLURAL NOUN** Your **responsibilities** are your duties. ❑ *He is busy with work and family responsibilities.*

re|spon|sible /rɪspɒnsɪb°l/

1 **ADJECTIVE** If you are **responsible for** something, it is your job or duty to deal with it. ❑ *I met the people who are responsible for sales and advertising.*

R

2 ADJECTIVE If someone or something is **responsible for** a particular event or situation, it is their fault. ❑ *He still felt responsible for her death.*

3 ADJECTIVE **Responsible** people behave in a proper and sensible way. ❑ *She's a responsible child who often helps around the house.*

rest /rɛst/ (**rests, resting, rested**)

1 VERB If you **rest**, you spend some time relaxing after doing something tiring. ❑ *He's tired, and the doctor advised him to rest.*

2 NOUN If you have a **rest**, you spend some time relaxing after doing something tiring. ❑ *You're exhausted—go home and get some rest.*

3 VERB If you **rest** something somewhere, you put it on another thing. ❑ *He rested his arms on the table.*

4 **The rest** is the parts of something that are left. ❑ *It was an experience I will remember for the rest of my life.*

5 PRONOUN **Rest** is also a pronoun. ❑ *I ate two cakes and saved the rest.*

→ look at **relax**

res|tau|rant /rɛstərənt, -tərɑnt, -trɑnt/ (**restaurants**) NOUN A **restaurant** is a place where you can buy and eat a meal. ❑ *We ate at an Italian restaurant.*

→ look at Picture Dictionary: **restaurant**

→ look at **city, eat**

rest|less /rɛstlɪs/ ADJECTIVE If you are **restless**, you are bored or nervous, and you want to move around. ❑ *I got restless and moved to San Francisco.* ❑ *My father seemed very restless and excited.*

re|store /rɪstɔr/ (**restores, restoring, restored**) VERB To **restore** someone or

something **to** a former condition means to put them in that condition again. ❑ *We will restore her to health.* ❑ *They are experts in restoring old buildings.*

re|strain /rɪstreɪn/ (**restrains, restraining, restrained**)

1 VERB If you **restrain** someone, you use force to stop them from doing something. ❑ *Wally held my arm to restrain me.*

2 VERB If you **restrain** an emotion, you prevent yourself from showing it. ❑ *She was unable to restrain her anger.*

re|strict /rɪstrɪkt/ (**restricts, restricting, restricted**)

1 VERB If you **restrict** something, you prevent it from becoming too great. ❑ *The school is restricting the number of students it accepts this year.*

2 VERB To **restrict** the actions of someone or something means to prevent them from acting freely. ❑ *The bandage restricts the movement in my right arm.* ● **re|stric|tion** /rɪstrɪkʃ°n/ (**restrictions**) NOUN ❑ *Are there any parking restrictions in this street?*

rest|room (**restrooms**) also **rest room** NOUN In a public place, a **restroom** is a room with toilets for people to use.

re|sult /rɪzʌlt/ (**results, resulting, resulted**)

1 NOUN A **result** is something that happens or exists because something else has happened. ❑ *People developed the disease as a direct result of their work.*

2 VERB If something **results in** a particular situation or event, it causes that situation or event. ❑ *Half of all road accidents result in head injuries.*

r

Picture Dictionary   **restaurant**

server / waitress

customer

glass

menu

spoon

plate   fork

table

tablecloth

knife   napkin

3 **VERB** If something **results from** a particular event or action, it is caused by that event or action. ❑ *Many health problems result from a poor diet.*

4 **NOUN** Results are facts such as a score that you get at the end of a competition or a test. ❑ *Are you happy with the election results?*

re|sume /rɪzum/ (resumes, resuming, resumed) **VERB** If you **resume** an activity, you begin it again. [FORMAL] ❑ *After the war he resumed his job at Wellesley College.* ❑ *The talks will resume on Tuesday.*

ré|su|mé /rɛzumeɪ/ (résumés) also **resume** **NOUN** Your **résumé** is a short description of your education and the jobs you have had.

re|tail /riteɪl/ **NONCOUNT NOUN** Retail is when a business sells goods directly to the public. ❑ *My sister works in retail, in a clothing store.*

re|tail|er /riteɪlər/ (retailers) **NOUN** A **retailer** is a business that sells goods directly to the public. ❑ *...a furniture retailer.*

re|tain /rɪteɪn/ (retains, retaining, retained) **VERB** To **retain** something means to continue to have it. [FORMAL] ❑ *He was looking for a way to retain control of his company.*

Word Builder **rethink**

re ≈ **again**

    re + cycle = recycle
    re + fresh = refresh
    re + think = rethink
    re + view = review
    re + write = rewrite

---

re|think /riθɪŋk/ (rethinks, rethinking, rethought) **VERB** If you **rethink** a problem or a plan, you think about it again and change it. ❑ *Both political parties are rethinking their programs.*

re|tire /rɪtaɪər/ (retires, retiring, retired) **VERB** When people **retire**, they leave their job and usually stop working completely. ❑ *He planned to retire at age 65.* • **re|tired** **ADJECTIVE** ❑ *I am a retired teacher.*

re|tire|ment /rɪtaɪərmənt/ **NONCOUNT NOUN** A person's **retirement** is the period in their life after they retire. ❑ *What do you plan to do during retirement?*

re|treat /rɪtrit/ (retreats, retreating, retreated) **VERB** If you **retreat**, you move away from something or someone.

❑ *I retreated from the room.* ❑ *The French soldiers were forced to retreat.*

re|turn /rɪtɜrn/ (returns, returning, returned)

1 **VERB** When you **return to** a place, you go back there. ❑ *He will return to Moscow tomorrow.*

2 **NOUN** Your **return** is when you arrive back at a place where you were before. ❑ *Kenny explained the reason for his return to Dallas.*

3 **VERB** If you **return** something that you borrowed or took, you give it back or put it back. ❑ *They will return the money later.*

4 **NOUN** Return is also a noun. ❑ *Marie demanded the return of the stolen money.*

5 If you do something **in return for** what someone did for you, you do it because they did that thing for you. ❑ *He smiled at Alison and she smiled in return.*

→ look at **shopping**

re|union /riyuniən/ (reunions) **NOUN** A **reunion** is a meeting between people who have not seen each other for a long time. ❑ *I am planning a family reunion.*

re|unite /riyunaɪt/ (reunites, reuniting, reunited) **VERB** If people **are reunited**, they see each other again after a long time. ❑ *She was finally reunited with her family.*

re|veal /rɪvil/ (reveals, revealing, revealed)

1 **VERB** To **reveal** something means to tell people something that they do not know already. ❑ *She has refused to reveal any more details.*

2 **VERB** If you **reveal** something, you show it by removing the thing that was covering it. ❑ *She smiled, revealing small white teeth.*

re|venge /rɪvɛndʒ/ **NONCOUNT NOUN** Revenge involves hurting or punishing someone who has hurt or harmed you. ❑ *He wanted revenge for the way they treated his mother.*

rev|enue /rɛvənyu/ (revenues) **NOUN** SOCIAL STUDIES Revenue is money that a company, an organization, or a government receives from people. ❑ *The company gets 98% of its revenue from Internet advertising.*

Rev|er|end /rɛvərənd/ **NOUN** Reverend is a title used before the name of a church leader. ❑ *The Reverend Jim Simons led the service.*

re|verse /rɪvɜrs/ (reverses, reversing, reversed)

1 **VERB** To **reverse** a decision or a situation means to change it to the opposite decision or situation. ❏ *They will not reverse the decision to increase prices.*

2 **VERB** If you **reverse** the order of a group of things, you arrange them in the opposite order. ❏ *You've made a spelling mistake. You need to reverse the "i" and the "e."*

3 **NONCOUNT NOUN** If your car is **in reverse**, you can drive it backward.

Word Builder   review

re ≈ **again**
    re + cycle = re**cycle**
    re + fresh = re**fresh**
    re + think = re**think**
    re + view = re**view**
    re + write = re**write**

---

re|view /rɪvyu/ (**reviews, reviewing, reviewed**)

1 **NOUN** A **review of** something is when you examine it to see if it needs changes. ❏ *The president ordered a review of the situation.*

2 **VERB** If you **review** something, you consider it carefully to see if it needs changes. ❏ *The new plan will be reviewed by the city council.*

3 **NOUN** A **review** is a report that gives your opinion of a book or a movie. ❏ *The movie got a good review in the magazine.*

4 **VERB** If someone **reviews** a book or a movie, they write a report that gives their opinion of it. ❏ *She reviews all the new DVDs.*

● **re|view|er** (**reviewers**) **NOUN** ❏ *He's a reviewer for the New York Times.*

5 **VERB** When you **review for** an exam, you study all the information about the subject again. ❏ *Review all your notes for each class.*

→ look at **grammar**

re|vise /rɪvaɪz/ (**revises, revising, revised**) **VERB** If you **revise** something, you change it in order to make it better or more correct. ❏ *Ask a friend to revise a paragraph that you have written.* ❏ *We are revising the rules.*

→ look at **writing**

re|vive /rɪvaɪv/ (**revives, reviving, revived**) **VERB** If you **revive** someone who has fainted, you do something to make them become conscious again. ❏ *A doctor revived the patient.*

re|volt /rɪvoʊlt/ (**revolts, revolting, revolted**)

1 **NOUN** A **revolt** is when a group of people fight against a person or an organization that has control. ❏ *It was a revolt by ordinary people against their leaders.*

2 **VERB** When people **revolt**, they fight against a person or an organization that has control. ❏ *Californian citizens revolted against higher taxes.*

re|volt|ing /rɪvoʊltɪŋ/ **ADJECTIVE** Revolting means extremely unpleasant. ❏ *The smell was revolting.*

revo|lu|tion /rɛvəluʃ°n/ (**revolutions**)

1 **NOUN** SOCIAL STUDIES A **revolution** is an attempt by a group of people to change their country's government by using force. ❏ *The period since the revolution has been peaceful.*

2 **NOUN** A **revolution** in a particular area of activity is an important change in that area. ❏ *There was a revolution in ship design in the nineteenth century.*

revo|lu|tion|ary /rɛvəluʃənɛri/

1 **ADJECTIVE** Revolutionary activities, organizations, or people try to cause a revolution. ❏ *Do you know anything about the revolutionary movement?*

2 **ADJECTIVE** Something that is **revolutionary** changes the way that something is done or made. ❏ *It is a revolutionary new product.*

re|volve /rɪvɒlv/ (**revolves, revolving, revolved**)

1 **VERB** If your life **revolves around** a particular thing, that thing is the most important part of your life. ❏ *Her life has revolved around sports.*

2 **VERB** When something **revolves**, it moves or turns in a circle. ❏ *The Earth revolves around the sun.*

→ look at **earth**

re|volv|er /rɪvɒlvər/ (**revolvers**) **NOUN** A **revolver** is a type of small gun.

re|ward /rɪwɔrd/ (**rewards, rewarding, rewarded**)

1 **NOUN** A **reward** is something that someone gives you because you have done something good. ❏ *The school gives rewards for good behavior.*

2 **VERB** If someone **rewards** you, they give you something because you have done something good. ❏ *She was rewarded for her years of hard work.*

re|ward|ing /rɪwɔrdɪŋ/ **ADJECTIVE** An experience or an action that is **rewarding** gives you satisfaction or brings you benefits. ❏ *I have a job that is very rewarding.*

r

Word Builder   **rewrite**

re ≈ again

    re + cycle = **re**cycle
    re + fresh = **re**fresh
    re + think = **re**think
    re + view = **re**view
    re + write = **re**write

---

re|write /riraɪt/ (**rewrites, rewriting, rewrote, rewritten**) **VERB** If someone **rewrites** a piece of writing, they write it in a different way in order to improve it. ❏ *She decided to rewrite her article.*

rhi|noc|er|os /raɪnɒsərəs/ (**rhinoceroses**) **NOUN** A **rhinoceros** is a large animal from Asia or Africa with a horn on its nose.

rhyme /raɪm/ (**rhymes, rhyming, rhymed**)
1 **VERB** LANGUAGE ARTS If one word **rhymes with** another, or if two words **rhyme**, they have a very similar sound. ❏ *June rhymes with moon.*
2 **NOUN** LANGUAGE ARTS A **rhyme** is a poem that has words that rhyme at the ends of its lines. ❏ *He was teaching Helen a rhyme.*

rhythm /rɪðəm/ (**rhythms**) **NOUN** MUSIC A **rhythm** is a regular pattern of sounds or movements. ❏ *Listen to the rhythms of jazz.*
→ look at **music**

rhyth|mic /rɪðmɪk/ or **rhythmical** /rɪðmɪkəl/ **ADJECTIVE** A **rhythmic** movement or sound is repeated in a regular pattern. ❏ *Good breathing is slow and rhythmic.*

rib /rɪb/ (**ribs**) **NOUN** SCIENCE Your **ribs** are the 12 pairs of curved bones that surround your chest. ❏ *Her heart was beating hard against her ribs.*

rib|bon /rɪbən/ (**ribbons**) **NOUN** A **ribbon** is a long, narrow piece of cloth that you use to tie things together, or as a decoration. ❏ *She tied her hair with a ribbon.*

rib cage (**rib cages**) **NOUN** SCIENCE Your **rib cage** is the structure of bones in your chest that protects your lungs and other organs.

rice /raɪs/ **NONCOUNT NOUN** Rice is white or brown grains from a plant that grows in wet areas. ❏ *The meal consisted of chicken, rice, and vegetables.*

rich /rɪtʃ/ (**richer, richest**)
1 **ADJECTIVE** A **rich** person has a lot of money or valuable possessions. ❏ *He was a very rich man.*
2 **PLURAL NOUN** The **rich** are rich people. ❏ *Only the rich can afford to live there.*

rid /rɪd/ (**rids, ridding, rid**) When you **get rid of** something or someone, you remove them completely or make them leave. ❏ *We had to get rid of our old car because it was too small.*

rid|den /rɪdən/ **Ridden** is a form of the verb **ride**.

rid|dle /rɪdəl/ (**riddles**) **NOUN** A **riddle** is a question that seems to be nonsense, but that has a clever answer.

ride /raɪd/ (**rides, riding, rode, ridden**)
1 **VERB** When you **ride** a bicycle or a horse, you sit on it, control it, and travel on it. ❏ *Riding a bike is great exercise.* ❏ *We passed three men riding on motorcycles.*
2 **VERB** When you **ride in** a vehicle, you travel in it. ❏ *He rode in the bus to the hotel.*
3 **NOUN** A **ride** is a trip on a horse or a bicycle, or in a vehicle. ❏ *She took some friends for a ride in the car.*
→ look at **route**

rid|er /raɪdər/ (**riders**) **NOUN** SPORTS A **rider** is someone who rides a horse, a bicycle, or a motorcycle. ❏ *She is a very good rider.*

ridge /rɪdʒ/ (**ridges**) **NOUN** SCIENCE GEOGRAPHY A **ridge** is a long, narrow part of something that is higher than the rest. ❏ *It's a high road along a mountain ridge.*

ri|dicu|lous /rɪdɪkyələs/ **ADJECTIVE** If something or someone is **ridiculous**, they are very silly or not serious. ❏ *They thought it was a ridiculous idea.*

rid|ing /raɪdɪŋ/ **NONCOUNT NOUN** SPORTS **Riding** is the activity or sport of riding horses. ❏ *The next morning we went riding.*

ri|fle /raɪfəl/ (**rifles**) **NOUN** A **rifle** is a long gun. ❏ *They shot him with a rifle.*

---

right

  ❶ CORRECT
  ❷ DIRECTION
  ❸ LAW
  ❹ EXACTLY OR IMMEDIATELY

Sound Partners   right, write

❶ right /raɪt/
1 **ADJECTIVE** If someone or something is **right**, they are correct. ❏ *Ron was right about the result of the election.* ❏ *"C" is the right answer.*

2 **ADVERB** **Right** is also an adverb. ❑ *If I'm going to do something, I want to do it right.*
3 You can use **right** to check whether you are correct. ❑ *"You're coming to the party, right?"*
4 **ADJECTIVE** The **right** action is the best one. ❑ *You made the right choice in moving to New York.*
5 **NONCOUNT NOUN** SOCIAL STUDIES You use **right** to talk about actions that are morally good and acceptable. ❑ *He knew right from wrong.*
6 **ADJECTIVE** **Right** is also an adjective. ❑ *It's not right to leave the children here alone.*

② **right** /raɪt/
1 **NOUN** The **right** is the side that is toward the east when you look north ❑ *On the right is a vegetable garden.*
2 **ADVERB** **Right** is also an adverb. ❑ *Turn right into the street.*
3 **ADJECTIVE** Your **right** arm or leg is the one that is on the right side of your body.

③ **right** /raɪt/ (**rights**) **NOUN** Your **rights** are the things that you are allowed to do morally, or by law. ❑ *Make sure you know your rights.* ❑ *We have the right to protest.*

④ **right** /raɪt/
1 **ADVERB** You can use **right** to say that something happens exactly in a particular place or at a particular time. ❑ *A car appeared right in front of him.* ❑ *Liz arrived right on time.*
2 **ADVERB** **I'll be right back** means that you will get back to a place in a very short time. ❑ *I'm going to get some water. I'll be right back.*
3 If you do something **right away**, you do it immediately. [INFORMAL] ❑ *He wants to see you right away.*

right an|gle (**right angles**) **NOUN** MATH A **right angle** is an angle that looks like a letter "L" and equals 90 degrees.
→ look at **geometry**

right-handed **ADJECTIVE** Someone who is **right-handed** uses their right hand rather than their left hand for activities such as writing and sports.

rig|id /rɪdʒɪd/
1 **ADJECTIVE** Laws or systems that are **rigid** cannot be changed. ❑ *We have rigid rules about student behavior.*
2 **ADJECTIVE** A **rigid** substance or object is stiff and does not bend, stretch, or twist easily. ❑ *Use rigid plastic containers.*

rim /rɪm/ (**rims**) **NOUN** The **rim** of a curved object is the edge of the object. ❑ *She looked at him over the rim of her glass.*

rind /raɪnd/ (**rinds**)
1 **NOUN** The **rind** of a fruit such as a lemon or an orange is its thick outside skin.
2 **NOUN** The **rind** of cheese is the hard outside edge that you do not eat.

ring /rɪŋ/ (**rings, ringing, rang, rung**)
1 **VERB** When a bell **rings**, it makes its sound. ❑ *The school bell rang.* ❑ *They rang the bell but nobody came to the door.*
2 **NOUN** **Ring** is also a noun. ❑ *There was a ring at the door.*
3 **NOUN** A **ring** is a small circle of metal that you wear on your finger. ❑ *She was wearing a gold wedding ring.*
4 **NOUN** A **ring** is something in the shape of a circle. ❑ *They built the fire in a ring of stones.*
→ look at **phone**

ringtone (**ringtones**) **NOUN** The **ringtone** is the sound made by your cellphone when someone calls you.

rink /rɪŋk/ (**rinks**) **NOUN** SPORTS A **rink** is a large area of ice where people go to ice-skate (= move over ice in special boots). ❑ *There were hundreds of skaters on the rink.*

rinse /rɪns/ (**rinses, rinsing, rinsed**) **VERB** When you **rinse** something, you wash it in order to remove dirt or soap from it. ❑ *Make sure you rinse all the shampoo out of your hair.*

riot /raɪət/ (**riots, rioting, rioted**)
1 **NOUN** When there is a **riot**, a group of people behave violently in a public place. ❑ *Twelve people were injured during a riot at the prison.*
2 **VERB** If people **riot**, they behave violently in a public place. ❑ *They rioted against the government.*

rip /rɪp/ (**rips, ripping, ripped**) **VERB** When you **rip** something, you tear it quickly. ❑ *I ripped my pants when I fell.*
▶ **rip up** If you **rip** something **up**, you tear it into small pieces. ❑ *He ripped up the letter and threw it in the fire.*

ripe /raɪp/ (**riper, ripest**) **ADJECTIVE** **Ripe** fruit or grain is ready to eat. ❑ *Choose firm but ripe fruit.*

rip|ple /rɪpᵊl/ (**ripples, rippling, rippled**)
1 **NOUN** **Ripples** are little waves on the surface of water.
2 **VERB** When the surface of water **ripples**, little waves appear on it. ❑ *If you throw a stone in a pool, it ripples.*

r

rise /raɪz/ (rises, rising, rose, risen)

1 **VERB** If something **rises**, it moves upward. ❑ *We could see black smoke rising from the chimney.*

2 **VERB** When you **rise**, you stand up. [FORMAL] ❑ *He rose slowly from the chair.*

3 **VERB** When you **rise**, you get out of bed. [FORMAL] ❑ *Tony rose early.*

4 **VERB** When the sun or the moon **rises**, it appears in the sky.

5 **VERB** If an amount or a number **rises**, it increases. ❑ *His income rose by $5,000.*

6 **NOUN** A **rise in** the amount of something is an increase in it. ❑ *There's been a rise in the price of oil.*

→ look at **greenhouse effect**

risk /rɪsk/ (risks, risking, risked)

1 **NOUN** If there is a **risk of** something bad, there is a possibility that it will happen. ❑ *There is a small risk of damage.*

2 **NOUN** If something that you do is a **risk**, it might have bad results. ❑ *You're taking a big risk by showing this to Robert.*

3 **NOUN** If something or someone is a **risk**, they are likely to harm you. ❑ *Being very fat is a health risk.*

4 **VERB** If you **risk** something bad, you do something knowing that the bad thing might happen as a result. ❑ *He risked breaking his leg when he jumped.*

5 **VERB** If you **risk** something important, you behave in a way that might result in it being lost or harmed. ❑ *She risked her own life to help him.*

6 To be **at risk** means to be in a situation where something bad might happen. ❑ *Our nation is at risk from an attack.*

risky /rɪski/ (riskier, riskiest) **ADJECTIVE** If an activity or an action is **risky**, it is dangerous or likely to fail. ❑ *They encourage young people to avoid risky behavior.*

ritu|al /rɪtʃuəl/ (rituals) **NOUN** A **ritual** is a series of actions that people perform in a particular order. ❑ *Every religion has holy days and rituals such as baptism.*

ri|val /raɪvᵊl/ (rivals) **NOUN** If people or groups are **rivals**, they compete against each other. ❑ *He was accused of spying on his political rivals.*

riv|er /rɪvər/ (rivers) **NOUN** SCIENCE GEOGRAPHY A **river** is a long line of water that flows into an ocean.

→ look at Picture Dictionary: **river**
→ look at **landform, water**

roach /roʊtʃ/ (roaches) **NOUN** A **roach** is the same as a **cockroach**.

road /roʊd/ (roads) **NOUN** A **road** is a long piece of hard ground that vehicles travel on. ❑ *There was very little traffic on the roads.*

→ look at **route**

roam /roʊm/ (roams, roaming, roamed) **VERB** If you **roam** an area, you move around it without planning where exactly you are going. ❑ *Children roamed the streets in groups.*

roar /rɔr/ (roars, roaring, roared)

1 **VERB** If a person, an animal, or a thing **roars**, they make a very loud noise. ❑ *The engine roared, and the vehicle moved forward.*

2 **NOUN** Roar is also a noun. ❑ *Who could forget the first time they heard the roar of a lion?*

roast /roʊst/ (roasts, roasting, roasted)

1 **VERB** When you **roast** meat or other food,

R

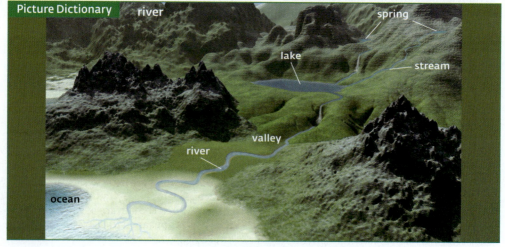

Picture Dictionary river

spring

lake

stream

valley

river

ocean

you cook it in an oven or over a fire. ❑ *He roasted the chicken.*

2 **ADJECTIVE** Roast meat is cooked in an oven or over a fire. ❑ *We had roast beef.*

→ look at **cook, meat**

rob /rɒb/ (robs, robbing, robbed) **VERB** If a person **is robbed**, someone steals money or property from them. ❑ *She was robbed of her watch.* ● **rob|ber** (robbers) **NOUN** ❑ *...a bank robber.*

rob|bery /rɒbəri/ (robberies) **NOUN** Robbery is when a person steals money or property from a place. ❑ *There have been several robberies in the area.*

robe /roʊb/ (robes)

1 **NOUN** A **robe** is a special piece of clothing that an important person wears during a ceremony. [FORMAL] ❑ *The judge was wearing a black robe.*

2 **NOUN** A **robe** is a piece of clothing that you wear in the house before you get dressed. ❑ *I put on a robe and went down to the kitchen.*

rob|in /rɒbɪn/ (robins) **NOUN** A **robin** is a brown bird with a red chest.

→ look at **bird**

ro|bot /roʊbət, -bɒt/ (robots) **NOUN** A **robot** is a machine that can move and perform tasks automatically. ❑ *We have robots that we could send to the moon.*

rock /rɒk/ (rocks, rocking, rocked)

1 **NONCOUNT NOUN** SCIENCE **Rock** is the hard substance that is in the ground and in mountains. ❑ *We tried to dig, but the ground was solid rock.*

2 **NOUN** A **rock** is a large piece of rock. ❑ *She sat on a rock and looked out across the ocean.*

3 **VERB** When something **rocks**, it moves slowly backward and forward. ❑ *His body rocked gently in the chair.* ❑ *She rocked the baby in her arms.*

4 **NONCOUNT NOUN** **Rock** is loud music with a strong beat that you play on electric instruments. ❑ *We went to a rock concert.*

→ look at **beach**

rock and roll also **rock'n'roll** **NONCOUNT NOUN** MUSIC **Rock and roll** is a type of music that was popular in the 1950s. ❑ *Elvis Presley was known as the King of Rock and Roll.*

rock|et /rɒkɪt/ (rockets)

1 **NOUN** A **rocket** is a vehicle that people use to travel into outer space. ❑ *This is the rocket that took them to the moon.*

2 **NOUN** A **rocket** is the same as a **missile**. ❑ *There was another rocket attack on the city.*

rocky /rɒki/ (rockier, rockiest) **ADJECTIVE** A **rocky** place has a lot of rocks in it. ❑ *The paths are very rocky.*

rod /rɒd/ (rods) **NOUN** A **rod** is a long, thin metal or wooden bar. ❑ *The roof was supported with steel rods.*

rode /roʊd/ **Rode** is a form of the verb **ride**.

ro|dent /roʊdᵊnt/ (rodents) **NOUN** **Rodents** are small animals such as mice, with sharp front teeth.

ro|deo /roʊdioʊ, roʊdeɪoʊ/ (rodeos) **NOUN** A **rodeo** is an event where you can watch people riding wild horses and catching animals with ropes.

Sound Partners	role, roll

role /roʊl/ (roles)

1 **NOUN** The **role** of someone or something in a situation is what they should do in it. ❑ *We discussed the role of parents in raising their children.*

2 **NOUN** A **role** is the character that an actor plays in a movie or a play. ❑ *Who plays the role of the doctor?*

Sound Partners	roll, role

roll /roʊl/ (rolls, rolling, rolled)

1 **VERB** When something **rolls**, it moves along a surface, turning over many times. ❑ *The pencil rolled off the desk.* ❑ *I rolled a ball to the baby.*

2 **VERB** If drops of liquid **roll** down a surface, they move quickly down it. ❑ *Tears rolled down her cheeks.*

3 If you **roll up** something, you form it into the shape of a ball or tube. ❑ *Steve rolled up the paper bag.*

4 **NOUN** A **roll of** paper is a long piece of it that you form into the shape of a ball or a tube. ❑ *There are twelve rolls of cloth here.*

5 **NOUN** A **roll** is an official list of the names of the people in a particular group. ❑ *If your name is not on the roll, you will not have a vote.*

6 **NOUN** A **roll** is a small piece of bread that is round or long. ❑ *He spread some butter on a roll.*

→ look at **bread**

r

roller-skate (roller-skates, roller-skating, roller-skated)

1 **NOUN** **Roller-skates** are boots with small wheels on the bottom. ❑ ...*a pair of roller skates.*

2 **VERB** If you **roller-skate**, you move over a flat surface wearing roller- skates. ❑ *Gary was roller-skating outside our house.*

Ro|man Catho|lic /roʊmən kæθlɪk/ (**Roman Catholics**)

1 **ADJECTIVE** The **Roman Catholic** Church is the same as the **Catholic** Church. ❑ *I am a Roman Catholic priest.*

2 **NOUN** A **Roman Catholic** is the same as a **Catholic**. ❑ *Maria was a Roman Catholic.*

ro|mance /roʊmæns, roʊmæns/ (**romances**)

1 **NOUN** A **romance** is a relationship between two people who love each other but who are not married. ❑ *After a short romance they got married.*

2 **NOUN** LANGUAGE ARTS A **romance** is a book or a movie about a romantic relationship. ❑ *Claire writes romances and young adult fiction.*

ro|man|tic /roʊmæntɪk/ **ADJECTIVE** You use **romantic** when you are talking about love and romance. ❑ *He was not interested in a romantic relationship with me.* ❑ *It is a lovely romantic movie.*
→ look at **movie**

roof /ruf/ (**roofs**)

> **PRONUNCIATION HELP**
> Pronounce the plural /rufs/ or /ruvz/.

1 **NOUN** The **roof** of a building is the top surface that covers it. ❑ *The house has a red roof.*

2 **NOUN** The **roof** of a vehicle is the top of it. ❑ *He listened to the rain on the roof of the car.*

room /rum/ (**rooms**)

1 **NOUN** A **room** is a separate area inside a building that has its own walls. ❑ *A minute later he left the room.*

2 **NONCOUNT NOUN** If there is **room** somewhere, there is enough empty space. ❑ *There is room for 80 guests.*
→ look at **house**

room|mate /rummeɪt/ (**roommates**) **NOUN** Your **roommate** is the person you share a room or an apartment with. ❑ *Dan and I were roommates in college.*

roost|er /rustər/ (**roosters**) **NOUN** A rooster is an adult male chicken.
→ look at **bird**

root /rut/ (**roots**) **NOUN** The **roots** of a plant are the parts of it that grow under the ground. ❑ *She dug a hole near the roots of an apple tree.*
→ look at **tree**

rope /roʊp/ (**ropes**) **NOUN** A **rope** is a type of very thick string that is made by twisting together several strings or wires. ❑ *He tied the rope around his waist.*

rose /roʊz/ (**roses**)

1 **Rose** is a form of the verb **rise**.

2 **NOUN** A **rose** is a flower with a pleasant smell. It has sharp points (= thorns) on its stems.

rot /rɒt/ (**rots, rotting, rotted**) **VERB** When food, wood, or another substance **rots**, it gets old and becomes softer, and sometimes smells bad. ❑ *The grain will start to rot after the rain.*

ro|tate /roʊteɪt/ (**rotates, rotating, rotated**) **VERB** When something **rotates**, it turns in a circle around a central line or point. ❑ *The Earth rotates every 24 hours.* ● **ro|ta|tion** /roʊteɪʃᵊn/ (**rotations**) **NOUN** ❑ *We learned about the daily rotation of the Earth.*
→ look at **earth**

rot|ten /rɒtᵊn/

1 **ADJECTIVE** If food, wood, or another substance is **rotten**, it has become old and soft, and sometimes smells bad. ❑ *The smell was very strong—like rotten eggs.*

2 **ADJECTIVE** If something is **rotten**, it is very unpleasant or bad. [INFORMAL] ❑ *I think it's a rotten idea.*

rough /rʌf/ (**rougher, roughest**)

1 **ADJECTIVE** If a surface is **rough**, it is not smooth or even. ❑ *His hands were rough.*

2 **ADJECTIVE** You say that people or their actions are **rough** when they use too much force. ❑ *Football's a rough game.* ● **rough|ly** **ADVERB** ❑ *They roughly pushed past him.*

3 **ADJECTIVE** A **rough** idea or guess is not exact or complete. ❑ *This is a rough guess of how much gas we need.* ● **rough|ly** **ADVERB** ❑ *Cancer kills roughly half a million people a year.*
→ look at **sense**

round /raʊnd/ (**rounds, rounder, roundest**)

1 **ADJECTIVE** Something that is **round** is shaped like a circle or ball. ❑ *She has a round face.*

R

2 **NOUN** In sports, a **round** is one game or a part of a competition. ❑ *The team went through to the fifth round of the competition.* ❑ *On Sundays, he has a round of golf at the club.*
→ look at **earth**

round|ed /ra͟ʊndɪd/ **ADJECTIVE** Something that is **rounded** is curved in shape, without any points or sharp edges. ❑ *We came to a low, rounded hill.*

round trip (round trips) **NOUN** If you make a **round trip**, you travel to a place and then back again. ❑ *The train makes the 2,400-mile round trip every week.*

route /ru͟t, ra͟ʊt/ (routes) **NOUN** A **route** is a way from one place to another. ❑ *Which is the most direct route to the center of the town?*
→ look at Word World: **route**

rou|tine /ruti͟n/ (routines) **NOUN** Your **routine** is the usual activities that you do every day. ❑ *The players changed their daily routine.*

Word Partners	Use **routine** with:
ADJ.	**daily** routine, **normal** routine, **regular** routine, **usual** routine
N.	**exercise** routine, **work** routine

row /ro͟ʊ/ (rows, rowing, rowed)
1 **NOUN** A **row** is a line of things or people. ❑ *They drove past a row of pretty little houses.*
2 **VERB** SPORTS When you **row**, you make a boat move through the water by using oars (= long pieces of wood with flat ends). ❑ *We rowed across the lake.*

row|boat /ro͟ʊboʊt/ (rowboats) **NOUN** A **rowboat** is a small boat that you move through the water by using oars (= long pieces of wood with flat ends).

roy|al /rɔ͟ɪəl/ **ADJECTIVE** **Royal** means to do with a king or queen. ❑ *We have an invitation to a royal garden party.*

roy|al|ty /rɔ͟ɪəlti/ **NONCOUNT NOUN** You sometimes use **royalty** when you are talking about the members of royal families. ❑ *He met royalty and government leaders from around the world.*

rub /rʌ͟b/ (rubs, rubbing, rubbed)
1 **VERB** If you **rub** something, you move a cloth or your fingers backward and forward over it. ❑ *He rubbed his stiff legs.* ❑ *She took off her glasses and rubbed them with a soft cloth.*
2 **VERB** If you **rub** a substance **into** a surface, you spread it over the surface using your hand. ❑ *He rubbed oil into my back.*
3 **VERB** If you **rub** two things **together**, they move backward and forward, and press against each other. ❑ *He rubbed his hands together.*

rub|ber /rʌ͟bər/ **NONCOUNT NOUN** **Rubber** is a strong substance used for making tires, boots, and other products. ❑ *I can smell burning rubber.*

rub|ber band (rubber bands) **NOUN** A **rubber band** is a thin circle of rubber that you put around things such as papers in order to keep them together. ❑ *Her blonde hair was tied back with a rubber band.*
→ look at **office**

ruby /ru͟bi/ (rubies) **NOUN** A **ruby** is a dark red stone that is used in jewelry. ❑ *I want a ruby ring.*

rude /ru͟d/ (ruder, rudest)
1 **ADJECTIVE** When people are **rude**, they are not polite. ❑ *He's so rude to her friends.*
● **rude|ly** **ADVERB** ❑ *Some hotel guests treat our employees rudely.* ● **rude|ness** **NONCOUNT NOUN** ❑ *Mom was annoyed at Cathy's rudeness.*
2 **ADJECTIVE** **Rude** words and behavior are likely to embarrass or offend people. ❑ *Fred keeps telling rude jokes.*

r

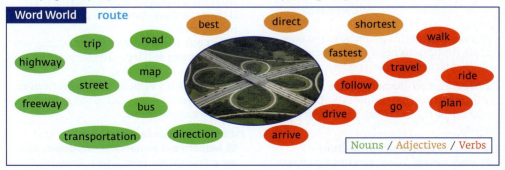

Word World route

best · direct · shortest · walk · trip · road · highway · map · fastest · street · travel · ride · freeway · bus · follow · go · plan · drive · transportation · direction · arrive

Nouns / Adjectives / Verbs

rug /rʌg/ (rugs) **NOUN** A rug is a piece of thick cloth that you put on a small area of a floor. ❑ *There was a beautiful red rug on the floor.*
→ look at **furniture**

rug|by /rʌgbi/ **NONCOUNT NOUN** SPORTS Rugby or rugby football is a game that is played by two teams who try to get a ball past a line at the end of the field.

ruin /ruɪn/ (ruins, ruining, ruined)
1 **VERB** To ruin something means to completely harm, damage, or spoil it. ❑ *My wife was ruining her health.*
2 **PLURAL NOUN** The ruins of a building are the parts of it that remain after something destroys the rest. ❑ *Police found two bodies in the ruins of the house.*
3 If a place is **in ruins**, only parts of it remain. ❑ *The church was in ruins.*
→ look at **pollution**

rule /rul/ (rules, ruling, ruled)
1 **NOUN** Rules are instructions that tell you what you must do or must not do. ❑ *I need a book that explains the rules of basketball.*
2 **VERB** The person or group that rules a country controls its affairs. ❑ *King Hussein ruled for 46 years.*
3 If you **rule out** a course of action, an idea, or a solution, you decide that it is impossible or not practical.
→ look at **grammar**

rul|er /rulər/ (rulers)
1 **NOUN** SOCIAL STUDIES The ruler of a country is the person who rules it. ❑ *He was the ruler of France at that time.*
2 **NOUN** MATH A ruler is a long, flat object that you use for measuring things and for drawing straight lines.
→ look at **measurement**

rum|ble /rʌmbᵊl/ (rumbles, rumbling, rumbled)
1 **NOUN** A rumble is a low, continuous noise. ❑ *We could hear the distant rumble of traffic.*
2 **VERB** If something rumbles, it makes a low, continuous noise. ❑ *Her stomach was rumbling because she did not eat breakfast.*

ru|mor /rumər/ (rumors) **NOUN** A rumor is information that people talk about, that may not be true. ❑ *There's a rumor that you're leaving.*

run /rʌn/ (runs, running, ran, run)
1 **VERB** SPORTS When you run, you move

very quickly on your legs. ❑ *It's very dangerous to run across the road.*
2 **NOUN** Run is also a noun. ❑ *After a six-mile run, Jackie went home for breakfast.* ● **run|ning** **NONCOUNT NOUN** ❑ *He goes running every morning.*
3 **VERB** If a road runs in a particular direction, it goes in that direction. ❑ *The road runs east from Highway 6 to Crownpoint.*
4 **VERB** If you run your hand **through** something, you move your hand through it. ❑ *He ran his fingers through his hair.*
5 **VERB** If you run a business or an activity, you are in charge of it. ❑ *She runs a restaurant in San Francisco.*
6 **VERB** When a machine **is running**, it is switched on and is working. ❑ *Sam waited in the car, with the engine running.*
7 **VERB** When vehicles run from one place to another, they take passengers between those two places. ❑ *A bus runs between the station and downtown.*
8 **VERB** If a liquid runs in a particular direction, it flows in that direction. ❑ *Tears were running down her cheeks.*
9 **NOUN** SPORTS A run is one point in the game of baseball. ❑ *The Blue Jays have scored 173 runs in their past 24 games.*
10 You use **in the long run**, to say what you think will happen over a long period of time in the future. ❑ *Spending more on education now will save money in the long run.*
→ look at **fitness**
▶ **run away** If you **run away**, you leave a place because you are unhappy or afraid there. ❑ *The girl turned and ran away.*
▶ **run into** **1** If you **run into** someone, you meet them unexpectedly. ❑ *He ran into William in the supermarket.*
2 If a vehicle **runs into** something, it hits it. ❑ *The driver was going too fast and ran into a tree.*
▶ **run off** If someone **runs off**, they go away from a place when they should stay there. ❑ *Our dog is always running off.* ❑ *The thief ran off with her purse.*
▶ **run out** If you **run out of** something, you have no more of it left. ❑ *We ran out of milk this morning.*
▶ **run over** If a vehicle **runs** someone **over**, it hits them and they fall to the ground. ❑ *A police car ran her over.*

run-down /rʌn daʊn/
1 **ADJECTIVE** If someone is **run-down**, they are tired or slightly sick. [INFORMAL]

2 **ADJECTIVE** A **run-down** building or area is in very bad condition. ❑ *He promised financial help for run-down areas.*

rung /rʌŋ/ (**rungs**)
1 **Rung** is a form of the verb **ring**.
2 **NOUN** The **rungs** of a ladder are the steps that you climb up.

run|ner /rʌnər/ (**runners**) **NOUN** **SPORTS**
A **runner** is a person who runs, or who is running. ❑ *He is the oldest runner in the race.*

runner-up (**runners-up**) **NOUN** A **runner-up** is the person who is in second place in a race or competition. ❑ *The runner-up will receive $500.*

run|ny /rʌni/ (**runnier, runniest**)
1 **ADJECTIVE** Something that is **runny** has more liquid than usual. ❑ *Warm the jelly until it is runny.*
2 **ADJECTIVE** If someone has a **runny** nose, a thick liquid flows from their nose.

run|way /rʌnweɪ/ (**runways**) **NOUN**
A **runway** is a long road that an aircraft travels on before it starts flying.

ru|ral /rʊərəl/ **ADJECTIVE** **Rural** places are not near cities or large towns. ❑ *The service is ideal for people who live in rural areas.*

rush /rʌʃ/ (**rushes, rushing, rushed**)
1 **VERB** If you **rush** somewhere, you go there quickly. ❑ *Emma rushed into the room.*
2 **VERB** If people **rush to** do something, they do it quickly. ❑ *Foreign banks rushed to buy as many dollars as they could.*
3 If you do something **in a rush**, you need to do it quickly. ❑ *The men left in a rush.*
4 **VERB** If you **rush** someone to a place, you take them there quickly. ❑ *They rushed him to a hospital.*

rush hour (**rush hours**) **NOUN** The **rush hour** is a period of the day when most people are traveling to or from their job. ❑ *Try to avoid traveling during the evening rush hour.*

rust /rʌst/ (**rusts, rusting, rusted**)
1 **NONCOUNT NOUN** **Rust** is a red-brown substance that forms on iron or steel when it is wet. ❑ *The old car was red with rust.*
2 **VERB** When a metal object **rusts**, rust starts to appear on it. ❑ *Iron rusts.*

rus|tle /rʌsəl/ (**rustles, rustling, rustled**)
1 **VERB** When something thin and dry **rustles**, it makes soft sounds as it moves. ❑ *The leaves rustled in the wind.*
2 **NOUN** **Rustle** is also a noun. ❑ *We listened to the rustle of leaves outside.*

rusty /rʌsti/ (**rustier, rustiest**) **ADJECTIVE**
A **rusty** metal object has some rust on it. ❑ *The house has a rusty iron gate.*

rut /rʌt/ (**ruts**)
1 **NOUN** If someone is **in a rut**, he or she has a particular way of doing things that is difficult to change. ❑ *I don't like being in a rut.*
2 **NOUN** A **rut** is a deep, narrow mark that the wheels of a vehicle make in the ground. ❑ *He drove slowly over the ruts in the road.*

ruth|less /ruːθlɪs/ **ADJECTIVE** If someone is **ruthless**, they are so determined to do something that they do not care if their actions harm other people. ❑ *...a ruthless dictator.*

rye /raɪ/ **NONCOUNT NOUN** **Rye** is a grain that you can use to make flour, bread, or other foods.
→ look at **bread**

r

Ss

sack /sæk/ (sacks) **NOUN** A **sack** is a large bag made of thick paper or rough material. ❑ ...a sack of potatoes.

sa|cred /seɪkrɪd/ **ADJECTIVE** Something that is **sacred** has a special religious meaning. ❑ The eagle is sacred to Native Americans.

sac|ri|fice /sækrɪfaɪs/ (sacrifices, sacrificing, sacrificed)

1 VERB If you **sacrifice** something that is valuable or important, you give it up in order to get something else for yourself or for other people. ❑ She sacrificed family life for her career.

2 NOUN Sacrifice is also a noun. ❑ The family made many sacrifices so that they could send the children to a good school.

3 VERB To **sacrifice** an animal or a person means to kill them in a special religious ceremony in order to say thank you to a god. ❑ The priest sacrificed a chicken.

sad /sæd/ (sadder, saddest)

1 ADJECTIVE If you are **sad**, you feel unhappy. ❑ I'm sad that Jason's leaving. ● **sad|ly** **ADVERB** ❑ "My girlfriend is moving away," he said sadly. ● **sad|ness** **NONCOUNT NOUN** ❑ I left with a mixture of sadness and joy.

2 ADJECTIVE If something is **sad**, it makes you feel sad. ❑ It was a sad ending to a great story. ❑ I have some sad news for you.

→ look at **feeling**

sad|dle /sæd³l/ (saddles)

1 NOUN A **saddle** is a leather seat that you put on the back of an animal. ❑ He put a saddle on the horse.

2 NOUN A **saddle** is a seat on a bicycle or a motorcycle.

sa|fa|ri /səfɑri/ (safaris) **NOUN** A **safari** is a trip to look at or hunt wild animals. ❑ She went on a seven-day African safari.

safe /seɪf/ (safer, safest, safes)

1 ADJECTIVE Something that is **safe** is not dangerous. ❑ We must try to make our roads safer.

2 ADJECTIVE If you are **safe**, you are not in danger. ❑ Where's Sophie? Is she safe? ● **safe|ly**

ADVERB ❑ "Drive safely," he said, waving goodbye.

3 NOUN A **safe** is a strong metal box with a lock, where you keep money or other valuable things. ❑ Who has the key to the safe?

→ look at **factory**

safe|ty /seɪfti/

1 NONCOUNT NOUN Safety is the state of not being in danger. ❑ We need to improve safety on our roads.

2 ADJECTIVE Safety equipment is intended to make something less dangerous. ❑ There are child safety locks on all the gates.

sag /sæg/ (sags, sagging, sagged) **VERB** When something **sags**, it hangs down loosely or folds in the middle. ❑ The dress won't sag or lose its shape after washing.

said /sɛd/ **Said** is a form of the verb **say**.

sail /seɪl/ (sails, sailing, sailed)

1 NOUN Sails are large pieces of cloth on a boat, that catch the wind and move the boat along.

2 VERB A boat **sails** when it moves over water. ❑ The ferry sails between Seattle and Bremerton.

3 VERB SPORTS If you **sail** a boat, you use its sails to move it across water. ❑ I'd like to buy a big boat and sail around the world.

→ look at **ocean**

sail|boat /seɪlboʊt/ (sailboats) **NOUN** SPORTS A **sailboat** is a boat with sails.

sail|ing /seɪlɪŋ/ **NONCOUNT NOUN** SPORTS Sailing is the activity or sport of sailing boats. ❑ There was swimming and sailing on the lake.

S

sail|or /seɪlər/ (**sailors**) NOUN A **sailor** is someone who works on a ship or sails a boat.

saint /seɪnt/ (**saints**) NOUN In certain religions, a **saint** is someone who has died, and whose life was a perfect example of the way people should live. ❑ *Every church here was named after a saint.*

sake /seɪk/ (**sakes**)
1 If you do something **for the sake of** something or someone, you do it because of them. ❑ *For the sake of peace, I am willing to forgive them.* ❑ *They stayed together for the sake of the children.*
2 If you do something **for** something's or someone's **sake**, you do it to help them or because of them. ❑ *For safety's sake, never stand directly behind a horse.* ❑ *Please do a good job, for Stan's sake.*

sal|ad /sæləd/ (**salads**) NOUN A **salad** is a mixture of foods, especially vegetables, that you usually serve cold. ❑ *She ordered a pasta and a green salad.*

sala|ry /sæləri/ (**salaries**) NOUN A **salary** is the money that you earn from your employer. ❑ *The lawyer was paid a huge salary.*

Sound Partners	sale, sail

sale /seɪl/ (**sales**)
1 NOUN The **sale** of something is the act of selling it for money. ❑ *He made a lot of money from the sale of the business.*
2 NOUN A **sale** is a time when a store sells things at less than their normal price. ❑ *Did you know the book store was having a sale?*
3 If something is **for sale**, it is available for people to buy. ❑ *The house had a "For Sale" sign in the yard.*
4 Products that are **on sale** are available for less than their normal price. ❑ *She bought the coat on sale at a department store.*
→ look at **shopping**

sales clerk (**sales clerks**) also **salesclerk** NOUN A **sales clerk** is a person who works in a store and sells things to customers.

sales|man /seɪlzmən/ (**salesmen**) NOUN A **salesman** is a man whose job is to sell things. ❑ *He's an insurance salesman.*

sales|person /seɪlzpɜrsᵊn/ (**salespeople** or **salespersons**) NOUN A **salesperson** is a person whose job is to sell things. ❑ *Be sure to ask the salesperson for help.*

sales|woman /seɪlzwʊmən/ (**saleswomen**) NOUN A **saleswoman** is a woman whose job is to sell things. ❑ *She spent three years as a traveling perfume saleswoman.*

sa|li|va /səlaɪvə/ NONCOUNT NOUN SCIENCE **Saliva** is the liquid in your mouth that helps you to swallow food.

salm|on /sæmən/ (**salmon**)
1 NOUN A **salmon** is a large fish with silver skin.
2 NONCOUNT NOUN **Salmon** is the pink flesh of this fish that you can eat. ❑ *He gave them a plate of salmon.*

sa|lon /səlɑn/ (**salons**) NOUN A **salon** is a place where you go to have your hair cut, or to have beauty treatments. ❑ *The club has a beauty salon and two swimming pools.*

salt /sɔlt/ NONCOUNT NOUN **Salt** is a white substance that you use to improve the flavor of food. ❑ *Now add salt and pepper.*

salty /sɔlti/ (**saltier, saltiest**) ADJECTIVE Something that is **salty** has salt in it or tastes of salt. ❑ *Ham and bacon are salty foods.*
→ look at **food, ocean, sense**

sa|lute /səlut/ (**salutes, saluting, saluted**)
1 VERB If you **salute** someone, you make a special sign to show your respect for them. Soldiers usually do this by raising their right hand to their head. ❑ *I saluted as the captain entered the room.*
2 NOUN **Salute** is also a noun. ❑ *He gave his salute and left.*

same /seɪm/
1 ADJECTIVE If two or more things are **the same**, they are very similar to each other in some way. ❑ *The houses are all the same.*
2 ADJECTIVE You use **same** to show that you are talking about only one thing, and not two different ones. ❑ *Jayden works at the same office as Gabrielle.* ❑ *He gets up at the same time every day.*

sam|ple /sæmpᵊl/ (**samples**) NOUN A **sample** is a small amount of something that shows you what the rest of it is like. ❑ *We're giving away 2,000 free samples.* ❑ *The doctor took a blood sample.*

sand /sænd/ NONCOUNT NOUN SCIENCE **Sand** is a powder made of very small

s

pieces of stone. Some deserts and most beaches are made of sand. ❑ *They walked across the sand to the water's edge.*
→ look at **beach**

san|dal /sænd³l/ (**sandals**) NOUN Sandals are light shoes that you wear in warm weather. ❑ *He put on a pair of old sandals.*

sand|wich /sænwɪtʃ, sænd-/ (**sandwiches**) NOUN A **sandwich** is two slices of bread with another food such as cheese or meat between them. ❑ *She ordered a ham sandwich.*

sandy /sændi/ (**sandier, sandiest**) ADJECTIVE A **sandy** area is covered with sand. ❑ *The island has long, sandy beaches.*

sane /seɪn/ (**saner, sanest**) ADJECTIVE Someone who is **sane** can think and behave normally and reasonably, and is not mad. ❑ *He seemed perfectly sane.*

sang /sæŋ/ **Sang** is a form of the verb **sing**.

sank /sæŋk/ **Sank** is a form of the verb **sink**.

sar|casm /sɑrkæzəm/ NONCOUNT NOUN If you say something with **sarcasm**, you say the opposite of what you mean in order to be rude to someone. ❑ *"How nice of you to join us,"*
he said with heavy sarcasm.

sar|cas|tic /sɑrkæstɪk/ ADJECTIVE If you say something in a **sarcastic** way, you say the opposite of what you really mean in order to be rude to someone. ❑ *He made some very sarcastic comments.*

sar|dine /sɑrdin/ (**sardines**) NOUN Sardines are small sea fish that you can eat. ❑ *They opened a can of sardines.*

sat /sæt/ **Sat** is a form of the verb **sit**.

sat|el|lite /sæt³laɪt/ (**satellites**)
1 NOUN TECHNOLOGY A **satellite** is a piece of electronic equipment that is sent into space in order to receive and send back information. ❑ *The rocket carried two communications satellites.*
2 ADJECTIVE Satellite navigation is a system that uses information from a satellite to help you to find your way. ❑ *Many of the boats have satellite navigation.*
→ look at **space**

sat|el|lite dish (**satellite dishes**) NOUN TECHNOLOGY A **satellite dish** is a piece of equipment that people put on their house in order to receive television signals from a satellite.

sat|el|lite tele|vi|sion NONCOUNT NOUN TECHNOLOGY **Satellite television** is a system of broadcasting television programs that are sent to your television from a satellite (= an object that moves around the Earth in space). ❑ *We have access to 49 satellite television channels.*
→ look at **television**

sat|in /sæt³n/ NONCOUNT NOUN Satin is a smooth, shiny type of cloth. ❑ *She's wearing a satin dress.*

sat|ire /sætaɪər/ (**satires**)
1 NONCOUNT NOUN Satire is the use of humor to criticize people's behavior or ideas. ❑ *He loved the book's humor and satire.*
2 NOUN LANGUAGE ARTS A **satire** is a play, a movie, or a piece of writing that uses humor to criticize people's behavior or ideas. ❑ *The movie is a satire on American politics.*

sat|is|fac|tion /sætɪsfækʃ³n/ NONCOUNT NOUN If you feel **satisfaction**, you feel pleased to do or get something. ❑ *It gives me a real sense of satisfaction when I help someone.*

sat|is|fac|tory /sætɪsfæktəri/ ADJECTIVE Something that is **satisfactory** is good enough for a particular purpose. ❑ *I never got a satisfactory answer.*

sat|is|fied /sætɪsfaɪd/ ADJECTIVE If you are **satisfied with** something, you are happy because you have what you wanted. ❑ *Doctors are satisfied with his condition.*

sat|is|fy /sætɪsfaɪ/ (**satisfies, satisfying, satisfied**) VERB If someone or something **satisfies** you, they give you enough of what you want or need. ❑ *Milk alone should satisfy your baby's hunger.*

sat|is|fy|ing /sætɪsfaɪɪŋ/ ADJECTIVE Something that is **satisfying** makes you feel happy because it is what you want. ❑ *Taking care of children can be very satisfying.*

Sat|ur|day /sætərdeɪ, -di/ (**Saturdays**) NOUN Saturday is the day after Friday and before Sunday. ❑ *He called her on Saturday morning.* ❑ *Every Saturday, Dad made soup.*

sauce /sɔs/ (**sauces**) NOUN A **sauce** is a thick liquid that you eat with other food. ❑ *The pasta is cooked in a garlic and tomato sauce.*

sauce|pan /sɔspæn/ (**saucepans**) NOUN A **saucepan** is a deep metal cooking pot, usually with a long handle and a lid. ❑ *Place the potatoes in a saucepan and boil them.*

S

sau|cer /sɔsər/ (saucers) NOUN A **saucer** is a small curved plate that you put under a cup.

sau|na /sɔnə/ (saunas) NOUN A **sauna** is a very hot room that is filled with steam, where people relax. ❏ *The hotel has a sauna and a swimming pool.*

sau|sage /sɔsɪdʒ/ (sausages) NOUN A **sausage** is a mixture of very small pieces of meat, spices, and other foods, inside a long thin skin. ❏ *They ate sausages for breakfast.*

sav|age /sævɪdʒ/ ADJECTIVE Someone or something that is **savage** is very cruel or violent. ❏ *This was a savage attack on a young girl.*

save /seɪv/ (saves, saving, saved)
1 VERB If you **save** someone or something, you help them to escape from a dangerous or bad situation. ❏ *We must save these children from disease and death.*
2 VERB If you **save**, you gradually collect money by spending less than you get. ❏ *Tim and Barbara are now saving for a house.* ❏ *I was saving money to go to college.*
3 **Save up** means the same as **save**. ❏ *Taylor was saving up for something special.*
4 VERB If you **save** time or money, you use less of it. ❏ *Going through the city by bike saves time.* ❏ *We're trying to save water.*
5 VERB If you **save** something, you keep it because you will need it later. ❏ *Save the vegetable water for making the sauce.*
6 VERB TECHNOLOGY If you **save** information in a computer, you give the computer an instruction to store the information. ❏ *It's important to save frequently when you are working on a document.*
7 NOUN SPORTS In a sports game, if you make a **save**, you stop someone from scoring a goal. ❏ *The goalkeeper made some great saves.*
→ look at **conservation, earth, email, energy**

sav|ings /seɪvɪŋz/ PLURAL NOUN Your **savings** are the money that you have saved, especially in a bank. ❏ *Her savings were in the First National Bank.*

sa|vory /seɪvəri/ ADJECTIVE **Savory** food has a salty flavor rather than a sweet one. ❏ *We had all sorts of sweet and savory breads.*

saw /sɔ/ (saws, sawing, sawed, sawed or sawn)
1 **Saw** is a form of the verb **see**.
2 NOUN A **saw** is a metal tool for cutting wood.
3 VERB If you **saw** something, you cut it with a saw. ❏ *He escaped by sawing through the*

bars of his jail cell. ❏ *I sawed the dead branches off the tree.*

saxo|phone /sæksəfoʊn/ (saxophones) NOUN MUSIC A **saxophone** is a musical instrument made of metal that you play by blowing into it.
→ look at **musical instrument**

say /seɪ/ (says /sɛz/, saying, said /sɛd/)
1 VERB When you **say** something, you speak words. ❏ *She said that they were very pleased.* ❏ *I packed and said goodbye to Charlie.*
2 NOUN If you have a **say in** something, you have the right to give your opinion. ❏ *He has the right to have a say in the decisions that affect his life.*
3 VERB If a notice or a clock **says** something, it gives information in writing or numbers. ❏ *The clock said four minutes past eleven.*
→ look at **communication**

say|ing /seɪɪŋ/ (sayings) NOUN A **saying** is something that people often say, that gives advice about life. ❏ *Remember that old saying: "Forgive and forget."*

scab /skæb/ (scabs) NOUN A **scab** is a hard, dry cover that forms over the surface of a wound. ❏ *After a few days, the spots become dry and form scabs.*

scaf|fold|ing /skæfəldɪŋ/ NONCOUNT NOUN **Scaffolding** is a frame of metal bars that people can stand on when they are working on the outside of a building. ❏ *Builders have put up scaffolding around the tower.*

scald /skɔld/ (scalds, scalding, scalded) VERB If you **scald yourself**, you burn yourself with very hot liquid or steam. ❏ *A patient scalded herself in the bath.*

scale /skeɪl/ (scales)
1 NOUN A **scale** is a machine that you use for weighing people or things. ❏ *He weighed himself on a bathroom scale.*
2 NOUN The **scale** of something is the size or level of it. ❏ *He doesn't realize the scale of the problem.*
3 NOUN A **scale** is a set of levels or numbers that you use to measure things. ❏ *The earthquake measured 5.5 on the Richter scale.*
4 NOUN SCIENCE **Scales** are small, flat pieces of hard skin that cover the body of animals like fish and snakes.
5 MUSIC A **scale** is a set of musical notes that are played in a fixed order. ❏ *...the scale of F major.* ❏ *Celia was practicing her scales on the piano.*

s

scal|lion /skǽlyən/ (**scallions**) NOUN
A **scallion** is a small onion with long green leaves.

scalp /skǽlp/ (**scalps**) NOUN SCIENCE Your **scalp** is the skin under the hair on your head. ❑ Try this treatment for beautiful thick hair and a healthy scalp.

scan /skǽn/ (**scans, scanning, scanned**)
1 VERB When you **scan** a piece of writing, you look through it quickly to find important or interesting information. ❑ She scanned the front page of the newspaper.
2 VERB If you **scan** a picture or a document, you make an electronic copy of it using a special piece of equipment (= a scanner). ❑ She scanned the images into her computer.

scan|dal /skǽnd³l/ (**scandals**) NOUN A **scandal** is a situation or an event that people think is shocking. ❑ It was a financial scandal.

scan|ner /skǽnər/ (**scanners**)
1 NOUN A **scanner** is a machine that you use to make an electronic copy of something, such as a picture or a document. ❑ Scan your photos using any desktop scanner.
2 NOUN TECHNOLOGY A **scanner** is a machine that gives a picture of the inside of something. ❑ His bag was passed through the airport X-ray scanner.

scar /skɑr/ (**scars, scarring, scarred**)
1 NOUN A **scar** is a mark that is left on the skin by an old wound. ❑ He had a scar on his forehead.
2 VERB If your skin **is scarred**, it is badly marked because of an old wound. ❑ He was scarred for life during a fight.

scarce /skɛərs/ (**scarcer, scarcest**) ADJECTIVE
If something is **scarce**, there is not enough of it. ❑ Food was scarce and expensive. ❑ Jobs are becoming scarce.
→ look at **water**

scarce|ly /skɛərsli/ ADVERB You use **scarcely** to emphasize that something is only just true. ❑ He could scarcely breathe.

scare /skɛər/ (**scares, scaring, scared**)
1 VERB If something **scares** you, it frightens or worries you. ❑ The thought of failure scares me.
2 NOUN If a sudden, unpleasant experience gives you a **scare**, it frightens you. ❑ You gave us a terrible scare!
3 NOUN A **scare** is a situation where many people are afraid or worried about something. ❑ The new drug was the subject of a recent health scare.

scared /skɛərd/ ADJECTIVE If you are **scared** of someone or something, you are frightened of them. ❑ I'm not scared of him.
→ look at **feeling**

scarf /skɑrf/ (**scarfs** or **scarves**) NOUN
A **scarf** is a piece of cloth that you wear around your neck or head. ❑ He loosened the scarf around his neck.

scary /skɛəri/ (**scarier, scariest**) ADJECTIVE
Something that is **scary** is frightening. [INFORMAL] ❑ The movie is too scary for children.
→ look at **movie**

scat|ter /skǽtər/ (**scatters, scattering, scattered**) VERB If you **scatter** things over an area, you throw or drop them so that they spread over it. ❑ She scattered the flowers over the grave.

scene /sin/ (**scenes**)
1 NOUN LANGUAGE ARTS A **scene** is a part of a play, a movie, or a book that happens in the same place. ❑ This is the opening scene of "Tom Sawyer."
2 NOUN You can call a place a **scene** when you are describing what is there. ❑ The photographs show scenes of everyday life in the village. ❑ It's a scene of complete horror.
3 NOUN The **scene of** an event is the place where it happened. ❑ Firefighters rushed to the scene of the car accident.

scen|ery /sínəri/
1 NONCOUNT NOUN The **scenery** in a country area is the land, water, or plants that you can see around you. ❑ Most visitors come for the island's beautiful scenery.
2 NONCOUNT NOUN In a theater, the **scenery** is the objects or the backgrounds that show where the action in the play is happening. ❑ The actors will move the scenery themselves.

Sound Partners scent, cent, sent

scent /sɛnt/ (**scents**) NOUN The **scent** of something is the pleasant smell that it has. ❑ This perfume gives off a heavy scent of roses.
● **scent|ed** ADJECTIVE ❑ ...scented soap.

sched|ule /skɛdʒul, -uəl/ (**schedules**)
1 NOUN A **schedule** is a plan that gives a list of the times when things will happen. ❑ For best results, plan a training schedule.
2 NONCOUNT NOUN If something happens

S

scheme 419 **scooter**

behind schedule, it happens after the planned time. ❏ *The project is about three months behind schedule.*
→ look at **calendar, day**

scheme /skim/ (**schemes, scheming, schemed**) **VERB** If people **are scheming**, they are making secret plans to do something. ❏ *The family was scheming to stop the wedding.*

schol|ar /skɒlər/ (**scholars**) **NOUN** A **scholar** is a person who studies an academic subject and knows a lot about it. [FORMAL] ❏ *The library is full of scholars and researchers.*

schol|ar|ship /skɒlərʃɪp/ (**scholarships**) **NOUN** If you win a **scholarship**, you receive money to help you to continue studying. ❏ *He got a scholarship to the Pratt Institute of Art.*

school /skul/ (**schools**)
1 **NOUN** A **school** is a place where people go to learn. ❏ *The school was built in the 1960s.*
2 **NONCOUNT NOUN** You can use **school** to talk about your time in school or college. ❏ *Parents want their kids to do well in school.* ❏ *Jack eventually graduated from school in 1998.*
→ look at Word World: **school**

school|room /skulrum/ (**schoolrooms**) **NOUN** A **schoolroom** is a classroom.

school|teacher /skultitʃər/ (**schoolteachers**) **NOUN** A **schoolteacher** is a teacher in a school.

school|work /skulwɜrk/ **NONCOUNT NOUN** Schoolwork is the work that a child does at school or work that teachers give children to do at home. ❏ *My mother always helps me with my schoolwork.*

school|yard /skulyɑrd/ (**schoolyards**) also **school yard** **NOUN** The **schoolyard** is the large area outside a school building, where the children can play. ❏ *Young children played in a nearby schoolyard.*

sci|ence /saɪəns/ **NONCOUNT NOUN** Science is the study of natural things. ❏ *He studied plant science in college.*
→ look at Word World: **science**

sci|ence fic|tion **NONCOUNT NOUN** Science fiction is stories in books, magazines, and movies about things that happen in the future or in other parts of the universe.

sci|en|tif|ic /saɪəntɪfɪk/ **ADJECTIVE** Scientific means to do with science. ❏ *He spends a lot of time conducting scientific research.*

sci|en|tist /saɪəntɪst/ (**scientists**) **NOUN** A **scientist** is someone whose job is to teach or do research in science. ❏ *Scientists have discovered a new gene.*
→ look at **science**

sci-fi /saɪ faɪ/ **NONCOUNT NOUN** Sci-fi is short for **science fiction**. [INFORMAL] ❏ *It's a two hour sci-fi movie.*

scis|sors /sɪzərz/ **PLURAL NOUN** Scissors are a small tool for cutting with two sharp parts that are joined together. ❏ *Cut the card using scissors.*
→ look at **office**

scold /skoʊld/ (**scolds, scolding, scolded**) **VERB** If you **scold** a person or an animal, you speak to them in an angry way because they have done something wrong. [FORMAL] ❏ *I could hear Barbara scolding the puppies outside.* ❏ *I scolded myself for talking so much.*

scoop /skup/ (**scoops, scooping, scooped**) **VERB** If you **scoop** something from a container, you remove it with your hand or with a spoon. ❏ *He was scooping dog food out of a can.*
▶ **scoop up** If you **scoop** something **up**, you put your hands under it and lift it. ❏ *Use both hands to scoop up the leaves.*

scoot|er /skutər/ (**scooters**)
1 **NOUN** A **scooter** is a small light motorcycle with a low seat.

s

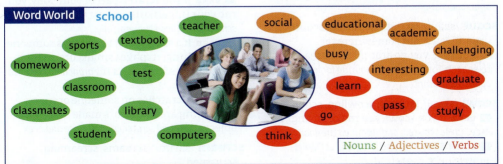

Word World **school**

Nouns / Adjectives / Verbs

teacher · social · educational · academic · sports · textbook · busy · challenging · homework · interesting · classroom · test · learn · graduate · classmates · library · pass · study · student · computers · go · think

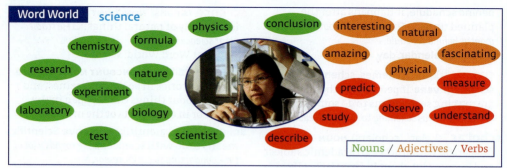

Word World   science

Nouns / Adjectives / Verbs

physics · conclusion · interesting · natural · chemistry · formula · amazing · fascinating · research · nature · physical · measure · experiment · predict · laboratory · biology · observe · understand · study · test · scientist · describe

---

2 **NOUN** A **scooter** is a child's vehicle with a long handle and two wheels joined by a long board.

scorch /skɔrtʃ/ (**scorches, scorching, scorched**) **VERB** To **scorch** something means to burn it slightly. ❑ *Many of my plants were scorched by the sun.*

score /skɔr/ (**scores, scoring, scored**)
1 **VERB** SPORTS In a sport or a game, if a player **scores** a goal or a point, they get a goal or a point. ❑ *Patten scored his second goal of the game.*
2 **VERB** If you **score** a particular amount on a test, you achieve that amount. ❑ *Kelly scored 88 on the test.*
3 **NOUN** Someone's **score** in a game or on a test is the number of points they have won. ❑ *Hogan won, with a score of 287.*
4 **NOUN** SPORTS The **score** in a game is the result. ❑ *The final score was 4–1.*

scorn /skɔrn/ **NONCOUNT NOUN** If you treat someone or something **with scorn**, you show that you do not like or respect them. ❑ *Her words attracted scorn and anger.*

scorn|ful /skɔrnfəl/ **ADJECTIVE** If you are **scornful of** someone or something, you show that you do not like or respect them. ❑ *He is deeply scornful of politicians.*
● **scorn|ful|ly** **ADVERB** ❑ *They laughed scornfully at his suggestion.*

scout /skaʊt/ (**scouts, scouting, scouted**) **VERB** If you **scout** somewhere **for** something, you go around that area in order to search for it. ❑ *She's scouting for locations to open a restaurant.*

scowl /skaʊl/ (**scowls, scowling, scowled**)
1 **VERB** If you **scowl**, you make an angry face. ❑ *He scowled, and slammed the door.*
2 **NOUN** **Scowl** is also a noun. ❑ *Daniel answered with a scowl.*

scram|ble /skræmbəl/ (**scrambles, scrambling, scrambled**)
1 **VERB** If you **scramble** over rocks or up a hill, you move quickly over them or up it, using your hands to help you. ❑ *Tourists were scrambling over the rocks to the beach.*
2 **VERB** If you **scramble** eggs, you break them, mix them together, and then cook them. ❑ *Make the toast and scramble the eggs.*
● **scram|bled** **ADJECTIVE** ❑ *We're having scrambled eggs and bacon.*

scrap /skræp/ (**scraps, scrapping, scrapped**)
1 **NOUN** A **scrap of** something is a very small piece or amount of it. ❑ *A scrap of red paper was found in her handbag.*
2 **VERB** If you **scrap** something, you get rid of it or cancel it. ❑ *The government has scrapped plans to build a new airport.*

scrape /skreɪp/ (**scrapes, scraping, scraped**)
1 **VERB** If you **scrape** a part of your body, you accidentally rub it against something hard and rough, and damage it slightly. ❑ *She fell, scraping her hands and knees.*
2 **VERB** If you **scrape** something from a surface, you remove it by moving a sharp object over the surface. ❑ *She scraped the frost off the car windows.*

scratch /skrætʃ/ (**scratches, scratching, scratched**)
1 **VERB** If you **scratch** part of your body, you rub your fingernails against your skin. ❑ *He scratched his head thoughtfully.*
2 **VERB** If a sharp object **scratches** someone or something, it makes small cuts on their skin or on its surface. ❑ *The branches scratched my face.*
3 **NOUN** **Scratches** on someone or something are small cuts made by a sharp object. ❑ *He had scratches on his face and neck.*

scream /skrim/ (**screams, screaming, screamed**)

1 **VERB** When you **scream**, you give a loud, high cry because you are hurt or frightened. ❏ *Women were screaming in the houses nearest the fire.*
2 **NOUN** Scream is also a noun. ❏ *Rose gave a loud scream.*

screech /skritʃ/ (**screeches, screeching, screeched**) **VERB** If a vehicle **screeches**, its tires make an unpleasant high sound on the road. ❏ *Two police cars screeched into the parking lot.*

screen /skrin/ (**screens**)
1 **NOUN** A **screen** is a flat surface on a piece of electronic equipment, such as a television or a computer, where you see pictures or words.
2 **NOUN** A **screen** is the flat area on the wall of a movie theater, where you see the movie. ❏ *The theater has 20 screens.*
→ look at **ATM, classroom, computer**

screen|saver /skrinseɪvər/ (**screensavers**) **NOUN** TECHNOLOGY A **screensaver** is a moving picture that appears on a computer screen when the computer is not being used.

screw /skru/ (**screws, screwing, screwed**)
1 **NOUN** A **screw** is a small metal object with a sharp end, that you use to join things together. ❏ *Each shelf is attached to the wall with screws.*
2 **VERB** If you **screw** something somewhere, you join it to another thing using a screw. ❏ *I screwed the shelf on the wall myself.*

screw|driver /skrudraɪvər/ (**screwdrivers**) **NOUN** A **screwdriver** is a tool that you use for turning screws.

scrib|ble /skrɪbᵊl/ (**scribbles, scribbling, scribbled**) **VERB** If you **scribble** something, you write or draw it quickly and roughly. ❏ *She scribbled a note to Mom.*

script /skrɪpt/ (**scripts**) **NOUN** LANGUAGE ARTS A **script** is the written words that actors speak in a play, a movie, or a television program. ❏ *Jenny's writing a movie script.*

scroll /skroʊl/ (**scrolls, scrolling, scrolled**) **VERB** TECHNOLOGY If you **scroll** through text on a computer screen, you move the text up or down to find the information that you need. ❏ *I scrolled down to find "United States of America."*

scrub /skrʌb/ (**scrubs, scrubbing, scrubbed**) **VERB** If you **scrub** something, you rub it hard in order to clean it. ❏ *Surgeons must scrub their hands and arms with soap and water.*

scruffy /skrʌfi/ (**scruffier, scruffiest**) **ADJECTIVE** Someone or something that is **scruffy** is dirty and messy. ❏ *The man was pale, scruffy and unshaven.*

sculp|tor /skʌlptər/ (**sculptors**) **NOUN** ARTS A **sculptor** is an artist who makes solid works of art out of stone, metal, or wood. ❏ *The sculptor carved the swan from a solid block of ice.*

sculp|ture /skʌlptʃər/ (**sculptures**)
1 **NOUN** ARTS A **sculpture** is a piece of art that is made into a shape from a material like stone or wood. ❏ *There were stone sculptures of different animals.*
2 **NONCOUNT NOUN** ARTS Sculpture is the art of creating objects (= sculptures) from a substance like stone or wood. ❏ *Both of them studied sculpture.*

Sound Partners	sea, see

sea /si/ (**seas**) **NOUN** A **sea** is a large area of salty water that is part of an ocean or is surrounded by land. ❏ *They swam in the warm Caribbean Sea.*

Word Partners	Use **sea** with:
PREP.	**above the** sea, **across the** sea, **below the** sea, **beneath the** sea, **by** sea, **from the** sea, **into the** sea, **near the** sea, **over the** sea
N.	sea **air**, sea **coast**, **land and** sea
ADJ.	**calm** sea, **deep** sea

sea|food /sifud/ **NONCOUNT NOUN** Seafood is fish and other small animals from the ocean that you can eat. ❏ *Let's find a seafood restaurant.*
→ look at **food**

sea|gull /sigʌl/ (**seagulls**) **NOUN** A **seagull** is a common type of bird with white or gray feathers that lives near the ocean.

Spelling Partners	**seal**

seal /sil/ (**seals, sealing, sealed**)
1 **VERB** When you **seal** an envelope, you close it by folding part of it and sticking it down. ❏ *He sealed the envelope and put on a stamp.*
2 **NOUN** A **seal** is a large animal with a rounded body and short fur that eats fish and lives near the ocean.

seam /sim/ (**seams**) **NOUN** A **seam** is a line where two pieces of cloth are joined together.

search /sɜrtʃ/ (**searches, searching, searched**)

1 **VERB** If you **search for** something or someone, you look carefully for them. ❏ *Police are already searching for the men.*

2 **VERB** If you **search** a place, you look carefully for something or someone there. ❏ *The police are searching the town for the missing men.*

3 **NOUN** A **search** is an attempt to find something or someone by looking for them carefully. ❏ *The search was stopped because of the heavy snow.*

→ look at **Internet**

search en|gine (**search engines**) **NOUN** TECHNOLOGY A **search engine** is a computer program that you use to search for information on the Internet.

sea|son /sizᵊn/ (**seasons**)

1 **NOUN** The **seasons** are the four parts of a year that have their own typical weather conditions. ❏ *Fall is my favorite season.*

2 **NOUN** You can use **season** to talk about a time each year when something happens. ❏ *The baseball season begins again soon.*

→ look at Word World: **season**

→ look at **climate**

seat /sit/ (**seats**)

1 **NOUN** A **seat** is something that you can sit on. ❏ *We had front-row seats at the concert.* ❏ *The car has comfortable leather seats.*

2 If you **take a seat**, you sit down. [FORMAL] ❏ *"Take a seat," he said.*

seat belt (**seat belts**) **NOUN** A **seat belt** is a long thin belt that you fasten around your body in a vehicle to keep you safe. ❏ *Please fasten your seat belts.*

sea|weed /siwid/ **NONCOUNT NOUN** Seaweed is a plant that grows in the ocean.

❏ *Seaweed is washed up on the beach.*

→ look at **beach, ocean**

sec|ond /sɛkənd/ (**seconds**)

1 **NOUN** MATH A **second** is a measurement of time. There are sixty seconds in one minute. ❏ *For a few seconds, nobody spoke.*

2 **ADJECTIVE** The **second** thing in a series is the one that you count as number two. ❏ *It was the second day of his visit to Florida.*

3 **ADVERB** Second is also an adverb. ❏ *Emma came in second in the race.*

→ look at **job, number, time**

sec|ond|ary /sɛkəndɛri/

1 **ADJECTIVE** If something is **secondary**, it is less important than something else. ❏ *Money is of secondary importance to them.*

2 **ADJECTIVE** **Secondary** education is given to students between the ages of 11 and 18. ❏ *They take examinations after five years of secondary education.*

second-hand /sɛkəndhænd/

1 **ADJECTIVE** **Second-hand** things are not new and have been used by another person. ❏ *They could just afford a second-hand car.*

2 **ADVERB** **Second-hand** is also an adverb. ❏ *They bought the furniture second-hand.*

sec|ond|ly /sɛkəndli/ **ADVERB** You say **secondly** when you want to talk about a second thing, or give a second reason for something. ❏ *Firstly, involve your children in planning the break, and secondly, ask your travel agent for family-friendly suggestions.*

se|cre|cy /sikrəsi/ **NONCOUNT NOUN** Secrecy is a situation in which you do not tell anyone about something. ❏ *They met in complete secrecy.*

se|cret /sikrɪt/ (**secrets**)

1 **ADJECTIVE** If something is **secret**, only a small number of people know about it, and they do not tell anyone else. ❏ *They tried to keep their marriage secret.*

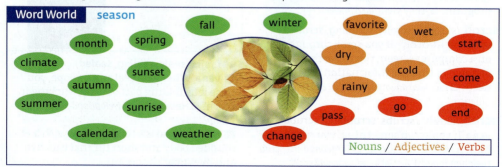

Word World   **season**

fall   winter   favorite   wet   start

month   spring   dry   cold   come

climate   sunset   rainy

autumn   pass   go   end

summer   sunrise

calendar   weather   change

Nouns / Adjectives / Verbs

2 NOUN A **secret** is something that only a small number of people know, and they do not tell anyone else. ❑ *Can you keep a secret?*

sec|re|tar|ial /sɛkrɪtɛəriəl/ **ADJECTIVE**
Secretarial work is typing letters, answering the telephone and other work that is done in an office. ❑ *I was doing temporary secretarial work.*

sec|re|tary /sɛkrɪteri/ (**secretaries**)
1 NOUN A **secretary** is a person whose job is to type letters, answer the telephone, and do other office work.
2 NOUN A **secretary** is a person with an important position in the government. ❑ *The defense secretary will meet with the president tomorrow.*

se|cre|tive /sikrətɪv, sɪkrit-/ **ADJECTIVE**
If you are **secretive**, you do not like to share your knowledge, feelings, or intentions. ❑ *She's very secretive about how much money she has.*

sec|tion /sɛkʃ°n/ (**sections**) **NOUN** A **section** of something is a particular part of it. ❑ *It is wrong to blame one section of society for all these problems.* ❑ *He works in the Georgetown section of Washington, D.C.*

se|cure /sɪkyʊər/
1 ADJECTIVE A **secure** place is well protected, so that people cannot enter it or leave it if you do not want them to. ❑ *We'll make our home as secure as possible.* ● **se|cure|ly** **ADVERB** ❑ *He locked the heavy door securely.*
2 ADJECTIVE If an object is **secure**, it is properly fixed in position. ❑ *The farmer made sure that the fence was always secure.* ● **se|cure|ly** **ADVERB** ❑ *He fastened his belt securely.*
3 ADJECTIVE If a job is **secure**, it will not end soon. ❑ *For the moment, his job is secure.*
4 ADJECTIVE If you feel **secure**, you feel safe and happy, and you are not worried about life. ❑ *She felt secure when she was with him.*
→ look at **email, Internet**

se|cu|rity /sɪkyʊərɪti/
1 NONCOUNT NOUN **Security** is everything that you do to protect a place. ❑ *They are improving airport security.*
2 NONCOUNT NOUN A feeling of **security** is a feeling of being safe and free from worry. ❑ *He loves the security of a happy home life.*

Sound Partners see, sea

see /si/ (**sees, seeing, saw, seen**)
1 VERB When you **see** something, you

notice it using your eyes. ❑ *The fog was so thick we couldn't see anything.* ❑ *Have you seen my keys?*
2 VERB If you **see** someone, you visit or meet them. ❑ *I saw him yesterday.*
3 VERB If you **see** a play, a movie, or a sports game, you watch it. ❑ *Let's go see a movie tonight.*
4 VERB If you **see** something, you understand it. ❑ *Oh, I see what you're saying.*
5 VERB If you **see** something, you find out information or a fact. ❑ *She looked around to see if anyone was listening.*
6 VERB If a person **sees** a particular event, they experience it. ❑ *I have seen many changes here over the past decade.*
7 People say "**I'll see**" or "**We'll see**" to show that they will decide something later. ❑ *"Can we go swimming tomorrow?"—"We'll see. Maybe."*
8 People say "**let's see**" when they are trying to remember something. ❑ *Let's see. Where did I leave my purse?*
9 "**See you**" and "**see you later**" are ways of saying goodbye to someone. [INFORMAL] ❑ *"Talk to you later."—"All right. See you."*
→ look at **movie, news, performance, sense**
▶ **see off** When you **see** someone **off**, you go with someone who is leaving to the station or airport, to say goodbye to them. ❑ *Ben saw Jackie off on her plane.*

seed /sid/ (**seeds**) **NOUN** A **seed** is the small, hard part of a plant from which a new plant grows. ❑ *Plant the seeds in small plastic pots.*
→ look at **fruit**

See|ing Eye dog (**Seeing Eye dogs**) **NOUN**
A **Seeing Eye dog** is a dog that is trained to lead a blind person. [TRADEMARK]
→ look at **disability**

seek /sik/ (**seeks, seeking, sought**) **VERB** If you **seek** something, you try to find it or get it. [FORMAL] ❑ *They are seeking work in hotels and bars.*

seem /sim/ (**seems, seeming, seemed**) **VERB**
If someone or something **seems** a particular way, they give that impression. ❑ *The thunder seemed quite close.* ❑ *They seemed a perfect couple to everyone who knew them.*

seen /sin/ **Seen** is a form of the verb **see**.

seg|ment /sɛgmənt/ (**segments**) **NOUN**
A **segment of** something is one part of it. ❑ *These people come from the poorer segments of society.*
→ look at **fruit**

S

seg|re|ga|tion /sɛgrɪgeɪʃ°n/ **NONCOUNT NOUN** SOCIAL STUDIES **Segregation** is the official practice of separating people, especially based on race or religion. ❑ *The report criticized the racial segregation of students in the school.*

seize /siz/ (**seizes, seizing, seized**) **VERB** If you **seize** something, you take hold of it quickly and firmly. ❑ *He seized my arm and pulled me closer.*

sel|dom /sɛldəm/ **ADVERB** If something **seldom** happens, it does not happen very often. ❑ *They seldom speak to each other.* ❑ *I've seldom felt so happy.*

se|lect /sɪlɛkt/ (**selects, selecting, selected**) **VERB** If you **select** something, you choose it from a group of similar things. ❑ *Only three players were selected for the Olympic team.* ❑ *Select "Save" from the File menu.*

se|lec|tion /sɪlɛkʃ°n/ (**selections**) **NOUN** A **selection** is a set of people or things that someone has chosen, or that you can choose from. ❑ *The singer will perform a selection of his favorite songs.* ❑ *Choose from our selection of fine wines.*

self /sɛlf/ (**selves**) **NOUN** Your **self** is your own personality or nature. ❑ *You're looking like your usual self again.*

self-confident **ADJECTIVE** Someone who is **self-confident** behaves confidently because they feel sure of their abilities or value. ❑ *She's become a very self-confident young woman.* ● **self-confidence** **NONCOUNT NOUN** ❑ *I lost all my self-confidence.*

self-conscious **ADJECTIVE** Someone who is **self-conscious** is easily embarrassed because they feel that everyone is judging them. ❑ *I felt a bit self-conscious in my bikini.*

self-control **NONCOUNT NOUN** **Self-control** is the ability to control yourself and your feelings. ❑ *She was told she must learn self-control.*

self-defense **NONCOUNT NOUN** **Self-defense** is the use of force to protect yourself against someone who is attacking you. ❑ *Use your weapon only in self-defense.*

self-employed **ADJECTIVE** If you are **self-employed**, you work for yourself, rather than for someone else. ❑ *If you are self-employed, it is easy to change the time you start work.*

self|ish /sɛlfɪʃ/ **ADJECTIVE** Someone who is **selfish** cares only about themselves, and not about other people. ❑ *I think I've been very selfish.* ● **self|ish|ly** **ADVERB** ❑ *Someone has selfishly emptied the cookie jar.* ● **self|ish|ness** **NONCOUNT NOUN** ❑ *Julie's selfishness shocked us.*

self-respect **NONCOUNT NOUN** If you have **self-respect** you feel confident about your own ability and value. ❑ *They have lost their jobs, their homes, and their self-respect.*

self-study **NONCOUNT NOUN** **Self-study** is study that you do on your own, without a teacher. ❑ *She's started a self-study course.*

Sound Partners	sell, cell

sell /sɛl/ (**sells, selling, sold**)
1 **VERB** If you **sell** something that you own, you let someone have it in return for money. ❑ *Emily sold the paintings to an art gallery.* ❑ *The directors sold the business for $14.8 million.*
2 **VERB** If a store **sells** a particular thing, it is available for people to buy there. ❑ *The store sells newspapers and candy bars.*
→ look at **shopping**
▶ **sell out** **1** If a store **sells out** of something, it sells all of its supply of it. ❑ *The supermarket sold out of milk in a single day.* **2** If a performance, a sports event, or another entertainment **sells out**, all the tickets for it are sold. ❑ *Football games often sell out fast.*

selves /sɛlvz/ **Selves** is the plural of **self**.

se|mes|ter /sɪmɛstər/ (**semesters**) **NOUN** A **semester** is half of a school or college year. ❑ *February 22nd is when most of their students begin their spring semester.*

semi|cir|cle /sɛmisɜrk°l, sɛmaɪ-/ (**semicircles**) **NOUN** MATH A **semicircle** is one half of a circle. ❑ *They sit in a semicircle and share stories.*

semi|co|lon /sɛmikoʊlən/ (**semicolons**) **NOUN** LANGUAGE ARTS A **semicolon** is the mark (;) that you use in writing to separate different parts of a sentence.
→ look at **punctuation**

semi|fi|nal /sɛmifaɪn°l, sɛmaɪ-/ (**semifinals**) **NOUN** SPORTS A **semifinal** is one of the two games in a competition that are played to decide who will play in the final part. ❑ *The basketball team lost in their semifinal yesterday.*

semi|nar /sɛmɪnɑr/ (**seminars**) **NOUN** A **seminar** is a class at a college or university in which the teacher and a small group of

S

students discuss a topic. ❏ *Students are asked to prepare material for the weekly seminars.*

Sen|ate /sɛnɪt/ (**Senates**) **NOUN**
SOCIAL STUDIES **The Senate** is the smaller and more important of the two parts of the legislature in some U.S. states and in some countries, for example, the United States and Australia. ❏ *That year the Republicans gained two Senate seats.*

sena|tor /sɛnɪtər/ (**senators**) **NOUN**
SOCIAL STUDIES A **senator** is a member of a Senate, for example, in the United States or Australia.
→ look at **vote**

send /sɛnd/ (**sends, sending, sent**)
1 **VERB** When you **send** someone a message or a package, you make it go to them. ❏ *I sent her an email this morning.* ❏ *Hannah sent me a letter last week.*
2 **VERB** If you **send** someone somewhere, you make them go there. ❏ *His parents sent him to the grocery store.*
→ look at **email**
▶ **send for** If you **send for** someone, you send them a message asking them to come and see you. ❏ *When he arrived in Portland, he sent for his wife and children.*

sen|ior /sinyər/ (**seniors**)
1 **ADJECTIVE** The **senior** people in an organization or a profession have the most important jobs. ❏ *He was a senior official in the Israeli government.*
2 **NOUN** **Seniors** are students in a high school, a university, or a college who are in their final year of study. ❏ *How many high school seniors go on to college?*

sen|ior citi|zen (**senior citizens**) **NOUN**
A **senior citizen** is an older person, especially someone over 65. ❏ *We want to improve healthcare services for senior citizens.*
→ look at **age**

sen|sa|tion /sɛnseɪʃ°n/ (**sensations**)
1 **NOUN** A **sensation** is a physical feeling. ❏ *Floating can be a pleasant sensation.*
2 **NOUN** If a person, an event, or a situation is a **sensation**, it causes great excitement or interest. ❏ *The movie was an overnight sensation.*

sen|sa|tion|al /sɛnseɪʃən°l/ **ADJECTIVE**
A **sensational** result, event, or situation causes great excitement and interest.
❏ *...a sensational victory.*

sense /sɛns/ (**senses**)
1 **NOUN** Your **senses** are your physical ability to see, smell, hear, touch, and taste. ❏ *Foxes have a strong sense of smell.*
2 **NOUN** If you have a **sense of** something, you feel it. ❏ *She felt a sense of relief as she crossed the finish line.*
3 **NONCOUNT NOUN** **Sense** is the ability to think carefully about something and do the right thing. ❏ *Now that he's older, he has a bit more sense.*
4 **NOUN** A **sense** of a word is one of its possible meanings. ❏ *This noun has four senses.*
5 If something **makes sense**, you can understand it. ❏ *Do these figures make sense to you?*

sense of hu|mor **NOUN** Someone who has a **sense of humor** often finds things funny, and is not serious all the time. ❏ *She has a good sense of humor.*

sen|sible /sɛnsɪb°l/ **ADJECTIVE** **Sensible** actions or decisions are good because they are based on reasons rather than emotions. ❏ *It might be sensible to get a lawyer.* ❏ *The sensible thing is to leave them alone.* ● **sen|sibly** /sɛnsɪbli/ **ADVERB** ❏ *He sensibly decided to hide for a while.*

sen|si|tive /sɛnsɪtɪv/
1 **ADJECTIVE** A person or thing that is **sensitive to** something is easily affected by it. ❏ *This chemical is sensitive to light.* ❏ *He is very sensitive to the cold.*

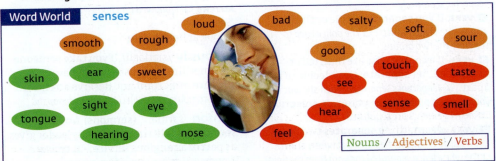

Word World   **senses**

loud · bad · salty · soft · sour · smooth · rough · good · touch · taste · skin · ear · sweet · see · sight · eye · sense · smell · tongue · hear · hearing · nose · feel

Nouns / Adjectives / Verbs

S

2 **ADJECTIVE** If you are **sensitive to** other people, you show that you understand their feelings. ❑ *The classroom teacher must be sensitive to a child's needs.*

3 **ADJECTIVE** If you are **sensitive about** something, you are easily worried and offended when people talk about it. ❑ *Young people are sensitive about their appearance.*

sent /sɛnt/ **Sent** is a form of the verb **send**.

sen|tence /sɛntəns/ (**sentences, sentencing, sentenced**)

1 **NOUN** LANGUAGE ARTS A **sentence** is a group of words that tells you something or asks a question. When a sentence is written, it begins with a capital letter and ends with a period. ❑ *After I've written each sentence, I read it aloud.*

2 **NOUN** In a law court, a **sentence** is the punishment that a person receives. ❑ *He was given a four-year sentence.*

3 **VERB** When a judge **sentences** someone, he or she tells the court what their punishment will be. ❑ *The court sentenced him to five years in prison.*

→ look at **grammar, writing**

sen|ti|ment|al /sɛntɪmɛntəl/ **ADJECTIVE** Someone or something that is **sentimental** feels or shows too much pity or love. ❑ *I'm trying not to be sentimental about the past.*

sepa|rate (**separates, separating, separated**)

PRONUNCIATION HELP
Pronounce the adjective /sɛpərɪt/.
Pronounce the verb /sɛpəreɪt/.

1 **ADJECTIVE** If one thing is **separate from** another, the two things are apart and are not connected. ❑ *Use separate surfaces for cutting raw meats and cooked meats.* ❑ *Men and women have separate exercise rooms.*

● **sepa|rate|ly** /sɛpərɪtli/ **ADVERB** ❑ *Cook each vegetable separately.*

2 **VERB** If you **separate** people or things, you move them apart. ❑ *The police tried to separate the two groups.*

3 **VERB** If a couple who are married or living together **separate**, they decide to live apart. ❑ *Her parents separated when she was very young.* ● **sepa|rat|ed** /sɛpəreɪtɪd/ **ADJECTIVE** ❑ *Rachel's parents are separated.*

4 **VERB** If something **separates** two people, groups, or things, it exists between them. ❑ *The white fence separated the yard from the field.*

Sep|tem|ber /sɛptɛmbər/ **NOUN** September is the ninth month of the year. ❑ *Her son was born in September.*

se|quence /sikwəns/ (**sequences**) **NOUN** A **sequence of** events or things is a number of them that come one after another. ❑ *This is the sequence of events that led to the murder.*

ser|geant /sɑrdʒənt/ (**sergeants**) **NOUN** A **sergeant** is an officer in the army or the police. ❑ *A police sergeant patrolling the area noticed the fire.*

se|rial /sɪəriəl/ (**serials**) **NOUN** A **serial** is a story that is told in a number of parts on television or radio, or in a magazine or newspaper. ❑ *The book was filmed as a six-part TV serial.*

se|ries /sɪəriz/ (**series**)

1 **NOUN** A **series of** things or events is a number of them that come one after another. ❑ *There will be a series of meetings with political leaders.*

2 **NOUN** A radio or television **series** is a set of programs. ❑ *The long-running TV series is filmed in Los Angeles.*

se|ri|ous /sɪəriəs/

1 **ADJECTIVE** **Serious** problems or situations are very bad, and they make people worried or afraid. ❑ *Crime is a serious problem in our society.* ● **se|ri|ous|ly** **ADVERB** ❑ *This law could seriously damage my business.* ● **se|ri|ous|ness** **NONCOUNT NOUN** ❑ *They don't realize the seriousness of the crisis.*

2 **ADJECTIVE** **Serious** matters are important, and people need to think about them carefully. ❑ *This is a very serious matter.*

3 **ADJECTIVE** If you are **serious about** something, you are not joking, and you really mean what you say. ❑ *You really are serious about this, aren't you?* ● **se|ri|ous|ly** **ADVERB** ❑ *"I followed him home," he said. "Seriously?"*

→ look at **health care**

se|ri|ous|ly /sɪəriəsli/ If you **take** someone or something **seriously**, you believe that they are important and deserve attention. ❑ *The company takes all complaints seriously.*

ser|mon /sɜrmən/ (**sermons**) **NOUN** A **sermon** is a talk that a religious leader gives as part of a religious service. ❑ *Cardinal Murphy will deliver the sermon on Sunday.*

serv|ant /sɜrvᵊnt/ (**servants**) **NOUN** A **servant** is someone who works at another person's home, doing work like cooking or cleaning. ❑ *The family employed several servants.*

serve /sɜrv/ (**serves, serving, served**)

1 **VERB** When you **serve** food and drinks, you give people food and drinks. ❑ *The restaurant serves breakfast, lunch, and dinner.*

2 **VERB** Someone who **serves** customers in a store or a bar helps them and provides them with what they want to buy. ❑ *Noah served me coffee and pie.*

3 **VERB** If you **serve** your country, an organization, or a person, you do useful work for them. ❑ *He spoke of the fine character of those who serve their country.*

serv|er /sɜrvər/ (**servers**)

1 **NOUN** TECHNOLOGY A **server** is a computer that stores information and supplies it to a number of computers on a network. ❑ *They couldn't send any emails because the mail server was down.*

2 **NOUN** A **server** is a person who works in a restaurant, serving people with food and drink. ❑ *A server came by with a tray of coffee cups.*
→ look at **restaurant**

ser|vice /sɜrvɪs/ (**services**)

1 **NOUN** A **service** is something that the public needs, such as transportation or energy supplies. ❑ *There is a regular local bus service to Yorkdale.*

2 **NONCOUNT NOUN** Service is the help that people in a restaurant or a store give you. ❑ *We always receive good service in that restaurant.*

3 **NONCOUNT NOUN** Service is the time that you spend working for someone else. ❑ *Most employees had long service with the company.*

4 **NOUN** A **service** is a religious ceremony. ❑ *After the service, his body was taken to a cemetery.*
→ look at **phone**

ses|sion /sɛʃᵊn/ (**sessions**) **NOUN** A **session** of a particular activity is a period of that activity. ❑ *The two leaders arrived for a photo session.*

set /sɛt/ (**sets, setting, set**)

1 **NOUN** A **set of** things is a number of things that belong together. ❑ *The table and chairs are normally bought as a set.* ❑ *I got a chess set for my birthday.*

2 **NOUN** The **set** for a movie is the place where it is made. ❑ *The place looked like the set of a James Bond movie.*

3 **NOUN** A television **set** is a television. ❑ *Children spend too much time in front of the television set.*

4 **VERB** If you **set** something somewhere, you put it there carefully. ❑ *She set the vase down gently on the table.*

5 **VERB** When you **set** a clock, you make it ready to use. ❑ *I set my alarm clock for seven o'clock every morning.*

6 **VERB** If you **set** a date or a price, you decide what it will be. ❑ *They have finally set the date of their wedding.*

7 **VERB** When the sun **sets**, it goes down in the sky until you can no longer see it. ❑ *They watched the sun set behind the hills.*

8 **VERB** When someone **sets** the table, they prepare it for a meal by putting plates, glasses, knives, forks, and spoons on it.

9 **ADJECTIVE** A **set** time is fixed and cannot be changed. ❑ *The kids have to be home at a set time every evening.*

10 **ADJECTIVE** If a movie or a story is **set** in a particular place or time, the events in it happen in that place or at that time. ❑ *The play is set in a small Midwestern town.*

11 If you **set fire to** something or **set** something **on fire**, you make it burn. ❑ *Angry protestors threw stones and set cars on fire.*

12 If you **set** someone **free**, you cause them to be free. ❑ *They agreed to set the prisoners free.*

▶ **set off** When you **set off**, you start going somewhere. ❑ *Nick set off for his farmhouse in Connecticut.*

▶ **set out** If you **set out to** do something, you start trying to do it. ❑ *He did what he set out to do.*

▶ **set up** If you **set** something **up**, you start or arrange it. ❑ *He plans to set up his own business.*

set|tle /sɛtᵊl/ (**settles, settling, settled**)

1 **VERB** If people **settle** an argument or a problem, they decide what to do by talking about it. ❑ *They agreed to try again to settle the dispute.*

2 **VERB** If something **is settled**, it has all been decided and arranged. ❑ *We feel the matter is now settled.*

3 **VERB** When people **settle** in a place, they start living there permanently. ❑ *He visited Paris and eventually settled there.*

4 **VERB** If you **settle** somewhere, you sit down and make yourself comfortable. ❑ *Brandon settled in front of the television.*

▶ **settle down** If a person **settles down**, they become calm after being excited.

s

❑ *Come on, kids. Time to settle down and go to sleep now.*

▶ **settle in** If you **settle in**, you become used to living in a new place, doing a new job, or going to a new school. ❑ *I enjoyed school once I settled in.*

set|tle|ment /sɛtᵊlmənt/ (**settlements**)

1 **NOUN** SOCIAL STUDIES A **settlement** is an official agreement between two people or groups after they have disagreed about something. ❑ *Officials are hoping for a peaceful settlement of the crisis.*

2 **NOUN** SOCIAL STUDIES A **settlement** is a place where people have come to live and have built homes. ❑ *The village is a settlement of just fifty houses.*

set|tler /sɛtlər, sɛtᵊl-/ (**settlers**) **NOUN**
SOCIAL STUDIES **Settlers** are people who go to live in a place where not many people live, and start a new life there. ❑ *He was one of the early settlers in North America.*

sev|en /sɛvᵊn/ MATH **Seven** is the number 7.
→ look at **number**

Word Builder **seventeen**

teen ≈ **plus ten, from 13-19**

eight + teen = eighteen
four + teen = fourteen
nine + teen = nineteen
seven + teen = seventeen
six + teen = sixteen
teen + age = teenage

---

sev|en|teen /sɛvᵊntin/ MATH **Seventeen** is the number 17.

sev|enth /sɛvᵊnθ/ (**sevenths**)

1 **ADJECTIVE, ADVERB** MATH The **seventh** item in a series is the one that you count as number seven. ❑ *I was the seventh child in the family.*

2 **NOUN** MATH A **seventh** is one of seven equal parts of something (⅟₇).
→ look at **number**

sev|en|ty /sɛvᵊnti/ MATH **Seventy** is the number 70.

sev|er|al /sɛvrəl/

1 **ADJECTIVE** You use **several** for talking about a number of people or things that is not large but is greater than two. ❑ *I spent several years in France.* ❑ *There were several blue boxes on the table.*

2 **PRONOUN** **Several** is also a pronoun.
❑ *The cakes were delicious, and we ate several before we left the party.*

se|vere /sɪvɪər/ (**severer, severest**)

1 **ADJECTIVE** You use **severe** to show that something is very bad. ❑ *The business is having severe financial problems.* ● **se|vere|ly** **ADVERB** ❑ *An aircraft crashed on the runway and was severely damaged.*

2 **ADJECTIVE** **Severe** punishments or criticisms are very strong. ❑ *A severe sentence is necessary for this type of crime.* ● **se|vere|ly** **ADVERB** ❑ *They want to punish dangerous drivers more severely.*

sew /soʊ/ (**sews, sewing, sewed, sewn**) **VERB**
When you **sew** pieces of cloth together, you join them using a needle and thread. ❑ *Anyone can sew a button onto a shirt.* ● **sew|ing** **NONCOUNT NOUN** ❑ *She lists her hobbies as cooking, sewing, and going to the movies.*

sew|er /suər/ (**sewers**) **NOUN** A **sewer** is a large pipe under the ground that carries waste and rain water away. ❑ *The rain water drains into the city's sewer system.*
→ look at **pollution**

sewn /soʊn/ **Sewn** is a form of the verb **sew**.

sex /sɛks/ (**sexes**)

1 **NOUN** The two **sexes** are the two groups, male and female, into which you can divide people and animals. ❑ *This movie appeals to both sexes.*

2 **NOUN** The **sex** of a person or an animal is their characteristic of being either male or female. ❑ *We can identify the sex of your unborn baby.*

3 **NONCOUNT NOUN** **Sex** is the physical activity by which people can produce children. ❑ *He was very open in his attitudes about sex.*

4 If two people **have sex**, they perform the act of sex.

sex|ual /sɛkʃuəl/

1 **ADJECTIVE** **Sexual** means connected with sex. ❑ *The clinic can provide information about sexual health.*

2 **ADJECTIVE** **Sexual** means relating to the differences between male and female people. ❑ *There are laws against sexual discrimination.*

3 **ADJECTIVE** **Sexual** means relating to the biological process by which people and animals produce young. ❑ *Girls usually reach sexual maturity earlier than boys.* ● **sex|ual|ly** **ADVERB** ❑ *These organisms can reproduce sexually.*

sexy /sɛksi/ (**sexier, sexiest**) **ADJECTIVE** **Sexy** describes people and things that you think are sexually attractive. ❑ *She is the sexiest woman I have ever seen.*

S

shab|by /ʃæbi/ (**shabbier, shabbiest**)
ADJECTIVE Shabby things or places look old and in bad condition. ❑ *His clothes were old and shabby.*

shade /ʃeɪd/ (**shades**)
1 **NOUN** A **shade of** a particular color is one of its different forms. ❑ *The walls were painted in two shades of green.*
2 **NONCOUNT NOUN** Shade is an area where direct sunlight does not reach. ❑ *Alexis was reading in the shade of a tree.*
3 **NOUN** A **shade** is a piece of material that you can pull down over a window. ❑ *Nancy left the shades down.*
→ look at **tree**

shad|ow /ʃædoʊ/ (**shadows**) **NOUN**
A **shadow** is a dark shape on a surface that is made when something blocks the light. ❑ *The long shadows of the trees fell across their path.*

shady /ʃeɪdi/ (**shadier, shadiest**) **ADJECTIVE**
A **shady** place is not in bright sunlight. ❑ *We stopped in a shady place under some trees.*

shake /ʃeɪk/ (**shakes, shaking, shook, shaken**)
1 **VERB** If someone or something **shakes**, they move quickly backward and forward or up and down. ❑ *My whole body was shaking with fear.*
2 **VERB** If you **shake** something, you hold it and move it quickly up and down. ❑ *Always shake the bottle before you pour out the medicine.*
3 **NOUN** Shake is also a noun. ❑ *We gave the children a gentle shake to wake them.*
4 **VERB** If you **shake** your **head**, you move it from side to side to say "no." ❑ *"Did you see Crystal?" Kathryn shook her head.*
5 If you **shake hands with** someone, you say hello or goodbye to them by holding their right hand in your own right hand and moving it up and down. You can also say that two people **shake hands**. ❑ *Michael shook hands with Burke.*

shaky /ʃeɪki/ (**shakier, shakiest**)
1 **ADJECTIVE** If a situation is **shaky**, it seems unlikely to be successful. ❑ *The couple's marriage is shaky.*
2 **ADJECTIVE** If your body or your voice is **shaky**, you cannot control it properly because you are sick or nervous. ❑ *Her voice was shaky and she was close to tears.* ● **shak|ily** **ADVERB** ❑ *"I don't feel well," she said shakily.*

shall /ʃəl, STRONG ʃæl/
1 **MODAL VERB** You use **shall** with "I" and "we" in questions to make offers or suggestions. ❑ *Shall I get the keys?* ❑ *Well, shall we go?*
2 **MODAL VERB** You use **shall**, usually with "I" and "we," when you are talking about something that will happen to you in the future. [FORMAL] ❑ *We shall be landing in Paris in sixteen minutes.* ❑ *I shall know more tomorrow.*

> **Usage** **shall**
> Use **shall** in only formal writing and speech. *The war **shall** end and there **shall** be peace.* In everyday English, use **will**. *We **will** be home after the movie.*

shal|low /ʃæloʊ/ (**shallower, shallowest**)
ADJECTIVE If something is **shallow**, it is not deep. ❑ *The river is very shallow here.*

shame /ʃeɪm/
1 **NONCOUNT NOUN** Shame is the very uncomfortable feeling that you have when you have done something wrong or stupid. ❑ *I was filled with shame.*
2 **NOUN** If you say that something is **a shame**, you feel sad or disappointed about it. ❑ *It was a shame about the weather, but the party was still a great success.*

shame|ful /ʃeɪmfəl/ **ADJECTIVE** If someone's behavior is **shameful**, it is very bad. ❑ *The government's treatment of the refugees was shameful.*

sham|poo /ʃæmpu/ (**shampoos, shampooing, shampooed**)
1 **NONCOUNT NOUN** Shampoo is a liquid soap that you use for washing your hair. ❑ *Don't forget to pack a towel, soap, and shampoo.*
2 **VERB** If you **shampoo** your hair, you wash it using shampoo. ❑ *I shampooed my hair and dried it, then I got dressed.*

shan't /ʃænt/ **Shan't** is short for "shall not."

shape /ʃeɪp/ (**shapes, shaping, shaped**)
1 **NOUN** The **shape of** something is its form or the appearance of its outside edges or surfaces. ❑ *Pasta comes in all different shapes and sizes.*
2 **NOUN** A **shape** is the form of something, for example a circle, a square, or a triangle.
3 **VERB** If you **shape** something, you give it a particular shape. ❑ *Shape the dough into a ball and place it in the bowl.*

s

4 If someone or something is **in shape**, or in **good shape**, they are in a good state of health or in a good condition. ❑ *He's 76 and still in good shape.*

5 If someone or something is **in bad shape**, they are in a bad state of health or in a bad condition. ❑ *The company is in bad shape.*

6 If you are **out of shape**, you are unhealthy and you are not able to do a lot of physical activity. ❑ *I weighed 245 pounds and I was out of shape.*

→ look at **geometry**

share /ʃɛər/ (**shares, sharing, shared**)
1 VERB If you **share** something **with** another person, you both have it or use it. ❑ *Jose shares an apartment with six other students.* ❑ *Maria and I shared a dessert.*
2 NOUN Your **share** of something is the part of it that you do or have. ❑ *I do my share of the housework.* ❑ *I need my share of the money now.*
3 NOUN A company's **shares** are the equal parts that its value is divided into. People can buy shares, so that they own a part of the company and have a part of its profit. ❑ *I've bought shares in my brother's new company.*

share|crop|per /ʃɛərkrɒpər/
(**sharecroppers**) NOUN SOCIAL STUDIES A **sharecropper** is a farmer who pays for his land with some of the crops that he produces. ● **share|crop|ping** NONCOUNT NOUN ❑ *Sharecropping is a contract between a land owner and a farm worker*

share|holder /ʃɛərhoʊldər/ (**shareholders**) NOUN A **shareholder** is a person who owns shares (= parts of a company's value).

shark /ʃɑrk/ (**sharks**) NOUN A **shark** is a very large fish. Some sharks have very sharp teeth and may attack people.
→ look at **animal**

sharp /ʃɑrp/ (**sharper, sharpest**)
1 ADJECTIVE A **sharp** point or edge is very thin and can cut through things very easily. ❑ *Cut the skin off the mango using a sharp knife.* ❑ *You'll need a sharp pencil and an eraser.*
2 ADJECTIVE A **sharp** bend or turn changes direction suddenly. ❑ *I came to a sharp bend in the road and had to brake quickly.*
3 ADVERB Sharp is also an adverb. ❑ *Do not cross the bridge but turn sharp left*

instead. ● **sharp|ly** ADVERB ❑ *After a mile, the road turns sharply to the right.*
4 ADJECTIVE If you are **sharp**, you are good at noticing and understanding things. ❑ *Dan's very sharp, and a quick thinker.*
5 ADJECTIVE If you say something in a **sharp** way, you say it suddenly and angrily. ❑ *His sharp reply surprised me.* ● **sharp|ly** ADVERB ❑ *"Why didn't you tell me?" she asked sharply.*
6 ADJECTIVE A **sharp** change or feeling happens suddenly and is very big or strong. ❑ *There's been a sharp rise in oil prices.* ❑ *I felt a sharp pain in my right leg.* ● **sharp|ly** ADVERB ❑ *Unemployment rose sharply last year.*
7 ADJECTIVE A **sharp** image is very clear and easy to see. ❑ *Digital TV offers sharper images than analog TV.*
8 ADVERB If something will happen at a particular time **sharp**, it will happen at that time exactly. ❑ *Be in my office tomorrow morning at eight o'clock sharp.*
9 ADJECTIVE MUSIC An F **sharp** or a G **sharp**, for example, is a note that is slightly higher than F or G. Compare with **flat**.

sharp|en /ʃɑrpən/ (**sharpens, sharpening, sharpened**) VERB If you **sharpen** something, you make its edge very thin or you make its end pointed. ❑ *What's the best way to sharpen a knife?* ❑ *Mike had to sharpen the pencils every morning.*

shat|ter /ʃætər/ (**shatters, shattering, shattered**) VERB If something **shatters**, it breaks into small pieces. ❑ *Megan dropped the glass, and it shattered on the floor.*

shave /ʃeɪv/ (**shaves, shaving, shaved**)
1 VERB If you **shave**, you remove hair from your face or body by cutting it off using a special knife (= a razor) or a piece of electric equipment (= a shaver). ❑ *Samuel took a bath and shaved.* ❑ *Many women shave their legs.*
2 NOUN Shave is also a noun. ❑ *I need a shave.*

shav|er /ʃeɪvər/ (**shavers**) NOUN A **shaver** is an electric piece of equipment that you use for shaving hair from your face and body. ❑ *In 1937 the company introduced the world's first electric shaver.*

shawl /ʃɔl/ (**shawls**) NOUN A **shawl** is a large piece of cloth that a woman wears over her shoulders or head.
→ look at **clothing**

she /ʃi, STRONG ʃi/ PRONOUN You use **she** to talk about a female person or animal when they are the subject of a sentence. ❑ *She's seventeen years old.*

shed /ʃɛd/ (sheds) **NOUN** A **shed** is a small building where you store things. ❑ *The house has a large shed in the backyard.*

she'd /ʃid, ʃɪd/
1 **She'd** is short for "she had." ❑ *She'd been all over the world.*
2 **She'd** is short for "she would." ❑ *She'd do anything for a bit of money.*

sheep /ʃip/ (sheep) **NOUN** A **sheep** is a farm animal with thick hair called wool. Farmers keep sheep for their wool or for their meat.
→ look at **farm**

sheet /ʃit/ (sheets)
1 **NOUN** A **sheet** is a large piece of cloth that you sleep on or cover yourself with in bed. ❑ *Once a week, we change the sheets.*
2 **NOUN** A **sheet of** paper is a piece of paper. ❑ *Sean folded the sheets of paper and put them in his briefcase.*

shelf /ʃɛlf/ (shelves) **NOUN** A **shelf** is a long flat piece of wood on a wall or in a cabinet that you can keep things on. ❑ *Dad took a book from the shelf.*

shell /ʃɛl/ (shells)
1 **NOUN** The **shell** of something is the hard part that surrounds it and protects it. ❑ *They cracked the nuts and removed their shells.*
2 **NOUN** The **shell** of an animal such as a snail is the hard part that covers its back and protects it.
3 **NOUN** **Shells** are hard outer parts of small sea creatures that you find on beaches. ❑ *I have gathered shells since I was a child.*
→ look at **beach, shellfish**

she'll /ʃil, ʃɪl/ **She'll** is short for "she will." ❑ *Sharon was wonderful. I know she'll be greatly missed.*

shell|fish /ʃɛlfɪʃ/ (shellfish) **NOUN** **Shellfish** are small creatures that live in the ocean

and have a shell. ❑ *The restaurant serves local fish and shellfish.*
→ look at Picture Dictionary: **shellfish**

shel|ter /ʃɛltər/ (shelters)
1 **NOUN** A **shelter** is a place that protects you from bad weather or danger. ❑ *...a bus shelter.*
2 **NONCOUNT NOUN** **Shelter** is protection from bad weather or danger. ❑ *They took shelter under a tree.*

sher|bet /ʃɜrbɪt/ **NONCOUNT NOUN** **Sherbet** is a frozen dessert made with fruit juice, sugar, and water. ❑ *...lemon sherbet.*

sher|iff /ʃɛrɪf/ (sheriffs) **NOUN** In the United States, a **sheriff** is a law enforcement officer (= a person who makes sure that people obey the law). A sheriff is usually responsible for a county (= a region). ❑ *Her father was the town sheriff.*

she's /ʃiz, ʃɪz/
1 **She's** is short for "she is." ❑ *She's a really good cook.*
2 **She's** is short for "she has." ❑ *She's been married for seven years.*

shield /ʃild/ (shields, shielding, shielded)
1 **VERB** If something or someone **shields** you **from** danger or injury, they protect you from it. ❑ *I shielded my eyes from the sun with my hands.*
2 **NOUN** A **shield** is a large piece of metal or leather that soldiers carried in the past to protect their bodies.

shift /ʃɪft/ (shifts, shifting, shifted)
1 **VERB** If you **shift** something, you move it from one place to another. ❑ *Please would you help me shift the table over to the window?*
2 **NOUN** A **shift** is one of the fixed periods of work in a factory or a hospital. ❑ *Nick works night shifts at the hospital.*
→ look at **job**

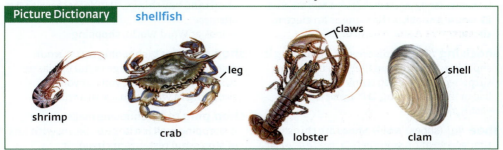

Picture Dictionary shellfish

claws

leg

shell

shrimp

crab

lobster

clam

shin /ʃɪn/ (shins) **NOUN** Your **shins** are the front parts of your legs between your knees and your ankles. ❏ *Ken suffered a bruised left shin.*

shine /ʃaɪn/ (shines, shining, shined or shone)
1 VERB When the sun or a light **shines**, it gives out bright light. ❏ *Today it's warm and the sun is shining.*
2 VERB If you **shine** a light somewhere, you point it there. ❏ *The guard shone a light in his face.*
3 VERB Something that **shines** is very bright because it is reflecting light. ❏ *The ocean shone in the silver moonlight.*

shiny /ʃaɪni/ (shinier, shiniest) **ADJECTIVE** If a surface is **shiny**, it is bright and it reflects light. ❏ *Her blonde hair was shiny and clean.*

ship /ʃɪp/ (ships, shipping, shipped)
1 NOUN A **ship** is a large boat that carries people or goods. ❏ *The ship was ready to sail.*
2 VERB If goods **are shipped** somewhere, they are sent there. ❏ *Our company ships orders worldwide.*
→ look at **ocean**

shirt /ʃɜrt/ (shirts) **NOUN** A **shirt** is a piece of clothing with a collar and buttons, that you wear on the top part of your body.
→ look at **clothing**

shiv|er /ʃɪvər/ (shivers, shivering, shivered) **1 VERB** If you **shiver**, your body shakes because you are cold, frightened, or sick. ❏ *She shivered with cold and fear.*
2 NOUN **Shiver** is also a noun. ❏ *She gave a small shiver.*

shock /ʃɒk/ (shocks, shocking, shocked)
1 NOUN If you have a **shock**, you suddenly feel very upset because something unpleasant has happened. ❏ *William never recovered from the shock of his brother's death.*
2 VERB If something **shocks** you, it suddenly makes you feel very upset because it is so unpleasant. ❏ *After forty years as a police officer, nothing shocks me.* ● **shocked ADJECTIVE** ❏ *She was deeply shocked when she heard the news.*
3 NOUN A **shock** is the same as an **electric shock**.

shock|ing /ʃɒkɪŋ/ **ADJECTIVE** If something is **shocking**, it makes you feel very upset and surprised because you think that it is very bad or morally wrong ❏ *Everyone found the photos shocking.*

shoe /ʃu/ (shoes) **NOUN** **Shoes** are things that you wear on your feet. ❏ *I need a new pair of shoes.* ❏ *I don't usually wear high-heeled shoes.*
→ look at **clothing**

shoe|lace /ʃuleɪs/ (shoelaces) **NOUN** **Shoelaces** are long, thick strings that you use to fasten your shoes. ❏ *He began to tie his shoelaces.*

shone /ʃoʊn/ **Shone** is a form of the verb **shine**.

shook /ʃʊk/ **Shook** is a form of the verb **shake**.

shoot /ʃut/ (shoots, shooting, shot)
1 VERB If someone **shoots** a person or an animal, they kill them or injure them by firing a gun at them. ❏ *The gunmen shot two policemen before they escaped.* ❏ *A man was shot dead during the robbery.*
2 VERB If someone **shoots**, they fire a bullet from a weapon. ❏ *He raised his arms above his head, and shouted, "Don't shoot!"*
3 VERB When people **shoot** a movie, they make a movie. ❏ *Tim wants to shoot his new movie in Mexico.*
4 NOUN **Shoots** are new parts that are growing from a plant or tree. ❏ *It was spring, and new shoots began to appear.*
5 VERB SPORTS In soccer or basketball, when you **shoot**, you kick or throw the ball toward the goal or net. ❏ *Brennan shot and missed.*

shop /ʃɒp/ (shops, shopping, shopped)
1 NOUN A **shop** is a small store that sells a particular type of thing. ❏ *Paul and his wife run a flower shop.*
2 VERB When you **shop**, you go to stores or shops and buy things. ❏ *He always shops on Saturday mornings.* ● **shop|per** (shoppers) **NOUN** ❏ *The streets were filled with crowds of shoppers.*
→ look at **shopping**

shop|ping /ʃɒpɪŋ/ **NONCOUNT NOUN** When you do **the shopping**, you go to stores or shops and buy things. ❏ *I'll do the shopping this afternoon.*
→ look at Word World: **shopping**

shop|ping cart (shopping carts) **NOUN** A **shopping cart** is a large metal or plastic basket on wheels that you put your shopping in while you are in a store.

shop|ping mall (shopping malls) **NOUN** A **shopping mall** is a large building with lots of stores and restaurants inside it.

Word World | shopping

debit card — new — expensive — medium — small — store — customer — cheap — large — sale — discount — online — return — exchange — mall — cash — sell — shop — store — pay — supermarket — credit card — buy

Nouns / Adjectives / Verbs

shore /ʃɔr/ (**shores**) **NOUN** GEOGRAPHY The **shore** of an ocean or a lake is the land along the edge of it. ❑ *They walked slowly down to the shore.*
→ look at **beach, ocean**

❶ **short** /ʃɔrt/ (**shorts, shorter, shortest**)
1 **ADJECTIVE** If something is **short**, it does not last very long. ❑ *Last year we all went to Miami Beach for a short vacation.*
2 **ADJECTIVE** Someone who is **short** is not tall. ❑ *She's a short woman with gray hair.*
3 **ADJECTIVE** Something that is **short** measures only a small amount from one end to the other. ❑ *The restaurant is only a short distance away.* ❑ *She has short, curly hair.*
4 **ADJECTIVE** If you are **short of** something, you do not have enough of it. ❑ *His family is very short of money.*
5 **ADJECTIVE** A word that is **short for** another word is a shorter way of saying it. ❑ *Her name's Jo—it's short for Josephine.*
6 **PLURAL NOUN** **Shorts** are pants with very short legs. ❑ *She was wearing pink shorts and a black t-shirt.*
→ look at **hair, route, writing**

Usage **short**
Short forms are very common in English. Usually you say the short form letter by letter. Some examples are **CD, DVD, USA,** and **WWW.**

short|age /ʃɔrtɪdʒ/ (**shortages**) **NOUN** If there is a **shortage of** something, there is not enough of it. ❑ *In this town there is a great shortage of cheap housing.*
→ look at **water**

short|en /ʃɔrtᵊn/ (**shortens, shortening, shortened**) **VERB** If you **shorten** something, you make it shorter. ❑ *The treatment shortens the length of the illness.*

short|ly /ʃɔrtli/ **ADVERB** If something is going to happen **shortly**, it is going to happen soon. ❑ *"Please take a seat. Dr. Garcia will see you shortly."*

short-term **ADJECTIVE** **Short-term** things last only for a short time, or have an effect soon rather than far in the future. ❑ *This is only a short-term solution.*

shot /ʃɒt/ (**shots**)
1 **Shot** is a form of the verb **shoot**.
2 **NOUN** A **shot** is an act of firing a gun. ❑ *The man was killed with a single shot.*
3 **NOUN** In sports, a **shot** is an act of kicking, hitting, or throwing the ball, to try to score a point. ❑ *Grant missed two shots at the goal.*
4 **NOUN** A **shot** is a photograph. ❑ *The photographer got some great shots of the bride.*

should /ʃəd, STRONG ʃʊd/
1 **MODAL VERB** You use **should** when you are saying what is the right thing to do. ❑ *I should exercise more.* ❑ *You shouldn't stay up so late.*
2 **MODAL VERB** You use **should** when you are saying that something is probably true or will probably happen. ❑ *The doctor said I should be fine by next week.* ❑ *You should have no problems with this exercise.*
3 **MODAL VERB** You use **should** in questions when you are asking someone for advice. ❑ *Should I ask for more help?* ❑ *What should I do?*

shoul|der /ʃoʊldər/ (**shoulders**) **NOUN** Your **shoulders** are the two parts of your body between your neck and the tops of your arms. ❑ *She put her arm round his shoulders.*
→ look at **body**

shouldn't /ʃʊdᵊnt/ **Shouldn't** is short for "should not."

should've /ʃʊdəv/ **Should've** is short for "should have."

shout /ʃaʊt/ (**shouts, shouting, shouted**)
1 **VERB** If you **shout**, you say something very loudly. ❑ *"She's alive!" he shouted.* ❑ *Andrew ran out of the house, shouting for help.*
2 **NOUN** **Shout** is also a noun. ❑ *There were angry shouts from the crowd.*

S

shove /ʃʌv/ (shoves, shoving, shoved)

1 **VERB** If you **shove** someone or something, you push them roughly. ❑ *The woman shoved the other customers out of the way.*
2 **NOUN** Shove is also a noun. ❑ *She gave Carrie a shove toward the house.*

shov|el /ʃʌvᵊl/ (shovels, shoveling, shoveled)

1 **NOUN** A **shovel** is a flat tool with a handle that is used for lifting and moving earth or snow. ❑ *I'll need the coal shovel.*
2 **VERB** If you **shovel** earth or snow, you lift it and move it with a shovel. ❑ *He had to shovel the snow away from the door.*

show /ʃoʊ/ (shows, showing, showed, shown)

1 **VERB** If information or a fact **shows that** a situation exists, it proves it. ❑ *Research shows that certain foods can help prevent headaches.*
2 **VERB** If you **show** someone something, you let them see it. ❑ *She showed me her engagement ring.*
3 **VERB** If you **show** someone how to do something, you teach them how to do it. ❑ *Claire showed us how to make pasta.*
4 **VERB** If something **shows**, it is easy to notice. ❑ *When I feel angry, it shows.*
5 **NOUN** A television or radio **show** is a program. ❑ *I never missed his TV show when I was a kid.*
6 **NOUN** A **show** in a theater is a performance. ❑ *How about going to see a show tomorrow?*
→ look at **identification, television**

▶ **show off** **1** If someone **is showing off**, they are trying to make people admire them. ❑ *He spent the entire evening showing off.*
2 If you **show off** something, you show it to a lot of people because you are proud of it. ❑ *Naomi was showing off her engagement ring.*

▶ **show up** If a person **shows up**, they arrive at the place where you agreed to meet them. ❑ *We waited until five, but he didn't show up.*

show busi|ness **NONCOUNT NOUN** Show business is the entertainment industry of movies, theater, and television. ❑ *His show business career lasted more than 45 years.*

Spelling Partners   **shower**

---

show|er /ʃaʊər/ (showers, showering, showered)

1 **NOUN** A **shower** is a thing that you stand

under, that covers you with water so you can wash yourself. ❑ *I was in the shower when the phone rang.*
2 **NOUN** If you take a **shower**, you wash yourself by standing under the water that comes from a shower. ❑ *I think I'll take a shower.*
3 **VERB** If you **shower**, you wash yourself by standing under the water that comes from a shower. ❑ *I was late and there wasn't time to shower.*
4 **NOUN** A **shower** is a short period of rain. ❑ *A few showers are expected in the Ohio Valley Saturday.*
5 **NOUN** A **shower** is a party for a woman who is getting married or having a baby. ❑ *Kelly's baby shower is on Thursday night.*
→ look at **bathroom**

shown /ʃoʊn/ **Shown** is a form of the verb **show**.

shrank /ʃræŋk/ **Shrank** is a form of the verb **shrink**.

shriek /ʃriːk/ (shrieks, shrieking, shrieked)

1 **VERB** If you **shriek**, you make a short, very loud cry. ❑ *Gwen shrieked with excitement when she heard the news.*
2 **NOUN** Shriek is also a noun. ❑ *He heard the boy shriek in terror.*

shrimp /ʃrɪmp/ (shrimp)

> **LANGUAGE HELP**
> The plural can also be **shrimps**.

NOUN Shrimp are small pink or gray sea animals, with long tails and many legs, that you can eat. ❑ *Add the shrimp and cook for 30 seconds.*
→ look at **shellfish**

shrine /ʃraɪn/ (shrines) **NOUN** A **shrine** is a religious place where people go to remember a holy person or event. ❑ *They visited the holy shrine of Mecca.*

shrink /ʃrɪŋk/ (shrinks, shrinking, shrank or shrunk) **VERB** If something **shrinks**, it becomes smaller in size. ❑ *Dad's pants shrank after just one wash.*

shrub /ʃrʌb/ (shrubs) **NOUN** A **shrub** is a small bush. ❑ *This books tells you how to choose shrubs for your backyard.*
→ look at **plant**

shrug /ʃrʌg/ (shrugs, shrugging, shrugged)

1 **VERB** If you **shrug**, you move your shoulders up to show that you do not know or care about something. ❑*Melissa just shrugged and replied, "I don't know."*

2 **NOUN** Shrug is also a noun. ❑*"Who cares?" said Anna with a shrug.*

shrunk /ʃrʌŋk/ Shrunk is a form of the verb **shrink.**

shud|der /ʃʌdər/ (shudders, shuddering, shuddered)

1 **VERB** If you **shudder**, your body shakes because you are frightened or cold, or because you feel disgust. ❑*Some people shudder at the idea of injections.*

2 **NOUN** Shudder is also a noun. ❑*"It was terrifying," she says with a shudder.*

shuf|fle /ʃʌfᵊl/ (shuffles, shuffling, shuffled)

1 **VERB** If you **shuffle**, you walk without lifting your feet off the ground. ❑*Moira shuffled across the kitchen.*

2 **VERB** If you **shuffle** playing cards, you mix them up before you begin a game. ❑*Aunt Mary shuffled the cards.*

shut /ʃʌt/ (shuts, shutting, shut)

1 **VERB** If you **shut** something, you close it. ❑*Please shut the gate.* ❑*Lucy shut her eyes and fell asleep at once.*

2 **ADJECTIVE** Shut is also an adjective. ❑*The police have told us to keep our doors and windows shut.* ❑*Her eyes were shut and she seemed to be asleep.*

▶ **shut down** If a factory or a business **shuts down**, it closes and work there stops. ❑*The factory was shut down last month and all the workers lost their jobs.*

▶ **shut up** If you say **"shut up"** to someone, you are asking them, in a rude way, to stop talking. ❑*Just shut up, will you?*

shut|ter /ʃʌtər/ (shutters) **NOUN** Shutters are wooden or metal covers on the outside of a window. ❑*She opened the shutters and looked out of the window.*

shut|tle /ʃʌtᵊl/ (shuttles)

1 **NOUN** A **shuttle** is the same as a **space shuttle.**

2 **NOUN** A **shuttle** is a plane, a bus, or a train that makes regular trips between two places. ❑*There is a free shuttle between the airport terminals.*

shy /ʃaɪ/ (shyer, shyest) **ADJECTIVE** If you are **shy**, you are nervous and embarrassed about talking to people that you do not know well. ❑*She was a shy, quiet girl.* ❑*I was too shy to say anything.* ● **shy|ly** **ADVERB** ❑*The children smiled shyly.* ● **shy|ness** **NONCOUNT NOUN** ❑*His shyness made it difficult for him to make friends.*

sib|ling /sɪblɪŋ/ (siblings) **NOUN** Your **siblings** are your brothers and sisters. [FORMAL] ❑*I often had to take care of my five younger siblings.*

sick /sɪk/ (sicker, sickest)

1 **ADJECTIVE** If you are **sick**, you are not well. ❑*He's very sick. He needs a doctor.*

2 **ADJECTIVE** If you are **sick of** something that has been happening for a long time, you are very annoyed by it and want it to stop happening. [INFORMAL] ❑*I am sick of all your complaints!*

3 If you are **out sick**, you are not at work because you are sick. ❑*Tom is out sick today.*

→ look at Word World: **sick**
→ look at **health care**

sick|ness /sɪknɪs/ **NONCOUNT NOUN** Sickness is the state of being unwell or unhealthy. ❑*Grandpa had only one week of sickness in fifty-two years.*

side /saɪd/ (sides)

1 **NOUN** The **side of** something is a position to the left or right of it. ❑*On the left side of the door there's a door bell.*

2 **NOUN** The **side** of an object is any part of it that is not its front, back, top, or bottom. ❑*He took me along the side of the house.*

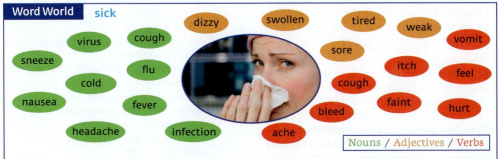

Word World | **sick**

dizzy · swollen · tired · weak · vomit · virus · cough · sore · itch · feel · sneeze · flu · cough · nausea · cold · faint · hurt · fever · bleed · headache · infection · ache

Nouns / Adjectives / Verbs

3 NOUN The **side of** something is its edge. ❏ *We parked on the side of the road.*

4 NOUN The **side of** something is one of its flat surfaces. ❏ *You should write on both sides of the paper.*

5 NOUN Your **sides** are the parts of your body from under your arms to the tops of your legs. ❏ *Hold your arms by your sides and bend your knees.*

6 NOUN The different **sides** in a war or a game are the groups of people who are fighting or playing against each other. ❏ *Both sides want the war to end.*

7 If you are **on** someone's **side**, or **taking** their **side**, you are supporting them in an argument. ❏ *Whose side are you on?*

8 If two people or things are **side by side**, they are next to each other. ❏ *The children were sitting side by side on the sofa.*

side|walk /ˈsaɪdwɔk/ (**sidewalks**) NOUN
A **sidewalk** is a path with a hard surface by the side of a road. ❏ *She was walking down the sidewalk toward him.*

side|ways /ˈsaɪdweɪz/
1 ADVERB If you do something **sideways**, you do it from or toward the side. ❏ *Pete looked sideways at her.*

2 ADJECTIVE **Sideways** is also an adjective. ❏ *Alfred gave him a sideways look.*

siege /sidʒ/ (**sieges**) NOUN A **siege** is when soldiers or police officers surround a place in order to force the people there to come out. ❏ *The siege has been going on for three days.*

sieve /sɪv/ (**sieves, sieving, sieved**)
1 NOUN A **sieve** is a tool with a fine metal net, that you use for separating solids from liquids. ❏ *Press the soup through a sieve into a bowl.*

2 VERB When you **sieve** a substance, you put it through a sieve. ❏ *Sieve the flour into a bowl.*

sigh /saɪ/ (**sighs, sighing, sighed**)
1 VERB If you **sigh**, you let out a deep breath because you are disappointed, tired, or pleased. ❏ *Roberta sighed with relief.*

2 NOUN **Sigh** is also a noun. ❏ *Maria kicked off her shoes and sat down with a sigh.*

sight /saɪt/ (**sights**)
1 NONCOUNT NOUN Your **sight** is your ability to see. ❏ *Grandpa has lost the sight in his right eye.*

2 NOUN The **sight of** something is the act of seeing it. ❏ *Liz can't bear the sight of blood.*

3 PLURAL NOUN The **sights** are the places that are interesting to see and that tourists often visit. ❏ *We saw the sights of Paris.*

4 If you **catch sight of** someone or something, you suddenly see them for a short period of time. ❏ *He caught sight of Helen in the crowd.*

5 If something is **in sight**, you can see it. If it is **out of sight**, you cannot see it. ❏ *At last the town was in sight.*

6 If you **lose sight of** someone or something, you can no longer see them. ❏ *The man ran off and I lost sight of him.*

→ look at **sense**

sight|see|ing /ˈsaɪtsiɪŋ/ NONCOUNT NOUN
If you go **sightseeing** or do some **sightseeing**, you travel around visiting the interesting places that tourists usually visit. ❏ *During our vacation, we had a day's sightseeing in Venice.*

Spelling Partners — **sign**

sign /saɪn/ (**signs, signing, signed**)
1 NOUN A **sign** is a mark, a shape or a movement that has a particular meaning. ❏ *In math, + is a plus sign and = is an equals sign.* ❏ *They gave me a sign to show that everything was OK.*

2 NOUN A **sign** is a piece of wood, metal, or plastic with words or pictures on it that warn you about something or give you information or an instruction. ❏ *The road signs here are in both English and French.* ❏ *The sign said, "Welcome to Hebron."*

3 NOUN If there is a **sign of** something, there is something that shows that it exists or is happening. ❏ *Matthew showed no sign of fear.*

4 VERB When you **sign** a document, you write your name on it. ❏ *World leaders have signed an agreement to protect the environment.*

	Word Partners Use **sign** with:
V.	**give a** sign **1**
	hang a sign, **read a** sign **2**
	see a sign **2** **3**
	refuse to sign **4**
N.	sign **on a door, neon** sign, **stop** sign, sign **in a window 2**
	sign **of progress,** sign **of trouble,** sign **of weakness 3**
	sign **an agreement,** sign **an autograph,** sign **a contract,** sign **legislation,** sign **your name,** sign **a treaty 4**
ADJ.	**bad** sign, **good** sign, **positive** sign, **warning** sign **3**

S

sig|nal /sɪgnəl/ (**signals, signaling, signaled**)

1 NOUN A **signal** is a movement, light, or sound that gives a particular message to the person who sees or hears it. ❑ *The captain gave the signal for the soldiers to attack.*

2 VERB If you **signal to** someone, you make a movement or sound to give them a particular message. ❑ *Mandy signaled to Jesse to follow her.*

sig|na|ture /sɪgnətʃər, -tʃʊər/ (**signatures**) **NOUN** Your **signature** is your name, written in your own special way. ❑ *I put my signature at the bottom of the page.*

sig|nifi|cance /sɪgnɪfɪkəns/ **NONCOUNT NOUN** The **significance** of something is its importance or meaning. ❑ *What do you think is the significance of this event?*

sig|nifi|cant /sɪgnɪfɪkənt/ **ADJECTIVE** If something is **significant**, it is important or large. ❑ *There has been a significant increase in the price of oil.* ● **sig|nifi|cant|ly ADVERB** ❑ *The temperature dropped significantly.*

Sikh /siːk/ (**Sikhs**) **NOUN** A **Sikh** is a person who follows the Indian religion called **Sikhism**. ❑ *Rebecca's husband is a Sikh.* ❑ *...a Sikh temple.*

si|lence /saɪləns/ (**silences**) **NOUN** If there is **silence**, no one is speaking. ❑ *They stood in silence.* ❑ *There was a long silence before Sarah replied.*

si|lent /saɪlənt/

1 ADJECTIVE If you are **silent**, you are not speaking. ❑ *Jessica was silent because she did not know what to say.* ● **si|lent|ly ADVERB** ❑ *She and Ned sat silently, enjoying the peace.*

2 ADJECTIVE If something is **silent**, it is completely quiet, with no sound at all. ❑ *The room was silent except for the TV.* ● **si|lent|ly ADVERB** ❑ *The thief moved silently across the room.*

sil|hou|ette /sɪluɛt/ (**silhouettes**) **NOUN** A **silhouette** is the dark shape that you see when someone or something has a bright light behind them. ❑ *She could see the distant silhouette of a castle.*

silk /sɪlk/ **NONCOUNT NOUN** **Silk** is a smooth, shiny cloth that is made from very thin threads. ❑ *Pauline was wearing a beautiful silk dress.*

silky /sɪlki/ (**silkier, silkiest**) **ADJECTIVE** If something is **silky**, it is smooth, soft, and shiny, like silk. ❑ *This shampoo makes your hair beautifully silky.*

sil|ly /sɪli/ (**sillier, silliest**) **ADJECTIVE** If you are **silly**, you do not behave in a sensible or serious way. ❑ *"Don't be so silly, darling!"* ❑ *I know it's silly to feel nervous but I can't help it.*

sil|ver /sɪlvər/

1 NONCOUNT NOUN **Silver** is a valuable pale gray metal that is used for making jewelry. ❑ *He bought her a bracelet made from silver.*

2 ADJECTIVE Something that is **silver** is shiny and pale gray in color. ❑ *He had thick silver hair.*

sil|ver med|al (**silver medals**) **NOUN** A **silver medal** is an award made of silver metal that you get as second prize in a competition. ❑ *Gillingham won the silver medal in the 200 meters.*

SIM card /sɪm kɑrd/ (**SIM cards**) **NOUN** A **SIM card** is a small electronic piece of equipment in a cellphone that connects it to a particular phone network. **SIM** is short for "Subscriber Identity Module."

simi|lar /sɪmɪlər/ **ADJECTIVE** If one thing is **similar to** another, or if two things are **similar**, they are the same in some ways but not in every way. ❑ *This cake tastes similar to carrot cake.* ❑ *Nowadays, cars all look very similar.*

simi|lar|ity /sɪmɪlærɪti/ (**similarities**) **NOUN** **Similarities** are things that are the same about two people or things. ❑ *There are many similarities between the two country's cultures.*

simi|le /sɪmɪli/ (**similes**) **NOUN** LANGUAGE ARTS A **simile** is an expression that describes a person or a thing by comparing it with another person or thing, using the words "like" or "as." An example of a simile is "She swims like a fish."

sim|mer /sɪmər/ (**simmers, simmering, simmered**) **VERB** If food **simmers**, it cooks gently in water that is just boiling. ❑ *Let the soup simmer for 15-20 minutes.*

sim|ple /sɪmpəl/ (**simpler, simplest**)

1 ADJECTIVE If something is **simple**, it is easy to understand. ❑ *The recipes in the book are simple and easy to follow.* ❑ *Just follow the simple instructions below.* ● **sim|ply ADVERB** ❑ *He explained his views simply and clearly.*

2 ADJECTIVE If something is **simple**, it has all the basic things it needs, but nothing more. ❑ *He ate a simple dinner of rice and beans.* ❑ *Amanda was wearing a simple black silk dress..* ● **sim|ply ADVERB** ❑ *Her house is decorated simply.*

s

sim|plic|ity /sɪmplɪsɪti/ **NONCOUNT NOUN**
Simplicity is the quality of being simple.
❏ *I love the simplicity of his designs.*

sim|pli|fy /sɪmplɪfaɪ/ (**simplifies,
simplifying, simplified**) **VERB** If you **simplify**
something, you make it easier to
understand or to do. ❏ *This program simplifies
the task of searching for information.*
● **sim|pli|fied ADJECTIVE** ❏ *We read a simplified
version of Shakespeare's "Hamlet."*

simp|ly /sɪmpli/ **ADVERB** You use **simply**
to emphasize what you are saying. ❏ *Your
behavior is simply unacceptable.*

sin /sɪn/ (**sins, sinning, sinned**)
1 **NOUN** A **sin** is an action or a type of
behavior that breaks a religious law.
❏ *They believe that lying is a sin.*
2 **VERB** If you **sin**, you do something that
breaks a religious law. ❏ *The Bible says that we
have all sinned.* ● **sin|ner** /sɪnər/ (**sinners**)
NOUN ❏ *Is she a sinner or a saint?*

since /sɪns/
1 **PREPOSITION** You use **since** when you are
talking about a time or an event that started
in the past, and that has continued from
then until now. ❏ *My uncle has lived in India
since 1995.*
2 **ADVERB** **Since** is also an adverb. ❏ *They
worked together in the 1980s, and have been friends
ever since.*
3 **CONJUNCTION** **Since** is also a conjunction.
❏ *I've lived here since I was six years old.*
4 **CONJUNCTION** **Since** means "because."
❏ *I'm always on a diet, since I put on weight easily.*

sin|cere /sɪnsɪər/ **ADJECTIVE** If you are
sincere, you are honest and you really mean
what you say. ❏ *Do you think Ryan's being
sincere?*

sin|cere|ly /sɪnsɪərli/
1 **ADVERB** If you say or feel something
sincerely, you really mean or feel it. ❏ *"Well
done!" he said sincerely.*
2 You write "**Sincerely yours**" or "**Sincerely**"
before your signature at the end of a formal
letter when you have addressed it to
someone by name. ❏ *Sincerely yours, Robbie
Weinz.*

sing /sɪŋ/ (**sings, singing, sang, sung**) **VERB**
MUSIC When you **sing**, you make music with
your voice. ❏ *I love singing.* ❏ *My brother and I
used to sing this song.*
→ look at **music**

sing|er /sɪŋər/ (**singers**) **NOUN** MUSIC
A **singer** is a person who sings, especially
as a job. ❏ *My mother was a singer in a band.*
→ look at **music, performance**

sin|gle /sɪŋɡᵊl/
1 **ADJECTIVE** You use **single** to show that you
are talking about only one thing. ❏ *She hasn't
said a single word about what happened.* ❏ *We sold
over two hundred pizzas in a single day.*
2 **ADJECTIVE** If you are **single**, you are not
married. ❏ *Joseph is a single man in his early
twenties.*
3 **ADJECTIVE** A **single** room or bed is for one
person only. ❏ *Would you like to reserve a single or
a double room?*

sin|gu|lar /sɪŋɡyələr/
1 **ADJECTIVE** LANGUAGE ARTS The **singular**
form of a word is the form that you use
when you are talking about one person or
thing. ❏ *The singular form of "mice" is "mouse."*
2 **NOUN** LANGUAGE ARTS The **singular** of a
noun is the form of it that you use when you
are talking about one person or thing.
❏ *What is the singular of "geese?"*

sink /sɪŋk/ (**sinks, sinking, sank, sunk**)
1 **NOUN** A **sink** is a large fixed container in a
kitchen or a bathroom that you can fill with
water. ❏ *The sink was filled with dirty dishes.*
❏ *The bathroom has a toilet, a shower, and a sink.*
2 **VERB** If a boat **sinks**, it goes below the
surface of the water. ❏ *The boat hit the rocks
and began to sink.*
3 **VERB** If something **sinks**, it moves slowly
down, to a lower level. ❏ *The sun was sinking in
the west.*
→ look at **bathroom, kitchen**

sip /sɪp/ (**sips, sipping, sipped**)
1 **VERB** If you **sip** a drink, you drink it
slowly, taking a small amount at a time.
❏ *Jessica sipped her drink slowly.*
2 **NOUN** A **sip** is a small amount of drink
that you take into your mouth. ❏ *Harry took
a sip of tea.*

sir /sɜr/ (**sirs**)
1 **NOUN** You use **sir** as a polite way of
talking to a man. ❏ *Excuse me sir, is this your car?*
2 You write **Dear Sir** at the beginning of a
formal letter or a business letter when you
are writing to a man. ❏ *Dear Sir, Thank you for
your letter.*

si|ren /saɪrən/ (**sirens**) **NOUN** A **siren** is a
piece of equipment that makes a long, loud

S

noise to warn people about something. Fire engines and police cars have sirens. ❏ *In the distance I could hear a siren.*

sis|ter /sɪstər/ (**sisters**) NOUN Your **sister** is a girl or woman who has the same parents as you. ❏ *This is my sister Sarah.*
→ look at **family**

sister-in-law (**sisters-in-law**) NOUN Someone's **sister-in-law** is the sister of their husband or wife, or the woman who is married to their brother.
→ look at **family**

sit /sɪt/ (**sits, sitting, sat**)
1 VERB If you **are sitting** in a chair, your bottom is resting on the chair and the upper part of your body is straight. ❏ *Mother was sitting in her chair in the kitchen.* ❏ *They sat watching television all evening.*
2 VERB When you **sit down**, you move your body down until you are sitting on something. ❏ *Kelly sat down on the bed and took off her shoes.* ❏ *Mom sat down beside me.*
▶ **sit up** If you **sit up**, you change the position of your body, so that you are sitting instead of lying down. ❏ *She felt dizzy when she sat up.*

site /saɪt/ (**sites**)
1 NOUN A **site** is a place where a particular thing happens. ❏ *Dad works on a building site.* ❏ *This city was the site of a terrible earthquake.*
2 NOUN TECHNOLOGY A **site** is the same as a **website**. ❏ *The site contains advice for new teachers.*

situ|at|ed /sɪtʃueɪtɪd/ ADJECTIVE If something is **situated** in a particular place, it is in that place. ❏ *The hotel is situated in the center of Berlin.*

situa|tion /sɪtʃueɪʃⁿn/ (**situations**) NOUN The **situation** is what is happening in a particular place at a particular time. ❏ *Army officers said the situation was under control.*

six /sɪks/ MATH **Six** is the number 6.
→ look at **number**

Word Builder **sixteen**

teen ≈ plus ten, from 13-19
    eight + teen = eighteen
    four + teen = fourteen
    nine + teen = nineteen
    seven + teen = seventeen
    six + teen = sixteen
    teen + age = teenage

---

six|teen /sɪkstin/ MATH **Sixteen** is the number 16.

sixth /sɪksθ/ (**sixths**)
1 ADJECTIVE, ADVERB MATH The **sixth** item in a series is the one that you count as number six. ❏ *The sixth round of the competition begins tomorrow.* ❏ *Brad came sixth in the swimming race.*
2 NOUN MATH A **sixth** is one of six equal parts of something (⅙).
→ look at **number**

six|ty /sɪksti/ MATH **Sixty** is the number 60.

size /saɪz/ (**sizes**)
1 NOUN The **size of** something is how big or small it is. ❏ *The size of the room is about 10 feet by 15 feet.* ❏ *The shelves contain books of various sizes.* ● **-sized** ADJECTIVE ❏ *I work for a medium-sized company in Chicago.*
2 NOUN A **size** is one of a series of particular measurements for clothes and shoes. ❏ *My sister is a size 12.* ❏ *What size are your feet?* ❏ *"Do you have these shoes in a size nine?"*

skate /skeɪt/ (**skates, skating, skated**)
1 NOUN SPORTS **Skates** (or **ice-skates**) are boots that have a long, sharp piece of metal on the bottom of them, so that you can move quickly and smoothly on ice when you are wearing them.
2 NOUN SPORTS **Skates** (or **roller-skates**) are boots that have wheels on the bottom of them, so that you can move quickly on the ground.
3 VERB SPORTS If you **skate**, you move around wearing skates. ❏ *When the pond froze, we skated on it.* ● **skat|ing** NONCOUNT NOUN ❏ *They all went skating together in the winter.* ● **skat|er** NOUN ❏ *The ice-rink was full of skaters.*

skate|board /skeɪtbɔrd/ (**skateboards**) NOUN SPORTS A **skateboard** is a narrow board with wheels at each end that you can stand on and ride.

skel|eton /skɛlɪtⁿn/ (**skeletons**) NOUN SCIENCE A **skeleton** is all the bones in a person's or an animal's body. ❏ *...a human skeleton.*

sketch /skɛtʃ/ (**sketches, sketching, sketched**)
1 NOUN ARTS A **sketch** is a drawing that you do quickly, without a lot of details. ❏ *He did a quick sketch of the building.*
2 VERB ARTS If you **sketch** something, you make a quick drawing of it. ❏ *She started*

s

sketching designs when she was six years old.
→ look at **draw**

ski /ski/ (**skis, skiing, skied**)
1 NOUN SPORTS **Skis** are long, flat, narrow pieces of wood, metal, or plastic that you fasten to your boots so that you can move easily on snow or water.
2 VERB SPORTS When you **ski**, you move over snow or water on skis. ❑ *They tried to ski down Mount Everest.* ● **ski|er** /skiər/ (**skiers**) NOUN ❑ *My dad's a very good skier.* ● **ski|ing** NONCOUNT NOUN ❑ *My hobbies are skiing and swimming.*

skid /skid/ (**skids, skidding, skidded**) VERB If a vehicle **skids**, it slides sideways or forward when you try to stop it suddenly. ❑ *The car skidded on the icy road.*

skill /skil/ (**skills**)
1 NOUN A **skill** is a job or an activity that needs special training and practice. ❑ *You're never too old to learn new skills.*
2 NONCOUNT NOUN **Skill** is your ability to do something well. ❑ *He shows great skill on the football field.*

skilled /skild/ ADJECTIVE If you are **skilled**, you have the knowledge and ability to do something well. ❑ *We need more skilled workers.*

skill|ful /skilfəl/ ADJECTIVE If you are **skillful** at something, you do it very well. ❑ *He was a highly skillful football player.* ● **skill|ful|ly** ADVERB ❑ *The story is skillfully written.*

skim /skim/ (**skims, skimming, skimmed**)
1 VERB If something **skims** a surface, it moves quickly just above it. ❑ *We watched seagulls skimming the waves.*
2 ADJECTIVE **Skim milk** is milk that has the fat removed from it. ❑ *You'll need half a cup of skim milk, one cup of yogurt, and some fruit.*

skin /skin/ (**skins**)
1 NONCOUNT NOUN SCIENCE **Skin** is the substance that covers the outside of a person's or an animal's body. ❑ *His skin is pale and smooth.* ❑ *...a crocodile skin handbag.*
2 NOUN The **skin** of a fruit or a vegetable is the outer part that covers it. ❑ *...a banana skin.*
→ look at **fruit, sense**

skin|ny /skini/ (**skinnier, skinniest**) ADJECTIVE Someone who is **skinny** is

extremely thin or too thin. [INFORMAL]
❑ *He was a skinny little boy.*

skip /skip/ (**skips, skipping, skipped**)
1 VERB If you **skip** along, you move forward quickly, jumping from one foot to the other. ❑ *We skipped down the street, talking and laughing.*
2 NOUN **Skip** is also a noun. ❑ *Joshua gave a little skip as he left the room.*
3 VERB If you **skip** something that you usually do, you decide not to do it. ❑ *Don't skip breakfast.*

skip rope (**skip ropes**) NOUN A **skip rope** is a piece of rope with handles at each end. You turn it and jump over it.

skirt /skɜrt/ (**skirts**) NOUN A **skirt** is a piece of clothing for women and girls. It hangs down from the waist and covers part of the legs.
→ look at **clothing**

skull /skʌl/ (**skulls**) NOUN SCIENCE A person's or an animal's **skull** is the bones of their head. ❑ *After the accident, they X-rayed his skull.*

skunk /skʌŋk/ (**skunks**) NOUN A **skunk** is a small black and white animal from North America with an unpleasant smell.

sky /skaɪ/ (**skies**) NOUN The **sky** is the space above the Earth that you can see when you stand outside and look upward. ❑ *The sun was shining in the sky.* ❑ *Today we have clear blue skies.*

sky|scraper /skaɪskreɪpər/ (**skyscrapers**) NOUN A **skyscraper** is a very tall building in a city.

slab /slæb/ (**slabs**) NOUN A **slab of** something is a thick, flat piece of it. ❑ *...slabs of stone.*

slack /slæk/ (**slacker, slackest**)
1 ADJECTIVE If something is **slack**, it is loose. ❑ *Suddenly, the rope went slack.*
2 ADJECTIVE If a business has a **slack** period, it is not busy. ❑ *The store has busy times and slack periods.*

slam /slæm/ (**slams, slamming, slammed**)
1 VERB If you **slam** a door, you shut it very noisily and roughly. ❑ *She slammed the door behind her.*
2 VERB If you **slam** something **down**, you put it there quickly and roughly. ❑ *Lauren slammed the phone down angrily.*

slang /slæŋ/ NONCOUNT NOUN **Slang** is informal words that you can use when you are talking to people you know very well. ❑ *The slang word for "money" is "dough."*

S

slant /slænt/ (**slants, slanting, slanted**) **VERB**
If something **slants**, it has one side higher than the other. ❏ *The roof of the house slants sharply.*

slap /slæp/ (**slaps, slapping, slapped**)
1 VERB If you **slap** someone, you hit them with the flat inside part of your hand. ❏ *I slapped him hard across the face.*
2 NOUN Slap is also a noun. ❏ *She gave him a slap on the face.*

slash /slæʃ/ (**slashes, slashing, slashed**)
1 VERB If you **slash** something, you make a long, deep cut in it. ❏ *Someone slashed my car tires in the night.*
2 NOUN LANGUAGE ARTS A **slash** is a line (/) that separates numbers, letters, or words in writing.

slaugh|ter /slɔtər/ (**slaughters, slaughtering, slaughtered**)
1 VERB If people **are slaughtered**, a very large number of them are killed violently. ❏ *So many innocent people have been slaughtered.*
2 NONCOUNT NOUN Slaughter is also a noun. ❏ *The slaughter of women and children was common.*
3 VERB To **slaughter** animals means to kill them for their meat. ❏ *The farmers here slaughter their own cows.*
4 NONCOUNT NOUN Slaughter is also a noun. ❏ *The sheep were taken away for slaughter.*

slave /sleɪv/ (**slaves, slaving, slaved**)
1 NOUN A **slave** is a person who belongs to another person and who works for them without being paid.
2 VERB If you **slave**, you work very hard. ❏ *He was slaving away in the hot kitchen.*

slav|ery /sleɪvəri, sleɪvri/ **NONCOUNT NOUN**
Slavery is when people belong to other people as slaves. ❏ *The United States abolished slavery in 1865.*

slave trade **NOUN** SOCIAL STUDIES The **slave trade** was the business of buying and selling slaves (= servants who are forced to work for someone). ❏ *Many people made money from the slave trade.*

sled /slɛd/ (**sleds**) **NOUN** A **sled** is an object that you sit on in order to travel over snow. ❏ *We pulled the children across the snow on a sled.*

sleep /slip/ (**sleeps, sleeping, slept**)
1 NONCOUNT NOUN Sleep is a person's or an animal's natural state of rest when their eyes are closed, and their body is not active. ❏ *You should try to get as much sleep as possible.*
2 VERB When you **are sleeping**, your eyes are closed and your mind and body are not active. ❏ *I didn't sleep well last night—it was too hot.*
3 NOUN A **sleep** is a period of sleeping. ❏ *Good morning, Pete. Did you have a good sleep?*
4 When you **go to sleep**, you start sleeping. ❏ *Be quiet and go to sleep!*
→ look at **relax**

sleep|ing bag (**sleeping bags**) **NOUN** A **sleeping bag** is a large warm bag for sleeping in when you go camping.

sleep|less /sliplɪs/ **ADJECTIVE** A **sleepless** night is one during which you do not sleep. ❏ *I have sleepless nights worrying about her.*

sleepy /slipi/ (**sleepier, sleepiest**) **ADJECTIVE**
If you are **sleepy**, you are very tired and are almost asleep. ❏ *The pills made me sleepy.*

sleet /slit/ **NONCOUNT NOUN Sleet** is a mixture of snow and rain. ❏ *The snow and sleet will continue overnight.*

sleeve /sliv/ (**sleeves**) **NOUN** The **sleeves** of a piece of clothing are the parts that cover your arms. ❏ *Rachel wore a blue dress with long sleeves.*

sleigh /sleɪ/ (**sleighs**) **NOUN** A **sleigh** is a vehicle with two pieces of wood or metal on the bottom, that you sit in to travel over snow. Sleighs are usually pulled by horses.

slept /slɛpt/ **Slept** is a form of the verb **sleep**.

slice /slaɪs/ (**slices, slicing, sliced**)
1 NOUN A **slice of** something is a thin piece that you cut from a larger piece. ❏ *Would you like a slice of bread?* ❏ *Nicole had a cup of coffee and a large slice of chocolate cake.*
2 VERB If you **slice** food, you cut it into thin pieces. ❏ *I blew out the candles and Mom sliced the cake.*
→ look at **bread**

slick /slɪk/ (**slicker, slickest**) **ADJECTIVE** A **slick** action is quick and smooth, and is done without any obvious effort. ❏ *We loved the slick way he passed the ball.*

slide /slaɪd/ (**slides, sliding, slid**)
1 VERB When someone or something **slides**, they move quickly and smoothly over a surface. ❏ *She slid across the ice on her stomach.*

2 **NOUN** A **slide** is a large metal frame that children can play on. They climb the steps at one side, and move down a smooth slope on their bottom.

slight /slaɪt/ **ADJECTIVE** Something that is **slight** is small and not important or serious. ❏ *The sun was shining and there was a slight breeze.* ❏ *The company has announced a slight increase in sales.*

slight|ly /slaɪtli/ **ADVERB** **Slightly** means just a little. ❏ *We've moved to a slightly larger house.* ❏ *Each person learns in a slightly different way.*

slim /slɪm/ (**slimmer, slimmest, slims, slimming, slimmed**) **ADJECTIVE** If you are **slim**, your body is thin in an attractive way. ❏ *The young woman was tall and slim.*

▶ **slim down** If you **slim down**, you lose weight and become thinner. ❏ *I've slimmed down a size or two.*

slime /slaɪm/ **NONCOUNT NOUN** **Slime** is a thick, wet substance that looks or smells unpleasant. ❏ *The rocks are slippery with mud and slime.*

sling /slɪŋ/ (**slings**) **NOUN** A **sling** is a piece of cloth that you wear around your neck and arm, to hold up your arm when it is broken or injured. ❏ *Emily had her arm in a sling.*

slip /slɪp/ (**slips, slipping, slipped**)
1 **VERB** If you **slip**, you accidentally slide and fall. ❏ *He slipped on the wet grass.*
2 **VERB** If something **slips**, it slides out of position. ❏ *Grandpa's glasses slipped down his nose.*
3 **VERB** If you **slip** somewhere, you go there quickly and quietly. ❏ *In the morning she quietly slipped out of the house.*
4 **VERB** If you **slip** something somewhere, you put it there quickly and quietly. ❏ *I slipped the letter into my pocket.*
5 **NOUN** A **slip** is a small mistake. ❏ *Even a tiny slip could ruin everything.*
6 **NOUN** A **slip of** paper is a small piece of paper. ❏ *He wrote our names on slips of paper.*

▶ **slip up** If you **slip up**, you make a mistake. ❏ *We slipped up a few times, but no-one noticed.*

slip|per /slɪpər/ (**slippers**) **NOUN** **Slippers** are loose, soft shoes that you wear indoors. ❏ *She put on a pair of slippers and went downstairs.*

slip|pery /slɪpəri/ **ADJECTIVE** If something is **slippery**, it is smooth or wet, and is difficult to walk on or to hold. ❏ *Be careful—the floor is slippery.*

slit /slɪt/ (**slits, slitting, slit**)
1 **VERB** If you **slit** something, you make a long narrow cut in it. ❏ *He slit open the envelope.*
2 **NOUN** A **slit** is a long narrow cut or opening in something. ❏ *Make a slit about half an inch long.*

slith|er /slɪðər/ (**slithers, slithering, slithered**) **VERB** If you **slither**, you move along the ground, sliding from side to side, like a snake. ❏ *Robert slithered down into the water.*

sliv|er /slɪvər/ (**slivers**) **NOUN** A **sliver of** something is a small thin piece of it. ❏ *A sliver of glass cut my foot.*

slo|gan /slougən/ (**slogans**) **NOUN** A **slogan** is a short phrase that you can remember easily. Slogans are used in advertisements and by political parties. ❏ *His campaign slogan was "Time for Action."*

slope /sloup/ (**slopes, sloping, sloped**)
1 **NOUN** A **slope** is the side of a mountain, hill, or valley. ❏ *A steep slope leads to the beach.*
2 **VERB** If a surface **slopes**, one end of it is higher than the other. ❏ *The land sloped down sharply to the river.* ● **slop|ing** **ADJECTIVE** ❏ *Our house has a sloping roof.*
3 **VERB** If something **slopes**, it leans to the right or to the left rather than being straight. ❏ *John's writing slopes backwards.*

slop|py /slɒpi/ (**sloppier, sloppiest**) **ADJECTIVE** If something is **sloppy**, it has been done in a careless and lazy way. ❏ *All teachers hate sloppy work from their students.*

slot /slɒt/ (**slots**) **NOUN** A **slot** is a long, narrow hole in something. ❏ *He dropped a coin into the slot and dialed the number.* ❏ *Please place your credit card in the slot.*
→ look at **ATM**

slow /slou/ (**slower, slowest, slows, slowing, slowed**)
1 **ADJECTIVE** If something is **slow**, it does not move or happen quickly. ❏ *His bike was heavy and slow.* ❏ *The investigation was a long and slow process.* ❏ *They danced to the slow rhythm of the music.* ● **slow|ly** **ADVERB** ❏ *He spoke slowly and clearly.*
2 **ADJECTIVE** If a clock or a watch is **slow**, it shows a time that is earlier than the correct time. ❏ *The clock is five minutes slow.*
→ look at **car, email**

▶ **slow down** If something **slows down**, it starts to move or happen more slowly. ❏ *The bus slowed down for the next stop.*

S

slow|down /sloʊdaʊn/ (slowdowns) NOUN
A **slowdown** is a reduction in speed or activity. ❑ *There has been a sharp slowdown in economic growth.*

slow mo|tion also **slow-motion**
NONCOUNT NOUN When film or television pictures are shown **in slow motion**, they are shown much more slowly than normal. ❑ *They played it again in slow motion.*

slug /slʌg/ (slugs) NOUN A **slug** is a small animal with a long soft body and no legs that moves very slowly.

slum /slʌm/ (slums) NOUN A **slum** is an area of a city where the buildings are in a bad condition and the people are very poor. ❑ *More than 2.4 million people live in the city's slums.*

slump /slʌmp/ (slumps, slumping, slumped)
1 VERB If the value of something **slumps**, it falls suddenly and by a large amount. ❑ *The company's profits slumped by 41% in a single year.*
2 NOUN Slump is also a noun. ❑ *There has been a slump in house prices.*
3 VERB If you **slump** somewhere, you fall or sit down suddenly and heavily. ❑ *She slumped into a chair and burst into tears.*

slur /slɜr/ (slurs, slurring, slurred) VERB
If you **slur** your words, you do not say each word clearly, because you are drunk, sick, or very tired. ❑ *He was slurring his words and I couldn't understand what he was saying.* ● **slurred** ADJECTIVE ❑ *Her speech was slurred and she was very pale.*

sly /slaɪ/ ADJECTIVE A **sly** look, expression, or remark shows that you know something that other people do not know or that was meant to be a secret. ❑ *He gave a sly smile.* ● **sly|ly** ADVERB ❑ *Anna grinned slyly.*

smack /smæk/ (smacks, smacking, smacked)
1 VERB If you **smack** someone, you hit them with your hand. ❑ *She smacked me on the side of the head.*
2 NOUN Smack is also a noun. ❑ *She gave him a smack.*

small /smɔl/ (smaller, smallest)
1 ADJECTIVE If something is **small**, it is not large in size or amount. ❑ *My daughter is small for her age.* ❑ *Fry the onions in a small amount of butter.*
2 ADJECTIVE A **small** child is a young child. ❑ *I have two small children.*

3 ADJECTIVE If something is **small**, it is not very serious or important. ❑ *It's a small problem, and we can easily solve it.*
→ look at **shopping**

small-scale ADJECTIVE A **small-scale** activity or organization is small in size and scale. ❑ *Most of the world's coffee beans are grown by small-scale farmers.*

smart /smɑrt/ (smarter, smartest)
ADJECTIVE If you are **smart**, you are clever or intelligent. ❑ *He's a very smart, intelligent player.*

smartphone (smartphones) NOUN
TECHNOLOGY A **smartphone** is a type of cellphone that can do many of the things that a computer does.

smash /smæʃ/ (smashes, smashing, smashed)
1 VERB If you **smash** something, it breaks into many pieces. ❑ *The gang started smashing windows in the street.* ❑ *I dropped the bottle and it smashed on the floor.*
2 NOUN Smash is also a noun. ❑ *I heard the smash of glass and I shouted, "Get down!"*

smear /smɪər/ (smears, smearing, smeared)
1 VERB If you **smear** a sticky substance on a surface, you spread the substance all over it. ❑ *My little sister smeared jam all over her face.*
● **smeared** ADJECTIVE ❑ *The child's clothes were smeared with dirt.*
2 NOUN A **smear** is a dirty mark on something. ❑ *There were smears of oil on his face.*

smell /smɛl/ (smells, smelling, smelled)
1 NOUN The **smell** of something is the quality of it that you notice when you breathe in through your nose. ❑ *I just love the smell of freshly baked bread.* ❑ *There was a horrible smell in the refrigerator.*
2 VERB If something **smells** a particular way, it has a quality that you notice by breathing in through your nose. ❑ *The room smelled of lemons.* ❑ *The soup smells delicious!*
3 VERB If something **smells**, it smells unpleasant. ❑ *My girlfriend says my feet smell.*
4 VERB If you **smell** something, you notice it when you breathe in through your nose. ❑ *As soon as we opened the front door, we could smell smoke.*
→ look at **sense**

smelly /smɛli/ (smellier, smelliest)
ADJECTIVE If something is **smelly**, it has an unpleasant smell. ❑ *...smelly socks.*

smile /smaɪl/ (smiles, smiling, smiled)

1 **VERB** If you **smile**, the corners of your mouth curve up because you are happy or you think that something is funny. ❑ *When he saw me, he smiled.* ❑ *The children were all smiling at her.*

2 **NOUN** A **smile** is the expression that you have on your face when you smile. ❑ *She gave a little smile.*

smog /smɒg/ **NONCOUNT NOUN** Smog is pollution in the air that is a mixture of fog (= thick cloud that forms close to the ground) and gases or smoke. ❑ *Winter smog was caused by people burning coal in their homes.* ❑ *A yellow smog hangs over the city on a hot Friday afternoon.*
→ look at **pollution**

smoke /smoʊk/ (smokes, smoking, smoked)

1 **NONCOUNT NOUN** Smoke is the black or white clouds of gas that you see in the air when something burns. ❑ *Thick black smoke blew over the city.*

2 **VERB** If you **smoke** a cigarette, you suck the smoke from it into your mouth and blow it out again. If you **smoke**, you regularly smoke cigarettes. ❑ *He smokes 20 cigarettes a day.* ❑ *You must quit smoking.* ● **smok|er** (smokers) **NOUN** ❑ *Smokers have a much higher risk of developing this disease.* ● **smok|ing** **NONCOUNT NOUN** ❑ *Smoking is banned in many restaurants.*
→ look at **pollution**

smoky /smoʊki/ (smokier, smokiest) also **smokey** **ADJECTIVE** If a place is **smoky**, there is a lot of smoke in the air. ❑ *The bar was dark, noisy, and smoky.*

smooth /smuð/ (smoother, smoothest)

1 **ADJECTIVE** If a surface is **smooth**, it is flat and has no rough parts, lumps, or holes. ❑ *The baby's skin was soft and smooth.* ❑ *The surface of the water is as smooth as glass.*

2 **ADJECTIVE** If a liquid is **smooth**, it has no lumps. ❑ *Stir the mixture until it is smooth.*

3 **ADJECTIVE** A **smooth** movement has no sudden changes in direction or speed. ❑ *The pilot made a very smooth landing.* ● **smooth|ly** **ADVERB** ❑ *The boat was traveling smoothly through the water.*

4 **ADJECTIVE** If a process is **smooth**, it goes well and has no problems. ❑ *We hope for a* smooth move to our new home. ● **smooth|ly** **ADVERB** ❑ *I hope your trip goes smoothly.*
→ look at **sense**

smoth|er /smʌðər/ (smothers, smothering, smothered)

1 **VERB** If you **smother** a fire, you cover it with something in order to stop it burning. ❑ *She tried to smother the flames with a blanket.*

2 **VERB** If you **smother** someone, you kill them by covering their face with something so that they cannot breathe. ❑ *She tried to smother him with a pillow.*

smudge /smʌdʒ/ (smudges, smudging, smudged)

1 **NOUN** A **smudge** is a dirty mark. ❑ *There was a dark smudge on his forehead.*

2 **VERB** If you **smudge** something, you make it dirty or messy by touching it. ❑ *Jennifer rubbed her eyes, smudging her make-up.*

smug /smʌg/ **ADJECTIVE** If you are **smug**, you are very pleased with yourself, in a way that other people find annoying. ❑ *"I have everything I need," he said with a smug little smile.* ● **smug|ly** **ADVERB** ❑ *Sue smiled smugly and sat down.*

smug|gle /smʌgəl/ (smuggles, smuggling, smuggled) **VERB** If you **smuggle** things or people into a place or out of it, you take them there illegally or secretly. ❑ *They smuggled goods into the country.* ● **smug|gler** (smugglers) **NOUN** ❑ *The police arrested the diamond smugglers yesterday.* ● **smug|gling** **NONCOUNT NOUN** ❑ *A pilot was arrested and charged with smuggling.*

snack /snæk/ (snacks, snacking, snacked)

1 **NOUN** A **snack** is a simple meal that is quick to prepare and to eat. ❑ *The kids have a snack when they come in from school.*

2 **VERB** If you **snack**, you eat a small amount of food between meals. ❑ *During the day, I snack on fruit and drink lots of water.*
→ look at **eat**

snag /snæg/ (snags) **NOUN** A **snag** is a small problem or difficulty. ❑ *There is one possible snag in his plans.*

snail /sneɪl/
(snails) **NOUN**
A **snail** is a small animal with a long, soft body, no legs, and a round shell on its back.

snake /sneɪk/ (**snakes**) **NOUN** A **snake** is a long, thin animal with no legs, that slides along the ground.

snap /snæp/ (**snaps, snapping, snapped**)

1 VERB If something **snaps**, it breaks with a short, loud noise. ❑ *Angrily, Matthew snapped the plastic pen in two.*

2 NOUN Snap is also a noun. ❑ *I heard a snap and a crash as the tree fell.*

3 VERB If you **snap at** someone, you speak to them in a sharp, angry way. ❑ *Sorry, I didn't mean to snap at you.*

4 VERB If a dog **snaps at** you, it tries to bite you. ❑ *The dog snapped at my ankle.*

snarl /snɑrl/ (**snarls, snarling, snarled**)

1 VERB If an animal **snarls**, it makes an angry sound in its throat while it shows its teeth. ❑ *The dog ran after them, barking and snarling.*

2 NOUN Snarl is also a noun. ❑ *With a snarl, the dog bit his leg.*

snatch /snætʃ/ (**snatches, snatching, snatched**) **VERB** If you **snatch** something, you take it away quickly and roughly. ❑ *Michael snatched the cards from Archie's hand.*

sneak /snik/ (**sneaks, sneaking, sneaked** or **snuck**)

> **LANGUAGE HELP**
> The form **snuck** is informal.

1 VERB If you **sneak** somewhere, you go there very quietly. ❑ *He sneaked out of his house late at night.*

2 VERB If you **sneak** a look at something, you secretly have a quick look at it. ❑ *She sneaked a look at her watch.*

sneak|er /snikər/ (**sneakers**) **NOUN** **Sneakers** are shoes that people wear especially for sports. ❑ *...a pair of sneakers.* → look at **clothing**

sneer /snɪər/ (**sneers, sneering, sneered**) **VERB** If you **sneer at** someone or something, your face shows that you do not like them. ❑ *"I don't need any help from you," he sneered.*

sneeze /sniz/ (**sneezes, sneezing, sneezed**)

1 VERB When you **sneeze**, you suddenly take in your breath and then blow it down your nose noisily, for example, because you have a cold. ❑ *Cover your nose and mouth when you sneeze.*

2 NOUN Sneeze is also a noun. ❑ *The disease is passed from person to person by a sneeze.* → look at **sick**

sniff /snɪf/ (**sniffs, sniffing, sniffed**)

1 VERB When you **sniff**, you suddenly and quickly breathe in air through your nose. ❑ *She dried her eyes and sniffed.*

2 NOUN Sniff is also a noun. ❑ *I could hear quiet sobs and sniffs.*

snig|ger /snɪɡər/ (**sniggers, sniggering, sniggered**)

1 VERB If someone **sniggers**, they laugh quietly in an unpleasant way. ❑ *Three kids started sniggering.*

2 NOUN Snigger is also a noun. ❑ *I heard a snigger, and looked around.*

snip /snɪp/ (**snips, snipping, snipped**) **VERB** If you **snip** something, you cut it quickly using sharp scissors. ❑ *Snip off the dead flowers with a pair of scissors.*

snob /snɒb/ (**snobs**) **NOUN** A **snob** is someone who feels that they are better than other people because of their behavior or social class. ❑ *Her parents did not like him because they were snobs.*

snore /snɔr/ (**snores, snoring, snored**)

1 VERB When someone **snores**, they make a loud noise each time they breathe when they are asleep. ❑ *His mouth was open, and he was snoring.*

2 NOUN Snore is also a noun. ❑ *We heard loud snores coming from the next room.*

snor|kel /snɔrkəl/ (**snorkels, snorkeling, snorkeled**)

1 NOUN A **snorkel** is a tube that a person swimming just under the surface of the ocean can breathe through.

2 VERB When someone **snorkels**, they swim under water using a snorkel. ❑ *You can snorkel off the side of the boat.*

snort /snɔrt/ (**snorts, snorting, snorted**)

1 VERB When people or animals **snort**, they breathe air noisily out through their noses. ❑ *Harrell snorted with laughter.*

2 NOUN Snort is also a noun. ❑ *Yana gave a snort of laughter.*

snout /snaʊt/ (**snouts**) **NOUN** The **snout** of an animal such as a pig is its long nose. ❑ *Two alligators rest their snouts on the water's surface.*

snow /snoʊ/ (**snows, snowing, snowed**)

1 NONCOUNT NOUN Snow is soft white frozen water that falls from the sky. ❑ *Six inches of snow fell.*

s

2 **VERB** When **it snows**, snow falls from the sky. ❑ *It snowed all night.*

→ look at **weather**

snow|ball /snoʊbɔl/ (**snowballs**) **NOUN** A **snowball** is a ball of snow.

snow|board|ing /snoʊbɔrdɪŋ/ **NONCOUNT NOUN** **SPORTS** **Snowboarding** is the sport of traveling down slopes that are covered with snow, with both your feet fastened to a board. ❑ *He loves skiing and snowboarding.*

● **snow|board|er** (**snowboarders**) **NOUN** ❑ *He's one of the world's top snowboarders.*

snow|man /snoʊmæn/ (**snowmen**) **NOUN** A **snowman** is a large shape like a person that is made out of snow.

snow|plow /snoʊplaʊ/ (**snowplows**) **NOUN** A **snowplow** is a vehicle that is used for pushing snow off roads or railroad tracks.

snowy /snoʊi/ (**snowier, snowiest**) **ADJECTIVE** **Snowy** means covered with snow. ❑ *...snowy mountains.*

snuck /snʌk/ **Snuck** is a form of the verb **sneak**. [INFORMAL]

snug|gle /snʌgəl/ (**snuggles, snuggling, snuggled**) **VERB** If you **snuggle** or **snuggle up** somewhere, you get into a warm, comfortable position, especially by moving closer to another person. ❑ *Jane snuggled up against his shoulder.*

so /soʊ/

1 **ADVERB** You use **so** to talk about something that has just been mentioned. ❑ *"Do you think they will stay together?"—"I hope so."* ❑ *If you don't like it, then say so.*

2 **ADVERB** You use **so** when you are saying that something is also true. ❑ *I enjoy Ann's company and so does Martin.* ❑ *They had a wonderful time and so did I.*

3 **CONJUNCTION** You use **so** to introduce the result of a situation. ❑ *I am shy and so I find it hard to talk to people.*

4 **CONJUNCTION** You use **so** and **so that** to introduce the reason for doing something. ❑ *Come to dinner so we can talk about what happened.* ❑ *They moved to the corner of the room so that nobody would hear them.*

5 **ADVERB** You can use **so** in conversations to introduce a new subject. ❑ *So how was your day?*

6 **ADVERB** You can use **so** in front of adjectives and adverbs to make them

stronger. ❑ *I'm surprised they're married—they seemed so different.*

7 You use **or so** when you are giving an approximate amount. ❑ *A ticket will cost you $20 or so.*

soak /soʊk/ (**soaks, soaking, soaked**)

1 **VERB** If you **soak** something, you put it into a liquid and leave it there. ❑ *Soak the beans for 2 hours.*

2 **VERB** If a liquid **soaks** something, it makes that thing very wet. ❑ *The water soaked his jacket.* ● **soaked** /soʊkt/ **ADJECTIVE** ❑ *The tent got completely soaked in the storm.*

● **soak|ing** **ADJECTIVE** ❑ *My raincoat was soaking wet.*

3 **VERB** If a liquid **soaks through** something, it passes through it. ❑ *Blood soaked through the bandages.*

▶ **soak up** If a soft or dry material **soaks up** a liquid, the liquid goes into it. ❑ *Use a towel to soak up the water.*

soap /soʊp/ **NONCOUNT NOUN** **Soap** is a substance that you use with water for washing yourself or for washing clothes. ❑ *...a bar of soap.*

→ look at **laundry**

soap op|era (**soap operas**) **NOUN** A **soap opera** is a popular television series about the daily lives and problems of a group of people who live in a particular place.

soar /sɔr/ (**soars, soaring, soared**)

1 **VERB** If the amount, the value, or the level of something **soars**, it quickly increases. ❑ *Prices soared in the first half of the year.*

2 **VERB** If a bird or an aircraft **soars** into the air, it goes quickly upward. ❑ *A golden eagle soared overhead.*

sob /sɒb/ (**sobs, sobbing, sobbed**)

1 **VERB** When someone **sobs**, they cry in a noisy way. ❑ *She began to sob.*

2 **NOUN** A **sob** is a noise that you make when you are crying. ❑ *She heard quiet sobs from the next room.*

so|ber /soʊbər/

1 **ADJECTIVE** A **sober** person is not drunk. ❑ *He was completely sober.*

2 **ADJECTIVE** **Sober** colors and clothes are plain and not bright. ❑ *He dresses in sober gray suits.*

so-called also **so called** **ADJECTIVE** You use **so-called** to show that you think a word or an expression is in fact wrong. ❑ *This so-called miracle never actually happened.*

S

soc|cer /sɒkər/ **NONCOUNT NOUN** SPORTS
Soccer is a game played by two teams of
eleven players using a round ball. Players
kick the ball to each other and try to score
goals by kicking the ball into a large net.
Outside the United States, this game is also
called **football**. ❑ *She plays soccer.*

so|cia|ble /souʃəbəl/ **ADJECTIVE** **Sociable**
people are friendly and enjoy talking to
other people. ❑ *She was extremely sociable.*

so|cial /souʃəl/
1 **ADJECTIVE** **Social** means relating to
society. ❑ *He sings about social problems like
poverty.* ● **so|cial|ly** **ADVERB** ❑ *It wasn't socially
acceptable to eat in the street.*
2 **ADJECTIVE** **Social** means relating to
enjoyable activities that involve meeting
other people. ❑ *We organize social events.*
● **so|cial|ly** **ADVERB** ❑ *We have known each other
socially for a long time.*
→ look at **school**

so|cial|ism /souʃəlɪzəm/ **NONCOUNT NOUN**
SOCIAL STUDIES **Socialism** is a set of political
principles whose general aim is to create a
system in which everyone has equal
chances to gain wealth and to own the
country's main industries.

so|cial|ist /souʃəlɪst/ (**socialists**)
1 **ADJECTIVE** SOCIAL STUDIES **Socialist** means
based on socialism or relating to socialism.
❑ *He's a member of the Socialist Party.*
2 **NOUN** SOCIAL STUDIES A **socialist** is a
person who believes in socialism. ❑ *His
grandparents were socialists.*

so|cial|ize /souʃəlaɪz/ (**socializes,
socializing, socialized**) **VERB** If you **socialize**,
you meet other people socially, for example
at parties. ❑ *I like socializing and making new
friends.*

so|cial life (**social lives**) **NOUN** Your **social life**
is the time you spend with your friends.
❑ *I was popular and had a busy social life.*

so|cial net|work|ing **NONCOUNT NOUN**
TECHNOLOGY **Social networking** is the activity
of contacting friends, sharing information,
and making new friends using links on
particular websites. ❑ *Have you used a social
networking site such as MySpace or Facebook?*

So|cial Se|cu|rity **NONCOUNT NOUN** Social
Security is a system by which workers and
employers in the U.S. have to pay money to

the government. The government can then
give money to people who are old, or who
cannot work.

so|cial stud|ies **NONCOUNT NOUN**
SOCIAL STUDIES **Social studies** is a school
subject that includes history, geography,
politics, and economics (= the study of how
a society organizes its money and trade).

so|cial work|er (**social workers**) **NOUN** A
social worker is a person whose job is to help
people who have social problems.

so|ci|ety /səsaɪɪti/ (**societies**)
1 **NOUN** **Society** consists of all the people
in a country, when you think about their
general behavior or problems. ❑ *These are
common problems in today's society.* ❑ *We live in an
unequal society.*
2 **NOUN** A **society** is an organization for
people who have the same interest or aim.
❑ *He's a member of the American Historical Society.*

sock /sɒk/ (**socks**) **NOUN** **Socks** are pieces of
clothing that cover your foot and ankle and
are worn inside shoes. ❑ *...a pair of red socks.*
→ look at **clothing**

sock|et /sɒkɪt/ (**sockets**) **NOUN** A **socket** is
a hole that something fits into to make a
connection. ❑ *He took the light bulb out of the
socket.* ❑ *There's an electric socket by every seat on
the train.*

soda /soudə/ (**sodas**)
1 **NONCOUNT NOUN** **Soda** is a sweet drink
that contains bubbles. ❑ *...a glass of soda.*
2 **NOUN** A **soda** is a bottle of soda. ❑ *We
bought sodas for the children.*

so|dium /soudiəm/ **NONCOUNT NOUN**
SCIENCE **Sodium** is a silvery white chemical
element such as salt, that combines with
other chemicals.

sofa /soufə/ (**sofas**) **NOUN** A **sofa** is a long,
comfortable seat with a back, and usually
with arms, that two or three people can
sit on.
→ look at **furniture**

soft /sɔft/ (**softer, softest**)
1 **ADJECTIVE** Something that is **soft** is
pleasant to touch, and not rough or hard.
❑ *Body lotion will keep your skin soft.* ❑ *She wiped
the baby's face with a soft cloth.*
2 **ADJECTIVE** Something that is **soft** changes
shape easily when you press it. ❑ *Add milk to
form a soft dough.*

s

3 **ADJECTIVE** A **soft** sound or light is very gentle. ❑ *There was a soft tapping on my door.* ● **soft|ly** **ADVERB** ❑ *She walked into the softly lit room.*

→ look at **music, sense**

soft|ball /sɔ̱ftbɔl/ (softballs)

1 **NONCOUNT NOUN** SPORTS Softball is a game similar to baseball, but it is played with a larger, softer ball.

2 **NOUN** SPORTS A softball is the ball used in the game of softball.

soft drink (soft drinks) **NOUN** A **soft drink** is a **soda**. ❑ *Can I get you some tea or coffee, or a soft drink?*

sof|ten /sɔ̱fªn/ (softens, softening, softened) **VERB** If you **soften** something, you make it less hard. ❑ *Soften the butter in a small saucepan, then add it to the flour.*

soft|ware /sɔ̱ftwɛər/ **NONCOUNT NOUN** TECHNOLOGY Computer programs are called **software**. Compare with **hardware**. ❑ *He writes computer software.*

sog|gy /sɒ̱gi/ (soggier, soggiest) **ADJECTIVE** Something that is **soggy** is unpleasantly wet. ❑ *The cheese and tomato sandwiches were soggy.*

soil /sɔ̱ɪl/ (soils) **NONCOUNT NOUN** SCIENCE **Soil** is the substance on the surface of the Earth in which plants grow. ❑ *The soil here is good for growing vegetables.*

so|lar /sɔ̱ʊlər/ **ADJECTIVE** SCIENCE **Solar** power is obtained from the sun's light and heat.

→ look at **energy**

so|lar col|lec|tor (solar collectors) **NOUN** TECHNOLOGY A **solar collector** is a piece of equipment that makes electricity from the heat from the sun. ❑ *Large homes should have solar collectors.*

sold /soʊld/ **Sold** is a form of the verb **sell**.

sol|dier /soʊ̱ldʒər/ (soldiers) **NOUN** A **soldier** is a member of an army.

sole /soʊl/ (soles)

1 **ADJECTIVE** The **sole** thing or person of a particular type is the only one of that type. ❑ *Their sole aim is to win.* ● **sole|ly** **ADVERB** ❑ *The money you earn belongs solely to you.*

2 **NOUN** The **sole** of your foot or of a shoe or sock is the underneath surface of it. ❑ *Wear shoes with thick soles.*

→ look at **foot**

sol|emn /sɒ̱ləm/ **ADJECTIVE** Someone or something that is **solemn** is very serious rather than cheerful or amusing. ❑ *His face looked solemn.* ● **sol|emn|ly** **ADVERB** ❑ *Her listeners nodded solemnly.*

sol|id /sɒ̱lɪd/ (solids)

1 **ADJECTIVE** A **solid** substance or object stays the same shape whether it is in a container or not. ❑ *The walls are made from solid concrete blocks.*

2 **NOUN** SCIENCE A **solid** is a hard substance. ❑ *Solids turn to liquids at certain temperatures.*

3 **ADJECTIVE** A substance that is **solid** is very hard or firm. ❑ *The lake was frozen solid.*

4 **ADJECTIVE** A **solid** object has no space inside it. ❑ *They had to cut through 50 feet of solid rock.*

→ look at **water**

soli|tary /sɒ̱lɪtɛri/

1 **ADJECTIVE** A **solitary** person or animal spends a lot of time alone. ❑ *Paul was a shy, solitary man.*

2 **ADJECTIVE** A **solitary** activity is one that you do alone. ❑ *He spent his evenings in solitary reading.*

solo /soʊ̱loʊ/ (solos)

1 **ADJECTIVE** You use **solo** when someone does something alone rather than with other people. ❑ *He has just recorded his first solo album.*

2 **ADVERB** **Solo** is also an adverb. ❑ *Lindbergh flew solo across the Atlantic.*

3 **NOUN** MUSIC A **solo** is a piece of music or a dance performed by one person. ❑ *The music teacher asked me to sing a solo.*

so|lu|tion /səlu̱ʃªn/ (solutions) **NOUN** A **solution to** a problem is a way of dealing with it. ❑ *They both want to find a peaceful solution.*

→ look at **fraction**

solve /sɒ̱lv/ (solves, solving, solved)

1 **VERB** If you **solve** a problem or a question, you find an answer to it. ❑ *They have not solved the problem of unemployment.*

2 **VERB** MATH If you **solve** a problem in math, you work out the answer.

Sound Partners some, sum

some /səm, STRONG sʌ̱m/

1 **ADJECTIVE** You use **some** to talk about an amount of something or a number of people or things. ❑ *Would you like some orange juice?* ❑ *He went to buy some books.*

2 **PRONOUN** **Some** is also a pronoun. ❑ *The apples are ripe, and we picked some today.*

3 **Some of** the people or things in a group means a few of them. **Some of** something means a part of it. ❑ *Some of the workers will lose their jobs.* ❑ *Put some of the sauce onto a plate.*

4 **PRONOUN** **Some** is also a pronoun. ❑ *When the chicken is cooked, I'll freeze some.*

5 **ADJECTIVE** If you talk about **some** person or thing, you mean that you do not know exactly which person or thing. ❑ *She wanted to talk to him about some problem she was having.*

some|body /sʌmbɑdi, -bʌdi/ **PRONOUN** **Somebody** means the same as **someone**.

some|day /sʌmdeɪ/ **ADVERB** **Someday** means at a date in the future that you do not yet know. ❑ *Someday I hope to become a pilot.*

some|how /sʌmhaʊ/ **ADVERB** You use **somehow** when you do not know or cannot say how something was done or will be done. ❑ *We'll manage somehow, I know we will.* ❑ *I somehow managed to finish the race.*

some|one /sʌmwʌn/

> **LANGUAGE HELP**
> The form **somebody** is also used.

PRONOUN You use **someone** to talk about a person without saying exactly who you mean. ❑ *I got a call from someone who wanted to rent the apartment.* ❑ *I need someone to help me.*

some|place /sʌmpleɪs/ **ADVERB** **Someplace** means the same as **somewhere**. ❑ *Maybe we could go someplace together.*

some|thing /sʌmθɪŋ/ **PRONOUN** You use **something** to talk about a thing or a situation, without saying exactly what it is. ❑ *He knew that there was something wrong.* ❑ *Was there something you wanted to ask me?*

some|time /sʌmtaɪm/ **ADVERB** You use **sometime** to talk about a time in the future or the past that is not known. ❑ *We will finish sometime next month.* ❑ *Why don't you come and see me sometime?*

some|times /sʌmtaɪmz/ **ADVERB** **Sometimes** means on some occasions rather than all the time. ❑ *I sometimes sit out in the garden and read.* ❑ *Sometimes he's a little rude.*

some|what /sʌmwʌt, -wɒt/ **ADVERB** **Somewhat** means "a little." [FORMAL] ❑ *She behaved somewhat differently when he was there.*

some|where /sʌmwɛər/ **ADVERB** You use **somewhere** to talk about a place without saying exactly where you mean. ❑ *I've seen him before somewhere.* ❑ *I needed somewhere to live.*

Sound Partners	son, sun

son /sʌn/ (**sons**) **NOUN** Someone's **son** is their male child. ❑ *Sam is the seven-year-old son of Eric Davies.*

song /sɔŋ/ (**songs**)
1 **NOUN** MUSIC A **song** is words and music sung together. ❑ *She sang a Spanish song.*
2 **NOUN** A bird's **song** is the pleasant, musical sounds that it makes. ❑ *It's lovely to hear a blackbird's song in the evening.*
→ look at **music**

son-in-law (**sons-in-law**) **NOUN** Someone's **son-in-law** is the husband of their daughter.

soon /sun/ (**sooner, soonest**)
1 **ADVERB** If something happens **soon**, it happens after a short time. ❑ *I'll call you soon.* ❑ *He arrived sooner than I expected.*
2 If something happens **as soon as** something else happens, it happens immediately after the other thing. ❑ *As soon as the weather improves we will go.*

soothe /suð/ (**soothes, soothing, soothed**)
1 **VERB** If you **soothe** someone who is angry or upset, you make them feel calmer. ❑ *He sang to her to soothe her.* ● **sooth|ing** **ADJECTIVE** ❑ *Put on some nice soothing music.*
2 **VERB** Something that **soothes** a part of your body where there is pain makes it feel better. ❑ *Use this lotion to soothe dry skin.*
● **sooth|ing** **ADJECTIVE** ❑ *Cold tea is very soothing for burns.*

so|phis|ti|cat|ed /səfɪstɪkeɪtɪd/
1 **ADJECTIVE** A **sophisticated** machine or system is complicated and highly developed. ❑ *Bees use a very sophisticated communication system.*
2 **ADJECTIVE** Someone who is **sophisticated** knows about things like culture and fashion. ❑ *Claude was a charming, sophisticated man.*

sopho|more /spfəmɔr/ (**sophomores**)
NOUN A **sophomore** is a student in the second year of college or high school.

so|pra|no /səprænoʊ, -prɑn-/ (**sopranos**)
NOUN MUSIC A **soprano** is a woman, girl, or boy with a high singing voice. ❑ *She was the main soprano at the theater.*

s

sore /sɔr/ (**sorer, sorest**) **ADJECTIVE** If part of your body is **sore**, it is painful and uncomfortable. ❑ *I had a sore throat and a cough.*
→ look at **sick**

sor|row /sɒroʊ/ **NONCOUNT NOUN** Sorrow is a feeling of deep sadness. ❑ *Words cannot express my sorrow.*

sor|ry /sɒri/ (**sorrier, sorriest**)
1 You say "**Sorry**" or "**I'm sorry**" to apologize for something that you have done. ❑ *"You're making too much noise."—"Sorry." ❑ Sorry I took so long.*
2 **ADJECTIVE** If you are **sorry** about a situation, you feel regret, sadness, or disappointment about it. ❑ *I'm sorry he's gone.*
3 You say "**I'm sorry**" to express your regret and sadness when you hear sad or unpleasant news. ❑ *"Robert's sick today."—"I'm sorry to hear that."*
4 **ADJECTIVE** If you feel **sorry for** someone, you feel sadness for them. ❑ *I felt sorry for him because nobody listened to him.*

sort /sɔrt/ (**sorts, sorting, sorted**)
1 **NOUN** A particular **sort of** thing is a type of thing that belongs to a larger group. ❑ *What sort of school did you go to? ❑ You can buy many different sorts of mushrooms.*
2 **VERB** If you **sort** things, you separate them into different groups. ❑ *He sorted the materials into their folders.*
3 You use **sort of** when your description of something is not very accurate. [INFORMAL] ❑ *"What's a sub?"—"Well, it's sort of a sandwich."*
▶ **sort out 1** If you **sort out** a group of things, you separate them into different groups. ❑ *Sort out all your bills as quickly as possible.*
2 If you **sort out** a problem, you deal with it successfully. ❑ *The two countries have sorted out their disagreement.*

sought /sɔt/ **Sought** is a form of the verb **seek**.

soul /soʊl/ (**souls**)
1 **NOUN** Your **soul** is the part of you that consists of your mind, character, thoughts, and feelings. Many people believe that your soul continues existing after your body is dead. ❑ *She prayed for the soul of her dead husband.*
2 **NONCOUNT NOUN** MUSIC **Soul** is the same as **soul music**. ❑ *The show stars American soul singer Anita Baker.*

soul music **NONCOUNT NOUN** MUSIC Soul music is a type of pop music performed mainly by African-American musicians. It often expresses deep emotions.

---

sound

❶ NOUN AND VERB USES
❷ ADJECTIVE AND ADVERB USES

---

❶ sound /saʊnd/ (**sounds, sounding, sounded**)
1 **NOUN** A **sound** is something that you hear. ❑ *Peter heard the sound of a car engine outside.*
2 **VERB** If a bell **sounds**, it makes a noise. ❑ *The fire alarm sounded at about 3:20 a.m.*
3 **VERB** When you are describing a noise, you can talk about the way it **sounds**. ❑ *They heard what sounded like a huge explosion.*
4 **VERB** The way someone **sounds** is how they seem when they speak. ❑ *She sounds very angry.*
5 **VERB** When you are describing your opinion of something, you can talk about the way it **sounds**. ❑ *It sounds like a wonderful idea to me.*
→ look at **language, music**

❷ sound /saʊnd/ (**sounder, soundest**)
1 **ADJECTIVE** If something is **sound**, it is in good condition. ❑ *The building is perfectly sound.*
2 **ADJECTIVE** **Sound** advice is sensible, and can be trusted. ❑ *Our experts will give you sound advice.*
3 **ADVERB** If someone is **sound** asleep, they are in a deep sleep. ❑ *He was lying in bed, sound asleep.*

sound|ly /saʊndli/ **ADVERB** If you sleep **soundly**, you sleep deeply and do not wake during your sleep. ❑ *How can he sleep soundly at night?*

soup /sup/ **NONCOUNT NOUN** Soup is liquid food made by boiling meat, fish, or vegetables in water. ❑ *...homemade chicken soup.*

sour /saʊər/
1 **ADJECTIVE** Something that is **sour** has a sharp, unpleasant taste like the taste of a lemon. ❑ *The stewed apple was sour.*
2 **ADJECTIVE** **Sour** milk is milk that has an unpleasant taste because it is no longer fresh. ❑ *I can smell sour milk.*
→ look at **sense**

source /sɔrs/ (**sources**)
1 **NOUN** The **source of** something is the person, place, or thing that it comes from.

S

❏ *Many adults use television as their major source of information.* ❏ *We are developing new sources of energy.*

2 **NOUN** SCIENCE The **source** of a river or a stream is the place where it begins. ❏ *...the source of the Tiber.*

→ look at **energy**

south /saʊθ/ also South

1 **NONCOUNT NOUN** GEOGRAPHY The **south** is the direction that is on your right when you are looking at the sun in the morning. ❏ *The town lies ten miles to the south.* ❏ *We organize vacations in the south of Mexico.*

2 **ADVERB** GEOGRAPHY If you go **south**, you travel toward the south. ❏ *I drove south on Highway 9.*

3 **ADJECTIVE** The **south** part of a place is the part that is toward the south. ❏ *We live on the south coast of Long Island.*

4 **ADJECTIVE** A **south** wind is a wind that blows from the south. ❏ *A mild south wind was blowing.*

→ look at **globe**

south|east /saʊθist/

1 **NONCOUNT NOUN** GEOGRAPHY The **southeast** is the direction that is between south and east. ❏ *The train left Colombo for Galle, 70 miles to the southeast.*

2 **ADJECTIVE** GEOGRAPHY **Southeast** means in or from the southeast. ❏ *I grew up in rural southeast Kansas.* ❏ *...Southeast Asia.*

south|eastern /saʊθistərn/ **ADJECTIVE** GEOGRAPHY **Southeastern** means in or from the southeast part of a place. ❏ *The city is on the southeastern edge of the United States.*

south|er|ly /sʌðərli/

1 **ADJECTIVE** GEOGRAPHY **Southerly** means to the south or toward the south. ❏ *We traveled in a southerly direction toward Arkansas.*

2 **ADJECTIVE** A **southerly** wind blows from the south. ❏ *...a strong southerly wind.*

south|ern /sʌðərn/ also Southern

ADJECTIVE GEOGRAPHY **Southern** means in or from the south of a place. ❏ *The Everglades National Park stretches across southern Florida.*

south|west /saʊθwɛst/

1 **NONCOUNT NOUN** GEOGRAPHY The **southwest** is the direction that is between south and west. ❏ *He lives about 500 miles to the southwest of Johannesburg.*

2 **ADJECTIVE** GEOGRAPHY **Southwest** means in or from the southwest. ❏ *...southwest Louisiana.*

south|western /saʊθwɛstərn/ **ADJECTIVE** GEOGRAPHY **Southwestern** means in or from the southwest part of a place. ❏ *They come from a small town in the southwestern part of the country.*

sou|venir /suvənɪər/ (souvenirs) **NOUN** A **souvenir** is something that you buy or keep to remind you of a place or event. ❏ *The cup was a souvenir of the summer of 1992.*

sov|er|eign|ty /sɒvrɪnti/ **NONCOUNT NOUN** SOCIAL STUDIES **Sovereignty** is the power that a country has to govern itself or another country. ❏ *It is important to protect our national sovereignty.*

sow /soʊ/ (sows, sowing, sowed, sown) **VERB** If you **sow** seeds, you plant them in the ground. ❏ *Sow the seed in a warm place in early March.*

soy /sɔɪ/ **NONCOUNT NOUN** **Soy** flour, butter, or other food is made from soybeans.

soy|bean /sɔɪbin/ (soybeans) also soy bean **NOUN** **Soybeans** are beans that can be eaten, or used for making flour, oil, or sauce.

spa /spɑ/ (spas)

1 **NOUN** A **spa** is a place where water comes out of the ground. ❏ *Buxton is a spa town that is famous for its water.*

2 **NOUN** A health **spa** is a place where people go to exercise and have special treatments in order to improve their health. ❏ *Hotel guests may use the health spa.*

space /speɪs/ (spaces, spacing, spaced)

1 **NOUN** You use **space** to talk about an area that is empty. ❏ *They cut down trees to make space for houses.* ❏ *The space under the bed could be used as a storage area.*

2 **NOUN** A **space of** time is a period of time. ❏ *They've come a long way in a short space of time.*

3 **NONCOUNT NOUN** SCIENCE **Space** is the area beyond the Earth's atmosphere, where the stars and planets are. ❏ *The six astronauts will spend ten days in space.*

4 **VERB** If you **space** a series of things, you separate them so that they are not all together. ❏ *Write the words down, spacing them evenly.*

5 **Space out** means the same as **space**. ❏ *He talks quite slowly and spaces his words out.*

→ look at Picture Dictionary: **space**

space|craft /speɪskræft/ (spacecraft) **NOUN** SCIENCE A **spacecraft** is a vehicle that can travel in space. ❏ *This is the world's largest and most expensive spacecraft.*

s

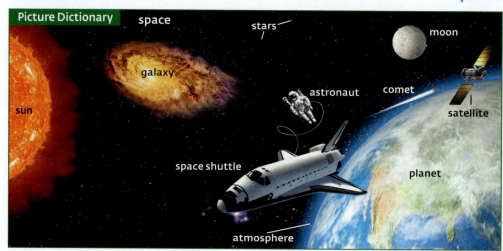

Picture Dictionary — space — stars — moon — galaxy — astronaut — comet — satellite — sun — space shuttle — planet — atmosphere

space|ship /speɪsʃɪp/ (spaceships) NOUN
SCIENCE A **spaceship** is the same as a
spacecraft.

space shut|tle (space shuttles) NOUN
SCIENCE A **space shuttle** is a vehicle that is
designed to travel into space and back to
Earth several times.
→ look at **space**

spa|cious /speɪʃəs/ ADJECTIVE A **spacious**
place is large, so that you can move around
easily in it. ❑ *The house has a spacious kitchen
and dining area.*

spade /speɪd/ (spades) NOUN A **spade** is
a tool that is used for digging. ❑ *...a garden
spade.*

spa|ghet|ti /spəgɛti/ NONCOUNT NOUN
Spaghetti is a type of pasta (= a food made
from flour and water) that looks like long
pieces of string.

spam /spæm/ NONCOUNT NOUN TECHNOLOGY
Spam is advertising messages that are sent
automatically by email to large numbers of
people. ❑ *Spam is becoming a major problem for
many Internet users.*
→ look at **email**

span /spæn/ (spans, spanning, spanned)
1 NOUN A **span** is a period of time. ❑ *The
batteries had a life span of six hours.*
2 VERB If something **spans** a long period
of time, it lasts for that period of time.
❑ *His professional career spanned 16 years.*
3 NOUN The **span** of something is the total
width of it from one side to the other.
❑ *The butterfly has a 2-inch wing span.*

4 VERB A bridge or other structure that **spans**
a river or a road, stretches right across it.
❑ *There is a footbridge that spans the little stream.*

spank /spæŋk/ (spanks, spanking, spanked)
VERB If someone **spanks** a child, they
punish them by hitting them on the bottom
with their hand. ❑ *When we were kids, our mom
never spanked us.*

spare /spɛər/ (spares, sparing, spared)
1 ADJECTIVE **Spare** things are extra things
that you keep in case you need them. ❑ *It's
useful to have a spare pair of glasses.* ❑ *I'll give you
the spare key.*
2 VERB If you **spare** time or money, you
make it available. ❑ *I can only spare 35 minutes
for this meeting.*

spare time NONCOUNT NOUN Your **spare
time** is the time when you do not have to work.
❑ *In her spare time she read books on cooking.*

spark /spɑrk/ (sparks)
1 NOUN A **spark** is a very
small piece of burning
material that comes out
of something that is
burning. ❑ *Sparks flew out
of the fire in all directions.*
2 NOUN A **spark** is a
flash of light caused by
electricity. ❑ *I saw a spark
when I connected the wires.*

spar|kle /spɑrkəl/ (sparkles, sparkling,
sparkled) VERB If something **sparkles**, it is
clear and bright, and it shines with a lot of
very small points of light. ❑ *The jewels on her
fingers sparkled.* ❑ *His bright eyes sparkled.*

S

spar|row /spǽroʊ/ (**sparrows**) **NOUN** A **sparrow** is a small brown bird that is very common in the United States.

sparse /spɑrs/ (**sparser, sparsest**) **ADJECTIVE** If something is **sparse**, there is not much of it and it is spread out over an area. ❑ *He was a fat little man in his fifties, with sparse hair.*
● **sparse|ly** **ADVERB** ❑ *This is a sparsely populated mountain region.*

speak /spik/ (**speaks, speaking, spoke, spoken**)
1 **VERB** When you **speak**, you use your voice in order to say something. ❑ *He opened his mouth to speak.* ❑ *I called the hotel and spoke to Louie.* ❑ *He often speaks about his mother.*
● **speak|er** (**speakers**) **NOUN** ❑ *You can understand a lot from the speaker's tone of voice.*
● **spo|ken** **ADJECTIVE** ❑ *They took tests in written and spoken English.*
2 **VERB** When someone **speaks**, they make a speech. ❑ *He will speak at the Democratic Convention.* ● **speak|er** **NOUN** ❑ *Bruce Wyatt will be the guest speaker at next month's meeting.*
3 **VERB** If you **speak** a foreign language, you know the language and are able to have a conversation in it. ❑ *He speaks English.*
→ look at **communication, language**
▶ **speak up** If you ask someone to **speak up**, you are asking them to speak more loudly. ❑ *I'm quite deaf—you'll have to speak up.*

Word Partners	Use **speak** with:
ADV.	speak **clearly**, speak **directly**, speak **louder**, speak **slowly** **1** speak **freely**, speak **publicly** **1** **2**
N.	**chance to** speak, **opportunity to** speak, speak **the truth** **1** **2** speak **English**, speak **French**, speak **Spanish**, speak **a foreign language** **3**

speak|er /spíkər/ (**speakers**) **NOUN** A **speaker** is a piece of electrical equipment that sound comes out of. ❑ *I bought a pair of speakers for my computer.*
→ look at **ATM**

spear /spɪər/ (**spears**) **NOUN** A **spear** is a weapon consisting of a long pole with a sharp metal point at the end.

spe|cial /spɛʃəl/
1 **ADJECTIVE** Someone or something that is **special** is better or more important than other people or things. ❑ *You're very special to me.* ❑ *My special guest will be Zac Efron.*
2 **ADJECTIVE** **Special** means different from

normal. ❑ *In special cases, a child can be educated at home.*

spe|cial|ist /spɛʃəlɪst/ (**specialists**) **NOUN** A **specialist** is a person who knows a lot about a particular subject. ❑ *Peckham is a cancer specialist.*

spe|cial|ize /spɛʃəlaɪz/ (**specializes, specializing, specialized**) **VERB** If you **specialize in** a subject, you concentrate a lot of your time and energy on it. ❑ *He's a professor who specializes in Russian history.*

spe|cial|ly /spɛʃəli/
1 **ADVERB** If something is **specially for** a particular person, it is only for that person. ❑ *This soap is specially designed for sensitive skin.*
2 **ADVERB** **Specially** means more than usual. [INFORMAL] ❑ *On his birthday I got up specially early.*

spe|cial|ty /spɛʃəlti/ (**specialties**)
1 **NOUN** Someone's **specialty** is a particular type of work that they do, or a subject that they know a lot about. ❑ *His specialty is international law.*
2 **NOUN** A **specialty** of a particular place is a special food or product that is always very good there. ❑ *Catfish is a Southern specialty.*

spe|cies /spíʃiz/ (**species**) **NOUN** SCIENCE A **species** is a related group of plants or animals. ❑ *Many species could disappear from our Earth.*
→ look at **conservation, earth**

spe|cif|ic /spɪsɪ́fɪk/
1 **ADJECTIVE** You use **specific** to talk about a particular subject. ❑ *Do you have pain in any specific part of your body?* ❑ *There are several specific problems.*
2 **ADJECTIVE** If someone is **specific**, they give a description that is exact and clear. ❑ *She refused to be more specific about her plans.*

spe|cifi|cal|ly /spɪsɪ́fɪkli/ **ADVERB** You use **specifically** to show that something is being considered separately. ❑ *The show is specifically for children.*

speci|fy /spɛ́sɪfaɪ/ (**specifies, specifying, specified**) **VERB** If you **specify** something, you explain it in an exact and detailed way. ❑ *Does the recipe specify the size of egg to be used?*

speci|men /spɛ́sɪmɪn/ (**specimens**) **NOUN** SCIENCE A **specimen of** something is an example or a small amount of it. ❑ *Job applicants have to give a specimen of handwriting.*

s

speck /spɛk/ (**specks**) **NOUN** A **speck** is a very small mark or piece of something. ❏ *There was a speck of dirt on his collar.*

spec|ta|cle /spɛktəkəl/ (**spectacles**) **NOUN** A **spectacle** is a big, wonderful sight or event. ❏ *The fireworks were an amazing spectacle.*

spec|tacu|lar /spɛktækyələr/ **ADJECTIVE** Something that is **spectacular** is big and dramatic. ❏ *We had spectacular views of Sugar Loaf Mountain.* ● **spec|tacu|lar|ly** **ADVERB** ❏ *Our sales increased spectacularly.*

spec|ta|tor /spɛkteɪtər/ (**spectators**) **NOUN** A **spectator** is someone who watches a sports event. ❏ *Thirty thousand spectators watched the game.*

specu|late /spɛkyəleɪt/ (**speculates, speculating, speculated**) **VERB** If you **speculate** about something, you make guesses about it. ❏ *Everyone has been speculating about why she left.* ● **specu|la|tion** /spɛkyəleɪʃən/ **NONCOUNT NOUN** ❏ *There has been a lot of speculation about the future of the band.*

sped /spɛd/ **Sped** is a form of the verb **speed**.

speech /spitʃ/ (**speeches**)
1 **NONCOUNT NOUN** Speech is the ability to speak or the act of speaking. ❏ *We are studying the development of speech in children.* ❏ *The medicine can affect speech.*
2 **NOUN** Your **speech** is the way in which you speak. ❏ *His speech became slow and unclear.*
3 **NOUN** A **speech** is a formal talk that someone gives to a group of people. ❏ *The president gave a speech to the nation.*

speech marks **PLURAL NOUN** **LANGUAGE ARTS** **Speech marks** are the same as **quotation marks**.

speed /spid/ (**speeds, speeding, sped** or **speeded**)

> **LANGUAGE HELP**
> Use **sped** in meaning **3** and **speeded** for the phrasal verb.

1 **NOUN** **SCIENCE** The **speed** of something is how fast it moves or is done. ❏ *He drove off at high speed.* ❏ *He invented a way to measure wind speeds.*
2 **NONCOUNT NOUN** Speed is very fast movement or travel. ❏ *Speed is essential for all athletes.*
3 **VERB** If you **speed** somewhere, you move or travel there quickly, usually in a vehicle. ❏ *Trains speed through the tunnel at 186 mph.*

4 **VERB** Someone who **is speeding** is driving a vehicle faster than the legal speed limit. ❏ *Police stopped him because he was speeding.*
● **speed|ing** **NONCOUNT NOUN** ❏ *He was fined for speeding.*
▶ **speed up** When something **speeds up**, it happens more quickly than before. ❏ *My breathing speeded up a bit.* ❏ *We need to speed up a solution to the problem.*

speedy /spidi/ (**speedier, speediest**) **ADJECTIVE** Something that is **speedy** happens or is done very quickly. ❏ *We wish Bill a speedy recovery.*

spell /spɛl/ (**spells, spelling, spelled**)
1 **VERB** **LANGUAGE ARTS** When you **spell** a word, you write or speak each letter in the correct order. ❏ *He spelled his name.* ❏ *How do you spell "potato?"*
2 **VERB** **LANGUAGE ARTS** Someone who can **spell** knows the correct order of letters in words. ❏ *He can't spell his own name.*
3 **NOUN** A **spell** is a set of magic words. ❏ *They say a witch cast a spell on her.*
→ look at **dictionary, writing**

spell|ing /spɛlɪŋ/ (**spellings**)
1 **NOUN** A **spelling** is the correct order of the letters in a word. ❏ *I'm not sure about the spelling of his name.*
2 **NONCOUNT NOUN** Spelling is the ability to spell words in the correct way. ❏ *His spelling is very bad.*

spend /spɛnd/ (**spends, spending, spent**)
1 **VERB** When you **spend** money, you pay money for things that you want or need. ❏ *I have spent all my money.*
2 **VERB** If you **spend** time doing something, you use your time doing it. ❏ *She spends hours working on her garden.*

spent /spɛnt/ **Spent** is a form of the verb **spend**.

sphere /sfɪər/ (**spheres**) **NOUN** A **sphere** is an object that is completely round in shape, like a ball. ❏ *A tennis ball is a regular sphere shape.*

spice /spaɪs/ (**spices**) **NOUN** A **spice** is a part of a plant that you put in food to give it flavor. ❏ *...herbs and spices.*

spicy /spaɪsi/ (**spicier, spiciest**) **ADJECTIVE** **Spicy** food is strongly flavored with spices. ❏ *Thai food is hot and spicy.*

spi|der /spaɪdər/ (**spiders**) **NOUN** A **spider** is a small animal with eight legs.

spike /spaɪk/ (**spikes**) **NOUN** A **spike** is a long piece of metal with a sharp point. ❑ *There was a high wall around the building with iron spikes at the top.*

spill /spɪl/ (**spills, spilling, spilled** or **spilt**) **VERB** If you **spill** a liquid, you accidentally make it flow over the edge of a container. ❑ *He always spilled the drinks.* ❑ *Oil spilled into the sea.*
→ look at **pollution**

spin /spɪn/ (**spins, spinning, spun**)
1 VERB If something **spins**, it turns quickly around a central point. ❑ *The disk spins 3,600 times a minute.* ❑ *He spun the steering wheel and turned the car around.*
2 VERB When people **spin**, they make thread by twisting together pieces of wool or cotton. ❑ *It's a machine for spinning wool.*

spin|ach /spɪnɪtʃ/ **NONCOUNT NOUN** Spinach is a vegetable with large dark green leaves.
→ look at **vegetable**

spine /spaɪn/ (**spines**) **NOUN** SCIENCE Your **spine** is the row of bones down your back. ❑ *He suffered injuries to his spine.*

spi|ral /spaɪrəl/ (**spirals, spiraling, spiraled**)
1 NOUN A **spiral** is a shape that winds around and around, with each curve above or outside the one before.
2 ADJECTIVE Spiral is also an adjective. ❑ *...a spiral staircase.*
3 VERB If something **spirals** somewhere, it grows or moves in a spiral curve. ❑ *Gray smoke spiraled up into the sky.*
4 VERB If an amount **spirals**, it rises quickly. ❑ *Prices began to spiral.*

spir|it /spɪrɪt/ (**spirits**)
1 NOUN Your **spirit** is the part of you that is not physical and that consists of your character and feelings. ❑ *The human spirit is hard to destroy.*
2 NOUN A person's **spirit** is the part of them that some people believe remains alive after their death. ❑ *He is gone, but his spirit is still with us.*
3 PLURAL NOUN Your **spirits** are your feelings at a particular time, especially feelings of happiness or unhappiness. ❑ *At supper, everyone was in high spirits.*

spir|itu|al /spɪrɪtʃuəl/
1 ADJECTIVE Spiritual means relating to people's thoughts and beliefs, rather than to their bodies. ❑ *She is a very spiritual person.*
2 ADJECTIVE Spiritual means relating to people's religious beliefs. ❑ *He is the spiritual leader of the world's Catholics.*

spit /spɪt/ (**spits, spitting, spit** or **spat**) **VERB** If you **spit** liquid or food somewhere, you force a small amount of it out of your mouth. ❑ *Spit out that gum.*

spite /spaɪt/
1 You use **in spite of** to introduce a fact that makes the rest of what you are saying seem surprising. ❑ *He hired her in spite of her lack of experience.*
2 NONCOUNT NOUN If you do something out of **spite**, you do it because you want to hurt or upset someone. ❑ *I didn't help him, out of spite I suppose.*

splash /splæʃ/ (**splashes, splashing, splashed**)
1 VERB If you **splash** in water, you hit the water in a noisy way. ❑ *People were splashing around in the water.*
2 VERB If a liquid **splashes**, some of it hits someone or something. ❑ *A little wave splashed in my face.*
3 NOUN A **splash** is the sound of something hitting water. ❑ *There was a splash as something fell into the water.*
→ look at **water**

splen|did /splendɪd/ **ADJECTIVE** If something is **splendid**, it is very good. ❑ *The book includes some splendid photographs.*

splin|ter /splɪntər/ (**splinters**) **NOUN** A **splinter** is a thin, sharp piece of wood or glass that has broken off from a larger piece. ❑ *We found splinters of the glass in our clothes.*

split /splɪt/ (**splits, splitting, split**)
1 VERB If something **splits**, it breaks into two or more parts. ❑ *The ship split in two during a storm.*
2 VERB If you **split** something, you divide it into two or more parts. ❑ *Split the chicken in half.*
3 VERB If wood or a piece of clothing **splits**, a long crack or tear appears in it. ❑ *My pants split while I was climbing over the wall.*
4 VERB If two or more people **split** something, they share it between them. ❑ *Let's split the bill.*
▶ **split up** If two people **split up**, they end their relationship. ❑ *His parents split up when*

he was ten. ❑ *I thought that nothing could ever split us up, but I was wrong.*

spoil /spɔɪl/ (**spoils, spoiling, spoiled** or **spoilt**)
1 **VERB** If you **spoil** something, you prevent it from being successful. ❑ *Don't let mistakes spoil your life.*
2 **VERB** If you **spoil** children, you give them everything they want or ask for.
❑ *Grandparents often like to spoil their grandchildren.*

spoke /spoʊk/ (**spokes**)
1 **Spoke** is a form of the verb **speak**.
2 **NOUN** The **spokes** of a wheel are the bars that connect the outer ring to the center.

spo|ken /spoʊkən/ **Spoken** is a form of the verb **speak**.

spokes|man /spoʊksmən/ (**spokesmen**)
NOUN A **spokesman** is a man who speaks as the representative of a group or an organization. ❑ *A spokesman said that food is on its way.*

spokes|person /spoʊkspɜrsən/
(**spokespersons** or **spokespeople**) **NOUN** A **spokesperson** is a person who speaks as the representative of a group or an organization.
❑ *...a White House spokesperson.*

spokes|woman /spoʊkswʊmən/
(**spokeswomen**) **NOUN** A **spokeswoman** is a woman who speaks as a representative of a group or an organization. ❑ *A hospital spokeswoman said he was recovering well.*

sponge /spʌndʒ/ (**sponges**) **NOUN** A **sponge** is a piece of a very light soft material with lots of little holes in it, that you use for washing yourself or for cleaning things.
❑ *He wiped the table with a sponge.*

spon|sor /spɒnsər/ (**sponsors, sponsoring, sponsored**)
1 **VERB** If an organization or a person **sponsors** an event, they pay for it. ❑ *A local bank is sponsoring the race.*
2 **VERB** If you **sponsor** someone who is doing something to raise money, you agree to give them money if they succeed in doing it. ❑ *The children asked friends and family to sponsor them.*
3 **NOUN** A **sponsor** is a person or an organization that pays for an event. ❑ *Our company is proud to be the sponsor of this event.*

spon|ta|neous /spɒnteɪniəs/ **ADJECTIVE**
Spontaneous acts are done because someone suddenly wants to do them. ❑ *He*

gave her a spontaneous hug. ● **spon|ta|neous|ly**
ADVERB ❑ *People spontaneously stood up and cheered.*

spooky /spuki/ (**spookier, spookiest**)
ADJECTIVE A place that is **spooky** seems frightening. [INFORMAL] ❑ *The house has a slightly spooky atmosphere.*

spoon /spun/ (**spoons**) **NOUN** A **spoon** is a long object with a round end that is used for eating, serving, or mixing food. ❑ *He stirred his coffee with a spoon.*
→ look at **restaurant**

spoon|ful /spunfʊl/ (**spoonfuls**) **NOUN**
A **spoonful of** food is an amount of food that a spoon holds. ❑ *He took a spoonful of the stew and ate it.*

sport /spɔrt/ (**sports**) **NOUN** **SPORTS** **Sports** are games and other activities that need physical effort and skill. ❑ *Basketball is my favorite sport.* ❑ *She is very good at sports.*
→ look at **fitness, play, school, television**

spot /spɒt/ (**spots, spotting, spotted**)
1 **NOUN** **Spots** are small, round, colored areas on a surface. ❑ *The leaves are yellow with orange spots.*
2 **NOUN** A particular place can be called a **spot**. ❑ *This is one of the country's top tourist spots.*
3 **VERB** If you **spot** something or someone, you notice them. ❑ *I didn't spot the mistake in his essay.*
4 If you do something **on the spot**, you do it immediately. ❑ *They offered him the job on the spot.*

spot|light /spɒtlaɪt/ (**spotlights**) **NOUN**
A **spotlight** is a powerful light that can be directed so that it lights up a small area.

spouse /spaʊs/ (**spouses**) **NOUN** Someone's **spouse** is their husband or wife. ❑ *You and your spouse must both sign the contract.*

sprang /spræŋ/ **Sprang** is a form of the verb **spring**.

spray /spreɪ/ (**sprays, spraying, sprayed**)
1 **NONCOUNT NOUN** **Spray** is a lot of small drops of water that are thrown into the air.
❑ *We were hit by spray from the waterfall.*
2 **NOUN** A **spray** is a liquid that comes out of a can or other container in very small drops when you press a button. ❑ *...hair spray.*
3 **VERB** If you **spray** a liquid somewhere, drops of the liquid cover a place. ❑ *Firefighters sprayed water on the fire.*

spread /sprɛd/ (**spreads, spreading, spread**)

1 **VERB** If you **spread** something somewhere, you open it out over a surface. ❑ *She spread a towel on the sand and lay on it.*

2 **Spread out** means the same as **spread**. ❑ *He spread the papers out on a table.*

3 **VERB** If you **spread** parts of your body, you stretch them out until they are far apart. ❑ *Sitting on the floor, spread your legs.*

4 **Spread out** means the same as **spread**. ❑ *David spread out his hands.*

5 **VERB** If you **spread** a substance on a surface, you put it all over the surface. ❑ *She was spreading butter on the bread.*

6 **VERB** If something **spreads**, it gradually reaches a larger area. ❑ *Information technology has spread across the world.*

7 **NOUN** **Spread** is also a noun. ❑ *We closed schools to stop the spread of the disease.*

▶ **spread out** If people **spread out**, they move apart from each other. ❑ *They spread out to search the area.*

spread|sheet /sprɛdʃit/ (**spreadsheets**) **NOUN** **TECHNOLOGY** A **spreadsheet** is a computer program that deals with numbers. Spreadsheets are mainly used for financial planning.

Spelling Partners   **spring**

---

spring /sprɪŋ/ (**springs, springing, sprang, sprung**)

1 **NOUN** **Spring** is the season between winter and summer when the weather becomes warmer and plants start to grow again. ❑ *They are getting married next spring.*

2 **NOUN** A **spring** is a long piece of metal that goes round and round. It goes back to the same shape after you pull it. ❑ *The springs in the bed were old and soft.*

3 **NOUN** A **spring** is a place where water comes up through the ground. ❑ *The town is famous for its hot springs.*

4 **VERB** When a person or an animal **springs** up or forward, they jump suddenly or quickly. ❑ *He sprang to his feet.*

→ look at **river, season**

sprin|kle /sprɪŋkəl/ (**sprinkles, sprinkling, sprinkled**) **VERB** If you **sprinkle** something **with** a liquid or powder, you drop a little of it over the surface. ❑ *Sprinkle the meat with salt before you cook it.*

sprin|kler /sprɪŋklər/ (**sprinklers**) **NOUN** A **sprinkler** is a machine that spreads drops of water over an area of grass or onto a fire.

sprint /sprɪnt/ (**sprints, sprinting, sprinted**)

1 **NOUN** **SPORTS** The **sprint** is a short, fast race. ❑ *Rob Harmeling won the sprint.*

2 **VERB** If you **sprint**, you run as fast as you can over a short distance. ❑ *Sergeant Adams sprinted to the car.*

sprout /spraʊt/ (**sprouts, sprouting, sprouted**)

1 **VERB** When plants, vegetables, or seeds **sprout**, they start to grow. ❑ *It only takes a few days for beans to sprout.*

2 **NOUN** **Sprouts** are small round green vegetables. They are also called **Brussels sprouts**.

sprung /sprʌŋ/ **Sprung** is a form of the verb **spring**.

spun /spʌn/ **Spun** is a form of the verb **spin**.

spy /spaɪ/ (**spies, spying, spied**)

1 **NOUN** A **spy** is a person whose job is to find out secret information about another country or organization. ❑ *He used to be a spy.*

2 **VERB** Someone who **spies** tries to find out secret information about another country or organization. ❑ *The two countries are still spying on one another.*

3 **VERB** If you **spy on** someone, you watch them secretly. ❑ *He spied on her while she was on her way to work.*

square /skwɛər/ (**squares**)

1 **NOUN** **MATH** A **square** is a shape with four straight sides that are all the same length. ❑ *Cut the cake in squares.*

2 **NOUN** In a town or city, a **square** is an open place with buildings around it. ❑ *The restaurant is in the town square.*

3 **ADJECTIVE** **MATH** Something that is **square** has four straight sides that are all the same length. ❑ *They sat at a square table.*

4 **ADJECTIVE** **MATH** **Square** is used for talking about the area of something. ❑ *The house covers an area of 3,000 square feet.*

5 **NOUN** **MATH** The **square of** a number is the number you get when you multiply that number by itself. ❑ *The square of 4 is 16.*

square root (**square roots**) **NOUN** **MATH** The **square root of** a number is another number that you multiply by itself to produce the first number. ❏ *The square root of 36 is 6.*

squash /skwɒʃ/ (**squashes, squashing, squashed**)

1 **VERB** If someone or something **is squashed**, they are pushed or pressed hard. ❏ *Robert was squashed against a fence by a car.*

2 **NONCOUNT NOUN** SPORTS **Squash** is a game in which two players hit a small rubber ball against the walls of a court. ❏ *I play squash once a week.*

3 **NOUN** A **squash** is a large vegetable with a thick skin.

→ look at **vegetable**

squeak /skwik/ (**squeaks, squeaking, squeaked**)

1 **VERB** If something or someone **squeaks**, they make a short, high sound. ❏ *My boots squeaked as I walked.*

2 **NOUN** **Squeak** is also a noun. ❏ *I heard a squeak, like a mouse.*

squeal /skwil/ (**squeals, squealing, squealed**)

1 **VERB** If someone or something **squeals**, they make a long, high sound. ❏ *Jennifer squealed with pleasure.*

2 **NOUN** **Squeal** is also a noun. ❏ *There was a squeal of brakes as the car suddenly stopped.*

squeeze /skwiz/ (**squeezes, squeezing, squeezed**)

1 **VERB** If you **squeeze** something, you press it firmly, usually with your hands. ❏ *He squeezed her arm gently.*

2 **NOUN** **Squeeze** is also a noun. ❏ *She took my hand and gave it a squeeze.*

3 **VERB** If you **squeeze** a soft substance out of a container, you get it out by pressing. ❏ *Joe squeezed some toothpaste out of the tube.*

squid /skwɪd/ (**squids**)

> **LANGUAGE HELP**
>
> The plural can also be **squid**.

1 **NOUN** A **squid** is a sea animal that has a long soft body and many soft arms called tentacles.

2 **NONCOUNT NOUN** **Squid** is pieces of this creature eaten as food. ❏ *Cook the squid for 2 minutes.*

squir|rel /skwɜrəl/ (**squirrels**) **NOUN** A **squirrel** is a small animal with a long thick tail. Squirrels live mainly in trees.

squirt /skwɜrt/ (**squirts, squirting, squirted**)

1 **VERB** If you **squirt** a liquid somewhere, it comes out of a narrow opening very quickly. ❏ *Norman squirted tomato sauce onto his plate.*

2 **VERB** If a liquid **squirts** somewhere, it comes out of a narrow opening very quickly. ❏ *The mustard squirted all over the front of my shirt.*

3 **NOUN** **Squirt** is also a noun. ❏ *It needs a little squirt of oil.*

stab /stæb/ (**stabs, stabbing, stabbed**) **VERB** If someone **stabs** you, they push a knife or sharp object into your body. ❏ *Someone stabbed him in the stomach.*

sta|ble /steɪbəl/ (**stabler, stablest, stables**)

1 **ADJECTIVE** If something is **stable**, it is not likely to change suddenly. ❏ *The price of oil has remained stable this month.* ● **sta|bil|ity** /stəbɪliti/ **NONCOUNT NOUN** ❏ *It was a time of political stability.*

2 **ADJECTIVE** If an object is **stable**, it is firmly fixed in position. ❏ *Make sure the ladder is stable.*

3 **NOUN** A **stable** or **stables** is a building in which horses are kept.

stack /stæk/ (**stacks, stacking, stacked**)

1 **NOUN** A **stack of** things is a pile of them. ❏ *There were stacks of books on the floor.*

2 **VERB** If you **stack** a number of things, you arrange them in piles. ❏ *He asked me to stack the dirty dishes.*

sta|dium /steɪdiəm/ (**stadiums**) **NOUN** SPORTS A **stadium** is a large sports field with rows of seats all around it. ❏ *...a baseball stadium.*

staff /stæf/ **NOUN** The **staff** of an organization are the people who work for it. ❏ *The hospital staff was very good.* ❏ *...staff members.*

stag /stæg/ (**stags**) **NOUN** A **stag** is an adult male deer (= a large wild animal that eats grass and leaves). **Stags** have horns that look like branches.

stage /steɪdʒ/ (**stages**)

1 **NOUN** A **stage of** an activity or a process is one part of it. ❏ *We are completing the first stage of the plan.*

2 **NOUN** In a theater, the **stage** is the area where people perform. ❏ *The band walked onto the stage.*

→ look at **performance**

stage|coach /steɪdʒkoʊtʃ/ (**stagecoaches**) **NOUN** In the past, **stagecoaches** were large

S

vehicles pulled by horses that carried passengers and mail.

stag|ger /stǽgər/ (**staggers, staggering, staggered**) VERB If you **stagger**, you cannot walk properly, for example because you are ill. ❑ *He staggered back and fell over.*

stain /steɪn/ (**stains, staining, stained**)

1 NOUN A **stain** is a mark on something that is difficult to remove. ❑ *How do you remove tea stains?*

2 VERB If a liquid **stains** something, it becomes colored or marked by the liquid. ❑ *Some foods can stain the teeth.* ● **stained** ADJECTIVE ❑ *His clothing was stained with mud.*
→ look at **laundry**

stair /steər/ (**stairs**)

1 PLURAL NOUN **Stairs** are a set of steps inside a building that go from one level to another. ❑ *Nancy began to climb the stairs.* ❑ *We walked up a flight of stairs.*

2 NOUN A **stair** is one of the steps in a set of stairs. ❑ *Terry was sitting on the bottom stair.*

stair|case /steərkeɪs/ (**staircases**) NOUN A **staircase** is a set of stairs inside a building. ❑ *They walked down the staircase together.*
→ look at **house**

stair|way /steərweɪ/ (**stairways**) NOUN A **stairway** is a set of steps, inside or outside a building. ❑ *The back stairway leads to the top floor.*

stake /steɪk/ (**stakes**)

1 If something is **at stake**, it might be lost if you are not successful. ❑ *There was so much at stake in this game.*

2 NOUN A **stake** is a pointed wooden pole that you push into the ground, for example in order to support a young tree. ❑ *She hung the clothes on a rope tied between two wooden stakes.*

stale /steɪl/ (**staler, stalest**) ADJECTIVE **Stale** food or air is no longer fresh. ❑ *....stale bread.*

stalk /stɔk/ (**stalks**) NOUN The **stalk** of a flower, a leaf, or a fruit is the thin part that joins it to the plant or tree. ❑ *A single flower grows on each long stalk.*

stam|mer /stǽmər/ (**stammers, stammering, stammered**) VERB If you **stammer**, you find it difficult to speak

without repeating words or sounds. ❑ *A lot of children stammer.* ❑ *"F-f-forgive me," I stammered.*

stamp /stæmp/ (**stamps, stamping, stamped**)

1 NOUN A **stamp** is a small piece of paper that you stick on an envelope before you mail it. ❑ *She put a stamp on the corner of the envelope.*

2 NOUN A **stamp** is a small block of wood or metal with words, numbers, or a pattern on it. You put ink on it, then press it onto a piece of paper. ❑ *...a date stamp.*

3 VERB If you **stamp** a mark or a word on an object, you press the mark or word onto it using a stamp. ❑ *They stamp a special number on new cars.*

4 VERB If you **stamp** your **foot**, you put your foot down very hard on the ground. ❑ *I stamped my foot in anger.*

stand /stænd/ (**stands, standing, stood**)

1 VERB When you **are standing**, you are on your feet. ❑ *She was standing beside my bed.*

2 VERB When someone **stands**, they move so that they are on their feet. ❑ *Becker stood and shook hands with Ben.*

3 **Stand up** means the same as **stand**. ❑ *When I walked in, they all stood up.*

4 VERB If you **stand aside** or **stand back**, you move a short distance away. ❑ *I stood aside to let her pass me.*

5 VERB If something **stands** somewhere, it is in that place. ❑ *The house stands alone on top of a hill.*

6 VERB If you cannot **stand** someone or something, you dislike them very strongly. [INFORMAL] ❑ *I can't stand that awful man.* ❑ *I can't stand that smell.*

7 NOUN A **stand** is a small structure where you can buy things like food, drink, and newspapers. ❑ *I bought a magazine from a newspaper stand.*

8 NOUN A **stand** is a small piece of furniture that you use to hold a particular thing. ❑ *Take the television set off the stand.*

▶ **stand by** **1** If you **are standing by**, you are ready to help. ❑ *Police officers are standing by in case of trouble.*

2 If you **stand by**, you do not do anything to stop something bad from happening. ❑ *I will not stand by and watch people suffering.*

▶ **stand for** Letters that **stand for** a particular word are a short form of that word. ❑ *U.S. stands for United States.*

▶ **stand out** If someone or something

S

stands out, they are very easy to see. ❏ *The black necklace stood out against her white dress.*

▶ **stand up for** If you **stand up for** a person or a belief, you support them. ❏ *Nelson Mandela stood up for his people and his beliefs.*

▶ **stand up to** If you **stand up to** someone who is more powerful than you, you defend yourself against them. ❏ *He was too afraid to stand up to her.*

stand\ard /stǽndərd/ (**standards**)
1 **NOUN** A **standard** is a level of quality. ❏ *The standard of his work is very low.*
2 **PLURAL NOUN** **Standards** are moral principles that guide people's behavior. ❏ *My father always had high moral standards.*
3 **ADJECTIVE** **Standard** describes things that are usual and normal. ❏ *It's just a standard size car.*

stand\ard of liv\ing (**standards of living**)
NOUN Your **standard of living** is the level of comfort and the amount of money that you have. ❏ *We're trying to improve our standard of living.*

stand\by /stǽndbaɪ/ (**standbys**) also **stand-by**
1 **NOUN** A **standby** is something or someone that is always ready to be used if they are needed. ❏ *Canned vegetables are a good standby.*
2 If someone or something is **on standby**, they are ready to be used if they are needed. ❏ *Five ambulances are on standby.*

stank /stǽŋk/ **Stank** is a form of the verb **stink**.

sta\ple /stéɪpᵊl/ (**staples, stapling, stapled**)
1 **ADJECTIVE** A **staple** food or product is one that is important in people's lives. ❏ *Rice is the staple food of more than half the world's population.*
2 **NOUN** A **staple** is a small piece of bent wire that holds sheets of paper together firmly. You put the staples into the paper using a stapler.
3 **VERB** If you **staple** something, you fix it in place using staples. ❏ *Staple some sheets of paper together.*

sta\pler /stéɪplər/ (**staplers**) **NOUN** A **stapler** is an instrument that is used for fastening sheets of paper together.
→ look at **office**

star /stɑ́r/ (**stars, starring, starred**)
1 **NOUN** SCIENCE A **star** is a large ball of burning gas in space. Stars look like small points of light in the sky. ❏ *Stars lit the sky.*

2 **NOUN** A **star** is a shape that has four, five, or more points sticking out of it in a regular pattern. ❏ *How many stars are there on the American flag?*
3 **NOUN** A **star** is a famous actor, musician, or sports player. ❏ *He's one of the stars of the TV series "Friends."*
4 **VERB** If an actor or an actress **stars in** a play or a movie, he or she has one of the most important parts in it. ❏ *Meryl Streep stars in the movie "The Devil Wears Prada."*
5 **VERB** If a play or a movie **stars** a famous actor or actress, he or she has one of the most important parts in it. ❏ *The movie stars Brad Pitt.*
→ look at **movie, space**

stare /stéər/ (**stares, staring, stared**)
1 **VERB** If you **stare at** someone or something, you look at them for a long time. ❏ *We all spend too much time staring at computer screens.*
2 **NOUN** **Stare** is also a noun. ❏ *Harry gave him a long stare.*

star\fish /stɑ́rfɪʃ/ (**starfish**) **NOUN** A **starfish** is a flat creature in the shape of a star, that lives in the ocean.

start /stɑ́rt/ (**starts, starting, started**)
1 **VERB** If you **start doing** something, you do something that you were not doing before. ❏ *Susanna started working in TV in 2005.*
2 **VERB** When something **starts**, it takes place from a particular time. ❏ *The fire started in an upstairs room.*
3 **NOUN** **Start** is also a noun. ❏ *It was 1918, four years after the start of the Great War.*
4 **VERB** When someone **starts** something, they create it or cause it to begin. ❏ *She has started a child care center in Ohio.*
5 **VERB** If you **start** an engine, a car, or a machine, you make it begin to work. ❏ *He started the car and drove off.*
6 You use **for a start** or **to start with** to introduce the first of a number of things. ❏ *For a start, you need her name and address.*
→ look at **car, day, job, season**
▶ **start off** If you **start off by** doing something, you do it as the first part of an activity. ❏ *She started off by clearing some space on the table.*
▶ **start over** If you **start over**, you begin something again from the beginning. ❏ *I did it all wrong and had to start over.*

star\tle /stɑ́rtᵊl/ (**startles, startling, startled**) **VERB** If something sudden and

S

unexpected **startles** you, it surprises and frightens you slightly. ❑ *The telephone startled him.* ● **star|tled ADJECTIVE** ❑ *Martha gave her a startled look.*

starve /stɑrv/ (**starves, starving, starved**)
1 VERB If people **starve**, they suffer greatly from lack of food, and may die. ❑ *A number of the prisoners are starving.* ● **star|va|tion** /stɑrveɪʃ°n/ **NONCOUNT NOUN** ❑ *Over three hundred people died of starvation.*
2 VERB To **starve** someone means not to give them any food. ❑ *He was starving himself.*

starv|ing /stɑrvɪŋ/ **ADJECTIVE** If you are **starving**, you are very hungry. [INFORMAL] ❑ *Does anyone have any food? I'm starving.*

state /steɪt/ (**states, stating, stated**)
1 NOUN SOCIAL STUDIES You can call countries **states**, particularly when you are talking about politics. ❑ *...a socialist state.*
2 NOUN Some large countries such as the U.S. are divided into smaller areas called **states**. ❑ *Leaders of the Southern states are meeting in Louisville.*
3 NOUN Some people say **the States** when they mean the U.S. [INFORMAL] ❑ *She bought it in the States.*
4 NOUN The state is the government of a country. ❑ *In Sweden, child care is provided by the state.*
5 NOUN When you talk about the **state of** someone or something, you mean the condition they are in. ❑ *After Daniel died, I was in a state of shock.*
6 VERB If you **state** something, you say it or write it in a formal or definite way. ❑ *Clearly state your address and telephone number.*

state|ment /steɪtmənt/ (**statements**)
NOUN A **statement** is something that you say or write that gives information in a formal way. ❑ *I was very angry when I made that statement.*

stat|ic /stætɪk/
1 ADJECTIVE Something that is **static** does not move or change. ❑ *House prices were static last month.*
2 NONCOUNT NOUN Static or **static electricity** is electricity that collects on things such as your body or metal objects.

sta|tion /steɪʃ°n/ (**stations**)
1 NOUN A **station** is a place where trains stop so that people can get on or off. ❑ *Ingrid went with him to the train station.*

2 NOUN A bus **station** is a place in a town or a city where a lot of buses stop, usually for a while. ❑ *I walked to the bus station and bought a ticket.*
3 NOUN A radio or television **station** is a company that broadcasts programs. ❑ *...a local radio station.*

sta|tion|ary /steɪʃənɛri/ **ADJECTIVE** Something that is **stationary** is not moving. ❑ *A bus crashed into the back of a stationary vehicle.*

sta|tion|ery /steɪʃənɛri/ **NONCOUNT NOUN** **Stationery** is paper, envelopes, and other materials or equipment used for writing and typing. ❑ *...office stationery.*
→ look at **office**

sta|tis|tic /stətɪstɪk/ (**statistics**) **NOUN** **Statistics** are facts that are expressed in numbers. ❑ *Statistics show that wages are rising.*

statue /stætʃu/ (**statues**) **NOUN** ARTS A **statue** is a large model of a person or an animal, made of stone or metal. ❑ *She gave me a stone statue of a horse.*
→ look at **city**

sta|tus /steɪtəs, stæt-/ **NONCOUNT NOUN** The **status** of someone or something is the importance that people give them. ❑ *Older family members enjoy high status in many societies.*

stay /steɪ/ (**stays, staying, stayed**)
1 VERB If you **stay** where you are, you continue to be there and do not leave. ❑ *"Stay here," Trish said. "I'll bring the car to you."*
2 VERB If you **stay** somewhere, you live there for a short time. ❑ *Gordon stayed at The Park Hotel, Milan.* ❑ *Can't you stay a for few more days?*
3 NOUN **Stay** is also a noun. ❑ *Please contact the hotel reception if you have any problems during your stay.*
4 VERB If someone or something **stays** in a particular state or situation, they continue to be in it. ❑ *Exercise is one of the best ways to stay healthy.*
5 VERB If you **stay away from** a place, you do not go there. ❑ *Most workers stayed away from work during the strike.*
▶ **stay in** If you **stay in**, you remain at home and do not go out. ❑ *We decided to stay in and have dinner at home.*
▶ **stay up** If you **stay up**, you do not go to bed at your usual time. ❑ *I used to stay up late with my mom and watch movies.*

S

steady /stɛdi/ (**steadier, steadiest, steadies, steadying, steadied**)

1 **ADJECTIVE** A **steady** situation continues or develops gradually and is not likely to change quickly. ❑ *Despite these problems there has been steady progress.* ● **steadi|ly** /stɛdɪli/ **ADVERB** ❑ *Prices have been rising steadily.*

2 **ADJECTIVE** If an object is **steady**, it is firm, and does not move around. ❑ *Hold the camera steady.*

3 **VERB** If you **steady** something, you stop it from moving around. ❑ *Two men were steadying the ladder.*

steak /steɪk/ (**steaks**)

1 **NOUN** A **steak** is a large flat piece of beef without much fat on it. ❑ *There was a steak cooking on the grill.*

2 **NOUN** A fish **steak** is a large piece of fish that does not contain many bones. ❑ *...fresh salmon steaks.*
→ look at **meat**

steal /stil/ (**steals, stealing, stole, stolen**)
VERB If you **steal** something **from** someone, you take it without their permission. ❑ *They said he stole a small boy's bicycle.* ❑ *It's wrong to steal.* ● **sto|len** /stoʊlən/ **ADJECTIVE** ❑ *We have now found the stolen car.*

steam /stim/ (**steams, steaming, steamed**)

1 **NONCOUNT NOUN**
Steam is the hot gas that forms when water boils. ❑ *The heat converts water into steam.*

2 **VERB** If you **steam** food, you cook it in steam rather than in water. ❑ *Steam the carrots until they are slightly soft.*
→ look at **cook, water**

steel /stil/ **NONCOUNT NOUN** Steel is a very strong metal that is made mainly from iron. ❑ *...steel pipes.* ❑ *...the steel industry.*

steep /stip/ (**steeper, steepest**)

1 **ADJECTIVE** A **steep** slope rises at a very sharp angle. ❑ *Some of the hills in San Francisco are very steep.* ● **steep|ly** **ADVERB** ❑ *The road climbs steeply.*

2 **ADJECTIVE** A **steep** rise in prices is a very big rise. ❑ *There have been steep price increases.* ● **steep|ly** **ADVERB** ❑ *Unemployment is rising steeply.*

steer /stɪər/ (**steers, steering, steered**) **VERB**
When you **steer** a vehicle, you control it so that it goes in the direction that you want. ❑ *What is it like to steer a big ship?*
→ look at **car**

steer|ing wheel (**steering wheels**) **NOUN**
In a car or other vehicle, the **steering wheel** is the wheel that the driver holds when he or she is driving.

stem /stɛm/ (**stems**) **NOUN** The **stem** of a plant is the long, thin part that the flowers and leaves grow on. ❑ *He cut the stem and gave her the flower.*

step /stɛp/ (**steps, stepping, stepped**)

1 **NOUN** If you take a **step**, you lift your foot and put it down in a different place. ❑ *I took a step toward him.* ❑ *She walked back a few steps.*

2 **VERB** If you **step on** something, you put your foot on it. ❑ *Neil Armstrong was the first man to step on the Moon.*

3 **NOUN** A **step** is a raised flat surface, that you put your feet on in order to walk up or down to a different level. ❑ *We went down some steps into the yard.* ❑ *A girl was sitting on the bottom step.*

4 **NOUN** A **step** is one of a series of actions that you take in a process. ❑ *We have taken the first step toward peace.*

5 If you do something **step by step**, you do it by progressing gradually from one stage to the next. ❑ *I am not rushing things. I'm taking it step by step.*

Word Partners	Use **step** with:
ADV.	step **ahead**, step **backward**, step **closer**, step **forward**, step **outside** **1** **4**
ADJ.	**big** step, **bold** step, **giant** step, **the right** step **4**

step|father /stɛpfɑðər/ (**stepfathers**) also **step-father** **NOUN** Someone's **stepfather** is the man who has married their mother but who is not their father.

step|mother /stɛpmʌðər/ (**stepmothers**) also **step-mother** **NOUN** Someone's **stepmother** is the woman who has married their father but who is not their mother.

ster|ile /stɛrəl/

1 **ADJECTIVE** Something that is **sterile** is completely clean. ❑ *Cover the cut with a sterile bandage.*

2 **ADJECTIVE** A person or an animal that is **sterile** is unable to produce babies. ❑ *The tests showed that George was sterile.*

S

stern /stɜrn/ (sterner, sternest)

1 **ADJECTIVE** **Stern** words or actions are very severe. ❏ *The AFL last night gave players a stern warning about their behavior.* ● **stern|ly** **ADVERB** ❏ *"We will punish anyone who breaks the rules," she said sternly.*

2 **ADJECTIVE** Someone who is **stern** is very serious and not friendly. ❏ *Her father was a stern man.*

stew /stu/ (stews, stewing, stewed)

1 **NOUN** A **stew** is a meal that you make by cooking meat and vegetables in liquid. ❏ *She gave him a bowl of beef stew.*

2 **VERB** When you **stew** meat, vegetables, or fruit, you cook them slowly in liquid. ❏ *Stew the apples for half an hour.*

stick /stɪk/ (sticks, sticking, stuck)

1 **NOUN** A **stick** is a thin branch from a tree. ❏ *She put some dry sticks on the fire.*

2 **NOUN** A **stick** is a long thin piece of wood that is used for a particular purpose. ❏ *He picked up his walking stick and walked away.*

3 **VERB** If you **stick** one thing to another, you join them together using a sticky substance. ❏ *Now stick your picture on a piece of paper.*

4 **VERB** If you **stick** a pointed object **into** something, you push it into it. ❏ *The doctor stuck the needle into Joe's arm.*

5 **VERB** If you **stick** something somewhere, you put it there. [INFORMAL] ❏ *He folded the papers and stuck them in his desk.*

6 **VERB** If one thing **sticks to** another, it becomes joined to it and is difficult to remove. ❏ *The paper sometimes sticks to the bottom of the cake.*

▶ **stick by** If you **stick by** someone, you continue to give them support. ❏ *All my friends stuck by me during the difficult times.*

▶ **stick out** **1** If something **sticks out**, it continues further than the main part of something. ❏ *His two front teeth stick out slightly.*

2 If you **stick** something **out**, you push it forward or away from you. ❏ *She stuck out her tongue at him.*

▶ **stick to** If you **stick to** a promise or a decision, you do not change your mind. ❏ *We are waiting to see if he sticks to his promise.*

▶ **stick up for** If you **stick up for** someone or something, you support them and say that they are right. ❏ *My father always sticks up for me.*

stick|er /stɪkər/ (stickers) **NOUN** A **sticker** is a small piece of paper with writing or a picture on one side, that you can stick onto a surface. ❏ *I bought a sticker that said, "I love Florida."*

sticky /stɪki/ (stickier, stickiest)

1 **ADJECTIVE** Something that is **sticky** sticks to other things. ❏ *The floor was sticky with spilled orange juice.* ❏ *If the mixture is sticky, add more flour.*

2 **ADJECTIVE** A **sticky** situation involves problems. [INFORMAL] ❏ *There were some sticky moments.*

stiff /stɪf/ (stiffer, stiffest)

1 **ADJECTIVE** Something that is **stiff** is firm or does not bend easily. ❏ *His jeans were new and stiff.* ● **stiff|ly** **ADVERB** ❏ *Moira sat stiffly in her chair.*

2 **ADJECTIVE** If you are **stiff**, your muscles or joints hurt when you move. ❏ *A hot bath is good for stiff muscles.*

3 **ADVERB** If you are bored **stiff** or worried **stiff**, you are extremely bored or worried. [INFORMAL] ❏ *Anna tried to look interested, but she was bored stiff.*

sti|fle /staɪfᵊl/ (stifles, stifling, stifled) **VERB** To **stifle** something means to stop it from happening or continuing. ❏ *He stifled a laugh.*

---

still

❶ ADVERB USES
❷ ADJECTIVE USES

---

❶ **still** /stɪl/

1 **ADVERB** If a situation that existed in the past **still** exists, it has continued and exists now. ❏ *Do you still live in Illinois?* ❏ *Donald is still teaching at the age of 89.*

2 **ADVERB** You use **still** to say that something is true, despite something else. ❏ *She says she still loves him even though he treats her badly.*

3 **ADVERB** You use **still** to make another word stronger. ❏ *It's good to travel, but it's better still to come home.*

❷ **still** /stɪl/ (stiller, stillest)

1 **ADJECTIVE** If you are **still**, you are not moving. ❏ *Please stand still and listen to me!*

2 **ADJECTIVE** If it is **still**, there is no wind. ❏ *It was a warm, still evening.*

stimu|late /stɪmyəleɪt/ (stimulates, stimulating, stimulated)

1 **VERB** To **stimulate** something means to make it more active. ❏ *America is trying to stimulate its economy.*

S

2 **VERB** If you **are stimulated by** something, it makes you feel full of ideas and enthusiasm. ❑ *Bill was stimulated by the challenge.* ● **stimu|lat|ing** **ADJECTIVE** ❑ *It is a stimulating book.* ● **stimu|la|tion** **NONCOUNT NOUN** ❑ *Children need stimulation, not relaxation.*

sting /stɪŋ/ (stings, stinging, stung)
1 **VERB** If a plant, an animal, or an insect **stings** you, a pointed part of it is pushed into your skin so that you feel a sharp pain. ❑ *She was stung by a bee.*
2 **NOUN** If you feel a **sting**, you feel a sharp pain in your skin. ❑ *This won't hurt—you will just feel a little sting.*
3 **VERB** If a part of your body **stings**, you feel a sharp pain there. ❑ *His cheeks were stinging from the cold wind.*

stink /stɪŋk/ (stinks, stinking, stank, stunk)
1 **VERB** To **stink** means to smell very bad. ❑ *We all stank and nobody cared.* ❑ *The kitchen stinks of fish.*
2 **NOUN** Stink is also a noun. ❑ *He was aware of the stink of onions on his breath.*

stir /stɜr/ (stirs, stirring, stirred)
1 **VERB** If you **stir** a liquid, you mix it in a container using a spoon. ❑ *Stir the soup for a few seconds.*
2 **VERB** If someone who is asleep **stirs**, they move slightly. ❑ *Eileen shook him, and he started to stir.*

stitch /stɪtʃ/ (stitches, stitching, stitched)
1 **VERB** If you **stitch** cloth, you sew it using a needle and thread. ❑ *Stitch the two pieces of fabric together.*
2 **NOUN** Stitches are the short lines of thread that have been sewn in a piece of cloth. ❑ *Sew a row of straight stitches.*
3 **VERB** When doctors **stitch** a wound, they use a special needle and thread to sew the skin together. ❑ *Jill washed and stitched the wound.*
4 **NOUN** A **stitch** is a line of thread that has been used for sewing the skin of a wound together. ❑ *He had six stitches in the cut.*

stock /stɒk/ (stocks, stocking, stocked)
1 **NOUN** Stocks are parts of the value of a business that may be owned by different people. ❑ *She works for a bank, buying and selling stocks and shares.*
2 **VERB** If a store **stocks** particular products, it keeps a supply of them to sell. ❑ *The store stocks everything from pens to TV sets.*
3 **NONCOUNT NOUN** A store's **stock** is the total amount of goods that it has available to sell. ❑ *Most of the stock was destroyed in the fire.*
4 If goods are **in stock**, a store has them available to sell. If they are **out of stock**, it does not. ❑ *Check that your size is in stock.*

stock ex|change (stock exchanges) **NOUN** A **stock exchange** is a place where people buy and sell stocks in companies. ❑ *...the New York stock exchange.*

stock|ing /stɒkɪŋ/ (stockings) **NOUN** Stockings are pieces of women's clothing that fit closely over their feet and legs. ❑ *...a pair of nylon stockings.*

stock mar|ket (stock markets) **NOUN** The **stock market** is the activity of buying shares (= parts of a company's value). ❑ *This is a practical guide to investing in the stock market.*

stole /stoʊl/ **Stole** is a form of the verb **steal**.

sto|len /stoʊlᵊn/ **Stolen** is a form of the verb **steal**.

stom|ach /stʌmək/ (stomachs)
1 **NOUN** **SCIENCE** Your **stomach** is the organ inside your body where food goes when you eat it. ❑ *He has stomach problems.*
2 **NOUN** **SCIENCE** Your **stomach** is the front part of your body below your waist. ❑ *The children lay down on their stomachs.*

stone /stoʊn/ (stones)
1 **NONCOUNT NOUN** Stone is a hard solid substance that is found in the ground and is often used for building. ❑ *...a stone floor.*
2 **NOUN** A **stone** is a small piece of rock that is found on the ground. ❑ *He removed a stone from his shoe.*
3 **NOUN** A **stone** is a piece of valuable rock in jewelry. ❑ *He gave her a diamond ring with three stones.*

stood /stʊd/ **Stood** is a form of the verb **stand**.

stool /stul/ (stools) **NOUN** A **stool** is a seat with legs and no support for your arms or back. ❑ *Kate sat on a stool and leaned on the counter.*

stop /stɒp/ (stops, stopping, stopped)
1 **VERB** If you **stop** doing something, you do not do it anymore. ❑ *Stop throwing those stones!* ❑ *She stopped and then continued eating.*
2 **VERB** If you **stop** something from happening, you prevent it from happening. ❑ *They are trying to find a way to stop the war.*

S

3 **VERB** If an activity or a process **stops**, it does not happen anymore. ❑ *The rain has stopped.*

4 **VERB** If a machine **stops**, it is no longer working. ❑ *The clock stopped at 11:59 Saturday night.*

5 **VERB** When a moving person or vehicle **stops**, they do not move anymore. ❑ *The car failed to stop at a stoplight.* ❑ *He stopped and waited for her.*

6 **NOUN** If something that is moving comes **to a stop**, it slows down and no longer moves. ❑ *Do not open the door before the train comes to a stop.*

7 **NOUN** A **stop** is a place where buses or trains regularly stop so that people can get on and off. ❑ *The nearest subway stop is Houston Street.*

8 If you **put a stop to** something, you prevent it from happening or continuing. ❑ *I'm going to put a stop to all this talk.*

stor|age /stɔrɪdʒ/ **NONCOUNT NOUN** Storage is keeping something in a special place until it is needed. ❑ *This room is used for storage.*

store /stɔr/ (**stores, storing, stored**)

1 **NOUN** A **store** is a place where things are sold. ❑ *She ran to the store to buy some cookies.* ❑ *...a grocery store.*

2 **VERB** When you **store** things, you put them somewhere and leave them there until they are needed. ❑ *Store the cookies in a box.*
→ look at **shopping**

storm /stɔrm/ (**storms**) **NOUN** A **storm** is very bad weather, with heavy rain and strong winds. ❑ *There will be violent storms along the East Coast.*

stormy /stɔrmi/ (**stormier, stormiest**) **ADJECTIVE** If the weather is **stormy**, there are strong winds and heavy rain. ❑ *Expect a night of stormy weather, with heavy rain and strong winds.*
→ look at **ocean**

sto|ry /stɔri/ (**stories**)

1 **NOUN** LANGUAGE ARTS A **story** is a description of imaginary people and events, that is intended to entertain people. ❑ *I'm going to tell you a story about four little rabbits.*

2 **NOUN** A **story** is a description of something that has happened. ❑ *The parents all had interesting stories about their children.*

3 **NOUN** A **story** of a building is one of its different levels. ❑ *Our apartment block is 25 stories high.*

story|book /stɔribʊk/ (**storybooks**) **NOUN** A **storybook** is a book of stories for children.

stove /stoʊv/ (**stoves**) **NOUN** A **stove** is a piece of equipment that provides heat, either for cooking or for heating a room. ❑ *She put the saucepan on the gas stove.*
→ look at **kitchen**

straight /streɪt/ (**straighter, straightest**)

1 **ADJECTIVE** If something is **straight**, it continues in one direction and does not bend or curve. ❑ *Keep the boat moving in a straight line.* ❑ *Grace had long straight hair.*

2 **ADVERB** **Straight** is also an adverb. ❑ *Stand straight and hold your arms out to the side.*

3 **ADVERB** If you go **straight** to a place, you go there immediately. ❑ *When he arrived, he went straight to his office.*

4 **ADJECTIVE** If you give someone a **straight** answer, you answer them clearly and honestly.

5 If you **get** something **straight**, you make sure that you understand it properly. [INFORMAL] ❑ *Now, let me get this straight: you say that you were here all evening?*
→ look at **geometry, hair**

straight|en /streɪtᵊn/ (**straightens, straightening, straightened**)

1 **VERB** If you **straighten** something, you make it neat or put it in its proper position. ❑ *She straightened a picture on the wall.*

2 **VERB** If you are standing and you **straighten**, you make your back or body straight. ❑ *The three men straightened and stood waiting.*

3 **Straighten up** means the same as **straighten**. ❑ *He straightened up and took his hands out of his pockets.*

4 **VERB** If you **straighten** something, you make it straight. ❑ *Straighten both legs.*

strain /streɪn/ (**strains, straining, strained**)

1 **NOUN** If **strain** is put **on** a person or an organization, they have to do more than they are able to do. ❑ *She couldn't cope with the stresses and strains of her career.*

2 **NOUN** A **strain** is an injury to a muscle in your body, caused by using it too much. ❑ *Avoid muscle strain by taking rests.*

3 **VERB** If you **strain** a muscle, you injure it by using it too much. ❑ *He strained his back playing tennis.*

4 **VERB** If you **strain to** do something, you make a great effort to do it. ❑ *I had to strain to hear her.*

s

5 **VERB** When you **strain** food, you separate the liquid part of it from the solid parts. ❑ *Strain the soup and put it back into the pan.*

strange /streɪndʒ/ (stranger, strangest)
1 **ADJECTIVE** Something that is **strange** is unusual or unexpected. ❑ *There was something strange about the way she spoke.* ● **strange|ly** **ADVERB** ❑ *She noticed he was acting strangely.*
2 **ADJECTIVE** A **strange** place is somewhere you have never been before. ❑ *I was alone in a strange city.*

stran|ger /streɪndʒər/ (strangers) **NOUN** A **stranger** is someone that you have never met before. ❑ *We don't want a complete stranger staying with us.*

stran|gle /stræŋgəl/ (strangles, strangling, strangled) **VERB** To **strangle** someone means to kill them by pressing their throat tightly so that they cannot breathe. ❑ *He tried to strangle a policeman.*

strap /stræp/ (straps, strapping, strapped)
1 **NOUN** A **strap** is a long, narrow piece of leather or other material. ❑ *Nancy held the strap of her bag.* ❑ *Her shoes had elastic ankle straps.*
2 **VERB** If you **strap** something somewhere, you fasten it there with a strap. ❑ *She strapped the baby seat into the car.*

strat|egy /strætədʒi/ (strategies) **NOUN** A **strategy** is a general plan or set of plans for the future. ❑ *Do you have a strategy for solving this type of problem?*

straw /strɔ/ (straws)
1 **NONCOUNT NOUN** Straw is the dried, yellow stems of crops. ❑ *The floor of the barn was covered with straw.* ❑ *...a straw hat.*
2 **NOUN** A **straw** is a thin tube that you use to suck a drink into your mouth. ❑ *I drank from a bottle of soda with a straw in it.*
3 If an event is **the last straw**, it is the last in a series of bad events, and it makes you feel that the situation is now impossible. ❑ *Patrick's crying was the last straw for his mother.*

straw|berry /strɔbɛri/ (strawberries) **NOUN** A **strawberry** is a small soft red fruit that has a lot of very small seeds on its skin. ❑ *...strawberries and cream.*

stray /streɪ/ (strays, straying, strayed)
1 **VERB** If someone **strays** somewhere, they go away from where they are supposed to be. ❑ *Be careful not to stray into dangerous parts of the city.*

2 **ADJECTIVE** A **stray** dog or cat has gone away from its owner's home. ❑ *A stray dog came up to him.*
3 **NOUN** Stray is also a noun. ❑ *The dog was a stray.*

streak /strik/ (streaks) **NOUN** A **streak** is a long mark on a surface. ❑ *There are dark streaks on the surface of the moon.*

stream /strim/ (streams, streaming, streamed)
1 **NOUN** SCIENCE A **stream** is a small narrow river. ❑ *There was a small stream at the end of the garden.*
2 **NOUN** A **stream of** things is a large number of them that come one after another. ❑ *The TV show caused a stream of complaints.*
3 **VERB** If something **streams** somewhere, it move there in large amounts. ❑ *Tears streamed down their faces.* ❑ *Sunlight was streaming into the room.*
→ look at **river**

street /strit/ (streets) **NOUN** A **street** is a road in a city or a town. ❑ *The streets were crowded with shoppers.* ❑ *He lived at 66 Bingfield Street.*
→ look at **car, route**

strength /strɛŋkθ, strɛŋθ/ (strengths)
1 **NONCOUNT NOUN** Your **strength** is how physically strong you are. ❑ *Swimming builds up the strength of your muscles.* ❑ *He threw the ball forward with all his strength.*
2 **NONCOUNT NOUN** Someone's **strength** is their confidence or courage. ❑ *He copes with his illness very well. His strength is amazing.*
3 **NOUN** The **strength** of an object or material is how strong it is. ❑ *He checked the strength of the rope.*
4 **NONCOUNT NOUN** If you talk about the **strength of** a feeling or a belief, you are talking about how deeply people feel it or believe it. ❑ *He was surprised at the strength of his own feeling.*
→ look at **fitness**

strength|en /strɛŋθᵊn/ (strengthens, strengthening, strengthened) **VERB** If you **strengthen** something, you make it stronger. ❑ *Cycling strengthens all the muscles of the body.*

stress /strɛs/ (stresses, stressing, stressed)
1 **VERB** If you **stress** a point in a discussion, you make it clear that it is very important. ❑ *He stressed that the problem was not serious.*

S

2 **NOUN** If you feel under **stress**, you are worried because of difficulties in your life. ❏ *I cannot think clearly when I'm under stress.*

3 **VERB** LANGUAGE ARTS If you **stress** a word or part of a word when you say it, you say it slightly more loudly. ❏ *She stressed the words "very important."*

4 **NOUN** Stress is also a noun. ❏ *The stress is on the first part of the word "animal."*
→ look at **feeling**

stressed /strɛst/ **ADJECTIVE** If you are **stressed**, you feel very worried because of difficulties in your life. ❏ *What situations make you feel stressed?*

Word Builder **stressful**

ful ≈ **filled with**

care + ful = careful
color + ful = colorful
help + ful = helpful
hope + ful = hopeful
stress + ful = stressful
use + ful = useful

---

stress|ful /strɛsfəl/ **ADJECTIVE** A **stressful** situation or experience can make you feel worried or upset. ❏ *I've got one of the most stressful jobs there is.*

stretch /strɛtʃ/ (**stretches, stretching, stretched**)

1 **VERB** Something that **stretches** over a distance covers all of it. ❏ *The line of cars stretched for several miles.*

2 **NOUN** A **stretch of** road, water, or land is a length or an area of it. ❏ *It's a very dangerous stretch of road.*

3 **VERB** When you **stretch**, you put your arms or legs out very straight. ❏ *He yawned and stretched.*

4 **VERB** When something soft **stretches**, it becomes longer and thinner. ❏ *Can you feel your leg muscles stretching?*
→ look at **fitness**

▶ **stretch out** **1** If you **stretch out**, you lie with your legs and body in a straight line. ❏ *The bathtub was too small to stretch out in.*

2 If you **stretch out** a part of your body, you hold it out straight. ❏ *He stretched out his hand to touch me.*

stretch|er /strɛtʃər/ (**stretchers**) **NOUN** A **stretcher** is a long piece of strong material with a pole along each side, that is used for carrying an injured or sick person. ❏ *They put him on a stretcher and put him in the ambulance.*

strict /strɪkt/ (**stricter, strictest**)

1 **ADJECTIVE** A **strict** rule or order is very clear and must be obeyed completely. ❏ *She gave them strict instructions not to get out of the car.* ❏ *The school's rules are very strict.* ● **strict|ly** **ADVERB** ❏ *The number of new members each year is strictly controlled.*

2 **ADJECTIVE** A **strict** person expects rules to be obeyed. ❏ *My parents were very strict.* ● **strict|ly** **ADVERB** ❏ *They brought their children up very strictly.*

stride /straɪd/ (**strides, striding, strode**)

1 **VERB** If you **stride** somewhere, you walk there with long steps. ❏ *The farmer came striding across the field.*

2 **NOUN** A **stride** is a long step that you take when you are walking or running. ❏ *He crossed the street with long, quick strides.*

strike /straɪk/ (**strikes, striking, struck**)

1 **VERB** If a person or a moving object **strikes** someone or something, they hit them. [FORMAL] ❏ *She took two steps forward and struck him across the face.* ❏ *His head struck the bottom when he dived into the pool.*

2 **VERB** Something that **strikes** has a quick and violent effect. ❏ *A storm struck the northeastern United States on Saturday.*

3 **VERB** If an idea **strikes** you, it suddenly comes into your mind. ❏ *A thought struck her. Was she jealous of her mother?*

4 **VERB** When a clock **strikes**, it makes a sound so that people know what the time is. ❏ *The clock struck nine.*

5 **VERB** When you **strike** a match, you make it produce a flame by moving it against something rough. ❏ *Robina struck a match and lit the fire.*

6 **NOUN** When there is a **strike**, workers stop working for a period of time, usually in order to try to get more money. ❏ *Staff at the hospital went on strike yesterday.*

7 **VERB** Strike is also a verb. ❏ *Workers have the right to strike.*

string /strɪŋ/ (**strings**)

1 **NOUN** String is thin rope that is made of twisted threads. ❏ *He held out a small bag tied with string.*

2 **NOUN** A **string of** things is a number of them on a piece of thread. ❏ *She wore a string of pearls around her neck.*

3 **NOUN** MUSIC The **strings** on a musical instrument are the thin pieces of wire that are stretched across it and that make sounds

S

when the instrument is played. ❑ *He changed a guitar string.*

stringed in|stru|ment (**stringed instruments**) NOUN MUSIC A **stringed instrument** is any musical instrument that has strings.

strip /strɪp/ (**strips, stripping, stripped**)
1 NOUN A **strip of** something is a long, narrow piece of it. ❑ *The rugs are made from strips of fabric.*
2 NOUN A **strip of** land or water is a long narrow area of it. ❑ *He owns a narrow strip of land along the coast.*
3 VERB If you **strip**, you take off your clothes. ❑ *They stripped and jumped into the pool.*
4 **Strip off** means the same as **strip**. ❑ *The children were stripping off and running into the ocean.*

stripe /straɪp/ (**stripes**) NOUN A **stripe** is a long line that is a different color from the areas next to it. ❑ *She wore a blue skirt with white stripes.*

striped /straɪpt/ ADJECTIVE Something that is **striped** has stripes on it. ❑ *...a striped tie.*

strode /stroʊd/ **Strode** is a form of the verb **stride**.

stroke /stroʊk/ (**strokes, stroking, stroked**)
1 VERB If you **stroke** someone or something, you move your hand slowly and gently over them. ❑ *Carla was stroking her cat.*
2 NOUN If someone has a **stroke**, the blood does not flow through their brain properly, which may kill them or make them unable to move one side of their body. ❑ *He had a stroke last year, and now he can't walk.*
3 NOUN The **strokes** of a pen or a brush are the movements or marks that you make with it. ❑ *She added a few brush strokes to the painting.*
4 NOUN SPORTS **Strokes** are the repeated movements that you make with your arms when you are swimming. ❑ *I turned and swam a few strokes further out to sea.*

stroll /stroʊl/ (**strolls, strolling, strolled**)
1 VERB If you **stroll** somewhere, you walk there in a slow, relaxed way. ❑ *We love strolling along by the river.*
2 NOUN **Stroll** is also a noun. ❑ *After dinner, I took a stroll around the city.*

stroll|er /stroʊlər/ (**strollers**) NOUN A **stroller** is a small chair on wheels, that a small child can be pushed around in.

strong /strɔŋ/ (**stronger** /strɔŋgər/, **strongest** /strɔŋgɪst/)
1 ADJECTIVE Someone who is **strong** is healthy with good muscles. ❑ *I'm not strong enough to carry him.*
2 ADJECTIVE Someone who is **strong** is confident and determined. ❑ *You have to be strong and do what you believe is right.*
3 ADJECTIVE **Strong** objects or materials do not break easily. ❑ *This strong plastic will not crack.* ● **strong|ly** ADVERB ❑ *The wall was very strongly built.*
4 ADJECTIVE **Strong** opinions are very definite opinions that you are willing to express or defend. ❑ *She has strong views on environmental issues.* ● **strong|ly** ADVERB ❑ *Obviously you feel very strongly about this.*
5 ADJECTIVE A **strong** drink, chemical, or drug contains a lot of the particular substance that makes it effective. ❑ *...a cup of strong coffee.*
6 ADJECTIVE A **strong** flavor, smell, or light is easily noticed. ❑ *Onions have a strong flavor.* ● **strong|ly** ADVERB ❑ *He smelled strongly of sweat.*
→ look at **fitness**

struck /strʌk/ **Struck** is a form of the verb **strike**.

struc|ture /strʌktʃər/ (**structures**)
1 NOUN The **structure of** something is the way in which it is made, built, or organized. ❑ *The typical family structure was two parents and two children.*
2 NOUN A **structure** is something that consists of parts that are connected together in an ordered way. ❑ *She had beautiful bone structure and great big eyes.* ❑ *Our experiences can change the structure of the brain.*
3 NOUN A **structure** is something that has been built. ❑ *This modern brick and glass structure was built in 1905.*

strug|gle /strʌgəl/ (**struggles, struggling, struggled**)
1 VERB If you **struggle to** do something, you try hard to do it, but you find it very difficult. ❑ *She struggled to find the right words.*
2 NOUN An action or activity that is a **struggle** is very difficult to do. ❑ *Losing weight was a terrible struggle.*
3 NOUN A **struggle** is a long and difficult attempt to achieve something such as freedom. ❑ *The movie is about a young boy's struggle to survive.*

S

4 **VERB** If you **struggle** when you are being held, you move violently in order to get free. ❏ *I struggled, but she was too strong for me.*

stub|born /stˈʌbərn/ **ADJECTIVE** Someone who is **stubborn** is determined to do what they want. ❏ *I am a very stubborn and determined person.* ● **stub|born|ly** **ADVERB** ❏ *He stubbornly refused to tell her the truth.*

stuck /stʌk/
1 **Stuck** is a form of the verb **stick**.
2 **ADJECTIVE** If something is **stuck** in a particular position, it is unable to move. ❏ *His car got stuck in the snow.*
3 **ADJECTIVE** If you are **stuck** in a place or in a boring or unpleasant situation, you want to get away from it, but are unable to. ❏ *I don't want to get stuck in another job like that.*
4 **ADJECTIVE** If you get **stuck**, you are unable to continue doing something because it is too difficult. ❏ *The teacher will help if you get stuck.*

stu|dent /stˈudənt/ (**students**) **NOUN** A **student** is a person who is studying at a school, college, or university. ❏ *Warren's eldest son is an art student.*
→ look at **school**

stu|dio /stˈudioʊ/ (**studios**)
1 **NOUN** ARTS A **studio** is a room where someone paints, draws, or takes photographs. ❏ *She was in her studio, painting on a large canvas.*
2 **NOUN** ARTS A **studio** is a room where people make radio or television programs, record CDs, or make movies. ❏ *She's much happier performing in a recording studio.*

study /stˈʌdi/ (**studies, studying, studied**)
1 **VERB** If you **study**, you spend time learning about a particular subject. ❏ *She spends most of her time studying.* ❏ *He studied History and Economics.*
2 **NONCOUNT NOUN** **Study** is the activity of studying. ❏ *What is the study of earthquakes called?*
3 **PLURAL NOUN** You can talk about education in a particular subject as that type of **studies**. ❏ *...a center for Islamic studies.*
4 **VERB** If you **study** something, you look at it or consider it very carefully. ❏ *Debbie studied her friend's face.*
5 **NOUN** A **study** is a room in a house that is used for reading, writing, and studying. ❏ *We sat together in his study.*
→ look at Word World: **study**

→ look at **climate, dictionary, grammar, history, language, school, science**

stuff /stʌf/ (**stuffs, stuffing, stuffed**)
1 **NONCOUNT NOUN** You can use **stuff** to talk about things in a general way. [INFORMAL] ❏ *He pointed to a bag. "That's my stuff."* ❏ *There is a huge amount of useful stuff on the Internet.*
2 **VERB** If you **stuff** something somewhere, you push it there quickly and roughly. ❏ *I stuffed the dollar bills into my pocket.*
3 **VERB** If you **stuff** food, you put a mixture of another type of food inside it. ❏ *Stuff the turkey and put it in the oven for 3 hours.* ❏ *...stuffed olives.*

stuffy /stˈʌfi/ (**stuffier, stuffiest**) **ADJECTIVE** A room that is **stuffy** feels unpleasant because it is warm and there is not enough fresh air. ❏ *It was hot and stuffy in the classroom.*

stum|ble /stˈʌmbəl/ (**stumbles, stumbling, stumbled**) **VERB** If you **stumble**, you nearly fall down while you are walking or running. ❏ *He stumbled and almost fell.*

stump /stʌmp/ (**stumps**) **NOUN** A **stump** is a small part of something that remains when the rest of it has been removed or broken off. ❏ *...a tree stump.*

stun /stʌn/ (**stuns, stunning, stunned**)
1 **VERB** If you **are stunned**, you are extremely shocked or surprised, so that you are unable to speak. ❏ *We're stunned by today's news.*
2 **VERB** If something **stuns** you, it makes you unconscious for a short time. ❏ *The blow to his head stunned him.*

stung /stʌŋ/ **Stung** is a form of the verb **sting**.

stunk /stʌŋk/ **Stunk** is a form of the verb **stink**.

stun|ning /stˈʌnɪŋ/ **ADJECTIVE** A **stunning** person or thing is extremely beautiful. ❏ *She was 55 and still a stunning woman.*

stunt /stʌnt/ (**stunts**) **NOUN** A **stunt** is a dangerous piece of action in a movie. ❏ *Sean Connery did his own stunts.*

stu|pid /stˈupɪd/ (**stupider, stupidest**) **ADJECTIVE** If someone or something is **stupid**, they are not at all sensible. ❏ *I'll never do anything so stupid again.* ❏ *I made a stupid mistake.* ● **stu|pid|ly** **ADVERB** ❏ *I'm sorry. I behaved stupidly.* ● **stu|pid|ity** /stupˈɪdɪti/ **NONCOUNT NOUN** ❏ *I was surprised by his stupidity.*

stur|dy /stˈɜrdi/ (**sturdier, sturdiest**) **ADJECTIVE** Someone or something that is **sturdy** looks strong and is unlikely to be

s

easily hurt or damaged. ❑ *She was a short, sturdy woman.* ● **stur|di|ly ADVERB** ❑ *The table was strong and sturdily built.*

stut|ter /stʌtər/ (**stutters, stuttering, stuttered**)

1 VERB Someone who **stutters** has difficulty speaking because they find it hard to say the first sound of a word. ❑ *"I ... I'm sorry," he stuttered.*

2 NOUN Stutter is also a noun. ❑ *He spoke with a stutter.*

style /staɪl/ (**styles**)

1 NOUN The **style** of something is the way in which it is done. ❑ *Children have different learning styles.* ❑ *I prefer the Indian style of cooking.*

2 NOUN The **style** of a product is its design. ❑ *These kids want everything in the latest style.*
→ look at **writing**

styl|ish /staɪlɪʃ/ **ADJECTIVE** Someone or something that is **stylish** is attractive and fashionable. ❑ *She was an attractive, stylish woman.*

Styro|foam /staɪrəfoʊm/ **NONCOUNT NOUN**
Styrofoam is a light plastic substance that is used for making things such as containers for food and drinks that you buy and take away to eat. ❑ *...a styrofoam cup.* [TRADEMARK]

sub|ject /sʌbdʒɪkt/ (**subjects**)

1 NOUN The **subject** of a conversation or a book is the thing that is being discussed. ❑ *I'd like to hear the president's own views on the subject.*

2 NOUN A **subject** is an area of knowledge that you study in school or college. ❑ *Math is my favorite subject.*

3 NOUN LANGUAGE ARTS In grammar, the **subject** is the noun that talks about the person or thing that is doing the action expressed by the verb. For example, in "My cat keeps catching birds," "my cat" is the subject.

4 NOUN ARTS The **subject** is the person or thing that is shown in a piece of art. ❑ *Spring flowers are a perfect subject for painting.*

sub|jec|tive /səbdʒɛktɪv/ **ADJECTIVE**
Something that is **subjective** is based on personal opinions and feelings rather than on facts. ❑ *Art is very subjective.*

sub|ma|rine /sʌbmərin/ (**submarines**)
NOUN A **submarine** is a type of ship that can travel below the surface of the ocean. ❑ *...a nuclear submarine.*

sub|mit /səbmɪt/ (**submits, submitting, submitted**) **VERB** If you **submit** a proposal, a report, or a request, you formally send it to someone so that they can consider it. ❑ *They submitted their reports yesterday.*

sub|scrip|tion /səbskrɪpʃ°n/ (**subscriptions**)
NOUN A **subscription** is an amount of money that you pay regularly in order to belong to an organization or to receive a service. ❑ *Members pay a subscription every year.*

sub|si|dy /sʌbsɪdi/ (**subsidies**) **NOUN** A **subsidy** is money that a government pays in order to help an industry or a business. ❑ *...farm subsidies.*

sub|stance /sʌbstəns/ (**substances**) **NOUN**
A **substance** is a solid, a powder, a liquid, or a gas. ❑ *The waste contained several unpleasant substances.*

sub|stan|tial /səbstænʃ°l/ **ADJECTIVE**
Substantial means very large. [FORMAL]
❑ *A substantial number of people disagree with the new plan.*

sub|sti|tute /sʌbstɪtut/ (**substitutes, substituting, substituted**)

1 VERB If you **substitute** one thing **for** another, it takes the place of the other thing. ❑ *You can substitute wholewheat flour for white flour.*

2 NOUN A **substitute** is something that you have or use instead of something else. ❑ *They are using calculators as a substitute for thinking.*

3 NOUN In team games, a **substitute** is a player who comes into a game to replace another player. ❑ *Jefferson entered as a substitute for the injured player.*

sub|tle /sʌt°l/ (**subtler, subtlest**)

1 ADJECTIVE Something that is **subtle** is not immediately obvious. ❑ *Subtle changes take place in all living things.* ● **sub|tly ADVERB** ❑ *The truth is subtly different.*

2 ADJECTIVE Subtle smells, tastes, sounds, or colors are pleasant and delicate. ❑ *Brown, gray, or subtle shades of purple are best.*

sub|tract /səbtrækt/ (**subtracts, subtracting, subtracted**) **VERB** MATH If you **subtract** one number **from** another, you take it away from the other number. For example, if you subtract 3 from 5, you get 2. ● **sub|trac|tion** /səbtrækʃ°n/ **NONCOUNT NOUN** ❑ *She's ready to learn subtraction.*
→ look at **fraction, math**

S

sub|urb /sˈʌbɜrb/ (suburbs) NOUN The **suburbs of** a city are the areas on the edge of it where people live. ❑ *Anna was born in a suburb of Philadelphia.* ❑ *His family lives in the suburbs.*

sub|ur|ban /səbˈɜrbən/ ADJECTIVE Suburban means relating to the suburbs. ❑ *They have a comfortable suburban home.*

sub|way /sˈʌbweɪ/ (subways) NOUN A **subway** is a railroad system that runs under the ground. ❑ *I don't ride the subway late at night.*
→ look at **transportation**

suc|ceed /səksˈid/ (succeeds, succeeding, succeeded) VERB If you **succeed**, you get the result that you wanted. ❑ *We have already succeeded in starting our own company.* ❑ *Do you think he will succeed?*

suc|cess /səksˈɛs/ (successes)
1 NONCOUNT NOUN Success is doing well and getting the result that you wanted. ❑ *Hard work is the key to success.* ❑ *We were surprised by the play's success.*
2 NOUN Someone or something that is a **success** does very well, or is admired very much. ❑ *We hope the movie will be a success.*

suc|cess|ful /səksˈɛsfəl/ ADJECTIVE Someone or something that is **successful** does or gets what they wanted. ❑ *How successful will this new treatment be?* ● **suc|cess|ful|ly** ADVERB ❑ *The disease can be successfully treated with drugs.*

suc|ces|sor /səksˈɛsər/ (successors) NOUN Someone's **successor** is the person who takes their job after they have left. ❑ *His successor is Dr. John Todd.*

such /sˈʌtʃ/
1 ADJECTIVE Such means like this or like that. ❑ *How could you do such a thing?*
2 ADJECTIVE You use **such** to make a noncount or plural noun stronger. ❑ *These roads are not designed for such heavy traffic.*
3 You use **such a** or **such an** to make a noun stronger. ❑ *It was such a pleasant surprise.*
4 You use **such as** to introduce an example. ❑ *Avoid fatty food such as butter and red meat.*

suck /sˈʌk/ (sucks, sucking, sucked)
1 VERB If you **suck** something, you hold it in your mouth for a long time. ❑ *They sucked their candies.* ❑ *Many young children suck their thumbs.*

2 VERB If you **suck** a liquid, you pull it into your mouth through your lips. ❑ *The baby sucked the milk from his bottle.*

sud|den /sˈʌdən/
1 ADJECTIVE Sudden means happening quickly and unexpectedly. ❑ *He was shocked by the sudden death of his father.* ❑ *It was all very sudden.* ● **sud|den|ly** ADVERB ❑ *Suddenly, she looked ten years older.* ❑ *Her expression suddenly changed.*
2 If something happens **all of a sudden**, it happens quickly and unexpectedly. ❑ *All of a sudden she didn't look tired anymore.*

suds /sˈʌdz/ PLURAL NOUN Suds are the bubbles on water that has soap in it. ❑ *He had soap suds in his ears.*

sue /sˈu/ (sues, suing, sued) VERB If you **sue** someone, you start a legal case against them, usually in order to get money from them because they have harmed you. ❑ *The couple are suing the company for $4.4 million.*

suf|fer /sˈʌfər/ (suffers, suffering, suffered)
1 VERB If you **suffer**, you feel pain, sadness, or worry. ❑ *She was very sick, and suffering great pain.* ❑ *He has suffered terribly the last few days.*
2 VERB If you **suffer from** an illness, you are affected by it. ❑ *He was suffering from cancer.* ● **suf|fer|er** (sufferers) NOUN ❑ *...asthma sufferers.*

suf|fer|ing /sˈʌfərɪŋ/ NOUN Suffering is pain, sadness, or worry that someone feels. ❑ *They began to recover from their pain and suffering.*

suf|fi|cient /səfˈɪʃənt/ ADJECTIVE If something is **sufficient for** a particular purpose, there is enough of it for the purpose. ❑ *The food we have is sufficient for 12 people.* ● **suf|fi|cient|ly** ADVERB ❑ *She recovered sufficiently to go on vacation.*

suf|fix /sˈʌfɪks/ (suffixes) NOUN A **suffix** is a letter or group of letters, for example "-ly" or "-ness," that is added to the end of a word in order to form a different word, often of a different word class. For example, the suffix "-ly" is added to "quick" to form "quickly." Compare with **prefix**.
→ look at **dictionary**

suf|fo|cate /sˈʌfəkeɪt/ (suffocates, suffocating, suffocated) VERB If someone **suffocates**, they die because there is no air

S

for them to breathe. ❑ *He either suffocated, or froze to death.*

suf|fra|gist /sʌfrədʒɪst/ (**suffragists**) **NOUN** SOCIAL STUDIES A **suffragist** is a person who believes that all adults in a particular country should have the right to vote. Suffragists often fight for women to be allowed to vote. → look at **vote**

sug|ar /ʃʊgər/ (**sugars**)
1 **NONCOUNT NOUN** Sugar is a sweet substance that is used for making food and drinks taste sweet. ❑ *Do you take sugar in your coffee?* ❑ *...a cup of brown sugar.*
2 **NOUN** If someone has one **sugar** in their tea or coffee, they have one small spoon of sugar in it. ❑ *How many sugars do you take?*

sug|gest /səgdʒɛst/ (**suggests, suggesting, suggested**) **VERB** If you **suggest** something, you tell someone what you think they should do. ❑ *I suggest you ask him some questions about his past.* ❑ *I suggested we go for a walk in the park.*

sug|ges|tion /səgdʒɛstʃən/ (**suggestions**) **NOUN** If you make a **suggestion**, you tell someone what you think they should do. ❑ *Do you have any suggestions for improving the service we provide?*

sui|cide /suɪsaɪd/ (**suicides**) **NOUN** Suicide is the act of killing yourself. ❑ *She tried to commit suicide several times.* ❑ *It was obviously a case of attempted suicide.*

suit /sut/ (**suits, suiting, suited**)
1 **NOUN** A **suit** consists of a jacket and pants or a skirt that are made from the same cloth. ❑ *...a dark business suit.*
2 **NOUN** A particular type of **suit** is a piece of clothing that you wear for a particular activity. ❑ *The divers wore special rubber suits.*
3 **VERB** If something **suits** you, it makes you look attractive. ❑ *Green suits you.* ❑ *Isabel's soft woolen dress suited her very well.*
4 **VERB** If something **suits** you, it is convenient for you. ❑ *With online shopping, you can do your shopping when it suits you.*
→ look at **clothing**

suit|able /sutəbəl/ **ADJECTIVE** Someone or something that is **suitable for** a particular purpose or occasion is right for it. ❑ *This film would be suitable for children 8-13 years.*
● **suit|ably** **ADVERB** ❑ *He was suitably dressed for the occasion.*

suit|case /sutkeɪs/ (**suitcases**) **NOUN** A **suitcase** is a case for carrying your clothes

when you are traveling. ❑ *It did not take Andrew long to pack a suitcase.*
→ look at **bag**

suite /swit/ (**suites**) **NOUN** A **suite** is a set of rooms in a hotel or other building. ❑ *They stayed in a suite at the Paris Hilton.*

sulk /sʌlk/ (**sulks, sulking, sulked**) **VERB** If you **sulk**, you are silent for a while because you are angry about something. ❑ *He turned his back and sulked.* ● **sulky** **ADJECTIVE** ❑ *I was a sulky, 14-year-old teenager.*

Sound Partners   sum, some

sum /sʌm/ (**sums**)
1 **NOUN** A **sum of** money is an amount of money. ❑ *Large sums of money were lost.*
2 **NOUN** MATH In mathematics, **the sum of** two or more numbers is the number that is obtained when they are added together. ❑ *Fourteen is the sum of eight and six.*

sum|ma|rize /sʌməraɪz/ (**summarizes, summarizing, summarized**) **VERB** If you **summarize** something, you give the most important points about it. ❑ *Now summarize the article in three sentences.*

sum|mary /sʌməri/ (**summaries**) **NOUN** LANGUAGE ARTS A **summary of** something is a short description of it, that gives the main points but not the details. ❑ *Here is a short summary of the process.*

sum|mer /sʌmər/ (**summers**) **NOUN** Summer is the season between spring and fall. In the summer, the weather is usually warm or hot. ❑ *I flew to Maine this summer.* ❑ *It was a perfect summer's day.*
→ look at **season**

sum|mit /sʌmɪt/ (**summits**)
1 **NOUN** A **summit** is a meeting between the leaders of two or more countries. ❑ *The topic will be discussed at next week's Washington summit.*
2 **NOUN** The **summit** of a mountain is the top of it. ❑ *He wanted to be the first man to reach the summit of Mount Everest.*

sum|mon /sʌmən/ (**summons, summoning, summoned**) **VERB** If you **summon** someone, you order them to come to you. [FORMAL] ❑ *Suddenly we were summoned to his office.*

Sound Partners   sun, son

sun /sʌn/
1 **NOUN** SCIENCE The **sun** is the ball of fire in the sky that gives us heat and light.

❏ *The sun was now high in the sky.* ❏ *Suddenly, the sun came out.*

2 **NOUN** **The sun** is the heat and light that comes from the sun. ❏ *They went outside to sit in the sun.*

→ look at **beach, space, weather**

sun|bathe /sʌnbeɪð/ (**sunbathes, sunbathing, sunbathed**) **VERB** When people **sunbathe**, they sit or lie in a place where the sun shines on them, so that their skin becomes browner. ❏ *Frank swam and sunbathed at the pool every morning.* ● **sun|bath|ing** **NONCOUNT NOUN** ❏ *The beach is perfect for sunbathing.*

sun|burn /sʌnbɜrn/ **NONCOUNT NOUN** If someone has **sunburn**, their skin is pink and sore because they have spent too much time in the sun. ❏ *Sunburn can damage your skin.*

sun|burned /sʌnbɜrnd/ also **sunburnt** **ADJECTIVE** Someone who is **sunburned** has pink, sore skin because they have spent too much time in the sun. ❏ *A badly sunburned face is extremely painful.*

sun|dae /sʌndeɪ, -di/ (**sundaes**) **NOUN** A **sundae** is a tall glass of ice cream (= a frozen sweet food) with cream and nuts or fruit on top. ❏ *We had ice cream sundaes for dessert.*

Sun|day /sʌndeɪ, -di/ (**Sundays**) **NOUN** **Sunday** is the day after Saturday and before Monday. ❏ *We went for a drive on Sunday.*

Word Builder **sundown**

down ≈ below, lower

down + hill = down hill
down + load = down load
down + stairs = down stairs
sun + down = sun down

---

sun|down /sʌndaʊn/ **NONCOUNT NOUN** **Sundown** is the time when the sun sets. ❏ *We got home about two hours after sundown.*

sun|flower /sʌnflaʊər/ (**sunflowers**) **NOUN** A **sunflower** is a very tall plant with large yellow flowers.

sung /sʌŋ/ **Sung** is a form of the verb **sing**.

sun|glasses /sʌnglæsɪz/ **PLURAL NOUN** **Sunglasses** are dark glasses that you wear to protect your eyes from bright light. ❏ *She put on a pair of sunglasses.*

sunk /sʌŋk/ **Sunk** is a form of the verb **sink**.

sun|light /sʌnlaɪt/ **NONCOUNT NOUN** **Sunlight** is the light that comes from the sun. ❏ *Sunlight filled the room.*

→ look at **greenhouse effect**

sun|ny /sʌni/ (**sunnier, sunniest**)
1 **ADJECTIVE** When it is **sunny**, the sun shines brightly. ❏ *The weather was warm and sunny.*

2 **ADJECTIVE** **Sunny** places are brightly lit by the sun. ❏ *...a sunny window seat.*

sun|rise /sʌnraɪz/ (**sunrises**)
1 **NONCOUNT NOUN** **Sunrise** is the time in the morning when the sun first appears in the sky. ❏ *The rain began before sunrise.*

2 **NOUN** A **sunrise** is the colors and light that you see in the sky when the sun first appears. ❏ *There was a beautiful sunrise yesterday morning.*

→ look at **season**

sun|screen /sʌnskrin/ **NONCOUNT NOUN** **Sunscreen** is a cream that protects your skin from the sun. ❏ *Use sunscreen when you go outside.*

sun|set /sʌnsɛt/ (**sunsets**)
1 **NONCOUNT NOUN** **Sunset** is the time in the evening when the sun goes down. ❏ *The party began at sunset.*

2 **NOUN** A **sunset** is the colors and light that you see in the sky when the sun disappears in the evening. ❏ *There was a red sunset over Paris.*

→ look at **season**

sun|shine /sʌnʃaɪn/ **NONCOUNT NOUN** **Sunshine** is the light and heat that comes from the sun. ❏ *She was sitting outside a cafe in bright sunshine.*

sun|tan /sʌntæn/ (**suntans**) **NOUN** If you have a **suntan**, the sun has made your skin darker. ❏ *They want to go to the Bahamas and get a suntan.*

su|per /supər/
1 **ADVERB** **Super** shows that someone or something has a lot of a particular quality. ❏ *...Beverly Hills, home of the rich and the super rich.*

2 **ADJECTIVE** **Super** shows that someone or something is larger or better than others. ❏ *My favorite characters were super heroes like Batman and Wonder Woman.*

su|perb /supɜrb/ **ADJECTIVE** If something is **superb**, it is very good. ❏ *There is a superb*

golf course 6 miles away. ● **su|perb|ly** ADVERB
❑ *The orchestra played superbly.*

super|in|ten|dent /su͟pərɪntɛndənt,
su͟prɪn-/ (**superintendents**)
1 NOUN A **superintendent** is a person who
is responsible for the work of a particular
department in an organization. ❑ *He became
superintendent of the bank's East African branches.*
2 NOUN A **superintendent** is a person
whose job is to take care of a large building
such as an apartment building. ❑ *The
superintendent opened the door with one of his keys.*

su|peri|or /su͟pɪəriər/
1 ADJECTIVE Someone or something that is
superior is better than other similar people
or things. ❑ *We want to create superior products
for our customers.* ❑ *...superior quality coffee.*
● **su|peri|or|ity** /su͟pɪəriɔ͟rɪti/ NONCOUNT
NOUN ❑ *Belonging to a powerful organization
gives them a feeling of superiority.*
2 NOUN Your **superior** at work is a person
who has a higher position than you.
❑ *They do not have much communication with their
superiors.*

super|la|tive /su͟pɜrlətɪv/ (**superlatives**)
1 ADJECTIVE LANGUAGE ARTS In grammar,
the **superlative** form of an adjective or
adverb is the form that shows that
something has more of a quality than
anything else in a group. For example,
"biggest" is the superlative form of "big."
Compare with **comparative**.
2 NOUN **Superlative** is also a noun. ❑ *His
writing contains many superlatives.*

super|mar|ket /su͟pərmɑrkɪt/
(**supermarkets**) NOUN A **supermarket** is a
large store that sells all kinds of food and
other products for the home. ❑ *Most of us do
our food shopping in the supermarket.*
→ look at **food, shopping**

super|sti|tion /su͟pərstɪ͟ʃ°n/ (**superstitions**)
NOUN A **superstition** is a belief that things
such as good and bad luck exist, even
though they cannot be explained. ❑ *Many
people have superstitions about numbers.*

super|sti|tious /su͟pərstɪ͟ʃəs/ ADJECTIVE
People who are **superstitious** believe in
things that cannot be exlpained. ❑ *Jean was
superstitious and believed that the color green
brought bad luck.*

super|vise /su͟pərvaɪz/ (**supervises,
supervising, supervised**) VERB If you

supervise an activity or a person, you make
sure that the activity is done correctly.
❑ *She cooks the supper, supervises the children's
homework, and puts them to bed.* ● **super|vi|sion**
/su͟pərvɪ͟ʒ°n/ NONCOUNT NOUN ❑ *Young
children need close supervision.* ● **super|vi|sor**
(**supervisors**) NOUN ❑ *He got a job as a
supervisor at a factory.*
→ look at **factory, job**

sup|per /sʌ͟pər/ (**suppers**) NONCOUNT NOUN
Supper is a meal that people eat in the
evening. ❑ *Would you like to join us for supper?*

sup|plement /sʌ͟plɪmənt/ (**supplements,
supplementing, supplemented**)
1 VERB If you **supplement** something, you
add something to it in order to improve it.
❑ *Some people do extra jobs to supplement their
incomes.*
2 NOUN **Supplement** is also a noun. ❑ *These
classes are a supplement to school study.*

sup|pli|er /səplaɪ͟ər/ (**suppliers**) NOUN
A **supplier** is a company that sells goods
or equipment to customers. ❑ *We are one of
the country's biggest food suppliers.*

sup|ply /səplaɪ͟/ (**supplies, supplying,
supplied**)
1 VERB If you **supply** someone with
something, you give them an amount of it.
❑ *The pipeline will supply Greece with Russian
natural gas.*
2 NOUN A **supply of** something is an
amount of it that is available for people
to use. ❑ *The brain needs a constant supply of
oxygen.*
3 PLURAL NOUN **Supplies** are food,
equipment, and other important things
that are provided for people. ❑ *What happens
when there are no more food supplies?*
→ look at **energy**

sup|port /səpɔ͟rt/ (**supports, supporting,
supported**)
1 VERB If you **support** someone or their
ideas, you agree with them, and perhaps
help them because you want them to
succeed. ❑ *We haven't found any evidence to
support that idea.*
2 NONCOUNT NOUN **Support** is also a noun.
❑ *The president gave his full support to the reforms.*
● **sup|port|er** (**supporters**) NOUN ❑ *...the
president's supporters.*
3 NONCOUNT NOUN If you give **support** to
someone, you help them. ❑ *She gave me a lot
of support when my husband died.*

4 **VERB** If you **support** someone, you provide them with money or the things that they need. ❏ *I have three children to support.*

5 **VERB** If something **supports** an object, it is under the object and holding it up. ❏ *Thick wooden posts supported the roof.*

6 **NOUN** A **support** is a bar or other object that supports something. ❏ *Each piece of metal was on wooden supports.*

sup|port|ive /səpɔrtɪv/ **ADJECTIVE** If you are **supportive**, you are kind and helpful to someone at a difficult or unhappy time in their life. ❏ *They were always supportive of each other.*

sup|pose /səpoʊz/ (**supposes, supposing, supposed**)

1 **VERB** You can use **suppose** or **supposing** before suggesting a situation that could happen. ❏ *Suppose someone gave you a check for $6 million. What would you do with it?*

2 **VERB** If you **suppose that** something is true, you imagine that it is probably true. ❏ *I suppose you're in high school, too?*

3 You can say "**I suppose**" when you are slightly uncertain about something. ❏ *I suppose you're right.* ❏ *"Is that the right way?"— "Yeah. I suppose so."*

Supreme Court /suprim kɔrt/

1 **NOUN** SOCIAL STUDIES The **Supreme Court** is the highest court of law in the United States.

2 **NOUN** SOCIAL STUDIES In each state, the **Supreme Court** is the most important law court in the state.

sure /ʃʊər/ (**surer, surest**)

1 **ADJECTIVE** If you are **sure** that something is true, you are certain about it. ❏ *He was not sure that he wanted to be a teacher.* ❏ *I'm not sure where he lives.*

2 **Sure** is an informal way of saying "yes" or "all right." ❏ *"Do you know where she lives?"— "Sure."*

3 If something is **for sure**, it is definitely true. ❏ *One thing's for sure, women still love Barry Manilow.*

4 If you **make sure that** something is the way that you want it to be, you check that it is that way. ❏ *He looked in the bathroom to make sure that he was alone.*

sure|ly /ʃʊərli/ **ADVERB** You use **surely** to show that you think something should be true. ❏ *You surely haven't forgotten Dr. Walters?*

surf /sɜrf/ (**surfs, surfing, surfed**)

1 **NONCOUNT NOUN** **Surf** is the mass of white bubbles on the top of waves in the ocean. ❏ *We watched the surf rolling onto the white sandy beach.*

2 **VERB** SPORTS If you **surf**, you ride on big waves in the ocean on a special board. ❏ *I'm going to buy a board and learn to surf.* ● **surf|er** (**surfers**) **NOUN** ❏ *This small fishing village continues to attract surfers.* ● **surf|ing** **NONCOUNT NOUN** ❏ *My favorite sport is surfing.*

3 **VERB** TECHNOLOGY If you **surf** the Internet, you spend time looking at different websites on the Internet. ❏ *No one knows how many people surf the Net.*

sur|face /sɜrfɪs/ (**surfaces**) **NOUN** The **surface** of something is the flat top part of it or the outside of it. ❏ *There were pen marks on the table's surface.* ❏ *Small waves moved on the surface of the water.*

→ look at **earth**

Word Partners	Use **surface** with:
N.	**Earth's** surface, surface **of the water**
ADJ.	**flat** surface, **rough** surface, **smooth** surface

surf|board /sɜrfbɔrd/ (**surfboards**) **NOUN** SPORTS A **surfboard** is a long narrow board that people use for surfing (= riding on ocean waves).

surge /sɜrdʒ/ (**surges, surging, surged**)

1 **NOUN** A **surge** is a sudden large increase in something. ❏ *...a surge in prices.*

2 **VERB** If a crowd of people **surge** forward, they suddenly move forward together. ❏ *The crowd surged forward into the store.*

sur|geon /sɜrdʒən/ (**surgeons**) **NOUN** A **surgeon** is a doctor who is specially trained to perform operations. ❏ *...a heart surgeon.*

sur|gery /sɜrdʒəri/ **NONCOUNT NOUN** **Surgery** is a process in which a doctor cuts open a patient's body in order to repair, remove, or replace a diseased or damaged part. ❏ *His father just had heart surgery.*

sur|gi|cal /sɜrdʒɪkəl/ **ADJECTIVE** **Surgical** equipment and clothing is used for doing operations. ❏ *...a collection of surgical instruments.*

sur|plus /sɜrplʌs, -pləs/ (**surpluses**)

1 **NOUN** If there is a **surplus of** something, there is more than you need. ❏ *The world has a surplus of food, but still people are hungry.*

2 **ADJECTIVE** **Surplus** describes something

s

that is extra or that is more than you need.
❑ *Few people have large sums of surplus cash.*

sur|prise /sərpraɪz/ (**surprises, surprising, surprised**)

1   **NOUN** A **surprise** is an unexpected event, fact, or piece of news. ❑ *I have a surprise for you: We are moving to Switzerland!*

2   **ADJECTIVE** **Surprise** is also an adjective. ❑ *Baxter arrived this afternoon, on a surprise visit.*

3   **NONCOUNT NOUN** **Surprise** is the feeling that you have when something that you do not expect happens. ❑ *The Pentagon has expressed surprise at his comments.*

4   **VERB** If something **surprises** you, it gives you a feeling of surprise. ❑ *We'll do the job ourselves and surprise everyone.* ❑ *It surprised me that he should make such a stupid mistake.*

sur|prised /sərpraɪzd/ **ADJECTIVE** If you are **surprised** at something, you have a feeling of surprise, because it is not expected. ❑ *I was surprised at how easy it was.*
→ look at **feeling**

sur|pris|ing /sərpraɪzɪŋ/ **ADJECTIVE** Something that is **surprising** is not expected and makes you feel surprised. ❑ *It is not surprising that children learn to read at different rates.* ● **sur|pris|ing|ly** **ADVERB** ❑ *The party was surprisingly good.*

sur|ren|der /sərɛndər/ (**surrenders, surrendering, surrendered**) **VERB** If you **surrender**, you stop fighting because you cannot win. ❑ *The army finally surrendered.*

sur|round /səraʊnd/ (**surrounds, surrounding, surrounded**) **VERB** If a person or thing **is surrounded** by something, that thing is all around them. ❑ *The church was surrounded by a low wall.*

sur|round|ings /səraʊndɪŋz/ **PLURAL NOUN** Your **surroundings** are everything around you or the place where you live. ❑ *He soon felt at home in his new surroundings.*

sur|vey /sɜrveɪ/ (**surveys**) **NOUN** If you do a **survey**, you try to find out information about a lot of different people by asking them questions. ❑ *They conducted a survey to see how students study.*

sur|viv|al /sərvaɪvəl/ **NONCOUNT NOUN** The **survival** of something or someone is the fact that they still exist after a difficult or dangerous time. ❑ *Many of these companies are now struggling for survival.*

sur|vive /sərvaɪv/ (**survives, surviving, survived**) **VERB** If a person or a living thing **survives** in a dangerous situation, they do not die. ❑ *It's a miracle that anyone survived.* ❑ *He survived heart surgery.* ● **sur|vi|vor** (**survivors**) **NOUN** ❑ *There were no survivors of the plane crash.*

sus|pect (**suspects, suspecting, suspected**)

> **PRONUNCIATION HELP**
> Pronounce the verb /səspɛkt/. Pronounce the noun /sʌspɛkt/.

1   **VERB** If you **suspect** that something is true, you think that it is true but you are not certain. ❑ *He suspected that she was telling lies.*

2   **VERB** If you **suspect** someone **of** doing something bad, you believe that they probably did it. ❑ *The police did not suspect him of anything.*

3   **NOUN** A **suspect** is a person who the police think may be guilty of a crime. ❑ *Police have arrested a suspect.*

sus|pend /səspɛnd/ (**suspends, suspending, suspended**)

1   **VERB** If you **suspend** something, you delay it or stop it from happening for a period of time. ❑ *The company will suspend production June 1st.*

2   **VERB** Something that **is suspended** from a high place is hanging from that place. ❑ *Three television screens were suspended from the ceiling.*

sus|pense /səspɛns/ **NONCOUNT NOUN** **Suspense** is a state of excitement about something that is going to happen very soon. ❑ *The suspense ended when the judges gave their decision.*

sus|pi|cion /səspɪʃən/ (**suspicions**) **NOUN** **Suspicion** is a belief or feeling that someone has done something wrong. ❑ *Don't do anything that might cause suspicion.*

sus|pi|cious /səspɪʃəs/

1   **ADJECTIVE** If you are **suspicious of** someone or something, you do not trust them. ❑ *He was suspicious of me at first.* ● **sus|pi|cious|ly** **ADVERB** ❑ *"What is it you want me to do?" Adams asked suspiciously.*

2   **ADJECTIVE** If someone or something is **suspicious**, there is something bad or wrong about them. ❑ *Please contact the police if you see any suspicious person in the area.* ● **sus|pi|cious|ly** **ADVERB** ❑ *Has anyone been acting suspiciously over the last few days?*

sus|tain /səsteɪn/ (**sustains, sustaining, sustained**)

1 VERB If you **sustain** something, you continue it for a period of time. ❑ *He has difficulty sustaining relationships.*

2 VERB If you **sustain** a loss or an injury, it happens to you. [FORMAL] ❑ *The aircraft sustained some damage.*

sus|tain|able /səsteɪnəbᵊl/ ADJECTIVE You use **sustainable** to talk about using natural products in a way that does not damage the environment. ❑ *The government introduced its program of sustainable development in 2006.*

● **sus|tain|abil|ity** /səsteɪnəbɪlɪti/ NONCOUNT NOUN ❑ *...environmental sustainability.*

→ look at **conservation**

swal|low /swɒloʊ/ (**swallows, swallowing, swallowed**)

1 VERB If you **swallow** something, you make it go from your mouth down into your stomach. ❑ *Polly took a bite of the apple and swallowed it.*

2 NOUN A **swallow** is a type of small bird with pointed wings and a split tail.

swam /swæm/ **Swam** is a form of the verb **swim**.

swan /swɒn/ (**swans**) NOUN A **swan** is a large white bird with a very long neck, that lives on rivers and lakes.

→ look at **bird**

swap /swɒp/ (**swaps, swapping, swapped**)

1 VERB If you **swap** something with someone, you give it to them and receive a different thing back from them. ❑ *Next week they will swap places.*

2 VERB If you **swap** one thing **for** another, you remove the first thing and replace it with the second. ❑ *He swapped his overalls for a suit and tie.* ❑ *I swapped my t-shirt for one of Karen's.*

sway /sweɪ/ (**sways, swaying, swayed**) VERB When people or things **sway**, they move slowly from one side to the other. ❑ *The people swayed back and forth singing.* ❑ *The tall grass was swaying in the wind.*

swear /sweər/ (**swears, swearing, swore, sworn**)

1 VERB If someone **swears**, they use language that is considered to be offensive. ❑ *It's wrong to swear and shout.*

2 VERB If you **swear to** do something, you promise in a serious way that you will do it. ❑ *I swear to do everything I can to help you.*

sweat /swɛt/ (**sweats, sweating, sweated**)

1 NONCOUNT NOUN **Sweat** is the liquid that comes out of your skin when you are hot, sick, or afraid. ❑ *Both horse and rider were dripping with sweat.*

2 VERB When you **sweat**, sweat comes out of your skin. ❑ *It's really hot. I'm sweating.*

3 PLURAL NOUN **Sweats** are loose, warm, comfortable pants, or pants and top that people wear to relax and do exercise. [INFORMAL]

sweat|er /swɛtər/ (**sweaters**) NOUN A **sweater** is a warm piece of clothing that covers the upper part of your body and your arms.

→ look at **clothing**

sweaty /swɛti/ (**sweatier, sweatiest**) ADJECTIVE If parts of your body or your clothes are **sweaty**, they are covered with sweat. ❑ *...hot, sweaty hands.* ❑ *...sweaty socks.*

→ look at **fitness**

sweep /swip/ (**sweeps, sweeping, swept**)

1 VERB If you **sweep** an area, you push dirt off it using a brush with a long handle. ❑ *The owner of the store was sweeping his floor.* ❑ *She was in the kitchen sweeping food off the floor.*

2 VERB If you **sweep** things off something, you push them off with a quick smooth movement of your arm. ❑ *She swept the cards from the table.*

→ look at **chore**

sweet /swit/ (**sweeter, sweetest, sweets**)

1 ADJECTIVE **Sweet** food and drink contains a lot of sugar. ❑ *...a cup of sweet tea.* ❑ *If the sauce is too sweet, add some salt.*

2 ADJECTIVE A **sweet** smell is a pleasant one. ❑ *I recognized the sweet smell of her perfume.*

3 ADJECTIVE A **sweet** sound is pleasant, smooth, and gentle. ❑ *The young girl's voice was soft and sweet.*

4 ADJECTIVE If someone is **sweet**, they are kind and gentle toward other people. ❑ *He was a sweet man.* ● **sweet|ly** ADVERB ❑ *I just smiled sweetly and said no.*

5 ADJECTIVE If a small person or thing is **sweet**, they are attractive in a simple way. [INFORMAL] ❑ *...a sweet little baby.*

6 PLURAL NOUN **Sweets** are foods that have a lot of sugar. ❑ *Eat more fruit and vegetables and less fat and sweets.*

→ look at **food, sense**

swell /swɛl/ (**swells, swelling, swelled, swollen**)

1 VERB If a part of your body **swells**, it

S

becomes larger and thicker than normal. ❑ *Do your legs swell at night?*

2 **Swell up** means the same as **swell**. ❑ *His eye swelled up.*

swept /swɛpt/ **Swept** is a form of the verb **sweep**.

swerve /swɜrv/ (**swerves, swerving, swerved**) **VERB** If a vehicle or other moving thing **swerves**, it suddenly changes direction. ❑ *Her car swerved off the road.*

swift /swɪft/ (**swifter, swiftest**)

1 **ADJECTIVE** A **swift** event or process happens very quickly or without delay. ❑ *We need to make a swift decision.* ● **swift|ly** **ADVERB** ❑ *We have to act as swiftly as we can.*

2 **ADJECTIVE** Something that is **swift** moves very quickly. ❑ *With a swift movement, Matthew sat up.* ● **swift|ly** **ADVERB** ❑ *Lenny moved swiftly and silently across the grass.*

swim /swɪm/ (**swims, swimming, swam, swum**)

1 **VERB** SPORTS When you **swim**, you move through water by making movements with your arms and legs. ❑ *She learned to swim when she was 10.* ❑ *I swim a mile a day.*

2 **NOUN** Swim is also a noun. ❑ *When can we go for a swim?* ● **swim|mer** (**swimmers**) **NOUN** ❑ *I'm a good swimmer.*

→ look at **fitness, ocean**

swim|ming /swɪmɪŋ/ **NONCOUNT NOUN** SPORTS **Swimming** is the activity of swimming, especially as a sport or for pleasure. ❑ *Swimming is a great form of exercise.*

swim|ming pool (**swimming pools**) **NOUN** SPORTS A **swimming pool** is a large hole filled with water that people can swim in.

swim|suit /swɪmsut/ (**swimsuits**) **NOUN** A **swimsuit** is a piece of clothing that you wear for swimming. A swimsuit is also called a **bathing suit**. ❑ *She refused to be photographed in a swimsuit.*

swing /swɪŋ/ (**swings, swinging, swung**)

1 **VERB** If something **swings**, it moves repeatedly backward and forward or from side to side through the air. ❑ *Amber walked beside him, her arms swinging.*

2 **NOUN** A **swing** is a seat that hangs by two ropes. You can sit on it and move forward and backward through the air. ❑ *I took the kids to the park to play on the swings.*

switch /swɪtʃ/ (**switches, switching, switched**)

1 **NOUN** A **switch** is a small control for turning electricity on or off. ❑ *She shut the dishwasher and pressed the switch.*

2 **VERB** If you **switch to** something different, you change to it. ❑ *Companies are switching to cleaner fuels.*

3 **VERB** If you **switch** two things, you replace one with the other. ❑ *They switched the keys, so Karen had the key to my room and I had the key to hers.*

▶ **switch off** If you **switch off** an electrical piece of equipment, you stop it from working by operating a switch. ❑ *She switched off the coffee machine.*

▶ **switch on** If you **switch on** an electrical piece of equipment, you make it start working by operating a switch. ❑ *He switched on the lamp.*

swol|len /swoʊlᵊn/

1 **ADJECTIVE** If a part of your body is **swollen**, it is larger and thicker than normal, usually as a result of injury or illness. ❑ *My eyes were swollen and I could hardly see.*

2 **Swollen** is a form of the verb **swell**.

→ look at **sick**

sword /sɔrd/ (**swords**) **NOUN** A **sword** is a weapon with a handle and a long sharp blade.

swore /swɔr/ **Swore** is a form of the verb **swear**.

sworn /swɔrn/ **Sworn** is a form of the verb **swear**.

swum /swʌm/ **Swum** is a form of the verb **swim**.

swung /swʌŋ/ **Swung** is a form of the verb **swing**.

syl|la|ble /sɪləbᵊl/ (**syllables**) **NOUN** LANGUAGE ARTS A **syllable** is a part of a word that contains a single vowel sound and that is pronounced as a unit. So, for example, "book" has one syllable, and "reading" has two syllables.

→ look at **dictionary, language**

syl|la|bus /sɪləbəs/ (**syllabuses**) **NOUN** A **syllabus** is a list of the subjects to be covered in a course. ❑ *The course syllabus consists mainly of novels by American writers.*

sym|bol /sɪmbᵊl/ (symbols) NOUN
LANGUAGE ARTS A **symbol for** something is a number, a letter, or a shape that represents that thing. ❑ *What's the chemical symbol for oxygen?*

sym|met|ri|cal /sɪmɛtrɪkᵊl/ ADJECTIVE If something is **symmetrical**, it has two halves that are exactly the same. ❑ *The rows of windows were perfectly symmetrical.*

sym|pa|thet|ic /sɪmpəθɛtɪk/ ADJECTIVE
A **sympathetic** person is kind and tries to understand other people's feelings. ❑ *Try talking about your problem with a sympathetic teacher.* ● **sym|pa|theti|cal|ly** /sɪmpəθɛtɪkli/ ADVERB ❑ *She nodded sympathetically.*

sym|pa|thize /sɪmpəθaɪz/ (sympathizes, sympathizing, sympathized) VERB If you **sympathize** with someone who is in a bad situation, you show that you are sorry for them. ❑ *It's terrible when a parent dies. I sympathize with you.*

sym|pa|thy /sɪmpəθi/ NONCOUNT NOUN
If you have **sympathy** for someone who is in a bad situation, you are sorry for them. ❑ *I get no sympathy from my family when I'm sick.*

sym|pho|ny /sɪmfəni/ (symphonies)
1 NOUN MUSIC A **symphony** is a piece of music that has been written to be played by an orchestra. ❑ *...Beethoven's Ninth Symphony.*
2 NOUN MUSIC A **symphony** orchestra is a large orchestra that plays classical music. ❑ *...the Boston Symphony Orchestra.*

symp|tom /sɪmptəm/ (symptoms) NOUN
A **symptom** of an illness is something that is wrong with you that is a sign of the illness. ❑ *All these patients have flu symptoms.*
→ look at **health care**

syna|gogue /sɪnəgɒg/ (synagogues) NOUN
A **synagogue** is a building where Jewish people go to pray.

syn|drome /sɪndroʊm/ (syndromes) NOUN
A **syndrome** is a medical condition. ❑ *No one knows what causes Sudden Infant Death Syndrome.*

syno|nym /sɪnənɪm/ (synonyms) NOUN
LANGUAGE ARTS A **synonym** is a word or an expression that means the same as another word or expression. ❑ *"Afraid" is a synonym for "frightened."*

syn|thet|ic /sɪnθɛtɪk/ ADJECTIVE Synthetic products are made from chemicals or artificial substances rather than from natural ones. ❑ *...synthetic rubber.*

sy|ringe /sɪrɪndʒ/ (syringes) NOUN A **syringe** is a small tube with a thin hollow needle at the end. It is used for putting medicine into a part of the body or for taking blood from your body.

syr|up /sɪrəp, sɜr-/ (syrups) NONCOUNT NOUN Syrup is a sweet liquid that is made by cooking sugar with water. ❑ *...canned fruit with syrup.*

sys|tem /sɪstəm/ (systems)
1 NOUN A **system** is a way of working, organizing, or doing something that follows a plan. ❑ *You need a better system for organizing your DVDs.*
2 NOUN A **system** is a set of equipment, parts, or instruments. ❑ *There's something wrong with the computer system.* ❑ *...a heating system.*
3 NOUN A **system** is a network of things that are linked together so that people or things can communicate with each other or travel from one place to another. ❑ *...Australia's road and rail system*

s

Tt

tab /tæb/ (**tabs**) **NOUN** A **tab** is a small piece of cloth, metal, or paper that is fixed to something, so that you can see it, hold it, or pull it. ❏ *He pushed back the tab on the can with his thumb and drank.*

ta|ble /teɪbᵊl/ (**tables**)
1 **NOUN** A **table** is a piece of furniture with a flat top that you put things on or sit at. ❏ *Mom was sitting at the kitchen table.*
2 **NOUN** A **table** is a set of facts or numbers that you arrange in neat rows. ❏ *See the table on page 104.*
→ look at **classroom, furniture, restaurant**

table|cloth /teɪbᵊlklɔθ/ (**tablecloths**) **NOUN** A **tablecloth** is a cloth that you use to cover a table.
→ look at **restaurant**

table|spoon /teɪbᵊlspun/ (**tablespoons**) **NOUN** A **tablespoon** is a large spoon that you use when you are cooking.

tab|let /tæblɪt/ (**tablets**) **NOUN** A **tablet** is a small solid piece of medicine that you swallow. ❏ *The doctor gave me a sleeping tablet to help me sleep.*

tack|le /tækᵊl/ (**tackles, tackling, tackled**)
1 **VERB** If you **tackle** a problem, you deal with it. ❏ *We discussed the best way to tackle the situation.*
2 **VERB** SPORTS If you **tackle** someone in a sports game, you try to take the ball away from them. ❏ *Foley tackled the quarterback.*
3 **NOUN** **Tackle** is also a noun. ❏ *A great tackle from Beckham saved the game.*

taco /tɑkoʊ/ (**tacos**) **NOUN** A **taco** is a type of Mexican bread that is folded in half and filled with meat, vegetables, and cheese.

tact|ful /tæktfəl/ **ADJECTIVE** If you are **tactful**, you are very careful not to do or say anything that will upset or embarrass other people. ❏ *Dan obviously overheard our argument but he was too tactful to mention it.* ● **tact|ful|ly** **ADVERB** ❏ *Tactfully, Jessica changed the subject.*

tac|tic /tæktɪk/ (**tactics**) **NOUN** Your **tactics** are the ways that you choose to do something when you are trying to succeed in a particular situation. ❏ *Things weren't going well, so I decided to change my tactics.*

tad|pole /tædpoʊl/ (**tadpoles**) **NOUN** **Tadpoles** are small water animals that look like fish, and that develop into frogs or toads (= small green or brown animals with long back legs).

tag /tæg/ (**tags**) **NOUN** A **tag** is a small piece of cardboard or cloth that is attached to something. It has information written on it. ❏ *The staff all wear name tags.* ❏ *There's no price tag on this purse.*

Sound Partners | tail, tale

tail /teɪl/ (**tails**)
1 **NOUN** The **tail** of an animal is the long thin part at the end of its body. ❏ *The dog barked and wagged its tail.*
2 **NOUN** A **tail** is the end or the back of something. ❏ *The plane's tail hit the runway while it was landing.*

tai|lor /teɪlər/ (**tailors**) **NOUN** A **tailor** is a person whose job is to make and repair clothes.

take /teɪk/ (**takes, taking, took, taken**)
1 **VERB** If you **take** something, you hold it or remove it. ❏ *Let me take your coat.* ❏ *He took a handkerchief from his pocket.*
2 **VERB** If you **take** something with you, you carry it with you. ❏ *Don't forget to take a map with you.*
3 **VERB** If a person or a vehicle **takes** someone somewhere, they transport them there. ❏ *Michael took me to the airport.*
4 **VERB** If you **take** something, you steal it. ❏ *They took my pocketbook.*
5 **VERB** If something **takes** an amount of time, it needs that time in order to happen. ❏ *The sauce takes 25 minutes to prepare.*
6 **VERB** If you **take** something that someone offers you, you accept it. ❏ *Sylvia has taken a job in Tokyo teaching English.* ❏ *I think you should take my advice.*

7 VERB If you **take** a road, you choose to travel along it. ❑ *Take a right at the stop sign.*

8 VERB If you **take** a vehicle, you use it to go from one place to another. ❑ *She took the train to New York.*

9 VERB You can use **take** to say that someone does something. ❑ *She was too tired to take a bath.* ❑ *Betty took a photograph of us.*

10 VERB If you **take** a subject at school, you study it. ❑ *Students can take European history and American history.*

11 VERB If you **take** an examination, you do it. ❑ *She took her driving test yesterday and passed.*

12 VERB If someone **takes** medicine, they swallow it. ❑ *I try not to take pills of any kind.*

▶ **take after** If you **take after** a member of your family, you look or behave like them. ❑ *Your mom was a smart, brave woman. You take after her.*

▶ **take away** If you **take** something **away**, you remove it. ❑ *The waitress took away the dirty dishes.*

▶ **take back** If you **take** something **back**, you return it. ❑ *If you don't like it, I'll take it back to the store.*

▶ **take off** **1** When an airplane **takes off**, it leaves the ground and starts flying. ❑ *We took off at 11 o'clock.*

2 If you **take** clothes **off**, you remove them. ❑ *Come in and take off your coat.*

3 If you **take** time **off**, you do not go to work for a time. ❑ *My husband was sick and I had to take time off work to look after him.*

→ look at **wear**

▶ **take out** If you **take** someone **out**, you take them somewhere enjoyable. ❑ *Sophia took me out to lunch today.*

▶ **take over** If people **take over** something, they get control of it. ❑ *I'm going to take over this company one day.*

▶ **take up** **1** If you **take up** an activity, you start doing it. ❑ *Peter took up tennis at the age of eight.*

2 If something **takes up** an amount of time or space, it uses that amount. ❑ *I don't want to take up too much of your time.* ❑ *The round wooden table takes up most of the kitchen.*

tak|en /ˈteɪkən/ **Taken** is a form of the verb **take**.

take|off /ˈteɪkɔf/ (**takeoffs**) also **take-off** NOUN **Takeoff** is the time when an aircraft leaves the ground and starts to fly. ❑ *What time is takeoff?*

take|out /ˈteɪkaʊt/ (**takeouts**)

1 NONCOUNT NOUN **Takeout** or **takeout** food is prepared food that you buy from a store or a restaurant and take away to eat somewhere else. ❑ *Let's just get a takeout pizza tonight.*

2 NOUN A **takeout** is a store or a restaurant that sells prepared food that you take away and eat somewhere else. ❑ *We took Kerry to her favorite Chinese takeout for her birthday.*

→ look at **eat**

Sound Partners	tale, tail

tale /teɪl/ (**tales**) NOUN A **tale** is a story. ❑ *It's a tale about the friendship between two boys.*

tal|ent /ˈtælənt/ (**talents**) NOUN **Talent** is your natural ability to do something well. ❑ *Both her children have a talent for music.* ❑ *He's got lots of talent, but he's rather lazy.*

tal|ent|ed /ˈtæləntɪd/ ADJECTIVE If you are **talented**, you have a natural ability to do something well. ❑ *Howard is a talented pianist.*

talk /tɔk/ (**talks, talking, talked**)

1 VERB If you **talk**, you say words, or speak to someone about your thoughts, ideas, or feelings. ❑ *After the fight, Mark was too upset to talk.* ❑ *Tom didn't talk until he was three years old.* ❑ *They were all talking about the movie.* ❑ *I talked to him yesterday.*

2 NONCOUNT NOUN **Talk** is also a noun. ❑ *I had a long talk with my father.*

3 NOUN **Talk** is also a noun. ❑ *She gave a brief talk on the history of the building.*

4 PLURAL NOUN **Talks** are formal discussions between different groups, to try to reach an agreement. ❑ *The government has begun peace talks with the rebels.*

→ look at **communication, phone**

tall /tɔl/ (**taller, tallest**)

1 ADJECTIVE If someone or something is **tall**, they are higher than other people or things. ❑ *John is very tall.* ❑ *The lighthouse is a tall square tower.*

2 ADJECTIVE You use **tall** when you are asking or talking about the height of someone or something. ❑ *"How tall are you?"—"I'm six foot five."*

→ look at **tree**

tam|bou|rine /ˌtæmbəˈrin/ (**tambourines**) NOUN MUSIC A **tambourine** is a round musical instrument that you shake or hit with your hand.

t

tame /teɪm/ (**tames, taming, tamed, tamer, tamest**)

1 **ADJECTIVE** If an animal is **tame**, it is not afraid of humans.

2 **VERB** If you **tame** a wild animal, you teach it not to be afraid of humans.

tan /tæn/ (**tans, tanning, tanned**)

1 **NOUN** If you have a **tan**, your skin has become darker because you have spent time in the sun. ❏ *She is tall and blonde, with a tan.*

2 **VERB** If your skin **tans**, it becomes darker because you have spent time in the sun. ❏ *I have very pale skin that never tans.* ● **tanned** **ADJECTIVE** ❏ *Becky's skin was deeply tanned.*

tan|gle /tæŋg³l/ (**tangles, tangling, tangled**)

1 **NOUN** A **tangle of** something is a mass of it that has become twisted together in a messy way. ❏ *A tangle of wires connected the two computers.*

2 **VERB** If something **is tangled** or **tangles**, it becomes twisted together in a messy way. ❏ *Her hair is curly and tangles easily.*

tank /tæŋk/ (**tanks**)

1 **NOUN** A **tank** is a large container for holding liquid or gas. ❏ *...a fuel tank.*

2 **NOUN** A **tank** is a heavy, strong military vehicle, with large guns. It moves on metal tracks that are fixed over the wheels.

tank|er /tæŋkər/ (**tankers**) **NOUN** A **tanker** is a large ship or truck that carries large amounts of gas or liquid. ❏ *...an oil tanker.*

tap /tæp/ (**taps, tapping, tapped**)

1 **VERB** If you **tap** something, you hit it or touch it quickly and lightly. ❏ *He tapped the table nervously with his fingers.* ❏ *Karen tapped on the bedroom door and went in.*

2 **NOUN** Tap is also a noun. ❏ *There was a tap on the door.*

3 A **tap** is an object that controls the flow of a liquid or a gas from a pipe.

tape /teɪp/ (**tapes, taping, taped**)

1 **NONCOUNT NOUN** Tape is a sticky strip of plastic used for sticking things together. ❏ *Attach the picture to the cardboard using sticky tape.*

2 **NONCOUNT NOUN** Tape is a long narrow plastic strip that you use to record music, sounds, or moving pictures.

3 **VERB** If you **tape** music, sounds, or moving pictures, you record them on a tape.

❏ *Ms. Pringle secretly taped her conversation with her boss.*

4 **VERB** If you **tape** one thing to another, you stick them together using tape. ❏ *I taped the envelope shut.*

→ look at **office**

tape re|cord|er (**tape recorders**) also **tape-recorder** **NOUN** A **tape recorder** is a machine that you use for recording and playing sound or music.

tar /tɑr/ **NONCOUNT NOUN** Tar is a thick, black, sticky substance that is used for making roads. ❏ *It was so hot that the tar melted on the roads.*

tar|get /tɑrgɪt/ (**targets**)

1 **NOUN** A **target** is something that you try to hit with a weapon or another object. ❏ *One of the missiles missed its target.*

2 **NOUN** Your **target** is the result that you are trying to achieve. ❏ *We failed to meet our sales targets last year.*

tar|mac /tɑrmæk/ **NONCOUNT NOUN** The **tarmac** is the long road that an aircraft travels on before it starts flying and when it lands. [TRADEMARK] ❏ *She closed her eyes as the plane hit the tarmac.*

tart /tɑrt/ (**tarts**) **NOUN** A **tart** is a type of food. It is a case made of flour, fat and water (= pastry) that you fill with fruit or vegetables and cook in an oven. ❏ *We had apple tarts, served with fresh cream.*

task /tæsk/ (**tasks**) **NOUN** A **task** is a piece of work that you have to do. ❏ *I had the task of cleaning the kitchen.*

task|bar /tæskbɑr/ (**taskbars**) also **task bar** **NOUN** The **taskbar** on a computer screen is a narrow strip at the bottom of the screen that shows you which windows are open.

taste /teɪst/ (**tastes, tasting, tasted**)

1 **NONCOUNT NOUN** Your sense of **taste** is your ability to recognize the flavor of things with your tongue. ❏ *Over the years my sense of taste has disappeared.*

2 **NOUN** The **taste** of something is the particular quality that it has when you put it in your mouth, for example whether it is sweet or salty. ❏ *I like the taste of chocolate.* ❏ *This medicine has a nasty taste.*

3 **VERB** If food or drink **tastes of** something, it has that particular flavor. ❏ *The water tasted of metal.* ❏ *The pizza tastes delicious.*

4 **VERB** If you **taste** some food or drink, you eat or drink a small amount of it in order to see what the flavor is like. ❏ *Don't add salt until you've tasted the food.*

5 **NOUN** Taste is also a noun. ❏ *Have a taste of this pie.*

6 **VERB** If you can **taste** something that you are eating or drinking, you are aware of its flavor. ❏ *Can you taste the onions in this dish?*

7 **NONCOUNT NOUN** Your **taste** is your choice **in** all the things that you like or buy. ❏ *Will's got great taste in clothes.*

→ look at **eat, food, sense**

taste|ful /teɪstfəl/ **ADJECTIVE** If something is **tasteful**, it is attractive, has a good design, and is of good quality. ❏ *Sarah was wearing a purple suit and tasteful jewelry.* ● **taste|ful|ly** **ADVERB** ❏ *They live in a large and tastefully decorated home.*

taste|less /teɪstlɪs/

1 **ADJECTIVE** If something is **tasteless**, it is unattractive, badly designed, and of poor quality. ❏ *Jim's house is full of tasteless furniture.*

2 **ADJECTIVE** If a remark or joke is **tasteless**, it is offensive. ❏ *That was a very tasteless remark.*

3 **ADJECTIVE** If food or drink is **tasteless**, it has no flavor. ❏ *The fish was tasteless.*

tasty /teɪsti/ (**tastier, tastiest**) **ADJECTIVE** If food is **tasty**, it has a pleasant flavor and is good to eat. ❏ *The food here is tasty and good value.*

tat|tle /tætᵊl/ (**tattles, tattling, tattled**) **VERB** If you **tattle on** someone, you give information to another person about something bad that they have done. ❏ *He was always tattling on people who broke the rules.*

tat|too /tætu/ (**tattoos, tattooing, tattooed**)

1 **NOUN** A **tattoo** is a design on a person's skin made with a needle and colored ink. ❏ *He has a tattoo of three stars on his arm.*

2 **VERB** If something **is tattooed** on your body, you have a tattoo there. ❏ *She has had a small black cat tattooed on one of her shoulders.*

taught /tɔt/ **Taught** is a form of the verb **teach**.

tax /tæks/ (**taxes, taxing, taxed**)

1 **NOUN** Tax is an amount of money that you have to pay to the government so that it can pay for public services such as roads and schools. ❏ *No one enjoys paying tax.* ❏ *The government has promised not to raise taxes this year.*

2 **VERB** When a person or company **is taxed**, they have to pay a part of their income to the government. ❏ *We are the most heavily taxed people in North America.*

taxa|tion /tækseɪʃᵊn/ **NONCOUNT NOUN** Taxation is when a government takes money from people and spends it on things such as education, health, and defense. ❏ *The council wants major changes in taxation.*

taxi /tæksi/ (**taxis**) **NOUN** A **taxi** is a car that you can hire, with its driver, to take you where you want to go. ❏ *We took a taxi back to our hotel.*

→ look at **transportation**

taxi|cab /tæksikæb/ (**taxicabs**) also **taxi-cab** **NOUN** A **taxicab** is the same as a **taxi**.

taxi stand (**taxi stands**) **NOUN** A taxi stand is a place where taxis wait for passengers, for example at an airport.

tax|payer /tækspeɪər/ (**taxpayers**) **NOUN** **Taxpayers** are people who pay tax. ❏ *The government has wasted taxpayers' money.*

tea /ti/

1 **NONCOUNT NOUN** Tea is a drink that you make by pouring boiling water on the dry leaves of a plant called the tea bush. ❏ *I made myself a cup of tea and sat down to watch TV.* ❏ *Would you like some tea?*

2 **NONCOUNT NOUN** Tea is the chopped dried leaves of the plant that tea is made from.

teach /titʃ/ (**teaches, teaching, taught**)

1 **VERB** If you **teach** someone something, you give them instructions so that they know about it or so that they know how to do it. ❏ *She taught me to read.* ❏ *George taught him how to ride a horse.*

2 **VERB** If you **teach**, you give lessons in a subject at a school or a college. ❏ *Christine teaches biology at Piper High.* ❏ *Mrs. Garcia has been teaching part-time for 16 years.* ● **teach|er** (**teachers**) **NOUN** ❏ *I was a teacher for 21 years.* ● **teach|ing** **NONCOUNT NOUN** ❏ *The quality of teaching in the school is excellent.*

→ look at **school**

team /tim/ (**teams**)

1 **NOUN** **SPORTS** A **team** is a group of people who play a particular sport or game against other groups of people. ❏ *Kate was on the school basketball team.*

2 **NOUN** A **team** is any group of people who work together. ❏ *A team of doctors visited the hospital yesterday.*

→ look at **play**

team|work /tɪ̱mwɜrk/ **NONCOUNT NOUN**
Teamwork is the ability that a group of people have to work well together. ❏ *She knows the importance of teamwork.*

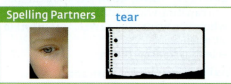

Spelling Partners **tear**

---

tear

1 CRYING
2 DAMAGING OR MOVING

❶ tear /tɪ̱ər/ (**tears**)
1 **NOUN** Tears are the drops of liquid that come out of your eyes when you are crying. ❏ *Her eyes filled with tears.*

2 If you are **in tears**, you are crying. ❏ *By the end of the movie, we were all in tears.*

3 If you **burst into tears**, you suddenly start crying. ❏ *She burst into tears and ran from the kitchen.*

❷ tear /tɛ̱ər/ (**tears, tearing, tore, torn**)
1 **VERB** If you **tear** something, you pull it into pieces or make a hole in it. ❏ *I tore my coat on a nail.* ❏ *She tore the letter into several pieces.*

2 **NOUN** Tear is also a noun. ❏ *I looked through a tear in the curtains.*

▶ **tear up** If you **tear up** a piece of paper, you tear it into small pieces. ❏ *He tore up the letter and threw it in the fire.*

tease /tɪ̱z/ (**teases, teasing, teased**) **VERB**
If you **tease** someone, you laugh at them or make jokes about them in order to embarrass them or annoy them. ❏ *Amber's brothers are always teasing her.*

tea|spoon /tɪ̱spun/ (**teaspoons**) **NOUN** A **teaspoon** is a small spoon that you use for putting sugar into tea or coffee. ❏ *Use a teaspoon to remove the seeds from the fruit.*

tech|ni|cal /tɛ̱knɪkəl/ **ADJECTIVE** Something that is **technical** involves machines, processes, and materials that are used in science and industry. ❏ *We still have to solve a number of technical problems.* ● **tech|ni|cal|ly** /tɛ̱knɪkli/ **ADVERB** ❏ *It is a very technically advanced car.*

tech|ni|cian /tɛknɪ̱ʃən/ (**technicians**) **NOUN**
A **technician** is someone whose job involves skillful use of scientific or medical equipment. ❏ *Joseph works as a laboratory technician at St. Thomas's Hospital.*

tech|nique /tɛknɪ̱k/ (**techniques**) **NOUN**
A **technique** is a special way of doing something practical. ❏ *Doctors have recently developed these new techniques.*

tech|nol|ogy /tɛknɒ̱lədʒi/ (**technologies**)
NOUN Technology is the way that scientific knowledge is used in a practical way. ❏ *Computer technology has developed fast during the last 10 years.*

Word Partners	Use **technology** with:
ADJ.	**available** technology, **educational** technology, **high** technology, **latest** technology, **medical** technology, **modern** technology, **new** technology, **wireless** technology
N.	**computer** technology, **information** technology, **science and** technology

ted|dy bear /tɛ̱di bɛ̱ər/ (**teddy bears**) **NOUN**
A **teddy bear** is a soft toy that looks like a bear.

te|di|ous /tɪ̱diəs/ **ADJECTIVE** If something is **tedious**, it continues for too long, and is not interesting. ❏ *The movie was very tedious.*

teen /tɪ̱n/ (**teens**)
1 **PLURAL NOUN** If you are in your **teens**, you are between thirteen and nineteen years old. ❏ *I met my husband when I was in my teens.*

2 **NOUN** A **teen** is a person who is in his or her teens.

Word Builder	**teenage**
teen ≈ plus ten, from 13-19	
eight + teen = eighteen	
four + teen = fourteen	
nine + teen = nineteen	
seven + teen = seventeen	
six + teen = sixteen	
teen + age = teenage	

teen|age /tɪ̱neɪdʒ/ **ADJECTIVE** Teenage children are aged between thirteen and nineteen years old. ❏ *Taylor is a typical teenage girl.*

teen|ager /tɪ̱neɪdʒər/ (**teenagers**) **NOUN**
A **teenager** is someone who is between thirteen and nineteen years old.

→ look at **age**

T

teeth /tiθ/ Teeth is the plural of **tooth**.
→ look at **face**

tele|com|mu|ni|ca|tions /tɛlɪkə myunɪkeɪʃᵊnz/ **NONCOUNT NOUN**
Telecommunications is the sending of signals and messages over long distances using electronic equipment. ❏ *Pete has 15 years' experience in the telecommunications industry.*

tele|phone /tɛlɪfoʊn/ (**telephones, telephoning, telephoned**)
1 NOUN A telephone is the piece of equipment that you use for speaking to someone who is in another place. ❏ *He got up and answered the telephone.*
2 VERB If you **telephone** someone, you speak to them using a telephone.
❏ *I telephoned my boyfriend to say I was sorry.*
❏ *He telephoned for a cab to take him to the airport.*
3 If you are **on the telephone**, you are speaking to someone by telephone. ❏ *Linda was on the telephone for three hours this evening.*
→ look at **phone**

tele|scope /tɛlɪskoʊp/ (**telescopes**) **NOUN**
A telescope is an instrument shaped like a tube. It has special glass inside it that makes things that are far away look bigger and nearer when you look through it.

tele|vi|sion /tɛlɪvɪʒᵊn, -vɪʒ-/ (**televisions**)
1 NOUN A television or a TV is a piece of electrical equipment with a screen on which you watch moving pictures with sound. ❏ *She turned the television on.*
2 NONCOUNT NOUN Television is the moving pictures and sounds that you watch and listen to on a television. ❏ *Michael spends too much time watching television.* ❏ *What's on television tonight?* ❏ *My favorite television program is about to start.*
→ look at Word World: **television**
→ look at **news**

tell /tɛl/ (**tells, telling, told**)
1 VERB If you **tell** someone something, you give them information. ❏ *I told Rachel I got the job.* ❏ *I called Anna to tell her how angry I was.*
❏ *Claire made me promise to tell her the truth.*
❏ *He told his story to The New York Times.*
2 VERB If you **tell** someone **to** do something, you order them to do it. ❏ *The police officer told him to get out of his car.*
3 VERB If you can **tell** what is happening or what is true, you are able to judge correctly what is happening or what is true. ❏ *I could tell that Tom was tired and bored.*
→ look at **communication**

tem|per /tɛmpər/
1 NONCOUNT NOUN If you have a **temper**, you become angry very easily. ❏ *Their mother had a terrible temper.*
2 NONCOUNT NOUN If you are **in** a bad **temper** you are likely to become angry very easily. ❏ *I was in a bad temper last night because I was so tired.*
3 If you **lose** your **temper**, you suddenly become angry. ❏ *Simon lost his temper and punched me.*

tem|pera|ture /tɛmprətʃər, -tʃʊər/ (**temperatures**)
1 NOUN The **temperature** of something is how hot or cold it is. ❏ *At night here, the temperature drops below freezing.*
2 NONCOUNT NOUN Your **temperature** is the temperature of your body, that shows whether you are healthy or not. ❏ *The baby's temperature continued to rise.*
3 If you **have a temperature**, your temperature is higher than it should be.
4 If someone **takes** your **temperature**, they use an instrument (= a thermometer) to measure the temperature of your body. ❏ *The nurse took my temperature.*
→ look at **climate, greenhouse effect**

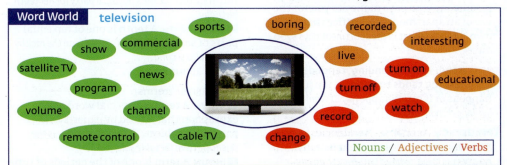

Word World | television

sports · boring · recorded · show · commercial · interesting · satellite TV · live · news · turn on · program · educational · volume · channel · turn off · watch · remote control · cable TV · record · change

Nouns / Adjectives / Verbs

Word Partners   Use **temperature** with:

ADJ.	**average** temperature **1**
	high temperature, **low** temperature, **normal** temperature **1** **2**
N.	**changes in** temperature, temperature **increase**, **ocean** temperature, **rise in** temperature, **room** temperature, **surface** temperature, **water** temperature **1**
	body temperature **2**

tem|ple /tɛmpəl/ (**temples**) **NOUN** A **temple** is a building where people pray to their god or gods. ❑ *We visited the biggest Sikh temple in India.*

tem|po|rary /tɛmpəreri/ **ADJECTIVE** If something is **temporary**, it lasts for only a certain time. ❑ *His job here is only temporary.*
● **tem|po|rari|ly** /tɛmpərɛərɪli/ **ADVERB** ❑ *Her website was temporarily shut down yesterday.*

tempt /tɛmpt/ (**tempts, tempting, tempted**) **VERB** If something **tempts** you, it attracts you and makes you want it, even though it may be wrong or harmful. ❑ *Credit cards can tempt people to buy things they can't afford.* ❑ *I was tempted to lie, but in the end I told the truth.*
● **tempt|ing** **ADJECTIVE** ❑ *The berries look tempting to children, but they're poisonous.*

temp|ta|tion /tɛmpteɪʃən/ **NONCOUNT NOUN** **Temptation** is the feeling that you want to do something or to have something, when you know that it is wrong. ❑ *Exercise regularly and resist the temptation to eat snacks.*

tempt|ed /tɛmptɪd/ **ADJECTIVE** If you are **tempted to** do something, you would like to do it although it may not be a good idea. ❑ *I was tempted to buy a car, but I paid off my debts instead.*

ten /tɛn/ **MATH** **Ten** is the number 10.
→ look at **number**

ten|ant /tɛnənt/ (**tenants**) **NOUN** A **tenant** is someone who pays money to you for the use of an apartment or an office that you own. ❑ *Each tenant in the apartment pays $200 a week.*

tend /tɛnd/ (**tends, tending, tended**) **VERB** If something **tends to** happen, it usually happens or it often happens. ❑ *Women tend to live longer than men.*

ten|den|cy /tɛndənsi/ (**tendencies**) **NOUN** A **tendency** is something that usually happens. ❑ *Laura has a tendency to gossip.*

ten|der /tɛndər/ (**tenderer, tenderest**)
1 **ADJECTIVE** Something that is **tender** is kind and gentle. ❑ *Her voice was tender.*
● **ten|der|ly** **ADVERB** ❑ *He kissed her tenderly.*
2 **ADJECTIVE** Meat that is **tender** is easy to cut or bite. ❑ *Cook for about 2 hours, until the meat is tender.*
3 **ADJECTIVE** If part of your body is **tender**, it is painful when you touch it. ❑ *My cheek felt very tender.*

ten|nis /tɛnɪs/ **NONCOUNT NOUN** **SPORTS** **Tennis** is a game for two or four players, who use rackets (= special bats) to hit a ball across a net between them.

tense /tɛns/ (**tenser, tensest, tenses**)
1 **ADJECTIVE** If you are **tense**, you are anxious and nervous, and you do not feel relaxed. ❑ *The team were very tense before the game.*
2 **ADJECTIVE** If your body is **tense**, your muscles are tight and not relaxed. ❑ *A bath can relax tense muscles.*
3 **NOUN** **LANGUAGE ARTS** The **tense** of a verb is the form that shows whether something is happening in the past, the present, or the future.
→ look at **grammar**

ten|sion /tɛnʃən/ **NONCOUNT NOUN** **Tension** is a feeling of worry and anxiety that makes it impossible for you to feel relaxed. ❑ *Physical exercise can reduce tension.*

tent /tɛnt/ (**tents**) **NOUN** A **tent** is a shelter made of thick cloth that is held up by poles and ropes. You sleep in a tent when you go camping.

tenth /tɛnθ/ (**tenths**)
1 **ADJECTIVE, ADVERB** **MATH** The **tenth** item in a series is the one that you count as number ten. ❑ *She's having a party for her tenth birthday.*
2 **NOUN** **MATH** A **tenth** is one of ten equal parts of something (¹⁄₁₀). ❑ *She won the race by a tenth of a second.*
→ look at **number**

term /tɜrm/ (**terms**)
1 **NOUN** A **term** is a special word or an expression that is used by experts in a particular subject. ❑ *Sodium chloride is the scientific term for table salt.*
2 **NOUN** A **term** is one of the periods of time

that a school, a college, or a university year is divided into. ❑ *The school's Principal, Mrs. Johnson, will retire at the end of the term.*

3 PLURAL NOUN The **terms** of an agreement are the conditions that all of the people involved in it must agree to. ❑ *The terms of the agreement are quite simple.*

ter|mi|nal /tɜrmɪnᵊl/ (**terminals**) **NOUN** A **terminal** is a place where people begin or end a trip by bus, aircraft, or ship. ❑ *Port Authority is the world's busiest bus terminal.*

ter|mi|nate /tɜrmɪneɪt/ (**terminates, terminating, terminated**) **VERB** If you **terminate** something, you end it. [FORMAL] ❑ *His contract was terminated early.*

ter|race /tɛrɪs/ (**terraces**) **NOUN** A **terrace** is a flat area next to a building, where people can sit. ❑ *Our house has a terrace overlooking the ocean.*

ter|ri|ble /tɛrɪbᵊl/
1 ADJECTIVE If something is **terrible**, it is extremely bad. ❑ *I have a terrible singing voice.* ● **ter|ri|bly ADVERB** ❑ *Our team played terribly today.*
2 ADJECTIVE If something is **terrible**, it causes great pain or sadness. ❑ *Thousands of people suffered terrible injuries.* ● **ter|ri|bly ADVERB** ❑ *These people have suffered terribly during 14 years of war.*

ter|rif|ic /tərɪfɪk/ **ADJECTIVE** If something is **terrific**, it is very good. [INFORMAL] ❑ *What a terrific idea!*

ter|ri|fy /tɛrɪfaɪ/ (**terrifies, terrifying, terrified**) **VERB** If something **terrifies** you, it makes you feel extremely afraid. ❑ *Flying terrifies him.* ● **ter|ri|fied ADJECTIVE** ❑ *Jacob is terrified of spiders.*

ter|ri|fy|ing /tɛrɪfaɪɪŋ/ **ADJECTIVE** If something is **terrifying**, it makes you very afraid. ❑ *That was a terrifying experience.*

ter|ri|tory /tɛrətɔri/ **NONCOUNT NOUN** SOCIAL STUDIES **Territory** is all the land that a particular country owns. ❑ *The central part of the Chimane forest is now Indian territory.*

ter|ror /tɛrər/ **NONCOUNT NOUN** **Terror** is very great fear. ❑ *I shook with terror.*

ter|ror|ism /tɛrərɪzəm/ **NONCOUNT NOUN** **Terrorism** is the use of violence to force a government to do something. ❑ *We need new laws to fight terrorism.*

ter|ror|ist /tɛrərɪst/ (**terrorists**) **NOUN** A **terrorist** is a person who uses violence to achieve their aims. ❑ *...terrorist attacks.* ● **ter|ror|ism NONCOUNT NOUN** ❑ *... global terrorism.*

test /tɛst/ (**tests, testing, tested**)
1 VERB If you **test** something, you use it or touch it to find out what condition it is in, or how well it works. ❑ *Test the temperature of the water with your wrist before you put your baby in the bath.* ❑ *The drug has only been tested on mice.*
2 NOUN **Test** is also a noun. ❑ *The car achieved great results in crash tests.*
3 VERB If you **test** someone, you ask them questions to find out how much they know about something. ❑ *The students were tested on grammar, spelling, and punctuation.*
4 NOUN **Test** is also a noun. ❑ *Only 15 of the 25 students passed the test.*
→ look at **school, science**

test tube (**test tubes**) **NOUN** SCIENCE A **test tube** is a small glass container in the shape of a tube. Test tubes are used in scientific experiments.

text /tɛkst/ (**texts, texting, texted**)
1 NONCOUNT NOUN **Text** is all the words in a book, a document, a newspaper, or a magazine. ❑ *You can insert text, delete text, or move text around.*
2 NOUN A **text** is an academic or scientific book or a short piece of writing. ❑ *The bookshelves were filled with religious texts.*
3 NOUN A **text** is the same as a **text message**. ❑ *The new system can send a text to a cellphone.*
4 VERB If you **text** someone, you send them a text message on a cellphone. ❑ *Mary texted me when she got home.*
→ look at **phone**

text|book /tɛkstbʊk/ (**textbooks**) also **text book NOUN** A **textbook** is a book containing facts about a particular subject that is used by people studying that subject. ❑ *Amy was in the library reading a textbook on international law.*
→ look at **school**

tex|tile /tɛkstaɪl/ (**textiles**) **NOUN** A **textile** is any type of cloth. ❑ *...the textile industry.*

text|ing /tɛkstɪŋ/ **NONCOUNT NOUN** TECHNOLOGY **Texting** is the same as **text messaging**.

text mes|sage (**text messages**) **NOUN** TECHNOLOGY A **text message** is a message

t

that you write and send using a cellphone. ❑ *Lauren sent her boyfriend a text message asking him to meet her at the diner at eight.*

t|ext mes|sag|ing NONCOUNT NOUN
TECHNOLOGY **Text messaging** is sending messages in writing using a cellphone. ❑ *Text messaging started to become widely used in 1998.*

tex|ture /tɛkstʃər/ (**textures**) NOUN ARTS
The **texture** of something is the way that it feels when you touch it. ❑ *The cheese has a soft, creamy texture.*

than /ðən, STRONG ðæn/
1 PREPOSITION You use **than** when you are comparing two people or things. ❑ *Tom is taller than his dad.* ❑ *Children learn faster than adults.* ❑ *They talked on the phone for more than an hour.*
2 CONJUNCTION **Than** is also a conjunction. ❑ *He should have helped her more than he did.*

thank /θæŋk/ (**thanks, thanking, thanked**)
1 You say **thank you** or, in more informal English, **thanks** when you want to show that you are grateful for something that someone has done for you. ❑ *Thank you very much for inviting me to your birthday party.* ❑ *Thanks for the information.* ❑ *"Would you like a cup of coffee?"—"Thank you, I'd love one."* ❑ *"Tea?"— "No thanks."*
2 VERB If you **thank** someone **for** something, you say "thank you" to show that you are grateful to them for it. ❑ *I thanked them for all their kindness to me.*
3 PLURAL NOUN If you express your **thanks** to someone, you say that you are grateful to them for something. ❑ *I would like to express my thanks and praise to the wonderful hospital staff.*
4 If something happens **thanks to** a particular person or thing, it happens because of them. ❑ *Thanks to Sean's courage, his dad survived.*

thank|ful /θæŋkfəl/ ADJECTIVE If you are **thankful**, you are very grateful and glad that something has happened. ❑ *I'm so thankful that they are all safe.*

thank|ful|ly /θæŋkfəli/ ADVERB You use **thankfully** in order to express approval or happiness about something. ❑ *Thankfully, she was not injured.*

Thanks|giving /θæŋksgɪvɪŋ/ NONCOUNT NOUN **Thanksgiving** or **Thanksgiving Day** is a public holiday in the United States on the fourth Thursday in November, and in

Canada on the second Monday in October. At Thanksgiving, families have a special meal together to celebrate all the good things in their lives. ❑ *Dad always managed to be home for Thanksgiving.*

that /ðæt/
1 ADJECTIVE You use **that** to talk about someone or something that is a distance away from you in position or time. ❑ *Look at that guy over there.*
2 PRONOUN **That** is also a pronoun. ❑ *What's that?*
3 PRONOUN You use **that** to talk about something that you have mentioned before. ❑ *They said you wanted to talk to me. Why was that?*
4 PRONOUN You use **that** to show which person or thing you are talking about. ❑ *There's the girl that I told you about.* ❑ *He hates the town that he lives in.*
5 CONJUNCTION You can use **that** to join two parts of a sentence. ❑ *He said that he and his wife were coming to New York.* ❑ *I felt sad that he was leaving.*
6 CONJUNCTION You use **that** after "so" and "such" to talk about the result of something. ❑ *I shouted so that they could hear me.*
7 ADVERB If something is **not that** bad, it is not as bad as it might be. ❑ *Well, actually, it's not that expensive.*
8 You can use **that's that** to say that you have finished with a particular subject. [INFORMAL] ❑ *If that's your final decision, I guess that's that.*

that's /ðæts/ **That's** is short for "that is."

thaw /θɔ/ (**thaws, thawing, thawed**) VERB
When ice or snow **thaws**, it melts. ❑ *We will leave when the snow thaws.* ❑ *How long does it take to thaw a frozen chicken?*

the

> **LANGUAGE HELP**
> Pronounce **the** /ði/ before a vowel (a, e, i, o, or u). Pronounce **the** /ðə/ before a consonant (all the other letters).

1 ARTICLE You use **the** before a noun when it is clear which person or thing you are talking about. ❑ *The office staff here are all British.* ❑ *It's always hard to think about the future.* ❑ *The doctor's on his way.*
2 ARTICLE You use **the** before a singular noun to talk about things of that type in general. ❑ *The computer has developed very fast in recent years.*

T

3 ARTICLE You use **the** with adjectives and plural nouns to talk about all people of a particular type or nationality. ❑ *...the British and the French.*

4 ARTICLE You use **the** in front of dates. ❑ *The meeting should take place on the fifth of May.*

5 ARTICLE You use **the** in front of superlative adjectives and adverbs. ❑ *Daily walks are the best exercise.*

thea|ter /θi̱ətər/ (**theaters**) NOUN ARTS A **theater** is a place where you go to see plays, shows, and movies. ❑ *Last evening, we went to the theater to see a play by Chekhov.* ❑ *A 14-screen movie theater opened in the town last November.* → look at **movie, performance**

theft /θɛ̱ft/ NONCOUNT NOUN Theft is the crime of stealing. ❑ *Martinez was arrested for car theft and assault.*

their /ðɛ̱ər/

1 ADJECTIVE You use **their** to show that something belongs to or relates to the group of people, animals, or things that you are talking about. ❑ *Janis and Kurt have announced their engagement.* ❑ *They took off their coats.*

2 ADJECTIVE You use **their** instead of "his or her" to show that something belongs or relates to a person, without saying if that person is a man or a woman. Some people think this use is incorrect. ❑ *Each student works at their own pace.*

> **Usage**   **their**, **there**, and **they're**
>
> **Their**, **there**, and **they're** sound the same but have very different meanings. **Their** is a possessive pronoun: *Their shoes are on the floor.* **There** can be the subject of *be* and can show location: *There are two seats here and another two over* **there**. **They're** is the contraction of **they are**: *They're studying English in Boston.*

theirs /ðɛ̱ərz/ PRONOUN You use **theirs** to show that something belongs or relates to the group of people, animals, or things that you are talking about. ❑ *The people at the table next to theirs were talking loudly.*

them /ðəm, STRONG ðɛm/

1 PRONOUN You use **them** to talk about more than one person, animal, or thing. ❑ *I've lost my keys. Have you seen them?*

2 PRONOUN You can use **them**, instead of "him or her", to talk about a person without saying whether that person is a man or a woman. ❑ *If anyone calls, tell them I'm out.*

theme /θi̱m/ (**themes**) NOUN The **theme** of a piece of writing or a discussion is its most important idea or its subject. ❑ *Progress was the main theme of his speech.*

them|selves /ðəmsɛ̱lvz/

1 PRONOUN You use **themselves** to talk about people, animals, or things that you have just talked about. ❑ *They all seemed to be enjoying themselves.*

2 PRONOUN If some people did something **themselves**, they did it, and not anyone else. ❑ *My parents designed our house themselves.*

then /ðɛ̱n/

1 ADVERB **Then** means at a particular time in the past or in the future. ❑ *I bought this apartment in 2005. Since then, house prices have fallen.*

2 ADVERB You use **then** to say that one thing happens after another. ❑ *Add the onion and then the garlic.*

3 ADVERB You can use **then** to start the second part of a sentence that begins with "if." ❑ *If you are not sure about this, then you must say so.*

theo|ry /θi̱əri/ (**theories**) NOUN A **theory** is an idea or a set of ideas that tries to explain something. ❑ *The Big Bang Theory explains the beginning of the universe.*

thera|pist /θɛ̱rəpɪst/ (**therapists**) NOUN A **therapist** is a person who helps people who have emotional or physical problems. ❑ *Scott saw a therapist after his marriage ended in 2004.*

thera|py /θɛ̱rəpi/

1 NONCOUNT NOUN **Therapy** is the process of talking to a person with special training about your problems and your relationships so that you can understand them and then change the way you feel and behave. ❑ *He returned to work, but he was still having therapy.*

2 NONCOUNT NOUN **Therapy** or a **therapy** is a treatment for a particular illness or condition. ❑ *Scientists are working on a therapy to slow down the aging process.*

there

> **PRONUNCIATION HELP**
> Pronounce /ðər, STRONG ðɛr/ for meaning **1**, and /ðɛ̱ər/ for meanings **2** to **4**.

1 PRONOUN You use **there** with the verb "be" to say that something exists or is happening. ❑ *There is a swimming pool in the backyard.* ❑ *Are there any cookies left?*

t

2 ADVERB You use **there** to talk about a place that has already been mentioned. ❑ *I'm going back to California. My family have lived there for many years.*

3 ADVERB You use **there** to talk about a place that you are pointing to or looking at. ❑ *"Where is Mr. Hernandez?"—"He's sitting over there."* ❑ *There she is, at the corner of the street.*

4 ADVERB You use **there** when you are speaking on the telephone, to ask if someone is available to speak to you. ❑ *Hello, is Tony there, please?*

there|fore /ðɛərfɔr/ ADVERB You use **therefore** when you are talking about the result of an action or a situation. ❑ *Matthew is injured and therefore will not play in Saturday's game.*

there's /ðɛərz/ **There's** is short for "there is."

ther|mom|eter /θərmɒmɪtər/ (**thermometers**) NOUN A **thermometer** is an instrument for measuring how hot or cold something is.

these

> **PRONUNCIATION HELP**
> Pronounce the adjective /ðiz/. Pronounce the pronoun /ðɪz/.

1 ADJECTIVE You use **these** to talk about people or things that are near you, especially when you touch them or point to them. ❑ *These scissors are heavy.*

2 PRONOUN **These** is also a pronoun. ❑ *Do you like these?*

3 ADJECTIVE You use **these** to talk about someone or something that you have already mentioned. ❑ *These people need more support.*

4 ADJECTIVE You use **these** to introduce people or things that you are going to talk about. ❑ *If you're looking for a builder, these phone numbers will be useful.*

they /ðeɪ/

1 PRONOUN You use **they** when you are talking about more than one person, animal, or thing. ❑ *She said goodbye to the children as they left for school.* ❑ *"Where are your toys?"—"They're in the garden."*

2 PRONOUN You can use **they** instead of "he or she" when you are talking about a person without saying whether that person is a man or a woman. ❑ *"Someone phoned. They said they would call back later."*

they'd /ðeɪd/

1 **They'd** is short for "they had." ❑ *They'd both lived on this road all their lives.*

2 **They'd** is short for "they would." ❑ *He agreed that they'd visit her later.*

they'll /ðeɪl/ **They'll** is short for "they will." ❑ *They'll probably be here Monday.*

they're /ðɛər/ **They're** is short for "they are." ❑ *People eat when they're depressed.*

they've /ðeɪv/ **They've** is short for "they have," especially when "have" is an auxiliary verb. ❑ *They've gone out.*

thick /θɪk/ (**thicker, thickest**)

1 ADJECTIVE If something is **thick**, it has a large distance between one side and the other. ❑ *I cut myself a thick slice of bread.*

2 ADJECTIVE You can use **thick** to say or ask how wide or deep something is. ❑ *The book is two inches thick.* ❑ *How thick are these walls?*

● **thick|ness** NONCOUNT NOUN ❑ *The cooking time depends on the thickness of the steaks.*

3 ADJECTIVE **Thick** hair consists of a lot of hairs growing closely together. ❑ *Jessica has thick dark curly hair.*

4 ADJECTIVE **Thick** smoke or cloud is difficult to see through. ❑ *The crash happened in thick fog.*

5 ADJECTIVE If a liquid is **thick**, it does not flow easily. ❑ *Cook the sauce until it is thick and creamy.*

Word Partners	Use **thick** with:
N.	thick **glass**, thick **ice**, thick **layer**, thick **lips**, thick **neck**, thick **slice**, thick **wall** **1**
	thick **beard**, thick **fur**, thick **hair** **3**
	thick **air**, thick **clouds**, thick **fog**, thick **smoke** **4**
ADV.	so thick, too thick, very thick **1** – **5**

thief /θif/ (**thieves** /θivz/) NOUN A **thief** is a person who steals something from another person. ❑ *The thieves took his camera.*

thigh /θaɪ/ (**thighs**) NOUN SCIENCE Your **thighs** are the top parts of your legs. ❑ *She's broken her thigh bone.*
→ look at **body**

thin /θɪn/ (**thinner, thinnest**)

1 ADJECTIVE If something is **thin**, there is a small distance between one side and the other. ❑ *His arms and legs were very thin.* ❑ *The book is printed on very thin paper.*

2 ADJECTIVE If a person or an animal is **thin**,

they have no extra fat on their body. ❑ *Bob was a tall, thin man.*

3 **ADJECTIVE** If a liquid is **thin**, it flows easily. ❑ *The soup was thin and tasteless.*

Word Partners	Use **thin** with:
N.	thin **ice**, thin **layer**, thin **line 1** thin **body**, thin **face**, thin **fingers**, thin **legs**, thin **man**, thin **woman 2**
ADJ.	**long and** thin **1** **tall and** thin **2**
ADV.	**extremely** thin, **too** thin, **very** thin **1** – **3**

thing /θɪŋ/ (**things**)

1 **NOUN** A **thing** is an object. ❑ *What's that thing in the middle of the road?*

2 **PLURAL NOUN** Your **things** are your possessions. ❑ *She told him to take all his things and not to return.*

3 **NOUN** A **thing** is something that happens or something that you think or talk about. ❑ *They were driving home when a strange thing happened.* ❑ *We had so many things to talk about.*

4 **PLURAL NOUN** You can use **things** to talk about life in general. ❑ *How are things with you?*

think /θɪŋk/ (**thinks, thinking, thought**)

1 **VERB** If you **think** something, you believe it or have an opinion about it. ❑ *I think that it will snow tomorrow.* ❑ *What do you think of my idea?*

2 **VERB** When you **think**, you use your mind to consider something. ❑ *She closed her eyes for a moment, trying to think.* ❑ *What are you thinking about?*

3 **VERB** If you **think of** something, it comes into your mind. ❑ *I know who he is but I can't think of his name.*

4 **VERB** If you **are thinking of** or **are thinking about** doing something, you are considering doing it. ❑ *I'm thinking of going to college next year.*

▶ **think over** If you **think** something **over**, you consider it carefully before you make a decision about it. ❑ *They've offered her the job but she said she needs time to think it over.*

→ look at **school**

third /θɜrd/ (**thirds**)

1 **ADJECTIVE, ADVERB** MATH The **third** item in a series is the one that you count as number three. ❑ *My office is the third door on the right.*

2 **NOUN** MATH A **third** is one of three equal parts of something (⅓).

→ look at **number**

thirst /θɜrst/ **NONCOUNT NOUN** Thirst is the feeling that you want to drink something.

❑ *Drink water to satisfy your thirst.*

thirsty /θɜrsti/ (**thirstier, thirstiest**)

ADJECTIVE If you are **thirsty**, you want to drink something. ❑ *Drink some water whenever you feel thirsty.*

thir|teen /θɜrtin/ MATH **Thirteen** is the number 13.

thir|ty /θɜrti/ MATH **Thirty** is the number 30.

this

PRONUNCIATION HELP
Pronounce the adjective /ðɪs/. Pronounce the pronoun /ðɪs/.

1 **ADJECTIVE** You use **this** to talk about a person or a thing that is near you, especially when you touch them or point to them. ❑ *I like this room much better than the other one.*

2 **PRONOUN** **This** is also a pronoun. ❑ *"Would you like a different one?"—"No, this is great."*

3 **ADJECTIVE** You use **this** to talk about someone or something that you have already mentioned. ❑ *How can we solve this problem?*

4 **PRONOUN** You use **this** to introduce someone or something that you are going to talk about. ❑ *This is what I will do. I will telephone Anna and explain.*

5 **ADJECTIVE** You use **this** to talk about the next day, month, or season. ❑ *We have tickets for this Sunday's performance.* ❑ *We're getting married this June.*

6 **PRONOUN** You use **this is** to say who you are when you are speaking on the telephone. ❑ *Hello, this is John Thompson.*

thorn /θɔrn/ (**thorns**)

NOUN Thorns are the sharp points on some plants and trees. ❑ *He removed a thorn from his foot.*

thor|ough /θɜroʊ/

ADJECTIVE If an action or an activity is **thorough**, it is done completely, and with great attention to detail. ❑ *There will be a thorough investigation into the cause of the crash.* ● **thor|ough|ly** **ADVERB** ❑ *The food must be thoroughly cooked.*

those

PRONUNCIATION HELP
Pronounce the adjective /ðoʊz/.
Pronounce the pronoun /ðoʊz/.

1 ADJECTIVE You use **those** when you are talking about people or things that are a distance away from you in position or time, especially when you point to them. ❏ *What are those buildings?*

2 PRONOUN Those is also a pronoun. ❏ *Those are nice shoes.*

3 ADJECTIVE You use **those** to talk about people or things that have already been mentioned. ❏ *I don't know any of those people you mentioned.*

though /ðoʊ/

1 CONJUNCTION Though means although, or despite the fact that. ❏ *I love him though I do not know him.* ❏ *Ashley plays in adult tennis games even though she is only 15.*

2 CONJUNCTION Though means but. ❏ *I think I left home at about seven thirty, though I could be wrong.*

thought /θɔt/ (thoughts)

1 Thought is a form of the verb **think**.

2 NOUN A **thought** is an idea or an opinion. ❏ *The thought of Nick made her sad.* ❏ *I just had a thought. Why don't you have a party?* ❏ *What are your thoughts about the political situation?*

3 NONCOUNT NOUN Thought is the activity of thinking, especially deeply and carefully. ❏ *Alice was deep in thought.*

thought|ful /θɔtfəl/

1 ADJECTIVE If you are **thoughtful**, you are quiet and serious because you are thinking about something. ❏ *Nancy paused, looking thoughtful.* ● **thought|ful|ly ADVERB** ❏ *Daniel nodded thoughtfully.*

2 ADJECTIVE If you are **thoughtful**, you think and care about other people's feelings. ❏ *Ben is a thoughtful and caring boy.*

thought|less /θɔtlɪs/ **ADJECTIVE** If you are **thoughtless**, you do not care or think about other people's feelings. ❏ *It was thoughtless of me to forget your birthday.*

thou|sand /θaʊzənd/ (thousands)

> **LANGUAGE HELP**
> The plural form is **thousand** after a number.

1 MATH A **thousand** or **one thousand** is the number 1,000. ❏ *Over five thousand people attended the conference.*

2 Thousands of things or people means a very large number of them. ❏ *I have been there thousands of times.*

thread /θrɛd/ (threads, threading, threaded)

1 NOUN Thread or a **thread** is a long, very thin piece of cotton, nylon, or silk, that you use for sewing. ❏ *... a needle and thread.*

2 VERB If you **thread** a needle, you put a piece of thread through the hole in the top of the needle so that you can sew with it. ❏ *I threaded a needle and sewed the button on the shirt.*

threat /θrɛt/ (threats)

1 NOUN If you **make a threat against** someone, you say that something bad will happen to them if they do not do what you want. ❏ *The two boys made death threats against a teacher.*

2 NOUN A **threat** is something that can harm someone or something ❏ *Stress is a threat to people's health.*

threat|en /θrɛtən/ (threatens, threatening, threatened)

1 VERB If you **threaten** someone, you say that you will hurt them if they do not do what you want. ❏ *Army officers threatened to destroy the town.* ❏ *If you threaten me, I will go to the police.* ● **threat|en|ing ADJECTIVE** ❏ *He was arrested for using threatening behavior toward police officers.*

2 VERB If something **threatens** people or things, it is likely to harm them. ❏ *The fire threatened more than 1,000 homes.*

three /θri/ **MATH Three** is the number 3. ❏ *We waited three months before going back.* → look at **number**

three-dimensional /θri dɪmɛnʃənᵊl/

1 ADJECTIVE ARTS A **three-dimensional** object is solid rather than flat. The short form **3D** is also used. ❏ *We made a three-dimensional model.*

2 ADJECTIVE ARTS A **three-dimensional** picture looks deep or solid rather than flat. ❏ *The software generates three-dimensional images.*

threw /θru/ **Threw** is a form of the verb **throw**.

thrill /θrɪl/ (thrills, thrilling, thrilled)

1 NOUN A **thrill** is a sudden feeling of great excitement. ❏ *I can remember the thrill of opening my birthday presents when I was a child.*

2 VERB If something **thrills** you, it gives you a feeling of great excitement. ❏ *The Yankees thrilled the crowd with a 7-5 victory.*

T

thrilled /θrɪld/ **ADJECTIVE** If you are **thrilled**, you are very happy and excited about something. ❑ *I was so thrilled to get a good grade on my math exam.*

thrill|er /θrɪlər/ (thrillers) **NOUN** A **thriller** is an exciting book, movie, or play about a crime. ❑ *The book is a historical thriller.*

thrill|ing /θrɪlɪŋ/ **ADJECTIVE** If something is **thrilling**, it is very exciting and enjoyable. ❑ *It was a thrilling finish to the tournament.*

thrive /θraɪv/ (thrives, thriving, thrived) **VERB** If someone or something **thrives**, they do well and they are successful, healthy, or strong. ❑ *Some plants thrive in the shade.* ❑ *Their national film industry is thriving. It produces thousands of films each year.*

throat /θroʊt/ (throats)
1 **NOUN** SCIENCE Your **throat** is the back of your mouth, where you swallow. ❑ *He spent two days at home with a sore throat.*
2 **NOUN** SCIENCE Your **throat** is the front part of your neck. ❑ *Mr. Williams grabbed him by the throat.*

throb /θrɒb/ (throbs, throbbing, throbbed)
1 **VERB** If something **throbs**, it beats regularly and very strongly, or it makes a regular sound, like your heart. ❑ *His heart throbbed with excitement.* ❑ *The ship's engines throbbed.*
2 **VERB** If part of your body **throbs**, it beats regularly with pain. ❑ *Kevin's head throbbed.*

throne /θroʊn/ (thrones) **NOUN** A **throne** is the special chair where a king or a queen sits on important official occasions.

through /θru/
1 **PREPOSITION** If someone or something goes **through** another thing, they go from one side of it to the other side. ❑ *The bullet went through the front windshield.* ❑ *We walked through the crowd.* ❑ *Alice looked through the window.*
2 **ADVERB** **Through** is also an adverb. ❑ *There was a hole in the wall and water was coming through.*
3 **PREPOSITION** Something that happens **through** a period of time happens from the beginning until the end of that period. ❑ *She kept quiet all through breakfast.*
4 **PREPOSITION** If something happens from a period of time **through** another, it starts at the first period and continues until the end of the second period. ❑ *The office is open Monday through Friday from 9 to 5.*

5 **PREPOSITION** Something that happens **through** something else happens because of it. ❑ *I only succeeded through hard work.*

through|out /θruaʊt/
1 **PREPOSITION** If something happens **throughout** a particular period of time, it happens during all of that period. ❑ *It rained heavily throughout the game.*
2 **PREPOSITION** If something happens or exists **throughout** a place, it happens or exists in all parts of that place. ❑ *Thousands of children throughout Africa suffer from the condition.*
3 **ADVERB** **Throughout** is also an adverb. ❑ *The apartment is painted white throughout.*

throw /θroʊ/ (throws, throwing, threw, thrown)
1 **VERB** If you **throw** an object that you are holding, you move your hand or arm quickly and let go of the object, so that it moves through the air. ❑ *The crowd began throwing stones at the police.*
2 **NOUN** **Throw** is also a noun. ❑ *That was a good throw.*
▶ **throw away** or **throw out** If you **throw away** or **throw out** something that you do not want, you get rid of it. ❑ *I never throw anything away.* ❑ *I've decided to throw out all the clothes I never wear.*
→ look at **pollution**

thrown /θroʊn/ **Thrown** is a form of the verb **throw**.

thud /θʌd/ (thuds) **NOUN** A **thud** is the sound that a heavy object makes when it hits the ground. ❑ *She tripped and fell with a thud.*

thumb /θʌm/ (thumbs) **NOUN** Your **thumb** is the short thick finger on your hand. ❑ *O'Donnell missed the game because of a broken thumb.*
→ look at **hand**

thumb|tack /θʌmtæk/ (thumbtacks) **NOUN** A **thumbtack** is a short pin with a broad, flat top that you use for fastening papers or pictures to a board or a wall.
→ look at **office**

thump /θʌmp/ (thumps, thumping, thumped)
1 **VERB** If you **thump** something, you hit it hard with your hand. ❑ *Ramon thumped the table with his fist.*
2 **VERB** If your heart **thumps**, it beats strongly and quickly because you are afraid

t

or excited. ❏ *Her heart was thumping loudly in her chest.*

thun|der /θˈʌndər/ (**thunders, thundering, thundered**)

1 NONCOUNT NOUN Thunder is the loud noise that you sometimes hear from the sky during a storm. ❏ *Last night there was thunder and lightning.*

2 VERB When **it thunders**, a loud noise comes from the sky during a storm. ❏ *It will probably thunder later.*

thunder|storm /θˈʌndərstɔrm/ (**thunderstorms**) **NOUN** A thunderstorm is a very noisy storm. ❏ *The tree was hit by lightning during a thunderstorm last night.*

Thurs|day /θˈɜrzdeɪ, -di/ (**Thursdays**) **NOUN** Thursday is the day after Wednesday and before Friday. ❏ *On Thursday Barbara invited me to her house for lunch.* ❏ *We go to the supermarket every Thursday morning.*

tick /tɪk/ (**ticks, ticking, ticked**)

1 VERB When a clock **ticks**, it makes a regular series of short sounds as it works. ❏ *An alarm clock ticked loudly on the bedside table.*

2 NOUN Tick is also a noun. ❏ *I could hear the tick of the clock in the hall.* ● **tick|ing NONCOUNT NOUN** ❏ *She could hear the ticking of a clock.*

tick|et /tˈɪkɪt/ (**tickets**) **NOUN** A ticket is a small piece of paper that shows that you have paid to go somewhere or to do something. ❏ *Where are the tickets for tonight's game?* ❏ *He had a first-class plane ticket for London.*

→ look at **movie**

tick|le /tˈɪkəl/ (**tickles, tickling, tickled**) **VERB** If you **tickle** someone, you move your fingers lightly over a part of their body to make them laugh. ❏ *Stephanie was cuddling the baby and tickling her toes*

tide /taɪd/ (**tides**) **NOUN SCIENCE** The tide is the regular change in the level of the ocean on the beach that happens twice a day. ❏ *The tide was going out.*

→ look at **ocean**

tidy /tˈaɪdi/ (**tidier, tidiest, tidies, tidying, tidied**)

1 ADJECTIVE Someone who is **tidy** likes everything to be in its correct place. ❏ *I'm not a very tidy person.*

2 ADJECTIVE Something that is **tidy** is neat, and is arranged in an organized way. ❏ *The room was neat and tidy.*

▶ **tidy up** When you **tidy up** a place, you organize it by putting things in their proper places. ❏ *You relax while I tidy up the house.*

tie /taɪ/ (**ties, tying, tied**)

1 VERB If you **tie** something, you fasten it or fix it, using string or a rope. ❏ *He tied the dog to the fence.* ❏ *She tied the ends of the two ropes together.* ❏ *She tied her scarf over her head.* ❏ *His hands were tied with rope.* ❏ *I bent down to tie my shoelaces.*

2 NOUN Tie up means the same as **tie**. ❏ *The woman tied up her dog outside the drugstore.*

3 NOUN A **tie** or a **necktie** is a long narrow piece of cloth that you tie a knot in and wear around your neck with a shirt. ❏ *Jason took off his jacket and loosened his tie.*

4 NOUN Ties are the connections that you have with people or a place. ❏ *Quebec has close ties to France.*

5 VERB SPORTS If two people or teams **tie** in a game, they have the same number of points at the end of the game. ❏ *The teams tied 2-2.*

6 NOUN Tie is also a noun. ❏ *The first game ended in a tie.*

→ look at **clothing, play**

ti|ger /tˈaɪgər/ (**tigers**) **NOUN** A **tiger** is a large wild animal of the cat family. Tigers are orange with black stripes.

tight /taɪt/ (**tighter, tightest**)

1 ADJECTIVE If clothes are **tight**, they are small, and they fit closely to your body. ❏ *Amanda was wearing a tight black dress.* ● **tight|ly ADVERB** ❏ *Her jacket fastened tightly at the waist.*

2 ADVERB If you hold someone or something **tight**, you hold them very firmly. ❏ *Richard put his arms around her and held her tight.* ❏ *Just hold tight to my hand and don't let go.*

3 ADJECTIVE Tight is also an adjective. ❏ *He kept a tight hold of her arm.* ● **tight|ly ADVERB** ❏ *The children hugged me tightly.*

→ look at **wear**

tight|en /tˈaɪtən/ (**tightens, tightening, tightened**) **VERB** If you **tighten** something, you make it tighter. ❏ *She tightened the belt on her robe.* ❏ *He tightened the last screw.*

tights /taɪts/ **PLURAL NOUN** Tights are a piece of tight clothing that covers the lower body, worn by women, girls, and dancers.

tile /taɪl/ (tiles) **NOUN** Tiles are flat, square objects that are used for covering floors, walls, or roofs.

tilt /tɪlt/ (tilts, tilting, tilted) **VERB** If something **tilts**, it has one end higher than the other. ❏ *The boat tilted as Eric leaned over the side.*
→ look at **earth**

tim|ber /tɪmbər/ **NONCOUNT NOUN** Timber is wood that is used for building and making things. ❏ *There are timber floors throughout the house.*

time /taɪm/ (times, timing, timed)
1 NONCOUNT NOUN Time is something that we measure in minutes, hours, days, and years. ❏ *Time passed, and still Mary did not come back.* ❏ *I've known Mr. Martin for a long time.* ❏ *Listen to me. I haven't got much time.*
2 NOUN You use **time** when you are talking about a particular point in the day, that you describe in hours and minutes. ❏ *"What time is it?"—"Eight o'clock."* ❏ *He asked me the time.*
3 NOUN The **time** is the point in the day when something happens. ❏ *Departure times are 08:15 from Baltimore, and 10:15 from Newark.* ❏ *It's time to go home.*
4 NOUN You use **time** or **times** to talk about a particular period of time in the past. ❏ *At that time there were no antibiotics.*
5 NOUN You use **time** to talk about an experience that you had. ❏ *Sarah and I had a great time at the party.*
6 NOUN You use **time** to talk about how often you do something. ❏ *Try to exercise at least three times a week.*
7 PLURAL NOUN You use **times** after numbers when you are showing how much bigger or smaller one thing is than another. ❏ *The sun is 400 times bigger than the moon.*
8 CONJUNCTION MATH You can use **times** when you are multiplying numbers. Three **times** five is written 3 x 5. ❏ *Four times six is 24.*
9 VERB If you **time** an activity, you measure how long it lasts. ❏ *Practice your speech and time yourself, so that you don't talk for too long.*
10 Something that happens **all the time** happens continually or very often. ❏ *We can't be together all the time.*
11 If things happen **at a time**, they happen together. ❏ *Patients may have two visitors at a time.*
12 Something that happens **at times**, happens sometimes. ❏ *Every job is boring at times.*
13 Something that is true **for the time being**, is true now, but only for a short time. ❏ *The situation is calm for the time being.*
14 If you do something **from time to time**, you do it sometimes but not often. ❏ *Her daughters visited her from time to time.*
15 If you are **in time for** something, you are not late. ❏ *I arrived just in time for my flight to Hawaii.*
16 Something that will happen **in** a week's or a month's **time**, for example, will happen a week or a month from now. ❏ *Presidential elections will be held in ten days' time.*
17 If someone or something is **on time**, they are not late or early. ❏ *The train arrived at the station on time at eleven thirty.*

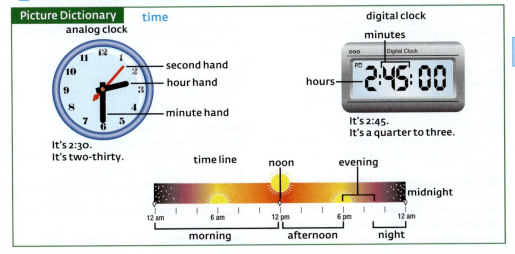

Picture Dictionary **time**

analog clock
second hand
hour hand
minute hand
It's 2:30.
It's two-thirty.

digital clock
minutes
hours
It's 2:45.
It's a quarter to three.

time line
noon
evening
midnight
12 am   6 am   12 pm   6 pm   12 am
morning   afternoon   night

t

18 If you **take** your **time**, you do something slowly. ❑ *"Take your time," Ted told him. "I'm in no hurry."*

→ look at Picture Dictionary: **time**

→ look at **relax**

time|line /taɪmlaɪn/ (**timelines**) also **time line** **NOUN** SOCIAL STUDIES A **timeline** is a picture that shows the order of historical events. ❑ *The timeline shows important events from the Earth's creation to the present day.*

→ look at **history**

time|table /taɪmteɪbᵊl/ (**timetables**) **NOUN** A **timetable** is a list of the times when trains, buses or airplanes arrive and depart. ❑ *Have you checked the bus timetable?*

time zone (**time zones**) **NOUN** GEOGRAPHY A **time zone** is one of the areas that the world is divided into for measuring time. ❑ *We were tired after a long flight across several time zones.*

tim|id /tɪmɪd/ **ADJECTIVE** If you are **timid**, you are shy and nervous, and you lack confidence in yourself. ❑ *I was a timid child.*

● **tim|id|ly** **ADVERB** ❑ *The little boy stepped forward timidly.*

tim|ing /taɪmɪŋ/ **NONCOUNT NOUN** Timing is the skill of judging the right moment to do something. ❑ *"Am I too early?"—"No, your timing is perfect."*

tin /tɪn/ **NONCOUNT NOUN** Tin is a type of soft metal. ❑ *...a tin can.*

tiny /taɪni/ (**tinier, tiniest**) **ADJECTIVE** If something or someone is **tiny**, they are extremely small. ❑ *The living room is tiny.*

tip /tɪp/ (**tips, tipping, tipped**)

1 **NOUN** The **tip** of something long and narrow is the end of it. ❑ *He pressed the tips of his fingers together.*

2 **VERB** If an object **tips**, it moves so that one end is higher than the other. ❑ *The baby carriage can tip backward if you hang bags on the handles.*

3 **VERB** If you **tip** something somewhere, you pour it there. ❑ *I picked up the bowl of cereal and tipped it over his head.*

4 **VERB** If you **tip** someone, you give them some money to thank them for a job they

have done for you. ❑ *At the end of the meal, he tipped the waiter.*

5 **NOUN** Tip is also a noun. ❑ *I gave the barber a tip.*

6 **NOUN** A **tip** is a useful piece of advice. ❑ *The article gives tips on applying for jobs.*

▶ **tip over** If you **tip** something **over**, you make it fall over. ❑ *He tipped the table over.*

tipi /tipi/ (**tipis**) **NOUN** SOCIAL STUDIES A **tipi** is a tall round tent made from animal skins, that some Native Americans traditionally lived in.

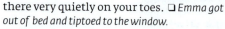

tip|toe /tɪptoʊ/ (**tiptoes, tiptoeing, tiptoed**)

1 **VERB** If you **tiptoe** somewhere, you walk there very quietly on your toes. ❑ *Emma got out of bed and tiptoed to the window.*

2 If you walk or stand **on tiptoe**, you walk or stand on your toes and you do not put your heels on the ground. ❑ *She stood on tiptoe to look over the wall.*

tire /taɪər/ (**tires, tiring, tired**)

1 **NOUN** A **tire** is a thick round piece of rubber that fits around the wheels of cars, buses, and bicycles.

2 **VERB** If something **tires** you, it makes you feel that you want to rest or sleep. ❑ *If driving tires you, take the train instead.*

tired /taɪərd/

1 **ADJECTIVE** If you are **tired**, you feel that you want to rest or sleep. ❑ *Michael is tired after his long flight.*

2 **ADJECTIVE** If you are **tired of** something, you do not want it to continue because you are bored with it. ❑ *I'm tired of waiting for him.*

→ look at **sick**

tir|ing /taɪərɪŋ/ **ADJECTIVE** If something is **tiring**, it makes you feel tired so that you want to rest or sleep. ❑ *It was a long and tiring day.* ❑ *Traveling is tiring.*

tis|sue /tɪʃu/ (**tissues**)

1 **NONCOUNT NOUN** SCIENCE Tissue is one of the substances that humans, animals, and plants are made of. ❑ *...brain tissue.*

2 **NONCOUNT NOUN** Tissue or tissue paper is thin paper that you use for wrapping things that break easily. ❑ *The package was wrapped in pink tissue paper.*

3 **NOUN** A **tissue** is a piece of thin, soft

T

paper that you use to wipe your nose. ❑ *He passed me a box of tissues.*

ti|tle /taɪtᵊl/ (**titles**)

1 NOUN LANGUAGE ARTS The **title** of a book, a play, a movie, or a piece of music is its name. ❑ *What is the title of the poem?*

2 NOUN Someone's **title** is a word such as "Mr." or "Dr." that is used in front of their own name.

Sound Partners   to, too, two

to /tə, tu, STRONG tu/

1 PREPOSITION You use **to** when you are talking about the position or direction of something. ❑ *Two friends and I drove to Florida.* ❑ *She went to the window and looked out.* ❑ *The bathroom is to the right.*

2 PREPOSITION When you give something **to** someone, they receive it. ❑ *He picked up the knife and gave it to me.*

3 PREPOSITION You use **to** when you are talking about how something changes. ❑ *The shouts of the crowd changed to laughter.*

4 PREPOSITION **To** means the last thing in a range. ❑ *I worked there from 1990 to 1996.* ❑ *I can count from 1 to 100 in Spanish.*

5 PREPOSITION You use **to** when you are saying how many minutes there are until the next hour. ❑ *At twenty to six I was waiting at the station.*

6 You use **to** before the infinitive (= the simple form of a verb). ❑ *We just want to help.* ❑ *It was time to leave.*

> **Usage**   to, too, and two
>
> It is easy to confuse the words **too**, **two**, and **to**. They sound the same but their meanings are very different. **Too** means "also" or "more than." *The sweater was **too** big for her.* **Two** is the number 2. *I have **two** brothers.* **To** is a preposition and is part of the infinitive verb form. *I need **to** go **to** the post office **to** mail this letter.*

toad /toʊd/ (**toads**) NOUN A **toad** is a small brown or green animal with long legs, that lives in water.

toast /toʊst/ (**toasts, toasting, toasted**)

1 NONCOUNT NOUN **Toast** is slices of bread that you have heated until they are brown. ❑ *For breakfast, he had toast and jam, and a cup of tea.*

2 VERB If you **toast** bread, you heat it so that it becomes brown. ❑ *Mom made us some delicious toasted sandwiches.*

3 NOUN If you drink a **toast to** someone,

you lift up your glass, wish them happiness, and drink. ❑ *We drank a toast to the bride and groom.*

4 VERB **Toast** is also a verb. ❑ *We all toasted the baby's health.*

→ look at **cook**

> **Word Builder**   **toaster**
>
> *er* ≈ something that does
>
> > clean + **er** = clean**er**
> > contain + **er** = contain**er**
> > dry + **er** = dry**er**
> > open + **er** = open**er**
> > print + **er** = print**er**
> > toast + **er** = toast**er**

toast|er /toʊstər/ (**toasters**) NOUN A **toaster** is a piece of electrical equipment that you use to heat bread.

to|bac|co /təbækoʊ/ NONCOUNT NOUN **Tobacco** is the dried leaves of a plant that people smoke in cigarettes.

to|day /tədeɪ/

1 ADVERB You use **today** when you are talking about the actual day on which you are speaking or writing. ❑ *How are you feeling today?*

2 NONCOUNT NOUN **Today** is also a noun. ❑ *Today is Friday, September 14th.*

3 ADVERB You can use **today** when you are talking about the present period of history. ❑ *More people have cars today.*

→ look at **day**

tod|dler /tɒdlər/ (**toddlers**) NOUN A **toddler** is a young child who has only just learned to walk. ❑ *Toddlers love activities that involve music and singing.*

→ look at **age**

toe /toʊ/ (**toes**) NOUN Your **toes** are the five parts at the end of your foot. ❑ *He is in the hospital with a broken toe.*

→ look at **foot**

toe|nail /toʊneɪl/ (**toenails**) NOUN Your **toenails** are the hard parts that cover the ends of each of your toes.

→ look at **foot**

to|geth|er /təgɛðər/

1 ADVERB If people do something **together**, they do it with each other. ❑ *We went on long walks together.* ❑ *Richard and I went to school together.*

2 ADVERB If things are joined **together**, they touch each other or make a single object, group, or mixture. ❑ *Beat the butter and sugar together.* ❑ *He joined the two pieces of wood together.* ❑ *We added all the numbers together.*

3 **ADVERB** If things or people are situated **together**, they are in the same place and are very near to each other. ❑ *The trees grew close together.* ❑ *Carol and Nick live together in Manhattan.*

4 **ADVERB** If two things happen **together**, they happen at the same time. ❑ *Patrick and Amanda arrived at the party together.*

toi|let /tɔɪlɪt/ (**toilets**) **NOUN** A **toilet** is a large bowl with a seat that you use when you want to get rid of waste from your body. ❑ *She flushed the toilet and went back into the bedroom.*

→ look at **bathroom**

toi|let pa|per or **toilet tissue** **NONCOUNT NOUN** **Toilet paper** is the thin, soft paper that you use to clean yourself after you have gotten rid of waste from your body.

→ look at **bathroom**

toi|let|ries /tɔɪlətriz/ **PLURAL NOUN** **Toiletries** are the things that you use when you are washing or taking care of your body, such as soap and toothpaste.

to|ken /toʊkən/ (**tokens**) **NOUN** A **token** is a round, flat piece of metal or plastic that you use in a machine instead of money. ❑ *The machine uses plastic tokens rather than coins.*

told /toʊld/ **Told** is a form of the verb **tell**.

tol|er|ant /tɒlərənt/ **ADJECTIVE** If you are **tolerant**, you are happy for other people to say, think, and do what they like even though you do not agree with them. ❑ *We all need to be tolerant of different points of view.*

● **tol|er|ance** **NONCOUNT NOUN** ❑ *They promote tolerance of all religions.*

tol|er|ate /tɒləreɪt/ (**tolerates, tolerating, tolerated**) **VERB** If you **tolerate** something or someone, you accept them although you do not like them very much. ❑ *The college will not tolerate such behavior.*

toll-free /toʊl fri/
1 **ADJECTIVE** A **toll-free** telephone number is a number that you can dial without having to pay for the call.
2 **ADVERB** **Toll-free** is also an adverb. ❑ *Call us toll-free 24 hours a day!*

to|ma|to /təmeɪtoʊ/ (**tomatoes**) **NOUN** A **tomato** is a soft, red fruit that you can eat raw in salads or cook like a vegetable.

→ look at **vegetable**

tomb /tum/ (**tombs**) **NOUN** A **tomb** is a stone grave where the body of a dead person is placed. ❑ *In Xian, we visited the emperor's tomb.*

tomb|stone /tumstoʊn/ (**tombstones**) **NOUN** A **tombstone** is a large stone on a person's grave, with words written on it, telling their name and the date that they were born and died.

to|mor|row /təmɔroʊ/
1 **ADVERB** **Tomorrow** is the day after today. ❑ *Bye, see you tomorrow.*
2 **NONCOUNT NOUN** **Tomorrow** is also a noun. ❑ *What's on your schedule for tomorrow?*
3 **ADVERB** You can talk about the future as **tomorrow**. ❑ *What is the world going to be like tomorrow?*
4 **NONCOUNT NOUN** **Tomorrow** is also a noun. ❑ *The children of today are the adults of tomorrow.*

→ look at **day**

ton /tʌn/ (**tons**) **NOUN** MATH A **ton** is a unit of weight. There are 2,000 pounds in a **ton**. ❑ *Hundreds of tons of oil spilled into the ocean.*

tone /toʊn/ (**tones**)
1 **NOUN** The **tone** of a sound is its particular quality. ❑ *Lisa has a deep tone to her voice.*
2 **NOUN** Someone's **tone** is the quality in their voice that shows what they are feeling or thinking. ❑ *I didn't like his tone of voice; he sounded angry.*

tongue /tʌŋ/ (**tongues**) **NOUN** SCIENCE Your **tongue** is the soft part inside your mouth that moves when you speak or eat.

→ look at **face, sense**

to|night /tənaɪt/
1 **ADVERB** **Tonight** is the evening of today. ❑ *I'm at home tonight.* ❑ *Tonight he showed what a great player he is.*
2 **NONCOUNT NOUN** **Tonight** is also a noun. ❑ *Tonight is a very important night for him.*

Sound Partners too, to, two

too /tu/
1 **ADVERB** **Too** means also. ❑ *I like swimming and tennis too.* ❑ *"Can we come too?"* ❑ *"I'm excited about the party."—"Me too."*
2 **ADVERB** You use **too** to mean more than you want or need. ❑ *She talks too much.* ❑ *Sorry, I can't stop. I'm too busy.*

took /tʊk/ **Took** is a form of the verb **take**.

tool /tul/ (**tools**) **NOUN** A **tool** is anything that you hold in your hands and use to do a particular type of work. ❑ *Do you have the right tools for the job?*

tool|bar /tu̲lbar/ (**toolbars**) NOUN A **toolbar** is a narrow strip across a computer screen that contains pictures (= icons) that represent different things that the computer can do.

toot /tu̲t/ (**toots, tooting, tooted**)
1 VERB If a car horn **toots**, or if you **toot** it, it makes a short sound. ❑ *The cars passed by with their horns tooting.* ❑ *The driver behind tooted his horn.*
2 NOUN Toot is also a noun. ❑ *The driver gave me a wave and a toot.*

tooth /tu̲θ/ (**teeth**)
1 NOUN Your **teeth** are the hard white objects in your mouth, that you use for biting and eating. ❑ *Brush your teeth at least twice a day.*
2 PLURAL NOUN The **teeth** of a comb (= an object you use to keep your hair neat) are the parts that stick out in a row on its edge.

tooth|brush /tu̲θbrʌʃ/ (**toothbrushes**) NOUN A **toothbrush** is a small brush that you use for cleaning your teeth.

tooth|paste /tu̲θpeɪst/ NONCOUNT NOUN **Toothpaste** is a thick substance that you put on a toothbrush and use to clean your teeth. ❑ *Don't forget to pack your toothpaste.*

top /tɒp/ (**tops**)
1 NOUN The **top** of something is its highest point. ❑ *We climbed the path up to the top of the hill.*
2 ADJECTIVE The **top** thing is the highest one. ❑ *I can't reach the top shelf.*
3 NOUN The **top** of something is its lid. ❑ *He twisted the top off the bottle and handed it to her.*
4 NOUN A **top** is a piece of clothing that you wear on the upper half of your body. [INFORMAL] ❑ *I was wearing a black skirt and a red top.*
5 If one thing is **on top** of another, it is placed on its highest part. ❑ *There was a clock on top of the television.*

top|ic /tɒpɪk/ (**topics**) NOUN A **topic** is a particular subject that you discuss or write about. ❑ *What is the topic of your essay?*

torch /tɔ̲rtʃ/ (**torches**) NOUN A **torch** is a long stick or object that has a flame at one end. ❑ *Wood carried the Olympic Torch in Sydney in 2002.*

tore /tɔ̲r/ **Tore** is a form of the verb **tear**.

torn /tɔ̲rn/ **Torn** is a form of the verb **tear**.

tor|na|do /tɔrne̲ɪdoʊ/ (**tornadoes** or **tornados**) NOUN SCIENCE A **tornado** is a storm with strong winds that spin around very fast and cause a lot of damage.

tor|til|la /tɔrti̲yə/ (**tortillas**) NOUN A **tortilla** is a piece of thin flat bread. ❑ *...soft flour tortillas filled with warm cheese.*
→ look at **bread**

tor|toise /tɔ̲rtəs/ (**tortoises**) NOUN A **tortoise** is an animal with a shell on its back. **Tortoises** move very slowly.

tor|ture /tɔ̲rtʃər/ (**tortures, torturing, tortured**)
1 VERB If someone **tortures** another person, they deliberately cause that person terrible pain.
2 NONCOUNT NOUN **Torture** is also a noun. ❑ *The use of torture is prohibited by international law.*

toss /tɔ̲s/ (**tosses, tossing, tossed**)
1 VERB If you **toss** something, you throw it. ❑ *Kate tossed the ball to Jessica.*
2 VERB If something **is tossed about** or **around**, it is made to move up and down, or from side to side, quickly and suddenly. ❑ *The huge waves tossed the boat about.*
3 VERB If you decide something by **tossing** a coin, you throw a coin into the air and guess which side of the coin will face upward when it lands. ❑ *We tossed a coin to decide who should go first.*

to|tal /to̲ʊtəl/ (**totals**)
1 NOUN A **total** is the number that you get when you add several numbers together. ❑ *Add all the amounts together, and subtract ten from the total.* ❑ *The three companies have a total of 1,776 employees.*
2 ADJECTIVE **Total** is also an adjective. ❑ *The total cost of the project was $240 million.*
3 ADJECTIVE **Total** means complete. ❑ *When I failed all my exams, I felt like a total failure.*
● **to|tal|ly** ADVERB ❑ *I accept that I am totally to blame.*

to|tali|tar|ian /toʊtælɪte̲əriən/ ADJECTIVE SOCIAL STUDIES A **totalitarian** political system is one in which there is only one political party that controls everything. ❑ *He promised that the country would never return to its totalitarian past.*

touch /tʌ̲tʃ/ (**touches, touching, touched**)
1 VERB If you **touch** something, you put your hand onto it. ❑ *Her little hands gently touched my face.*

t

2 NOUN **Touch** is also a noun. ❑ *She felt the touch of his hand on her arm.*

3 VERB If one thing **touches** another, there is no space between them. ❑ *Their knees were touching.* ❑ *Her feet just touched the floor.*

4 NONCOUNT NOUN Your sense of **touch** is your ability to tell what something is like when you feel it with your hands. ❑ *A baby's sense of touch is fully developed at birth.*

5 If you are **in touch with** someone, you write or speak to them regularly. ❑ *My brother and I keep in touch by phone.*

6 If you **get in touch with** someone, you write to them or telephone them. ❑ *We'll get in touch with you if we have any news of your brother.*

7 If you **lose touch with** someone, you gradually stop writing or speaking to them. ❑ *When he went to college, I lost touch with him.*
→ look at **sense**

touch|down /tʌtʃdaʊn/ (**touchdowns**)
1 NOUN SPORTS A **touchdown** is an act of scoring points in football, by taking the ball over the other team's goal line. ❑ *Taylor scored three touchdowns in the last five minutes of the game.*

2 NONCOUNT NOUN **Touchdown** is when an aircraft lands. ❑ *The pilot reported problems just a few minutes before touchdown.*

tough /tʌf/ (**tougher, toughest**)
1 ADJECTIVE If you are **tough**, you are strong and determined. ❑ *Paul has a reputation as a tough businessman.*

2 ADJECTIVE If a task is **tough**, it is difficult to do. ❑ *We will have to make some tough decisions.*

3 ADJECTIVE If a substance is **tough**, it is strong, and it is difficult to break or cut. ❑ *The bag is made from a tough and waterproof nylon material.* ❑ *The meat was tough and chewy.*
→ look at **job**

Word Partners	Use **tough** with:
N.	tough **guy** **1**
	tough **conditions**, tough **fight**, tough **job**, tough **question**, tough **situation** **2**
V.	**get** tough **1**
	make the tough **decisions** **2**

tour /tʊər/ (**tours, touring, toured**)
1 VERB When musicians or performers **tour**, they go to several different places, where they perform. ❑ *A few years ago the band toured Europe.*

2 NOUN **Tour** is also a noun. ❑ *The band is*

planning a national tour. ❑ *Next year, the orchestra will be going on tour.*

3 NOUN A **tour** is a trip to an interesting place or around several interesting places. ❑ *Michael took me on a tour of the nearby islands.* ❑ *We went on a tour of the new office building.*

4 VERB If you **tour** a place, you go on a trip around it. ❑ *Tour the museum with a guide for $5 per person.*

tour|ism /tʊərɪzəm/ NONCOUNT NOUN **Tourism** is the business of providing hotels, restaurants, trips, and activities for people who are on vacation. ❑ *Tourism is the island's main industry.*

tour|ist /tʊərɪst/ (**tourists**) NOUN A **tourist** is a person who is visiting a place on vacation. ❑ *About 75,000 tourists visit the town each year.*

tour|na|ment /tʊərnəmənt, tɜr-/ (**tournaments**) NOUN SPORTS A **tournament** is a sports competition. Each player who wins a game plays another game, until just one person or team remains. They win the competition. ❑ *Tiger Woods won the tournament in 2000.*

tow /toʊ/ (**tows, towing, towed**) VERB If one vehicle **tows** another vehicle, it pulls it along behind it. ❑ *He uses the truck to tow his trailer.*

to|ward /tɔrd/ also **towards**
1 PREPOSITION If you move **toward** something or someone, you move in their direction. ❑ *They drove toward Lake Ladoga in silence.*

2 PREPOSITION If you have a particular attitude **toward** something or someone, that is the way you feel about them. ❑ *How do you feel toward the man who stole your purse?*

3 PREPOSITION If something happens **toward** a particular time, it happens just before that time. ❑ *We're having another meeting toward the end of the month.*

4 PREPOSITION If you give money **toward** something, you give it to help pay for that thing. ❑ *My husband's parents gave us $50,000 toward our first house.*

tow|el /taʊəl/ (**towels**) NOUN A **towel** is a piece of thick, soft cloth that you use to dry yourself. ❑ *I've put clean towels in the bathroom.*
→ look at **bathroom**

tow|er /taʊər/ (**towers**) NOUN A **tower** is a tall, narrow building, or a tall part of another building. ❑ *He looked up at the clock in the church tower. It was ten o'clock.*

T

town /taʊn/ (**towns**) **NOUN** A **town** is a place with many streets, buildings, and stores, where people live and work. ❑ *Larry comes from a small town near the Canadian border.* ❑ *We met in town at around eight.*

tox|ic /tɒksɪk/ **ADJECTIVE** If a substance is **toxic**, it is poisonous. ❑ *The leaves of the plant are highly toxic.*

toy /tɔɪ/ (**toys**) **NOUN** A **toy** is an object that children play with. ❑ *Sophie went to sleep holding her favorite toy.*

trace /treɪs/ (**traces, tracing, traced**)
1 **VERB** If you **trace** someone or something, you find them after looking for them. ❑ *The police quickly traced the owner of the car.*
2 **VERB** If you **trace** a picture, you make a copy of it by covering it with a piece of transparent paper and drawing over the lines below. ❑ *Linda learned to draw by tracing pictures in books.* → look at **draw**

track /træk/ (**tracks, tracking, tracked**)
1 **NOUN** A **track** is a rough road or path. ❑ *We walked along a track in the forest.*
2 **NOUN** SPORTS A **track** is a piece of ground that is used for races. ❑ *The university's facilities include a 400-meter running track.*
3 **NOUN** Railroad **tracks** are the metal lines that trains travel along.
4 **NOUN** A **track** is one of the songs or pieces of music on a CD. ❑ *I only like two of the tracks on this CD.*
5 **PLURAL NOUN** **Tracks** are the marks that an animal leaves on the ground. ❑ *William found fresh bear tracks in the snow.*
6 **VERB** If you **track** animals or people, you try to find them by following the signs or marks that they leave behind. ❑ *We all got up early to track deer in the woods.*
7 If you **keep track of** someone or something, you have information about them all the time. ❑ *Keep track of what you spend while you're on vacation.*
8 If you **lose track of** someone or something, you no longer know where they are or what is happening. ❑ *I'm sorry I'm late. I lost track of time.*
▶ **track down** If you **track down** someone or something, you find them after a difficult or long search. ❑ *She spent years trying to track down her parents.*

trac|tor /træktər/ (**tractors**) **NOUN** A **tractor** is a vehicle that a farmer uses to pull farm machinery.
→ look at **farm**

trade /treɪd/ (**trades, trading, traded**)
1 **VERB** If people or countries **trade**, they buy and sell goods. ❑ *We have been trading with this company for over thirty years.*
2 **NONCOUNT NOUN** **Trade** is also a noun. ❑ *Texas has a long history of trade with Mexico.*
3 **VERB** If you **trade** one thing **for** another, you give someone that thing and get something else from them in exchange. ❑ *He traded his car for a motorcycle.*

trade|mark /treɪdmɑrk/ (**trademarks**) **NOUN** A **trademark** is a special name or a symbol that a company owns and uses on its products. ❑ *Kodak is a trademark of Eastman Kodak Company.*

tra|di|tion /trədɪʃᵊn/ (**traditions**) **NOUN** A **tradition** is a type of behavior or a belief that has existed for a long time. ❑ *Thanksgiving dinner is an American tradition.* ● **tra|di|tion|al** /trədɪʃᵊnᵊl/ **ADJECTIVE** ❑ *The band plays a lot of traditional Scottish music.* ● **tra|di|tion|al|ly** **ADVERB** ❑ *Christmas is traditionally a time for families.*

traf|fic /træfɪk/
1 **NONCOUNT NOUN** **Traffic** is all the vehicles that are on a particular road at one time. ❑ *There was heavy traffic on the roads.* ❑ *Yesterday, traffic was light on the freeway.*
2 **NONCOUNT NOUN** **Traffic** is the movement of ships, trains, or aircraft between one place and another. ❑ *No commercial air traffic was allowed out of the airport.*
→ look at **car**

Word Partners	Use **traffic** with:
ADJ.	**heavy** traffic, **light** traffic, **stuck in** traffic **1**
N.	traffic **accident**, **city** traffic, traffic **flow**, traffic **pollution**, traffic **problems**, **rush hour** traffic, traffic **safety**, traffic **signals**, traffic **violation** **1** **air** traffic **2**

traf|fic jam (**traffic jams**) **NOUN** A **traffic jam** is a long line of vehicles that cannot move forward, or can only move very slowly.

traf|fic light (**traffic lights**) **NOUN** **Traffic lights** are colored lights that control the flow of traffic.

trag|edy /trædʒɪdi/ (**tragedies**)
1 **NOUN** A **tragedy** is an extremely sad event or situation. ❑ *They have suffered a terrible personal tragedy.*

2 **NOUN** LANGUAGE ARTS **Tragedy** is a type of serious play, that usually ends with the death of the main character. ❑ ...the tragedies of Shakespeare.

trag|ic /trædʒɪk/ **ADJECTIVE** A **tragic** event or situation is extremely sad. ❑ It was a tragic accident. ●**tragi|cal|ly** /trædʒɪkli/ **ADVERB** ❑ He died tragically in a car accident.

trail /treɪl/ (**trails**)
1 **NOUN** A **trail** is a rough path. ❑ He was walking along a trail through the trees.
2 **NOUN** A **trail** is a series of marks that is left by someone or something as they move around. ❑ Everywhere in the house was a sticky trail of orange juice.

trail|er /treɪlər/ (**trailers**)
1 **NOUN** A **trailer** is a long narrow house that can be moved to a place where it becomes a permanent home.
2 **NOUN** A **trailer** is a vacation home that is pulled by a car.
3 **NOUN** A **trailer** is a large container on wheels that is pulled by a truck or another vehicle.

train /treɪn/ (**trains, training, trained**)
1 **NOUN** A **train** is a long vehicle that is pulled by an engine along a railroad. ❑ We caught the early morning train. ❑ He came to New York by train.
2 **VERB** If you **train to** do something, you learn the skills that you need in order to do it. ❑ Stephen is training to be a teacher.
●**train|ing** **NONCOUNT NOUN** ❑ Kennedy had no formal training as an artist.
3 **VERB** SPORTS If you **train for** a sports competition, you prepare for it. ❑ She spent six hours a day training for the race. ●**train|ing** **NONCOUNT NOUN** ❑ He keeps fit through exercise and training.
→ look at **transportation**

trai|tor /treɪtər/ (**traitors**) **NOUN** A **traitor** is someone who harms a group that they belong to by helping its enemies. ❑ There were traitors among us who were sending messages to the enemy.

tram /træm/ (**trams**) **NOUN** A **tram** is a public transportation vehicle that travels along rails in the surface of a street. ❑ You can get to the beach by tram.

trans|con|ti|nen|tal rail|road
/trænskɒntɪnɛntˀl reɪlroʊd/ (**transcontinental railroads**) **NOUN** SOCIAL STUDIES The **transcontinental railroad** is a railroad that crosses from one side of North America to

the other side. ❑ The first transcontinental railroad opened in 1869.

trans|fer (**transfers, transferring, transferred**)

> **PRONUNCIATION HELP**
> Pronounce the verb /trænsfɜr/. Pronounce the noun /trænsfɜr/.

1 **VERB** If you **transfer** something or someone **from** one place **to** another place, you make them go from the first place to the second place. ❑ Transfer the meat to a dish.
2 **NOUN** **Transfer** is also a noun. ❑ Arrange for the transfer of medical records to your new doctor.

trans|form /trænsfɔrm/ (**transforms, transforming, transformed**) **VERB** To **transform** someone or something means to change them completely. ❑ The railroad transformed America. ❑ Your body transforms food into energy.
●**trans|for|ma|tion** /trænsfərmeɪʃˀn/ (**transformations**) **NOUN** ❑ The TV show follows the transformation of a bedroom into an office.

tran|si|tive /trænzɪtɪv/ **ADJECTIVE** A **transitive** verb has a direct object.

trans|late /trænzleɪt/ (**translates, translating, translated**) **VERB** If something that someone says or writes **is translated**, it is said or written again in a different language. ❑ A small number of Kadare's books have been translated into English. ●**trans|la|tor** (**translators**) **NOUN** ❑ She works as a translator.
→ look at **language**

trans|la|tion /trænzleɪʃˀn/ (**translations**) **NOUN** A **translation** is a piece of writing or speech that has been put into a different language. ❑ ...a translation of the Bible.

trans|par|ent /trænspɛərənt, -pær-/ **ADJECTIVE** If an object or a substance is **transparent**, you can see through it. ❑ We used a sheet of transparent plastic.

trans|plant /trænsplænt/ (**transplants**) **NOUN** A **transplant** is a medical operation in which a part of a person's body is replaced because it is damaged or has a disease. ❑ ...a heart transplant.

> **Word Builder** **transport**
>
> *port* ≈ **carry**
>   air + port = airport
>   ex + port = export
>   im + port = import
>   port + able = portable
>   trans + port = transport

T

trans|port /trænsport/ (transports, transporting, transported) **VERB** To **transport** people or goods somewhere is to take them from one place to another place in a vehicle. ❑ *Buses transported passengers to the town.*

trans|por|ta|tion /trænspərteɪʃᵊn/
1 **NONCOUNT NOUN** **Transportation** means any type of vehicle that you can travel in or carry goods in. ❑ *The company will provide transportation.*
2 **NONCOUNT NOUN** **Transportation** is the activity of taking goods or people from one place to another place in a vehicle. ❑ *...transportation costs.*
→ look at Picture Dictionary: **transportation**
→ look at **route**

trap /træp/ (traps, trapping, trapped)
1 **NOUN** A **trap** is a piece of equipment for catching animals. ❑ *Nathan's dog got caught in a trap.*
2 **VERB** To **trap** animals means to catch them using traps. ❑ *They survived by trapping and killing wild animals.*
3 **NOUN** A **trap** is a trick that is intended to catch someone. ❑ *He hesitated, wondering if there was a trap in the question.*
4 **VERB** If someone **traps** you, they trick you so that you do or say something that you do not want to do or say. ❑ *Were you trying to trap her into confessing?*
5 **VERB** If you **are trapped** somewhere, something prevents you from moving. ❑ *The car turned over, trapping both men.*

trash /træʃ/ **NONCOUNT NOUN** **Trash** consists of things that people no longer want.

trash can (trash cans) **NOUN** A **trash can** is a large round container where people put things that they no longer want, or waste from their homes.

trav|el /trævᵊl/ (travels, traveling, traveled)
1 **VERB** If you **travel**, you go from one place to another, often to a place that is far away. ❑ *I've been traveling all day.* ❑ *People often travel hundreds of miles to get here.*
2 **NONCOUNT NOUN** **Travel** is the activity of traveling. ❑ *He hated air travel.*
→ look at **route**

trav|el|er /trævələr/ (travelers) also **traveller** **NOUN** A **traveler** is a person who is on a trip or a person who travels a lot. ❑ *...airline travelers.*

tray /treɪ/ (trays) **NOUN** A **tray** is a flat piece of wood, plastic, or metal that is used for carrying things, especially food and drinks. ❑ *He took her a glass of water on a small silver tray.*

tread /trɛd/ (treads, treading, trod, trodden) **VERB** If you **tread** in a particular way, you walk that way. ❑ *There is no safety railing here, so tread carefully.*

treas|ure /trɛʒər/ **NONCOUNT NOUN** In children's stories, **treasure** is a collection of valuable old objects, such as gold coins and jewelry. ❑ *...buried treasure.*

treat /triːt/ (treats, treating, treated)
1 **VERB** If you **treat** someone or something in a particular way, you behave toward them in that way. ❑ *Stop treating me like a child.*
2 **VERB** When a doctor or a nurse **treats** a patient or an illness, he or she tries to make the patient well again. ❑ *The boy was treated for a minor head wound.*
3 **VERB** If you **treat** someone **to** something special, you buy it or arrange it for them. ❑ *She was always treating him to ice cream.*
4 **NOUN** **Treat** is also a noun. ❑ *Lesley returned from town with a special treat for him.*
→ look at **health care**

t

Picture Dictionary transportation

taxi   airplane   car   bicycle   subway

train   bus   ferry   truck   motorcycle

treat|ment /trítmənt/ (**treatments**)

1 NOUN Treatment is medical attention that is given to a sick or injured person or animal. ❑ *Many patients are not getting the medical treatment they need.*

2 NONCOUNT NOUN Your **treatment** of someone is the way you behave toward them or deal with them. ❑ *We don't want any special treatment.*

→ look at **health care**

trea|ty /tríti/ (**treaties**) **NOUN** SOCIAL STUDIES A **treaty** is a written agreement between countries. ❑ *...a treaty on global warming.*

tree /tri/ (**trees**) **NOUN** A **tree** is a tall plant that lives for a long time. It has a hard central part (= a trunk), branches, and leaves. ❑ *...apple trees.*

→ look at Word World: **tree**

→ look at **plant**

trek /trɛk/ (**treks, trekking, trekked**)

1 VERB If you **trek** somewhere, you go on a journey across difficult country, usually on foot. ❑ *We trekked through the jungle.*

2 NOUN Trek is also a noun. ❑ *We went on a trek through the desert.*

trem|ble /trɛmbəl/ (**trembles, trembling, trembled**)

1 VERB If you **tremble**, you shake slightly. ❑ *Lisa was white and trembling with anger.*

2 VERB If something **trembles**, it shakes slightly. ❑ *He felt the earth tremble under him.*

tre|men|dous /trɪmɛndəs/

1 ADJECTIVE You use **tremendous** to show how strong a feeling or a quality is, or how large an amount is. ❑ *My students have all made tremendous progress recently.*

● **tre|men|dous|ly ADVERB** ❑ *I thought they played tremendously well, didn't you?*

2 ADJECTIVE If someone or something is **tremendous**, they are very good. ❑ *I thought her performance was absolutely tremendous.*

trend /trɛnd/ (**trends**) **NOUN** A **trend** is a change or a development toward something different. ❑ *The restaurant is responding to the trend toward healthier eating.*

trendy /trɛndi/ (**trendier, trendiest**) **ADJECTIVE** If something or someone is **trendy**, they are fashionable and modern. [INFORMAL] ❑ *...a trendy Seattle night club.*

tri|al /traɪəl/ (**trials**)

1 NOUN A **trial** is a formal meeting in a law court, at which a judge decides whether a person is guilty of a crime. ❑ *New evidence showed the witness lied at the trial.* ❑ *He is on trial for murder.*

2 NOUN A **trial** is an experiment in which you test something by using it or doing it for a period of time to see how well it works. ❑ *The drug is being tested in clinical trials.*

tri|an|gle /traɪæŋgəl/ (**triangles**) **NOUN** MATH A **triangle** is a shape with three straight sides. ❑ *On a piece of paper, draw a triangle like the one below.* ● **tri|an|gu|lar** /traɪæŋgyələr/ **ADJECTIVE** ❑ *...a triangular roof.*

tribe /traɪb/ (**tribes**) **NOUN** The word **tribe** is sometimes used for talking about a group of people of the same race, language, and culture, especially in a developing country. Some people disapprove of this use. ❑ *...three hundred members of the Xhosa tribe.* ● **trib|al** /traɪbəl/ **ADJECTIVE** ❑ *...tribal lands.*

trib|ute /trɪbyut/ (**tributes**) **NOUN** A **tribute** is something that you say, do, or make to show that you admire and respect someone. ❑ *The song is a tribute to Roy Orbison.*

trick /trɪk/ (**tricks, tricking, tricked**)

1 VERB If someone **tricks** you, they do something dishonest in order to make you do something. ❑ *Stephen is going to be very upset when he finds out how you tricked him.* ❑ *They tricked him into signing the contract.*

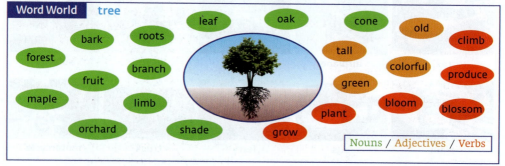

Word World tree

leaf · oak · cone · old · climb · bark · roots · tall · forest · branch · colorful · produce · fruit · green · maple · limb · bloom · blossom · plant · orchard · shade · grow · blossom

Nouns / Adjectives / Verbs

T

2 NOUN Trick is also a noun. ❏ *Andy has a son who loves to play tricks on him.*

3 NOUN A **trick** is a clever or skillful action that someone does in order to entertain people. ❏ *He showed me some card tricks.*

trick|le /trɪkᵊl/ (**trickles, trickling, trickled**)
1 VERB When a liquid **trickles**, a small amount of it flows slowly. ❏ *A tear trickled down the old man's cheek.*
2 NOUN Trickle is also a noun. ❏ *There was not even a trickle of water.*

tricky /trɪki/ (**trickier, trickiest**) **ADJECTIVE** A **tricky** task or problem is difficult to deal with. ❏ *Parking can be tricky downtown.*

tri|cy|cle /traɪsɪkᵊl/ (**tricycles**) **NOUN** A **tricycle** is a bicycle with three wheels.

trig|ger /trɪgər/ (**triggers**) **NOUN** The **trigger** of a gun is the part that you pull to make it shoot. ❏ *A man pointed a gun at them and pulled the trigger.*

trim /trɪm/ (**trims, trimming, trimmed**)
1 VERB If you **trim** something, you cut off small amounts of it in order to make it look neater. ❏ *My friend trims my hair every eight weeks.*
2 NOUN Trim is also a noun. ❏ *His hair needed a trim.*

trio /triːoʊ/ (**trios**) **NOUN** MUSIC A **trio** is a group of three people, especially musicians or singers.

trip /trɪp/ (**trips, tripping, tripped**)
1 NOUN A **trip** is a journey that you make to a particular place. ❏ *She has just returned from a week-long trip to Montana.*
2 VERB If you **trip** when you are walking, you knock your foot against something and fall or nearly fall. ❏ *She tripped and broke her hip.*
→ look at **car, route**

tri|ple /trɪpᵊl/ (**triples, tripling, tripled**)
1 ADJECTIVE Triple means consisting of three things or parts. ❏ *The property includes a triple garage.*
2 VERB Something that **triples** becomes three times as large. ❏ *I got a fantastic new job and my salary tripled.*

tri|plet /trɪplɪt/ (**triplets**) **NOUN** Triplets are three children that are born at the same time to the same mother.

tri|umph /traɪʌmf/ (**triumphs**)
1 NOUN A **triumph** is a great success. ❏ *The championships were a personal triumph for the coach.*

2 NONCOUNT NOUN Triumph is a feeling of great satisfaction after a great success. ❏ *She felt a sense of triumph.*

triv|ial /trɪviəl/ **ADJECTIVE** Something that is **trivial** is not important or serious. ❏ *I was not interested in the trivial details of his daily life.*

trod /trɒd/ Trod is a form of the verb **tread**.

trod|den /trɒdᵊn/ Trodden is a form of the verb **tread**.

trol|ley /trɒli/ (**trolleys**) **NOUN** A **trolley** or a **trolley car** is an electric vehicle for carrying people. A trolley travels on rails in the streets of a city. ❏ *He took a northbound trolley on State Street.*

trom|bone /trɒmboʊn/ (**trombones**) **NOUN** MUSIC A **trombone** is a metal musical instrument that you play by blowing into it and sliding part of it backward and forward. ❏ *Her husband plays the trombone.*

troop /truːp/ (**troops**) **PLURAL NOUN** Troops are soldiers. ❏ *35,000 troops from a dozen countries are already there.*

tro|phy /troʊfi/ (**trophies**) **NOUN** A **trophy** is a prize that is given to the winner of a competition. ❏ *The special trophy for the best rider went to Chris Read.*

tropi|cal /trɒpɪkᵊl/ **ADJECTIVE** GEOGRAPHY **Tropical** means belonging to or typical of the hot, wet areas of the world. ❏ *...tropical diseases.*
→ look at **climate**

trop|ics /trɒpɪks/ **PLURAL NOUN** The tropics are the hottest parts of the world, where it is hot and wet.

trot /trɒt/ (**trots, trotting, trotted**)
1 VERB If you **trot** somewhere, you move at a speed between walking and running. ❏ *I trotted down the steps and out to the garden.*
2 VERB When an animal such as a horse **trots**, it moves fairly fast, taking quick small steps. ❏ *My horse was soon trotting around the field.*

trou|ble /trʌbᵊl/ (**troubles, troubling, troubled**)
1 NONCOUNT NOUN Trouble is problems or difficulties. ❏ *I had trouble parking.* ❏ *You've caused us a lot of trouble.*
2 NONCOUNT NOUN If there is **trouble**, people are arguing or fighting. ❏ *Police were sent to the city to prevent trouble.*

t

3 **VERB** If something **troubles** you, it makes you feel worried. ❑ *Is anything troubling you?*

4 If someone is **in trouble**, they have broken a rule or a law, and they are likely to be punished. ❑ *He was in trouble with his teachers.*

trouble|maker /trʌbəlmeɪkər/ (**troublemakers**) **NOUN** A **troublemaker** is someone who causes trouble. ❑ *She has always been a troublemaker.*

trou|sers /trauzərz/ **PLURAL NOUN** Trousers are a piece of clothing that covers the body from the waist downward, and that covers each leg separately. [FORMAL] ❑ *He was dressed in a shirt, dark trousers and boots.*

truck /trʌk/ (**trucks**)
1 **NOUN** A **truck** is a large vehicle that is used for transporting goods by road. ❑ *The fire started on a truck that was carrying paint.* ❑ *My dad is a truck driver.*
2 **NOUN** A **truck** is a vehicle with a large area with low sides in the back for carrying things. ❑ *There are only two seats in the truck.*
→ look at **transportation**

true /tru/ (**truer, truest**)
1 **ADJECTIVE** If something is **true**, it is based on facts, and is not invented or imagined. ❑ *Everything she said was true.* ❑ *The movie is based on a true story.*
2 If a dream or wish **comes true**, it actually happens. ❑ *When I was 13, my dream came true and I got my first horse.*

tru|ly /truli/
1 **ADVERB** **Truly** means really and completely. ❑ *We want a truly democratic system.* ❑ *Believe me, Susan, I am truly sorry.*
2 You can write **Yours truly** before your name at the end of a letter to someone you do not know very well. ❑ *Yours truly, Phil Turner.*

trum|pet /trʌmpɪt/ (**trumpets**) **NOUN** MUSIC A **trumpet** is a metal musical instrument that you blow. ❑ *I played the trumpet in the school orchestra.*
→ look at **musical instrument**

trunk /trʌŋk/ (**trunks**)
1 **NOUN** The **trunk** of a tree is the large main stem from which the branches grow. ❑ *The tree trunk was more than five feet across.*
2 **NOUN** The **trunk** of a car is a covered space at the back in which you put bags or other things. ❑ *She opened the trunk of the car and took out a bag of groceries.*

3 **NOUN** A **trunk** is a large, strong box that is used for storing things. ❑ *Maloney unlocked his trunk and took out some clothing.*
4 **NOUN** An elephant's **trunk** is its long nose.

trust /trʌst/ (**trusts, trusting, trusted**)
1 **VERB** If you **trust** someone, you believe that they are honest and that they will not deliberately do anything to harm you. ❑ *"I trust you completely," he said.*
2 **NONCOUNT NOUN** Trust is also a noun. ❑ *He destroyed my trust in men.* ❑ *There was a shared feeling of trust amongst the members of the team.*
3 **VERB** If you **trust** someone **to** do something, you believe that they will do it. ❑ *I trust you to keep this secret.*
4 **VERB** If you do not **trust** something, you feel that it is not safe. ❑ *She nodded, not trusting her own voice.*

trust|worthy /trʌstwɜrði/ **ADJECTIVE** A **trustworthy** person is responsible and can be trusted completely. ❑ *He is a trustworthy leader.*

truth /truθ/ **NONCOUNT NOUN** The truth about something is all the facts about it, rather than things that are imagined or invented. ❑ *There is no truth in this story.* ❑ *Are you telling me the truth?*

truth|ful /truθfəl/ **ADJECTIVE** A **truthful** person or answer is honest. ❑ *She was always completely truthful with us.* ❑ *The truthful answer is that I don't know.* ● **truth|ful|ly** **ADVERB** ❑ *I answered all their questions truthfully.*
● **truth|ful|ness** **NONCOUNT NOUN** ❑ *I can say, with absolute truthfulness, that I did my best.*

try /traɪ/ (**tries, trying, tried**)
1 **VERB** If you **try** to do something, you make an effort to do it. ❑ *He tried to help her at work.* ❑ *She doesn't seem to try hard enough.* ❑ *I must try and see him.*
2 **NOUN** Try is also a noun. ❑ *It was a good try.*
3 **VERB** If you **try** something new or different, you use it or do it in order to discover what it is like. ❑ *You could try a little cheese melted on the top.*
4 **NOUN** Try is also a noun. ❑ *All we're asking is that you give it a try.*
5 **VERB** If you **try** a particular place or person, you go to them because you think that they may be able to give you what you need. ❑ *Have you tried the local music stores?*
6 **VERB** When a person **is tried**, he or she appears in a law court where a judge decides

if they are guilty of a crime. ❑ *They were arrested and tried for murder.*

▶ **try on** If you **try on** a piece of clothing, you put it on in order to see if it fits you or if it looks nice. ❑ *Try on the shoes to make sure they fit.*

▶ **try out** If you **try** something **out**, you test it in order to find out how useful or effective it is. ❑ *I want to try the boat out next weekend.*

T-shirt (T-shirts) also **tee-shirt** NOUN A **T-shirt** is a simple shirt with no collar and short sleeves.
→ look at **clothing**

tsu|na|mi /tsʊnɑmi/ (tsunamis) NOUN SCIENCE A **tsunami** is a very large wave that flows onto the land and can cause a lot of damage.

tub /tʌb/ (tubs)
1 NOUN A **tub** is the same as a **bathtub**. ❑ *I went into the bathroom to fill the tub.*
2 NOUN A **tub** is a deep container of any size. ❑ *We ate four tubs of ice cream between us.*

tuba /tubə/ (tubas) NOUN MUSIC A **tuba** is a large round metal musical instrument with one wide end, that produces very low notes when you blow into it.

tube /tub/ (tubes)
1 NOUN A **tube** is a long hollow object that is usually round, like a pipe. ❑ *He is fed by a tube that enters his nose.*
2 NOUN A **tube of** something is a long, thin container that you can press in order to force the substance out. ❑ *...a tube of toothpaste.*
→ look at **container**

tuck /tʌk/ (tucks, tucking, tucked) VERB If you **tuck** something somewhere, you put it there so that it is safe, comfortable, or neat. ❑ *He tucked his shirt inside his pants.*

Tues|day /tuzdeɪ, -di/ (Tuesdays) NOUN **Tuesday** is the day after Monday and before Wednesday. ❑ *He phoned on Tuesday, just before you arrived.* ❑ *Work on the project will start next Tuesday.*

tug /tʌg/ (tugs, tugging, tugged)
1 VERB If you **tug** something, you give it a quick, strong pull. ❑ *A little boy tugged at his sleeve excitedly.*
2 NOUN Tug is also a noun. ❑ *I felt a tug at my sleeve.*

tugboat /tʌgboʊt/ (tugboats) NOUN A **tugboat** is a small powerful boat that pulls large ships. ❑ *The 76,000-ton barge was pulled by five tugboats.*

tu|lip /tulɪp/ (tulips) NOUN **Tulips** are flowers that grow in the spring and are shaped like cups.

tum|ble /tʌmbəl/ (tumbles, tumbling, tumbled)
1 VERB If someone or something **tumbles**, they fall with a rolling movement. ❑ *A small boy tumbled off the step.*
2 NOUN Tumble is also a noun. ❑ *He took a tumble down the stairs.*

tum|my /tʌmi/ (tummies) NOUN Your **tummy** is your stomach. ❑ *Your baby's tummy should feel warm, but not hot.*

tu|mor /tumər/ (tumors) NOUN SCIENCE A **tumor** is an unusual lump that has grown in a person's or an animal's body. ❑ *...a brain tumor.*

tuna /tunə/ (tuna or tunas)

> **LANGUAGE HELP**
> The plural can be either **tuna** or **tunas**.

1 NOUN **Tuna** or **tuna fish** are large fish that live in warm seas.
2 NONCOUNT NOUN **Tuna** or **tuna fish** is this fish when it is eaten as food. ❑ *She opened a can of tuna.*

tune /tun/ (tunes, tuning, tuned)
1 NOUN MUSIC A **tune** is a series of musical notes that is pleasant to listen to. ❑ *She was humming a little tune.*
2 VERB MUSIC When someone **tunes** a musical instrument, they adjust it so that it produces the right notes. ❑ *We tune our guitars before we go on stage.*
3 **Tune up** means the same as **tune**. ❑ *Others were quietly tuning up their instruments.*
4 MUSIC A singer or a musical instrument that is **in tune** produces exactly the right notes. A person or a musical instrument that is **out of tune** does not produce exactly the right notes. ❑ *It was just an ordinary voice, but he sang in tune.*

tun|nel /tʌnəl/ (tunnels) NOUN A **tunnel** is a long passage that has been made under the ground, usually through a hill or under the sea.

tur|key /tɜrki/ (turkeys)
1 NOUN A **turkey** is a large bird that is kept on a farm for its meat.
2 NONCOUNT NOUN **Turkey** is the meat of this bird when it is eaten as food.

turn /tɜrn/ (turns, turning, turned)
1 VERB If someone or something **turns**,

t

they move in a different direction. ❏ *He turned and walked away.* ❏ *Then we turned right, off the highway.*

2 **NOUN** Turn is also a noun. ❏ *You can't do a right-hand turn here.*

3 **VERB** When something **turns**, it moves around in a circle. ❏ *The wheels turned very slowly.* ❏ *Turn the key to the right.*

4 **VERB** If you **turn** a page in a book, you move it so that you can look at the next page. ❏ *He turned the pages of his photo album.*

5 **VERB** If you **turn to** a particular page in a book, you open it and find that page. ❏ *Please turn to page 236.*

6 **VERB** If you **turn to** someone, you ask them for their help. ❏ *She turned to him for support when she lost her job.*

7 **VERB** If something **turns into** something else, it becomes something different. ❏ *The sky turned pale pink.* ❏ *In the story, the prince turns into a frog.*

8 **VERB** When you **turn** a particular age, you reach that age. ❏ *He made a million dollars before he turned thirty.*

9 **NOUN** Your **turn to** do something is the time when you can do it. ❏ *Tonight it's my turn to cook.*

10 If two people **take turns**, they do something one after the other several times. ❏ *It's a long way to Washington, so we took turns driving.*

→ look at **earth, play**

▶ **turn down** **1** If you **turn down** an offer, you refuse it. ❏ *The company offered me a new contract, but I turned it down.*

2 When you **turn down** a piece of equipment, you make it produce less sound or heat. ❏ *Please turn the TV down!* ❏ *I'll turn down the central heating.*

▶ **turn off** When you **turn off** a piece of equipment, you make it stop working. ❏ *The light's a bit bright. Can you turn it off?* ❏ *When the tub was full, she turned off the faucet.*

→ look at **conservation, television**

▶ **turn on** When you **turn on** a piece of equipment, you make it start working. ❏ *I turned on the television.*

→ look at **television**

▶ **turn out** **1** The way that something **turns out** is the way that it happens. ❏ *I didn't know my life was going to turn out like this.*

2 When you **turn out** a light, you switch it off. ❏ *Remember to turn the lights out when you leave the building.*

▶ **turn over** If you **turn** something **over**, you move it so that the top part is on the bottom. ❏ *Liz picked up the envelope and turned it over.* ❏ *The car turned over and landed in a river.*

▶ **turn up** **1** If someone **turns up**, they arrive. ❏ *They finally turned up at nearly midnight.*

2 When you **turn up** a piece of equipment, you make it produce more sound or heat. ❏ *I turned the volume up.*

tur|nip /tɜrnɪp/ (**turnips**) **NOUN** A **turnip** is a round white vegetable that grows under the ground.

turn|out /tɜrnaʊt/ (**turnouts**) **NOUN** The **turnout** at an event is the number of people who go to it. ❏ *It was a great afternoon with a huge turnout of people.*

turn|over /tɜrnoʊvər/ (**turnovers**) **NOUN** The **turnover** of a company is the value of the goods or services that are sold during a particular period of time. ❏ *The company had a turnover of $3.8 million.*

turn sig|nal (**turn signals**) **NOUN** A car's **turn signals** are its lights that flash in order to show that it is going to turn left or right. ❏ *Check the turn signals to make sure they're working.*

tur|quoise /tɜrkwɔɪz/ **ADJECTIVE** Something that is **turquoise** is of a light greenish-blue color. ❏ *...the clear turquoise ocean.*

tur|tle /tɜrtəl/ (**turtles**) **NOUN** A **turtle** is an animal that has a thick shell around its body, and may live on land or in water. ❏ *Seabirds and sea turtles live on the island.*

tusk /tʌsk/ (**tusks**) **NOUN** **Tusks** are two very long, curved, pointed teeth that grow beside the mouth of an elephant (= a very large gray animal that lives in Africa and Asia).

tu|tor /tutər/ (**tutors**) **NOUN** A **tutor** is someone who gives private lessons to one student or to a very small group of students. ❏ *...a math tutor.*

tux|edo /tʌksidoʊ/ (**tuxedos**) **NOUN** A **tuxedo** is a suit or a jacket, usually black, that some men wear for formal social events.

TV /ti vi/ (**TVs**) **NOUN** **TV** means the same as **television**. ❏ *The TV was on.* ❏ *What's on TV?* ❏ *They watch too much TV.*

→ look at **movie**

twee|zers /twiːzərz/ **PLURAL NOUN** Tweezers are a small tool that you use for picking up or removing small objects. Tweezers consist of two thin pieces of metal joined together at one end. ❑ ...*a pair of tweezers.*

twelfth /twɛlfθ/ (**twelfths**)

1 **ADJECTIVE, ADVERB** The **twelfth** item in a series is the one that you count as number twelve. ❑ *They're celebrating the twelfth anniversary of the revolution.*

2 **NOUN** MATH A **twelfth** is one of twelve equal parts of something (¹⁄₁₂). ❑ *She will get a twelfth of her father's money.*
→ look at **number**

twelve /twɛlv/ MATH **Twelve** is the number 12.
→ look at **number**

twen|ty /twɛnti/ MATH **Twenty** is the number 20.

24-7 /twɛntifɔrsɛvᵊn/ also **twenty-four seven**

1 **ADVERB** If something happens **24-7**, it happens all the time. **24-7** means twenty-four hours a day, seven days a week. [INFORMAL] ❑ *I feel like sleeping 24-7.*

2 **ADJECTIVE** **24-7** is also an adjective. ❑ ...*a 24-7 radio station.*

twice /twaɪs/

1 **ADVERB** If something happens **twice**, it happens two times. ❑ *He visited me twice last week.* ❑ *I phoned twice a day.*

2 **ADVERB** If one thing is **twice as** big **as** another, the first thing is double the size of the second. ❑ *Budapest is twice as big as my home town.*

twig /twɪɡ/ (**twigs**) **NOUN** A **twig** is a very small thin branch that grows out from a main branch of a tree or a bush.

twi|light /twaɪlaɪt/ **NONCOUNT NOUN** **Twilight** is the time just before night when the light of the day has almost gone. ❑ *They returned at twilight.*

twin /twɪn/ (**twins**)

1 **NOUN** **Twins** are two people who were born at the same time from the same mother. ❑ *Sarah was looking after the twins.*

2 **ADJECTIVE** **Twin** describes a pair of things that look the same and are close together. ❑ *The boat's twin engines make the trip fast and safe.* ❑ *Carter booked a room with twin beds.*

twin|kle /twɪŋkᵊl/ (**twinkles, twinkling, twinkled**) **VERB** If a star or a light **twinkles**, it shines with a light that continuously becomes brighter and then weaker. ❑ *Lights twinkled across the valley.*

twirl /twɜrl/ (**twirls, twirling, twirled**)

1 **VERB** If you **twirl** something, you turn it around several times very quickly. ❑ *Bonnie twirled her empty glass in her fingers.*

2 **VERB** If you **twirl**, you turn around several times quickly. ❑ *The dancers twirled around the dance floor.*

twist /twɪst/ (**twists, twisting, twisted**)

1 **VERB** If you **twist** something, you turn it to make it into a different shape. ❑ *She sat twisting the handles of the bag, and looking worried.*

2 **VERB** If you **twist** part of your body such as your head or your shoulders, you turn that part while keeping the rest of your body still. ❑ *She twisted her head around to look at him.*

3 **VERB** If you **twist** a part of your body, you injure it by turning it too suddenly, or in an unusual direction. ❑ *He fell and twisted his ankle.*

4 **VERB** If you **twist** something, you turn it so that it turns. ❑ *She was twisting the ring on her finger.*

twitch /twɪtʃ/ (**twitches, twitching, twitched**)

1 **VERB** If a part of your body **twitches**, it makes a little jumping movement. ❑ *Her right eye began to twitch.*

2 **NOUN** **Twitch** is also a noun. ❑ *He had a nervous twitch.*

Sound Partners	two, to, too

two /tuː/ MATH **Two** is the number 2.
→ look at **number**

two-dimensional /tuː dɪmɛnʃənᵊl/ **ADJECTIVE** ARTS A **two-dimensional** object or figure is flat.

type /taɪp/ (**types, typing, typed**)

1 **NOUN** A **type of** something is a particular kind of it. ❑ *I like most types of music.* ❑ *Have you done this type of work before?*

2 **VERB** If you **type** something, you write it using a machine like a computer. ❑ *I can type your essays for you.* ❑ *You should learn to type properly.*

type|writ|er /taɪpraɪtər/ (**typewriters**) **NOUN** A **typewriter** is a machine with keys

t

that you press in order to print writing onto paper.

typi|cal /tɪpɪkᵊl/

1 **ADJECTIVE** A **typical** person or thing is a good example of that type of person or thing. ❑ *Tell me about your typical day.* ❑ *In some ways, Jo is just a typical 12-year old.*

2 **ADJECTIVE** If something is **typical of** someone, it shows their usual qualities or characteristics. ❑ *The bear had thick, creamy white fur, typical of polar bears.*

typi|cal|ly /tɪpɪkli/

1 **ADVERB** You use **typically** to say that something is a good example of a particular type of person or thing. ❑ *The food is typically American.*

2 **ADVERB** You can use **typically** when you mean usually. ❑ *The day typically begins with swimming.*

typ|ist /taɪpɪst/ (**typists**) **NOUN** A **typist** is someone who works in an office typing letters and other documents.

ty|rant /taɪrənt/ (**tyrants**) **NOUN** A **tyrant** is someone who has a lot of power and treats people in a cruel and unfair way. ❑ *His staff all thought he was a tyrant.*

Uu

ugly /ˈʌgli/ (uglier, ugliest) **ADJECTIVE** If someone or something is **ugly**, they are very unpleasant to look at. ❑ *He had an ugly scar across the side of his face.* ❑ *She was wearing an ugly little hat.*

ul|ti|mate /ˈʌltɪmɪt/ **ADJECTIVE** You use **ultimate** when you are talking about the final result of a long series of events. ❑ *Our ultimate goal is to win the gold medal.* ❑ *The ultimate aim is to keep the kids in school.*

ul|ti|mate|ly /ˈʌltɪmɪtli/ **ADVERB** Ultimately means finally, after a long series of events. ❑ *Who, ultimately, is going to pay?*

ultra|vio|let /ˌʌltrəˈvaɪəlɪt/ **ADJECTIVE** Ultraviolet light makes your skin become darker in color. ❑ *Although it is invisible, ultraviolet light is extremely powerful.*

um|brel|la /ʌmˈbrɛlə/ (**umbrellas**) **NOUN** An **umbrella** is a long stick with a cloth or plastic cover that you use to protect yourself from the rain. ❑ *Harry held an umbrella over Denise.*

um|pire /ˈʌmpaɪr/ (**umpires**) **NOUN** SPORTS An **umpire** is a person whose job is to watch a sports game to make sure that the rules are not broken. ❑ *The umpire's decision is final.*

Word Builder	unable
un ≈ **not**	
un + able = unable	
un + fair = unfair	
un + happy = unhappy	
un + healthy = unhealthy	
un + like = unlike	
un + safe = unsafe	

---

un|able /ʌnˈeɪbəl/ **ADJECTIVE** If you are **unable to** do something, you are not able to do it. ❑ *After the car accident, Jacob was unable to walk.* → look at **disability**

Word Partners	Use **unable** with:
V.	unable **to afford**, unable **to agree**, unable **to attend**, unable **to control**, unable **to cope**, unable **to decide**, unable **to explain**, unable **to find**, unable **to hold**, unable **to identify**, unable **to make**, unable **to move**, unable **to pay**, unable **to reach**, unable **to speak**, unable **to walk**, unable **to work**
ADV.	**physically** unable

---

un|ac|cep|table /ˌʌnəkˈsɛptəbəl/ **ADJECTIVE** If something is **unacceptable**, it is bad or wrong and you cannot accept it or allow it. ❑ *This behavior is unacceptable and will be punished.*

unani|mous /yuˈnænɪməs/ **ADJECTIVE** When a group of people are **unanimous**, they all agree about something. ❑ *Their decision was unanimous.* ● **unani|mous|ly ADVERB** ❑ *The board unanimously approved the project last week.*

un|armed /ʌnˈɑrmd/ **ADJECTIVE** An **unarmed** person is not carrying a gun or any weapon. ❑ *The soldiers were unarmed.*

un|at|trac|tive /ˌʌnəˈtræktɪv/ **ADJECTIVE** **Unattractive** people and things are not beautiful or attractive. ❑ *I felt lonely and unattractive.* ❑ *The walls were painted an unattractive orange color.*

un|avail|able /ˌʌnəˈveɪləbəl/
1 ADJECTIVE When people are **unavailable**, you cannot meet them or contact them. ❑ *She was making a film in Canada, and was unavailable for comment.*
2 ADJECTIVE If something is unavailable, you cannot have it or obtain it. ❑ *Figures are unavailable for the period April–June.*

un|avoid|able /ˌʌnəˈvɔɪdəbəl/ **ADJECTIVE** If something is **unavoidable**, you cannot avoid it or stop it from happening. ❑ *Mr. Earnhardt said that the accident was unavoidable.*

un|aware /ˌʌnəˈwɛər/ **ADJECTIVE** If you are **unaware** of something, you do not know about it. ❑ *Many people are unaware that they have the disease.*

u

un|bear|able /ʌnbɛərəbᵊl/ **ADJECTIVE** If something is **unbearable**, it is so unpleasant that you cannot deal with it. ❑ *The pain was unbearable.* ● **un|bear|ably** /ʌnbɛərəbli/ **ADVERB** ❑ *In the afternoon, the sun became unbearably hot.*

un|be|liev|able /ʌnbɪliːvəbᵊl/

1 **ADJECTIVE** If something is **unbelievable**, it is very hard to believe. ❑ *The movie was good, but the story was unbelievable.*

2 **ADJECTIVE** If something is **unbelievable**, it is very good or bad. ❑ *It's a beautiful island, with unbelievable views.* ● **un|be|liev|ably** /ʌnbɪliːvəbli/ **ADVERB** ❑ *Jarrod is an unbelievably brave guy.*

un|born /ʌnbɔrn/ **ADJECTIVE** An **unborn** child has not yet been born. ❑ *This is a disease that can harm an unborn child.*

un|cer|tain /ʌnsɜrtᵊn/ **ADJECTIVE** If you are **uncertain** about something, you are not sure about it. ❑ *If you're uncertain about anything, you must ask.*

un|cle /ʌŋkᵊl/ (uncles) **NOUN** Your **uncle** is the brother of your mother or father, or the husband of your aunt. ❑ *My uncle was the mayor of Memphis.* ❑ *An email from Uncle Fred arrived.*
→ look at **family**

un|clear /ʌnklɪər/

1 **ADJECTIVE** If something is **unclear**, it is not known. ❑ *It is unclear who tried to kill the president.*

2 **ADJECTIVE** If you are **unclear** about something, you do not understand it well or are not sure about it. ❑ *People are unclear about the present situation.*

un|com|fort|able /ʌnkʌmftəbᵊl, -kʌmfərtə-/

1 **ADJECTIVE** If you are **uncomfortable**, you are slightly worried or embarrassed, and not relaxed and confident. ❑ *The request for money made them feel uncomfortable.* ❑ *She was uncomfortable with the situation.*

● **un|com|fort|ably** /ʌnkʌmftəbli, -kʌmfərtə-/ **ADVERB** ❑ *Sam's face was uncomfortably close.*

2 **ADJECTIVE** Something such as a bed or a chair that is **uncomfortable** does not make you feel relaxed when you use it. ❑ *This is an extremely uncomfortable chair.*

un|con|scious /ʌnkɒnʃəs/ **ADJECTIVE** Someone who is **unconscious** is not awake and not aware of what is happening around

them because of illness or a serious injury. ❑ *When the ambulance arrived, he was unconscious.*

● **un|con|scious|ness** **NONCOUNT NOUN** ❑ *Breathing in this toxic gas can cause unconsciousness and death.*

un|con|sti|tu|tion|al /ʌnkɒnstɪtuʃənᵊl/ **ADJECTIVE** SOCIAL STUDIES If something is **unconstitutional**, it does not follow the rules of a constitution (= the laws of a country or organization). ❑ *They believe that these laws are unconstitutional.*

un|con|trol|lable /ʌnkəntroʊləbᵊl/ **ADJECTIVE** If a feeling or a physical action is **uncontrollable**, you cannot stop yourself from feeling it or doing it. ❑ *She felt an almost uncontrollable excitement.* ● **un|con|trol|lably** /ʌnkəntroʊləbli/ **ADVERB** ❑ *I started shaking uncontrollably.*

Word Builder   uncover

un ≈ **reverse**
     un + cover = un**cover**
     un + do = un**do**
     un + dress = un**dress**
     un + fold = un**fold**

---

un|cov|er /ʌnkʌvər/ (uncovers, uncovering, uncovered)

1 **VERB** If you **uncover** something, you take away something that is covering it. ❑ *Uncover the dish and cook the chicken for about 15 minutes.*

2 **VERB** If you **uncover** something secret, you find out about it. ❑ *They want to uncover the truth of what happened that night.*

un|de|cid|ed /ʌndɪsaɪdɪd/ **ADJECTIVE** If you are **undecided** about something, you have not decided about it. ❑ *Mary is still undecided about her future.*

un|der /ʌndər/

1 **PREPOSITION** If a person or a thing is **under** something, they are below it. ❑ *There are hundreds of tunnels under the ground.* ❑ *The two girls were sitting under a tree.* ❑ *There was a big splash and she disappeared under the water.*

2 **PREPOSITION** If something or someone is **under** a particular age or amount, they are less than that age or amount. ❑ *Sarah has three children under ten years of age.*

3 **ADVERB** **Under** is also an adverb. ❑ *Children (14 years and under) get in to the show free if accompanied by an adult.*
→ look at **location**

U

under|go /ˌʌndərˈgoʊ/ (**undergoes, undergoing, underwent, undergone**) **VERB**
If you **undergo** something unpleasant, it happens to you. ❑ *Mia is undergoing treatment for cancer.*

under|gradu|ate /ˌʌndərˈgrædʒuɪt/ (**undergraduates**) **NOUN** An **undergraduate** is a student in their first, second, third, or fourth year at a college. ❑ *More than 55 percent of undergraduates are female.*

under|ground

> **PRONUNCIATION HELP**
> Pronounce the adverb /ˌʌndərˈgraʊnd/.
> Pronounce the adjective /ˈʌndərgraʊnd/.

1 **ADVERB** Something that is **underground** is below the surface of the ground. ❑ *Much of the White House is built underground.*
2 **ADJECTIVE** **Underground** is also an adjective. ❑ *The new library has an underground parking garage for 143 vehicles.*

under|line /ˌʌndərˈlaɪn/ (**underlines, underlining, underlined**) **VERB** If you **underline** a word or a sentence, you draw a line under it. ❑ *She underlined her name.*
→ look at **answer**

under|neath /ˌʌndərˈniθ/
1 **PREPOSITION** If one thing is **underneath** another, it is below or under it. ❑ *The bomb exploded underneath a van.*
2 **ADVERB** **Underneath** is also an adverb. ❑ *He was wearing a blue sweater with a white T-shirt underneath.*
→ look at **location**

under|pants /ˈʌndərpænts/ **PLURAL NOUN** **Underpants** are a short piece of underwear that covers the area between your waist and the top of your legs. ❑ *Richard packed a spare shirt, socks and underpants.*

under|shirt /ˈʌndərʃɜrt/ (**undershirts**) **NOUN** You wear an **undershirt** on the top half of your body next to your skin to keep yourself warm. ❑ *Luis put on a pair of shorts and an undershirt.*

under|stand /ˌʌndərˈstænd/ (**understands, understanding, understood**)
1 **VERB** If you **understand** something, you know what it means, or why or how it happens. ❑ *Toni can speak and understand Russian.* ❑ *"Do you understand what I'm telling you, Sean?"*

2 **VERB** You say that you **understand** something when you know why or how it happens. ❑ *They are too young to understand what is going on.* ❑ *I don't understand why you're so afraid of her.*
3 **VERB** If you **understand** that something is true, you believe it is true because you have been given information about it. ❑ *I understand that you're leaving tomorrow.*
→ look at **communication, science**

under|stand|ing /ˌʌndərˈstændɪŋ/ (**understandings**)
1 **NOUN** If you have an **understanding of** something, you know how it works or know what it means. ❑ *Children need to have an understanding of right and wrong.*
2 **ADJECTIVE** If you are **understanding**, you are kind to other people and you always try to understand their feelings. ❑ *He was very understanding when we told him about our mistake.*

un|der|stood /ˌʌndərˈstʊd/ **Understood** is a form of the verb **understand**.

under|take /ˌʌndərˈteɪk/ (**undertakes, undertaking, undertook, undertaken**) **VERB** When you **undertake** some work, you start doing it. ❑ *The company has undertaken two large projects in Dubai.*

un|der|took /ˌʌndərˈtʊk/ **Undertook** is a form of the verb **undertake**.

under|wa|ter /ˌʌndərˈwɔtər/
1 **ADVERB** Something that exists or happens **underwater** exists or happens below the surface of the ocean, a river, or a lake. ❑ *Submarines are able to travel at high speeds underwater.*
2 **ADJECTIVE** **Underwater** is also an adjective. ❑ *The divers were using underwater cameras.*

under|wear /ˈʌndərwɛər/ **NONCOUNT NOUN** **Underwear** is clothes that you wear next to your skin, under your other clothes. ❑ *I bought some new underwear for the children.*
→ look at **wear**

un|der|went /ˌʌndərˈwɛnt/ **Underwent** is a form of the verb **undergo**.

un|did /ʌnˈdɪd/ **Undid** is a form of the verb **undo**.

u

Word Builder	undo

un ≈ **reverse**

un + cover = uncover
un + do = undo
un + dress = undress
un + fold = unfold

undo /ʌndu/ (**undoes, undoing, undid, undone**) **VERB** If you **undo** something that was tied or fastened, you untie it or make it loose. ❏ *I managed to undo a corner of the package.* ❏ *I undid the buttons of my shirt.*

Word Builder	undress

un ≈ **reverse**

un + cover = uncover
un + do = undo
un + dress = undress
un + fold = unfold

un|dress /ʌndrɛs/ (**undresses, undressing, undressed**) **VERB** When you **undress**, you take off your clothes. ❏ *Emily undressed, got into bed and turned off the light.* ❏ *Often young babies don't like being undressed and bathed.*
● **un|dressed** **ADJECTIVE** ❏ *Fifteen minutes later Brandon was undressed and in bed.*

un|easy /ʌnizi/ **ADJECTIVE** If you are **uneasy**, you are anxious or afraid about something. ❏ *Madison looked uneasy and refused to answer questions.* ● **un|easi|ly** /ʌnizili/ **ADVERB** ❏ *Meg looked at her watch and moved uneasily on her chair.*

un|em|ployed /ʌnɪmplɔɪd/
 1 **ADJECTIVE** If you are **unemployed**, you are able to work but you do not have a job. ❏ *Millions of people are unemployed.* ❏ *This course helps young unemployed people to find work.*
 2 **PLURAL NOUN** The **unemployed** are people who are unemployed. ❏ *We want to create jobs for the unemployed.*

un|em|ploy|ment /ʌnɪmplɔɪmənt/
 1 **NONCOUNT NOUN** **Unemployment** is when people who want to work cannot work, because there are not enough jobs. ❏ *Robert's family live in an area of high unemployment.*
 2 **NONCOUNT NOUN** **Unemployment** is money that is paid by the government to people who do not have a job. ❏ *She gets $413 a week in unemployment.*

un|equal /ʌnikwəl/ **ADJECTIVE** An **unequal** system or situation is unfair because one person or group receives better treatment than another. ❏ *Unequal pay is a serious problem in this industry.*

un|even /ʌnivən/ **ADJECTIVE** An **uneven** surface is not flat or smooth. ❏ *The ground was uneven and he fell off his bike.*

un|ex|pec|ted /ʌnɪkspɛktɪd/ **ADJECTIVE** If something is **unexpected**, it surprises you because you did not think that it was likely to happen. ❏ *Scientists have made an unexpected discovery.* ● **un|ex|pect|ed|ly** **ADVERB** ❏ *April was unexpectedly hot.*

Word Builder	unfair

un ≈ **not**

un + able = unable
un + fair = unfair
un + happy = unhappy
un + healthy = unhealthy
un + like = unlike
un + safe = unsafe

un|fair /ʌnfɛər/ **ADJECTIVE** If something is **unfair**, it does not treat people in an equal way or in the right way. ❏ *It's unfair to expect a child to behave like an adult.* ❏ *They claimed that the test was unfair.* ● **un|fair|ly** **ADVERB** ❏ *She feels they treated her unfairly.* ● **un|fair|ness** **NONCOUNT NOUN** ❏ *I joined the police to tackle unfairness in society.*

un|fa|mil|iar /ʌnfəmɪlyər/ **ADJECTIVE** If something is **unfamiliar to** you, you do not know it, and it is strange to you. ❏ *The woman's voice was unfamiliar to me.*

un|fit /ʌnfɪt/
 1 **ADJECTIVE** If someone or something is **unfit** for a particular purpose, they are not good enough for that purpose. ❏ *The water was unfit for drinking.*
 2 **ADJECTIVE** If you are **unfit**, your body is not healthy or strong. ❏ *Many children are so unfit they cannot do even basic exercises.*

Word Builder	unfold

un ≈ **reverse**

un + cover = uncover
un + do = undo
un + dress = undress
un + fold = unfold

un|fold /ʌnfoʊld/ (**unfolds, unfolding, unfolded**) **VERB** If you **unfold** something that has been folded, you open it out and make it flat. ❏ *Mom unfolded the piece of paper.*

un|for|tu|nate /ʌnfɔrtʃənɪt/
 1 **ADJECTIVE** If someone is **unfortunate**, something unpleasant or unlucky has

U

happened to them. ❏ *We were very unfortunate to lose the game.*

2 **ADJECTIVE** An **unfortunate** event is one that you did not want to happen. ❏ *We made some unfortunate mistakes in the past.*

un|for|tu|nate|ly /ʌnfɔ̱rtʃənɪtli/ **ADVERB**
You say **unfortunately** when you are sorry about something. ❏ *Unfortunately, I don't have time to stay.*

un|friend|ly /ʌnfrɛ̱ndli/ **ADJECTIVE** If someone is **unfriendly**, they behave in an unkind or unpleasant way. ❏ *The people he met there were unfriendly and rude.*

Word Builder   **unhappy**

un ≈ **not**

    un + able = un**able**
    un + fair = un**fair**
    un + happy = un**happy**
    un + healthy = un**healthy**
    un + like = un**like**
    un + safe = un**safe**

---

un|hap|py /ʌnhæ̱pi/ (**unhappier, unhappiest**)

1 **ADJECTIVE** If you are **unhappy**, you are sad. ❏ *Christopher was a shy, unhappy man.*

● **un|hap|pi|ly** **ADVERB** ❏ *Jean shook her head unhappily.* ● **un|hap|pi|ness** **NONCOUNT NOUN** ❏ *There was a lot of unhappiness in my childhood.*

2 **ADJECTIVE** If you are **unhappy about** something, you are not satisfied with it. ❏ *Our coach was unhappy with the way we played on Friday.*

Word Builder   **unhealthy**

un ≈ **not**

    un + able = un**able**
    un + fair = un**fair**
    un + happy = un**happy**
    un + healthy = un**healthy**
    un + like = un**like**
    un + safe = un**safe**

---

un|healthy /ʌnhɛ̱lθi/ (**unhealthier, unhealthiest**)

1 **ADJECTIVE** If you are **unhealthy**, you are sick, or not in good physical condition. ❏ *A pale, unhealthy looking man walked into the store.*

2 **ADJECTIVE** Something that is **unhealthy** can make you ill or harm your health. ❏ *Avoid unhealthy foods such as hamburgers and fries.*

→ look at **eat, health care**

un|help|ful /ʌnhɛ̱lpfəl/ **ADJECTIVE** If someone or something is **unhelpful**, they do not help you or make things better. ❏ *Josh was rude and unhelpful to Della.*

uni|form /yu̱nɪfɔrm/ (**uniforms**) **NOUN** A **uniform** is the special clothes that some people wear to work in, and that some children wear in school. ❏ *The police wear blue uniforms.* ❏ *Daniel was dressed in his school uniform.*

→ look at **wear**

un|im|por|tant /ʌnɪmpɔ̱rtⁿnt/ **ADJECTIVE** Something or someone that is **unimportant** is not important. ❏ *Abigail always remembers unimportant details*

un|ion /yu̱nyən/ (**unions**)

1 **NOUN** A **union** is a workers' organization that tries to improve working conditions. ❏ *Ten new members joined the union.*

2 **NOUN** SOCIAL STUDIES A **union** is a group of states or countries that join together. ❏ *The United Kingdom is a union of nations.*

→ look at **factory**

unique /yuni̱k/ **ADJECTIVE** Something that is **unique** is the only one of its kind. ❏ *Each person's signature is unique.*

unit /yu̱nɪt/ (**units**)

1 **NOUN** A **unit** is a single, complete thing that can belong to something larger. ❏ *The building is divided into twelve units.*

2 **NOUN** MATH A **unit** is a measurement. ❏ *An inch is a unit of measurement.*

unite /yuna̱ɪt/ (**unites, uniting, united**) **VERB** If different people or things **unite**, they join together and act as a group. ❏ *The world must unite to fight this disease.* ❏ *Only the president can unite the people.*

uni|ver|sal /yu̱nɪvɜ̱rsəl/ **ADJECTIVE** Something that is **universal** includes or affects everyone. ❏ *Love is a universal emotion.*

● **uni|ver|sal|ly** /yu̱nɪvɜ̱rsəli/ **ADVERB** ❏ *Reading is universally accepted as being good for kids.*

uni|verse /yu̱nɪvɜrs/ (**universes**) **NOUN** SCIENCE The **universe** is everything, including the Earth, the sun, the moon, the planets, and the stars, that exists in space. ❏ *Can you tell us how the universe began?*

u

uni|ver|sity /yunɪvɜrsɪti/ (**universities**)
NOUN A **university** is a place where you can study after high school. ❑ *Maria goes to Duke University.* ❑ *Robert's mother is a university professor.*

un|just /ʌndʒʌst/ **ADJECTIVE** If something is **unjust**, it is not fair or right. ❑ *He was an unjust ruler, responsible for the deaths of thousands of people.* ● **un|just|ly ADVERB** ❑ *Megan was unjustly accused of stealing money.*

un|kind /ʌnkaɪnd/ (**unkinder, unkindest**)
ADJECTIVE If you are **unkind**, you behave in an unpleasant and unfriendly way. ❑ *Tyler was unkind to his sister all evening.*

un|known /ʌnnoʊn/
1 ADJECTIVE If something is **unknown** to you, you do not know it. ❑ *The child's age is unknown.*
2 ADJECTIVE An **unknown** person is not famous. ❑ *Ten years ago he was an unknown writer but now he is a celebrity.*

un|less /ʌnlɛs/ **CONJUNCTION** **Unless** means "if the thing mentioned does not happen." ❑ *Ryan says he won't go to the party, unless I go too.*

Word Builder unlike

un ≈ **not**

    un + able = unable
    un + fair = unfair
    un + happy = unhappy
    un + healthy = unhealthy
    un + like = unlike
    un + safe = unsafe

---

un|like /ʌnlaɪk/ **PREPOSITION** If one thing is **unlike** another thing, the two things are different. ❑ *You're so unlike your father!*

un|like|ly /ʌnlaɪkli/ (**unlikelier, unlikeliest**)
ADJECTIVE If something is **unlikely**, it will probably not happen. ❑ *The boys are unlikely to arrive before nine o'clock.*

un|load /ʌnloʊd/ (**unloads, unloading, unloaded**)
1 VERB If you **unload** goods from a ship or a vehicle, you remove them from it. ❑ *We unloaded everything from the car.*
2 VERB If you **unload** a ship or a vehicle, you remove things from it. ❑ *The men started unloading the truck.*

un|lock /ʌnlɒk/ (**unlocks, unlocking, unlocked**) **VERB** If you **unlock** something, you open it using a key. ❑ *Taylor unlocked the car and threw the coat on to the back seat.*

un|lucky /ʌnlʌki/ (**unluckier, unluckiest**)
1 ADJECTIVE If someone is **unlucky**, something bad has happened to them, and it is not their fault. ❑ *Michael was very unlucky not to be chosen for the team.*
2 ADJECTIVE If something is **unlucky**, it will bring bad luck. ❑ *Four is an unlucky number in the Far East.*

un|mis|tak|able /ʌnmɪsteɪkəbəl/ also **unmistakeable ADJECTIVE** If something is **unmistakable**, it is so obvious that it is easy to recognize. ❑ *A few minutes later, we heard Sherrie's unmistakable voice.*

un|natu|ral /ʌnnætʃərəl/ **ADJECTIVE** Something that is **unnatural** is different from what you usually expect. ❑ *His eyes were an unnatural shade of blue.*

un|nec|es|sary /ʌnnɛsəsɛri/ **ADJECTIVE** If something is **unnecessary**, it is not needed or does not have to be done. ❑ *It is unnecessary to spend huge amounts of money on Christmas presents.*

un|of|fi|cial /ʌnəfɪʃəl/ **ADJECTIVE** Something that is **unofficial** is not organized or approved by an official person or group. ❑ *Unofficial reports say at least one police officer was killed.*

un|pack /ʌnpæk/ (**unpacks, unpacking, unpacked**) **VERB** When you **unpack** a suitcase or a box, you take things out of it. ❑ *He unpacked his bag.* ❑ *Bill helped his daughter to unpack.*

un|paid /ʌnpeɪd/
1 ADJECTIVE If you do **unpaid** work, you do a job without receiving any money for it. ❑ *Most of the work I do is unpaid.*
2 ADJECTIVE **Unpaid** taxes or bills have not been paid yet.

un|pleas|ant /ʌnplɛzənt/
1 ADJECTIVE If something is **unpleasant**, it gives you a bad feeling because it makes you feel upset or uncomfortable. ❑ *The plant has an unpleasant smell.* ● **un|pleas|ant|ly ADVERB** ❑ *She stayed in the bathtub until the water became unpleasantly cold.*
2 ADJECTIVE An **unpleasant** person is very unfriendly and rude. ❑ *He is such an unpleasant man!*

un|plug /ʌnplʌg/ (**unplugs, unplugging, unplugged**) **VERB** If you **unplug** electrical equipment, you take it from its electrical

U

supply, so that it stops working. ❏ *Whenever there's a storm, I unplug my computer.*

un|popu|lar /ʌnpɒpyələr/ **ADJECTIVE** If something or someone is **unpopular**, most people do not like them. ❏ *It was an unpopular decision.* ❏ *I was very unpopular in high school.*

un|pre|dict|able /ʌnprɪdɪktəbəl/ **ADJECTIVE** If someone or something is **unpredictable**, you never know what they are going to do. ❏ *Karen is completely unpredictable.*

un|pre|pared /ʌnprɪpɛərd/ **ADJECTIVE** If you are **unprepared for** something, you are not ready for it. ❏ *I was totally unprepared for the news.*

un|rea|son|able /ʌnriɪzənəbəl/ **ADJECTIVE** If someone is **unreasonable**, they behave in a way that is not fair or sensible. ❏ *It's unreasonable to expect a child to behave well all the time.*

un|re|li|able /ʌnrɪlaɪəbəl/ **ADJECTIVE** If someone or something is **unreliable**, you cannot trust them. ❏ *My old car is very slow and unreliable.* ❏ *The law protects people from unreliable builders.*

un|ru|ly /ʌnruli/ **ADJECTIVE** If people are **unruly**, they are difficult to control. ❏ *He was arrested for unruly behavior.*

Word Builder **unsafe**

un ≈ **not**

    un + able = unable
    un + fair = unfair
    un + happy = unhappy
    un + healthy = unhealthy
    un + like = unlike
    un + safe = unsafe

---

un|safe /ʌnseɪf/ **ADJECTIVE** If something is **unsafe**, it is dangerous. ❏ *The building is unsafe and beyond repair.* ❏ *The water here is unsafe to drink.*

un|sat|is|fac|tory /ʌnsætɪsfæktəri/ **ADJECTIVE** If something is **unsatisfactory**, it is not good enough. ❏ *I found his answer unsatisfactory.*

un|steady /ʌnstɛdi/ **ADJECTIVE** If you are **unsteady**, you are likely to fall. ❏ *My grandma is unsteady on her feet.*

un|suc|cess|ful /ʌnsəksɛsfəl/ **ADJECTIVE** If you are **unsuccessful**, you do not manage to do what you want to do. ❏ *They tried to save the man's life, but they were unsuccessful.*

un|suit|able /ʌnsutəbəl/ **ADJECTIVE** Someone or something that is **unsuitable** is not right for someone or something. ❏ *This movie is unsuitable for children.*

un|sure /ʌnʃuər/ **ADJECTIVE** If you are **unsure about** something, you are not certain about it. ❏ *Police are unsure exactly when the items were stolen.*

un|sym|pa|thet|ic /ʌnsɪmpəθɛtɪk/ **ADJECTIVE** An **unsympathetic** person is not kind or helpful to someone who is having problems. ❏ *Jane's husband was unsympathetic and she felt she had no one to talk to.*

un|til /ʌntɪl/
1 **PREPOSITION** If something happens **until** a particular time, it happens before that time and stops at that time. ❏ *Until 2004, Julie lived in Canada.*
2 **CONJUNCTION** **Until** is also a conjunction. ❏ *I waited until it got dark.*
3 **PREPOSITION** If something does not happen **until** a particular time, it does not happen before that time and only starts happening at that time. ❏ *I won't arrive in New York until Saturday.*
4 **CONJUNCTION** **Until** is also a conjunction. ❏ *They won't be safe until they get out of the country.*

un|true /ʌntru/ **ADJECTIVE** Something that is **untrue** is not true or correct. ❏ *Bryant said the story was untrue.*

un|usual /ʌnyuʒuəl/ **ADJECTIVE** If something is **unusual**, it does not happen very often or you do not see it or hear it very often. ❏ *It's unusual for our teacher to make a mistake.*
● **un|usu|al|ly** /ʌnyuʒuəli/ **ADVERB** ❏ *It was an unusually cold winter.*

un|want|ed /ʌnwɒntɪd/
1 **ADJECTIVE** If something or someone is **unwanted**, you do not want them. ❏ *Every day I have to delete unwanted emails from my computer.*
2 **ADJECTIVE** If something or someone is **unwanted**, nobody wants them. ❏ *Emily felt unwanted and unloved.*

un|wel|come /ʌnwɛlkəm/ **ADJECTIVE** If someone or something is **unwelcome**, you do not want to see them or have them. ❏ *We were clearly unwelcome guests.*

un|well /ʌnwɛl/ **ADJECTIVE** If you are **unwell**, you are sick. ❏ *Grandpa was feeling unwell and had to stay at home.*

u

un|will|ing /ʌnwɪlɪŋ/ **ADJECTIVE** If you are **unwilling** to do something, you do not want to do it. ❑ *Many people are unwilling to change their email addresses.*

un|wind /ʌnwaɪnd/ (**unwinds, unwinding, unwound**)

1 **VERB** If you **unwind** something that is wrapped around something else, you make it loose and straight. ❑ *She unwound the scarf from her neck.*

2 **VERB** When you **unwind**, you do something relaxing after you have been working hard or worrying about something. ❑ *Dad needs to unwind after a busy day at work.*

un|wise /ʌnwaɪz/ **ADJECTIVE** Something that is **unwise** is not sensible. ❑ *It would be unwise of me to comment.* ● **un|wise|ly** **ADVERB** ❑ *She understands that she acted unwisely.*

un|wrap /ʌnræp/ (**unwraps, unwrapping, unwrapped**) **VERB** When you **unwrap** something, you take off the paper or plastic that is around it. ❑ *I untied the ribbon and unwrapped the small box.*

un|zip /ʌnzɪp/ (**unzips, unzipping, unzipped**)

1 **VERB** TECHNOLOGY If you **unzip** a computer file, you make it go back to its original size after it has been zipped (= reduced using a special program). ❑ *Use the "Unzip" command to unzip the file.*

2 **VERB** If you **unzip** clothing, you undo the metal strip (= a zipper) that is fastening it. ❑ *Pete unzipped his leather jacket and sat down.*

up

PRONUNCIATION HELP
Pronounce the preposition /ʌp/.
Pronounce the adverb and adjective /ʌp/.

1 **PREPOSITION** Up means toward a higher place. ❑ *They were climbing up a mountain road.* ❑ *I ran up the stairs.*

2 **ADVERB** Up is also an adverb. ❑ *Keep your head up.*

3 **ADVERB** If someone stands **up**, they move from sitting or lying down, so that they are standing. ❑ *He stood up and went to the window.*

4 **PREPOSITION** If you go **up** a road, you go along it. ❑ *A dark blue truck came up the road.*

5 **ADVERB** If you go **up** to something or someone, you move to the place where they are. ❑ *He came up to me and gave me a big hug.*

6 **ADVERB** If something goes **up**, it increases. ❑ *Gasoline prices went up in June.*

7 **ADJECTIVE** If you are **up**, you are not in bed. ❑ *They were up very early to get to the airport on time.*

8 **ADJECTIVE** A period of time is **up** when it comes to an end. ❑ *When the half-hour was up, Brian left.*

9 If it is **up to** someone to do something, they must do it. ❑ *It's up to you to solve your own problems.*

10 If you are **up against** something, you have a difficult situation to deal with. ❑ *They were up against a good team, but did very well.*

11 **What's up?** is an informal way of saying "Hello" or "How are you?" ❑ *"Hey, guys, what's up?"*

up|bring|ing /ʌpbrɪŋɪŋ/ **NONCOUNT NOUN** Your **upbringing** is the way that your parents treat you and the things that they teach you when you are growing up. ❑ *I had a strict upbringing.*

up|date (**updates, updating, updated**)

PRONUNCIATION HELP
Pronounce the verb /ʌpdeɪt/. Pronounce the noun /ʌpdeɪt/.

1 **VERB** If you **update** something, you make it more modern or add new information to it. ❑ *We update our news reports regularly.*

2 **NOUN** An **update** is when someone provides the most recent information about a particular situation. ❑ *Now here's a weather update.*

up|grade /ʌpgreɪd, -greɪd/ (**upgrades, upgrading, upgraded**)

1 **VERB** If you **upgrade** something, you improve it or replace it with a better one. ❑ *The road into town is being upgraded.* ❑ *I recently upgraded my computer.*

2 **NOUN** Upgrade is also a noun. ❑ *...a software upgrade.*

up|hill /ʌphɪl/

1 **ADVERB** If something or someone is moving **uphill**, they are going up a slope. ❑ *He ran uphill a long way.*

2 **ADJECTIVE** Uphill is also an adjective. ❑ *It was a long, uphill journey.*

up|load /ʌploʊd/ (**uploads, uploading, uploaded**) **VERB** TECHNOLOGY If you **upload** a document or a program, you move it from your computer to another one, using the Internet. ❑ *Next, upload the files on to your website.*

U

upon /əpɒn/ **PREPOSITION** Upon means on. [FORMAL] ❑ *The decision was based upon science and fact.*

up|per /ʌpər/ **ADJECTIVE** Upper describes something that is in a higher area. ❑ *There is a good restaurant on the upper floor of the building.* ❑ *The soldier was shot in the upper back.*

upper case /ʌpərkeɪs/ **NONCOUNT NOUN** LANGUAGE ARTS Upper case is the form that you use to write or type the larger letters at the beginning of sentences or people's names. Examples of upper case letters are "A," "D," and "M." These are also called "capital letters." Compare with **lower case**. ❑ *Typing an email using upper case letters is like shouting at someone.*

up|right /ʌpraɪt/ **ADJECTIVE** If someone or something is standing **upright**, they are standing up straight. ❑ *John offered Andrew a seat, but he remained upright.*

up|set /ʌpsɛt/ (upsets, upsetting, upset)
1 **ADJECTIVE** If you are **upset**, you are unhappy because something bad has happened. ❑ *After Grandma died, I was very, very upset.* ❑ *Marta looked upset.*
2 **VERB** If something **upsets** you, it makes you feel worried or unhappy. ❑ *What you said in your letter really upset me.*
3 **VERB** If something **upsets** your plans, it makes them go wrong. ❑ *Heavy rain upset our plans for a barbecue on the beach.*
4 **ADJECTIVE** An **upset** stomach is a slight sickness in your stomach. ❑ *Paul was sick last night with an upset stomach.*

up|set|ting /ʌpsɛtɪŋ/ **ADJECTIVE** Something that is **upsetting** makes you feel unhappy or worried. ❑ *The death of a family pet is always upsetting.*

up|side down /ʌpsaɪd daʊn/
1 **ADVERB** If something is **upside down**, the part that is usually at the bottom is at the top. ❑ *The painting was hanging upside down.*
2 **ADJECTIVE** Upside-down is also an adjective. ❑ *Paul drew an upside-down triangle and colored it in.*

up|stairs /ʌpstɛərz/
1 **ADVERB** If you go **upstairs** in a building, you walk up the stairs to a higher floor. ❑ *He went upstairs and changed his clothes.*
2 **ADVERB** If something or someone is **upstairs** in a building, they are on a higher

floor. ❑ *The restaurant is upstairs.*
3 **ADJECTIVE** An **upstairs** room or object is on a floor of a building that is higher than the ground floor. ❑ *Mark lived in the upstairs apartment.*

up-to-date also **up to date**
1 **ADJECTIVE** If something is **up-to-date**, it is the most recent thing of its kind. ❑ *We need some up-to-date weather information.*
2 **ADJECTIVE** If you are **up-to-date** on something, you have the latest information about it. ❑ *We'll keep you up to date with any news.*

up|ward /ʌpwərd/ **ADVERB** If someone moves or looks **upward**, they move or look up toward a higher place. ❑ *She turned her face upward.*

ur|ban /ɜrbən/ **ADJECTIVE** Urban means relating to a city or a town. ❑ *Mission High School is situated in an urban neighborhood of San Francisco.*

urge /ɜrdʒ/ (urges, urging, urged)
1 **VERB** If you **urge** someone **to** do something, you try hard to persuade them to do it. ❑ *Doctors urged my uncle to change his diet.*
2 **NOUN** An **urge** is a strong feeling that you want to do or have something. ❑ *He felt a sudden urge to call Mary.*

ur|gent /ɜrdʒənt/ **ADJECTIVE** If something is **urgent**, it needs attention as soon as possible. ❑ *The refugees have an urgent need for food and water.* ● **ur|gent|ly** **ADVERB** ❑ *These people urgently need medical supplies.*

Word Partners	Use **urgent** with:
N.	urgent **action**, urgent **business**, urgent **matter**, urgent **meeting**, urgent **message**, urgent **mission**, urgent **need**, urgent **problem**

URL /yu ar ɛl/ (URLs) **NOUN** TECHNOLOGY A **URL** is an address that shows where you can find a particular page on the World Wide Web. **URL** is short for "Uniform Resource Locator." ❑ *The URL for Collins Dictionaries is http://www.collinslanguage.com.* → look at **Internet**

Usage	URL

When you read URLs or web addresses out loud you say the : as **colon** and // as **backslash backslash**. For example, http://www. collinslanguage.com sounds like **h-t-t-p colon backslash backslash w-w-w dot collins language dot com.**

u

us /əs, STRONG ʌs/

1 **PRONOUN** You use **us** to talk about yourself and the person or people with you. ❑ *William's girlfriend has invited us for lunch.*

2 **PRONOUN** You use **us** to talk about yourself and another person or other people who are not with you. ❑ *Heather went to the kitchen to get drinks for us.*

USB /yu ɛs bi/ (USBs) **NOUN** TECHNOLOGY A **USB** or **USB port** on a computer is a part where you can attach another piece of equipment. **USB** is short for "Universal Serial Bus." ❑ *The printer plugs into the computer's USB port.*

use (uses, using, used)

> **PRONUNCIATION HELP**
> Pronounce the verb /yuz/. Pronounce the noun /yus/.

1 **VERB** If you **use** something, you do something with it. ❑ *They wouldn't let him use the phone.* ❑ *She used the money to help her family.*

2 **VERB** If you **use** something, you finish it so that none of it is left. ❑ *She used all the shampoo.*

3 **Use up** means the same as **use**. ❑ *If you use up the milk, please buy some more.*

4 **NONCOUNT NOUN** The **use** of something is the action of using it. ❑ *We encourage the use of computers in the classroom.*

5 **NOUN** The **uses** of something are the ways in which you can use it. ❑ *Bamboo has many uses.*

6 **NONCOUNT NOUN** If you have the **use of** something, you are able to use it. ❑ *My sister has the use of Mom's car one night a week.*

7 You say **it's no use** when you stop doing something because you believe that it is impossible to succeed. ❑ *"It's no use asking him what happened," said Kate. "He won't tell us."*

→ look at **disability, energy, phone**

> **used**
> **1** MODAL USES AND PHRASES
> **2** ADJECTIVE USE

1 used /yust/

1 You use **used to** to talk about something that was true in the past but is not true now. ❑ *I used to live in Los Angeles.* ❑ *He used to be one of my teachers.*

2 If you **are used to** something, you are familiar with it because you have done it many times before. ❑ *I'm used to hard work.*

3 If you **get used to** something, you become familiar with it. ❑ *This is how we do things here. You'll soon get used to it.*

2 used /yuzd/ **ADJECTIVE** **Used** objects are not new. ❑ *If you are buying a used car, you will need to check it carefully.*

> **Word Builder** useful
>
> *ful* ≈ **filled with**
>
> care + ful = careful
> color + ful = colorful
> help + ful = helpful
> hope + ful = hopeful
> stress + ful = stressful
> use + ful = useful

use|ful /yusfəl/ **ADJECTIVE** If something is **useful**, it helps you in some way. ❑ *The book is full of useful advice about growing fruit and vegetables.* ● **use|ful|ly** **ADVERB** ❑ *The students used their extra time usefully, doing homework or playing sports.*

→ look at **dictionary**

> **Word Builder** useless
>
> *less* ≈ **without**
>
> care + less = careless
> end + less = endless
> help + less = helpless
> home + less = homeless
> use + less = useless
> wire + less = wireless

use|less /yuslɪs/

1 **ADJECTIVE** If something is **useless**, it has no use. ❑ *My leather jacket is useless in the rain.*

2 **ADJECTIVE** If an action is **useless**, it does not have the result you would like. ❑ *Christina knew it was useless to argue with the police officer.*

user /yuzər/ (users) **NOUN** A **user** is a person who uses something. ❑ *Some young Internet users spend up to 70 hours a week online.* ❑ *I'm a regular user of the subway.*

user-friendly **ADJECTIVE** If a piece of equipment or a system is **user-friendly**, it is well designed and easy to use. ❑ *This is a well designed and user-friendly website.*

user|name /yuzərneɪm/ (usernames) **NOUN** TECHNOLOGY Your **username** is the name that you type onto your screen each time you open a particular computer program or website. ❑ *You have to log in with a username and a password.*

U

usu|al /yuʒuəl/

1 **ADJECTIVE** **Usual** describes what happens most often. ❏ *It is a large city with the usual problems.* ❏ *February was warmer than usual.*

2 If something happens **as usual**, it happens in the way that it normally does. ❏ *Dad's late, as usual.*

usu|al|ly /yuʒuəli/ **ADVERB** If something **usually** happens, it is the thing that most often happens. ❏ *We usually eat in the kitchen.*

uten|sil /yutɛnsᵊl/ (**utensils**) **NOUN** Utensils are tools or objects that you use when you are preparing or eating

food. ❏ *Always wash cooking utensils after handling raw meat.*

uter|us /yutərəs/ (**uteruses**) **NOUN** **SCIENCE** The **uterus** is the part of the female body where babies grow.

ut|ter /ʌtər/ (**utters, uttering, uttered**)

1 **VERB** If you **utter** sounds or words, you say them. [FORMAL] ❏ *He finally uttered the words "I'm sorry."*

2 **ADJECTIVE** **Utter** means complete. ❏ *This is utter nonsense.*

ut|ter|ly /ʌtərli/ **ADVERB** **Utterly** means completely or very. ❏ *Their behavior was utterly stupid.* ❏ *Patrick felt completely and utterly alone.*

u

Vv

v. v. is short for **versus**.

va|can|cy /veɪkənsi/ (**vacancies**)

1 NOUN If there are **vacancies** at a hotel, some of the rooms are empty. ❑ *The hotel still has a few vacancies.*

2 NOUN A **vacancy** is a job that has not been filled. ❑ *We have a vacancy for an assistant.*

va|cant /veɪkənt/ ADJECTIVE If something is **vacant**, it is not being used by anyone. ❑ *They saw two vacant seats in the center.*

va|ca|tion /veɪkeɪʃⁿn/ (**vacations**)

1 NOUN A **vacation** is a period of time when you relax and enjoy yourself, often away from home. ❑ *They planned a vacation in Europe.*

2 NOUN A **vacation** is a period of the year when schools, universities, and colleges are officially closed. ❑ *During his summer vacation he visited Russia.*

→ look at **relax**

vac|ci|nate /væksɪneɪt/ (**vaccinates, vaccinating, vaccinated**) VERB If a person or animal **is vaccinated**, they are given a substance to prevent them from getting a disease. ❑ *Has your child been vaccinated against measles?* ● **vac|ci|na|tion** /væksɪneɪʃⁿn/ (**vaccinations**) NOUN ❑ *I got my flu vaccination last week.*

vac|cine /væksin/ (**vaccines**) NOUN A **vaccine** is a substance containing a harmless form a particular disease. It is given to people to prevent them from getting that disease. ❑ *The flu vaccine is free for those aged 65 years and over.*

vac|uum /vækyum, -yuəm/ (**vacuums, vacuuming, vacuumed**)

1 VERB When you **vacuum** a room or a surface, you clean it using a **vacuum cleaner**.

2 NOUN SCIENCE A **vacuum** is a space that does not contain any air or other gas. ❑ *...a vacuum caused by hot air rising.*

→ look at **chore**

vacuum clean|er (**vacuum cleaners**) NOUN A **vacuum cleaner** or a **vacuum** is an electric machine that cleans surfaces by sucking up dust and dirt.

va|gi|na /vədʒaɪnə/ (**vaginas**) NOUN A woman's or girl's **vagina** is the passage that leads from the outside of the body to the uterus (= the place where babies grow).

vague /veɪg/ (**vaguer, vaguest**) ADJECTIVE If something written or spoken is **vague**, it does not explain things clearly. ❑ *The description was pretty vague.*

vague|ly /veɪgli/ ADVERB **Vaguely** means to a small degree. ❑ *The voice on the phone was vaguely familiar.*

vain /veɪn/ (**vainer, vainest**)

1 ADJECTIVE A **vain** attempt does not achieve what was intended.

2 ADJECTIVE If someone is **vain**, they are too proud of the way they look. ❑ *He was so vain he spent hours in front of the mirror.*

3 If you do something **in vain**, you do not succeed in doing what you want. ❑ *She tried in vain to open the door.*

val|en|tine /væləntaɪn/ (**valentines**) NOUN A **valentine** or a **valentine card** is a card that you send to someone who you are in love with, or who you like very much, on Valentine's Day, February 14. ❑ *I didn't receive any valentine cards this year.*

val|id /vælɪd/ ADJECTIVE If a ticket is **valid**, it can be used and will be accepted. ❑ *All tickets are valid for two months.*

val|ley /væli/ (**valleys**) NOUN GEOGRAPHY A **valley** is a low area of land between hills. ❑ *...a steep mountain valley.*

→ look at **landform, river**

valu|able /vælyuəbⁿl/

1 ADJECTIVE If something is **valuable**, it is very useful. ❑ *Television can be a valuable tool in the classroom.*

2 ADJECTIVE **Valuable** objects are worth a lot of money. ❑ *Do not leave any valuable items in your hotel room.*

V

value /vǽlyu/ (values, valuing, valued)
1 **NONCOUNT NOUN** The **value** of something is its importance or usefulness. ❏ *They didn't recognize the value of language learning.*
2 **VERB** If you **value** something or someone, you think that they are important. ❏ *I value my husband's opinion.*
3 **NOUN** The **value** of something is how much money it is worth. ❏ *The value of the house rose by $50,000 in a year.*
4 **PLURAL NOUN** The **values** of a person or group are their moral principles and beliefs. ❏ *The countries of South Asia share many common values.*

valve /vǽlv/ (valves) **NOUN** A **valve** is an object that controls the flow of air or liquid through the tube.

vam|pire /vǽmpaɪər/ (vampires) **NOUN** In stories, **vampires** are monsters that come out at night and suck the blood of living people.

van /vǽn/ (vans)
NOUN A **van** is a vehicle with space for carrying things in the back.

van|dal /vǽndəl/ (vandals) **NOUN** A **vandal** is someone who deliberately damages property. ❏ *The street lights were broken by vandals.*

van|dal|ism /vǽndəlɪzəm/ **NONCOUNT NOUN** **Vandalism** is the act of deliberately damaging property. ❏ *What can be done to stop school vandalism?*

van|dal|ize /vǽndəlaɪz/ (vandalizes, vandalizing, vandalized) **VERB** If something **is vandalized** by someone, it is damaged on purpose. ❏ *The walls were vandalized with spray paint.*

va|nil|la /vənɪ́lə/ **NONCOUNT NOUN** Vanilla is a flavor used in sweet food.

van|ish /vǽnɪʃ/ (vanishes, vanishing, vanished) **VERB** If someone or something **vanishes**, they go away suddenly or in a way that cannot be explained. ❏ *He vanished ten years ago and was never seen again.*

va|por /véɪpər/ **NONCOUNT NOUN** SCIENCE **Vapor** consists of tiny drops of water or other liquids in the air. ❏ *Water vapor rises from Earth and falls again as rain.*
→ look at **greenhouse effect**

vari|able /vɛ́əriəbəl/ **ADJECTIVE** Something that is **variable** changes quite often. ❏ *The quality of his work is very variable.*

vari|ation /vɛ̀əriéɪʃən/ (variations)
1 **NOUN** A **variation on** something is the same thing presented in a slightly different form. ❏ *This is a delicious variation on an omelet.*
2 **NOUN** A **variation** is a change or difference in a level or amount. ❏ *Can you explain the wide variation in your prices?*

var|ied /vɛ́ərid/ **ADJECTIVE** Something that is **varied** consists of different types of things. ❏ *Your diet should be varied.*

va|ri|ety /vəráɪɪti/ **NONCOUNT NOUN** If something has **variety**, it consists of things that are different from each other. ❏ *Susan wanted variety in her lifestyle.*

vari|ous /vɛ́əriəs/ **ADJECTIVE** If you talk about **various** things, you mean many different things of the type mentioned. ❏ *He spent the day doing various jobs around the house.*

var|nish /vɑ́rnɪʃ/ (varnishes) **NONCOUNT NOUN** Varnish is a thick, clear liquid that is painted onto things to give them a shiny surface.

var|si|ty /vɑ́rsɪti/ (varsities) **NOUN** The **varsity** or the **varsity** team is the main team that plays a particular sport for a school or a university. ❏ *He plays for the varsity basketball team.*

vary /vɛ́əri/ (varies, varying, varied)
1 **VERB** If things **vary**, they are different from each other. ❏ *The bowls are handmade, so they vary slightly.*
2 **VERB** If something **varies** or if you **vary** it, it becomes different or changed. ❏ *Be sure to vary the topics you write about.*

vase /véɪs, vɑ́z/ (vases) **NOUN** A **vase** is a container that is used for holding flowers. ❏ *There was a small vase of flowers on the table.*

vast /vǽst/ (vaster, vastest) **ADJECTIVE** Something that is **vast** is extremely large. ❏ *Australia is a vast continent.* ❏ *Suddenly they have a vast amount of cash.*
→ look at **Internet**

vault /vɔ́lt/ (vaults, vaulting, vaulted)
1 **NOUN** A **vault** is a room where money and other valuable things can be kept safely. ❏ *The jewels were kept in a bank vault.*

v

Picture Dictionary **vegetables**

asparagus

broccoli pepper squash onion

spinach

eggplant cauliflower

carrots

corn on the cob peas potatoes cucumber tomatoes

2 **VERB** If you **vault** something or **vault over** it, you jump quickly over it. ❑ *He could easily vault the wall.*

veg|eta|ble /vɛdʒtəbᵊl, vɛdʒɪ-/ (**vegetables**) **NOUN** Vegetables are plants that you can cook and eat.
→ look at Picture Dictionary: **vegetables**
→ look at **food**

veg|etar|ian /vɛdʒɪtɛəriən/ (**vegetarians**)
1 **ADJECTIVE** Vegetarian food does not contain meat or fish. ❑ *They did not keep a strict vegetarian diet.* ❑ *...a vegetarian dish.*
2 **NOUN** A **vegetarian** is someone who never eats meat or fish. ❑ *When did you decide to become a vegetarian?*

veg|eta|tion /vɛdʒɪteɪʃᵊn/ **NONCOUNT NOUN** Plants, trees, and flowers can be called **vegetation**. [FORMAL] ❑ *...tropical vegetation.*

ve|hi|cle /viːɪkᵊl/ (**vehicles**) **NOUN** A **vehicle** is a machine that carries people or things from one place to another. ❑ *There are too many vehicles on the road.* ❑ *The car hit another vehicle that was parked nearby.*

veil /veɪl/ (**veils**) **NOUN** A **veil** is a piece of thin soft cloth that women sometimes wear over their heads to cover their faces. ❑ *She wore a veil over her face.*

vein /veɪn/ (**veins**) **NOUN** Your **veins** are the thin tubes in your body that your blood flows through. Compare with **artery**.

vel|vet /vɛlvɪt/ (**velvets**) **NONCOUNT NOUN** Velvet is soft cloth that is thick on one side. ❑ *...red velvet drapes.*

vent /vɛnt/ (**vents, venting, vented**)
1 **NOUN** A **vent** is a hole that allows clean air to come in, and smoke or gas to go out. ❑ *Vents in the walls allow fresh air to enter the house.*
2 **VERB** If you **vent** your feelings, you express them strongly. ❑ *She telephoned her best friend to vent her anger.*

ven|ti|late /vɛntᵊleɪt/ (**ventilates, ventilating, ventilated**) **VERB** If you **ventilate** a room, you allow fresh air to get into it. ❑ *You must ventilate the room well when painting.* ● **ven|ti|la|tion** /vɛntᵊleɪʃᵊn/ **NONCOUNT NOUN** ❑ *The only ventilation came from one small window.*

venue /vɛnyu/ (**venues**) **NOUN** The **venue** for an event or an activity is the place where it will happen. ❑ *Fenway Park will be used as a venue for the rock concert.*

verb /vɜrb/ (**verbs**) **NOUN** LANGUAGE ARTS A **verb** is a word such as "sing," "feel," or "eat" that is used for saying what someone or something does.
→ look at **grammar**

ver|bal /vɜrbᵊl/ **ADJECTIVE** You use **verbal** to show that something is expressed in speech. ❑ *We will not tolerate verbal abuse.*
● **ver|bal|ly** **ADVERB** ❑ *We complained both verbally and in writing.*
→ look at **communication**

ver|dict /vɜrdɪkt/ (**verdicts**) **NOUN** The **verdict** is the decision that is given in a court of law. ❑ *The jury delivered a verdict of "not guilty."*

V

verge /vɜrdʒ/ If you are **on the verge of** something, you are going to do it very soon. ❑ *Carole was on the verge of tears (= she was nearly crying).*

veri|fy /vɛrɪfaɪ/ (**verifies, verifying, verified**) **VERB** If you **verify** something, you check that it is true. [FORMAL] ❑ *We haven't yet verified his information.*
→ look at **identification**

ver|sa|tile /vɜrsətəl/ **ADJECTIVE** A **versatile** person has many different skills. ❑ *He was one of our most versatile athletes.*

verse /vɜrs/ (**verses**)
1 **NONCOUNT NOUN** LANGUAGE ARTS **Verse** is poetry. ❑ *The story was written in verse.*
2 **NOUN** LANGUAGE ARTS A **verse** is one of the parts into which a poem or song is divided.

ver|sion /vɜrʒən/ (**versions**)
1 **NOUN** A **version of** something is a particular form of it. ❑ *He is bringing out a new version of his book.*
2 **NOUN** Someone's **version of** an event is their own description of it. ❑ *Her version of the story was different from Jack's.*

ver|sus /vɜrsəs/ **PREPOSITION** SPORTS **Versus** is used for showing that two teams or people are on different sides in a sports event. The short forms **vs.** and **v.** are also used. ❑ *It will be the U.S. versus Belgium in tomorrow's game.*

ver|te|brate /vɜrtɪbrɪt/ (**vertebrates**)
1 **NOUN** SCIENCE A **vertebrate** is an animal that has a spine (= bones in its back). Compare with **invertebrate**.
2 **ADJECTIVE** **Vertebrate** is also an adjective. ❑ *...a vertebrate animal.*

ver|ti|cal /vɜrtɪkəl/ **ADJECTIVE** Something that is **vertical** stands or points straight up. ❑ *The climber moved up a vertical wall of rock.*

very /vɛri/ **ADVERB** **Very** is used before an adjective to make it stronger. ❑ *The answer is very simple.* ❑ *I'm very sorry.*

ves|sel /vɛsəl/ (**vessels**) **NOUN** A **vessel** is a ship or a large boat. [FORMAL] ❑ *The vessel sank in 10 meters of water.*

vest /vɛst/ (**vests**) **NOUN** A **vest** is a piece of clothing without sleeves that people usually wear over a shirt.

vet /vɛt/ (**vets**) **NOUN** A **vet** is a person whose job is to treat sick or injured animals. **Vet** is short for **veterinarian**. [INFORMAL]

vet|er|an /vɛtərən/ (**veterans**)
1 **NOUN** A **veteran** is someone who has fought for their country during a war. ❑ *He's a veteran of the Vietnam War.*
2 **NOUN** You use **veteran** to talk about someone who has been doing a particular activity for a long time. ❑ *...a veteran teacher.*

vet|eri|nar|ian /vɛtərɪnɛəriən/ (**veterinarians**) **NOUN** A **veterinarian** is a person whose job is to treat sick or injured animals.

veto /vitoʊ/ (**vetoes, vetoing, vetoed**)
1 **VERB** SOCIAL STUDIES If someone **vetoes** something, they stop it from happening. ❑ *The president vetoed the proposal.*
2 **NONCOUNT NOUN** SOCIAL STUDIES **Veto** is the power that someone has to stop something from happening. ❑ *The president has power of veto over the matter.*

via /vaɪə, viə/ **PREPOSITION** If you go somewhere **via** a particular place, you go through that place on the way. ❑ *I'm flying to Sweden via New York.*

vi|brate /vaɪbreɪt/ (**vibrates, vibrating, vibrated**) **VERB** If something **vibrates**, it shakes with repeated small, quick movements. ❑ *There was a loud bang and the ground seemed to vibrate.* ● **vi|bra|tion** /vaɪbreɪʃən/ (**vibrations**) **NOUN** ❑ *Vibrations from the train made the house shake.*

vice /vaɪs/ (**vices**)
1 **NONCOUNT NOUN** **Vice** is criminal activity connected with sex and drugs.
2 **NOUN** A **vice** is a habit that is seen as a weakness. ❑ *My only vice is that I spend too much on clothes.*

vice ver|sa /vaɪsə vɜrsə, vaɪs/ **Vice versa** shows the opposite of what you have said. ❑ *The government exists to serve us, and not vice versa.*

vi|cious /vɪʃəs/
1 **ADJECTIVE** A **vicious** person is violent and cruel. ❑ *He was a cruel and vicious man.*
2 **ADJECTIVE** A **vicious** remark is cruel and intended to upset someone. ❑ *That wasn't true; it was just a vicious rumour.*

vic|tim /vɪktəm/ (**victims**) **NOUN** A **victim** is someone who has been hurt or killed. ❑ *The driver apologized to the victim's family.*

v

vic|to|ri|ous /vɪktɔriəs/ **ADJECTIVE**
Victorious describes someone who has won in a war or a competition. ❏ *The Canadian team was victorious in all four games.*

vic|to|ry /vɪktəri, vɪktri/ (**victories**) **NOUN**
A **victory** is a success in a war or a competition. ❏ *The Democrats are celebrating their victory.*

video /vɪdioʊ/ (**videos**)
1 **NOUN** A **video** is an event that has been recorded. ❏ *We watched a video of my first birthday party.*
2 **NOUN** A **video** is a movie that you can watch at home. ❏ *You can rent a video for two dollars and watch it at home.*
3 **NONCOUNT NOUN** TECHNOLOGY **Video** is the system of recording movies and events in this way. ❏ *She has watched the show on video.*

video game (**video games**) **NOUN** A **video game** is an electronic game that you play on your television or on a computer screen.
→ look at **play**

view /vyu/ (**views**)
1 **NOUN** Your **views** are the opinions that you have about something. ❏ *We have similar views on politics.*
2 **NOUN** The **view** from a window or a high place is everything that you can see from there. ❏ *From our hotel room we had a great view of the ocean.*
3 **NOUN** If you have a **view of** something, you can see it. ❏ *He stood up to get a better view of the blackboard.*
4 If a painting is **on view**, it is in a public place for people to look at. ❏ *Her paintings are on view at the Portland Gallery.*

view|er /vyuər/ (**viewers**) **NOUN** Viewers are people who are watching a particular program on television. ❏ *Twelve million viewers watch the show every week.*

vig|or|ous /vɪgərəs/ **ADJECTIVE** Vigorous physical actions involve using a lot of energy. ❏ *You should have an hour of vigorous exercise three times a week.* ● **vig|or|ous|ly** **ADVERB** ❏ *He shook his head vigorously.*

vil|lage /vɪlɪdʒ/ (**villages**) **NOUN** GEOGRAPHY
A **village** is a small town in the countryside.

vil|lain /vɪlən/ (**villains**) **NOUN** A **villain** is someone who deliberately harms other people or breaks the law . ❏ *They called him a villain and a murderer.*

vine /vaɪn/ (**vines**) **NOUN**
A **vine** is a plant that grows up or over things. ❏ *...a grape vine.*

vin|egar /vɪnɪgər/
NONCOUNT NOUN Vinegar is a sour, sharp-tasting liquid that is used in cooking.

vine|yard /vɪnyərd/ (**vineyards**) **NOUN** A **vineyard** is an area of land where grape vines are grown in order to produce wine.

vi|nyl /vaɪnɪl/ **NONCOUNT NOUN** Vinyl is a strong plastic that is used for making things like floor coverings and furniture. ❏ *...vinyl floor covering.*

vio|la /vioʊlə/ (**violas**) **NOUN** MUSIC A **viola** is a musical instrument with four strings that produces low notes. You hold it under your chin, and play it by moving a long stick (= a bow) across the strings. ❏ *She plays the viola in several different orchestras.*

vio|late /vaɪəleɪt/ (**violates, violating, violated**) **VERB** If someone **violates** an agreement or a law, they break it. [FORMAL] ❏ *The company has violated international law.* ● **vio|la|tion** /vaɪəleɪʃn/ (**violations**) **NOUN** ❏ *This is a violation of state law.*

vio|lence /vaɪələns/ **NONCOUNT NOUN**
Violence is behavior that is intended to hurt or kill people. ❏ *Twenty people died in the violence.*

vio|lent /vaɪələnt/ **ADJECTIVE** If someone is **violent**, or if they do something that is **violent**, they use physical force to hurt or kill other people. ❏ *These men have committed violent crimes.* ● **vio|lent|ly** **ADVERB** ❏ *The woman was violently attacked while out walking.*

Word Partners	Use **violent** with:
N.	violent **attacks**, violent **behavior**, violent **crime**, violent **criminals**, violent **films**, violent **movies**, violent **offenders**
ADV.	**extremely** violent, **increasingly** violent

vio|let /vaɪəlɪt/ (**violets**)
1 **NOUN** A **violet** is a small plant that has purple or white flowers in the spring.
2 **ADJECTIVE** Something that is **violet** is of a blue-purple color. ❏ *...a violet dress.*

V

vio|lin /vaɪəlɪn/ (violins) **NOUN** MUSIC
A **violin** is a musical instrument made of wood with four strings. You hold it under your chin, and play it by moving a long stick (= a bow) across the strings. ❑ *Lizzie plays the violin.*
→ look at **musical instrument**

VIP /vi aɪ pi/ (VIPs) **NOUN** A **VIP** is someone who is given better treatment than ordinary people because they are famous or important. **VIP** is short for "very important person." ❑ *Five hundred celebrities and VIPs attended the concert.*

vir|tual /vɜrtʃuəl/
1 **ADJECTIVE** You can use **virtual** to show that something is nearly true. ❑ *He was a virtual prisoner in his own home.* ● **vir|tu|al|ly** /vɜrtʃuəli/ **ADVERB** ❑ *She does virtually all the cooking.*
2 **ADJECTIVE** TECHNOLOGY **Virtual** objects and activities are made by a computer to seem like real objects and activities. ❑ *The virtual world sometimes seems more attractive than the real one.*

vir|tual re|al|ity **NONCOUNT NOUN** Virtual reality is an environment that is produced by a computer to seem very like it is real to the person experiencing it. ❑ *...a virtual reality game.*

vir|tue /vɜrtʃu/ (virtues)
1 **NONCOUNT NOUN** Virtue is thinking good thoughts and doing what is right. ❑ *The priests talked to us about virtue.*
2 **NOUN** A **virtue** is a good quality or way of acting. ❑ *His greatest virtue is patience.*

vi|rus /vaɪrəs/ (viruses)
1 **NOUN** A **virus** is a very small living thing that can enter your body and cause you to be sick. ❑ *There are thousands of different types of virus, and they change all the time.*
2 **NOUN** TECHNOLOGY In computer technology, a **virus** is a program that enters a system and changes or destroys the information held there. ❑ *You should protect your computer against viruses.*
→ look at **sick**

visa /vizə/ (visas) **NOUN** A **visa** is an official document or a stamp put in your passport, that allows you to enter a particular country.

vis|ibil|ity /vɪzɪbɪlɪti/ **NONCOUNT NOUN** Visibility means how far or how clearly you can see in particular weather conditions. ❑ *Visibility was poor.*

vis|ible /vɪzɪbəl/ **ADJECTIVE** If something is **visible**, it can be seen. ❑ *The warning lights were clearly visible.*

vi|sion /vɪʒən/ (visions)
1 **NOUN** Your **vision of** a future situation or society is what you imagine or hope it will be like. ❑ *I have a vision of world peace.*
2 **NONCOUNT NOUN** Your **vision** is your ability to see clearly with your eyes. ❑ *He's suffering from loss of vision.*

vis|it /vɪzɪt/ (visits, visiting, visited)
1 **VERB** If you **visit** someone, you go to see them in order to spend time with them. ❑ *He wanted to visit his brother.* ❑ *In the evenings, friends often visit.*
2 **NOUN** Visit is also a noun. ❑ *I recently had a visit from an English relative.*
3 **VERB** If you **visit** a place, you go there for a short time. ❑ *He'll be visiting four cities on his trip.*

Word Partners	Use **visit** with:
ADJ.	**brief** visit, **last** visit, **next** visit, **recent** visit, **short** visit, **surprise** visit **1** **2**
V.	**come to** visit, **go to** visit, **invite** *someone* **to** visit, **plan to** visit **1** **2**
N.	visit **family**, visit **friends**, visit **your mother**, visit **relatives** **1** visit **a museum**, **weekend** visit **2**

visi|tor /vɪzɪtər/ (visitors) **NOUN** A **visitor** is someone who is visiting a person or place. ❑ *We had some visitors from Milwaukee.*

vis|ual /vɪʒuəl/ **ADJECTIVE** Visual means relating to sight, or to things that you can see. ❑ *The movie's visual effects are amazing.*

vi|tal /vaɪtəl/ **ADJECTIVE** If something is **vital**, it is very important. ❑ *It is vital that children attend school regularly.*

vita|min /vaɪtəmɪn/ (vitamins) **NOUN** Vitamins are substances in food that you need in order to stay healthy. ❑ *These problems are caused by lack of vitamin D.*

viv|id /vɪvɪd/
1 **ADJECTIVE** Vivid memories and description are very clear and detailed. ❑ *I had a very vivid dream last night.* ● **viv|id|ly** **ADVERB** ❑ *I can vividly remember the first time I saw him.*
2 **ADJECTIVE** Something that is **vivid** is very bright in color. ❑ *She was dressed in a vivid pink jacket.*

V

vo|cabu|lary /voʊkǽbyələri/ (**vocabularies**)

1 **NOUN** LANGUAGE ARTS Your **vocabulary** is all the words you know in a particular language. ❑ *He has a very large vocabulary.*

2 **NOUN** LANGUAGE ARTS The **vocabulary** of a language is all the words in it. ❑ *English has the biggest vocabulary of any language.*

→ look at **dictionary, language**

vo|cal /voʊkəl/

1 **ADJECTIVE** Someone who is **vocal** gives their opinion very strongly. ❑ *Local people were very vocal about the problem.*

2 **ADJECTIVE** **Vocal** means using the human voice, especially in singing. ❑ *She has an interesting vocal style.*

voice /vɔɪs/ (**voices**) **NOUN** Someone's **voice** is the sound that comes from their mouth when they speak or sing. ❑ *She spoke in a soft voice.* ❑ *Lucinda sings in the choir and has a beautiful voice.*

void /vɔɪd/ (**voids**) **NOUN** A **void** is an empty feeling. ❑ *His death left a void in her life.*

vol|ca|no /vɒlkeɪnoʊ/ (**volcanoes**) **NOUN** SCIENCE A **volcano** is a mountain that throws out hot, liquid rock and fire. ❑ *The volcano erupted last year.*

→ look at **disaster**

volley|ball /vɒlibɔl/ **NONCOUNT NOUN** SPORTS **Volleyball** is a game in which two teams hit a large ball over a high net with their arms or hands.

volt /voʊlt/ (**volts**) **NOUN** SCIENCE A **volt** is a unit used for measuring electricity.

vol|ume /vɒlyum/ (**volumes**)

1 **NOUN** MATH The **volume** of an object is the amount of space that it contains. ❑ *What is the volume of a cube with sides of length 3 cm?*

2 **NOUN** A **volume** is one book in a series of books. ❑ *We read the first volume of his autobiography.*

3 **NONCOUNT NOUN** The **volume** of a sound is how loud or quiet it is. ❑ *He turned down the volume.*

→ look at **television**

vol|un|tary /vɒlənteri/

1 **ADJECTIVE** **Voluntary** actions or activities are done because someone wants to do them and not because they must. ❑ *Participation is completely voluntary.* ● **vol|un|tar|ily** /vɒləntɛərɪli/ **ADVERB** ❑ *I would never leave here voluntarily.*

2 **ADJECTIVE** **Voluntary** work is done by people who are not paid for it, but who do it because they want to do it. ❑ *I do voluntary work with handicapped children.*

vol|un|teer /vɒləntɪər/ (**volunteers, volunteering, volunteered**)

1 **NOUN** A **volunteer** is someone who does work without being paid for it, because they want to do it. ❑ *She helps in a local school as a volunteer.*

2 **VERB** If you **volunteer** to do something, you offer to do it without being forced to do it. ❑ *Mary volunteered to clean up the kitchen.*

vom|it /vɒmɪt/ (**vomits, vomiting, vomited**)

1 **VERB** If you **vomit**, food and drink comes back up from your stomach and out through your mouth. ❑ *Milk made him vomit.*

2 **NONCOUNT NOUN** **Vomit** is partly digested food and drink that comes out of your mouth when you vomit.

→ look at **sick**

vote /voʊt/ (**votes, voting, voted**)

1 **NOUN** SOCIAL STUDIES A **vote** is a choice made by a particular person or group in a meeting or an election. ❑ *Mr. Reynolds won the election by 102 votes to 60.*

2 **VERB** When you **vote**, you show your choice officially at a meeting or in an election. ❑ *The workers voted to strike.*

● **vot|er** (**voters**) **NOUN** ❑ *The state has*

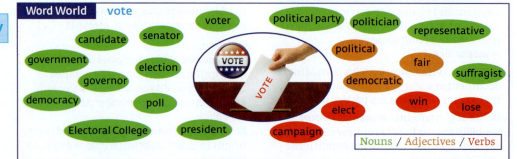

Word World vote

voter, political party, politician, representative, candidate, senator, political, government, election, fair, suffragist, governor, democratic, democracy, poll, win, lose, elect, Electoral College, president, campaign

VOTE

Nouns / Adjectives / Verbs

2.1 million registered voters.

→ look at Word World: **vote**

vow /vaʊ/ (**vows, vowing, vowed**)

1 **VERB** If you **vow** to do something, you make a serious promise or decision that you will do it. ❑ *She vowed to continue the fight.* ❑ *I vowed that someday I would go back to Europe.*

2 **NOUN** A **vow** is a serious promise or decision to do a particular thing. ❑ *I made a vow to be more careful in the future.*

vow|el /vaʊəl/ (**vowels**) **NOUN** LANGUAGE ARTS A **vowel** is a sound such as

the ones written as **a**, **e**, **i**, **o** and **u**, and sometimes **y**.

→ look at **language**

voy|age /vɔɪɪdʒ/ (**voyages**) **NOUN** A **voyage** is a long trip on a ship or in a spacecraft. ❑ *They began the long voyage down the river.*

vs. SPORTS **vs.** is short for **versus**. ❑ *We were watching the Yankees vs. the Red Sox.*

vul|ner|able /vʌlnərəbᵊl/ **ADJECTIVE** Someone who is **vulnerable** is weak and without protection. ❑ *Older people are particularly vulnerable to colds and flu in cold weather.*

v

Ww

wade /weɪd/ (**wades, wading, waded**) **VERB**
If you **wade** through water, you walk through it with difficulty. ❏ *I waded across the river to reach them.*

waf|fle /wɒfᵊl/ (**waffles**) **NOUN** A **waffle** is a flat, sweet cake with a pattern of squares on it that is usually eaten warm with syrup (= a thick, sweet liquid) for breakfast.

wag /wæg/ (**wags, wagging, wagged**) **VERB**
When a dog **wags** its tail, it moves its tail from side to side.

wage /weɪdʒ/ (**wages**) **NOUN** Someone's **wages** are the amount of money that is paid to them for the work that they do. ❏ *His wages have gone up.*
→ look at **factory**

<table>
<tr><td colspan="2">Word Partners   Use wage with:</td></tr>
<tr><td>ADJ.</td><td>average wage, high wage, hourly wage, low wage</td></tr>
<tr><td>N.</td><td>wage cuts, wage earners, wage increases, wage rates</td></tr>
<tr><td>V.</td><td>offer a wage, pay a wage, raise a wage</td></tr>
</table>

wag|on /wægən/ (**wagons**) **NOUN** A **wagon** is a strong vehicle with four wheels, usually pulled by animals.

Sound Partners	waist, waste

waist /weɪst/ (**waists**)
1 **NOUN** Your **waist** is the middle part of your body. ❏ *Ricky put his arm around her waist.*
2 **NOUN** The **waist** of a pair of pants is the part of it that goes around the middle part of your body. ❏ *The waist of these pants is a little tight.*
→ look at **body**

Sound Partners	wait, weight

wait /weɪt/ (**waits, waiting, waited**)
1 **VERB** When you **wait** for something or someone, you spend time doing very little, before something happens. ❏ *I walked to the street corner and waited for the school bus.* ❏ *I waited to hear what she said.* ❏ *We had to wait a week before we got the results.*
2 **NOUN** A **wait** is a period of time in which you do very little, before something happens. ❏ *There was a four-hour wait at the airport.*
3 **VERB** If something **is waiting for** you, it is ready for you to use, have, or do. ❏ *There'll be a car waiting for you.*
4 **VERB** If you say that something can **wait**, you mean that it is not very important, so you will do it later. ❏ *I want to talk to you, but it can wait.*
5 If you **can't wait** to do something, you are very excited about it. ❏ *We can't wait to get started.*

<table>
<tr><td colspan="2">Word Partners   Use wait with:</td></tr>
<tr><td>N.</td><td>wait for an answer, wait days, wait hours, wait a long time, wait your turn 1</td></tr>
<tr><td>V.</td><td>can wait, can't afford to wait, couldn't wait, have to wait, wait to hear, wait to say, will wait, won't wait, wouldn't wait 1
can't wait 5</td></tr>
</table>

wait|er /weɪtər/ (**waiters**) **NOUN** A **waiter** is a man whose job is to serve food in a restaurant.

wait|ing room (**waiting rooms**) **NOUN** A **waiting room** is a room where people can sit down while they wait. ❏ *She sat for half an hour in the dentist's waiting room.*

wait|ress /weɪtrɪs/ (**waitresses**) **NOUN** A **waitress** is a woman whose job is to serve food in a restaurant.
→ look at **restaurant**

wake /weɪk/ (**wakes, waking, woke, woken**)
1 **VERB** When you **wake**, you stop sleeping. ❏ *It was cold and dark when I woke at 6:30.*
2 **VERB** When someone or something **wakes** you, they make you stop sleeping. ❏ *Betty woke me when she left.*
3 **Wake up** means the same as **wake**. ❏ *We woke up early to a perfect summer morning.*

walk /wɔk/ (**walks, walking, walked**)
1 **VERB** When you **walk**, you move forward by putting one foot in front of the other. ❏ *She walked two miles to school every day.*

W

❑ *We walked into the hall.* ❑ *I walked a few steps toward the fence.*
2 **NOUN** A **walk** is a trip that you make by walking, usually for pleasure. ❑ *I went for a walk after lunch.*
→ look at **fitness, route**
▶ **walk out** If you **walk out of** a situation, you leave it suddenly, to show that you are angry or bored. ❑ *Several people walked out of the meeting in protest.*

Word Partners	Use **walk** with:
ADV.	walk **alone**, walk **away**, walk **back**, walk **home**, walk **slowly** **1**
V.	**begin to** walk, **start to** walk **1** **go for a** walk, **take a** walk **2**
N.	walk **a dog** **2**
ADJ.	**long** walk, **short** walk **2**

wall /wɔl/ (**walls**)
1 **NOUN** A **wall** is one of the sides of a building or a room. ❑ *His bedroom walls are covered with pictures of cars.*
2 **NOUN** A **wall** is a long narrow structure made of stone or brick that divides an area of land. ❑ *He sat on the wall in the sun.*

wal|let /wɒlɪt/ (**wallets**) **NOUN** A **wallet** is a small case in which you can keep money and cards.

wall|paper /wɔlpeɪpər/ (**wallpapers, wallpapering, wallpapered**)
1 **NONCOUNT NOUN** Wallpaper is colored or patterned paper that is used for decorating the walls of rooms.
2 **VERB** If someone **wallpapers** a room, they cover the walls with wallpaper.

wal|nut /wɔlnʌt, -nət/ (**walnuts**) **NOUN** Walnuts are nuts that are hard and round, with a rough texture.

wan|der /wɒndər/ (**wanders, wandering, wandered**) **VERB** If you **wander**, you walk around, often without intending to go in any particular direction. ❑ *When he got bored he wandered around the park.*

want /wɒnt/ (**wants, wanting, wanted**)
VERB If you **want** something, you feel a need for it. ❑ *I want a drink.* ❑ *People wanted to know who she was.* ❑ *They wanted their father to be the same as other dads.*

war /wɔr/ (**wars**) **NOUN** A **war** is a period of fighting between countries or groups. ❑ *He spent part of the war in France.*
→ look at **history**

ward /wɔrd/ (**wards**) **NOUN** A **ward** is a room in a hospital that has beds for many people. ❑ *They took her to the children's ward.*

ward|robe /wɔrdroʊb/ (**wardrobes**) **NOUN** Someone's **wardrobe** is the clothes that they have. ❑ *Ingrid bought a new wardrobe for the trip.*

ware|house /wɛərhaʊs/ (**warehouses**) **NOUN** A **warehouse** is a large building where goods are stored before they are sold.
→ look at **factory**

war|fare /wɔrfɛər/ **NONCOUNT NOUN** Warfare is the activity of fighting a war. ❑ *His men were trained in desert warfare.*

warm /wɔrm/ (**warmer, warmest, warms, warming, warmed**)
1 **ADJECTIVE** Something that is **warm** has some heat, but is not hot. ❑ *On warm summer days, she would sit outside.* ❑ *Because it was warm, David wore only a white cotton shirt.*
2 **ADJECTIVE** Warm clothes and blankets are made of a material that protects you from the cold. ● **warm|ly** **ADVERB** ❑ *Remember to dress warmly on cold days.*
3 **ADJECTIVE** A **warm** person is friendly. ❑ *She was a warm and loving mother.* ● **warm|ly** **ADVERB** ❑ *We warmly welcome new members.*
→ look at **climate, greenhouse effect, wear**
▶ **warm up** If you **warm** something **up**, you make it less cold. ❑ *He blew on his hands to warm them up.*

Word Partners	Use **warm** with:
N.	warm **air**, warm **bath**, warm **breeze**, warm **hands**, warm **water**, warm **weather** **1** warm **clothes** **2** warm **smile**, warm **welcome** **3**
ADJ.	warm **and dry**, warm **and sunny** **1** **soft and** warm **2** warm **and friendly** **3**

warmth /wɔrmθ/
1 **NONCOUNT NOUN** The **warmth** of something is the heat that it produces. ❑ *Feel the warmth of the sun on your skin.*
2 **NONCOUNT NOUN** Warmth is friendly behavior toward other people. ❑ *They treated us with warmth and kindness.*

w

warm-up (**warm-ups**) **NOUN** A warm-up is a period of gentle exercise that you do to prepare yourself for a particular sport or activity. ❏ *Training consists of a 20-minute warm-up, followed by ball practice.*

warn /wɔrn/ (**warns, warning, warned**) **VERB** If you **warn** someone about a possible danger, you tell them about it. ❏ *They warned him of the dangers of sailing alone.*

warn|ing /wɔrnɪŋ/ (**warnings**) **NOUN** A **warning** is something that tells people of a possible danger. ❏ *It was a warning that we should be careful.* ❏ *Suddenly and without warning, a car crash changed her life.*

war|rant /wɔrənt/ (**warrants**) **NOUN** A **warrant** is a legal document that allows someone to do something. ❏ *Police issued a warrant for his arrest.*

war|ran|ty /wɔrənti/ (**warranties**) **NOUN** A **warranty** is a promise by a company that if you buy something that does not work, they will repair or replace it. ❏ *The TV comes with a twelve-month warranty.*

wary /wɛəri/ (**warier, wariest**) **ADJECTIVE** If you are **wary of** something or someone, you are careful because you do not know much about them and you think they may be dangerous. ❏ *People teach their children to be wary of strangers.*

was /wəz, STRONG wʌz, wɒz/ **Was** is a form of the verb **be**.

wash /wɒʃ/ (**washes, washing, washed**)
1 **VERB** If you **wash** something, you clean it using water and soap. ❏ *She finished her dinner and washed the dishes.* ❏ *It took a long time to wash the dirt out of his hair.*
2 **VERB** If you **wash**, you clean your body using soap and water. ❏ *I haven't washed for days.* ❏ *She washed her face with cold water.*
3 If an item of clothing **is in the wash**, it is being washed. [INFORMAL] ❏ *Your jeans are in the wash.*
→ look at **chore, food, laundry**
▶ **wash up** If you **wash up**, you clean part of your body with soap and water, especially your hands and face. ❏ *He went to the bathroom to wash up.*

wash|cloth /wɒʃklɔθ/ (**washcloths**) **NOUN** A **washcloth** is a small cloth that you use for washing yourself.
→ look at **bathroom**

wash|ing ma|chine (**washing machines**) **NOUN** A **washing machine** is a machine that you use to wash clothes in. ❏ *Dan put his shirts in the washing machine.*
→ look at **laundry**

wasn't /wʌzᵊnt, wɒz-/ **Wasn't** is short for "was not."

wasp /wɒsp/ (**wasps**) **NOUN** A **wasp** is an insect with wings and yellow and black stripes across its body. Wasps can sting people.

| Sound Partners | waste, waist |

waste /weɪst/ (**wastes, wasting, wasted**)
1 **VERB** If you **waste** time, money, or energy, you use too much of it doing something that is not important. ❏ *She didn't want to waste time looking at old cars.* ❏ *I decided not to waste money on a hotel.*
2 **NOUN** Waste is also a noun. ❏ *It is a waste of time complaining about it.*
3 **NONCOUNT NOUN** Waste is material that is no longer wanted because the valuable or useful part of it has been taken out. ❏ *Waste materials such as paper and aluminum cans can be recycled.*
→ look at **energy, pollution**

waste|basket /weɪstbæskɪt/ (**wastebaskets**) **NOUN** A **wastebasket** is a container for things that you no longer want, especially paper. ❏ *He emptied the wastebasket and found her letter.*

watch /wɒtʃ/ (**watches, watching, watched**)
1 **VERB** If you **watch** someone or something, you look at them for a period of time. ❏ *A man stood in the doorway, watching me.* ❏ *I stayed up late to watch the movie.*
2 **VERB** If you **watch** someone or something, you take care of them for a period of time. ❏ *Could you watch my bags? I need to go to the bathroom.*
3 **NOUN** A **watch** is a small clock that you wear on your wrist. ❏ *Dan gave me a watch for my birthday.*

4 If someone **keeps watch**, they keep looking and listening so that they can warn other people of danger. ❏ *Josh climbed a tree to keep watch.*
→ look at **movie, news, performance, television**
▶ **watch for** or **watch out for** If you **watch**

for something or **watch out for** it, you pay attention so that you will notice it if it happens. ❏ *You should watch carefully for signs of the illness.*

▶ **watch out** If you tell someone to **watch out**, you are warning them to be careful. ❏ *Police warned shoppers to watch out for thieves.*

Word Partners	Use **watch** with:
N.	watch **a DVD**, watch **a film**, watch **a game**, watch a **movie**, watch **the news**, watch **people**, watch **television**, watch **TV**, watch **a video** **1** watch **children** **2**
ADV.	watch **carefully**, watch **closely** **1** **2** **4**
V.	**check** *your* watch, **glance at** *your* watch, **look at** *your* watch **3**

wa|ter /wɔtər/ (**waters, watering, watered**)
1 **NONCOUNT NOUN** Water is a clear thin liquid that has no color or taste. It falls from clouds as rain. ❏ *Get me a glass of water, please.*
2 **VERB** If you **water** plants, you pour water over them in order to help them to grow.
3 **VERB** If your eyes **water**, tears build up in them because they are hurting, or because you are upset.
→ look at Word World: **water**
→ look at **conservation, greenhouse effect, ocean**

water|color /wɔtərkʌlər/ (**watercolors**)
1 **NOUN** ARTS **Watercolors** are colored paints that are mixed with water and used for painting pictures. ❏ *Campbell painted with watercolors.*
2 **NOUN** ARTS A **watercolor** is a picture that has been painted with watercolors. ❏ *...a watercolor by Andrew Wyeth.*

water|fall /wɔtərfɔl/ (**waterfalls**) **NOUN**
SCIENCE A **waterfall** is a place where water flows over the edge of a steep part of hills or mountains, and falls into a pool below.
→ look at **water**

water|melon /wɔtərmɛlən/ (**watermelons**)
NOUN A **watermelon** is a large, heavy fruit with green skin, pink flesh, and black seeds.
→ look at **fruit**

water|proof /wɔtərpruf/ **ADJECTIVE**
Something that is **waterproof** does not let water pass through it. ❏ *You'll need to take waterproof clothing when you go camping.*

watt /wɒt/ (**watts**) **NOUN** SCIENCE A **watt** is a unit of measurement of electrical power.
❏ *The lamp takes a 60 watt lightbulb.*

Spelling Partners	**wave**

wave /weɪv/ (**waves, waving, waved**)
1 **VERB** If you **wave** your hand, you hold your hand up and move it from side to side, usually in order to say hello or goodbye to someone. ❏ *Jessica saw Lois and waved to her.* ❏ *He smiled, waved, and said, "Hi!"*
2 **NOUN** **Wave** is also a noun. ❏ *Steve stopped him with a wave of the hand.*
3 **VERB** If you **wave** something, you hold it up and move it from side to side. ❏ *More than 4,000 people waved flags and sang songs.*
4 **NOUN** SCIENCE A **wave** is a higher part of water on the surface of the ocean. **Waves** are caused by the wind blowing on the surface of the water. ❏ *I fell asleep to the sound of waves hitting the rocks.*
5 **NOUN** SCIENCE **Waves** are the form in which things such as sound, light, and radio signals travel. ❏ *...sound waves.* ❏ *...radio waves.*
→ look at **beach, ocean**

wave|length /weɪvlɛŋθ/ (**wavelengths**)
1 **NOUN** SCIENCE A **wavelength** is the size of a radio wave that a particular radio station

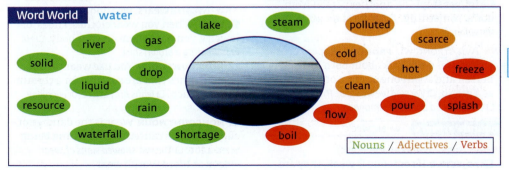

Word World   water

lake · steam · polluted · scarce · river · gas · cold · solid · drop · hot · freeze · liquid · clean · resource · rain · flow · pour · splash · waterfall · shortage · boil

Nouns / Adjectives / Verbs

W

uses to broadcast its programs. ❑ *She found the station's wavelength on her radio.*

2 If two people are **on the same wavelength**, they find it easy to understand each other because they share similar interests or opinions. ❑ *We often finished each other's sentences—we were on the same wavelength.*

wavy /we͟ɪvi/ (**wavier, waviest**) **ADJECTIVE** Wavy hair is not straight or curly, but curves slightly. ❑ *She had short, wavy brown hair.*
→ look at **hair**

wax /wæ͟ks/ **NONCOUNT NOUN** Wax is a solid, slightly shiny substance that is used for making candles (= sticks that you burn for light) and polish for furniture. ❑ *The candle wax melted in the heat.*

way /we͟ɪ/ (**ways**)
1 **NOUN** A **way** of doing something is the action that you take to do it. ❑ *One way of making friends is to go to an evening class.* ❑ *She smiled in a friendly way.*
2 **NOUN** The **way** to a place is the route that you take in order to get there. ❑ *Do you know the way to the post office?*
3 **NOUN** If you go a particular **way**, you go in that direction. ❑ *Which way do we go now—left or right?*
4 **NOUN** A **long way** is a long distance. ❑ *It's a long way from New York to Nashville.*
5 You say **by the way** when you are going to talk about something different. ❑ *By the way, how is your back?*
6 If you **get** your **way** or **have** your **way**, nobody stops you from doing what you want to do. ❑ *He likes to get his own way.*
7 If someone **is in the way**, they are in the same place as you, and so they stop you from doing something. ❑ *Please can you move? You're in the way.*
8 If someone **gets out of the way**, they are no longer stopping another person from doing something. ❑ *Get out of the way of the ambulance!*

we /wi, STRONG wi͟/ **PRONOUN** A speaker or writer uses **we** to talk about both himself or herself and about one or more other people as a group. ❑ *We said we would be friends for ever.* ❑ *We bought a bottle of lemonade.*

weak /wi͟k/ (**weaker, weakest**)
1 **ADJECTIVE** If someone is **weak**, they are

not healthy, or they do not have strong muscles. ❑ *I was too weak to move.* ● **weak|ly** **ADVERB** ❑ *"I'm all right," Max said weakly.*
● **weak|ness** **NONCOUNT NOUN** ❑ *Symptoms of the disease include weakness in the arms.*
2 **ADJECTIVE** A **weak** drink, chemical, or drug contains very little of a particular substance. ❑ *We sat at the table drinking weak coffee.*
3 **ADJECTIVE** A **weak** person does not have much determination, and it is easy to influence them. ❑ *He was weak, but he was not a bad man.* ● **weak|ness** **NONCOUNT NOUN** ❑ *Some people think that crying is a sign of weakness.*
→ look at **sick**

weak|en /wi͟kən/ (**weakens, weakening, weakened**) **VERB** If something **weakens**, it becomes less strong. ❑ *The economy weakened in early 2001.*

weak|ness /wi͟knɪs/ (**weaknesses**) **NOUN** If you have a **weakness for** something, you like it very much. ❑ *Stephen had a weakness for chocolate.*

wealth /we͟lθ/ **NONCOUNT NOUN** Wealth is a large amount of money, property, or other valuable things ❑ *He used his wealth to help others.*

wealthy /we͟lθi/ (**wealthier, wealthiest**)
1 **ADJECTIVE** Someone who is **wealthy** has a large amount of money, property, or valuable possessions. ❑ *She's going to be a very wealthy woman someday.*
2 **PLURAL NOUN** The **wealthy** are people who are wealthy. ❑ *Good education should be available to everyone, not just the wealthy.*

weap|on /we͟pən/ (**weapons**) **NOUN** A **weapon** is an object such as a gun, that is used for killing or hurting people. ❑ *He was charged with carrying a dangerous weapon.*

wear /we͟ər/ (**wears, wearing, wore, worn**)
1 **VERB** When you **wear** clothes, shoes, or jewelry, you have them on your body. ❑ *He was wearing a brown shirt.*
2 **NONCOUNT NOUN** You use **wear** to talk about clothes that are suitable for a certain time or place. ❑ *Jeans are perfect for everyday wear.*
3 **NONCOUNT NOUN** Wear is the damage or change that is caused by something being used a lot. ❑ *The suit showed signs of wear.*
→ look at Word World: **wear**

W

Word World   wear

glasses · bathrobe · casual · dress · pajamas · uniform · outfit · bathing suit · underwear · old · new · tight · comfortable · warm · loose · hang up · fit · iron · change · take off · put on

Nouns / Adjectives / Verbs

▶ **wear down** If something **wears down**, it becomes flatter or smoother because it as been rubbing against something. ❑ *The heels on my shoes have worn down.*

▶ **wear off** If a sensation, or feeling **wears off**, it disappears slowly. ❑ *The excitement of having a new job soon wore off.*

▶ **wear out** If something **wears** you **out**, it makes you feel extremely tired. [INFORMAL] ❑ *The kids wore themselves out playing soccer all afternoon.*

wea|ry /wɪ̱əri/ (wearier, weariest)

1 **ADJECTIVE** If you are **weary**, you are very tired. ❑ *Rachel looked pale and weary.*

2 **ADJECTIVE** If you are **weary of** something, you have become tired of it. ❑ *They were all growing a bit weary of the game.*

weath|er /we̱ðər/ **NONCOUNT NOUN** SCIENCE The **weather** is the temperature and conditions outside, for example if it is raining, hot, or windy. ❑ *The weather was bad.* ❑ *I like cold weather.*
→ look at Picture Dictionary: **weather**
→ look at **climate, season**

Word Partners   Use **weather** with:

ADJ.   **bad** weather, **clear** weather, **cold** weather, **cool** weather, **dry** weather, **fair** weather, **good** weather, **hot** weather, **nice** weather, **rainy** weather, **severe** weather, **stormy** weather, **sunny** weather, **warm** weather, **wet** weather

N.   weather **conditions**, weather **report**

weave /wi̱v/ (weaves, weaving, wove, woven) **VERB** If you **weave** cloth, you make it by crossing threads over and under each other. ❑ *We gathered wool and learned how to weave it into cloth.*

web /we̱b/ (webs)

1 **NOUN** TECHNOLOGY The **Web** is a computer system that helps you find information. You can use it anywhere in the world. It is also called the **World Wide Web**. ❑ *The handbook is available on the Web.*

2 **NOUN** A **web** is the thin net made by a spider from a string that comes out of its body. ❑ *...a spider's web.*

Picture Dictionary   weather

sun

clouds

wind

snow

fog

rain

w

web|cam /wɛbkæm/ (**webcams**) **NOUN**
TECHNOLOGY A **webcam** is a camera on a computer that produces images that can be seen on a website.

web page (**web pages**) **NOUN** TECHNOLOGY
A **web page** is a set of information that you can see on a computer screen as part of a website.

web|site /wɛbsaɪt/ (**websites**) also **web site**
NOUN TECHNOLOGY A **website** is a set of information about a particular subject that is available on the Internet.
→ look at **news**

wed|ding /wɛdɪŋ/ (**weddings**) **NOUN**
A **wedding** is a marriage ceremony and the party that often takes place after the ceremony. ❑ *Many couples want a big wedding.*

Wednes|day /wɛnzdeɪ, -di/ (**Wednesdays**)
NOUN Wednesday is the day after Tuesday and before Thursday. ❑ *Come and have supper with us on Wednesday.*

weed /wid/ (**weeds, weeding, weeded**)
1 **NOUN** A **weed** is a plant that grows where you do not want it. ❑ *The garden was full of weeds.*
2 **VERB** If you **weed** an area, you remove the weeds from it. ❑ *Try not to walk on the flowerbeds while you are weeding.*
→ look at **plant**

Sound Partners   week, weak

week /wik/ (**weeks**)
1 **NOUN** A **week** is a period of seven days.
❑ *I thought about it all week.*
2 **NOUN** Your working **week** is the hours that you spend at work during a week.
❑ *I work a 40-hour week.*
→ look at **calendar**

week|day /wikdeɪ/ (**weekdays**) **NOUN**
A **weekday** is any of the days of the week except Saturday and Sunday.
→ look at **calendar, day**

week|end /wikɛnd/ (**weekends**) **NOUN**
The **weekend** is Saturday and Sunday. ❑ *I had dinner with Tim last weekend.*
→ look at **calendar, day, job, relax**

week|ly /wikli/
1 **ADJECTIVE** A **weekly** event happens once a week or every week. ❑ *We do the weekly shopping every Thursday.*
2 **ADVERB** Weekly is also an adverb. ❑ *The group meets weekly.*
→ look at **calendar**

weep /wip/ (**weeps, weeping, wept**) **VERB**
If someone **weeps**, they cry. ❑ *She wept tears of joy.*

Sound Partners   weigh, way

weigh /weɪ/ (**weighs, weighing, weighed**)
1 **VERB** If someone or something **weighs** a particular amount, this amount is how heavy they are. ❑ *She weighs nearly 120 pounds.*
2 **VERB** If you **weigh** something or someone, you measure how heavy they are.
❑ *Lisa weighed the boxes for postage.*

Sound Partners   weight, wait

weight /weɪt/ (**weights**)
1 **NOUN** The **weight** of a person or thing is how heavy they are. ❑ *What is your height and weight?*
2 **NOUN** Weights are objects that people lift as a form of exercise. ❑ *I was in the gym lifting weights.*
3 If someone **loses weight**, they become thinner. If they **gain weight** or **put on weight**, they become fatter. ❑ *I'm lucky because I never put on weight.*
→ look at **fitness**

Word Partners	Use **weight** with:
ADJ.	**excess** weight, **healthy** weight, **ideal** weight, **normal** weight **1**
N.	**body** weight, weight **gain**, weight **loss**, **height and** weight, **size and** weight **1** weight **training 2**
V.	**gain** weight, **lose** weight, **put on** weight **3**

weird /wɪərd/ (**weirder, weirdest**) **ADJECTIVE**
If something or someone is **weird**, they are strange. [INFORMAL] ❑ *He's a very weird guy.*

wel|come /wɛlkəm/ (**welcomes, welcoming, welcomed**)
1 **VERB** If you **welcome** someone, you act in a friendly way when they arrive somewhere.
❑ *She was there to welcome him home.*
2 **NOUN** Welcome is also a noun. ❑ *They gave him a warm welcome.*
3 You use **welcome** to be friendly to someone who has just arrived somewhere.
❑ *Welcome to Washington.*
4 You say "**You're welcome**" to someone who has thanked you for something.
❑ *"Thank you for dinner."—"You're welcome."*

wel|fare /wɛlfɛər/
1 **NONCOUNT NOUN** The **welfare** of a person or group is their health and happiness.

❏ *I don't believe he is thinking of Emma's welfare.*

2 NONCOUNT NOUN Welfare is money that the government pays to people who are poor or sick. ❏ *Some states are making cuts in welfare.*

---

well

❶ INTRODUCING STATEMENTS
❷ ADVERB USES
❸ PHRASES
❹ ADJECTIVE USE
❺ NOUN USE

---

❶ **well** /wɛl/

1 ADVERB You often say **well** before you begin to speak, or when you are surprised about something. ❏ *Well, it's a pleasure to meet you.* ❏ *Well, I didn't expect to see you here!*

2 You say **oh well** to show that you accept a situation, even though you are not very happy about it. ❏ *Oh well, I guess it could be worse.*

❷ **well** /wɛl/ (**better, best**)

1 ADVERB If you do something **well**, you do it in an effective way. ❏ *The team played well last week.* ❏ *He speaks English well.* ❏ *Did you sleep well last night?*

2 ADVERB If you do something **well**, you do it in a complete way. ❏ *Mix the butter and sugar well.* ❏ *Do you know him well?*

3 If you **do well**, you are successful. ❏ *If she does well in her exams, she will go to college.*

4 You say **well done!** to someone when they have done something good. ❏ *This is excellent work. Well done!*

❸ **well** /wɛl/

1 As well means also. ❏ *Everywhere he went, I went as well.*

2 As well as means and also. ❏ *Adults as well as children will enjoy the movie.*

3 If you say that you **may as well** do something, you mean that you will do it because there is nothing better to do. ❏ *Anyway, you're here now—you may as well stay.*

❹ **well** /wɛl/ **ADJECTIVE** If you are **well**, you are healthy. ❏ *"How are you?"—"I'm very well, thank you."* ❏ *He said he wasn't feeling well.*

❺ **well** /wɛl/ (**wells**) **NOUN** A **well** is a deep hole in the ground from which people take water or oil. ❏ *The women and children were carrying water from the well.*

we'll /wɪl, STRONG wil/ **We'll** is short for "we shall" or "we will." ❏ *Don't worry, we'll be fine.*

well done

1 Something that is **well done** is properly done, with good results. ❏ *Many thanks for a job well done.*

2 ADJECTIVE If meat is **well done**, it has been cooked thoroughly. ❏ *I like lamb well done.*

well-known ADJECTIVE A **well-known** person or thing is famous. ❏ *She was a very well-known author.*

well-off ADJECTIVE Someone who is **well-off** is rich. [INFORMAL]

went /wɛnt/ **Went** is a form of the verb **go**.

wept /wɛpt/ **Wept** is a form of the verb **weep**.

were /wər, STRONG wɜr/

1 Were is a form of the verb **be**.

2 Were is sometimes used instead of "was" in conditional sentences or after the verb "wish." [FORMAL] ❏ *Jerry wished he were back in Washington.*

we're /wɪər/ **We're** is short for "we are." ❏ *We're going to the theater tonight.*

weren't /wɜrnt, wɜrənt/ **Weren't** is short for "were not."

west /wɛst/ also **West**

1 NONCOUNT NOUN GEOGRAPHY The **west** is the direction that is in front of you when you look at the sun in the evening. ❏ *I drove to Flagstaff, a hundred miles to the west.* ❏ *Many of the buildings in the west of the city are on fire.*

2 ADJECTIVE GEOGRAPHY **West** is also an adjective. ❏ *...the west coast.*

3 ADVERB If you go **west**, you travel toward the west. ❏ *We are going west to California.*

4 ADJECTIVE A **west** wind blows from the west.

5 NOUN GEOGRAPHY **The West** is the United States, Canada, and the countries of Western Europe. ❏ *...relations between Japan and the West.*

→ look at **globe**

west|er|ly /wɛstərli/

1 ADJECTIVE GEOGRAPHY **Westerly** means to the west or toward the west. ❏ *They walked in a westerly direction along the riverbank.*

2 ADJECTIVE A **westerly** wind blows from the west. ❏ *...a strong westerly wind.*

west|ern /wɛstərn/ (**westerns**) also **Western**

1 ADJECTIVE GEOGRAPHY **Western** means in or from the west of a place. ❏ *...Western Europe.*

2 ADJECTIVE SOCIAL STUDIES **Western**

w

describes things, people, or ideas that come from the United States, Canada, and the countries of Western Europe. ❑ *They need billions of dollars from Western governments.*

3 **NOUN** A **western** is a movie about life in the western United States in the past.

wet /wɛt/ (**wetter, wettest, wets, wetting, wet** or **wetted**)

1 **ADJECTIVE** If something is **wet**, it is covered in liquid. ❑ *He dried his wet hair with a towel.*

2 **VERB** To **wet** something means to put water or some other liquid over it. ❑ *She wet a cloth and wiped the child's face.*

3 **ADJECTIVE** If the weather is **wet**, it is raining. ❑ *It's cold and wet outside.*
→ look at **climate, laundry, season**

we've /wiv, STRONG wiv/ **We've** is short for "we have." ❑ *We've never been to the cinema together.*

whale /weɪl/
(**whales**) **NOUN**
Whales are very large mammals that live in the ocean.
→ look at **ocean**

what /wʌt, wɒt/

1 **PRONOUN** You use **what** in questions when you ask for information. ❑ *What do you want?* ❑ *"Has something happened?"—"Yes."—"What?"*

2 **ADJECTIVE** **What** is also an adjective. ❑ *What time is it?*

3 **CONJUNCTION** **What** means "the thing that." ❑ *I want to know what happened to Norman.*

4 You use **what a** or **what an** in exclamations to an opinion or reaction stronger. ❑ *What a horrible thing to do!*

5 **ADJECTIVE** **What** is also an adjective. ❑ *What pretty hair she has!*

6 You use **what about** when you make a suggestion, an offer, or a request. ❑ *What about going to see a movie?*

7 You say **what if** at the beginning of a question when you ask about something that might happen. ❑ *What if this doesn't work?*

what|ev|er /wʌtɛvər, wɒt-/

1 **CONJUNCTION** You use **whatever** to talk about anything or everything of a particular type. ❑ *Frank was free to do whatever he wanted.*

2 **ADJECTIVE** **Whatever** is also an adjective. ❑ *He has to accept whatever punishment they give him.*

3 **CONJUNCTION** You use **whatever** to say that something is the case in all situations. ❑ *I will always love you, whatever happens.*

what's /wʌts, wɒts/ **What's** is short for "what is" or "what has." ❑ *What's that?* ❑ *What's happened?*

wheat /wit/ **NONCOUNT NOUN** **Wheat** is a crop that is grown for food. It is made into flour and used for making bread.
→ look at **bread**

wheel /wil/ (**wheels, wheeling, wheeled**)

1 **NOUN** The **wheels** of a vehicle are the round objects under it that allow it to move along the ground. ❑ *The car's wheels slipped on the wet road.*

2 **NOUN** The **wheel** of a vehicle is the round object that you turn to make the vehicle go in different directions. ❑ *He sat down behind the wheel and started the engine.*

3 **VERB** If you **wheel** an object somewhere, you push it along on its wheels. ❑ *He wheeled his bike into the alley.*
→ look at **color**

wheel|barrow /wilbæroʊ/ (**wheelbarrows**) **NOUN** A **wheelbarrow** is an open container with one wheel and two handles, that is used for moving things such as bricks, earth, or plants.

wheel|chair /wiltʃɛər/ (**wheelchairs**) **NOUN** A **wheelchair** is a chair with wheels that you use if you cannot walk very well.
→ look at **disability**

when /wɛn/

1 **PRONOUN** You use **when** to ask questions about the time at which things happen. ❑ *When are you going home?* ❑ *When did you get married?*

2 **CONJUNCTION** You use **when** to talk about something that happens during a situation. ❑ *When I met Jill, I was living on my own.*

3 **CONJUNCTION** You use **when** to introduce the part of the sentence where you mention the time at which something happens. ❑ *I asked him when he was coming back.*

when|ever /wɛnɛvər/ **CONJUNCTION** You use **whenever** to talk about any time or every time that something happens. ❑ *Whenever I talked to him, he seemed quite nice.* ❑ *You can stay at my house whenever you like.*

W

Sound Partners	where, wear

where /wɛər/

1 **PRONOUN** You use **where** to ask questions about the place someone or something is in. ❑ *Where did you meet him?* ❑ *Where's Anna?*

2 **CONJUNCTION** You use **where** to talk about the place in which something happens. ❑ *People were looking to see where the noise was coming from.* ❑ *He knew where Henry was.*

3 **PRONOUN** **Where** is also a pronoun. ❑ *This is the room where I work.*

where's /wɛərz/ **Where's** is short for "where is."

wher|ever /wɛrɛvər/

1 **CONJUNCTION** You use **wherever** to say that something happens in any place or situation. ❑ *Some people enjoy themselves wherever they are.*

2 **CONJUNCTION** You use **wherever** when you say that you do not know where a person or place is. ❑ *I'd like to be with my children, wherever they are.*

wheth|er /wɛðər/

1 **CONJUNCTION** You use **whether** when you are talking about a choice between two or more things. ❑ *They now have two weeks to decide whether or not to buy the house.*

2 **CONJUNCTION** You use **whether** to say that something is true in any of the situations that you mention. ❑ *You are part of this family whether you like it or not.*

which /wɪtʃ/

1 **ADJECTIVE** You use **which** to talk about a choice between two or more possible people or things. ❑ *I want to know which school you went to.* ❑ *"You go down that road."—"Which one?"* ❑ *Which teacher do you like best?*

2 **PRONOUN** You use **which** when you want to show the exact thing that you are talking about. ❑ *Police stopped a car which didn't stop at a red light.*

3 **PRONOUN** You use **which** to talk about something that you have just said. ❑ *She spoke extremely good English, which was not surprising.*

which|ever /wɪtʃɛvər/

1 **ADJECTIVE** **Whichever** means any person or thing. ❑ *Whichever way we do this, it isn't going to work.*

2 **CONJUNCTION** **Whichever** is also a conjunction. ❑ *You can order by phone or from our website—whichever you prefer.*

while /waɪl/

1 **CONJUNCTION** If one thing happens **while** another thing is happening, the two things are happening at the same time. ❑ *His wife got up while he was in bed asleep.*

2 **NOUN** A **while** is a period of time. ❑ *They walked on in silence for a while.*

whine /waɪn/ (whines, whining, whined)

1 **VERB** If something or someone **whines**, they make a long high noise that sounds sad or unpleasant. ❑ *He could hear the dog barking and whining in the background.*

2 **VERB** If someone **whines**, they complain in an annoying way about something unimportant. ❑ *People were complaining and whining.*

whip /wɪp/ (whips, whipping, whipped)

1 **NOUN** A **whip** is a long thin piece of material attached to a handle. It is used for hitting people or animals.

2 **VERB** If someone **whips** a person or an animal, they hit them with a whip. ❑ *Mr. Melton whipped the horse several times.*

3 **VERB** When you **whip** cream or egg, you stir it very fast until it is thick or stiff. ❑ *Whip the cream until it is thick.*

whirl /wɜrl/ (whirls, whirling, whirled) **VERB** If something or someone **whirls**, they turn around very quickly. ❑ *She whirled around to look at him.*

whisk /wɪsk/ (whisks, whisking, whisked)

1 **VERB** If you **whisk** someone or something somewhere, you take them or move them there quickly. ❑ *He whisked her across the dance floor.*

2 **VERB** If you **whisk** eggs or cream, you stir them very fast.

3 **NOUN** A **whisk** is a kitchen tool used for whisking eggs or cream.

whisk|er /wɪskər/ (whiskers) **NOUN** The **whiskers** of an animal such as a cat or a mouse are the long stiff hairs that grow near its mouth.

whis|per /wɪspər/ (whispers, whispering, whispered)

1 **VERB** When you **whisper**, you say something very quietly. ❑ *"Be quiet," I whispered.* ❑ *He whispered in her ear.*

2 **NOUN** **Whisper** is also a noun. ❑ *People were talking in whispers.*

whis|tle /wɪsəl/ (whistles, whistling, whistled)

1 **VERB** When you **whistle**, you make

w

musical sounds by blowing your breath out between your lips. ❑ *He was whistling softly to himself.*

2 **NOUN** A **whistle** is a small tube that you blow in order to produce a loud sound. ❑ *The guard blew his whistle and the train started to move.*

white /waɪt/ (**whiter**, **whitest**, **whites**)

1 **ADJECTIVE** Something that is **white** is the color of snow or milk. ❑ *He had nice white teeth.*

2 **NOUN** White is also a noun. ❑ *He was dressed in white from head to toe.*

3 **ADJECTIVE** A **white** person has a pale skin. ❑ *A family of white people moved into a house up the street.*

4 **NOUN** **Whites** are white people. ❑ *The school has brought blacks and whites together.*
→ look at **bread**, **color**

white|board /waɪtbɔrd/ (**whiteboards**)
NOUN A **whiteboard** is a shiny white board that you can draw or write on, using special pens. Teachers often use whiteboards.
→ look at **classroom**

White House **NOUN** SOCIAL STUDIES
The White House is the official home in Washington DC of the president of the United States. You can also use **the White House** to talk about the president of the United States and his or her officials. ❑ *He drove to the White House.* ❑ *The White House welcomed the decision.*

whiz /wɪz/ (**whizzes**, **whizzing**, **whizzed**) also **whizz** **VERB** If something **whizzes** somewhere, it moves there very fast. [INFORMAL] ❑ *Stewart felt a bottle whiz past his head.*

who /hu/

> **PRONUNCIATION HELP**
> Pronounce /hu/ for meaning **2**.

1 **PRONOUN** You use **who** in questions when you ask about the name of a person or a group of people. ❑ *Who's there?* ❑ *Who is the strongest man around here?* ❑ *"You remind me of someone."—"Who?"*

2 **CONJUNCTION** You use **who** in the part of a sentence before you talk about a person or a group of people. ❑ *Police have not found out who did it.*

who'd /hud, hud/
1 **Who'd** is short for "who had." ❑ *I met someone who'd been waiting for three hours.*
2 **Who'd** is short for "who would." ❑ *Who'd like a coffee?*

who|ever /huɛvər/
1 **CONJUNCTION** You use **whoever** to talk about someone when you do not know who they are. ❑ *Whoever wins the prize is going to be famous for life.*
2 **CONJUNCTION** You use **whoever** to talk about any person. ❑ *You can have whoever you like visit you.*

> **Sound Partners** whole, hole

whole /hoʊl/
1 **The whole of** something means all of it. ❑ *This is a problem for the whole of society.*
2 **ADJECTIVE** **Whole** is also an adjective. ❑ *We spent the whole summer in Italy that year.*
3 **On the whole** means in general. ❑ *On the whole I agree with him.*

who'll /hul, hul/ **Who'll** is short for "who will" or "who shall." ❑ *I need to talk to someone who'll listen.*

whom /hum/ **PRONOUN** **Whom** is used in formal or written English instead of "who" when it is the object of a verb or preposition. ❑ *The book is about her husband, Denis, whom she married in 1951.* ❑ *To whom am I speaking?*

who's /huz, huz/ **Who's** is short for "who is" or "who has." ❑ *Who's going to argue with that?* ❑ *Who's been using my cup?*

whose /huz/
1 **PRONOUN** You use **whose** in questions to ask about the person that something belongs to. ❑ *"Whose is this?"—"It's mine."*
2 **ADJECTIVE** **Whose** is also an adjective. ❑ *Whose daughter is she?* ❑ *I can't remember whose idea it was.*
3 **PRONOUN** You use **whose** when you mention something that belongs to the person or thing mentioned before. ❑ *That's the driver whose car was blocking the street.*

who've /huv, huv/ **Who've** is short for "who have." ❑ *These are people who've never used a computer before.*

why /waɪ/

> **PRONUNCIATION HELP**
> Pronounce the conjunction and the pronoun /waɪ/.

1 **PRONOUN** You use **why** in questions when you ask about the reasons for something. ❑ *Why is she here?* ❑ *Why are you laughing?*
2 **CONJUNCTION** You use **why** at the beginning of a statement in which you talk

W

about the reasons for something. ❑ *He wondered why she was late.*
3 **ADVERB** **Why** is also an adverb. ❑ *I liked him - I don't know why.*
4 **ADVERB** You use **why** with "not" in questions in order to introduce a suggestion. ❑ *Why not give Jenny a call?*

wick|ed /wɪkɪd/ **ADJECTIVE** If something or someone is **wicked**, they are very bad. ❑ *That's a wicked lie!*

wide /waɪd/ (**wider, widest**)
1 **ADJECTIVE** Something that is **wide** is a large distance from one side to the other. ❑ *The bed is too wide for this room.*
2 **ADJECTIVE** If you open something **wide**, you open it as far as possible. ❑ *"It was huge,"* he announced, spreading his arms *wide*.
3 **ADJECTIVE** You use **wide** to talk or ask about how much something measures from one side to the other. ❑ *The lake was over a mile wide.*

wid|en /waɪdən/ (**widens, widening, widened**) **VERB** If you **widen** something, you make it bigger from one side or edge to the other. ❑ *They are planning to widen the road.*

wide|screen /waɪdskrin/ **ADJECTIVE** A **widescreen** television or computer has a screen that is wide in relation to its height.

wide|spread /waɪdsprɛd/ **ADJECTIVE** Something that is **widespread** happens over a large area, or to a great extent. ❑ *Food shortages are widespread.*

wid|ow /wɪdoʊ/ (**widows**) **NOUN** A **widow** is a woman whose husband has died. ❑ *She became a widow a year ago.*

wid|ow|er /wɪdoʊər/ (**widowers**) **NOUN** A **widower** is a man whose wife has died.

width /wɪdθ, wɪtθ/ (**widths**) **NOUN** The **width** of something is the distance from one side of it to the other. ❑ *Measure the full width of the window.*
→ look at **geometry**

wife /waɪf/ (**wives**) **NOUN** A man's **wife** is the woman he is married to. ❑ *He married his wife, Jane, 37 years ago.*
→ look at **family**

wig /wɪg/ (**wigs**) **NOUN** A **wig** is a covering of artificial hair that you wear on your head.

wig|gle /wɪgəl/ (**wiggles, wiggling, wiggled**) **VERB** If you **wiggle** something, you make it move up and down or from side to side in

small quick movements. ❑ *She wiggled her finger.*

wild /waɪld/ (**wilder, wildest**)
1 **ADJECTIVE** **Wild** animals or plants live or grow in nature, and people do not take care of them. ❑ *We could hear the calls of wild animals in the jungle.*
2 **ADJECTIVE** **Wild** behavior is uncontrolled or excited. ❑ *The crowds went wild when they saw him.* ● **wild|ly** **ADVERB** ❑ *As she finished each song, the crowd clapped wildly.*

wil|der|ness /wɪldərnɛs/ (**wildernesses**) **NOUN** A **wilderness** is a desert or other area of natural land that is not used by people. ❑ *There will be no wilderness left on the planet within 30 years.*

wild|life /waɪldlaɪf/ **NONCOUNT NOUN** You can use **wildlife** to talk about the animals and other living things that live in nature. ❑ *The area is rich in wildlife.*
→ look at **conservation**

---
will
❶ MODAL VERB USES
❷ NOUN USES
---

❶ will /wɪl/

> **LANGUAGE HELP**
> When you are speaking, you can use the short forms **I'll** for **I will** and **won't** for **will not**.

1 **MODAL VERB** You use **will** to talk about things that are going to happen in the future. ❑ *I'm sure things will get better.* ❑ *The concert will finish at about 10:30 p.m.* ❑ *One day I will come to visit you in Toronto.*
2 **MODAL VERB** You use **will** when you are asking someone to do something. ❑ *Please will you be quiet?*
3 **MODAL VERB** You use **will** when you offer to do something. ❑ *No, don't call a cab. I'll drive you home.*

❷ will /wɪl/ (**wills**)
1 **NOUN** Your **will** is the ability that you have to decide to do something difficult. ❑ *I have a strong will and I'm sure I'll succeed.*
2 **NOUN** A **will** is a legal document that says who will receive your money when you die. ❑ *He left $8 million in his will to the University of Alabama.*

will|ing /wɪlɪŋ/ **ADJECTIVE** If someone is **willing**, they are happy about doing

w

something. ❏ *He was a natural and willing learner.* ❏ *She's willing to answer questions.*
● **willingly** ADVERB ❏ *Bryant talked willingly to the police.* ● **willingness** NONCOUNT NOUN ❏ *She showed her willingness to work hard.*

win /wɪn/ (**wins, winning, won**)
1 VERB SPORTS If you **win** a competition, a fight, or an argument, you do better than everyone else involved. ❏ *He does not have a chance of winning the fight.* ❏ *The four local teams all won their games.*
2 NOUN Win is also a noun. ❏ *They played eight games without a win.*
3 VERB If you **win** a prize, you get it because you have done better than everyone else. ❏ *The first correct entry wins the prize.*
→ look at **play, vote**

Spelling Partners   **wind**

wind

1 AIR
2 TURNING

1 wind /wɪnd/ (**winds**) NOUN SCIENCE Wind is air that moves. ❏ *A strong wind was blowing from the north.*
→ look at **weather, climate, energy**

2 wind /waɪnd/ (**winds, winding, wound**)
1 VERB If a road **winds**, it has a lot of bends in it. ❏ *From here, the river winds through attractive countryside.*
2 VERB When you **wind** something long around something else, you wrap it around several times. ❏ *She wound the rope around her waist.*
3 VERB When you **wind** a clock or a watch, you turn part of it several times in order to make it work. ❏ *Did you remember to wind the clock?*

wind in|stru|ment /wɪnd ɪnstrəmənt/ (**wind instruments**) NOUN MUSIC A **wind instrument** is any musical instrument that you blow into to produce sounds.

wind|mill /wɪndmɪl/ (**windmills**) NOUN A **windmill** is a building with long flat parts on the outside that turn as the wind blows to make machinery move inside. **Windmills** are used for grinding grain or to pump water.

win|dow /wɪndoʊ/ (**windows**)
1 NOUN A **window** is a space in the wall of a building or in the side of a vehicle that has glass in it. ❏ *He looked out of the window.*
2 NOUN TECHNOLOGY On a computer screen, a **window** is one of the work areas that the screen can be divided into. ❏ *Open the document in a new window.*

Word Partners	Use **window** with:
ADJ.	**broken** window, **dark** window, **large** window, **narrow** window, **small** window, **open** window **1**
N.	**car** window, window **curtains**, **kitchen** window, **store** window **1**
V.	**close a** window, **open a** window, **look out a** window **1**

wind|shield /wɪndʃild/ (**windshields**) NOUN The **windshield** of a vehicle is the glass window at the front.

wind|shield wip|er /wɪndʃild waɪpər/ (**windshield wipers**) NOUN A **windshield wiper** is a part that wipes rain from a vehicle's front window.

wind|surf|ing /wɪndsɜrfɪŋ/ NONCOUNT NOUN SPORTS **Windsurfing** is a sport in which you move across water on a long narrow board with a sail on it.

windy /wɪndi/ (**windier, windiest**) ADJECTIVE If it is **windy**, the wind is blowing a lot. ❏ *It was a wet and windy day.*

wine /waɪn/ (**wines**) NOUN **Wine** is an alcoholic drink made from grapes (= small green or purple fruit). ❏ *...a bottle of white wine.*

wing /wɪŋ/ (**wings**)
1 NOUN The **wings** of a bird or an insect are the two parts of its body that it uses for flying. ❏ *The bird flapped its wings.*
2 NOUN The **wings** of an airplane are the long flat parts at the side that support it while it is flying.

wink /wɪŋk/ (**winks, winking, winked**)
1 VERB When you **wink at** someone, you look at them and close one eye quickly, usually as a sign that something is a joke or a secret.
2 NOUN Wink is also a noun. ❏ *I gave her a wink.*

W

win|ner /wɪnər/ (**winners**) **NOUN** The **winner** of a prize, a race, or a competition is the one that wins it. ❑ *She will present the prizes to the winners.*

win|ter /wɪntər/ (**winters**) **NOUN** Winter is the season between fall and spring. In the winter the weather is usually cold. ❑ *In winter the nights are long and cold.*
→ look at **season**

wipe /waɪp/ (**wipes, wiping, wiped**)
1 **VERB** If you **wipe** something, you rub its surface with a cloth to remove dirt or liquid from it. ❑ *I'll just wipe my hands.*
2 **NOUN** Wipe is also a noun. ❑ *The table's dirty – could you give it a wipe, please?*
3 **VERB** If you **wipe** dirt or liquid from something, you remove it by using a cloth or your hand. ❑ *Gary wiped the sweat from his face.*
▶ **wipe out** To **wipe out** something means to destroy it completely. ❑ *The disease wiped out thousands of birds.*

wire /waɪər/ (**wires**) **NOUN** A wire is a long thin piece of metal. ❑ *Eleven birds were sitting on a telephone wire.* ❑ *...a wire fence.*

Word Builder   **wireless**

less ≈ **without**
    care + less = careless
    end + less = endless
    help + less = helpless
    home + less = homeless
    use + less = useless
    wire + less = wireless

---

wire|less /waɪərlɪs/ **ADJECTIVE** Wireless equipment uses radio waves (= a form of power that travels through the air) instead of wires. ❑ *I have a wireless Internet connection for my laptop.*
→ look at **communication**

wis|dom /wɪzdəm/ **NONCOUNT NOUN** Wisdom is the ability to use your experience and knowledge to make sensible decisions or judgments. ❑ *He has the wisdom that comes from old age.*

wise /waɪz/ (**wiser, wisest**) **ADJECTIVE** A wise person is able to use their experience and knowledge to make sensible decisions and judgments. ❑ *She's a wise woman.* ● **wise|ly** **ADVERB** ❑ *They spent their money wisely.*

wish /wɪʃ/ (**wishes, wishing, wished**)
1 **NOUN** If something is your **wish**, you would like it. ❑ *Her wish is to become a doctor.*

2 **VERB** If you **wish** to do something, you want to do it. [FORMAL] ❑ *I wish to leave a message.*
3 **VERB** If you **wish** something were true, you would like it to be true, even though you know that it is impossible or unlikely. ❑ *I wish I could do that.*
4 **VERB** If you **wish for** something, you say in your mind that you want that thing, and then hope that it will happen. ❑ *Every birthday I closed my eyes and wished for a guitar.*
5 **NOUN** Wish is also a noun. ❑ *Did you make a wish?*
6 **VERB** If you **wish** someone luck or happiness, you express the hope that they will be lucky or happy. ❑ *I wish you both a good trip.*
7 **PLURAL NOUN** If you express your good **wishes** toward someone, you are politely expressing your friendly feelings toward them and your hope that they will be successful or happy. ❑ *Please give him my best wishes.*

wit /wɪt/ **NONCOUNT NOUN** Wit is the ability to use words or ideas in an amusing and clever way. ❑ *He writes with great wit.*

witch /wɪtʃ/ (**witches**) **NOUN** In children's stories, a **witch** is a woman who has magic powers that she uses to do bad things.

witch-hunt (**witch-hunts**) **NOUN** SOCIAL STUDIES When people organize a **witch-hunt**, they try to find and punish people that they think have a bad influence on everyone else.

with /wɪð, wɪθ/
1 **PREPOSITION** If one person is **with** another, they are together in one place. ❑ *Her son and daughter were with her.*
2 **PREPOSITION** If you discuss something **with** someone, or if you fight or argue **with** someone, you are both involved in a discussion, a fight, or an argument. ❑ *We didn't discuss it with each other.* ❑ *About a thousand students fought with police.*
3 **PREPOSITION** If you do something **with** a particular tool, object, or substance, you do it using that tool, object, or substance. ❑ *Turn the meat over with a fork.* ❑ *I don't allow my children to eat with their fingers.*
4 **PREPOSITION** If someone stands or goes somewhere **with** something, they are carrying it. ❑ *A woman came in with a cup of coffee.*

w

5 PREPOSITION Someone or something **with** a particular feature or possession has that feature or possession. ❏ *He was tall, with blue eyes.*

with|draw /wɪðdrɔ, wɪθ-/ (**withdraws, withdrawing, withdrew, withdrawn**)

1 VERB If you **withdraw** something from a place, you remove it or take it away. [FORMAL] ❏ *He reached into his pocket and withdrew a sheet of paper.*

2 VERB When groups of people such as troops **withdraw**, they leave the place where they are fighting and return nearer home. ❏ *The army will withdraw as soon as the war ends.*

3 VERB If you **withdraw** money from a bank account, you take it out of that account. ❏ *He withdrew $750 from his account.*

4 VERB If you **withdraw from** an activity or an organization, you stop taking part in it. ❏ *She's the second tennis player to withdraw from the games.*

with|drawn /wɪðdrɔn, wɪθ-/ **Withdrawn** is a form of the verb **withdraw**.

with|drew /wɪðdru, wɪθ-/ **Withdrew** is a form of the verb **withdraw**.

with|in /wɪðɪn, wɪθ-/

1 PREPOSITION If something is **within** a place, area, or object, it is inside it or surrounded by it. [FORMAL] ❏ *The sports fields must be within the city.*

2 PREPOSITION If you are **within** a particular distance of a place, you are less than that distance from it. ❏ *The man was within a few feet of him.*

3 PREPOSITION **Within** a particular length of time means before the end of it. ❏ *Within twenty-four hours I had the money.*

with|out /wɪðaʊt, wɪθ-/

1 PREPOSITION You use **without** to show that someone or something does not have or use the thing mentioned. ❏ *I prefer tea without milk.* ❏ *You shouldn't drive without a seat belt.*

2 PREPOSITION If one thing happens **without** another thing, the second thing does not happen. ❏ *He left without speaking to me.* ❏ *They worked without stopping.*

3 PREPOSITION If you do something **without** someone else, they are not in the same place as you are, or they are not involved in the same action as you. ❏ *I told Frank to start dinner without me.*

wit|ness /wɪtnɪs/ (**witnesses, witnessing, witnessed**)

1 NOUN A **witness** is a person who saw a particular event such as an accident or a crime. ❏ *Witnesses say they saw an explosion.*

2 VERB If you **witness** something, you see it happen. ❏ *Anyone who witnessed the attack should call the police.*

3 NOUN A **witness** is someone who appears in a court of law to say what they know about a crime or other event. ❏ *Eleven witnesses appeared in court.*

wit|ty /wɪti/ (**wittier, wittiest**) ADJECTIVE Someone or something that is **witty** is amusing in a clever way. ❏ *His books were very witty.*

wives /waɪvz/ **Wives** is the plural of **wife**.

wiz|ard /wɪzərd/ (**wizards**) NOUN In children's stories, a **wizard** is a man who has magic powers.

wob|bly /wɒbli/ ADJECTIVE Something that is **wobbly** is not steady and moves from side to side. ❏ *He sat on a wobbly plastic chair.*

woke /woʊk/ **Woke** is a form of the verb **wake**.

wok|en /woʊkən/ **Woken** is a form of the verb **wake**.

wolf /wʊlf/ (**wolves**) NOUN A **wolf** is a wild animal that looks like a large dog.

wom|an /wʊmən/ (**women**) NOUN A **woman** is an adult female human being. ❏ *My favorite woman is my mother.*
→ look at **age**

wom|en /wɪmɪn/ **Women** is the plural of **woman**.

wom|en's room (**women's rooms**) NOUN The **women's room** is a bathroom for women in a public building.

Sound Partners | won, one

won /wʌn/ **Won** is a form of the verb **win**.

won|der /wʌndər/ (**wonders, wondering, wondered**)

1 VERB If you **wonder** about something, you think about it, and try to guess or understand more about it. ❏ *I wondered what the noise was.*

2 NOUN If it is a **wonder that** something happened, it is very surprising and unexpected. ❏ *It's a wonder that we're still friends.*

W

3 NONCOUNT NOUN **Wonder** is a feeling of great surprise and pleasure. ❏ *My eyes opened wide in wonder at the view.*

4 NOUN A **wonder** is something that causes people to feel great surprise or admiration. ❏ *He loved to read about the wonders of nature.*

won|der|ful /wʌndərfəl/ ADJECTIVE If something or someone is **wonderful**, they are extremely good. ❏ *The cold air felt wonderful on his face.* ❏ *It's wonderful to see you.*

won't /wount/ **Won't** is short for "will not." ❏ *I won't hurt you.*

Sound Partners   wood, would

wood /wʊd/ (**woods**)

1 NONCOUNT NOUN **Wood** is the hard material that trees are made of. ❏ *Some houses are made of wood.*

2 NOUN A **wood** or **woods** is a large area of trees growing near each other. ❏ *We went for a walk in the woods.*

wood|en /wʊdᵊn/ ADJECTIVE **Wooden** objects are made of wood. ❏ *She sat in a wooden chair.*

wood|wind /wʊdwɪnd/ NONCOUNT NOUN MUSIC **Woodwind** instruments are the group of musical instruments that are mainly made of wood, that you play by blowing into them.

wool /wʊl/

1 NONCOUNT NOUN **Wool** is the hair that grows on sheep and on some other animals.

2 NONCOUNT NOUN **Wool** is a material made from animal's wool that is used for making things such as clothes. ❏ *The socks are made of wool.*

word /wɜrd/ (**words**)

1 NOUN LANGUAGE ARTS A **word** is a unit of language with meaning. ❏ *The Italian word for "love" is "amore."*

2 NOUN If you have **a word** with someone, you have a short conversation with them. ❏ *Could I have a word with you in my office, please?*

3 NOUN A **word** is something that you say. ❏ *John didn't say a word all the way home.*

4 You say **in other words** before you repeat something in a different way. ❏ *Ray is in charge of the office. In other words, he's my boss.*

5 If you repeat something **word for word**, you say it using exactly the same words. ❏ *I learned the song word for word.*

→ look at **communication, dictionary, grammar, writing**

Word docu|ment (**Word documents**) NOUN TECHNOLOGY A **Word document** is a document that you create on a computer using a program for writing text. [TRADEMARK]

wore /wɔr/ **Wore** is a form of the verb **wear**.

work /wɜrk/ (**works, working, worked**)

1 VERB People who **work** have a job and earn money for it. ❏ *He worked as a teacher for 40 years.* ❏ *I can't talk to you right now—I'm working.*

2 VERB If you **work**, you do an activity that uses a lot of your time or effort. ❏ *You should work harder at school.*

3 VERB If a machine **works**, it operates correctly. ❏ *My cellphone isn't working.*

4 VERB If a way of doing something **works**, it is successful. ❏ *Our plan worked perfectly.*

5 VERB If you **work** a machine, you use or control it. ❏ *Do you know how to work the DVD player?*

6 NONCOUNT NOUN Your **work** is the job that you do to earn money. ❏ *I start work at 8:30 a.m. and finish at 7 p.m.*

7 NONCOUNT NOUN **Work** is the place where you do your job. ❏ *I'm lucky. I can walk to work.*

8 NONCOUNT NOUN **Work** is any activity that uses a lot of your time or effort. ❏ *I did some work in the backyard this weekend.*

9 NOUN A **work** is a painting, a book, or a piece of music that someone has produced. ❏ *My uncle bought me the complete works of William Shakespeare for Christmas.* ❏ *...a work of art.*

→ look at **factory, job**

▶ **work out** **1** If you **work out** a solution to a problem, you discover the solution by thinking. ❏ *It took me some time to work out the answer.*

2 If a situation **works out**, it develops in a way that is good for you. ❏ *I hope everything works out for you in Australia.*

3 If you **work out**, you do physical exercises in order to make your body healthy. ❏ *I work out at a gym twice a week.*

Word Builder   worker

er ≈ **someone who does**
    climb + er = climb**er**
    farm + er = farm**er**
    lead + er = lead**er**
    own + er = own**er**
    play + er = play**er**
    work + er = work**er**

work|er /wɜrkər/ (**workers**)

1 NOUN **Workers** are people who work, who

w

are below the level of a manager. ❑ *His parents were factory workers.*

2 **NOUN** You can use **worker** to say how well or badly someone works. ❑ *He is a hard worker.*
→ look at **factory**

work|force /wɜrkfɔrs/ (**workforces**)
1 **NOUN** The **workforce** is the total number of people in a country or region who are able to do a job and who are available for work. ❑ *Half the workforce is unemployed.*
2 **NOUN** The **workforce** is the total number of people who are employed by a particular company. ❑ *The company employs of a very large workforce.*

work|out /wɜrkaʊt/ (**workouts**) **NOUN**
A **workout** is a period of physical exercise or training. ❑ *She does a 35-minute workout every day.*
→ look at **fitness**

work|place /wɜrkpleɪs/ (**workplaces**) also **work place** **NOUN** Your **workplace** is the place where you work. ❑ *This new law will make the workplace safer for everyone.*

work|shop /wɜrkʃɒp/ (**workshops**)
1 **NOUN** A **workshop** is a time when people share their knowledge or experience on a particular subject. ❑ *A music workshop for beginners will be held in the town hall.*
2 **NOUN** A **workshop** is a place where people make or repair things. ❑ *He works as a mechanic in the workshop.*

work|station /wɜrksteɪʃ°n/ (**workstations**) also **work station**
1 **NOUN** Your **workstation** is the desk and computer that you sit at when you are at work.
2 **NOUN** A **workstation** is a screen and keyboard that are part of an office computer system.
→ look at **office**

world /wɜrld/ (**worlds**) **NOUN** GEOGRAPHY
The **world** is the planet that we live on.
→ look at **earth, history**

Word Partners	Use **world** with:
PREP.	**all over the** world, **anywhere in the** world, **around the** world
N.	world **history**, world **peace**, world **premiere**, world **record**
V.	**travel the** world

world|wide /wɜrldwaɪd/
1 **ADVERB** If something exists or happens **worldwide**, it exists or happens throughout the world. ❑ *His books have sold more than 20 million copies worldwide.*

2 **ADJECTIVE** **Worldwide** is also an adjective. ❑ *They made $20 billion in worldwide sales last year.*

World Wide Web **NOUN** TECHNOLOGY The **World Wide Web** is a computer system that allows you to see information from all over the world on your computer. The short forms **WWW** and the **Web** are often used.
→ look at **Internet**

worm /wɜrm/ (**worms**) **NOUN** A **worm** is a small animal with a long thin body, no bones, and no legs.

worn /wɔrn/
1 **Worn** is a form of the verb **wear**.
2 **ADJECTIVE** **Worn** describes something that is damaged or thin because it is old and you have used it a lot. ❑ *There was a worn blue carpet on the floor.*

wor|ry /wɜri, wʌri/ (**worries, worrying, worried**)
1 **VERB** If you **worry**, you keep thinking about problems that you have or about unpleasant things that might happen. ❑ *Don't worry, I'm sure he'll be fine.* ❑ *I worry about her all the time.* ❑ *They worry that he works too hard.* ● **wor|ried** **ADJECTIVE** ❑ *He seemed very worried.*
2 **VERB** If someone or something **worries** you, they make you anxious because you keep thinking about problems or unpleasant things that might be connected with them. ❑ *"Why didn't you tell us?"—"I didn't want to worry you."*
3 **NONCOUNT NOUN** **Worry** is the state or feeling of anxiety and unhappiness caused by the problems that you have or by thinking about unpleasant things that might happen. ❑ *Modern life is full of worry.*
4 **NOUN** A **worry** is a problem that you keep thinking about and that makes you unhappy. ❑ *My parents had a lot of worries.*
→ look at **feeling**

worse /wɜrs/
1 **Worse** is a form of the adjective **bad**.
2 **Worse** is a form of the adverb **badly**.
3 If a situation changes **for the worse**, it becomes more unpleasant or more difficult. ❑ *My luck changed for the worse.*

wor|ship /wɜrʃɪp/ (**worships, worshiping, worshiped**)
1 **VERB** If you **worship**, you show your respect to God or a god, for example, by

saying prayers. ❑ *He likes to worship in his own home.* ❑ *We talked about different ways of worshiping God.*

2 **NONCOUNT NOUN** **Worship** is also a noun. ❑ *This was his family's place of worship.*

3 **VERB** If you **worship** someone or something, you love them or admire them very much. ❑ *She worshiped him for many years.*

worst /wɜrst/

1 **Worst** is the superlative of **bad**.

2 **Worst** is the superlative of **badly**.

3 **NOUN** The **worst** is the most unpleasant thing that could happen or does happen. ❑ *Many people still fear the worst.*

worth /wɜrθ/

1 **VERB** If something is **worth** a particular amount of money, you can sell it for that amount or you think that it has that value. ❑ *The picture is worth $500.*

2 If you talk about a particular amount of money**'s worth of** something, you mean how much of it that you can buy for that amount of money. ❑ *I went and bought six dollars' worth of potato chips.*

3 **VERB** If something is **worth** having, it is pleasant or useful, and a good thing to have. ❑ *He decided to see if the house was worth buying.*

worth|less /wɜrθlɪs/ **ADJECTIVE** Something that is **worthless** has no value or use. ❑ *He had nothing but a worthless piece of paper.*

worth|while /wɜrθwaɪl/ **ADJECTIVE** If something is **worthwhile**, it is enjoyable or useful, and worth the time, money, or effort that you spend on it. ❑ *The president's trip was worthwhile.*

Sound Partners	would, wood

would /wəd, STRONG wʊd/

1 **MODAL VERB** You use **would**, usually in questions with "like," when you are making a polite offer or invitation. ❑ *Would you like a drink?*

2 **MODAL VERB** You use **would** with "if" clauses. ❑ *If I had more money, I would go traveling.* ❑ *Would it be all right if I opened a window?*

3 **MODAL VERB** You use **would** when you are saying what someone believed, hoped, or expected to happen. ❑ *We all hoped you would come.*

4 **MODAL VERB** You use **would** to say that someone was willing to do something. You

use **would not** to say that they refused to do something. ❑ *He said he would help her.* ❑ *She wouldn't say where she bought her shoes.*

5 **MODAL VERB** You use **would** to talk about something that someone often did in the past. ❑ *He would sit by the window, watching people go by.*

wouldn't /wʊdᵊnt/ **Wouldn't** is short for "would not." ❑ *My parents wouldn't allow me to stay up late.*

would've /wʊdəv/ **Would've** is short for "would have." ❑ *I would've loved to go to the concert.*

wound /wund/ (**wounds, wounding, wounded**)

> **PRONUNCIATION HELP**
> Pronounce /waʊnd/ for meaning **1**.

1 **Wound** is a form of the verb **wind**.

2 **NOUN** A **wound** is damage to part of your body caused by a gun or something sharp like a knife. ❑ *The wound is healing nicely.*

3 **VERB** If a weapon or something sharp **wounds** you, it damages your body. ❑ *He killed one man with a knife and wounded five other people.*

wow /waʊ/ **EXCLAMATION** You can say "**wow**" when you think something is very good or surprising. [INFORMAL] ❑ *I thought, "Wow, what a good idea."*

wrap /ræp/ (**wraps, wrapping, wrapped**)

1 **VERB** When you **wrap** something, you fold paper or cloth tightly around it to cover it.

2 **Wrap up** means the same as **wrap**. ❑ *Diana is wrapping up the presents.*

3 **VERB** When you **wrap** a piece of paper or cloth around another thing, you put it around it. ❑ *She wrapped a cloth around her hand.*

wrap|per /ræpər/ (**wrappers**) **NOUN** A **wrapper** is a piece of paper or plastic that covers something that you buy, especially food. ❑ *There were candy wrappers on the floor.*

wreck /rɛk/ (**wrecks, wrecking, wrecked**)

1 **VERB** To **wreck** something means to completely destroy or ruin it. ❑ *The storm wrecked the garden.*

2 **NOUN** A **wreck** is a ship, a car, a plane, or a building that has been destroyed, usually in an accident. ❑ *They discovered the wreck of a sailing ship.*

w

wrench /rɛntʃ/ (**wrenches**) **NOUN** A **wrench** is a metal tool that you use for turning small pieces of metal (= nuts) to make them tighter.

wres|tle /rɛsəl/ (**wrestles, wrestling, wrestled**) **VERB** SPORTS If you **wrestle** with someone, you fight them by trying to throw them to the ground. Some people wrestle as a sport. ❏ *My father taught me to wrestle.*

wrin|kle /rɪŋkəl/ (**wrinkles, wrinkling, wrinkled**)

1 **NOUN** **Wrinkles** are lines that form on your face as you grow old.

2 **VERB** If cloth **wrinkles**, it gets folds or lines in it. ❏ *Her stockings wrinkled at the ankles.*

● **wrin|kled** **ADJECTIVE** ❏ *His suit was wrinkled and he looked very tired.*

→ look at **laundry**

wrist /rɪst/ (**wrists**) **NOUN** Your **wrist** is the part between your hand and your arm that bends when you move your hand. ❏ *She fell over and broke her wrist.*

→ look at **body, hand**

| **Sound Partners** | write, right |

write /raɪt/ (**writes, writing, wrote, written**)

1 **VERB** When you **write**, you use a pen or a pencil to produce words, letters, or numbers. ❏ *Write your name and address on a postcard and send it to us.* ❏ *I'm teaching her to read and write.*

2 **VERB** LANGUAGE ARTS If you **write** a book, a poem, or a piece of music, you create it. ❏ *She wrote articles for French newspapers.*

3 **VERB** When you **write to** someone you give them information, ask them something, or express your feelings in a letter or an email. ❏ *She wrote to her aunt asking for help.* ❏ *I wrote a letter to the manager.*

→ look at **communication, language, music, writing**

▶ **write down** When you **write** something **down**, you record it on a piece of paper using a pen or pencil. ❏ *I wrote down what I thought was good about the program.*

writ|er /raɪtər/ (**writers**) **NOUN** LANGUAGE ARTS A **writer** is a person whose job is to write books, stories, or articles. ❏ *She enjoys reading detective stories by American writers.*

writ|ing /raɪtɪŋ/

1 **NONCOUNT NOUN** **Writing** is something that has been written or printed. ❏ *Joe tried to read the writing on the next page.*

2 **NONCOUNT NOUN** LANGUAGE ARTS You can call any piece of written work **writing**, especially when you are considering the style of language used in it. ❏ *The writing is very funny.*

3 **NONCOUNT NOUN** LANGUAGE ARTS **Writing** is the activity of writing, especially of writing books for money. ❏ *She was bored with writing books about the same thing.*

4 **NONCOUNT NOUN** Your **writing** is the way that you write with a pen or pencil. ❏ *It's difficult to read your writing.*

→ look at Word World: **writing**

writ|ten /rɪtən/ **Written** is a form of the verb **write**.

→ look at **communication**

wrong /rɔŋ/

1 **ADJECTIVE** If there is something **wrong**, there is something that is not as it should be. ❏ *Pain is the body's way of telling us that something is wrong.* ❏ *What's wrong with him?*

2 **ADJECTIVE** If you choose the **wrong** thing, person, or method, you make a mistake and do not choose the one that you really want. ❏ *He went to the wrong house.*

3 **ADJECTIVE** If a decision is **the wrong** one, it is not the best or most suitable one. ❏ *I made the wrong decision.*

4 **ADJECTIVE** If something is **wrong**, it is not correct. ❏ *I did not know if Mark's answer was right or wrong.*

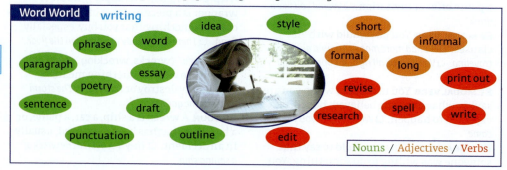

Word World   **writing**

idea — style — short — informal — phrase — word — formal — long — paragraph — essay — poetry — revise — print out — sentence — draft — research — spell — write — punctuation — outline — edit

Nouns / Adjectives / Verbs

W

5 **ADVERB** Wrong is also an adverb. ❑ *I must have added it up wrong.* ● **wrong|ly** **ADVERB** ❑ *He is an innocent man who was wrongly accused of stealing.*

6 **ADJECTIVE** If you are **wrong** about something, what you say or think about it is not correct. ❑ *I was wrong about the time of the meeting.*

7 **ADJECTIVE** If you say that something someone does is **wrong**, you mean that it is bad. ❑ *She was wrong to leave her child alone.*

8 **NONCOUNT NOUN** Wrong describes activities or actions that are considered to be morally bad. ❑ *He can't tell the difference between right and wrong.*

9 If a situation **goes wrong**, it stops progressing in the way that you expected or intended, and becomes much worse. ❑ *We will do everything to make sure that nothing goes wrong.*

wrote /roʊt/ **Wrote** is a form of the verb **write**.

WWW /dʌbᵊlyu dʌbᵊlyu dʌbᵊlyu/ TECHNOLOGY WWW is short for **World Wide Web**. It appears at the beginning of website addresses in the form **www**. ❑ *Check our website at www.collinslanguage.com.*

w

Xx

X-ray (**X-rays, X-raying, X-rayed**) also **x-ray**
1 **NOUN** SCIENCE An **X-ray** is a picture that is made by sending a special type of light through something, usually someone's body. ❑ *She had a chest X-ray at the hospital.*
2 **VERB** If someone or something **is**

X-rayed, an X-ray picture is taken of them.
❑ *All hand baggage must be x-rayed.*

xy|lo|phone /zaɪləfoʊn/ (**xylophones**) **NOUN**
MUSIC A **xylophone** is a musical instrument with a row of wooden bars of different lengths that you play with special hammers.
→ look at **musical instrument**

Yy

yacht /yɒt/ (yachts) **NOUN** A **yacht** is a large boat with sails or a motor, used for racing or for pleasure trips.

yam /yæm/ (yams) **NOUN** A **yam** is a vegetable that is similar to a sweet potato. ❑ *Peel and boil the yams, and then mash them.*

yank /yæŋk/ (yanks, yanking, yanked)
1 **VERB** If you **yank** someone or something, you pull them hard. ❑ *She yanked open the drawer.*
2 **NOUN** Yank is also a noun. ❑ *Shirley grabbed the rope and gave it a yank.*

Yan|kee /yæŋki/ (Yankees)
1 **NOUN** A **Yankee** is a person from the north or north-east of the United States.
2 **NOUN** Sometimes people use **Yankee** to talk about anyone from the United States of America.

yard /yɑrd/ (yards)
1 **NOUN** A **yard** is a unit for measuring length. There are 91.4 centimeters in a yard. ❑ *The bomb exploded 500 yards from where he was standing.*
2 **NOUN** A **yard** is a piece of land next to a house, with grass and plants growing in it.
→ look at **measurement**

yard|stick /yɑrdstɪk/ (yardsticks) **NOUN** A **yardstick** is a stick that is one yard (= 36 inches) long, that is used for measuring things.

yarn /yɑrn/ **NONCOUNT NOUN** Yarn is thick cotton or wool thread. ❑ *She brought me a bag of yarn and some knitting needles.*

yawn /yɔn/ (yawns, yawning, yawned)
1 **VERB** If you **yawn**, you open your mouth very wide and breathe in more air than usual because you are tired. ❑ *She yawned, and stretched lazily.*
2 **NOUN** Yawn is also a noun. ❑ *Sophia woke and gave a huge yawn.*

yeah /yɛə/ Yeah means yes. [INFORMAL]
❑ *"Don't forget your library book."—"Oh, yeah."*
❑ *"Anybody want my ice cream?"—"Um, yeah sure."*

year /yɪər/ (years)
1 **NOUN** A **year** is a period of twelve months, beginning on the first of January and ending on the thirty-first of December. ❑ *The year was 1840.* ❑ *We had an election last year.*
2 **NOUN** A **year** is any period of twelve months. ❑ *Graceland has more than 650,000 visitors a year.*
3 **PLURAL NOUN** You use **years** to talk about a long time. ❑ *I lived here years ago.*
4 If something happens **all year round**, it happens for the whole year. ❑ *The hotel is open all year round.*
→ look at **calendar**

year|ly /yɪərli/
1 **ADJECTIVE** A **yearly** event happens once a year or every year. ❑ *The company dinner is a yearly event.*
2 **ADVERB** Yearly is also an adverb. ❑ *Students may pay fees yearly or by semester.*

yeast /yist/ **NONCOUNT NOUN** Yeast is the substance that makes bread rise. ❑ *Add the yeast to the flour in the bowl.*

yell /yɛl/ (yells, yelling, yelled)
1 **VERB** If you **yell**, you shout loudly. ❑ *"Eva!" he yelled.*
2 **NOUN** A **yell** is a loud shout. ❑ *I heard a yell and the sound of something falling.*

yel|low /yɛlou/
1 **ADJECTIVE** Something that is **yellow** is the color of lemons or butter. ❑ *She was wearing a yellow dress.*
2 **NOUN** Yellow is also a noun. ❑ *Her favorite color is yellow.*
→ look at **color**

Yel|low Pages **NOUN** The **Yellow Pages** is a book that has the telephone numbers for businesses and organizations in a particular area. [TRADEMARK] ❑ *I looked for a plumber in the Yellow Pages.*

yes /yɛs/
1 You use **yes** to give a positive answer to a question. ❑ *"Are you a friend of Nick's?"—"Yes."*
2 You use **yes** to accept an offer or a request, or to give permission. ❑ *"More coffee?"—"Yes please."*

yes|ter|day /yɛstərdeɪ, -di/

1 **ADVERB** You use **yesterday** to talk about the day before today. ❏ *She left yesterday.*

2 **NONCOUNT NOUN** Yesterday is also a noun. ❏ *In yesterday's game, the Cowboys were the winners.*

→ look at **day**

yet /yɛt/

1 **ADVERB** You use **yet** when something has not happened up to the present time, although it probably will happen. ❏ *They haven't finished yet.* ❏ *They haven't yet set a date for their wedding.*

2 **ADVERB** You can use **yet** in questions to ask if something has happened before the present time. ❏ *Have they finished yet?*

3 **ADVERB** If something should not or cannot be done **yet**, it should not or cannot be done now, although it will have to be done at a later time. ❏ *Don't get up yet.* ❏ *You can't go home just yet.*

4 **CONJUNCTION** You can use **yet** to add a fact that is surprising. ❏ *He's a champion tennis player yet he is very modest.*

yield /yiːld/ (yields, yielding, yielded)

1 **VERB** If fields, trees or plants **yield** crops, fruit or vegetables, they produce them. ❏ *Each tree yields about 40 pounds of apples.*

2 **VERB** If you **yield**, you finally agree to do what someone wants you to do. ❏ *Finally, he yielded to his parents' demands.*

3 **VERB** If a driver **yields**, they slow down or stop in order to allow people or other vehicles to pass in front of them. ❏ *Drivers must yield to buses.*

yoga /yoʊgə/ **NONCOUNT NOUN** **SPORTS** Yoga
is a type of exercise in which you move your body into various positions in order to become more fit, and to relax your body and your mind. ❏ *I do yoga twice a week.*

→ look at **fitness, relax**

yo|gurt /yoʊgərt/ (yogurts) also yoghurt
NOUN Yogurt is a thick liquid food that is made from milk. ❏ *Frozen yogurt is $2 per cup.*

yolk /yoʊk/ (yolks) **NOUN**
The **yolk** of an egg is the yellow part in the middle. ❏ *Only the yolk contains cholesterol.*

you /yu/

1 **PRONOUN** A speaker or writer uses **you** when they mean the person or people that

they are talking to or writing to. ❏ *Hurry up! You are really late.* ❏ *I'll call you tonight.*

2 **PRONOUN** In spoken English and informal written English, **you** can sometimes mean people in general. ❏ *Getting good results gives you confidence.* ❏ *In those days you did what you were told.*

you'd /yud, STRONG yud/

1 **You'd** is short for "you had." ❏ *I think you'd better tell us what you want.*

2 **You'd** is short for "you would." ❏ *You'd look good in red.*

you'll /yul, STRONG yul/ **You'll** is short for
"you will." ❏ *Promise me you'll take care of yourself.*

young /yʌŋ/ (younger /yʌŋgər/, youngest /yʌŋgɪst/)

1 **ADJECTIVE** A **young** person, animal, or plant has not lived for very long. ❏ *There is plenty of information on this for young people.* ❏ *...a field of young corn.*

2 **PLURAL NOUN** The **young** are people who are young. ❏ *Everyone from the young to the elderly can enjoy yoga.*

3 **PLURAL NOUN** An animal's **young** are its babies. ❏ *You can watch birds feed their young with this wireless camera.*

→ look at **age**

young|ster /yʌŋstər/ (youngsters) **NOUN**
Youngsters are young people, especially children. ❏ *The children's club will keep the youngsters occupied.*

your /yɔr, yʊər/

1 **ADJECTIVE** You use **your** to show that something belongs or relates to the person or people that you are talking or writing to. ❏ *Are you taller than your brother?* ❏ *I left your newspaper on your desk.*

2 **ADJECTIVE** You can use **your** to show that something belongs to or relates to people in general. ❏ *You should always wash your hands after touching raw meat.*

you're /yɔr, yʊər/ **You're** is short for "you
are." ❏ *Tell him you're sorry.*

yours /yɔrz, yʊərz/

1 **PRONOUN** You use **yours** when you mean something that belongs or relates to the person or people that they are talking to. ❏ *I believe Paul is a friend of yours.*

2 People write **yours**, **yours sincerely**, or **yours truly** at the end of a letter before they sign their name. ❏ *I hope to see you soon. Yours truly, George.*

Y

your|self /yɔrsɛlf, yʊər-, yər-/ (**yourselves**)

1 **PRONOUN** A speaker or writer uses **yourself** to mean the person that they are talking or writing to. ❑ *Be careful with that knife - you might cut yourself.*

2 **PRONOUN** You use **yourself** to make "you" stronger. ❑ *You don't know anything about it—you said so yourself.*

3 **PRONOUN** If you do something **yourself** or **by yourself**, you, and not anyone else, does it. ❑ *Don't do all of that yourself – let me help you.*

youth /yuθ/ (**youths** /yuðz/)

1 **NONCOUNT NOUN** Someone's **youth** is the period of their life when they are a child, before they become an adult. ❑ *In my youth, my ambition was to be a dancer.*

2 **NONCOUNT NOUN** **Youth** is the quality or state of being young. ❑ *Youth is not an excuse for bad behavior.*

3 **NOUN** A **youth** is a young man.

❑ *A 17-year-old youth was arrested yesterday.*

4 **PLURAL NOUN** The **youth** are young people when they are considered as a group. ❑ *The youth of today are just as caring as we were.*

Word Partners	Use **youth** with:
N.	youth **center**, youth **culture**, youth **groups**, youth **organizations**, youth **programs**, youth **services** **4**

you've /yuv/ **You've** is short for "you have." ❑ *You've got to see it to believe it.*

yo-yo /joʊ joʊ/ (**yo-yos**)
NOUN A **yo-yo** is a round wooden or plastic toy that you hold in your hand. You make it go up and down on a piece of string.

yup /jʌp/ **Yup** is a very informal word for **yes**. ❑ *"Are you ready to leave?"—"Yup!"*

Zz

zeb|ra /zíbrə/ (**zebras** or **zebra**) **NOUN**
A **zebra** is a wild horse with black and white stripes that lives in Africa.
→ look at **animal**

zero /zíərou/ (**zeros** or **zeroes**)
1 **Zero** is the number 0.
2 **NONCOUNT NOUN** SCIENCE **Zero** is a temperature of 0° C, at which water freezes.
❑ ...*a few degrees above zero*.

zig|zag /zígzæg/ (**zigzags**) also **zig-zag**
NOUN A **zigzag** is a line that has angles in it like a series of Ws.

zinc /zíŋk/ **NONCOUNT NOUN** SCIENCE **Zinc** is a blue-white metal.

zip /zíp/ (**zips, zipping, zipped**) **VERB** When you **zip** a computer file, you use a special program to reduce its size so that it is easier to send it to someone using the Internet.
❑ *This is how to zip files so that you can send them via email.* TECHNOLOGY
▶ **zip up** If you **zip up** a piece of clothing, you fasten it using its zipper. ❑ *He zipped up his jeans.*

zip code (**zip codes**) **NOUN** Your **zip code** is a short series of numbers at the end of your address that helps the post office to sort the mail.

zip|per /zípər/ (**zippers**) **NOUN**
A **zipper** is a part of a piece of clothing or a bag that has two rows of metal or plastic teeth with a small part that you use to open and close it.

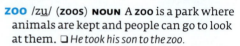

zone /zóun/ (**zones**) **NOUN**
A **zone** is an area where something particular happens. ❑ *The area is a disaster zone.*

zoo /zú/ (**zoos**) **NOUN** A **zoo** is a park where animals are kept and people can go to look at them. ❑ *He took his son to the zoo.*

zoom /zúm/ (**zooms, zooming, zoomed**)
VERB If you **zoom** somewhere, you go there very quickly. [INFORMAL] ❑ *Trucks zoomed past at 70 miles per hour.*

zuc|chi|ni /zukíni/ (**zucchini** or **zucchinis**)
NOUN **Zucchini** are long thin vegetables with a dark green skin.

LIST OF VOCABULARY BUILDERS

Picture Dictionary
age
animals
answer
area
ATM
bags
bathroom
beach
birds
body
bread
chores
city
classroom
clothing
color
computer
containers
cook
draw
face
family
farm
foot
fractions
fruit
furniture
globe
hair
hand
house
kitchen
landforms
location
measurements
musical instruments
natural disasters
numbers
office
payments
plants
punctuation
restaurant
river
shellfish
space
time
transportation
vegetable
weather

Sound Partners
ate
bare
be
bear
beat

bee
beet
blew
blue
brake
break
buy
by
bye
cell
cent
cereal
dear
deer
dew
do
due
eight
flour
flower
for
four
heal
hear
heel
here
hole
hour
know
meat
meet
no
one
our
peace
piece
poor
pour
right
role
roll
sail
sale
scent
sea
see
sell
sent
serial
some
son
sum
sun
tail
tale
to
too
two

waist
wait
waste
way
weak
wear
week
weigh
weight
where
whole
won
wood
would
write

Spelling Partners
back
bank
base
beam
block
bow
box
check
chip
close
deck
foot
glass
hood
horn
iron
jam
key
letter
light
line
match
mole
pitcher
seal
shower
sign
spring
tear
wave
wind

Usage
a
an
at
aunt
both
Celsius
dot
each
even

Fahrenheit
female
for
girl
its
many
minus
much
o'clock
plus
shall
short
their
times
to
URL

Word Builders
accountant
airport
artist
assistant
attendant
careful
careless
championship
cleaner
climber
colorful
comfortable
consultant
container
contestant
dependable
disagree
disappear
disconnect
dishonest
disobey
disorganized
downhill
download
downloadable
downstairs
dryer
eighteen
enable
endless
enjoy
enjoyable
enlarge
ensure
export
farmer
fourteen
friendship
guitarist
helpful

helpless
homeless
honorable
hopeful
immature
impatient
imperfect
import
impossible
inbox
incomplete
incorrect
independent
indirect
indoors
inland
input
insecure
inside
invisible
irrational
irregular
irrelevant
irresponsible
journalist
leader
leadership
membership
misbehavior
misfortune
mislead
misspell
mistrust
misunderstand
nineteen
nonfat
nonfiction
nonsense
nonstop
novelist
opener
overcrowded
overdue
overflow
overheat
oversleep
overweight
owner
ownership
player
portable
printer
recycle
refresh
relationship
rethink
review
rewrite

seventeen
sixteen
stressful
sundown
teenage
toaster
transport
unable
uncover
undo
undress
unfair
unfold
unhappy
unhealthy
unlike
unsafe
useful
useless
wireless
worker

Word Partners
accident
account
address
advice
afford
another
application
baby
ball
beach
bed
bill
bottom
break
business
button
buy
call
careful
catch
chance
change
charity
check
close
cold
correct
dance
decision
diet
empty
environment
experiment
finish
follow

forget
freedom
friend
future
goal
hair
healthy
home
house
idea
information
laboratory
land
learn
lie
meal
memory
mistake
nervous
news
next
note
obvious
opportunity
outside
paper
popular
prepare
process
question
quiet
rate
read
reason
refuse
regular
remember
routine
safe
sea
sign
speak
step
surface
technology
temperature
thick
thin
tough
traffic
unable
urgent
violent
visit
wage
wait
walk
warm

watch
weather
weight
window
world
youth

Word Worlds
calendar
car
climate
communication
conservation
day
dictionary
disability
earth
eat
e-mail
energy
factory
feeling
fitness
food
geometry
grammar
greenhouse effect
health care
history
identification
internet
job
language
laundry
math
meat
movie
music
news
ocean
performance
phone
play
pollution
relax
route
school
science
seasons
senses
shopping
sick
television
tree
vote
water
wear
writing

LIST OF HEADWORDS BY SUBJECT AREA

Arts

abstract
acrylic
act
acting
actor
actress
aesthetic
animation
art
art gallery
artist
background
ballet
canvas
carve
ceramic
chalk
charcoal
classic
clay
collage
costume
culture
dance
dancer
design
designer
director
drama
draw
drawing
easel
exhibit
exhibition
festival
film
fine art
folk
foreground
gallery
graphics
landscape
marble
masterpiece
media
medium
mime
model
mosaic
multimedia
museum
nude
oil painting
paint
painter
painting
pastel

pattern
pencil
perspective
photograph
photography
picture
play
portrait
pottery
primary color
proportion
rehearsal
rehearse
relief
sculptor
sculpture
sketch
statue
studio
subject
texture
theater
three-dimensional
two-dimensional
watercolor

Geography

altitude
atlas
bay
canal
capital
channel
coast
coastline
compass
continent
country
desert
earth
east
easterly
eastern
equator
equatorial
forest
geography
globe
gulf
hemisphere
hill
island
lake
land
landform
latitude
longitude
map

mountain
mouth
north
northeast
northeastern
northerly
northern
northwest
northwestern
oasis
ocean
peninsula
plateau
polar
pole
port
prairie
rainforest
region
reservoir
ridge
river
shore
south
southeast
southeastern
southerly
southern
southwest
southwestern
time zone
tropical
valley
village
west
westerly
western
world

Language Arts

abbreviation
accent
acknowledgment
active
acute accent
adjective
adverb
alphabet
antonym
apostrophe
appendix
article
author
autobiography
auxiliary
biography
book
bracket

capital
chapter
character
clause
colon
comedy
comma
comparative
compound
conclusion
conditional
conjunction
consonant
continuous
contraction
count
count noun
dash
definite article
definition
dialogue
dictionary
direct object
draft
drama
emphasis
English
epic
epilogue
essay
exclamation point
fable
fairytale
feminine
fiction
foreword
form
future tense
glossary
grammar
grammatical
hero
heroine
hyphen
idiom
imperative
indefinite article
index
indirect object
infinitive
intransitive
introduction
irony
irregular
journal
language
legend
letter

literature	satire	division	ninety
lowercase	scene	eight	ninth
main clause	script	eighteen	number
masculine	semicolon	eighth	numeral
metaphor	sentence	eighty	oblong
modal	simile	eleven	odd
moral	singular	equal	one
mystery	slash	equal sign	ounce
myth	speech marks	equation	oz.
narrator	spell	even	parallel
negative	story	fifteen	pentagon
noncount noun	stress	fifth	percent
nonfiction	subject	fifty	percentage
noun	summary	figure	perimeter
novel	superlative	five	plus
novelist	syllable	formula	positive
object	symbol	forty	power
paragraph	synonym	four	probability
parody	tense	fourteen	pyramid
participle	title	fourth	qt.
part of speech	tragedy	fraction	quart
passage	uppercase	gallon	quarter
passive	verb	geometry	radius
past tense	verse	gram	ratio
perfect tense	vocabulary	graph	rectangle
period	vowel	half	right angle
phrasal verb	word	hemisphere	ruler
phrase	write	hexagon	second
playwright	writer	hundred	semicircle
plot	writing	inch	seven
plural		kg	seventeen
poem		kilo	seventh
poet	**Math**	kilogram	seventy
poetry	acute angle	kilometer	six
possessive	add	km	sixteen
preface	addition	lb.	sixth
prefix	algebra	liter	sixty
preposition	angle	math	solve
present continuous	area	mathematical	square
present perfect	arithmetic	mathematics	square root
present tense	average	mean	subtract
prologue	axis	median	sum
pronoun	calculate	meter	ten
pronunciation	calculation	metric	tenth
proper noun	circle	mg	third
prose	circumference	mile	thirteen
punctuation	cone	milligram	thirty
punctuation mark	cube	milliliter	thousand
question mark	cubic	millimeter	three
quotation	cylinder	million	time
quotation mark	decimal	minus	ton
read	decimal point	ml	triangle
reader	degree	mm	twelfth
reflexive pronoun	diagonal	mph	twelve
reflexive verb	diameter	multiply	twenty
regular	digit	negative	two
rhyme	dimension	nine	unit
romance	divide	nineteen	volume

Music

accompany
accordion
band
banjo
bass
bassoon
baton
beat
blue
bow
brass
carol
cello
choir
chord
chorus
clarinet
classical
compose
composer
composition
concert
conduct
conductor
cymbal
double bass
drum
duet
duo
flat
flute
folk music
French horn
gospel
guitar
guitarist
harmony
harp
hip-hop
horn
hymn
instrument
instrumental
jazz
key
keyboard
lyrics
major
melody
minor
music
musical
musical instrument
musician
note
oboe
octave

opera
orchestra
organ
percussion
pianist
piano
piccolo
play
player
quartet
rap
recorder
reggae
rhythm
rock and roll
saxophone
scale
sharp
sing
singer
solo
song
soprano
soul
soul music
string
stringed instrument
symphony
tambourine
trio
trombone
trumpet
tuba
tune
viola
violin
wind instrument
woodwind
xylophone

Science

abdomen
absorb
acid
air
air pollution
alkali
animal
antenna
anus
appendix
artery
astronaut
astronomy
atmosphere
atom
atomic
attract

avalanche
axis
backbone
bacteria
bark
beach
beam
biceps
big bang theory
biological
bladder
blood
blood vessel
boiling point
bone
botany
bowel
brain
breast
breathe
breed
bud
bulb
calorie
canyon
cape
carbohydrate
carbon dioxide
carbon monoxide
cardio-
carnivore
cave
cell
Celsius
Centrifugal force
charge
chemical
chemist
chemistry
chest
cholesterol
chromosome
circuit
circulation
cliff
climate
coast
coastline
cocoon
collarbone
colon
comet
compound
conduct
conservation
core
crater
crystal

current
cycle
degree
dense
density
dental
desert
digest
dilute
dissect
dissolve
drug
dune
eardrum
earth
earthquake
echo
eclipse
ecology
ecosystem
electric
electricity
element
embryo
endangered species
energy
environment
erupt
esophagus
evaporate
evolution
evolve
experiment
extinct
eyeball
Fahrenheit
fault
female
fertile
fetus
filter
fir
food chain
force
formation
formula
fossil
fossil fuel
freeze
frequency
fungus
galaxy
gas
gene
genetic
genetically modified
genetics
genus

geology
glacier
global warming
gram
gravity
greenhouse effect
greenhouse gas
gum
gut
habitat
hail
heart
heartbeat
helium
herbivore
hibernation
hill
hormone
human being
hurricane
hybrid
iceberg
insulate
invertebrate
iris
island
jaw
joint
kg
kHz
kidney
kilo
kilogram
kilohertz
kilowatt
kW
lab
laboratory
lake
landform
laser
lava
lens
lifecycle
light
lightning
liter
liquid
live
liver
lung
magnet
magnetic
male
mammal
marsh
mass
mate

melting point
mercury
meteor
metric
metric ton
mg
microbe
microscope
milligram
milk
mineral
mix
ml
molecule
monsoon
moon
mountain
mouth
muscle
nature
nerve
nostril
nuclear
nucleus
nutrient
omnivore
orbit
organ
organic
organism
oxygen
ozone layer
pelvis
photosynthesis
physics
planet
plant
pollen
power
predator
pressure
prey
psychology
pulse
radar
radiation
radio wave
rain
rainfall
ray
reef
reproduce
respiration
rib
ribcage
ridge
river
rock

saliva
sand
scale
scalp
skeleton
skin
skull
sodium
soil
solar
solid
source
space
spacecraft
spaceship
space shuttle
species
specimen
speed
spine
star
stomach
stream
sun
test tube
thigh
throat
tide
tissue
tongue
tornado
tsunami
tumor
universe
uterus
vacuum
vapor
vertebrate
volcano
volt
waterfall
watt
wave
wavelength
weather
wind
X-ray
zero
zinc

Social Studies
abolitionist
AD
amendment
American
ancestor
archeology
assassinate

BC
bill
Bill of Rights
border
boycott
cabinet
capitalism
capitalist
capitol
carpetbagger
cavalry
cease-fire
census
charter
circumnavigate
citizen
civilization
civil rights
civil war
classic
Cold War
colony
commonwealth
communism
Congress
congressman
congresswoman
conquer
constituency
constituent
constitution
country
crown
culture
currency
Declaration of
    Independence
delegate
democracy
democrat
democratic
depression
descendant
dictator
discriminate
discrimination
eastern
economics
economist
economy
elect
election
Electoral College
Electoral vote
emancipation
emperor
empire
ethnic

European
executive branch
export
federal
federal government
federalism
feminism
feminist
First Lady
forty-niner
frontier
general election
global economy
globalization
govern
government
governor
gross national
  product
head of state
history
holocaust
house
human rights
immigrant
impeach
imperialism
import
inaugurate
indentured servant
independence
Indian
industrial
industry
judicial branch
king
kingdom
knight
labor
legislative branch
legislature
mayor
medieval
Middle Ages
middle class
migrant
migrate
Minuteman
monarchy
monopoly
monument
municipal
nation
nationalism
nationality
Native American
naturalization

neutral
parliament
pass
patriot
Pentagon
petition
pilgrim
pioneer
policy
political
political party
politics
population
prejudice
president
primary
prime minister
prohibition
propaganda
proslavery
public office
Puritan
queen
racetrack
racism
rebellion
Reconstruction
reform
regulate
reign
religious freedom
representation
representative
representative
  government
republic
Republican
revenue
revolution
right
ruler
segregation
Senate
senator
settlement
settler
sharecropper
slave trade
socialism
socialist
social studies
sovereignty
state
suffragist
Supreme Court
territory
timeline

tipi
totalitarian
transcontinental
  railroad
treaty
unconstitutional
union
veto
vote
western
White House
witch-hunt

Sports

ace
aerobics
athlete
backstroke
badminton
ball
ballgame
ballpark
base
baseball
basket
basketball
bat
baton
batter
beat
bicycle
bike
box
boxing
breaststroke
captain
catch
champion
championship
cheerleader
climber
climbing
coach
course
court
crawl
cross
cycle
cyclist
dart
defender
defense
defensive
discus
dive
diving board
exercise

field
final
fishing
fishing rod
football
foul
game
goal
goalkeeper
goalpost
golf
golf club
golf course
gym
gymnasium
gymnastics
halftime
high jump
hockey
hockey stick
horseback
  riding
horseracing
hurdle
ice hockey
in
javelin
jockey
jog
judo
karate
lap
league
long jump
major leagues
marathon
match
meet
mountain bike
net
opponent
paddle
penalty
physical education
Pilates
Ping-Pong
pitcher
play
player
push-up
race
racket
referee
relay
rider
riding
rink

row
rugby
run
runner
sail
sailboat
sailing
save
score
semifinal
shoot
skate
skateboard
ski
snowboarding
soccer
softball
sport
sprint
squash
stadium
stroke
surf
surfboard
swim
swimming
swimming pool
tackle
team
tennis
tie
touchdown
tournament
track
train
umpire
versus
volleyball
vs.
win
windsurfing
wrestle
yoga

Technology
account
address
address book
analog
application
artificial intelligence
attachment
avatar
back
backup
bit
blackberry

blog
blogosphere
Bluetooth
bookmark
boot
broadband
browse
browser
bug
bulletin board
byte
camera phone
CD
CD burner
CD player
CD-ROM
cellphone
chat room
click
code
command
compact disc
computer
corrupt
crash
cursor
cut and paste
cyberspace
data
database
delete
desktop
dialog box
dial-up
digital
disk
disk drive
document
domain name
double-click
down
download
downloadable
drag and drop
drop-down menu
DVD
DVD burner
DVD player
email
FAQ
file
filename
file-sharing
flash drive
floppy disk
folder
format

forward slash
game console
gigabyte
Google
graphics
hard disk
hard drive
hardware
HDTV
high tech
homepage
HTML
hybrid
hyperlink
icon
IM
inbox
information
 technology
instant messaging
Internet
intranet
iPod
ISP
I.T.
KB
key
keyboard
keyword
kilobyte
laptop
laser printer
log
mailbox
megabyte
memory
memory card
memory stick
menu
message
message board
microchip
modem
mouse
mouse pad
MP3
MP3 player
navigate
net
network
notebook
offline
online
operating system
password
PC
PDF

personal computer
plasma screen
podcast
post
program
RAM
reboot
satellite
satellite dish
satellite television
save
scanner
screensaver
scroll
search engine
server
site
smart phone
social
 networking
software
solar collector
spam
spreadsheet
surf
texting
text message
text messaging
unzip
upload
URL
USB
username
video
virtual
virus
web
webcam
webpage
website
window
Word document
World Wide Web
WWW
zip

DEFINING VOCABULARY

A

a
a few
a little
ability
able
about
above
abroad
absence
absent
absorb
academic
accent
accept
acceptable
accident
accidentally
according to
account
accurately
acid
across
act
action
active
activity
actor
actress
actual
add
addition
address
admiration
admire
admit
adult
advance
advantage
adventure
advertise
advertisement
advertising
advice
advise
affair
affect
afford
afraid

after
afternoon
afterward
again
against
age
ago
agree
agreement
ahead
aim
air
aircraft
airplane
airport
alcohol
alcoholic
alive
all
allow
almost
alone
along
aloud
alphabet
already
also
although
altogether
always
among
amount
amuse
amusing
an
ancient
and
anger
angle
angry
animal
ankle
annoy
annoyed
annoying
another
answer
anxiety
anxious

any
anyone
anything
anyway
anywhere
apart
apartment
apologize
appear
appearance
apple
apply
appoint
appropriate
approval
approve
approximate
approximately
area
argue
argument
arm
arms
army
around
arrange
arrangement
arrest
arrival
arrive
art
article
artificial
artist
artistic
as
ashamed
aside
aside from
ask
asleep
association
at
atom
attack
attempt
attend
attention
attract

attractive
aunt
automatic
automatically
autumn
available
average
avoid
awake
award
aware
away

B

baby
back
background
backward
bacteria
bad
badly
bag
baggage
bake
balance
ball
banana
band
bank
bar
base
bat
bath
bathroom
battle
be
be called
be going to
be sick
beach
beak
bear
beard
beat
beautiful
beauty
because
because of
become

bed
bedroom
beer
before
begin
beginning
behave
behavior
behind
belief
believe
bell
belong
below
belt
bend
beneath
benefit
bent
beside
best
better
between
beyond
bicycle
big
bill
bin
bird
birth
birthday
bit
bite
bitter
black
blade
blame
blank
blind
block
blood
blow
blue
board
boat
body
boil
bomb
bone

book	button	certainly	clothes	confusing
boot	buy	chain	clothing	confusion
border	buyer	chair	cloud	connect
bored	by	chance	club	connection
born		change	coal	conscious
borrow	**C**	character	coast	consider
boss	cable	characteristic	coat	consist of
both	cake	charge	coffee	contact
bottle	calculate	chase	coin	contain
bottom	call	cheat	cold	container
bowl	calm	check	collect	contents
box	camera	cheek	collection	continue
boy	camp	cheerful	college	continuous
boyfriend	camping	cheese	color	continuously
brain	can	chemical	colored	contract
branch	cancel	chemistry	combination	control
brave	cancer	chest	combine	convenient
bread	candy	chicken	come	conversation
break	cap	chief	comfort	cook
breakfast	capital	child	comfortable	cookie
breast	captain	chin	command	cooking
breath	car	chocolate	commit	cool
breathe	card	choice	committee	copy
breed	cardboard	choose	common	corner
brick	care	church	communicate	correct
bridge	careful	cigarette	communication	correctly
bright	carefully	cinema	company	cost
brightly	careless	circle	compare	cotton
bring	carelessly	citizen	comparison	cough
broad	carrot	city	compete	could
broadcast	carry	claim	competition	council
broken	case	clap	complain	count
brother	castle	class	complaint	country
brown	cat	classroom	complete	countryside
brush	catch	clean	completely	courage
bubble	cause	clear	complicated	course
build	CD	clearly	computer	court
building	ceiling	clerk	concentrate	cover
bullet	celebrate	clever	concentration	covered
bunch	celebration	click	concern	cow
burn	cell	climb	concerning	crack
burst	cellphone	climbing	concert	crash
bury	cent	clock	concrete	cream
bus	center	close	condition	create
bush	centimeter	close	confidence	creature
business	central	closed	confident	crime
busy	century	closely	confidently	criminal
but	ceremony	closet	confuse	criticism
butter	certain	cloth	confused	criticize

crop	defend	discover	**E**	encouragement
cross	defense	discovery	each	end
crowd	degree	discuss	each other	ending
cruel	delay	discussion	ear	enemy
cry	deliberate	disease	early	energy
cultural	deliberately	disgust	earn	engine
culture	delicate	dish	earth	engineer
cup	delight	dishonest	easily	enjoy
cupboard	deliver	dishonestly	east	enjoyable
cure	demand	disk	eastern	enjoyment
curl	department	dislike	easy	enough
curly	depend	dismiss	eat	enter
current	depth	distance	economic	entertain
curtain	describe	divide	economy	entertainer
curve	description	division	edge	entertainment
curved	desert	divorce	educate	enthusiasm
customer	deserve	divorced	educated	enthusiastic
cut	design	do	education	entrance
cycle	desk	doctor	effect	envelope
	despite	document	effective	environment
D	destroy	dog	effectively	environmental
daily	destruction	dollar	effort	equal
damage	detail	door	egg	equally
dance	determination	dot	either	equipment
dancer	determined	double	elbow	escape
dancing	develop	doubt	elect	especially
danger	device	down	election	establish
dangerous	diamond	drag	electric	even
dare	dictionary	dramatic	electrical	evening
dark	die	draw	electricity	event
date	difference	drawer	electronic	ever
daughter	different	drawing	element	every
day	differently	dream	else	everyone
dead	difficult	dress	email	everything
deaf	difficulty	dressed	email	everywhere
deal	dig	drink	embarrass	evil
deal with	dinner	drive	embarrassed	exact
dear	direct	driver	embarrassing	exactly
death	direction	driving	emergency	exam
debt	directly	drop	emotion	examination
decay	dirt	drug	emotional	examine
decide	dirty	drugstore	emotionally	example
decision	disadvantage	drum	emphasis	excellent
declare	disagree	drunk	emphasize	except
decorate	disappear	dry	employ	exchange
decoration	disappoint	dull	employee	excite
decorative	disappointed	during	employer	excited
decrease	disappointing	dust	employment	excitement
deep	disapproval	duty	empty	exciting
defeat	disapprove	DVD	encourage	excuse

exercise
exist
existence
expect
expensive
experience
experiment
expert
explain
explanation
explode
explosion
express
expression
extra
extremely
eye

F

face
fact
factory
fail
failure
faint
fair
fairly
faith
faithful
fall
fall over
fame
familiar
family
famous
fancy
far
farm
farmer
farming
fashion
fashionable
fast
fasten
fat
father
fault
favor
favorite

fear
feather
feed
feel
feeling
fellow
female
fence
fever
few
field
fifth
fight
fighting
figure
fill
final
finance
financial
find
find out sth
fine
finger
finish
fire
firm
firmly
first
fish
fishing
fit
fix
fixed
flag
flame
flash
flat
flavor
flesh
flight
float
flood
floor
flour
flow
flower
fly
flying
fold
follow

food
foot
football
for
forever
force
foreign
forest
forget
forgive
fork
form
formal
formally
former
formerly
fortune
forward
forwards
fourth
frame
free
freedom
freeze
frequent
fresh
friend
friendly
frighten
frightening
from
front
fruit
full
fun
funeral
funny
fur
furniture
farther
farthest
future

G

gain
game
garage
garbage
garbage can

garden
gas
gasoline
gate
gather
gear
general
generally
generous
gentle
gentleman
gently
geography
get
get off
get on
gift
girl
girlfriend
give
glad
glass
glasses
glue
go
go down
go up
go wrong
goal
god
gold
good
good at
goodbye
goods
govern
government
gradual
gradually
grain
gram
grammar
grand
grandchild
granddaughter
grandfather
grandmother
grandparent
grandson
grass

grateful
grave
gray
great
green
ground
group
grow
grow up
growth
guard
guess
guest
guide
guilty
gun

H

habit
hair
half
hall
hammer
hand
handle
hang
happen
happily
happiness
happy
hard
hardly
harm
harmful
harmless
hat
hate
hatred
have
have to
he
head
health
healthy
hear
heart
heat
heating
heaven

heavy	**I**	inside	**K**	leave
heel	ice	instead	keen	leave out
height	idea	instruction	keep	left
hello	if	instrument	key	leg
help	illegal	insult	keyboard	legal
helpful	illegally	insulting	kick	legally
her	illness	insurance	kill	legislature
here	image	intelligence	kilo	lemon
hers	imaginary	intelligent	kilogram	lend
herself	imagination	intend	kilometer	length
hide	imagine	intention	kind	less
high	immediate	interest	kindly	lesson
highway	immediately	interested	kindness	let
hill	importance	interesting	king	letter
him	important	international	kiss	level
himself	importantly	Internet	kitchen	library
hire	impossible	interrupt	knee	lid
his	improve	interruption	knife	lie
historical	improvement	into	knock	life
history	in	introduce	knot	lift
hit	in a hurry	introduction	know	light
hobby	in charge of	invent	knowledge	lightly
hold	in exchange for	invention		like
hole	in fact	invitation	**L**	likely
holiday	in general	invite	labor	limit
hollow	in order to	involve	laboratory	line
holy	in public	involvement	lack	lip
home	include	iron	lady	liquid
honest	including	island	lake	list
honestly	income	it	lamp	listen
honor	increase	its	land	liter
hook	indoor	itself	language	literature
hope	indoors		large	little
horizontal	industrial		last	live
horn	industry	**J**	last name	live
horse	inexpensive	jacket	late	load
hospital	infect	jealous	later	local
host	infection	jelly	latest	lock
hot	infectious	jewelry	laugh	lonely
hotel	influence	job	law	long
hour	inform	join	lawyer	look
house	informal	joint	lay	look at
how	information	joke	lazy	look for
human	injure	joy	lead	loose
humor	injured	judge	leader	loosely
hungry	injury	judgment	leaf	lord
hunt	ink	juice	lean	lose
hurry	inner	jump	learn	loss
hurt	inquiry	just	least	lost
husband	insect	justice	leather	lot

loud	meat	move	newspaper	often
loudly	medical	movement	next	oil
love	medicine	movie	next to	old
low	meet	movie theater	nice	old-fashioned
loyal	meeting	much	night	on
luck	melt	mud	no	once
lucky	member	multiply	noon	one
lump	memory	murder	no one	onion
lunch	mention	muscle	noise	only
lung	menu	museum	noisily	open
	message	music	noisy	operate
M	messy	musical	none	operation
machine	metal	musician	nonsense	opinion
machinery	meter	must	nor	opponent
mad	method	my	normal	opportunity
magazine	middle	myself	normally	oppose
magic	midnight	mysterious	north	opposite
mail	might	mystery	northern	opposition
main	mile		nose	or
mainly	military	**N**	not	orange
make	milk	nail	note	order
make-up	mind	naked	nothing	ordinary
male	mine	name	notice	organ
man	mineral	narrow	noticeable	organization
manage	minister	nation	now	organize
management	minute	national	nowhere	organized
manager	mirror	natural	nuclear	origin
manner	miss	naturally	number	original
many	mistake	nature	nurse	originally
map	mix	navy	nut	other
march	mixture	near		otherwise
mark	model	nearly	**O**	our
market	modern	neat	obey	ours
marriage	moment	necessary	object	ourselves
married	money	neck	obtain	out
marry	month	need	obvious	outdoor
mass	mood	needle	obviously	outdoors
master	moon	negative	occasion	outer
match	moral	neighbor	ocean	outside
material	morally	neighborhood	o'clock	oven
mathematics	more	neither	of	over
matter	morning	nerve	off	owe
may	most	nervous	offend	own
me	mostly	nervously	offense	owner
meal	mother	nest	offensive	
mean	motor	net	offer	**P**
meaning	motorcycle	network	office	pack
means	mountain	never	officer	package
measure	mouse	new	official	packet
measurement	mouth	news	officially	page

pain	personal	polite	principle	queen
painful	personality	politely	print	question
paint	persuade	political	printer	quick
painting	pet	politically	printing	quickly
pair	photograph	politician	prison	quiet
palace	photography	politics	prisoner	quietly
pale	phrase	pollution	private	
pan	physical	pool	privately	**R**
pants	physically	poor	prize	race
paper	physics	pop music	probable	radio
parallel	piano	popular	probably	railroad
parent	pick	population	problem	rain
park	pick sth up	port	process	raise
part	picture	position	produce	range
particular	piece	positive	product	rank
partly	pig	possess	production	rare
partner	pile	possession	profession	rate
party	pill	possibility	profit	rather
pass	pilot	possible	program	rather than
passage	pin	possibly	progress	raw
passenger	pink	post	promise	reach
past	pipe	pot	pronounce	react
path	pity	potato	pronunciation	reaction
patience	place	pound	proof	read
patient	plain	pour	proper	reader
pattern	plan	powder	property	reading
pause	planet	power	protect	ready
pay	plant	powerful	protection	real
payment	plastic	practical	proud	really
peace	plate	practice	proudly	reason
peaceful	play	praise	prove	reasonable
pen	player	prayer	provide	reasonably
pence	pleasant	prefer	public	receive
pencil	pleasantly	pregnant	publish	recent
people	please	preparation	pull	recently
pepper	pleased	prepare	punish	recognition
per	pleasure	presence	punishment	recognize
perfect	plenty	present	pure	record
perfectly	pocket	preserve	purple	red
perform	poem	president	purpose	reduce
performance	poetry	press	push	reduction
performer	point	pressure	put	refrigerator
perhaps	pointed	pretend	put sth on	refusal
period	poison	pretty		refuse
permanent	poisonous	prevent	**Q**	regular
permanently	pole	price	qualification	regularly
permission	police	priest	quality	related
permit	police officer	prince	quantity	related to
person	polish	princess	quarter	relating to

relation	root	score	sheep	sixth
relationship	rope	scratch	sheet	size
relative	rough	screen	shelf	-sized
relaxed	roughly	screw	shell	skill
relaxing	round	search	shelter	skillful
religion	rounded	season	shine	skillfully
religious	route	seat	shiny	skin
remain	row	second	ship	skirt
remark	royal	secret	shirt	sky
remember	rub	secretary	shock	sleep
remind	rubber	secretly	shocked	sleeve
remove	rude	see	shocking	slide
rent	rudely	seed	shoe	slight
repair	ruin	seem	shoot	slightly
repeat	rule	sell	shopping	slip
repeated	ruler	send	short	slope
repeatedly	run	sense	shot	slow
reply	runner	sensible	should	slowly
report	running	sensitive	shoulder	small
represent	rush	sentence	shout	smell
representative		separate	show	smile
request	**S**	series	shower	smoke
respect	sad	serious	shut	smooth
responsibility	sadness	seriously	shy	snake
responsible	safe	servant	sick	snow
rest	safely	serve	side	so
restaurant	safety	service	sideways	so that
result	sail	set	sight	soap
return	salad	set fire to	sign	soccer
reward	salary	settle	signal	social
rhythm	sale	seventh	signature	socially
rice	salt	several	silence	society
rich	salty	severe	silent	sock
rid	same	severely	silly	soft
ride	sand	sew	silver	software
rider	satisfaction	sex	similar	soil
riding	satisfied	sexual	simple	soldier
right	satisfy	sexually	simply	solid
ring	sauce	shade	since	solution
rise	save	shadow	sincere	solve
risk	say	shake	sincerely	some
river	scale	shall	sing	somehow
road	schedule	shame	singer	someone
rob	scene	shape	single	something
rock	school	shaped	sink	sometimes
roll	science	share	sister	somewhere
romantic	scientific	sharp	sit	son
roof	scientist	shave	sit down	song
room	scissors	she	situation	soon

sore	sticky	supermarket	tell	tie
sorry	stiff	supply	temperature	tight
soul	still	support	temporary	tightly
sound	sting	supporter	tend	time
soup	stomach	suppose	tendency	tin
sour	stone	sure	tent	tire
south	stop	surface	term	tired
southern	store	surprise	terrible	title
space	storm	surprised	test	to
speak	story	surprising	text	today
special	stove	surround	than	toe
specialist	straight	swallow	thank	together
speech	strange	swear	thank you	tomato
speed	strangely	sweep	that	tomorrow
spell	stranger	sweet	the	tongue
spend	stream	swell	the rest	tonight
spice	street	swim	the Web	too
spicy	strength	swimming	theater	tool
spider	stretch	swing	their	tooth
spin	strike	switch	theirs	top
spirit	string	switch sth off	them	total
split	strip	switch sth on	themselves	touch
spoil	stripe	symbol	then	tour
spoon	stroke	sympathetic	theory	tourist
sport	strong	sympathy	there	toward
spot	strongly	system	therefore	tower
spread	structure		they	town
spring	struggle	**T**	thick	toy
square	student		thief	track
stage	study	table	thin	trade
stair	stupid	tail	thing	tradition
stamp	style	take	think	traditional
stand	subject	take care (of)	third	traditionally
stand up	substance	take part	thirsty	traffic
standard	succeed	take sth off	this	train
star	success	talk	thorough	training
start	successful	tall	though	translate
state	such	task	thought	transparent
station	suck	taste	thread	transport
stay	sudden	tax	threat	transportation
steady	suddenly	taxi	threaten	trap
steal	suffer	tea	throat	travel
steam	sugar	teach	through	traveler
steel	suggest	teacher	throw	treat
steep	suggestion	teaching	throw sth away	treatment
stem	suit	team	thumb	tree
step	sum	tear	thus	triangle
stick	summer	technical	ticket	trick
stick out	sun	telephone	tidy	trip
		television		

tropical
trouble
truck
true
trust
truth
try
tube
tune
turn
twice
twist
type
typical
typically

U

ugly
unable
uncertain
uncle
uncomfortable
unconscious
under
understand
underwear
undo
unemployed
unexpected
unexpectedly
unfair
unfairly
unhappiness
unhappy
uniform
union
unit
unite
universe
university
unkind
unlikely
unlucky
unpleasant
unreasonable
unsuccessful
until
unusual
unwilling

unwillingly
up
upper
upset
upside down
upstairs
upward
urge
urgent
us
use
useful
useless
user
usual
usually

V

vacation
valley
valuable
value
variety
various
vary
vegetable
vehicle
very
victory
view
village
violence
violent
violently
visit
visitor
voice
volume
vomit
vote

W

waist
wait
waiter
wake
walk
walking
wall

wander
want
war
warm
warmth
warn
warning
wash
washing
waste
watch
water
wave
way
we
weak
weakness
wealth
weapon
wear
weather
website
wedding
week
weekly
weigh
weight
welcome
well
west
western
wet
what
whatever
wheel
when
whenever
where
whether
which
while
whisper
whistle
white
who
whoever
whole
whose
why

wide
width
wife
wild
will
willing
win
wind
window
wine
wing
winner
winter
wipe
wire
wise
wish
with
within
without
woman
wonder
wood
wooden
wool
word
work
worker
working
world
worried
worry
worse
worship
worst
worth
would
wound
wrap
wrist
write
writer
writing
wrong
wrongly

Y

yard
year

yellow
yes
yesterday
yet
you
young
your
yours
yourself
youth

Z

zero

Texting Abbreviations

1	used to replace *"-one"*: *NE1* = anyone		**GL**	**good luck**
			GF	**girlfriend**
2	**to** or **too**: *it's up 2 U* = it's up to you; *me 2* = me too used to replace **"to-"**: *2day* = today		**HHIS**	**hanging head in shame**: used for showing that you are embarassed
2DAY	**today**		**IB**	**I'm back**
2MORO	**tomorrow**		**IC**	**I see**
2NITE	**tonight**		**IDK**	**I don't know**
4	**for**: *4 U* = for you used to replace **"-fore"**: *B4* = before		**IYSS**	**if you say so**
			K	**OK**
			KNO	**know**
411	**information**: *TNX4 the 411*		**L8**	**late**
8	used to replace **"-ate"** or **"-eat"**: *GR8* = great; *C U L8R* = see you later		**L8R**	**later**: *CUL8R* = see you later
			LOL	**laughing out loud**: used for showing that you think something is funny
86	discard, get rid of		**MSG**	**message**
AFAIK	**as far as I know**		**MYOB**	**mind your own business**: for telling people not to ask questions about something that you do not want them to know about
B	**be**: used to replace **"be-"** in other words: *B4* = before			
B4	**before**			
B4N	**bye for now**			
BC	**because**		**N**	**no**
BF	**boyfriend**		**NE**	**any**
BRB	**be right back**		**NE1**	**anyone**
BTW	**by the way**		**NO1**	**no one**
C	**see**: *C U 2moro* = see you tomorrow		**NETHING**	**anything**
			NP	**no problem**
CID	**consider it done**		**OIC**	**Oh, I see**
CU	**see you**		**OTOH**	**on the other hand**
CUL8R	**call you later**		**PCM**	**please call me**
D8	**date**		**PLS**	**please**
EZ	**easy**		**prolly**	**probably**
FWIW	**for what it's worth**: used for saying that someone may or may not be interested in what you have to say		**PWB**	**please write back**
			R	**are**: *RU free 2nite* = Are you free tonight?
			RUCMNG	**Are you coming?**
			RUOK?	**Are you OK?**
FYI	**for your information**: used as a way of introducing useful information		**SPK**	**speak**
			SRY	**sorry**
			TBD	**to be decided/determined**
GR8	**great**		**THNQ**	**thank you**: *THNQ for visiting my home page.*
G2G	**got to go**			

THX/TX	**thanks:** *THX4 the info.*
TTUL/TTYL	**talk to you later**
TY	**thank you**
TYVM	**thank you very much**
U	**you:** *CUL8R* = see you later
URW	**You're welcome.**
W8	**wait**
WAN2	**want to**
WRK	**work**
XLNT	**excellent**
Y	**yes**
Y?	**why?**
Y/N?	**yes or no?**
YR	**your**
ZZZZ	**sleeping**

EMOTICONS HORIZONTAL →

:-)	smiling; agreeing
:-D	laughing
|-)	hee hee
|-D	ho ho
'-) or ;-)	winking; just kidding
:*)	clowning
:-(	frowning; sad
:(	sad
:'-(	crying and really sad
>:-< or :-||	angry
:-@	screaming
:-V	shouting
:-p or :-r	sticking tongue out
|-O	yawning
:*	kiss
((((name))))	hug
@-{----	rose
<3	heart
</3	broken heart

EMOTICONS VERTICAL ↓

(^_^)	smiling
(`_^) or (^_~)	winking
(>_<)	angry, or ouch
(-_-)zzz	sleeping
\(^o^)/	very excited (raising hands)
(-_-;) or (^_^')	nervous, or sweatdrop (embarrassed; semicolon can be repeated)
d-_-b title.mp3	listening to music, labelling title afterwards
\m/	rocker fingers
\m/(>_<)\m/	rocker dude

List of Basic Vocabulary

This list includes all of the words on Dr. Robert J. Marzano's basic vocabulary lists 1, 2, and 3.

A

a
able
aboard
above
accept
accident
accuse
across
act
action
active
activity
actor
actress
add
addition
address
adjective
adult
adverb
advice
advise
afloat
afraid
afternoon
afterward
afterwards
against
age
ago
agree
ah
aha
ahead
ahead of
ain't
air
aircraft
airline
airplane
airport
alarm
alert

alike
alive
all
alley
alligator
allow
almond
almost
alone
along
aloud
alphabet
already
always
am
amaze
ambulance
among
amount
an
analyze
anchor
ancient
and
angel
anger
angle
angry
animal
ankle
another
answer
ant
any
anybody
anymore
anyone
anywhere
apart
apartment
appeal
appear
appearance
applause

apple
appoint
approach
April
apron
aquarium
are
area
aren't
argue
arm
army
around
arrive
arrow
art
artist
as
ash
aside
ask
asleep
aspirin
astronaut
at
athlete
athletic
attach
attention
attract
audience
August
aunt
author
automobile
avalanche
avenue
average
avocado
awake
award
away
awful
awhile

ax
axe

B

baa
baby
babysitter
back
backward
backwards
bacon
bad
badge
badly
bag
bake
baker
bakery
balance
bald
ball
ballet
balloon
banana
band
bandage
bandit
bang
banjo
bank
banner
bar
barbecue
barber
barefoot
bark
barn
barrel
base
baseball
basement
bashful
basket

basketball
bat
bath
bathrobe
bathroom
batter
battery
battle
bathtub
bay
be
beach
beak
bean
bear
beard
beat
beautiful
beauty
beaver
because
because of
become
bed
bedroom
bedspread
bedtime
bee
beef
beehive
been
beep
beer
before
beg
begin
beginner
beginning
behave
behind
being
belief
believe
bell

belly	blow	bright	**C**	catch
belong	blue	brilliant	cab	catcher
below	blueberry	bring	cable	caterpillar
belt	board	broil	cafeteria	catsup
bench	boat	broke	caffeine	cause
bend	body	broomstick	cage	cave
beneath	boil	brother	cake	caveman
bent	bologna	brown	calculate	ceiling
berry	bomb	brownie	calendar	celebrate
beside	bone	bruise	calf	celebrity
best	book	brush	call	celery
bet	bookcase	bubble	calm	cellar
better	booklet	buck	camera	cent
between	bookstore	bucket	camp	center
beyond	boom	buckle	campfire	century
bible	boot	bug	can	cereal
bicycle	born	build	can't	certain
big	borrow	building	canal	certainly
bike	boss	bull	candidate	chain
bill	both	bulldog	candle	chair
billion	bother	bullet	candlestick	chalk
bird	bottle	bully	candy	chalkboard
birdhouse	bottom	bumblebee	cannot	champion
birthday	boulder	bump	canoe	chance
biscuit	bounce	bumpy	canyon	change
bit	bowl	bun	cap	change
bite	bowling	bunch	cape	chapter
black	box	bunny	capture	chase
blackboard	boxer	burn	car	chat
blade	boxing	bury	caramel	cheap
blame	boy	bus	card	cheat
blank	boyfriend	bush	cardboard	check
blanket	brag	business	care	cheer
blast	braid	busy	career	cheese
bleed	brain	but	careful	cherry
bless	brake	butcher	carpet	chest
blind	branch	butter	carrot	chew
blink	brave	butterfly	carry	chicken
blister	bread	butterscotch	cartoon	child
blizzard	break	button	carve	chili
block	breakfast	buy	cash	chill
blonde	breath	buzz	cashew	chimney
blood	brick	by	castle	chin
blossom	bridge	bye	cat	chips

chocolate	coat	cookie	crop	dangerous
choice	cockroach	cool	cross	dare
choir	cocoa	cooperate	crouch	dark
choke	coconut	copy	crow	dash
choose	cocoon	cork	crowd	date
chop	coffee	corn	crown	daughter
chopsticks	coffeepot	corner	cruel	day
chore	coin	correct	cruise	daydream
chubby	cold	cost	crumb	daytime
chuckle	cold	costume	crumble	dead
church	coleslaw	cotton	crumple	deaf
circle	collar	couch	crush	dear
circus	collect	cough	crust	decade
citizen	collie	could	crutch	December
city	color	couldn't	cry	decide
clap	colorful	count	cub	decimal
clasp	comb	counter	cube	deep
class	combine	counterclockwise	cucumber	deer
classify	come	country	cuddle	defeat
classmate	comedy	county	cue	define
classroom	comma	couple	cup	delay
claw	command	courage	cupboard	delicate
clay	common	court	cupcake	deliver
clean	community	courteous	cupid	demand
clear	compare	cousin	curl	democracy
click	complain	cover	curtain	dent
cliff	complete	cow	curve	dentist
climb	compliment	cowboy	cushion	depart
clip	compose	crack	custodian	depth
clock	comprehend	cracker	customer	describe
clockwise	computer	cradle	cut	desert
close	conclude	cranberry	cute	design
closet	confident	crash	cylinder	desk
cloth	confuse	crate		dessert
clothes	connect	crawl		destroy
clothing	considerate	crayon	**D**	develop
cloud	consonant	crazy	dad	devil
clown	container	creak	daily	diagram
club	contest	cream	dam	dial
cluck	continent	create	damage	diameter
clue	control	creek	dance	diamond
clumsy	convince	crib	dancer	diaper
coach	cook	criminal	dandelion	diary
coast	cookbook	crooked	danger	dictionary

did	doorstep	eagle	except	feel
die	doorway	ear	excite	feet
difference	dot	early	excuse	female
different	doubt	earn	exercise	fence
difficult	dough	earth	exhale	fender
dig	doughnut	earthquake	exit	fever
dime	down	east	expand	few
dinner	downhill	easy	expect	fiction
dinnertime	downpour	eat	expensive	fidget
dinosaur	downstairs	echo	experiment	field
direct	downtown	edge	expert	fifteen
direction	downward	effect	explain	fifty
dirt	dozen	egg	explode	fight
disagree	draft	eight	explore	fill
disappear	drag	eighteen	extra	film
discover	dragon	eighty	eye	fin
discuss	drain	either	eyebrow	find
disease	draw	elbow	eyelash	fine
dish	drawer	elephant		finger
dishonest	drawing	eleven		finish
dislike	dream	elf		fire
disobey	dress	else	**F**	firecracker
ditch	dribble	empty	face	firefighter
dive	drill	encourage	fact	fireworks
divide	drink	end	fail	firm
division	drip	enemy	fair	first
divorce	drive	engine	fairy	fish
dizzy	driveway	enjoy	fall	fit
do	drop	enormous	familiar	five
dock	drugstore	enough	family	fix
doctor	drum	enter	fan	flag
does	drummer	equal	fancy	flake
doesn't	dry	equator	far	flame
dog	duck	error	farm	flap
doggie	dull	essay	fast	flat
doing	dump	estimate	fasten	flavor
doll	during	even	fat	flea
dollar	dust	evening	father	flipper
don't	dwarf	event	faucet	float
done		ever	fault	flood
donkey		every	fear	floor
door	**E**	evil	feather	floss
doorbell	each	exam	February	flour
doorknob	eager	example	feed	flower

flush	furnace	goose	hair	height
fly	future	gorilla	half	helicopter
fog		grab	hall	helium
fold	**G**	grade	hallway	hello
folder	gallon	graduate	ham	helmet
follow	gallop	grandparent	hamburger	help
food	game	granny	hammer	hemisphere
foot	garage	grape	hamper	hen
football	garbage	grapefruit	hamster	her
for	garbageman	graph	hand	herd
forbid	garden	grass	handkerchief	here
force	gas	grasshopper	handle	here's
forehead	gate	grateful	handshake	hero
forest	gather	gravy	handsome	heroic
forever	gee	gray	handwriting	hers
forget	generation	grease	happen	herself
forgive	gentle	great	happiness	hey
fork	geography	green	happy	hi
fort	germ	greet	hard	hide
forty	get	grill	hardly	high
forward	ghetto	grin	harm	highway
four	ghost	grocery	has	hike
fourteen	giant	grouch	hasn't	hill
fowl	gift	ground	hat	hillside
fox	gigantic	groundhog	hatch	him
freckle	giggle	group	hate	himself
free	giraffe	grow	haul	hip
freeway	girl	growl	have	hire
freeze	give	grown-up	have to	his
frequent	glad	grumpy	haven't	history
fresh	glass	guard	he	hit
Friday	glasses	guess	he'd	hive
friend	glide	guest	he'll	ho
frog	glove	guilt	he's	hockey
from	glue	guitar	head	hold
front	go	gum	heal	hole
frown	goal	gun	health	holiday
fruit	gobble	guy	hear	holler
fry	god	gym	heart	hollow
fudge	gold		heat	holy
fuel	golf	**H**	heater	home
full	good	ha	heaven	homework
fun	good-bye	had	heavy	honest
fur	goodnight	hail	heel	honestly

honey
hood
hoof
hop
hope
hopeful
hopefully
horn
horse
horseshoe
hose
hospital
hot
hotdog
hotel
hour
hourly
house
housewife
housework
how
hug
huge
human
humor
hundred
hunger
hungry
hunt
hurricane
hurry
husband
hut

I

I
I'd
I'll
I'm
I've
ice
icicle
idea
if

ill
image
imagine
important
impossible
improve
in
inch
include
individual
indoor
indoors
inform
information
injure
injury
ink
insect
inside
instead
instruct
instrument
interest
into
invent
invention
investigate
invisible
iron
is
island
isn't
it
it's
itch
its

J

jacket
jail
jam
janitor
January
jar

jaw
jay
jealous
jeans
jelly
jet
jewel
jewelry
job
join
joint
joke
jolly
journal
journey
joy
joyful
judge
jug
juggle
juice
juicy
July
jumbo
jump
June
jungle
junk
just

K

kangaroo
keep
kerchief
key
keyboard
kick
kid
kill
killer
kind
kindergarten
king
kiss

kitchen
kite
kitten
knee
kneel
knife
knight
knob
knock
knot
know

L

labor
lace
ladder
lady
ladybug
lake
lamb
lamp
land
language
lap
large
last
late
lately
later
latter
laugh
laughter
law
lawn
lawnmower
lawyer
lay
lazy
leader
leaf
leak
lean
leap
learn

leash
leather
leave
left
leg
legend
lemon
length
less
lesson
let
letter
lettuce
level
liar
liberty
library
lick
licorice
lid
lie
life
lift
light
lightbulb
lightening
like
likely
limb
limit
limp
line
lion
lip
liquid
list
listen
literature
litter
little
live
loaf
lobster
location

lock	man	mile	mouse	neighbor
locomotive	manhole	military	mouse	neighborhood
log	many	milk	mouth	neither
lollipop	map	million	mouthful	nephew
long	marble	mind	move	nervous
look	March	mine	movie	nest
loop	march	minister	mow	net
loose-leaf	margarine	minus	much	never
lose	margin	minute	mud	new
loser	mark	miracle	muffin	news
loss	marriage	mirror	mug	newspaper
lot	marry	miss	multiplication	next
loud	marshmallow	misspell	multiply	nice
love	mask	mistake	murder	nickel
lovely	math	mittens	muscle	nickname
low	May	mix	museum	niece
loyal	may	model	music	night
luck	maybe	mom	music	nightgown
luckily	maybe	Monday	must	nine
lucky	mayonnaise	money	mustard	nineteen
lullaby	mayor	monitor	my	ninety
lunch	me	monkey	myself	ninth
lunchroom	meal	monster	mystery	no
lunchtime	mean	month	myth	no one
	measure	monument		nobody
M	meat	moo	**N**	nod
ma	medal	moon	nail	noise
macaroni	medicine	moose	naked	none
machine	meet	mop	name	noodle
mad	melody	more	nap	noon
magazine	melon	more	napkin	normal
magic	melt	morning	narrow	north
magician	member	mosquito	nation	nose
magnet	memory	most	nature	nostril
magnify	mention	most	naughty	not
maid	meow	mostly	navy	note
mail	mermaid	motel	near	notebook
mailbox	merry	moth	nearby	nothing
mailman	message	mother	nearly	noun
make	metal	motion	neat	novel
male	meteor	motor	neck	November
mall	middle	motorcycle	necklace	now
mama	midnight	mound	need	nowhere
mammy	might	mountain	needle	number

numeral
nun
nurse
nursery
nut
nylon

O

o'clock
oar
oatmeal
obedient
obey
object
occur
ocean
October
odd
of
off
offer
office
officer
official
often
oh
oil
ok
okay
old
olive
omelet
on
once
one
onion
only
onto
ooh
open
opener
opinion
opposite
or

orange
orchestra
order
ordinary
organize
origin
other
our
ours
out
outcome
outdoors
outer
outline
outside
outsmart
outstanding
oval
oven
over
overcast
overheard
overnight
owe
owl
own
owner
oxygen

P

pack
package
paddle
page
pail
pain
paint
paintbrush
painter
painting
pair
pajamas
pal

palace
pan
pancake
pants
papa
paper
paperboy
parade
parchute
parent
park
parrot
part
partner
party
pass
passenger
past
paste
pastor
pat
patch
path
patio
pattern
pause
paw
pay
payment
peace
peach
peanut
pear
peas
pebble
pedal
peek
peel
peep
pen
pencil
penny
people
pepper

perfect
perfume
period
permit
person
persuade
pet
phone
photo
photograph
piano
pick
pickle
picnic
picture
pie
piece
pig
pigtail
pile
pill
pillow
pillowcase
pilot
pin
pinch
pineapple
pink
pioneer
pipe
pirate
pit
pitcher
pizza
place
plain
plan
plane
planet
plant
plastic
plate
play
playground

playmate
playpen
playroom
please
plenty
plop
plum
plumber
plus
pocket
pocketknife
poem
poetry
point
police
policeman
polite
pond
pony
pool
poor
pop
popcorn
pope
popular
porch
pork
portion
position
possess
possible
possibly
post
postcard
poster
pot
potato
pound
pour
poverty
power
practice
prairie
praise

pray	put	real	rice	sad
prediction	puzzle	really	rich	saddle
prepare	pyramid	rear	riddle	safe
present		reason	ride	sail
president	**Q**	recess	right	salad
pretend	quack	recipe	ring	sale
pretty	quarrel	recite	rinse	salmon
pretzel	quart	recommend	rip	salt
price	quarter	record	ripe	salute
priest	queen	recording	rise	same
prince	question	recreation	risk	sand
princess	quick	rectangle	river	sandal
principal	quiet	red	road	sandwich
print	quit	reflect	roar	Saturday
prisoner		refrigerator	roast	sauce
private	**R**	refuse	robe	sausage
prize	rabbit	region	robin	save
problem	raccoon	regular	robot	savings
proceed	race	regulation	rock	saw
process	racetrack	reindeer	rocket	say
produce	racing	relax	roll	scab
profession	radio	religion	roof	scar
promise	radius	remain	room	scare
protect	raft	remember	rooster	scarf
proud	rag	remind	root	scene
prove	railroad	remove	rope	school
prune	rain	rent	rose	schoolboy
publish	rainbow	repair	rotate	schoolgirl
pudding	raincoat	repairman	rough	schoolroom
puddle	raindrop	repeat	round	schoolteacher
pull	rainfall	reply	route	schoolwork
pumpkin	raise	request	routine	schoolyard
punch	raisin	require	row	science
punish	rake	respectful	rub	scissors
pup	ramp	respond	rude	scold
pupil	ranch	responsible	rug	scoop
puppet	rank	rest	ruin	scooter
puppy	rare	restaurant	rule	scratch
purchase	rash	result	run	scream
purple	raspberry	return	runner	screw
purpose	rat	revolution	rush	screwdriver
purr	rattle	reward		scribble
purse	read	rhyme	**S**	scrub
push	ready	ribbon	sack	sea

seafood	sharp	sight	sleigh	soda
seal	shave	sign	slice	sofa
search	she	signal	slick	soft
season	she'd	silence	slide	softball
seat	she'll	silent	slim	soil
seatbelt	she's	silk	slip	soldier
second	shed	silly	slipper	solo
secret	sheep	silver	slippery	solve
secretary	sheet	similar	sliver	some
section	shelf	simple	sloth	somebody
see	shell	simply	slow	someday
seed	shelter	since	slowdown	someone
seem	sherbet	sing	slug	someplace
seldom	sheriff	singer	slum	something
select	shine	single	slump	sometimes
self	shiny	sink	small	somewhere
selfish	ship	sip	smart	son
sell	shirt	sir	smash	song
send	shiver	siren	smell	soon
sentence	shoe	sister	smile	sorry
separate	shoelace	sit	smoke	sort
September	shoot	six	smooth	sound
sequence	shop	sixteen	snack	soup
seriously	shore	sixth	snail	sour
servant	short	sixty	snake	south
serve	shorten	size	snap	space
set	shorts	skate	sneeze	spacecraft
seven	should	skating	sniff	spaghetti
seventeen	shoulders	skeleton	snip	spank
seventh	shouldn't	skid	snore	spark
seventy	shout	skiing	snort	speak
several	shove	skill	snow	speaker
sew	shovel	skim	snowball	special
sewer	show	skin	snowman	speech
shade	shrimp	skinny	snowplow	speed
shadow	shrine	skip	snuggle	spell
shake	shrink	skirt	so	spend
shall	shut	skunk	so	spider
shallow	shy	sky	soak	spill
shame	sibling	slam	soap	spin
shampoo	sick	slap	soar	spinach
shape	side	sled	soccer	spit
share	sidewalk	sleep	society	splash
shark	sideways	sleeve	sock	splinter

split	steep	sudden	taco	that's
sponge	step	suds	tadpole	the
spoon	stew	sugar	tail	theater
spoonful	stick	suggest	take	their
sport	still	suit	tale	theirs
spot	sting	suitcase	talent	them
spray	stink	sum	talk	then
spread	stir	summary	tall	there
spring	stocking	summer	tap	there's
sprinkle	stomach	sun	tape	thermometer
sprinkler	stone	sunburn	task	these
spy	stool	sundae	taste	they
square	stop	Sunday	tasty	they'd
squash	store	sundown	tattle	they'll
squat	storm	sunglasses	taxi	they're
squeak	story	sunny	taxicab	they've
squeeze	storybook	sunrise	tea	thick
squirrel	straight	sunset	teach	thief
squirt	strange	sunshine	teacher	thin
stab	stranger	super	team	thing
stack	strap	supper	tear	think
stadium	strawberry	suppose	tease	third
stage	stream	sure	teaspoon	thirst
stagecoach	street	surprise	technology	thirsty
stair	strength	surround	teenager	thirteen
staircase	stretch	survive	teeth	thirty
stairs	strict	swallow	telephone	this
stairway	string	sweat	television	those
stamp	stripe	sweater	tell	though
stand	strong	sweep	temperature	thousand
star	student	sweet	temple	thread
stare	study	sweets	ten	three
starfish	stumble	swim	tennis	throat
start	stump	swimming	tent	through
starve	stupid	swing	tenth	throughout
state	subject	switch	terrible	throw
statement	submarine	sword	territory	thumb
station	subtract	symbol	test	thunder
statue	subtraction	syrup	text	thunderstorm
stay	suburb		textbook	Thursday
steak	subway	**T**	than	tick
steal	succeed	table	thank	ticket
steam	such	tablecloth	thankful	tickle
steel	suck	tablespoon	that	tie

tiger	tractor	twig	vanilla	waste
tight	trade	twin	vase	watch
tighten	trail	twinkle	vegetables	water
tights	trailer	twirl	vegetation	wave
timber	train	twist	verb	we
time	trap	two	very	we'll
tiny	trash	type	vibrate	we're
tip	travel		video	we've
tiptoe	tray	**U**	view	weak
tire	treasure	ugly	village	weakness
title	treat	umbrella	villain	wear
to	tree	uncle	vine	weather
toad	triangle	under	violent	wedding
toast	triangular	underline	violin	Wednesday
today	tribe	underneath	visit	weed
toddler	trick	understand	visitor	week
toe	trickle	unequal	vitamin	weekday
together	tricycle	unfair	vocabulary	weekend
tomato	trigger	unfortunately	voice	weekly
tomorrow	trip	unhappy	volleyball	weigh
tongue	trot	uniform	vote	weird
tonight	trouble	universe	vowel	welcome
too	truck	unkind		well
tool	true	unless	**W**	were
toot	truly	unlike	waffle	weren't
tooth	trunk	unsafe	wag	west
toothbrush	trust	until	wagon	wet
toothpaste	truth	up	waist	whale
top	try	upon	wait	what
topic	tub	upright	waiter	what's
tornado	tube	upset	waitress	wheat
tortilla	Tuesday	upside-down	wake	wheel
toss	tugboat	upstairs	walk	wheelbarrow
total	tumble	upward	wall	when
touch	tuna	us	wallet	where
touchdown	tunnel	use	walnut	where's
toward	turkey	useful	wander	whether
towel	turn	usual	want	which
tower	turtle		war	while
town	tweezers	**V**	warm	whisker
toy	twelve	vacation	warn	whisper
toys	twenty	valentine	was	whistle
trace	twice	valley	wash	white
track	twice	van	wasp	who

whole	wipe	world	**Y**	young
why	wire	worm	yacht	your
wicked	wise	worry	yank	yours
wide	wish	worse	yard	yourself
width	witch	worst	yardstick	
wife	with	would	yawn	**Z**
wiggle	within	wouldn't	year	zebra
wild	without	wow	yell	zero
wildlife	wizard	wrap	yellow	zip
will	wolf	wreck	yes	zipper
win	woman	wrestle	yesterday	zone
wind	won't	wrestling	yet	zoo
window	wonder	wrinkle	yolk	zoom
wine	wood	wrist	you	
wing	wool	write	you'd	
wink	word	writer	you'll	
winner	work	writing	you're	
winter	worker	wrong	you've	

VOCABULARY NOTEBOOK

A vocabulary notebook is an important tool for English language learners. It allows learners to create a record of their own language development. Learners should keep individual vocabulary notebooks and review the vocabulary often. In addition to new vocabulary, students should maintain words they have already learned by including related vocabulary, phrases, collocates, and other information as their language learning progresses.

A vocabulary notebook is very easy to use. (Please see the example below.) In the top left box learners write the new word and its meaning (in their own words). In the box on the right learners draw a picture or some visual representation of the new word. The lower left box is for words and phrases related to the new word.

| Word:

farm
food is from a farm
there are cows and pigs.

Related words:
food   corn
chicken   field
farmer | Picture:

 |

The vocabulary notebook description and example is adapted from the work of Dr. Robert J. Marzano and is included in his book *Teaching Basic and Advanced Vocabulary: A Framework for Direct Instruction.*

The following pages include blank diagrams for students to create their own vocabulary notebooks. Or, if this book is being shared in a classroom, these pages (590–597) are photocopiable for use with this dictionary.

| Word:

Related words: | Picture: |

Word:	Picture:
Related words:	

Word:	Picture:
Related words:	

Word:	Picture:
Related words:	

Word:

Picture:

Related words:

Word:

Picture:

Related words:

Word:

Picture:

Related words:

Word:	Picture:
Related words:	

Word:	Picture:
Related words:	

Word:	Picture:
Related words:	

Word:	Picture:
Related words:	

Word:	Picture:
Related words:	

Word:	Picture:
Related words:	

Word:

Picture:

Related words:

Word:

Picture:

Related words:

Word:

Picture:

Related words:

Word:	Picture:
Related words:	

Word:	Picture:
Related words:	

Word:	Picture:
Related words:	

Word:	Picture:
Related words:	

Word:	Picture:
Related words:	

Word:	Picture:
Related words:	

Word:

Picture:

Related words:

Word:

Picture:

Related words:

Word:

Picture:

Related words:

CREDITS

Illustrations:

Higgins Bond: pp. 102, 280, 431, 524 ; © Higgins Bond/Anita Grien
Richard Carbajal: pp. 91, 495 ; © Richard Carbajal/illustrationOnLine.com
Ron Carboni: pp. 96, 293 ; © Ron Carboni/Anita Grien
Patrick Gnan: pp. 311, 328 (right), 408 ; © Patric Gnan/illustrationOnLine.com
Sharon and Joel Harris: pp. 52, 187, 218 ; © Sharon and Joel Harris/illustrationOnLine.com
Philip Howe: pp. 169 ; © Philip Howe/illustrationOnLine.com
Robert Kayganich: pp. 57, 266, 452, 503 ; © Robert Kayganich/illustrationOnLine.com
Stephen Peringer: pp. 88, 105 ; © Stephen Peringer/illustrationOnLine.com
Precision Graphics: pp. 535 ; © Precision Graphics
Alan Reingold: pp. 82, 144, 216, 403 ; © Alan Reingold /Anita Grien
Beryl Simon: pp. 135 ; © Beryl Simon
Rob Shuster: pp. 347 ; © Rob Shuster
Gerard Taylor: pp. 10, 172, 535 ; © Gerard Taylor/illustrationOnLine.com
Ralph Voltz: pp. 28, 85, 197, 232, 262 ; © Ralph Voltz/illustrationOnLine.com
Brad Walker: pp. 83 ; © Brad Walker
Cam Wilson: pp. 157, 205 ; © Cam Wilson/illustrationOnLine.com
Phil Wilson: pp. 17, 41, 47 ; © Phil Wilson

Photos:

3: Evgeny Murtola/Shutterstock; **12:** (top) Michael G Smith/Shutterstock, (bottom) Branislav Senic/Shutterstock; **13:** Elmarie Dreyer/Shutterstock; **16:** Stephen Coburn/Shutterstock; **17:** Perov Stanislav/Shutterstock; **19:** (left) Lebanmax/Shutterstock, (right) Piotr Adamski(Shutterstock); **22:** (top) Uwe Bumann/Shutterstock, (middle) Dmitrijs Mihejevs/Shutterstock, (bottom) Mitch Aunger/Shutterstock; **32:** Baloncic/Shutterstock; **33:** (left) Jupiterimages/photos.com, (middle) Jupiterimages/photos.com, (right) Perov Stanislav/Shutterstock; **35:** (top) Aleksandr Frovolov/Shutterstock, (top row, l to r) Norman Pogson/Dreamstime, Igor Terekhov/Dreamstime, Tatiana Popova/Shutterstock, magicoven/Shutterstock, Photka/Dreamstime, Adeek/Dreamstime, (bottom row, l to r) Colour59/Dreamstime, Graca Victoria/Shutterstock, Karkas/Shutterstock; **36:** mypokcik/Shutterstock; **37:** (left) ilbusca/istockphoto, (right) Marbo/dreamstime; **38:** (bottom) StudioThreeDots/istockphoto, (top left) Shanin/dreamstime, (top right) kromedomio/istockphoto; **39:** Craig Dingle/Shutterstock; **41:** (top) Clarence S Lewis/Shutterstock, (bottom left) asiseeit/istockphoto, (bottom middle) Olga Chernetskaya & Leonid Yastremsky/Shutterstock, (bottom right) John Wollwerth/Shutterstock, (middle) CLFProductions/Shutterstock; **44:** (left) Madeleine Openshaw/Shutterstock, (top right) Karkas/Shutterstock, (top left) Trinacria Photo/Shutterstock; **46:** Wellmony/dreamstime; **49:** blackred/istockphoto; **50:** (left) Vaide Seskauskiene/Shutterstock, (middle) iofoto/Shutterstock, (right) Joseph McCullar/Shutterstock; **51:** Wd/dreamstime; **52:** Steven Coling/Shutterstock; **53:** Rodionov/Shutterstock; **55:** (l to r) Wizdata, Inc/Shutterstock, Caramaria/dreamstime, freelanceartist/Shutterstock, Sasa Petkovic/Shutterstock, Peter Hansen/Shutterstock, Andrea Danti/Shutterstock, Steven Pepple/Shutterstock, (top) gilas/istockphoto; **58:** Jgroup/dreamstime; **60:** (top) Konstantynov/dreamstime, (bottom) vnlit/Shutterstock; **63:** marti157900/istockphoto; **64:** hardtmuth/Shutterstock; **66:** Michael ledrey/Shutterstock; **67:** Benjamin Albiach Galan/istockphoto; **69:** (top) Joel Blit/Shutterstock, (bottom) Natalia Bratslavsky/Shutterstock; **70:** Jupiterimages/photos.com; **72:** (top) Sean Gladwell/Shutterstock, (bottom) Eric Isselee/Shutterstock; **78:** (left) v.o./Shutterstock, (middle) DNY59/istockphoto, (right) Jill Battaglia/Shutterstock; **80:** (bottom) sonya etchison/Shutterstock, (top) timsa/istockphoto, GodfriedEdelman/istockphoto; **81:** Pablo H Caridad/Shutterstock; **84:** aida ricciardiello/Shutterstock; **86:** Jupiterimages/photos.com; **87:** (l to r) dscz/istockphoto, RBFried/istockphoto, Yelena Panyukova/Shutterstock; **93:** Chris Schmidt/istockphoto; **100:** sweetym/istockphoto; **106:** Terry Weaver/Shutterstock; **109:** Brian Chase/Shutterstock; **112:** (l to r) Lipsky/Shutterstock, James Steidl/Shutterstock; **117:** Colin Stitt/Shutterstock; **119:** Prawny/Dreamstime; **121:** (l to r) dbvirago/Dreamstime, James Brey/istockphoto, Macdsean/Dreamstime; **131:** Scott Richardson/Shutterstock; **134:** Jacom Stevens/istockphoto; **139:** Matthew Cole/Shutterstock; **140:** (top) Ariel Bravy/Shutterstock, (bottom) Sparkling Moments Photography/Shutterstock; **141:** (top) Studio 37/Shutterstock, (middle) David Eby/Shutterstock, (bottom) Chistophe Testi/Shutterstock; **145:** Galushko Sergey/Shutterstock;